Childe Hassam

American Impressionist

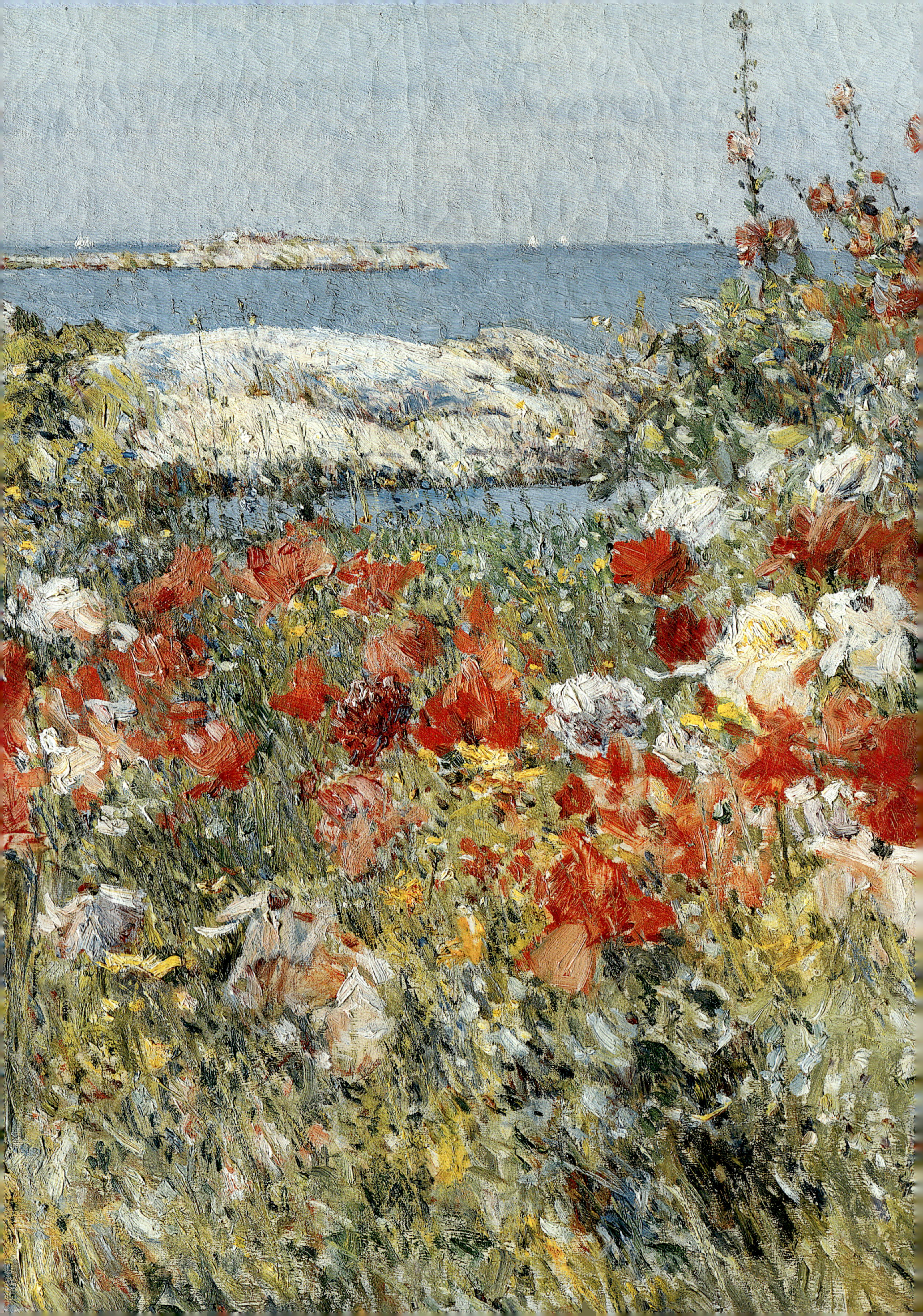

Childe Hassam

American Impressionist

H. Barbara Weinberg

WITH CONTRIBUTIONS BY

Elizabeth E. Barker, Elizabeth Block, Elizabeth Broun, Kathleen M. Burnside, Stephanie L. Herdrich, Erica E. Hirshler, Megan Holloway, Susan G. Larkin, Lisa Miller, Kimberly Orcutt, Dana Pilson, and Carol Troyen

The Metropolitan Museum of Art, New York

Yale University Press, New Haven and London

This volume has been published in conjunction with the exhibition "Childe Hassam, American Impressionist," organized by The Metropolitan Museum of Art, New York, and held there from June 10 to September 12, 2004.

The exhibition is made possible by
THE PETER JAY SHARP FOUNDATION and
THE BANK OF NEW YORK.

Additional support has been provided by the
Marguerite and Frank A. Cosgrove Jr. Fund.

Published by The Metropolitan Museum of Art, New York

John P. O'Neill, Editor in Chief
Carol Fuerstein, Editor
Bruce Campbell, Designer
Sally VanDevanter, Production
Minjee Cho, Desktop Publishing
Jean Wagner, Bibliographer

New photography of works in the Metropolitan Museum collection by Mark Morosse, Juan Trujillo, and Peter Zeray, the Photograph Studio, The Metropolitan Museum of Art

Typeset in Galliard and Bauer Bodoni

Printed on 130 gsm Lumisilk

Separations by Professional Graphics, Rockford, Illinois

Printed and bound by CS Graphics PTE Ltd., Singapore

Jacket/cover illustration: detail, fig. 232. *Allies Day, May 1917*

Frontispiece: detail, fig. 9. *Celia Thaxter's Garden, Isles of Shoals, Maine*

Library of Congress Cataloging-in-Publication Data

Weinberg, H. Barbara (Helene Barbara)
Childe Hassam, American impressionist / H. Barbara Weinberg; with contributions by Elizabeth E. Barker . . . [et al.].
p. cm.
Includes bibliographical references and index.
ISBN 1-58839-119-1 (hardcover)—ISBN 1-58839-120-5 (pbk.)—
ISBN 0-300-10293-3 (Yale University Press)
1. Hassam, Childe, 1859–1935—Exhibitions. 2. Impressionism (Art)—United States—Exhibitions.
I. Barker, Elizabeth E. II. Title.
N6537.H367A4 2004
759.13–dc22 2004004299

Contents

Sponsor's Statement

THE PETER JAY SHARP FOUNDATION

The Peter Jay Sharp Foundation is honored to support the exhibition *Childe Hassam, American Impressionist* at The Metropolitan Museum of Art. This important and quintessentially American painter was much admired by the late Peter Jay Sharp, a unique patron of the arts who benefited from a traditional American upbringing and education. Mr. Sharp was eager to support innovative efforts in education and culture, especially in the New York City area. His long association with the Metropolitan makes this sponsorship particularly appropriate. The support of this extraordinary exhibition would have pleased him, as it pleases all of us at the Foundation.

The Foundation depends on the work and oversight of its Board of Directors. Individual board members have taken the responsibility of ensuring that organizations of high quality are funded, that they carry out their program commitments, and that they achieve a reasonable degree of effectiveness. Over the years, this technique has led the Foundation to support educational institutions, opera and other music, art, theater, museums, libraries, medical research, environmental organizations, and other activities that Peter Sharp, with his widely varied interests, would have deemed appropriate.

In general, the Foundation was designed to function after Mr. Sharp's death as it would have if Peter were alive and presiding from the chairman's seat. The Board of Directors has not established formal guidelines but pursues interests based on initiatives from its four directors. While New York City has been the center of most of our activity, other areas of commitment have been schools and institutions ranging in scope from the Princeton University Art Museum to the Washington-based Conservation Fund, which is concerned with the environment.

The Peter Jay Sharp Foundation thanks Philippe de Montebello and the staff of the Metropolitan Museum for bringing this remarkable exhibition to the City of New York. They have been extremely efficient and caring in organizing this exhibition. In his works, Childe Hassam celebrated the city and honored the American scene and American traditions. We are delighted to help in presenting this grand display of his finest paintings, watercolors, drawings, and prints at this particularly fitting moment in our nation's history.

Norman L. Peck
President and Director
The Peter Jay Sharp Foundation

Sponsor's Statement

The Bank of New York

By 1900 Childe Hassam had come to be recognized as the leading exponent of the Impressionist movement in the United States. While adept at capturing the charm of the countryside in dazzling evocations of rural light and color, he was one of the first artists to see the city, particularly New York City, as a place of beauty and a source of inspiration. From 1890 through World War I, he painted New York's fashionable avenues and parks, as well as the city's burgeoning skyline. Hassam believed that "the man who will go down to posterity is the man who paints his own time and the scenes of every-day life around him." Works such as *The Hovel and the Skyscraper,* 1904 (Pennsylvania Academy of the Fine Arts, Philadelphia), and *Allies Day, May 1917,* 1917 (National Gallery of Art, Washington, D.C.), characterized New York's transition to the modern age and highlighted its exceptional dynamism.

We at The Bank of New York, which has been a part of this vibrant city since 1784, share Hassam's fascination with our city's diversity, energy, and truly unique character. While we are very proud of our role in New York's financial and commercial growth over the years, we are equally proud of our contributions to the city's cultural fabric. The Bank's relationship with The Metropolitan Museum of Art spans more than a century. We are honored and privileged to reaffirm our support of the Metropolitan through sponsorship of *Childe Hassam, American Impressionist,* a retrospective of the artist's finest works. This extraordinary exhibition invites visitors from around the world, as well as New Yorkers, to celebrate Childe Hassam's remarkable talent.

Thomas A. Renyi
Chairman and Chief Executive Officer
The Bank of New York

Director's Foreword

The Metropolitan Museum's collection is notable for the breadth and quality of its works by the American Impressionists. Represented by vivid and engaging paintings, watercolors, drawings, and prints are Mary Cassatt, William Merritt Chase, Theodore Robinson, John Singer Sargent, and others who depicted aspects of modern life abroad and at home about 1900. Expatriates Cassatt and Sargent caught the spirit of the new French painting during the late 1870s. Among the repatriated American Impressionists, Childe Hassam (1859–1935) was exceptional in adopting the style while he was still a student in Paris, between 1886 and 1889. Settling in New York in 1889, Hassam became the city's principal American Impressionist chronicler, influenced many of his contemporaries, and earned the praise of critics. Between 1890 and 1918 he made long, productive visits to picturesque villages along the New England coast, and, after 1919, he spent summers working in stylish East Hampton, New York.

To the 1909 gift of its first canvas by Hassam, the Metropolitan added oils, watercolors, and prints through gifts and purchases, establishing an excellent record of the artist's accomplishments. In 1932 the Museum even produced a short silent film on Hassam, the first in a series devoted to living American artists. Generous gifts of three striking landscapes bestowed between 1994 and 1996 helped to make Hassam the American Impressionist best represented at the Metropolitan after Cassatt and Sargent. The excitement generated by these notable recent acquisitions inspired us to plan the first major retrospective exhibition of the artist's work held in a museum since 1972 (when the museum at the University of Arizona organized a display). Recent scholarship—including the research associated with our groundbreaking exhibition of 1994, *American Impressionism and Realism: The Painting of Modern Life, 1885–1915*—revealed Hassam to be a paradigmatic American Impressionist and confirmed our belief that his career deserved reexamination.

In this exhibition and its accompanying publication, the insights of H. Barbara Weinberg, the Metropolitan's Alice Pratt Brown Curator of American Paintings and Sculpture, and other expert contributors shed new light on Hassam's achievements. Reconsidered, for example, are his formative period in Boston and his student years in Paris, where he was a neighbor of avant-garde artists in Montmartre. Hassam's urban and rural scenes, analyzed in terms of their Impressionist composition, palette, and brushwork, are also measured in light of his credo, announced in 1892: "I believe the man who will go down to posterity is the man who paints his own time and the scenes of every-day life around him." His genteel portrayals of New York, for example, are shown to have become increasingly euphemistic as the city and its populations became ever more dynamic and heterogeneous after 1900. And his New England views, which offer a composite portrait of the region that preserved American traditions in the face of daunting change, are examined for the first time in relation to the attributes of the locales he visited. Hassam's watercolors, etchings, and lithographs have also merited fresh scrutiny both independently and in comparison to his oils. Unique to this volume are an account of Hassam's lifelong campaign to market his art, a study of the frames he selected and designed for his paintings, and an unprecedented lifetime exhibition record.

Both the exhibition and the catalogue depended on the assistance of generous supporters. Many public institutions and private collectors lent treasured works to this exhibition, and we are profoundly grateful for their indispensable participation. We deeply appreciate the inspired sponsorship of The Peter Jay Sharp Foundation and The Bank of New York and the additional assistance given by the Marguerite and Frank A. Cosgrove Jr. Fund and the William Cullen Bryant Fellows of the American Wing, which enabled us to undertake and realize this important project.

Philippe de Montebello
Director
The Metropolitan Museum of Art

Acknowledgments

We welcome the opportunity to thank many people who helped us realize this project. Philippe de Montebello, the Metropolitan Museum's Director, recognized the importance of American Impressionism to our collection and our audiences and encouraged us. Mahrukh Tarapor, Associate Director for Exhibitions, coordinated preparations with help from Martha Deese. Doralynn Pines, Associate Director for Administration, supported our efforts. Emily Kernan Rafferty, Senior Vice President for External Affairs, Nina McN. Diefenbach, Deputy Vice President for External Affairs and Chief Development Officer, and their associates in the Development Department secured splendid sponsorship from The Peter Jay Sharp Foundation and The Bank of New York and coordinated contributions from the Marguerite and Frank A. Cosgrove Jr. Fund and the William Cullen Bryant Fellows of the American Wing. Kerstin M. Larsen, Christine Scornavacca, Claire Gylphé, Andrea Kann, and Rosayn D. Anderson of the Development Department were especially helpful. Harold Holzer, Vice President for Communications and Marketing, and John O'Keefe, O'Keefe and Associates, introduced the Museum to The Peter Jay Sharp Foundation and assured media coverage for the exhibition.

Our plans were implemented by many skilled colleagues. Nina S. Maruca, Associate Registrar, managed registration. Conservators Dorothy Mahon, George Bisacca, Pascale Patris, and Marjorie Shelley cared for works on loan and from our own collection. Linda M. Sylling, Manager for Special Exhibitions and Gallery Installations, oversaw our handsome installation in collaboration with Michael Langley and Connie Norkin, our gifted exhibition designer and graphic designer, respectively; Jeffrey L. Daly, Chief Designer, gave welcome advice. Taylor Miller supervised construction, and Clint Coller and Rich Lichte worked their magic with lighting. Gerald P. Lunney and his colleagues in the Office of the Registrar made key contributions. American Wing technicians Don E. Templeton, Gary Burnett, Sean Farrell, and Rob Davis brought their professionalism to the task of installing the exhibition, as did David del Gaizo and Ricky Luna, technicians in the Department of Drawings and Prints. Morrison H. Heckscher, Lawrence A. Fleischman Chairman of the American Wing, and curators Kevin J. Avery, Carrie Rebora Barratt, Alice Cooney Frelinghuysen, Peter M. Kenny, Amelia Peck, Frances Gruber Safford, Thayer Tolles, and Beth Carver Wees cheered us on; Katie Banser, Elaine Bradson, Catherine Scandalis, and Kathryn Sill attended to details. Colleagues from other departments who provided expertise were Elisabeth R. Baldwin, Barbara W. File, and Jeanie M. James, Archives; Elyssa Schram and Melinda Webber, Costume Institute; Marilyn Jenkins-Madina, Islamic Art; and Douglas Eklund, Photographs.

We depended upon numerous institutions and individuals for information and assistance. Repositories that deserve special notice are: Archives of American Art, Smithsonian Institution, Washington, D.C.; Columbia University Libraries, New York; Frick Art Reference Library, New York; Library of Congress, Washington, D.C.; Museum of the City of New York; New-York Historical Society; and New York Public Library. Foremost among those who have earned our gratitude are Stuart P. Feld and Kathleen M. Burnside, Hirschl and Adler Galleries, New York, who shared documentation and insights gained during years spent in pursuit of research on Hassam. Also generous with their knowledge and resources were Warren Adelson, Cynthia Bird, and Elizabeth Oustinoff, Adelson Galleries, New York; Trina Weckley and Joy Weiner, Archives of American Art; John Driscoll, Babcock Galleries, New York; Bruce Weber, Berry-Hill Galleries, New York; Aaron Schmidt, Boston Public Library; Peter Kloman, Paul Provost, and Eric Widing, Christie's, New York; Jerry E. Patterson, William Doyle Galleries, New York; Diana Dayton and Dorothy King, Long Island Collection, East Hampton Library; Angela Mack, Gibbes Museum of Art, Charleston, South Carolina; M. P. Naud, Tom Parker, and Zachary Ross, Hirschl and Adler Galleries, New York; Carol A. Irish, the late Vance Jordan, and Kendall Scully, Vance Jordan Fine Art, New York; Martha Fleischman, Kennedy Galleries, New York;

Larry Shar, Julius Lowy Frame and Restoring Company, New York; Marguerite Ladden and Eileen Morales, Museum of the City of New York; Kenneth Maddox, Newington Cropsey Foundation, Hastings-on-Hudson, New York; Robert Karr, Osaka Garden, Jackson Park, Chicago; Margaret Bullock and Karen Christenson, Portland Art Museum, Oregon; Ursula S. Wright, Portsmouth Athenaeum, New Hampshire; Colleene Fesko and Anne E. Poling, Skinner Auctions, Boston; Dara Mitchell, Colin J. Montgomery, and Alexis Thoman, Sotheby's, New York; Bill Fiddler, Lisa N. Peters, Judy Salerno, and Ira Spanierman, Spanierman Gallery, New York; Bridget Byrne and Priscilla Sapienza, Star Island Corporation, Portsmouth, New Hampshire; Robert C. Vose III and Siobhan M. Wheeler, Vose Galleries of Boston; Thomas Denenberg, Wadsworth Atheneum, Hartford; and Lynne Addison, Amy Freedberg, and Lisa Hodemarski, Yale University Art Gallery, New Haven. We benefited as well from the help of Thomas W. Barwick, Douglas Blackburn, Jonathan Boos, Thomas Folk, Robert Hamburger, Ulrich W. Hiesinger, Emilie Kilgore, Rita Krauss, Lisa Kunik, Maan Z. Madina, Dorothy Manville and Richard Manville, David Nisinson, Meg J. Perlman, Ignacio Cano Rivera, Cheryl Robledo, Christina Ryan, Nicolás Salas, Jenny Spoonberg, Juliana Terian, Mike Wallace, Linda Cohen Wassong, Deedee Wigmore, Eli Wilner and Suzanne Smeaton, and the late Richard York.

Our lenders not only sacrificed their own enjoyment of their pictures for the duration of the exhibition but also furnished information about them. We are grateful to all for their generous responses to our requests and offer particular thanks to the following individuals and their associates: Adam Weinberg, Susan C. Faxon, and Emily Schreiner, Addison Gallery of American Art, Phillips Academy, Andover, Massachusetts; Douglas G. Schultz and Douglas Dreishpoon, Albright-Knox Art Gallery, Buffalo; Virginia Dajani, Kathy Kienholz, and Souhad Rafey, American Academy of Arts and Letters, New York; Rick Stewart, Jane Myers, and Patricia Junker, Amon Carter Museum, Fort Worth; Alain Joyaux and Nancy M. Huth, Ball State University Museum of Art, Muncie, Indiana; Doreen Bolger and Sona Johnston, Baltimore Museum of Art; Patricia C. Willis and Ellen Cordes, Beinecke Rare Book and Manuscript Library, Yale University, New Haven; Arnold Lehman, Linda Ferber, Kevin L. Stayton, Barbara Gallati, and Teresa Carbone, Brooklyn Museum of Art; Richard Armstrong and Louise Lippincott, Carnegie Museum of Art, Pittsburgh; William J. Hennessey and Lynne Marsden-Atlass, Chrysler Museum of Art, Norfolk, Virginia; David C. Levy, Jacquelyn Serwer, and Sarah Cash, Corcoran Gallery of Art, Washington, D.C.; John R. Lane and Eleanor Jones Harvey, Dallas Museum of Art; Graham W. J. Beal and James Tottis, Detroit Institute of Arts; Richard V. West and Debra J. Byrne, Frye Art Museum, Seattle; Anne Hawley, Alan Chong, and Mario Pereira, Isabella Stewart Gardner Museum, Boston; Jeffrey Andersen, Florence Griswold Museum, Old Lyme, Connecticut; Ruth Appelhof, Farrin Cary, and Simon Taylor, Guild Hall Museum, East Hampton, New York; Tod Ruhstaller and Susan Benedetti, Haggin Museum, Stockton, California; Richard Andrews, Elizabeth Brown, and Judy Darlene Sourakli, Henry Art Gallery, University of Washington, Seattle; Mitchell A. Codding and Marcus B. Burke, Hispanic Society of America, New York; Randall Suffolk and Erin Budis Coe, Hyde Collection, Glens Falls, New York; Franklin Robinson and Andrew C. Weislogel, Herbert F. Johnson Museum of Art, Cornell University, Ithaca, New York; J. Brooks Joyner, Claudia Einecke, and Marsha V. Gallagher, Joslyn Art Museum, Omaha; Andrea L. Rich, Bruce Robertson, and Leslie Furth, Los Angeles County Museum of Art; Sharon Bradham and Michael J. Beam, Mitchell Museum at Cedarhurst, Mount Vernon, Illinois; Patterson Sims, Gail Stavitsky, and Rosemary Vence, Montclair Art Museum, New Jersey; Malcolm Rogers, Elliot Bostwick Davis, Sue Welsh Reed, Carol Troyen, Erica E. Hirshler, and Janet Comey, Museum of Fine Arts, Boston; Earl A. Powell III, Nicolai Cikovsky Jr., Franklin Kelly, and Anne Halpern, National Gallery of Art, Washington, D.C.; Marc F. Wilson, Margaret Conrads, and Randall Griffey, Nelson-Atkins Museum of Art, Kansas City, Missouri; Mary Sue Sweeney Price, Joseph Jacobs, and Miesha Hardison, Newark Museum; Kenneth T. Jackson and Jan Seidler Ramirez, New-York Historical Society; Christina Orr-Cahall, Roger Ward, Kevin Sharp, and Elizabeth Heard, Norton Museum of Art, West Palm Beach, Florida; Trudy C. Kramer, Alicia Longwell, and Novella Laspia, Parrish Art Museum, Southampton, New York; Derek A. Gillman and Kim Sajet, Pennsylvania Academy of the Fine Arts, Philadelphia; Jay Gates, Eliza Rathbone, and Hannah Byers, Phillips Collection, Washington, D.C.; John Hallmark Neff and Marla Binker, Reynolda House, Museum of American Art, Winston-Salem, North Carolina; Joseph D. Ketner and Leila Amalfitano, Rose Art Museum, Brandeis University, Waltham, Massachusetts; Brent R. Benjamin and Connie

Homburg, Saint Louis Art Museum; Robert H. Frankel, Robert Henning, and Marshall Price, Santa Barbara Museum of Art; Suzannah Fabing, Linda Muehlig, and Michael Goodison, Smith College Museum of Art, Northampton, Massachusetts; Elizabeth Broun and Joann Moser, Smithsonian American Art Museum, Washington, D.C.; Elizabeth Glassman, Catherine L. Ricciardelli, Elizabeth Kennedy, and Sophie Levy, Terra Museum of American Art, Chicago; Roger M. Berkowitz and Lawrence W. Nichols, Toledo Museum of Art; Michael Brand, David Park Curry, and Elizabeth O'Leary, Virginia Museum of Fine Arts, Richmond; Charles Steiner and Stephen Gleissner, Wichita Art Museum; James A. Welu and David Brigham, Worcester Art Museum, Massachusetts.

Essential to the lasting importance of our exhibition is this publication. A key chapter was contributed by Stephanie L. Herdrich, and another was written by Susan G. Larkin, who also served as a perceptive consultant. Essays that shed new light on Hassam were written by Elizabeth E. Barker, Elizabeth Broun, Kathleen M. Burnside, Erica E. Hirshler, Larkin, Lisa Miller, Kimberly Orcutt, Dana Pilson, and Carol Troyen. In the museum, Elizabeth Block, Herdrich, Megan Holloway, and Pilson of the American Wing were indefatigable researchers who also compiled invaluable chronologies. Miller and Orcutt volunteered as researchers; Cynthia Van Allen Schaffner, Gene Silbert, and Lori Zabar pursued queries. Jennie Choi and Michele M. Lussier of Information Systems and Technology helped us manage information. Mark Morosse, Juan Trujillo, and Peter Zeray of the Photograph Studio contributed their skills. We were assisted in the area of information retrieval by the staff of the Thomas J. Watson Library, especially Deborah Vincelli. Deanna D. Cross and Carol Lekarew of the Photograph and Slide Library helped us collect transparencies and made slides.

It is impossible to thank adequately the extraordinary team in the Metropolitan's Editorial Department, which transformed our manuscripts and illustrations into this publication. John P. O'Neill, Editor in Chief and General Manager of Publications, championed the project and offered astute counsel. Carol Fuerstein brought her experience, exceptional tact, and unsurpassed literary gifts to the task of preparing the texts for publication. She was ably assisted in this regard by editors Margaret Donovan, Joan K. Holt, and Ruth Lurie Kozodoy and bibliographer Jean Wagner and in the production phase by Barbara Cavaliere and Sue Potter. Bruce Campbell devised the striking design, balancing scholarly imperatives with our desire for a beautiful presentation. He worked closely with our skillful production manager, Sally VanDevanter, and with other members of the production team: Peter Antony, Robert Weisberg, and especially Minjee Cho, who meticulously handled the desktop publishing. Margaret Chace and Connie Harper-Castle coordinated details. For the wisdom, patience, and devotion of these talented professionals we are deeply grateful.

Many people in the Metropolitan were dedicated to our goal of reaching the widest possible audience. Egle Žygas was our skilled press officer, working with Elyse Topalian, Jennifer Oetting, and other members of the Communications staff. Led by Kent Lydecker, Associate Director for Education, educators planned programs, for which special thanks are owed to Deborah Howes, Nicholas Ruocco, Catherine Fukushima, Elizabeth Hammer, Alice Schwarz, Nancy Thompson, Tomlyn Barns, Merantine Hens, Vivian Wick, Rebecca McGinnis, and Michael Norris. Hilde Limondjian, Lisa Musco Doyle, Mikel Frank, Felix Cotto, and Stephen Rotker of Concerts and Lectures staged subscription lectures. Eti Bonn-Muller and Osamu "Sam" Takahashi managed our representation on the Museum's website. The staff of Merchandising Activities prepared exhibition-related products, and we thank for their creativity Valerie Troyansky, Robie Rogge, William Lach, Sarah Kirtland, Eugénie Roussel, Karrie Witkin, Sheila Bernstein, Marilyn Jensen, Steve Zane, and Helga Lose.

To situate Hassam in a broader context, Elizabeth E. Barker, Elizabeth Block, and Megan Holloway, in consultation with H. Barbara Weinberg, organized the concurrent exhibition *American Impressions, 1865–1925: Prints, Drawings, and Watercolors from the Collection* in The Henry R. Luce Center for the Study of American Art. That exhibition was designed by Michael Batista in collaboration with Barbara Weiss; related education programs were arranged by Amy Silva.

Finally, we again thank our sponsors for their enlightened interest in American art and their commitment to presenting the accomplishments of an artist who absorbed and articulated in so many engaging works the dynamic and challenging spirit of the America of his time.

H. Barbara Weinberg
Alice Pratt Brown Curator of
American Paintings and Sculpture

Lenders to the Exhibition

Addison Gallery of American Art, Andover, Massachusetts 78
Albright-Knox Art Gallery, Buffalo 26
American Academy of Arts and Letters, New York 32, 80, 135
Amon Carter Museum, Fort Worth 45
Ball State University Museum of Art, Muncie, Indiana 13
The Baltimore Museum of Art 112
Beinecke Rare Book and Manuscript Library, Yale University Library, New Haven 41, 141
Brooklyn Museum of Art, New York 11, 60, 75
Carnegie Museum of Art, Pittsburgh 42
The Chrysler Museum of Art, Norfolk, Virginia 8
The Corcoran Gallery of Art, Washington, D.C. 88
Dallas Museum of Art 4
The Detroit Institute of Arts 90
Frye Art Museum, Seattle 97
Isabella Stewart Gardner Museum, Boston 87
Florence Griswold Museum, Old Lyme, Connecticut 124
Guild Hall Museum, East Hampton, New York 79
The Haggin Museum, Stockton, California 17
Henry Art Gallery, Seattle 93
The Hispanic Society of America, New York 20, 118
The Hyde Collection, Glens Falls, New York 54
Herbert F. Johnson Museum of Art, Ithaca, New York 82
Joslyn Art Museum, Omaha 7
Los Angeles County Museum of Art 99
The Metropolitan Museum of Art, New York 9, 14, 15, 21, 24, 25, 28, 31, 33, 35, 40, 43, 53, 59, 62, 73, 74, 77, 86, 91, 94, 98, 103, 104, 107, 115, 117, 119, 121, 127, 128, 132, 140, 142, 143
Mitchell Museum at Cedarhurst, Mount Vernon, Illinois 130
The Montclair Art Museum, New Jersey 123
Museum of Fine Arts, Boston 12, 23, 61, 89, 92
National Gallery of Art, Washington, D.C. 2, 96, 102
The Nelson-Atkins Museum of Art, Kansas City, Missouri 113
The Newark Museum 56
The New-York Historical Society 44
The New York Public Library, Astor, Lenox, and Tilden Foundations 3, 120, 139
Norton Museum of Art, West Palm Beach, Florida 58
The Parrish Art Museum, Southampton, New York 27
Pennsylvania Academy of the Fine Arts, Philadelphia 19, 65
The Phillips Collection, Washington, D.C. 138
Reynolda House, Museum of American Art, Winston-Salem, North Carolina 55
Rose Art Museum, Brandeis University, Waltham, Massachusetts 126
The Saint Louis Art Museum 122
Santa Barbara Museum of Art 83
Smith College Museum of Art, Northampton, Massachusetts 16, 133
Smithsonian American Art Museum, Washington, D.C. 52, 68, 114, 134
Terra Museum of American Art, Chicago 10, 50, 64, 85
The Toledo Museum of Art 108
Virginia Museum of Fine Arts, Richmond 71
Wichita Art Museum 38, 72
Worcester Art Museum, Massachusetts 129

Ms. Cheryl Chase and Mr. Stuart Bear 95
Curtis Galleries, Minneapolis 51
Mrs. Douglas Dillon 140
Marie and Hugh Halff 30
Margaret and Raymond Horowitz 102
Tom James Company / Oxxford Clothes 105
Mrs. George M. Kaufman 46
Mr. and Mrs. Theodore N. Lerner 131
Cornelia and Meredith Long 145
Manoogian Collection 63
May Family Collection, Christopher T. May, Sterling A. May, Meredith M. Smith, Laura May, Trustees 109
Mr. and Mrs. Samuel P. Peabody 29
Lord and Lady Ridley-Tree 66
Senator and Mrs. John D. Rockefeller IV 48, 111
Mr. and Mrs. Thomas A. Rosse 137
Robert Rubin 116
Lewis and Ali Sanders 69, 70
Fayez Sarofim 1
Slavin Family 106
Howard and Susan Sosin 84

Anonymous lenders 5, 6, 18, 22, 34, 36, 37, 39, 47, 49, 57, 67, 76, 81, 100, 101, 110, 125, 136, 144

Contributors to the Catalogue

Elizabeth E. Barker, Assistant Curator, Drawings and Prints
The Metropolitan Museum of Art

Elizabeth Block, Research Assistant, American Paintings and Sculpture
The Metropolitan Museum of Art

Elizabeth Broun, Margaret and Terry Stent Director
Smithsonian American Art Museum, Washington, D.C.

Kathleen M. Burnside, independent scholar and
coauthor, Childe Hassam catalogue raisonné
Hirschl and Adler Galleries, New York

Stephanie L. Herdrich, independent scholar

Erica E. Hirshler, Croll Senior Curator of Paintings, Art of the Americas
Museum of Fine Arts, Boston

Megan Holloway, Research Assistant, American Paintings and Sculpture
The Metropolitan Museum of Art

Susan G. Larkin, independent scholar

Lisa Miller, independent scholar

Kimberly Orcutt, Assistant Curator of American Art, Fogg Art Museum
Harvard University, Cambridge, Massachusetts

Dana Pilson, independent scholar

Carol Troyen, John Moors Cabot Curator of Paintings, Art of the Americas
Museum of Fine Arts, Boston

H. Barbara Weinberg,
Alice Pratt Brown Curator of American Paintings and Sculpture
The Metropolitan Museum of Art

Childe Hassam

American Impressionist

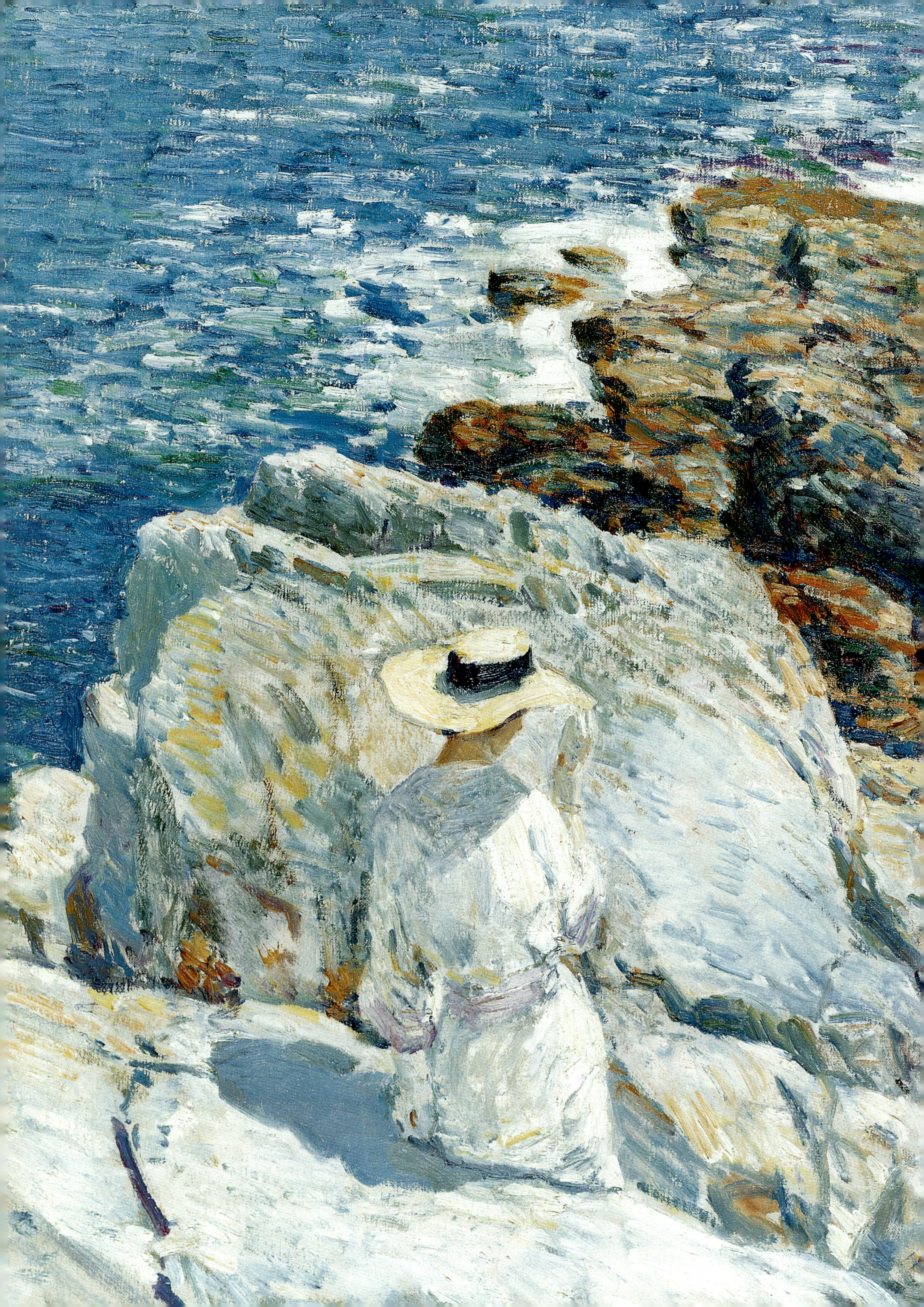

Introduction

H. Barbara Weinberg

Childe Hassam (1859–1935) was a pioneer of American Impressionism and perhaps its most devoted, prolific, and successful practitioner. He caught the spirit of the new painting in Paris in the late 1880s, while most of his compatriots were still ignoring it. He contributed to the full flowering of American Impressionism in the United States in the 1890s and rode the great wave of enthusiasm for the style to fame and fortune. In the publication accompanying the Metropolitan's 1994 exhibition *American Impressionism and Realism: The Painting of Modern Life, 1885–1915*, we posited that leaders of the two allied movements responded to a period of exciting yet bewildering political, economic, and cultural change with an art characterized by optimism, euphemism, nationalism, and nostalgia.[1] Specializing in genteel New York street scenes and bucolic New England landscapes, Hassam epitomized that response. The present retrospective reviews his fifty-year career of ceaseless activity. It reveals that he was a much more distinctive artist than we had anticipated and a more complex one than its title—*Childe Hassam, American Impressionist*—suggests.

First, there is the matter of his name. Frederick Childe Hassam was born on October 17, 1859, in historic Dorchester, Massachusetts, then an independent village just outside Boston.[2] His mother, Rosa Delia Hathorne (1834–1891 or 1892), was descended from William Hathorne, who settled in Salem in 1630 and moved to Dorchester the following year.[3] His father, Frederick Fitch Hassam (1825–1912), a cutlery merchant, was descended from William Horsham, who had arrived in Manchester, Massachusetts, before April 1684.[4] "Hassam is a corruption of the English surname Horsham," reported the family genealogist in 1870.[5] The future artist was named Frederick for his father and Childe—"the Saxon word for shield or knight"—for an uncle.[6] Proud of his Puritan pedigree, especially as increasing immigration to the United States challenged the Anglo-Saxon hegemony, the artist often commented on the roots of the name Hassam (correctly pronounced HASS-am). For example, he told an interviewer in East Hampton, New York, in 1923: "My ancestors were just like yours—New England farmers and sailors. Our family name was once Horseham [*sic*]—how it came to be changed to Oriental-sounding Hassam, I don't know—probably because they couldn't spell."[7] He also boasted of his family ties to celebrated New Englanders, painter William Morris Hunt and writer Nathaniel Hawthorne.[8] Sympathetic commentators often invoked Hassam's Yankee roots and self-conscious identification with American traditions to explain his artistic outlook.[9]

Raised as a Unitarian but utterly indifferent to religion,[10] Hassam enjoyed the confusion created by the Arabic pronunciation of his name (Hass-AM). For all his Yankee swagger, he pointed out his swarthy complexion and allowed friends to call him Muley, a play on the Arabic Mawlā (Lord or Master).[11] He recalled in an interview of 1927 with DeWitt McClellan Lockman: "Frederick [*sic*] Remington had been reading the Granada and the History of Rome, and he said my name must have come from the Arabic, and so they called me Muley Hassam. And [ever] since I am called by the painters Muley Hassam. My wife even uses it."[12] "The Granada" was Washington Irving's durably popular *The Alhambra* (1832), which recounts the reign of Muley Abul Hassan, who succeeded to the Muslim throne at Granada in 1465.[13]

Detail, fig. 146. *The South Ledges, Appledore*

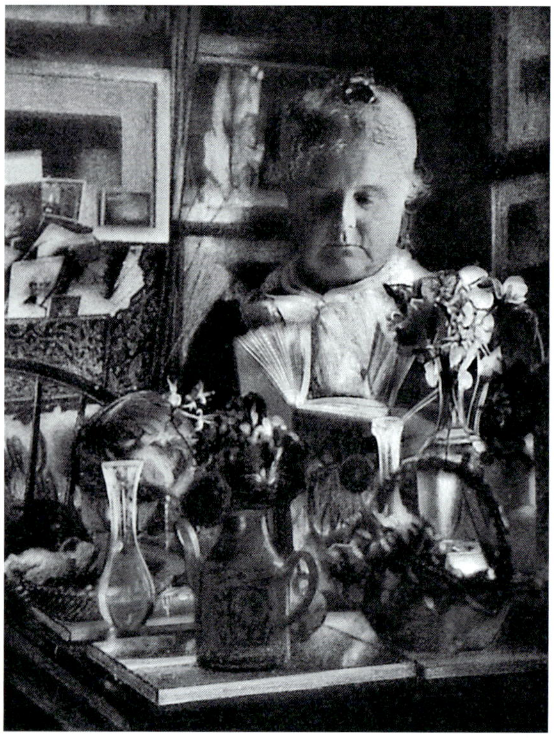

At the urging of poet Celia Laighton Thaxter, whom Hassam recalled meeting "when [he] was not much past twenty," he discarded his prosaic given name in favor of his unusual, presumably more marketable middle name.[14] After signing himself "F. Childe Hassam" for a while, he dropped the initial in 1883 and became "Childe Hassam."[15] About 1885 he also placed before his signature a crescent, at first rendered carefully and later more cursorily. The crescent's meaning for Hassam is not definitively known, although it is said by one author to refer to the crescent-shaped silver hair ornament that Thaxter often wore (fig. 1).[16] Symbolizing the waxing moon and Turkish power, the crescent must also have reinforced the Islamic associations provoked by Hassam's

Fig. 1. Celia Thaxter at her painting table, ca. 1890. Courtesy Portsmouth Athenaeum, New Hampshire

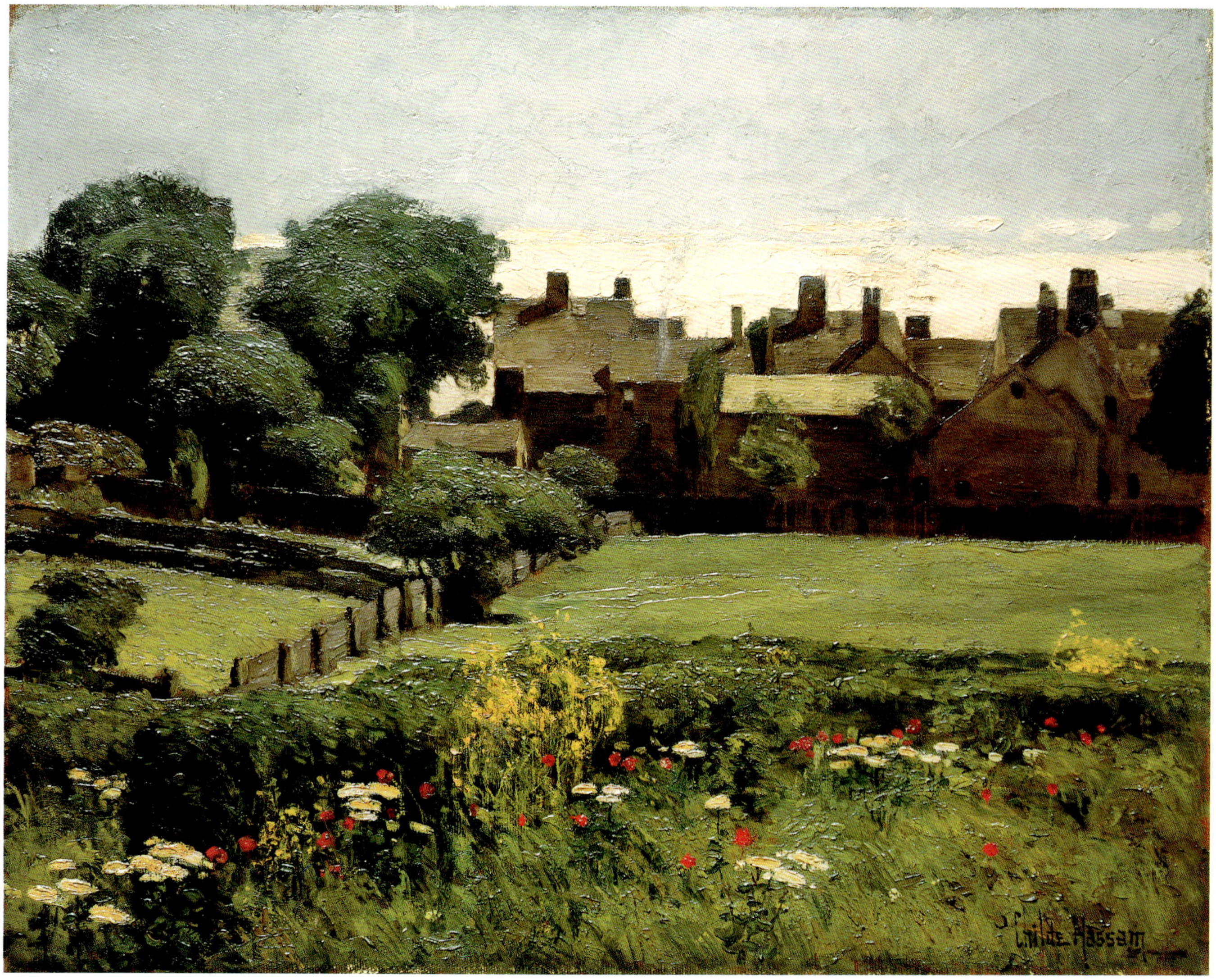

Fig. 2. Childe Hassam. *Village Scene,* 1883-85. Oil on canvas, 17¼ x 22¼ in. (43.8 x 56.5 cm). Mr. and Mrs. Thomas A. Rosse

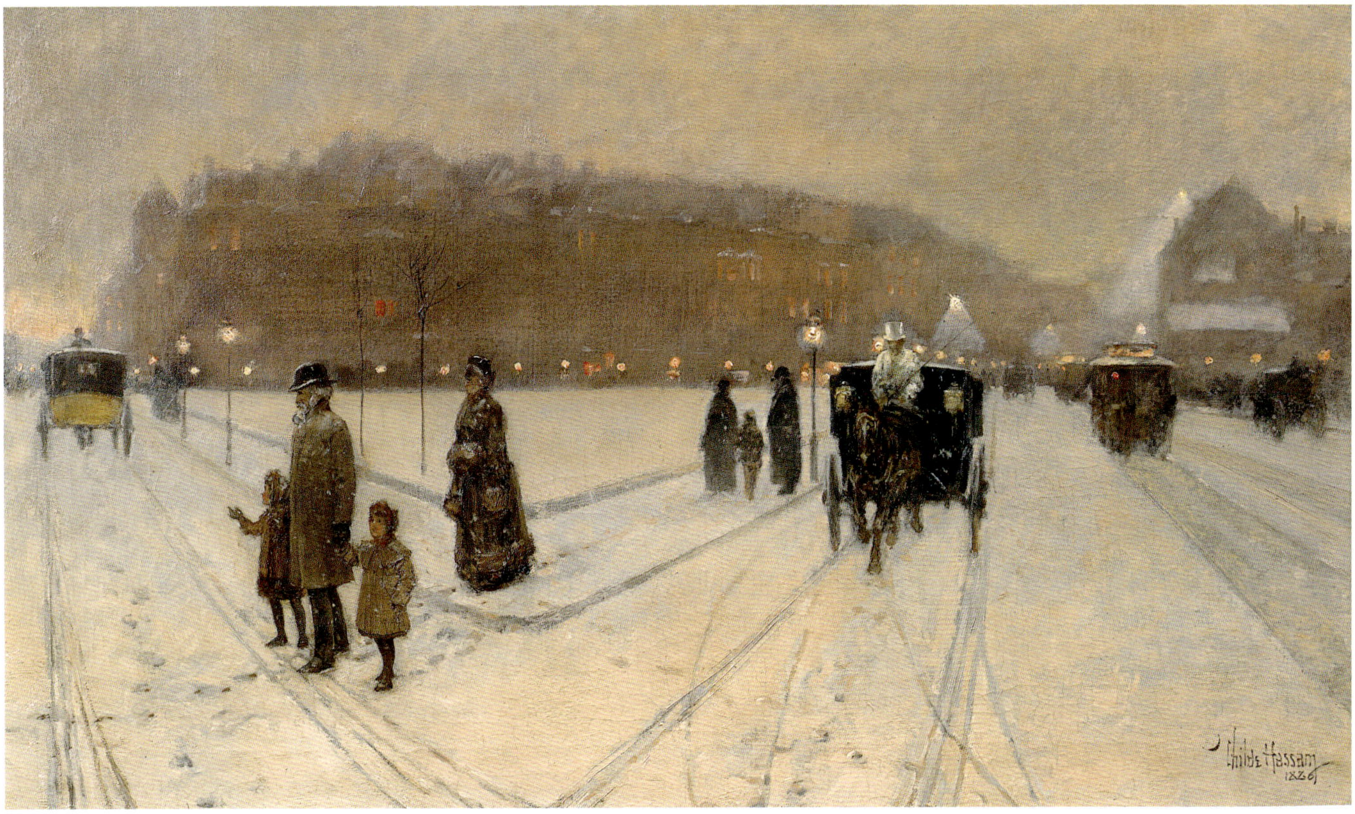

Fig. 3. Childe Hassam. *A City Fairyland,* 1886. Oil on canvas, 20 x 33 in. (50.8 x 83.8 cm). Mr. and Mrs. Samuel P. Peabody

surname. The ambiguous surname and the crescent—notwithstanding their juxtaposition with the "Childe" of Anglo-Saxon connections—provoked persistent rumors of Hassam's Middle Eastern origins.

Like his name, Hassam's Impressionism is more complex than it at first appears: it is an Impressionism formulated in response to diverse influences and developed with a commitment sometimes to candor and sometimes to contrivance. Trained initially in Dorchester and Boston as a watercolorist and illustrator, Hassam learned oil painting at several practical schools and through contact with various artists. He had no meaningful instruction in anatomy, which explains his often schematic rendering of figures. He made his first trip to Europe in July and August 1883, not to study but to see the sights in Great Britain, France, Spain, and elsewhere on the Continent. In Europe, he later claimed, he was more engaged by nature than by art; he admitted to an interest in J. M. W. Turner's watercolors, however, and painted his own as he traveled.[17] His New England oils and watercolors, especially those made after his trip abroad (see fig. 2), focus on verdant pastoral landscape and evocative colonial architecture. Apparent in these nostalgic visions of rural life is Hassam's attraction to the naturalistic Barbizon scenes that Boston collectors were acquiring and such American painters as William Morris Hunt, Winslow Homer, G. Ruger Donoho, and George Fuller had been emulating since 1855.

On February 1, 1884, Hassam married Montreal-born Kathleen Maud Doane (1862–1946).[18] She traced her lineage back to Deacon John Doane, who had arrived in the Plymouth Colony in 1630 and served as the governor's assistant.[19] The couple moved to a "French flat" on Columbus Avenue in Boston's newly expanded South End. Here Hassam was inspired to paint his most remarkable early works, a series of street scenes in the South End and the even more fashionable Back Bay, Boston's two new neighborhoods (see fig. 3).[20] These poetic cityscapes, which reveal an illustrator's concern with genre details, echo the subjects of the watercolors of Swiss esplanades and Venetian piazzas Hassam made during his European travels but are focused on American urban life. They also suggest the influence of European painters of the juste-milieu, among them Giuseppe de Nittis, Jean Béraud, Edmond-Georges Grandjean, and Jean-François Raffaëlli, who used conservative styles to render Impressionist subjects. Hassam could have seen some of their works, which were reproduced in books and magazines and shown in Boston, New York, and Paris in the early 1880s.[21] He could also have encountered French Impressionist canvases in Boston's *Foreign Exhibition* and New York's *Pedestal Fund Art Loan Exhibition,* both held in late 1883, as well as on his summer 1883 trip to Europe and in the immense exhibition of French Impressionist art shown in New York in spring 1886.[22] These works would have reinforced his interest in modern subjects and capturing the effects of light by painting out of doors (see fig. 4).

Three years after Hassam returned from his grand tour, he went back to Europe to study. Accompanied by his wife,

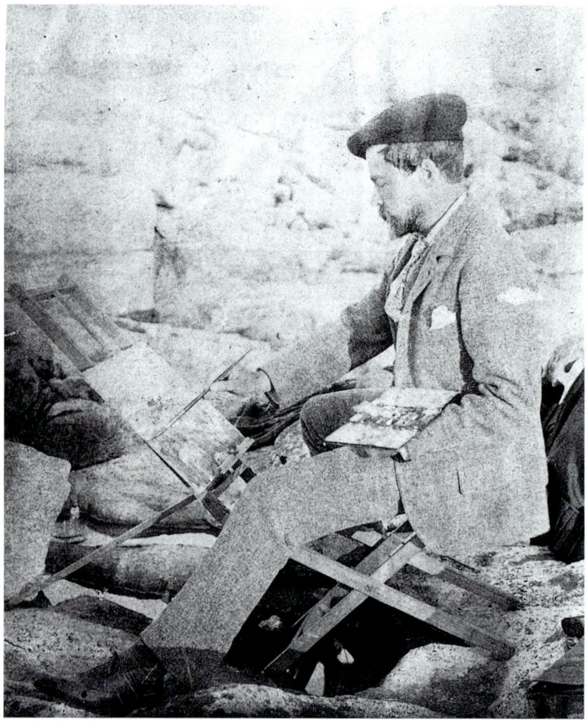

Fig. 4. Hassam painting at Appledore, Isles of Shoals, ca. 1886. Boston Public Library/Rare Book Department–Courtesy of the Trustees

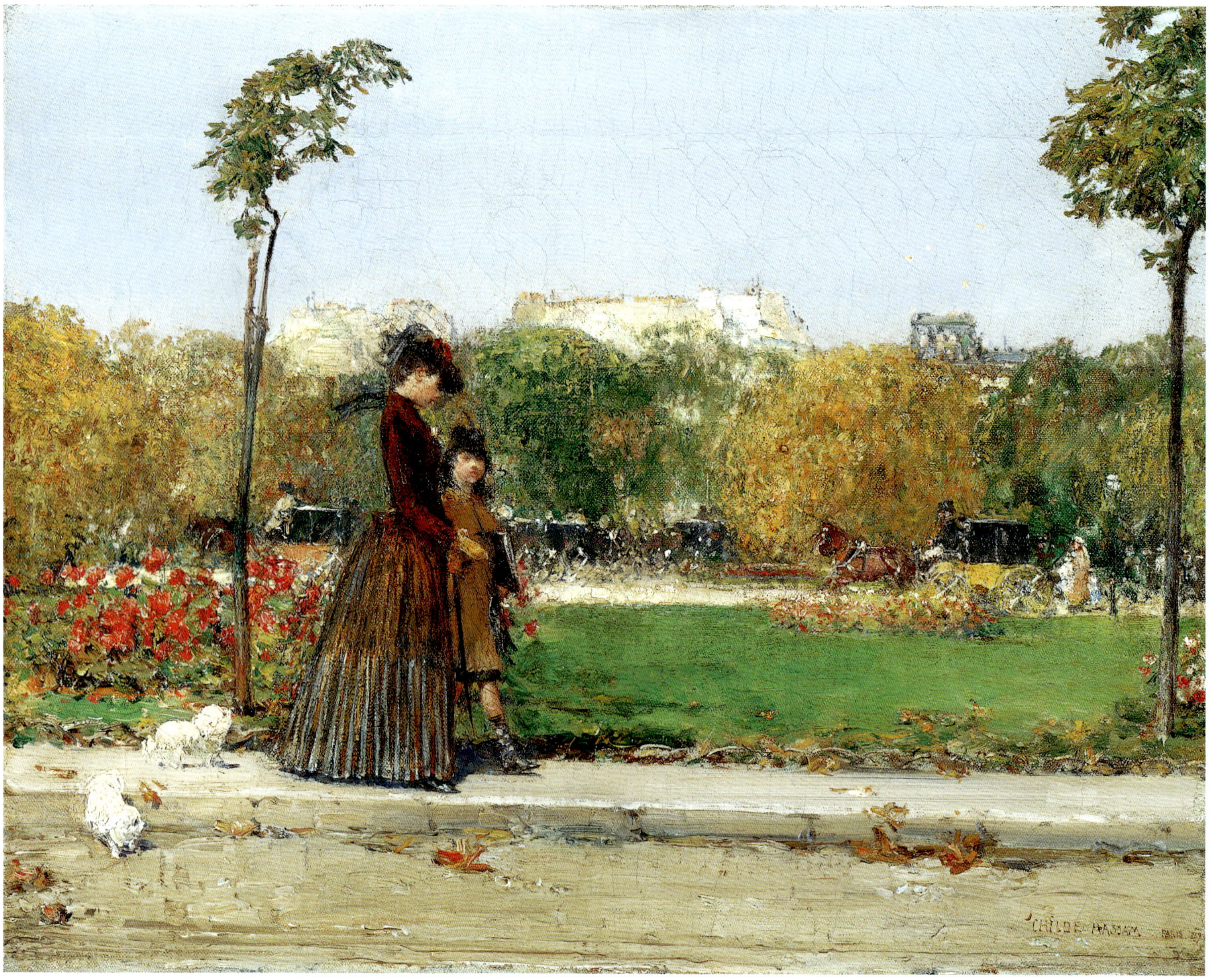

Fig. 5. Childe Hassam. *In the Park,* 1889. Oil on canvas, 12¾ x 16⅜ in. (32.4 x 41.6 cm). Lewis and Ali Sanders

he arrived in Paris in the fall of 1886, rented an apartment with an adjoining studio, and enrolled in the popular Académie Julian. By his own account, he worked hard,[23] but, diligence notwithstanding, he did not remedy his halting command of human anatomy. Hassam would always portray costumed men and women more convincingly than nudes, although he often enlisted professional nude models.

By the later 1880s instruction in Paris was de rigueur for aspiring American painters. Most of Hassam's compatriots went to Paris early in their careers and paid attention only to their academic studies. By contrast, when Hassam arrived in Paris he had already established a reputation, and he responded to the multiplicity of styles on display. He appears to have found inspiration not only in the work of juste-milieu painters and Impressionists, whose paintings were just finding an American market, but also in traditionalists such as Pierre Puvis de Chavannes, whose generalized figures may have validated for him his own schematic human forms, and even, perhaps, Postimpressionists such as Georges Seurat. Although Hassam liberated his brushwork in Paris and frequently lightened his palette to record brilliant sunlight (see fig. 5), he as often reiterated the tonal manner he had used in Boston (see fig. 6). His attraction to both conservatives and the avant-garde was like that of Pierre-Auguste Renoir, who embraced academic as well as Impressionist impulses, and whom Hassam esteemed without acknowledging his influence.[24]

Hassam maintained that he appreciated few artists other than the Dutch painter Johan Barthold Jongkind; British landscapists Turner, Richard Bonington, and John Constable; and Impressionist Alfred Sisley, whose English origins he emphasized.[25] He disavowed Claude Monet's influence, a manifestation of his annoyance at constantly being called the French master's American disciple, especially as his own reputation grew, and the influence of French Impressionists in general.[26] By contrast, his acknowledgment of his English and Dutch favorites is an expression of his unfailing appreciation of the Anglo-Dutch traditions upon which America was founded.

By the time Hassam settled in New York at the end of 1889, he was committed to Impressionism (see figs. 7, 8). Inspired by that style, he adopted informal compositions and high vantage points, used rapid strokes, and portrayed commonplace subjects in familiar metropolitan surroundings, albeit in a palette still alternately chromatic and tonal. He voiced his credo in 1892: "I believe the man who will go down to posterity is the man who paints his own time and the scenes of every-day life around him. . . . A true historical painter, it seems to me, is one who paints the life he sees about him, and so makes a record of his own epoch."[27] Hassam was more willing than William Merritt Chase, for example, to leave the bucolic parks and step onto New York's bustling boulevards. As the foremost Impressionist chronicler of the American urban scene, Hassam responded to Charles Baudelaire's prescription of 1863: "For the perfect *flâneur*, for the passionate spectator, it is an immense joy to set up house in the heart of the multitude, amid the ebb and flow of movement, in the midst of the fugitive and the infinite."[28] Hassam, however, always selected his subjects from the "heart of the multitude" with an eye to fashion and emphasized the "more smiling aspects of life," as William Dean Howells had urged novelists to do in 1891.[29] He exemplified the buoyant spirit of most of the American Impressionists, ignoring social ferment and viewing his dynamic and complicated period as if through rose-colored glasses.

Beginning in 1890 Hassam made long visits to New England locales that served artists and other city dwellers as retreats from modern urban pressures (see fig. 9). The same cheerful elitism and escapism that identify his city views mark the rural scenes he painted in these places.[30] Upon his death, critic Elisabeth Luther Cary observed: "Childe Hassam has gone and with him something irreplaceable has left American art. I know of no other painter with his power to make the world look convincingly joyous with its own joy, and this he seemed always able to do."[31] A few years later A. Hyatt Mayor, the Metropolitan Museum's curator of prints, noted: "Hassam's art reached its peak when he found in the New England freshness just the note that vibrated in sympathy with his delicately happy temperament."[32]

After his return to New York from a yearlong trip to Europe in 1897, Hassam began to reconsider his approach to Impressionist subjects. While he continued to portray New York, he eschewed the gritty themes preferred by the Ash Can School, retreated from the boulevards to depict secluded parks and elegant apartments (see fig. 10), and romanticized emblematic modern structures such as skyscrapers. Only when Fifth Avenue was festooned with colorful flags between 1916 and 1919 did he again celebrate the grand thoroughfare he had often described in earlier moments (see fig. 11).

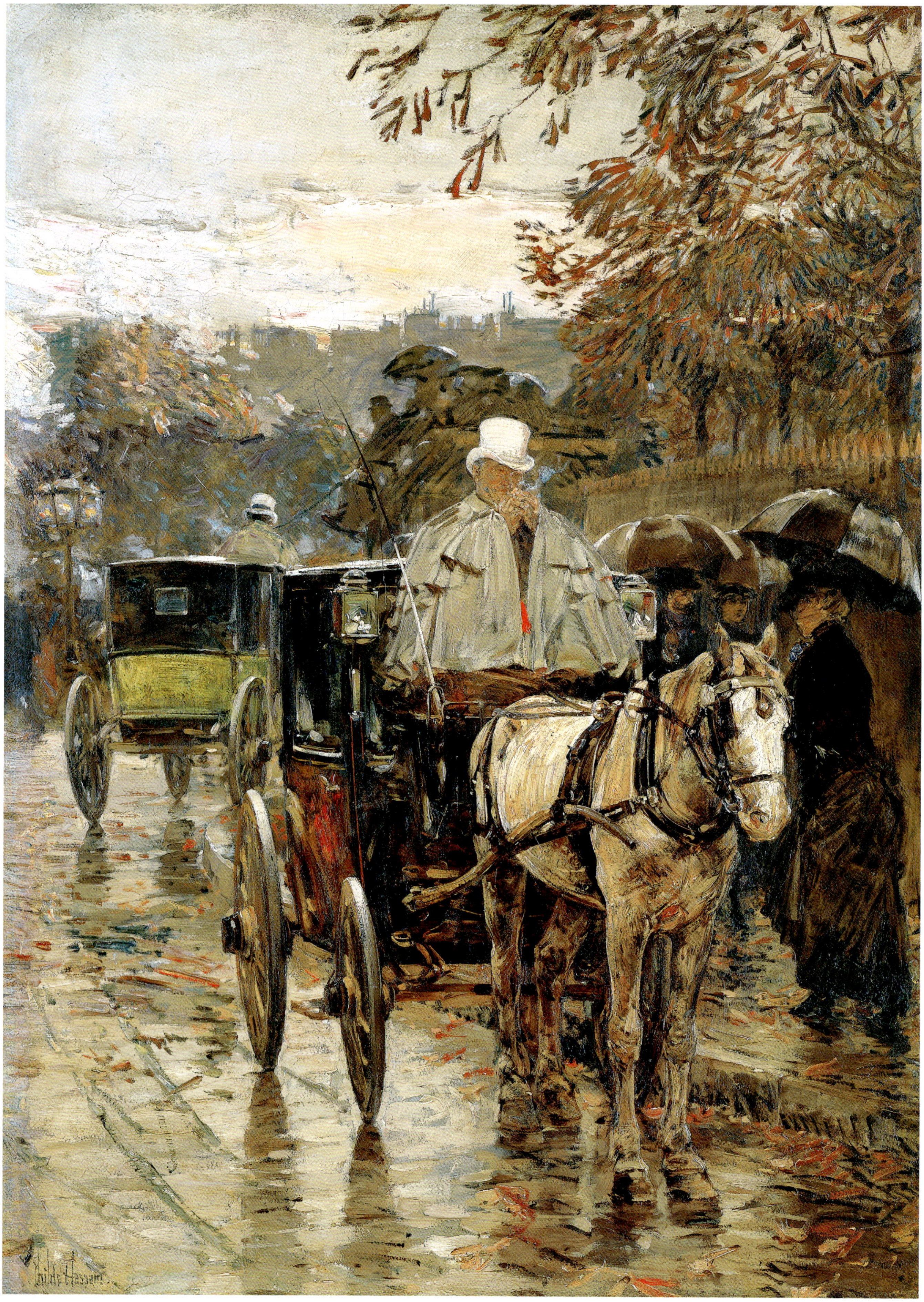

Fig. 6. Childe Hassam. *Carriage, Rue Bonaparte,* 1888. Oil on canvas, 41 x 30½ in. (104.1 x 77.5 cm). Private collection

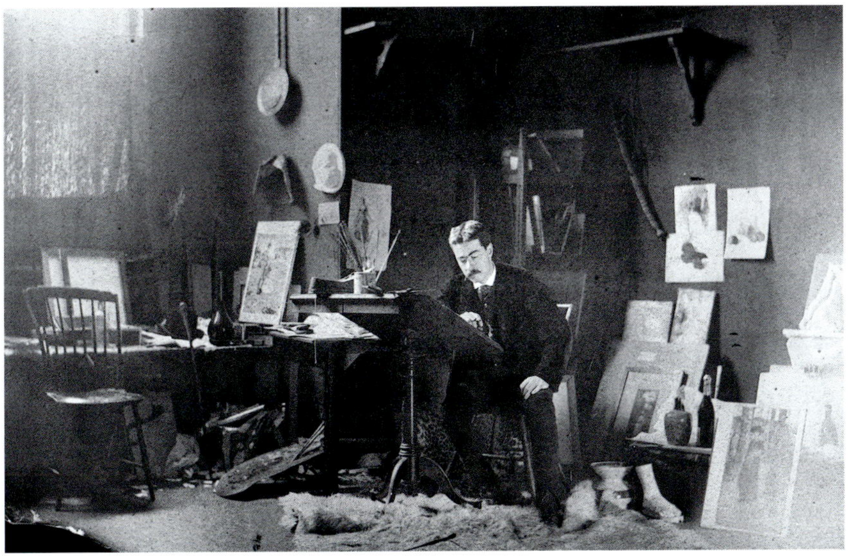

Fig. 7. Hassam in his studio, ca. 1890. Courtesy Portsmouth Athenaeum, New Hampshire

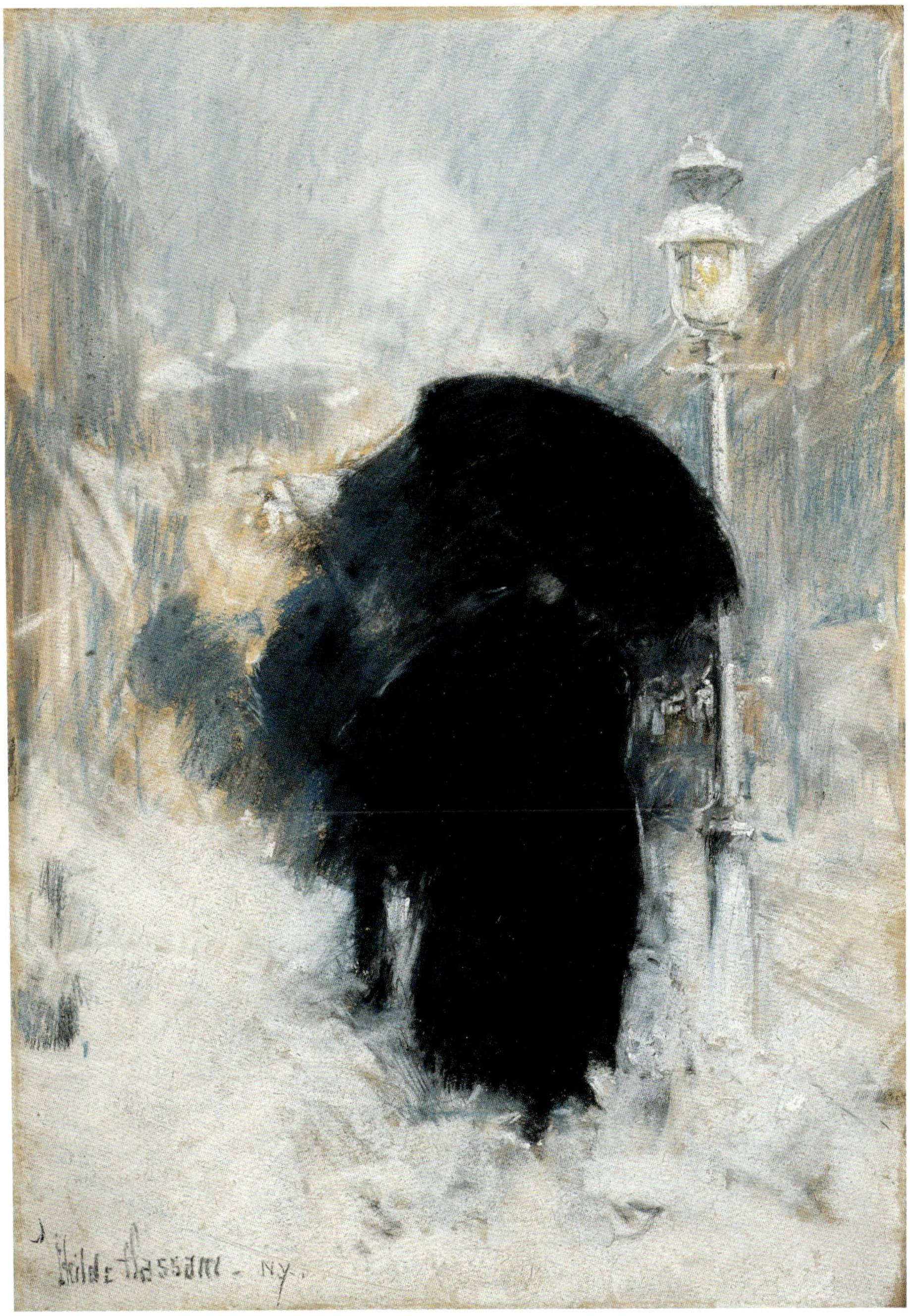

Fig. 8. Childe Hassam. *A New York Blizzard*, ca. 1890. Pastel on gray paper, 13¾ x 9½ in. (34.9 x 24.1 cm). Isabella Stewart Gardner Museum, Boston

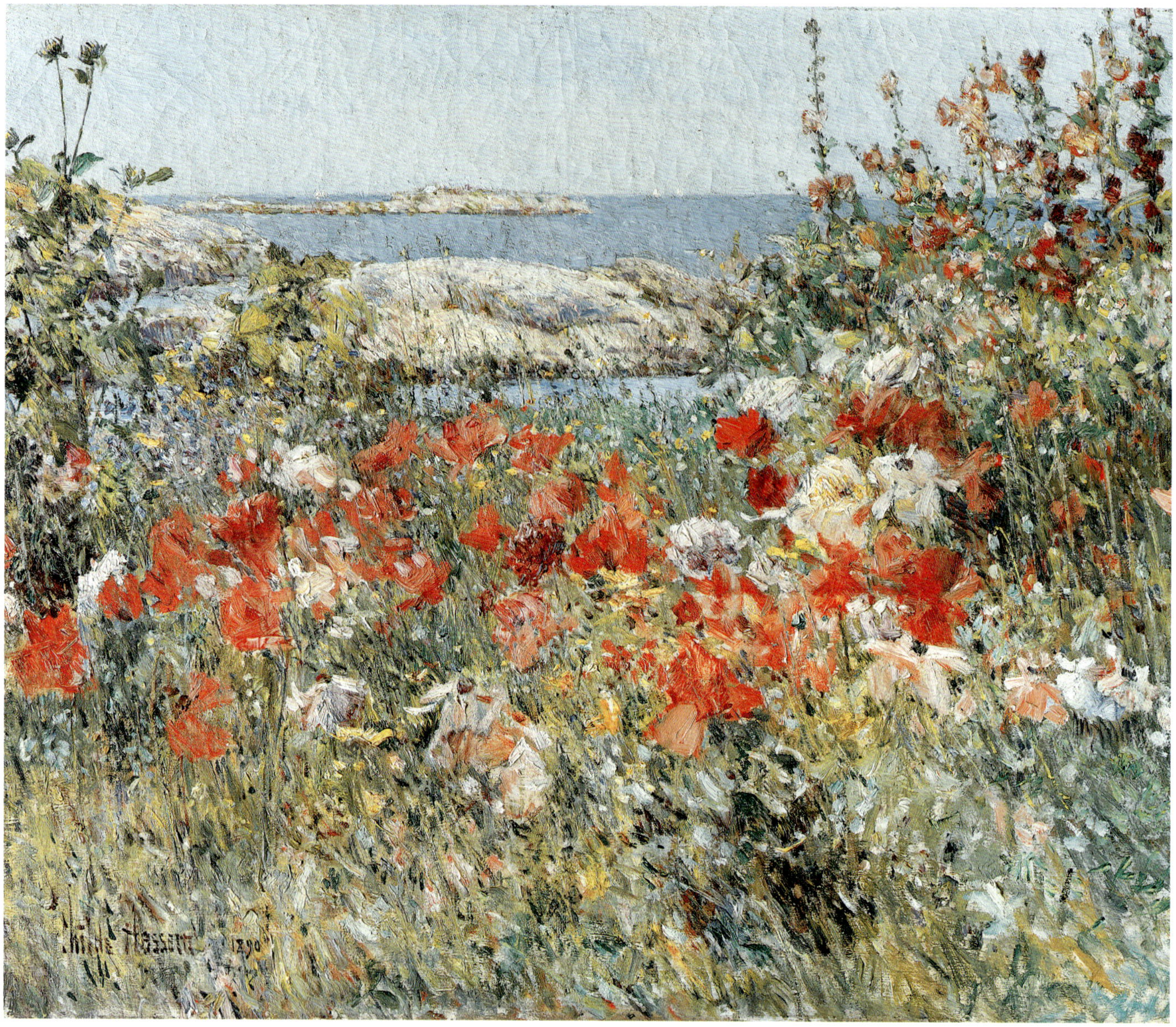

Fig. 9. Childe Hassam. *Celia Thaxter's Garden, Isles of Shoals, Maine,* 1890. Oil on canvas, 17 ¾ x 21 ½ in. (45.1 x 54.6 cm). The Metropolitan Museum of Art, New York. Anonymous Gift, 1994 1994.567

Beginning in 1898 Hassam added to his repertoire images of nude figures that embody symbolic and mythical ideals (see fig. 12).[33] The rapid pace of cultural change and the emergence of modern styles he found unfathomable may have motivated his decision to mine history and tradition. Critic James William Pattison remarked in 1908 of Hassam's works of this new kind, "It looks very much as if Hassam were seeking to hand his name down to posterity as a great

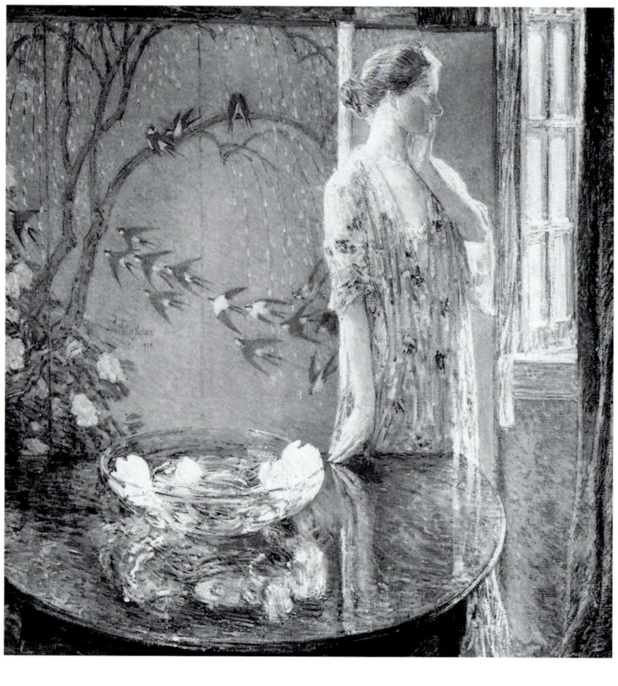

Fig. 10. Childe Hassam. *Spring Morning,* 1909. Oil on canvas, 42 x 40¼ in. (106.7 x 102.2 cm). Carnegie Museum of Art, Pittsburgh, Museum Purchase

Fig. 11. Childe Hassam. *The Avenue in the Rain,* February 1917. Oil on canvas, 42 x 22¼ in. (106.7 x 56.5 cm). White House Historical Association (White House Collection), Washington, D.C.

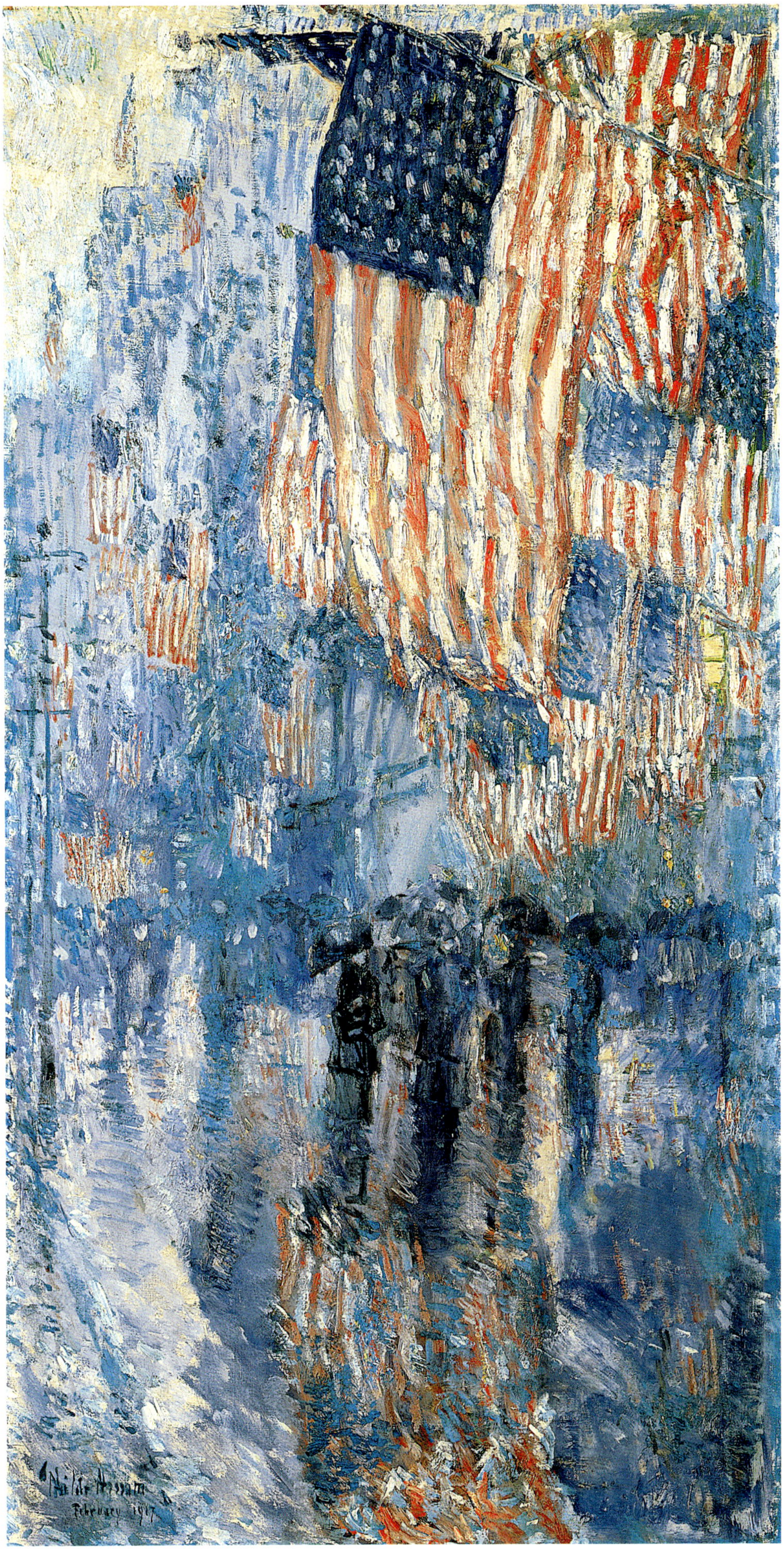

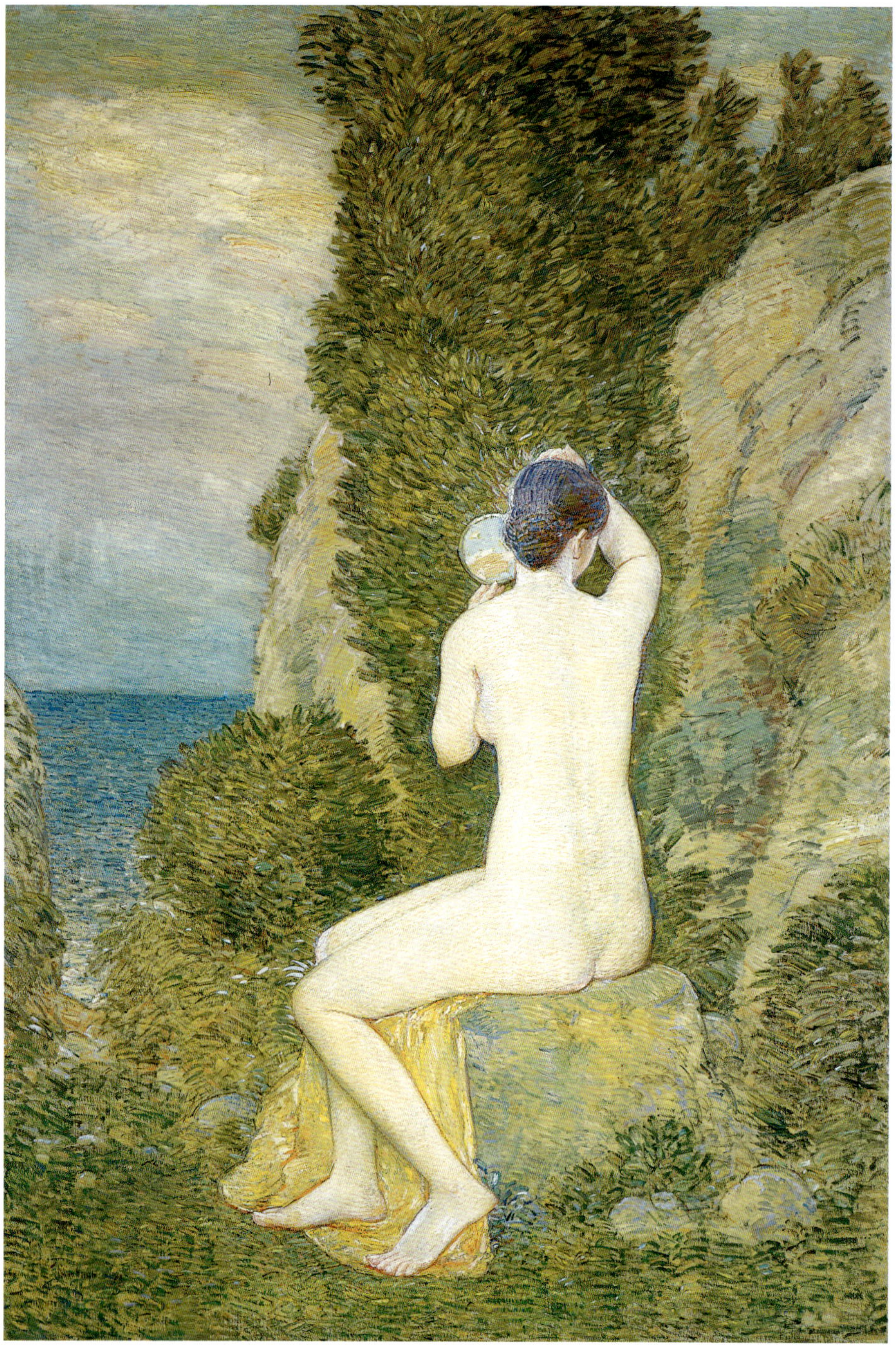

Fig. 12. Childe Hassam. *Aphrodite, Appledore,* 1908. Oil on canvas, 82 x 56 in. (208.3 x 142.2 cm). American Academy of Arts and Letters, New York

academical man, rather than a painter of light and air."[34] Numerous other influences also seem to have encouraged him to "hand his name down to posterity" by painting universal themes. He had recently studied great old master paintings in Europe and could have seen contemporary Symbolist works there as well. Moreover, he was increasingly in contact with members of Ten American Painters, the exhibiting organization he helped to found just after his return home in 1897.[35] The Ten included Robert Reid and Edward E. Simmons, painters of allegorical murals, and Thomas W. Dewing, who was producing Tonalist images of evocative feminine subjects. Hassam was drawn to their work and also respected the leaders of the contemporaneous American Renaissance movement, especially John La Farge and Kenyon Cox, who were reviving classical traditions. He admired the murals by Puvis de Chavannes in the Boston Public Library, the paradigmatic American Renaissance monument, and knew of John Singer Sargent's midcareer self-reinvention, epitomized in the esoteric murals he painted for that building.[36]

Although he was stimulated by the work of these contemporaries, Hassam was unusual among his peers in pursuing a goal he described as "treating the modern with the classic," often setting his nudes in identifiable Impressionistic

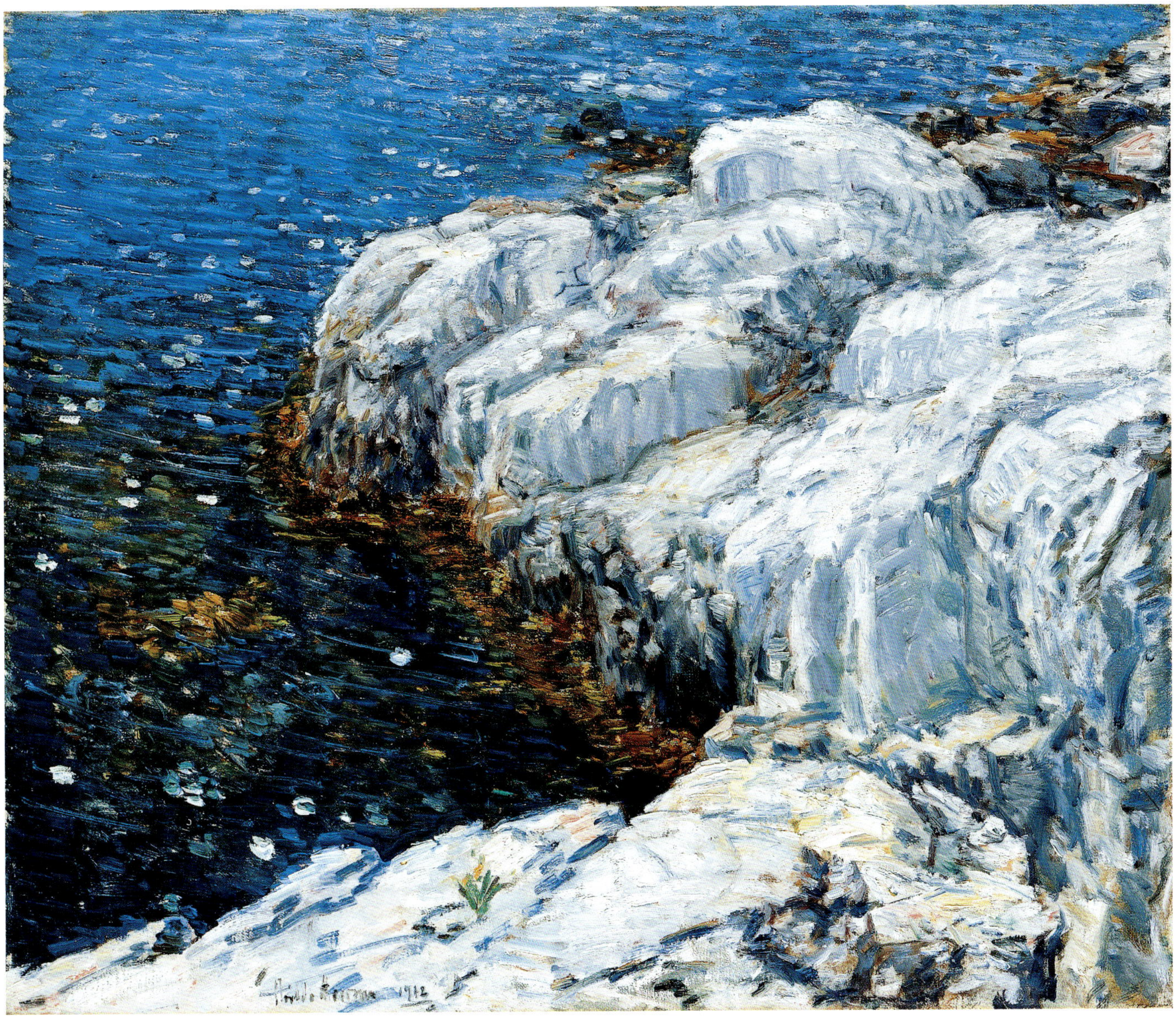

Fig. 13. Childe Hassam. *Jelly Fish,* 1912. Oil on canvas, 20⅛ x 24⅛ in. (51.1 x 61.3 cm). The John W. and Mildred L. Graves Collection, Wichita Art Museum, Kansas

landscapes.[37] Given his lack of academic training, however, his paintings of nudes recall the efforts of the inarticulate Demosthenes to be a great orator. But they were less successful than Demosthenes' attempts and bewildered many critics, who tended to prefer his more naturalistic works.[38]

Whatever his subjects, Hassam never renounced Impressionism's staccato brushwork (see fig. 13). However, some canvases done about the turn of the century—for example, his European scenes of 1897—reveal him experimenting with painting very thinly (see fig. 330), and others show him seeking a thick, tapestried effect (see fig. 141). In a story that Hassam enjoyed recounting, his artist friend Frederic Remington reacted to a plein air work, probably of the latter sort: "Well! I have an aunt up state who can knit a better picture than that."[39] Responding more gently to Hassam's technique, Pattison observed in 1908: "The manner of painting used by Childe Hassam is so distinctly individual that it may be truthfully said that it is like no other."[40]

In his twentieth-century works Hassam often generalized figures; tightened the structure and control of his compositions; emphasized flattened surfaces over three-dimensional illusions, distilling urban and rural views, nudes, and still-life setups into decorative arrangements (see fig. 14); and experimented with bolder design and vibrant, even arbitrary color. However, in contrast to Monet, whose audacious late style expanded earlier ideas and explored new possibilities, Hassam—like J. Alden Weir, Maurice Prendergast, and many of his other American contemporaries—fell short of

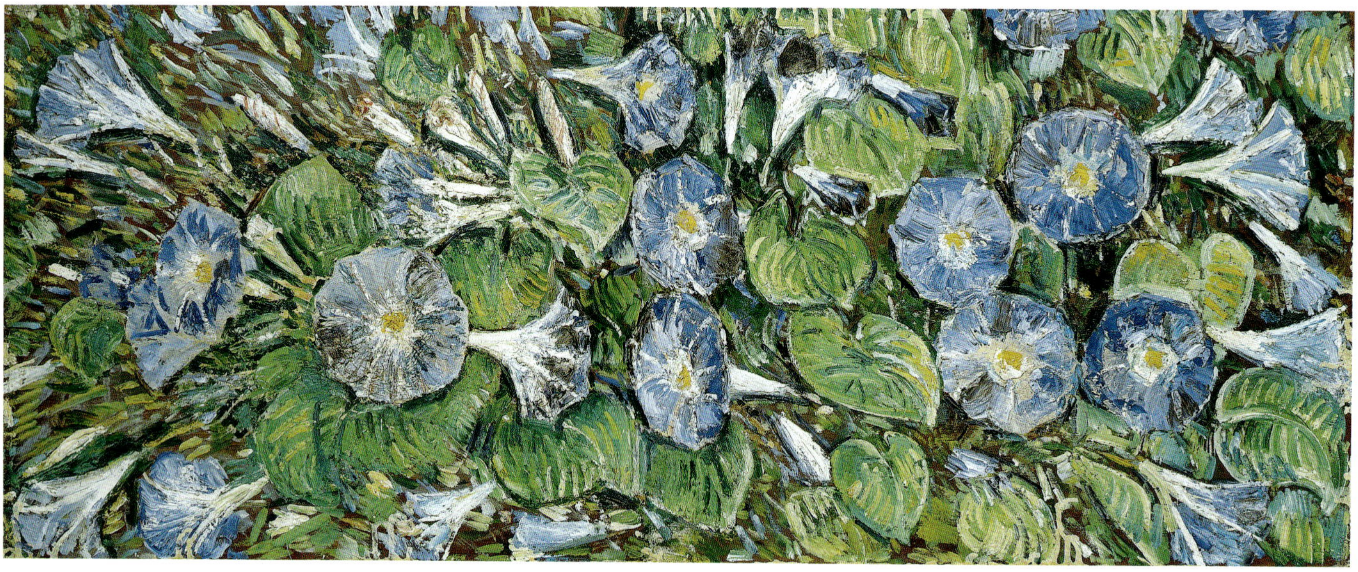

Fig. 14. Childe Hassam. *Heavenly Blues,* 1931. Oil on canvas, 13 x 33½ in. (33 x 85.1 cm). American Academy of Arts and Letters, New York

his previous standard of inventiveness and technical finesse in his late works. For example, his wooden golfers—who should invoke the legacy of Homer's croquet players, Thomas Eakins's scullers, and George Bellows's prizefighters—often discredit his enthusiasm for the sport.

Among Hassam's most successful late works are many of the etchings to which he turned his attention beginning in 1912 and more seriously in 1915 and which engaged him for the rest of his life (see fig. 15).[41] His interest in this popular medium echoed that of James McNeill Whistler and Francis Seymour Haden, both based in London, and friends in America such as Weir, Joseph Pennell, and Frank W. Benson. A factor in Hassam's attraction to etchings was their origins in seventeenth-century Dutch printmaking and their concomitant evocation of America's colonial period—all aspects of which appealed to him. His historicist's devotion to the medium prompted him to print etchings on antique papers and to display only them, not his paintings, in his colonial house in East Hampton.[42]

Hassam and his wife (see fig. 16) were childless but nevertheless had substantial financial needs. They maintained a gracious lifestyle, occupying a series of spacious, well-located

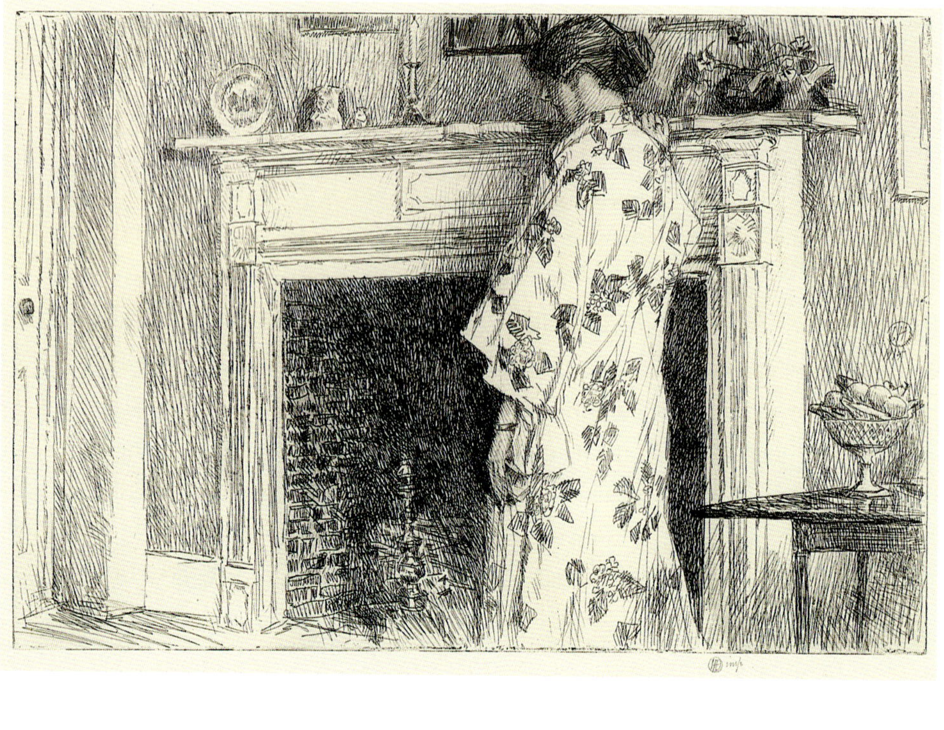

Fig. 15. Childe Hassam. *The White Kimono,* 1915. Etching and drypoint on cream laid paper (French, Ingres d'Arches, *MBM* watermark), 7⅜ x 10⅞ in. (18.7 x 27.6 cm). The Metropolitan Museum of Art, New York. Harris Brisbane Dick Fund, 1917 17.3.494 (C47)

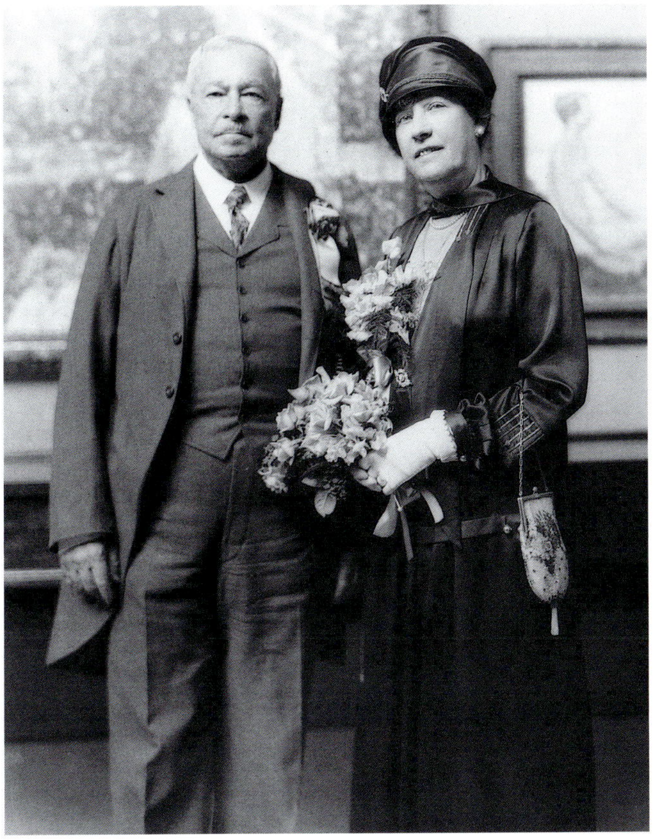

apartments with adjacent studios in Manhattan and spending summers in New England; in August 1919, at the end of Hassam's most successful decade, they purchased a house and land in fashionable East Hampton. Energized by necessity as well as by competence in and curiosity about many media, the versatile artist rendered an impressive range of subjects—landscapes, cityscapes, still lifes, and figures—in more than two thousand oils, watercolors (see fig. 17), and pastels and other drawings, as well as illustrations for articles and books. His prints included more than four hundred etchings (see fig. 18), lithographs, and lithotints. During a period when most American artists supplemented their incomes by teaching, taking on commissions for portraits or

Fig. 16. Hassam and his wife, Maud, at the opening of his 1927 retrospective exhibition at the American Academy of Arts and Letters. American Academy of Arts and Letters, New York

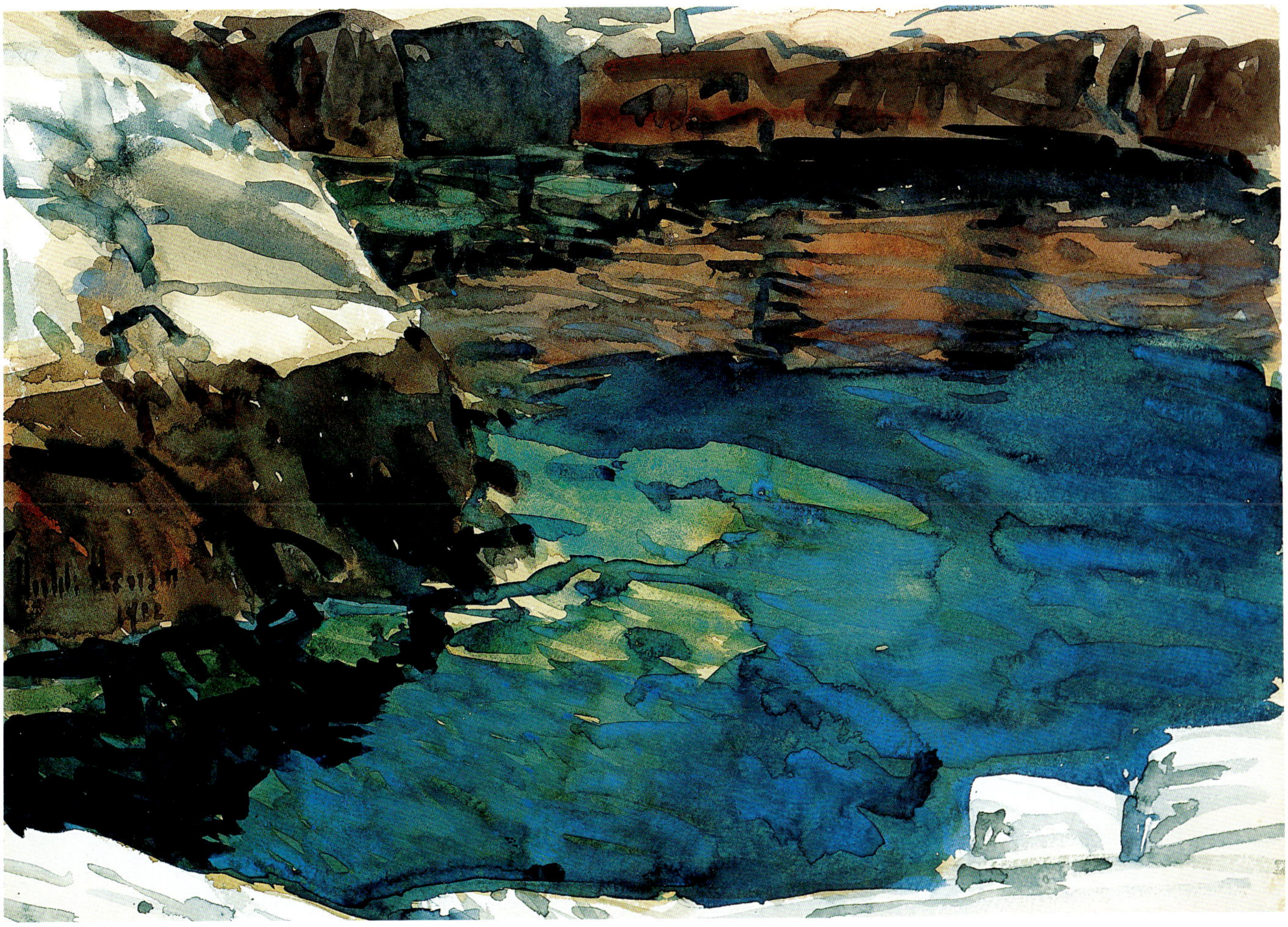

Fig. 17. Childe Hassam. *The Cove,* 1912. Watercolor on paper, 14 x 20 in. (35.6 x 50.8 cm). The John W. and Mildred L. Graves Collection, Wichita Art Museum, Kansas

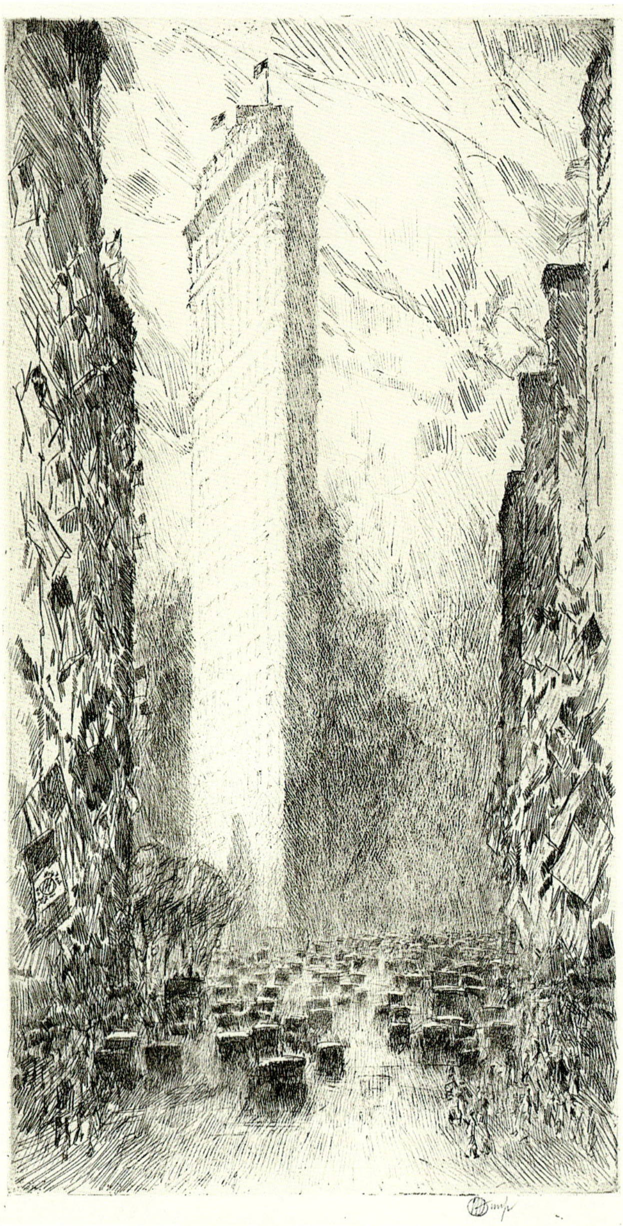

Fig. 18. Childe Hassam. *Washington's Birthday, Fifth Avenue and 23rd Street,* 1916. Etching, 12⅞ x 8¼ in. (32.7 x 21 cm). Print Collection, Miriam and Ira D. Wallach Division of Art, Prints, and Photographs, The New York Public Library, Astor, Lenox, and Tilden Foundations (C68)

murals, or relying on work as illustrators, Hassam depended on marketing his large and varied output.

By 1911 Hassam's paintings were included in the collections of the leading museums of many American cities. His works could also be seen far and wide in the United States in commercial galleries, annual shows of professional organizations and clubs, fairs, and other diverse exhibitions. He had at least one one-man show in a museum or commercial gallery every year between 1905 and 1935 except 1921 and 1931; sometimes thirty or forty of his works were on display simultaneously. "In 1920 he said the revenue from his brush that year was $100,000," according to a 1935 report.[43] Painter Jerome Myers wrote in 1940: "In the army of artists, Childe Hassam was like a major general, covered with medals and honors, with stripes of long service [fig. 19]. He commanded the art dealers, issuing his orders of the day, supervising the galleries, a general whose word was law to 57th Street. He was an artist to salute for his excellent record, in full possession of his power of production and—what is a major point—with a keen knowledge of distribution, the tactical ability to place his work."[44] At his death in 1935, Hassam's gross estate, comprising mainly stocks and bonds—and exclusive of the many works of art he bequeathed to the American Academy of Arts and Letters—was appraised at $212,710, equivalent to about $2,790,655 in 2002.[45]

Hassam's zealous self-promotion helped his colleagues, an example being his spearheading the formation of the Ten (fig. 20). The painters who joined this group were members of the National Academy of Design and/or the Society of American Artists and to varying degrees were committed to Impressionism.[46] Dissatisfied with the constraints and miscellaneous look of the annual exhibitions of the established organizations, they resigned from them presumably under

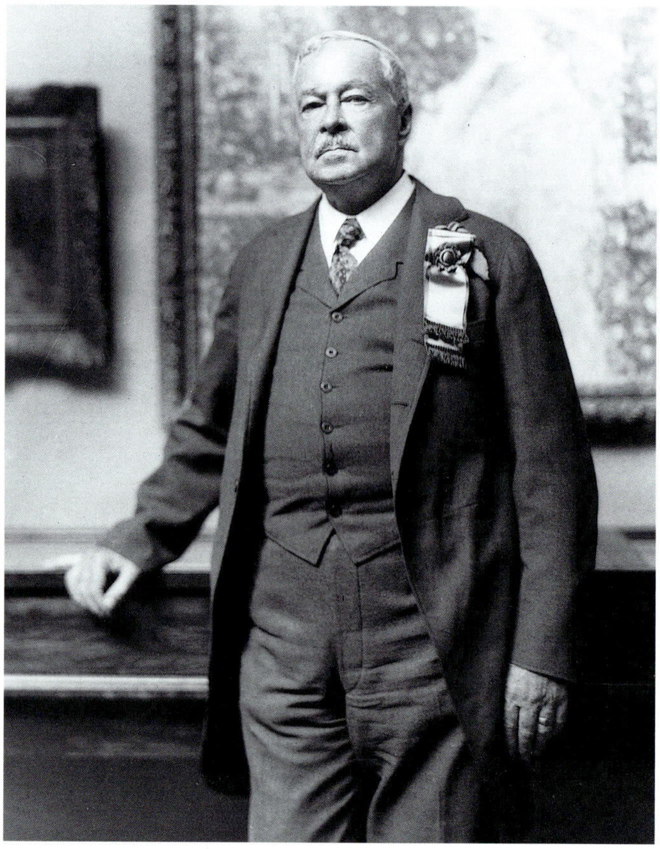

Fig. 19. Hassam at the opening of his 1927 retrospective exhibition at the American Academy of Arts and Letters. American Academy of Arts and Letters, New York

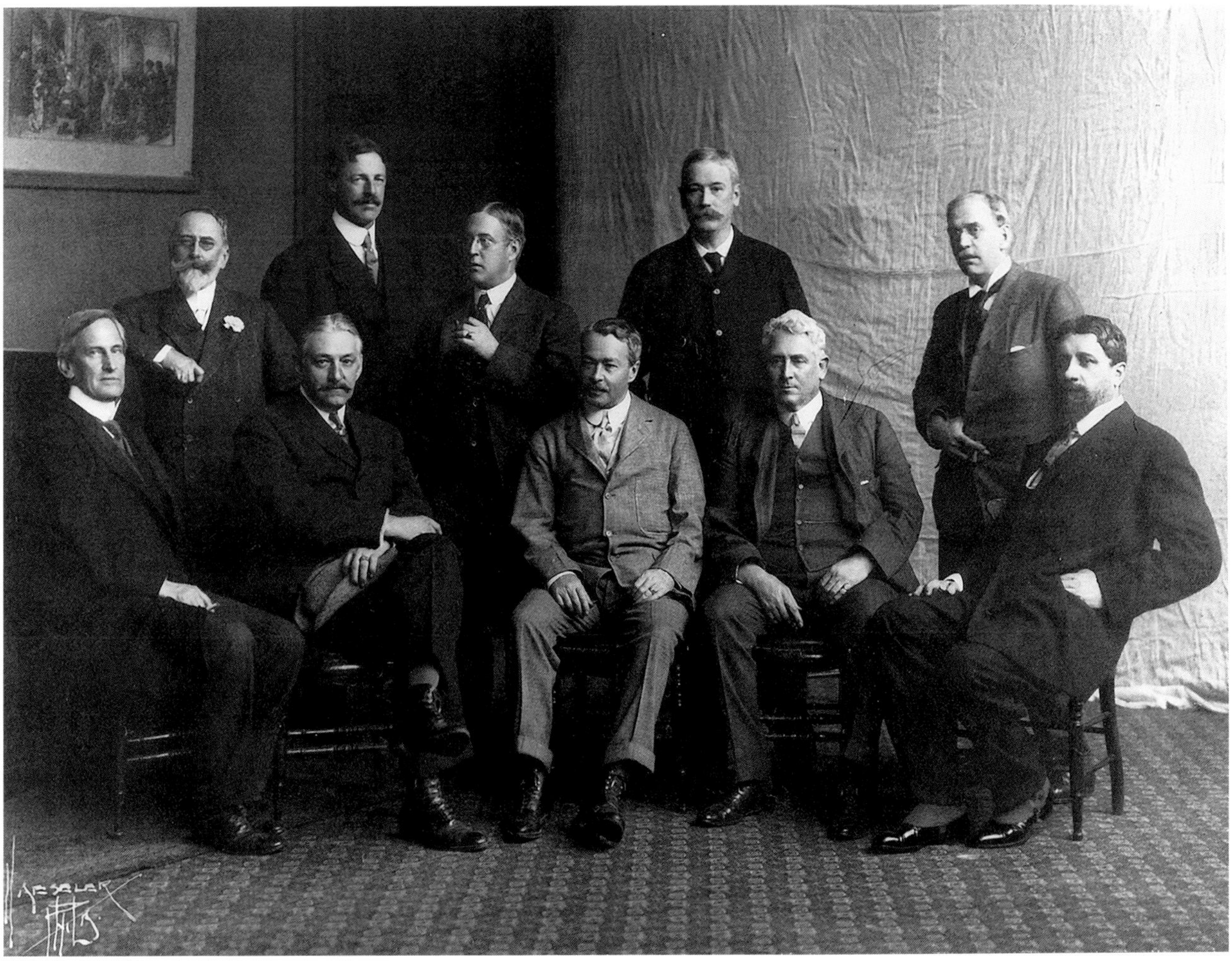

Fig. 20. The Ten, 1908. Left to right, seated: Edward Simmons, Willard L. Metcalf, Childe Hassam, J. Alden Weir, Robert Reid; standing: William Merritt Chase, Frank W. Benson, Edmund C. Tarbell, Thomas W. Dewing, Joseph R. DeCamp. Milch Gallery Records, 1911–1980, Archives of American Art, Smithsonian Institution, Washington, D.C.

the leadership of Hassam—who was aided by Weir and John H. Twachtman. Guided by these three, they incorporated the Ten on December 17, 1897, and held annual shows in New York (and occasionally other cities) between 1898 and 1919. Hassam was the only member to contribute to all the annual displays, which he sometimes dominated.[47]

Some of Hassam's friends admired his awesome productivity. Weir, his closest comrade, for example, noted in a November 13, 1910, letter to Colonel Charles Erskine Scott Wood, a Portland, Oregon, lawyer and collector: "He [Hassam] produces more canvases than any man I know, thirty or forty in a season seem nothing to him. I wish I had that power. I count on six or eight and think I am doing well."[48] Weir reiterated to Wood two months later: "He is the greatest producer of any I know."[49] But others worried that he was too facile. Theodore Robinson jotted in his diary in February 1896: "To the A[merican] A[rt] A[ssociation] to see Hassam's pictures. After a certain astonishment at the cleverness of his painting of detail, one is struck by its superficiality, the glitter and nothing beside, 'tinsel' sort of art, a lack of something, not of endeavor, of a certain kind."[50] Jerome Myers called Hassam "a brilliant but incessant painter" and griped, "Between us there was a gulf of income."[51] Critics also disparaged Hassam's industriousness. A reviewer of the 1906 exhibition of the Ten, which included only four of his works, declared that "probably Mr. Hassam paints too many pictures."[52]

A sociable fellow, Hassam belonged to numerous clubs, served on countless art juries, won every imaginable award and honor, and was elected to virtually every distinguished art society.[53] His identification with Impressionism, however, marked him as an artist of the nineteenth century, although he lived and worked through the first third of the twentieth. He was recognized as a dean of American art but may yet have felt marginalized as his style diverged from modern approaches. While he appears to have responded to Postimpressionism and Symbolism—in the form of paintings by Seurat, van Gogh, and Arthur B. Davies, for example—he disappointed critics who were coming to terms with Cubism, Fauvism, Surrealism, and abstraction. His increasing detachment from "the heart of the multitude," heavy drinking, and diatribes against modernism may have reflected his discontent.

Some friends described Hassam's problem drinking (and others may have hesitated to mention it). For example, while Hassam was at the Holley House in Cos Cob, Connecticut, in October and November 1902, Constant Holley MacRae referred to his excessive drinking in letters to her mother, who owned the boardinghouse. On October 1, for instance, MacRae wrote: "Muley has straightened himself out—about time."[54] But his sobriety was erratic. In an undated interview Mrs. MacRae and her painter husband, Elmer MacRae, recalled: "Another time he [Hassam] came back [to the Holley House] when he had had too much to drink & was carefully coming up the steps in front of the house, pulling himself up by the rails, suddenly one gave way & he went rolling down among the lilac bushes."[55] And in February 1904 Weir worried about Hassam's drinking in a letter to their mutual friend Colonel Wood: "Old Hassam has been off on a bat for three weeks but is all right again."[56] During Hassam's visit to Oregon later the same year, Wood was vexed, telling his daughter: "Mr. Hassam has taken advantage of the trip to have an attack, and I hope to bring him back in a clear and sane condition. Poor fellow. My heart aches for one with such cravings."[57]

Hassam despised most modern art. He was one of the two oldest American painters represented in the landmark Armory Show of 1913 (the other was Weir), displaying six oils, five pastels, and one drawing. But he ridiculed the innovative exhibitors. These artists, he told Lockman in 1927, "went to the extreme" by showing "not very beautiful things, with one eye in the top of the head and the other in the chin, and all the absurdities in an attempt to attract attention."[58] In a 1928 article chronicling his likes (fellow American painters such as Weir and Twachtman, Albert Pinkham Ryder and Winslow Homer) and dislikes (foreign artists, collectors of their works, and critics and institutions favorably disposed to them), Hassam again damned the Armory Show: "It was successful, enormously so on account of the shockingly foolish things there. It was so idiotic in spots that it captured the public. Barnum would have been tickled to death with it."[59]

Even more reactionary tirades against modern art punctuate Hassam's later conversations. As Homer Saint-Gaudens observed in 1941: "Like so many other men who were revolutionists in their youth, in his age he developed an almost malignant intolerance of any fresh group who wished to give a new approach, a new style, or a new meaning to a new world."[60] In a 1932 birthday interview, for example, Hassam proclaimed his aversion to the creators, purveyors, and supporters of contemporary European art, grumbling: "Our own art is as good as any other in the world today . . . , and it certainly should be the most important to us, in spite of all the little snobs who come out of college and litter the land with encomiums on every dab of paint that comes out of dressmaking Paris." He added: "Art in America is managed, directed and run by old women. It's a racket for foreign art dealers, and our native painters, every whit as good and usually better than the Europeans, haven't a chance." Of critics he fulminated: "Everybody is writing about art today, and none of them knows what he is talking about. There are a few competent critics: Royal Cortissoz and Elizabeth [*sic*] Luther Cary. The rest are dolts, asses, dullards."[61]

Asked in 1933 "what he thought of the so-called modernistic art," Hassam read extracts from a tribute to his friend the late Gari Melchers, which he was preparing for delivery at the American Academy of Arts and Letters. He noted that Melchers "abhorred what I call the cult of the incompetent, and what a valued writer of the Academy characterized years ago as Ellis Island art."[62] Just as cranky in 1934, Hassam told an interviewer: "If modern art means the formless atrocities which are turned out by incompetents and sold under the guise of art by designing foreign dealers, then I have no use for it."[63]

Hassam's strident defense of American art, which he insisted was unjustly ignored in favor of the foreign product, amplified the spirit of isolationism and cultural nationalism that surfaced in the United States in the 1920s and 1930s. That he equated modern art with foreign art and blamed its success on aggressive European dealers also imply that his patriotic pride in his Puritan heritage had evolved into xenophobia and nativism.[64] He expressed his support of American art more constructively by bequeathing to New York's American Academy of Arts and Letters his studio contents—ultimately 326 oil paintings (including 19 decorative panels), 89 watercolors, and 33 pastels—and recommending that proceeds from their sale enrich the

Hassam Fund, with which works by American and Canadian artists would be purchased for presentation to American and Canadian museums.[65]

Despite his alienation from advanced art and forward-looking commentators, Hassam retained faithful advocates, including conservative critics Cortissoz, Cary, and Frederic Newlin Price, and his death at the age of seventy-five, on August 27, 1935, provoked effusive obituaries. One writer even argued that his works were still pertinent in relation to contemporary art: "Long before the days when the American scene became popular, Hassam found his favorite themes in [New] England, New York, and Long Island."[66]

The later 1930s witnessed both the unraveling of Hassam's reputation and the collapse of interest in American Impressionism. Although an appreciative biography of Hassam by Adeline Adams appeared in 1938 and the American Academy of Arts and Letters featured his works in an exhibition held at the time of the 1939 New York World's Fair,[67] a less positive note was struck in the publication accompanying the Brooklyn Museum's 1937 exhibition *Leaders of American Impressionism*. The curator, John I. H. Baur, asserted that Hassam, along with Weir, Twachtman, and Mary Cassatt, were the "pioneer Impressionists" who had "contributed most to the inauguration and development of Impressionism in America." Baur explained, however, that with Hassam's death "the movement is dead, for Hassam outlived it in this country just as Monet [did] in France."[68]

During the 1940s and 1950s, as modernism burgeoned, attracting an increasingly appreciative audience, and cultural nationalism continued to flourish, American Impressionism received only occasional attention. In spring 1943 a display of twenty-one oils and thirty-three watercolors by Hassam appeared at New York's Milch Galleries, where it was deemed more successful than concurrent exhibitions featuring Ernest Lawson and Theodore Robinson.[69] In March 1948, when Hassam's etchings were shown in New York at the Grand Central Art Galleries, he was called a "belated Impressionist," and demand and prices for his erstwhile popular prints were said to be "down considerably."[70] The conservative journal *American Artist* kept Hassam's name alive during the 1950s with laudatory articles on his watercolors and prints, but even in those pages he was ranked among the "abandoned geniuses" by 1960.[71] *Art News* slammed a February 1958 exhibition of Hassam's 1932–33 Long Island paintings at Milch Galleries, maintaining that they "represent[ed his] first, timid efforts to go beyond Impressionism" and mocking his attempt to Americanize the French style. "He did put some American soft-drink bottles in his still-lifes," the reviewer sneered.[72] The *New York Times* was more complimentary but nevertheless concluded: "Hassam, as good an impressionist as America ever produced, cooled his fires in later years. . . . The sparkle of his early work dwindled to sunlit glimpses from the seventeenth tee."[73]

The revival of Hassam's reputation began in the mid-1960s. A February 1964 display of thirty-seven works at New York's Hirschl and Adler Galleries was called "the first important exhibition in a long time" by a sympathetic critic, the sculptor (and Weir's son-in-law) Mahonri Sharp Young.[74] A gathering of seventy-five works, organized in 1965 by the Corcoran Gallery of Art, Washington, D.C., traveled to the Museum of Fine Arts, Boston; the Currier Gallery of Art, Manchester, New Hampshire; and the Gallery of Modern Art, New York. The Corcoran's director, Charles E. Buckley, noted that this was the "first comprehensive exhibition of his work held in an American museum" since the 1929 retrospective at the Albright Art Gallery in Buffalo.[75] Also during the 1960s pioneering collectors—Mr. and Mrs. Arthur G. Altschul, Mr. and Mrs. Irving Mitchell Felt, Mr. and Mrs. Daniel Fraad, Mr. and Mrs. Raymond J. Horowitz, and Mr. and Mrs. Meyer P. Potamkin, for example—began to acquire American Impressionist pictures, which reflected and encouraged interest in the style.

Commercial and scholarly attention to Hassam and American Impressionism grew rapidly in the early 1970s as cultural nationalism subsided and available French Impressionist works became scarce and increasingly expensive. An immense exhibition entitled *French Impressionists Influence American Artists* was held at the Lowe Art Museum in Coral Gables, Florida, in spring 1971; the museum's director introduced the catalogue by remarking, "A style in American art that has received little attention is that of American Impressionism."[76] The following year Donelson F. Hoopes published an overview of American Impressionism, and 130 of Hassam's works appeared in a retrospective organized by the University of Arizona Museum of Art and shown also at the Santa Barbara Museum of Art.[77] In 1973 a major exhibition of American Impressionism was organized by the National Gallery of Art, Washington, D.C., and traveled to New York, Cincinnati, and Raleigh. Hassam's *Duck Island*, 1906 (Dallas Museum of Art), appeared on the catalogue's cover.[78] Also in 1973 The Metropolitan Museum of Art hosted an exhibition of the Horowitz collection, and in 1974 Richard J. Boyle's survey of American Impressionism appeared.[79] All these displays and publications signaled the beginning of the commercial and scholarly industry in American Impressionism that has flourished for the last thirty years.[80]

The Metropolitan Museum of Art, which accessioned its first canvas by Hassam in 1909, had manifested little interest in American Impressionism until that date. A few paintings by artists associated with American Impressionism had entered the collection between 1888 and 1893, but these canvases were conservative and tonal.[81] In 1898 the Museum's Art Committee signaled its disdain for more radical American Impressionism when it declined the gift of the late Theodore Robinson's *Port Ben, Delaware and Hudson Canal,* 1892 (Pennsylvania Academy of the Fine Arts, Philadelphia), from the Society of American Artists, declaring that the canvas "represented a class of painting that should not be encouraged."[82] In April 1899 William T. Evans, a leading collector of American art, offered the Museum Robinson's *Valley of the Seine from Giverny Heights,* 1892 (Corcoran Gallery of Art, Washington, D.C.). However, Evans offended the Metropolitan's director by obtaining the Society of American Artists' endorsement before proposing the gift to the trustees, and this second effort to memorialize Robinson at the Metropolitan failed.[83] In 1906 the Museum reversed itself on Robinson, perhaps in deference to Evans, accepting his gift of the artist's lifesize—and relatively conservative—Giverny figure painting *A Girl and Cow* (*La Vachère*) (fig. 21).[84]

Much more significant for the representation of American Impressionism at the Metropolitan was the establishment in January 1906 of the George A. Hearn Fund, intended to finance the Museum's purchase of works by living American artists.[85] Hearn, a Museum trustee and passionate collector and supporter of American art, served as the institution's de facto curator of American paintings, directed his endowment fund's expenditures, and gave some paintings outright. Under his influence the full spectrum of American Impressionist canvases slowly began to enter the Metropolitan's collection. In 1907 the Museum purchased with the Hearn Fund Robert Reid's *Fleur de Lis,* ca. 1895–1900 (07.140). In 1909 it accepted two gifts from Hearn: Hassam's *Coast Scene, Isles of Shoals* (fig. 22), which Hearn had bought in 1908, and Twachtman's *Waterfall,* ca. 1889–91 (09.25.2); it also purchased with the Hearn Fund Walter Elmer Schofield's *Sand Dunes near Lelant, Cornwall, England,* 1905 (09.26.1) and Cassatt's *Mother and Child* (*Baby Getting Up from His Nap*), ca. 1899 (09.27).[86]

Soon after Hearn gave *Coast Scene, Isles of Shoals* to the Metropolitan, Hassam expressed his wish that the Museum more fully recognize living American artists. Writing to a friend in October 1909 of his keen anticipation of a large display of his art at the Carnegie Institute's annual exhibition the following spring, he added: "It proves that there is interest enough in the work of a living American painter for them to go to the great expense and trouble of collecting his most important works and showing them properly in an adequate space—a large gallery. If the Metropolitan Museum would do this, it would at least be original and

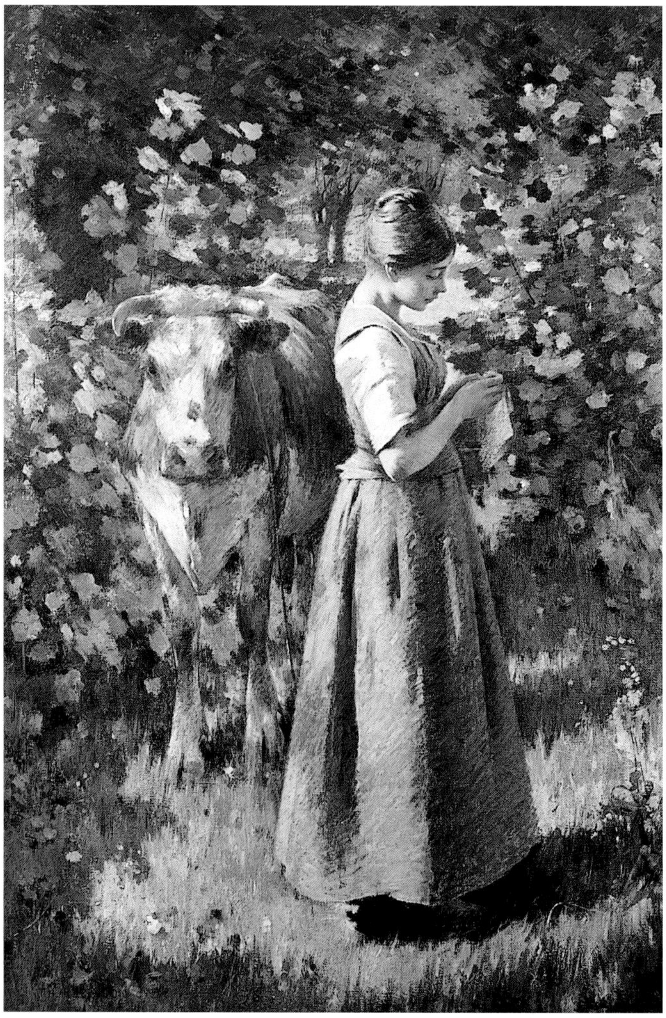

Fig. 21. Theodore Robinson. *A Girl and Cow (La Vachère),* 1888. Oil on canvas, 86⅜ x 59⅝ in. (219.4 x 151.4 cm). The Baltimore Museum of Art: Given in Memory of Joseph Katz by his Children BMA 1966.46

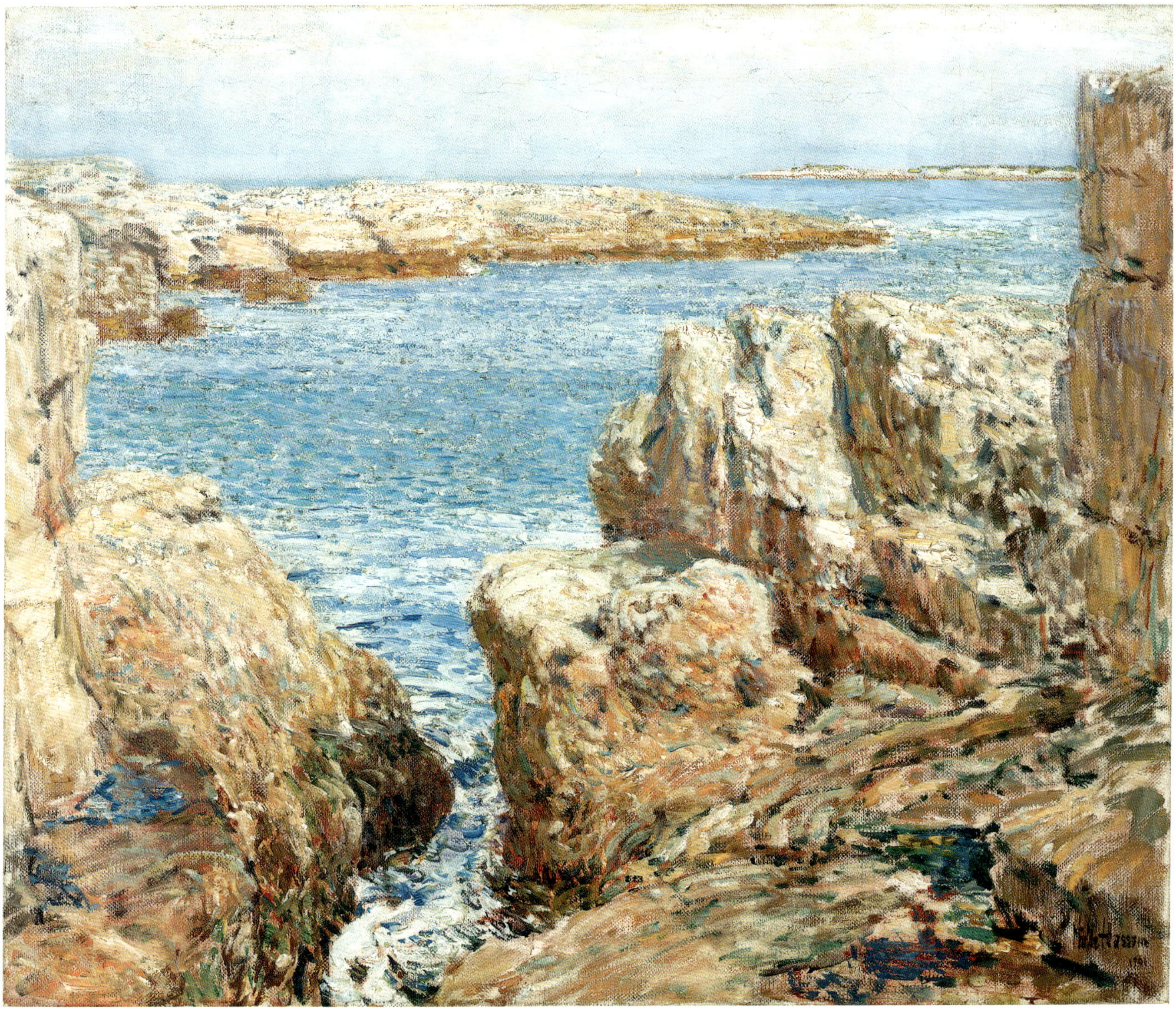

Fig. 22. Childe Hassam. *Coast Scene, Isles of Shoals,* 1901. Oil on canvas, 24 ⅞ x 30 ⅛ in. (63.2 x 76.5 cm). The Metropolitan Museum of Art, New York. Gift of George A. Hearn, 1909 09.72.6

most interesting to the people who enjoy good painting. . . . They would do it at once for a second rate European painter of course!"[87]

While the Metropolitan would not honor Hassam's wish for a major exhibition for almost a century, it steadily acquired his works.[88] Highlights of this initiative during the artist's lifetime were the purchase in 1911 of his Oregon landscape *Golden Afternoon* (fig. 336) and the purchase in 1925 and 1929, respectively, of oils *The Church at Gloucester* (fig. 184) and *July Fourteenth, Rue Daunou, 1910* (fig. 205).[89] In March 1940 Maud Hassam donated to the Metropolitan thirty-eight etchings and twelve lithographs by her late husband; these constitute the majority of Hassam's prints owned by the Museum.[90] In 1943 two fine New York street scenes in oil—*Winter in Union Square* (fig. 89) and *Spring Morning in the Heart of the City* (fig. 91)—which had appeared in the Metropolitan's landmark exhibition *Life in America* in 1939—were received as gifts.[91] In 1967 two more of his oils—*Broadway and 42nd Street* (fig. 214) and *Avenue of the Allies, Great Britain, 1918* (fig. 347)—were included in a major bequest. Between 1994 and 1996 three beautiful and important landscapes by Hassam were accepted as gifts: *The Water Garden* (fig. 241); *Celia Thaxter's Garden, Isles of Shoals, Maine* (fig. 9); and *Surf, Isles of Shoals* (fig. 139). After the expatriates Cassatt and Sargent, Hassam is the American Impressionist best represented at the Metropolitan.

Acquisitions were not the only signs of the Metropolitan's support of Hassam; another was the production by the

Museum of a film about him. As the *New York Times* reported in January 1932: "The Metropolitan Museum of Art has begun a series of one-reel motion-picture films illustrating the theory and practice of contemporary American painters, sculptors, etchers and workers in other fields of art. The first film, already finished, is devoted to Childe Hassam. . . . Several scenes were taken last Summer at Mr. Hassam's country home in East Hampton, L.I."[92] In the film Hassam is shown swimming at the Maidstone Club and later on the beach wearing a robe of antique Chinese silk; appearing to paint *Long Island Pebbles and Fruit* (fig. 350) in his studio; working on correspondence with his secretary (his wife's grandniece), Virginia Rook; and painting out of doors. Mrs. Hassam and Rook sit in the garden perusing an album of Hassam's works, and he plays golf. Finally, he visits the Metropolitan Museum and examines his *Coast Scene, Isles of Shoals; July Fourteenth, Rue Daunou, 1910;* and *The Church at Gloucester.* In July 1940 the Museum again affirmed its interest in Hassam, when it celebrated Mrs. Hassam's gift of prints by installing them for a month in the Room of Recent Accessions and publishing in its *Bulletin* a sympathetic article on the artist.[93] Another exhibition, *Childe Hassam as Printmaker: A Selection in Various Media,* was held at the Museum in 1977.[94]

Like all exhibitions, the present one is selective. We admit a bias for what we deem to be Hassam's strongest periods, those in which he was most engaged with everyday life. Other aspects of his production we consider only in this catalogue. Having benefited from recent scholarship on Hassam, especially Ulrich W. Hiesinger's 1994 monograph, we have eschewed a biographical framework. Instead, we have proceeded chrono-thematically, treating, for example, Hassam's concurrent interests in urban and rural American themes between 1889 and 1918–19 in parallel sections, rather than following his annual peregrinations. We have limited our treatment of the Ten, which has received ample attention, and of two major episodes of Hassam's career—his engagement with the Isles of Shoals and his Flag series—trusting that readers will consult the admirable publications on these subjects by David Park Curry and Ilene Susan Fort, respectively.[95] Like all scholars of Hassam's career, we are indebted to the huge bibliography of lifetime and posthumous exhibition catalogues, reviews, and articles; published interviews dating from the 1890s through the 1930s, especially the invaluable series recorded by Lockman in 1927; and troves of other archival material.

The seven chapters that follow, written by H. Barbara Weinberg, Susan G. Larkin, and Stephanie L. Herdrich, provide an overview of Hassam's career. Nine additional texts, essays by both established scholars of American Impressionism and talented contributors newer to the field, explore Hassam's techniques and subjects, and the presentation, marketing, and reception of his works. Carol Troyen and Elizabeth Barker, respectively, review his accomplishments as watercolorist and printmaker. Elizabeth Broun examines his reflections of his self-image as a Puritan; Erica E. Hirshler studies his interest in architecture; Lisa Miller reviews his fascination with gardens; and Kimberly Orcutt comments on his late ideal themes. Susan G. Larkin discusses his framing of his paintings, and Dana Pilson and Kathleen M. Burnside investigate, respectively, Hassam's self promotion and critics' responses to his art.

A chronology of Hassam's career and a chronology of exhibitions held during his lifetime follow the chapters and essays. Given the difficulties of assigning titles (and dates) to many of Hassam's works, we present in the chronologies only the names under which they were shown, allowing readers to draw their own inferences with respect to shifting titles.[96] In the chapters and essays, we use the titles supplied by the current owners. Like all scholars in this field, we eagerly await publication of the catalogue raisonné upon which Stuart P. Feld and Kathleen M. Burnside have been laboring since the late 1970s.

Our present effort honors the wish Hassam voiced in 1909 for a retrospective at the Metropolitan and a critic's recommendation of 1929: "In due season there should be a splendid retrospective exhibition of Mr. Hassam's works conducted by the Metropolitan Museum of Art or whatever organization is best fitted to the task, an exhibition that will give us gallery upon gallery of his best and largest paintings of all periods."[97]

1. Weinberg, Bolger, and Curry 1994.
2. Dorchester was annexed to Boston in 1870. See Elizabeth Broun, "Hassam's Pride in His Ancestry," in this publication, pp. 285–86. Genealogical information is from J. T. Hassam 1870, pp. 3–4. See also J. T. Hassam 1880, 1889, and 1896. Lockman interview, January 25, 1927, pp. 2–4. DeWitt McClellan Lockman was a New York portrait painter, recording secretary of the New-York Historical Society (1936–57), and president of the National Academy of Design (1949–50). His campaign of interviewing eighty-six artists associated with the National Academy of Design was conducted in 1926 and 1927. Hassam had five interviews between January 25 and February 10, 1927. While the typescripts of his interviews are riddled with errors of spelling, grammar, and fact, they remain a valuable resource. See also Childe Hassam, Autobiographical notes, 1934, Hassam Papers, reel NAA1, frame 739.
3. Hassam said that his mother "would be one hundred years old this year as Mr. Whistler [born in 1834] would be if he were living." Hassam, Autobiographical notes, 1934, Hassam Papers, reel NAA1, frame 739. (We infer the date of Hassam's autobiographical notes from this statement.) "[Lockman] Do you know the date of your mother's death? [Hassam]: No. It would have been 1891 or 1892." Lockman interview, February 3, 1927, p. 16.
4. The life dates of Hassam's father are given in Frederick Adams Virkus, ed., *The Abridged Compendium of American Genealogy: First Families of America; a Genealogical Encyclopedia of the United States* (1925; reprint, Baltimore: Genealogical Publishing Co., 1987), vol. 1, p. 319.
5. J. T. Hassam 1870, pp. 3–4.
6. For Hassam's given names, see Hassam, Autobiographical notes, 1934, Hassam Papers, reel NAA1, frame 739. See also Cortissoz 1939, p. 8.
7. Rattray 1923, p. 6. See also Hassam, Autobiographical notes, 1934, Hassam Papers, reel NAA1, frame 739.
8. Hassam, Autobiographical notes, 1934, Hassam Papers, reel NAA1, frame 739.
9. See, for example, White 1911, pp. XXIX–XXXIII, and Ernest Haskell's introduction to Pousette-Dart 1922, p. vii. Fort (1993, p. viii) summarizes critics' characterizations of Hassam as a Puritan.
10. For a discussion of Hassam's indifference to religion, see Susan G. Larkin, "Hassam in New England, 1889–1918," in this publication, pp. 158, 162.
11. Mawlā is used, for example, in the customary invocation "izz li-Mawlānā al-sultān" (Glory to our lord, the sultan). The author thanks Dr. Maan Z. Madina, Professor Emeritus of Middle East and Asian Languages and Cultures, Columbia University, and Dr. Marilyn Jenkins-Madina, Research Curator of Islamic Art, The Metropolitan Museum of Art, for their scholarly advice and the transliteration. Lockman interview, January 25, 1927, p. 13: "Most people think I am a Turk—when they hear Hassam. Some think I am an Egyptian. Isn't that funny. It's New England. But they think it's Turkish."
12. Lockman interview, January 31, 1927, p. 28. See n. 2 above. Young (1960, p. 197, note) mentions that Remington had given Hassam the nickname. Adams 1938, p. 5: "To the end of his life, his intimate friends called him Muley Hassam, a double compliment proclaiming both his stubbornness of will and his touch of the exotic."
13. Washington Irving, *The Alhambra,* edited by William T. Lenehan and Andrew B. Myers (London and New York, 1832; Boston: Twayne Publishers, 1983), p. 81. Irving also described Muley Abul Hassan in the chapter entitled "The Abencerrages," pp. 84–92, passim.
14. Hassam, Letter to Miss Farmer, 1933, p. 5, Hassam Papers, reel NAA1, frame 747.
15. See Stephanie L. Herdrich, "Hassam in Boston, 1859–1886," in this publication, p. 49, n. 25. *Promenade* (fig. 26), dated 1883, is signed "Childe Hassam." Hassam's grave marker in Cedar Lawn Cemetery, East Hampton, New York, is inscribed *Frederick Childe Hassam.* The author thanks Cynthia Schaffner, Research Assistant, Department of American Decorative Arts, The Metropolitan Museum of Art, for providing photographs.
16. Curry 1990, p. 31.
17. Lockman interview, January 31, 1927, pp. 6–8.
18. As there has been some confusion about the spelling of the names Maud and Doane, the author relies on the following authorities: Mrs. Hassam's signature as Maud Doane Hassam on autograph letters, including Maud Doane Hassam, New York, March 31, 1935, to [Grace L.] Venamee, Secretary to the President, American Academy of Arts and Letters, New York, Hassam Papers, reel NAA1, frames 811–12; and Mrs. Hassam's grave marker in Cedar Lawn Cemetery, East Hampton, New York, for photographs of which the author is indebted to Cynthia Schaffner, Research Assistant, Department of American Decorative Arts.
19. Virkus, *Abridged Compendium of American Genealogy,* vol. 1, p. 319.
20. Bienenstock (1980, p. 169) notes the few American antecedents of Hassam's Boston scenes: topographical views such as Edward Lamson Henry, *Saint George Chapel, Beekman and Cliff Street, New York,* 1875 (The Metropolitan Museum of Art, New York, 33.136.2), and evocative vignettes such as J. Alden Weir, *Mercer Street, Snow,* 1881 (location unknown), and Louis Comfort Tiffany, *Duane Street,* 1878 (The Brooklyn Museum of Art).
21. Ibid., pp. 168–71.
22. C. B. Norton, *Official Catalogue: Foreign Exhibition* (Boston: George Coolidge, 1883); Maureen C. O'Brien, *In Support of Liberty: European Paintings at the Pedestal Fund Art Loan Exhibition,* exh. cat. (Southampton, N.Y.: Parrish Art Museum, 1986). The *Foreign Exhibition* opened on September 3, 1883; the *Pedestal Fund Art Loan Exhibition* opened on December 4, 1883. *Special Exhibition. Works in Oil and Pastel by the Impressionists of Paris* opened in New York on April 10, 1886, and was expanded and reopened on May 25, 1886. See Herdich, "Hassam in Boston, 1859–1886," in this publication, pp. 47–48.
23. Childe Hassam, 11, boulevard de Clichy, Paris, January 11, 1887, to William Howe Downes, Boston, Downes Papers, MSS L337, transcribed in Hiesinger 1994, p. 177: "I am drawing like a slave at Julians and shall until Spring."
24. Recalling an encounter with Renoir's works in Paris in 1889, Hassam claimed: "I knew that he was trying for the same thing that I was trying for." Lockman interview, January 31, 1927, p. 20.
25. For Jongkind, see Lockman interview, February 3, 1927, p. 15: "Jongkind was the best [p]ainter in France within the period from say 1860 to 1880." For the English painters, see S. J. Woolf, "Hassam Speaks Out for American Art," *New York Times Magazine,* October 14, 1934, p. 7: "As a young man I was influenced by these Englishmen." For Sisley, see Hassam 1928, p. 27, in which he calls Sisley "surely one of the best of the landscape painters of the nineteenth century," mentions his own appreciation of Jongkind and the British artists, and denies the importance of French painting.

26. For example, Forbes Watson, "Childe Hassam," *New York Evening Post Illustrated Magazine,* February 28, 1914, p. 11: "Stemming from Monet he has made the formula of Impressionism his own and imbued it with the native tang of our own soil." Buchanan 1916, pp. LXXXV–LXXXVI: "When we go into a roomful of Monets, we experience something of the same sensation that we experience when we encounter these hundred or more pictures of Mr. Hassam's." "'Avenue of the Allies' at Durand-Ruel's," *American Art News* 17, no. 7 (November 23, 1918), p. 2: "It will hardly be denied that Mr. Hassam is, as far as technique goes, a disciple of Claude Monet." "Childe Hassam's Work in Various Mediums," *New York Times Magazine,* November 16, 1919, p. 12: "He does more consistently than Monet what Monet tried to do with color." Ameen Rihani, "Landscape Painting in America, Part II," *International Studio* 71 (July 1920), pp. VIII–IX: "One would say that he is the principal exponent in this country of the impressionism that was fathered by Monet." Hassam's denial of French influence is expressed most fully in Childe Hassam, [New York], December 3, 1934, to Ellery Sedgwick, Boston, Hassam Papers, reel NAA2, frame 244: "I have to de-bunk the idea that I learned to paint in France. I learned to paint in Boston before I ever went to France. I have to de-bunk the idea that I use dots of color, so called, or what is known as impressionism (everybody who paints and sees is probably an impressionist) but none of those men who are supposed to have painted with dots and dashes ever really did do just that. There are only two or three who ever tried it and they gave it right up."
27. Ives 1892, p. 116.
28. Charles Baudelaire, "Le peintre de la vie moderne" (1863), in *The Painter of Modern Life and Other Essays,* trans. and ed. Jonathan Mayne (London: Phaidon, 1964), p. 9.
29. W[illiam] D[ean] Howells, *Criticism and Fiction* (New York: Harper and Brothers, 1891), p. 128. Howells, whom Hassam may have met through their mutual friend Celia Thaxter, was more than twenty years older than Hassam, but he is an apt literary counterpart. He moved from Boston, where he spent his early career, to New York in 1891 and bridged the divide between Romanticism and Realism, especially in his portrayals of middle-class life. Hassam made seven watercolors for reproduction as illustrations in the new edition of Howells's 1866 *Venetian Life,* 2 vols. (Boston and New York: Houghton, Mifflin & Co., 1892); watercolors by Ross Turner, F. Hopkinson Smith, and Rhoda Holmes Nicholls were also included.
30. Elizabeth Broun, "Childe Hassam's America," *American Art* 13, no. 3 (fall 1999), pp. 32–57, discusses Hassam's simultaneous embrace and avoidance of unpleasant turn-of-the-century realities.
31. Elisabeth Luther Cary, "Childe Hassam, Sterling Artist: An Appreciation," *New York Times,* September 1, 1935, p. 9.
32. Mayor 1940, pp. 138–39. Mayor eloquently likens Hassam's etchings of New England to Henry James's evocations of his "childhood haunts" in *The American Scene* (New York: Harper and Brothers, 1907): "Their impressions of New England are so similar as to be like words and pictures put forth by a single mind, though Hassam began to etch seriously a decade after James had written."
33. In *The First Exhibition: Ten American Painters* (New York: Durand-Ruel Galleries, March 31–April 16, 1898), Hassam showed a canvas that presumably depicted a nude (no. 26, *The Bather*). Located nudes painted by Hassam in the early twentieth century include *Pomona,* 1900 (Smithsonian American Art Museum, Washington, D.C.); *The Butterfly,* (fig. 323); *The Lorelei,* 1904 (The Walters Art Gallery, Baltimore); *June* (fig. 321); *Aphrodite, Appledore* (fig. 12), and *The Nymph of the Beryl Gorge* (fig. 322).
34. Pattison 1908, p. 19.
35. For Hassam's association with the Ten, see pp. 16–17, below.
36. Hassam praised Weir for recommending that Puvis paint murals for the Boston Public Library and called the result "one of the most beautiful mural decorations in the world." See Childe Hassam, "Reminiscences of Weir," in Duncan Phillips et al., *Julian Alden Weir: An Appreciation of His Life and Works,* Phillips Publications, no. 1 (1921; New York: E. P. Dutton, 1922), pp. 71–72. Hassam remarked on La Farge in Lockman interview, February 2, 1927, pp. 12–13; and on Cox in Lockman interviews, February 2, 1927, pp. 17–18, and February 3, 1927, p. 27. His appreciation of Sargent is noted in Childe Hassam, "Gari Melchers," in *Commemorative Tributes of the American Academy of Arts and Letters, 1905–1941* (New York: The Academy, 1942), pp. 284–85, and Hassam 1928, p. 22. Hassam realized that he was quite different in temperament from some of his more genteel associates. Childe Hassam, New York, December 13, 1904, to C. E. S. Wood, Wood Papers (Berkeley): "I was photographed the other day with John La Farge in the center and [Edwin] Blashfield on the other wing (we were serving on a jury). I never saw anything with such striking contrasts: They look good and kind and refined—I look tough—rough and knownothing."
37. Lockman interview, February 2, 1927, p. 27.
38. Referring to two images of nudes that Hassam showed at the exhibition of Ten American Painters in New York in March 1902, a critic wrote: "We shall find ourselves viewing Childe Hassam's group with qualified acceptance. Two [works] . . . we must dismiss as the amiable vagaries of a painter who insists upon sandwiching in between his wonderfully truthful pictures examples of how things do not appear to average sane minds." "Exhibition of Ten American Painters," *New York Sun,* April 1, 1902, p. 6, quoted in Burnside 1990, p. 105.
39. Price 1923, p. 5. Hassam tells the same story in Lockman interview, January 31, 1927, p. 28: "One day Remington came to my studio at #95 Fifth Avenue and looked at one of my pictures. He said 'Hell, I have an old aunt up state who can knit a better picture than that.'" Directories of The Players indicate that Hassam and Remington both joined in 1890, so it is possible that Remington's observation preceded 1892, when Hassam moved from 95 Fifth Avenue.
40. Pattison 1908, p. 19.
41. Lockman interview, February 2, 1927, p. 20, and January 31, 1927, p. 35. Memorandum from Elizabeth Barker, March 26, 2003, to the author: "The catalogue raisonné of Hassam's etched work (Cortissoz) lists no prints later than 1934. It seems reasonable to imagine, however, that he would have continued to work on plates as long as his health permitted, even in the year of his death, 1935." For Hassam's prints, see Elizabeth Barker, "'A truly learned weaving of light and dark': Hassam's Prints," in this publication.
42. Rattray 1923, p. 6.
43. "Art Fund Created by Hassam's Will," *New York Times,* November 13, 1935, p. 18. The 2002 equivalent is $896,000 according to http://www.eh.net/ehresources/howmuch/dollarq.php.
44. Myers 1940, p. 101.
45. "Petition in the Matter of the Tax Upon the Estate of Frederick Childe Hassam, April 30, 1936, Schedule A," Surrogate's Court, Suffolk County, New York. See also "Hassam Estate is Appraised at $212,710," *East Hampton Star,* July 9, 1936, p. 2. For the 2002 equivalent, see http://www.eh.net/ehresources/howmuch/dollarq.php.

46. Hassam, Weir, John H. Twachtman, and Willard L. Metcalf usually worked in an Impressionist style. Edmund C. Tarbell and Benson experimented with Impressionism but painted portraits in an increasingly traditional manner, as did their Boston colleague Joseph R. DeCamp; Simmons and Reid had considerable experience as muralists, although they painted some Impressionist scenes; Dewing painted feminine subjects in a Tonalist style. In 1905 Chase replaced Twachtman, who had died in 1902.
47. Hassam first claimed credit for inventing the Ten in "Reminiscences of Weir," in *Julian Alden Weir*, pp. 67–68. His claim cannot be verified, but it has not been disputed. For the organization, see Gerdts et al. 1990 and Hiesinger 1991. For a summary of Hassam's involvement, see Burnside 1990, pp. 103–8. An "Index to the Exhibitions of the Ten," which lists dates and venues for the exhibitions held from 1898 to 1919, compiled by Carol Lowrey, appears in Gerdts et al. 1990, p. 177.
48. J. Alden Weir, Windham, Connecticut, November 13, 1910, to C. E. S. Wood, Wood Papers (San Marino). Weir painted the portrait of Hassam that was required upon Hassam's election as an associate of the National Academy of Design; see J. Alden Weir, *Childe Hassam*, 1902–3 (National Academy of Design, New York; reproduced in Doreen Bolger Burke, *J. Alden Weir: An American Impressionist* [Newark: University of Delaware Press; New York, London, and Toronto: Cornwall Books, 1983], p. 252, fig. 6.36).
49. J. Alden Weir, New York, January 13, 1911, to C. E. S. Wood, Wood Papers (San Marino).
50. Theodore Robinson, Diaries, 1892–1896, February 7, 1896, Frick Art Reference Library, New York.
51. Myers 1940, pp. 83, 102.
52. "Annual Show of The Ten Painters," *New York Evening Mail*, March 21, 1906, p. 7, col. 5, quoted in Burnside 1990, p. 103. Burnside (1990) quotes other similar comments. See also, for example, Buchanan 1916, pp. LXXXIII–LXXXVI.
53. Hassam was a member of the following Boston social clubs and arts organizations: Paint and Clay Club (from 1883) and Boston Art Club. He belonged to the following New York social clubs and arts organizations: American Watercolor Society (1890–1935); New York Water Color Club (1890–1935); Players Club (1890–1931); Society of American Artists (1890–97); Ten American Painters (1897–1919); National Institute of Arts and Letters (1898–1935); Salmagundi Club (1900–35); National Academy of Design (Associate 1902–6, Academician, 1906–35); Lotos Club (at least 1909–16 or 1917); Coffee House (1916–27; 1928–35, nonresident member); American Academy of Arts and Letters (1920–35); Union Club (1928–35); and Painter-Gravers of America. He was also a member of the Pennsylvania Academy of the Fine Arts; Louisville Art League (possibly); Société Nationale des Beaux-Arts, Paris (from May 1897); Munich Secession (corresponding member). Sources for the foregoing information are *American Art Annual* (1898–1933), *Social Register of New York* (1908–35), *Who's Who* (1923–36), the records of the Salmagundi Club, and Hiesinger 1994, passim. Although editions of *Who's Who* for 1924–27 list Hassam as a member of the Century Club, New York, he did not belong to it and was never proposed for membership. Jonathan Harding, Century Club archivist and curator, conversation with Megan Holloway, Research Assistant, Department of American Paintings and Sculpture, The Metropolitan Museum of Art, November 25, 2002.
54. Constant Holley MacRae, Cos Cob, Connecticut, October 1, 1902, to Josephine Holley, Rock, Massachusetts, Holley/MacRae Papers, William E. Finch Archives, Historical Society of the Town of Greenwich, Cos Cob, Connecticut. The author thanks Susan G. Larkin for calling this material to her attention.
55. Typescript (probably by Dorothy Weir Young) of notes from an undated interview with Elmer and Constant Holley MacRae, Dorothy Weir Young, Research papers, tub 3, "Holley Farm" folder, archives, Weir Farm National Historic Site, Wilton, Connecticut. The author thanks Susan G. Larkin for calling this material to her attention.
56. J. Alden Weir, February 1904, to C. E. S. Wood, quoted in Young 1960, pp. 221–22.
57. C. E. S. Wood, Seattle, September 19, 1904, to his daughter Nancy, Wood Papers (San Marino), quoted in Hiesinger 1994, p. 126. See also Nannie Moale Wood [Wood's wife], "Personal Recollections: Dictated to Dean Fischer, Her Nurse and Companion," ca. 1932, p. 41, quoted in Robert Hamburger, *Two Rooms: The Life of Charles Erskine Scott Wood* (Lincoln: University of Nebraska Press, 1998), p. 142. For the empty beer, wine, and liquor bottles unearthed by archaeologists from the crawl space beneath the doorsill of Hassam's studio at the Florence Griswold House, Old Lyme, Connecticut, see Larkin, "Hassam in New England, 1889–1918," in this publication, p. 157.
58. Lockman interview, February 2, 1927, p. 25. Ironically, as Susan G. Larkin has remarked to the author, the Armory Show was masterminded by two of Hassam's Cos Cob associates, Elmer MacRae and Henry Fitch Taylor, who were open to new ideas.
59. Hassam 1928, p. 22. Although Hassam fulminated against modernism, he took little notice in print of the Ash Can School. He expressed mild contempt when he was approached for comment about a proposed book on Robert Henri, and he wrote to the publisher: "Your idea of getting out a series of books on American artists is a good one, I am sure. I have said for some years past there are books on all the modern European mediocrities in art, and none on really great modern artists, who have worked and passed their lives in America, notably my old friend Twachtman. I might make a wicked epigram now—There are books on all the European mediocrities in art, and now we are going to have some on the Americans." Quoted in Price 1923, p. 6.
60. Saint-Gaudens 1941, pp. 196–97.
61. "Childe Hassam Observed 73rd Birthday Mon.," *East Hampton Star*, October 21, 1932, p. 1, quoting "an interview by a staff correspondent of the New York Herald-Tribune, with Mr. Hassam last Saturday."
62. "Childe Hassam Observed 74th Birthday Tues.," *East Hampton Star*, October 20, 1933, p. 3. The hand-annotated typescript of Hassam's tribute is preserved in Hassam Papers, reel NAA2, frames 77–78. In the transcript of the November 1933 speech published later by the Academy, Hassam's unfortunate reference is expanded to describe "the cult of the incompetent, now known as the Ellis Island School." Hassam explains: "Cortissoz had years ago called these European absurdities Ellis Island Art. It is now a school and it tears down, or rather tries to tear down, all of the older established art." See Hassam, "Gari Melchers," p. 285.
63. Woolf, "Hassam Speaks Out for American Art," p. 7.
64. Webster's III defines nativism as "the attitude or policy of favoring the native inhabitants of a country as against immigrants." An early diatribe against foreign art appears in Childe Hassam, New York, November 30, 1906, to C. E. S. Wood, Wood Papers (Berkeley): "These damned picture dealer sharks are reaping the harvest of good times by selling the public spuriosities (how is that for a new word?) of the Early English, Dutch and Barbizon schools—and even an occasional rare Spaniard or Italian.

El Greco seems to have their attention just now. . . . Of course no body is any good over here. Who the hell has heard of Weir or Hassam?" For Hassam's aversion to foreigners, see Hassam, Autobiographical notes, 1934, Hassam Papers, reel NAA1, frame 740, in which he describes Dorchester as "the ugly suburb of a large city" and declares "that part of Boston now has anything but an American population, a good many French Canadians, and a good many more Middle Europeans of all kinds—none of the old English names of families persist." In Hassam, Letter to Miss Farmer, 1933, p. 8, Hassam Papers, reel NAA1, frame 749, he complains about the destruction of the pleasant Dorchester countryside and expostulates: "Now look at it! I do not think that I care to again—or the mongrels who live there, mostly Kanucks from Canada." Hassam's sentiments were shared by his friend Remington, of whom critic Holland Cotter has observed: "His letters and diaries are records of a vexed man in a world that was rapidly changing around him as cities expanded, communications advanced and new populations—Jews, Italians, Irish and blacks moving north—poured through the country." Holland Cotter, "Art Review, 'Frederic Remington': A Painter Who Tried to Change with a Changing World," *New York Times,* April 11, 2003, sec. E, p. 35.

65. Hassam, Will, dated December 20, 1934, and "Petition in the Matter of the Tax Upon the Estate of Frederick Childe Hassam, April 30, 1936, Schedule A," Surrogate's Court, Suffolk County, New York. See also Receipt, dated January 7, 1936, Hassam Papers, reel NAA2, frame 323. "Art Fund Created by Hassam's Will," *New York Times,* November 13, 1935, p. 18. Hassam may have included Canadian artists and Canadian museums in recognition of Maud Hassam's origins in Montreal. Having raised more than $1 million from the sale of Hassam's works, the Academy imposed a moratorium on October 24, 1968 (Minutes of the board meeting, October 24, 1968, of the American Academy of Arts and Letters). Nancy A. Johnson observed in Lillian B. Miller and Nancy A. Johnson, *Portraits from the American Academy and Institute of Arts and Letters,* exh. cat. (Washington, D.C.: National Portrait Gallery, Smithsonian Institution, 1987), p. 64: "By 1946 a great many of Hassam's paintings had been sold, and the Fund had accumulated enough capital to carry out the artist's plan. That year the first distribution was made and, in four decades since, the Academy-Institute has spent $1.2 million for more than 750 paintings, drawings, and graphic works by living artists, which are now in the permanent collection of more than five-hundred museums nationwide." The National Institute of Arts and Letters was founded in 1898 and incorporated by Act of Congress in 1913 for the purpose of furthering literature and the fine arts in the United States. Its membership was limited to 250 artists, musicians, and writers. The National Institute of Arts and Letters served as the parent body for the American Academy of Arts and Letters, founded in 1904 and incorporated by Act of Congress in 1916. Its membership was limited to 50 people chosen for special honor from those who at any time were members of the institute. Membership in the institute did not lapse when an individual was elected to the academy. The two organizations were combined in 1976, becoming the American Academy and Institute of Arts and Letters. Membership in the institute is limited to 250 native or naturalized United States citizens, of whom 50 are elected to the academy.

66. "Brilliant Career of Childe Hassam Comes to a Close," *Art News* 34 (September 14, 1935), p. 12. See also Royal Cortissoz, "The Traits of the Late Childe Hassam," *New York Herald Tribune,* October 6, 1935, sec. 5, p. 10; Cary, "Childe Hassam, Sterling Artist," p. 9.

67. Adams 1938; the author was the wife of sculptor Herbert Adams. A reviewer explained in "American Academy Show," *New York Times,* May 21, 1939, p. X7: "It is triple-barreled, the World's Fair salute sponsored by the American Academy of Arts and Letters. . . . In the main building the permanent collection . . . has been opened to the public. Here, likewise, will be found selected work by Edwin Austin Abbey, lent by Yale. And the regular exhibition gallery houses a memorial show of paintings, watercolors, and prints by Childe Hassam." See also "Special Art Show Opens Tomorrow, Display at American Academy to Last through Summer as Fair Attraction," *New York Times,* May 13, 1939, p. 27.

68. John I. H. Baur, *Leaders of American Impressionism,* exh. cat. (Brooklyn: Brooklyn Museum, 1937), p. 3.

69. *Paintings and Watercolors by Childe Hassam* (New York: Milch Galleries, April 26–May 15, 1943). R. B. H., "Revaluing Hassam, U.S. Impressionist," *Art News* 42 (May 1–14, 1943), p. 12; M[aude] R[iley], "Noted American Impressionists—Lawson, Robinson, Hassam—Exhibited," *Art Digest* 17 (April 15, 1943), pp. 5–7, 30.

70. "Childe Hassam," *Art News* 47 (March 8, 1948), p. 47. The exhibition was *Childe Hassam Etchings* (New York: Grand Central Art Galleries, March 9–20, 1948).

71. Jacob Getlar Smith, "Watercolors of Childe Hassam," *American Artist* 19 (November 1955), p. 51; Grant Reynard, "The Prints of Childe Hassam, 1859–1935," *American Artist* 24 (November 1960), pp. 42–47.

72. L. C., "Childe Hassam," *Art News* 57 (March 1958), pp. 13–14. The exhibition was *Long Island Paintings by Childe Hassam* (New York: Milch Galleries, February 10–March 8, 1958).

73. Stuart Preston, "Magic to Modern," *New York Times,* February 16, 1958, p. 14X.

74. Mahonri Sharp Young, "A Quiet American," *Apollo,* n.s., 79 (May 1964), pp. 401–2. The exhibition was *Childe Hassam* (New York: Hirschl and Adler Galleries, February 18–March 7, 1964). Other exhibitions of Hassam's works held between 1935 and 1964 are listed in Hassam (Tucson) 1972, p. 149.

75. Hassam (Washington, D.C.) 1965, p. 5.

76. John J. Baratte, "Preface," in *French Impressionists Influence American Artists,* exh. cat. (Coral Gables, Fla.: Lowe Art Museum, University of Miami, 1971), p. 3. The catalogue includes 196 works by French and American painters.

77. Hoopes 1972; Hassam (Tucson) 1972. The University of Arizona Museum of Art is now known as the Arizona State Museum, University of Arizona.

78. Moussa M. Domit, *American Impressionist Painting,* exh. cat. (Washington, D.C.: National Gallery of Art, 1973). The venues were the Whitney Museum of American Art, New York; Cincinnati Art Museum; and North Carolina Museum of Art, Raleigh.

79. Dianne H. Pilgrim, *American Impressionist and Realist Paintings and Drawings, from the Collection of Mr. and Mrs. Raymond J. Horowitz,* exh. cat. (New York: The Metropolitan Museum of Art, 1973); Boyle 1974.

80. A brief historiography of American Impressionism appears in Gerdts 1980, pp. 9–10. This landmark exhibition inaugurated the American Impressionist studies of the 1980s, which yielded the still indispensable William H. Gerdts, *American Impressionism* (New York: Abbeville Press, 1984), and copious publications by numerous authors.

81. J. Alden Weir, *Idle Hours,* 1888 (88.7, Gift of Several Gentlemen, 1888); William Merritt Chase, *Lady in Black,* 1888 (91.11, Gift of William Merritt Chase, 1891); Dennis Miller Bunker, *Eleanor Hardy Bunker,* 1890 (93.20, Gift of Several Gentlemen, 1893).

82. "Refused Offered Picture," *New York Times,* December 30, 1898, p. 1. Robinson had died in 1896.

83. Luigi di Cesnola, Director, Metropolitan Museum, New York, April 19, 1899, to Samuel P. Avery, Chairman of the Art Committee, and related correspondence, The Metropolitan Museum of Art Archives. The painting, which Evans had purchased from Robinson's Estate sale in 1898, appeared in *Catalogue of American Paintings Belonging to William T. Evans,* . . . sale cat. (New York: American Art Association, January 31, February 1, 2, 1900), lot 250 (February 2). It was purchased from the Evans sale by the Corcoran Gallery of Art for $600. For Evans, who, between 1907 and 1915, founded the collection now known as the Smithsonian American Art Museum, Washington, D.C., see William H. Truettner, "William T. Evans, Collector of American Paintings," *American Art Journal* 3 (fall 1971), pp. 50–79.

84. William T. Evans, New York, March 9, 1906, to Edward Robinson, Director, Metropolitan Museum, calls Robinson's *A Girl and Cow* the artist's magnum opus; Robert W. de Forest, Secretary, Metropolitan Museum, April 11, 1906, to William T. Evans, New York, indicates that the trustees have accepted the gift. Both letters are in The Metropolitan Museum of Art Archives. See also Florence N. Levy, "Theodore Robinson," *Bulletin of The Metropolitan Museum of Art* 1 (July 1906), pp. 111–12. *A Girl and Cow* (06.1263) was deaccessioned by the Metropolitan and sold in 1956. See *Objets de Vertu . . . Primitive, Old Master and XIX Century Paintings . . . from the Collections of The Metropolitan Museum of Art, Sold by Order of the Board of Trustees, Part Three,* . . . sale cat. (New York: Parke-Bernet Galleries, Inc., October 24–26, 1956), lot 398, *La Vachère* (October 25). Levy notes ("Theodore Robinson," p. 111) that Robinson's *A Winter Landscape,* 1889 (Terra Foundation for the Arts, Daniel J. Terra Collection, Chicago), lent by James [*sic*] Mortimer Lichtenauer, had "been on view [at the Metropolitan] for some years." J. Mortimer Lichtenauer, executor of Joseph M. Lichtenauer's estate, New York, February 12, 1913, to Bryson Burroughs, Curator, Metropolitan Museum, requests the return of the painting for the estate sale at the American Art Association, February 27–28, 1913. Letter and related correspondence in The Metropolitan Museum of Art Archives.

85. See Carrie Rebora Barratt, "George A. Hearn: 'Good American pictures can hold their own,'" *Magazine Antiques* 157, no. 1 (January 2000), pp. 219–28.

86. More conservative canvases by American Impressionists acquired in this period are William Merritt Chase, *Seventeenth Century Lady,* ca. 1895 (06.1220, George A. Hearn Fund, 1906); Frank W. Benson, *Portrait of a Lady,* 1901 (06.1221, George A. Hearn Fund, 1906); J. Alden Weir, *The Green Bodice,* by 1898 (06.1302, Gift of George A. Hearn, 1906). Tonalist paintings were acquired in greater numbers than American Impressionist canvases at this time.

87. Childe Hassam, October 18, 1909, to Miss Cornelia B. Sage, archives of the Albright-Knox Art Gallery, Buffalo, quoted in Hiesinger 1994, p. 141.

88. Information about the Metropolitan's acquisition of Hassam's oils before 1980 is recorded in Burke 1980, pp. 353–65, passim.

89. On June 3, 1925, curator Bryson Burroughs recommended purchase of Hassam's *Garden at Ermont, France,* 1897, from Durand-Ruel for $5,000, arguing: "We would do well to have another picture by Hassam and this is the most charming example of his work I have found for sale in years." The trustees rejected Burroughs's recommendation but instead purchased *The Church at Gloucester* from the Macbeth Gallery for $4,500 on July 3, 1925. "Recommendation of Purchase," June 3, 1925, and July 3, 1925, respectively. Robert W. Macbeth, New York, May 17, 1929, to Bryson Burroughs, offered to the Metropolitan Hassam's *July Fourteenth, Rue Daunou, 1910* (fig. 205) for $3,550; an initialed handwritten note on the letter, dated May 18, 1929, indicates that Harry B. Wehle negotiated the price down to $3,200. All documents are in The Metropolitan Museum of Art Archives.

90. The Executive Committee of the Metropolitan's Trustees accepted the gift on March 18, 1940. See Mayor 1940, pp. 138–39.

91. *Life in America: A Special Loan Exhibition of Paintings, Held During the Period of the New York World's Fair,* exh. cat. (New York: The Metropolitan Museum of Art, 1939), no. 272 (*Union Square, New York,* Lent by Ethelyn McKinney), no. 273 (*Madison Square, New York,* Lent by Ethelyn McKinney). Hassam was also represented in *Life in America* by no. 274, *Spring in West 78th Street, New York,* 1905 (private collection). In 1943 Ethelyn McKinney, who gave to the Metropolitan Hassam's views of Union Square and Madison Square, also gave his *Allies Day, May 1917* (fig. 232) to the National Gallery of Art, Washington, D.C.

92. *Childe Hassam, Artist* (New York: The Metropolitan Museum of Art, 1932), one-reel silent film; "Artists at Work Filmed by Museum," *New York Times,* January 18, 1932, p. 17.

93. "Childe Hassam Exhibit to Open at Metropolitan," *New York Herald Tribune,* July 20, 1940, p. 11. Mayor 1940, pp. 138–39.

94. Burke and Kiehl 1977.

95. For Ten American Painters, see nn. 46, 47, above; Curry 1990; and Fort 1988.

96. Hassam scholar and art dealer Stuart P. Feld summarizes the problems encountered in dating Hassam's paintings: the dates are often difficult to read and not always reliable, as some works were signed and dated some time after they were completed, when Hassam had forgotten when he had painted them; some undated pictures have been assigned dates to make them more desirable commercially; and some works have had their dates removed. Stuart P. Feld, "Childe Hassam—A Retrospective View in Progress," in Hassam (East Hampton) 1981, p. 10.

97. Ralph Flint, "In New York Galleries," *Christian Science Monitor,* May 13, 1929, p. 9, reviewing *Exhibition of Paintings by Childe Hassam, N.A., Covering the Period from 1888 to 1919, Together with Etchings, Water Colors and Pastels* (New York: Macbeth Gallery, April 16–29, 1929).

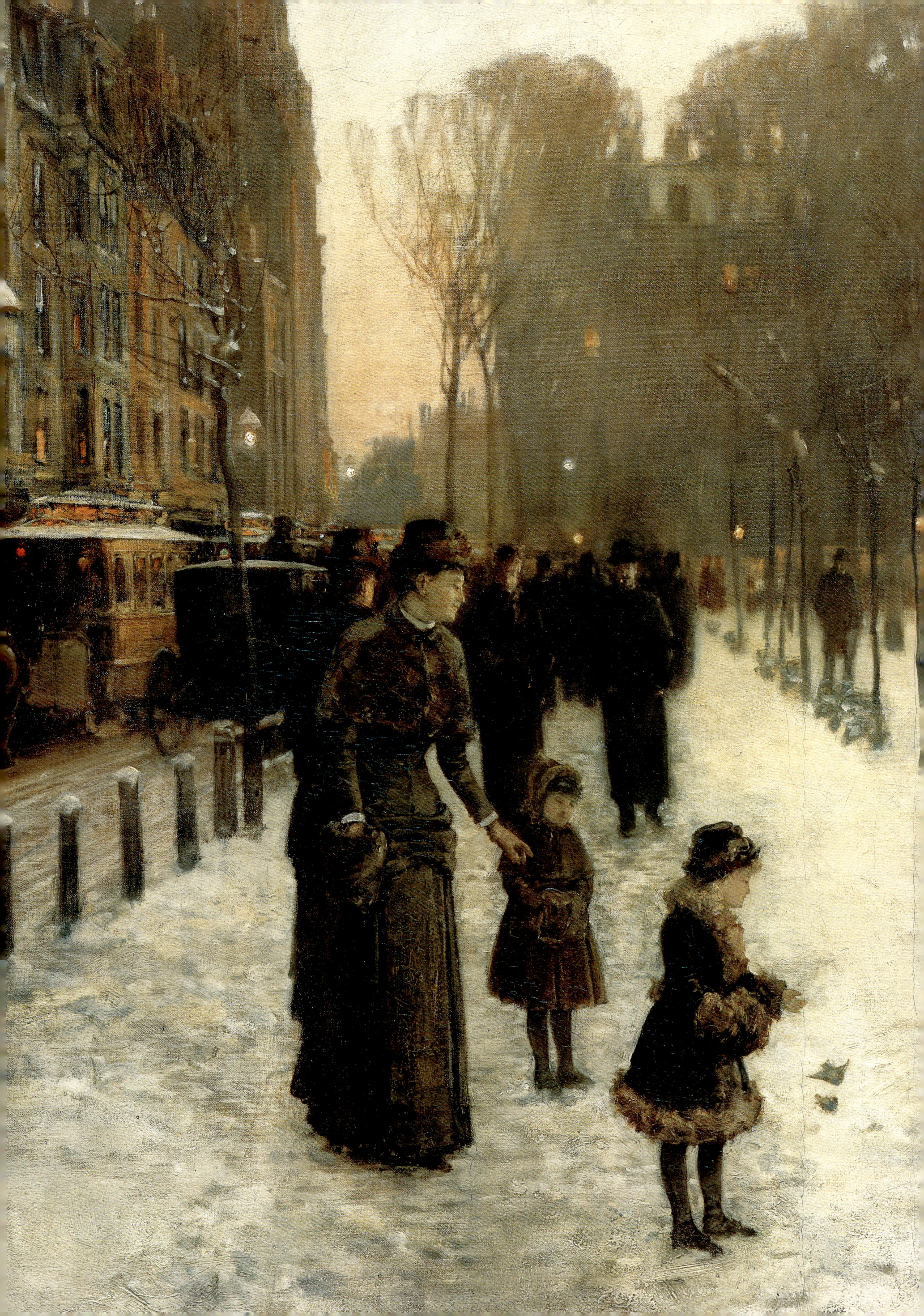

CHAPTER ONE

Hassam in Boston, 1859–1886

Stephanie L. Herdrich

Between 1879, when Hassam began his professional career as an illustrator, and 1886, when he went to Paris to pursue academic training as a fine artist, he established himself in his native Boston as what a critic writing in 1887 deemed "one of the men destined to hold high place in the landscape art of the century."[1] During these years Hassam took advantage of some of the art classes that were available in Boston, became an important member of the city's community of artists, and gradually synthesized the influences of the dominant styles of the moment to produce works that were distinctively his own. Moreover, beginning in 1884, he created a series of compelling and novel images of urban life that are landmarks in American art.

Frederick Childe Hassam was born just outside Boston in Dorchester, Massachusetts, in 1859 to Frederick Fitch Hassam (1825–1912), a New Hampshire native who was a cutlery merchant by trade, and Rosa Delia Hathorne (1834–1891 or 1892) of Maine. He traced his family's origins back to 1630 in Salem, Massachusetts, on his mother's side and on his father's side to before 1684—when the first Hassam arrived in New England.[2] Hassam was fiercely proud of his family's New England heritage and his American ancestry. His enthusiasm for New England would become a lifelong theme in his oeuvre. The firstborn of seven children, he was particularly proud of his paternal great-grandfather, who had served in the Revolutionary War. These facts and much else of what is known of the artist's childhood and early years are recorded in a series of five interviews conducted by DeWitt McClellan Lockman in January and February 1927.[3] In this account—whose tone and details make evident Hassam's regard for his heritage—the artist described his father as a devoted collector of "Americana—old furniture."[4] He recalled making his first sketches from the back of a historic coach in the collection. "One of the early stories is that they found me sitting [in the coach] trying to make a drawing of one of the prints on the wall. It was probably one of those sporting prints of horses, etc. I had artists' material given me as early as I can remember. . . . Water colors, colored crayons, etc. . . . I could not have been much over five or six years," he recounted.[5]

Hassam's mother and his aunt Delia recognized his talent and enthusiasm and "thought [he] ought to be encouraged,"[6] he said. His aunt did so by introducing him to local artists. Hassam told Lockman that when he was a child he saw painters working outdoors and "the first man that I saw using paint in the field was Frank Myrick. It was at the back of my house and was surrounded by trees. I was probably eight, ten, or twelve years old at that time."[7] Although relatively little is known about Boston painter and illustrator Frank Myrick and his work, it is clear that his impulse to paint outdoors, directly from nature, left an impression on the young Hassam, who would paint en plein air throughout his career. Hassam also told his interviewer that, like all children who attended public schools in Massachusetts after 1870, he received instruction in drawing as part of the curriculum.[8] And, as he revealed to a local historian in a letter, he learned to paint in watercolor at Dorchester High School, although he left before graduating.[9]

After Hassam's father lost his hardware business in the Boston fire of November 6, 1872, he was forced to dispose of his collection of Americana. While the financial impact of this disaster—and of the depression that began in 1873—on the Hassam family is not clear, it may have been long lasting and

Detail, fig. 39. *Boston Common at Twilight*

perhaps explains Hassam's abbreviated high school studies. Although he wished to pursue a career in art, he went to work in the accounting division of Little, Brown and Company, the Boston publishing firm. Hassam's aptitude was not for numbers, he explained to Lockman: "They said I would not do. I told them I wanted to keep on in art, and they put me in a wood engraver's office and instead of becoming a prosperous business man I drew on wood, and the moment they found I was more useful as a draughtsman . . . they sent me to George E. Johnston [*sic*], called a wood engraver."[10] Hassam produced commercial designs and letterheads for Johnson, probably from 1879 until about 1881. In 1879 and 1880 Hassam was listed in *The Boston Directory* as "draughtsman" at 9 Milk Street, the address of one of Johnson's offices in the city center, near Boston Common, and was commuting into the city from Dorchester or Hyde Park. By July 1, 1882 he had a studio of his own at 28 School Street, not far from his former employer on Milk Street, and was listed as "artist."[11]

Hassam's ability to maintain his own studio reflects a degree of financial and professional success, and, indeed, throughout the 1880s his work as an illustrator provided him with a steady income. Signed illustrations by Hassam first appear in 1883, in such diverse publications as *The High Tide on the Coast of Lincolnshire, 1571* and *The Belle of Australia; or, Who Am I?*[12] Between 1884 and 1887 he would regularly contribute illustrations to the children's magazine *Wide Awake.*[13] And in the 1890s his efforts were also included in prestigious and more widely read serials such as *Harper's Weekly, Scribner's Monthly,* and *Century.*

While working as an illustrator, Hassam pursued the limited opportunities for formal artistic training available to him in Boston. The School of the Museum of Fine Arts, which was based on such models as the National Academy of Design in New York and the Pennsylvania Academy of the Fine Arts in Philadelphia and their European antecedents, opened in 1877. Boston's first art school, it featured a curriculum that began with a basic drawing class and varied depending on the student's intended profession. However, Hassam, who needed to support himself, would not have been able to attend the Museum school's day classes, and its night classes, when offered, were few.[14]

Like aspiring artists in Boston before the founding of the Museum school and his contemporaries who could not afford to go to its day classes, Hassam fashioned a course of instruction from various resources. These included his apprenticeship in the print shop (a common starting point for artists in Boston during this period) and, presumably, study of works of art in local venues. He told Lockman that he "went to the Lowell Institute Drawing Class in the evening," and that he "had instruction in painting in the Lowell Institute,"[15] doubtless referring to the institution on Boylston Street formally known as the Lowell School of Practical Design, a division of the Massachusetts Institute of Technology. According to *The United States Art Directory and Year-Book* of 1884, the curriculum at Lowell consisted of nine courses given over four years that were intended to aid "the advancement, development, and practical application of sciences in connection with the arts, agriculture, manufacture, and commerce. . . . But provision has also been made for those who desire to pursue special or partial courses."[16] One such provision was the School of Practical Design, maintained by the trustees of the Lowell Institute, which, *The United States Art Directory and Year-Book* explained, offered free evening instruction to men and women "in a variety of subjects, including drawing and architecture."[17] The exact dates of Hassam's attendance are not known.

Not only Hassam's training but also his early professional relationships were important to his fledgling career and the development of his work.[18] As he told Lockman, he received advice early on from John B. Johnston, George Fuller, J. Foxcroft Cole, and Thomas Robinson,[19] all Boston artists influenced by the popular taste for modern French painting as interpreted by William Morris Hunt. Hunt, the city's leading painter, teacher, and tastemaker during the 1860s and 1870s, had studied in Paris with Thomas Couture and had worked at Barbizon with Jean-François Millet. Couture espoused an antiacademic method—the free style and glazed colors of the great sixteenth-century Venetian painters—and favored allegorical and historical themes. Millet found his subject matter in the rural landscape and peasants and represented them in a style not unlike Couture's, painting generalized figures and repudiating academic compositional conventions (see fig. 29). In his own art Hunt combined lessons from Couture and Millet. He also collected works by Millet and other Barbizon artists, which he popularized in Boston. After his marriage in 1855 into a prominent New England family, Hunt was ideally positioned to promote the naturalism of the Barbizon painters among Boston's collectors and artists.[20] Although he died in September 1879, his taste dominated the Boston art scene well into the 1880s, when

Hassam was setting out as a painter. Hassam and Hunt were distantly related, yet they never met.[21] Thus it was through such mentors as Johnston, Cole, and Robinson and exposure to the artistic environment of the day that Hunt's influence reached Hassam.

A clear picture of that environment emerges from the content of the important *Exhibition of Contemporary Art* held at the Museum of Fine Arts in April 1879. This exhibition constituted a synopsis of current trends in American art and a snapshot of contemporary taste in Boston. In its range and size it was an unprecedented display for Boston, and an aspiring young artist such as Hassam probably would have attended. The Barbizon painters were shown, Millet being the most fully represented, with eleven paintings and twenty-one drawings. The roster of European academic artists included Dutch-born Lawrence Alma-Tadema from England and Léon Bonnat from France. The works of Hunt and his followers, among them J. Appleton Brown and J. Foxcroft Cole, were prominent, and a visitor to the exhibition could also have seen contributions by Winslow Homer and by European-trained Americans John La Farge, Elihu Vedder, William Merritt Chase, Thomas W. Dewing, Frank Duveneck, Thomas Eakins, and James McNeill Whistler. On display as well were pictures by Hudson River School painters, including Albert Bierstadt, Frederic E. Church, Sanford R. Gifford, and John F. Kensett. A reviewer for the *Boston Transcript* observed, "Here is afforded to all classes a full view of contemporary American art. . . . The loan collection of foreign masters in the present exhibition is exceedingly rich and a boon to all lovers of pictures."[22]

Hassam started to show and sell his paintings in the early 1880s, exhibiting them in what a reviewer described as "galleries connected with our art stores."[23] It was also at this time that he began his long association with the Boston Art Club, founded in 1855 and one of the city's older and more venerable art establishments.[24] The club's regular exhibitions, which were open to the public, made it an important element in Boston's cultural scene. In 1882 Hassam made his first submission to the club, sending two oil paintings, *A May Morning* (location unknown) and *A Daisy Field* (location unknown), to its twenty-fifth exhibition, which opened in February.[25] And to its *Twenty-sixth Exhibition of Water Colors and Works in Black and White,* which opened 1882, he sent two watercolors, *Harbinger of Spring—In the City and in the Country* (location unknown) and *Bit of Autumn* (location unknown). By showing at this established institution, which was expanding in this period, Hassam found a large audience, began receiving critical attention, and inaugurated a lifelong practice of exhibiting in annuals throughout the country.

Hassam's early exhibition history reveals that he worked in both oil and watercolor from the beginning of his career; however, in the early 1880s he favored watercolor, as he seems to have been better trained and more experienced in its use. By autumn 1882 he had produced a considerable body of watercolors, many of which he displayed in his first solo exhibition. This was held at the Williams and Everett Gallery, Boston's oldest and most established gallery and the first to import works by foreign artists and by Americans who painted abroad.[26] The exhibition catalogue reveals that Hassam's preferred subject matter was the New England countryside. At least eight of the watercolors listed were painted at Nantucket, where Hassam had spent part of his summer holiday in 1882.[27] Other sites represented were Sudbury, Beverly, and Swampscott in Massachusetts, and North Conway in New Hampshire. However, the majority of titles do not refer to specific locations but rather suggest picturesque vignettes in generalized settings: *Shelling Peas, The River-Bank,* and *Sheep Pasture* are examples. One unidentified reviewer remarked that the exhibition, which included fifty-one watercolors and three black-and-white sketches, "introduces to the public a young artist of exceptional talent and of more than ordinary promise." Noting that it contained "faithful studies from nature, marked by accurate drawing, strong color and artistic feeling," the writer praised its "fresh 'outdoor' feeling."[28]

These early titles reveal an unresolved difficulty for Hassam scholarship. Since many suggest time rather than place—*September, Morning; Winter Twilight; One Afternoon; Sunday Morning,* for example[29]—and sheets are, moreover, rarely identified with inscriptions, it is often impossible to connect located works with their original titles. Further complicating the matter is the fact that Hassam often painted several images of related motifs, as demonstrated by the following titles from the Williams and Everett catalogue: no. 37, *Study of an Apple-Tree*; no. 43, *Early Blossoms*; no. 48, *Apple-Blossoms.* Despite such confusion, Hassam's titles and the works themselves make clear his overriding preoccupation with nature, the seasons, and their transitory effects.

The charming *Country Road* (fig. 23) epitomizes Hassam's early efforts in watercolor as well as the problems attached to

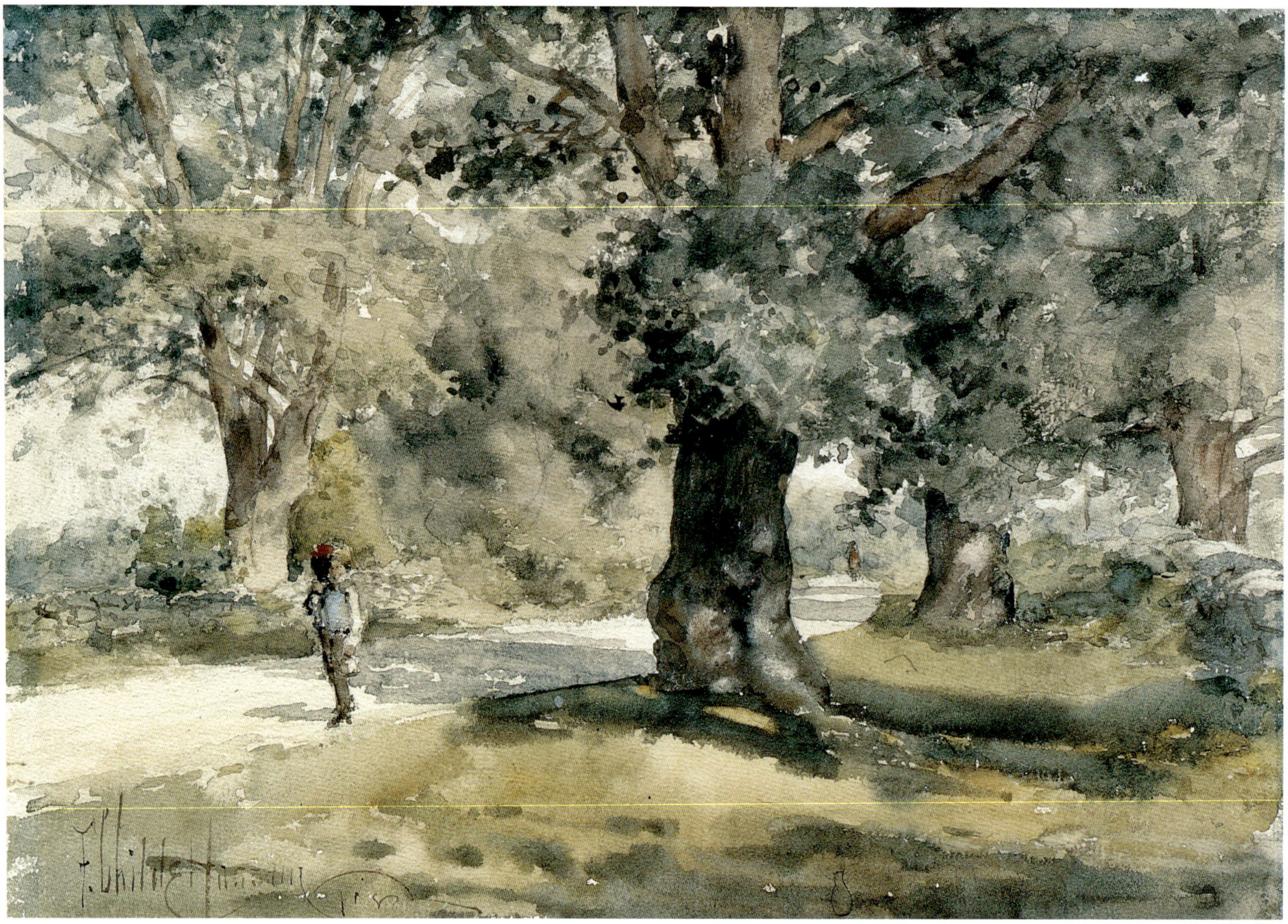

Fig. 23. Childe Hassam. *Country Road*, 1882. Watercolor on paper, 9½ x 14 in. (24.1 x 35.6 cm). Private collection

identifying them. In recent scholarship this work has been called *Wayside Inn, Sudbury, Massachusetts,* referring to the historic inn in Sudbury, about twenty miles west of central Boston.[30] However, this idyllic landscape, which depicts a gently curving country road lined with massive trees, contains no details connected with a particular place, and the sheet bears no identifying inscription. Hassam's inclusion of narrative elements, such as the two diminutive figures walking along the road at some distance from each other, suggests a specific moment, but the primary subject is atmospheric effects: the illusion of light shown filtering through leaves that cast shadows. He also explored the tonal range of his green and brown palette, gently layering pools of color with a soft, brushy technique that infuses the scene with a moody feeling. Given Hassam's delicate and calligraphic signature and the date, 1882, inscribed at the lower left of the sheet, this watercolor may well have been included in the solo exhibition of autumn 1882 at the Williams and Everett Gallery; if so, it probably bore one of Hassam's more poetic titles that referred to a moment in time.

In *Old House, Nantucket* (fig. 24)[31] Hassam pursued themes he would favor throughout his long career: domestic architecture and lush landscape both cultivated and wild—the former represented here by the flowering vines growing up the side of the house, the latter as seen in the woodsy background. The carefully drawn architecture with its delicately executed details reveals Hassam's training as an illustrator. Moreover, the bucolic setting and the absence of narrative create a sense of serenity and timelessness he would reiterate in later images such as *Little Old Cottage, Egypt Lane, East Hampton* (fig. 246).

Perhaps encouraged by the critical and financial success of the Williams and Everett exhibition of autumn 1882, Hassam made a number of significant decisions in 1883. These demonstrated his seriousness of purpose and resulted in his forging important personal and professional relationships. He joined Boston's Paint and Clay Club, founded three years earlier as an alternative to the Boston Art Club. In the late 1870s, in an effort to remain financially stable, the Art Club

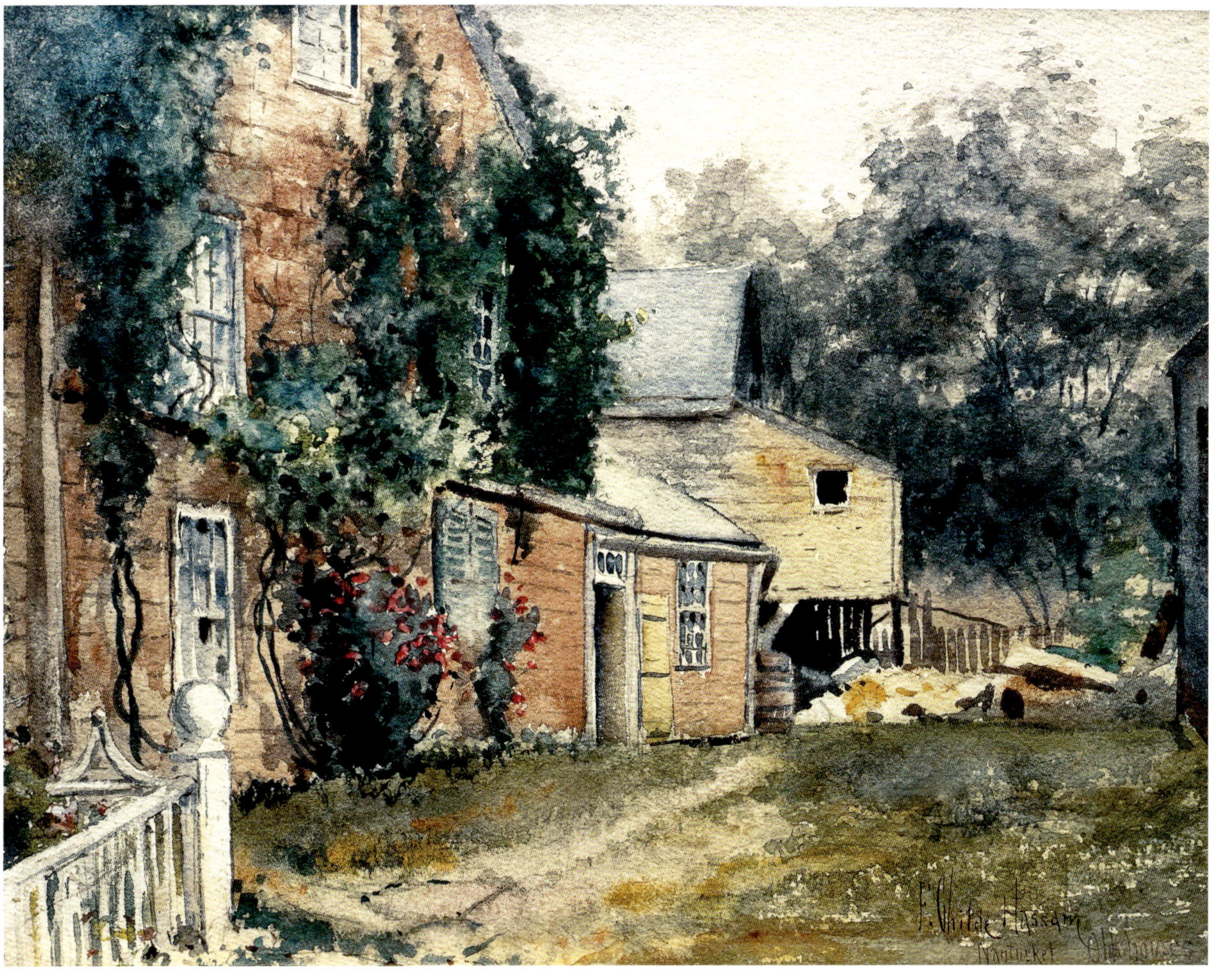

Fig. 24. Childe Hassam. *Old House, Nantucket,* ca. 1882. Watercolor on paper, 9¾ x 11¾ in. (24.8 x 29.8 cm). Vose Galleries of Boston

had expanded its membership to allow nonartists to join. As a consequence, by 1880, "lay members outnumbered artists eight to one," according to Trevor Fairbrother.[32] By contrast, the membership of the new Paint and Clay Club was restricted to practicing artists, and its roster comprised Boston's up-and-coming young professionals, including Dennis Miller Bunker, Edmund C. Tarbell, and Frank W. Benson. By January 1883 Hassam also rented a studio at 149A Tremont Street on the eastern edge of Boston Common (fig. 25). This same year—in connection with a documented stay in Portsmouth, New Hampshire—he probably made his first trip to the nearby Isles of Shoals to visit his friend Celia Laighton Thaxter, whom he had likely met about 1879.[33]

In 1883 as well Hassam traveled to Europe for the first time, accompanied by his friend and colleague the illustrator Edmund Henry Garrett. Planning to spend two months abroad, the pair sailed on the SS *Anchoria* on June 30.[34] Hassam visited Scotland, England, the Netherlands, France, Switzerland, Italy, and Spain before he returned to New York via Naples

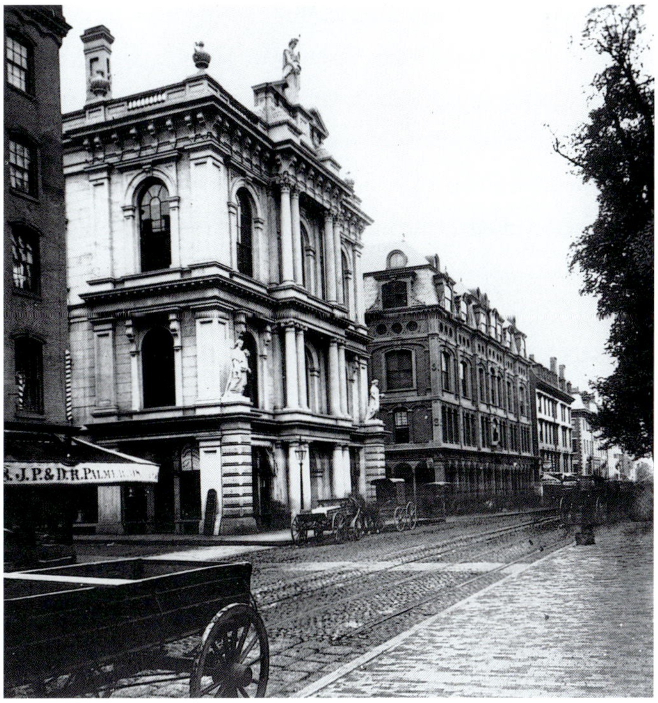

Fig. 25. John P. Soule. Horticultural and Studio Buildings, Tremont Street, Boston, ca. 1870s. Society for the Preservation of New England Antiquities, Boston

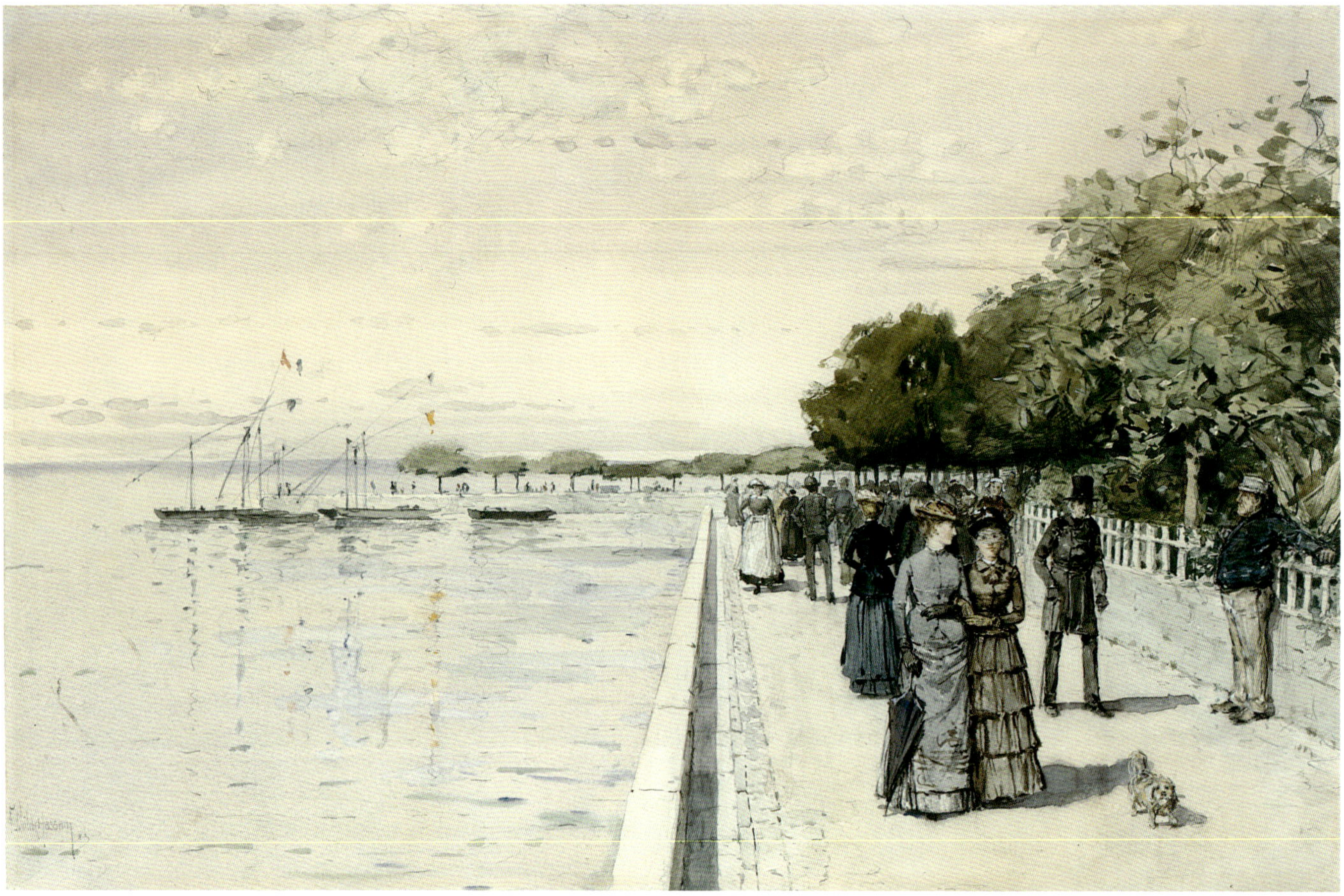

Fig. 26. Childe Hassam. *Promenade,* 1883. Watercolor, gouache, and graphite on off-white wove paper, 16 15/16 x 25 13/16 in. (43 x 65.6 cm). The Metropolitan Museum of Art, New York. Gift of Mr. and Mrs. Arthur G. Altschul, 1971 1971.246.2

in late August or early September. However, the order in which he visited these countries and the duration of his stays at the various locales are unknown. Years later, when he discussed the trip with Lockman, he distinguished it from his subsequent pursuit of formal academic study in Paris but described it in the most general terms: "I did not go into the schools. I went around and saw things. I just looked at the galleries. I spent most of my time in London and Paris. . . . I would advise any boy to do just what I did—to go to the great studios."[35] He did not indicate which studios he visited or what exhibitions he attended, and when Lockman asked him about his impression of the "old pictures" he saw, Hassam insisted they had no influence on him. "I was greatly interested in the aspect of nature," he explained.[36] He admitted only that he remembered "being impressed by Turner's Water Colors and his drawings."[37] Here it should be noted that Hassam's esteem for Turner reflects the influence of Hunt, who was a great admirer of the British master and had declared: "One hundred years from now, Turner will be counted among the greatest men who have ever lived!"[38]

Exploiting the portability of the medium, Hassam chronicled his trip in a series of watercolors.[39] In the ambitious *Promenade* (fig. 26), he announced his interest in depicting aspects of urban life while demonstrating his illustrator's habit of capturing details. Representing elegant strollers as well as picturesque local types on an esplanade along a lake, he carefully described the diverse costumes of the characters. Of particular note is the woman in the distance garbed in an apron and a pointed hat, a costume Hassam almost certainly intended to be a charming signifier of an "exotic" locale, perhaps a spot near the port of Ouchy on Lake Geneva, near Lausanne.[40] According to one guidebook, Ouchy was remarkable for its "shady quay, its handsome promenade skirting the lake, and its fine views," features Hassam was able to transcribe with skill.[41] In composition and subject this watercolor is an important precursor of Hassam's Boston cityscapes of the mid-1880s. It is also one of his earliest portrayals of the strolling pedestrians who would become lifelong subjects, appearing in many later works, among them *Lower Fifth Avenue* (fig. 95), *The*

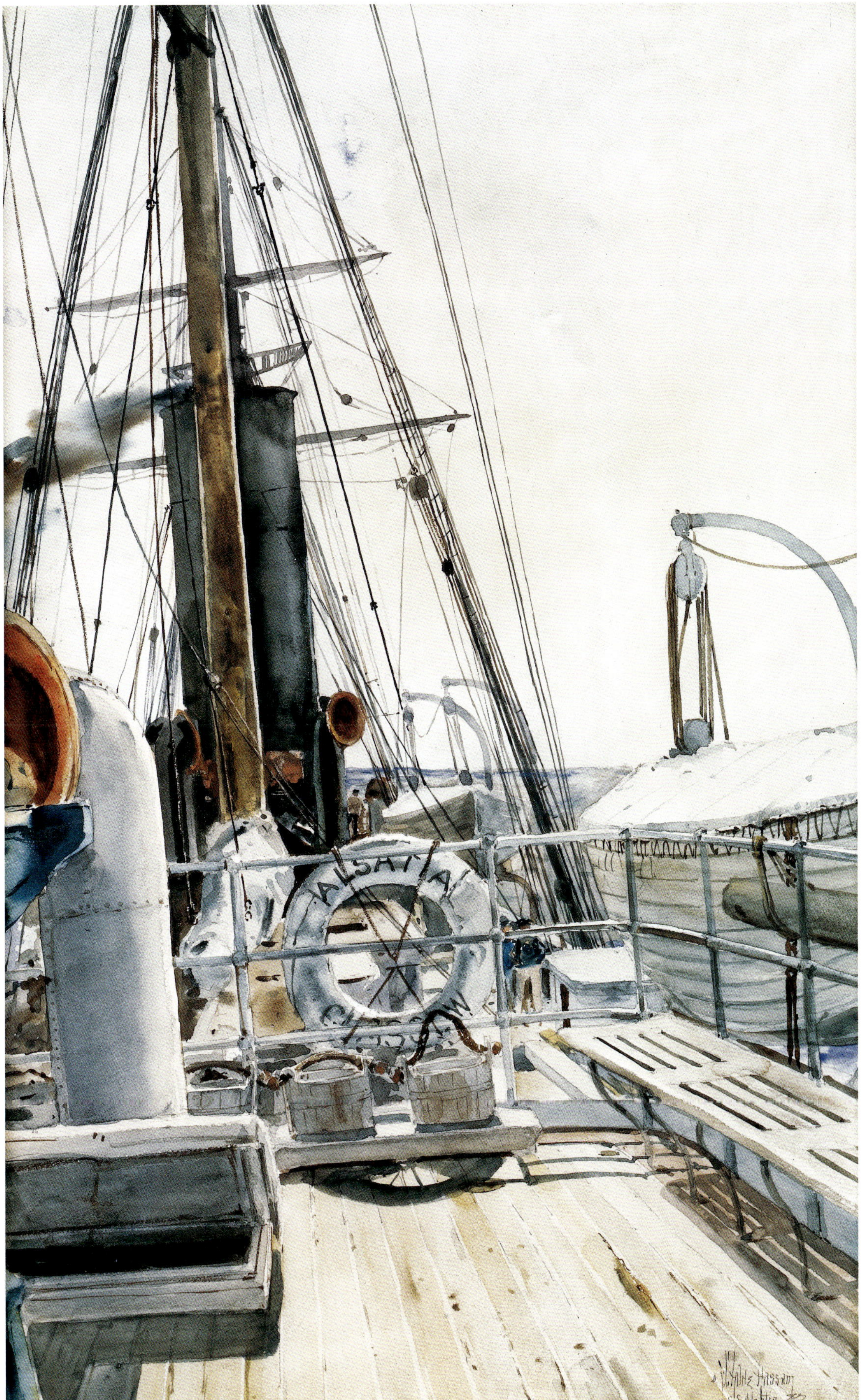

Fig. 27. Childe Hassam. *On the Deck,* 1883. Watercolor on paper, 18⅞ x 12¼ in. (47.9 x 31.1 cm). Ms. Cheryl Chase and Mr. Stuart Bear

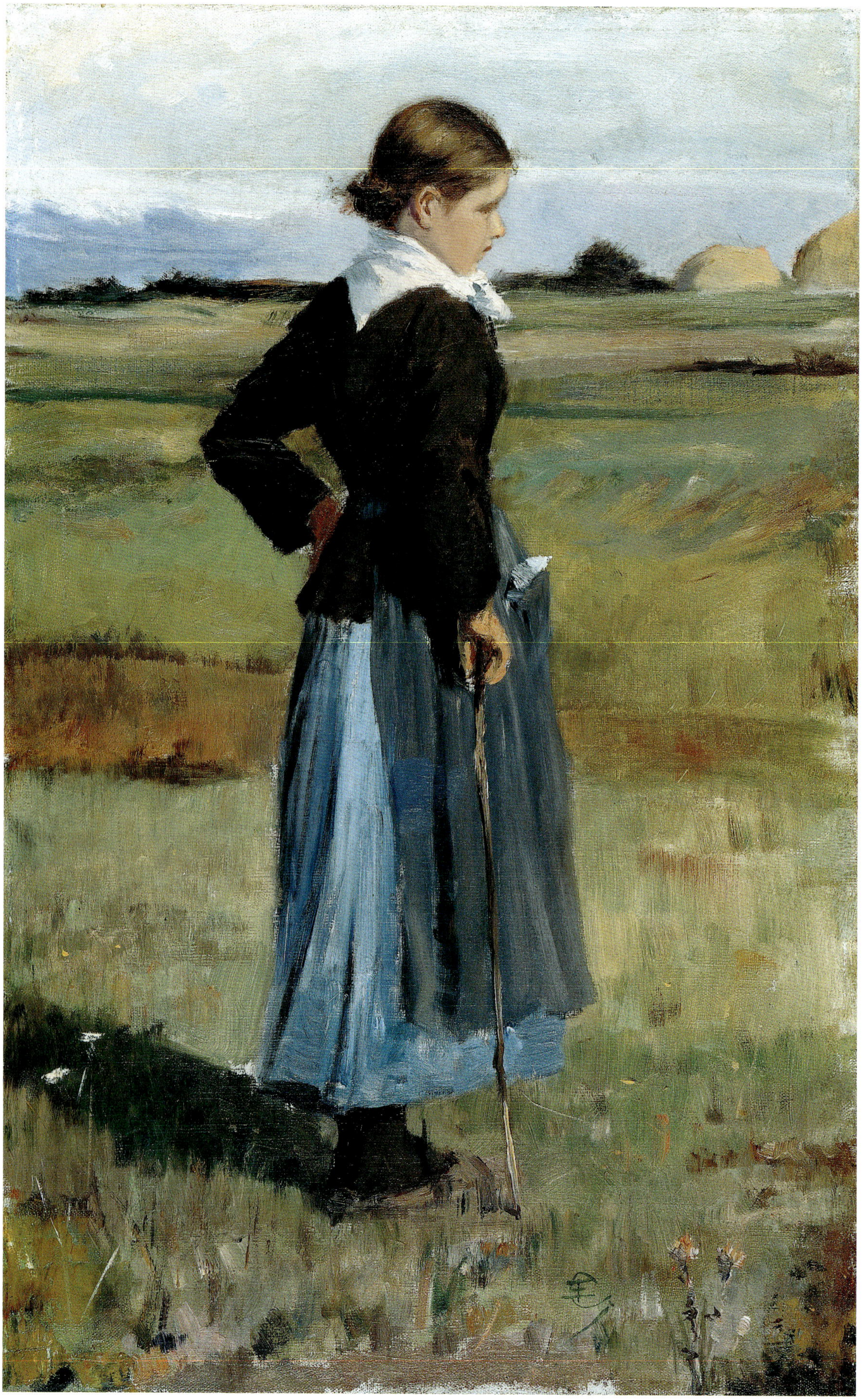

Fig. 28. Childe Hassam. *French Peasant Girl,* ca. 1883. Oil on canvas, 21⅝ x 13⅞ in. (54.9 x 35.2 cm). Terra Foundation for the Arts, Chicago, Daniel J. Terra Collection

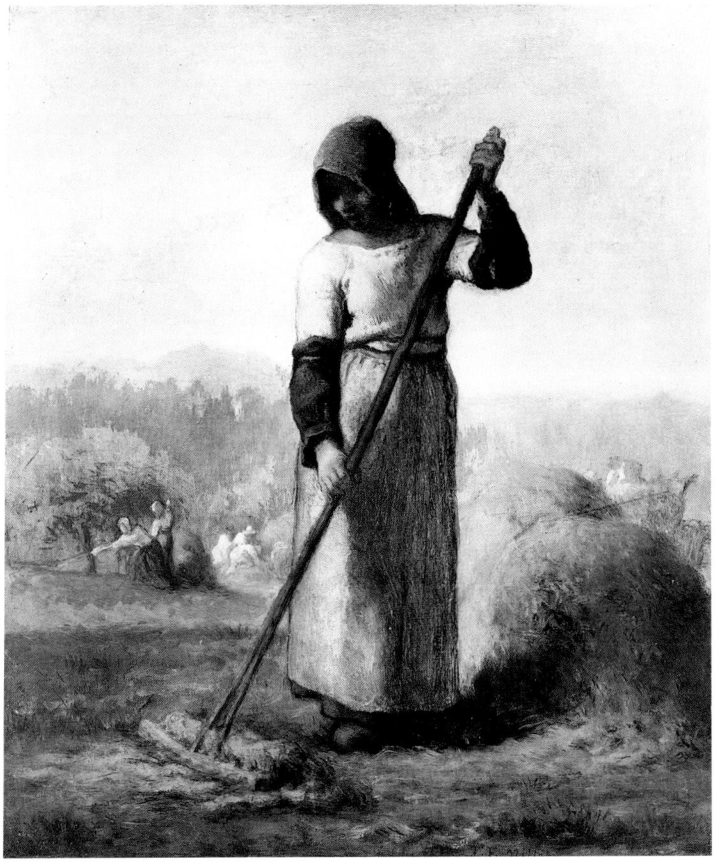

Fig. 29. Jean-François Millet. *Woman with a Rake,* probably 1856–57. Oil on canvas, 15⅝ x 13½ in. (39.7 x 34.3 cm). The Metropolitan Museum of Art, New York. Gift of Stephen C. Clark, 1938 38.75

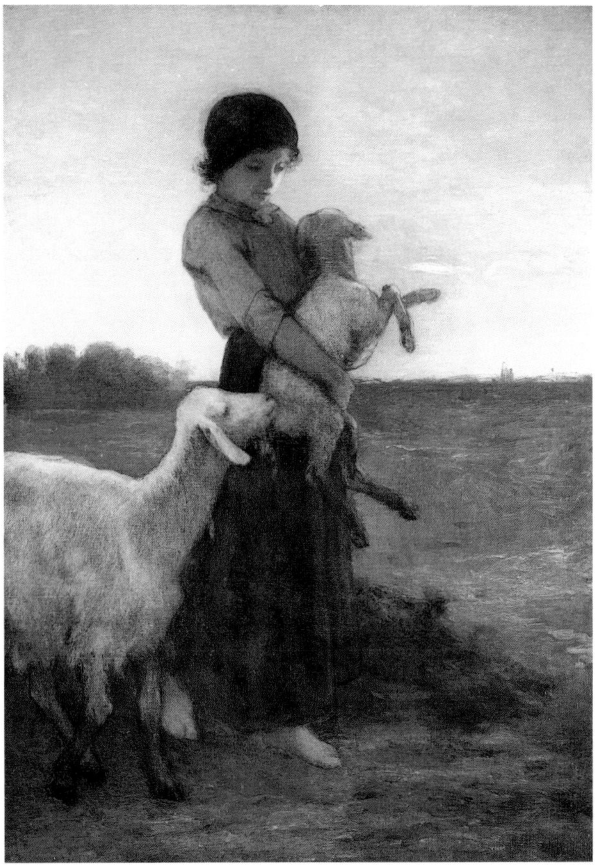

Fig. 30. William Morris Hunt. *The Belated Kid,* ca. 1854–57. Oil on canvas, 54¼ x 38¾ in. (137.8 x 98.4 cm). The Museum of Fine Arts, Boston. Bequest of Miss Elizabeth Howes

Manhattan Club (The Stewart Mansion) (fig. 99), and *Washington Arch, Spring* (fig. 97).

The oil *Village Scene* (fig. 2) has often been associated with Hassam's first European sojourn, although its picturesque locale is unidentified. In this canvas, as in *Old House, Nantucket,* Hassam explored the theme of rural architecture and landscape. Again nature is both wild and cultivated: here the lush, long grasses and flowers of the verdant foreground are contrasted with a manicured pasture beyond. A puff of smoke rising from one of the chimneys in the distance emphasizes the bucolic mood.

Hassam memorialized his return voyage to New York aboard the SS *Alsatia* in the closely observed watercolor *On the Deck* (fig. 27), a study of the ship's deck and riggings. His training as an illustrator is evident in the controlled linearity and articulation of the details, and his preoccupation with tone and harmony is apparent in the subtle coloration.[42]

Although certainly inspired by his travels, *French Peasant Girl* (fig. 28) could have been made after Hassam's return to Boston. In this oil he experimented with a broader and freer application of pigment than he had employed in *Village Scene* and other earlier works. One of his first depictions of what would be an enduring theme for him—women shown out of doors—*French Peasant Girl* reflects Hassam's adoption of the Barbizon aesthetic in both its subject and its style. In particular, the painting treats the theme of peasant labor as portrayed by Millet and popularized by Hunt. For inspiration Hassam may have looked to such models as Millet's *Woman with a Rake* (fig. 29) or Hunt's *Belated Kid* (fig. 30) or *French Girl Raking,* about 1854 (location unknown).[43] Like Millet and Hunt, Hassam depicted his figure against a spare landscape background. However, he departed from these presumed prototypes by employing a higher vantage point and eschewing the overt representation of labor, showing the woman leaning against her walking stick.

Back in Boston, Hassam continued his artistic training by enrolling in the life classes at the new School of Drawing at the Boston Art Club, which had opened in December 1883.[44] The instructor was Tommaso Juglaris, an Italian painter who had worked under Couture in Paris.[45]

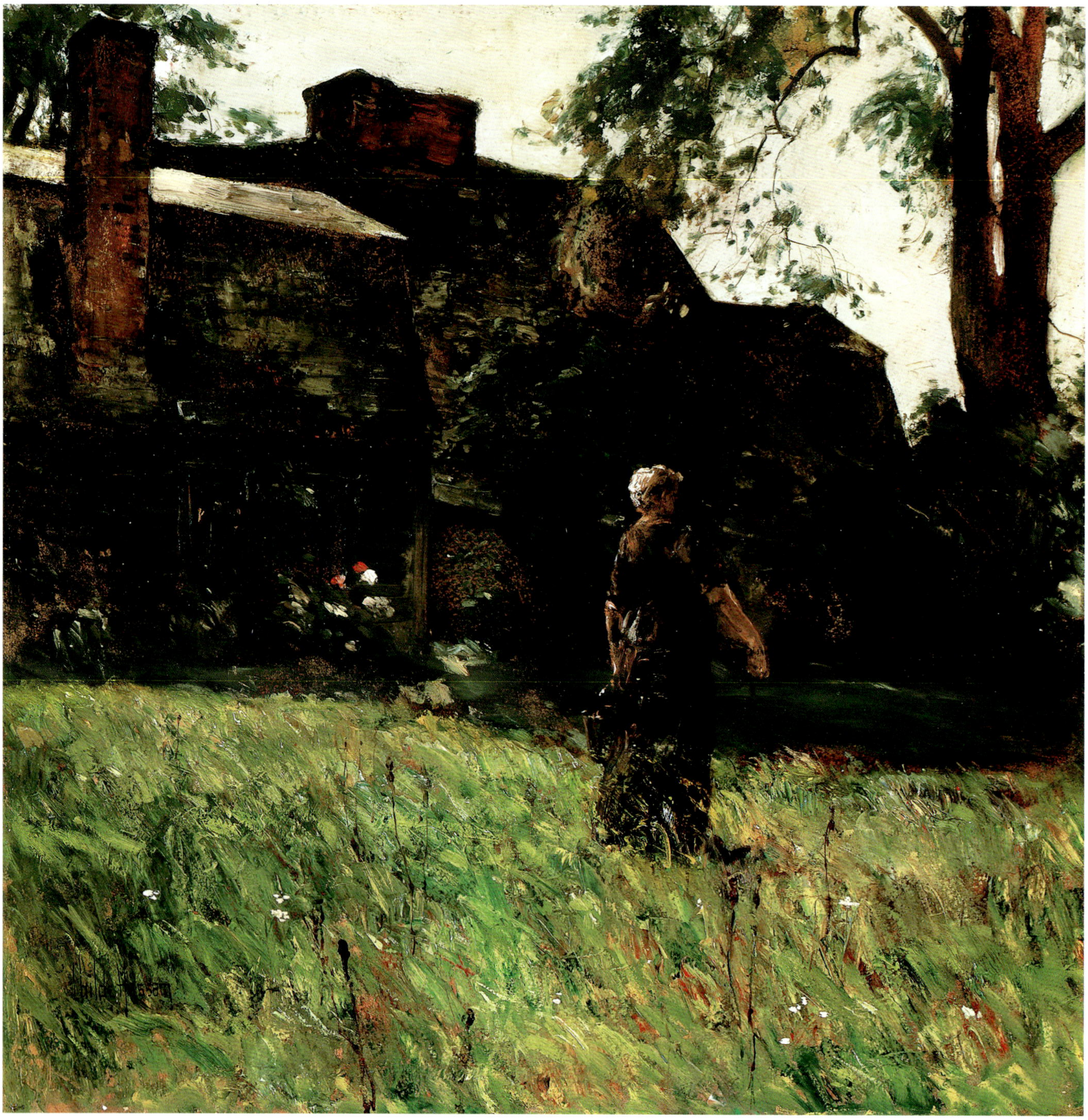

Fig. 31. Childe Hassam. *The Old Fairbanks House, Dedham, Massachusetts,* ca. 1884. Oil on canvas, 22⅛ x 22 in. (56.2 x 55.9 cm). The Museum of Fine Arts, Boston. Bequest of Kate Talbot Hopkins

Juglaris's impact on Hassam was significant. After his return to Boston, Hassam painted more often in oil, producing larger, more impressive and ambitious works, a development probably inspired by his exposure to great European art, but no doubt it also reflected an increased confidence in his use of the medium that Juglaris's teaching would have instilled. Juglaris's influence must have reinforced that of Hunt and the Barbizon aesthetic, which had already left its mark on Hassam and perhaps provided the primary impetus for the creation of *French Peasant Girl.*

Hassam displayed sixty-seven watercolors executed during his European tour in his second solo exhibition, which, like his first, took place at the Williams and Everett Gallery.[46] The show, held in 1884, was well received: as Hassam recalled, "the prices were low. But it was quite successful."[47] One critic praised the works for their "free, out-door feeling" and lauded

> *the local color which Mr. Hassam has very happily succeeded in catching. . . . There are some crudenesses here and there, sometimes in the drawing or posing of a figure, sometimes*

in its proportions, and rarely in the coloring. But these are so much overbalanced by the freedom and abandon of the outdoor scenes, the clever technical facility with which the artist has handled difficulties now and then, and an occasional originality in the way of looking at things that they are almost forgotten.[48]

In a series of canvases painted about 1884, Hassam renounced specificity and revealed his fully evolved personal version of the Barbizon manner. *The Old Fairbanks House, Dedham, Massachusetts* (fig. 31) epitomizes his treatment of familiar pastoral vignettes in the series. For this picture he chose a historic backdrop—the oldest wooden-frame house in North America—whose age he emphasized by including the word "old" in the painting's title.[49] In Hassam's day the house was still occupied by the family that had built it in 1636, and he underscored the fact of its continuing use by including a woman engaged in the quotidian task of carrying a bucket up the grassy hill. She is a New England counterpart of the noble peasants of Millet and Hunt.

Hassam's choice of subject not only reflects his affinity for the Barbizon works of Millet and Hunt; it also accords with the prevailing American enthusiasm for rural imagery. Homer, for example, had popularized the theme of rustic America in his paintings in the 1870s, and as several critics have observed, it became his hallmark. Thus, in 1877 a writer for the *Art Journal* remarked that Homer "likes the men, the women, the boys, and the girls, of the rustic by-ways of our land."[50] And in 1879 a commentator for *Appleton's Journal* declared that he was "wholly en rapport with American life."[51] Hassam would have been acquainted with Homer's work, which was well known in Boston. In particular, Hassam had notable opportunities to see Homer's paintings in 1879 in Boston's *Contemporary Exhibition* and in December 1880, when a large display of his watercolors was installed at the Doll and Richards Gallery.[52]

Although Homer's *Gloucester Farm* (fig. 32) was not included in these Boston venues and in fact was not exhibited until 1884—when it was shown at New York's Palette Club—it reveals striking parallels to *The Old Fairbanks House*. Both paintings share a rural site, the figure of a woman carrying a bucket, and the use of a low vantage point from which a vernacular structure on high ground is viewed. Hassam, however, avoided the overt narrative content of Homer's image. And by portraying a local landmark, he added to his genre subject a specific reference to historical New England, thus distinguishing his interpretation of Barbizon prototypes from Homer's. *The Old Fairbanks House* shows development in Hassam's approach: in it he abandoned the subtle coloration of his early works to represent strong sunlight, which silhouettes the house and, to a

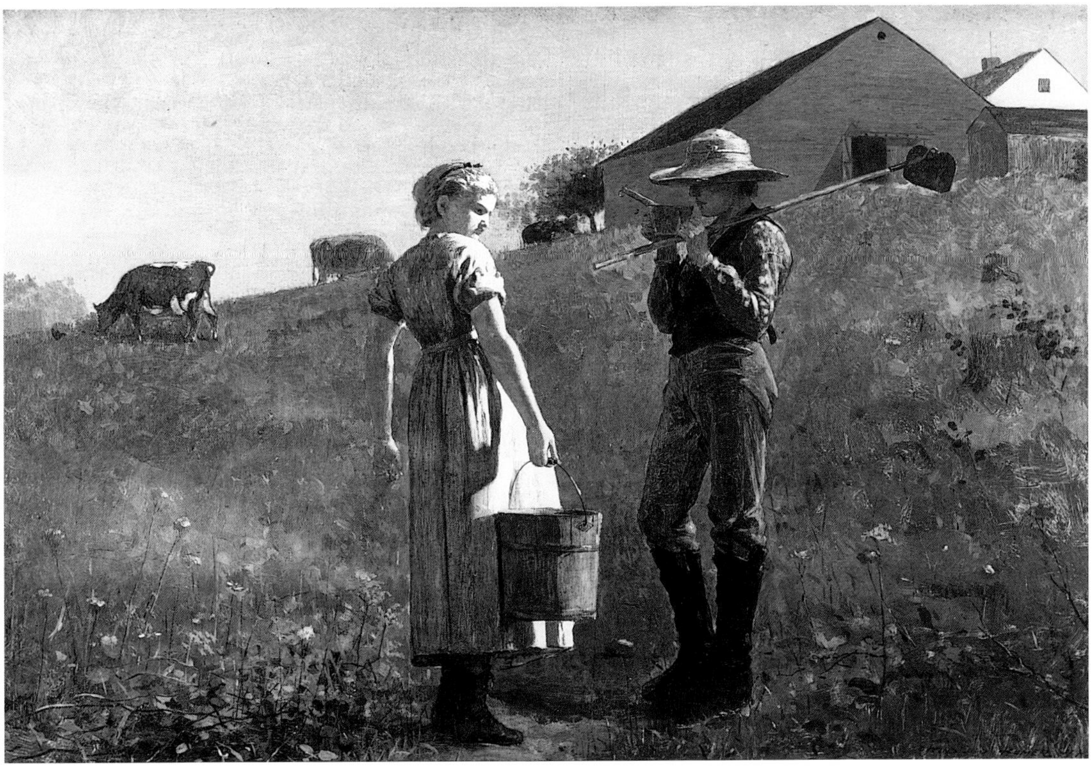

Fig. 32. Winslow Homer. *Gloucester Farm*, 1874. Oil on canvas, 20¾ x 30⅛ in. (52.7 x 76.5 cm). Philadelphia Museum of Art: Purchased: John H. McFadden Collection

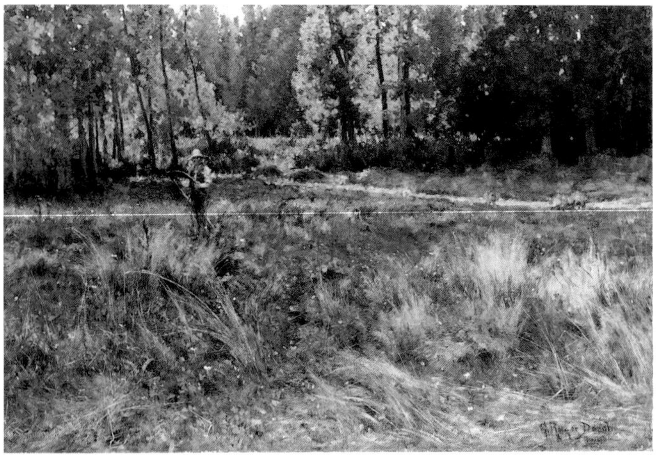

Fig. 33. G. Ruger Donoho. *La Marcellerie,* ca. 1882. Oil on canvas, 51⅜ x 77⅛ in. (130.5 x 195.9 cm). Brooklyn Museum of Art, Gift of George A. Hearn 11.533

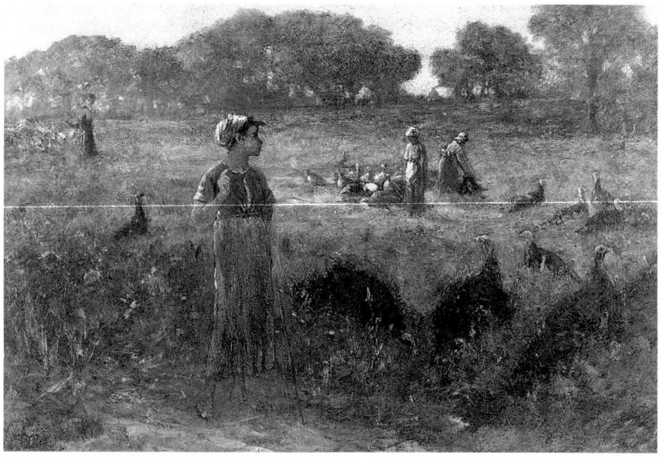

Fig. 34. George Fuller. *The Turkey Pasture,* 1878. Oil on canvas, 27½ x 40¾ in. (69.9 x 103.5 cm). Chrysler Museum of Art, Norfolk, Virginia, Gift of Walter Chrysler, Jr. 71.649

lesser degree, the figure amid the bright green of the grass. When Hassam's painting was exhibited before the auction at Noyes, Cobb and Company in Boston in March 1887, one critic praised the "just relation between the black house and the vivid sky" and called its style "poetic."[53]

Hassam certainly knew and appreciated the Barbizon-style landscapes of American artists other than Homer. One such painting, G. Ruger Donoho's verdant landscape *La Marcellerie* (fig. 33), he described to Lockman as "probably the best out-of door picture painted by an American painter at that time."[54] Donoho, who would become Hassam's friend and painting companion in East Hampton after 1898, studied in Paris at the Académie Julian from 1879 to 1887 and worked at Barbizon and Grez-sur-Loing in the 1880s. *La Marcellerie* was widely exhibited and acclaimed: it was shown in 1882 at the Paris Salon, in 1883 at the National Academy of Design, New York, in 1884 at the Society of American Artists, New York, and in 1889 at the Exposition Universelle, Paris, where it won a silver medal. Hassam doubtless knew the painting by 1884, when he encountered it at the Society of American Artists,[55] but he also could have seen it a year earlier at the National Academy, where his own *Spring Blossoms* (location unknown) was shown. Donoho's broadly painted composition, with its rather tonal palette and solitary figure that conveys a solemn mood, is echoed in Hassam's landscapes from this period.

Another painter who probably influenced Hassam was George Fuller, who, like Donoho, achieved renown for his images of rural life in both Boston and New York. The two artists had met in 1883 when Hassam rented the studio at 149A Tremont Street, where Fuller also worked.[56] In one of his interviews with Lockman, Hassam made note of the importance of Fuller's friendship during his early career.[57] It may well be then that Hassam looked to *The Turkey Pasture* (fig. 34) and similar examples by Fuller as images of idyllic rural life and labor in the tradition of Hunt.

A Back Road (fig. 35) represents the culmination of Hassam's exploration of Barbizon-inspired naturalism. With the lone figure shown in the distance riding up the hill in a cart, he continued to interpret the theme of rural labor, but this detail is secondary to the landscape, which attains a new monumentality. Hassam must have recognized the exceptional quality of the canvas, because in January 1885 at the Boston Art Club, he offered it for $500, a much higher price than he had asked for his earlier oils. The picture's merit and pedigree were recognized by one contemporary Boston critic, who placed *A Back Road* firmly within the tradition of French landscape painting as practiced by such masters as Corot and Courbet. She asked rhetorically, "What wonder that the Boston taste for landscape painting, founded on this sound French school, is the one vital, positive, productive and distinctive tendency among our artists today." Remarking that "the latest development of the school . . . embodies the realism and naturalism . . . of everything in French art nowadays," she added:

> *The two most notable landscapes at the current Art Club exhibition are evidently inspired by this cult, the "Upland Ranche"* [sic] *of* [John Randolph] *Stites, and the sunny*

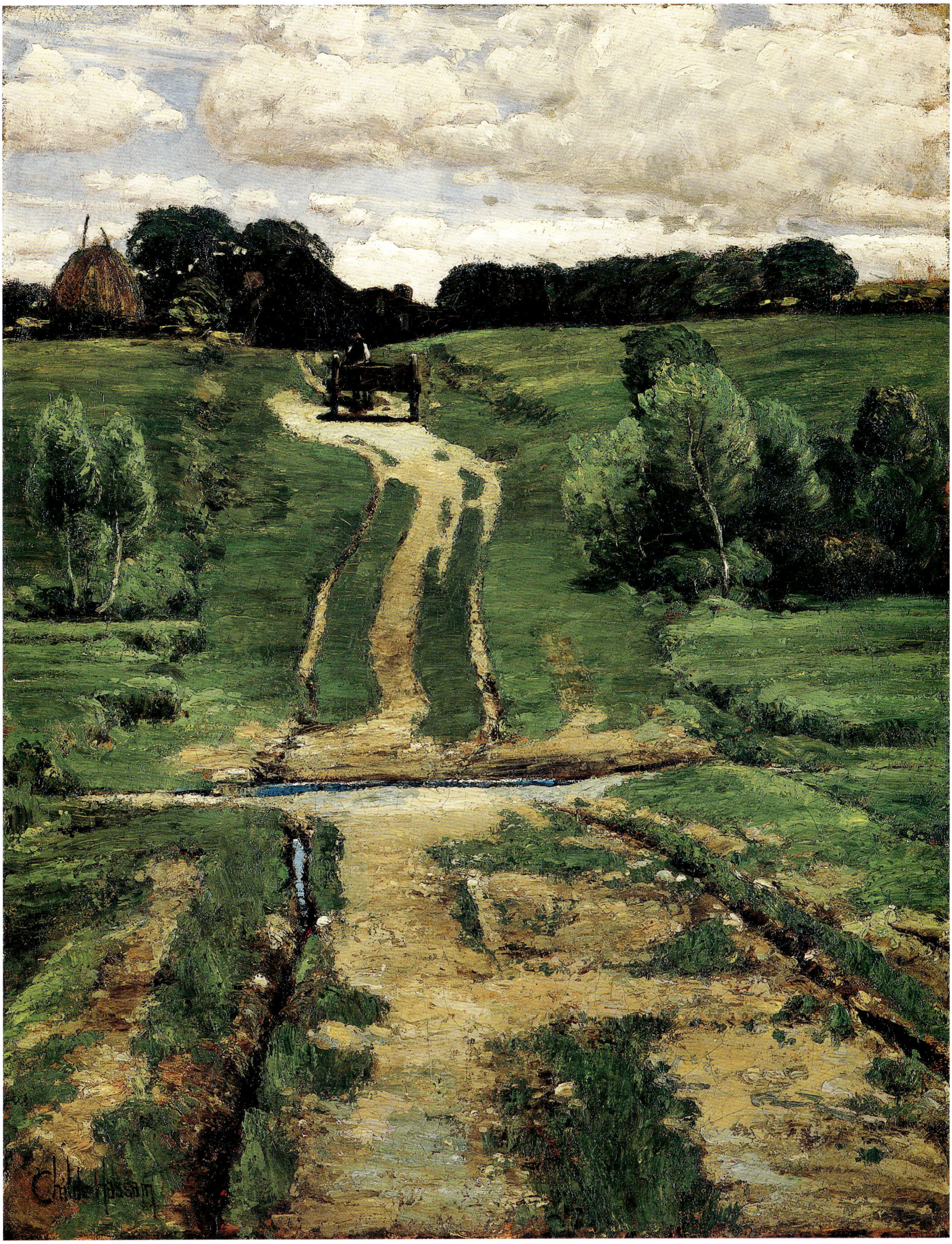

Fig. 35. Childe Hassam. *A Back Road,* 1884. Oil on canvas, 31¼ x 25 in. (79.4 x 63.5 cm). Brooklyn Museum of Art, Caroline H. Polhemus Fund 47.122

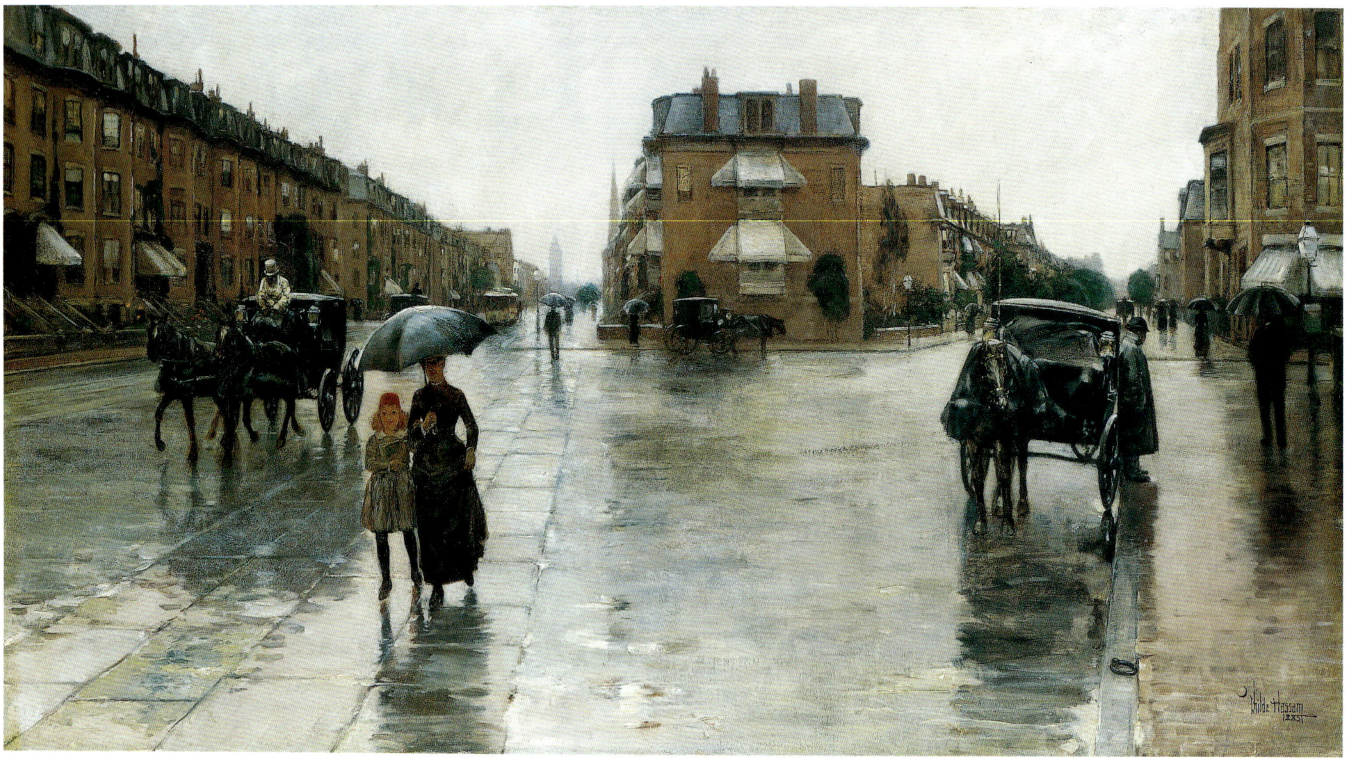

Fig. 36. Childe Hassam. *Rainy Day, Columbus Avenue, Boston,* 1885. Oil on canvas, 26 ⅛ x 48 in. (66.4 x 121.9 cm). Toledo Museum of Art; Purchased with funds from the Florence Scott Libbey Bequest in Memory of her Father, Maurice A. Scott

> *rough country-road of Childe Hassam. . . . Both are boldly, strongly, realistically true, frank and unconventional in their delineation of the facts of nature. The truth is poetry enough for these radicals of the new school. It is a healthy, manly, muscular kind of art, having the courage of its convictions, and must continue to flourish and exert a vitalizing influence.*[58]

Recently, Teresa A. Carbone has suggested specific sources of inspiration for *A Back Road* among the paintings of Hunt and the early landscapes of Camille Pissarro, the latter of which Hassam could have seen in France in 1883.[59]

After marrying Kathleen Maud Doane on February 1, 1884, Hassam took an apartment in The Albemarle at 282 Columbus Avenue, the main thoroughfare of Boston's newly enlarged South End. Like the creation of the Back Bay, the expansion of the South End was a response to Boston's dramatic population growth in the second quarter of the nineteenth century. As waves of immigrants came to live in the older parts of the city, the established, more prosperous residents began to move elsewhere. The filling of the Back Bay tidal estuary in the 1850s created two distinct districts to accommodate the displaced Bostonians: the expanded South End and the new Back Bay, both designed on grid plans based on Baron Georges-Eugène Haussmann's new Paris. Columbus Avenue was laid out in 1869. One of its most striking characteristics was its great width, which made it "one of the finest thoroughfares in Boston," according to a contemporary guidebook.[60] Such broad avenues were in marked contrast to the winding streets of the old city center.

After Hassam moved to Columbus Avenue, he began painting an impressive series of large, tonal canvases depicting urban life under various atmospheric conditions. The scale and ambition of these paintings were unanticipated in his oeuvre, and the subject was quite novel in American art.[61] In *Rainy Day, Columbus Avenue, Boston* (fig. 36), the earliest of these major Boston street scenes, Hassam presented a dramatic perspectival experiment, a masterly tonal study of the city under gray skies, and a portrait of the new Boston. The site, viewed from West Canton Street, is the intersection of Columbus Avenue, at the left, and Appleton Street, on the right, not far from Hassam's new apartment.[62] Hassam emphasized the broad scale of the intersection and the width of the streets by creating a panoramic view from a relatively low vantage point and leaving the center foreground empty except for the scattered pedestrians and cabs. The dramatic

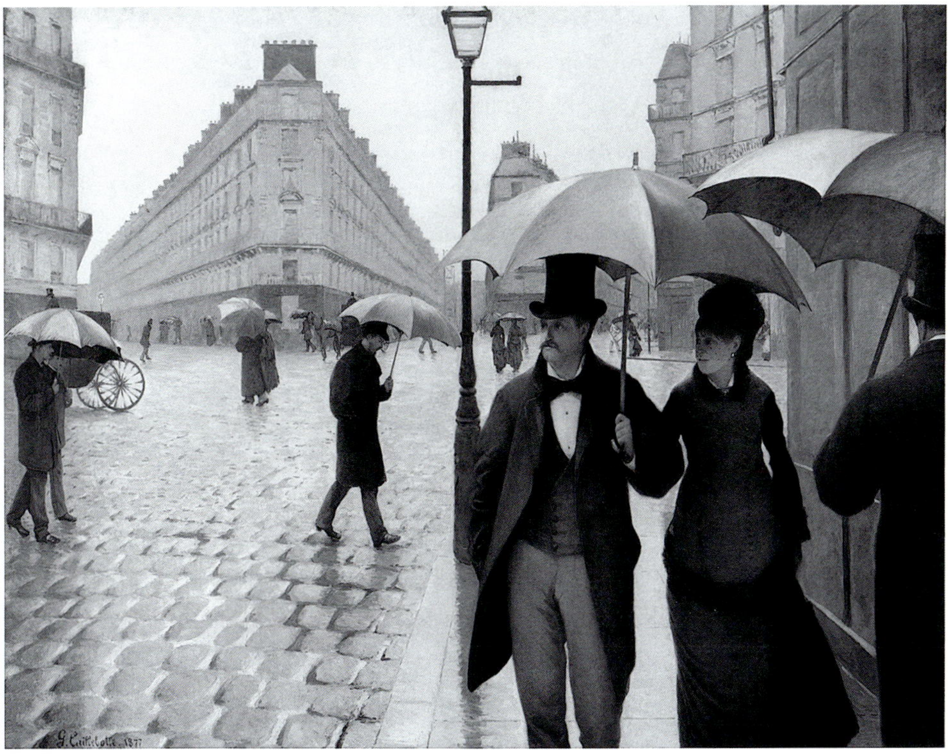

Fig. 37. Gustave Caillebotte. *Paris Street; Rainy Day,* 1876–77. Oil on canvas, 83½ x 108¾ in. (212.1 x 276.2 cm). The Art Institute of Chicago, Charles H. and Mary F. S. Worcester Collection

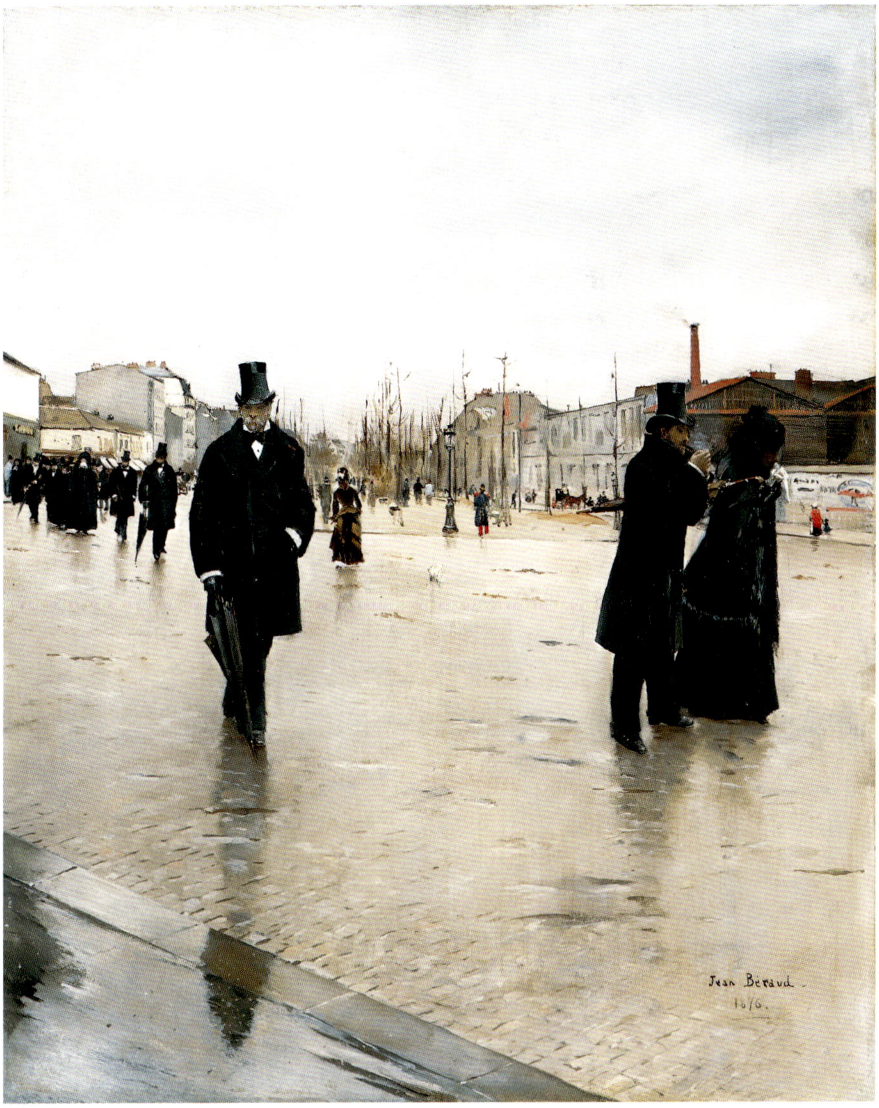

Fig. 38. Jean Béraud. *Le Retour de l'enterrement (After the Funeral),* 1876. Oil on canvas, 26 x 21 in. (66 x 53.3 cm). Private collection

divergence of the receding streets, which accentuates the breadth of the intersection, has led some scholars to propose that the painting resembles a stereographic photograph and that its composition may have been inspired by such views.[63]

Asked in 1892 how he had begun painting street scenes, Hassam recalled: "I lived in Columbus Avenue in Boston. The street was all paved in asphalt, and I used to think it very pretty when it was wet and shining, and caught the reflections of passing people and vehicles. I was always interested in the movements of humanity in the street."[64] Indeed, in his rendering of the intersection, Hassam skillfully explored effects of the shiny wet pavement and subtle reflections under dull skies. He experimented with similar imagery in the painting *Columbus Avenue, Rainy Day,* 1885 (Worcester Art Museum), a view of Columbus Avenue from a closer vantage point.

By 1885, when Hassam painted *Rainy Day, Columbus Avenue, Boston* and *Columbus Avenue, Rainy Day,* the elegant tone of the South End was already fading. Many of its private residences had been converted to lodging houses inhabited by young couples and aspiring immigrants. In 1886 Henry James caught the popular perception of the district's divided quality when he wrote of the South End home of a character in *The Bostonians* as having "a peculiar look of being both new and faded—a kind of modern fatigue—like certain articles of commerce which are sold at a reduction as shop-worn."[65] While Hassam's broad boulevards chronicle the new Boston, his muted palette, gray skies, and quiet streets evoke the "modern fatigue" that James described.

Hassam showed a view of Boston in the rain in his May 1886 debut at the Society of American Artists in New York. One critic writing about such pictures in 1888 suggested that Hassam had transformed commonplace scenes into something poetic and acknowledged the novelty of his subject, asking: "Did he not make some of the prosaic thoroughfares of the south district of Boston pictorially poetic, and impress on our memories a new way of viewing street life?"[66]

In interviews and articles Hassam remained extremely vague about his early artistic role models, suggesting that he was inspired simply by the beauty of the city to paint what he saw. Yet in choosing to portray urban life he seems to have responded to a variety of prototypes. His *Rainy Day, Columbus Avenue, Boston,* for example, has a strikingly close analogue in the French Impressionist Gustave Caillebotte's *Paris Street; Rainy Day* (fig. 37). While the paintings are remarkably similar in subject and composition, Hassam probably did not know Caillebotte's monumental picture. However, he had many opportunities to see works by other Impressionists as well as by more conservative artists who were committed to urban imagery, and he presumably sought inspiration in them. He may well have seen the seventeen works by Camille Pissarro, Alfred Sisley, Pierre-Auguste Renoir, and Claude Monet shown at the *Foreign Exhibition,* which opened in Boston on September 3, 1883 (there were, however, no urban scenes among them).[67] And he could have attended or read about the highly publicized *Pedestal Fund Art Loan Exhibition,* which opened in New York on September 4, 1883, and included a sampling of works by Impressionists.[68]

As Jennifer Bienenstock has pointed out, Hassam's Boston cityscapes of the mid-1880s show strong affinities with the work of the conservative artists of the juste-milieu.[69] These painters, who worked in France and included Giuseppe de Nittis and Jean Béraud, combined Impressionist subject matter with more traditional academic techniques.[70] Beginning in the 1870s de Nittis and Béraud enjoyed international recognition. De Nittis's plein air subjects and his participation in the first Impressionist exhibition in 1874 established his reputation among contemporary critics. In addition, his conservative interpretation of Impressionism was more acceptable to much of the public than the radical versions of Monet, Renoir, and other standard-bearers of the movement. Béraud became widely known after his painting *Le Retour de l'enterrement (After the Funeral)* (fig. 38) was applauded at the 1876 Paris Salon. His particular focus was on the people and customs of Paris, and it was his habit to record street life from a cab. As a critic wrote in 1880: "Jean Béraud has the strangest life imaginable. He spends all his time in carriages. It is not unusual to see a cab parked at the corner of a street for hours on end, with an artist sitting inside, firing off rapid sketches. That's Jean Béraud, in search of a scene, drawing a small fragment of Paris. Almost all the cab drivers in the city know him."[71] Hassam would adopt—and become well known for—a similar practice by the early 1890s.[72]

During the 1880s works by de Nittis and Béraud were becoming popular in the United States and could be found in several private collections. Examples were reproduced in Edward Strahan's *Art Treasures of America* (1879–82) as well as in other publications of the early 1880s.[73] De Nittis showed *Place de la Concorde,* 1875 (location unknown),[74] a rainy urban view, in the 1883 *Pedestal Fund Art Loan Exhibition.* Hassam could have seen these and perhaps other works by de Nittis

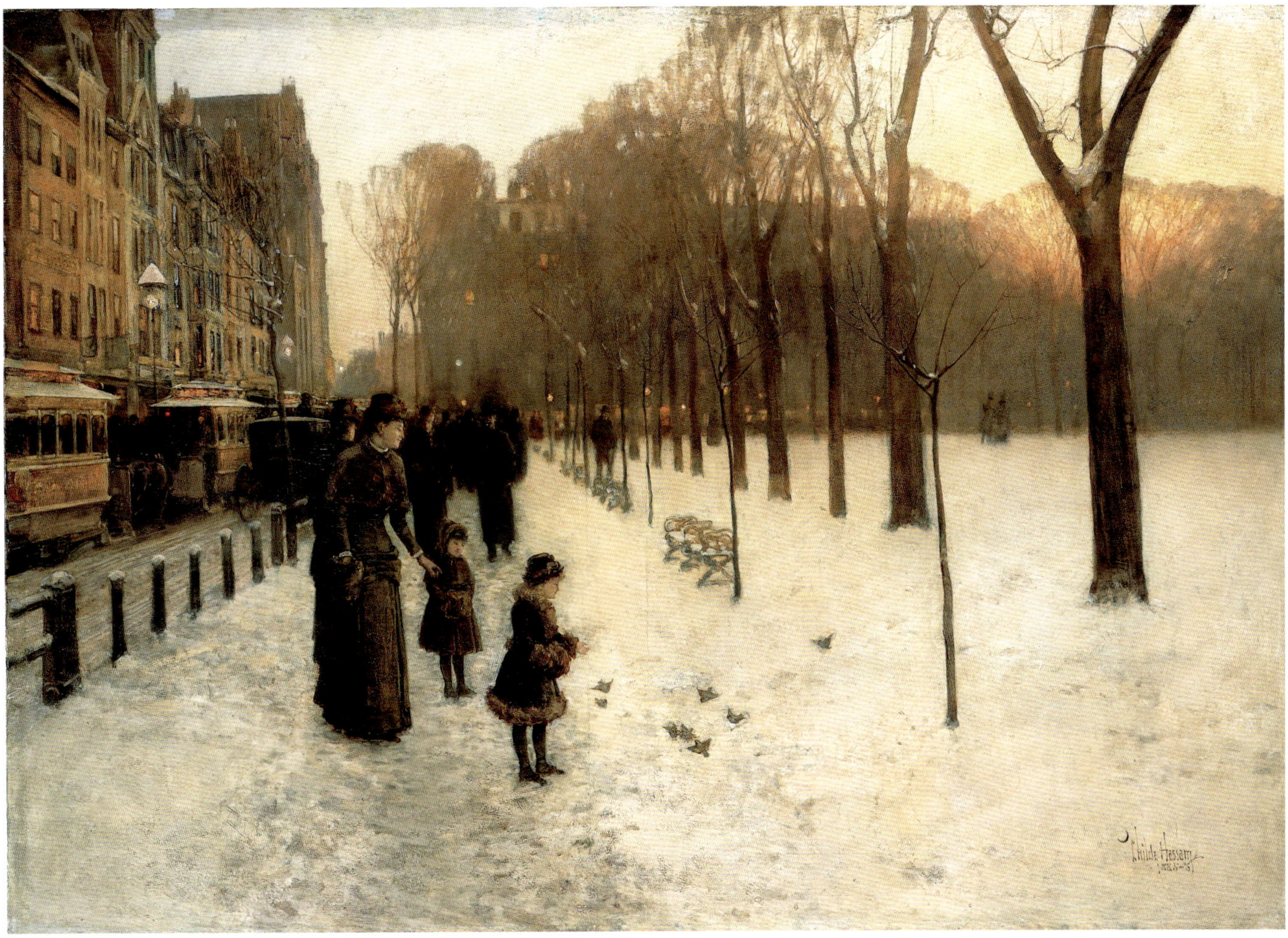

Fig. 39. Childe Hassam. *Boston Common at Twilight,* 1885–86. Oil on canvas, 42 x 60 in. (106.7 x 152.4 cm). The Museum of Fine Arts, Boston. Gift of Mrs. Maud E. Appleton

during his 1883 visit to Paris, when de Nittis's *Place des Pyramides,* 1883 (location unknown), for example, was on view at the Musée du Luxembourg.[75] Several works by Béraud were displayed in Munich and Amsterdam during Hassam's stay in Europe.[76] However, Hassam does not seem to have gone to Germany in 1883, and it is unclear whether he traveled to Amsterdam. Thus his exposure to Béraud's paintings may have been limited to written accounts and reproductions.

Hassam would have found in de Nittis's and Béraud's versions of Impressionism appropriate models to adapt for his conservative Boston audience, which until the later 1880s usually rejected Impressionism in favor of Barbizon-style landscapes. Indeed, the broad, open foreground, wet pavement, isolated pedestrians, and sober tone of *Rainy Day, Columbus Avenue, Boston* recall like features in de Nittis's *Place de la Concorde.* And the rendering of mood in Hassam's picture may also have been inspired by its counterpart in works by Béraud, including *Le Retour de l'enterrement,* which Hassam could have known from reproductions.[77]

Although Hassam never acknowledged the influence of de Nittis or Béraud, he did express admiration for the Dutch artist Johan Barthold Jongkind, whose urban scenes paralleled those of the Impressionists in their exploitation of dramatic perspective and elaboration of atmospheric effects realized through plein air painting. In an interview of 1927 Hassam recalled that he had discovered Jongkind through the followers of Hunt. Here he paraphrased Hunt's opinion of Jongkind: "'Jongkind [is] the modern man, who paints out-of-door scenes right, as I think it ought to be done.'" He concluded, "Jongkind was the best painter in France within the period from say 1860 to 1880."[78] Elsewhere he declared that he admired the Dutch artist's naturalistic palette and preferred it to that of Monet and other French painters.[79] And in 1928 he credited Jongkind as the first

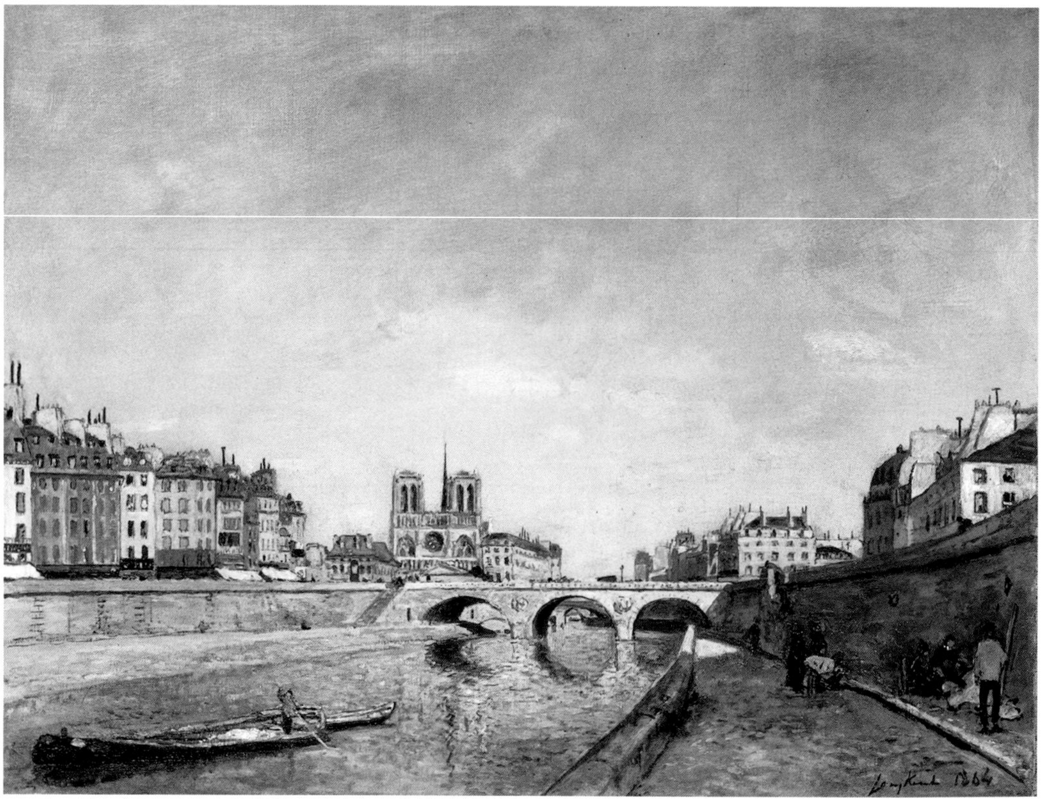

Fig. 40. Johan Barthold Jongkind. *The Seine and Notre-Dame, Seen from the Quai des Grands Augustins and the Pont Saint-Michel,* 1864. Oil on canvas, $11\frac{1}{4}$ x $16\frac{1}{2}$ in. (42 x 56.5 cm). Musée d'Orsay, Paris

painter "who tried for light, and large form out of doors" in his watercolors.[80]

In *Boston Common at Twilight* (fig. 39) Hassam sought to record the effect of fading daylight on the snow-covered park near his Tremont Street studio. Again he used a dramatic perspective, here framed by the repetitive forms of town houses and the trolley cars of Tremont Street on the left and tall bare trees that line the Common on the right. In many respects the picture recalls de Nittis's *A Winter's Promenade.*[81] Although it is unclear whether Hassam knew this particular painting or a related one, his elegant pedestrians at the edge of the park and de Nittis's figure are extremely close in conception, and the rendering of the birds against the snow, the large public space lined with town houses, and the bare trees are remarkably similar in both paintings. In its composition and use of perspective, however, Hassam's canvas is very like works by Jongkind, among them *The Seine and Notre-Dame, Seen from the Quai des Grands Augustins and the Pont Saint-Michel* (fig. 40) and *The Boulevard de Pont Royal, Paris,* 1877 (National Gallery, London). *Boston Common at Twilight* incorporates anecdotal scenes of modern life represented with an illustrator's precision in an image that captures the atmospheric effects of a specific moment during the day—thus synthesizing the hallmarks of Hassam's Boston period.

Hassam explored related themes in his monumental watercolor *The Public Garden (Boston Common)* (fig. 41).[82] Boston's Public Garden, established by legislative act in 1856, is one of the oldest botanical gardens in the United States. When Hassam made the garden the subject of this watercolor in the 1880s, it was being incorporated into the Boston Public Park system, the so-called Emerald Necklace designed by Frederick Law Olmsted between 1878 and 1896. Like the enlarged South End and the new Back Bay, this grand park system was a response to Boston's overcrowding and rapid growth.

As in *Boston Common at Twilight,* Hassam accentuated the dramatic recessions of Boston's avenues in *The Public Garden.* And here, as in the oil painting, he balanced his preoccupation with specifics of time and place with his interest in rendering atmospheric effects. The thinly planted flower bed at right, as well as the still-bare tree branches in the center of the composition, may suggest spring. One of the garden's distinctive features in the 1880s was its use of hothouse plants, which were continually rotated, a detail that Hassam perhaps indicated by including empty and overturned clay pots in the center foreground. Presumably, their contents had recently been transplanted to the nearby flower beds.[83]

In *A City Fairyland* (fig. 3), the last of the major Boston street scenes Hassam painted before he departed for study in Paris, he returned to the splayed perspective of *Rainy Day, Columbus Avenue, Boston*. Here, however, he represented the city under falling snow and fading daylight and accentuated spatial recession with the tracks of carriages and trolleys in the fresh snow. Although the site has been identified by some writers as Copley Square,[84] the heart of the Back Bay, the gentle light and the veil of snow combine to create a soft-focus image whose obscured details preclude certain recognition of place. Erica E. Hirshler has suggested that the location is probably in the enlarged South End.[85] She argues that the buildings in the background, with their relatively uniform rooflines, appear to be row houses typical of both the Back Bay and the South End but that three-sided intersections like the one shown are characteristic of the South End.[85] Rather than portraying a particular place, Hassam's main preoccupation, as in his earliest works, was to present the transitory effects of nature: the falling snow and muted light transforming the city into an otherworldly and ethereal fairyland.

Encouraged by his successes and having earned enough to support himself and his wife, Hassam determined to finish his artistic education in Paris. Before he left for Europe with Maud in autumn 1886, he had an unprecedented opportunity to see the kind of contemporary French art he would encounter abroad. About 290 French Impressionist oils and pastels came to New York for an exhibition that opened on April 10, 1886. This show was sponsored by the American Art Association and the Parisian dealer Durand-Ruel and was so popular that an expanded version, *Works in Oil and Pastel by the Impressionists of Paris*, was organized. Numbering 310 works, the larger exhibition opened on May 25 at the National Academy of Design. Included in this monumental display were seventeen works by Manet, twenty-three by Degas, forty-eight by Monet, forty-two by Pissarro, and ten by Caillebotte. Although it is not known whether Hassam

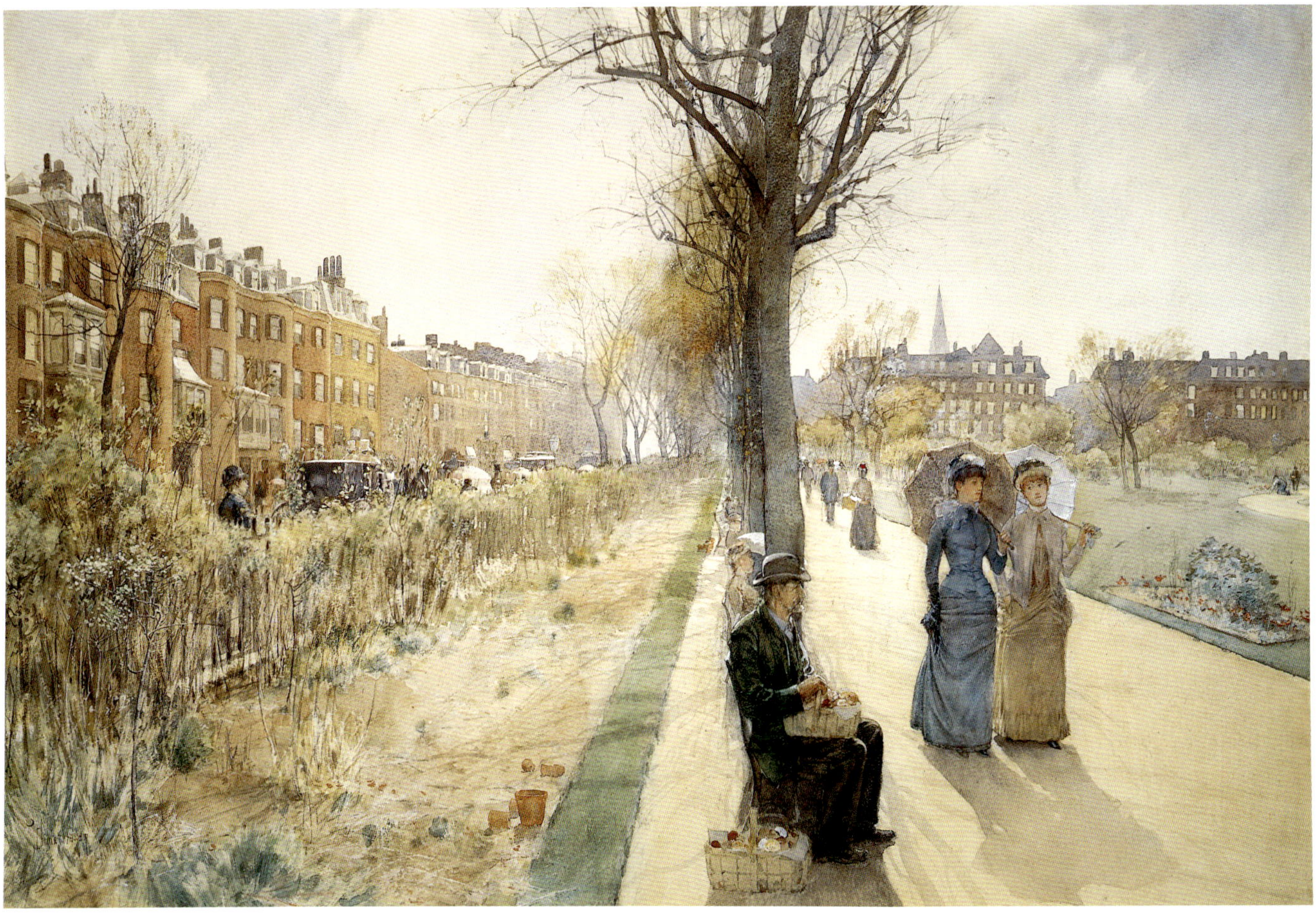

Fig. 41. Childe Hassam. *The Public Garden (Boston Common)*, ca. 1885. Watercolor on paper, 26⅛ x 38⅛ in. (66.4 x 96.8 cm). Slavin Family

visited the exhibition, he would certainly have been aware of it, as it received widespread attention in the press.[86]

When Hassam departed for Europe, he left behind a considerable body of paintings to be auctioned at Noyes, Cobb and Company in March 1887. The works constituted a veritable retrospective of his early career. In reviewing the exhibition that was held before the auction, the critic for the *Boston Evening Transcript* observed:

> *Childe Hassam is a strong painter, one of the men destined to hold high place in the landscape art of the century. . . . He has a breadth that is commensurate with Nature, he is keenly alive to all manner of natural and pictorial impressions; his sympathy is very wide. He takes true pleasure in everything that is beautiful, although, like so many modern painters, his feeling for effects of light is embryonic. Withal, his love of beauty is not for the trivial, broad and superficial, but for the more subtle and delicate effects. . . . There is always the very closest connection between Nature, his impression and his handling. The work is fresh, spontaneous, keenly interested; if anything, there seems almost too much catholicity, amounting to a lack of conviction, but this is due to his excessive breadth of sympathy; one can see in his latest pictures a growing personality.*

He concluded, presciently, "When Mr. Hassam gets home from Europe he will hold an artistic position second to almost no one."[87]

1. "Childe Hassam's Work at Noyes & Cobb's," undated clipping, labeled "*Boston Transcript*, [March] 1887," Hassam Papers, reel NAA1, frame 508. The exhibition and sale were held March 9 and 10, 1887. Although the clipping is undated, it must date from early March, as the unidentified author had seen the exhibition but the sale had not yet taken place when the review was written.
2. Hassam discussed his parents' genealogies in Lockman interview, January 25, 1927, pp. 2–4. The genealogies as reported by Hassam are confirmed in Frederick Adams Virkus, ed., *The Abridged Compendium of American Genealogy: First Families of America; a Genealogical Encyclopedia of the United States* (1925; reprint, Baltimore: Genealogical Publishing Co., 1987), vol. 1, p. 319.
3. See H. Barbara Weinberg, "Introduction," in this publication, p. 23, n. 2, for more information on Lockman.
4. Lockman interview, January 25, 1927, p. 1.
5. Ibid., pp. 6–7.
6. Ibid., January 31, 1927, p. 1.
7. Ibid.
8. Ibid., January 25, 1927, p. 9. In 1870 the Commonwealth of Massachusetts passed a legislative act requiring the teaching of drawing in the public schools. See Diana Korzenik, *Drawn to Art: A Nineteenth-Century American Dream* (Hanover, N.H.: University Press of New England, 1985), pp. 153–55.
9. Hassam, Letter to Miss Farmer, p. 3, 1933, Hassam Papers, reel NAA1, frame 746. According to Hassam's notes (reel NAA1, frame 743) accompanying it, "This letter was written in answer to a request from Miss Farmer who was making a record of the Graduates of the Dorchester High School."
10. Lockman interview, January 25, 1927, p. 9. Hassam both elaborated and condensed the story in his Autobiographical notes, typescript, n.d. [probably mid-1930s], Hassam Papers, reel NAA2, frame 227: "I prepared for college at the Dorchester High School and as I wanted to follow along the pathway of the Fine Arts in my third year at the High School I was put in a Boston wood engravers charge."
11. *The Boston Directory: Containing the City Record, a Directory of the Citizens, and Business Directory, for the Year Commencing July 1, 1879* (Boston: Sampson, Davenport, and Company, 1879), p. 433: "Hassam, Fred. C., draughtsman, 9 Milk, bds. Michigan av., Dorch."; *The Boston Directory, . . . for the Year Commencing July 1, 1880* (Boston: Sampson, Davenport, and Company, 1880), p. 454: "Hassam, Fred. C., draughtsman, 9 Milk, bds at Hyde Park"; *The Boston Directory, . . . for the Year Commencing July 1, 1882* (Boston: Sampson, Davenport, and Company, 1882), p. 489: "Hassam, Fred. C., artist, 28 School, rm. 56, bds. at Hyde Park." The 1882 directory, p. 561, lists "Johnson, George E. (Johnson & Co.), engraver, 9 Milk and 28 School, rm. 64, house at Waltham."
12. Jean Ingelow, *The High Tide on the Coast of Lincolnshire, 1571* (Boston: Roberts Brothers, 1883); William H. Thomes, *The Belle of Australia; or, Who Am I?* (Boston: DeWolfe, Fiske and Company, 1883).
13. Hiesinger (1994, p. 14) suggests that Hassam supported himself in the early 1880s by selling illustrations to such periodicals as *Babyland, Wide Awake, Saint Nicholas, "Harper's,"* and *"Scribner's."* However, a search of these publications revealed no signed illustrations by him prior to 1884. I am grateful to David B. Dearinger for providing us with a copy of his unpublished paper "The Book Illustrations of Childe Hassam" (Graduate Center, City University of New York, fall 1984).
14. For example, in 1879 the school's annual report noted that special evening classes would be offered during the 1879–80 school year only "until the evenings become too short." Museum of Fine Arts, *School of Drawing and Painting, Third Annual Report* (Boston: Alfred Mudge and Son, Printers, 1879), p. 23.
15. Lockman interview, January 25, 1927, pp. 9, 11.
16. *The United States Art Directory and Year-Book (Second Year)*, compiled by S. R. Koehler (New York, London, and Paris: Cassell and Company, 1884), pp. 67–68.
17. Ibid.
18. Hiesinger (1994, p. 18) offers a detailed account of the importance of Hassam's early professional relationships.

19. Hassam told Lockman: "I was very fortunate, I think, in being brought up in Boston, which was the centre of culture, for I had the advice of my fellow painters in my youth. There was Fuller, Johnson [*sic*], Cole and Robinson." Lockman interview, February 3, 1927, p. 15.
20. Hunt married Louisa Dumaresq Perkins. For a discussion of her family and its social prominence in Boston, see Sally Webster, *William Morris Hunt* (Cambridge: Cambridge University Press, 1991), pp. 39–40.
21. Hassam told Lockman, "My father's mother was Mary Hunt. Mary Hunt was the daughter of Roswell Hunt. Her grandsons were Richard Morris Hunt and William Morris Hunt. William Morris Hunt besides being a very able painter, probably left as deep an imprint on art culture of his city as anybody that ever lived in it." Lockman interview, February 3, 1927, p. 23. In an earlier interview Hassam had said, "My kinsman William Hunt I never actually met. But I saw him once walking through his studio where he had on exhibition his Niagara Falls picture. He was my relative but I did not pay any attention to it at all." Lockman interview, January 31, 1927, pp. 2–3.
22. "The Art Museum Exhibition," *Boston [Evening] Transcript*, April 29, 1879, p. 4. Although no catalogue has been found for this exhibition, the review includes an extensive discussion of the participating artists and their works. I am grateful to Trevor Fairbrother for providing a copy of this article. Fairbrother (1986, p. 39) discusses the exhibition.
23. Unidentified clipping, [autumn 1882], Hassam Papers, reel NAA1, frame 508. The clipping is undated, but the review pertains to the Williams and Everett exhibition of Hassam's work held in autumn 1882.
24. The Boston Art Club was founded with a membership of twenty people. By 1881 there were more than eight hundred members and a large new clubhouse was being built in the Back Bay. See Fairbrother 1986, p. 40.
25. Hassam exhibited in the 1882 Boston Art Club show as F. Childe Hassam. In 1883 he seems, for the most part, to have dropped the "F." *Promenade* is signed Childe Hassam. He did, however, continue to show under the name F. Childe Hassam at the Boston Art Club until 1887. Hassam recalled, "When I was not much past twenty I met Celia Thaxter who liked as so many others did . . . to paint in water colors. She said to me one day 'You should not with an unusual name like yours fail to take advantage of its unique character'" (Hassam, Letter to Miss Farmer, 1933, p. 5, Hassam Papers, reel NAA1, frame 747). For further discussion of his friendship with Thaxter, see Susan G. Larkin, "Hassam in New England, 1889–1918," in this publication, pp. 120–37.
26. Fairbrother 1986, p. 32.
27. *Water Colors by Fred C. Hassam*, exh. cat. (Boston: Williams and Everett, 1882).
28. Unidentified clipping, [autumn 1882], Hassam Papers, reel NAA1, frame 508.
29. These titles are from the 1882 Williams and Everett exhibition catalogue *Water Colors by Fred C. Hassam.*
30. Hiesinger 1994, p. 15, fig. 3. According to the records of the Vose Galleries, Boston, *Country Road* was shown in the 1882 Williams and Everett exhibition as no. 9, *Road Leading to Wayside Inn, Sudbury.* However, the basis of this identification is unknown. A sheet sold at Parke-Bernet Galleries, New York, on February 20, 1963, as *Wayside Inn, Sudbury, Mass.* (lot 8), seems more likely to be the watercolor from the Williams and Everett exhibition because it features a building. I am grateful to Kathleen M. Burnside for the reference to the Parke-Bernet sale. Hassam exhibited a watercolor called *The Red Horse Tavern (Longfellow's "Wayside Inn")* at the Boston Art Club in April 1884.
31. This watercolor may have been exhibited at Williams and Everett in autumn 1882 as no. 10, *Old House, Nantucket.*
32. Fairbrother 1986, p. 41.
33. Hassam's watercolor *Church Point, Portsmouth, New Hampshire,* inscribed *1883*, is reproduced in Curry 1990, p. 32. For Hassam's friendship with Thaxter, see n. 25, above.
34. "Studio Notes," *Studio* 1 (June 16, 1883), p. 265, and "Studio Notes," *Studio* 2 (July 1883), p. 33.
35. Lockman interview, January 31, 1927, p. 3. In the interview Hassam mistakenly said he went to Europe in 1882. Although he also remarked, "I did not go to Holland," a number of watercolors exhibited at Williams and Everett in 1884 include references to Holland and locales in the Netherlands in their titles. See, for example, no. 10, *Towing—Holland;* no. 19, *On the River, near Rotterdam;* no. 22, *On the Beach Scheveningen;* and no. 34, *Dutch Fisherman.*
36. Lockman asked: "Do you think these old pictures changed your viewpoint?" Hassam responded: "No, I cannot say that they had any influence." Lockman interview, January 31, 1927, p. 8.
37. Ibid., p. 6.
38. William Morris Hunt, *Talks on Art* (1896–98; reprint, with the title *On Painting and Drawing,* New York: Dover, 1976), p. 136, quoted in Fairbrother 1986, p. 35.
39. As Hassam explained, "I was working all the time by myself making water color paintings. I painted in water color mostly on that trip. It is the easiest way in which you can carry material." Lockman interview, January 31, 1927, p. 4.
40. The identification of this site is based on information from Hassam's exhibition *Water Colors by Hassam,* held at Williams and Everett in 1884, which included sixty-seven watercolors from his European travels. No. 23 was *The Promenade, Ouchy, Switzerland.* The ambitious format and the sophisticated and dramatic spatial construction of *The Promenade* suggest that Hassam planned it as a work for exhibition and that it may be the piece shown as no. 23.
41. The Blue Guides, *Switzerland, with Chamonix and the Italian Lakes,* edited by Findlay Muirhead (London: Macmillan and Company, 1923), p. 84.
42. Hassam may have been referring to this watercolor when he said to Lockman: "That was a trip without incident, and as I remember we had very wonderful weather. I made a water color of the ALSATIA, which is owned by a friend of mine. Let's see whether I can think of his name. I met him in Charleston, S.C. two winters ago. I recalled this water color and would like to get it again. What is his name? He is a painter. Mrs. Hassam can give me his name. He has that water color. It is very carefully done." Lockman: "What did you call it?" Hassam: "SS ALSATIA." Lockman interview, January 31, 1927, p. 10.
43. *French Girl Baking* is reproduced in Laura L. Meixner, *An International Episode: Millet, Monet, and Their North American Counterparts,* exh. cat. (Memphis, Tenn.: Dixon Gallery and Gardens, 1982), p. 23, fig. 9.
44. *United States Art Directory and Year-Book* 1884, p. 62–63.
45. Hassam recollected that, in 1884: "I was working in a life class. Always drawing from life under [Tommaso] Juglaris. He was an Italian painter who came over. He was a pleasant blond Italian. . . . I worked steadily in the life class. I worked out of doors everywhere that I could." Lockman interview, January 31, 1927, p. 11. In an interview a few days earlier Hassam had recalled: "I had instruction at the Lowell Institute. In the evening class and at the Boston Art Club. . . . There was an Italian by the name of Juglaress [*sic*] who instructed later, but who the other man was I cannot remember." Lockman interview, January 25, 1927, p. 11. Details of

Juglaris's biography are scarce. His life dates, 1844–1925, are given in Peter Hastings Falk, ed., *Who Was Who in American Art* (Madison, Conn.: Sound View Press, 1985), p. 1773. He studied first at the Academy in Turin and then with Thomas Couture in Paris, starting in 1871. In 1879 he went to Boston to become artistic director of Prang and Company, a firm that reproduced works of art in the form of engravings, a position he left after six months in order to work independently. Further biographical details can be found in *Allgemeines Lexikon der bildenden Künstler von der Antike bis zur Gegenwart begründet von Ulrich Thieme und Felix Becker,* edited by Hans Vollmer, vol. 19 (Leipzig: E. A. Seemann, 1926), p. 301. The Hassam literature often mentions his studies with the German-émigré painter Ignaz Marcel Gaugengigl. Yet Hassam named only Juglaris as his teacher in Boston, and no contemporary sources about either Hassam or Gaugengigl mention a student-teacher relationship. The first reference to Gaugengigl as Hassam's teacher appears in Adams 1938, pp. 19–20: "He studied at the Lowell Institute. Then, when a young German artist, Mr. I. M. Gaugengigl, opened a class on painting from the model, and proved to be an excellent instructor, Hassam worked under his careful counsels. The studio was less crowded than that at the Lowell Institute, and he made good progress." Hiesinger (1994, p. 16) concluded: "Hassam apparently mentioned studying for a time with the German painter Ignaz Gaugengigl," adding (p. 28, n. 19): "Adams, op. cit., p. 19, is the only source for this information; she may have confused Gaugengigl's name with that of Juglaris." Hiesinger's conclusion, with which we concur, is especially compelling since Adams never mentioned Juglaris, whom Hassam acknowledged twice in the Lockman interviews. Hassam's reference to "the other man" in the Lockman interview, January 25, 1927, p. 11, leaves room for speculation. However, Gaugengigl had a long career in Boston, and Hassam would probably have remembered his name. If Hassam did study with Gaugengigl, little of his influence is apparent in his works, which are more closely aligned with the tradition of Couture as transmitted by Juglaris than with the German artist's Munich-based realism.

46. The exact dates of this exhibition are unknown.
47. Lockman interview, January 31, 1927, p. 10.
48. "Mr. Hassam's Water Colors," undated clipping, labeled "*Boston Globe,*" Hassam Papers, reel NAA1, frame 508.
49. This title can be traced back to 1887. The painting was included in *Exhibition and Sale of Works in Oil and Water Color by Childe Hassam* held at Noyes, Cobb and Company, Boston, March 9–10, 1887, as no. 72, *Old Fairbanks House. Dedham.* A related work is *Old House, Dorchester,* 1884 (location unknown; illustrated in William H. Gerdts, *American Impressionism* [New York: Abbeville Press, 1984], p. 93, fig. 95). In this painting, as in *The Old Fairbanks House,* Hassam showed local rural architecture from a low vantage point. Here, however, a flowering tree occupies the center foreground. The result is a plein air study that is more sophisticated in composition and handling than earlier works such as *Old House, Nantucket* (fig. 24).
50. "The Academy Exhibition," *Art Journal* 3 (1877), p. 159, quoted in Nicolai Cikovsky Jr. and Franklin Kelly, *Winslow Homer,* exh. cat. (Washington, D.C.: National Gallery of Art; New Haven: Yale University Press, 1995), p. 95.
51. "Editor's Table," *Appleton's Journal* 6 (May 1879), p. 471, quoted in Cikovsky and Kelly, *Winslow Homer,* p. 95.
52. See under December 1880 in "Exhibitions in Homer's Lifetime," in Cikovsky and Kelly, *Winslow Homer,* p. 409.
53. "Childe Hassam's Work at Noyes & Cobb's," undated clipping, labeled "*Boston Transcript,* [March] 1887."
54. Lockman interview, February 2, 1927, p. 10.
55. In 1916 Hassam recalled seeing *La Marcellerie* at the Society of American Artists in 1884; Childe Hassam, "Foreword," in *Memorial Exhibition, Paintings by the Late Ruger Donoho,* exh. cat. (New York: The Macbeth Gallery, 1916).
56. Hassam told Lockman: "I made illustrations and thought that I had to have a studio. I took one it only cost about $250. a year. It was at 149 Tremont Street, Boston, and that was a small studio. I suppose I paid $250. a year for it. Then I met George Fuller, he had a studio in the same building." Lockman interview, January 25, 1927, pp. 10–11.
57. See n. 19 above. Fuller encouraged Hassam to exhibit his paintings: "Fuller insisted on showing one of my paintings with a group of Boston painters that was exhibited in New York City. . . . I [was] a boy of 21." Lockman interview, January 25, 1927, p. 11. The exhibition referred to has not been identified. See also Lockman interview, February 3, 1927, p. 15, as discussed in Hiesinger 1994, p. 18.
58. Greta [pseud.], "Boston Correspondence," *Art Amateur* 12 (March 1885), p. 82, quoted in Hiesinger 1994, p. 20.
59. Teresa A. Carbone, *American Paintings in the Brooklyn Museum of Art: Artists Born by 1876,* forthcoming, 2004. Carbone cites Hunt's *Sand Dunes, Newbury, Massachusetts,* 1875 (Mead Art Museum, Amherst, Massachusetts), and Pissarro's *Jalais Hill, Pontoise,* 1867 (The Metropolitan Museum of Art, New York, 51.30.2). I am grateful to Dr. Carbone for making available a draft of her catalogue entry for this painting.
60. Prolific guidebook author Moses King observed in 1881 that the avenue was eighty feet wide, and "the sidewalks, being each eighteen feet wide, give the avenue virtually a width of one hundred and sixteen feet, and make of it one of the finest thoroughfares in Boston." Moses King, *The Back-Bay District and the Vendome,* 3rd ed. (Boston: N.p., 1881), p. 7.
61. See Bienenstock 1980, p. 169, and H. Barbara Weinberg, "Introduction," in this publication, p. 23, n. 20.
62. The site is identified in the catalogue entry for this painting in Susan E. Strickler, *The Toledo Museum of Art, American Paintings* (Toledo, Ohio: Toledo Museum of Art, 1979), p. 58. Much of the discussion of this painting that follows is based on Weinberg, Bolger, and Curry 1994, pp. 173–75.
63. Hiesinger (1994, p. 24) mentions the resemblance only in passing. Michael J. Murphy discusses the subject at greater length in "The Rejecting Embrace: Urban Modernity and Childe Hassam's *Rainy Day, Boston*" (Master's thesis, Washington University, Saint Louis, 1998), chap. 2. However, Hassam denied the influence of photography. He told A. E. Ives, "I have been asked if I did not think photographic views were great helps to the artist in this branch of study. Undoubtedly they might be, but they have not been so to me. I never owned a camera or pressed the button of a Kodak in my life." Ives 1892, p. 117.
64. Ives 1892, p. 117.
65. Henry James, *The Bostonians* (1886; London and New York: Penguin Books, 1984), p. 54. *The Bostonians* was first serialized in *Century* 29–31 (February 1885–February 1886).
66. It is unclear which of Hassam's several tonal views of Boston on a rainy day was shown at the Society of American Artists from May to October 1886 or at the National Academy of Design in April 1886. Frank T. Robinson, *Living New England Artists: Biographical Sketches* (Boston: Samuel E. Cassino, 1888; reprint, New York: Garland Publishing Co., 1977), p. 102.
67. *Official Catalogue: Foreign Exhibition,* compiled by C. B. Norton (Boston: George Coolidge, 1883).

68. Maureen C. O'Brien, *In Support of Liberty: European Paintings at the 1883 Pedestal Fund Art Loan Exhibition,* exh. cat. (Southampton, N.Y.: Parrish Art Museum, 1986).
69. Bienenstock 1980, pp. 168–71.
70. Albert Boime, *The Academy and French Painting in the Nineteenth Century* (London: Phaidon, 1971), pp. 15–21, discusses the juste-milieu.
71. Paul Hourie, "Jean Béraud," *L'estafette,* September 13, 1880, page not given, as translated in Patrick Offenstadt, *Jean Béraud, 1849–1935; the Belle Epoque: A Dream of Times Gone By; Catalogue Raisonné* (Cologne: Benedikt Taschen for the Wildenstein Institute, 1999), p. 9.
72. "'I paint from cabs a good deal,' said Mr. Childe Hassam, when asked how he got his spirited sketches of street life. 'I select my point of view and set up my canvas, or wooden panel, on the little seat in front of me, which forms an admirable easel.'" Ives 1892, p. 116.
73. Edward Strahan [Earl Shinn], ed., *The Art Treasures of America: Being the Choicest Works of Art in the Public and Private Collections of North America* 3 vols. (Philadelphia: G. Barrie, [1879–82]; reprint, New York: Garland Publishing Co., 1977), reproduces Giuseppe de Nittis's *"Isn't It Cold?"* (collection of Chauncey J. Blair, Chicago) in vol. 3, opp. p. 67, and Jean Béraud's, *A Funeral at the Madeleine* (collection of Henry Hilton, New York) in vol. 2, p. 51.
74. Reproduced in O'Brien, *In Support of Liberty,* fig. 20.
75. As Bienenstock mentions, de Nittis showed street scenes at both the *Exposition internationale de peinture* at the Galerie Georges Petit, Paris, held May 11–June 10, 1883, and at an exhibition at the Palais des Champs-Elysées, which opened in September 1883 (*Catalogue officiel des ouvrages de peinture, sculpture, architecture, gravure et lithographie des artistes vivants exposés au Palais des Champs-Elysées, le 15 septembre 1883* [Paris: Réunies, 1883]). However, Hassam does not seem to have been in Paris while either of those exhibitions was open. Bienenstock 1980, p. 170.
76. Béraud exhibited at the *Exposition universelle de la Section des Beaux-Arts,* Amsterdam, May 1–October 31, 1883, and at the *International Kunstausstellung,* Munich, July 15–October 15, 1883. Offenstadt, *Jean Béraud,* p. 360.
77. Hassam's connection with other conservative French painters of modern life calls for further investigation. One artist to whom he may have looked is Firmin-Girard (Firmin Marie-François Girard), whose *The Flower Market, Paris,* is illustrated in Strahan's *Art Treasures of America,* vol. 3, opp. p. 115. Another whose works invite comparison is Norbert Goeneutte; see his *Boulevard de Clichy under Snow* (fig. 45).
78. Lockman interview, February 3, 1927, p. 15.
79. Hassam also told Lockman: "All this patter about the Frenchmen and all about Monet cleaning up the Pallet [*sic*]. He never discovered that at all. It was the Dutchman Jonkind [*sic*] who William Hunt brought to Boston. Jonkind [*sic*] was the first man who painted in that way, and I saw him in Boston." Lockman interview, January 25, 1927, p. 12.

The estate of Jongkind's most important collector, Theodore Bascle, was auctioned at the Hôtel Drouot, Paris, April 12–14, 1883. The results indicate Jongkind's popularity at that time. The collection, which included eighty-three canvases and twenty-one watercolors by Jongkind, was admired and sold for the considerable sum of 193,000 francs. Some details about the auction can be found in Victorine Hefting, *Jongkind: Sa vie, son oevure, son époque* (Paris: Arts et Métiers Graphiques, 1975), p. 386. Hassam was not in Paris in April 1883 and could not, therefore, have attended the sale.
80. Hassam 1928, p. 27. The influence of Jongkind on Hassam is mentioned as early as 1906: "He found his first inspiration in Jongkind, one of the earliest champions of a lighter key and looser handling, a few of whose pictures had strayed to Boston." S[adakichi] H[artman], "Studio-Talk: [Childe Hassam]," *International Studio* 29 (September 1906), p. 267.
81. Sotheby's, New York, sale cat., May 24, 1995, lot 245.
82. This watercolor was previously published as *Boston Common,* ca. 1886–91. For example, see Adelson, Cantor, and Gerdts 1999–2000, p. 126, fig. 134. However, in 1890 it was reproduced as *The Public Garden* in Clarence Pullen, "The Boston Park and Parkway System," *Harper's Weekly* 34 (September 27, 1890), p. 747. The watercolor was probably exhibited as *In the Public Garden* at the Boston Art Club (no. 129) in April 1885 and in the Noyes and Cobb sale (no. 48) in March 1887. A review of the Noyes, Cobb and Company exhibition mentions "'In the Public Garden,' a large water color which was much admired in the American Water Color Society exhibition of 1886." No catalogue has been found to confirm that it was included in the latter show. "Mr. Hassam's Exhibition," undated clipping, labeled "*Boston Advertiser,* 1887," Hassam Papers, reel NAA1, frame 508. Hassam sent a work titled *The Public Garden (Spring)* for exhibition at the St. Botolph Club, Boston, in April 1886. However, the medium was not specified in the catalogue; it is unlikely that it was a watercolor, as it was offered for sale at $350, an unrealistically high price for a work in the medium in this period.
83. For more information about the Boston Public Garden and its history, see *The Public Garden Boston* (Boston: Friends of the Public Garden and Common, 1988) and M[ariana] G[riswold] Van Rensselaer, "Correspondence:—The Boston Public Garden," *Garden and Forest* 1 (September 12, 1888), pp. 345–46.
84. For example, see Hiesinger 1994, p. 26.
85. Erica E. Hirshler, e-mail message to author, September 15, 2002.
86. It is possible, and tempting to imagine, that Hassam traveled to New York during the spring of 1886 and thus would have had a chance to see the Durand-Ruel exhibition. He showed a painting at the National Academy of Design (April 5–May 15, 1886) and made his debut with a painting at the Society of American Artists (May 5–October 15, 1886). For further discussion of the Durand-Ruel exhibition and some of the critical reaction to it, see Gerdts, *American Impressionism,* pp. 51–53.
87. "Childe Hassam's Work at Noyes & Cobb's," undated clipping, labeled "*Boston Transcript,* 1887."

CHAPTER TWO

Hassam in Paris, 1886–1889

H. Barbara Weinberg

By 1886 Hassam had crafted from random resources a credible technique and an appealing range of subjects and had begun to attract favorable notices for his work. Having supported himself by making watercolors and illustrations, he decided to commit himself to painting by going to Paris to study. "I was well paid," he told DeWitt McClellan Lockman in January 1927, "I said to myself if you're going to paint let's stop. So I stopped."[1] While this recollection exaggerated Hassam's renunciation of illustration—even while he was in Paris he would seek income from illustrating and, until about 1895, would make watercolors for reproduction in journals and books—he was, apparently, determined to work primarily as a painter.[2]

Hassam sailed for Europe in the autumn of 1886 with his wife, Maud. A commentator wrote in the *Art Amateur* of November of that year: "Childe Hassam, the audacious and brilliant watercolorist and landscapist, is off for three years study in Paris [see fig. 42]."[3] The successful sale of Hassam's works in the Boston galleries of Noyes, Cobb and Company in March 1887 vindicated this critic's assessment and financed the trip.

Although Hassam was much more mature artistically than most of his American colleagues by the time he went to Paris to study, his decision to do so was inevitable. For about twenty years American art had been redefined by French influence. Emulating the French contemporaries with whom

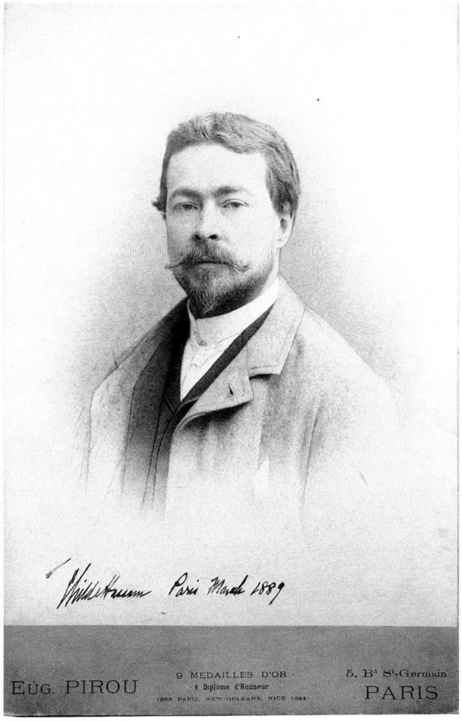

Fig. 42. Eugène Pirou. Hassam in Paris, March 1889. American Academy of Arts and Letters, New York

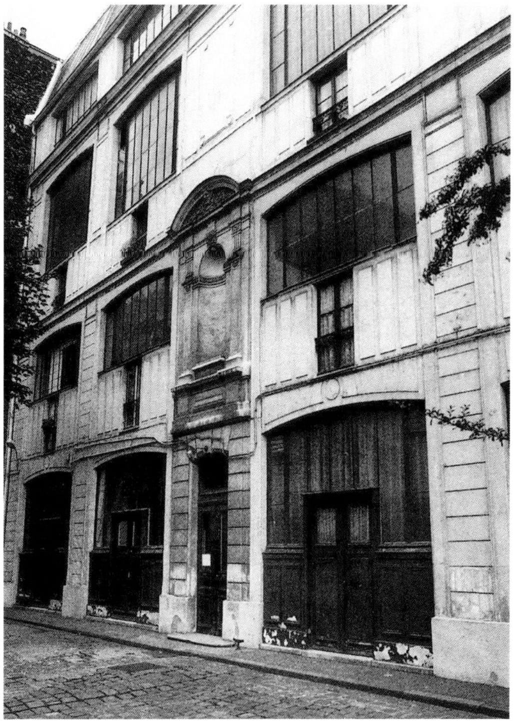

Fig. 43. Hassam's studio at 11, boulevard de Clichy, Montmartre

Detail, fig. 57. *Along the Seine, Winter*

they had to compete for patronage, American painters abandoned expansive views for intimate, poetic landscapes in the Barbizon manner and explored the historical, ideal, and exotic subjects that had brought acclaim to academic masters such as Jean-Léon Gérôme and Alexandre Cabanel.[4] American artists of Hassam's generation deemed training in Paris to be the essential capstone to preliminary work in local schools that had been formed or re-formed according to the French instructional model.

Hassam and his wife settled into an apartment with an adjoining studio at 11, boulevard de Clichy in Montmartre (fig. 43). Hassam recalled that it was "right in the quarter of the painters that were called 'arrived painters.' When you think of the assumption [*sic*] of this young man to go there to live! Of course if you had the price—you could live there. You could have an apartment."[5] The boulevard de Clichy—which runs eastward from the place de Clichy through the place Blanche to the place Pigalle, where it becomes the boulevard Rochechouart—was the boundary between Montmartre and the Paris of the *grands boulevards* to the south.[6] During the late 1880s the Clichy district was evolving into an artistic quarter and a center for bars and cabarets. Along the boulevard de Clichy were establishments in which artists gathered, among them the Restaurant du Chalet and Café du Tambourin, at no. 43 and no. 62, respectively. The Moulin Rouge, featuring an open-air café chantant and astonishing dancing, opened on place Blanche in May 1889 to attract visitors to the Exposition Universelle of that year. Landmarks of the boulevard Rochechouart were the Élysées Montmartre and Mirliton dance halls and the Cirque Fernando, which Edgar Degas and Henri de Toulouse-Lautrec had painted.

North of the boulevards de Clichy and Rochechouart, the steep streets of Montmartre retained the spirit of a rural village. Sacré-Cœur, the great basilica that was still rising on the butte de Montmartre, would welcome worshipers in 1891. Its domes would accent the northern Paris skyline as the new Eiffel Tower, constructed for the 1889 Exposition, would punctuate the southern. The neighborhood was rich with artistic ferment.

Occupants of studios in the quarter in the same period that Hassam lived at the edge of Montmartre were numerous and diverse. They included, on the boulevard de Clichy alone, Paul Signac, a practitioner and later a theorist of Neoimpressionism, who worked at no. 130 from 1886 to 1888; Georges Seurat at no. 128 bis from 1887 to 1891; muralist Fernand Cormon, who ran a teaching studio at no. 104 and instructed Montmartre denizens van Gogh and Toulouse-Lautrec; Swedish portraitist and printmaker Anders Zorn at no. 71 from about 1888 to 1896; renowned academic Gérôme at no. 65; and American-born Impressionist Mary Cassatt at no. 6. Among the residents of Hassam's building were portraitist Giovanni Boldini, historical genre painter Henri Pille, and Frank Boggs, an American painter of urban subjects, among them *La Place de la Bastille* (fig. 44) and *Paris Street Scene,* 1893 (The Metropolitan Museum of Art, New York, 1971.246.1).

Artists of various persuasions captured the half-built, ancient-modern character of the boulevard de Clichy about the time of Hassam's residence there. Their views record the boulevard's mix of two-story wooden dwellings juxtaposed

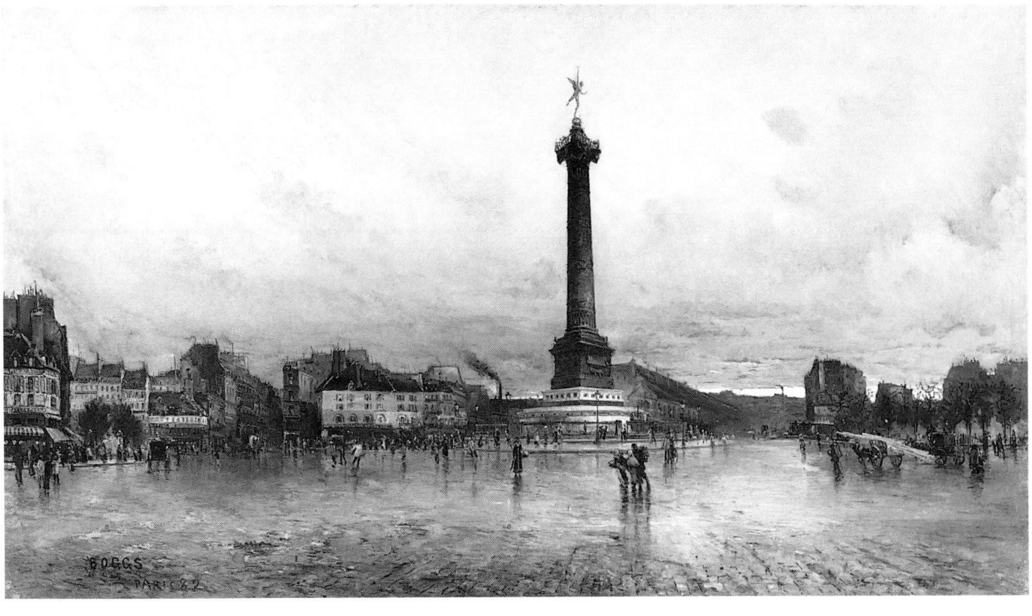

Fig. 44. Frank Boggs. *La Place de la Bastille,* 1882. Oil on canvas, 55⅛ x 98⅜ in. (140 x 249.9 cm). Musée de La Coopération Franco-Américaine, Blérancourt, France

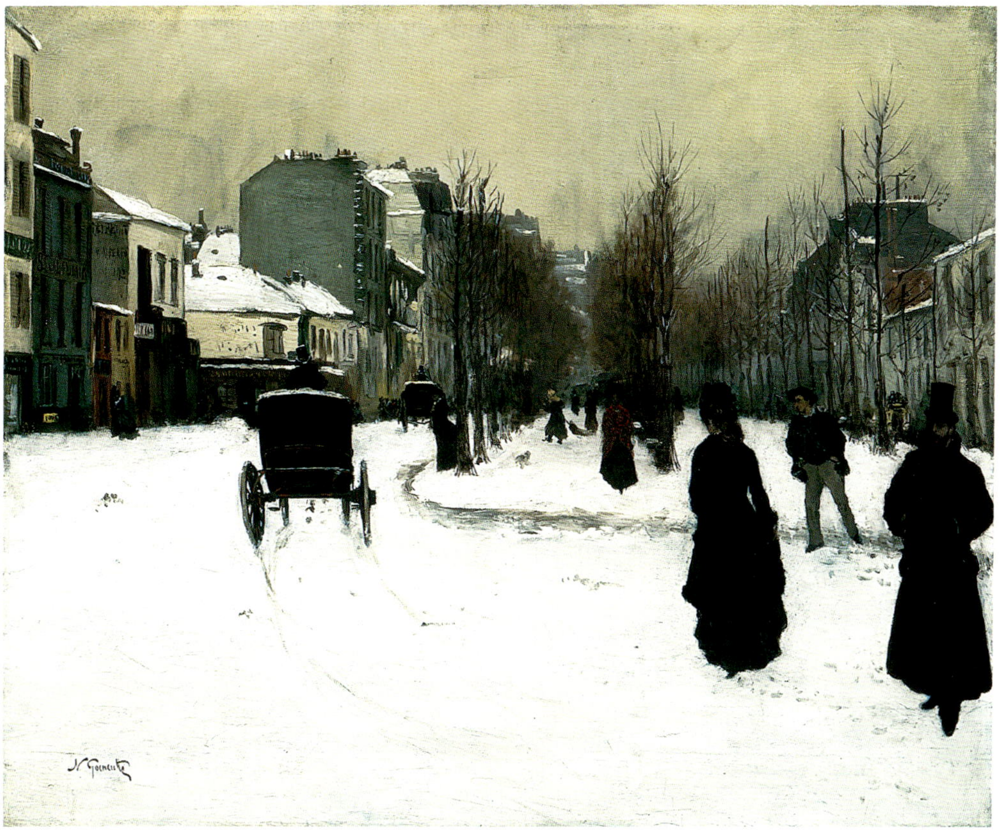

Fig. 45. Norbert Goeneutte. *The Boulevard de Clichy under Snow,* 1876. Oil on canvas, 23 ⅝ x 28 ⅞ in. (60 x 73.3 cm). Tate, London

with new mansard-roofed studios and its wide median, planted with young trees. Pertinent to Hassam's own paintings of Paris streets are Norbert Goeneutte's detailed *Boulevard de Clichy under Snow* (fig. 45); Signac's Pointillist *Snow, Boulevard de Clichy, Paris* (fig. 46); and van Gogh's *Boulevard de Clichy, Paris* (fig. 47).

On November 20, 1886, Hassam wrote to Rose Lamb, a Boston portrait painter: "We have arrived safely and have at last found a nice little apartment—with a tremendously fine large studio connected. It is fifty feet square and as high, I should think. . . . We are on high ground and look down on Paris,—i.e. the Grand Opera and finest boulevards are at the foot of the hill (Montmartre). We shall be first rate and snug when we are fixed up a little more."[7] An attentive, recently wed husband, Hassam was sensitive to his wife's response to Paris and yielded to her practical dictates. "Mrs. Maude [*sic*]

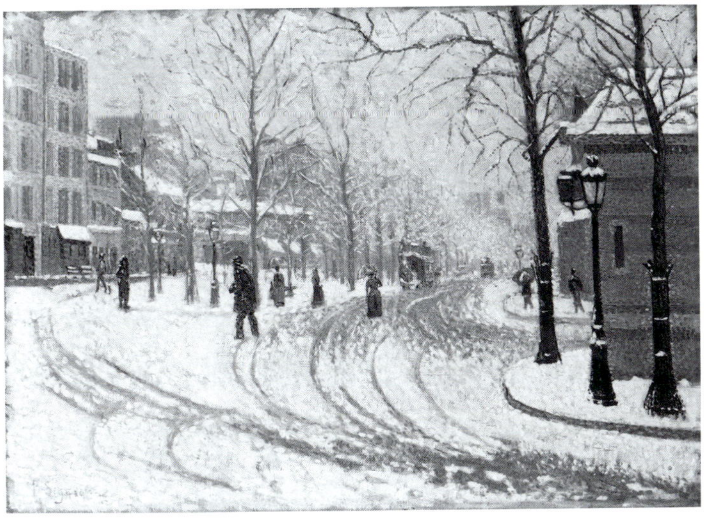

Fig. 46. Paul Signac. *Snow, Boulevard de Clichy, Paris,* 1886. Oil on canvas, 19 x 25 ⅞ in. (48.3 x 65.7 cm). The Minneapolis Institute of Arts, Bequest of Putnam Dana McMillan

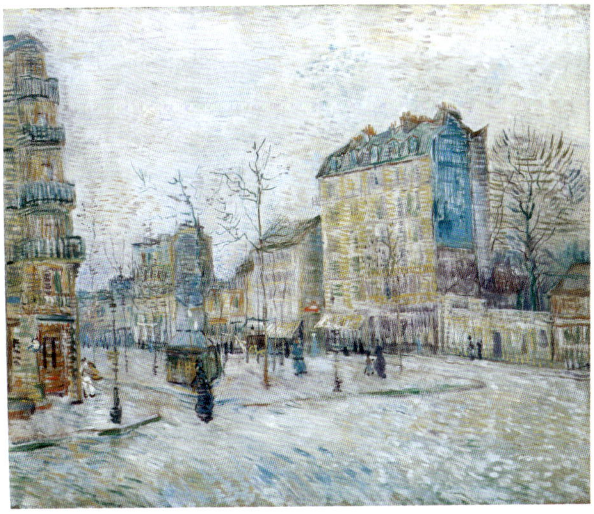

Fig. 47. Vincent van Gogh. *Boulevard de Clichy, Paris,* 1887. Oil on canvas, 17 ⅞ x 21⅝ in. (45.4 x 54.9 cm). Van Gogh Museum (Vincent van Gogh Foundation), Amsterdam

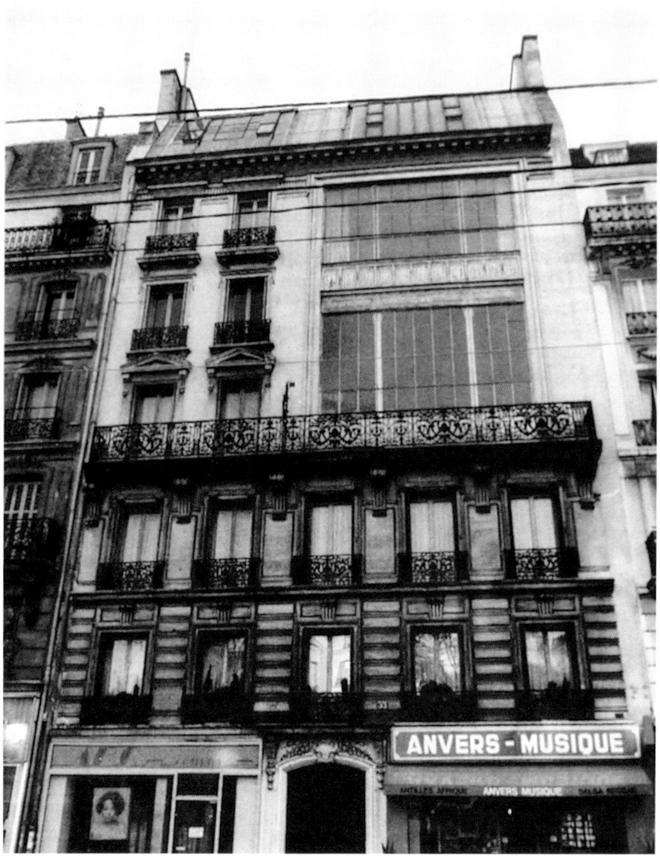

Fig. 48. Hassam's studio at 35, boulevard Rochechouart

likes Paris only pretty well as yet. She will be sure to like it better," he told Lamb. He admitted: "Mrs. Maude [*sic*] gave me a fine scolding because I came home one day with two fine old 'prayer rugs' and a little Moorish table inlaid with Mother of Pearl. . . . She says if I keep on I will not have enough money to buy actual necessities in the way of furniture, and as she is my business manager, legal adviser and wife all in one, I find I have to stop."[8] Boston artist and writer Susan Hale visited Hassam and "his pretty, charming little wife" in 1887 and reported: "The Hassams have a rosey apartment which includes a big studio with an admirable light, hung about with rugs and things which they know how to select."[9]

By late autumn 1887 Hassam and his wife had moved to a new studio at 35, boulevard Rochechouart (fig. 48). "I am," he wrote to Lamb on November 29, 1887, "only a stone's throw from the other place. We like our new quarters much better—the studio is no better, but the living rooms are more connected and it is pleasanter in winter on that account."[10] He told Lockman in January 1927: "I led a very quiet life. Of course, we saw the Mont Martre life around us. The Elysee–Mont Martre was just across the way. It did not interest me much."[11] Many avant-garde artists who lived in Hassam's neighborhood were, of course, inspired to depict the entertainments available along the boulevard de Clichy and the boulevard Rochechouart: their paintings of the subject include Louis Anquetin's *La Place Clichy* (fig. 49); van Gogh's *Woman at a Table in the Café du Tambourin,* 1887 (van Gogh Museum, Amsterdam); and Toulouse-Lautrec's *Equestrienne (At the Circus Fernando),* 1887–88 (Art Institute of Chicago). It may be that Hassam looked back and exaggerated his detachment from Montmartre's lively scene when he spoke to Lockman in 1927. If so, his denial perhaps reflects his puritanism, his durable tendency to portray himself as self-invented, and the repudiation of foreign influence that prevailed in America during the isolationist 1920s. Whether or not he exaggerated, the works Hassam produced in Paris do bear witness to his aesthetic distance from the world of van Gogh, Toulouse-Lautrec, and his other Montmartre neighbors, despite his physical presence in it.

Hassam's utterly bourgeois living arrangements and apparent puritanical temperament set him apart even from his compatriots, many of whom arrived in Paris younger than he and were unmarried, friendlier with one another, and more engaged with the city's bohemian elements. "We had a French maid and lived there like a very proper worth-while family. . . . We lived among French people, spoke French. It was a French house and we wanted to speak French," Hassam later recalled, suggesting that his isolation from his fellow Americans was intentional. Indeed, when he was asked, "You did not meet many of the American men at this time?" Hassam replied, "No, I met almost nobody."[12] The fact that Hassam and his wife did not travel during their stay in France perhaps indicates not only that they needed and tried to limit expenses but also his indifference to hobnobbing with other artists.[13] Although the American colony at Giverny, for example, was beginning to burgeon with the extended or occasional presence of Theodore Robinson, Willard L. Metcalf, and John Singer Sargent, Hassam did not venture there, to Barbizon, or to other artists' colonies.

Hassam did, however, follow the most common course of study for Americans by enrolling, probably as soon as he was settled, in the Académie Julian, a popular training ground

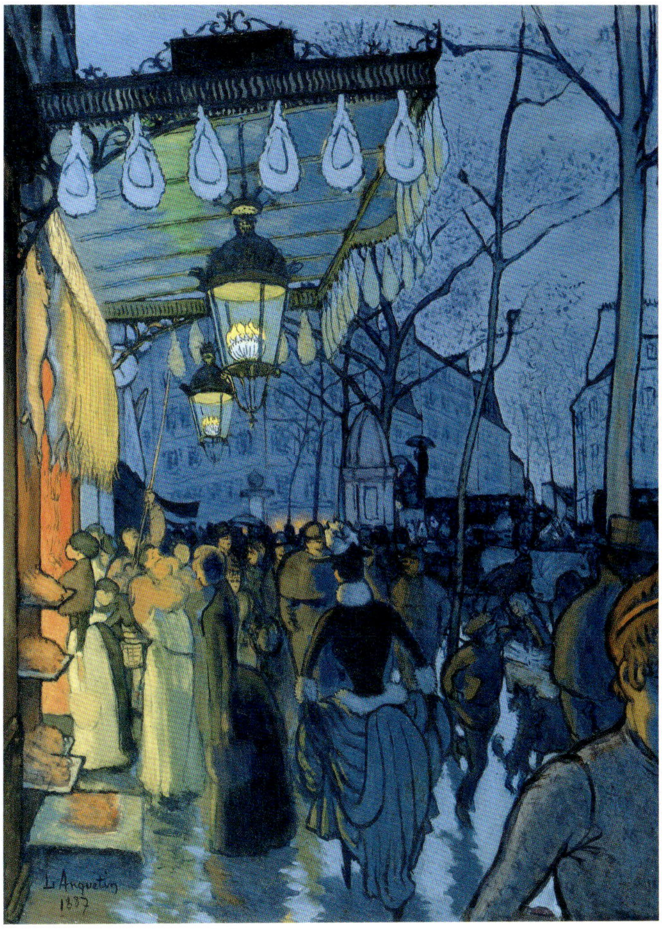

Fig. 49. Louis Anquetin. *La Place Clichy,* 1887. Oil on canvas, 27⅛ x 21 in. (68.9 x 53.3 cm). Wadsworth Atheneum, Hartford, The Ella Gallup Sumner and Mary Catlin Sumner Collection Fund

for students from all over the world. Founded in 1868 to prepare aspirants for the entrance examinations at the French government's École des Beaux-Arts, Julian's had become a profitable rival academy, with studios for men and women installed throughout Paris. The tuition-free government school (limited to men until 1897) required an application to one of the three *chefs d'atelier* for painting for admission to the teacher's studio, or success in a rigorous semiannual examination for matriculation and access to the daily drawing class. By contrast, entrance to Julian's depended merely on the ability to pay monthly tuition. Julian's taught only practical skills, unlike the government school, where lectures on history and archaeology, art history and aesthetics, anatomy, and other subjects accompanied technical training. The painting styles of Julian's instructors were identical to those of the École's *chefs d'atelier,* whose influence on the annual Salon juries they also matched. Assigned in pairs to the various studios, Julian's instructors were expected to visit their classes twice weekly, usually in alternating months, to critique *académies*—single-figure studies of nude models—which were either drawn or painted, depending the student's level of advancement.[14]

The most popular atelier for Americans at Julian's in the late 1880s—and, ultimately, for most American Impressionists of Hassam's generation—was overseen by Gustave-Rodolphe Boulanger, a successful Orientalist, and Jules-Joseph Lefebvre, a history painter. Located at 48, rue du faubourg Saint-Denis in the tenth arrondissement, not far from the gare de l'Est and from Hassam's residence, the studio had already attracted several of Hassam's Boston contemporaries by the time he started there. Frank W. Benson, for example, had studied from about 1880 to 1883 at the School of the Museum of Fine Arts, Boston, before entering Julian's, where he worked under Boulanger and Lefebvre from 1883 to 1885. Hassam's friend Edmund C. Tarbell followed the same path but remained at Julian's a year longer. Metcalf had attended several Boston art schools, including the Massachusetts Normal Art School, the Lowell Institute, and the School of the Museum of Fine Arts, before he studied at Julian's under Boulanger and Lefebvre in 1883–84. Albert Henry Munsell, a graduate of and instructor at the Massachusetts Normal Art School, began working under Boulanger and Lefebvre in 1885.[15]

By the time Hassam arrived in Paris, although he had received less formal training at home than had most of his compatriots, he was not only more advanced as a painter but also more widely traveled than they. Thanks to the favor he had gained in Boston for his outdoor scenes of contemporary life, he must have felt that he had mastered composition and perspective. Probably, however, he perceived a need for additional study of figure drawing and figure painting, the key academic tasks. Whether he deemed his studies in Paris to be essential to his mastery of the figure or a pro forma professional obligation, he worked hard as a student.

Years later Hassam recalled entering Julian's: "Albert E. [*sic*] Munsell was there at the time and he introduced me into Julians' Academy, and I remember that they gave me out of compliment a seat in the front row, looking up at this model, and my first drawing was done under Jules Le Fevre. . . . And they said: 'Why you don't want to do this any more.' It was a very careful academic drawing. After that I could do as I wanted to. . . . Although I made a few paintings from [life] in Julian's I made any number of drawings from life, as I believed in a careful academic training whatever you are going to do."[16] And he wrote to Boston critic William Howe

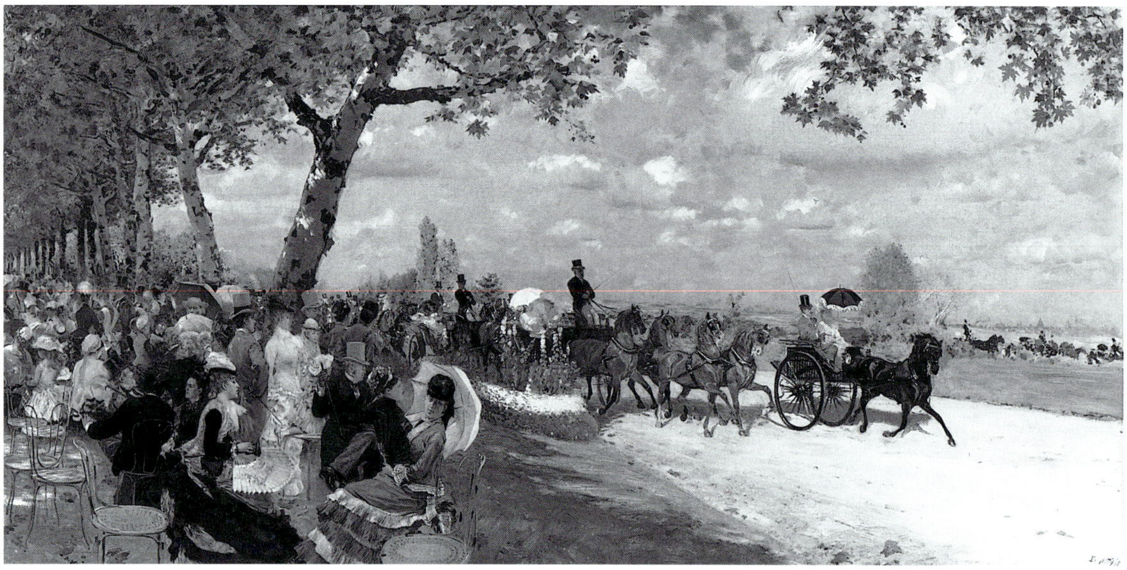

Fig. 50. Giuseppe de Nittis. *Return from the Races,* 1875. Oil on canvas, 22⅞ x 54⅛ in. (58.1 x 137.5 cm). Philadelphia Museum of Art; W. P. Wilstach Collection

Downes on January 11, 1887, "I am drawing like a slave at Julians and shall until Spring." But, perhaps convinced that he could not learn all he needed to know in the time he had committed to staying in Paris, he was already frustrated with academic instruction. He continued to Downes: "I don't believe all that there is in the academy is good. It teaches whoever comes within to draw mechanically exact—That's about all but it is of importance of course as far as it goes."[17] By his own account Hassam worked at Julian's for a year and a half, until the spring of 1888.[18] Toward the end of his sojourn in Paris, he complained in a long letter to Downes that Lefebvre was "*supposed* to teach two mornings in the week at Julians men's school one month and women's the month following but—note this he is never there half of the time," and expostulated: "The Julian Academy is the personification of routine, and with the Beaux Arts has spoilt more than one artist who goes there *too long*."[19] By the turn of the century Hassam had concluded that "his Boston art education was preliminary and his Paris instruction was superfluous."[20]

What was not superfluous was the artistic variety Paris offered in museums, galleries, and numerous exhibitions, where a broad spectrum of styles and subjects was on display.[21] Much of this rich array left its mark on Hassam's development. Visible in Hassam's Paris paintings, for example, are echoes from works by Giuseppe de Nittis (see fig. 50) and Jean Béraud (see figs. 38, 51), juste-milieu artists whose detailed city scenes seem already to have influenced him in Boston. Other masters of the juste-milieu—including Gustave Caillebotte (see fig. 37), Norbert Goeneutte (see fig. 45), Luigi Loir, Louis Marie de Schryver (see fig. 70), Federico Zandomeneghi, and Anders Zorn—who, like de Nittis and Béraud, interpreted modern subjects in conservative styles, also produced works that anticipate or parallel Hassam's Paris scenes. Of apparent interest to Hassam, too, were paintings by Jules Bastien-Lepage, a master of Naturalism who specialized in portraying peasants and pearly light, and leading Impressionists, whose

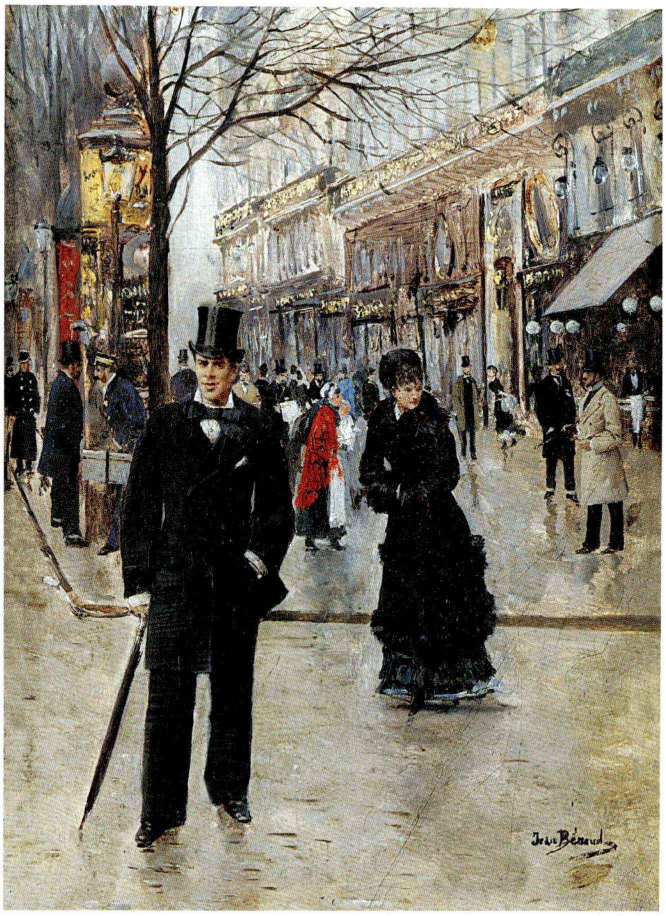

Fig. 51. Jean Béraud. *Paris Boulevard,* 1885. Oil on canvas, 33 x 25 in. (83.8 x 63.5 cm). Musée de la Ville de Paris, Musée Carnavalet, Paris

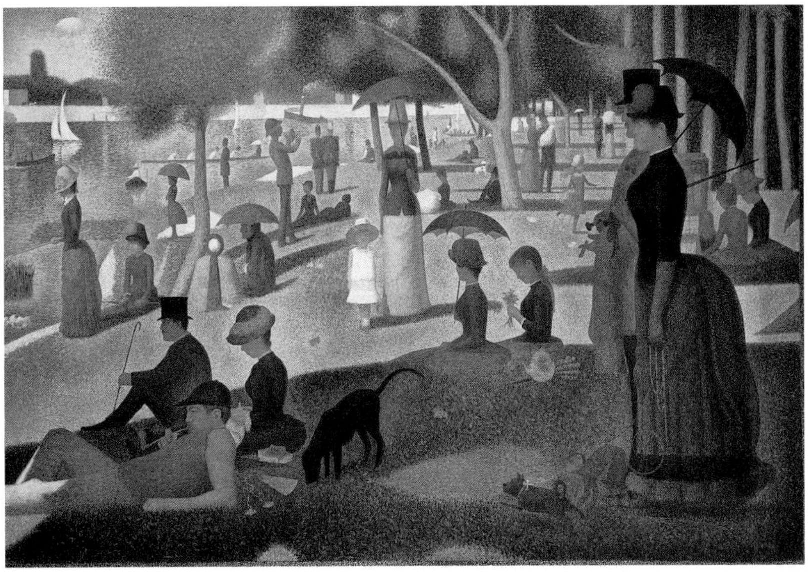

Fig. 52. Georges Seurat. A *Sunday on La Grande Jatte–1884*, 1884–86. Oil on canvas, 81¾ x 121¼ in. (207.6 x 308 cm). The Art Institute of Chicago, Helen Birch Barlett Memorial Collection 1926.224

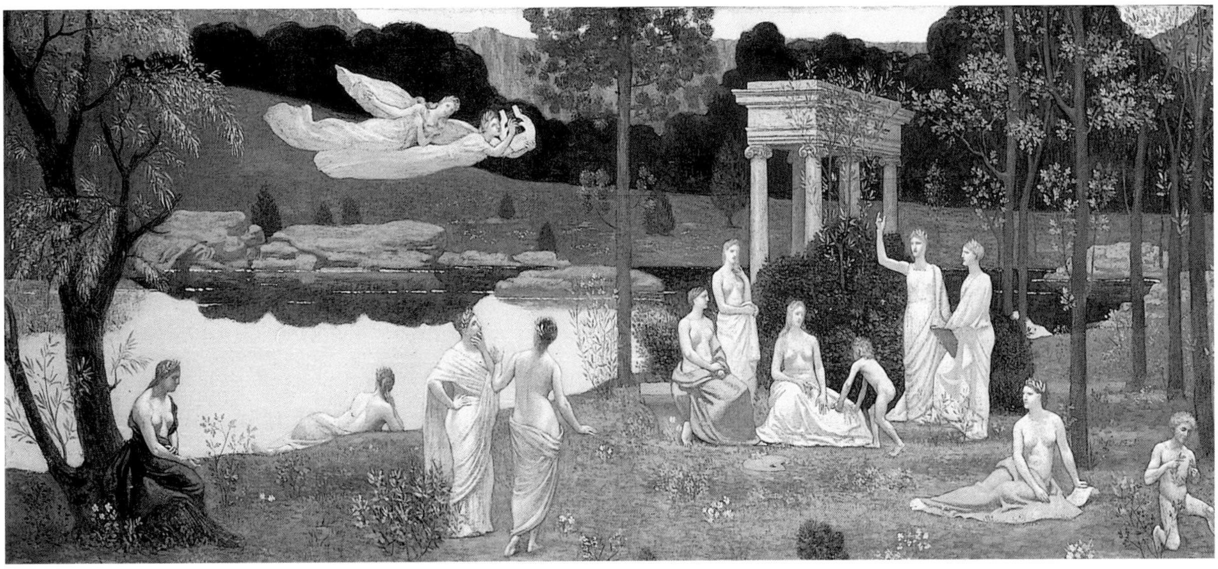

Fig. 53. Pierre Puvis de Chavannes. *The Sacred Grove, Beloved of the Arts and Muses,* 1884–89. Oil on canvas, 36 ⅝ x 90 ⅞ in. (93 x 230.8 cm). The Art Institute of Chicago, Mr. and Mrs. Potter Palmer Collection 1922.445

works were often on view at Galerie Georges Petit, Galerie Durand-Ruel, and Galerie Boussod Valadon. He seems to have been attracted as well to Neoimpressionists, especially Seurat, whose revolutionary *Sunday on La Grande Jatte—1884* (fig. 52) had been included in the last Impressionist group exhibition, in spring 1886, and who showed consistently at the Société des Artistes Indépendants between 1886 and 1889. Also important to him was easel painter and muralist Pierre Puvis de Chavannes (see fig. 53), like Seurat a Montmartre neighbor and a seeker of simple geometries beneath the accidents of appearance.[22] The modern classicism of both of these artists may have inspired some of Hassam's tubular figures or validated his tendency to generalize human anatomy. In addition, the paintings of Boggs, one of the few Americans with whom Hassam recalled having contact, in some respects paralleled his own city scenes.[23]

Writing to Downes toward the end of his French studies, Hassam mentioned with appreciation Jean-Jacques Henner, Jean-Charles Cazin, John Singer Sargent, George Inness, and James McNeill Whistler, all current or former residents of Paris. Of the Impressionists, he said: "Even Claude Monet, Sisley, Pissaro [*sic*] and the school of extreme impressionists do some things that are charming and that will live, and even the major part of their work, although they are not always serious, and some time they try too much to 'étonner le bourg[e]ois.'"[24]

Hassam's Parisian works suggest that he was much more inclined than were most of his compatriots to interpret in a personal and vital way the styles of the modern French painters—the artists of the juste-milieu, Impressionists, and Neoimpressionists—and to celebrate urban life. He often brightened his palette, loosened his brushwork, and showed

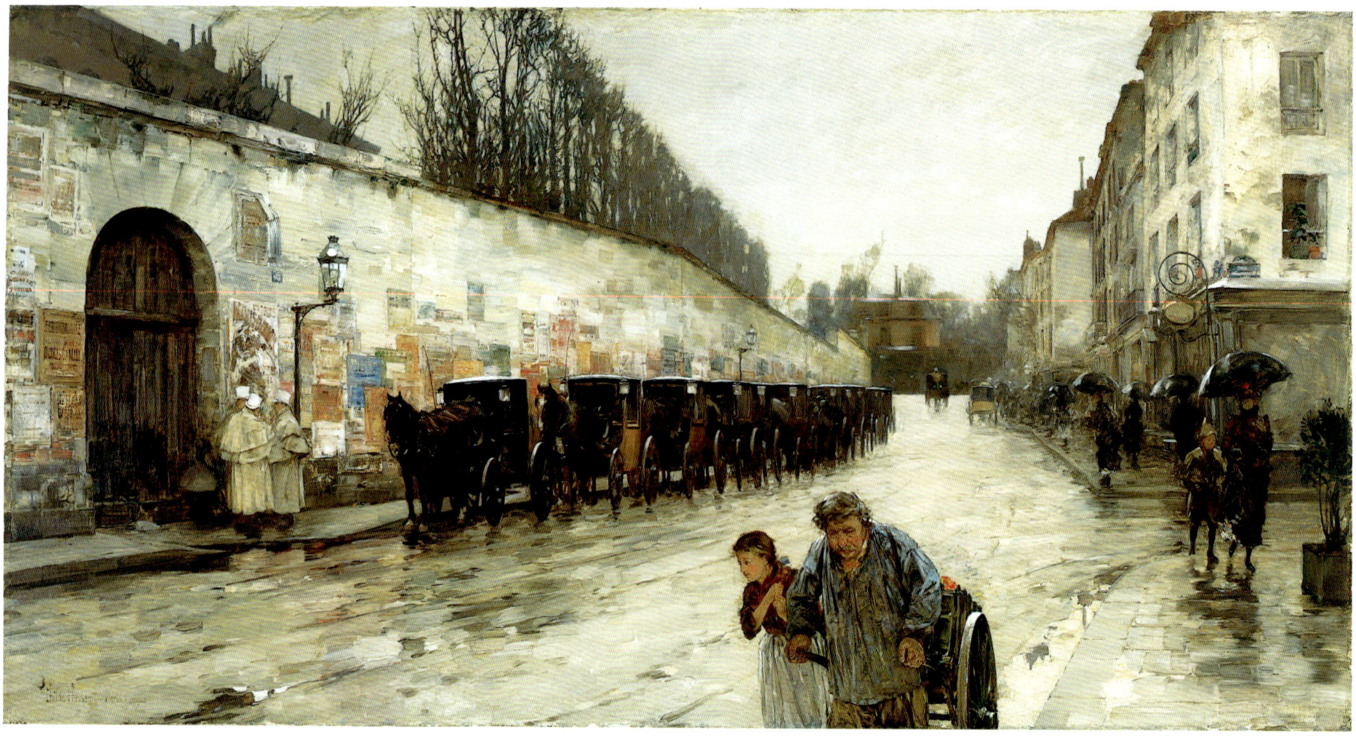

Fig. 54. Childe Hassam. *Une Averse—rue Bonaparte,* 1887. Oil on canvas, 40⅜ x 77½ in. (102.6 x 196.9 cm). Terra Foundation for the Arts, Chicago, Daniel J. Terra Collection

the effects of brilliant sunlight in oils and watercolors that record the spectacle of Paris. Yet, inklings of Impressionism notwithstanding, Hassam sometimes enlisted the tonal palette he had used in Boston, and he consistently maintained traditional volumetric armatures and careful outlines in rendering forms. His stylistic position between the avant-garde and the academy was like that of Pierre-Auguste Renoir, whose work he particularly esteemed. Hassam vividly expressed his feeling of kinship with the French painter in a recollection of 1927; in this account he explained that, in preparation for his return home in 1889, he had given up his studio apartment on the boulevard Rochechouart and rented a smaller one that Renoir had occupied: "In this place were all sorts of little experiments. I did not know anything about Renoir or care anything about Renoir. I looked at these experiments in pure color and saw it was what I was trying to do myself. He was a very able painter and his finished things are academically complete. . . . I was a young man under thirt[y] and I had never heard of Renoir. . . . But I knew that he was trying for the same thing that I was trying for."[25]

Hassam's Paris paintings disclose a bourgeois gentility that echoes his lifestyle and typifies the cheerful euphemism that helps define American Impressionism.[26] In them he assumed the role of *flâneur,* the archetypal urban observer described by Charles Baudelaire as a "passionate spectator" for whom "it is an immense joy to set up house in the heart of the multitude."[27] Indeed, when Hassam was asked in 1927 what his "greatest amusement" had been, he replied: "To go about Paris."[28] But, although he embraced the subject of modern Paris much more fully than most of his fellow Americans, Hassam went about the city and recorded it only selectively. He emphasized the features of Third Republic Paris, just as he had earlier focused on highlights of the new Boston. He was interested principally in broad new boulevards and fashionable residents, although he did sometimes portray the winding old streets of Montmartre and his picturesque working-class neighbors. "The man who will go down to posterity is the man who paints his own time and the scenes of every-day life around him," Hassam insisted in 1892,[29] but he would have had to admit that he chose to present very limited aspects of "every-day life" in Paris.

Une Averse—rue Bonaparte (fig. 54), the painting that occupied Hassam during the winter of 1886–87, exemplifies his views of Paris.[30] Here, on one of his largest canvases, he recapitulated the near-monochromatic gray palette, plunging perspective, wet pavement, and figures carrying umbrellas he had shown in *Rainy Day, Columbus Avenue, Boston* (fig. 36). Once again atmospheric effects were a major concern, a fact recognized by contemporary critic Susan Hale, who wrote enthusiastically: "The whole tone of the picture is not only grey, it is dripping."[31] In the Paris picture Hassam did not record his own neighborhood, as he had done in the Boston view. Rather, he portrayed the artistic epicenter of the Left Bank, the street on which the École des Beaux-Arts is situated, seen from the place Saint-Sulpice looking south toward the rue du Luxembourg and the Jardin du Luxembourg. However, in both works he captured the insistent ordinariness of his scene. As Donelson F. Hoopes notes, "This prospect of the Rue Bonaparte ignores the more colorful Place St. Sulpice, with its magnificent 17th-century church and the renowned Medici Fountain, although it is just to the left of the view he has chosen to paint. . . . The subject of this painting is really the poignant bleakness of this street."[32]

The Barbizon painters, Bastien-Lepage, and Manet all showed an interest in shabby types, which Hassam echoed in the two figures he included in the foreground of *Une Averse—rue Bonaparte*. These are a child and a weathered laborer pulling a handcart; the man, Hassam explained to Lamb, is "aided by his little girl," adding "they are both bare-headed according to their custom—rain or shine."[33] These rustic embodiments of outdoor manual labor are bracketed by distinctive urbanites. At the left are three cochers, or cabdrivers, in double-caped light raincoats chatting near a large wooden door in the long, bill-plastered wall in front of the seminary of Saint-Sulpice.[34] On the sidewalk at the right are what Hassam described to Lamb as "better dressed and more fortunate wayfarers with umbrellas."[35] The shabby folks, liveried cabdrivers, and well-heeled pedestrians recall the range of urban characters Manet portrayed in *The Rue Mosnier with Flags* (fig. 55): a worker carrying a ladder, a hunched amputee on crutches, and elegant passengers in carriages. More pointedly than in any other painting, Hassam signaled in *Une Averse—rue Bonaparte* the coexistence of hardship and prosperity in the modern city and the demise of rural traditions that accompanied urban growth.[36] He also announced the city's variety and complexity with the dialogue between the austere seminary wall and the posters advertising Parisian amusements.

Hassam's gentle social commentary notwithstanding, the true focus of *Une Averse—rue Bonaparte* is the rain-slicked Latin Quarter street and the line of fiacres. These small, four-wheeled hackney coaches, whose tops Hale characterized as shining "like the backs of turtles drying themselves on a big stone,"[37] stand ready to relieve city dwellers of their burdens. Thus, the painting literally diagrams Hassam's preference for portraying urban privilege, not poverty, and his attraction to the pleasing aspects of modern city life.

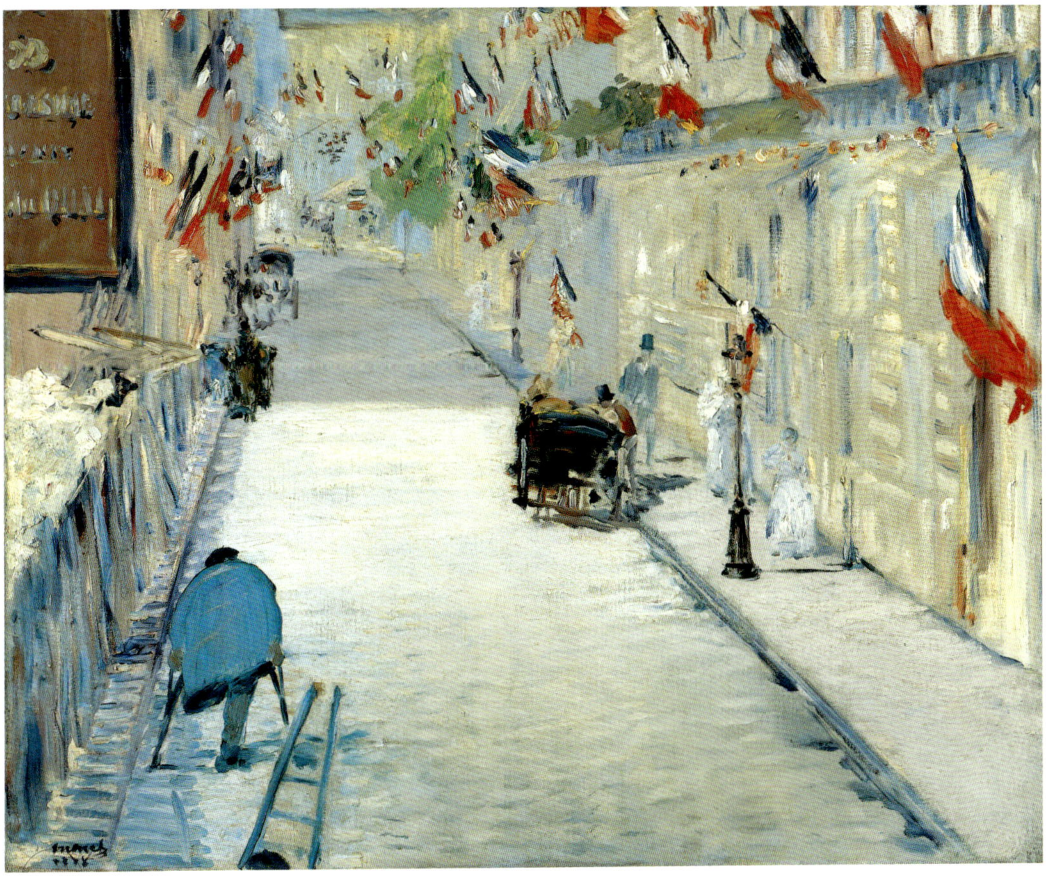

Fig. 55. Édouard Manet. *The Rue Mosnier with Flags*, 1878. Oil on canvas, 25¾ x 31¾ in. (65.4 x 80.6 cm). The J. Paul Getty Museum, Los Angeles 89.PA71

Hassam made an auspicious Salon debut in May 1887 with *Une Averse—rue Bonaparte*. With this exhibition he extended to Paris his Boston habit of seeking every opportunity to display his works. He would become an aggressive and successful Salon exhibitor, showing annually during his student years and leaving pictures for presentation the year after his return home. By comparison, Tarbell showed only once (in 1886), Metcalf only once (in 1888), and Benson not at all. Robert Reid, however, also a product of the School of the Museum of Fine Arts, Boston, and a student of Boulanger's and Lefebvre's during Hassam's years at the Académie Julian, exhibited in the Salons of 1887, 1888, and 1889.

Une Averse—rue Bonaparte was keenly appreciated by the critics. In an article describing only a few of the works in the large American Salon display, a writer for *American Art Illustrated* noted that Hassam's canvas "has been received by the Frenchmen with very marked and discriminating endorsement of those qualities that were so conspicuous in this artist's work of similar motive, done before he went to Europe."[38] Another writer reproduced the painting and commented: "This picture is very good, and gives great promise, inasmuch as it displays on the part of the artist delicate faculties of vision, and a sensitiveness to the values of objects in ambient atmosphere, which are, unfortunately rare."[39] Hassam recounted to Lamb: "My picture was exposed at Goupil's for a week after the Salon closed. This is my luckiest stroke since I have been here. While it was in the 'Salon' I had notices in four French journals—all favorable, (this surprised me)."[40]

Favorite subjects of Hassam's were fiacres and other horse-drawn vehicles, and he often painted them in picturesque weather conditions. In *Carriage, Rue Bonaparte* (fig. 6), a portrayal of a cab whose driver pauses to light a pipe, passengers huddle under umbrellas on the crowded upper deck of a large

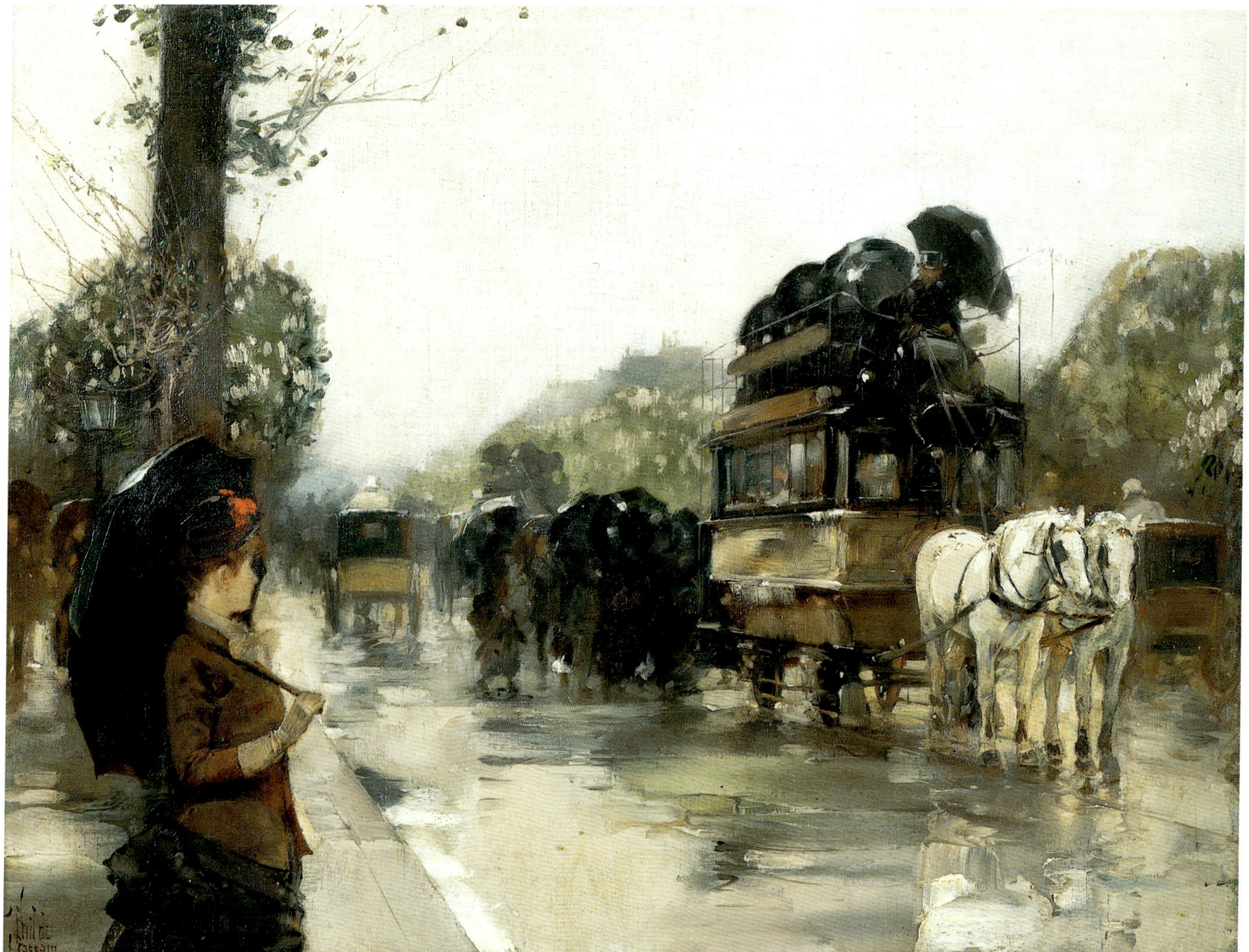

Fig. 56. Childe Hassam. *April Showers, Champs Élysées, Paris,* 1888. Oil on canvas, 12½ x 16⅝ in. (31.8 x 42.2 cm). Joslyn Art Museum, Omaha JAM1946.30

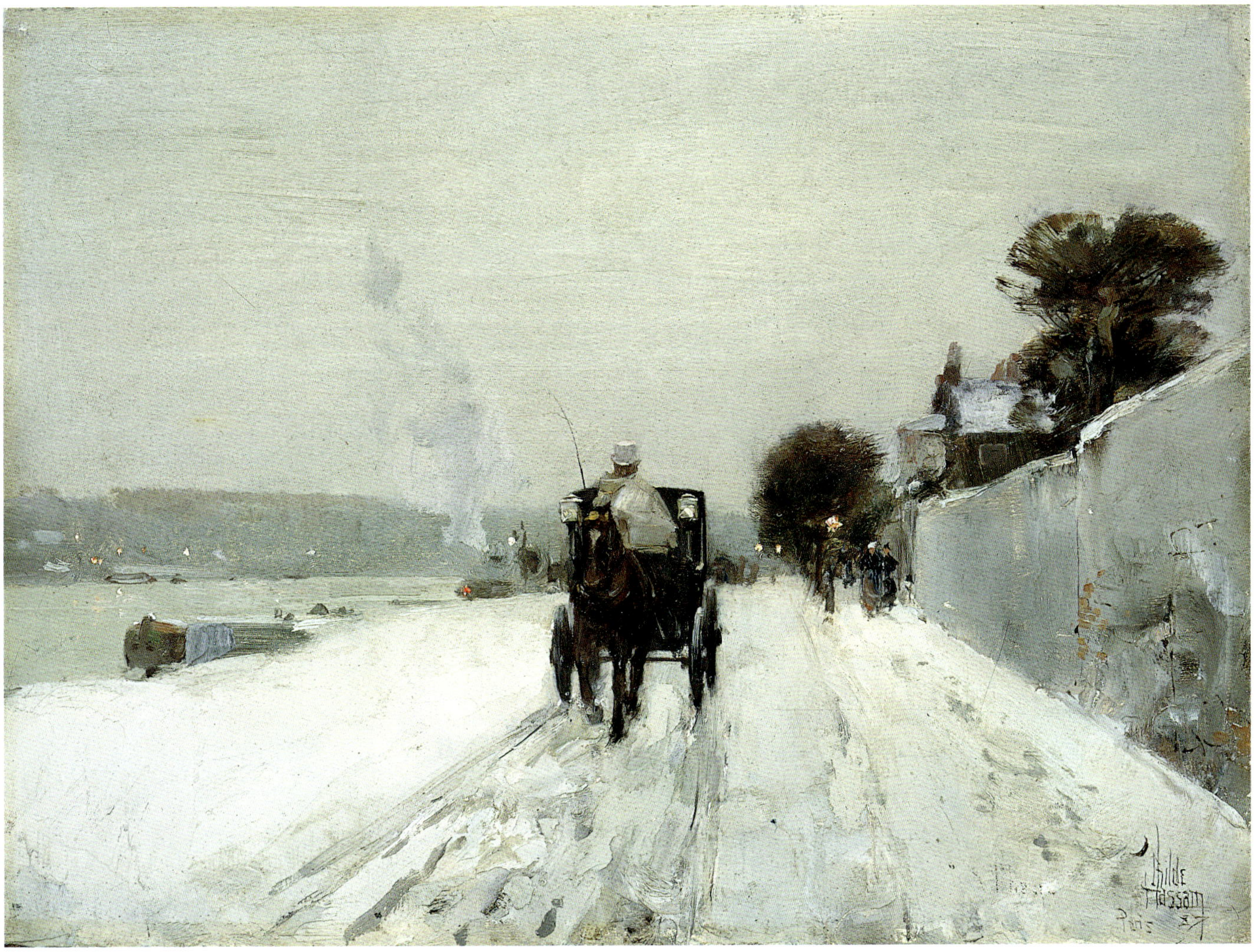

Fig. 57. Childe Hassam. *Along the Seine, Winter,* 1887. Oil on cardboard, 8 x 11 in. (20.3 x 27.9 cm). Dallas Museum of Art, bequest of Joel T. Howard

public omnibus in the background as pedestrians carrying umbrellas make their way along a rain-slicked sidewalk. Hassam's lively strokes suggest reflections on wet pavement and energize the subtle near-monochrome gray that dominates the composition, while a pearly pink color in the sky indicates that the rain will soon end. The brushwork here, like that in *April Showers, Champs-Élysées, Paris* (fig. 56), implies Hassam's awareness of Manet's technique. In subject as well as in technique *Carriage, Rue Bonaparte* relates to *April Showers, Champs-Élysées, Paris,* whose focus is an omnibus filled with passengers who shield themselves with umbrellas. That the rain Hassam shows is merely April showers or drizzle is conveyed by the demeanor of the young woman in a flower-bedecked bonnet who rests the shaft of her umbrella on her shoulder as she observes the crowded coach.

In his scenes of Paris on gray and rainy days, Hassam denied that the weather was disagreeable by including figures, often graceful women, who make their way easily along the wet pavements. Moreover, by using phrases such as *April Showers* in his titles, he reminded viewers that rainy days were characteristic of the metropolis. Yet Hassam's wet-weather views irritated at least one critic, who complained (of *Une Averse—rue Bonaparte*): "Childe Hassam ought to 'come in out of the rain,'" and warned that "one will have to take a dose of quinine as an antidote against the dampness that pervades Mr. Hassam's artistic environment."[41]

In the delightful oil sketch *Along the Seine, Winter* (fig. 57), viscous white pigment inflected with various warm and cool grays re-creates the thick snow that must have muted the clattering wheels of the fiacre seen on the quai. Such spontaneous and intimate works are as typical of Hassam's Parisian painting campaign as are his larger, more complex Salon submissions. It is to such a "little Paris thing of the streets" that he must have been referring when he wrote to

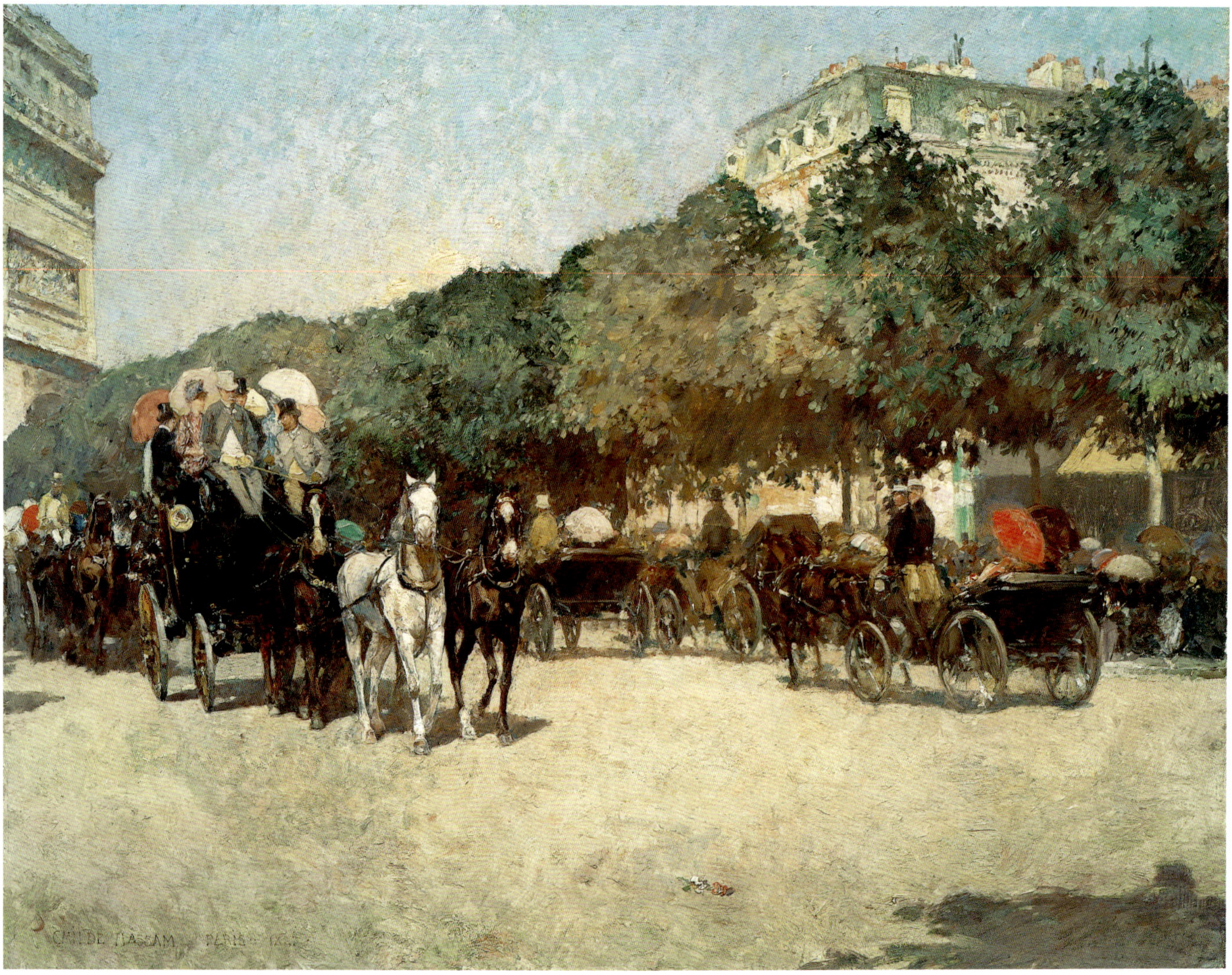

Fig. 58. Childe Hassam, *Grand Prix Day,* 1887. Oil on canvas, 24⅛ x 31 in. (61.3 x 78.7 cm). The Museum of Fine Arts, Boston. Ernest Wadsworth Longfellow Fund

Downes in January 1887: "I have unquestionably arrived at my selection of subjects."[42]

For *Grand Prix Day* (fig. 58), conceived in June 1887, Hassam came "in out of the rain" and the snow to portray a sparkling, sun-drenched scene with vibrant Impressionist hues and flecked brushwork that announce his departure from the tonal palette he had brought to Paris from Boston. His revised chromatic range is also apparent in the second version of the scene (fig. 359), intended for the 1888 Salon. Painting this second, larger canvas in his new studio on boulevard Rochechouart in late autumn, Hassam seems to have amplified remembered June sunlight. He told Lamb on November 29, 1887: "The studio is good in this way, that one side is all glass nearly to the floor, so that I can paint a figure here the same as on the street. . . . Just now, by the way, I am painting sunlight," and then he described the Grand Prix day image.[43]

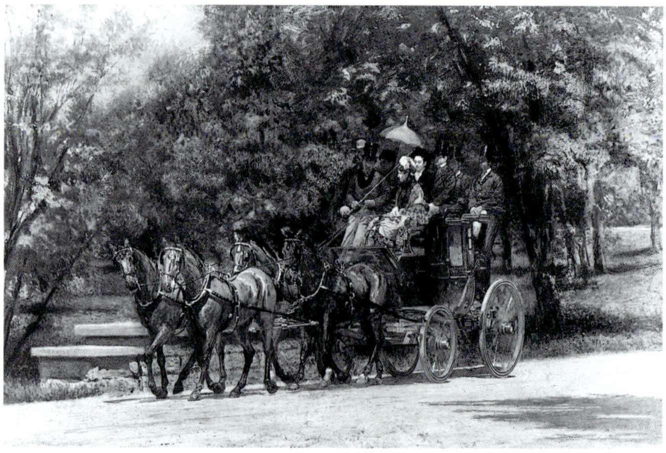

Fig. 59. Thomas Eakins. *A May Morning in the Park (The Fairman Rogers Four-in-Hand),* 1879. Oil on canvas, 23¾ x 36 in. (60.3 x 91.4 cm). Philadelphia Museum of Art: Gift of William Alexander Dick

In both oil versions of *Grand Prix Day,* Hassam may have been inspired by Monet for his tonalities and brushwork and perhaps took his cue from Degas and Caillebotte for the asymmetry and cropping of the composition and for the empty foreground. However, he maintained an academic armature for major forms, whose clarity resists the effects of corrosive sunlight. The strong volumes and precise detail in *Grand Prix Day* suggest the influence of Thomas Eakins's *A May Morning in the Park (The Fairman Rogers Four-in-Hand)* (fig. 59), which Hassam could have seen at the Boston Art Club in 1881.[44] They also align the scene with stylistically conservative juste-milieu images such as de Nittis's *Return from the Races* (fig. 50) and make it seem deliberate by comparison with candid French Impressionist works, for example Monet's *Boulevard des Capucines* (fig. 60).[45]

Grand Prix Day also reveals Hassam's preference for depicting urban elegance, which stands in contrast to the emphasis on urban anonymity of Monet and other French Impressionists. It betokens as well his special fondness for equestrian themes, which, along with tranquil parks, he far preferred as subjects to cafés, theaters, or other urban entertainments. In *Grand Prix Day* Hassam celebrated a triumphantly modern neighborhood, the prestigious eighth arrondissement, which Baron Georges-Eugène Haussmann had renovated during the Second Empire by cutting several new boulevards that converged on the Étoile. Presented here is the glamorous noonday promenade of elaborate equipages near the Arc de Triomphe on the first Sunday in June 1887, before their procession to the Bois de Boulogne for the great international horse race, run at about 3 P.M. in the Hippodrôme de Longchamp.[46] Hassam portrayed in brilliant sunlight the dynamic spectacle of two lines of carriages proceeding in opposite directions. Toward the left, near the Arc de Triomphe, a modish four-in-hand drag or a mail coach,[47]

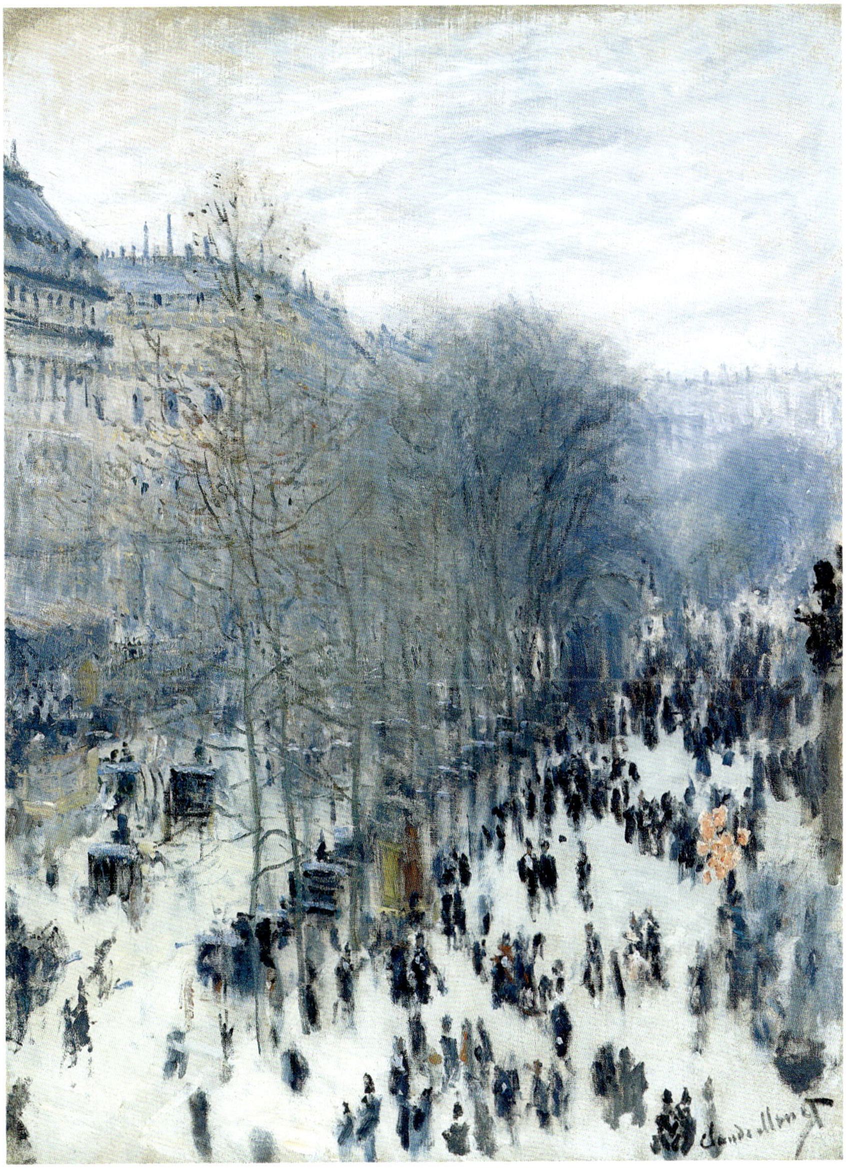

Fig. 60. Claude Monet. *Boulevard des Capucines,* 1873–74. Oil on canvas, 31⅝ x 23¾ in. (80.3 x 60.3 cm). The Nelson-Atkins Museum of Art, Kansas City, Missouri (Purchase: acquired through the Kenneth A. and Helen F. Spencer Foundation Acquisition Fund) F72–35

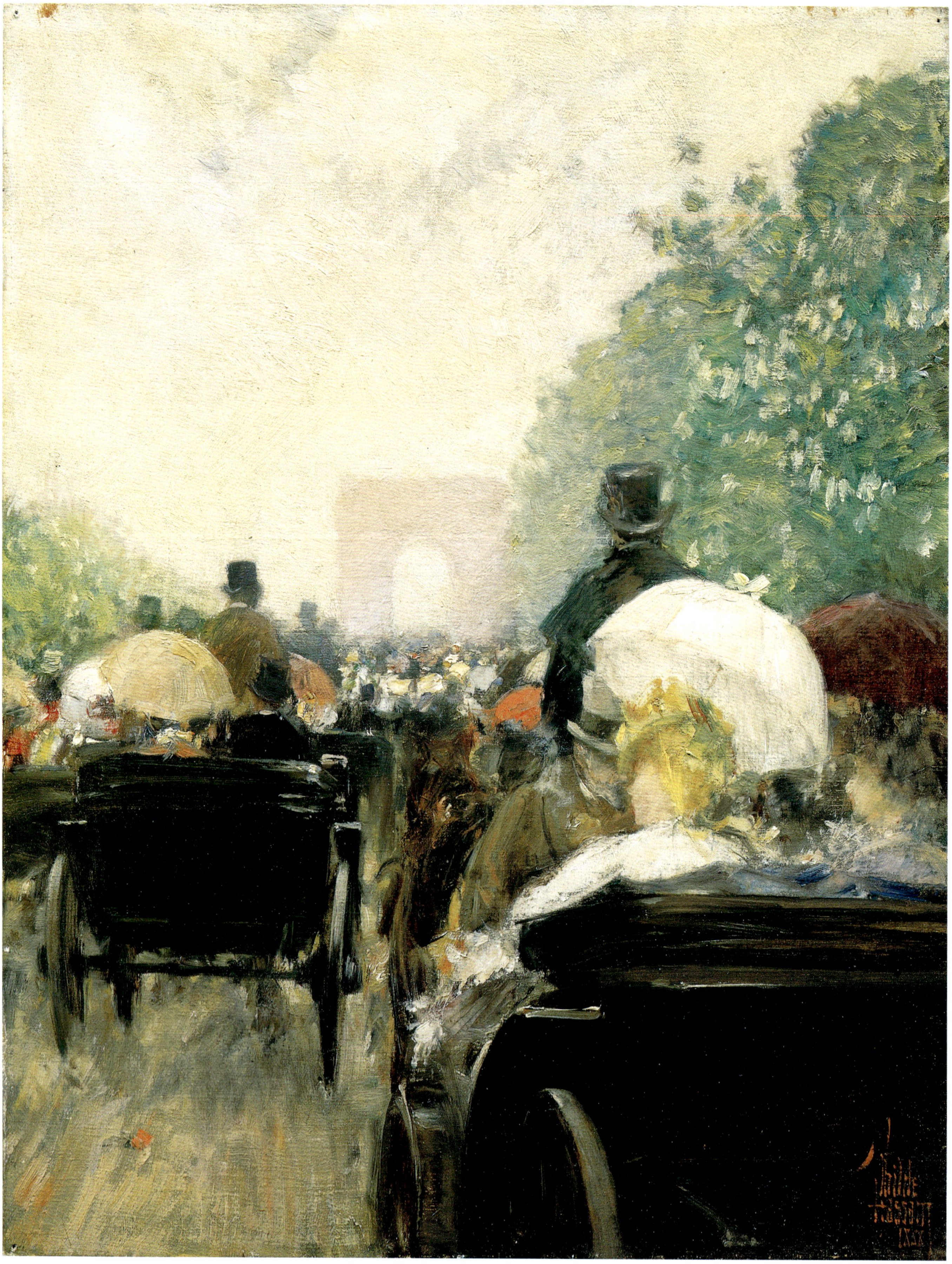

Fig. 61. Childe Hassam. *Carriage Parade,* 1888. Oil on canvas, 15 x 12 in. (38.1 x 30.5 cm). Haggin Collection, The Haggin Museum, Stockton, California

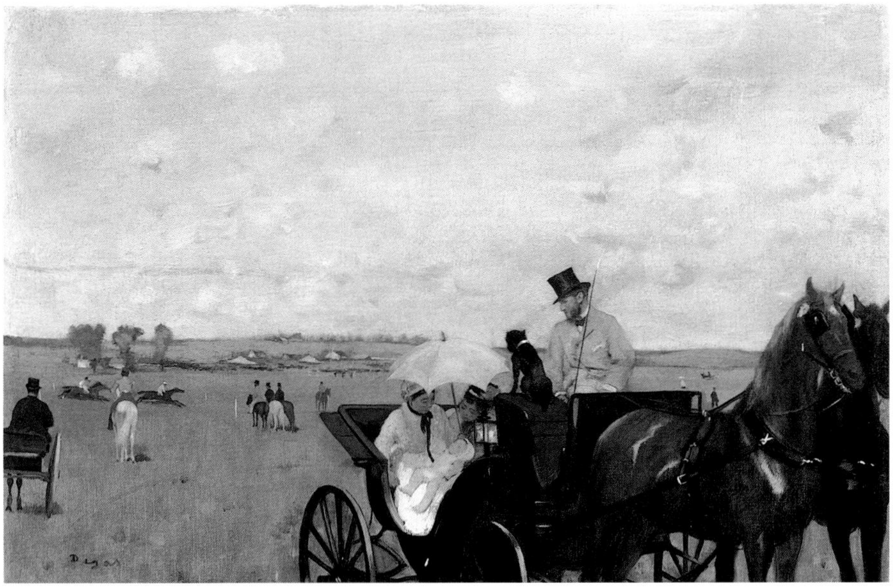

Fig. 62. Edgar Degas. *At the Races in the Countryside,* 1869. Oil on canvas, 14⅜ x 22 in. (36.5 x 55.9 cm). The Museum of Fine Arts, Boston. 1931 Purchase Fund

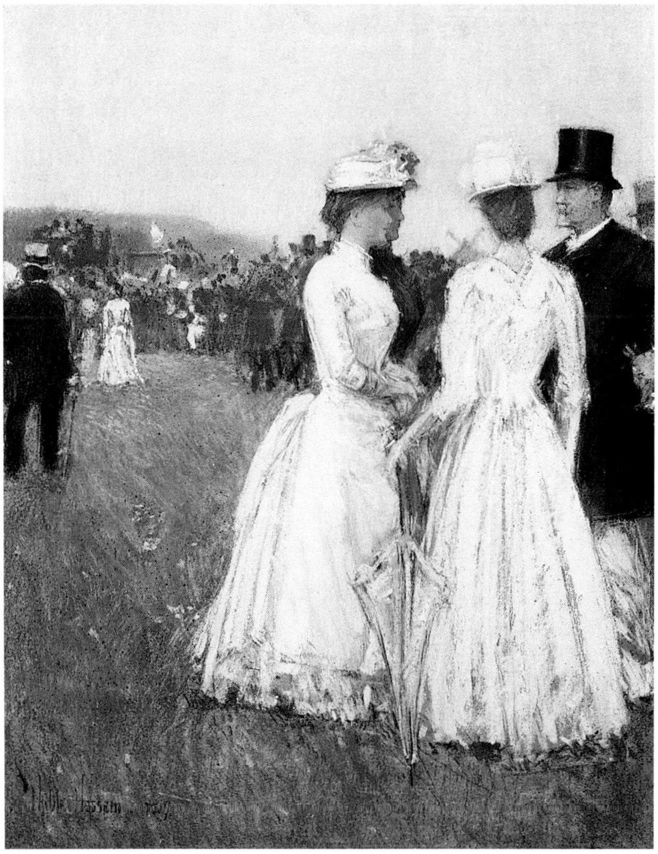

Fig. 63. Childe Hassam. *Au Grand Prix de Paris,* 1887. Pastel and pencil on tan board, 15⅞ x 12½ in. (40.3 x 31.8 cm). The Corcoran Gallery of Art, Washington, D.C. Bequest of James Parmelee 41.12

drawn by four graceful white and brown horses, advances, carrying on its high seats gentlemen attired in brown and gray and ladies wearing pastel dresses and narrow-brimmed hats and holding parasols. The feminine fashions provide a scintillating contrast to the somber male costumes and the shiny black coach. The foreground space apparently has just been vacated, perhaps by a carriage from which a rose that lies on the pavement has fallen. A second line of carriages—two-passenger victorias and four-passenger landaus—moves toward the arch. Spectators fill the sidewalks, which are shaded by sun-dappled horse-chestnut trees Haussmann had planted, their foliage rendered as freely as any forms Hassam had yet painted.[48]

In *Carriage Parade* (fig. 61) Hassam cropped principal forms at one side and at the bottom edge of the canvas, as Degas had done in such paintings as *At the Races in the Countryside* (fig. 62). By cutting off parts of the vehicle in this way, showing it on the picture plane and from the rear, Hassam invited the viewer to enjoy the procession toward the Arc de Triomphe from a seat in a carriage following a landau. He recorded the scene at the Longchamp track itself in a pastel, *Au Grand Prix de Paris* (fig. 63). Unlike Manet and Degas, who focused on jockeys and their mounts in their Longchamp pictures, Hassam showed only stylish spectators in his versions of the theme—here three young women and a top-hatted gentleman chatting on the turf.[49]

Hassam depicted fashionable Parisians in a variety of settings. In the delightful *Promenade at Sunset, Paris* (fig. 64), for example, a trim young woman seen from behind lifts the hem of her striped skirt to avoid a puddle as she tiptoes onto a sidewalk filled with other modish types out for a stroll after a rain. The charming *In the Park* (fig. 5) features a slender young woman dressed in a skirt with a very large bustle and a bodice of heavy material—an elegant outfit, but not the most up-to-date[50]—and a younger schoolgirl carrying a notebook. Two small white dogs accompany them as they stroll along a sidewalk. The greensward beyond them, punctuated by newly planted trees and beds of pink and red flowers, separates the pedestrian path from a carriage road in the middle distance.

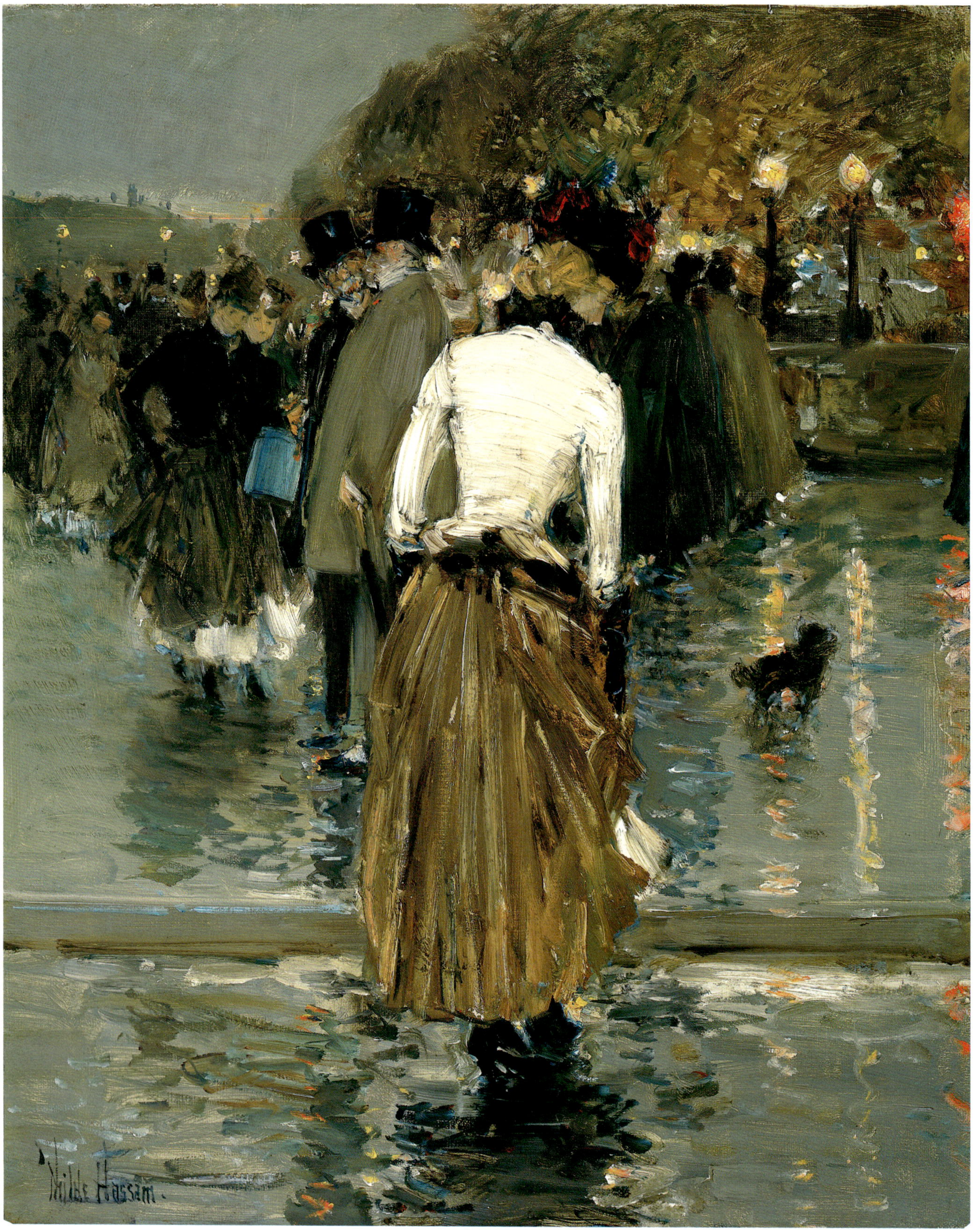

Fig. 64. Childe Hassam. *Promenade at Sunset, Paris,* 1888–89. Oil on canvas, 18⅛ x 15⅛ in. (46 x 38.4 cm). Tom James Company / Oxxford Clothes

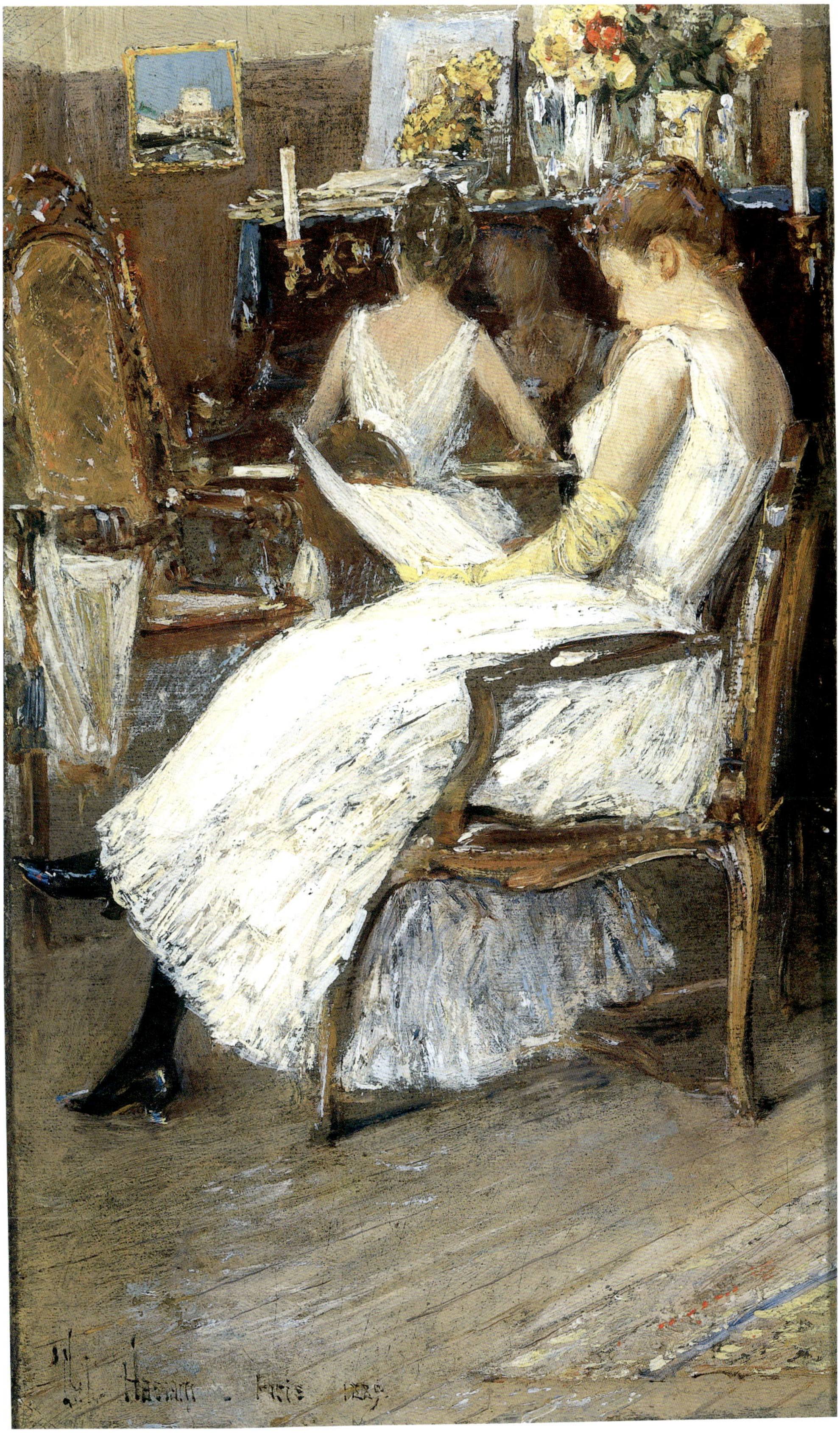

Fig. 65. Childe Hassam. *Mrs. Hassam and Her Sister,* 1889. Oil on canvas, $9\frac{7}{8}$ x $6\frac{1}{8}$ in. (25.1 x 15.6 cm). Terra Foundation for the Arts, Daniel J. Terra Collection, Chicago

While the specific site—perhaps the Champs-Élysées or Jardin des Tuileries—resists identification, the line of carriages and the mansard roofs seen over the treetops denote the locale as Paris. In the intimate *Mrs. Hassam and Her Sister* (fig. 65) the artist's wife, seated and viewed in profile, and his sister-in-law, playing the spinet piano, enjoy a quiet moment, apparently in his studio residence on the boulevard Rochechouart.[51] That the two women are shown clad in undergarments—chemises, corsets, camisoles, and petticoats (perhaps with day skirts over them)—suggests the private intention of the work. Mrs. Hassam wears long yellow gloves with her undergarments, and black daytime shoes and stockings together with evening décolletage. These unlikely combinations probably indicate that Hassam was dressing up his models for a studio exercise, not recording a moment in their daily routine.

Although Hassam was devoted to painting people and their activities in Paris, he occasionally focused on architecture, as had Johan Barthold Jongkind (see fig. 40) and Frank Boggs (see fig. 44). One picture in which architecture is central is *Notre Dame Cathedral, Paris, 1888* (fig. 66), a view of the great church as seen from the quai de Montebello, alongside which rise clouds of steam from the unseen boats on the river below.[52] The emphasis on the cathedral notwithstanding, the painting discloses Hassam's commitment to depicting quotidian life through its inclusion of the fiacre at curbside and the assorted pedestrians who make their way along the quai. The combination of architecture with dramatically rendered industrial steam in this scene parallels that in views of the Pont de l'Europe and the Gare Saint-Lazare by many of Hassam's contemporaries, including Monet, Anquetin,

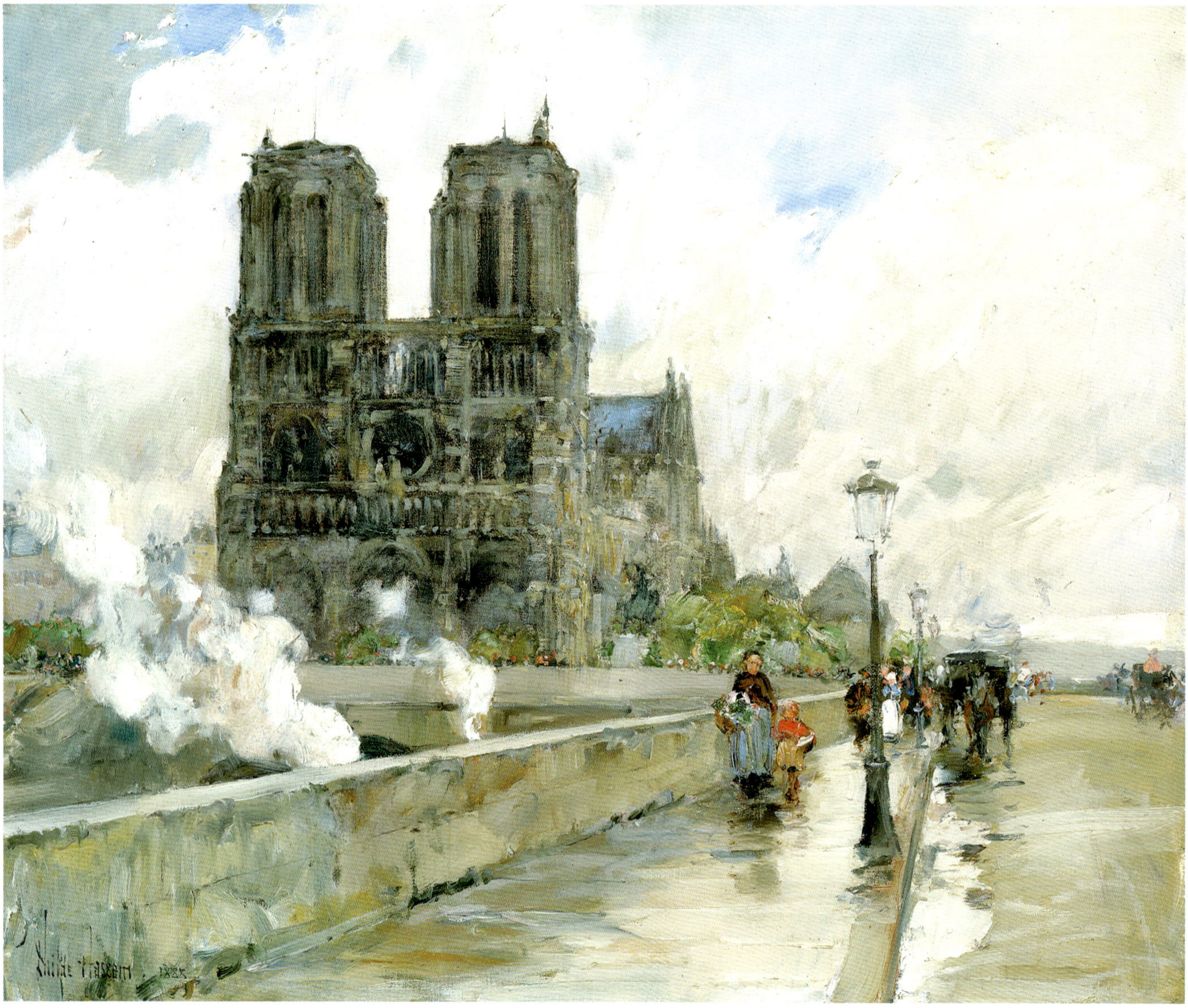

Fig. 66. Childe Hassam. *Notre Dame Cathedral, Paris, 1888*, 1888. Oil on canvas, 17½ x 21½ in. (44.5 x 54.6 cm). The Detroit Institute of Arts. Founders Society Purchase, Robert H. Tannahill Foundation Fund

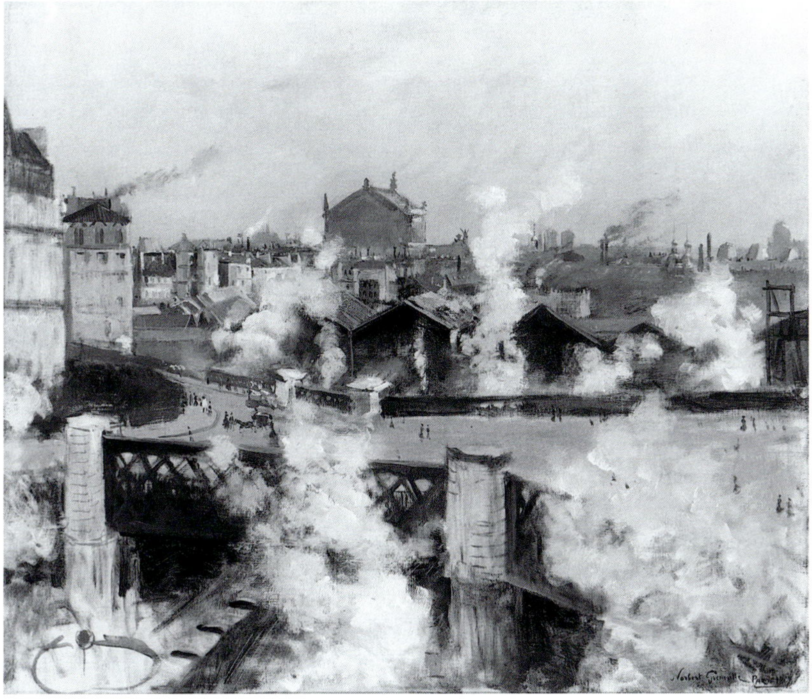

Fig. 67. Norbert Goeneutte. *View of St. Lazare Railway Station, Paris,* 1887. Oil on canvas, 18¾ x 22¼ in. (47.6 x 56.5 cm). The Baltimore Museum of Art: The George A. Lucas Collection, purchased with Funds from the State of Maryland, the Bequest of Laurence Bendann, and Contributions from individuals, foundations, and corporations through the Baltimore community BMA1996.45.118

Béraud, and Goeneutte, whose *View of St. Lazare Railway Station, Paris* (fig. 67) probably appeared (as *Nightfall*) in the 1888 Salon.[53]

Among Hassam's signature themes were graceful young Parisian shopkeepers and flower vendors as well as rougher types of female merchants, familiar figures along the quais of the Seine and on the streets of picturesque Montmartre. "There," as Ulrich W. Hiesinger has noted, "in an atmosphere more reminiscent of a French rural village than a great metropolis, Hassam roamed purposefully, recording the shop fronts with their colorful displays and the earthy characters who tended their businesses and watched from doorways."[54] *La Bouquetière et la Laitière* (fig. 68), among Hassam's most impressive watercolors, features one such earthy character, a dairywoman set off by the grid of mullioned windows of her shop and the line of milk cans on the sidewalk. She observes a flower seller kneeling to arrange her basket of blooms.[55] Another that makes use of a similar device is *La Fruitière*

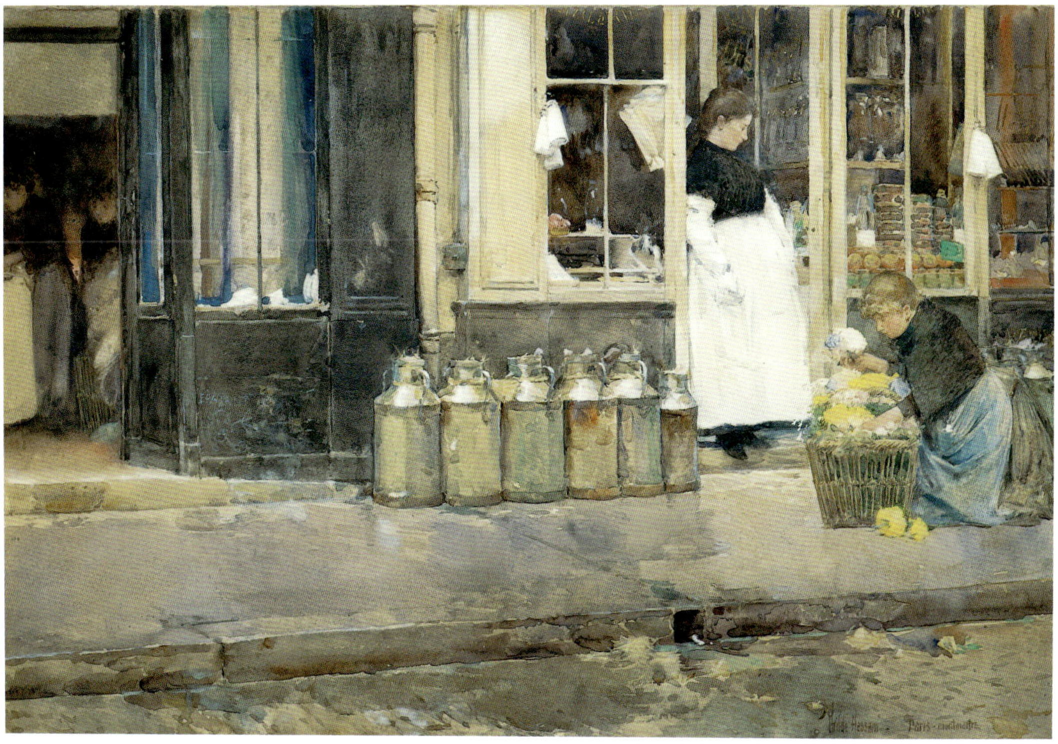

Fig. 68. Childe Hassam. *La Bouquetière et la Laitière,* ca. 1888. Watercolor on paper, 17 x 26 in. (43.2 x 66 cm). Private collection

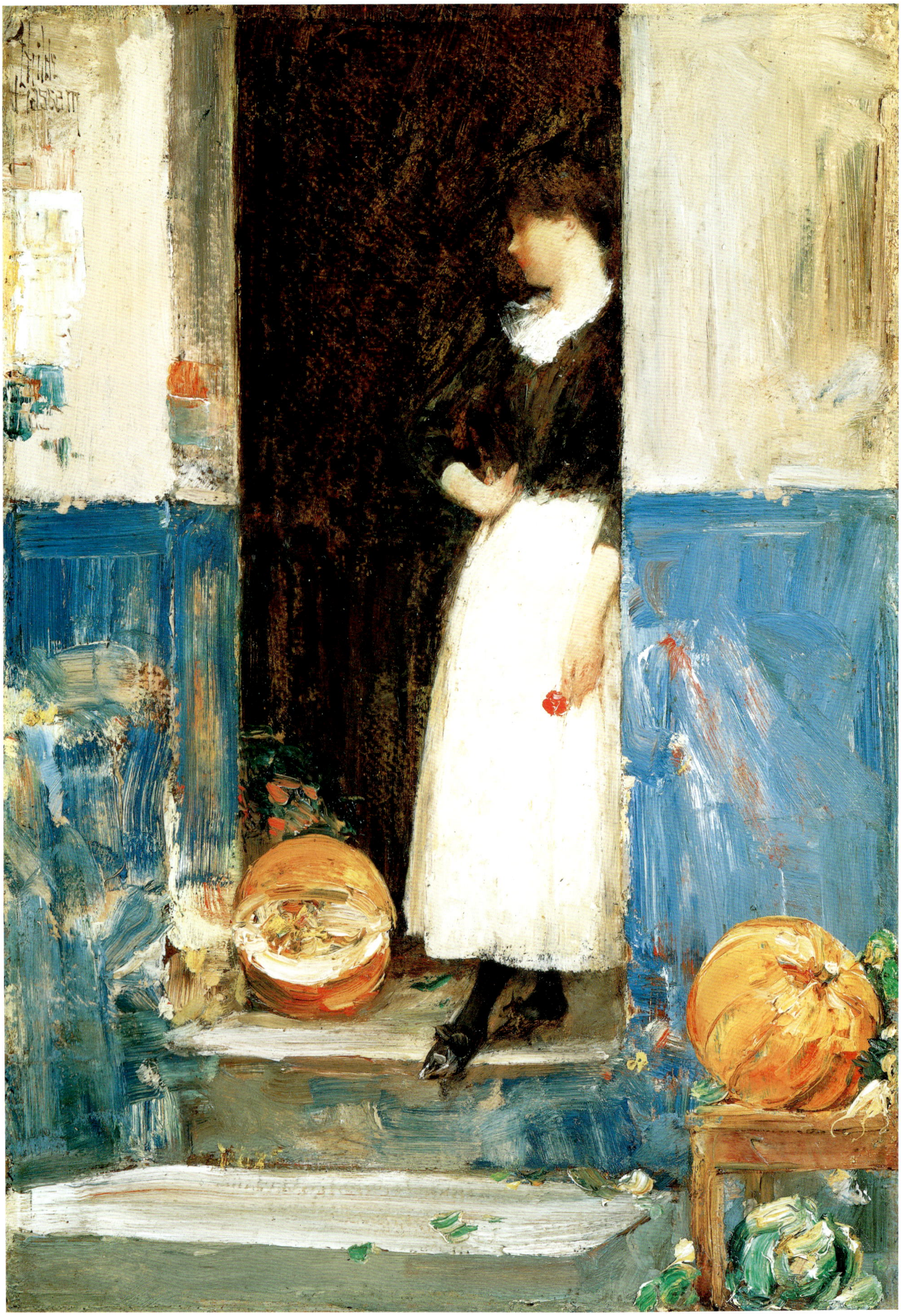

Fig. 69. Childe Hassam. *La Fruitière,* ca. 1888–89. Oil on composition board, 14¼ x 10¼ in. (36.2 x 26 cm). Curtis Galleries, Minneapolis

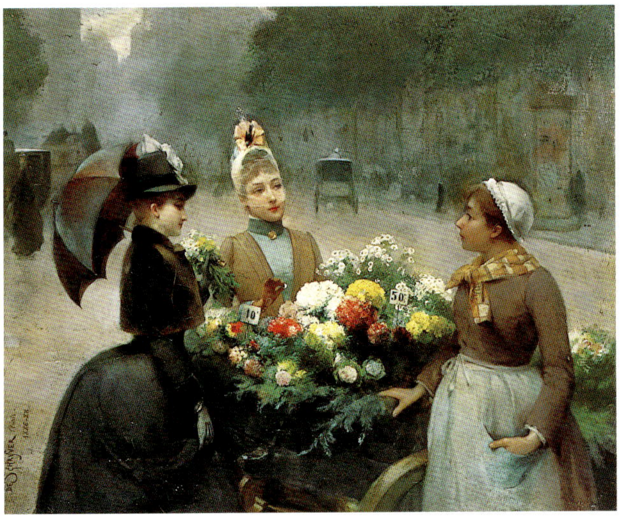

Fig. 70. Louis Marie de Schryver. *The Flower Seller,* 1886–88. Oil on canvas, 20 x 24¼ in. (50.8 x 61.5 cm). Private collection

(fig. 69), an engaging, sketchy oil study of a young woman framed in a doorway. The composition is enlivened by the contrasts between brilliant blue and white walls and two huge orange muskmelons.[56]

Hassam shared an interest in the subject of flower sellers with artists of the juste-milieu, including Louis Marie de Schryver (see fig. 70). These women appear in many of Hassam's Paris works, their wares affording him an opportunity to capture brilliant color accents in otherwise dull-hued scenes. In *Flower Girl* (fig. 71) Hassam depicted at the edge of a curb a young vendor clad in a simple dress and apron to which have been added fashionable elements including a bow at the neck

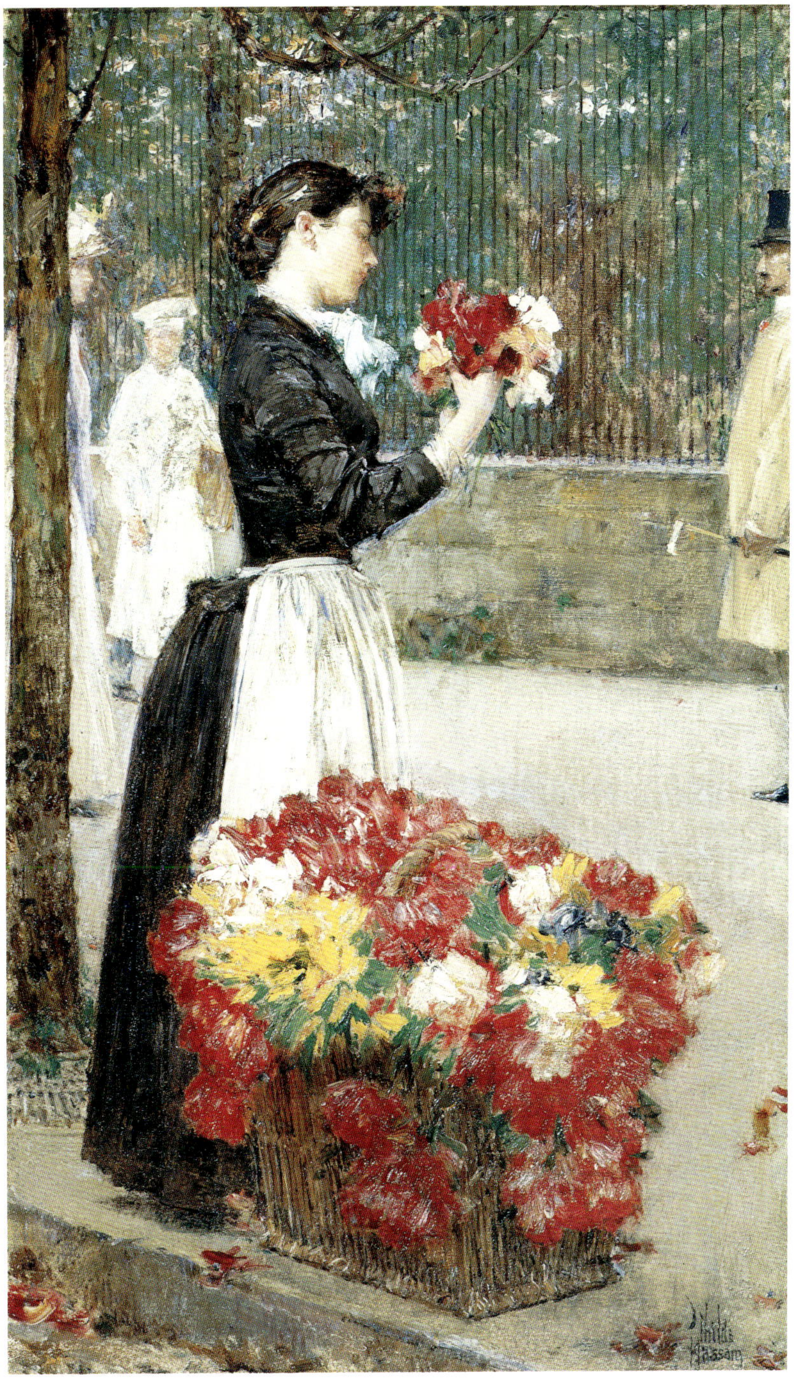

Fig. 71. Childe Hassam. *Flower Girl,* ca. 1887–89. Oil on canvas, 14¼ x 8⅝ in. (36.2 x 21.9 cm). Senator and Mrs. John D. Rockefeller IV

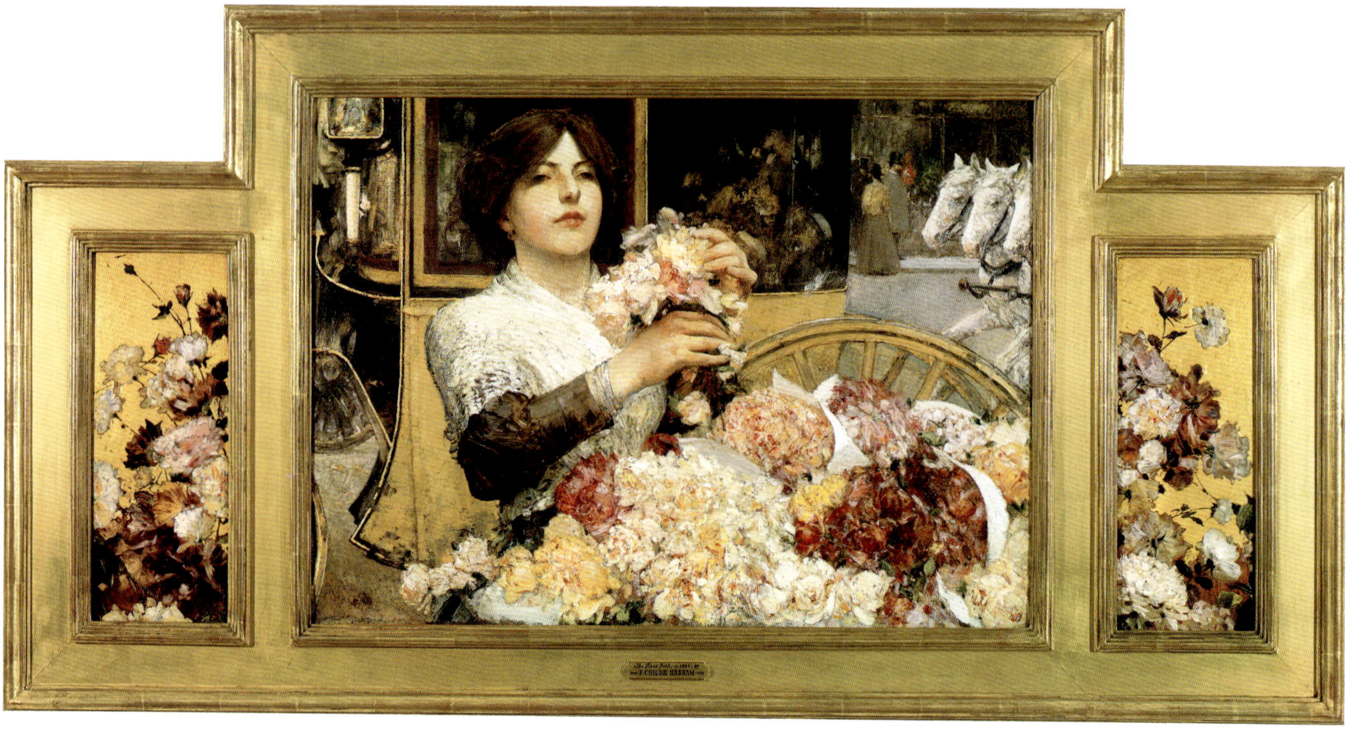

Fig. 72. Childe Hassam. *The Rose Girl,* ca. 1888. Center panel, oil on canvas with gold leaf, 21¾ x 30⅛ in. (55.2 x 76.5 cm); side panels, oil on wood with gold leaf, each 15¼ x 6¼ in. (38.7 x 15.9 cm). Senator and Mrs. John D. Rockefeller IV

and a small bustle. She selects a bouquet from her immense basket of blooms. A well-dressed woman emerging from the left, a chef, and, at the right, a handsome man wearing a top hat and carrying a cane suggest a range of Parisian types. Hassam hints that disparities of social class pale by comparison with the beauty of the young vendor and her sumptuous display of flowers.

In *The Rose Girl* (fig. 72) a flower vendor offering a bouquet to the viewer becomes almost heroic. Like the mirror behind the barmaid in Manet's *Bar at the Folies-Bergère* (fig. 73), the reflective coach windows that set off the young woman's head implicate space in front of the picture plane. A critic for the *New York Times* noted in 1890: "The versatility of Mr. Childe Hassam is indeed surprising. *The Rose Girl* is a composition in the manner of James Tissot, the flower girl and her masses of flowers, the yellow cab and passers-by being painted with a solid insistence not generally found in Mr. Hassam's other works."[57] Hassam quoted the golden panels of the coach's doors in flower-filled gilded side panels and placed all three elements within what the same critic described as "a wonderful frame," which has since been replaced.[58] The triptych format and gilding in *The Rose Girl* imply that a modern secular subject is as worthy as the sacred figures who appear in religious altarpieces.

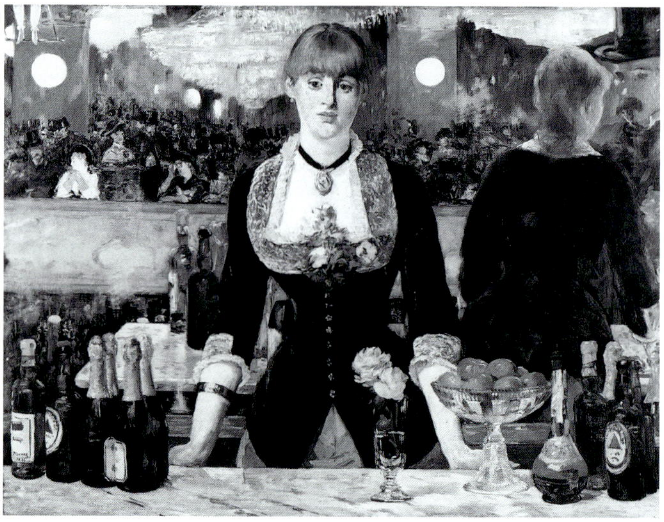

Fig. 73. Édouard Manet. *A Bar at the Folies-Bergère,* 1881. Oil on canvas, 37¾ x 51⅛ in. (95.9 x 129.9 cm). Courtauld Institute Galleries, Courtauld Institute of Art, London

Hassam favored a high-key palette and loose brushwork for most of his Parisian scenes, but—as he demonstrated in *The Rose Girl* and a number of other pictures—he could pick and choose any point along a stylistic spectrum from academic to Impressionist according to the occasion. In 1888, for example, he painted on a canvas about eleven feet wide a somber late-afternoon scene entitled *Autumn* (fig. 74). Here, in one of Hassam's most sentimental works, an aged street

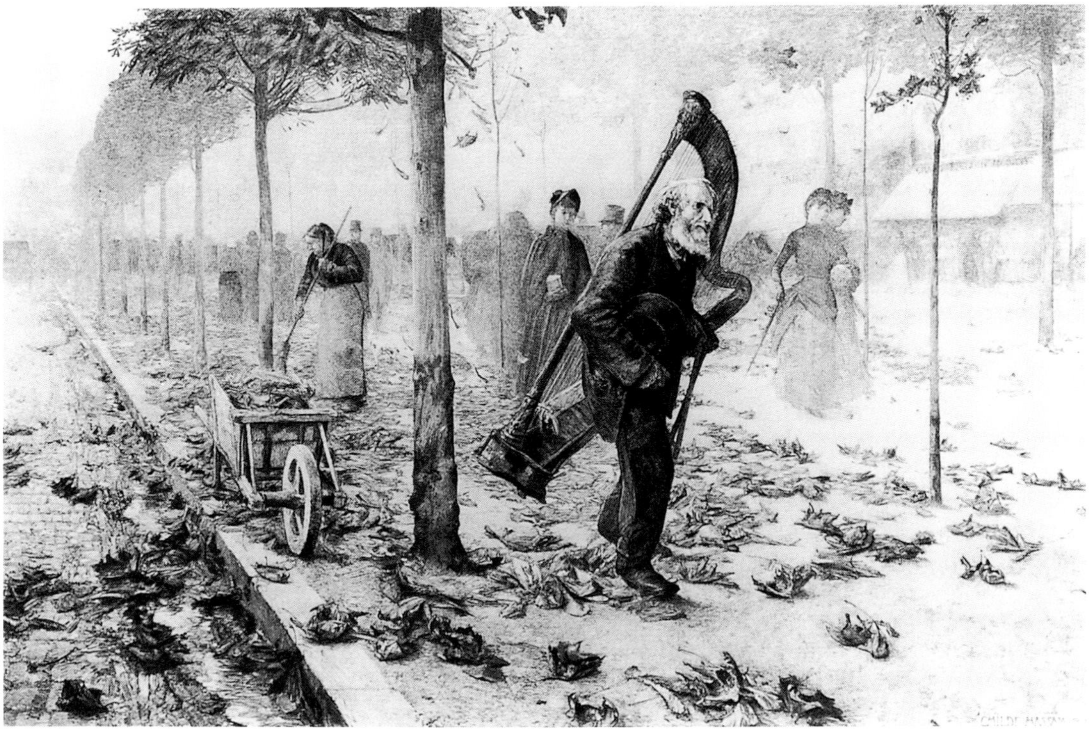

Fig. 74. Childe Hassam. *Autumn,* 1888. Oil on canvas. Location unknown

musician bent under the weight of a harp makes his way along a leaf-strewn Parisian boulevard on which are also seen fashionable pedestrians and a woman working as a street sweeper. Hassam's intention was clearly metaphorical: to echo the waning of the minstrel's life in the waning of the day and the year. When *Autumn* appeared in the 1889 Salon, critics especially appreciated Hassam's mastery of atmospheric effects, one noting "the delicate pearly effect of Parisian autumn twilight"[59] and another remarking on "the pearly evening mist [that] gives mystery to the distance."[60] In both subject and setting the picture is distant from Hassam's usual lighthearted genre scenes.

Another of Hassam's monumental Parisian canvases is the more cheerful *At the Florist* (fig. 75), for which he again employed a traditional composition and technique: here a stagelike space, volumetric forms, crisp detail, and an almost illusionistic rendering of flowerpots and puddles. The approach seems extremely conventional, especially by contrast with his slightly earlier *Gathering Flowers in a French Garden* (fig. 315), a large but very informal image of a similar subject. In conceiving *At the Florist* Hassam may well have been seeking a conservative stylistic statement appropriate to the 1890 Salon, in which the canvas appeared after his return home.[61] The subject is a large flower stall overseen by a young woman in rural garb who serves a well-dressed customer attired in a black jacket and flowing sheer scarf over a light skirt. The vendor embodies country life, and her wares—flowering plants, some pruned to a standard, and all wrapped for clean and easy transport—suggest the accommodation of rural nature to urban life. Hassam was also proposing that the young flower vendor herself is analogous to her wares. As Jefferson C. Harrison has suggested, she "wears a long white work apron whose shape and hue are echoed in the brilliant white paper cones encircling the bouquets and flowering plants. The significance of the analogy could not be more obvious: the girl herself is a living, breathing bouquet, her flawless face merely the crowning blossom in the armful of flowers she holds."[62] While fashionable urbanites dominate Hassam's Parisian works, he could, as here and in *La Bouquetière et la Laitière* and *La Fruitière,* interpret with dignity the rural types who work in the city.

In the three summers from 1887 through 1889 Hassam and his wife visited Villiers-le-Bel, about ten miles northeast of Paris in the Oise Valley near Ecouen. Their hosts were Ernest Blumenthal, a cosmopolitan and successful German businessman resident in Paris, and his wife, who had become Maud Hassam's closest friend in the city.[63] The Blumenthals occupied a house on an estate owned by a daughter of the French painter Thomas Couture.[64] In a June 1888 letter to Lamb, Hassam recited these details: "I wish we were at the Shoals for this summer, but we will really go to Vdliers [*sic*]-le-bel and I shall paint in a charming old French garden. That is where Couture lived and painted. Hunt must have been [t]here. The proprietor of the property that my friend lives [on], married one of Couture's daughters, and has a houseful of his works. I wish very much to see them some day and will."[65] Mentor for years to Manet and briefly to Cassatt, among others, Couture interested Hassam because he had taught not only his Boston instructor Tommaso Juglaris but also the influential Boston painter William Morris Hunt, Hassam's distant relative and Celia Thaxter's close friend.[66]

The garden scenes Hassam painted at the Blumenthals' country retreat anticipate, generally, his tendency to create works in series and, more specifically, his later images of Thaxter's Appledore Island garden. "The Blumenthal[s]," Hassam recalled, "had a French gardener, who kept the things beautiful."[67] The gardener and his employers favored terraces, raised flower beds, potted plants, and shrubs clipped to standards. In these walled formal gardens Hassam painted a series of works showing both servants, who were the suburban counterparts of his Parisian flower vendors, and more privileged women, including his wife, Maud. These women tend or enjoy plantings that are as detached from wild nature as the wrapped bouquets sold in Paris. *After Breakfast* (fig. 76), one of the earliest and most ambitious of these scenes, focuses on a slender maid watering a potted oleander and set off by tiers of bright red potted geraniums, like the one Hassam had featured in *Summer Evening* (fig. 115), painted at Appledore a year earlier. *After Breakfast* shows, seated at a breakfast table on a terrace to the right, a young woman at leisure who reads the morning paper. The inclusion in the servant's costume of elements of fashion (for example, a shirtwaist that was, perhaps, a castoff from her employer), her lovely face, and her captivating pose that echoes the posture of the woman reading all indicate Hassam's wish to express the two women's kinship in grace, despite disparities of wealth and social class. The asymmetrical composition and the newspaper—which signals engagement with the modern world—are examples of Hassam's adoption of devices used by Degas in *The Ballet Class* (fig. 77) and like works. Comparison of *After Breakfast* with Degas's image, however,

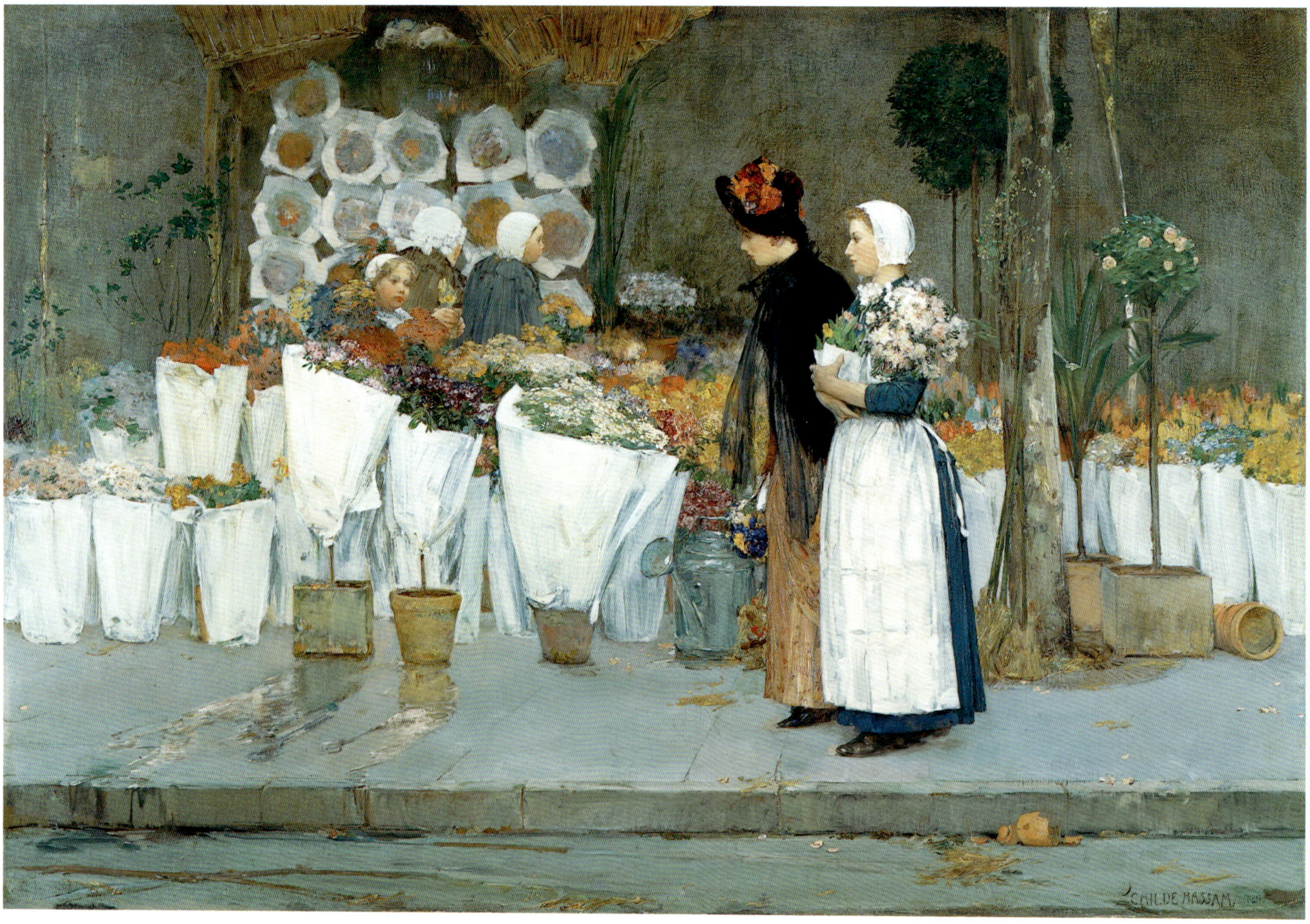

Fig. 75. Childe Hassam. *At the Florist,* 1889. Oil on canvas, 36¾ x 54¼ in. (93.4 x 137.8 cm). Chrysler Museum of Art, Norfolk, Virginia; Gift of Walter P. Chrysler, Jr. This work of art is dedicated by the Museum Trustees to Linda Kaufman in gratitude for the time, talent and resources she has so generously given to the Chrysler. June 1999

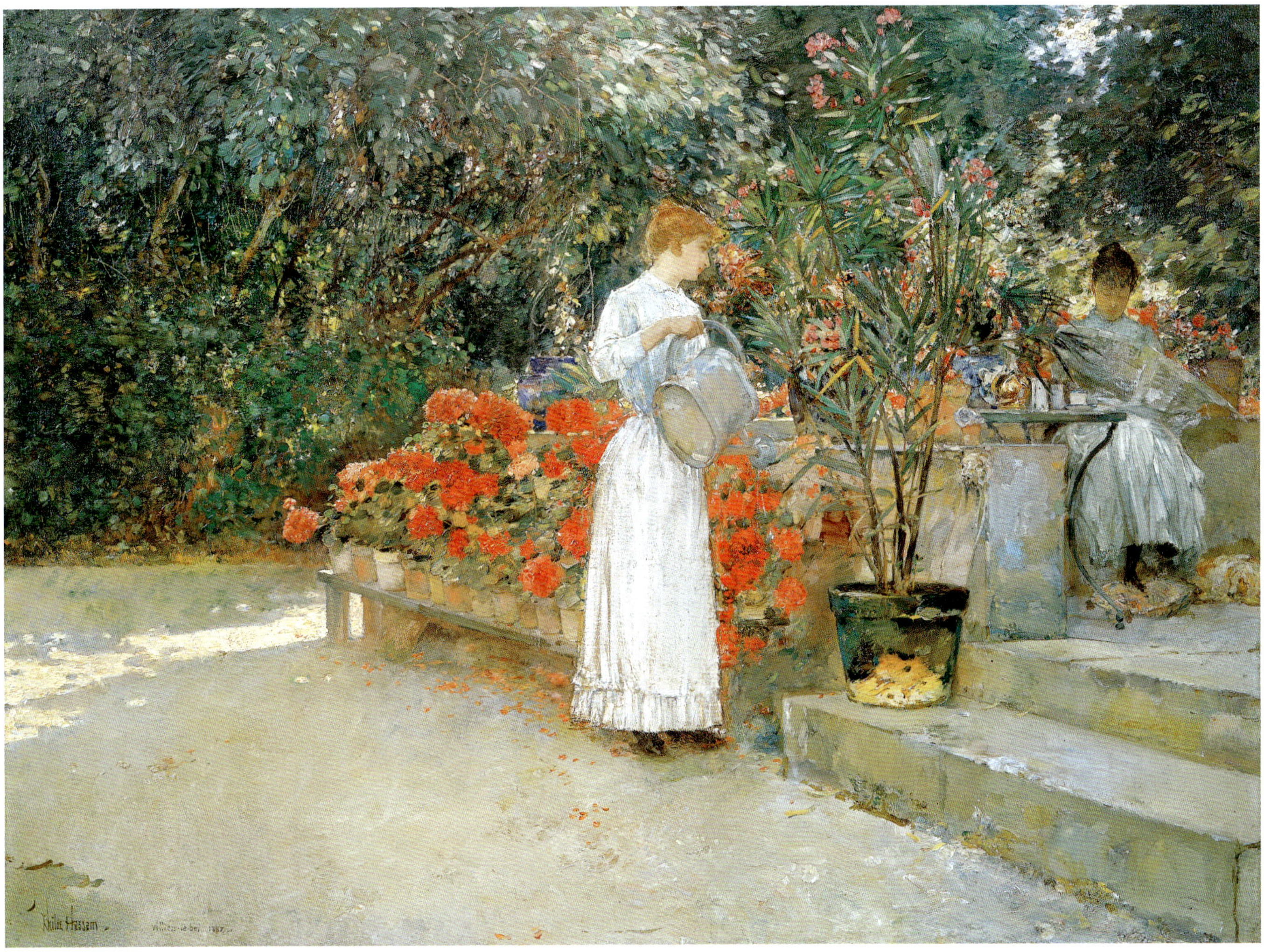

Fig. 76. Childe Hassam. *After Breakfast,* 1887. Oil on canvas, 28¾ x 39⅝ in. (73 x 100.6 cm). Collection of Fayez Sarofim

reveals Hassam's reluctance to crop forms radically and his preference for more ingratiating, bourgeois subject matter. Moreover, the even more striking similarities between *After Breakfast* and canvases such as de Schryver's *Woman in a Garden* (fig. 78) suggest Hassam's greater susceptibility to influence from the Parisian juste-milieu painters.

Hassam also recalled de Schryver in *Geraniums* (fig. 79), which Hassam showed in the 1889 Salon as *Soleil et fleurs.* Here pots of brilliant red geraniums are set on a deep window ledge and on two steps of a terrace,[68] and a large potted oleander like the one tended in *After Breakfast* stands at the right. The geraniums create a dazzling screen of color behind which appears a beautifully rendered sunlit wall to the right. To the left, under a glass awning that is announced by the shadows

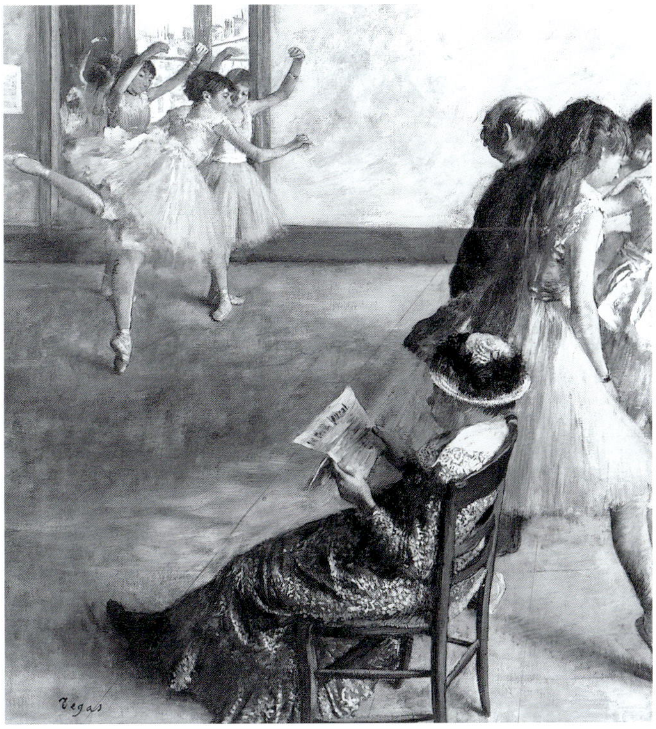

Fig. 77. Edgar Degas. *The Ballet Class,* ca. 1880. Oil on canvas, 32⅜ x 30¼ in. (82.2 x 77.2 cm). Philadelphia Museum of Art: Purchased with the W. P. Wilsach Fund

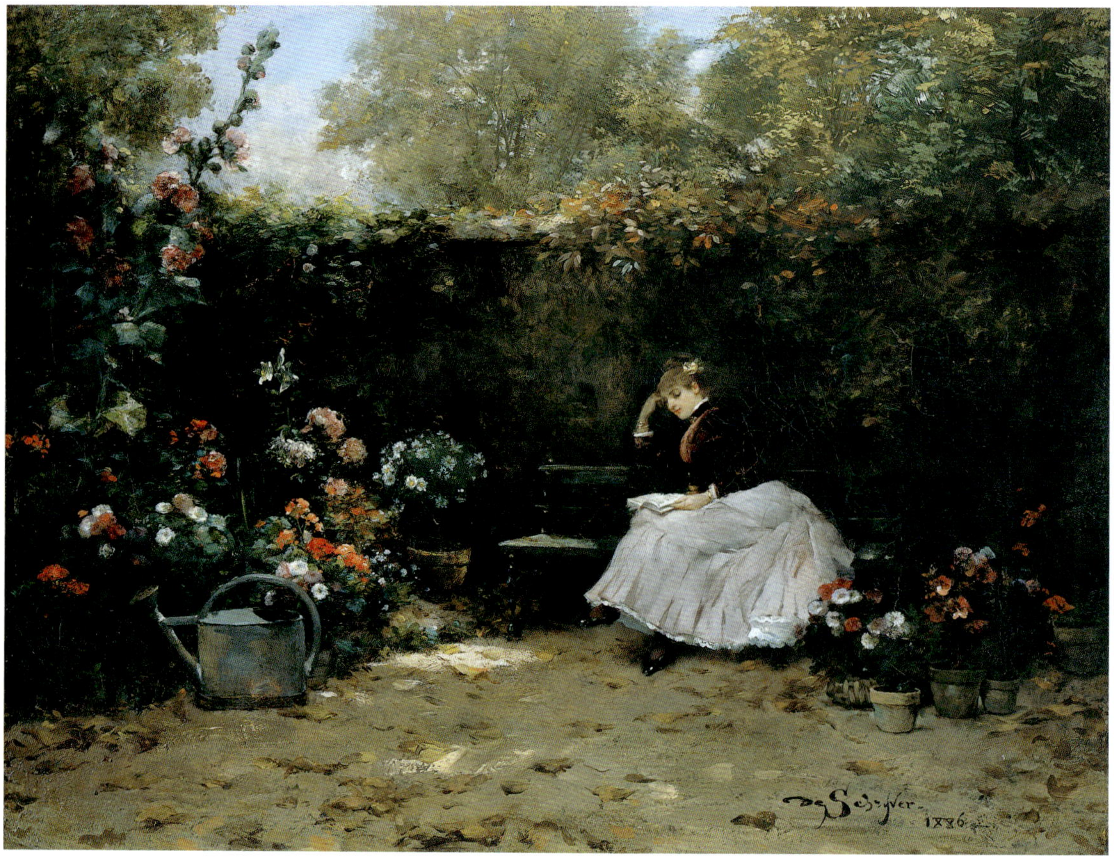

Fig. 78. Louis Marie de Schryver. *Woman in a Garden*, 1886. Oil on canvas, 14¾ x 18¾ in. (37.5 x 47.6 cm). Collection of the Modern Art Museum of Fort Worth, Bequest of Mrs. Benjamin J. Tillar

it casts, Mrs. Hassam is seen sewing.[69] The accord between the flowers and the woman is emphasized by the blossoms that encircle her head: all are in bloom. Two large watering cans that occupy the foreground manifest Hassam's gift for placing and painting still-life objects, a gift in evidence in many of his later works as well. The subject of the charming small oil *In the Garden* (fig. 80) is a young woman perched on a low stone terrace wall and set off by a screen of lilacs accented by poppies that line the wall's edge. The model's fresh pale pink cotton day dress is the utilitarian attire of a maid, suggesting again, as Hassam had in *After Breakfast* and other works, that social class is irrelevant to feminine beauty and grace.

Just as Hassam recorded few topographical views of Paris, he painted few simple landscapes in the French countryside. An exquisite rare landscape is *Peach Blossoms—Villiers-le-Bel* (fig. 81), which shows an overgrown peach tree in an orchard near the Blumenthals' country home. Here Hassam celebrated the beauty of cultivated nature now gone wild, playing off the bent Y-shaped trunk against the tangled veil of blooming branches that surmounts it. The unruly peach tree is delectably dynamic, especially in contrast to the controlled nature that usually preoccupied Hassam at Villiers-le-Bel.[70]

Hassam's French city and country scenes quickly found an appreciative audience. For example, in his influential book *Recent Ideals of American Art*, published in 1888, the important critic George William Sheldon singled out Hassam from the multitude of artists who preferred historical, exotic, and peasant subjects:

> *The only American who makes a practice of painting life in the cities—in the parks, in the streets, and on the house-tops—is Mr. Childe Hassam. Sometimes he reproduces the flower-gardens of country-houses, where the women are so charming, and, above all, so "paintable"; but it is in the cities that he chiefly finds his subjects, where the women in out-door costumes are not less charming, and where the correlated atmospheric effects appeal to the artist's pencil. Mr. Hassam's pictures tell interesting stories and at the same time record the most delicate play of light and shade.*[71]

Frank T. Robinson was equally enthusiastic, publishing a long description of Hassam's accomplishments at home and abroad in another book of 1888, his *Living New England Artists: Biographical Sketches*. He concluded: "It is safe to predict that Hassam is sure to become one of the strongest painters this country has produced."[72]

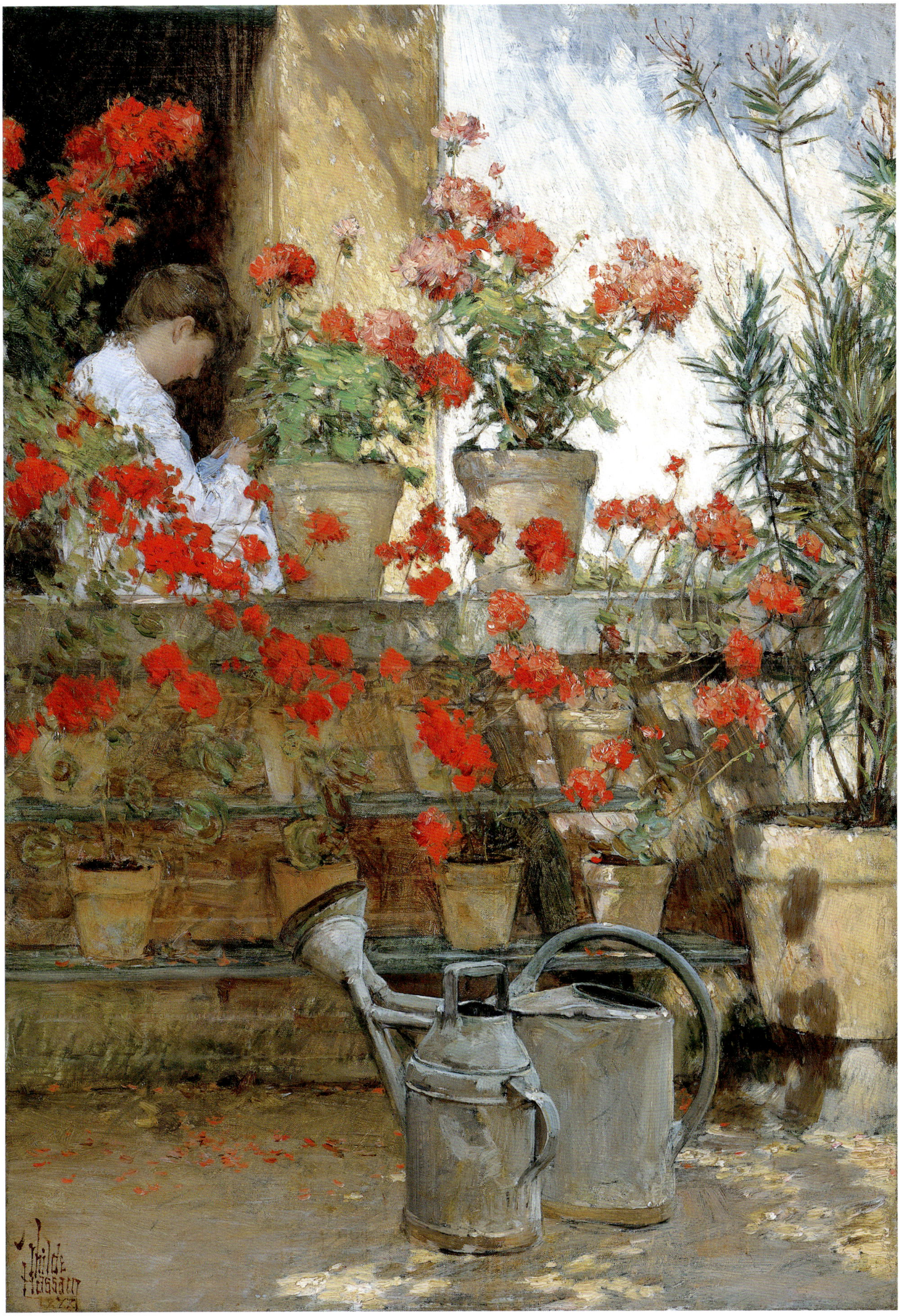

Fig. 79. Childe Hassam. *Geraniums,* 1888–89. Oil on canvas, 18¼ x 13 in. (46.4 x 33 cm). The Hyde Collection, Glens Falls, New York

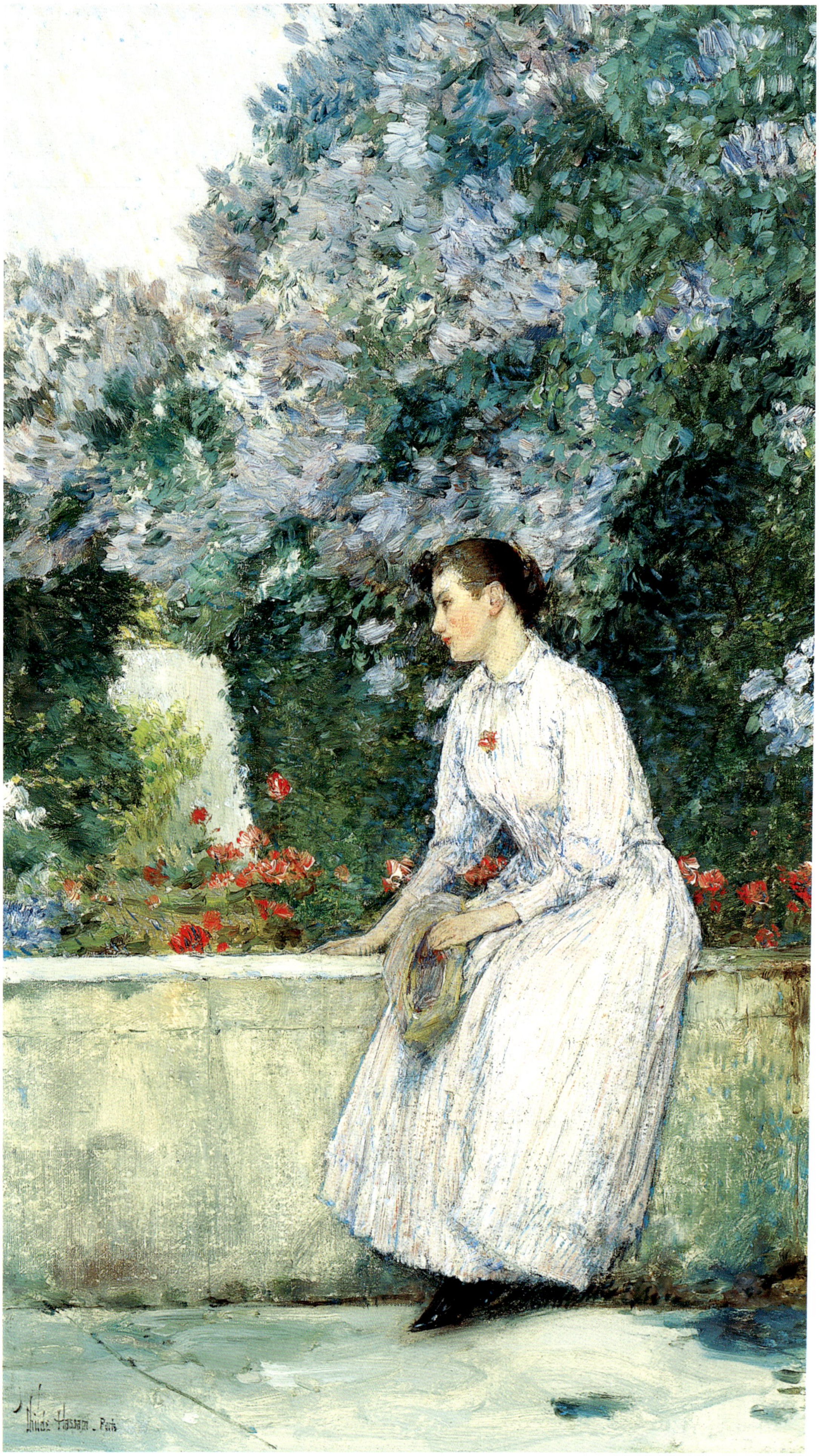

Fig. 80. Childe Hassam. *In the Garden*, ca. 1888–89. Oil on canvas, 18 x 10¾ in. (45.7 x 27.3 cm). Private collection

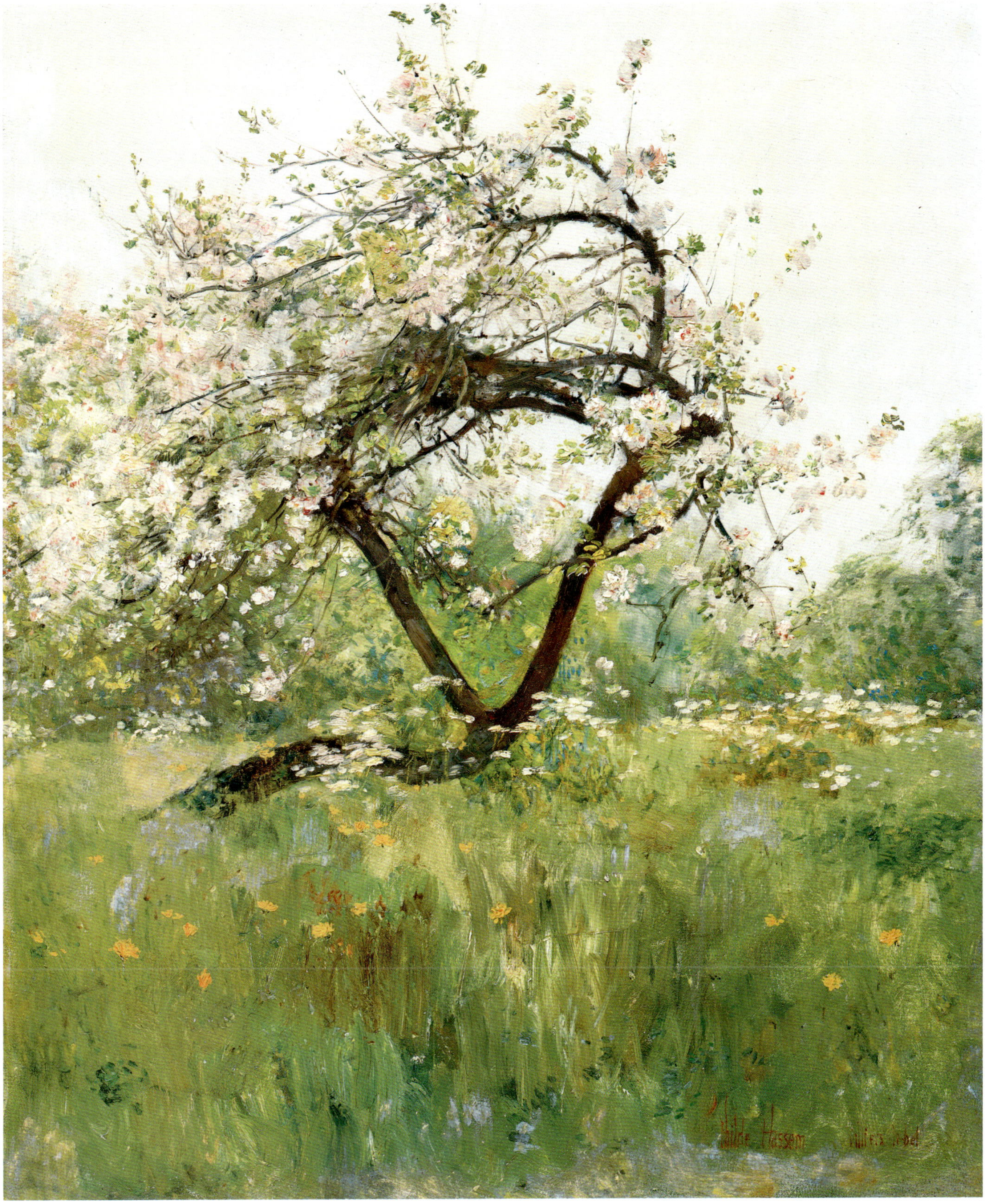

Fig. 81. Childe Hassam. *Peach Blossoms—Villiers-le-Bel*, ca. 1887–89. Oil on canvas, $18\frac{1}{8}$ x $21\frac{1}{2}$ in. (46 x 54.6 cm). The Metropolitan Museum of Art, New York. Gift of Mrs. J. Augustus Barnard, 1979 1979.490.9

In March 1889, about six months before he returned home, Hassam showed thirty-five of his Parisian works at Noyes, Cobb and Company, Boston. The favorable reviews that greeted the exhibition, like Sheldon's appraisal, endorsed Hassam's dedication to painting modern life in a modern style. As the critic for the *Boston Evening Transcript* wrote:

> *The exhibition . . . is full of gayety and brightness, and has a truly Parisian savor. Mr. Hassam has been in Paris two or three years, and his pictures are largely of the streets, gardens and environs of that capital. Since he left Boston he has made a very noticeable gain, especially in color, and he has never painted so well as now. . . . It is refreshing to note that Mr. Hassam, in the midst of so many good, bad and indifferent art currents, seems to be paddling his own canoe with a good deal of independence and method. When his Boston pictures of three years ago . . . are compared with the more recent works . . . , it may be seen how he has progressed.*[73]

Also in the spring of 1889 Hassam showed two paintings in the Salon and four in the Exposition Universelle.[74] These works demonstrated his commitment to painting contemporary life, and the award of a bronze medal at the Exposition recognized his efforts. That summer Hassam and his wife visited London, Broadstairs, Canterbury, Chiswick, and other towns in England and made a last journey to Villiers-le-Bel. It was upon their return to Paris that they resided for a short time in the studio and apartment that Renoir had occupied. In a letter of October 1 Hassam shared his plans with a Boston acquaintance: "By the time you receive this I shall be on the way over to 'Yankee Doodle.' I shall locate in New York. . . . I am come back with the firm intention to create a capital and erect a summer castle somewhere in New England or New York."[75] He would celebrate his thirtieth birthday on shipboard on October 17.[76]

Five months before this birthday Hassam had summed up the lessons of his Parisian sojourn in a long letter to Downes. Of "the Academy and the Prix de Rome system" he wrote: "It is nonsense. It crushes all originality out of the growing men. It tends to put them in a rut and it keeps them in it." Far preferable was adherence to his credo: "An artist should paint his own time and treat nature as he feels it, not repeat the same stupidities of his predecessors." He added: "The American Section in the Universal [Exposition] has convinced me for ever of the capability of Americans to claim a school. . . . But as long as a crowd of apostates from America who have more money than brains continue to go to France to study for such a long time, . . . there will be little growth of an American school."[77]

Having experienced a modicum of academic training, confirmed his commitment to recording everyday life, and achieved critical success in Paris, Hassam came home in the late summer, by way of England, to help create "an American school."

1. Lockman interview, January 31, 1927, p. 12
2. Childe Hassam, Paris, November 2, 1888, to [Charles Stuart] Pratt, [probably Boston], George Henry Sargent Autograph Collection, Manuscript Division, New York Public Library, microfilm, Archives of American Art, reel N25, frames 1373–74: "I am going to turn my attention again to illustration. In devoting all my time to paintings I like all American painters (whether they care to admit it or not) produce more work than I can sell and sales come too often a long time after the work is completed. You can understand this readily enough. Now I am going to do less painting and give a large share of my time to serious illustrating." Hassam goes on to propose that he provide to Pratt two drawings a month. Mr. Pratt was almost certainly Charles Stuart Pratt (1854–1921), an author and an editor at D. Lothrop and Company, Boston, publishers of *Babyland* and *Wide Awake*, periodicals for children. Hassam provided illustrations for Pratt's book *Bye-o-Baby Ballads* (Boston: D. Lothrop and Co., 1886).
3. Greta [pseud.], "Art in Boston, . . ." *Art Amateur* 15 (November 1886), p. 113, quoted in Hiesinger 1994, p. 31.
4. See, for example, Peter Bermingham, *American Art in the Barbizon Mood*, exh. cat. (Washington, D.C.: National Collection of Fine Arts, Smithsonian Institution, 1975); Laura L. Meixner, *An International Episode: Millet, Monet, and Their North American Counterparts*, exh. cat. (Memphis, Tenn.: Dixon Gallery and Gardens, 1982); and H. Barbara Weinberg, *The Lure of Paris: Nineteenth-Century American Painters and Their French Teachers* (New York: Abbeville Press, 1991).
5. Lockman interview, January 31, 1927, p. 13. Adams 1938, p. 26, records: "Aware that patriotic Americans are inclined to flock by themselves in a foreign city, thus missing much of the very culture they had crossed the ocean to find, the Hassams thought it best not to live in the classic Latin Quarter, with its many American students. After a short stay at the *Hôtel de l'Univers et de Portugal*, more magnificent in name than in fact, they crossed the river, and explored Montmartre."
6. The boulevard de Clichy and the boulevard Rochechouart literally divide the ninth from the eighteenth arrondissement. The odd-numbered buildings on both boulevards are in the ninth arrondissement. This summary description of the boulevard de Clichy and the boulevard Rochechouart and their residents is indebted to the excellent account in John Milner,

The Studios of Paris: The Capital of Art in the Late Nineteenth Century (New Haven: Yale University Press, 1988), pp. 132–47. For the development of avant-garde painting in the quarter during the late 1880s, see Cornelia Homburg, *Vincent Van Gogh and the Painters of the Petit Boulevard,* exh. cat. (Saint Louis: Saint Louis Art Museum in association with Rizzoli International Publications, 2001).

7. Childe Hassam, 11, boulevard de Clichy, Paris, November 20, 1886, to Miss Rose Lamb, 83 Mt. Vernon Street, Boston, Isles of Shoals Collection, Ms. 58. Lamb studied with William Morris Hunt and Helen Knowlton beginning about 1876 and edited and published the letters of poet Celia Laighton Thaxter in 1895. She was best known for portraits of children but gave up painting about 1900 because of illness. Peter Hastings Falk, ed., *Who Was Who in American Art, 1564–1975,* vol. 2 (Madison, Conn.: Sound View Press, 1999), p. 1932.
8. Hassam, November 20, 1886, to Lamb. The misspellings of Maud's name are attributable to the typist who transcribed the lost manuscript letters.
9. Susan Hale, untitled, undated clipping, labeled "*Boston Transcript,* 1887," Hassam Papers, reel NAA1, frame 489.
10. Childe Hassam, 35, boulevard Rochechouart, Paris, November 29, 1887, to Miss Rose Lamb, 83 Mt. Vernon Street, Boston, Isles of Shoals Collection, Ms. 58.
11. Lockman interview, January 31, 1927, p. 17.
12. Ibid., pp. 17, 19. Hassam mentioned in the same interview (passim) the following among the Americans he did encounter in Paris: Ernest L. Major, Albert Henry Munsell, Ogden Wood, Moses White, Frank Boggs, Gari Melchers, and Edward E. Simmons.
13. Hoopes (1979, p. 14) suggests that Hassam was constrained from travel principally by financial considerations.
14. For the Académie Julian, see Catherine Fehrer, "New Light on the Académie Julian and Its Founder (Rodolphe Julian)," *Gazette des beaux-arts,* ser. 6, 126 (May–June 1984), pp. 207–16; Robert Kashey and Elisabeth Kashey, *The Julian Academy, Paris, 1868–1939,* essay by Catherine Fehrer, exh. cat. (New York: Shepherd Gallery, 1989); Weinberg, *Lure of Paris,* chap. 9; and Gabriel P. Weisberg and Jane R. Becker, eds., *Overcoming All Obstacles: The Women of the Académie Julian,* exh. cat. (New York: Dahesh Museum; New Brunswick, N.J.: Rutgers University Press, 1999).
15. Lockman interview, January 31, 1927, p. 13. The recent bibliography on Benson, Tarbell, and Metcalf is extensive; for Munsell, see *National Cyclopaedia of American Biography* 36 (1950), pp. 337–38.
16. Lockman interview, January 31, 1927, p. 13. Hassam may have mistaken the "compliment" given to him with the front-row seat. In most Parisian teaching ateliers students chose working places according to their seniority in the studio or their success in studio competitions. Usually it was the more advanced students who chose positions farthest from the model—where they could paint at full length—and the beginners who were relegated to the close-up, worm's-eye views, which permitted only head-and-shoulder studies. See Weinberg, *Lure of Paris,* p. 91.
17. Childe Hassam, 11, boulevard de Clichy, Paris, January 11, 1887, to William Howe Downes, Boston, Downes Papers, MSS L337, transcribed in Hiesinger 1994, p. 177.
18. Lockman interview, January 31, 1927, p. 14.
19. Childe Hassam, 35, boulevard Rochechouart, Paris, May 28, 1889, to William Howe Downes, Boston, Downes Papers, MSS L337, transcribed in Hiesinger 1994, p. 179.
20. Frederick W. Morton, "Childe Hassam, Impressionist," *Brush and Pencil* 8 (June 1901), p. 146.
21. A listing of "Art Exhibitions in Paris, 1886–1889," other than the Salons appears in Alain G. Joyaux, Brian A. Moore, and Ned H. Griner, *Childe Hassam in Indiana,* exh. cat. (Muncie, Ind.: Ball State University Art Gallery, November 3–December 8, 1985; Oxford, Ohio: Miami University Art Museum, January 11–March 16, 1986), pp. 23–24.
22. The painting by Puvis in Chicago is a reduction of a large mural for the Musée des Beaux-Arts, Lyon, 1884. See also, for example, Pierre Puvis de Chavannes, *A Vision of Antiquity—Symbol of Form,* ca. 1887–90 (Carnegie Museum of Art, Pittsburgh), a reduction of a large mural for the Palais des Arts, Lyon, 1885.
23. Hassam recalled of Boggs: "He had a studio in the building. . . . He painted Paris subjects. The same things that I did at the time." Lockman interview, January 31, 1927, p. 16.
24. Hassam, May 28, 1889, to Downes, transcribed in Hiesinger 1994, p. 179.
25. Lockman interview, January 31, 1927, pp. 19–20. According to John House et al., *Renoir,* exh. cat. (London: Arts Council of Great Britain, 1985), p. 303, Renoir occupied an apartment and a studio at 35, boulevard Rochechouart for about a year beginning October 15, 1886. Maurice Hamel, a French critic, described the American display at the 1889 Exposition Universelle, where Hassam showed four paintings. He observed the pervasiveness of French influence and cited the example of Hassam, "qui pense à Renoir." Maurice Hamel, "Les écoles étrangères," *Gazette des beaux-arts,* ser. 3, 31 (October 1889), p. 382. The comment was exaggerated in the English translation of a portion of Hamel's remarks ("Hassam, who is always thinking of Renoir"). See "American Art at the Paris Exposition: A French Criticism," *Studio* 4 (November 1889), p. 181.
26. For the American Impressionists' euphemism, nationalism, optimism, and nostalgia, see Weinberg, Bolger, and Curry 1994, pp. 3–33.
27. Charles Baudelaire, "Le peintre de la vie moderne" (1863), in *The Painter of Modern Life and Other Essays,* trans. Jonathan Mayne (London: Phaidon, 1964), p. 9.
28. Lockman interview, January 31, 1927, p. 17.
29. Quoted in Ives 1892, p. 116.
30. Hassam painted a smaller version, almost certainly before he executed the final canvas. See *Rue Bonaparte,* oil on canvas, 19 x 25¼ in. (48.3 x 64.1 cm), reproduced in *Lines of Different Character: American Art from 1727 to 1947,* exh. cat. (New York: Hirschl and Adler Galleries, 1982), no. 46.
31. Hale, untitled, undated clipping, labeled "*Boston Transcript,* 1887," Hassam Papers, reel NAA1, frame 489.
32. Hoopes 1979, p. 26.
33. Childe Hassam, 11, boulevard de Clichy, Paris, July 21, 1887, to Rose Lamb, Thaxter Cottage, Isles of Shoals, Isles of Shoals Collection, Ms. 58.
34. Hoopes (1979, p. 26) identifies the seminary. John House et al., *Landscapes of France: Impressionism and Its Rivals,* exh. cat. (Boston: Museum of Fine Arts; London: Hayward Gallery, 1995), p. 168, note that Saint-Sulpice was "one of the leading institutions in Paris for the training of priests." For Paris cochers, see Frédéric Mayer, "The Paris Cocher," *Harper's Weekly,* July 28, 1900, pp. 698–99, and Vance Thompson, "The Paris Cabman," *Outing* 43 (December 1903), pp. 241–51; both sources are cited in William H. Gerdts, "Three Themes," in Adelson, Cantor, and Gerdts 1999, p. 225, nn. 28, 30.
35. Hassam, July 21, 1887, to Lamb.
36. Elizabeth Broun, "Childe Hassam's America," *American Art* 13, no. 3 (fall 1999), p. 35, suggests "the old pushcart vendor and his daughter seem out of place. . . . They exit the scene almost as if they were crowded out by modernization."

37. Hale, in an untitled, undated clipping, labeled "*Boston Transcript,* 1887," Hassam Papers, reel NAA1, frame 489. The driver of a fiacre sat in front of the passenger box.
38. H. T. Woolf, "American Artists in the Salon," *American Art Illustrated* 1, no. 9 (1887), p. 262. Hassam was one of 116 Americans who exhibited paintings in the 1887 Salon.
39. Theodore Child, "The Paris Salon of 1887," *Art Amateur* 16 (May 1887), p. 126. The illustration of the painting (p. 126) is captioned "A Summer Shower."
40. Hassam, July 21, 1887, to Lamb. See also Child, "Paris Salon of 1887," p. 126.
41. Unidentified clipping, signed "E.W.M.," labeled "*Boston Transcript,* 1887," Hassam Papers, reel NAA1, frame 509.
42. Hassam, January 11, 1887, to Downes, transcribed in Hiesinger 1994, p. 177.
43. Hassam explained that he had been urged by friends to paint a larger version of the first canvas. He added: "I hope I shall do it as well as the smaller one which I thought was successful in some ways." Hassam, November 29, 1887, to Lamb. Hassam also repeated the composition of *Grand Prix Day* in a pastel; this work, *At the "Grand Prix de Paris,"* shown at Doll and Richards Gallery, Boston, in February 1891 (no. 43), has not been located. See Carol Troyen, *The Boston Tradition: American Paintings from the Museum of Fine Arts, Boston,* exh. cat. (New York: American Federation of Arts, 1980), p. 164.
44. Hiesinger 1994, p. 39.
45. Hassam's composition is uncannily similar to Ernest Gutierrez (Spanish, 19th–20th century), *A Street Scene by the Arc de Triomphe, Paris,* Sotheby's, London, sale cat., June 17, 1992, lot 609. Little is known about Gutierrez, and the circumstances surrounding the relationship between his painting and Hassam's scenes of Grand Prix day remain elusive.
46. The short shadows in Hassam's paintings imply that the sun is at its apogee and therefore suggest that the horse parade shown precedes the race. Warren Adelson ("Childe Hassam: Cosmopolitan and Patriot," in Adelson, Cantor, and Gerdts 1999, p. 22) argues that Hassam depicted "a time in the afternoon after the race when the parade of swells returned from this annual event in the Bois de Boulogne." Gerdts ("Three Themes," p. 133) makes the same claim. The identity of the avenue shown is not certain. In 1889 Hassam exhibited the large version of the scene as *The Champs-Élysées, Day of the Grand Prix;* see *Exhibition and Private Sale of Paintings by Mr. Childe Hassam* (Boston: Noyes, Cobb and Co., March 1889), no. 16. However, he had previously told Lamb that the site was the avenue de la Grande Armée, the continuation of the Champs-Élysées on the northwest side of the Étoile. Hassam, November 29, 1887, to Lamb. A columnist for the *New York Herald,* undated clipping, labeled "1888," noted that the painting shown in the Salon depicts "the avenue du Bois de Boulogne with the Arc de Triomphe in the distance"; Hassam Papers, reel NAA1, frame 509. Susan G. Larkin concludes that "the angle at which the avenue approaches the Arc suggests that it was the Avenue Foch [formerly the Avenue du Bois de Boulogne], the broad thoroughfare that leads directly from the *place* to the Bois de Boulogne." Catalogue entry in *New Britain Museum of American Art: Highlights of the Collection: Volume I* (New Britain, Conn.: New Britain Museum of American Art, 1999), p. 83. Larkin's catalogue entry (pp. 82–83) contains much interesting information about the Grand Prix race of 1887. Gerdts ("Three Themes," pp. 132–33), relying on a letter from Robert Herbert, maintains that avenue Foch is depicted. Hiesinger (1994, p. 39) claims: "It is probable that Hassam used the term 'Grand Prix' in its generic sense," studied the fashionable parade in April 1887, and painted it in the autumn, which accounts for "the dark-colored foliage of the chestnut trees in the picture."
47. Undated clipping, labeled "*New York Herald,* 1888," Hassam Papers, reel NAA1, frame 509, states that the painting shown in the Salon depicts "a four-in-hand drag." Coincidentally, Eakins had depicted a four-in-hand drag in *A May Morning in the Park (The Fairman Rogers Four-in-Hand)* (fig. 59). Larkin (catalogue entry, in *New Britain Museum of American Art,* p. 82) identifies the large carriage in Hassam's Salon painting as a mail coach and notes that it "was an obvious sign of wealth."
48. For additional commentary on the first version of the scene, see Troyen, *Boston Tradition,* p. 164, and William H. Gerdts, *American Impressionism: Masterworks from Public and Private Collections in the United States* (Lugano-Castagnola: Thyssen-Bornemisza Foundation, 1990), p. 52.
49. Hassam portrayed groups of elegant men and women watching the races at Longchamp from atop their carriages in a watercolor, *Spectators at the Grand Prix,* 1888 (National Gallery of Art, Washington, D.C.), and a pastel, *At the Grand Prix,* 1889 (location unknown), illustrated in Hiesinger 1994, p. 42, fig. 35. Among many examples by French painters, see Édouard Manet, *Race Track near Paris (Courses à Longchamp),* 1864 (Art Institute of Chicago), and the watercolor *Race Course at Longchamp,* 1864 (Fogg Art Museum, Harvard University Art Museums, Cambridge, Massachusetts); and Edgar Degas, *Racehorses at Longchamp,* ca. 1871 (Museum of Fine Arts, Boston).
50. The author thanks Elyssa Schram, Research Assistant, and Melinda Webber, Collection Assistant, Costume Institute, The Metropolitan Museum of Art, for information on the costumes in Hassam's Paris paintings.
51. *The Doane Family and Their Descendants* (Boston: Alfred Adler Doane, 1902), p. 374, gives Maud's birth date as June 26, 1862; her sister Cora Napeth's as August 13, 1856. Letter (in the possession of the Terra Foundation for the Arts, Chicago), New England Historic Genealogical Society Research Service, Boston, April 1, 1985, to Mrs. John Barringer, states that Cora Napeth Doane married Oliver D. Stimpson on September 30, 1874, and speculates that she was widowed and was remarried (between 1881 and 1889) to George H. Cotton. Mrs. Hassam and her sister, who returned from Paris with the Hassams in 1889 (Lockman interview, February 3, 1927, p. 18), also posed for *Twilight (Le Crépuscule)* (fig. 313), a large oil on canvas that Hassam exhibited in the 1889 Exposition Universelle. Hassam described the painting in Lockman interview, January 31, 1927, p. 14.
52. *Scene on Left Bank, Paris,* 1887, oil on canvas, 18¾ x 22¼ in. (private collection?), Selkirk's Auction House, Saint Louis, *Winter Gallery Auction,* sale cat., December 1–3, 1996, lot 387, as *Quai St. Michel,* reproduced in Hassam (Tucson) 1972, p. 65, pl. 27, shows the same view on a rainy twilit evening with several pedestrians on the sidewalk.
53. Juliet Wilson-Bareau, *Manet, Monet, and the Gare Saint-Lazare,* exh. cat. (Washington, D.C.: National Gallery of Art, 1998), pp. 94–101, passim, illustrates other pertinent works by these artists. The dialogue between old architecture and modern elements also anticipates that in Hassam's *Charles River and Beacon Hill* (fig. 84).
54. Hiesinger 1994, p. 44.
55. The scale and carefully rendered details of *La Bouquetière et la Laitière* suggest that it may be the work that Hassam exhibited in the 1890 Salon

as *Une Cremière—aquarelle* (no. D-2978). A work of unspecified medium entitled *La Cremière et la Bouquetière* appeared in the 13th Annual Exhibition, Rochester Art Club, Rochester, New York, May 25–June 4, 1892, no. 102, suggesting that Hassam used the terms of *La Cremière* and *La Laitière* interchangeably. The author thanks Kathleen M. Burnside for the reference.

56. Similar in scale and spirit is *L'Épicerie,* 1889, oil on wood panel (The Dumbarton Oaks Collections, Washington, D.C.).

57. "Society of American Artists," *New York Times,* May 23, 1890, p. 4, col. 6.

58. Ibid.: "The picture is in a wonderful frame, which takes under its wings two smaller panels with flowers." The current frame is based on the illustration of the painting in *Auction: Important Oil Paintings,* sale cat. (New York: O'Reilly's Plaza Art Galleries, October 4, 1962), in which the painting appeared as lot 60; information supplied to owner by Hirschl and Adler Galleries, New York, September 21, 1992. About 1963–64, when the side panels were separated from the central scene, the original frame was probably destroyed. According to the same source, Hassam used the triptych format twice more: in *Still Life,* 1908, oil on canvas (Portland Art Museum, Oregon), and *Chicory,* 1922, oil on wood panel (private collection).

59. "American Artists at the Paris Salon," clipping, labeled "*Harper's Weekly,* 1889," Hassam Papers, reel NAA1, frame 510.

60. Theodore Child, "The Paris Salon of 1889: Third and Concluding Notice," *Art Amateur* 21 (July 1889), p. 27.

61. A related work, *Corner Flower Shop,* an informal sketch now in a private collection, illustrated in *American Paintings VI 1990* (New York: Berry-Hill Galleries, 1990), is inscribed *Paris May 1889*. In the catalogue of the 1890 Salon, no. 1178, *At the Florist (Chez la fleuriste),* and no. 2978, *Une Cremière* (see n. 55, above) were referred to as the property of M. Guichard-Fourniret. *Explication des ouvrages de peinture, sculpture . . . exposés au Palais des Champs-Élysées le 1er mai 1890* (Paris, 1890). Adelson, "Childe Hassam: Cosmopolitan and Patriot," p. 30: For the moment "he abandoned his painterly Impressionist brushwork and tilted toward the more popular technique of de Nittis and Tissot."

62. Jefferson C. Harrison, *The Chrysler Museum: Handbook of the European and American Collections, Selected Paintings, Sculpture and Drawings* (Norfolk, Va.: Chrysler Museum, 1991), p. 149.

63. Lockman interview, January 31, 1927, p. 15: "Then there was M. and Mme. Blumenthal. Mme. Blumenthal had married a German from Frankfort, who was a remarkable linguist. He spoke German, French, English, Italian and Spanish. He spoke English so well. And could speak French without an accent. The people said (that is the French people) that you could not tell whether he was French or not. This man was a well-to-do merchant. He had an apartment in another part of Paris in the well-to-do section." Ibid., p. 18: "She [Maud Hassam] was interested in looking about Paris and going shopping. Her friend Mrs. Blumenthal was a great pleasure and a great delight to her. You see she took her about. They were both really charming to us. She is still, we write to her. He is dead."

64. Couture's two daughters were Berthe-Geneviève (1860–1932) and Jean-Cécile, the Baroness Risler (1862–1936). The author thanks Professor Albert Boime, University of California at Los Angeles, for information regarding Couture's family. See also Marie-José Salmon, ed., *Thomas Couture, 1815–1879,* exh. cat. (Senlis: Association pour la Sauvegarde de Senlis, 1978–79), no. 13.

65. Childe Hassam, Paris, June 27, 1888, to Miss Rose Lamb, Isles of Shoals, Isles of Shoals Collection, Ms. 58. In Lockman interview, January 31, 1927, pp. 15–16, Hassam noted: "They [the Blumenthals] were absolutely good friends of our[s]. Having no children, they said "Your [*sic*] will do us a great kindness to come out here and stay a week or ten days, or a month. But we liked to travel about." The following sources incorrectly state or imply that Mrs. Blumenthal was Couture's daughter: Hiesinger 1994, pp. 31, 50; Adelson, "Childe Hassam: Cosmopolitan and Patriot," p. 23; and Gerdts, "Three Themes," pp. 171 and 228 n. 104.

66. For Hunt's relationship to Hassam, see Stephanie L. Herdrich, "Hassam in Boston, 1859–1886," in this publication, p. 49, n. 21. Hassam mentioned Hunt and his connection with Thaxter in Lockman interview, January 31, 1927, pp. 24–25. Hunt had died by drowning in the waters off the Isles of Shoals in September 1879.

67. Lockman interview, January 31, 1927, p. 15.

68. The canvas is signed and dated at the lower left: *Childe Hassam 1888,* and is also signed in monogram and dated on the back in red paint: *C H 1889*. A stamp on the back of the painting reads *1889/Salon*. James K. Kettlewell, *The Hyde Collection Catalogue* (Glens Falls, N.Y.: Hyde Collection, 1981), p. 215.

69. Recalling paintings done at Villiers-le-Bel, Hassam remarked: "One is of Mrs. Hassam seated under a glass awning. Of course, the awning does not show. The geraniums are banked on a series of two or three steps." Lockman interview, January 31, 1927, p. 15.

70. For additional commentary on the painting, see the catalogue entry by Susan G. Larkin in H. Barbara Weinberg and Susan G. Larkin, *American Impressionists Abroad and At Home: Paintings from the Collection of The Metropolitan Museum of Art,* exh. cat. (New York: American Federation of Arts, 2000), p. 56.

71. George William Sheldon, *Recent Ideals of American Art* (New York and London: D. Appleton and Company, 1888; reprint, New York: Garland Publishing Co., 1977), p. 146. *Twilight (Le Crépuscule)* (fig. 313) appears following p. 140 and *Autumn* (captioned *Autumn in Paris*) (fig. 74) appears following p. 148.

72. Frank T. Robinson, *Living New England Artists: Biographical Sketches* (Boston: Samuel E. Cassino, 1888; reprint, New York: Garland Publishing Co., 1977), p. 105. Robinson's account of Hassam fills pages 101–8.

73. "Fine Arts. Exhibition of Mr. Hassam's Paintings at Noyes, Cobb & Co.'s Gallery," undated clipping, labeled "*Boston Transcript,*" [March 1889], Hassam Papers, reel NAA1, frame 509.

74. At the Exposition Universelle, which ran from May 5 to November 5, 1889, Hassam exhibited *Twilight (Le Crépuscule)* (fig. 313; see n. 71 above); *After Breakfast;* and two unlocated paintings: *Rue Lafayette, Winter Evening;* and *Letter from America*. See Annettte Blaugrund et al., *Paris 1889: American Artists at the Universal Exposition,* exh. cat. (Philadelphia: Pennsylvania Academy of the Fine Arts; New York: Harry N. Abrams, 1989). *Rue Lafayette, Winter Evening* was called "a delicate rendering of Parisian atmosphere" in Theodore Child, "American Artists at the Paris Exposition," *Harper's New Monthly Magazine* 74 (September 1889), p. 518.

75. Childe Hassam, Paris, October 1, 1889, to [Charles Stuart] Pratt, [probably Boston], George Henry Sargent Autograph Collection, Manuscript Division, New York Public Library, microfilm, Archives of American Art, reel N25, frame 1370. See n. 2, above.

76. Lockman interview, January 31, 1927, p. 18: "I remember having a birthday on the steamer."

77. Hassam, May 28, 1889, to Downes, transcribed in Hiesinger 1994, p. 179.

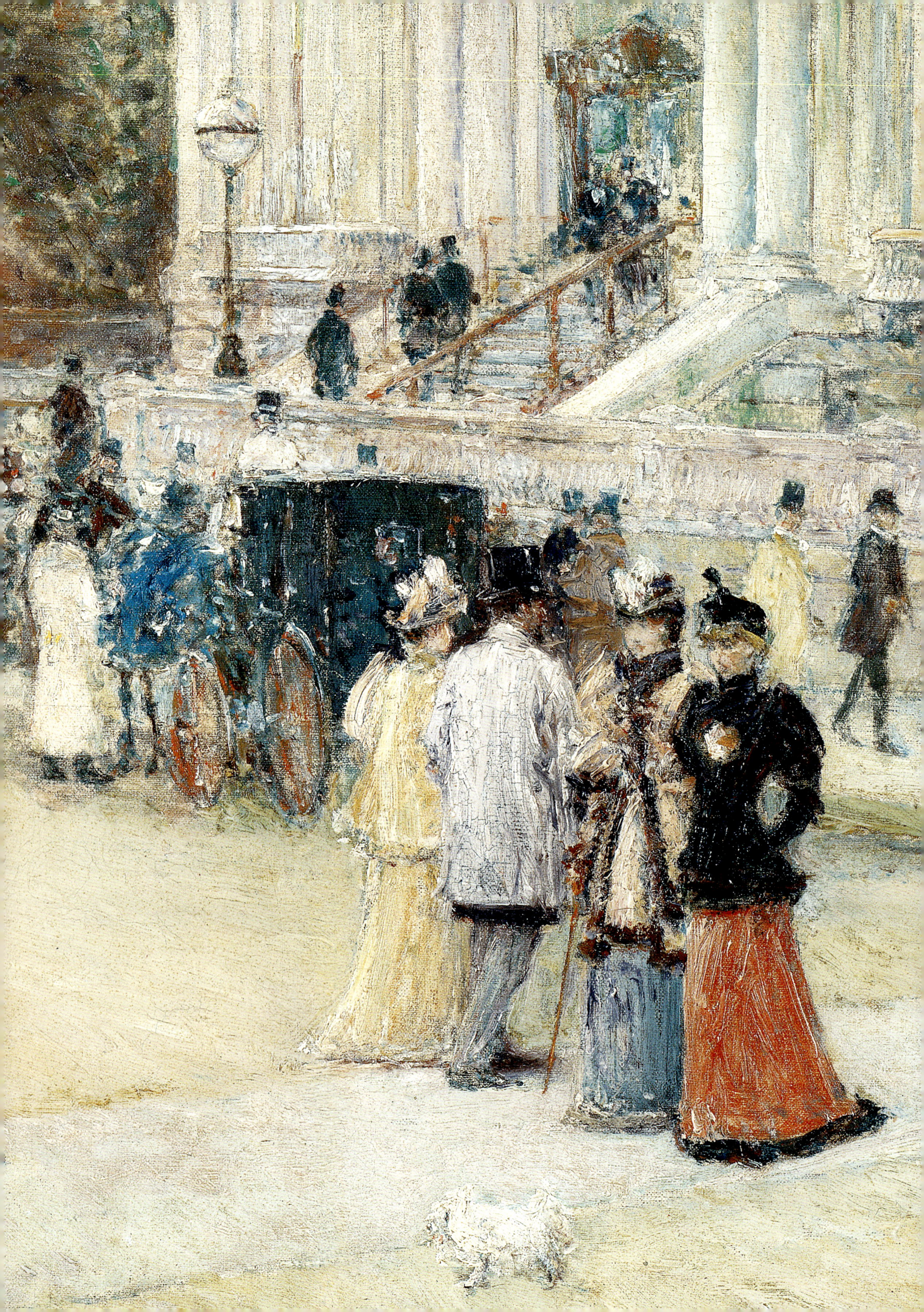

CHAPTER THREE

Hassam in New York, 1889–1896

H. Barbara Weinberg

Years after his return to the United States in late October 1889, Hassam recalled: "I never had any desire to remain permanently on the other side. America represented to me the highest opportunity. When I came back I came to New York, though I always considered Boston my home. To me New York is the most wonderful and most beautiful city in the world. All life is in it. . . . No street, no section of Paris or any other city I have seen is equal to New York."[1]

When Hassam came back home, he went first to Boston—apparently to prepare to move—and "sometime before December" settled in New York City.[2] He probably anticipated greater commercial success in New York than in his hometown: New York had supplanted Boston as America's cultural and artistic epicenter.[3] Thereafter he made New York his personal headquarters and principal subject for oils, watercolors, and pastels, alternating long creative seasons in the city with working summers along the New England shore. Using the candid compositions, rapid stroke, and varied palettes with which he had experimented in Boston and Paris, Hassam would produce unprecedented impressions of the city's thoroughfares, parks, and skyline. He enjoyed the energy and uniqueness of modern New York. As he remarked in 1898: "The old part, the Bowery, etc., is not so interesting as the new. The old part is picturesque, but it is not picturesque in an original way. The new part is unlike any other place. It is distinguished, vital and picturesque in its own way. It has character and force, and that is why I like it."[4]

Hassam recalled his search for housing in New York: "We wanted a studio and apartment about the same accommodation that we had had in Paris. We could not find anything just like that of course." He considered the Rembrandt at 152 West Fifty-seventh Street, but found that it was "a way up town, . . . away out in the country."[5] Instead of going uptown, he and his wife rented quarters at 95 Fifth Avenue on the southeast corner of Seventeenth Street, "one of the very first houses residences [*sic*] that went into apartments," he later noted.[6] In late 1892 they moved to the Chelsea Hotel at 222 West Twenty-third Street, remaining there for a year, and in 1893 established themselves at the Rembrandt,[7] which apparently no longer seemed "away out in the country." In October 1901 the couple moved to the Holbein Studio Building at 139 West Fifty-fifth Street, and in late March 1903—after a short stay at the Sherwood Studio Building at 58 West Fifty-seventh Street—they went to live in a studio building at 27 West Sixty-seventh Street. By January 1909 they had settled permanently in a new cooperative studio building at 130 West Fifty-seventh Street.

Hassam knew few New York artists at first but soon became active in several art organizations and initiated many sustaining professional relationships. He was a founder of the New York Water Color Club in 1890[8] and a member of the American Water Color Society, at whose January 1890 exhibition he first met J. Alden Weir and John H. Twachtman, who both became close friends.[9] In 1890 Hassam also joined the Players Club and was elected to the Society of American Artists, key social and exhibiting organizations for progressive painters, and in 1897 he helped found Ten American Painters. Since Hassam hardly ever taught or painted on commission to supplement his income, his involvement in these and other groups was crucial, as they abetted his lifelong campaign to show and sell his works through regular exhibitions.

Detail, fig. 99. *The Manhattan Club (The Stewart Mansion)*

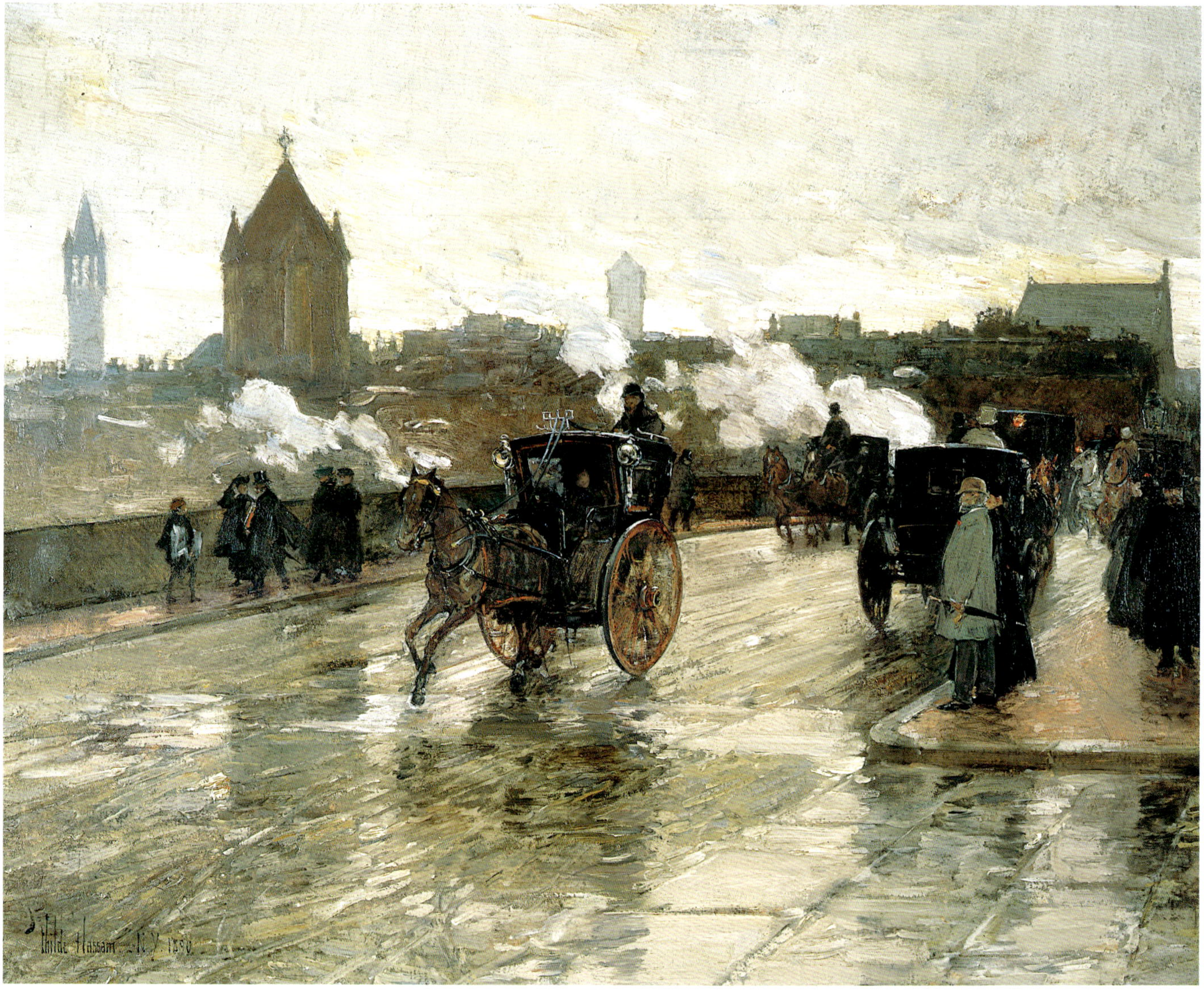

Fig. 82. Childe Hassam. *Clearing Sunset (Corner of Berkeley Street and Columbus Avenue)*, 1890. Oil on canvas, 25 x 30½ in. (63.5 x 77.5 cm). Marie and Hugh Halff

In New York, Hassam continued to build his reputation as a delineator of modern urban flux and fashions. In so doing he anticipated by several years the exhortation that "art must step out of the picture gallery, out of the school room, out of the boudoir, and go into the streets," which was expressed by a writer for the September 1897 *Brush and Pencil.*[10] As early as his January 1893 exhibition at Boston's Doll and Richards Gallery, a reviewer recognized that street scenes were "a class of motives which the artist has made his specialty for some years, and in which he has attained a rare degree of success."[11] By 1898 a leading critic would call him New York's "street painter par excellence."[12]

Although Hassam based his activities in New York, he maintained ties to Boston, exhibiting and selling works there. As he had done before his sojourn in Paris, he turned a

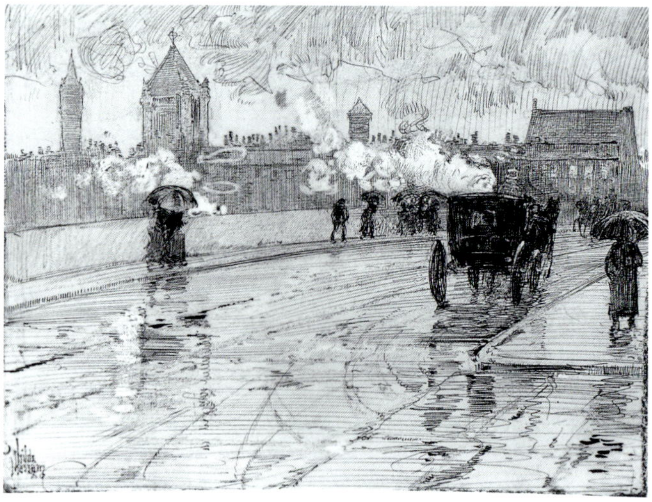

Fig. 83. Childe Hassam. *Rainy Day, Boston*, 1886. Black ink and black crayon or chalk heightened with Chinese white on off-white paper, 10³⁄₁₆ x 12½ in. (25.9 x 31.8 cm). The Corcoran Gallery of Art, Washington, D.C. Bequest of Bessie Potter Vonnoh Keyes 55.56

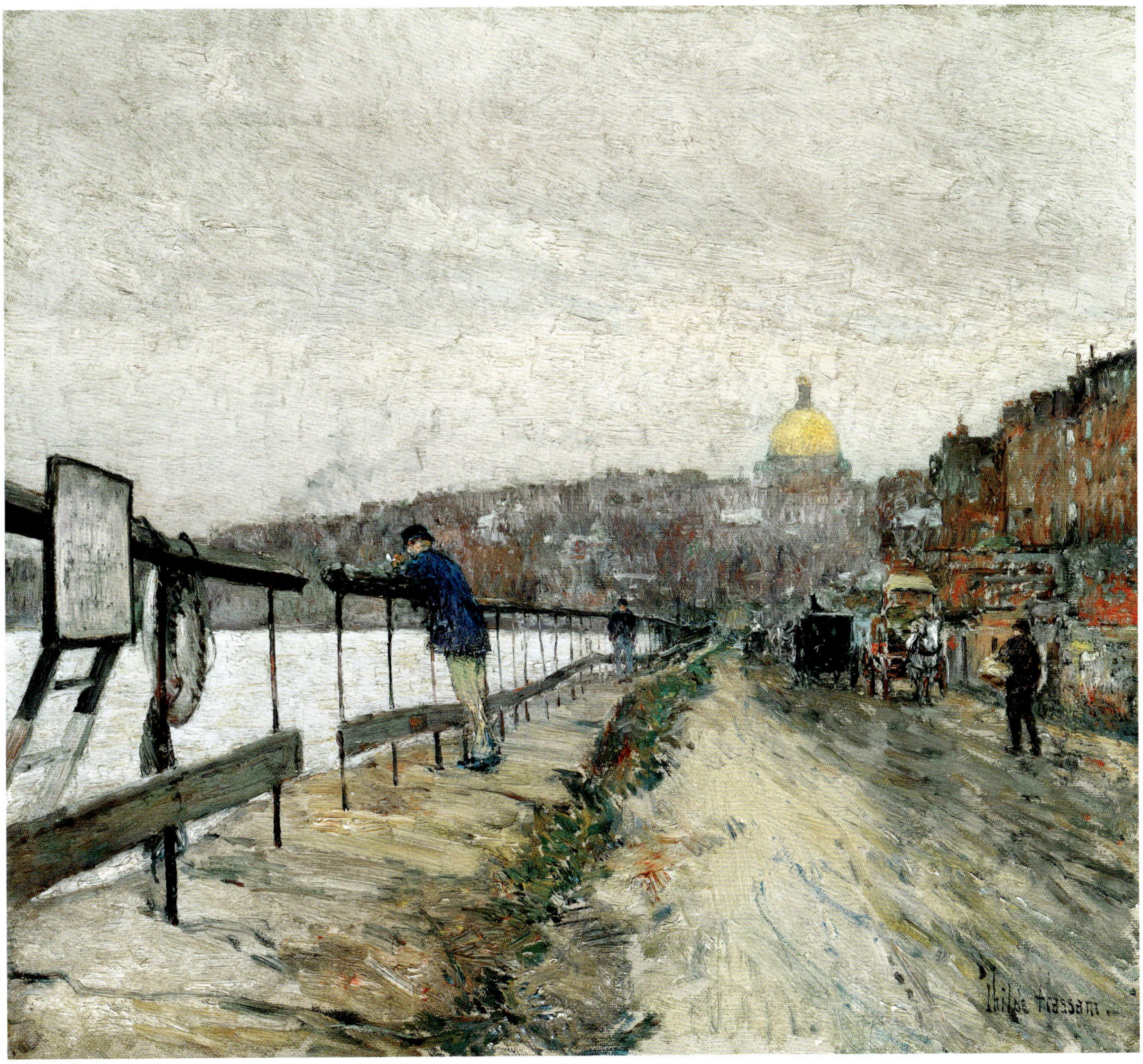

Fig. 84. Childe Hassam. *Charles River and Beacon Hill*, ca. 1892. Oil on canvas, 16⅛ x 18 in. (41 x 45.7 cm). The Museum of Fine Arts, Boston. Tompkins Collection

lively eye to the social spectacle in Boston's newly developed neighborhoods. *Clearing Sunset (Corner of Berkeley Street and Columbus Avenue)* (fig. 82), for example, depicts a busy intersection in Boston's South End. Based upon *Rainy Day, Boston* (fig. 83), an 1886 sketch, the oil may, in fact, have been among the first that Hassam painted in New York. His earlier drawing would have enabled him to begin work as soon as he arrived in the city, rather than prowl New York's cold streets searching for subjects in the winter of 1889–90. Moreover, the familiar Boston scene may have offered Hassam a convenient bridge back to American imagery after his time in Paris.

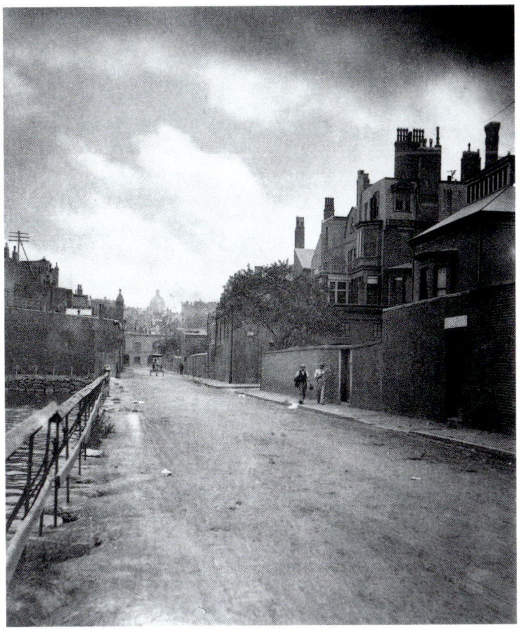

Fig. 85. James A. Wells. Along the Charles River, Beacon Street, Boston, 1880s. Society for the Preservation of New England Antiquities, Boston

In *Clearing Sunset,* Berkeley Street recedes toward the right background, where there appears a bulky gabled building, probably the Boston Young Men's Christian Association; Columbus Avenue cuts across the portion of Berkeley Street shown in the foreground. The view to the northwest highlights landmarks of Boston's Back Bay silhouetted against the opalescent twilit sky.[13] The reduced palette, the setting in the South End neighborhood where Hassam had lived from 1884 to 1886, "wet and shining pavement,"[14] newly popular Hansom cabs,[15] and well-dressed urbanites parading on the sidewalks all recall his earlier Boston works. However, the steam seen rising from the railroad tracks that run beneath Berkeley Street toward the Boston and Providence passenger and freight depots echoes the steam rising from river barges along the Seine in Hassam's *Notre Dame Cathedral, Paris, 1888* (fig. 66) and brings to mind Monet's renditions of the steam locomotives in the Gare Saint-Lazare.

About 1892 some two years after he completed *Clearing Sunset,* Hassam set up his easel in the Back Bay to paint *Charles River and Beacon Hill* (fig. 84). A testament to modern engineering and technology and a supreme example of American city planning, the Back Bay is the 450-acre salt marsh that had been developed as Boston's second great landfill project in response to the explosive population growth of the mid-nineteenth century.[16] The neighborhood, which doubled the size of the original city, became Boston's "Throne of Wealth":[17] its broad streets and rational plan distinguished it from old Boston, and its architectural styles documented changing taste as the district evolved block by block from east to west.[18]

Hassam's vantage point for *Charles River and Beacon Hill*—and that of the male observer he portrayed in the picture—is the Charles River Esplanade, which runs along the Charles River Basin (fig. 85). The view is east toward Beacon Hill, over present-day Storrow Drive.[19] In a dialogue between old and new Boston, the golden State House dome in the distance (the far away, the past) contrasts with the new Back Bay buildings in the foreground. At the right are the backs of houses along lower Beacon Street. It was such a house that transfixed Silas Lapham, William Dean Howells's nouveau-riche protagonist, whose heart's desire was to possess a dwelling "on the water side of Beacon."[20] That the Back Bay was new and about to develop even further is signaled by the esplanade's unfinished pavement and the rough walkway along the embankment. Perfectly suited to expressing the Back Bay's modernity are Hassam's Impressionist devices: an asymmetrical composition in which space recedes sharply; a large, empty foreground area; rapid paint application; and radically cropped forms.[21]

Hassam's visits to Boston (and Chicago, in 1892)[22] yielded a few urban scenes, but it was New York that truly engaged him beginning in the early 1890s. No other American city could have better stimulated the repatriation of his Parisian imagery. New York concentrated American culture, as Paris concentrated French culture, and in this period was increasingly deemed a world capital.[23] The city was often said to resemble Paris, especially in its new architecture and urban design, which reflected the recent Beaux-Arts training of many American architects. A writer for *Harper's Weekly,* remarking in 1891 on the affinity between the two cities, concluded that Paris is "naturally a New-Yorker's paradise, and every New-Yorker feels very much at home there. . . . So it came that one New-Yorker over there said to me, 'I don't know how to explain it, but the only thing here that seems foreign is the language.'"[24] Critics would observe that Hassam applied the French painters' ideas to New York subjects. One declared in 1895: "Hassam is a brilliant painter, a sort of Watteau of the Boulevards, with unlimited sparkle and gaiety, movement and animation. He suggests a crowd well; he gives you the color of the streets and the tone of the city."[25] New York more than any other American city compelled the use of Impressionist devices to convey its spirit. Describing the city in 1909, critic John C. Van Dyke signaled the suitability of candid composition and rapid brushwork for its portrayal: "In a swift-expanding city like New York everything is more or less confused by movement, by casual phenomena, by want to definition."[26]

Hassam expressed his nationalistic pride in America's new cultural capital and a city as alluring as Paris when he told A. E. Ives, a writer for *Art Amateur,* in 1892: "I believe the thoroughfares of the great French metropolis are not one whit more interesting than the streets of New York. There are days here when the sky and atmosphere are exactly those of Paris, and when the squares and parks are every bit as beautiful in color and grouping." It was to this same writer in this same interview of 1892 that Hassam proclaimed his Baudelairean commitment to "paint[ing] his own time and the scenes of every-day life around him."[27] Hassam also contributed to the growing tendency to rank New York among the world's greatest urban centers with the 1899

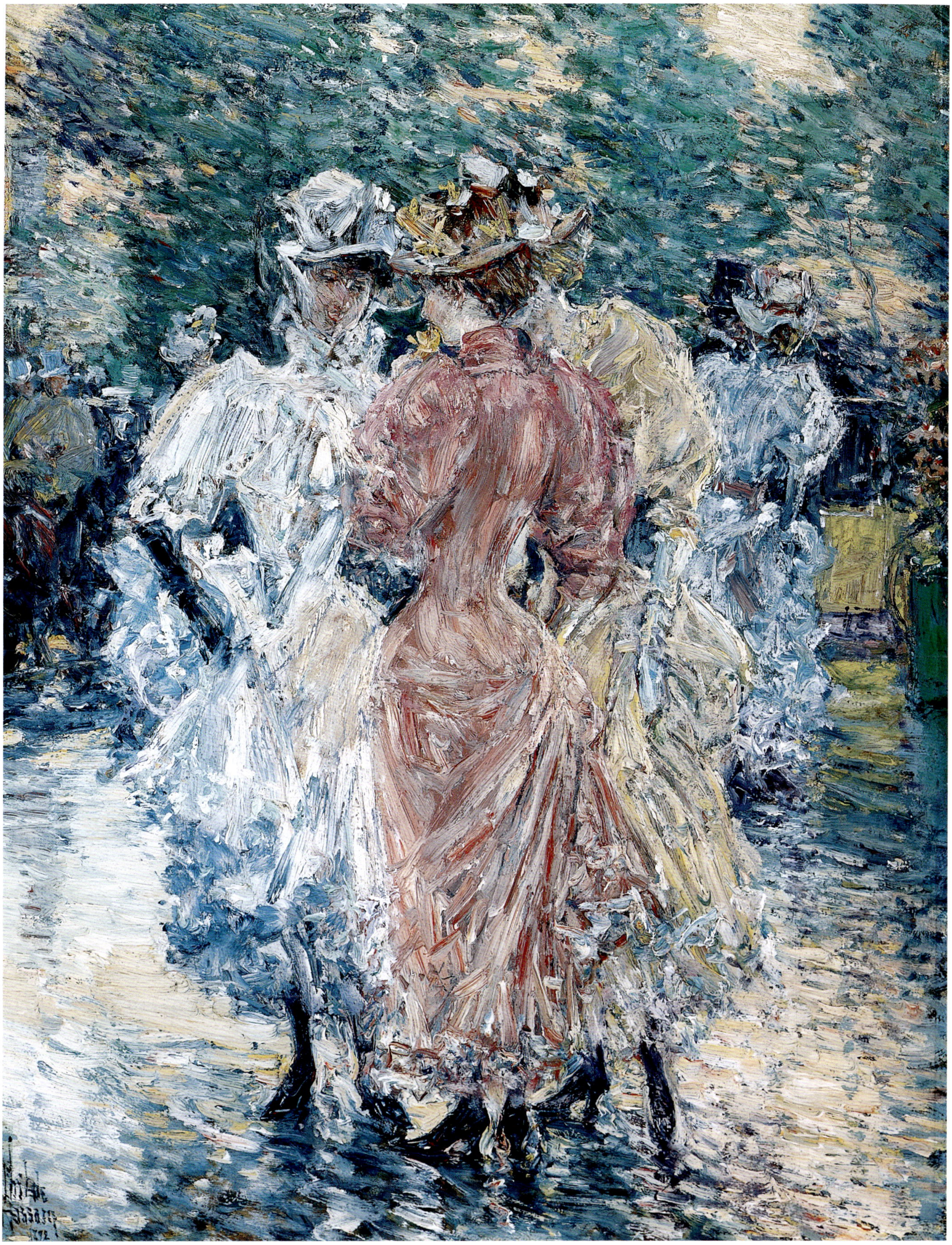

Fig. 86. Childe Hassam. *Conversation on the Avenue,* 1892. Oil on board, 15¾ x 12½ in. (40 x 31.8 cm). Private collection

publication of his *Three Cities*, a folio volume containing fifty of his oils, watercolors, pastels, and drawings that treat New York, Paris, and London with equal enthusiasm.[28] Describing Hassam's New York scenes in 1911, a critic summarized the artist's patriotic appreciation of his adopted city: "It is a delight to talk to Mr. Hassam about New York. To him it is simply the handsomest city in the world. He is big enough, modern enough, imaginative enough to prefer it to London or Paris."[29]

In New York's bustling urban spectacle Hassam found the grand thoroughfares, parks, churches, cabs, and other subjects of the sort that had interested him in Paris. Thus the slender young New Yorkers in bright stylish dresses he chose to paint—for example the trio in *Conversation on the Avenue* (fig. 86)—echo the charming girls he had depicted in the French capital at the same time they illustrate his claim that "New York women are sometimes the finest-dressed women in the world."[30] But more than Paris, New York displayed immense energy and tremendous contrasts. It was a place that could generate in the same year—1890, the first full year Hassam lived there—commentaries as disparate as Ward McAllister's *Society As I Have Found It* and Jacob Riis's *How the Other Half Lives:* the first recording the extremes of conspicuous consumption among the city's Four Hundred, the second documenting in prose and photographs the sordid poverty that pervaded the city's tenements.[31]

New York's population grew from about 60,500 citizens in 1800; to about 515,600 in 1850; to 3.437 million in 1900, following the consolidation of Brooklyn with Manhattan and part of the Bronx in 1898.[32] Low-rise brick and brownstone buildings were giving way to the more numerous, more closely packed skyscrapers that limited land elicited and modern technology permitted.[33] By 1907 Henry James would complain in *The American Scene* that Manhattan's "multitudinous skyscrapers" resembled "extravagant pins in a cushion already overplanted."[34] New construction brought unprecedented density of both building and population to business and residential districts and ever increasing congestion to their streets. The modern urban scene also included impressive new churches, clubhouses, hotels, monuments, and parks; extraordinary mansions built in every historical style; newly formed and re-formed cultural institutions and recreational facilities; an increasingly heterogeneous populace reflecting immigration and domestic migrations; and crowds of workers arriving daily from expanding suburbs. These developments—along with motor buses that replaced horse-drawn trolleys; electrified subways and elevated railroads that supplanted steam engines; electric streetlights that superseded gas lamps; automobiles that were rendering obsolete horse-drawn cabs—all altered New York's appearance, light and air, rhythm and sound, and changed the patterns of neighborhood use. There were more—and more diverse—people with more to do at a faster pace, and there were more places and hours in which they could do it.

New York was described and celebrated in new and newly vigorous magazines published in the city for national circulation and in dozens of self-congratulatory books.[35] These publications documented New York's history and recorded the current scene in prose and in illustrations by Hassam and other artists.[36] This New York literature of the 1890s aimed to bear witness to a past that was quickly disappearing and to survey the present before the future—the new century—began. Hassam was praised as New York's chronicler almost immediately upon his arrival in the city. A critic observed in 1891: "When he wants a subject to paint, Mr. Hassam looks about him, and does not get out his sketches in Normandy or Holland. More than that he does not have to go to Niagara or the Rocky Mountains, nor even to the country or the seaside. He simply looks out of his window upon the city streets, up Broadway or Madison Avenue in New York."[37] All these developments reflected and reinforced Hassam's belief in New York's vitality and his interest in its pictorial possibilities, to which he responded in his art and in his words in numerous interviews, such as the one conducted by A. E. Ives in 1892.

Given Hassam's euphemistic portrayals of bourgeois Boston and Paris, it is not surprising that he maintained a genteel view of New York and held at arm's length the city's unpleasant realities. His depiction of Fifth Avenue as uniformly elegant, for example, is at odds with the variety that a writer observed in 1915: "In the entire length of Fifth Avenue is not one thing, but everything. . . . It is a study in progressive sociology with mansions and factories, libraries, museums, vacant lots, hospitals, parks, and slums."[38]

Hassam's escapist celebrations of New York highlight the most pleasing elements of attractive neighborhoods and their refined residents and convey the optimistic tone of contemporary accounts of the city's growth and energy. Thus they are conceived in the spirit of McAllister rather than of Riis. Hassam did not "indulge in the sentimental aspect of squalor, or look with sympathetic gaze upon the picturesque life of the humble," as artist-critic Eliot Clark noted in 1920.[39]

He avoided the ethnic enclaves that would engage the Ash Can School, sought scenes that resonated with his own middle-class Anglo-Saxon background, and was attuned to his affluent patrons' likely preferences: Hassam knew such subjects were more apt than cheerless images to attract praise and buyers from a prosperous urban clientele.

His works almost always suggest that New York was civilized and hospitable despite its rapid growth, and that if it was crowded and confusing, it was still picturesque. "The portrait of a city," Hassam claimed, "is in a way like the portrait of a person—the difficulty is to catch not only the superficial resemblance but the inner self . . . one should strive to portray the soul of a city with the same care as the soul of a sitter."[40] His flattering portraits of New York are more like portraits of people by John Singer Sargent than those by Thomas Eakins. They record the vestigial Gilded Age gentility that would vanish with the advent of an even more heterogeneous, even more modern metropolis as the new century unfolded.

During the 1890s Hassam produced more than fifty paintings, watercolors, and pastels portraying New York's fashionable residential precincts.[41] Typical are genre scenes set along the grand, bustling spine of Gilded Age Manhattan—Fifth Avenue from Greenwich Village to about Fifty-ninth Street—and in the adjacent squares, Union, Madison, and Washington, which offered respite from urban hurly-burly and provoked civic pride. He viewed about half of his New York scenes from street level, the others from higher vantage points, always remaining a bit detached from his genteel subjects. Rather than intruding on their activities, revealing intimacies, demanding reciprocal gazes, or immersing himself in urban disorder—as his Ash Can School successors would do—Hassam respected and preserved the boundaries of nineteenth-century upper-class decorum.[42] While his images of New York are one-dimensional and uniform from a sociocultural standpoint, they vary in the seasons and times of day depicted. The contrasting moods of snow-blanketed parks, streets lined with budding trees, avenues ablaze in sunlight, and tall buildings seen at dusk all engaged him.

Hassam's first New York studio was close to Greenwich Village on the south, Union Square on the east, Madison Square on the north, and Ladies' Mile—the strip of stylish dry-goods emporiums running along Broadway from Tenth Street to Madison Square at Twenty-third Street—on the west. These locales provided subjects analogous to those he had portrayed in Paris.

Perhaps painted as early as Hassam's first winter in the city is *Fifth Avenue in Winter* (fig. 87),[43] one of the artist's many tributes to New York's Champs-Élysées. Hassam recalled that this view of well-dressed pedestrians, a large horse-drawn stage, and coaches was recorded from his first New York studio.[44] His elevated vantage point, a device familiar from French Impressionist paintings—for example Monet's *Boulevard des Capucines* (fig. 60)—was one whose potential Hassam had not explored in Boston or Paris. That vantage point encoded the experience of the tall buildings that were becoming New York's distinguishing landmarks and must have seemed to Hassam a way to express the fundamental spirit of the new metropolis. Beginning in 1890 he enlisted it often for his New York scenes.

The high vantage point in *Fifth Avenue in Winter* allowed Hassam to emphasize the pavement of the block on Fifth Avenue's east side and focus on the attractive stoops and other street-level details on its west side (see fig. 88). At the northwest corner of Fifth Avenue and Eighteenth Street was George B. Post's Chickering Hall, whose distinctive red-brick facade, arched windows trimmed in brownstone and gray marble, and framed performance notices are visible in the center background of Hassam's painting.[45]

The artful distribution of the dark figures against the snowy pavement in the picture suggests that Hassam made use of a process of intentional selection and arrangement, which he described in 1892: "I do not always find the streets interesting, so I wait until I see picturesque groups, and those that compose well in relation to the whole."[46] Although Hassam may occasionally have recorded awaited impressions, he preferred forms that were more solid and specific than the fleeting ones of French prototypes such as Monet's *Boulevard des Capucines*. *Fifth Avenue in Winter* earned Hassam praise in Paris, where it was displayed in early summer 1891 at the Galerie Durand-Ruel and admired by the critic for *Le Figaro* for its good color, solid execution, and American character.[47] It became the second painting he sold to a museum when the Carnegie Institute (predecessor of the Carnegie Museum of Art) purchased it from the 1899 Carnegie International exhibition.[48]

Winter in Union Square (fig. 89) is another painting that probably dates from Hassam's first winter in New York. By the 1880s Union Square was the center of New York intellectual life, home to leading writers, among them Richard Watson Gilder.[49] Gilder's magazine, *The Century*, occupied opulent offices—a showplace and rendezvous for writers—next door

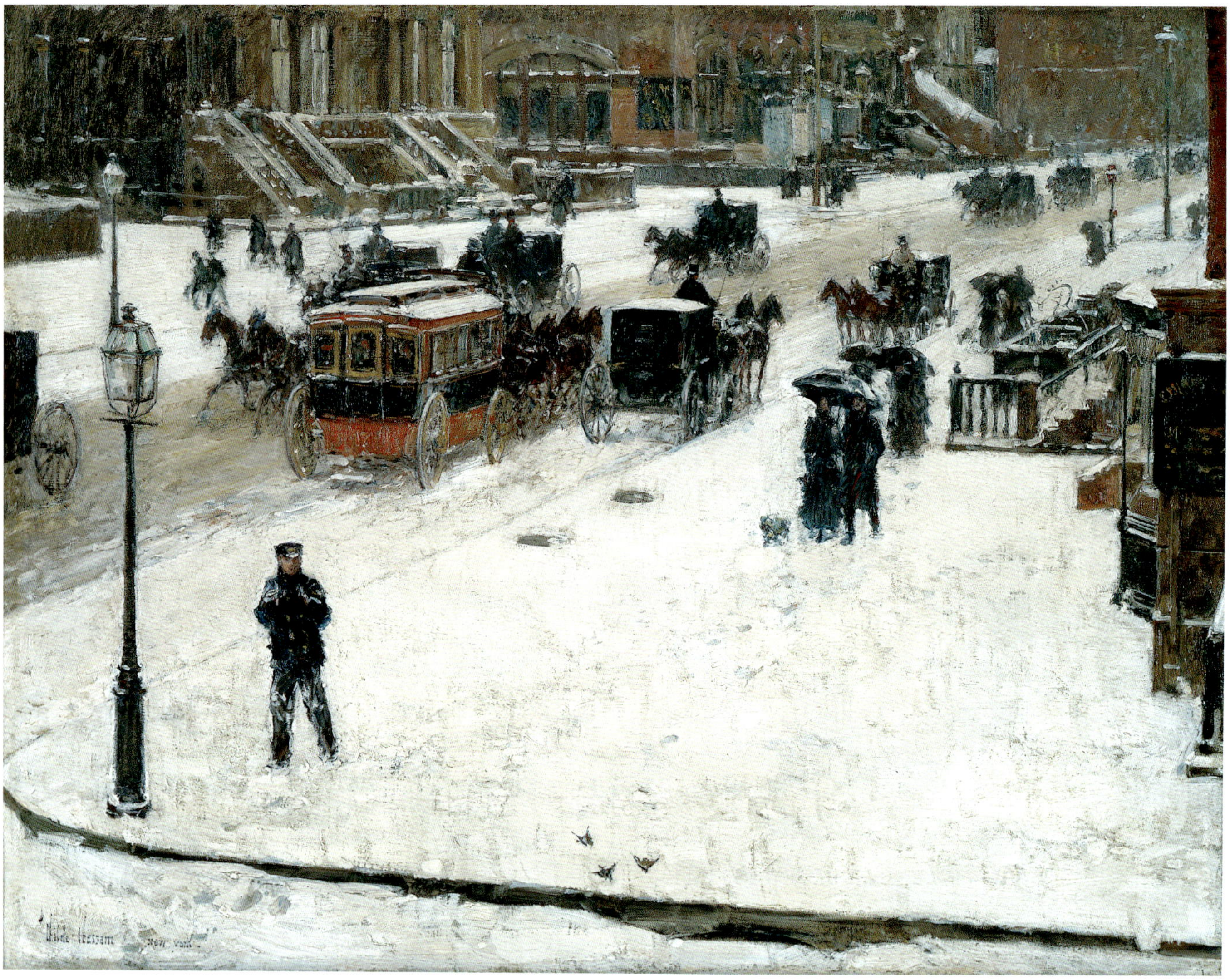

Fig. 87. Childe Hassam. *Fifth Avenue in Winter,* ca. 1890. Oil on canvas, 21⅝ x 28 in. (54.9 x 71.1 cm). Carnegie Museum of Art, Pittsburgh; Museum purchase 00.2

to the Everett House Hotel at 33 East Seventeenth Street, or Union Square North. Painters, sculptors, and photographers were tenants in the upper-floor studios of buildings along Union Square West.[50] As Hassam's friend the painter Edward E. Simmons recalled in his memoirs, "Most of the life of those days [the 1890s] centered about Union Square, with tentacles reaching down to Washington and up to Madison Squares."[51] Increasingly, however, commercial use had impinged upon the residential character of Union Square.[52] Private homes were converted to businesses or torn down and replaced by stores. The Domestic Sewing Machine Building (1872–73) exemplified the area's new manufacturing and mercantile function and, as the city's tallest building, symbolized New York's new architectural and urban energy.[53]

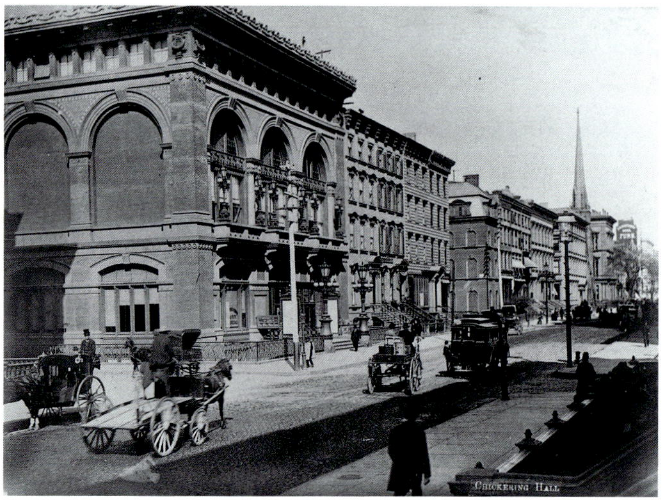

Fig. 88. Fifth Avenue looking north, including Chickering Hall. Collection of The New-York Historical Society

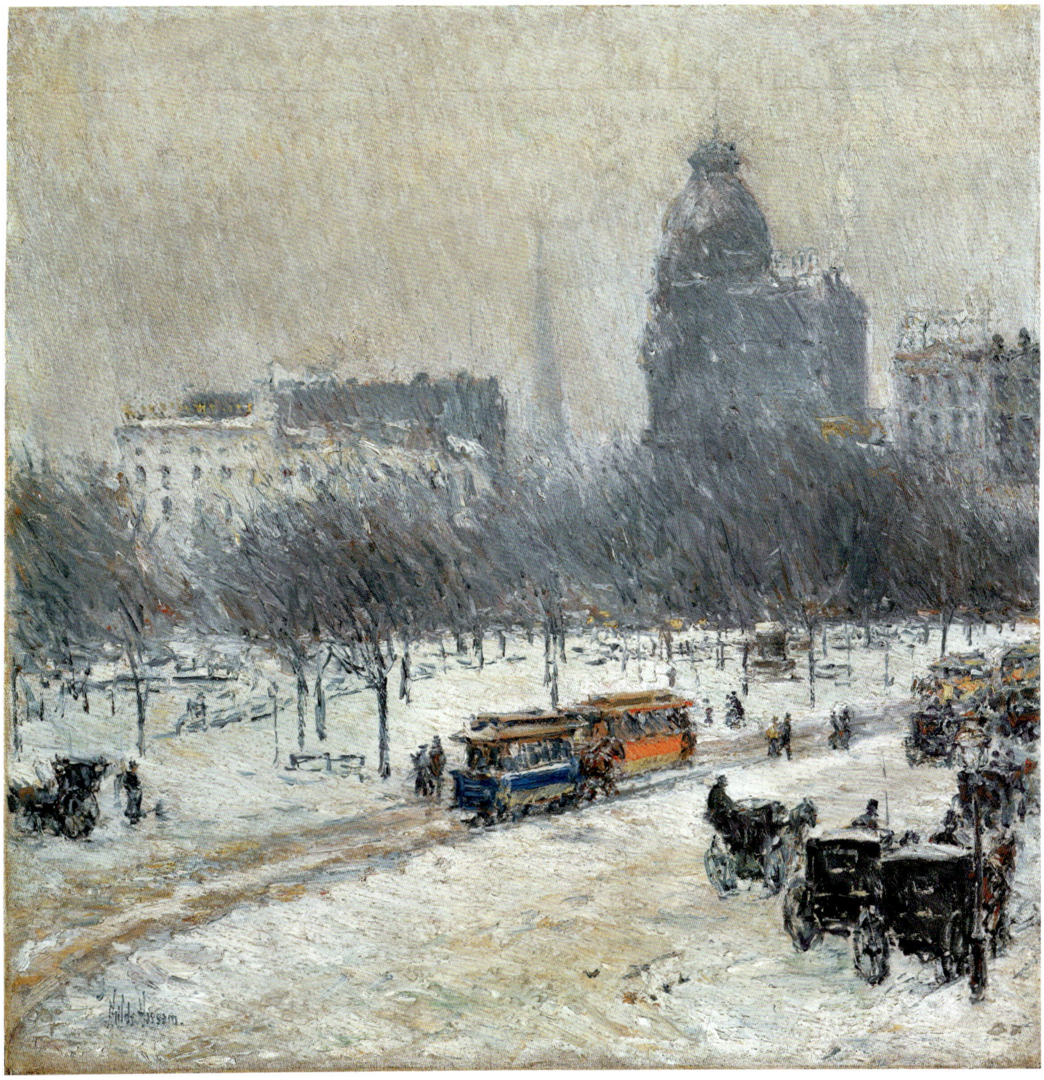

Fig. 89. Childe Hassam. *Winter in Union Square,* 1889–90. Oil on canvas, 18¼ x 18 in. (46.4 x 45.7 cm). The Metropolitan Museum of Art, New York. Gift of Ethelyn McKinney, in memory of her brother, Glenn Ford McKinney, 1943 43.116.2

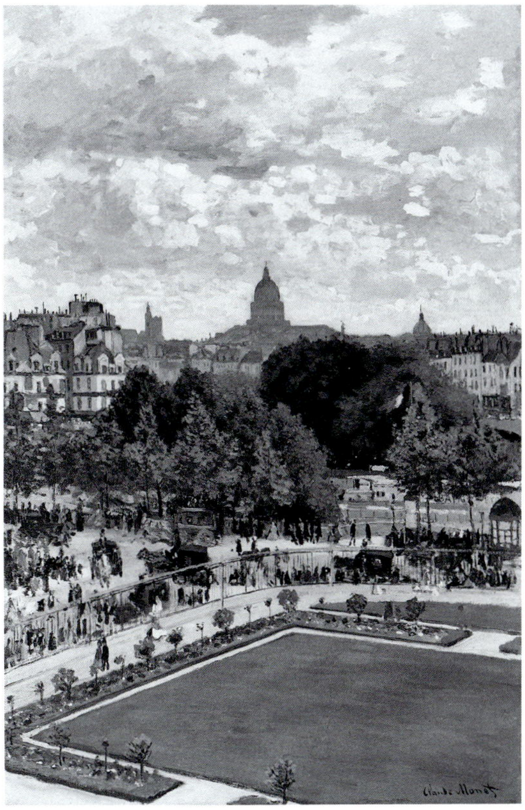

Fig. 90. Claude Monet. *The Garden of the Princess, Louvre,* 1867. Oil on canvas, 36⅛ x 24⅜ in. (91.8 x 61.9 cm). Allen Memorial Art Museum, Oberlin College, Ohio; R. T. Miller, Jr. Fund, 1948

Union Square had also redefined itself as an entertainment center by the 1870s. It would remain the focus of the city's theatrical and musical life, surrounded by hotels, restaurants, theaters, concert halls, and the activities that supported entertainment, until it was superseded by Times Square at the end of the century.[54] Originally named for marking the "union" between Fourth Avenue and Broadway, which broke Manhattan's street grid, and then associated with the Union cause during the Civil War, the square was now linked as well with unionization: with the economic unrest engendered by the Depression of 1873 to 1898, it became the site of labor union activities, including rallies and, beginning in 1890, May Day parades.[55] As the square's connections with commercial and labor interests grew, it faded as a fashionable residential and entertainment center. Yet Union Square, accessible from the Third Avenue and Sixth Avenue elevated railroad lines, would remain a lively crossroads at the junction of two major north-south avenues and bustling Fourteenth Street.

For his painting *Winter in Union Square,* Hassam took a high, panoramic diagonal view, as Monet had often done for urban images, for example, *The Garden of the Princess, Louvre* (fig. 90).[56] Utilizing the modern format of a square canvas, Hassam looked south across Union Square from a vantage point on Union Square West at Seventeenth Street (fig. 108), just a block from his studio.[57] The Morton House Hotel, which occupied the blockfront on Fourteenth Street between Fourth Avenue and Broadway, is shown in the left background; the domed Domestic Sewing Machine Company, on the southwest corner of Fourteenth Street and Broadway, is at the right. These two structures bracket the barely visible stone spire of the Gothic Revival Grace Church (James Renwick, 1847), at Broadway and Tenth Street, in the distance.[58] Cabs awaiting patrons are gathered in the right foreground, along Union Square West, where horse-drawn trolleys crisscross. *Charity,* the huge bronze figure group designed by Karl Adolph Donndorf and placed as a drinking fountain alongside Union Square West, between Sixteenth and Fifteenth Streets, appears in the right middle ground.[59]

Working more freely than ever before, Hassam sketched, rather than delineated, the site, distancing himself from dreary realities: he used snow to soften sharp edges of buildings and vehicles and suggest the muffling of the sound of the city, and he emphasized the locale's picturesque qualities. Hassam defended his choice of palette and rendering of atmosphere in this and other related paintings when he remarked to Ives: "I suppose a great many people think my pictures are too blue. . . . To me, there is nothing so beautiful as truth. This blue that I see in the atmosphere is beautiful, because it is one of the conditions of this wonderful nature all about us. If you are looking toward any distant object, there will be between you and that object air, and the deeper or denser the volume of air, the bluer it will be. People would know and see this if the quality of observation was not dead in them."[60]

Apparently painted during Hassam's first spring in New York, but reworked between 1895 and 1899, was *Spring Morning in the Heart of the City* (fig. 91), for which he also used a raised vantage point. The subject is Madison Square, a seven-acre park bounded by Twenty-sixth Street on the north and Twenty-third Street on the south and by Madison Avenue on the east and Fifth Avenue on the west.[61] Hassam's expansive view shows the point where Broadway cuts across Fifth Avenue to form a wide triangular area, "one of the busiest centres of the city,"[62] before each broad avenue resumes its separate identity south of Twenty-third Street (fig. 92).

Madison Square had been the centerpiece of an affluent neighborhood filled with stylish brownstones in which such patricians as Theodore Roosevelt and Edith Wharton were born in 1858 and 1862, respectively. In September 1859 the luxurious Fifth Avenue Hotel opened at 200 Fifth Avenue between Twenty-third and Twenty-fourth Streets. (Its entrance—denoted by a classical portico, a large circular clock, and two curbside gas lamps—appears in the lower left corner of Hassam's painting.) With the hotel's construction, Madison Square began to develop as one of the city's most vibrant centers for tourism and entertainment. A rival to the Fifth Avenue Hotel in the 1890s was the Hoffman House, one block north, boasting opulent interior furnishings, among them Adolphe-William Bouguereau's famous *Nymphs and Satyr,* 1873 (Sterling and Francine Clark Art Institute, Williamstown, Massachusetts), which hung over the bar. The new Madison Square Garden opened in 1890 on Madison Avenue at Twenty-sixth Street.[63] There were numerous theaters, concert halls, and restaurants—including the legendary Delmonico's at Fifth Avenue and Twenty-sixth Street—all of which attracted pedestrian and vehicular traffic to the square. As Mrs. Van Rensselaer declared in 1893, Madison Square was "socially the most interesting spot on the avenue . . . the true center of idle New York, as Wall Street is the center of busy New York."[64]

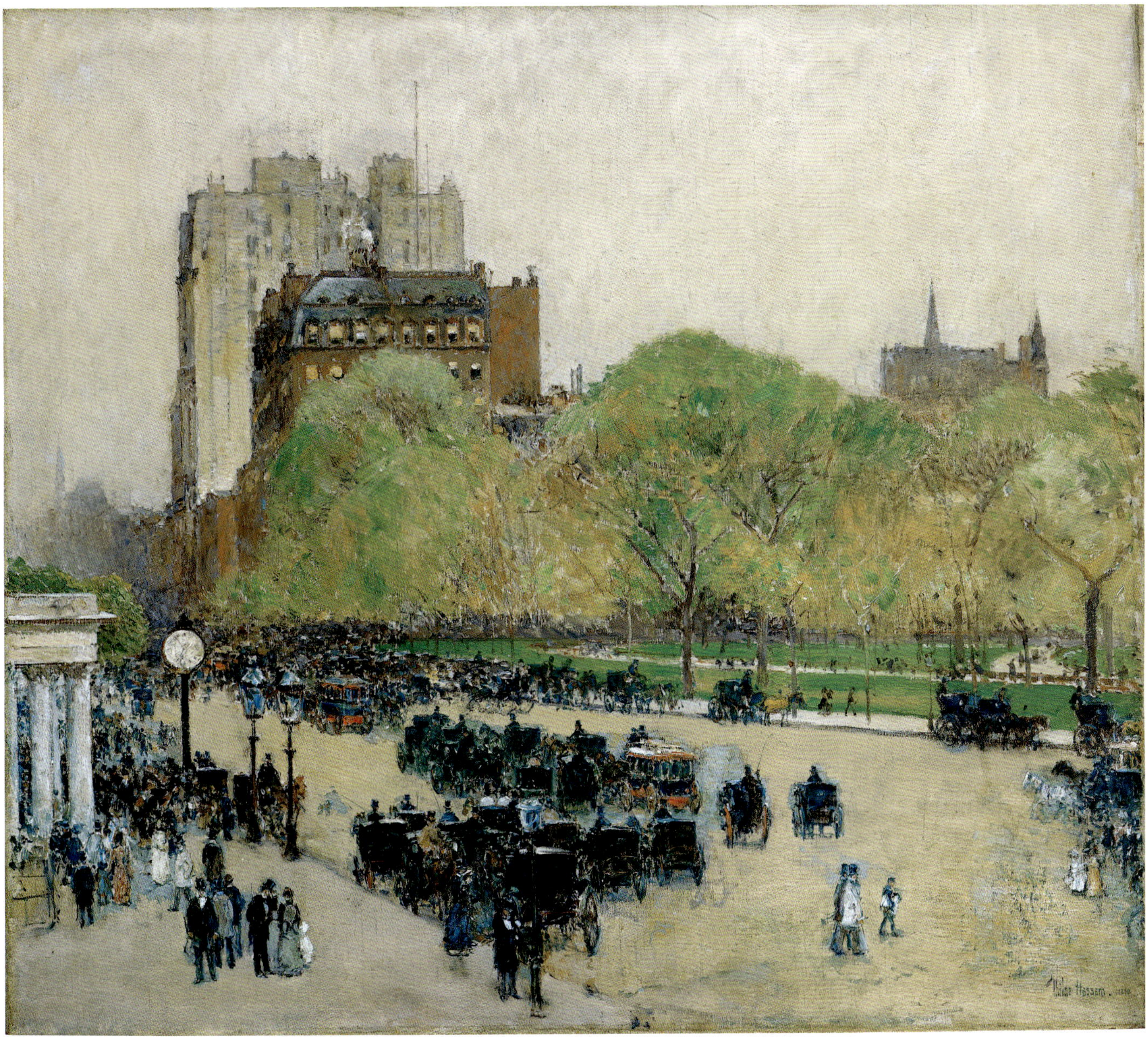

Fig. 91. Childe Hassam. *Spring Morning in the Heart of the City,* 1890, reworked 1895–99. Oil on canvas, 18⅛ x 20¾ in. (46 x 52.7 cm). The Metropolitan Museum of Art, New York. Gift of Ethelyn McKinney, in memory of her brother, Glenn Ford McKinney, 1943 43.116.1

Hassam told Ives in 1892 that for *Spring Morning in the Heart of the City* he had worked from "the second-story window in Dunlap's about fifteen feet from the ground." His principal aim, he said, had been to focus on the group of cabs in the foreground and let "the lines in the composition radiate and generally fade out from this centre." He added that the strollers and vehicles "didn't arrange themselves and stand

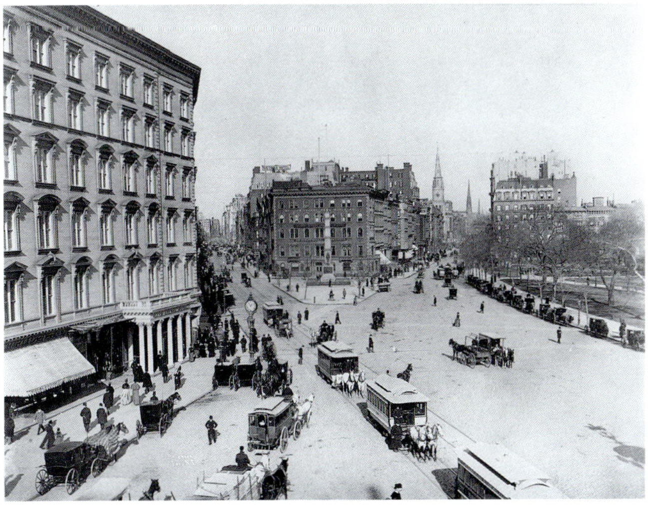

Fig. 92. Rockwood. Madison Square, ca. 1888–89. Museum of the City of New York. Gift of Elwin M. Eldredge

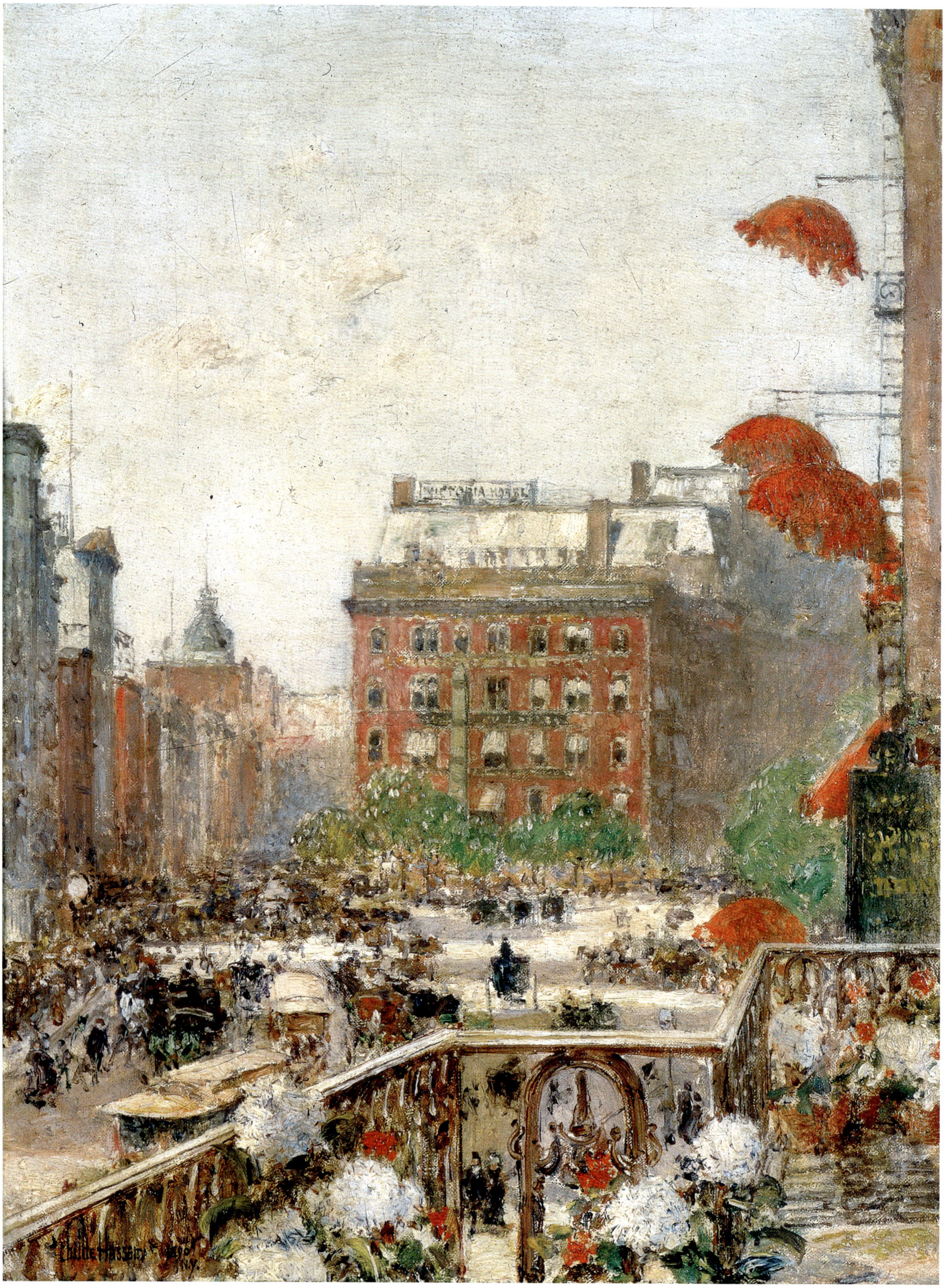

Fig. 93. Childe Hassam. *View of Broadway and Fifth Avenue,* 1890. Oil on canvas, 13¾ x 10½ in. (34.9 x 26.7 cm). Private collection, Pennsylvania

still in these groupings for my especial benefit," so he had "to catch them, bit by bit, as they flitted past."[65] Hassam concentrated on bands of animated pedestrians and horse-drawn vehicles, bright lime-green foliage, and large buildings. These buildings included, north of the square, the mansard-roofed Hotel Brunswick, silhouetted against what Mrs. Van Rensselaer called the "cliff-like background of the Knickerbocker apartment-house."[66] Hassam ignored most of the landmarks and activities associated with "the true center of idle New York"—notably Madison Square Garden, just completed to the east of the scene he chose to depict.[67] Nevertheless, a critic writing for the *Boston Evening Transcript* in 1893 found in the painting "probably the best delineation of a subject of the sort that anybody has made" and claimed that Hassam had captured the spirit of the area:

> *The wide street and sidewalks are fairly swarming with cabs, omnibuses, drags, cars and foot passengers, like the great human hive that New York is, and there arises from this vivid instantaneous glimpse of seething streets, to the ear of fancy, that muffled road of traffic which is the incessant voice of the metropolis. Nothing could be gayer or more characteristic of that part of the city which visitors are likely to know, and nothing could be more appropriate to the theme, th[a]n Mr. Hassam's sprightly and sparkling style.*[68]

View of Broadway and Fifth Avenue (fig. 93) depicts the same busy site from the eastern side of the broad intersection, a vantage point opposite the Fifth Avenue Hotel looking north. Hassam painted on a balcony that was one of many on the Hotel Bartholdi, located on the southeast corner of Broadway and Twenty-third Street (fig. 94).[69] Red umbrellas advertising the wares of the adjacent shop echo the red of geraniums that decorate the balcony, along with potted blue hydrangeas. The shift of his vantage point allowed Hassam to portray the line of buildings on the Broadway side of Madison Square north of the Fifth Avenue Hotel and, superimposed upon each other from north to south between Broadway and Fifth Avenue, the distinctive mansard roof of the Victoria Hotel, identified by its roof sign; the red-brick facade of the Madison Square Bank building; and the triangular traffic island with the obelisk dedicated in 1857 to Major General William Jenkins Worth, a hero of the Mexican War. The lively space where Broadway and Fifth Avenue cross is filled with vehicles and pedestrians.

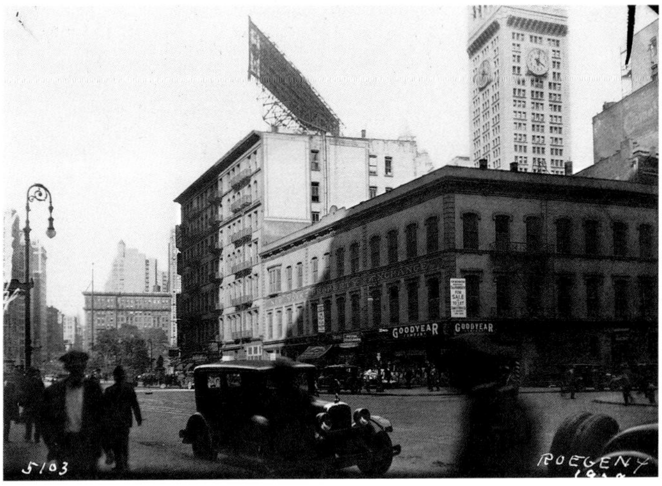

Fig. 94. Roege. East side of Broadway, from 22nd to 25th Streets, 1928. Collection of The New-York Historical Society

Paintings such as *Spring Morning in the Heart of the City* and *View of Broadway and Fifth Avenue* reveal Hassam's increasing commitment to seemingly candid compositions with objects cropped at their edges, distant views that justify the dissolution of solid forms—especially people who become mere notations of paint—and a high-key palette with which he rendered brilliant light. His experiments with these Impressionist devices were stimulated by a variety of factors: his friendships with Weir and Twachtman, who were working in the Impressionist style; his participation in exhibitions that included Impressionist pictures; and his awareness of Monet's paintings and principles gained through Theodore Robinson, who worked alternately in Giverny with the French master and in New York between 1888 and 1892. It was thanks in large part to the adaptations of French models by Hassam and his colleagues Weir, Twachtman, and Robinson, as well as a number of other like-minded compatriots, that American Impressionism reached its apogee during the 1890s and became a mainstream style by the turn of the century.

Another attractive district was the subject of Hassam's *Lower Fifth Avenue* (fig. 95), apparently painted in spring 1890. For this canvas Hassam eschewed the elevated viewpoint he had used in *Spring Morning in the Heart of the City* and *View of Broadway and Fifth Avenue* for a more intimate one. This was the street-level vantage point of the east sidewalk of Fifth Avenue at about Thirteenth Street looking across the avenue and southwest toward the First Presbyterian Church (Joseph C. Wells, 1844–46) at Twelfth Street and the Church of the Ascension (Richard Upjohn, 1841) at Tenth Street (fig. 96).[70] The English Gothic Revival style of these buildings silhouetted

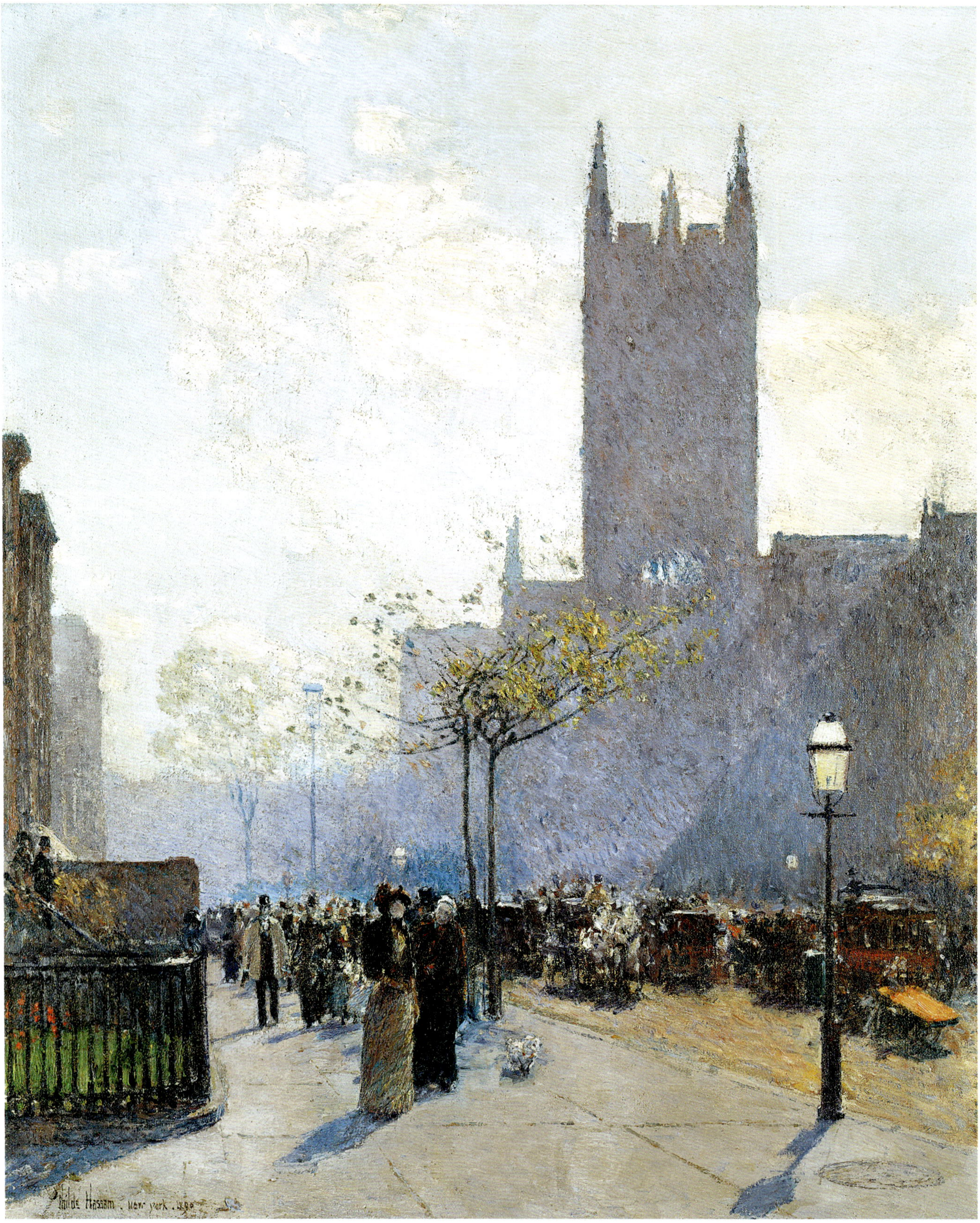

Fig. 95. Childe Hassam. *Lower Fifth Avenue,* 1890. Oil on canvas, 25¼ x 21 in. (64.1 x 53.3 cm). Private collection

against an opalescent afternoon sky and the old-fashioned gas lamp in the right foreground invoke tradition in Hassam's painting. The busy sidewalk, lined with wrought-iron railings to the left and trees in spring bloom at curbside, is filled by a multitude of well-dressed pedestrians. Jarring metropolitan bustle is confined to the roadway crowded with all sorts of horse-drawn vehicles. The unobtrusiveness of this traffic confirms the observations of a writer who claimed in 1891 that this stretch of Fifth Avenue retained its traditional gentility:

> *Cut off from the residential district to the northward by the river of traffic that flows along Fourteenth Street, the lower end of Fifth Avenue forms a picturesque oasis, where the aristocratic air of old Knickerbocker stateliness lingers amid a commonplace environment. The six blocks between Washington Square and Thirteenth Street are a unique corner of New York. Their architecture is that of a generation that has now passed away. . . . The trees that line the street . . . help to make this one of the most picturesque points of Fifth Avenue.*[71]

Like *Lower Fifth Avenue,* Hassam's Greenwich Village scene *Washington Arch, Spring* (fig. 97) proposes that New York at the end of the Gilded Age was still a picturesque town. Emblematic of many of his urban images in its cheerful optimism, euphemism, nationalism, and nostalgia, the canvas portrays the triumphal arch—New York's Arc de Triomphe—that was dedicated upon the centennial of George Washington's inauguration as the first president of the United States. Hassam painted from a vantage point on the west sidewalk of lower Fifth Avenue, looking south toward the arch, which is screened by budding trees and which frames a partial view of the red-brick structures on the south side of Washington Square.[72] Long shadows crossing the pavement indicate that the scene was captured early on a spring morning. It is a bright new day in what Mrs. Van Rensselaer called the "clear, pure, crystalline air" of the new New York in the season of rebirth.[73]

Carriages clatter along the avenue; one with a liveried coachman has stopped beside the curb; a street sweeper—a member of the White Angels[74]—cleans the gutter between this carriage and his wheeled cart. A baby nurse—a familiar type on lower Fifth Avenue, where wealthy households employed many domestic servants—wheels a perambulator. Such nursemaids, along with newsboys, messengers, cabdrivers, and construction workers, are stock characters in many of Hassam's works, providing foils for more affluent urbanites and allowing him to indulge in gentle social commentary. The fashionable pedestrians who join the procession uptown in *Washington Arch, Spring* embody the urban spirit that Hassam told Ives he so much enjoyed: "There is nothing so interesting to me as people. I am never tired of observing them in everyday life, as they . . . saunter down the promenade on pleasure. Humanity in motion is a continual study to me."[75]

In *Washington Arch, Spring,* Hassam described a venerable New York locale with historical and patriotic significance. The area south of the lower end of Fifth Avenue had been converted to a park and military parade ground in 1826 and named Washington Square after the first president to commemorate the fiftieth anniversary of the signing of the Declaration of Independence. A fine row of Greek Revival town houses, their style consonant with the democratic associations of the square, was built on its north edge in 1832 and occupied by prominent New Yorkers, prompting improvements around the square and in the adjacent streets. The construction of New York University and the Reformed Dutch Church on Washington Square East in the 1830s confirmed the distinction of the area. Although a north-south drive was cut through the square in 1871, the district remained a refuge from city clamor. Greenwich Village's winding streets discouraged development, and their picturesque quality attracted artists to the neighborhood.[76] Mrs. Van Rensselaer remarked in 1893: "When I think how things have happened elsewhere in New York, I am ready to affirm that Washington Square has thus far led a reasonably conservative life."[77]

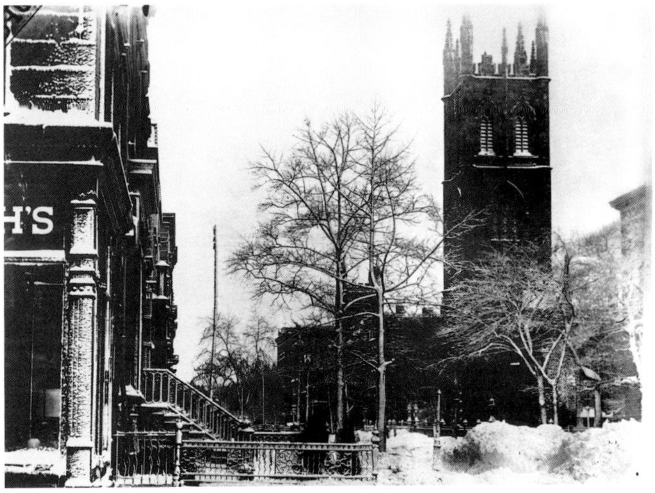

Fig. 96. Fifth Avenue looking to the southwest from 13th Street, with a view of the First Presbyterian Church. Collection of The New-York Historical Society

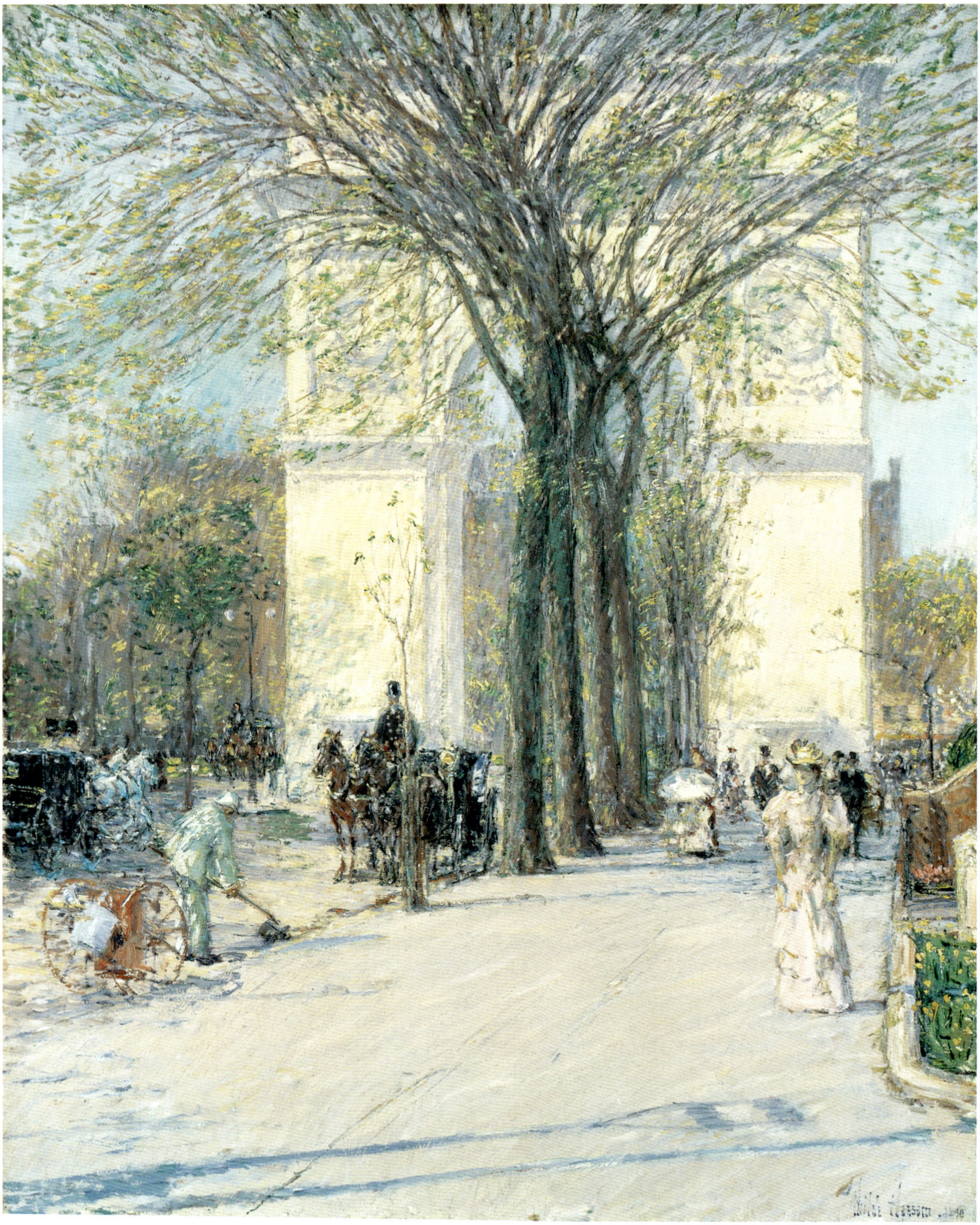

Fig. 97. Childe Hassam. *Washington Arch, Spring,* ca. 1893 (inscribed *1890*). Oil on canvas, 27⅛ x 22½ in. (68.9 x 57.2 cm). The Phillips Collection, Washington, D.C.

Although elegant Washington Square North was somewhat immune to incursions of lower-class populations, after the Civil War it grew less and less appealing to the city's elite, who were migrating uptown. By 1890 the fashionable associations of the square were being challenged by commercial activity, brothels, tenements for the burgeoning population of immigrants in the streets to the south and east, and the conversion of some of the town houses ringing it to apartment hotels, boardinghouses, cafés, and shops.[78] This was the sort of Washington Square that confronted Isabel and Basil March, transplanted Bostonians in William Dean Howells's *Hazard of New Fortunes* (1890), when, searching for a flat to rent, they "met Italian faces, French faces, Spanish faces." They commented on "the old-fashioned American respectability which keeps the north side of the square in vast mansions of red brick, and the international shabbiness which has invaded the southern border, and broken it up into lodging houses, shops, beer gardens and studios."[79]

Hassam ignored this evolution and celebrated the Washington Arch, a symbol of American tradition holding fast in the face of change. The monument, designed by Stanford White, originated in plans developed in 1884 to commemorate the centennial of the first president's inauguration, in 1789.[80] Its first incarnation, straddling Fifth Avenue at Washington Mews, about one hundred feet north of the square, was in wood and plaster, ornamented in papier-mâché, painted white to imitate marble, and crowned with a balustrade and a wooden statue of Washington (fig. 98). It was ready in time for the elaborate Centennial Celebration held from April 29 to May 1, 1889. Shortly thereafter a committee of distinguished citizens raised funds to allow replication of the arch in white Tuckahoe marble in the square itself. The marble arch confirmed pride in Washington and national values and was expected to inspire patriotism in the neighborhood's immigrant tenement-dwellers.[81]

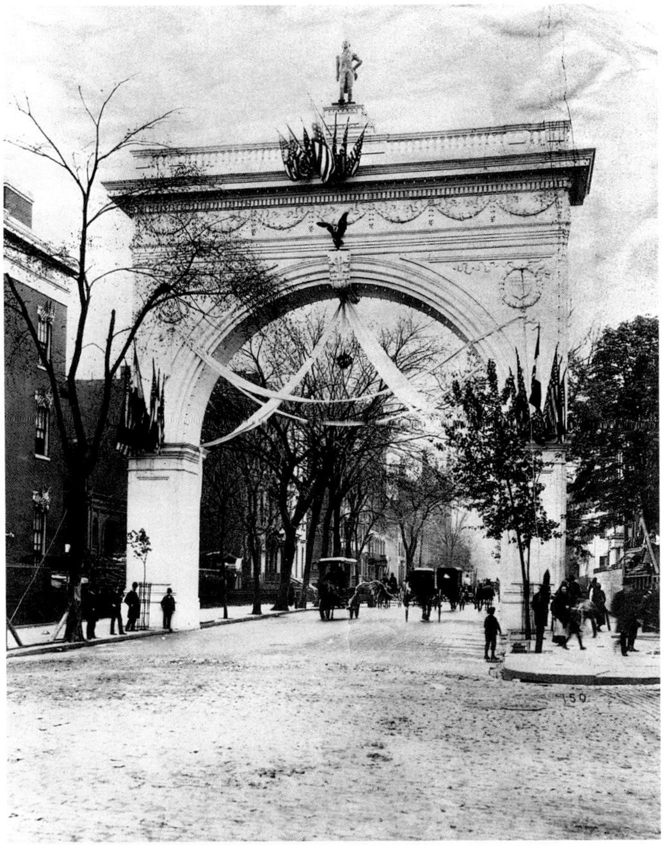

Fig. 98. Paul C. Oscanyan. *Fifth Avenue at Washington Square,* 1889. Museum of the City of New York

Although Hassam's painting bears a date of 1890 and has been said to represent the temporary arch,[82] the structure shown resembles the bulkier permanent version and lacks the first monument's wooden statue of Washington. Hassam, whose studio was a few blocks north of Washington Square on Fifth Avenue, could easily have visited the area not only to view the temporary arch but also to witness the construction of its successor between May 1890 and April 1892. That the carved trophy panels he depicted on the second story of the north face of the arch were not installed on the marble monument until February 1893 is significant for the dating of the picture.[83] This, together with the fact that the painting was exhibited in early 1895, means that Hassam must have executed it in spring 1893 or spring 1894.[84] In the picture the handsome new-old classical triumphal arch invokes the neighborhood's links to the foundations of America, its first president, and the Greco-Roman heritage. Other elements provide a backdrop of optimistic references to the new New York—productive immigrants who drive carriages, wheel perambulators, and sweep the streets.[85] Rather than documenting the deterioration of lower Fifth Avenue, Hassam's painting shows the hoped-for regeneration of the neighborhood and offers a harmonious, sunny, optimistic, patriotic image of the new New York, unified despite its complications. His city is a place where tranquillity and energy coexist and where democracy reconciles the rich and the working class, the new and the old.[86]

Hassam depicted another chic neighborhood in transition in *The Manhattan Club (The Stewart Mansion)* (fig. 99). The backdrop for the scene is the grandiose marble mansion

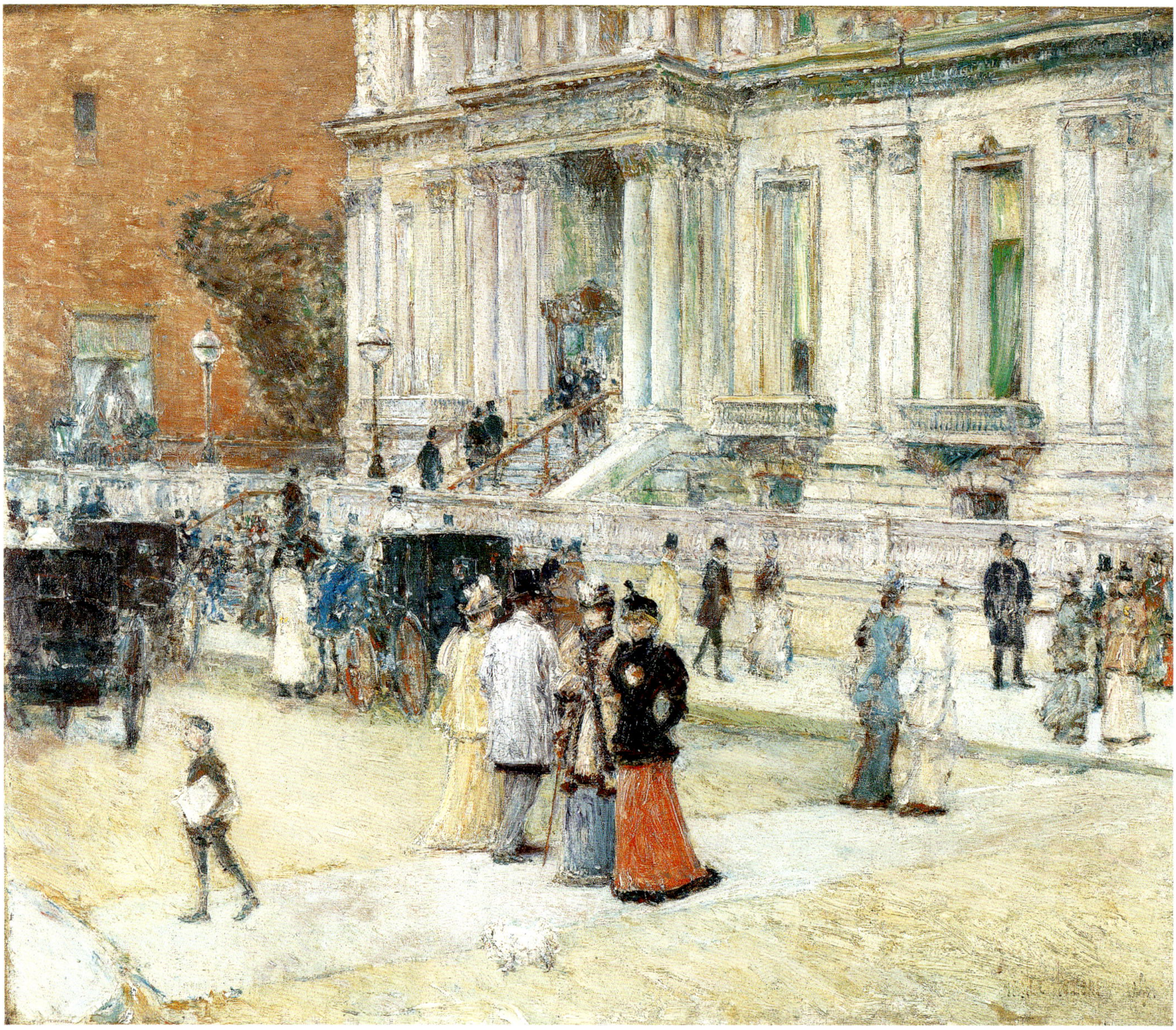

Fig. 99. Childe Hassam. *The Manhattan Club (The Stewart Mansion)*, ca. 1891. Oil on canvas, 18¼ x 22⅛ in. (46.4 x 56.2 cm). Santa Barbara Museum of Art, Gift of Mrs. Sterling Morton to the Preston Morton Collection

erected for dry-goods magnate Alexander Turney Stewart in 1869 on the northwest corner of Thirty-fourth Street and Fifth Avenue (fig. 100).[87] Stewart's palace, designed by John Kellum, was built of Carrara marble in the French Second Empire style and incorporated a ground-floor picture gallery for its owner's immense collection of contemporary academic art. It stood opposite the much more modest 1856 brownstone on the southwest corner of Fifth Avenue in which Mrs. William B. Astor II presided over the ballroom that could hold the Four Hundred who defined New York society. Stewart's two-million-dollar marble pile,[88] the cynosure of post–Civil War wealth and cultural striving, ushered in the new era of ostentatious residential construction that would ultimately extend as far north as Ninety-sixth Street.

After the death of Stewart's widow, in 1886, the house remained empty until it was leased in 1890 to the Manhattan Club, which occupied it until 1899. In 1892 a reporter deemed the club "the home of swallowtail Democracy," explaining "to the Democratic Party it is what the Union League Club is to the Republican Party." Perhaps the fact that "the members wear fine linen, have many changes of raiment, and are partial to patent-leathers and silk-woven galoshes" and that "there [were] brains and culture in the Club"[89] prompted Hassam to paint it. A member-patron might find a portrait of the club's distinguished new home appealing enough to buy. Stewart's Marble Palace was demolished in 1903 and replaced by the Corinthian-columned Knickerbocker Trust Company, which was oriented toward Fifth Avenue rather than Thirty-fourth Street.[90]

For *The Manhattan Club (The Stewart Mansion),* Hassam adopted a composition employed by juste-milieu artist Jean Béraud in paintings such as *The Church of Saint-Philippe-du-Roule, Paris* (fig. 101), in which a major architectural form provides a receding stage set for figures arrayed along a foreground sidewalk. Hassam's vantage point is at the southwest corner of Fifth Avenue, looking north across Thirty-fourth Street. The neighborhood's ongoing transition to commercial use was familiar to Hassam, who would have visited the nearby Fifth Avenue Art Galleries, at 366 Fifth Avenue, and M. Knoedler and Company, on the northeast corner of Fifth Avenue and Thirty-fourth Street.[91] In 1897 the Astor residence would give way to the new Astoria Hotel, which completed the conversion of the block initiated in 1893 by the construction of the Waldorf Hotel on the Thirty-third Street corner.[92]

Hassam was well aware of New York's men's social-club culture.[93] On familiar ground with his subject, he signaled the Stewart mansion's new identity as a private men's social club by the procession of men in dark suits and top hats on the entrance stairs. A fashionable throng and a newsboy—one of Hassam's favorite stock figures—appear in the foreground. The mild social commentary here, limited to a portrayal of the contrast between the wealthy crowd and a working-class character, is typical for Hassam. His slightly elevated vantage point suggests that he may have set up his canvas in a cab.

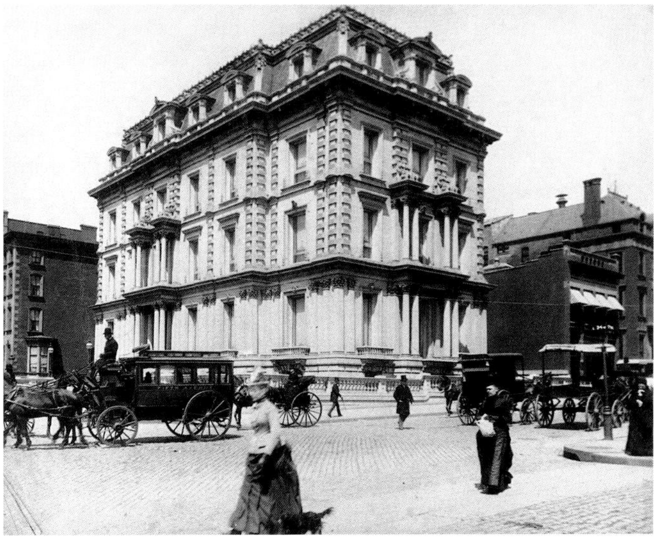

Fig. 100. A. T. Stewart Mansion, northwest corner of Fifth Avenue and 34th Street, ca. 1889. Collection of The New-York Historical Society

"I paint from cabs a good deal," Hassam told Ives in 1892. "I paint from a cab window when I want to be on a level with the people in the street and wish to get comparatively near views of them, as you would see them if walking in the street."[94]

Hassam's habit of obscuring facial features and elongating figures is manifest in *The Manhattan Club (The Stewart Mansion)*. This practice may reflect his belief that painting an "impression" demanded a rejection of precise physiognomy.

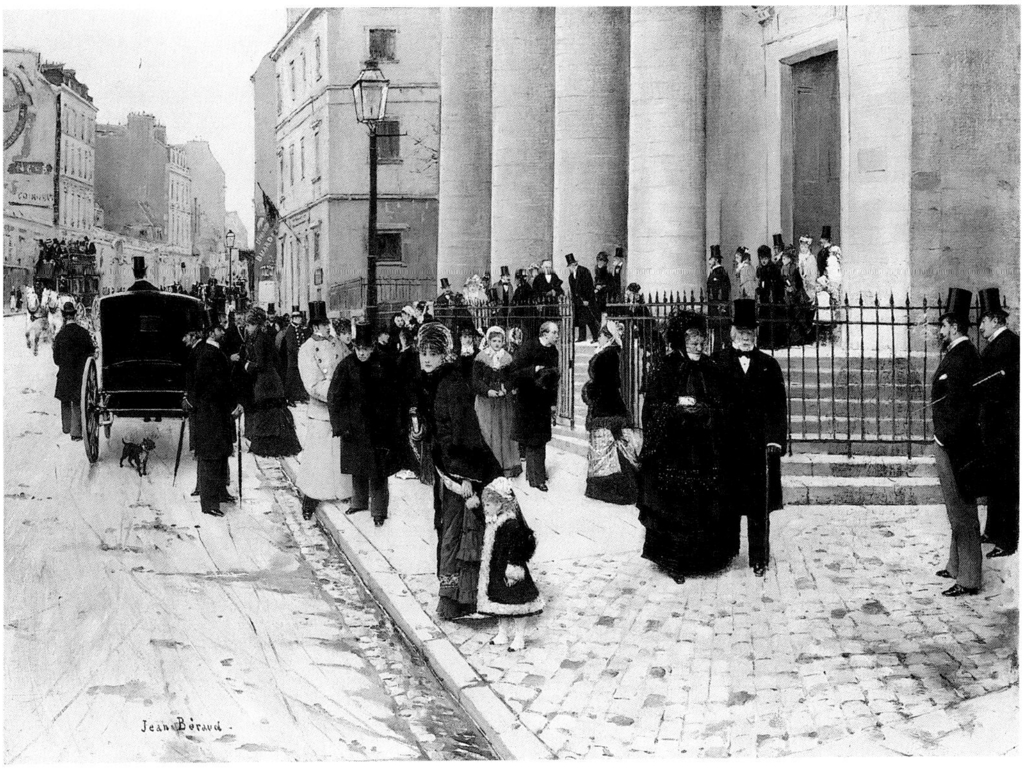

Fig. 101. Jean Béraud. *The Church of Saint-Philippe-du-Roule, Paris,* 1877. Oil on canvas, 23 ⅜ x 31 ⅞ in. (59.4 x 81 cm). The Metropolitan Museum of Art, New York. Gift of Mr. and Mrs. William B. Jaffe, 1955 55.35

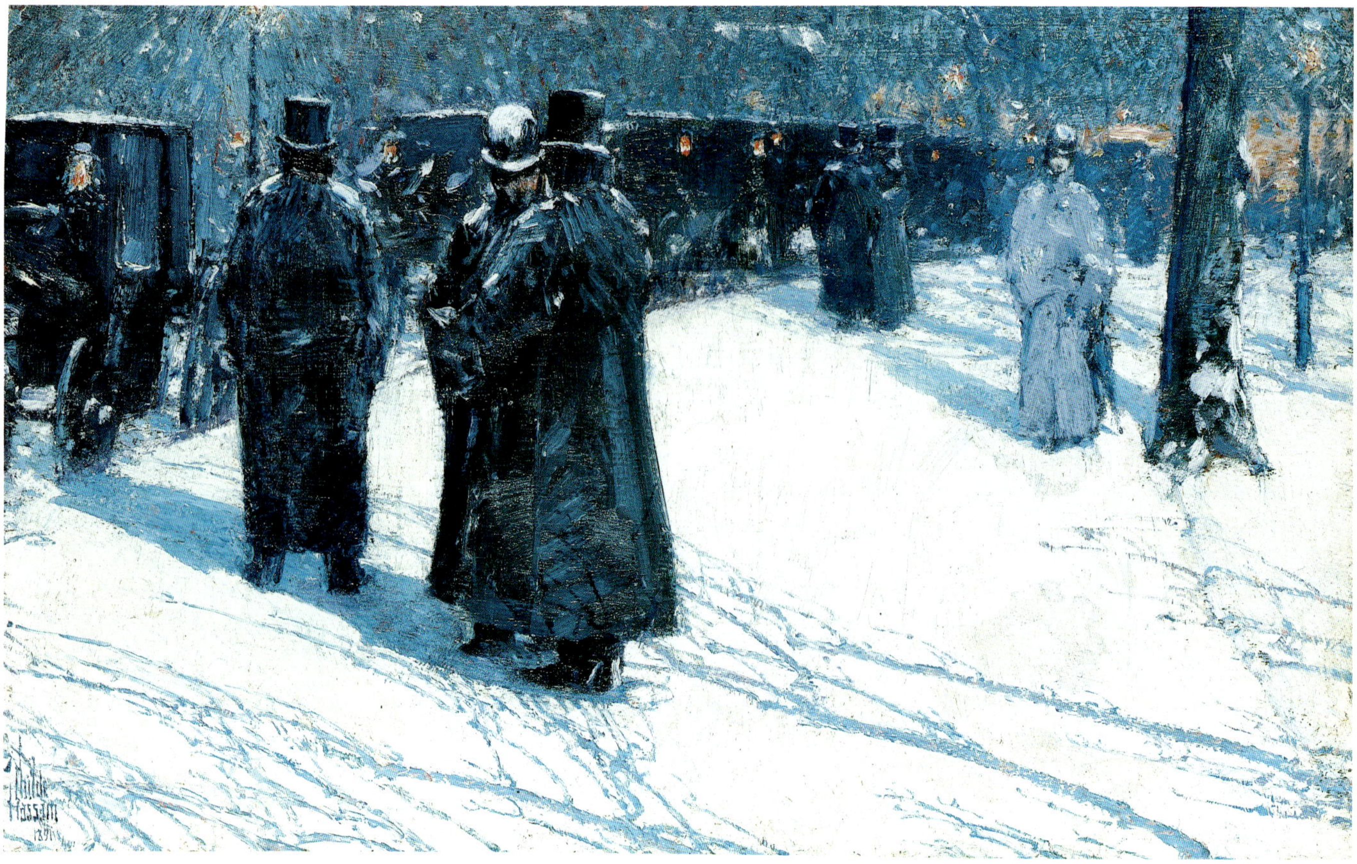

Fig. 102. Childe Hassam. *Cab Stand at Night, Madison Square,* 1891. Oil on paper, 9 x 14 3/8 in. (22.9 x 36.5 cm). Smith College Museum of Art, Northampton, Massachusetts. Bequest of Annie Swan Coburn (Mrs. Lewis Larned Coburn)

He declared to Ives: "If you looked down a street and saw at one glance a moving throng of people, say fifty or one hundred feet away, it would not be true that you would see the details of their features or dress. Any one who paints a scene of that sort, and gives you such details, is not painting from the impression he gets on the spot, but from preconceived ideas he has formed from sketching studio models and figures near at hand. Such a man is an analyst, not an artist."[95]

In another work from his early years in New York, *Cab Stand at Night, Madison Square* (fig. 102), Hassam portrayed the line of hackneys opposite the Fifth Avenue Hotel along Madison Square's western edge (fig. 103) that he had painted in *Spring Morning in the Heart of the City.*[96] In *Cab Stand at Night, Madison Square* Hassam quoted the long diagonal line of cabs at curbside and three hackneys seen to the left of the composition from his *Une Averse—rue Bonaparte* (fig. 54). Using a more intimate vantage point, he reinterpreted the expansive autumnal Paris scene for this small picture depicting a vignette of winter in New York, replacing the Latin Quarter with Fifth Avenue, the cochers with heavily cloaked New York cabbies who huddle together, and the shiny wet pavement with snow embroidered by the blue shadows of saplings. And the lady walking in Paris with a companion and shielding herself with an umbrella has become in New York an unaccompanied woman who proceeds along the wide sidewalk at the right of the composition, carrying her umbrella at her side.

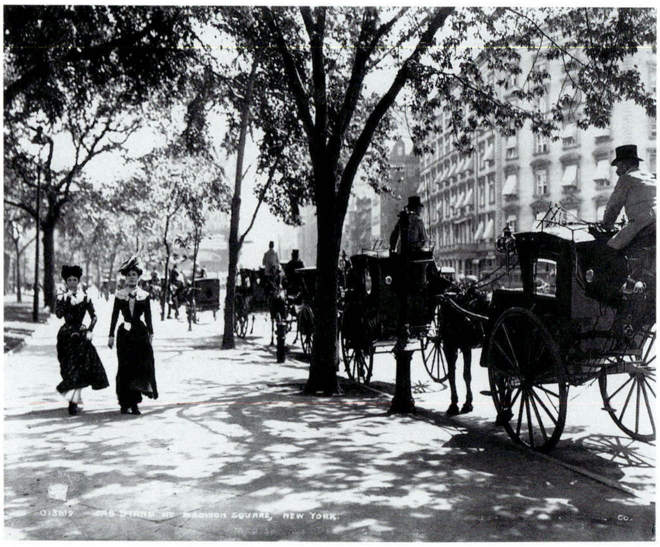

Fig. 103. Cab stand at Madison Square, ca. 1900. Collections of the Library of Congress, Washington, D.C.

Hassam recorded with economical painterly means in *Cab Stand at Night, Madison Square* the forms and gestures of the cabdrivers awaiting fares. These characters fascinated him, as he explained in 1892: "There is no end of material in the cabbies. Their backs are quite as expressive as their faces. They live so much in their clothes, that they get to be like thick shells, and take on every angle and curve of their tempers as well as their forms. They interest me immensely."[97] Hassam was intrigued as well by night effects, and in this picture he explored the contrast between the dim glow of a gas lamp in the right background and the metallic glare from unseen electric streetlights—an innovation that had become increasingly common in the city since the 1880s—which cast strong shadows.[98] Perhaps in reference to this work, in 1892 Hassam described how he captured the look of lights and night: "If I want to observe night effects carefully, I stand out in the street with my little sketch-book, draw figures and shadows, and note down in colored crayons the tones seen in the sky, in the snow, in the reflections or in a gas lamp shining through the haze. I worked in that way for this bit of street scene in winter under the electric light."[99]

Hassam silhouetted dark forms against wintry New York streets in several other works. In one, *A New York Blizzard* (fig. 8), he evoked with vivid calligraphy a few well-dressed pedestrians buffeted by blowing snow. So hastily did he draw the scene that one can even imagine him working outdoors during a blizzard! This lively sheet reiterates motifs that had already appeared in Hassam's earliest Boston scenes. Well-dressed figures are challenged by but do not suffer in the snow, which softens sharp edges of buildings and seems to muffle urban clatter. The prominent gas lamp, a vestige of older lighting methods that would soon give way to electricity, provides a nostalgic note. The strictly reduced palette, limited to the triad of black, in the silhouetted coats and umbrellas, white, in the snow, and gray, in the paper, emphasizes pared-down flat pattern and abstract design, which accords with Hassam's preference for a selective rather than a journalistic interpretation of his own time. In *Winter, Midnight* (fig. 104) Hassam featured the radiance of a gas lamp "shining through the haze" and described a street along which horse-drawn cabs struggle to make their way through snow and slush. He thus anticipated both the mood and the painterly intensity of Realist works such as Robert Henri's *Street Scene with Snow (57th Street, N.Y.C.)* (fig. 105) and George Luks's *Butcher Cart* (fig. 106).

By contrast with Hassam's muted and coloristically reduced *Winter in Union Square*, his *Union Square in Spring* (fig. 107) vibrates with vernal sunlight.[100] The effect is the chromatic, peculiarly American one that critic Mrs. Van Rensselaer described in an article published in 1892 in *Century*:

> *The modern artist . . . has washed the old traditional palette, and set it anew with fresh, cheerful colors; he has learned how to portray the brightest sunshine; and he can rejoice in a place where he must paint sunlight falling on clear whites and yellows, bold reds, bright browns, and vivid greens, no less than one where, as in London, he can confine himself to neutral tones, or where, as in Paris, he can veil his whites, his pale light blues, his soft greens, and occasional notes of a more brilliant kind, with a delicate gauze of airiest gray.*[101]

In *Union Square in Spring* Hassam adopted a steeper view than he had used for any earlier urban scene, implying a vantage point in a modern skyscraper. In fact, he may have worked from the seven-story headquarters of the Century Company in the Century Building on Union Square North.[102] He looked down on Union Square from such a precipitous angle (see fig. 108) that the ground plane tilts radically upward, the horizon appears at the very top of the canvas, and decorative pattern rather than traditional perspective dominates the composition. The abstract effect, which is similar to that seen in cityscapes by Monet and Pissarro—such as the latter's *Place du Théâtre* (fig. 109)—is amplified by the square shape of Hassam's canvas. Although Hassam's treatment of space is in sharp contrast to that of the academic stage set in *At the Florist* (fig. 75), *Union Square in Spring* restates the earlier painting's dialogue between the artificial and the natural in an urban context. In *At the Florist* blooms were wrapped in paper; in Union Square nature is "wrapped" into bright green oases and organized by curvilinear pathways.

Hassam captured in the foreground the gabled roof of the small public comfort station just inside the park.[103] Beyond appear the park's lozenges of green lawn, seen as if they were floating on a golden asphalt sea. The energy of this disposition of larger forms is echoed in the rapid strokes that roughly define architectural surfaces and delineate the delicate trees with the first hints of spring foliage. Across Union Square, on Fourteenth Street between Fourth Avenue at the left and Broadway at the right, is the Morton House Hotel, which was made up of several buildings and contained the Union Square Theatre.

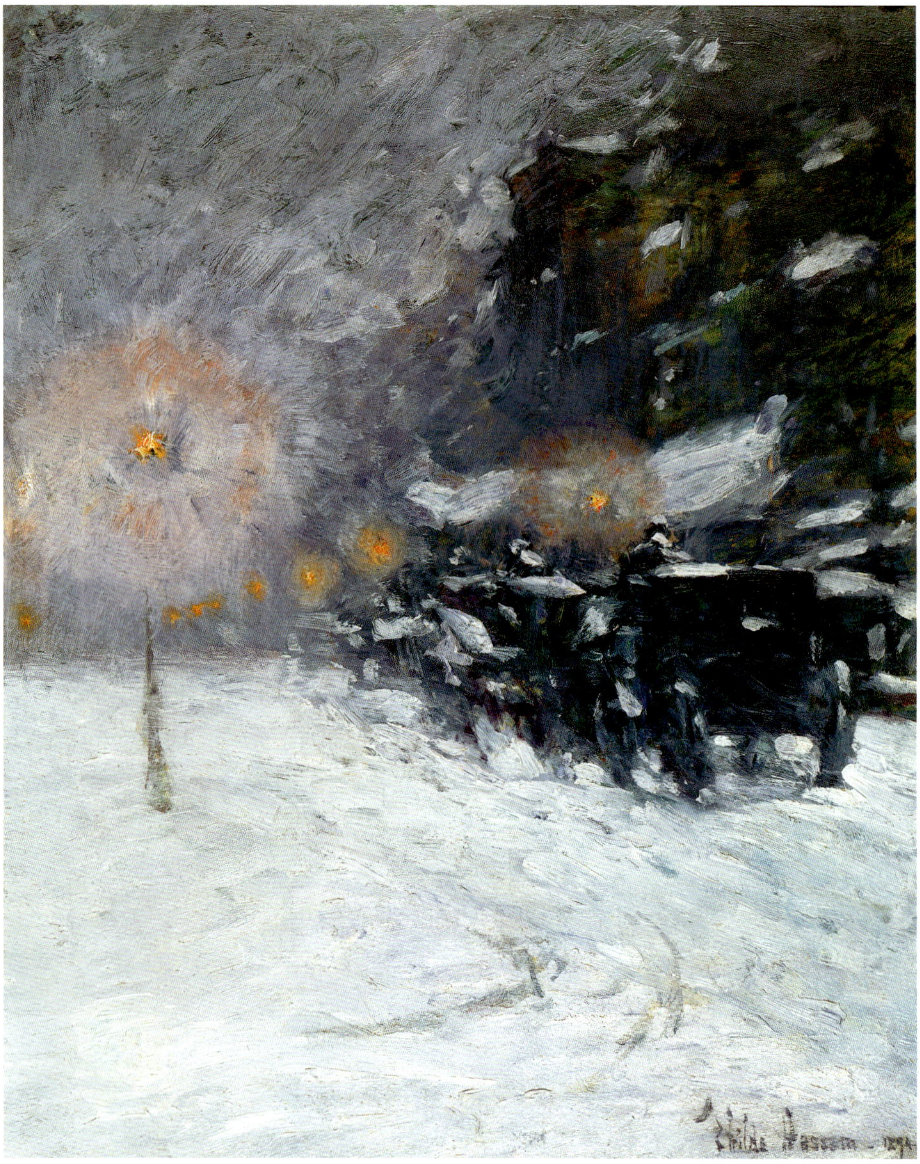

Fig. 104. Childe Hassam. *Winter, Midnight,* 1894. Oil on canvas, 21½ x 17½ in. (54.6 x 44.5 cm). Private collection

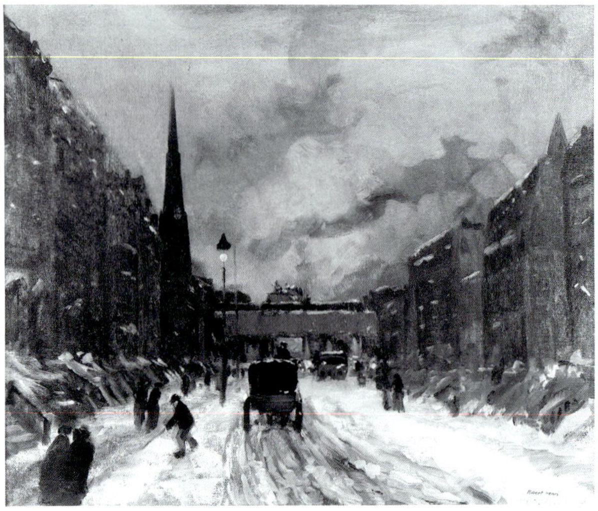

Fig. 105. Robert Henri. *Street Scene with Snow (57th Street, N.Y.C.),* 1902. Oil on canvas, 26 x 32 in. (66 x 81.3 cm). Yale University Art Gallery, New Haven, Mabel Brady Garvan Collection

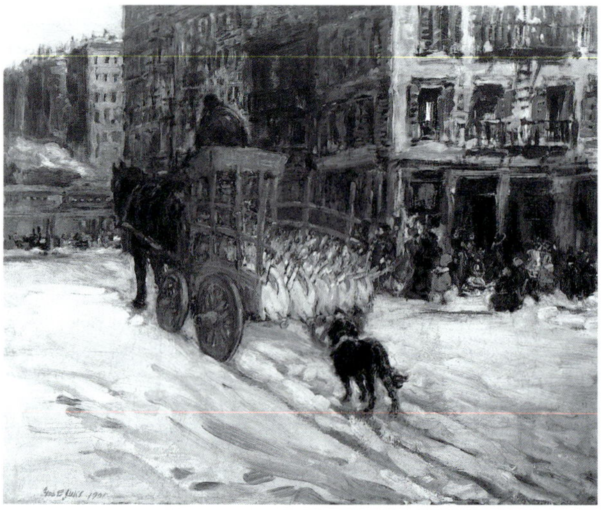

Fig. 106. George Luks. *The Butcher Cart,* 1901. Oil on canvas, 22 x 27 in. (55.9 x 68.6 cm). The Art Institute of Chicago, Friends of American Art Collection 1941.825

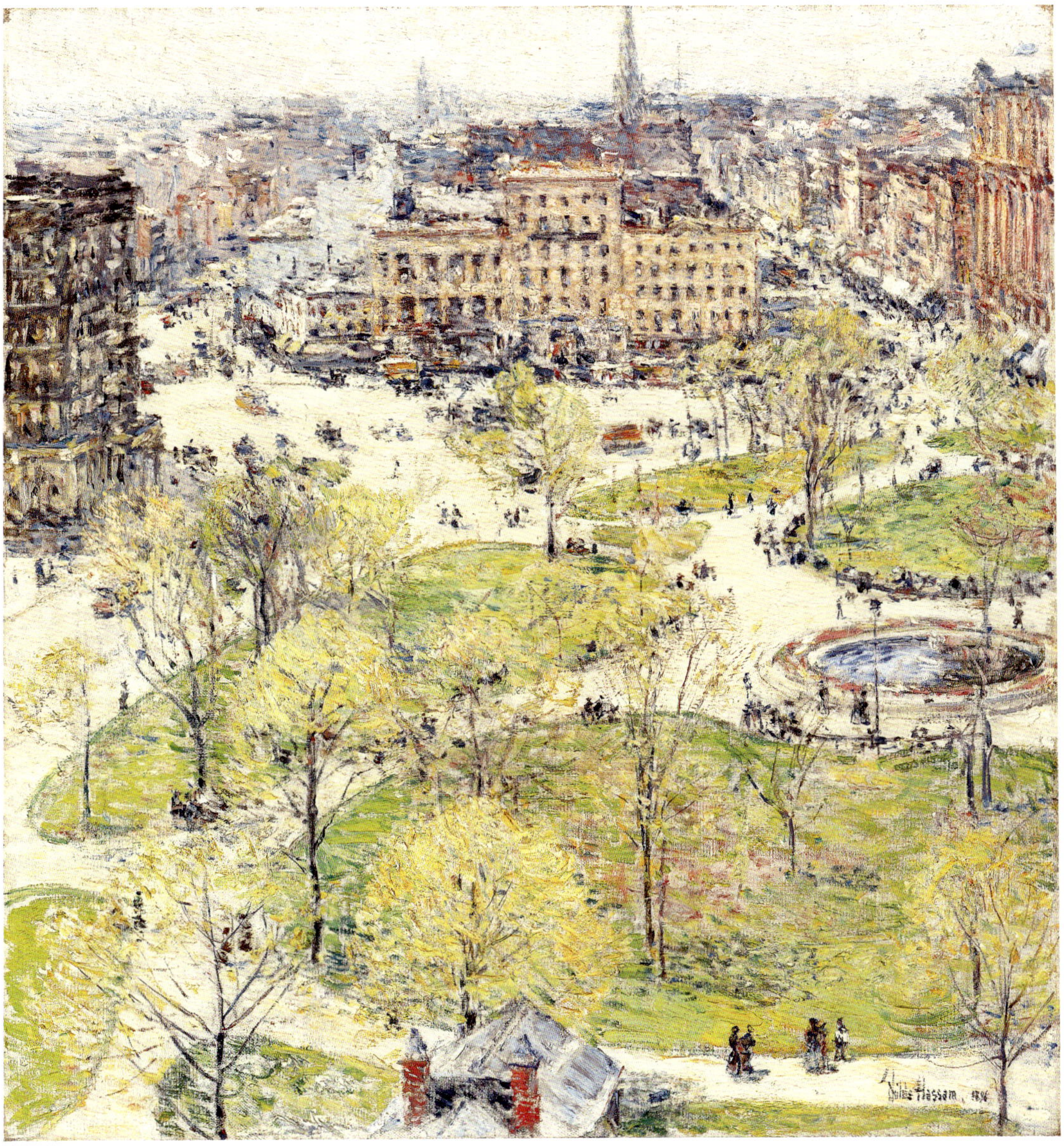

Fig. 107. Childe Hassam. *Union Square in Spring*, 1896. Oil on canvas, 21½ x 21 in. (54.6 x 53.3 cm). Smith College Museum of Art, Northampton, Massachusetts. Purchased

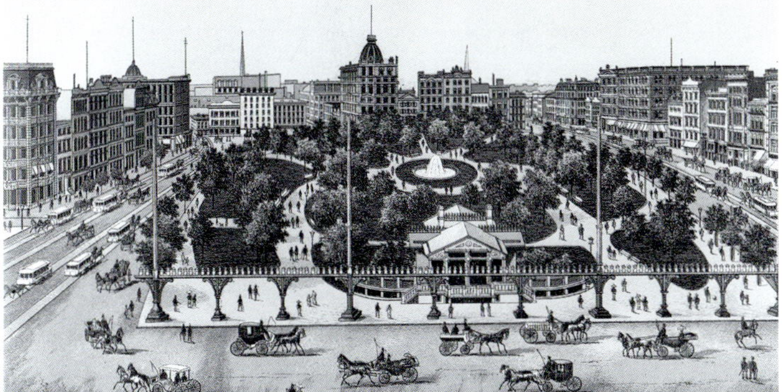

Fig. 108. Union Square, view of the park, undated postcard. Museum of the City of New York

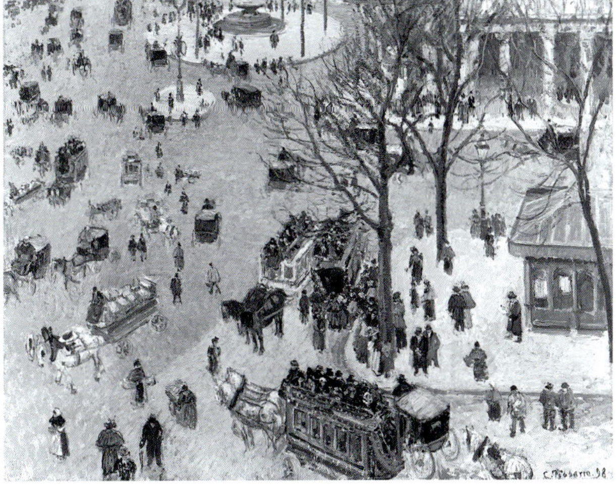

Fig. 109. Camille Pissarro. *Place du Théâtre*, 1898. Oil on canvas, 28½ x 36½ in. (72.4 x 92.7 cm). Los Angeles County Museum of Art, Mr. and Mrs. George Gard de Sylva Collection

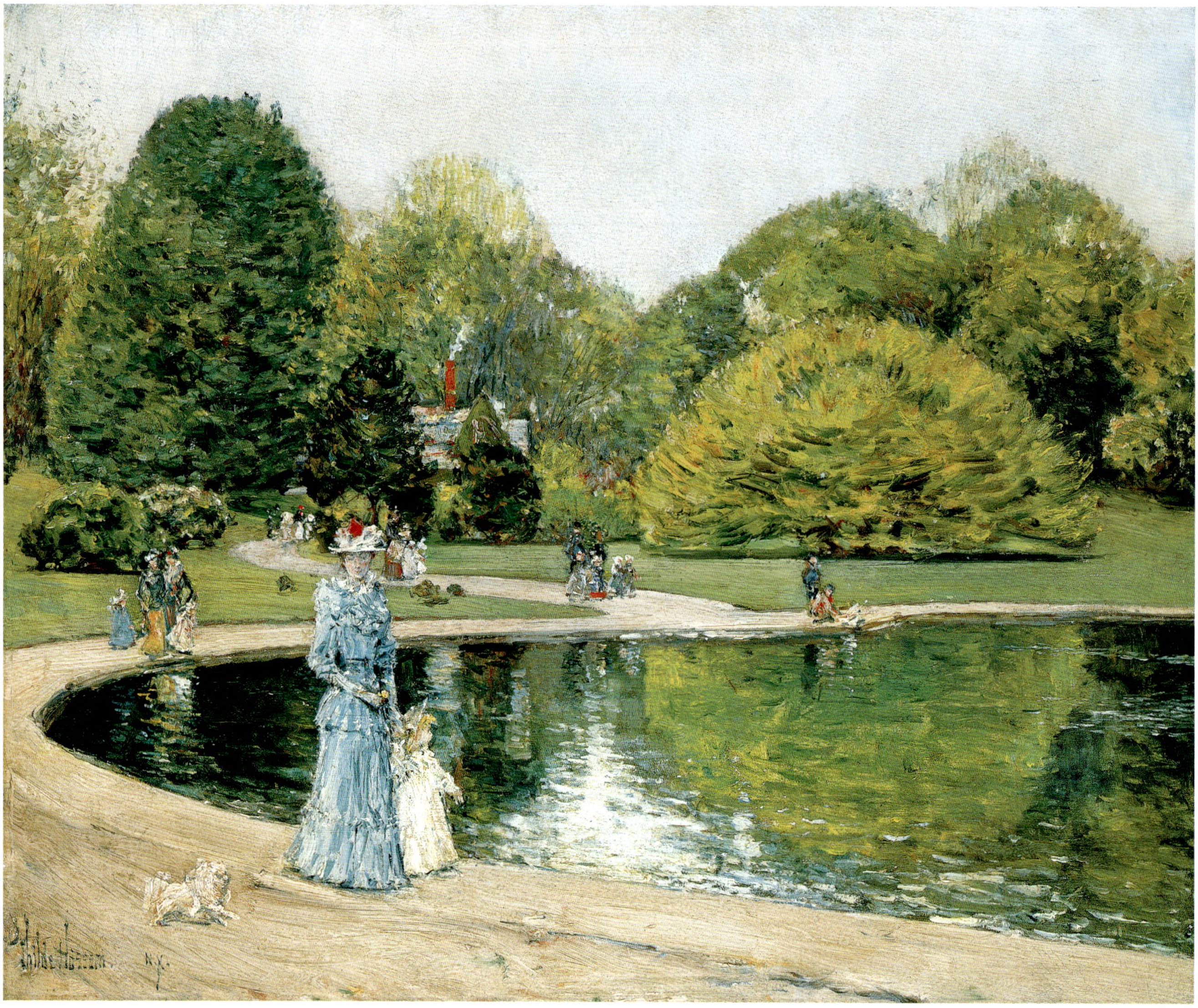

Fig. 110. Childe Hassam. *Central Park,* 1892. Oil on canvas, 18 x 22½ in. (45.7 x 57.2 cm). Private collection

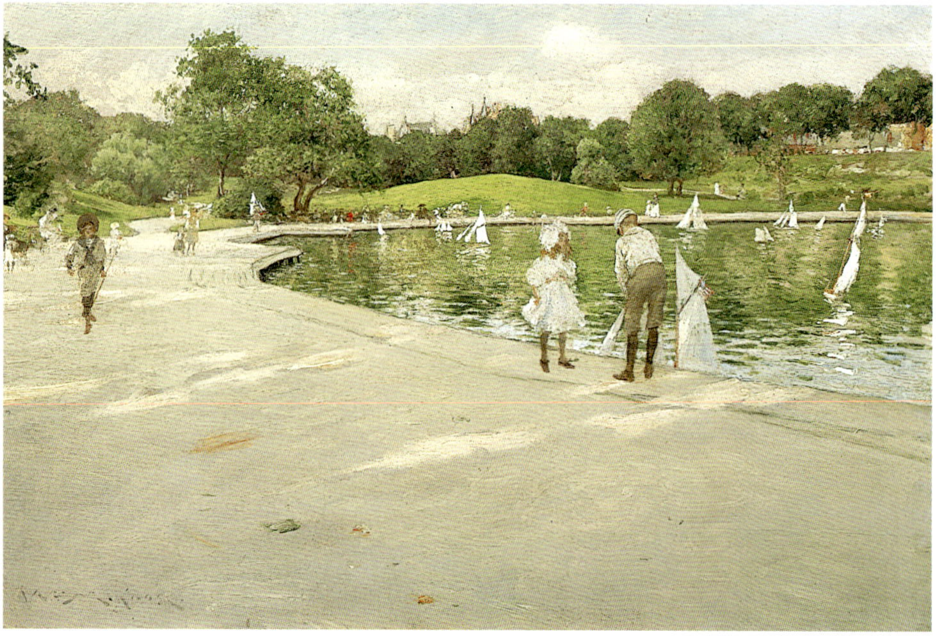

Fig. 111. William Merritt Chase. *The Lake for Miniature Yachts,* ca. 1890. Oil on canvas, 16 x 24 in. (40.6 x 61 cm). Collection of Mrs. Peter G. Terian, New York

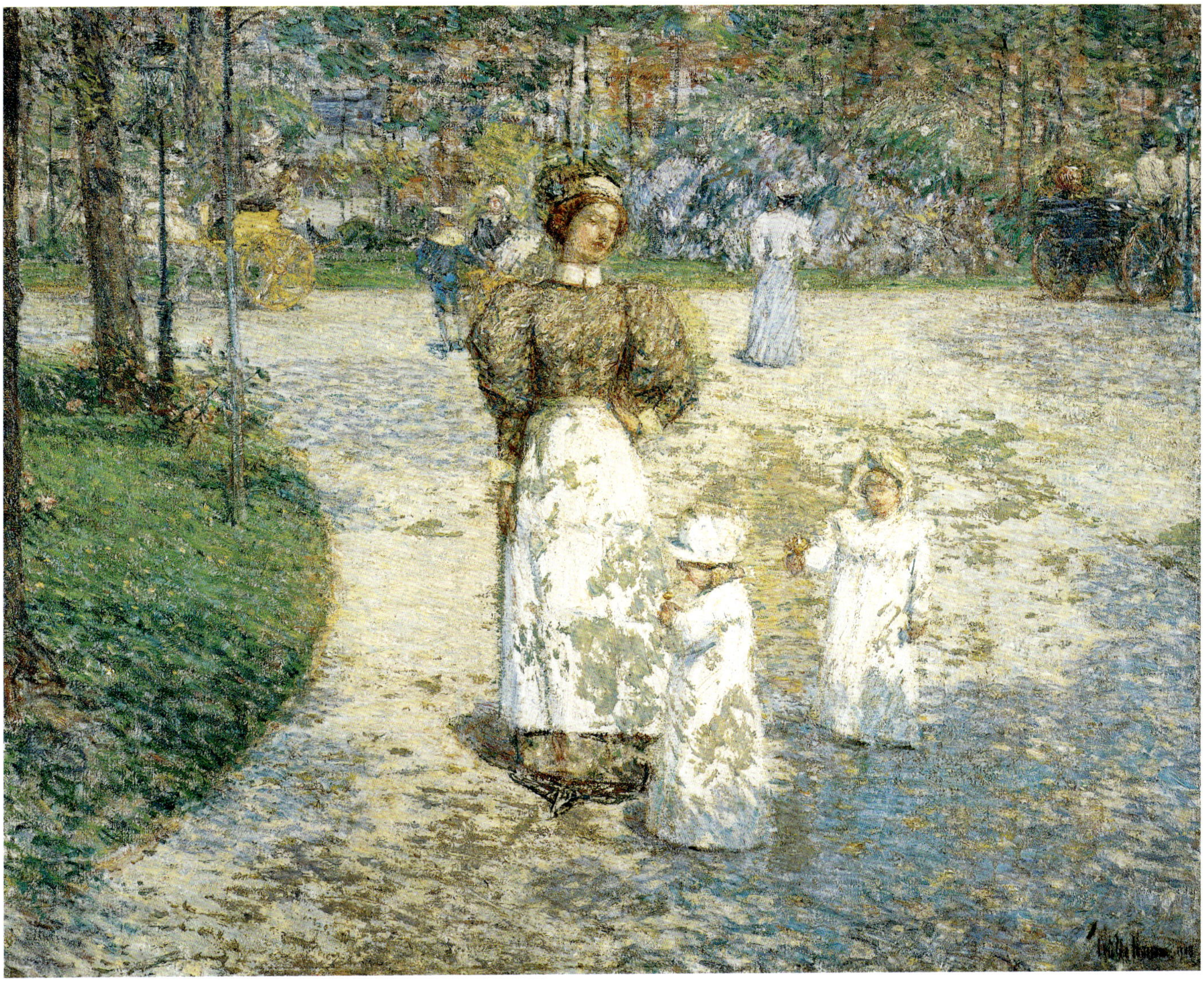

Fig. 112. Childe Hassam. *Spring in Central Park (Springtime),* 1898. Oil on canvas, 29 ½ x 37 ½ in. (74.9 x 95.3 cm). Robert Rubin

Bracketing the canvas are, to the left, the gray facade of the porticoed six-story Union Square Hotel on Fourth Avenue at Fifteenth Street, and, to the right, on Broadway, the double-colonnaded facade of the Domestic Sewing Machine Company, edited by Hassam to exclude its distinctive dome. In the distance, emerging against the hazy horizon of lower Manhattan, are church steeples, unidentifiable except for the prominent one of Grace Church. These monuments stand in contrast to the secular cathedrals of modern commerce and entertainment that defined Union Square.

Like the great squares along Fifth Avenue, Central Park inspired Hassam to paint a variety of compositions. In one of these, *Central Park* (fig. 110), he recorded well-dressed people promenading on the park's pathways and along the perimeter of the Conservatory Water just off Fifth Avenue at Seventy-third Street. Like William Merritt Chase, who was the first American Impressionist to respond to Central Park's pictorial potential—and who had painted the same site in *The Lake for Miniature Yachts* (fig. 111)—Hassam focused on a genteel spot then most often frequented by families from the adjacent affluent neighborhood.

After a trip to Europe from December 1896 to November 1897, Hassam would resume his role as New York's most devoted memoirist, rededicating himself to recording city views but also demonstrating an impressive new authority in his handling of composition and his execution. *Spring in Central Park (Springtime)* (fig. 112), depicting a nurse and her two young charges, provides an engaging record of costumes and mores of a privileged element of New York society in the

1890s. It reveals as well Hassam's growing inventiveness and skill, here displayed in his ability to play off the volumes of the figures against the flat patterns of the pathway and adjacent lawn, capture the sparkling sunlight and shadows that fall randomly across the setting and figures, and balance the requirements of depiction with those of design. These are concerns that would inform many of his twentieth-century works.

1. Hassam quoted in John Kimberly Mumford, "Who's Who in New York—No. 75," *New York Herald Tribune,* August 30, 1925, sec. 2, p. 3. Oddly, Hassam had hinted at a willingness to stay in Paris in Hassam, 35, boulevard Rochechouart, Paris, to Celia Thaxter, Isles of Shoals, June 13, 1888, private collection; transcribed in Hiesinger 1994, p. 178: "We may come back to America some day. It is Mrs. Hassam's dream."
2. Lockman interview, January 31, 1927, p. 20.
3. During his stay in Paris, Hassam had expressed doubts about his commercial success in Boston. For example, Hassam to Thaxter, June 13, 1888; transcribed in Hiesinger 1994, p. 178: "I may send some pictures over to Boston next winter. I am not sure though, it is such a doubtful market. I will not send my large ones certainly."
4. Hassam quoted in "New York Beautiful," 1898, p. 9. The best contemporaneous account of the city that Hassam experienced is John C. Van Dyke, *The New New York: A Commentary on the Place and the People* (New York: Macmillan Company, 1909). Recent analyses of the spirit of the new New York include Wanda M. Corn, "The New New York," *Art in America* 61 (July-August 1973), pp. 58–65, and Erica E. Hirshler, "The 'New New York' and the Park Row Building," *American Art Journal* 21 (1989), pp. 26–45.
5. Lockman interview, January 31, 1927, pp. 20–23 passim.
6. Childe Hassam, Autobiographical notes, n. d., Hassam Papers, reel NAA1, frame 689. Mariana Griswold Van Rensselaer recalled in 1893: "No one much younger than I can realize what a wail went up when the first shop-window was cut on the [Fifth] avenue—if I am not mistaken, at the south-east corner of Seventeenth street." M[ariana] G[riswold] Van Rensselaer, "Fifth Avenue, with Pictures by Childe Hassam," *Century* 47, n.s. 25 (November 1893), p. 12.
7. Lockman interview, January 31, 1927, p. 22.
8. Ibid., February 3, 1927, p. 5: "I started the Water Color Club, and I was its first President. . . . That happened because we wanted to have another exhibit in the Fall. Water colors were so low in price, and it was a more democratic art, as water colors could be sold for much lower prices than the oil paintings and it was the medium of the English speaking people."
9. Ibid., January 31, 1927, pp. 21–22. For additional records of the Hassam-Weir friendship, see Young 1960, passim. Information on the Hassam-Twachtman friendship is more scattered, but the relationship is mentioned throughout the Twachtman literature, including, for example, John Douglas Hale, "The Life and Creative Development of John H. Twachtman," 2 vols. (Ph.D. diss., Ohio State University, Columbus, 1957), passim. Childe Hassam, *Two Children* (1897, Cincinnati Art Museum) is said to depict the interior of Twachtman's Greenwich, Connecticut, home and two of his daughters. Hassam often praised Weir and Twachtman in his assessments of American art. See, for example, Hassam 1928, pp. 22, 27, and Childe Hassam, "John H. Twachtman: An Estimation," *North American Review* 176 (April 1903), pp. 555–57.
10. George R. Sparks, "Something about Posters," *Brush and Pencil* 1 (September 1897), p. 14.
11. "The Fine Arts: Mr. Hassam's Exhibition," *Boston Evening Transcript,* January 28, 1893, p. 4.
12. Sadakichi Hartmann, "Art Talk," *The Criterion,* January 8, 1898, p. 17, quoted in Fort 1993, p. vii.
13. From left to right, the steeples are those of the New Old South Church (Cummings and Sears, 1874–75), Trinity Church (H. H. Richardson, 1872–77), and Brattle Square Church (H. H. Richardson, 1869–73).
14. Quoted in Ives 1892, p. 117.
15. The two-wheeled, one-horse Hansom cab, whose driver was mounted on an elevated seat behind the passenger compartment, was patented in England by J. A. Hansom in 1834 and introduced in the United States in the 1890s. Edward B. Watson, *New York Then and Now: 83 Manhattan Sites Photographed in the Past and in the Present* (New York: Dover Publications, 1976), p. 38. Hassam's enthusiasm for Hansom cabs and their drivers is expressed in Ives 1892, p. 116.
16. Cynthia Zaitzevsky, *Frederick Law Olmsted and the Boston Park System* (Cambridge, Mass.: Harvard University Press, 1982), p. 10. The residential area of the Back Bay, which occupies about two hundred acres, runs west from Arlington Street, the boundary of the Public Garden, to Fenway Park, and from the Charles River on the north to Copley Square and Boylston Street on the south.
17. Walter Blackburn Harte, "The Back Bay: Boston's Throne of Wealth," *The Arena* 10 (June 1894), pp. 1–22. For the development of the Back Bay in general, see Moses King, *The Back-Bay District and the Vendome,* 3rd ed. (Boston, 1881); Edwin M. Bacon, *King's Dictionary of Boston* (Cambridge, Mass.: Moses King, 1883); Bainbridge Bunting, *Houses of Boston's Back Bay: An Architectural History, 1840–1917* (Cambridge, Mass.: The Belknap Press of Harvard University Press, 1967); Walter Muir Whitehill, *Boston: A Topographical History,* 2nd ed., enl. (Cambridge, Mass.: Harvard University Press, 1968), chap. 7, pp. 141–73; and Lewis Mumford and Walter Muir Whitehill, *Back Bay Boston: The City as a Work of Art,* exh. cat. (Boston: Museum of Fine Arts, 1969). Sam Bass Warner Jr., *Streetcar Suburbs: The Process of Growth in Boston, 1870–1900,* 2nd ed. (Cambridge, Mass.: Harvard University Press, 1978) discusses late-nineteenth-century changes in Boston, including the development of the Back Bay and the emergence of its suburbs. Recent urban histories of Boston include Robert Campbell and Peter Vanderwarker, *Cityscapes of Boston: An American City through Time* (Boston: Houghton Mifflin Company, 1992), and Lawrence W. Kennedy, *Planning the City upon a Hill: Boston since 1630* (Amherst: University of Massachusetts Press, 1992).
18. "A pedestrian starting at the Public Garden and walking westward can review American architectural development of half a century within the confines of a single street." Bunting, *Houses of Boston's Back Bay,* p. 6.
19. Carol Troyen, *The Boston Tradition: American Paintings from the Museum of Fine Arts, Boston,* exh. cat. (New York: American Federation of Arts, 1980), p. 166: "The artist stood just beyond Massachusetts Avenue at the point where the river bends northward and the land mass widens, providing a dramatically foreshortened view into the city."

20. William Dean Howells, *The Rise of Silas Lapham* (1885; New York: Viking Penguin, 1986), p. 32.
21. Troyen (*Boston Tradition*, p. 166) notes that the receding rail with uprights at broad intervals that rises from the perpendicular stone sea wall along the Charles River and the observer who directs attention away from the center of the composition echo devices in Gustave Caillebotte's *Pont d'Europe*, 1876 (Musée d'Art Moderne de Renoir à Picasso, Petit Palais, Geneva). There is no evidence that Hassam saw Caillebotte's painting, which remained in the French artist's possession after its appearance in the third Impressionist exhibition in 1877.
22. Hassam's 1892 visit to Chicago is discussed in H. Barbara Weinberg, "Hassam's Travels, 1892–1914," in this publication, pp. 179–82.
23. The outspoken protagonist of Rupert Hughes's novel *The Real New York* asserted that "compared with New York, every other city in the world is a squat little village." Rupert Hughes, *The Real New York* (New York and London: Smart Set Publishing Company, 1904), p. 21; quoted in Kathleen M. Burnside, "New York City as Subject in the Gilded Age: The Proliferation of Genteel and Picturesque Urban Imagery" (manuscript, Graduate Center, City University of New York, 1989), p. 29, n. 15.
24. Julian Ralph, "Eight Days in Paris," *Harper's Weekly*, July 4, 1891, p. 507, quoted in Burnside, "New York City as Subject," pp. 7–8. M[ariana] G[riswold] Van Rensselaer, "Picturesque New York," *Century* 45, n.s. 23 (December 1892), pp. 164–75, noted (p. 166) the affinities between the two cities, deciding that, although New York might lack the beauty of Paris, it had a character that would reward an artist's consideration. Charles Henry White, "In the Street," *Harper's New Monthly Magazine* 110 (February 1905), pp. 365–76, also described the picturesque elements of New York and its potential for artists. Louis Baury, "The Message of Manhattan," *Bookman* 33 (August 1911), pp. 592–601, surveyed artists' attitudes toward New York.
25. [William Henry] Howe in [William Henry] Howe and [George] Torrey, "Childe Hassam," *Art Interchange* 34 (May 1895), p. 133. In the same article, coauthor Torrey dissented from Howe's favorable assessment, claiming: "Hassam's sentiment is thin; much of his work is not what you can call serious. It is doubtful if he will ever do serious work; he does not see the need of it."
26. Van Dyke, *New New York*, p. vii.
27. Ives 1892, pp. 117, 116. See H. Barbara Weinberg, "Introduction," in this publication, p. 7. Hassam expressed similar sentiments when he compared the atmosphere of New York to that of Paris in "New York Beautiful" 1898, p. 9, and its boulevards with those of Paris (and London) in "New York the Beauty City," *New York Morning Sun*, February 23, 1913, p. 16. Ives's article provides a useful account by Hassam of his Impressionist technique.
28. Hassam 1899.
29. Annie Nathan Meyer, "A City Picture: Hassam's Latest Painting of New York," *Art and Progress* 2 (March 1911), p. 139.
30. Hassam quoted in "New York Beautiful" 1898, p. 9. Hassam added: "They are apt to overdress, but when they succeed they succeed beautifully."
31. See Ward McAllister, *Society As I Have Found It* (New York: Cassell Publishing Company, 1890), and Jacob A. Riis, *How the Other Half Lives: Studies among the Tenements of New York* (New York: Charles Scribner's Sons, 1890).
32. Walter Wellman, "Rise of the American City: The Wonderful Story of the Census of 1900," *McClure's Magazine* 17 (September 1901), p. 471; Kenneth T. Jackson, ed., *The Encyclopedia of New York City* (New Haven: Yale University Press, 1995), pp. 922–23.
33. Crucial engineering developments were steel-skeleton framing, mechanical elevators, and fireproof construction. A fine overview of turn-of-the-century architectural innovations is Robert A. M. Stern, Gregory Gilmartin, and John Montague Massengale, *New York 1900: Metropolitan Architecture and Urbanism 1890–1915* (New York: Rizzoli, 1983).
34. Henry James, *The American Scene* (New York: Harper and Brothers, 1907), quoted in Alan Trachtenberg, "Image and Ideology: New York in the Photographer's Eye," *Journal of Urban History* 10 (August 1984), p. 456.
35. For the celebratory iconography of New York in the 1890s, see, for example, *King's Handbook of New York City: An Outline History and Description of the American Metropolis* (Boston: Moses King, 1892; 2nd ed., Boston: Moses King, 1893); Corolyn Faville Ober and Cynthia M. Westover, *Manhattan Historic and Artistic: A Six Day Tour of New York City* (New York: Lovell, Coryell and Co., 1892); Frank Moss, *The American Metropolis: From Knickerbocker Days to the Present Time. New York City Life in All Its Various Phases: An Historiograph of New York*, 3 vols. (New York: Peter Fenelon Collier, 1897); and Van Dyke, *New New York*. A comprehensive annotated bibliography of books on New York published between 1853 and 1976 is Alan Burnham, *New York City, the Development of the Metropolis: An Annotated Bibliography* (New York: Garland Publishing, 1988). Corollary material includes numerous turn-of-the-century articles recommending remedies for the problems of cities, especially New York, and proposals for urban beautification. The recent bibliography—scholarly and popular—on the history and development of the American city, New York in particular, is vast. Among useful sources, see Gunther Barth, *City People: The Rise of Modern City Culture in Nineteenth-Century America* (New York: Oxford University Press, 1980); Howard Gillette Jr. and Zane L. Miller, eds., *American Urbanism: A Historiographical Review* (New York: Greenwood Press, 1987); and Raymond A. Mohl, ed., *The Making of Urban America* (Wilmington, Del.: Scholarly Resources Books, 1988).
36. Hassam's illustrations and reproductions of his New York paintings appeared in Thomas Curtis Clarke, "Rapid Transit in Cities. I—The Problem," *Scribner's Magazine* 11 (May 1892), pp. 566–78, and "Rapid Transit in Cities. II—The Solution," *Scribner's Magazine* 11 (June 1892), pp. 743–58; Van Rensselaer, "Fifth Avenue, with Pictures by Hassam," pp. 5–18 (which also includes illustrations by Theodore Robinson); and Royal Cortissoz, "Landmarks of Manhattan," *Scribner's Magazine* 18 (November 1895), pp. 531–44.
37. "Greta" [pseud.], "The Etching Club Exhibition," *Art Amateur* 24 (March 1891), p. 92.
38. Simeon Strunsky, "The Lane That Has No Turning," *Harper's New Monthly Magazine* 131 (September 1915), p. 490, quoted in William H. Gerdts, *Impressionist New York* (New York: Abbeville Press, 1994), pp. 45–46.
39. Eliot Clark, "Childe Hassam," *Art in America* 8 (June 1920), p. 173.
40. Quoted in "New York the Beauty City," *New York Morning Sun*, February 23, 1913, p. 16.
41. Kathleen M. Burnside, "New York City in the 1890's: The Cityscapes of Childe Hassam," in *Sotheby's Art at Auction 1988–89* (New York: Sotheby's Publications, 1989), p. 169.
42. Fort (1993, p. vii) remarks on Hassam's reserve. Fort's astute reading of Hassam's New York scenes was a great help to the author of the present essay.
43. Hiesinger (1994, p. 105, n. 8) suggests that "this is most likely the canvas Hassam exhibited at the Art Institute of Chicago from June 9 to July 30, 1890,

under the title *Fifth Avenue and the Snow*," and (ibid., p. 65) as the painting Hassam showed under the same title at Galerie Durand-Ruel, Paris, in June-July 1891; see n. 47, below. Diana Strazdes, *American Paintings and Sculpture to 1945 in the Carnegie Museum of Art* (New York: Hudson Hills Press in Association with the Carnegie Museum of Art, 1992), p. 233, had dated the painting "ca. 1892." It was reproduced in Van Rensselaer, "Fifth Avenue, with Pictures by Hassam," p. 8, as *A Winter Morning (Fifth Avenue and Seventeenth Street)*. Hassam's illustrations, which are images of New York based on his paintings, are not integral to Van Rensselaer's text, which is personal and retrospective.

44. Lockman interview, January 31, 1927, p. 23. Mrs. Van Rensselaer remembered the Fifth Avenue of her youth: "There was a line of stages which turned into the avenue from Broadway at Thirteenth street, and stopped finally at Forty-second. These stages were gaily colored, and had big pictures on each side." Van Rensselaer, "Fifth Avenue, with Pictures by Hassam," p. 8.

45. Jackson, *Encyclopedia of New York City*, p. 691. One of New York's leading concert venues from its opening in 1875 until it was converted entirely to retail use in 1893, the four-story Chickering Hall contained piano showrooms and an auditorium that seated an audience of 1,450 for concerts and lectures. William H. Gerdts, "Three Themes," in Adelson, Cantor, and Gerdts 1999, p. 140, notes that Chickering Hall was home to the Mendelssohn Glee Club and Boston Symphony Society and was the site of concerts and lectures by Franz Liszt, Ignace Paderewski, Oscar Wilde, and Mark Twain, among others.

46. Ives 1892, p. 116.

47. *Exposition de peintures et sculptures par un groupe d'artistes américains*, exh. cat. (Paris: Galerie Durand-Ruel, June 4–July 13, 1891). For the review see an unidentified clipping, Hassam Papers, quoted in Hiesinger 1994, p. 106, n. 9 (where the source is given as *Le Figaro* and the date as June 10, 1891): "Mais je cherche dans l'exposition américaine quelques passages vraiment américaines: ils sont rares, il faut avouer; cependant M. Child Hassam, un des artistes les plus aimés des Etats-Unis, me donne une impression vraiment interessante avec un coin de New-York sous la neige, qu'il appelle Cinquième Avenue en hiver; bonne couleur: solidement peinte, cette toile est une des plus appréciées de l'Exposition Durand-Ruel." A variant of *Fifth Avenue in Winter* is *Street Scene, Christmas Morning*, 1892 (Smith College Museum of Art, Northampton, Massachusetts), which appeared in National Academy of Design, New York, *Catalogue Loan Collection 1893, Including Twelfth Annual Exhibition*, exh. cat. (New York: National Academy of Design, December 4, 1893–January 13, 1894), no. 172, as *Christmas Morning—Fifth Avenue*. According to Strazdes (*American Paintings and Sculpture the Carnegie Museum*, p. 234), Hassam later painted at least three other views of the same street corner, all now in private collections.

48. The first painting purchased by a museum was *Pont Royal* (fig. 330), acquired by the Cincinnati Art Museum from its summer 1899 annual. Hassam misremembered when he said of *Fifth Avenue in Winter*: "It was the first picture that was bought by a museum, that was the Carnegie Institute, and it paid me $800. It was a large price for a painting in those days, and it hangs there now." Lockman interview, January 31, 1927, p. 23. Hassam's relationship with the Carnegie Institute is the subject of Gail Stavitsky, "Childe Hassam and the Carnegie Institute: A Correspondence," *Archives of American Art Journal* 22, no. 3 (1982), pp. 2–7.

49. Hassam suggested he knew Gilder at the time he lived at 95 Fifth Avenue. "I was near Union Square. There was Alexander Drake of the Century, and of course Gilder." He also recalled: "Gilder came to the Isle of Shoals. I met him at the [*sic*] Appledore." Lockman interview, January 31, 1927, pp. 23–24, 26.

50. M. Christine Boyer, *Manhattan Manners: Architecture and Style, 1850–1900* (New York: Rizzoli, 1985), pp. 76–77. See also Thomas Bender, *New York Intellect: A History of Intellectual Life in New York City, from 1750 to the Beginnings of Our Own Time* (New York: Alfred A. Knopf, 1987), pp. 216–22.

51. Edward Simmons, *From Seven to Seventy: Memories of a Painter and a Yankee* (New York: Harper and Brothers, 1922; reprint, New York: Garland Publishing, 1976), p. 203.

52. For commercial development around Union Square and on nearby Broadway, see Robert A. M. Stern, Thomas Mellins, and David Fishman, *New York 1880: Architecture and Urbanism in the Gilded Age* (New York: Monacelli Press, 1999), pp. 711–22.

53. See Watson, *New York Then and Now*, p. 154.

54. See Mary C. Henderson, *The City and the Theatre: New York Playhouses from Bowling Green to Times Square* (Clifton, N.J.: James T. White and Co., 1973), pp. 139–49, and John W. Frick, *New York's First Theatrical Center: The Rialto at Union Square* (Ann Arbor: UMI Research Press, 1985).

55. Joseph G. Rayback, *A History of American Labor, Expanded and Updated* (New York: MacMillan, 1968), p. 169.

56. Hassam's painting appeared in *Catalogue of the Ninth Autumn Exhibition of the National Academy of Design*, exh. cat. (New York: National Academy of Design, 1890), no. 64, as *Winter Morning, Union Square*. "The Academy of Design," *Art Amateur* 24 (January 1891), p. 31, is the only review of this exhibition thus far located that describes Hassam's painting; while the remarks do not definitively identify *Winter in Union Square*, they relate more closely to it than to any other known painting by him. The writer declared: "It is by far the best thing we have yet seen from this painter."

57. The painting was illustrated in Hassam 1899 (unpaged) as *Winter in Union Square (Seventeenth Street and Broadway, looking south)*. For the significance of the square canvas format, see William H. Gerdts, "The Square Format and Proto-Modernism in American Painting," *Arts Magazine* 50 (June 1978), pp. 70–75. Gerdts observes (p. 74) that Hassam "made fairly extensive use of this format," as did Twachtman, Emil Carlsen, Frederick C. Frieseke, and Willard L. Metcalf.

58. Burke 1980, p. 356.

59. Margot Gayle and Michele Cohen, *The Art Commission and the Municipal Art Society Guide to Manhattan's Outdoor Sculpture* (New York: Prentice-Hall Press, 1988), pp. 90–97, identifies and documents *Charity* and other sculptures in Union Square.

60. Ives 1892, p. 116.

61. A 240-acre tract, called the Parade, had been set aside between the Bloomingdale Road (Broadway) and the Boston Post Road (Third Avenue) in 1807 for an arsenal, barracks, and burial ground. It was pared to 90 acres and renamed for President James Madison in 1814 and then reduced again and opened in 1847. See Jackson, *Encyclopedia of New York City*, pp. 711–12.

62. Moses King, *King's Views of New York, 1896–1915 and Brooklyn, 1905* (Boston, 1896–1915; reprint, New York: Benjamin Blom, 1974), p. 60.

63. The new Madison Square Garden, designed by Stanford White, contained an eight-thousand-seat auditorium and was surmounted by a huge Moorish-style tower (the second-tallest building in New York City) crowned with Augustus Saint-Gaudens's gilded weather vane *Diana*, first

version, 1891 (location unknown); second version, 1894 (Philadelphia Museum of Art). Madison Square Garden replaced an 1879 building with the same name and function. White's building was razed in 1925. Jackson, *Encyclopedia of New York City*, pp. 711–12.

64. Van Rensselaer, "Fifth Avenue, with Pictures by Hassam," p. 15.
65. Ives 1892, pp. 116–17. "Dunlap's" was almost certainly R. Dunlap and Company, a two-story hat store at 178 Fifth Avenue between Twenty-second and Twenty-third Streets; Hiesinger 1994, p. 68.
66. Van Rensselaer, "Fifth Avenue, with Pictures by Hassam," p. 14.
67. Hassam shifted his vantage point to paint *Madison Square in Snow*, 1893 (Peabody Art Collection, Maryland Commission on Artistic Property of the Maryland State Archives), which includes White's Madison Square Garden and the seated bronze memorial to William Henry Seward by Randolph Rogers, installed at the southwest corner of the square in 1876. Gerdts ("Three Themes," p. 138) suggests that Hassam's vantage point was the two-story Erie Railroad Office on the triangular site later occupied by the Fuller ("Flatiron") Building.
68. "The Fine Arts: Mr. Hassam's Exhibition," *Boston Evening Transcript*, January 28, 1893, p. 4, reviewing the exhibition of Hassam's works at Doll and Richards Gallery, Boston. For additional information on *Spring Morning in the Heart of the City*, see Burke 1980, pp. 353–55. Burke explains that the most noticeable change Hassam made when he reworked the painting between 1895 and 1899 was the removal of a group of people crossing the street in the right foreground; the pentimento is quite apparent. The canvas before repainting is illustrated in Van Rensselaer, "Fifth Avenue, with Pictures by Hassam," p. 10.
69. The painting appeared in *Catalogue of the Ninth Autumn Exhibition of the National Academy of Design*, no. 120, as *Broadway and Madison Square, from a balcony, May*. The anonymous author of "The Academy of Design," *Art Amateur* 24 (January 1891), p. 31, noted: "The effect of May weather in the city is felt and to some degree rendered. . . . it seems to us that the multiplied red touches, in the flowers, the red umbrellas, the brick buildings, are rather raw than gay." Just south of the Hotel Bartholdi was the American Art Galleries at 940–952 Broadway, which Hassam would have visited. Hassam had been in New York in 1883, when the American Art Association took over the American Art Galleries at 6 East Twenty-third Street and presented a full year of important exhibitions. In November 1884 the association annexed gallery space at 940–952 Broadway and presented an inaugural exhibition that included two works by Hassam. In winter 1889–90 the American Art Association presented a blockbuster exhibition, *The Works of Antoine-Louis Barye, His Friends, and His Contemporaries*, to raise funds for the Barye Monument in Paris. This exhibition included Millet's *Angelus*, 1857–59 (Musée d'Orsay, Paris). The American Art Association grossed close to $200,000 on the New York show and tour, and more than four hundred thousand people came to see Millet's painting. Also in 1890 at the American Art Galleries were the exhibition of the Society of American Artists and the first exhibition of the New York Water Color Club, of which Hassam was the founding president. See Gerald D. Bolas, "The Early Years of the American Art Association, 1879–1900" (Ph.D. diss., Graduate Center, City University of New York, 1998), passim.
70. The Gothic Revival chapel of the First Presbyterian Church, set back from the corner of Eleventh Street, was designed by McKim, Mead, and White and constructed in 1893–94. See *Guide to New York City Landmarks*, 2nd ed. (New York: John Wiley and Sons, 1998), p. 44. Hassam made urban churches the subject of several works, including *Saint Marks in the Bowery*, 1910 (Yale University Art Gallery, New Haven), and the following paintings now in private collections, for which illustration sources are listed: *The Cathedral and Fifth Avenue in June*, 1893 (Christie's, New York, sale cat., May 26, 1999, lot 31); *Calvary Church in the Snow*, 1893 (Adelson, Cantor, and Gerdts 1999, p. 201); *Church of the Paulist Fathers*, n.d. (Christie's, New York, sale cat., May 21, 1998, lot 59).
71. R[ichard] H. Titherington, "Picturesque Points of Fifth," *Munsey's Magazine* 6 (November 1891), pp. 125–26.
72. Useful sources on this include Edmund T. Delaney, *New York's Greenwich Village* (Barre, Mass.: Barre Publishers, 1968); Mindy Cantor, ed., *Around the Square, 1830–1890: Essays on Life, Letters, and Architecture in Greenwich Village* (New York: New York University, 1982); Gina d'Angelo, "Childe Hassam's *Washington Arch, Spring*" (manuscript, Graduate Center, City University of New York, 1990); Bruce Weber, *Homage to the Square: Picturing Washington Square, 1890–1965*, exh. cat. (New York: Berry Hill Galleries, 2001); and Emily Kies Folpe, *It Happened on Washington Square* (Baltimore: Johns Hopkins University Press, 2002). The picture was shown as *Fifth Avenue and the Washington Arch in May* in *Exhibition and Private Sale of Oil Paintings by Mr. Childe Hassam at the Art Gallery of Messrs Doll & Richards* (Boston: Doll and Richards Gallery, February 23–March 6, 1895), no. 15, and as *Washington Arch, May* in *Exhibition of Paintings by Childe Hassam* (Boston: St. Botolph Club, October 29–November 17, 1900), no. 17. A related painting that appeared in *Catalogue of the Ninth Autumn Exhibition of the National Academy of Design*, no. 73, *Fifth Avenue at Washington Square (May)*, is apparently the work illustrated as *Fifth Avenue at Washington Square* in Van Rensselaer, "Fifth Avenue, with Pictures by Hassam," p. 5, an article that offers Van Rensselaer's reminiscences of patrician Washington Square.
73. The painting captures the characteristic atmosphere of the city, which Mrs. Van Rensselaer described: "the clear, pure, crystalline air of New York, which seems to sparkle with Atlantic salt. . . . our brilliant sky, our crisp lights, and our strong sharp shadows." Van Rensselaer, "Picturesque New York," p. 166.
74. These street sweepers flourished in the 1890s, especially after the appointment in 1895 of Colonel George E. Waring Jr. as commissioner of the Street-Cleaning Department. See William W. Ellsworth, "Colonel Waring's 'White Angels': A Sketch of the Street-Cleaning Department of New York," *Outlook* 53 (June 27, 1896), pp. 1191–94. Hassam called Colonel Waring "one of the greatest citizens of New York," along with Richard Watson Gilder, and noted: "I rented my studio one year [1897] to Colonel Waring's daughter and went abroad." Lockman interview, January 31, 1927, pp. 26–27; regarding the sublet, see also ibid., p. 33.
75. Ives 1892, pp. 116–17.
76. Richard Morris Hunt's Tenth Street Studio Building opened at 15 (later 51) West Tenth Street in 1858 and housed numerous, usually well-established, painters, including Winslow Homer and William Merritt Chase. Other artists worked in the New York University building on Washington Square. By about 1910 the identity of Greenwich Village as New York's Bohemia or Latin Quarter began to develop in earnest, with more and more artists and writers, teachers, and settlement-house workers moving into the neighborhood's quaint, and, by then, ethnically diverse and inexpensive mews. The Salmagundi Club, a popular artists' gathering place, settled at 47 Fifth Avenue in 1917.
77. Van Rensselaer, "Fifth Avenue, with Pictures by Hassam," p. 10.

78. The tragic fire that took 146 lives at the Triangle Shirtwaist Company on March 25, 1911, occurred in the Asch Building on Washington Place, one block east of Washington Square.
79. William Dean Howells, *A Hazard of New Fortunes* (1890; New York: New American Library, 1983), p. 48; see pp. 158–59 for Basil March's additional thoughts on the picturesqueness of immigrants. Jan Seidler Ramirez calls attention to *A Hazard of New Fortunes,* Howells's first delineation of New York, in "Within Bohemia's Borders: Greenwich Village, 1830–1930," interpretive script accompanying an exhibition (New York: Museum of the City of New York, [1990]), p. 8. Leaders of the Ash Can School—William Glackens, John Sloan, George Luks, and Everett Shinn—would also settle in Greenwich Village, finding inspiration in the neighborhood's ethnic types and street scenes, and work as illustrators for such Village-based journals as *The Masses.* An overview of the migration of artists to Greenwich Village appears in Steven Watson, *Strange Bedfellows: The First American Avant-Garde* (New York: Abbeville Press, 1991), "Village I: New Bohemia on Washington Square," pp. 122–65.
80. Information regarding the centennial celebration and the Washington Arch is derived from *The History of Washington Arch in Washington Square* (New York: Ford and Garnett Publishers, 1896), and John Tauranac, *Elegant New York: The Builders and The Buildings, 1885–1915* (New York: Abbeville Press, 1985), pp. 47–48.
81. See the remarks of Henry G. Marquand, chairman of the Washington Arch Memorial Committee, in "In Honor of Washington: Laying the Cornerstone of the Memorial Arch," *New York Times,* May 31, 1890, pp. 1–7; quoted in d'Angelo, "Childe Hassam's *Washington Arch, Spring,*" p. 6.
82. See, for example, William H. Gerdts, *American Impressionism: Masterworks from Public and Private Collections in the United States* (Lugano-Castagnola: Thyssen-Bornemisza Foundation, 1990), p. 54. Gerdts ("Three Themes," p. 142) gives the date of the painting as ca. 1893 and notes (p. 144) that it portrays the permanent arch.
83. The painting was reproduced in Van Rensselaer, "Fifth Avenue, with Pictures by Hassam," p. 6. D'Angelo ("Childe Hassam's *Washington Arch, Spring*") demonstrates that Hassam depicted the permanent arch. An unattributed photograph of the temporary arch (Collection of the New-York Historical Society, negative #59539) is reproduced in Weber, *Homage to the Square,* p. 30. The permanent arch was dedicated on May 4, 1895. An entry on the painting appears in Erika D. Passantino, ed., *The Eye of Duncan Phillips: A Collection in the Making* (Washington, D.C.: Phillips Collection in Association with Yale University Press, New Haven, 1999), p. 161, but it does not discuss the disparity between the date on the canvas and the date on which the north trophy panels were installed. The fact that Hassam's signature was applied in blue paint and the date, 1890, was written in black paint supports the possibility that the incorrect date was added to the canvas some time after its completion.
84. The painting was exhibited at Doll and Richards Gallery, Boston, in February 1895.
85. The street sweepers, who preoccupied Hassam in several canvases, were remarked to be "able-bodied, strapping fellows between the ages of twenty-five and forty years . . . of various nationalities, Irish, German, and Italian." *New York Times,* February 17, 1891, p. 8; quoted in d'Angelo, "Childe Hassam's *Washington Arch, Spring,*" p. 14.
86. Arthur M. Barnes, "Washington Square," *Harper's Weekly* 38 (July 14, 1894), p. 660, remarked on the marble arch's "power to quicken patriotism." Hassam painted the temporary arch, which was constructed at Fifth Avenue and Twenty-fourth Street to celebrate Admiral George Dewey's return to New York following his victory over the Spanish fleet in Manila Bay during the Spanish-American War. *Dewey's Arch,* 1900, gouache and watercolor, is illustrated (p. 161) in Adelson, Cantor, and Gerdts 1999 and discussed there (pp. 159, 161).
87. For the Stewart house, see Jay E. Cantor, "A Monument of Trade: A. T. Stewart and the Rise of the Millionaire's Mansion in New York," *Winterthur Portfolio* 10 (1975), pp. 165–97; and Stern, Mellins, and Fishman, *New York 1880,* pp. 570–77.
88. The price—the highest that had ever been spent for a dwelling in New York City—is given in *Harper's Weekly,* August 14, 1869, pp. 525–26, quoted in Gerdts, *Impressionist New York,* p. 106.
89. Edward G. Riggs, *New York Sun,* April 23, 1892; quoted in Henry Watterson, *History of the Manhattan Club: A Narrative of the Activities of Half a Century* (New York: Manhattan Club, 1915), p. xxiii.
90. For an anecdotal summary of the history of the site, see Arthur Bartlett Maurice, *Fifth Avenue* (New York: Dodd, Mead and Company, 1918; reprint, New York: Arno Press, 1975), pp. 244–45. Hassam painted the Knickerbocker Trust Company in *Flags on the Waldorf, 1916* (fig. 230), which is discussed in H. Barbara Weinberg, "Hassam in New York, 1897–1919," in this publication, p. 218.
91. Shortly after the turn of the century the neighborhood replaced Fourteenth Street and Ladies' Mile as the center for large retail establishments. Macy's and Gimbel Brothers opened their stores in 1904 and 1909, respectively, on Broadway between Thirty-second and Thirty-fifth Streets, just a block to the west; Fifth Avenue between Thirty-fourth and Thirty-seventh Streets became home to department stores B. Altman (1906–13), Arnold Constable (1914), and Lord and Taylor (1914); Jackson, *Encyclopedia of New York City,* pp. 327–28. By 1906 B. Altman and Company occupied most of the block between Thirty-fourth and Thirty-fifth Streets and between Fifth and Madison Avenues. M. Knoedler and Company remained on the northeast corner of Fifth Avenue at Thirty-fourth Street until 1911, when it moved up to 556 Fifth Avenue at Forty-sixth Street. Christopher Gray, ed., *Fifth Avenue, 1911, from Start to Finish in Historic Block-by-Block Photographs* (New York: Dover Publications, 1994), p. vii, pls. 32, 45.
92. Jackson, *Encyclopedia of New York City,* pp. 1232–33.
93. Hassam also painted *Union League Club,* 1893, watercolor (Union League Club, New York); used the Union League Club as the background in *Allied Flags, April 1917,* 1917 (private collection; illustrated in Fort 1988, p. 45); and included the University Club on Fifth Avenue in *Allies Day, May 1917* (fig. 232).
94. Ives 1892, p. 116.
95. Ibid.
96. This cabstand, seen from a slightly greater distance, also appears in *Winter Mist (Madison Square, looking south),* a watercolor reproduced in Hassam 1899 (unpaged); the obelisk commemorating Major General William Jenkins Worth is shown at the right. The cabstand is recorded in the foreground of Edward Steichen's photograph *The Flatiron* (fig. 213).
97. Ives 1892, p. 116.
98. According to Gerdts ("Three Themes," p. 146), "this area of New York—Broadway between Madison and Union Squares—was the first to be electrified, in 1880." Gerdts relies on Edward Robb Ellis, *The Epic of New York City: A Narrative History* (New York: Coward-McCann, 1966), p. 363,

and Bayrd Still, *Mirror for Gotham* (New York: University Press, 1956), p. 209.

99. Ives 1892, p. 116. Regarding *Cab Stand at Night, Madison Square,* curatorial notes, Smith College Museum of Art, Northampton, Massachusetts, indicate: "inscribed on back of panel, upside down, in pencil, across entire height and width of panel: *Electric Light* [illegible]." The same source adds that this painting may have been shown at the *13th Annual Exhibition* (New York: Society of American Artists, April 27–May 23, 1891), no. 113, *Electric Light*; and at *Exhibition and Private Sale of Paintings by Childe Hassam,* exh. cat. (Boston: Doll and Richards Gallery, March 1893), no. 17, *Effect of Electric Light on the Snow [Madison Square]*; and sold at American Art Association, New York, February 7, 1896, no. 123, *Effect of Electric Light on the Snow, Madison Square.* Hassam's painting appears as an illustration in Van Rensselaer, "Fifth Avenue, with Pictures by Hassam," p. 9. For recent discussions of the painting, see Deborah Chotner, catalogue entry in *Masterworks of American Painting and Sculpture from the Smith College Museum of Art,* edited by Linda Muehlig (New York: Hudson Hills Press in association with the Smith College Museum of Art, Northampton, Mass., 1999), pp. 116–18, and John Davis, catalogue entry in *The Smith College Museum of Art: European and American Painting and Sculpture, 1760–1960,* by John Davis and Jaroslaw Leshko (New York: Hudson Hills Press in association with the Smith College Museum of Art, Northampton, Mass., 2000), p. 172.

100. A noteworthy account of *Union Square in Spring* appears in John Davis, catalogue entry in Davis and Leshko, *Smith College Museum of Art,* p. 174.

101. Van Rensselaer, "Picturesque New York," p. 167.

102. The painting is reproduced as *Spring in Union Square, looking south* [sic] *from a tall building* in Hassam 1899 (unpaged). For offices of the Century Company, designed by Stanford White, see Arthur John, *Best Years of the Century: Richard Watson Gilder,* Scribner's Monthly, *and the* Century Magazine, *1870–1909* (Urbana: University of Illinois Press, 1981), pp. 140–41. The address is given in John F. Trow, *Trow's New York City Directory* (New York: Trow City Directory Co., 1885–86, 1890, and 1900). For Hassam's acquaintance with Richard Watson Gilder, editor of *The Century,* see n. 49, above.

103. "At just the time this work was painted, such facilities were receiving much publicity, reflecting the city's growing concern for public amenities," according to Gerdts, "Three Themes," p. 138, citing Committee of Seventy, New York, *Preliminary Report of Sub-Committee on Baths and Lavatories* (New York, 1895), and Albert Shaw, "The Higher Life of New York City," *Outlook,* January 25, 1896, p. 134.

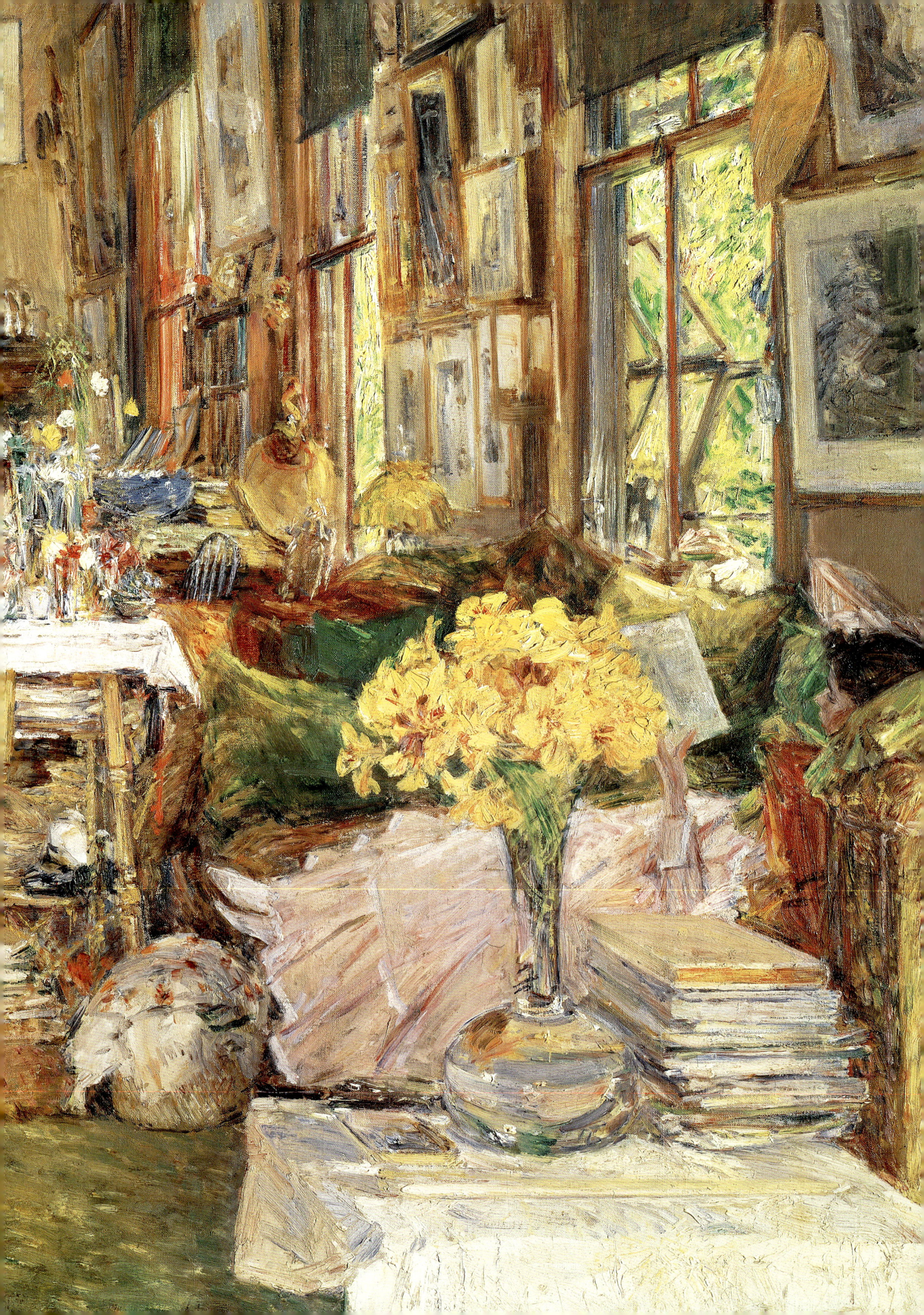

CHAPTER FOUR

Hassam in New England, 1889–1918

Susan G. Larkin

When Hassam settled in New York on his return from Europe in 1889, he resumed the summer painting excursions along the New England shore that he had initiated as a young artist starting out in Boston. He spent the warm months of nearly every year roaming that coast until he purchased his own country home in East Hampton on New York's Long Island in 1919. In scores of paintings, drawings, pastels, watercolors, and etchings, he expressed and promoted prevailing cultural values, especially the widely shared conviction that New England represented the essence of America.[1] Hassam identified personally with that heritage. He prided himself on his family's deep New England roots, which he believed made him more truly American than later arrivals. Echoing Ulysses S. Grant's exclamation "I am an American!" Hassam declared, "I would rather have that said of me than anything else. And I believe I have more right to say it than most people."[2] Although Hassam considered the old sections of New York "not so interesting as the new,"[3] it was the old in New England that kept him coming back year after year.

Hassam's desire for stimulating companionship narrowed his choices of painting sites. In a letter from Paris he confessed that he missed the glorious sunsets at the Isles of Shoals but added, "the surroundings of pleasant people is equal always to that of nature."[4] At the Shoals, as in Cos Cob, Old Lyme, and Gloucester, Hassam joined enclaves of artists who energized his work and enriched his leisure. Although he protested later that he had visited Old Lyme "in the fall before the artists got there and after they had left," photographs taken there—like others from Appledore in the Isles of Shoals and Cos Cob—show him surrounded by smiling colleagues.[5]

A healthful environment, escape from the city's heat, and recreation were also powerful attractions. An advertisement of the 1890s for the Isles of Shoals played to those motivations, promising an ideal "rest cure" in a clean, quiet resort with an average midday temperature of sixty-five degrees, "perfectly safe bathing and, of course, boating and tennis."[6] Hassam loved swimming, a pastime that somewhat offset his voracious enjoyment of good food. Like visitors to New England since the Pilgrims, he savored seafood fresh from the Atlantic. At Appledore he claimed to "eat the north side of a haddock for breakfast a bucket of fish chowder for dinner and a few broiled live lobsters for supper."[7] In Cos Cob he got into the kitchen himself to make "a real Boston clam chowder" for a party at the Holley House.[8]

Play was important to the gregarious Hassam, but work governed his New England sojourns. He seems never to have visited a place solely for vacation; instead, recreation and companionship complemented days of productive activity. Above all, Hassam sought subject matter in New England. Ignoring, for the most part, evidence of change or modernity, he captured on his canvases picturesque villages, white-columned churches, old-fashioned gardens, demure women, and rugged seacoasts. Such themes represented qualities Hassam cherished and struck a chord with potential collectors who discerned in them assurance of enduring values.

Hassam found those collectors, more frequently than has been recognized, at the same places in which he worked. In most of the sites we will consider in this chapter, he enjoyed opportunities to exhibit and sell his pictures. The galleries that are as common as clam shacks in seaside resorts today had their precedents in a variety of improvised art venues a century ago.

Detail, fig. 118. *The Room of Flowers*

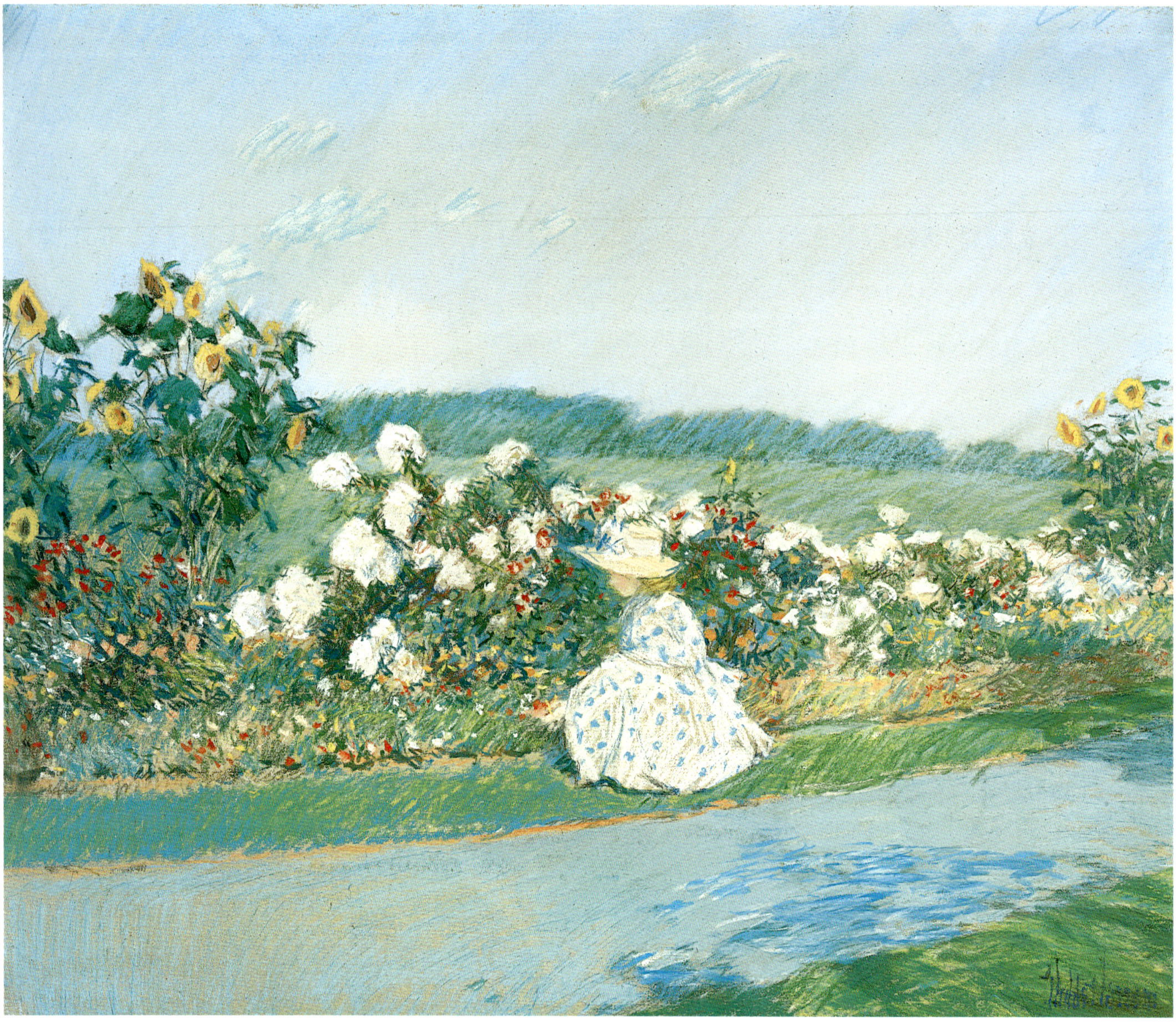

Fig. 113. Childe Hassam. *Summertime*, 1891. Pastel on canvas, 20 x 24 in. (50.8 x 61 cm). Private collection

These summer outlets supplemented the winter season in urban galleries, enabling artists to market their work year-round.

While tradition, congenial companionship, recreation, subject matter, and, to varying degrees, marketing opportunities were offered in all the New England places Hassam favored, each of them claimed a distinct identity. Appledore was an island resort; Cos Cob, a rustic village; Gloucester, a commercial seaport. In depicting them Hassam created a composite portrait of New England. Only a few of his pictures resist identification by locale. *A Country Road* (fig. 328) distills classic Yankee elements—elm tree, brook, horse and buggy on a dirt road—in a generalized image redolent of a rural hamlet. *Summertime* (fig. 113), with a little girl in her Sunday best kneeling to admire blossoms, could represent a flower-bordered driveway on almost any suburban estate. However, most of Hassam's New England views are site-specific, as are the titles he gave them.

The Isles of Shoals, a cluster of rocky islands nine miles off the New Hampshire and Maine coast, attracted Hassam from about 1886 until about 1916.[9] That thirty-year span saw him develop from a twenty-four-year-old embarking on a career to one of the most famous artists in America. Hassam's sojourns on the Isles of Shoals contributed greatly to this success.

On Appledore, the largest of the islands, a hotel owned by the Laighton family accommodated four hundred guests. Poet Celia Laighton Thaxter (fig. 114), who helped her

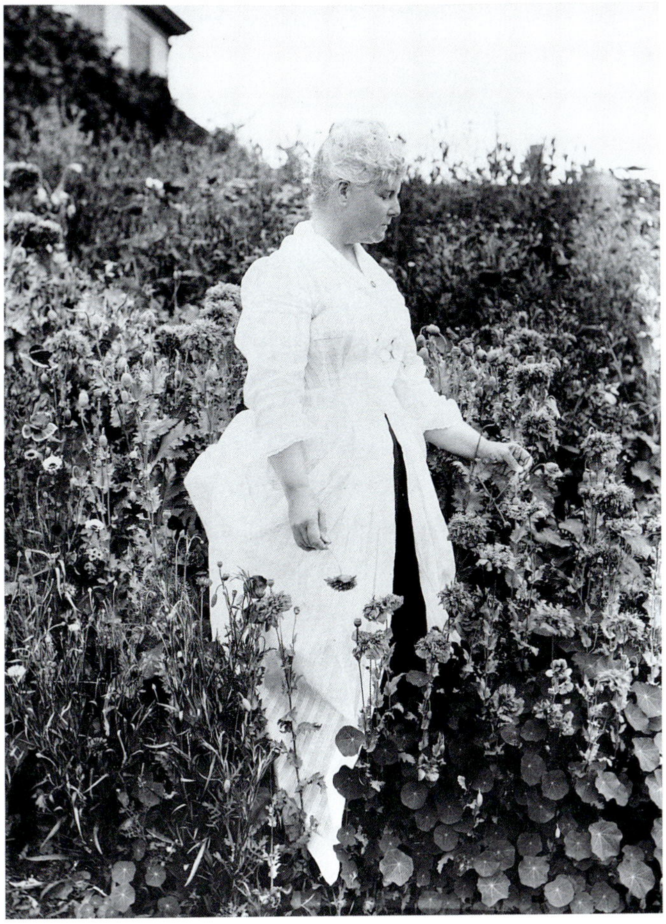

brothers manage Appledore House, hosted a lively salon of writers, artists, and musicians on the island from the 1860s. Among those who visited her at the Shoals were Hassam's distant relatives novelist Nathaniel Hawthorne and painter William Morris Hunt. Hassam recalled later that he met Thaxter, twenty-five years his senior, in Boston when he was "not much past twenty."[10] They perhaps were introduced by Hassam's painter friend Ross Sterling Turner, who frequented Appledore. Hassam sketched Thaxter's winter home in Kittery, Maine, in 1881, substituted for Turner as her watercolor instructor in 1883 (when he may have first visited Appledore), and illustrated some of her publications by 1884. On her shrewd advice, he dropped his first name, Frederick, to exploit the marketing advantage of Childe, his unusual middle name.[11] By the time Hassam made his first documented visit to the Shoals, in 1886, he and Thaxter had established both an emotional and a professional bond that would last until her death, in 1894.

Fig. 114. Celia Thaxter in her garden, ca. 1892. Courtesy Portsmouth Athenaeum, New Hampshire

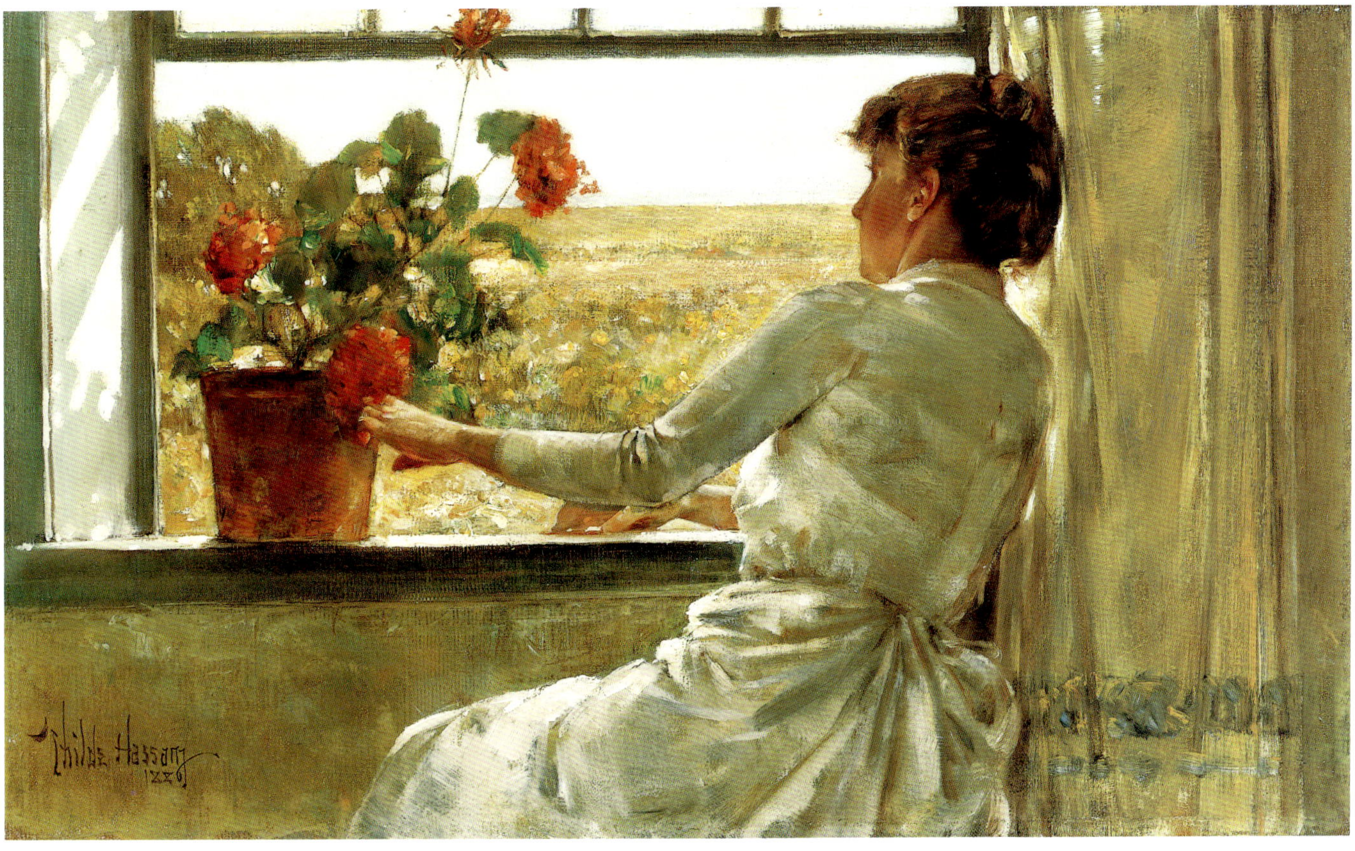

Fig. 115. Childe Hassam. *Summer Evening*, 1886. Oil on canvas, 12⅛ x 20⅜ in. (30.8 x 51.8 cm). Florence Griswold Museum, Old Lyme, Connecticut; Gift of the Hartford Steam Boiler Inspection and Insurance Company

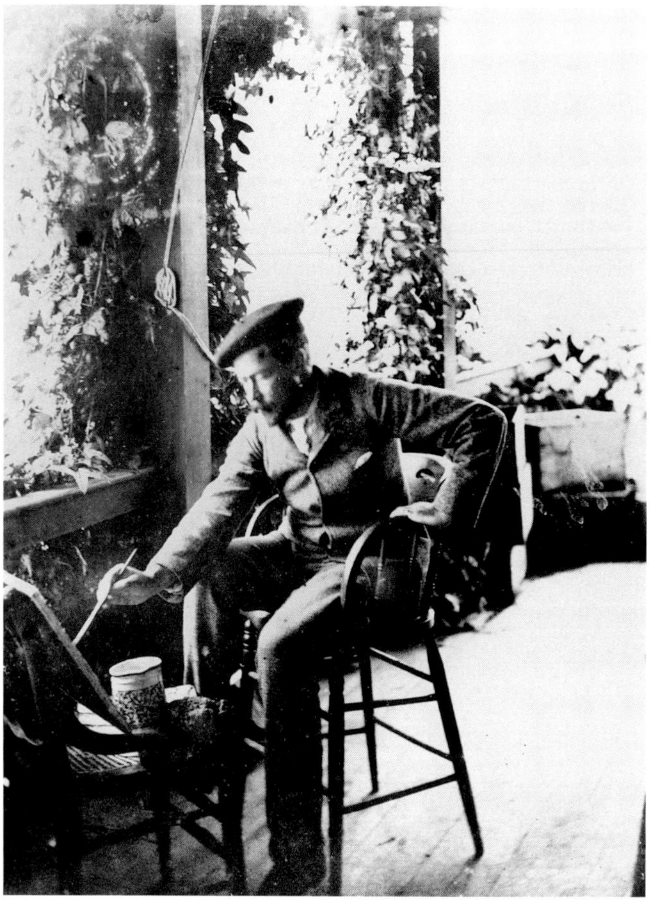

Fig. 116. Karl Thaxter. Hassam painting on Celia Thaxter's porch, ca. 1886. Courtesy Portsmouth Athenaeum, New Hampshire

Appledore was heavily populated during the summer. Thaxter advised her friend the writer William Dean Howells to "come early in the season, because after July Fourth every corner of the Islands will be crowded full, so that there will not be a single nook in which I can find a place for you. . . . From early July until September, there is a chaos of humanity let loose upon Appledore."[12] None of that "chaos of humanity" appears in the hundreds of oils, watercolors, and pastels Hassam produced at the Isles of Shoals. *Summer Evening* (fig. 115), dated 1886, sets out three of the themes that would occupy him there during the next three decades: flowers, the female figure, and the sea. In *Summer Evening* Hassam used the window to establish a geometric framework for his composition and, in a manner recalling devices of Japanese woodblock prints and the etchings of James McNeill Whistler, set up oppositions between foreground and distance, shadow and light. The model, who resembles his wife, Maud Doane Hassam, shelters in the cool, shady interior; only her hands venture into the glaring sun. The potted geranium—a tender plant, needing special protection to survive in the Shoals' harsh climate—is both counterbalance and equivalent to the young woman. Its rosy blossoms and diagonal slant echo her complexion and posture. Beyond the open window an expansive field stretches to the

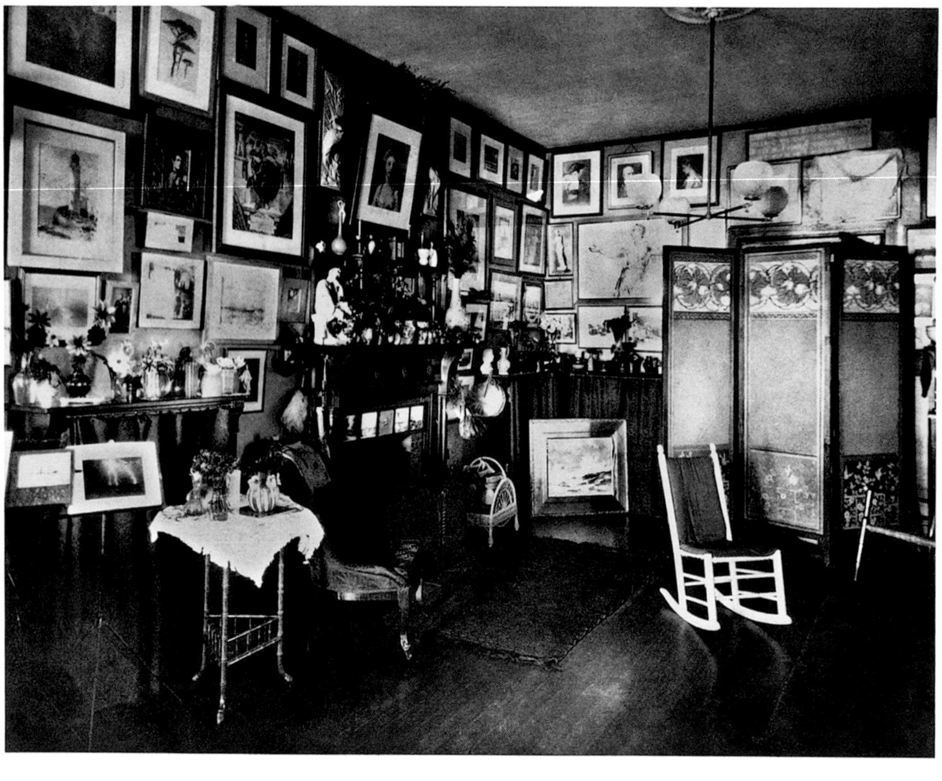

Fig. 117. Celia Thaxter's parlor. Courtesy Portsmouth Athenaeum, New Hampshire

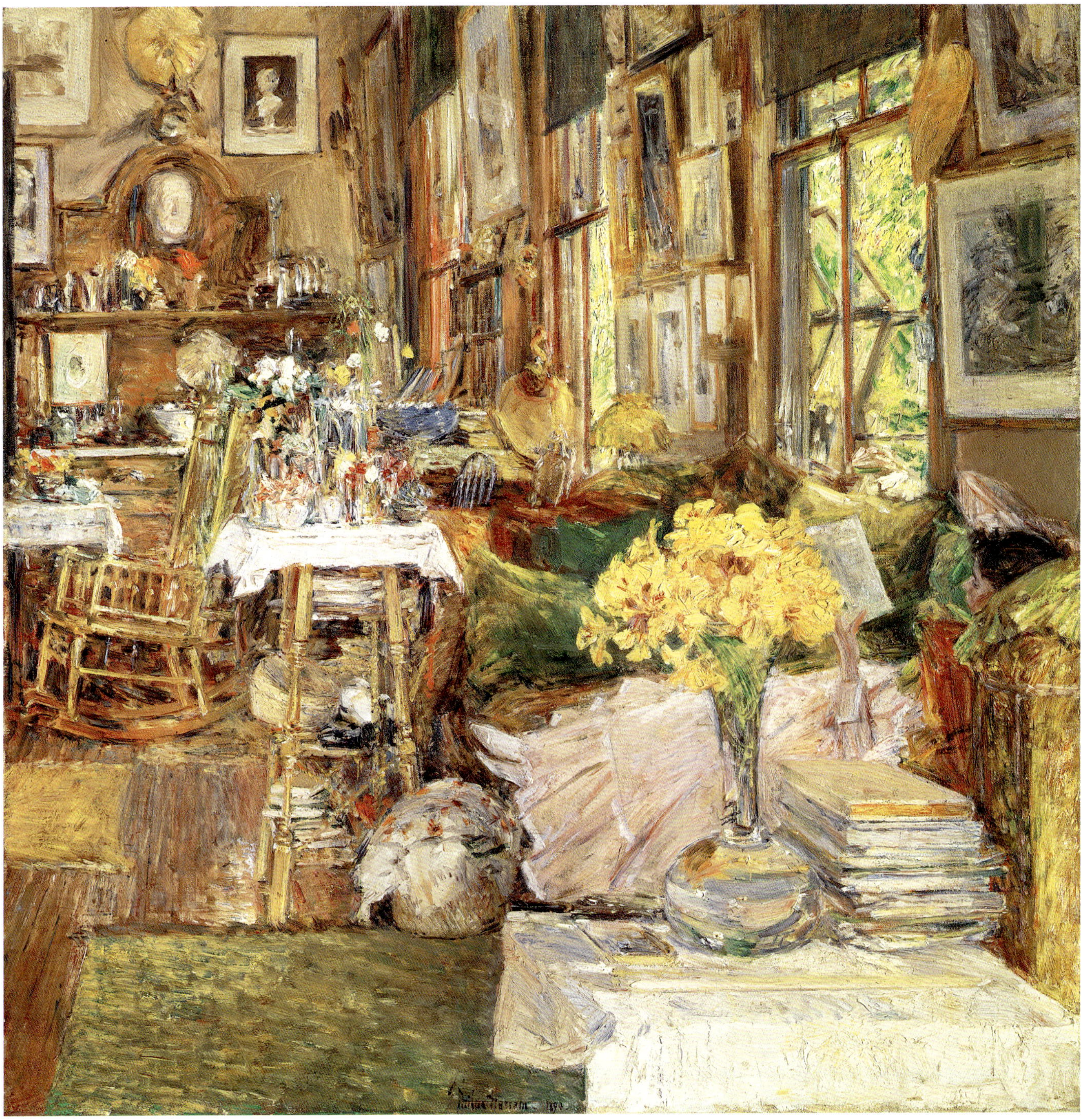

Fig. 118. Childe Hassam. *The Room of Flowers,* 1894. Oil on canvas, 34 x 34 in. (86.4 x 86.4 cm). Private collection

sea, dotted with tiny white sails. In contrast to the hermetic New York interiors Hassam would paint two decades later, this room—like those he would subsequently depict in Connecticut—seems a pleasant retreat in which the woman retains her connection to nature.

Hassam may have worked on *Summer Evening* in Celia Thaxter's cottage, where her son Karl photographed him painting on the porch about 1886 (fig. 116).[13] Thaxter could accommodate ten or twelve paying guests in her house next door to the hotel. Most were musicians, writers, or painters, but occasionally she extended the privilege of lodging with her to others. One young woman, visiting the island with her parents, recalled that she "nearly died of joy when, the second day after my meeting her, [Thaxter] said, 'Child, I like you! You may come and stay here in my cottage—I believe there is one empty room left.'"[14] In addition to those who roomed at Thaxter's house, "favored guests from the cottages and hotel" could join the inner circle for mornings and evenings

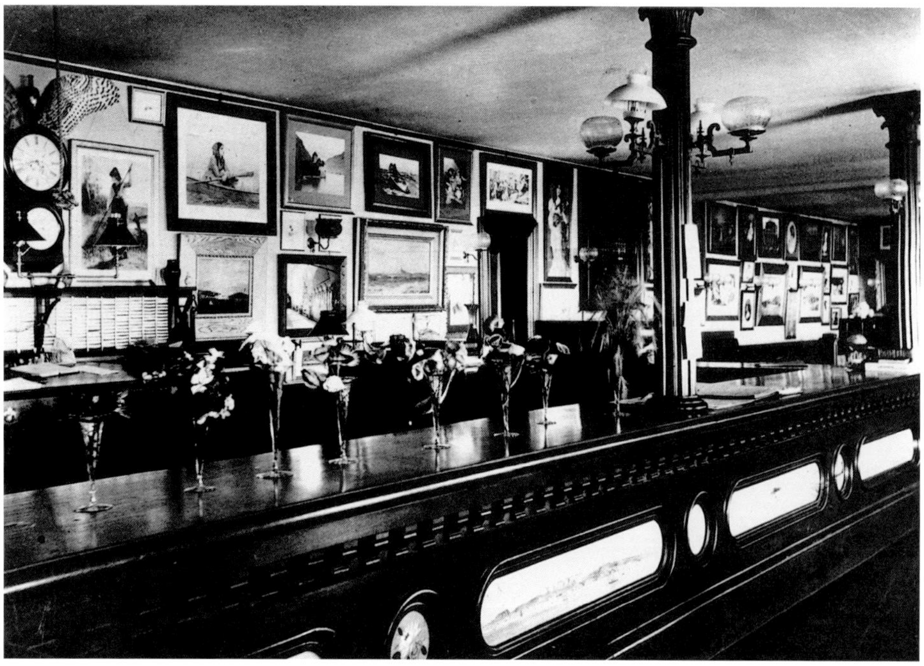

Fig. 119. The Appledore House lobby and desk. Collection of the Vaughn Cottage Memorial Library and Museum, Isles of Shoals, Star Island Corporation, Portsmouth, New Hampshire

of music, readings, and conversation.[15] Celia Thaxter's parlor (fig. 117) was, one visitor wrote, "a fitting framework for musicales and conversations. With walls literally covered with pictures . . . , with the desk of the poet in one corner and her table filled with materials for china and water-color painting at a window, with flowers banked upon the mantel-piece and in jars and vases upon tables and shelves, with books and bric-a-brac, music and open piano, it is as pleasant a summer parlor as one could wish."[16]

Hassam depicted the famous parlor in his masterly oil *The Room of Flowers* (fig. 118). The square canvas explodes with flowers, books, and pictures, all splashed with sunlight pouring through uncurtained windows. Beethoven's death mask hanging over the sideboard evokes the musicales held every morning, when guests rushed for comfortable seats to enjoy the piano compositions of the Romantics. Here, however, Hassam captures a solitary moment: a young woman reclines on a sofa, absorbed in a book. For her the parlor is a place of liberating comfort, where she can put up her feet and lose herself in the world of ideas and imagination.

Celia Thaxter's parlor is one of the most celebrated interiors in American cultural history. It was, as many have remarked, a place where art of various types was produced and enjoyed; few have noticed that it was also a place where art was sold. The aura Thaxter created was essential to the latter function. An acquaintance recalled that the poet was "not very polite to strangers unless they came introduced, or if they played or wrote or did something else interesting."[17] That exclusivity

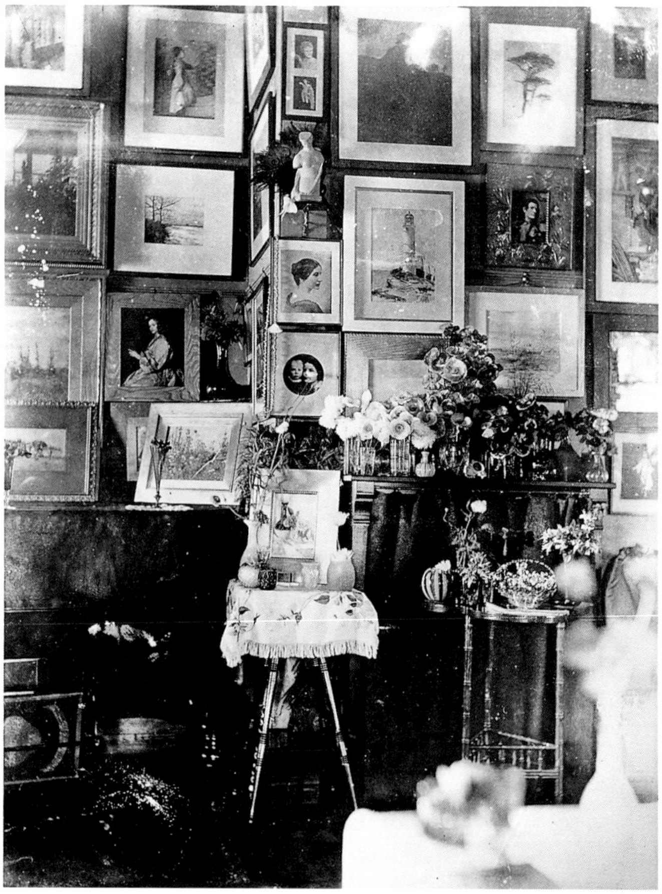

Fig. 120. A corner of Celia Thaxter's parlor, Appledore Island, ca. 1890. University of New Hampshire, Durham, Isles of Shoals Collection, courtesy of Rosamond Thaxter

Fig. 121. Childe Hassam. *The Altar and Shrine*, 1892. Watercolor on paper, 15½ x 12¼ in. (39.4 x 31.1 cm). Private collection, loaned courtesy Spanierman Gallery, New York

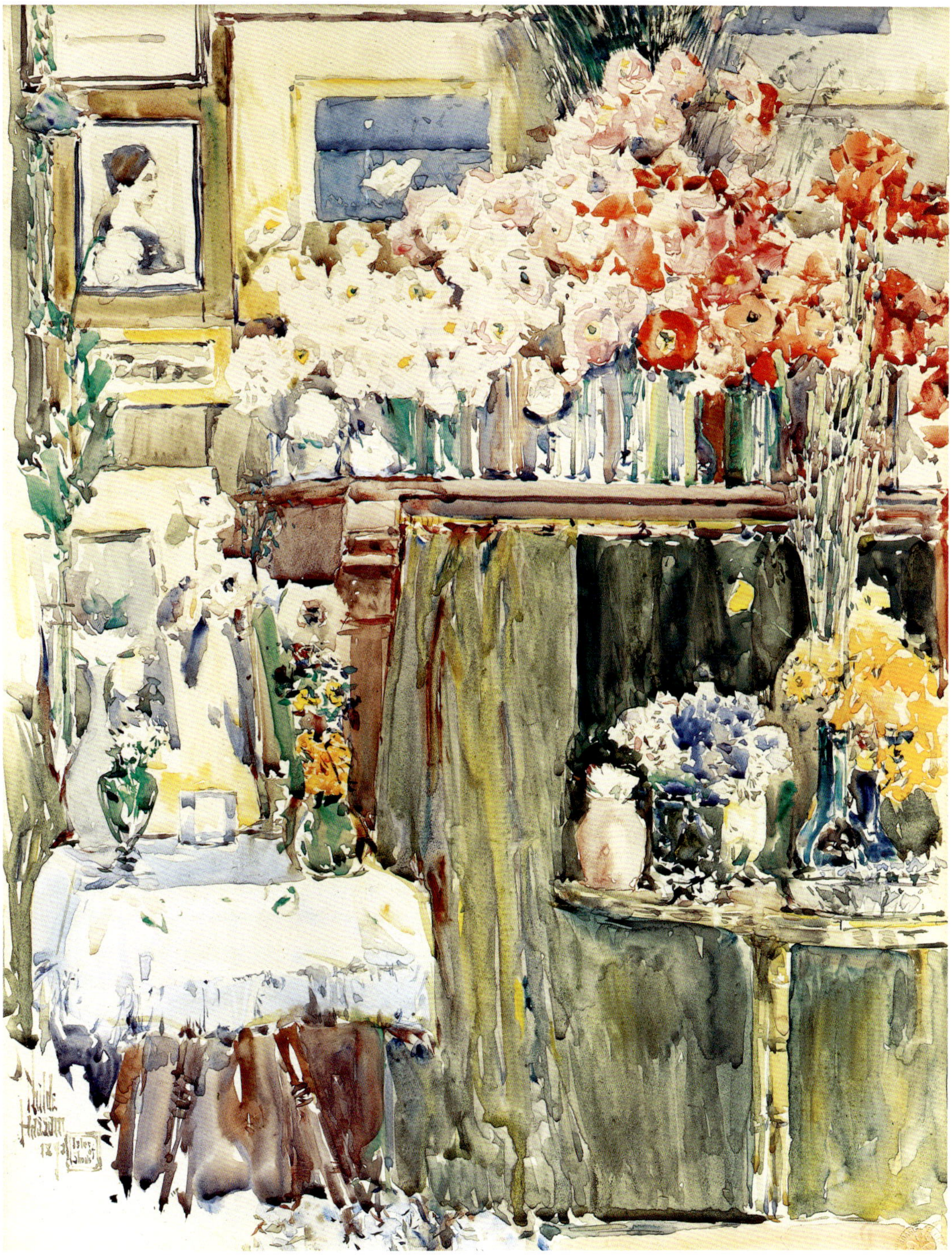

made an invitation to her parlor all the more coveted. Moreover, a strict protocol heightened the rarefied atmosphere. One regular described the morning routine:

> *You were not supposed to go up and speak to Mrs. Thaxter when you entered, as she was always busy with her sketching, illustrating her books printed on water color paper, which were often sold for fifty dollars before she could finish them. The guests slipped quietly into a cushioned window seat, or an old-fashioned chair, and were soon lost in admiration of some new picture placed upon the easel by the artist for Mrs. Thaxter's criticism, and with the privilege of purchase by the guests. Meanwhile William Mason or John K. Payne would be transporting us into musical heights.*[18]

Even the flowers were for sale. "At first, the garden was started entirely for pleasure," that same visitor related, "but in after years it became quite a source of revenue, as the hotel guests gladly availed themselves of the privilege to possess the lovely corsage bouquets arranged by her own hands."[19] So crucial were Celia Thaxter's parlor and garden in attracting visitors to Appledore that her brothers' hotel failed after her death.[20]

In an era when few women of her class earned an independent income, Thaxter supported herself not only by writing and by selling bouquets but also by selling her painted china and illuminated manuscripts. The souvenirs of Thaxter's aesthetic environment that guests were privileged to acquire extended to the paintings she displayed on an easel and propped up around the room.[21] She reminded Turner, who was preparing for a visit, "You must not forget to bring frames and mats and have one of your pictures always for sale in my room, on the easel, and others beside. That is the place where they will sell best, because so many eyes will see them."[22] The hotel lobby may have served as an adjunct gallery. A photograph (fig. 119) shows the desk decorated with flower arrangements like Thaxter's and the wall densely hung with pictures, one of which (second from the left, bottom row) might be by Hassam.

When the commercial gallery system in the United States was still in its infancy, Celia Thaxter's parlor was an important outlet for her artist friends. A visitor to the parlor in July 1893 wrote to a friend, "Childe Hassam has some very fine pictures over there."[23] A photograph of a corner of the room (fig. 120), taken about 1890, shows three works by Hassam: a pastel of Celia Thaxter's garden stands on the piano, a watercolor of the White Island lighthouse hangs on the wall, and a minimalist seascape appears under the picture of the lighthouse.[24]

Hassam depicted the same corner in the watercolor *The Altar and Shrine* (fig. 121). In the watercolor, as in the photograph, flower-filled vases are set on three surfaces: the top of a low, curtained bookcase; a small cloth-covered table to its left; and a small bamboo table to the right. In *An Island Garden,* published in 1894 with illustrations by Hassam—including *The Altar and Shrine*—Thaxter wrote about the enormous effort it took to achieve the studied informality of her arrangements. To create the "roseate cloud" of Shirley poppies atop the bookcase, she arose at dawn to cut the flowers while they were still covered with dew. Back in the parlor, she arranged the blossoms in thirty-two vases, working from left to right in chromatic sequence. She described the effect: "The color gathers, softly flushing from the snow white at one end, through all rose, pink, cherry, and crimson shades, to the note of darkest red."[25]

The Sonata (fig. 122) probably was not painted at Appledore, but its combination of music, art, and flowers evokes the aesthetic atmosphere of the place that enchanted Hassam and others in Thaxter's circle. Hassam exhibited *The Sonata* under two different titles: *Beethoven's Sonata Appassionata* in his March 1929 retrospective in Buffalo and *The Maréchal Niel Rose* at the American Academy of Arts and Letters in New York in November 1930. Beethoven was Celia Thaxter's favorite composer, and his Sonata in F Minor, popularly called the "Appassionata," is considered to represent the epitome of his heroic style.[26] The tempestuous piece culminates in a frenzied finale that might explain the subtly erotic exhaustion of Hassam's young model. The snuffed candle and overblown rose augment the sense of spent emotion. Although the Maréchal Niel rose probably did not grow at Appledore, two yellow tea roses Hassam sketched for an illustration in *An Island Garden* (fig. 123) have that variety's heavy voluptuousness.[27]

Hassam signed *The Sonata* in the corner of the picture shown hanging over the piano. That picture-within-the-picture resembles several nocturnes he produced at Appledore, especially *The Evening Star* (fig. 124). With the simplest of means Hassam suggested the vast night sky, punctuated only by a single star, and the star's reflection in the calm water. He created the starlit sea and the darker sky with energetic slanting strokes of blue pastel. A dot represents Venus; a vertical series of short, curved dashes traces its path across the water. In his economy Hassam surpassed even Whistler, whose influence is evident here. By comparison with *The Evening Star,* Whistler's *Nocturne: Blue and Silver—Battersea Reach* (fig. 125) is packed with information: not only a star but also a barge, factory smokestacks, a church steeple, and artificial lights dotting the riverbank.

The Evening Star, dated 1891, may be the pastel Hassam exhibited in Boston that autumn as *Eternity.*[28] Reporters described *Eternity* in terms that perfectly match *The Evening Star.* One observed, "It is a calm peaceful scene of a placid sea and cloudless sky. One star alone sheds a ray of light, and, reflected in the water beneath, is the only break to the otherwise endless stretch of blue sea and bluer sky."[29] Nothing else in the exhibition attracted as much attention. The title encouraged viewers to seek symbolism in the unorthodox composition. "Blue, endless sea, blue, deep, vibrating sky, a track of far-reaching light on the water . . . these things probably come as near to representing eternity as anything else that an artist can attain to," one critic wrote.[30] "The picture is remarkable and grows upon you as you gaze until you seem to be looking indeed into eternity," another commented.[31] A third called the pastel one of Hassam's

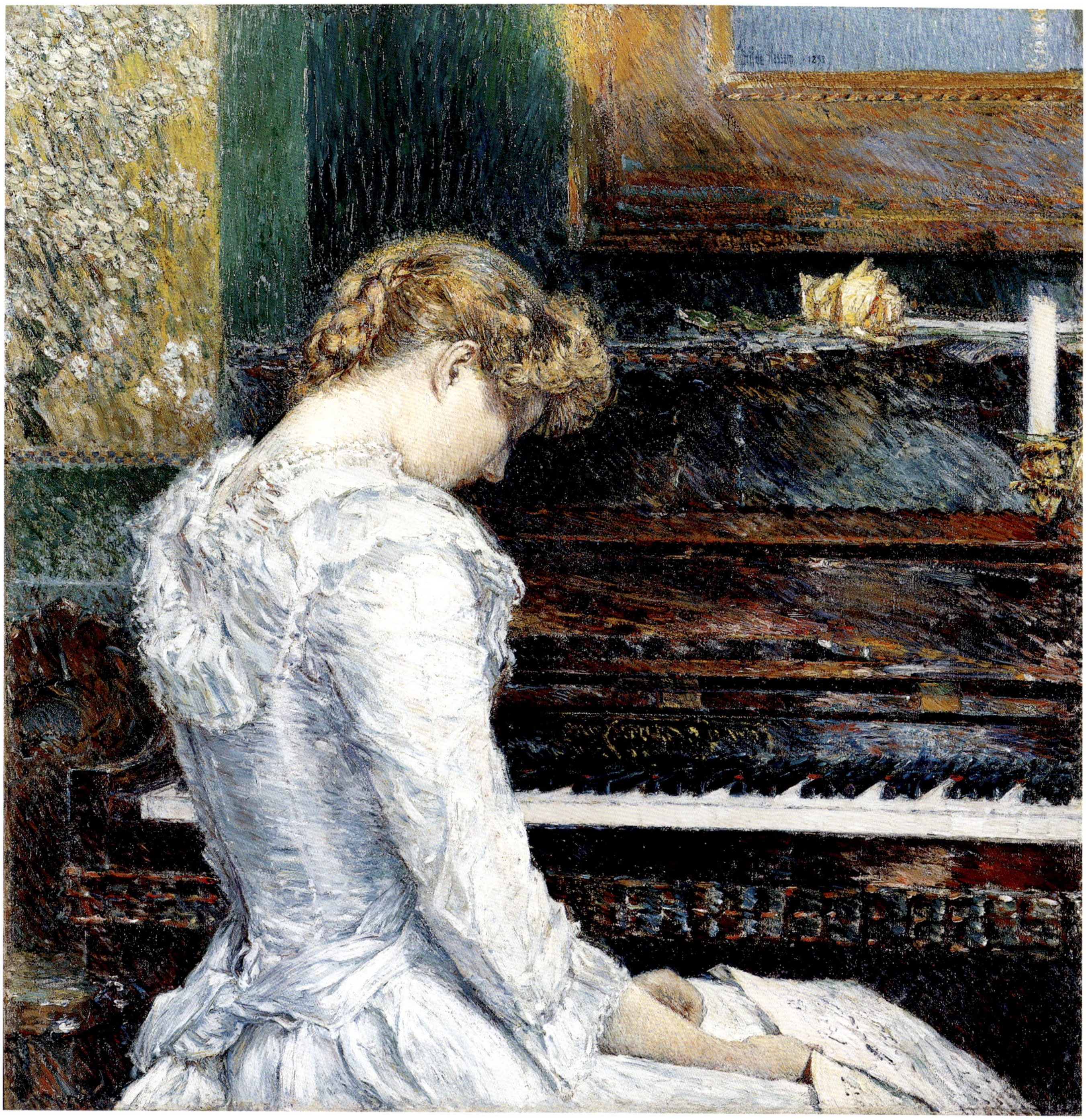

Fig. 122. Childe Hassam. *The Sonata,* 1893. Oil on canvas, 32 x 32 in. (81.3 x 81.3 cm). The Nelson-Atkins Museum of Art, Kansas City, Missouri (Gift of Mr. and Mrs. Joseph S. Atha) 52-5

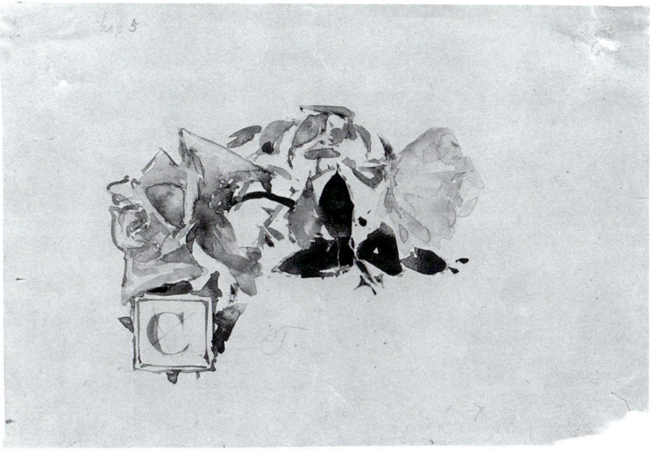

Fig. 123. Childe Hassam. *Tea Roses,* headpiece in Celia Thaxter's *An Island Garden* (Boston, 1894). Photograph. Boston Public Library, Print Department

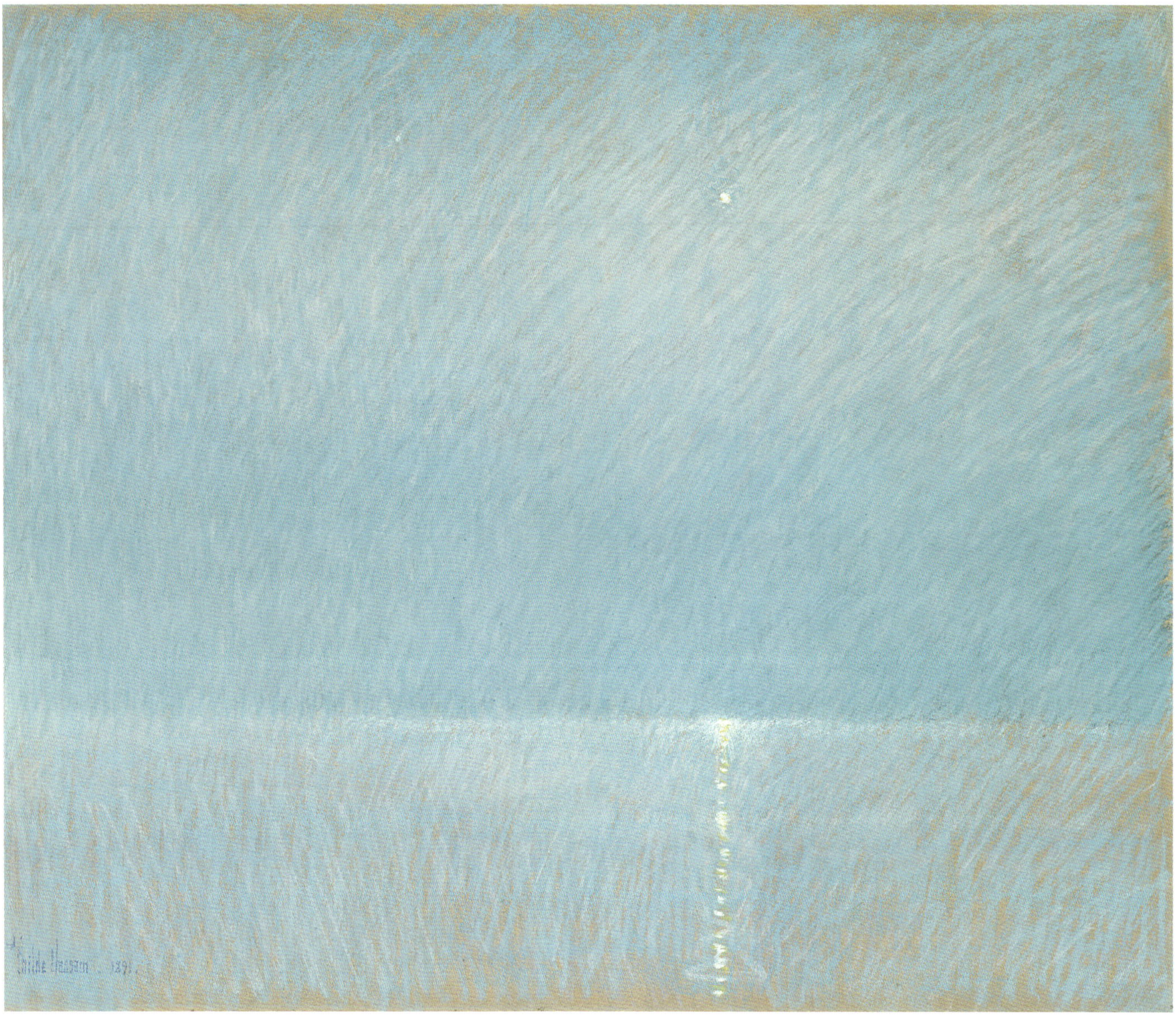

Fig. 124. Childe Hassam. *The Evening Star,* 1891. Pastel on tan paper, 20 x 24 in. (50.8 x 61 cm). Yale Collection of American Literature, Beinecke Rare Book and Manuscript Library, New Haven

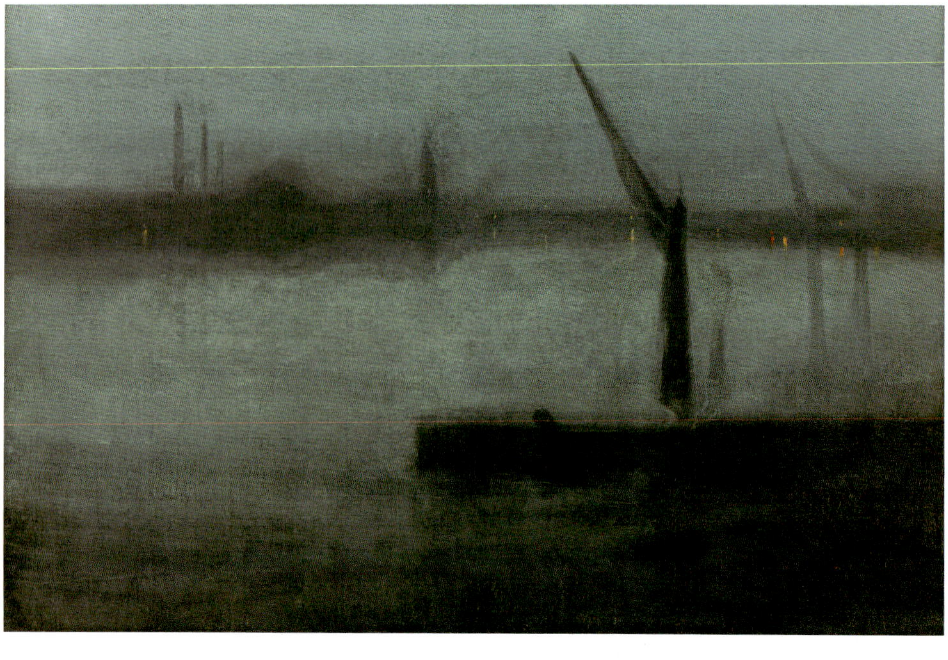

Fig. 125. James McNeill Whistler. *Nocturne: Blue and Silver—Battersea Reach,* ca. 1870–75. Oil on canvas, 19⅝ x 30⅛ in. (49.8 x 76.5 cm). Freer Gallery of Art, Smithsonian Institution, Washington, D.C.: Gift of Charles Lang Freer F1902.97

"specimens of audacity" that may "startle old fogies" and irreverently proposed "Blue Monday" as an alternate title.[32]

Sunlight, not starlight, illuminates the paintings and drawings of Thaxter's garden that Hassam produced between about 1889 and 1894. The poet defied the island's poor soil and harsh winds to create what she called in one of her verses "a tiny space of tangled bloom."[33] She fenced a fifteen-by-fifty-foot plot in front of her house, edged rectangular beds with boards, and covered every vertical surface with vines. A photograph of her cottage (fig. 126) reveals the surprisingly small size of the fenced garden and the barrenness of the surrounding landscape. The garden was set within a densely built environment, next door to the sprawling three-story hotel and behind a tennis court (fig. 127). But Hassam disguised the limited size and crowded environs of Thaxter's garden by excluding all buildings from his paintings of it. The red barn in the background of *Flower Garden* (fig. 128) indicates that it is not the poet's plot that is depicted, although she may have supplied the white lilies and blue larkspur, a combination she favored. Like most gardeners, Thaxter enjoyed sharing plants. One sunny morning she rowed to a nearby island, her dory loaded with seedlings to give her neighbors.[34]

Hassam captured the luxuriance Thaxter introduced to the windswept island in *The Garden in Its Glory* (fig. 129). He sat with his watercolor pad just outside the open gate, where the land slopes gently to the sea, and looked through the narrow garden up at Thaxter and her small grandson enshrined in the cottage doorway. Vines smother the trellis and clamber over the porch; hollyhocks shoot up beside the gate; coreopsis and poppies spill over the path. More poppies blaze outside the enclosure and sweet peas cloak the rough board fence.

In its varied colors, heights, and textures, the garden contrasted dramatically with the rocky landscape. Hassam exploited that contrast. *In the Garden (Celia Thaxter in Her Garden)* (fig. 130) sets the flowery space that swirls around the white-haired, white-gowned poet against the open sea and sky. Thaxter (tall and stately, but more slender in Hassam's portrayal than she was in fact) stands within the garden: she is "the goddess of Appledore."[35] Masses of vibrant poppies, accented by coreopsis, dianthuses, and roses, reach nearly to the waist of this horticultural deity. Hassam preserved the spatial distinction between her Yankee paradise and the world beyond by showing only seed heads on the poppies outside the gate.

Hassam usually disguised the garden's underpinnings. *Home of the Hummingbird* (fig. 131) is a rare exception, recording the vertical supports for the string, netting, or chicken wire that protected and staked the plants. In the pastel *Poppies, Isles of Shoals* (fig. 132) and the watercolor *Flower Garden, Isles of Shoals* (fig. 133), on the other hand, the low, close-up viewpoint hides any hint of human intervention. Such images prompted the misconception that wildflowers are represented. On the contrary, Thaxter painstakingly cultivated her flowers, starting seedlings in eggshells, importing toads to devour insect pests, and rising in the middle of the night to ring plants with slug-deterring lime.

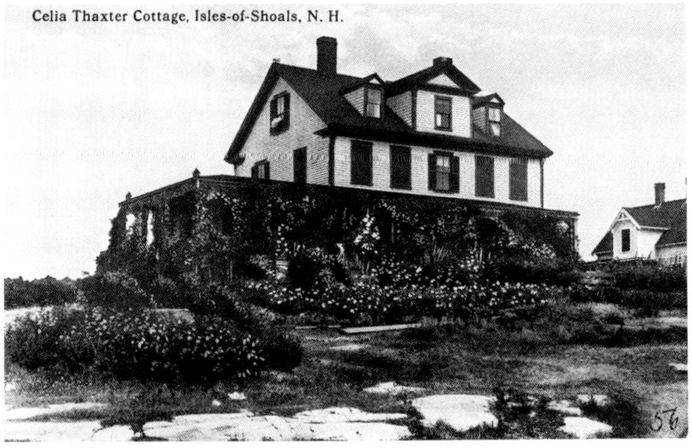

Fig. 126. Celia Thaxter's cottage, Isles of Shoals, ca. 1887. Courtesy Portsmouth Athenaeum, New Hampshire

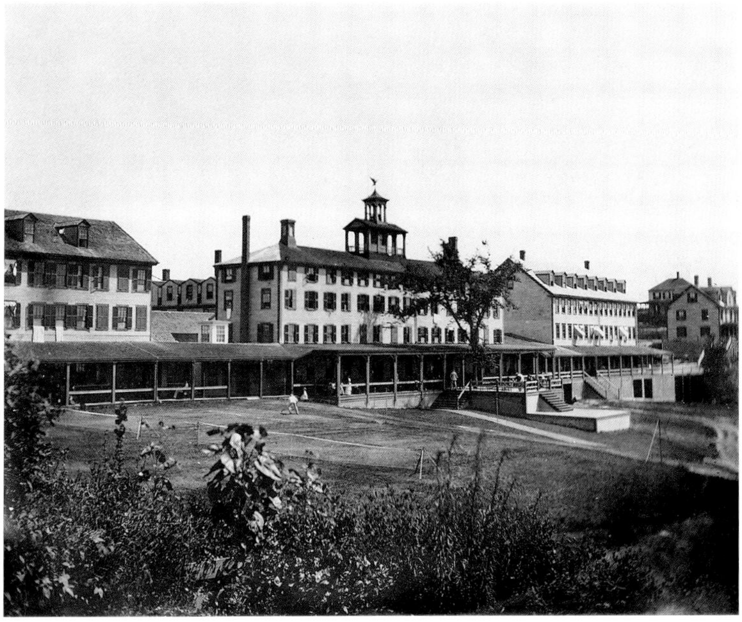

Fig. 127. Karl Thaxter. Appledore House from Celia Thaxter's cottage, ca. 1890. Courtesy Portsmouth Athenaeum, New Hampshire

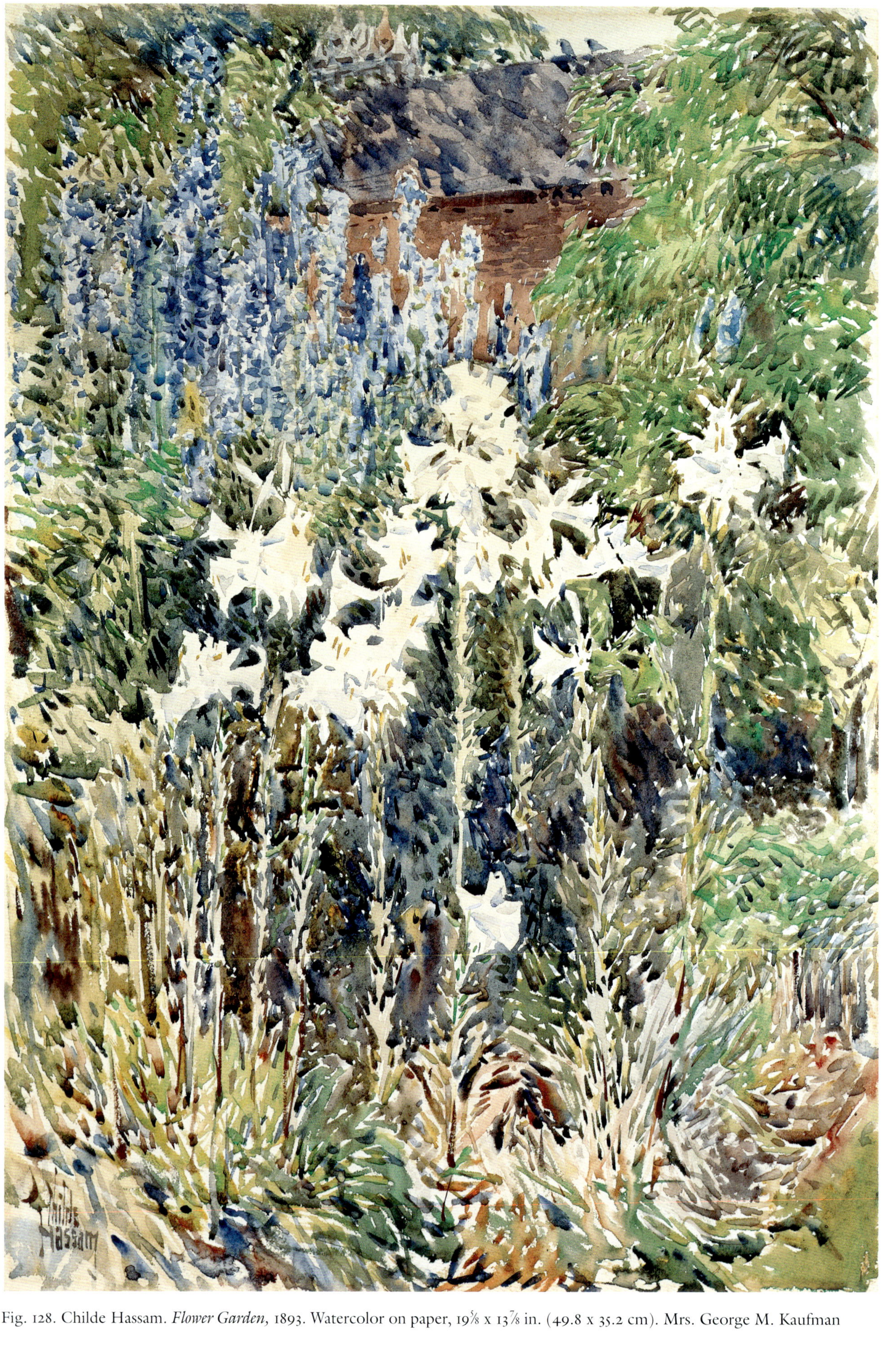

Fig. 128. Childe Hassam. *Flower Garden,* 1893. Watercolor on paper, $19\frac{5}{8}$ x $13\frac{7}{8}$ in. (49.8 x 35.2 cm). Mrs. George M. Kaufman

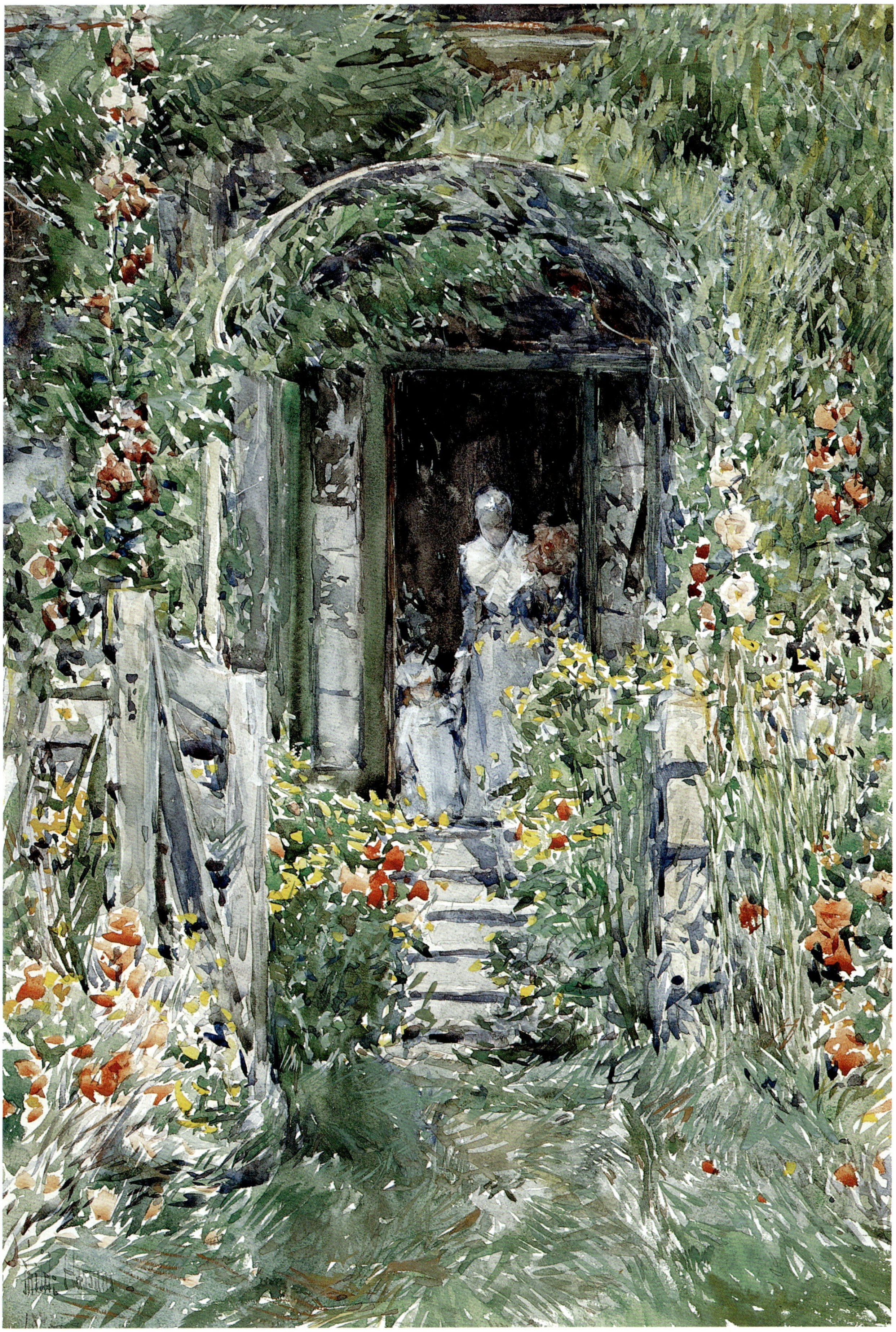

Fig. 129. Childe Hassam. *The Garden in Its Glory*, 1892. Watercolor on paper, 19⅞ x 13⅞ in. (50.5 x 35.2 cm). Smithsonian American Art Museum, Washington, D.C. Gift of John Gellatly

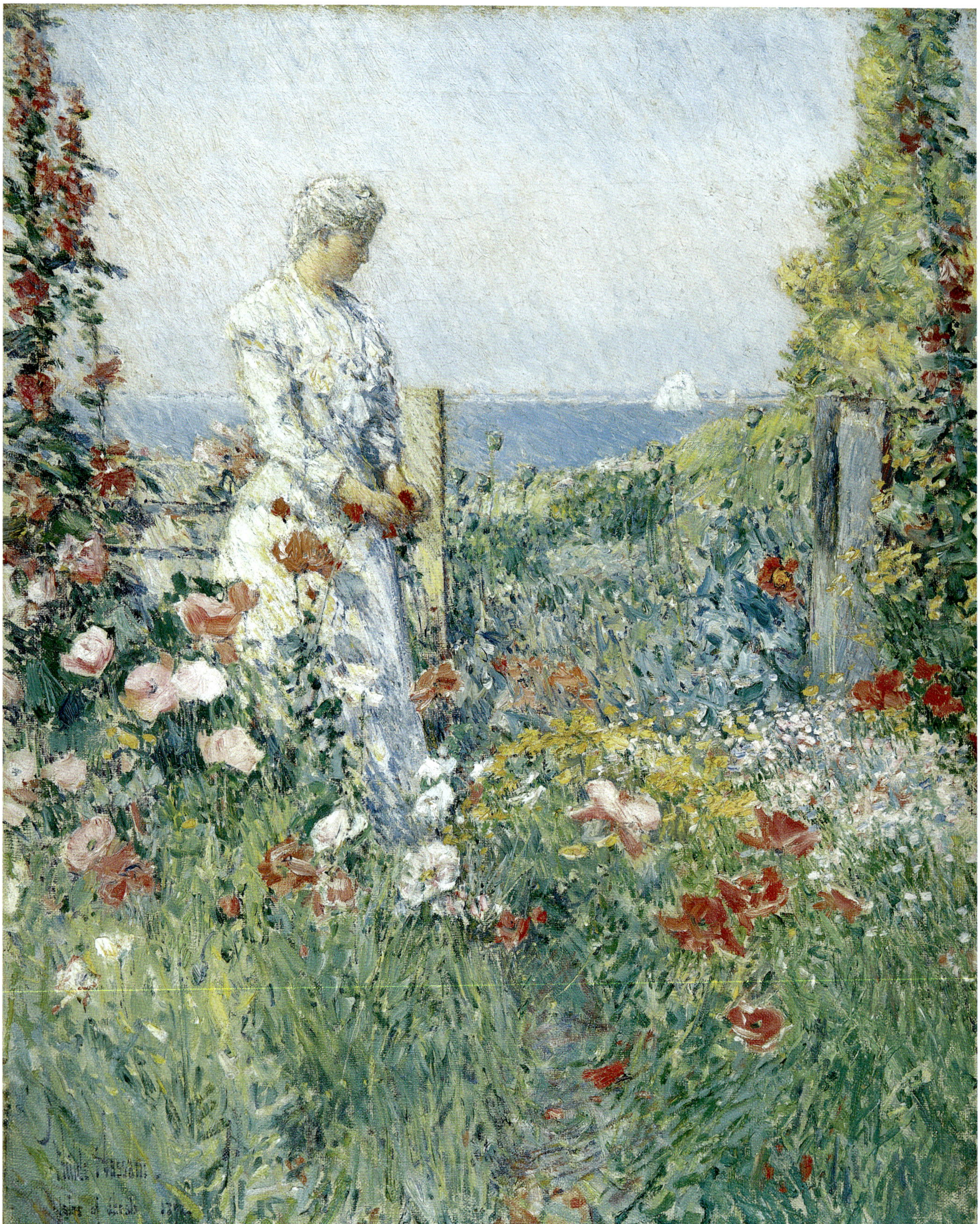

Fig. 130. Childe Hassam. *In the Garden (Celia Thaxter in Her Garden),* 1892. Oil on canvas, 22¼ x 18 in. (56.5 x 45.7 cm). Smithsonian American Art Museum, Washington, D.C. Gift of John Gellatly

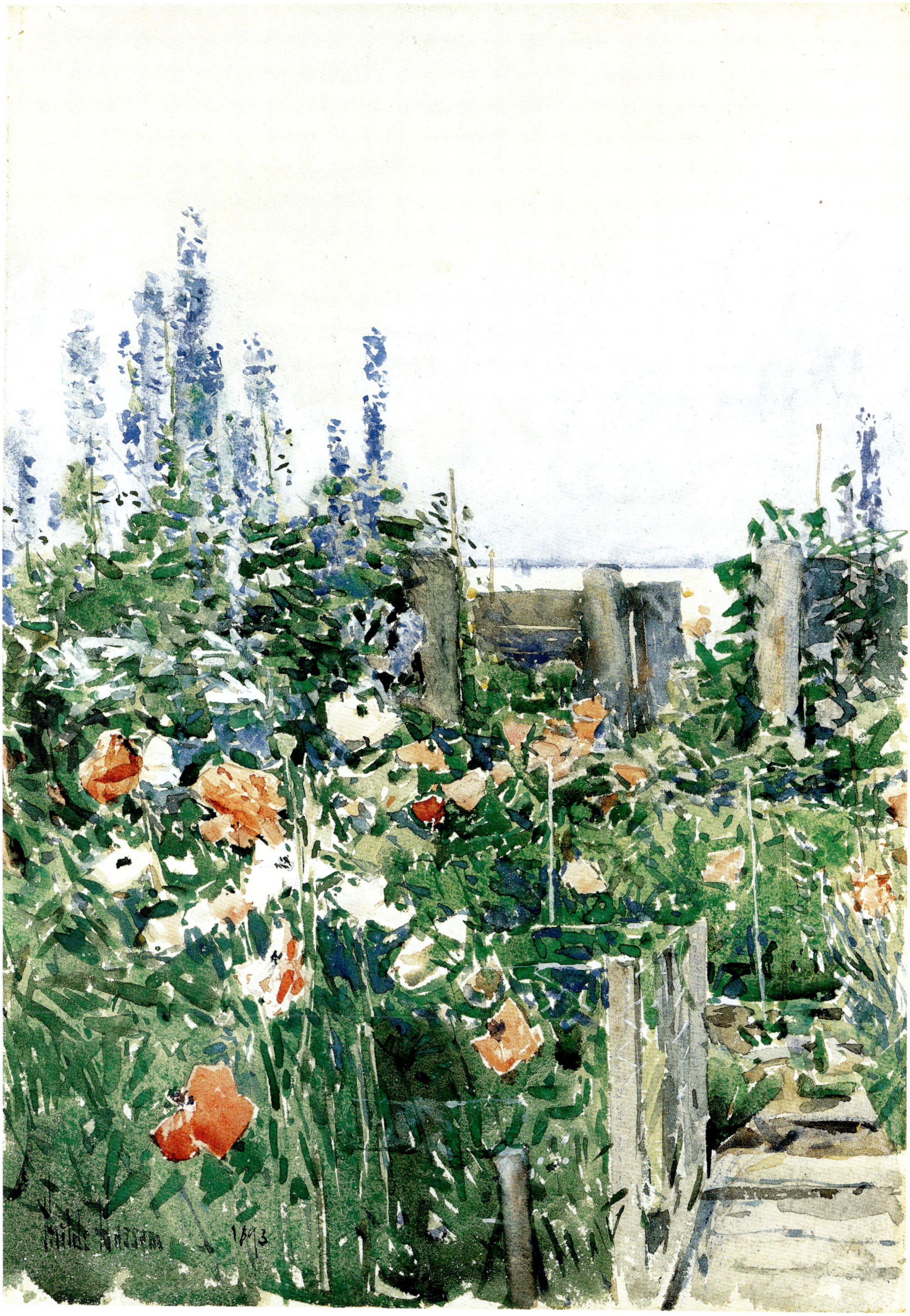

Fig. 131. Childe Hassam. *Home of the Hummingbird,* 1893. Watercolor on paper, $13\frac{3}{4}$ x $10\frac{1}{8}$ in. (34.9 x 25.7 cm). Manoogian Collection

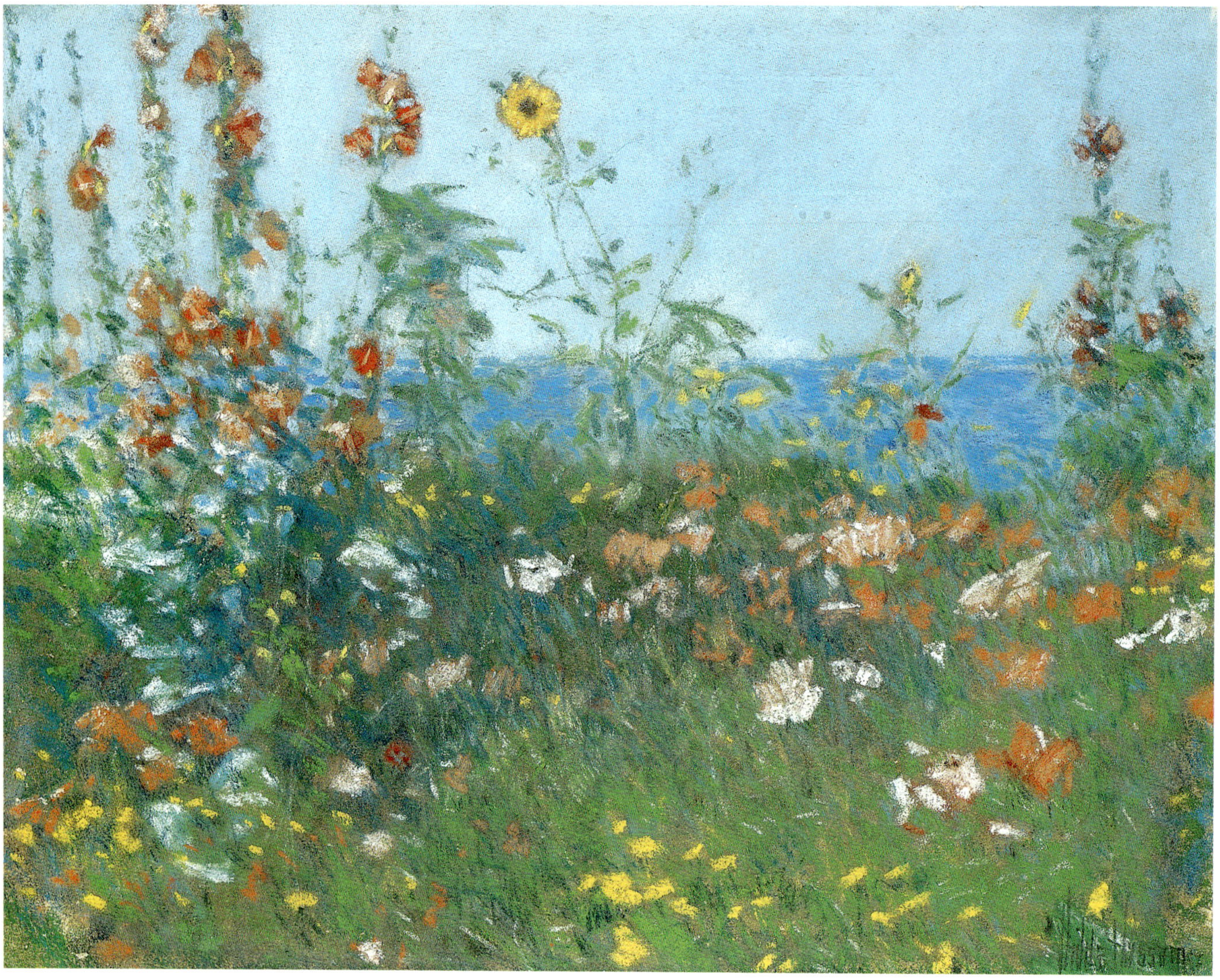

Fig. 132. Childe Hassam. *Poppies, Isles of Shoals,* ca. 1890. Pastel on paper, 9 x 12 in. (22.9 x 30.5 cm). Private collection

Her island garden was as artificial as a formal *potager* in Kansas. But Thaxter created a wild effect by extending her plantings beyond the fenced enclosure. In early May 1893 she noted in her journal that she had seeded poppies all over the bank sloping down to the sea. "I am always planting Shirley Poppies somewhere!" she wrote enthusiastically. "One never can have enough of them."[36]

Celia Thaxter's Garden, Isles of Shoals, Maine (fig. 9) presents the view from the garden to Babb's Rock, the rounded form in the center of the composition. Hassam sat so low in the flower beds that the garden fence is hidden. Painting the same view a year later in the oil *Poppies, Isles of Shoals* (fig. 134), he moved closer to the shoreline to depict a mass of poppies Thaxter had sown outside the enclosure. In both works Hassam excluded the swimming pool and related structures that stood just to the left of the site he represented. However, a photograph Karl Thaxter shot from approximately the same viewpoint (fig. 135) reveals the flagpole, platform, and bathhouses that flanked the pool. Hassam treated such evidence of resort life at the Shoals only after Celia Thaxter's death. In *Bathing Pool, Appledore* (fig. 136), dated 1907, for example, Babb's Rock seems less a geological outcropping than a convenient spot for sunbathing. The brightly colored bathhouses edge the pool, dotted with swimmers, while women and children in white stroll the ocean path.

Celia Thaxter died at her cottage on August 26, 1894. That year had been especially significant in the fruitful Thaxter–Hassam relationship. Their collaboration, *An Island Garden,* was published in the spring. The exquisite book, with full-page chromolithographs after Hassam's watercolors and his specially designed headpieces (see figs. 123, 137), brilliantly culminated his years as an illustrator. From then on he would support

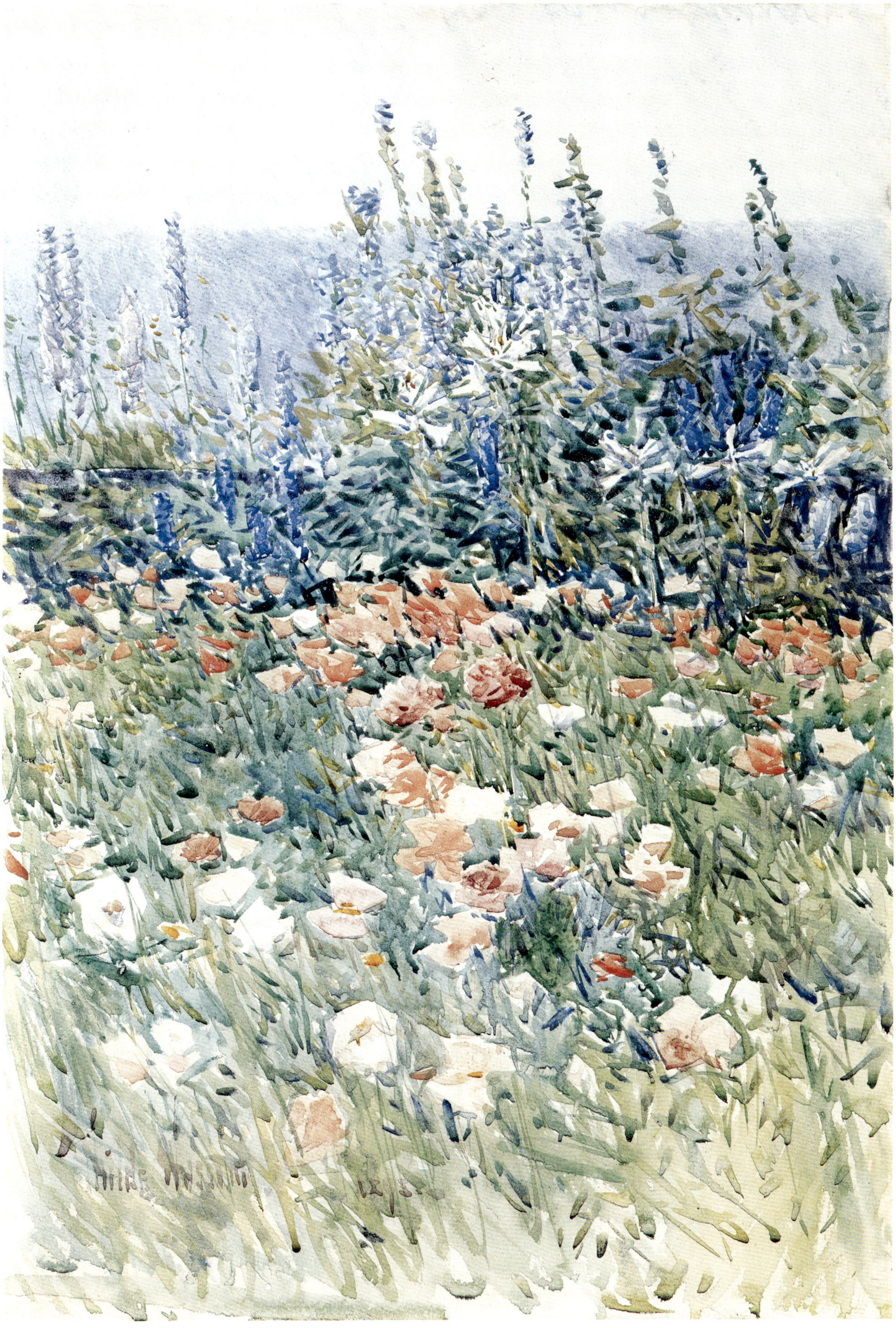

Fig. 133. Childe Hassam. *Flower Garden, Isles of Shoals,* 1893. Watercolor on paper, 19½ x 13½ in. (49.5 x 34.3 cm). Private collection, New York

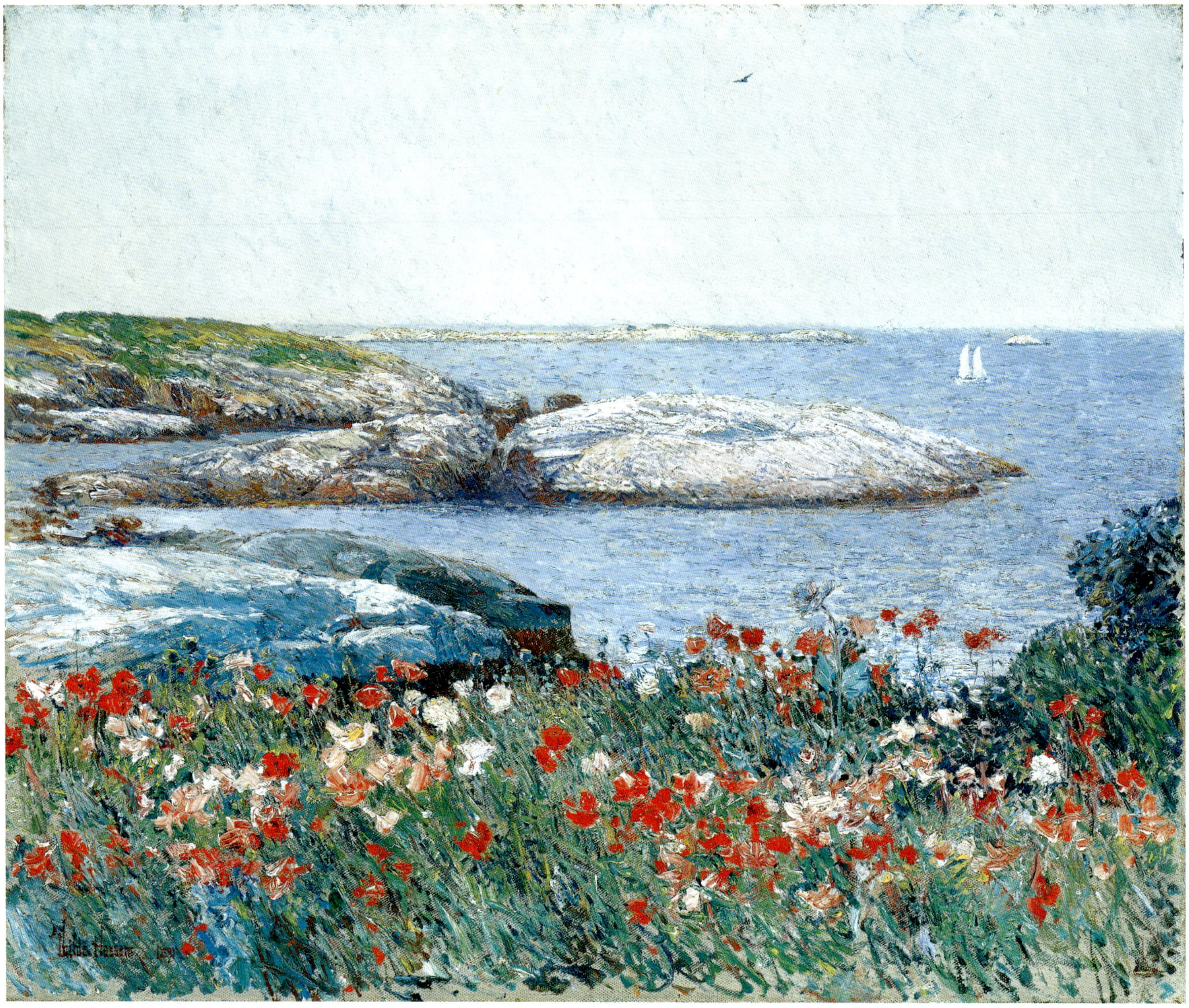

Fig. 134. Childe Hassam. *Poppies, Isles of Shoals,* 1891. Oil on canvas, 19¾ x 24 in. (50.2 x 61 cm). National Gallery of Art, Washington, D.C. Gift (Partial and Promised) of Margaret and Raymond Horowitz 1997.135.1

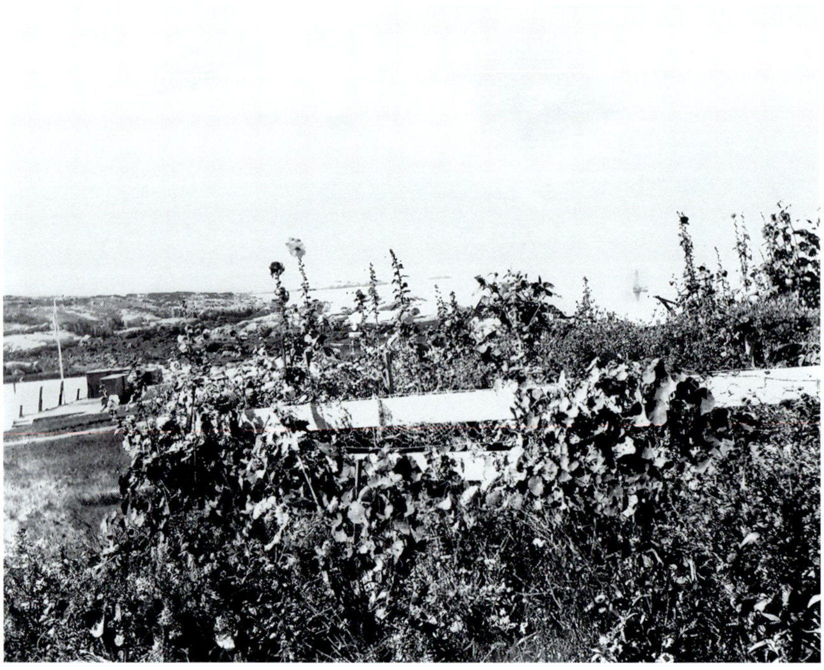

Fig. 135. Karl Thaxter. View from Celia Thaxter's front porch, looking southwest to the bathing pool, ca. 1890. Courtesy Portsmouth Athenaeum, New Hampshire

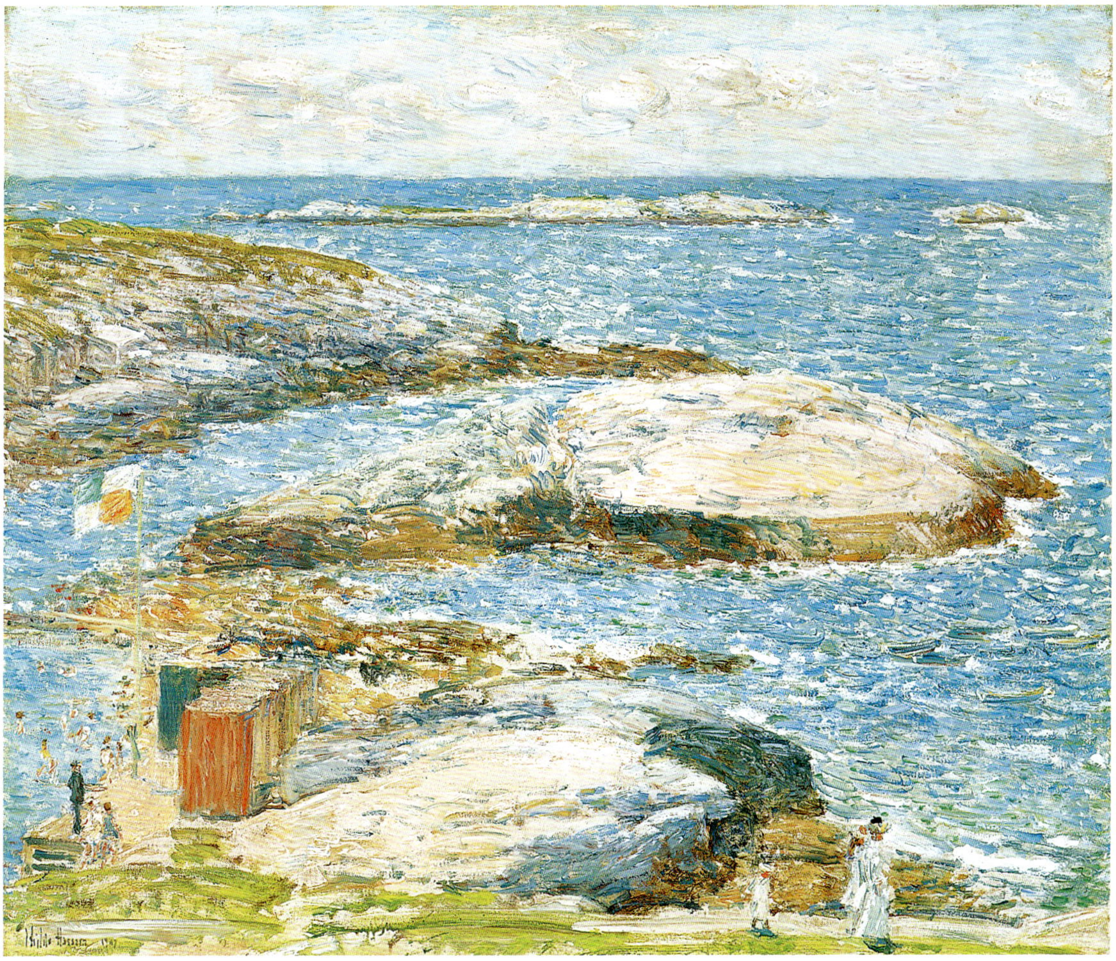

Fig. 136. Childe Hassam. *Bathing Pool, Appledore,* 1907. Oil on canvas, 24⅞ x 29¾ in. (63.2 x 75.6 cm). The Museum of Fine Arts, Boston. Ernest Wadsworth Longfellow Fund

himself entirely through the sales of his art.[37] Celia Thaxter had contributed to that transition, praising the young artist in at least two poems, securing him commissions for illustrations, and providing a venue for the sales of his paintings. In the summer of 1894, before Thaxter's death, Hassam had painted *The Room of Flowers* (fig. 118), celebrating the parlor where her intimates had gathered for three decades. The morning after she died, he helped decorate the room for her simple funeral, which closed a significant phase in his career.

Hassam returned to Appledore in the summer of 1895, as he and others in her circle had pledged to do after the funeral, and then stayed away for a few years.[38] During a visit in 1903 he confessed to his friend J. Alden Weir, "I felt pretty

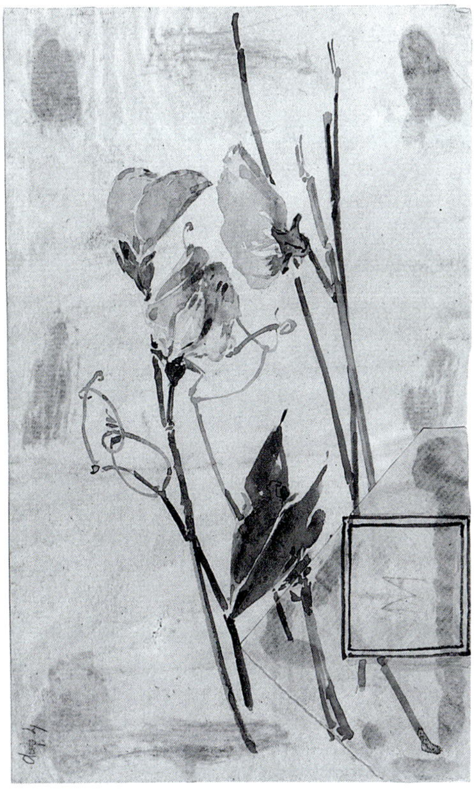

Fig. 137. Childe Hassam. *Sweet Peas,* headpiece in Celia Thaxter's *An Island Garden* (Boston, 1894). Photograph. Boston Public Library, Print Department

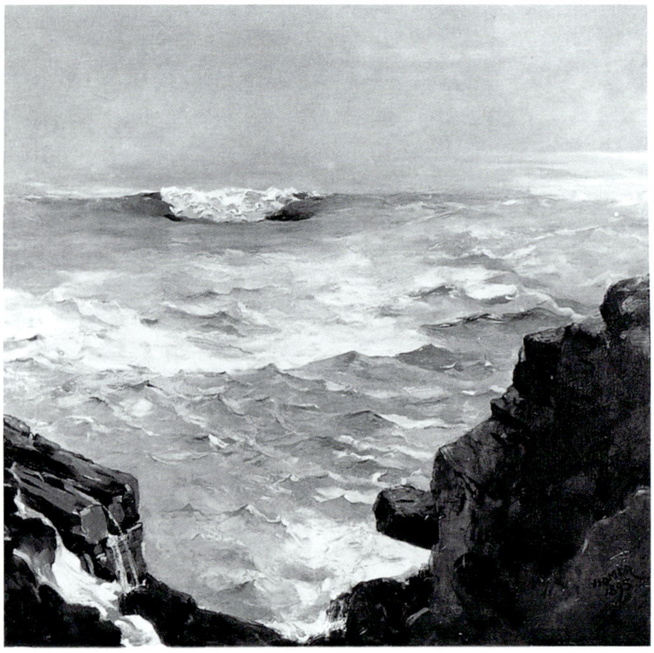

blue here for the first few days, the place is filled with ghosts . . . and a good many of the people I know can just hobble about. I was very young when I came here first."[39] But Hassam's irrepressible ebullience, relish for ocean swimming, and love of the islands drew him back. On his return he found a newly compelling subject, the rugged coastline. "The rocks and the sea are the few things that do not change and they are wonderfully beautiful—more so than ever!" he told Weir.[40]

While Hassam was painting at Appledore, Winslow Homer was also preoccupied with "the rocks and the sea,"

Fig. 138. Winslow Homer. *Cannon Rock,* 1895. Oil on canvas, 40 x 40 in. (101.6 x 101.6 cm). The Metropolitan Museum of Art, New York. Gift of George A. Hearn, 1906 06.1281

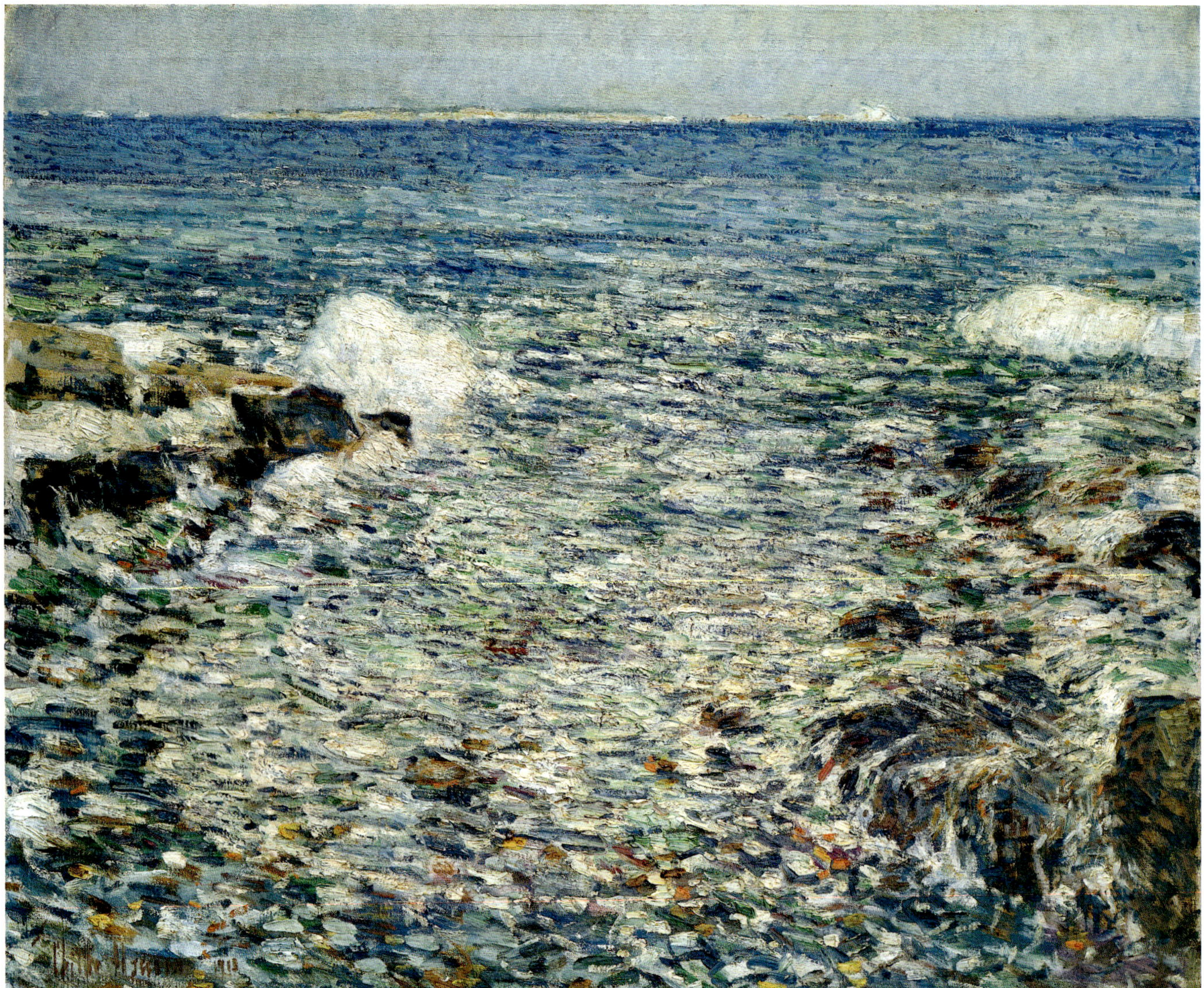

Fig. 139. Childe Hassam. *Surf, Isles of Shoals,* 1913. Oil on canvas, 28¼ x 35¼ in. (71.8 x 89.5 cm). The Metropolitan Museum of Art, New York. Gift of Dr. and Mrs. Sheldon C. Sommers, 1996 1996.382

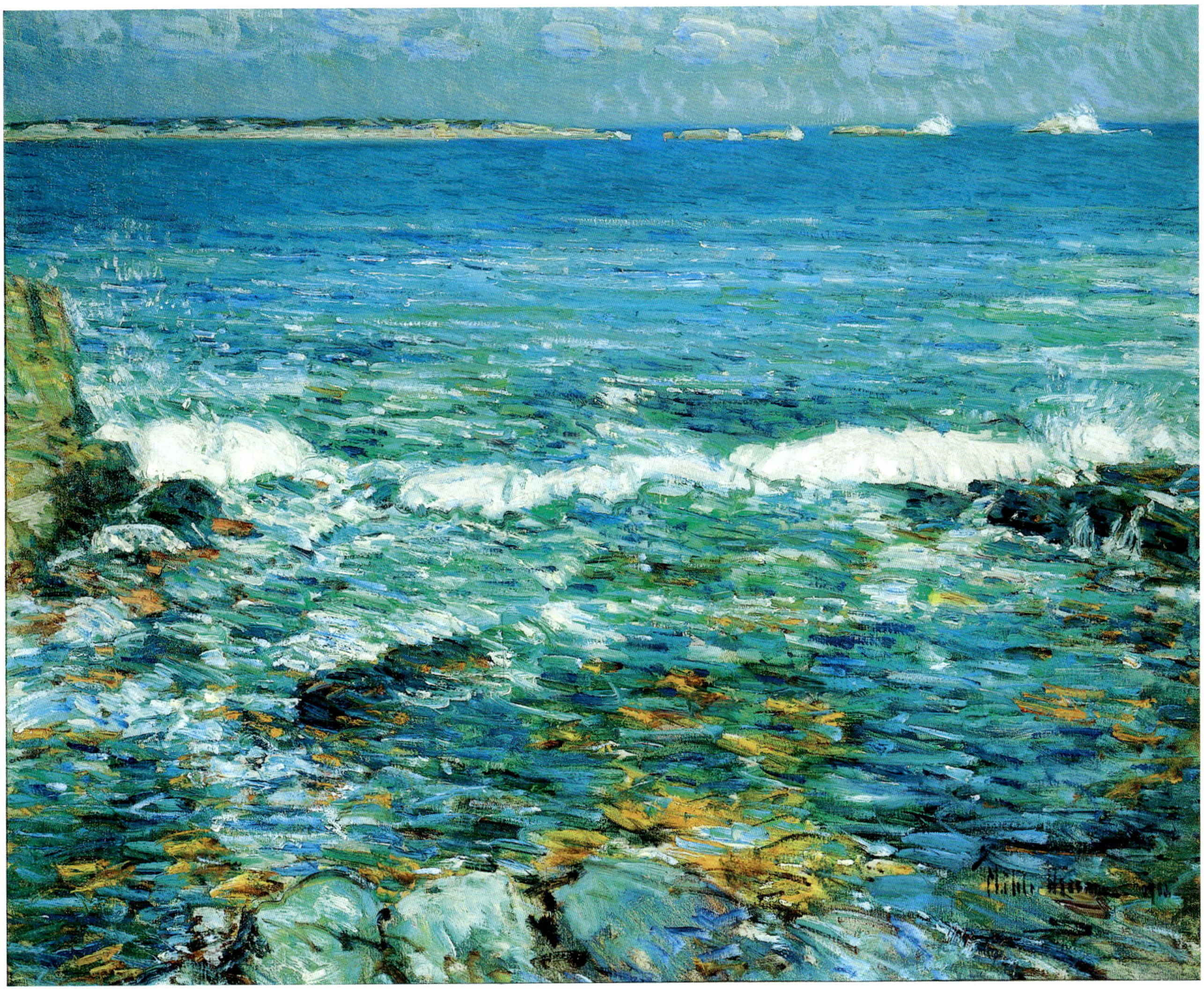

Fig. 140. Childe Hassam. *Duck Island from Appledore,* 1911. Oil on canvas, 28¼ x 35¾ in. (71.8 x 90.8 cm). Private collection

portraying them at nearby Prouts Neck, Maine. Homer exhibited regularly in New York, where Hassam no doubt saw his elemental seascapes. One of these, *Cannon Rock* (fig. 138), received a rave review when it was shown at the Society of American Artists in New York in 1903. "Seldom has even Homer expressed with greater simplicity and truth the grandeur of the ocean," the *New York Times* critic wrote, declaring Homer "in some ways the greatest living marine painter of the age."[41]

Hassam's *Surf, Isles of Shoals* (fig. 139) resembles *Cannon Rock* in composition and subject matter but differs dramatically in emotional tone. In Homer's painting dark rocks, rough water, and brooding sky convey nature's terrifying power. To increase the sense of danger, Homer combined different tide levels: the breaker shown appears only at low tide and the brimming foreground cleft fills only at high tide.[42] The churning water threatens to crash through the jagged V formed by the silhouetted rocks, engulfing the viewer poised on the brink. The somber palette, heavily impastoed wave, and fog-shrouded horizon dramatize the confrontation with onrushing natural forces. In Hassam's painting, by contrast, sunlight dances over the water. The rocks embrace the shallows in a protective curve, and the breakers embellish the edges of the composition, posing no hazard to the viewer. The sea deepens from a multicolored mosaic in the foreground through a medium blue to a deeper, darker band. Distant islands gleam under a cloudless sky. Nature does not threaten but cajoles.

Hassam moved farther out on the cliffs to depict the same scene in *Duck Island from Appledore* (fig. 140). A froth of breakers divides the canvas in half; the waves crashing against the distant rocks are rendered as cloudlike puffs. Duck Island's ledges, which Celia Thaxter called "dreadful," caused numerous shipwrecks.[43] Whereas Homer would have

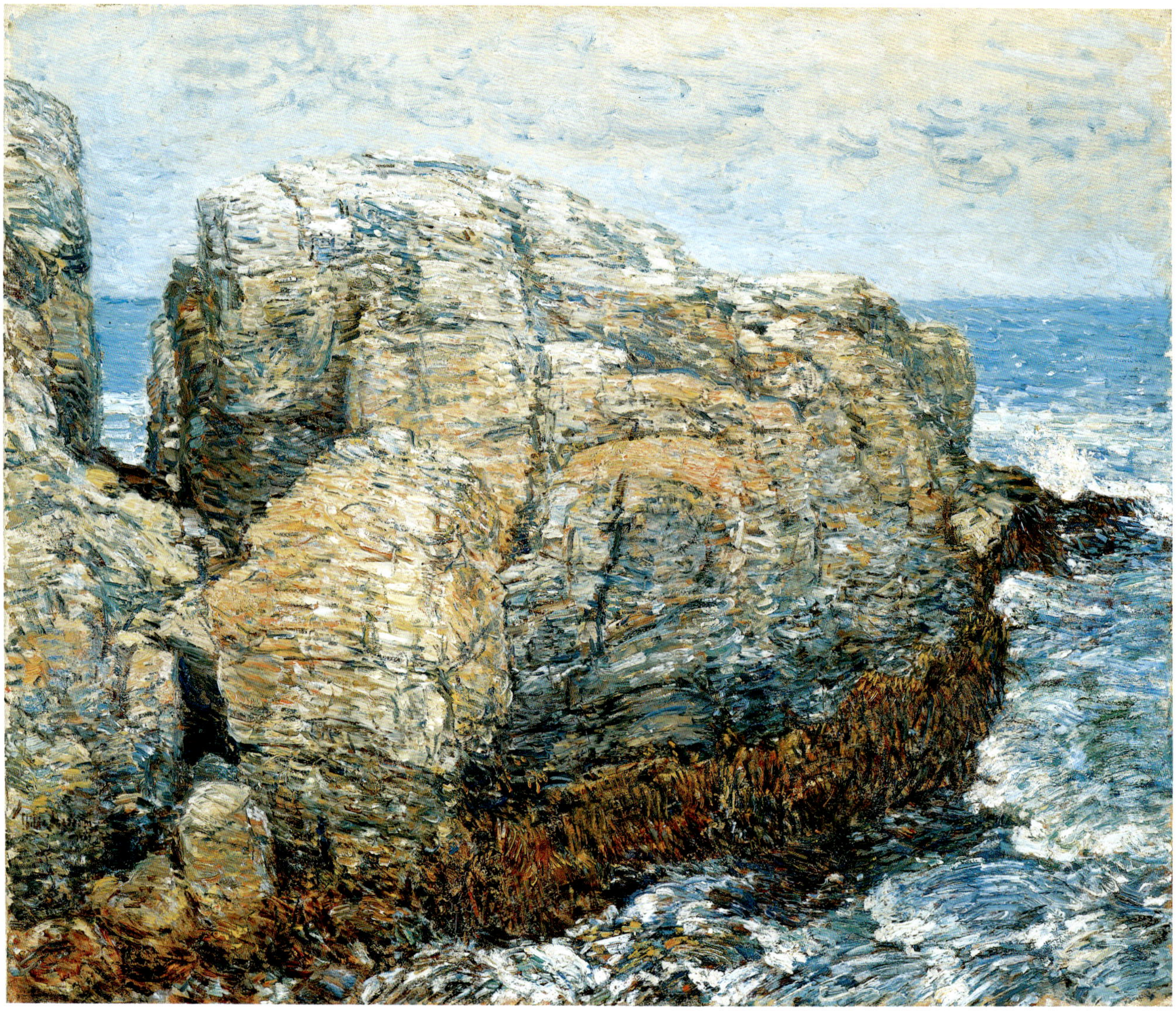

Fig. 141. Childe Hassam. *Sylph's Rock, Appledore,* 1907. Oil on canvas, 25 x 30 in. (63.5 x 76.2 cm). Worcester Art Museum, Massachusetts, Gift of Charlotte E. W. Buffington in memory of her husband

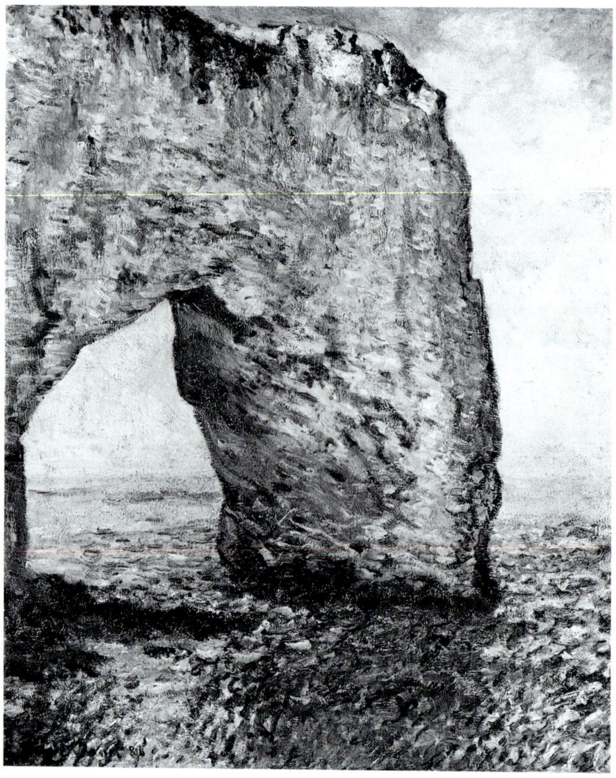

Fig. 142. Claude Monet. *The Manneporte near Étretat,* 1886. Oil on canvas, 32 x 25¾ in. (81.3 x 65.4 cm). The Metropolitan Museum of Art, New York. Bequest of Lillie P. Bliss, 1931 31.67.11

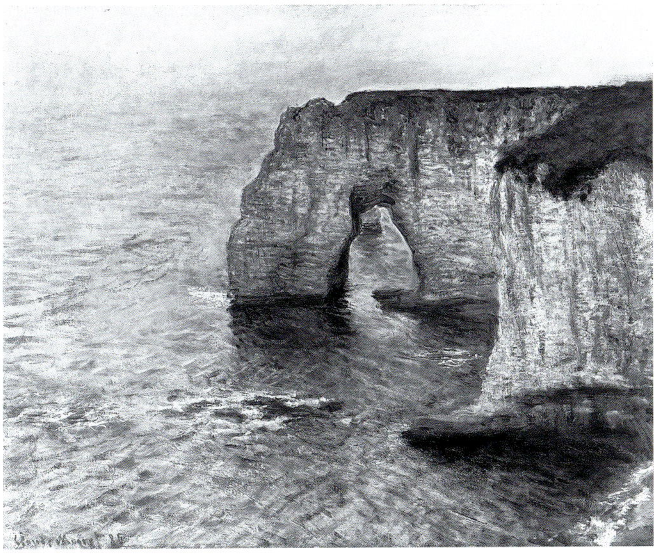

Fig. 143. Claude Monet. *Manne-Porte, Étretat,* 1885. Oil on canvas, 25¾ x 32 in. (65.4 x 81.3 cm). Philadelphia Museum of Art: John G. Johnson Collection, 1917

conveyed their menace, Hassam created a sparkling tapestry of benign rocks, water, and sky.

Hassam's treatment of rocks and sea allies him not with the American Homer but the French painter Claude Monet. *Sylph's Rock, Appledore* (fig. 141) by Hassam recalls Monet's *Manneporte near Étretat* (fig. 142) in its bold focus on a geological formation and the use of a high-keyed palette to capture the myriad colors of stone, sea, and sky. Although it was painted two decades earlier than Hassam's picture, Monet's composition is more modern. But at least one observer applauded Hassam's daring when he exhibited his canvas in 1907. "Some painters would have classified 'The Sylph's Rock at Appledore' as among the unpaintable things," the *New York Herald* reviewer wrote, "but Mr. Hassam has presented it amid the swirl of waters in a way which appeals to imagination and sentiment."[44]

For *Coast Scene, Isles of Shoals* (fig. 22), Hassam chose a high vantage point, as Monet had done for many paintings of Étretat in the 1880s, including *Manne-Porte, Étretat* (fig. 143). Hassam provided a comfortable perch on the foreground rocks, while Monet dangled the viewer in the air. Monet

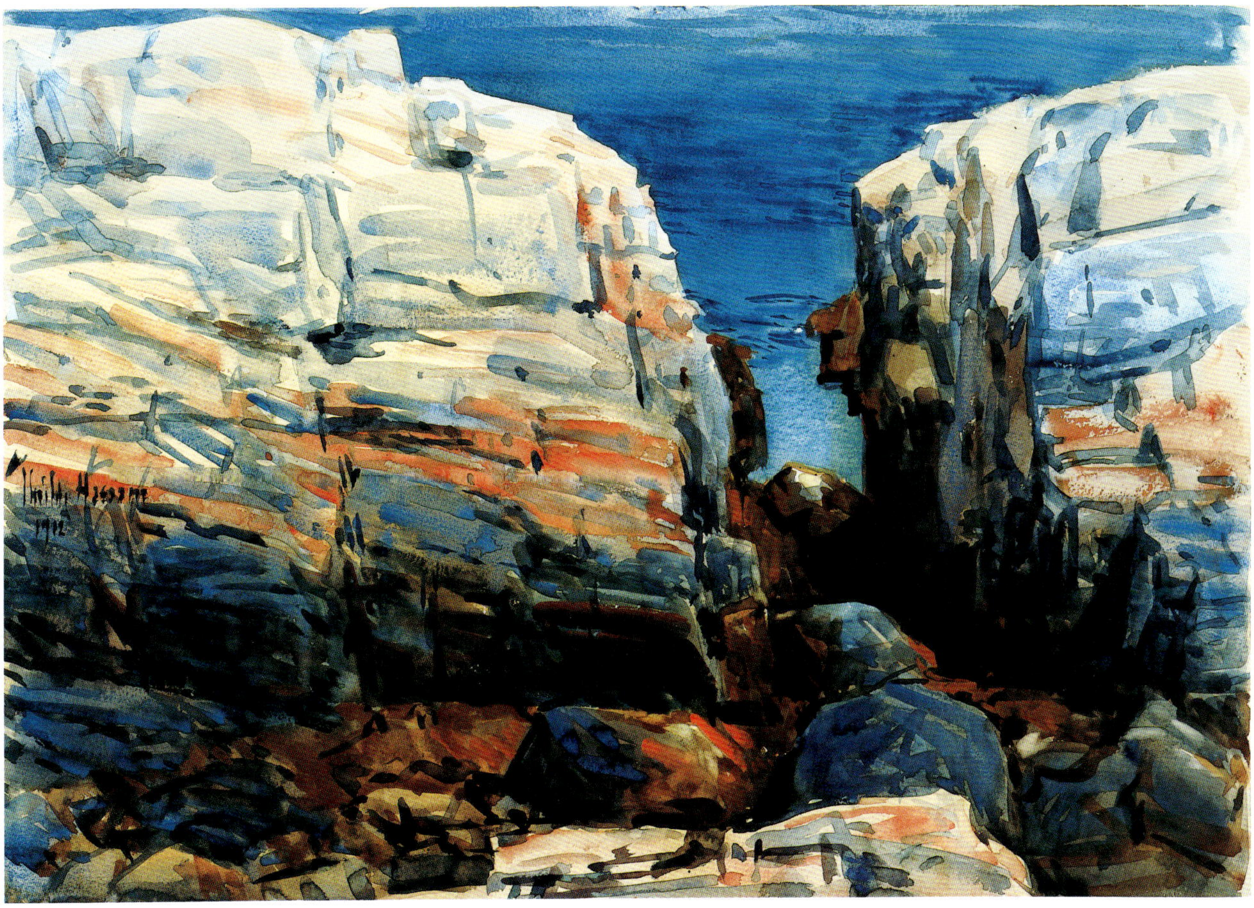

Fig. 144. Childe Hassam. *The Gorge, Appledore,* 1912. Watercolor on paper, 13¾ x 19⅞ in. (34.9 x 50.5 cm). Brooklyn Museum of Art, Museum Collection Fund 24.103

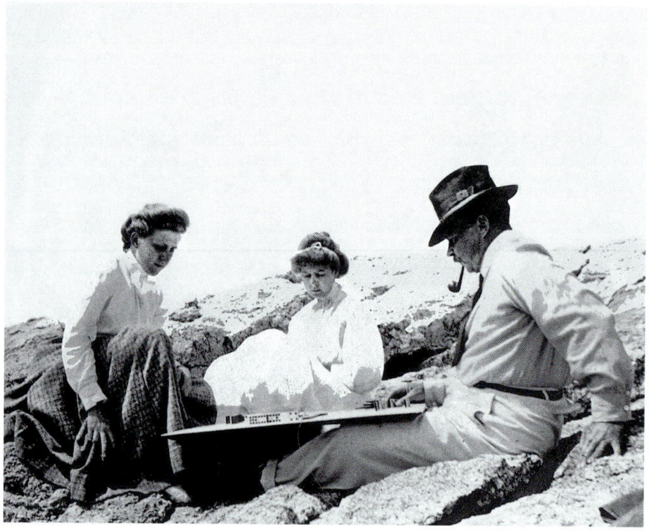

Fig. 145. Hassam with two women on the rocks, ca. 1905. Collection of the Vaughn Cottage Memorial Library and Museum, Isles of Shoals, Star Island Corporation, Portsmouth, New Hampshire

Fig. 146. Childe Hassam. *The South Ledges, Appledore,* 1913. Oil on canvas, 34¼ x 36⅛ in. (87 x 91.8 cm). Smithsonian American Art Museum, Washington, D.C. Gift of John Gellatly

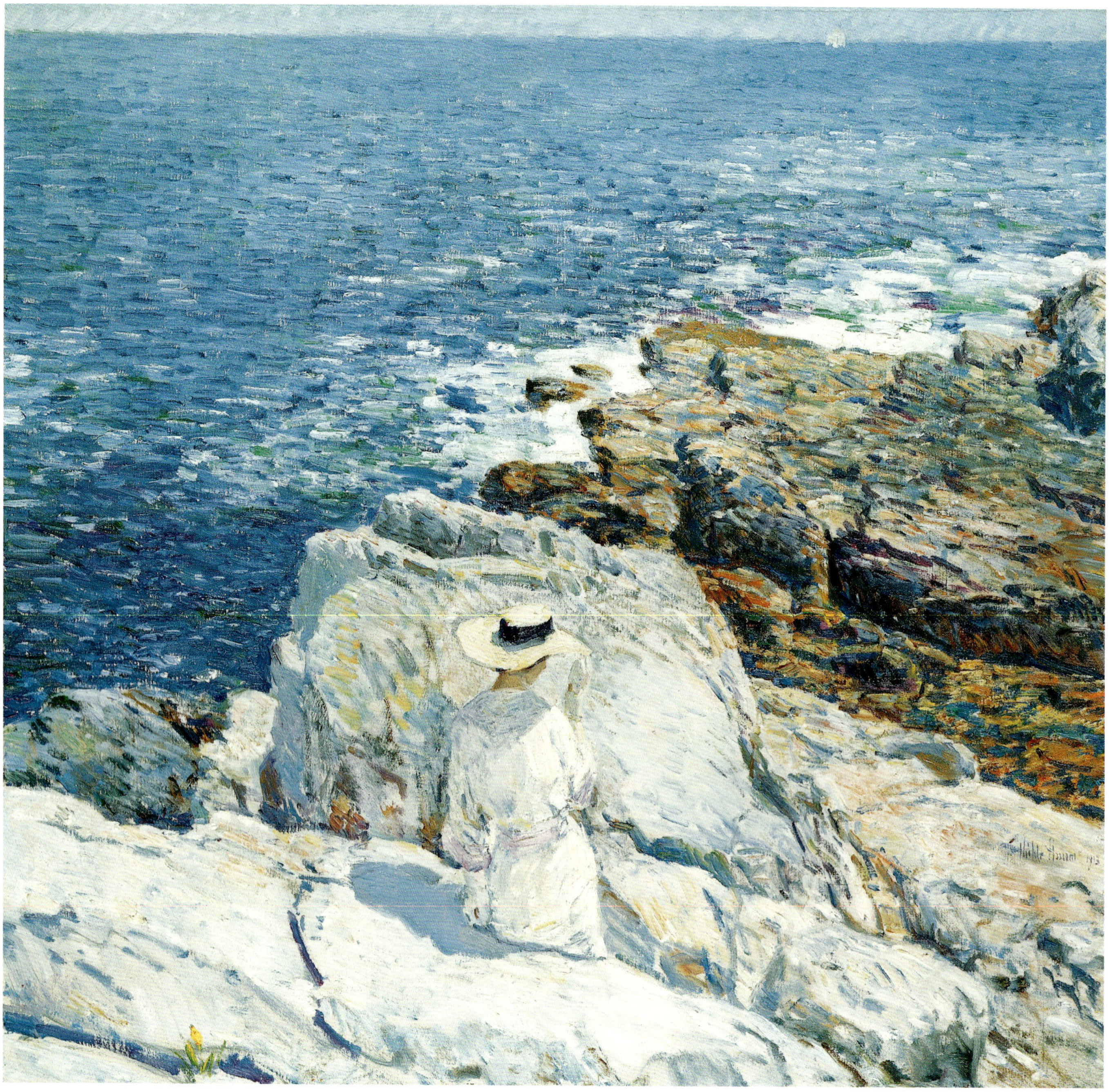

abstracted the subject, blurring details and obscuring the horizon line in a haze of violet, blue, and green. Hassam's treatment seems more realistic, but David Park Curry has found that, possibly working in his studio, the artist combined two views that were separated by about a quarter mile.[45]

Hassam reduced his palette and simplified forms in *Jelly Fish* (fig. 13). Celia Thaxter shared his appreciation of the weird beauty of the diaphanous jellyfish, "colored like a great melting opal in the pale-green, translucent water."[46] In Hassam's painting these creatures stud the sapphire sea with pearl and turquoise. The saturated hues of the picture, an oil dated 1912, suggest the influence of the vibrant watercolors Hassam produced at the Shoals that year.[47] In *The Cove* (fig. 17) the transparent, liquid medium corresponds perfectly with the subject matter. For another watercolor, *The Gorge, Appledore* (fig. 144), Hassam used the white paper to imply the sun-bleached rocks, building up variations of light and shadow on their faceted surfaces with horizontal slashes of yellow, orange, rust, and blue.

Appledore's rocks—remnants of the Ice Age in a place where evidence of human history was limited—were tourist attractions, and Hassam enjoyed them as much as did any other summer visitor. Old photographs show him exploring the craggy ledges, even playing a game of dominoes there (fig. 145). One of his companions in those snapshots may have posed for *The South Ledges, Appledore* (fig. 146). Hassam's

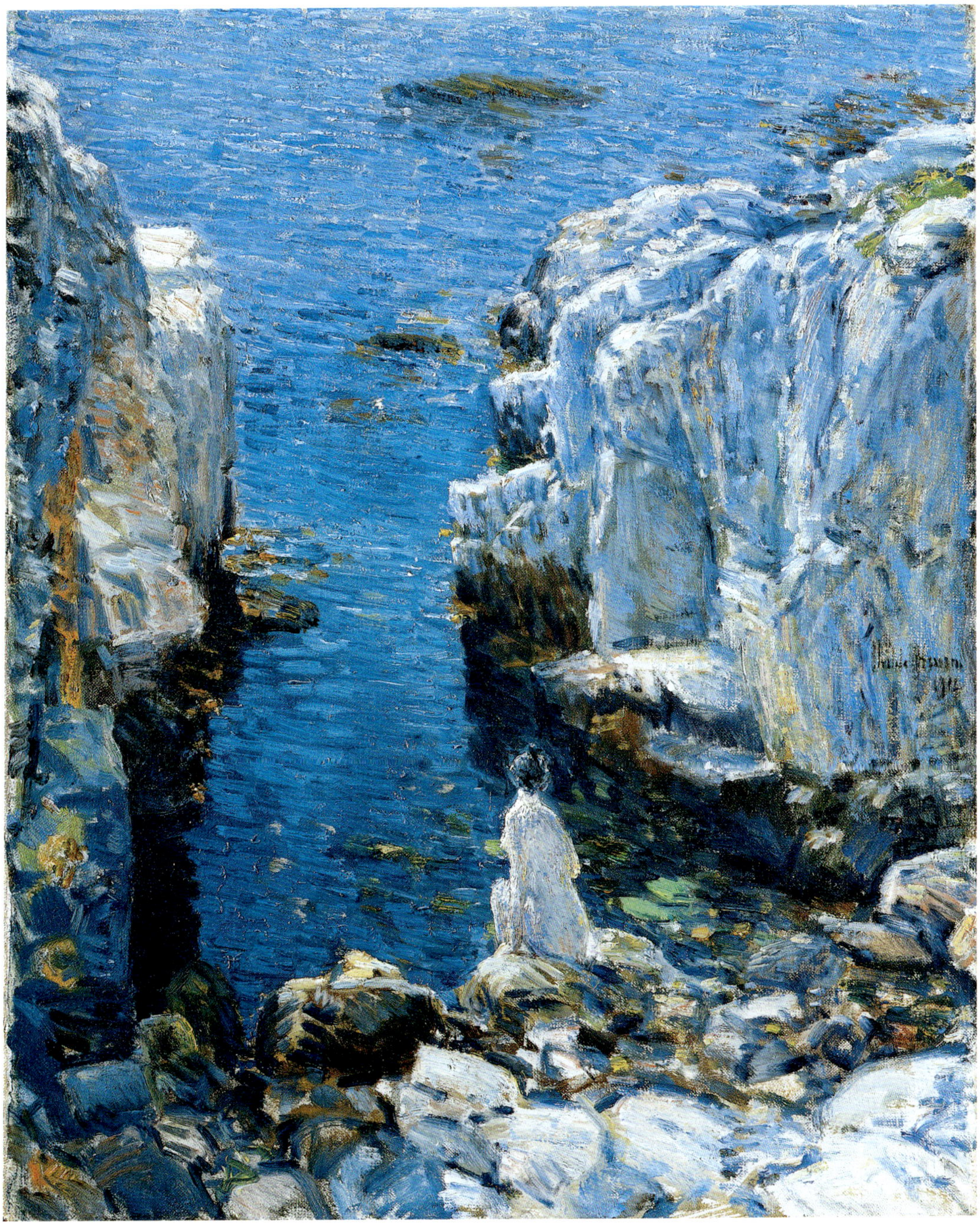

Fig. 147. Childe Hassam. *The Isles of Shoals*, 1912. Oil on canvas, 22 x 18 in. (55.9 x 45.7 cm). Virginia Museum of Fine Arts, Richmond, The Adolph D. and Wilkins C. Williams Fund

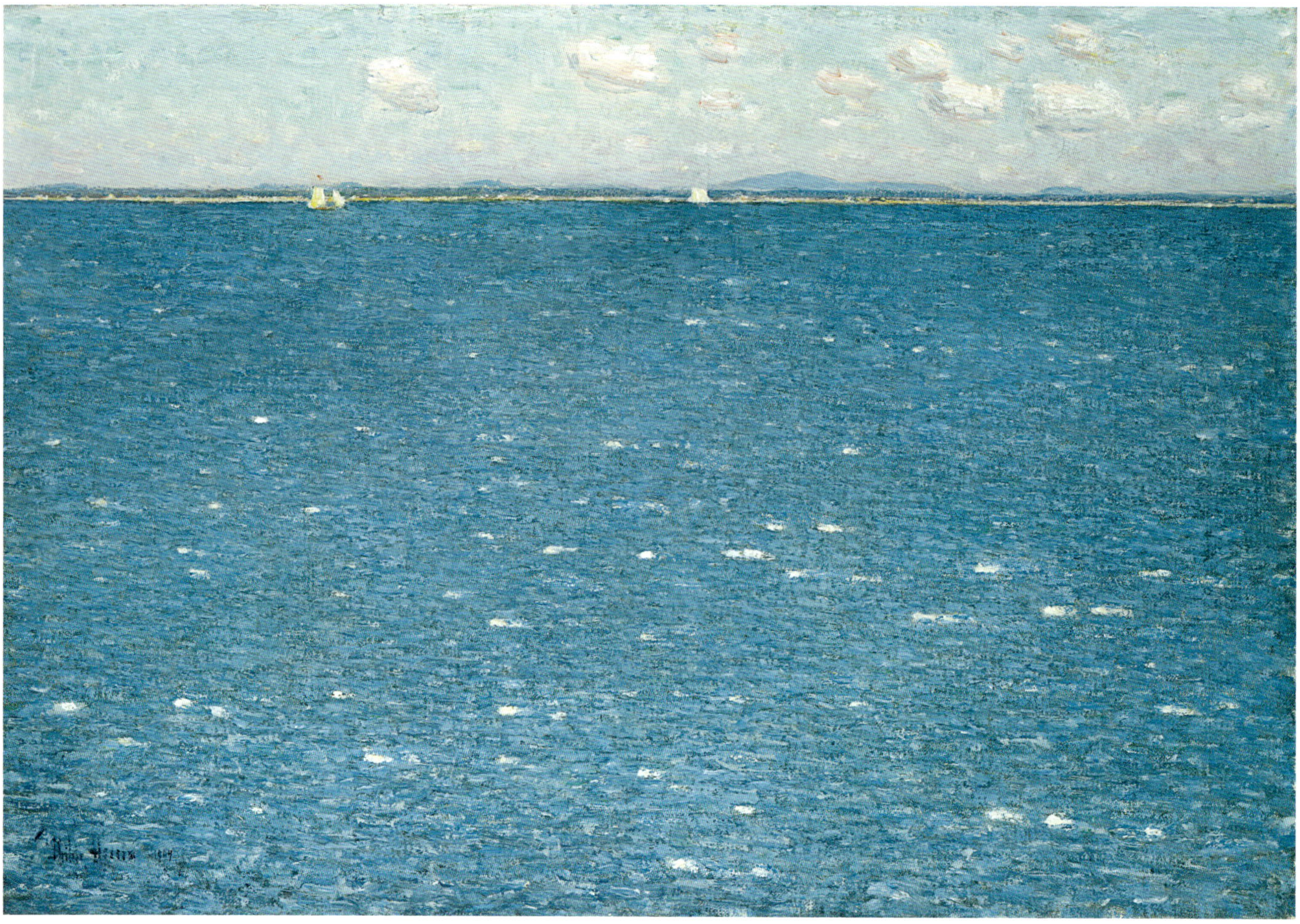

Fig. 148. Childe Hassam. *The West Wind, Isles of Shoals,* 1904. Oil on canvas, 15 x 22 in. (38.1 x 55.9 cm). Yale Collection of American Literature, Beinecke Rare Book and Manuscript Library, New Haven

composition places her in nature while shielding her from it. Firmly contained by the rocks, she sits high and dry, adjusting her wide-brimmed hat with a gloved hand. Her white costume merges with the chalky cliffs; only her blue shadow and purple hatband announce her presence.

The nude model in *The Isles of Shoals* (fig. 147) is even more sheltered. Her body projects against the sea, which is calm. The gorge forms an open-air boudoir, its entrance doubly sealed by two rocks high in the composition. The absence of a horizon line obliterates the world beyond this intimate space. Hassam repeated the nude's flesh tones in the rocks, warming their timeworn surfaces with peach, pink, and rose.

In marked contrast to the sense of confinement in those pictures is the exhilarating spaciousness of *The West Wind, Isles of Shoals* (fig. 148) . Eliminating figure and foreground, Hassam offered a gull's-eye view of the sea, the distant shore, and the blue hills beyond. Tiny sails speed the viewer's gaze over the whitecap-flecked Atlantic. Hassam produced economical, near-abstract works of this kind periodically throughout his years at Appledore. The spare *Sunset at Sea* (fig. 149) injects a Whistlerian composition with intense Postimpressionist color. The stylization of clouds and water into decorative striations recalls Georges Seurat's *Lighthouse at Honfleur* (fig. 150). Although Hassam did not adopt Seurat's Pointillist brushstroke, he exploited the coarse weave of the canvas to catch dabs of brilliant pigment, creating a tapestry of color like that produced by his French contemporary. Hassam almost certainly saw the works of Seurat, Paul Gauguin, Pierre Bonnard, Édouard Vuillard, and other Postimpressionists during his stays in Europe, including his last, in 1910, the year before he painted *Sunset at Sea*. Although he disavowed the influence of French art with mounting vehemence, its effect is evident in his paintings.

A fire swept Appledore in 1914, destroying the hotel and cottages, including Hassam's studio. He may have returned for the last time in 1916, but other, more accessible places had already claimed his attention. The trip to Appledore required a train journey of 270 miles from New York, followed

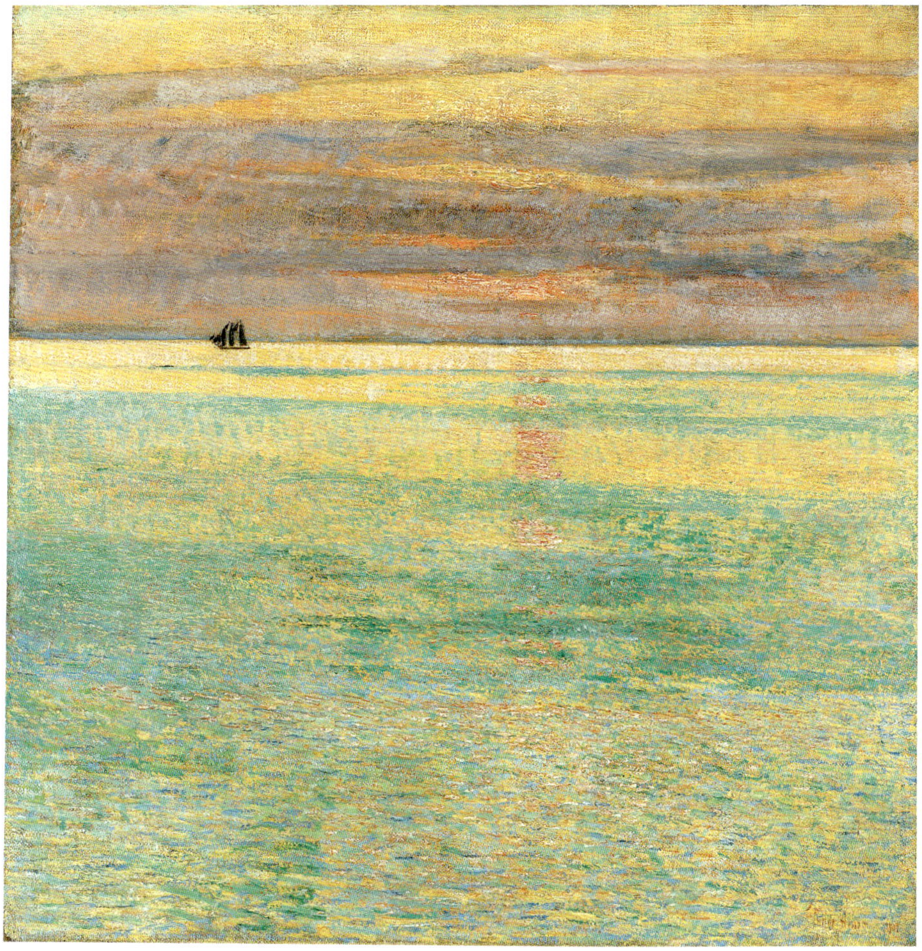

Fig. 149. Childe Hassam. *Sunset at Sea,* 1911. Oil on canvas, 34 x 34 in. (86.4 x 86.4 cm). Collection of The Rose Art Museum, Brandeis University, Waltham, Massachusetts, Gift of Mr. and Mrs. Monroe Geller

by an hour-long steamship voyage from Portsmouth, New Hampshire. By necessity and choice, Hassam broke the trip with sojourns in other coastal outposts. The closest was Cos Cob, Connecticut, a modest waterfront section of Greenwich that was "as unspoiled by the summer visitor," a contemporary reported, "as if it were miles back in the country instead of being forty minutes by train from New York."[48]

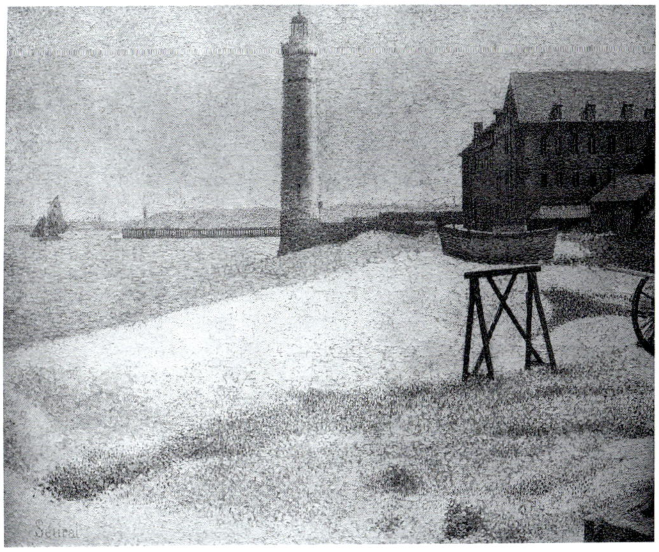

Fig. 150. Georges Seurat. *The Lighthouse at Honfleur,* 1886. Oil on canvas, 26¼ x 32¼ in. (66.7 x 81.9 cm). National Gallery of Art, Washington, D.C. Collection of Mr. and Mrs. Paul Mellon 1983.1.33

Hassam's first recorded visit to Greenwich was in 1894, when Theodore Robinson noted in his diary that Hassam was helping their mutual friend John H. Twachtman lay the foundation for an addition to Twachtman's house.[49] From the time Twachtman settled in Greenwich, in 1889, colleagues had taken the train out to Connecticut to paint with him. By 1891 he established summer painting classes in Cos Cob, about three miles from his home (fig. 151). Like its counterpart at the Isles of Shoals, the Cos Cob art colony included writers, editors, and musicians as well as painters. Willa Cather mentioned the village in one of her novels; crusading journalist Lincoln Steffens devoted a chapter of his best-selling autobiography to the art colony.[50] During the 1890s Twachtman, Robinson, Weir, Henry Fitch Taylor, and Hassam were the art colony's leaders. After Robinson's and Twachtman's untimely deaths, in 1896 and 1902, respectively,

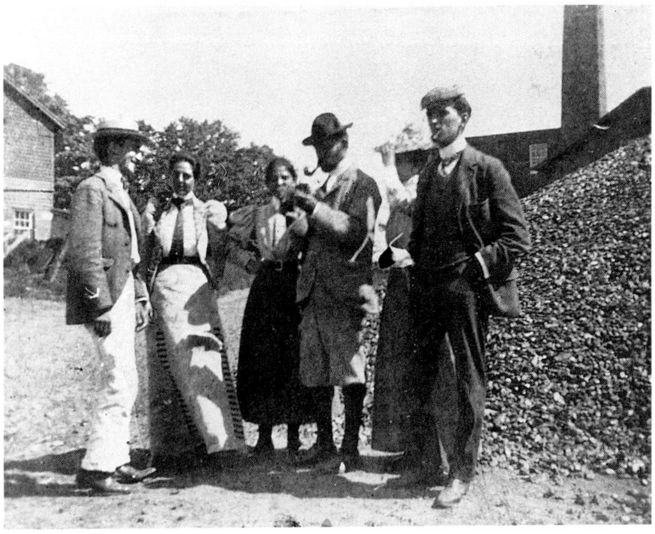

Fig. 151. John H. Twachtman (center) with summer students in the Palmer and Duff Shipyard, Cos Cob, Connecticut, ca. 1897. Courtesy of the William E. Finch, Jr. Archives, The Historical Society of the Town of Greenwich

artists continued to visit the rustic village; Hassam returned frequently until 1918.

The art colonists congregated at a rambling old saltbox overlooking Cos Cob's small harbor that was operated as a genteel boardinghouse by Josephine Lyon Holley and her daughter Constant (figs. 152, 153). Students mingled with mature artists at the Holley House. (Now called the Bush-Holley House, the artists' former gathering place is a museum operated by the Historical Society of the Town of Greenwich.) Constant's marriage in 1900 to Twachtman's student Elmer MacRae ensured the art colony's survival for another generation. The Holleys, one student wrote,

> *are charming, cultivated people, and their good taste is apparent everywhere. The walls are hung with photographs of the old masters; the living room is furnished in mahogany and the dining table is set with old silver and quaint blue china. There are four huge fireplaces where on cold evenings the students gather, telling stories, popping corn and making "fudge." On warm evenings there is plenty of amusement, with bicycles for land and boats on the water. As we row in at night from the Riverside Yacht Club the old house with its gayly lighted paper lanterns looks almost Japanese . . . while the Italian workingmen, skimming past us in other boats, singing their songs, make us think of Venice.*[51]

Twachtman's students installed end-of-summer exhibitions in the Holleys' barn, and MacRae filled The Old House, as it was often called, with displays of his work. Otherwise, the Holleys seem not to have served as agents for their artist-boarders. They may have wanted to avoid creating competition for the struggling MacRae; furthermore, the art colony's aloofness from the wealthy new residents of Greenwich was not conducive to cultivating local patronage. "We talked art, and we had a contempt for people who talked

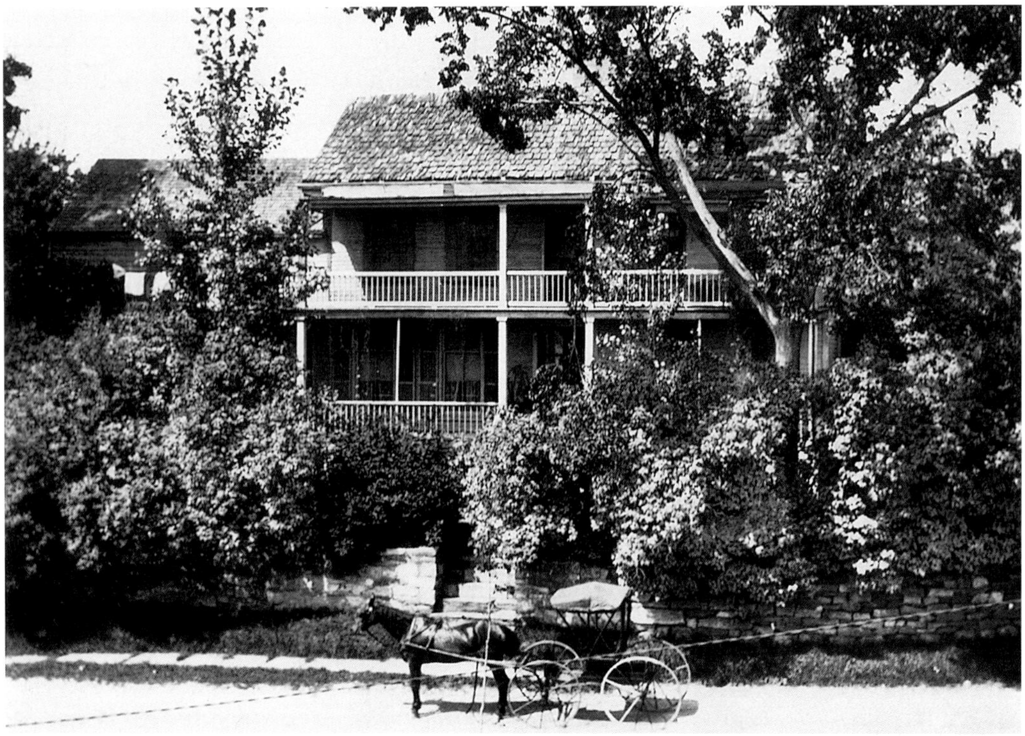

Fig. 152. The Holley House, Cos Cob, Connecticut, ca. 1890. William E. Finch, Jr. Archives, The Historical Society of the Town of Greenwich

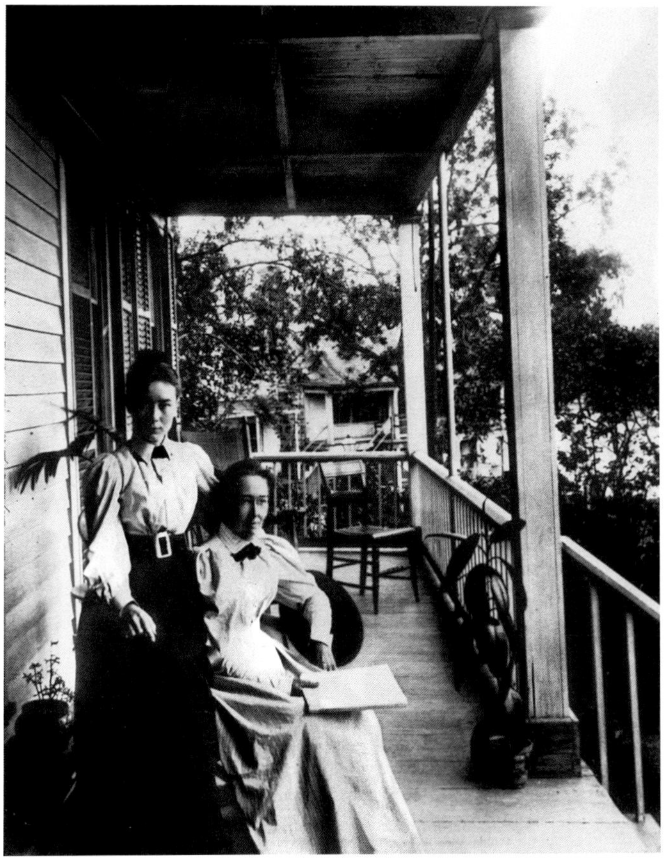

Fig. 153. Josephine Lyon Holley and Constant Holley on the front porch of the Holley House, Cos Cob, Connecticut, ca. 1895. Courtesy of the William E. Finch, Jr. Archives, The Historical Society of the Town of Greenwich

business and politics," Steffens wrote of the art colony. "The townspeople and fishermen were all right; they fitted into the land- and seascapes, but toward the . . . successful New Yorkers who were buying up Greenwich and modernizing that lovely old town, we were such snobs that after cutting us and then discovering that we were cutting them, they used to try to get in with us. And they couldn't."[52]

That attitude would change in time. Meanwhile, the artists relished the bohemian atmosphere of the Holley House. Hassam visited so often that he seemed like a member of the family. Constant Holley MacRae organized "a clambake . . . to celebrate Muley's [Hassam's] birthday—down the river on Captain Knapp's island. Two boat loads."[53] When firewood ran short, he cut up a fallen cedar a neighbor had offered. "Mr. Hassam is fine on the chop," Constant reported to her mother; "we are all going over with apples and saws and bring the tree home."[54]

The subject matter Hassam favored in Cos Cob differed dramatically from the sea and rocks he painted at Appledore. And although the Holleys and MacRaes grew their own fruits and vegetables, cultivated extensive flower borders, and filled the house with bouquets, Hassam ignored garden images there. He focused now on architectural and figural subjects, and he found most of them without even leaving the Holley House. From its upper porch, a contemporary wrote, artists "could see the whole village; the irregular, dusty 'green,' with its bordering stores and the three or four old white dwelling houses. They could look across the creek to the old mossy dock, and the dull red factory, which is always as quiet as a church. They could see the shipyard beyond it; the rusty ways and the weather-beaten oyster sloops. They could look across the mill race . . . and see the mill pond and the red lilies that grow along its edges."[55]

The old houses, barns, mill, and shipyard inspired so many pictures that Hassam nicknamed the art colony "the Cos Cob Clapboard School."[56] But he, more frequently than anyone else, depicted the rustic vernacular architecture. Not surprisingly, the Holley House itself was one of Hassam's favorite subjects; he rendered it no fewer than seventeen times, in oil, watercolor, pastel, and etching. As if to emphasize its age—and to present it as a paradigm of American tradition—he used its popular name, "The Old House," in most of his titles. The house was not as old as Hassam and his contemporaries believed, however. Recent research dates construction of its earliest part to about 1732, not to the mid-1600s, as they thought. Regardless of its exact age, the house represented steadfast endurance, as emphasized in an article published in 1898: "The big cedar shingles and siding, nearly 250 years old, are still in place, and look as though they might last many years longer. They are grooved by the rains and snow; they are a rusty brown, faded by the sun; they are moss grown and worm eaten, but they stay; they are staunch and true, and the big, iron hand wrought nails, rusty and old, still hold them in place."[57]

The Holley Farm (fig. 154), one of about twenty pastels Hassam produced at Cos Cob in 1902, clearly documents the house's double porches, uneven roofline, and two flights of steps down to the road, as well as the mass of shrubbery in front of it. For *Summer at Cos Cob* (fig. 155) he adopted a less conventional viewpoint, positioning himself between the house and the lilac bushes—traditional companions to New England farmhouses. The eye sweeps from the dappled shadows up the sun-splashed white facade, festooned with wisteria vines and accented with a box of red geraniums. A pair of trees (the one on the left an American elm) rhymes with the white columns. The rooftop and chimneys in the

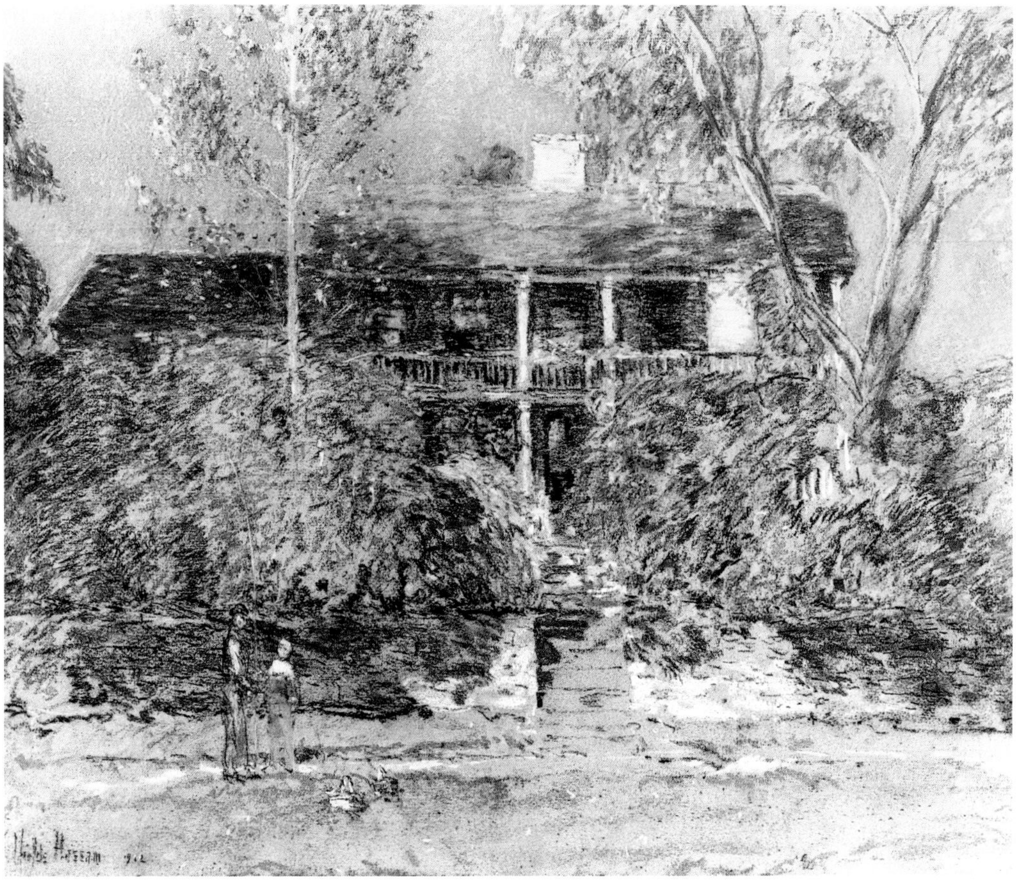

Fig. 154. Childe Hassam. *The Holley Farm,* 1902. Pastel on paper, 18 x 22 in. (45.7 x 55.9 cm). Diplomatic Reception Rooms, U.S. Department of State, Washington, D.C.

background acknowledge the closely built community and indicate another of Hassam's favorite subjects, the Brush house.

Just across the road from the Holley House, the Brush house was built sometime between 1751 and 1784. Its resident during the art-colony period, Joseph E. B. Brush, was a living link to the past. A descendant of one of the oldest families in town, he had worked on the packet boats that sailed between Cos Cob and New York until the railroad put them out of business. If the Holley House was full, artists sometimes roomed at Brush's, but its ramshackle condition made it more desirable as the subject of a picture than as a place to stay. In a pastel dated 1902 (fig. 156) Hassam captured the play of light and shadow over the old house and the adjacent country store. Depicting the same house in watercolor fourteen years later (fig. 157), he eliminated the store but retained his focus on the network of shadows on the steep roof. He left the paper bare in some areas to suggest patches of sunlight; in others he brushed wet-into-wet to produce veils of color.

Hassam stood on the upper porch of the Holley House to paint *Oyster Sloop, Cos Cob* (fig. 158), a view of the shipyard just across the inlet that the house overlooked. The transitory elements (a boatman sculling past, a worker approaching the sloop), animated brushwork, bright colors, and cropped forms suggest that it is an unedited snapshot of observed reality. Hassam's composition, however, was calculated to preserve the appearance of tradition in a place undergoing modernization. The sailboat's mast and rigging form a pyramid that lends satisfying stability to the canvas. The hulls of such workboats were usually coated with tar, but Hassam rendered this one in a luscious blue-green that secures its position as the painting's focal point. Greenwich oystermen clung to sail-powered craft long after their competitors up the coast had converted to more efficient steamboats. The oyster sloop was as outdated as Hassam's romantic notion of the shipyard. By cropping the mustard yellow building, he excluded the thriving new factory, producing gasoline engines and launches, that had opened on the adjacent property the year before he painted his picture. Although Hassam chose to ignore it, the modern plant fascinated Weir. Weir toured it eagerly with MacRae, afterward remarking to the younger artist, "My, isn't our job a fussy one?"[58]

Hassam had not traveled to the Connecticut shore to celebrate industrial progress, however. Perhaps to avoid evidence of change in Cos Cob, in the second decade of the twentieth century he often retreated inside the Holley House to paint female models; the canvases that resulted are country

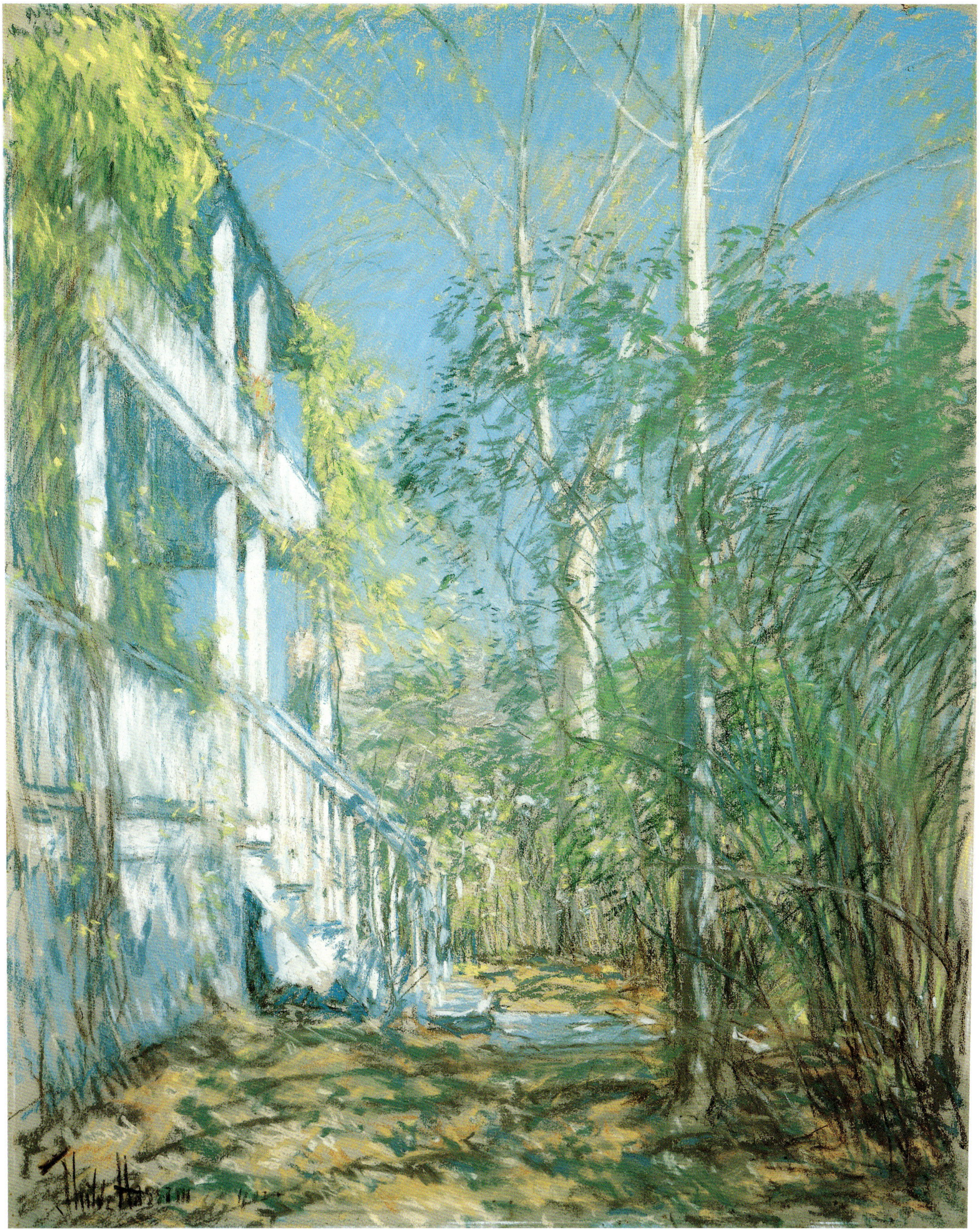

Fig. 155. Childe Hassam. *Summer at Cos Cob,* 1902. Pastel on paper, 22 x 18 in. (55.9 x 45.7 cm). The Montclair Art Museum, Gift of William T. Evans 1915.24

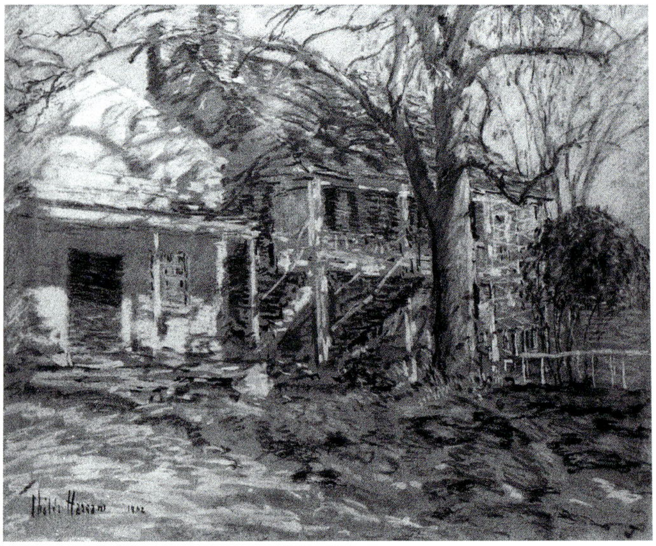

Fig. 156. Childe Hassam. *The Brush House,* 1902. Pastel on paper, 18 1/16 x 22 1/8 in. (45.8 x 56.2 cm). Courtesy of the Canajoharie Library and Art Gallery, New York

Fig. 157. Childe Hassam. *The Brush House,* 1916. Watercolor and graphite on off-white wove paper, 15 5/16 x 22 5/16 in. (38.9 x 56.7 cm). The Metropolitan Museum of Art, New York. Rogers Fund, 1917 17.31.1

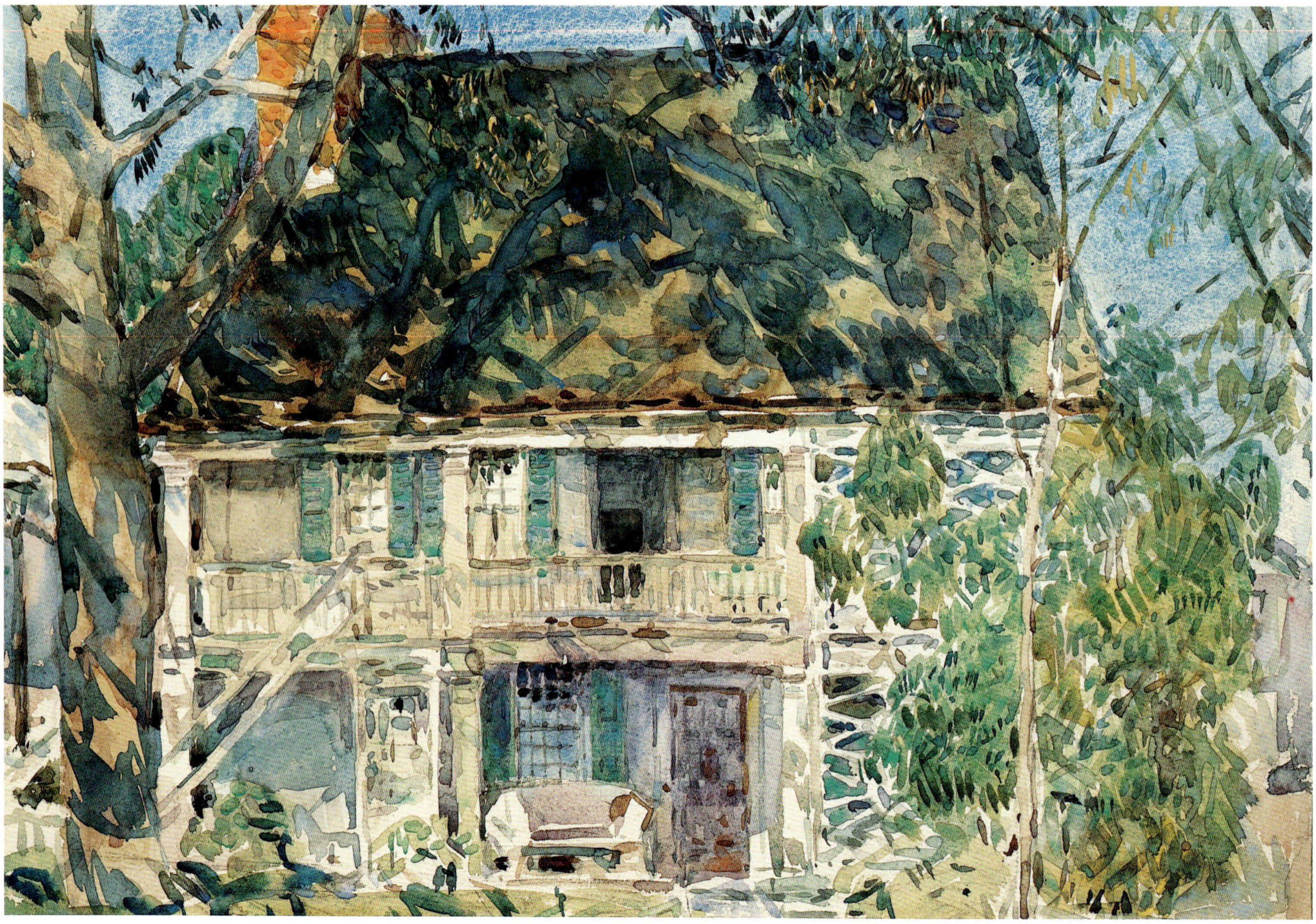

counterparts of a series he began in his Manhattan studio about 1909. He seemed to invite comparison of one city–country pair, *The New York Window* (fig. 227) and *Bowl of Goldfish* (fig. 159), by sending them to the prestigious annual exhibition at the Corcoran Gallery of Art in Washington, D.C., in December 1912.[59] Had they been hung side by side, their strong formal similarities would not have escaped critical notice. Both use the window format to play off the tension between interior and exterior, both include a prominent still-life element, and in both the woman's individuality is muted by a blurring of features, a turn of the head.

Those similarities highlight the differences between the two paintings. In *The New York Window* the closed and curtained windows completely separate the model from the world beyond. Absorbed in reverie, she turns inward, her slumped form contrasting with the vigorous verticals of the skyscrapers glimpsed outside. The emphatically divided space opposes the home—feminine, traditional—to the city—masculine, modern. The Cos Cob windows, by contrast, are flung open; curtains frame the view without obstructing it, and space flows freely from indoors to outdoors. The model, who in her erect posture echoes the slender tree

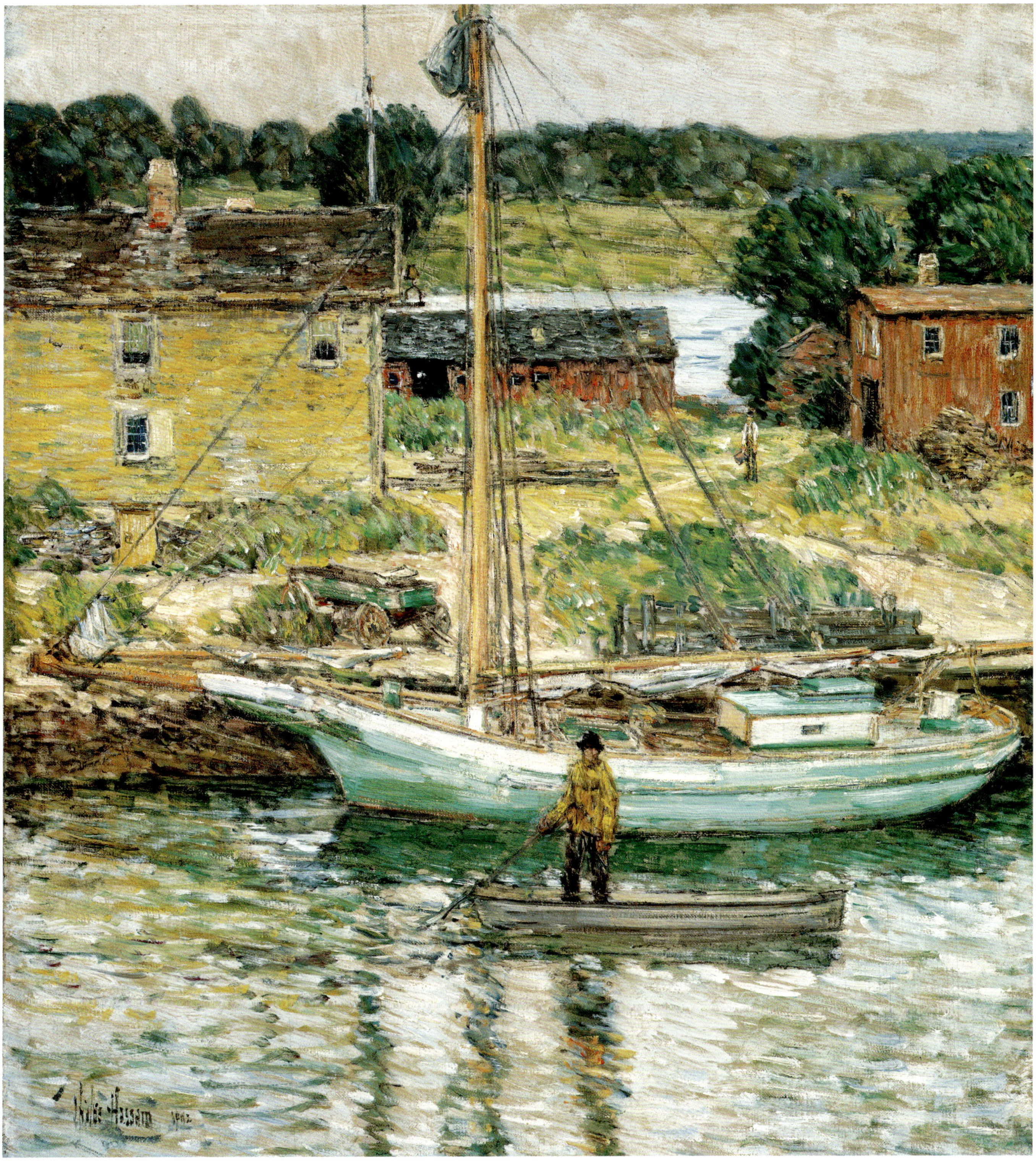

Fig. 158. Childe Hassam. *Oyster Sloop, Cos Cob,* 1902. Oil on canvas, $24\frac{3}{8}$ x $22\frac{3}{8}$ in. (61.9 x 56.8 cm). National Gallery of Art, Washington, D.C. Ailsa Mellon Bruce Collection 1970.17.100

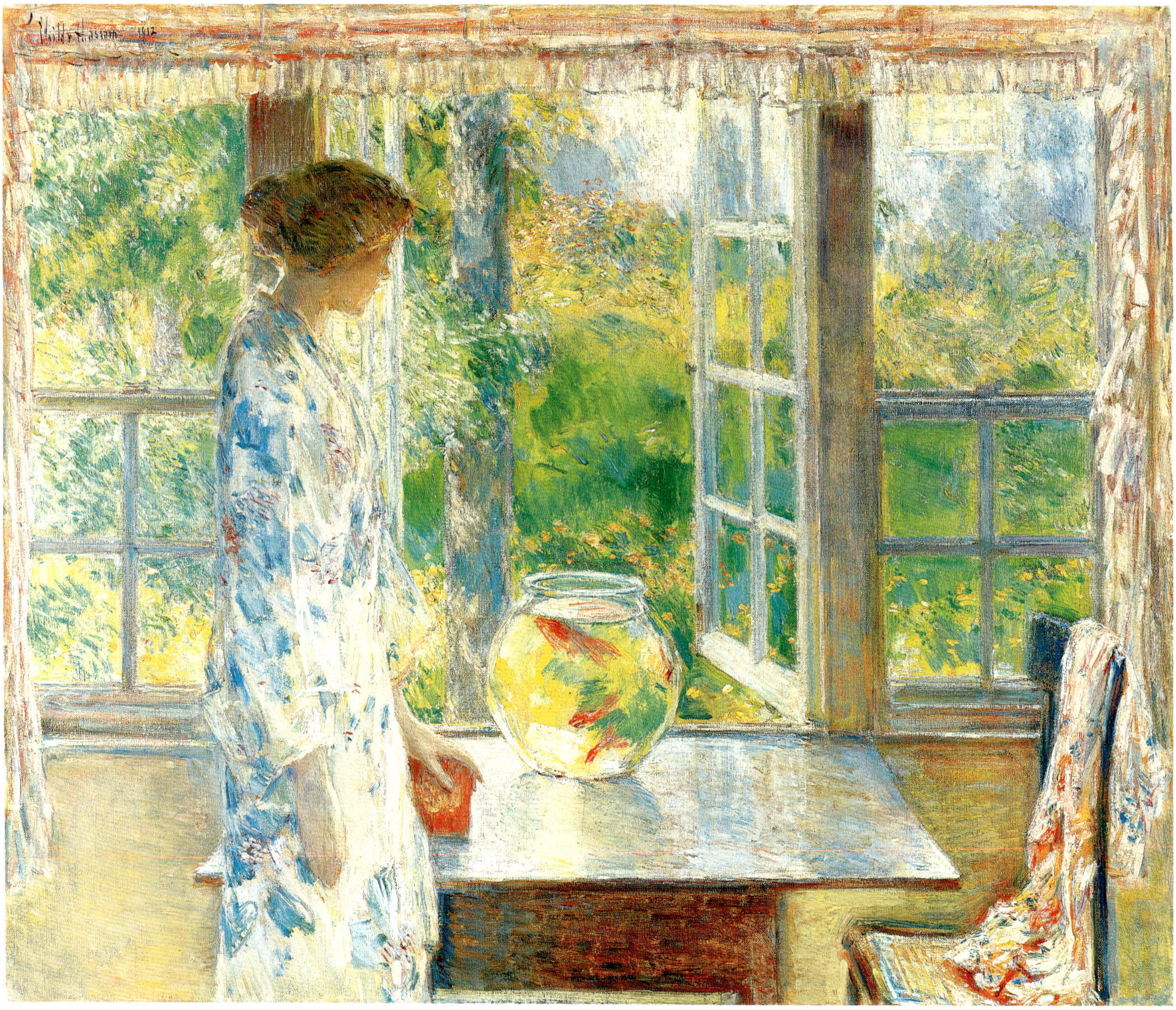

Fig. 159. Childe Hassam. *Bowl of Goldfish,* 1912. Oil on canvas, 25⅛ x 30¼ in. (63.8 x 76.8 cm). Ball State University Museum of Art, Muncie, Indiana, Frank C. Ball Collection, partial gift and promised gift of the Ball Brothers Foundation

trunk, gazes out the window. Her flowered kimono seems an extension of the garden; the bowl of swirling goldfish—no *nature morte*—captures the world of nature and brings it into the domestic sphere.

Helen Burke, the teenage daughter of Cos Cob's Irish-born tavern keeper, posed for *Bowl of Goldfish.* In 1914 Hassam hired her to pose again, this time for *In the Old House* (fig. 160), painted in a first-floor chamber of the Holley House.[60] The mood is more subdued than that of the goldfish painting: America would soon enter World War I, and Hassam's comfortable world faced challenges from all sides. A rising tide of immigrants threatened Anglo-Saxon hegemony, the Armory Show of 1913 made Impressionism look *retardataire,* and the career-oriented New Woman of the day undermined conventions of feminine demeanor. In this unsettled climate, the image of a demure woman at the hearth of an old house offered reassurance of enduring values.

But Hassam yearned for continuity, not mere antiquity. Antiquarian and photographer Wallace Nutting had photographed the same room a decade earlier, posing his model before the Federal-period mantelpiece and dressing her in an eighteenth-century gown (fig. 161).[61] Hassam's model, by contrast, wears contemporary clothing. Both images record Holley family heirlooms: antique andirons, brass candlesticks, a pink lusterware tea set, and a small iridescent vase filled with nasturtiums. The minor changes made over the years separating the two images reflect a new cosmopolitanism. The sampler has yielded its privileged position over the

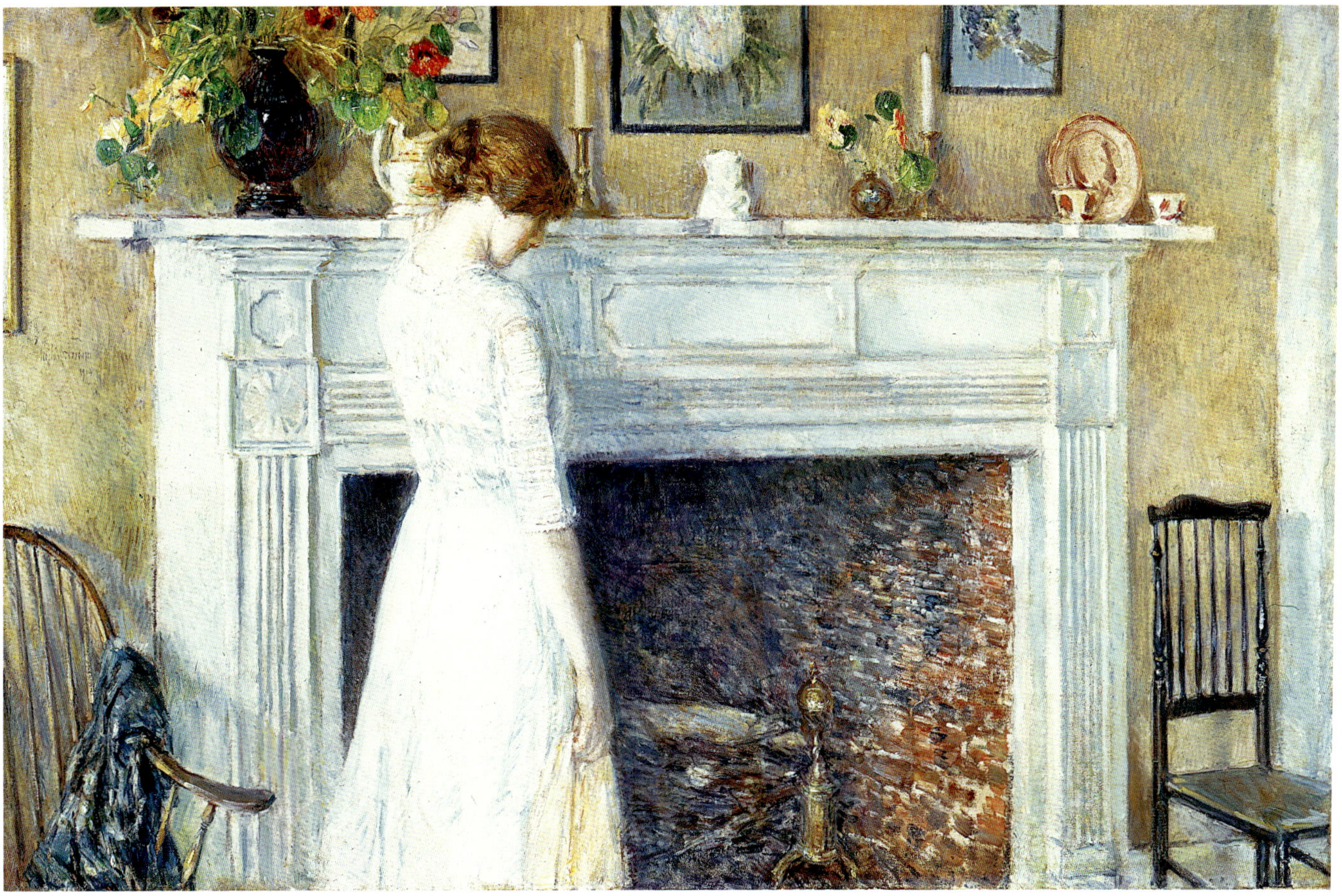

Fig. 160. Childe Hassam. *In the Old House,* 1914. Oil on canvas, 31¼ x 48 in. (79.4 x 121.9 cm). Lewis and Ali Sanders

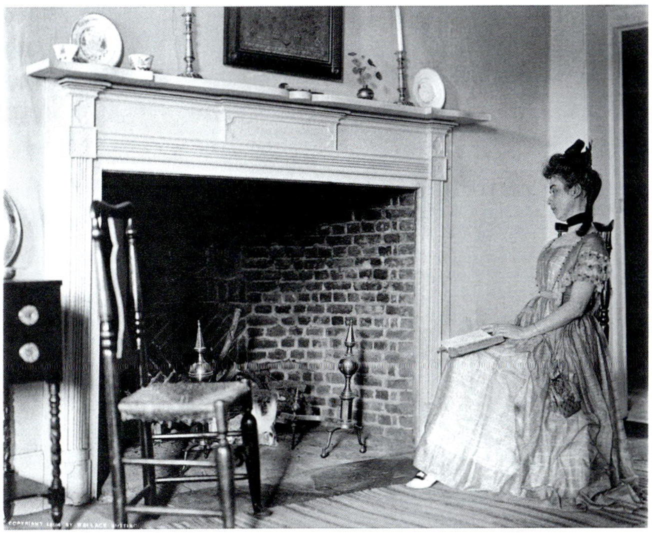

Fig. 161. Wallace Nutting. *Reflections Are Ever Best,* 1904. Platinum print. Courtesy of the William E. Finch, Jr. Archives, The Historical Society of the Town of Greenwich

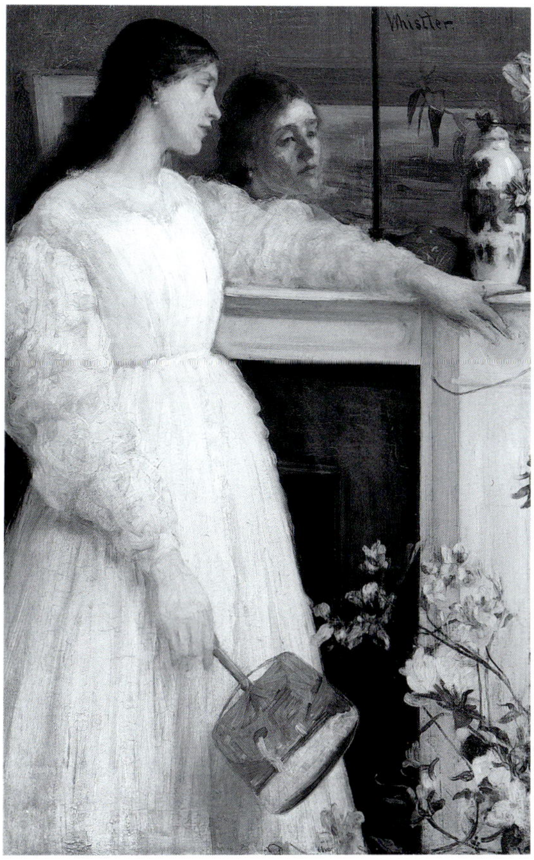

Fig. 162. James McNeill Whistler. *Symphony in White, No. 2: The Little White Girl,* 1864. Oil on canvas, 30 x 20 in. (76.2 x 50.8 cm). Tate, London

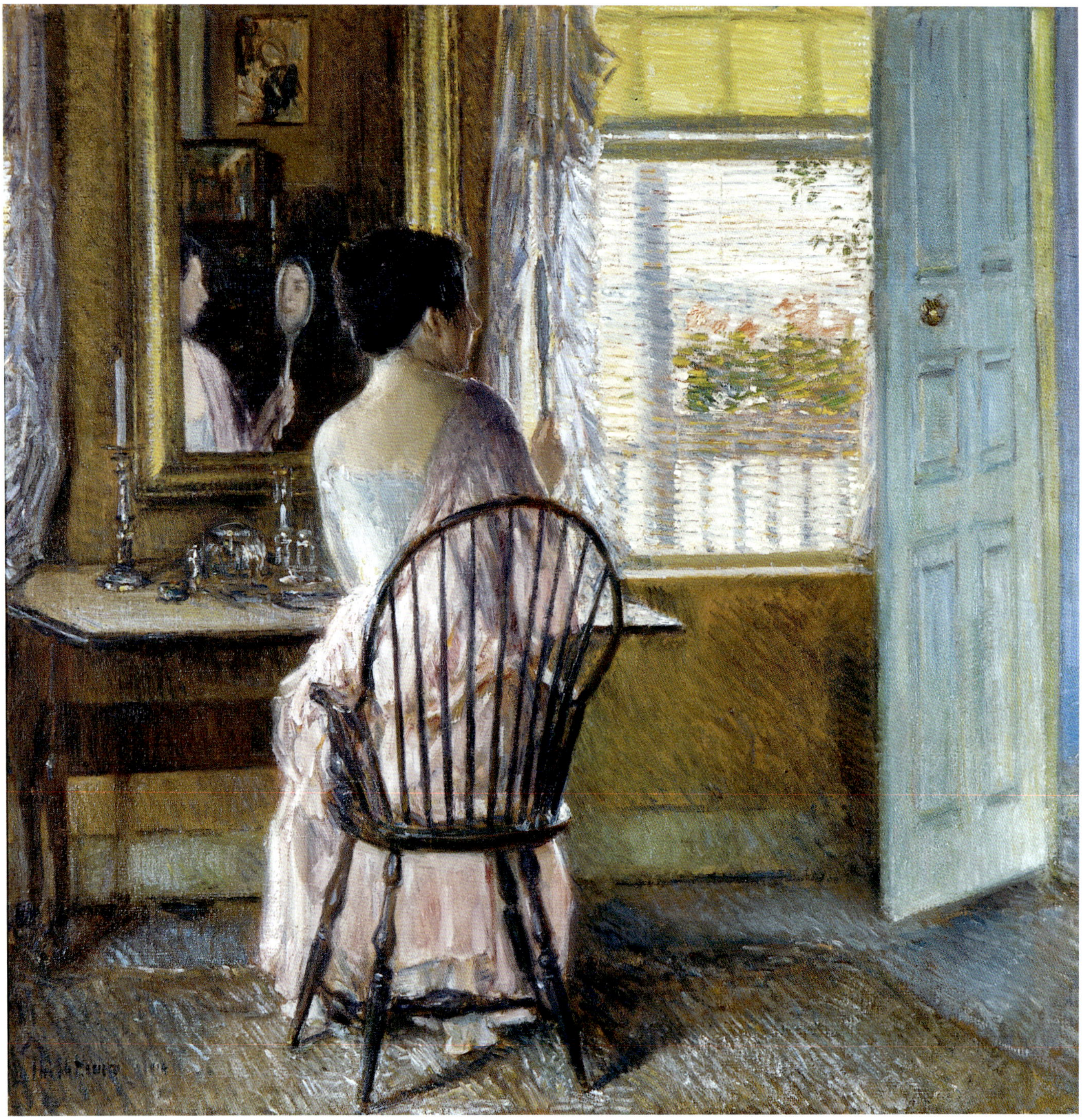

Fig. 163. Childe Hassam. *Morning Light,* 1914. Oil on canvas, 34 x 34 in. (86.4 x 86.4 cm). Howard and Susan Sosin

fireplace to a group of Japanesque flower studies by MacRae, and the old china has been supplemented by a large aubergine-purple vase by art-potter Leon Volkmar. Hassam combined the homespun quality of Nutting's photograph with the aestheticism of Whistler's *Symphony in White, No. 2: The Little White Girl* (fig. 162), but he went further than either of them in equating the female figure with hearth and home. Helen's lacy dress and pale skin merge with the white fireplace surround. Her auburn hair, echoing the color of centuries-old bricks and the small vase, is aligned with the mantelshelf; like the ornaments displayed there, she is an objet d'art.

Maud Hassam posed for *Morning Light* (fig. 163), painted in the north bedroom of the Holley House in the summer of 1914. The model's identity lends the picture an element of urbanity and eroticism that is absent or subdued in the paintings for which young Helen Burke posed. We glimpse Mrs. Hassam at her toilette—an intimate moment a genteel woman of her era would share only with her husband.

Hassam set up a game of reflections, fragmenting his wife's image in three mirrors. He also played with varieties of illumination, as his title indicates. A matchstick blind suspended from the upper porch filters the morning light, flattening the view into a scrap of patterned fabric. An old-fashioned shade, raised nearly to the top of the window, imparts an amber glow. Light from the unseen north window caresses the nape of Mrs. Hassam's neck, her left shoulder, white bodice, and pink peignoir and picks out highlights on her silver and glass dressing-table set.

Surprisingly, Hassam did not send *Morning Light* or any other Cos Cob paintings to exhibitions in Greenwich. In 1912 the art colonists had belatedly recognized the wealthy newcomers as a potential market for their work. They organized as the Greenwich Society of Artists, established a category of associate members that included collector Louisine Havemeyer, and mounted their first exhibition, at Greenwich's fledgling Bruce Museum. Hassam exhibited with the society in 1914, 1919, and 1922, sending works painted in Appledore, New York, and East Hampton. He may have speculated that unfamiliar subjects would have more appeal to the town's New York–based elite than images of the well-known environs of rustic Cos Cob.

The exhibitions mounted by resident artists in Old Lyme, by contrast with those of Cos Cob's colony, featured work done only in that region. The art colony in Old Lyme, about seventy-five miles up the Connecticut coast from Greenwich, got its start in 1900. In that year Tonalist Henry Ward Ranger decided to make the quiet community the American counterpart of Barbizon, the village on the edge of the Fontainebleau forest where Jean-François Millet, Théodore Rousseau, and their followers gathered in the mid-nineteenth century to paint the local peasants, their livestock, and the unremarkable countryside.[62] In Old Lyme, as in Appledore and Cos Cob, the artists congregated at an unpretentious but aesthetic house presided over by a welcoming hostess (figs. 164, 165). Florence Griswold, who had struggled to support herself and maintain her handsome family home, happily provided accommodations for the artists Ranger recruited to join him in Old Lyme. (The house, built in 1817, is today part of the Florence Griswold Museum.)

Like Celia Thaxter, Florence Griswold encouraged the sale of her boarders' paintings. "Not only was Miss Florence interested in the work of her guests, but she was forever trying to sell it, and help along the prosperity of her artists," one of them recalled.[63] A guidebook related that the Griswold House contained "many framed pictures and other works of art which the visitor can have for a consideration."[64] The front hall functioned as an informal gallery, where paintings and old furniture were offered for sale.

To complement Griswold's discreet promotion of their work, the artists began mounting summer exhibitions just two years after the colony was founded. The first, held in the local library in late August 1902, featured twelve artists, all working in the Tonalist style. The Hartford paper reported that the library was "thronged" by visitors from "Hartford, New Haven, Middletown, New York, New London, Boston, Chicago, Springfield and other places."[65]

It seems no accident that Hassam, always alert to market opportunities, first stayed in Old Lyme the following year.

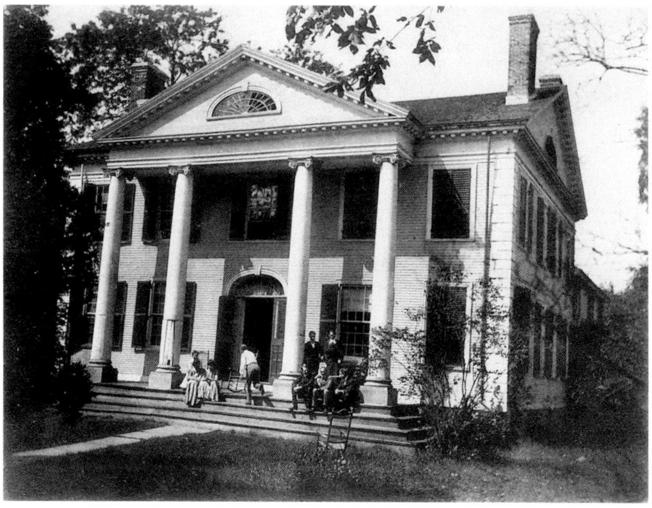

Fig. 164. Artists and friends gathered on the front steps of the Florence Griswold House, ca. 1905. Florence Griswold Museum, Old Lyme, Connecticut; Lyme Historical Society Archives

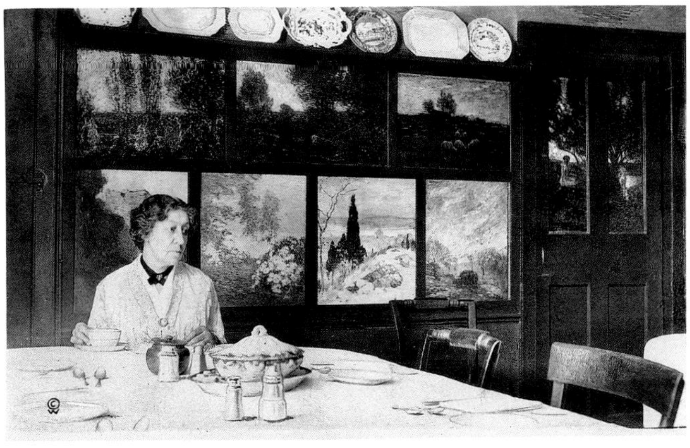

Fig. 165. Miss Florence seated in her dining room at the Florence Griswold House, ca. 1920. Florence Griswold Museum, Old Lyme, Connecticut; Lyme Historical Society Archives. Hassam's panels depicting nudes in a landscape are visible on the door at the right

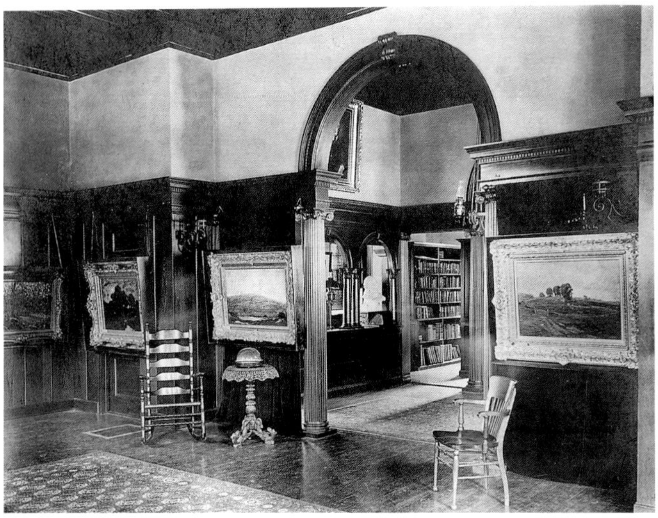

Fig. 166. *Second Annual Library Exhibition,* in what was then the main reading room, 1903. Old Lyme Phoebe Griffin Noyes Library, Old Lyme, Connecticut

During that visit he painted a view of the humpbacked bridge over the Lieutenant River (fig. 167), leaving it behind for the September exhibition (fig. 166) when he continued on to Appledore. Both the *New York Times* and the *Hartford Courant* commented that Hassam's painting was the only Impressionist work in the show.[66] A Pittsburgh paper singled out *The Old Lyme Bridge* as a "noticeable exception" to the "wonderful harmony" of Tonalist paintings, calling it "a delightful bit of open-air realism and strangely prominent in lieu of its environment."[67]

Although there is no information about sales made at the early exhibitions in Old Lyme, we know these shows were public-relations successes, securing Hassam and other participants career-enhancing attention from the press and the public. The annual became a popular destination for visitors from New York, Hartford, and surrounding communities. Its duration increased from three days in 1902 to six by 1910. Hassam participated in most of the Old Lyme exhibitions between 1903 and 1912, showing even in the years he did not paint there. Florence Griswold acted as his agent, arranging

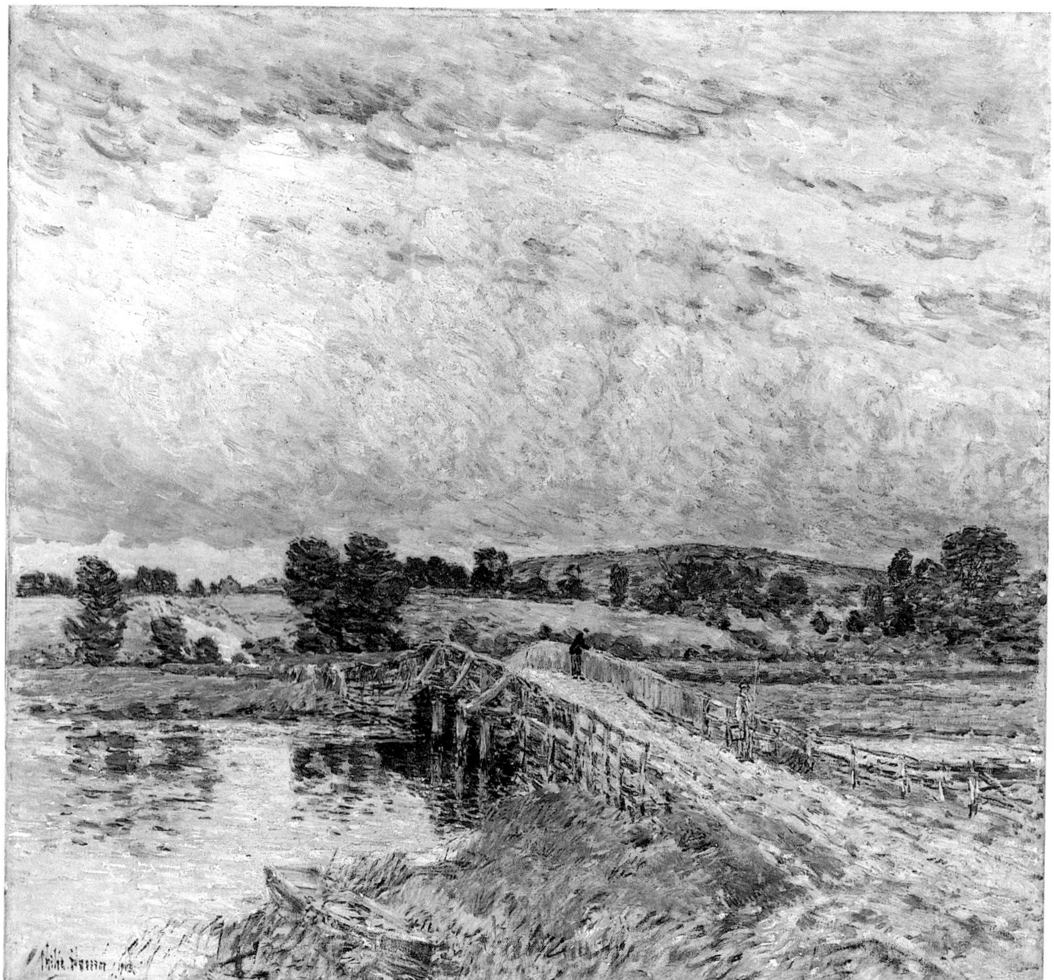

Fig. 167. Childe Hassam. *The Old Lyme Bridge,* July 1903. Oil on canvas, 24½ x 26 in. (62.2 x 66 cm). Ball State University Museum of Art, Muncie, Indiana, Gift of the Edmund Burke Ball heirs 1980.010.06

for his paintings to be transported to the library and accepting a commission on those that sold.[68]

Hassam visited Old Lyme over a relatively short time span—between 1903 and 1909—but his involvement helped draw attention to the art colony and hastened the shift in its makeup from Tonalists to Impressionists.[69] By 1907 one critic observed that the Old Lyme exhibitions were "thoroughly impressionistic. Ranger oaks are seen through Hassam eyes, and the Connecticut River flows blue through canvases instead of yellow."[70]

When he stayed at the Griswold House, Hassam kept his materials in one of the studios, converted from barns and sheds, that stood between the boardinghouse and the Lieutenant River. "I wish I might have appeared with the fruit buds," he wrote to Florence Griswold in late April 1905. "However if I may have my studio in the garden (that I had before) and a room I will be happy."[71] Ensconced in Old Lyme that July, he wrote jubilantly to Weir, who had a well-equipped workroom on his own farm in Branchville, Connecticut, "You are all well I hope and of course you are enjoying that bully studio! You should see mine here, just the place for high thinking and low living."[72]

Hassam depicted his studio in the background of *Apple Trees in Bloom, Old Lyme* (fig. 168). A photograph shows the artist, sleeves rolled up, with the canvas on his easel (fig. 169). A vigorous young apple tree takes center stage in his composition; a taller, older one fans its branches over the sapling and the ramshackle shed that was the studio. Harry Hoffman depicted the same scene five years later (fig. 170); like Hassam, he took artistic license in setting the outbuilding closer to the river than it actually was. A recent archaeological survey reveals that no structure stood as close to the riverbank.[73] However, in the northwest corner of the orchard archaeologists discovered the likely site of Hassam's studio, an outbuilding measuring about twelve by twenty-four feet, probably converted from agricultural use about 1900. The "low living" to which Hassam alluded may be reflected in the stash of empty beer, wine, and liquor bottles they unearthed in the crawl space under the doorsill.[74]

The motif of a blossoming fruit tree had long appealed to Hassam. He gave it a Japanesque treatment in *Peach Blossoms—Villiers-le-Bel* (fig. 81), painted in France in the late 1880s. *Apple Trees in Bloom, Old Lyme,* on the other hand, speaks with a Yankee accent. The fruit, better able to endure New England winters than the peach or the pear, became the region's major agricultural product during the eighteenth century. As New England turned to industry from farming, for which its rocky soil is ill suited, the remnants of old orchards inspired nostalgic treatment by artists as diverse as Jasper Francis Cropsey, Martin Johnson Heade, and Winslow Homer.[75] Wallace Nutting devoted 75 of the 304 illustrations in his book *Connecticut Beautiful* to blossoming fruit trees.[76] His hand-tinted photograph *Decked as a Bride* (fig. 171), recording a country lane winding past an apple orchard in full bloom, was a popular wedding present.[77] In Hassam's painting the rustic shed and wire fence suggest a farm, not a studio. The combination of an old tree and a young one, implying the past and the future, conveys the nostalgia and optimism that permeated American culture at the turn of the last century.

In Old Lyme, as elsewhere, the female figure was one of Hassam's major themes. *The Victorian Chair* (fig. 172), thought to have been painted during Hassam's visit to Old Lyme in the autumn of 1906, may portray Katherine Langhorne Adams.[78] Only twenty-one at the time, she had studied under Twachtman at the Art Students League in New York and possibly also in the summer school at Cos Cob. Hassam posed the model seated in profile in a balloon-back armchair in the Rococo style.[79] Such chairs, produced in the United States in the mid-nineteenth century, lack the aura of antiquity that Hassam usually sought in his New England subjects. However, its upholstery printed with huge red roses creates an indoor garden for the brunette beauty, whose embroidered white dress reiterates the floral motif.

Twenty-sixth of June, Old Lyme (fig. 173) emphasizes, in title and subject matter, a specific time and place. The date was Maud Hassam's birthday (she was fifty in 1912, the year the picture was painted), and the vase of mountain laurel establishes the Old Lyme setting. Connecticut's official flower, laurel grows throughout the state, but it flourishes in particular in Old Lyme's rocky ledges and became a favorite of Hassam's and of other artists there. (One of them, Edward F. Rook, attached cotton balls to the shrubs so that he could continue painting them after the blossoms faded.)[80] In *Twenty-sixth of June, Old Lyme* Maud Hassam adopted the same pose, costume, and hairstyle as the model in *The Table Garden* (fig. 226), painted in New York two years earlier. The vertical elements in the city painting—expressed in the skyscrapers, angular folds in the sheer curtains, and leggy foliage on the potted bulbs—give way in the country picture to more rounded forms rendered in looser brushwork.

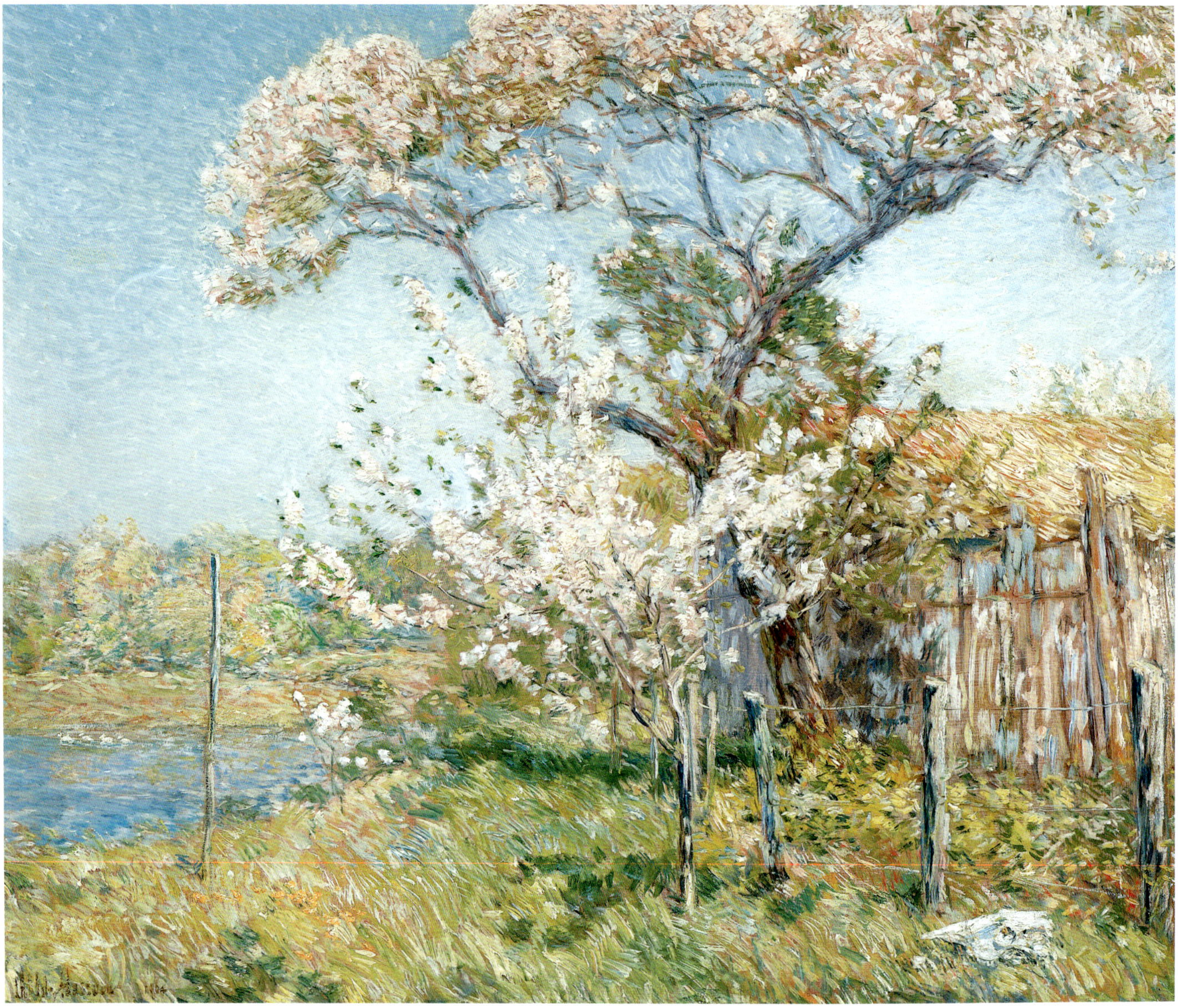

Fig. 168. Childe Hassam. *Apple Trees in Bloom, Old Lyme,* 1904. Oil on panel, 25 x 30½ in. (63.5 x 77.5 cm). Private collection, New York City

Most of Hassam's Old Lyme paintings of the female figure depict nudes in the open air, a subject he treated occasionally at Appledore and more frequently in East Hampton, bringing models out to Long Island from New York City.[81] Hassam considered his nudes to be among his finest works, but few critics, then or now, have shared his opinion. Both of his paintings in the 1906 Old Lyme exhibition portrayed "nude figures among green foliage."[82] The same description applies to a pair of panels (fig. 174) he had painted in the Griswold House dining room three years earlier. An invitation from the art colony's founders to decorate panels in this room was an honor, and it was one extended to Hassam during his first visit. Covering the doors and walls, most of the thirty-odd panels are landscapes, although the colony's Barbizon component is well represented by images of sheep and cattle (see fig. 165). Hassam collaborated on one such pastoral scene with Walter Griffin and Henry Rankin Poore and also painted a bouquet of dahlias on a narrow panel beside the fireplace. His lumpen figures, the only nudes in the room, do not disturb the ensemble's charm.

Hassam's most significant Old Lyme subject was the First Congregational Church, designed by Samuel Belcher of Ellington, Connecticut, and built in 1817.[83] He depicted it seven times, in oil, pastel, and etching. The best-known versions, painted in 1903, 1905, and 1906 (figs. 175, 176, 177), show him shifting from side to side as if seeking the most flattering angle for a portrait. All share the same vertical format, truncated steeple, and absence of figures. This church is portrayed without a congregation, and as such is an expression of Hassam's own religious attitude. As a boy he attended a

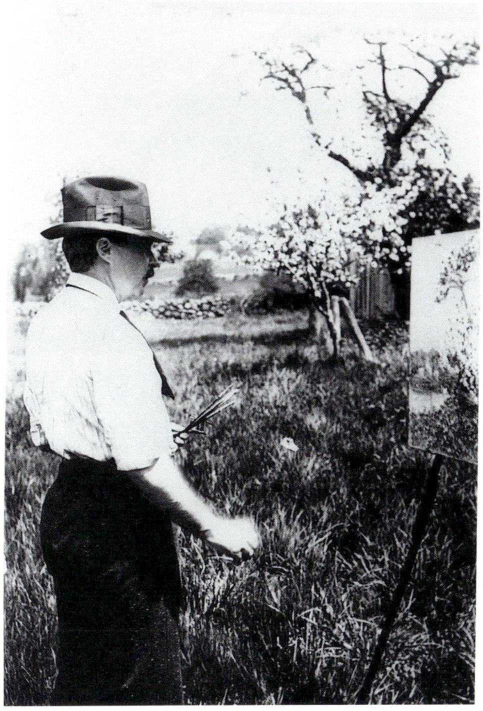

Fig. 169. Hassam, with *Apple Trees in Bloom, Old Lyme* on his easel, painting in the orchard behind Florence Griswold's house, 1904. Florence Griswold Museum, Old Lyme, Connecticut; Lyme Historical Society Archives

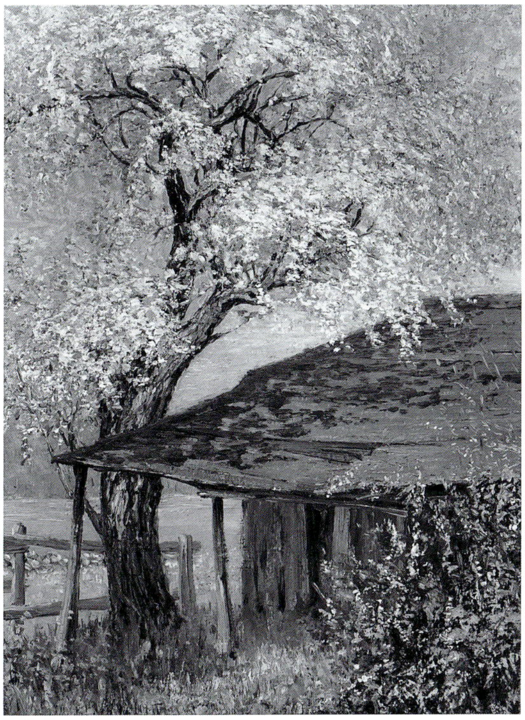

Fig. 170. Harry Hoffman. *Childe Hassam's Studio,* 1909. Oil on canvas, 24 x 18 in. (61.0 x 45.7 cm). Florence Griswold Museum, Old Lyme, Connecticut; Gift of the Artist

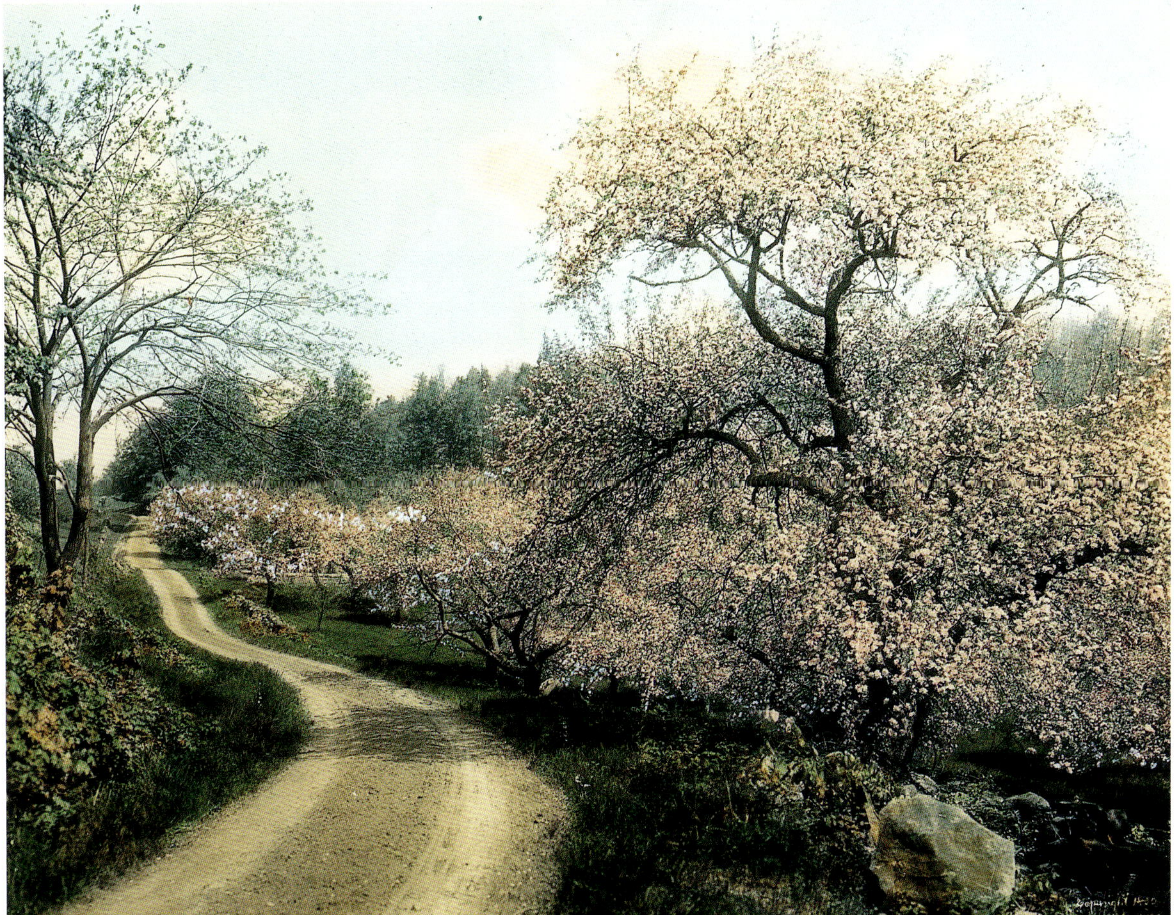

Fig. 171. Wallace Nutting. *Decked as a Bride,* 1910. Hand-tinted platinum print. Dorothy and Richard Manville, Southbury, Connecticut

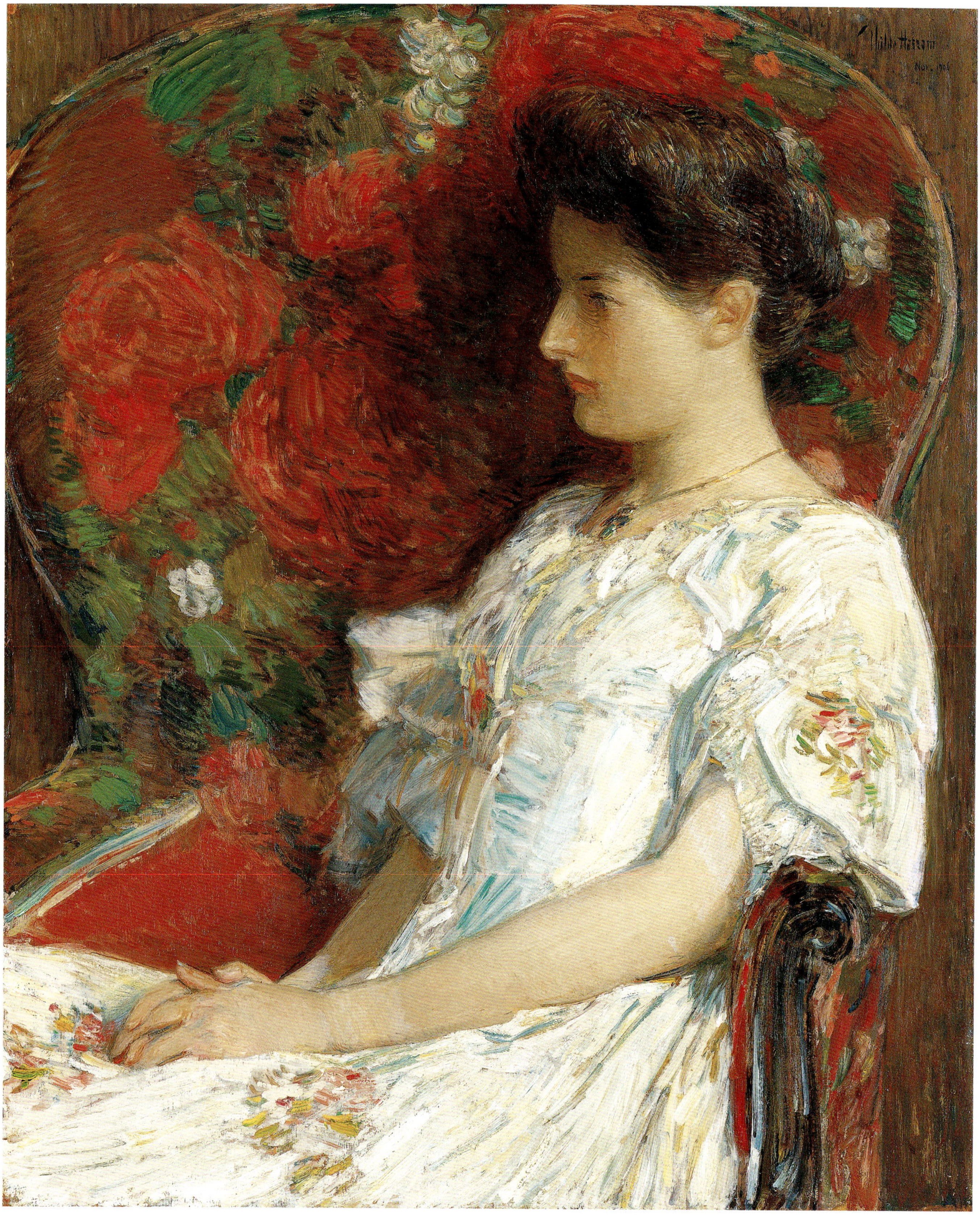

Fig. 172. Childe Hassam. *The Victorian Chair,* 1906. Oil on wood, 30⅛ x 25 in. (76.5 x 63.5 cm). Smithsonian American Art Museum, Washington, D.C. Gift of William T. Evans

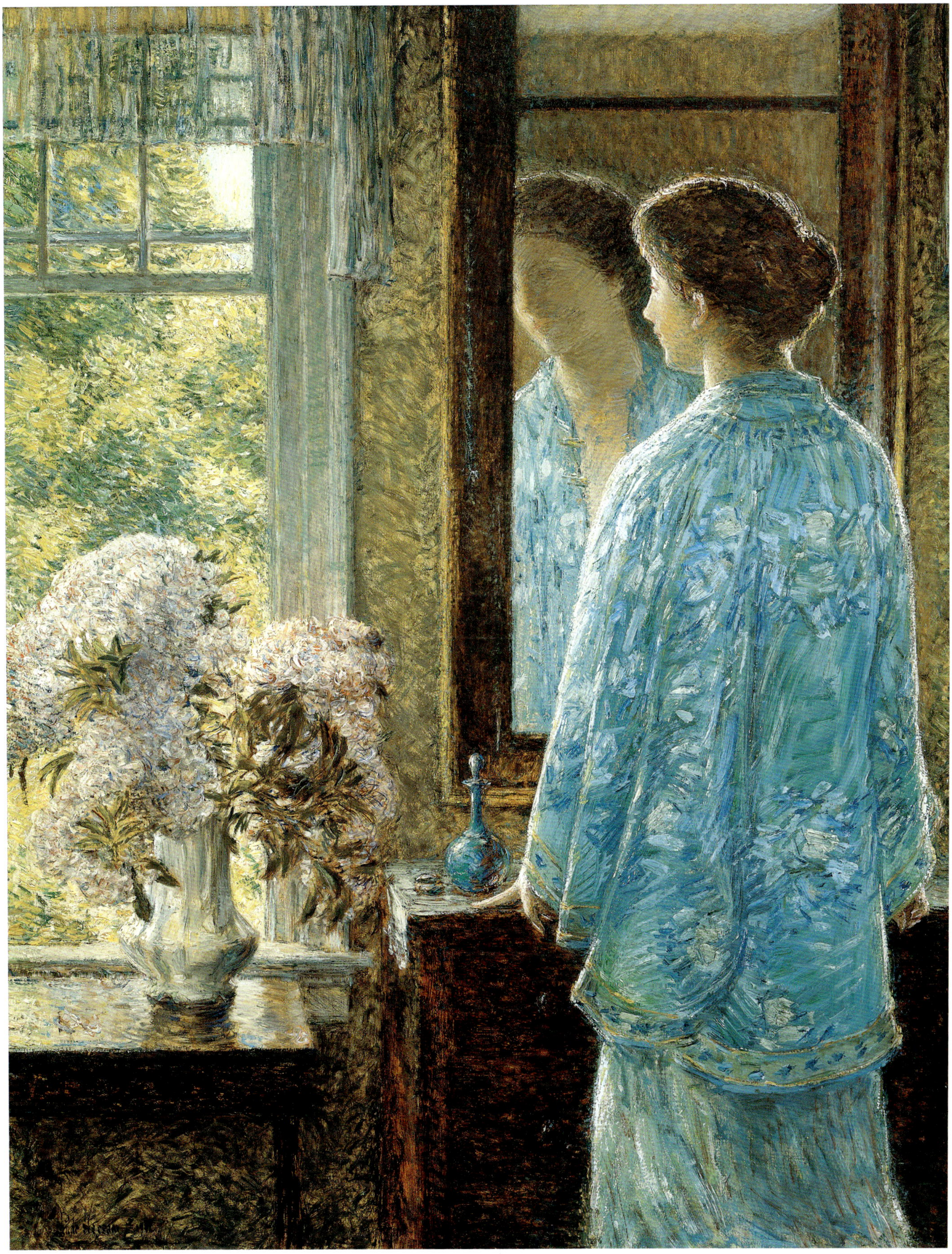

Fig. 173. Childe Hassam. *Twenty-sixth of June, Old Lyme,* 1912. Oil on canvas, 31¾ x 24½ in. (80.6 x 62.2 cm). Mr. and Mrs. Theodore N. Lerner

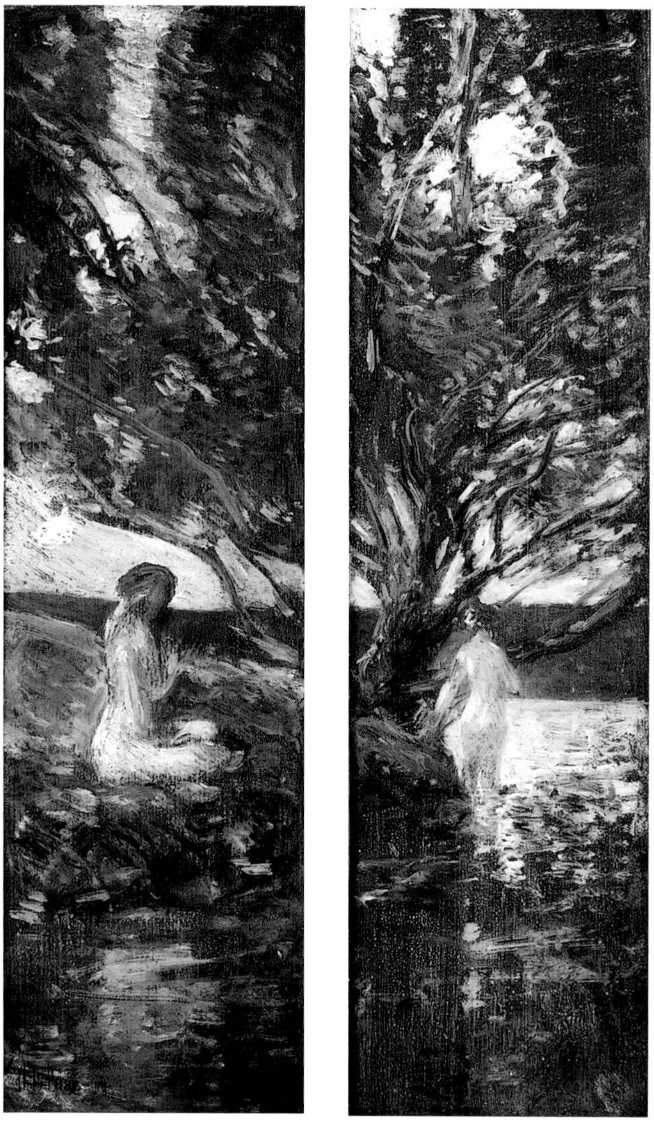

Fig. 174. Childe Hassam. *The Bathers,* 1903. Oil on panel, each of two panels, 31 x 9 in. (78.7 x 22.9 cm). Florence Griswold Museum, Old Lyme, Connecticut; Gift of the Artist

Unitarian church; after his death an Episcopal priest officiated at his funeral.[84] In the intervening years religion seems to have played no part in his life. A friend's suggestion that he might actually kneel to pray on the "two fine old 'prayer rugs'" he had bought for his Paris apartment prompted his amused response, "I hasten to defend myself against the 'Prayer' idea! That is so funny! I haven't said a prayer or thought one since I was a boy."[85] He prided himself that, whereas his wife's family tree included many ministers, "his own forbears were more by way of being sailors and privateersmen, or even pirates, and that he liked them so."[86] In an autobiographical sketch Hassam named two pivotal occurrences of the year of his birth: John Brown's raid at Harper's Ferry and the publication of Charles Darwin's *Origin of Species,* declaring, "the one event was to free the world of human slavery and the other was to free it from theological slavery of thought—or mental slavery."[87]

For Hassam the New England meetinghouse represented not a place of worship but an emblem of beauty and of Anglo-American tradition. He traced its appeal to his boyhood in Dorchester. "Some of the white churches were actual . . . masterpieces of architecture," he wrote:

> *and the white church on Meeting House hill . . . was no exception. Painting as I often have the white New England church tower in its setting preferably of American elms, sometimes with the color of our glorious American autumn . . . I can look back and very truly say that probably and all unconsciously I as a very young boy looked at this New England church and without knowing it appreciated partly its great beauty as it stood there then against one of our radiant North American clear blue skies. And as it still stands there now.*[88]

The knowledge that "it still stands there now" reassured him during a period of increasing immigration to America, mostly from Catholic countries. The absence of figures enhances the timelessness of his Old Lyme Church paintings; worshipers' clothing would have anchored the images in a specific period. The banishing of figures also promotes an aura of exclusivity, as William H. Truettner and Thomas Andrew Denenberg have suggested.[89] Few are admitted to pure Yankeeism. One must be born to it, as was Hassam.

Hassam asserted that "New England churches have the same kind of beauty as Greek temples."[90] The Greek temple facade of the Old Lyme church is most evident in the canvas now in the Albright-Knox Art Gallery, Buffalo (fig. 176). Hassam dated it with the exact month and day of its completion—October 17, 1905—as if to emphasize that he had worked before the subject, accurately capturing the gleam of its white Ionic columns in the sunlight. Autumn permits a better view of the architecture than does summer and strengthens the identification with New England, whose fall foliage has attracted generations of leaf-peepers. When the painting was exhibited at the National Academy of Design in New York in March 1907, one reviewer called it "in essence a phase of consecrated New England."[91]

For the version now at the Parrish Art Museum, Southampton, New York (fig. 177), Hassam chose a vantage point that included most of the steeple. He sent it to the Old Lyme exhibition in late August 1908, the year after the

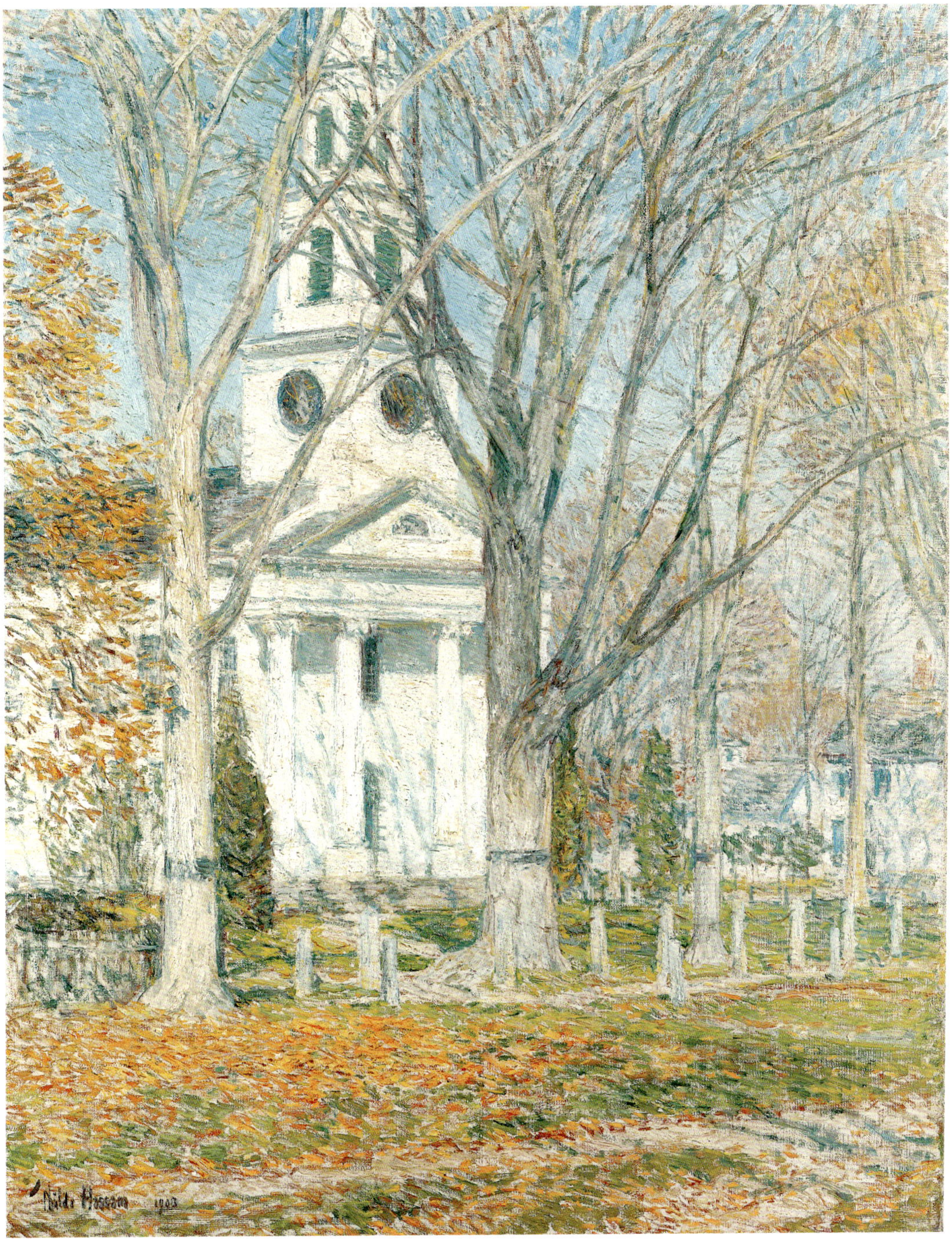

Fig. 175. Childe Hassam. *Church at Old Lyme,* 1903. Oil on canvas, 36½ x 28½ in. (92.7 x 72.4 cm). Private collection

church had been destroyed by fire. "I always had a real and pagan delight in the . . . old church," he wrote to Florence Griswold when he heard of the fire. "They cannot rebuild it—never! And the fine and immemorial elms—Oh! It is a pity."[92] The church was quickly rebuilt, however, partly with proceeds from the 1907 exhibition.

Hassam usually went to several sites each summer. Gloucester, just one hour from Boston by train, was easily accessible to the young artist, who first visited there in 1880 or 1881. After he moved to New York, Gloucester was a convenient stopover on his journeys to Appledore, and he stayed there at least five times in the 1890s. In July 1894 he sent an urgent request to New York dealer William Macbeth to send more than thirty of his matted watercolors to his East Gloucester hotel, where he apparently intended to display them.[93] At the time it was only in such improvised exhibitions that artists could present their work to Gloucester's summer visitors and prosperous year-round residents.

Gloucester combines colonial architecture, a picturesque setting, and a bustling harbor. America's largest fishing port during Hassam's time, it also supported granite quarrying, ironworking, shipbuilding, fish-drying, and fish-packing industries. Tourism developed there rapidly, beginning about 1835.[94] Among the town's summer visitors were many artists.

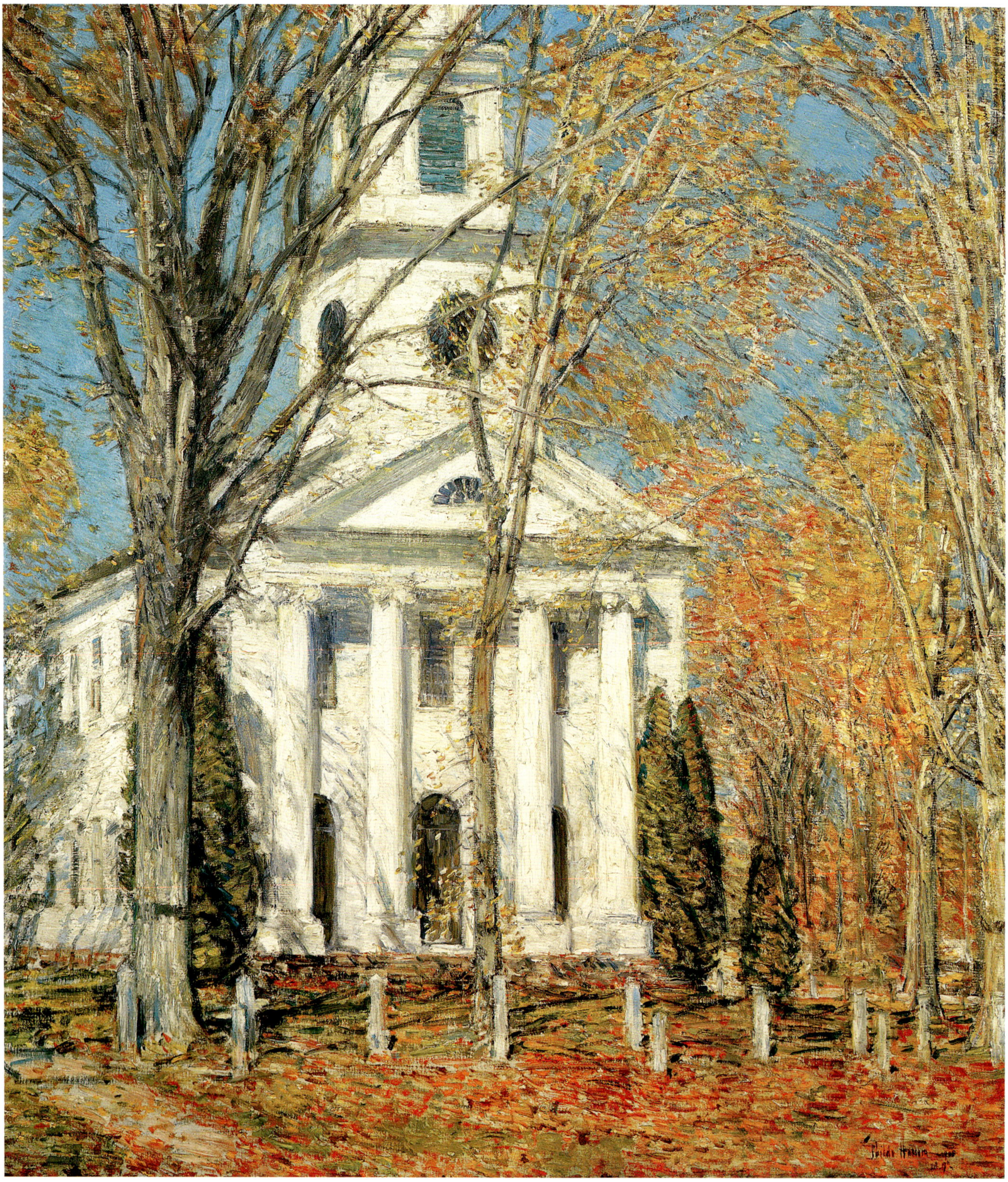

Fig. 176. Childe Hassam. *Church at Old Lyme*, 1905. Oil on canvas, 36¼ x 32¼ in. (92.1 x 81.9 cm). Albright-Knox Art Gallery, Buffalo, Albert H. Tracy Fund, 1909

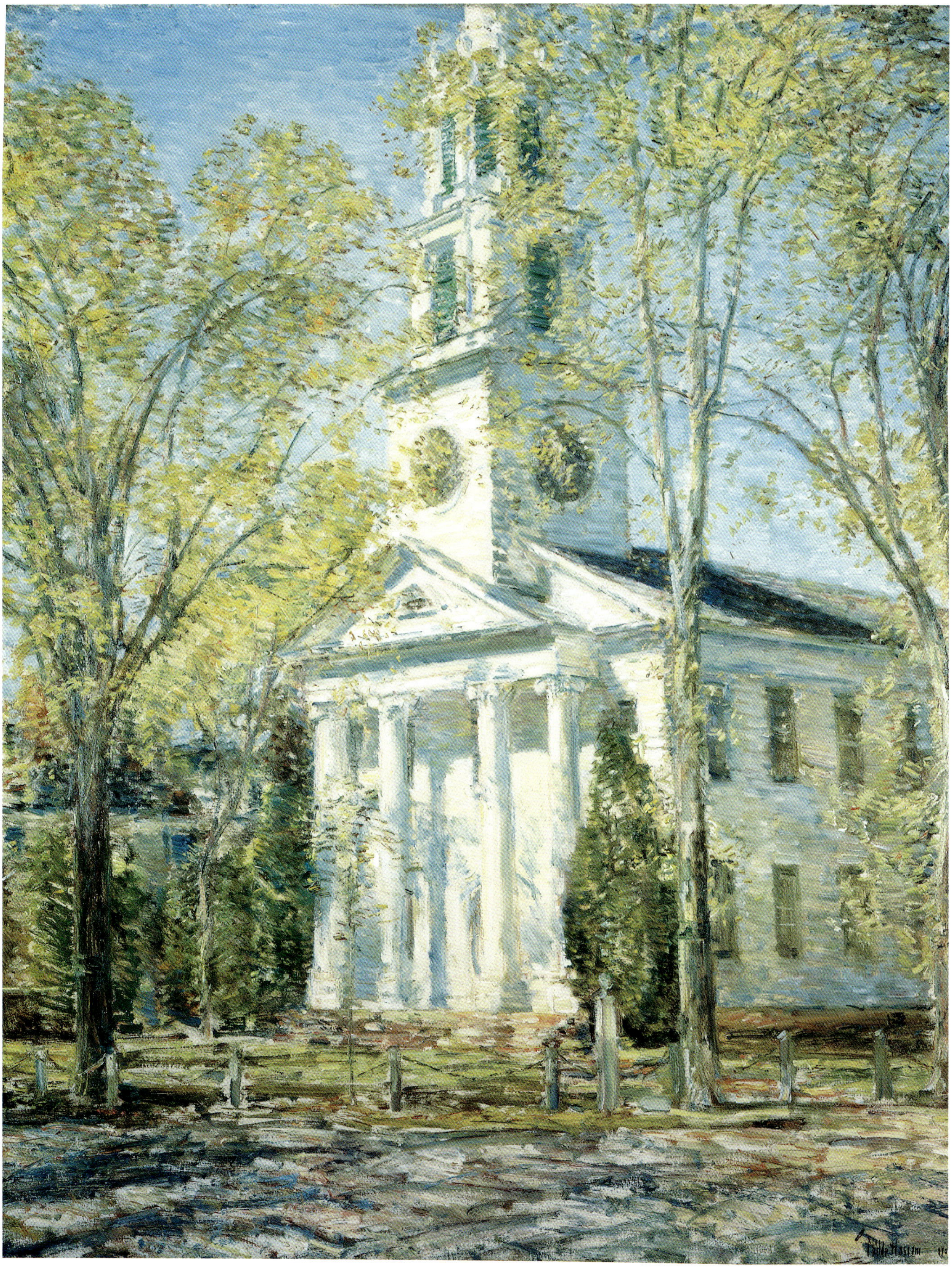

Fig. 177. Childe Hassam. *Church at Old Lyme,* 1906. Oil on canvas, 30⅛ x 25¼ in. (76.5 x 64.1 cm). The Parrish Art Museum, Southampton, New York, Littlejohn Collection

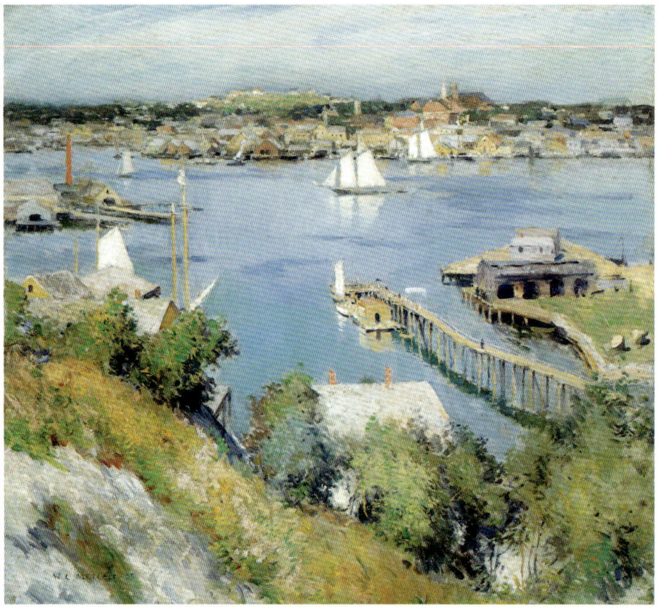

Fitz Hugh Lane, a native son, and Martin Johnson Heade painted there in the mid-nineteenth century. Homer and Hunt followed them after the Civil War, and Twachtman, Charles H. Davis, Joseph R. DeCamp, Frank Duveneck, Willard L. Metcalf, and Edward Henry Potthast joined the flood of artists working in Gloucester at the turn of the last century.[95] Unlike Appledore, Cos Cob, and Old Lyme, in each of which one aesthetic boardinghouse served as the art colony's principal gathering place, in Gloucester the artists dispersed among widely scattered hotels, boardinghouses, and rental cottages.

Fig. 178. Willard Metcalf. *Gloucester Harbor,* 1895. Oil on canvas, 26⅛ x 29¼ in. (66.4 x 74.3 cm). Mead Art Museum, Amherst College, Massachusetts, Gift of George D. Pratt, Class of 1893 AC P.1932.16

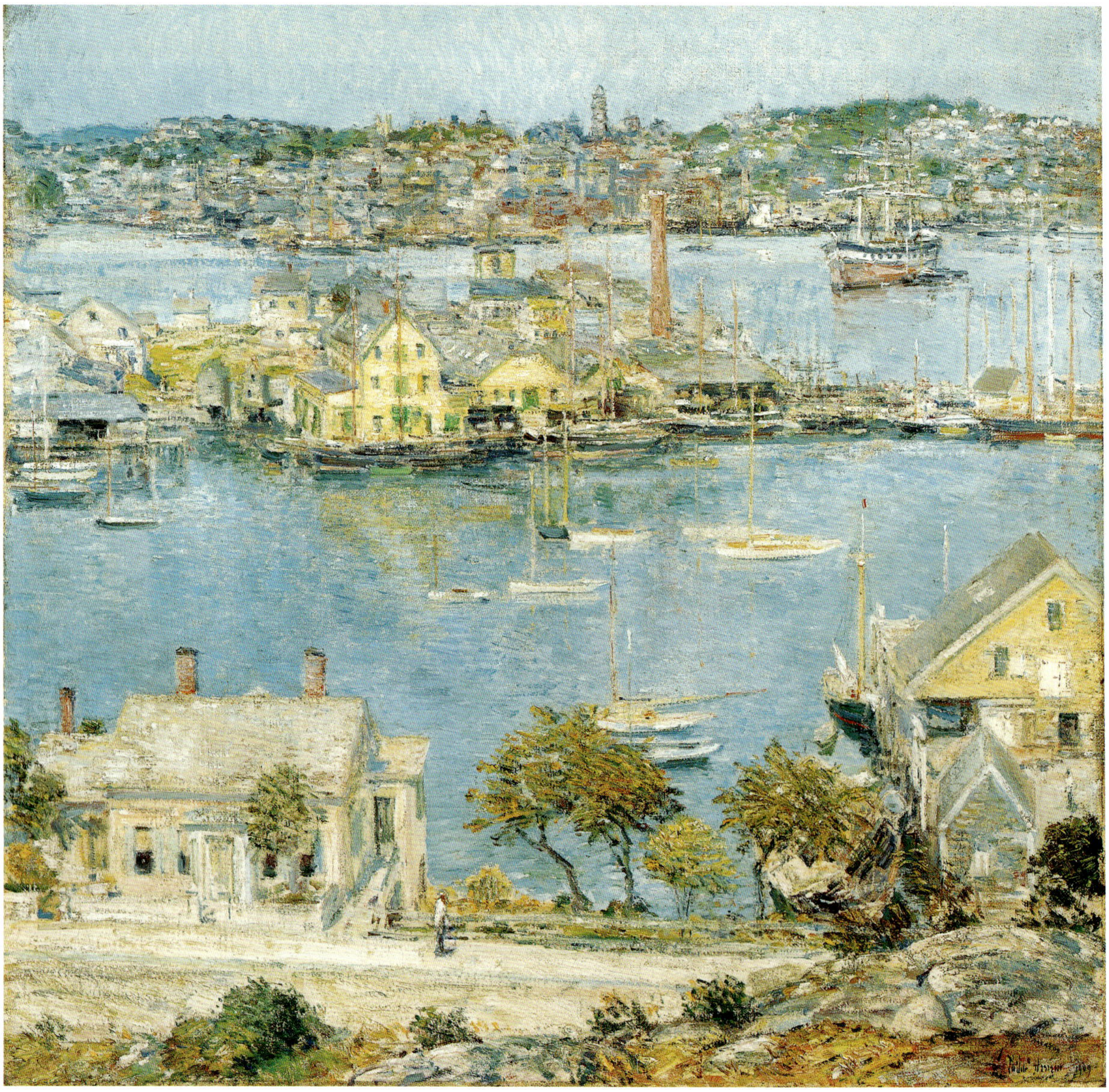

Fig. 179. Childe Hassam. *Gloucester Harbor,* 1899 (inscribed *1909*). Oil on canvas, 25 x 26 in. (63.5 x 66 cm). Norton Museum of Art, West Palm Beach, Florida

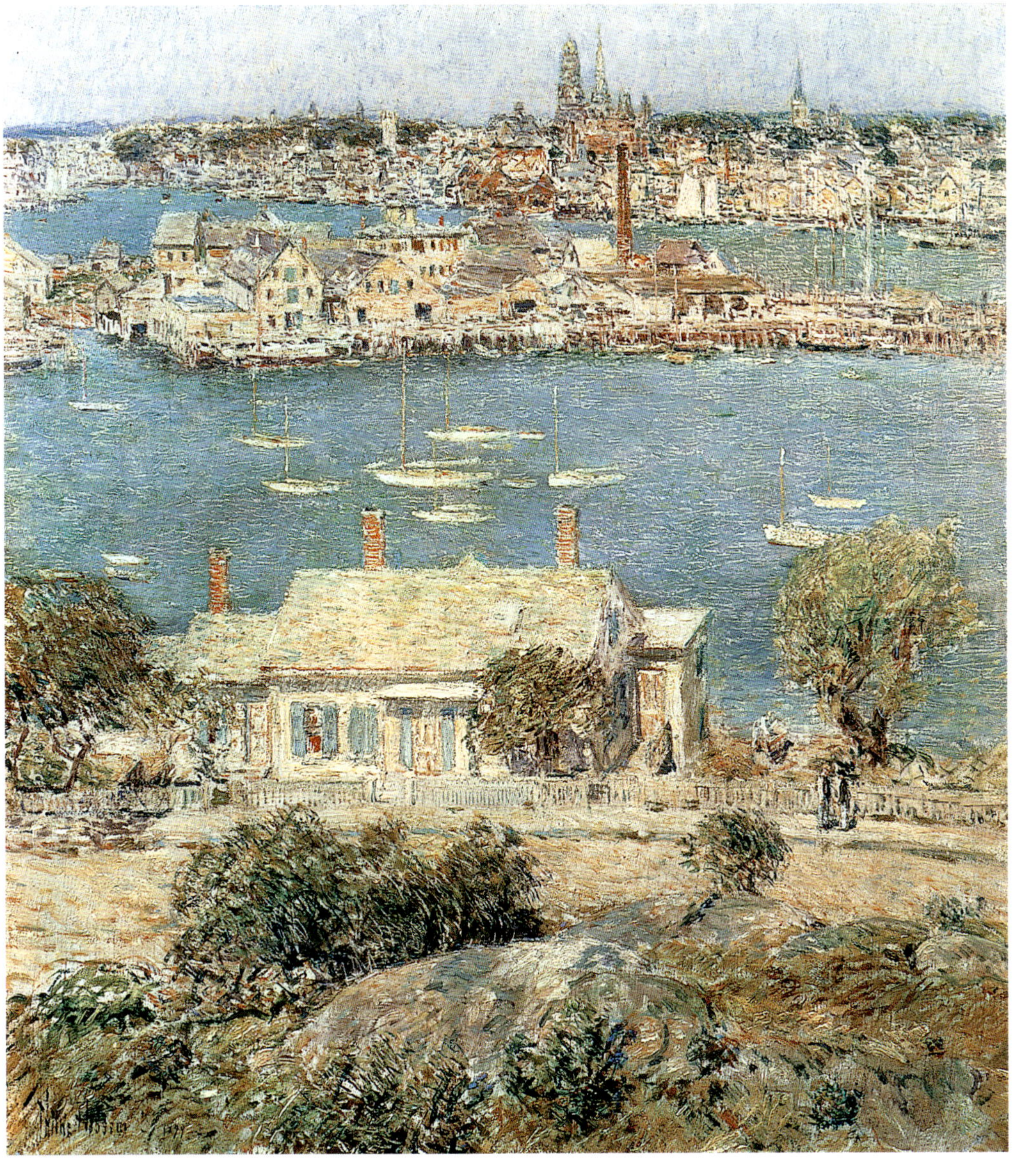

Fig. 180. Childe Hassam. *Gloucester Harbor,* 1899. Oil on canvas, 24½ x 22½ in. (62.2 x 57.2 cm). Private collection

Hassam often planned his sojourns in Gloucester to coincide with those of his friends. In 1895 he visited with Metcalf, who had been working in a Barbizon-influenced style but adopted a more Impressionist manner that summer. "It was the beginning of his success," Hassam boasted later, taking credit for influencing the transformation.[96] In *Gloucester Harbor* (fig. 178) Metcalf glamorized the old seaport. The foreground of rocks and foliage implies a rural vantage point. A delicate pier angles into the harbor, whose placid blue water is punctuated by gleaming white sails. A red smokestack is a pleasing accent rather than an industrial intrusion. Green fills the foreground, underlines the pier, and threads a verdant ribbon through the distant city.

In comparison with Metcalf's canvas, Hassam's *Gloucester Harbor* in the Norton Museum of Art (fig. 179), painted in summer 1899, smacks of Yankee plain speaking. Straightforward horizontal bands replace Metcalf's artful diagonals, the foreground acknowledges the urban setting, and the limited use of green admits to a populous city. Hassam's shift westward affords a clear view of the fish canneries on Rocky Neck, the peninsula in the middle ground. The prominent chimney of the Marine Railways power plant staples the island to the distant city, echoing the vertical of the landmark city-hall clock tower. Pleasure craft drift at their moorings in Smith's Cove, but the ship anchored in the Inner Harbor testifies to the business of Gloucester. (The ship may be one of the Italian barks that imported salt for fish processing.) The panoramic viewpoint, which recalls that device in Hassam's New York paintings, captures the varied elements that made Gloucester so appealing to him.

Hassam may have painted his canvas from the upper story of the Hawthorne Inn, where he sometimes stayed. For a

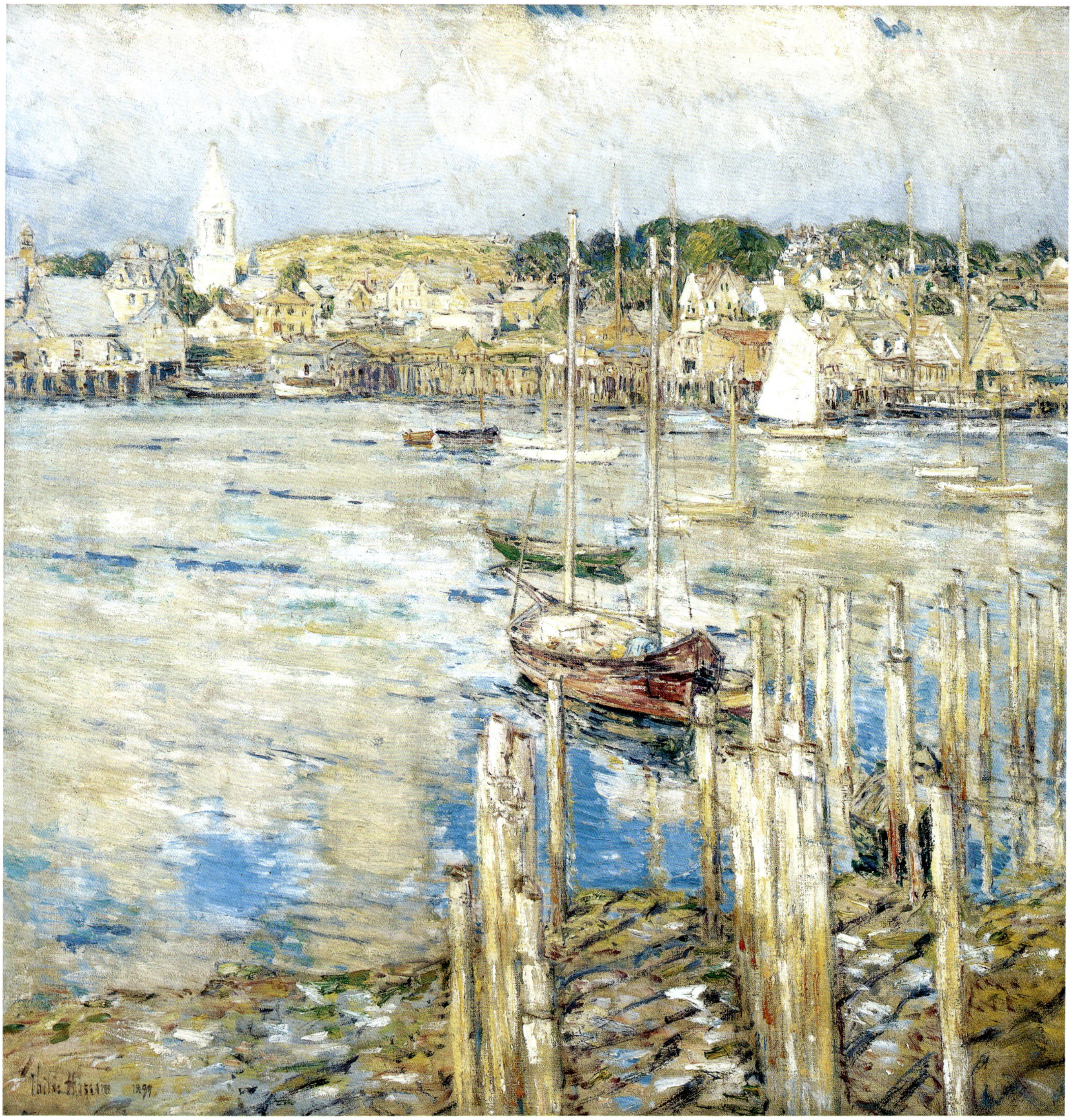

Fig. 181. Childe Hassam. *Gloucester,* 1899. Oil on canvas, 32 x 32 in. (81.3 x 81.3 cm). Collection of The Newark Museum, Gift of Mr. and Mrs. J. Russell Parsons, 1973

closely related variant, also titled *Gloucester Harbor* (fig. 180), he seems to have set his easel on the ground and somewhat to the left, eliminating the yellow building at the lower right edge of the Norton picture. Although the two canvases are nearly the same size, their different proportions produce subtly divergent effects. The Norton painting's square format counters the illusion of depth, focusing the viewer's attention on the surface of the picture plane. The other picture's vertical orientation, by contrast, speeds the eye from the shimmering foliage in the foreground, across the water, to the spires rising above the horizon line.

In both of these versions of *Gloucester Harbor,* Hassam edited out the trolley tracks and power lines that are visible in contemporary photographs of the site. *Gloucester* (fig. 181), a third painting of the waterfront, is till more euphemistic. Repeated verticals direct the eye past the pilings and masts in the lower right and across a stretch of open water to the white church lifting its slender steeple over the clustered

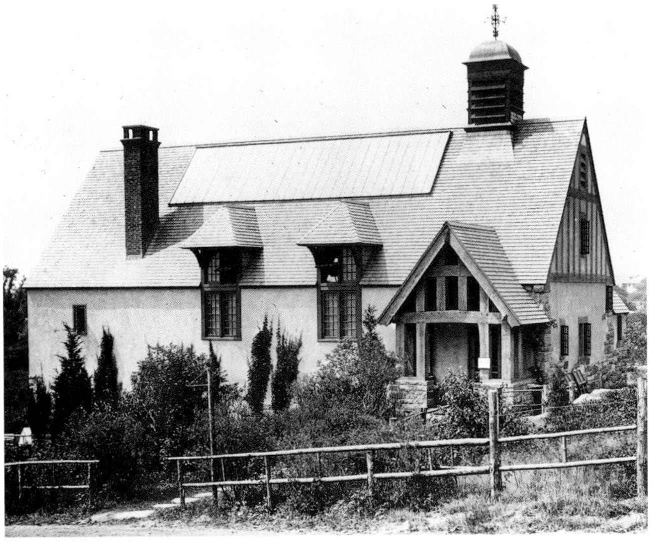

Fig. 182. Gallery-on-the-Moors, East Gloucester, Massachusetts, 1919. Cape Ann Historical Museum, Gloucester, Massachusetts

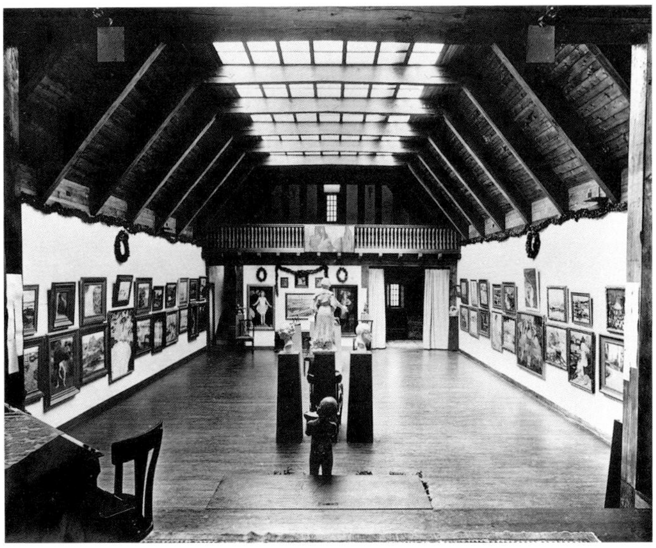

Fig. 183. Installation view, *First Annual Exhibition*, Gallery-on-the-Moors, 1916. Cape Ann Historical Museum, Gloucester, Massachusetts

houses and warehouses in the distance. Such paintings of Gloucester prompted critic Ernest Haskell's comment, "Before I had seen Hassam's pictures, [Gloucester] seemed a fishy little city, now as I pass through it I feel Hassam. The schooners beating in and out, the wharves, the sea, the sky, these belong to Hassam."[97]

After an absence of several years, Hassam returned to Gloucester in 1909. The tourist industry had burgeoned, but Hassam reported to Weir that "after ten years I'm in this port again and it is really as beautiful as ever. They have put up a few more 'Crabcroft's' and 'Lobster Lodges' but it is not spoiled yet."[98] He came back in 1916, the year William and Emmeline Atwood opened the Gallery-on-the-Moors in East Gloucester (figs. 182, 183), Cape Ann's first purpose-built exhibition space. The Atwoods bore all the expenses of the nonprofit gallery and, taking no commission on sales, invited selected artists to exhibit there during the six years of its operation.[99] Hassam apparently liked what he saw there. In the gallery's third annual exhibition, in August 1918, he showed seven of the lithographs he had produced in Gloucester that summer. In July 1919 he was featured in a smaller group show, along with his contemporary Maurice Prendergast and some of the younger Realists then working in Gloucester.[100] Hassam calculated the impact of the exhibition in a letter to dealers Edward and Albert Milch. "'The Alders' is to go to Mr. Atwood," he instructed them. "Nothing will happen to it up there but I am sure that a few people will see it. . . . The 'Gallery on the Moors' this time has a group exhibition of six or eight men only so it will not be shown to disadvantage. . . . Send any checks right along up here!"[101]

Hassam's lightheartedness contrasted with his mood of the previous summer, when he was preoccupied with news about World War I. The war front edged close to Gloucester that summer, as German submarines prowled the Atlantic coast, threatening civilian as well as military vessels. Clergymen spurred their congregations to hardened resolve when U-boats attacked American passenger ships. Acknowledging that "we in America did not fully realize what the war means to us until the German submarines appeared off the Jersey coast," one preacher nevertheless declared that the kaiser "has no power to create a cowering fear in the heart of an American."[102] The sinking of a Canadian hospital ship, reported in early July, fanned American outrage.[103] Hassam wrote to MacRae, asking what Viola Roseboro', a highly respected editor who was a member of the Cos Cob art colony, thought about the sinking. "If you want to hear some real war talk," he continued, "you should get out on a wharf here as I did yesterday and hear some of the Yankee sailor stock talk. New England is pretty real."[104]

In the war talk of the stalwart Gloucester fishermen, tested by a lifetime of battling the elements, Hassam found reassurance that bedrock American values would endure. He expressed his heightened patriotism in his rendering of Gloucester's Universalist meetinghouse. Although *The Church at Gloucester* (fig. 184) shares obvious similarities with

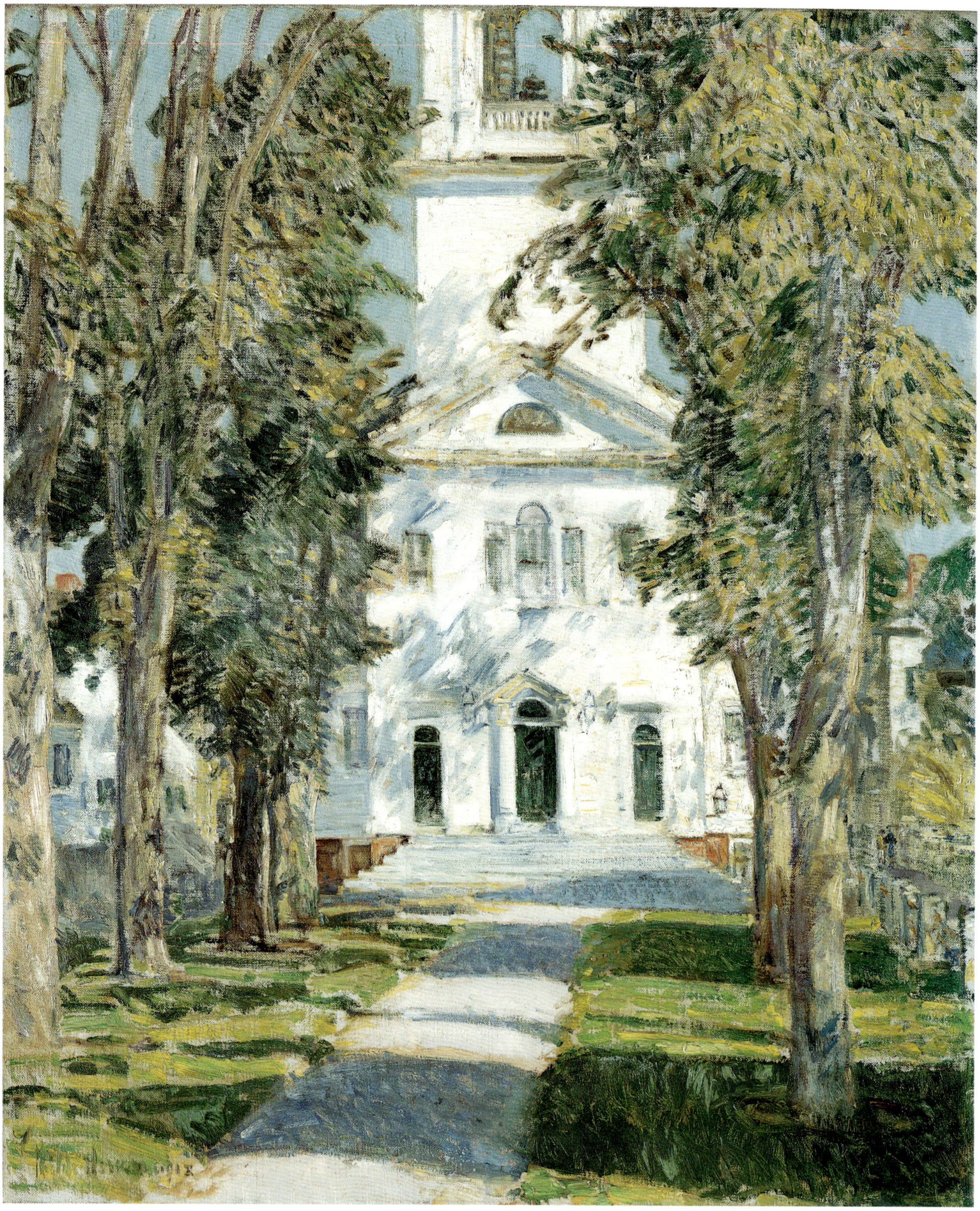

Fig. 184. Childe Hassam. *The Church at Gloucester,* 1918. Oil on canvas, 30 x 25 in. (76.2 x 63.5 cm). The Metropolitan Museum of Art, New York. Arthur Hoppock Hearn Fund, 1925 25.206

the views of the Old Lyme church Hassam had executed a decade earlier, the differences reflect the changed mood of a country at war. Painted in peacetime, in all its versions the Old Lyme church turns a graceful oblique shoulder to the viewer. No path invites us to approach, a low post-and-chain fence bars access, and in the Parrish picture the door is hidden. The Old Lyme meetinghouse seems to belong not to us but to other people, another time. In 1918, by contrast, Hassam set the Gloucester church squarely before us. The path and steps form an arrow pointing to the unobstructed door. Comparison of the painting with an early photograph (fig. 185) reveals that Hassam widened the walkway, converting

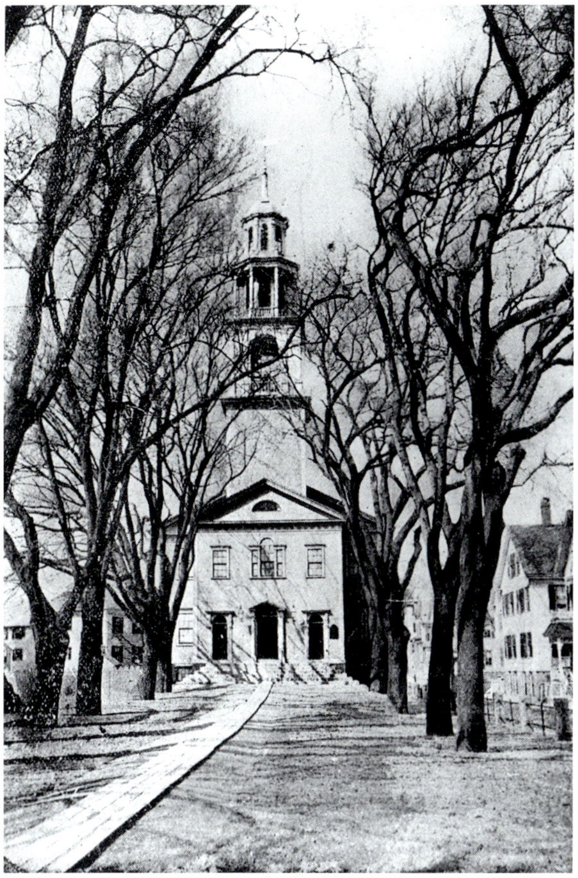

Fig. 185. Independent Christian Church, Gloucester, Massachusetts, 1905. Cape Ann Historical Museum, Gloucester, Massachusetts

Fig. 186. Childe Hassam. *Colonial Church, Gloucester,* 1918. Lithograph on lightweight beige wove paper (Japanese, foliate watermark), 13¾ x 10⅜ in. (34.9 x 26.4 cm). The Metropolitan Museum of Art, New York. Gift of Mrs. Childe Hassam, 1940 40.30.40 (G41)

it from the proverbial straight-and-narrow to a more inviting processional. American elms flank the path, their trunks and shadows measuring our progress to this temple of freedom. Such double rows of elms invested "the very air with a sense of peace and serenity," according to one of Hassam's contemporaries.[105] Hassam concentrated attention on the sun-blessed facade of the Gloucester church by cropping its steeple even more closely than Old Lyme's. Ironically, the truncated steeple implies a greater height than the fully delineated spire in the related lithograph (fig. 186).

The Universalist Church had emerged out of struggles for the separation of church and state in colonial Gloucester and remained committed to religious liberty for all. A freed slave was among its charter members, and the denomination was the first to ordain women.[106] The building Hassam depicted was the congregation's second home, dedicated in 1806. Partly visible near the top of the painting is its famous bell, cast at Paul Revere's foundry. By virtue of its close associations with early American struggles for freedom, Hassam's *Church at Gloucester* is an icon of patriotism, a New England counterpart to his New York Flag paintings (see figs. 233, 234).

A church also figures in *Cat Boats, Newport* (fig. 187). Although the brushwork here is apparently quick and spontaneous, a related sketch (fig. 188) reveals that Hassam carefully plotted his composition. He replaced the drawing's horizontal format with a nearly square canvas, in which the masts' receding verticals counter the town's horizontal sweep. The asymmetrically placed cluster of sailboats balances the steeple of Trinity Church, a Christopher Wren–inspired building dedicated in 1726. On this canvas, one of his first to enter a museum collection, Hassam summarized the features that attracted him to Newport: a scenic harbor, eighteenth-century architecture, and a leafy town center.[107]

Hassam spent an extended time in Newport only once, in 1901. He ignored the palatial new "cottages" along Cliff Walk, concentrating instead on the town's oldest neighborhood, near the harbor. Of the seven large paintings he executed in Newport, all but one show the town from the harbor, crowned by the spire of Trinity Church.[108] In an etching of

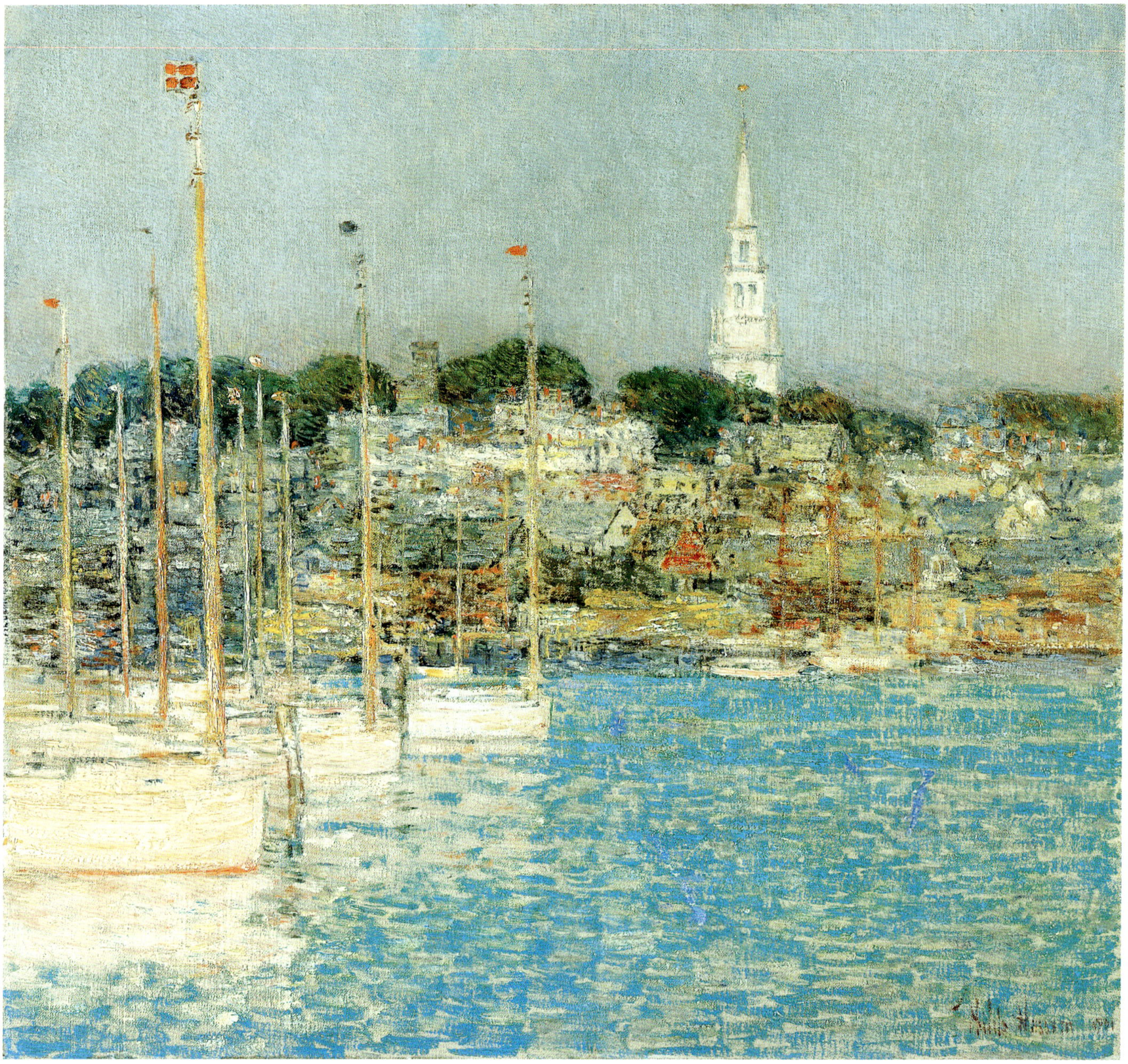

Fig. 187. Childe Hassam. *Cat Boats, Newport,* 1901. Oil on canvas, 24⅛ x 26⅛ in. (61.3 x 66.4 cm). Courtesy of the Pennsylvania Academy of the Fine Arts, Philadelphia. Joseph E. Temple Fund

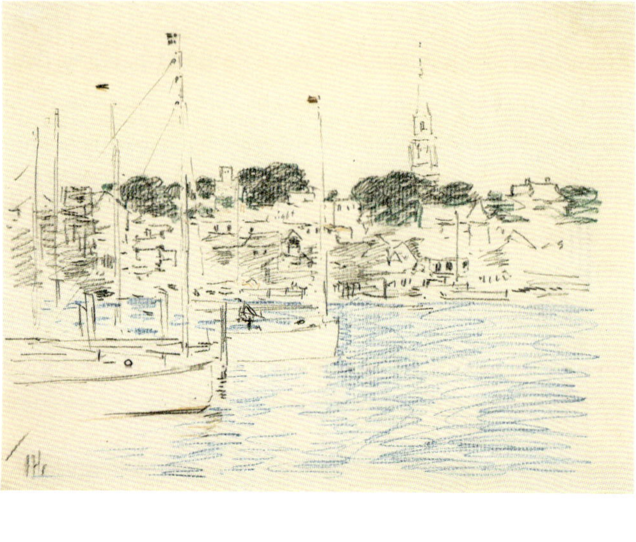

Fig. 188. Childe Hassam. *Cat Boats, Newport Harbor,* 1901. Chalk on paper, 8 x 10 ¾ in. (20.3 x 27.3 cm). Carnegie Museum of Art, Pittsburgh; Andrew Carnegie Fund 07.14.6

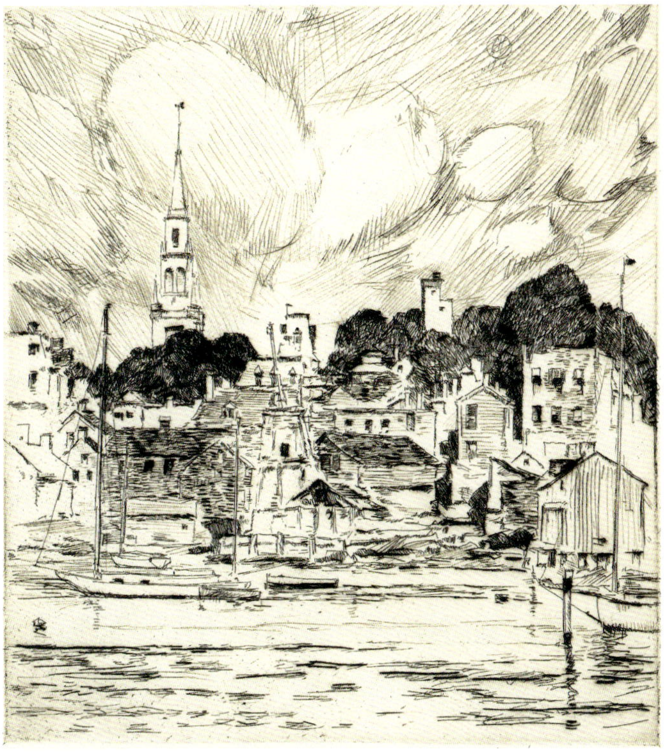

the same subject dated 1916 (fig. 189), his treatment of the sky behind the church recalls the radiance of religious paintings.

The classic white frame church was, for Hassam, an essential element of the ideal New England community—so much so that he once "restored" a burned church in order to incorporate it in his composition. Hassam painted this picture, *Street in Portsmouth* (fig. 190), during a visit to that New Hampshire seaport in 1916. The meetinghouse that was actually visible from his vantage point was a Romanesque brick structure with an unadorned pyramidal tower. It had been built just twenty years earlier to replace the First Universalist church on the site, whose white, louvered campanile closely resembled the structure that commands

Fig. 189. Childe Hassam. *Newport Harbor,* 1916. Etching, 6⅞ x 6¼ in. (17.5 x 15.9 cm). American Academy of Arts and Letters, New York (C105)

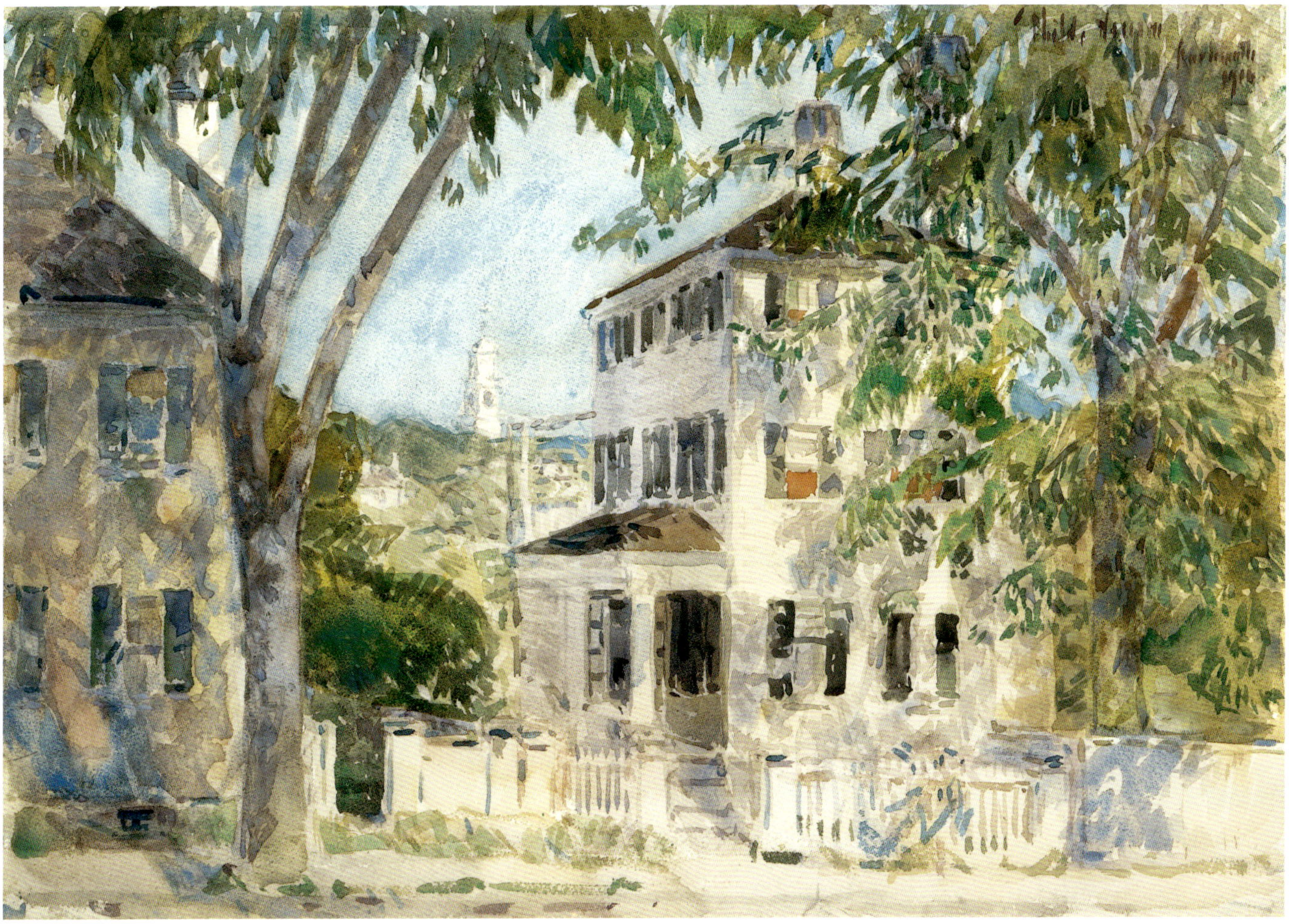

Fig. 190. Childe Hassam. *Street in Portsmouth,* 1916. Watercolor on off-white wove paper, 15⅛ x 22 in. (38.4 x 55.9 cm). The Metropolitan Museum of Art, New York. Rogers Fund, 1917 17.31.2

the distance in Hassam's watercolor.[109] The earlier church exemplified "New England's pine-wood Palladianism" that, as distinguished curator A. Hyatt Mayor wrote, "vibrated in sympathy with [Hassam's] delicately happy temperament" and evoked the best of his art.[110]

Hassam responded enthusiastically not just to fine Federal churches; even the simplest buildings could move his spirit and his brush. The three-story clapboard house in *Street in Portsmouth* was built about 1810 on a narrow lot near the South Mill Pond. Hassam presented the unpretentious house and its neighbor, with their white picket fences and elm trees framing the distant church and a glimpse of the water, as a microcosm of New England.

Hassam's summer excursions would soon end, as he settled into his own place in East Hampton, Long Island.[111] Unlike his friends Twachtman and Weir, who years earlier had found their signature subject matter on their private country properties, Hassam waited until late in life to acquire his own summer retreat. His belated rootedness proved a blessing. For most of his long career the varied seaports and villages of the New England coast inspired some of his most compelling images and shaped the enduring vision of the region as quintessential America.

1. For a provocative study of those values, see Truettner and Stein 1999.
2. Quoted in J. Walter McSpadden, *Famous Painters of America* (New York: Dodd, Mead and Company, 1916), p. 397. That passage reads more fully: "'I am an American!' thus exclaims General Grant in his 'Memoirs'—and the same keynote is struck by Childe Hassam, one of the most typically native of all our artists past or present. 'I would rather have that said of me,' says Mr. Hassam, referring to the Grant quotation, 'than anything else. And I believe I have more right to say it than most people.'"
3. "New York Beautiful" 1898.
4. Childe Hassam, 35, boulevard Rochechouart, Paris, June 13, 1888, to Celia Thaxter, Isles of Shoals, private collection, transcribed in Hiesinger 1994, p. 178. This attitude is in marked contrast to the indifference to the companionship of American artists that he professed while he was in Paris, for which see H. Barbara Weinberg, "Hassam in Paris, 1886–1889," in this publication, p. 56.
5. Hassam's comment is taken from Lockman interview, February 2, 1927, p. 28. In his later years Hassam seemed to remain aloof from art colonies—possibly to avoid fraternizing with artists who were younger and less established than he. On July 7, 1918, he wrote from Gloucester, Mass., to Elmer MacRae in Cos Cob (Holley/MacRae Family Papers, William E. Finch Archives, Historical Society of the Town of Greenwich, Cos Cob, Connecticut), "I am away from the 'art colony' back out on the cape so that I don't have to talk to the tabbys." Hassam was then staying at The Moorland in Bass Rocks, some distance from the harbor area and East Gloucester, his base on earlier visits. In addition to its relative isolation, Bass Rocks offered the enticement of a golf course.
6. The broadside, from about 1898, is reproduced in Curry 1990, p. 22.
7. Childe Hassam, Appledore, Isles of Shoals, N.H., July 1907, to Florence Griswold, Old Lyme, archives, Florence Griswold Museum, Old Lyme, Connecticut.
8. Constant Holley MacRae, Cos Cob, October 28, 1902, to Josephine Holley, Rock, Mass., Holley/MacRae Family Papers.
9. It is impossible to pin down the years of Hassam's first and last visits to the Isles of Shoals. When interviewer DeWitt McClellan Lockman asked where he had lived during World War I, Hassam said, "I lived in New York and I think I went to the Shoals for the last time the year of the outbreak in 1916. The old Appledore Hotel burned down. Mrs. Thaxter's cottage and other places were swept clear." Lockman interview, February 2, 1927, p. 27. The fire to which Hassam referred destroyed most of the buildings on Appledore on September 13, 1914. If he returned to the Isles of Shoals after that date, he probably stayed on Star Island. The definitive study of Hassam on Appledore is Curry 1990. Another valuable reference is Susan C. Faxon, Alice Downey, and Peter Bermingham, *A Stern and Lovely Scene: A Visual History of the Isles of Shoals*, exh. cat. (Durham, N.H.: University Art Galleries, University of New Hampshire, 1978). The Isles of Shoals are divided between Maine and New Hampshire. Five of the nine islands, including Appledore, are located in Maine; the rest are in New Hampshire. Notwithstanding the official location of Appledore in Maine, Hassam and others often referred to the Isles of Shoals, New Hampshire. The Web site www.islesofshoals.com includes ferry schedules and links to the Shoals Marine Laboratory site, which provides information on visiting Celia Thaxter's restored garden on Appledore (www.sml.cornell.edu/garden).
10. In his interview with Lockman, January 31, 1927, p. 24, Hassam said of Thaxter, "I met her in Boston." In Hassam, Letter to Miss Farmer, 1933, p. 5, he wrote, "When I was not much past twenty I met Celia Thaxter."
11. For more on Hassam's name change, see Stephanie L. Herdrich, "Hassam in Boston, 1859–1886," in this publication, p. 49, n. 25, and Dana Pilson, "'On the crest of the wave': Hassam and the Marketing of His Art," in this publication, p. 343.
12. Quoted in Rosamond Thaxter, *Sandpiper: The Life and Letters of Celia Thaxter and Her Home on the Isles of Shoals, Her Family, Friends, and Favorite Poems*, rev. ed. (Francestown, N.H.: M. Jones Co., 1963; reprint, Portsmouth, N.H.: Peter E. Randall, 1999), p. 107.
13. Maud Appleton McDowell identified Hassam as one of the artists who stayed at Thaxter's cottage; Maud Appleton McDowell, "Girlhood Memories of Celia Thaxter," in Celia Thaxter, *The Heavenly Guest, with Other Unpublished Writings*, edited by Oscar Laighton (Andover, Mass.: Smith and Coutts Co., 1935), pp. 125, 127. Hassam built his own studio on Appledore about 1890, according to Peter Bermingham, "Art on the Shoals," in Faxon, Downey, and Bermingham, *Stern and Lovely Scene*, p. 121, and Curry 1990, pp. 37–38.
14. McDowell, "Girlhood Memories of Celia Thaxter," p. 127.
15. A Visitor, "Domesticana," in C. Thaxter, *Heavenly Guest*, p. 131.
16. Ibid.
17. Diary of Charlotte Goodrich Smith (Mrs. R. Smith of Peabody, Mass.); MS 547.1, Jessie Donahue Collection, Vaughn Museum and Library, Star Island, Isles of Shoals. According to Thaxter's granddaughter, Rosamond

Thaxter, "Celia was very careful that only her especial and invited friends should invade her sanctuary." R. Thaxter, *Sandpiper,* p. 199.

18. Emma M. Anderson, "Celia Thaxter and Her Gardens," in C. Thaxter, *Heavenly Guest,* pp. 121–22.
19. Ibid., pp. 119–20.
20. Oscar Laighton wrote years after Thaxter's death, "After we lost our sister there was a change in the fortunes of Appledore. Her beautiful garden and the attraction of her parlor were greatly missed." Oscar Laighton, *Ninety Years at the Isles of Shoals* (Boston: Beacon Press, 1930), pp. 144–45, quoted in Susan Faxon, "A History of the Isles of Shoals," in Faxon, Downey, and Bermingham, *Stern and Lovely Scene,* p. 66.
21. According to family accounts, "Standing on the floor and easels were watercolors, oils and pastels painted by artists who hoped for a sale." R. Thaxter, *Sandpiper,* p. 199.
22. Celia Thaxter, March 14, 1888, to Ross Turner, quoted in R. Thaxter, *Sandpiper,* p. 226.
23. Marie Walther, Isles of Shoals, July 8, 1893, to Charlotte Briggs, William Page Papers, Archives of American Art, Smithsonian Institution, reel 23, frame 4125, quoted in Curry 1990, p. 34.
24. According to Candace Wheeler, "a little picture of the sea, one of Childe Hassam's" hung "over the white end of this bank of flowers"—the position this work occupies both in the photograph and in Hassam's watercolor *The Altar and Shrine* (fig. 121). Candace Wheeler, *Content in a Garden* (Boston and New York: Houghton Mifflin and Co., 1901), pp. 56–60, quoted in Adelson, Cantor, and Gerdts 1999, p. 192.
25. Thaxter 1894, pp. 94, 96.
26. Charles Rosen, *Beethoven's Piano Sonatas: A Short Companion* (New Haven: Yale University Press, 2002), p. 192.
27. The Maréchal Niel rose, introduced in 1864, was probably too modern to have been included in Celia Thaxter's old-fashioned garden. Furthermore, that tender variety was unsuited to Appledore's harsh climate. See Mrs. Frederick Love Keays, *Old Roses* (New York: Macmillan, 1935), p. 132.
28. See *Exhibition and Private Sale of Pastel and Watercolor Drawings by Childe Hassam* (Boston: Doll and Richards Gallery, November 13–25, 1891), no. 8, *Eternity.* If *Eternity,* the pastel exhibited to such acclaim in 1891, is *The Evening Star,* the title had changed by 1936, when the American Academy of Arts and Letters, New York, received the Hassam bequest. The list of works in the bequest includes a pastel titled *The Evening Star* but nothing titled *Eternity.* Hassam had stipulated that the Academy sell works from the bequest and use the proceeds to buy pictures by living artists for dispersal to museums in the United States and Canada. Sinclair Lewis purchased *The Evening Star* from the Academy; he in turn bequeathed it to Yale.
29. "Eternity," *Weymouth Gazette,* November 20, 1891, clipping, Hassam Papers, reel NAA1, frame 525.
30. Undated clipping, labeled "Transcript," Hassam Papers, reel NAA1, frame 481.
31. "Eternity," *Weymouth Gazette,* November 20, 1891.
32. "The Fine Arts. Exhibition of Pastels and Watercolors by Mr. Childe Hassam," undated clipping, labeled "Transcript," p. 6, Hassam Papers, reel NAA1, frame 492. Thanks are due to Kathleen M. Burnside for calling attention to the article.
33. For the poem, "My Garden," see R. Thaxter, *Sandpiper,* pp. 282–83.
34. Thaxter 1894, p. 55. At least one of Thaxter's brothers kept a garden (ibid., p. 53). For alerting me that *Flower Garden* does not represent Celia Thaxter's garden, I am grateful to Stephanie L. Herdrich, Lisa Miller, Virginia Chisholm of the Rye, New Hampshire, Driftwood Garden Club, and Bob Tuttle, Shoals historian.
35. Celia Thaxter was often called the goddess of Appledore, according to a visitor to the Shoals and one of her obituaries. See A Visitor, "Domesticana," p. 129, and "Celia Thaxter, Sweet 'Poet Goddess' of the Isle [*sic*] of Shoals," unidentified clipping, Hassam Papers, reel NAA1, frame 619. Thaxter weighed 236 pounds when she was fifty-two; R. Thaxter, *Sandpiper,* p. 197.
36. Thaxter 1894, p. 50.
37. Hassam produced a few illustrations in 1895 and 1896, and *Three Cities,* with illustrations based on his paintings, was published in 1899. However, *An Island Garden* was his major work as an illustrator and nearly the last.
38. Typescript of a letter from Martha Stowell, Appledore, October 1, 1894, to Mrs. L. E. (Edna) Walrath, Cooperstown, N.Y., MS #58, box 7, folder 11, Archives, Portsmouth Athenaeum, Portsmouth, N.H. After the funeral, the letter relates, Celia Thaxter's family and close friends returned to the parlor. "Her intimate friends retain their rooms for next year. . . . All of her near friends promised to come and do all that was possible to make it cheerful. . . . Mr. Mason said he would send his piano as usual and Hassam and Broan [*sic;* Brown] would do all they could, so that is the prospect for another summer."
39. Childe Hassam, Appledore, August 12, 1903, to J. Alden Weir, Branchville or Windham, Conn., quoted in Young 1960, p. 218.
40. Childe Hassam, Appledore, July 20, 1911, to J. Alden Weir, Branchville or Windham, Conn., Hassam Papers, reel NAA1, frame 66.
41. *New York Times,* March 29, 1903, p. 7, quoted in Natalie Spassky et al., *American Paintings in The Metropolitan Museum of Art, Volume II, A Catalogue of Works by Artists Born between 1816 and 1845* (New York: The Metropolitan Museum of Art, 1985), p. 476. For additional information on *Cannon Rock,* see Nicolai Cikovsky Jr. and Franklin Kelly, *Winslow Homer,* exh. cat. (Washington, D.C.: National Gallery of Art; New Haven: Yale University Press, 1995), p. 331.
42. Philip C. Beam et al., *Winslow Homer in the 1890s: Prout's Neck Observed,* exh. cat. (Rochester: Memorial Art Gallery of the University of Rochester; New York: Hudson Hills Press, 1990), p. 132.
43. Celia Thaxter, *Among the Isles of Shoals* (1873; reprint, Bowie, Md., and Hampton, N.H.: Heritage Books, 1978), pp. 143–44.
44. "Childe Hassam's Work," clipping, labeled "*New York Herald,* December 12, 1907," Hassam Papers, reel NAA1, frame 547. See *Exhibition of Pictures by Childe Hassam* (New York: Montross Gallery, December 11–28, 1907), exh. cat. no. 13, *Sylph's Rock—Appledore.*
45. Curry 1990, p. 180. Curry calls the painting *Isles of Shoals,* but his reference to the illustration, whose caption includes the complete title, makes clear that he means *Coast Scene, Isles of Shoals.*
46. Thaxter 1894, p. 125.
47. A watercolor closely related to *Jelly Fish* may represent Hassam's first impression of the subject, which he subsequently translated into oil. That watercolor, *East Headland, Isles of Shoals,* 1912 (collection of Mr. and Mrs. Perry T. Rathbone), is reproduced in Curry 1990, p. 188. It is not known, however, which work Hassam painted first.
48. "An Art School at Cos Cob," *Art Interchange* 43 (September 1899), p. 56.
49. Hassam visited Cos Cob, central Greenwich, or both in 1894, 1896–99, 1901–3, 1907, and 1911–18. Note that more years are included here than in Susan G. Larkin, *The Cos Cob Art Colony: Impressionists on the Connecticut*

Shore, exh. cat. (New York: National Academy of Design; New Haven: Yale University Press, 2001), app. A, p. 213.

50. Cather mentions Cos Cob in *The Song of the Lark* (Boston: Houghton Mifflin, 1915 and 1943), p. 537. Lincoln Steffens, "Cos Cob: An Art Colony," chap. 11 in *The Autobiography of Lincoln Steffens,* 2 vols. (1931; New York and London: Harcourt Brace Jovanovich, 1958), vol. 2, pp. 436–42. For more writers and performing artists who were members of the Cos Cob art colony, see Larkin, *Cos Cob Art Colony,* app. B, pp. 218–21.
51. "Art School at Cos Cob," p. 56.
52. Steffens, *Autobiography,* vol. 2, pp. 436–37.
53. Constant Holley MacRae, Cos Cob, October 20, 1902, to Josephine Holley, Rock, Mass., Holley MacRae Family Papers
54. MacRae, October 28, 1902, to Holley.
55. "A Small Art Colony," *Commercial Advertiser* (New York), July 22, 1899, p. 1, clipping in Holley/MacRae Family Papers.
56. The term "the Cos Cob Clapboard School" was published for the first time in Hassam 1928, p. 28. It is repeated in Adams 1938, p. 93.
57. "The Oldest House in Town," *Greenwich Graphic,* January 29, 1898, p. 1.
58. Typescript (probably by Dorothy Weir Young) of notes from an undated interview with Elmer and Constant Holley MacRae, Dorothy Weir Young research papers, tub 3, "Holley Farm" folder, archives, Weir Farm National Historic Site, Wilton, Connecticut.
59. See *Fourth Exhibition Oil Paintings by Contemporary Artists,* exh. cat. (Washingtion, D.C.: Corcoran Gallery of Art, December 17, 1912–January 26, 1913), no. 136, *The Bowl of Gold Fish;* no. 165, *The New York Window.* For the New York Window series, see H. Barbara Weinberg, "Hassam in New York, 1897–1919," in this publication, pp. 211–16. For a more extensive comparison of the New York and Cos Cob images of women, see "Familiar Faces: Images of Women and Children," chap. 4 of Larkin, *Cos Cob Art Colony.*
60. The room served various purposes. During the art colony's heyday it was one of the best bedrooms. Hassam and his wife, Maud, often stayed there.
61. For more on Nutting, see Thomas Andrew Denenberg, *Wallace Nutting and the Invention of Old America,* exh. cat. (Hartford, Conn.: Wadsworth Athenaeum Museum of Art; New Haven: Yale University Press, 2003).
62. For the Tonalists in the art colony, see Jeffrey W. Andersen and Barbara J. MacAdam, *Old Lyme: The American Barbizon,* exh. cat. (Old Lyme, Conn.: Lyme Historical Society, Florence Griswold Museum, 1982). For the Impressionists who came later to Old Lyme, see Jeffrey W. Andersen, "The Art Colony at Old Lyme," in Harold Spencer, Susan G. Larkin, and Jeffrey W. Andersen, *Connecticut and American Impressionism,* exh. cat. (Storrs, Conn.: William Benton Museum of Art, 1980), pp. 114–37. Jeffrey W. Andersen's essay "A Season in Lyme: Life among the Artists," in *En Plein Air: The Art Colonies at East Hampton and Old Lyme, 1880–1930,* exh. cat. (Old Lyme: Florence Griswold Museum; East Hampton: Guild Hall Museum, 1989), pp. 25–32, covers both Tonalists and Impressionists.
63. Arthur Heming, *Miss Florence and the Artists of Old Lyme* (Essex, Conn.: Pequot Press, 1971), p. 19. The commissions she earned supplemented her modest income.
64. Thomas D. Murphy, *New England Highways and Byways from a Motorcar; Sunrise Highways* (Boston: L. C. Page and Company, 1924), p. 279. I am grateful to Jeffrey W. Andersen for bringing this quotation to my attention.
65. "The Lyme Art Show," *Hartford Daily Courant,* September 2, 1902, archives, Florence Griswold Museum. The article ran the following day in the *New London Day.*
66. "Notable Artistic Exhibit," *New York Times,* September 6, 1903, p. 7, and "Paintings at Lyme," *Hartford Daily Courant,* September 4, 1903; archives, Florence Griswold Museum.
67. Anthony H. Euwer, "Old Lyme, Connecticut: The American Barbizon," *Sound Breeze,* April 2, 1904, quoted in Andersen, "Art Colony at Old Lyme," p. 123. The article originally appeared in the *Pittsburgh Index.* I am grateful to Jeffrey W. Andersen for this information.
68. Childe Hassam, Appledore, August 16 and 21, 1906, to Florence Griswold, Old Lyme, archives, Florence Griswold Museum. Hassam's appearance in Old Lyme exhibitions between 1903 and 1912 are noted in the exhibition chronology in this publication.
69. Hassam is known to have visited Old Lyme in 1903, 1904, 1905, 1906, and 1909. He may also have stayed there in 1907 (the only evidence for this is the date *1907* inscribed on the door panel in the Griswold House dining room he painted with Henry Rankin Poore and Walter Griffin [see p. 158]) and in 1908, when his paintings were shown in Old Lyme. The chronologies in Hiesinger 1994, Adelson, Cantor, and Gerdts 1999, and this publication also place him in Old Lyme in September 1915. That stay seems not to have resulted in significant work, however. An etching, *The Ox-Cart* (C17), dated 1915, was based on a drawing made at Old Lyme, possibly years earlier.
70. Lillian Baynes Griffin, "Art Colony at Old Lyme Expands," *Hartford Courant,* ca. July 4, 1907, archives, Florence Griswold Museum. Lillian Baynes Griffin was married to painter Walter Griffin, Hassam's friend.
71. Childe Hassam, New York, April 29, 1905, to Florence Griswold, Old Lyme, archives, Florence Griswold Museum.
72. Childe Hassam, Old Lyme, July 3, 1905, to J. Alden Weir, probably Branchville, archives, Florence Griswold Museum; also available in Hassam Papers, reel NAA2, frame 72.
73. Stuart A. Reeve, Laurie Bradt, Harold Juli, and Robert Gradie, "The Archaeology of the Lyme Art Colony, Florence Griswold Museum, Old Lyme, Connecticut," *Connecticut College Archaeology Laboratory Report,* no. 11 (April 2000), pp. 128–68. I am grateful to Jeffrey W. Andersen and Laurie Bradt for providing me with a copy of the report and sharing their insights about the studios. The report revises earlier ideas about the location of Hassam's studio. In the schematic map on p. 126 of Spencer, Larkin, and Andersen, *Connecticut and American Impressionism,* the site designated as "Small Studio (known as 'Hassam's Studio')" is now understood to have been clear of buildings.
74. In addition to the bottles, a full complement of artists' materials (some in fragments) was discovered at the site: a paint box, paint tubes and bottles, brushes, palettes, varnish bottles, a palette knife, an easel, and painted fabric, possibly the remains of a discarded painting. Others who used the studio when Hassam was not in residence include Matilda Browne, Louis Paul Dessar, Allen B. Talcott, and Mrs. Woodrow Wilson.
75. For more on this theme, see Bruce Weber, *The Apple of America: The Apple in 19th Century American Art,* exh. cat. (New York: Berry-Hill Galleries, 1993).
76. Wallace Nutting, *Connecticut Beautiful* (Framingham, Mass.: Old America Co., 1923).
77. See Denenberg, *Wallace Nutting and Invention of Old America,* pp. 74–77.
78. Adams stated that she was the model in a visit of 1965 and a phone call of 1968 to the National Collection of Fine Arts, Washington, D.C. (now the Smithsonian American Art Museum). According to Adams, the painting was executed in Florence Griswold's garden in September 1906.

(Information from curatorial files, Smithsonian American Art Museum.) However, the painting is inscribed with the date *November 1906,* and the setting is clearly an interior, not a garden.

79. Robert Bishop, *Centuries and Styles of the American Chair, 1640–1970* (New York: E. P. Dutton and Co., 1972), pp. 336–37; Thomas H. Ormsbee, *Field Guide to American Victorian Furniture* (Boston: Little, Brown and Co., 1952), pp. 56–57.
80. Rook's niece, Virginia Rook, was Maud Hassam's grandniece and later Childe Hassam's secretary. See Diane Pietrucha Fischer, *Edward F. Rook, 1870–1960: American Impressionist,* exh. cat. (Old Lyme: Florence Griswold Museum, 1987), pp. 14, 19, n. 22.
81. Lockman interview, February 2, 1927, p. 30. For more on this subject, see H. Barbara Weinberg, "Hassam in East Hampton, 1898–1935," in this publication, pp. 243–45.
82. "Many Pictures of Old Lyme Shown," *Hartford Daily Courant,* August 31, 1906.
83. Belcher also designed the Griswold House, built the same year.
84. Hassam attended Sunday school and services at a Unitarian church in Dorchester, according to autobiographical notes he wrote in 1934 (Hassam Papers, reel NAA1, frame 742). The *East Hampton Star* reported, "Rev. William Grainger, rector of St. Luke's Episcopal Church here, read the simple prayer-book service" at the artist's home. "Funeral Services Held Here for Childe Hassam," *East Hampton Star,* September 5, 1935, clipping, Hassam Papers, reel NAA1, frame 651.
85. Childe Hassam, Paris, November 20, 1886, and March 19, 1887, to Rose Lamb, Boston, Isles of Shoals Collection, Ms. 58, transcribed in Hiesinger 1994, p. 177.
86. Adams 1938, p. 25.
87. Childe Hassam, Autobiographical notes, 1934, Hassam Papers, reel NAA1, frame 739.
88. Ibid., frames 741–42.
89. William H. Truettner and Thomas Andrew Denenberg, "The Discreet Charm of the Colonial," in Truettner and Stein 1999, p. 99.
90. Quoted by Young 1960, p. 192.
91. Frank Fowler, "Art: Impressions of Spring Academy," *Nation* 84 (March 28, 1907), p. 298, quoted in William H. Gerdts, "Three Themes," in Adelson, Cantor, and Gerdts 1999, pp. 205, 230, n. 155.
92. Childe Hassam, Appledore, probably July 9, 1907, to Florence Griswold, Old Lyme, archives, Florence Griswold Museum.
93. Childe Hassam, East Gloucester, July 8, 1894, to William Macbeth, New York, Macbeth Gallery Papers, Archives of American Art, Smithsonian Institution, reel NMc7, frame 385. Hassam instructed Macbeth to pack the watercolors in a box that he could reuse "for taking them on their next journey," which was to Appledore.
94. James R. Coffin, "Le Beau Port: The Sea-Browned Fishing Town of Gloucester," *New England Magazine* 42 (April 1910), p. 168.
95. For surveys of artists in Gloucester, see John Wilmerding, "Interpretations of Place: Views of Gloucester, Mass., by American Artists," *Essex Institute Historical Collections* 103 (January 1967), pp. 53–65, and Lisa N. Peters and Karen Quinn, *Painters of Cape Ann, 1840–1940,* exh. cat. (New York: Spanierman Gallery, 1996).
96. Lockman interview, February 2, 1917, p. 14.
97. Ernest Haskell, introduction to Pousette-Dart 1922, p. viii.
98. Childe Hassam, Gloucester, September 14, 1909, to J. Alden Weir, quoted in Hiesinger 1994, p. 141.
99. James F. O'Gorman, "Parnassus on Ledge Road: The Life and Times of East Gloucester's Gallery-on-the-Moors, 1916–1922," in *This Other Gloucester: Occasional Papers on the Arts of Cape Ann Massachusetts* (Boston: O'Gorman, 1976). I am grateful to Kathleen Kienholz for giving me a copy of this article.
100. Ibid., p. 89. The exhibition presented twenty-three works by eight artists: William Glackens, Hassam, Charles Hopkinson, Louis Kronberg, Hayley Lever, Jonas Lie, Maurice Prendergast, and John Sloan. Jennifer Joseph of the Cape Ann Historical Museum graciously supplied the checklist and related information.
101. Childe Hassam, Bass Rocks, Gloucester, July 15, 1919, to E. and A. Milch, New York, Milch Gallery Records, 1911–1980, Archives of American Art, Smithsonian Institution, reel 4420, frame 270.
102. "Churches Denounce U-Boat Attack Here," *New York Times,* June 10, 1918, p. 20.
103. "British Admiralty's Graphic Report of Sinking of the Llandovery Castle," *New York Times,* July 2, 1918, p. 1, and "Abhor Violation of Hospital Ship," *New York Times,* July 3, 1918, p. 1.
104. Childe Hassam, Bass Rocks, Gloucester, July 7, [1918], to Elmer MacRae, Cos Cob, Holley/MacRae Family Papers. Hassam dated the letter July 7, 1917, however, the envelope is postmarked July 7, 1918. Later that month New England fishing boats came under attack from German submarines. See, for example, "U Boat Sinks Ship Off Maine Coast," *New York Times,* July 24, 1918, p. 1, and "Sure He Hailed German Raider," *New York Times,* July 25, 1918, p. 1.
105. Frank French, "Trees," *Scribner's Magazine* 28 (July 1900), p. 32, quoted in Michael Kammen, *Meadows of Memory: Images of Time and Tradition in American Art and Culture* (Austin: University of Texas Press, 1992), p. 175, n. 30.
106. For more on this church, see Edwin A. Start, "Round about Gloucester," *New England Magazine* 6 (August 1892), pp. 692–96, and Weinberg, Bolger, and Curry 1994, pp. 131–33. Additional information is available at www.uua.org/info/origins.html.
107. *Cat Boats, Newport* was included in the seventy-first annual exhibition of the Pennsylvania Academy of the Fine Arts, Philadelphia, which ran from January 20 to March 1, 1902. On the recommendation of Harrison S. Morris, PAFA's secretary and managing director from 1892 to 1905, the painting was purchased on March 2, 1902, for the academy's permanent collection.
108. The paintings, listed by Kathleen M. Burnside in Gerdts et al. 1990, p. 155, n. 1, are: *Newport* (private collection, on deposit at The Fine Arts Museums of San Francisco), *Newport Harbor* (Flint Institute of Arts, Michigan), *The White Church, Newport* (no further information given), *Catboats, Newport* (Pennsylvania Academy of the Fine Arts, Philadelphia), *Bailey's Beach, Newport* (Art Institute of Chicago), *Duke Street, Newport* (private collection), and *Newport—October Sundown* (private collection).
109. Correspondence between Kevin Avery, Metropolitan Museum, New York, and Jane Porter, Portsmouth Athenaeum, March 16 and 19, 1994, curatorial files, Department of American Paintings and Sculpture, The Metropolitan Museum of Art. A photograph of the "Old Universalist Church" is reproduced in C. S. Gurney, *Portsmouth, Historic and Picturesque* (Portsmouth, N.H.: C. S. Gurney, 1902), p. 146. The church built in 1896 to replace it is shown in a photograph on the same page.
110. Mayor 1940, p. 139.
111. See Weinberg, "Hassam in East Hampton, 1898–1935," in this publication.

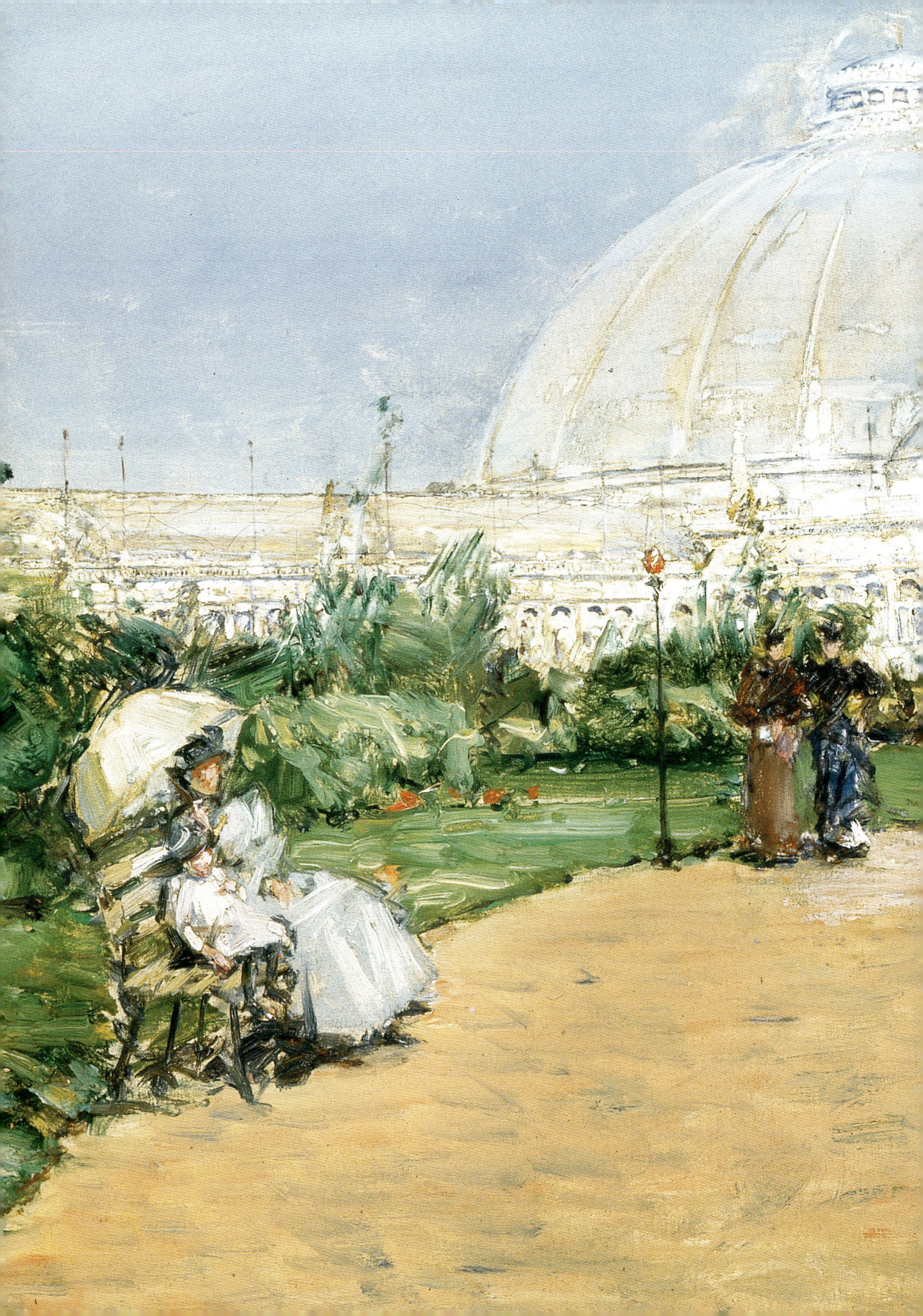

CHAPTER FIVE

Hassam's Travels, 1892–1914

H. Barbara Weinberg

Hassam's pattern of spending winters in New York and summers in New England and, later, East Hampton on Long Island refreshed his spirit and artistic imagination. Although he proclaimed, "I am the Marco Polo of the painters,"[1] he went to Europe less often than did a number of other American artists—William Merritt Chase and Theodore Robinson, for example—and he avoided European artists' colonies and had little interest in foreign exhibitions. Asked whether he had met "many American painters" during his 1910 journey to Europe, Hassam exclaimed: "I avoided artists. Always kept by myself and never went to artistic colony."[2] In the same interview he recounted that after his return home from Paris in 1911, a woman asked: "Do you go to the Salon Mr. Hassam?" to which he replied: "Why no, I would be no painter to go to the Salon. I am too old to look at other men."[3]

Hassam did, however, make several trips that stimulated him to paint significant works: one to Chicago (1892), others to more distant locales: Havana (1895), Europe (1883, 1896–97, 1910, 1911), Oregon (1904, 1908), and California (1914).[4] In many of the images executed during these journeys, he sacrificed simple descriptiveness to a more decorative approach. The subjects he encountered in unfamiliar places perhaps liberated him to engage more with formal issues than was his custom at home. The need to paint quickly to accommodate a travel schedule may also have encouraged him to adopt the more advanced style of the pictures he made when he was away. Whatever prompted these experiments, they are often reflected as well in works Hassam painted after he returned to familiar terrain.

Hassam's 1892 visit to Chicago in connection with the World's Columbian Exposition provoked some distinctive images. In order to supplement his income, Hassam undertook two commercial assignments associated with the fair, which would open on May 1, 1893.[5] He added backgrounds and figures to a group of existing architectural drawings by other artists, which were then reproduced as a series of chromolithographs entitled *Gems of the White City;* made original views of the Exposition buildings in watercolor and gouache;[6] and painted a few other watercolors and oils on Chicago themes. One of the last group, the superb Whistlerian *Nocturne, Railway Crossing, Chicago* (fig. 191), manifests Hassam's watercolor technique at its most sophisticated.[7] This handsome sheet reveals his ability to evoke forms and effects with the most economical painterly means: here the layering of subtle monochromatic washes accented with brilliant highlights to suggest glowing streetlights, carriage lamps, and streetcars and their reflections in the wet pavement.

Horticulture Building, World's Columbian Exposition, Chicago (fig. 192) portrays in oil the exceptional structure designed by Chicago architects William LeBaron Jenney and W. B. Mundie (fig. 193). The building, which occupied a broad site facing the Exposition's Lagoon, was separated from the other exhibitions by ornamental gardens and parterres. Intended to display "nearly every specimen of the plant life of the world," as a contemporary boasted,[8] the Horticulture Building was based on greenhouse or conservatory design. The standard configuration was, however, modified to include two-storied end pavilions, one-storied glazed galleries, several low supporting domes, and an immense central dome that housed palm trees, bamboo, and other large exotic botanical specimens. Especially in contrast to

Detail, fig. 192. *Horticulture Building, World's Columbian Exposition, Chicago*

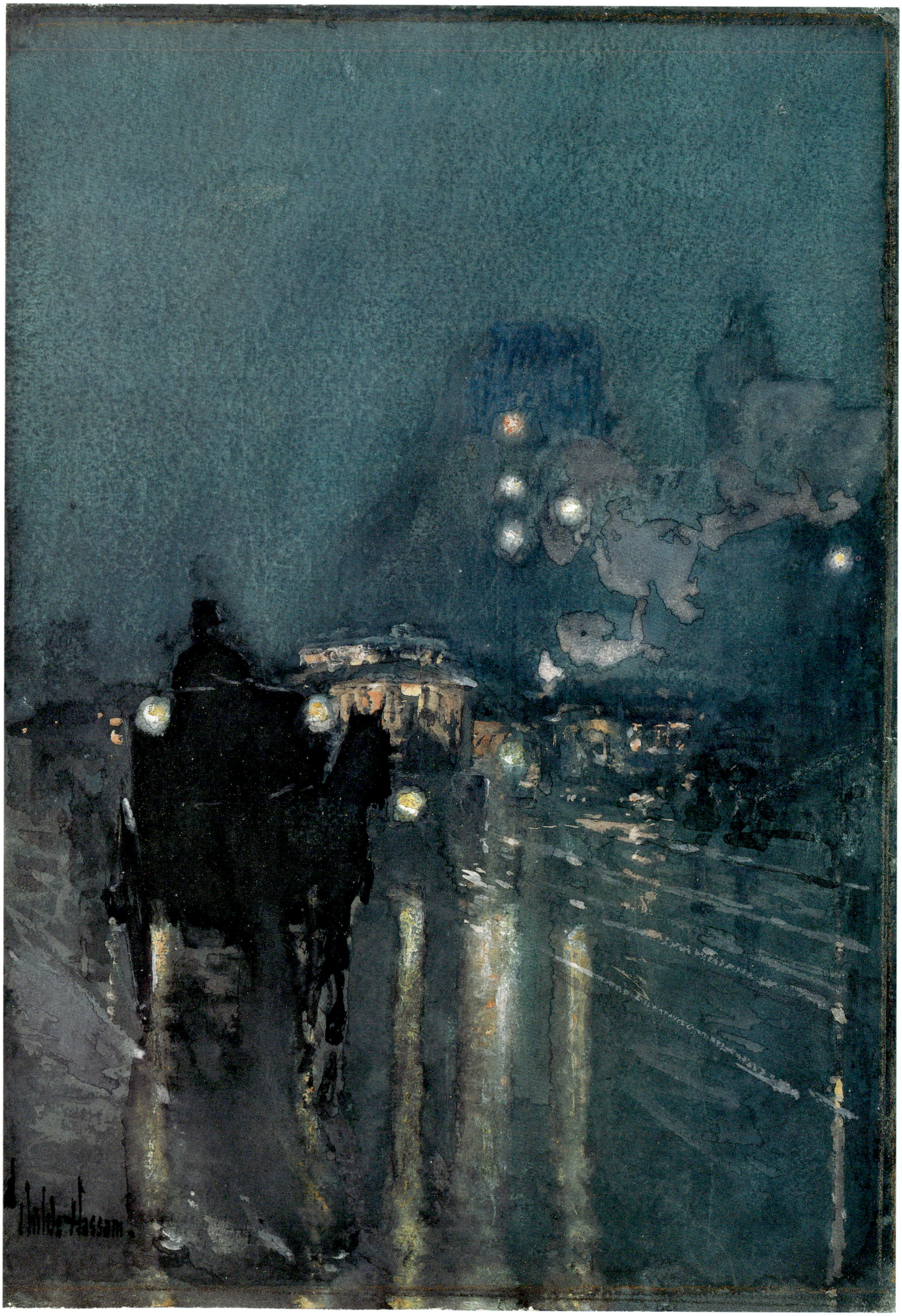

Fig. 191. Childe Hassam. *Nocturne, Railway Crossing, Chicago,* 1893. Watercolor on paper, 16 x 11¾ in. (40.6 x 29.8 cm). The Museum of Fine Arts, Boston. The Hayden Collection. Charles Henry Hayden Fund

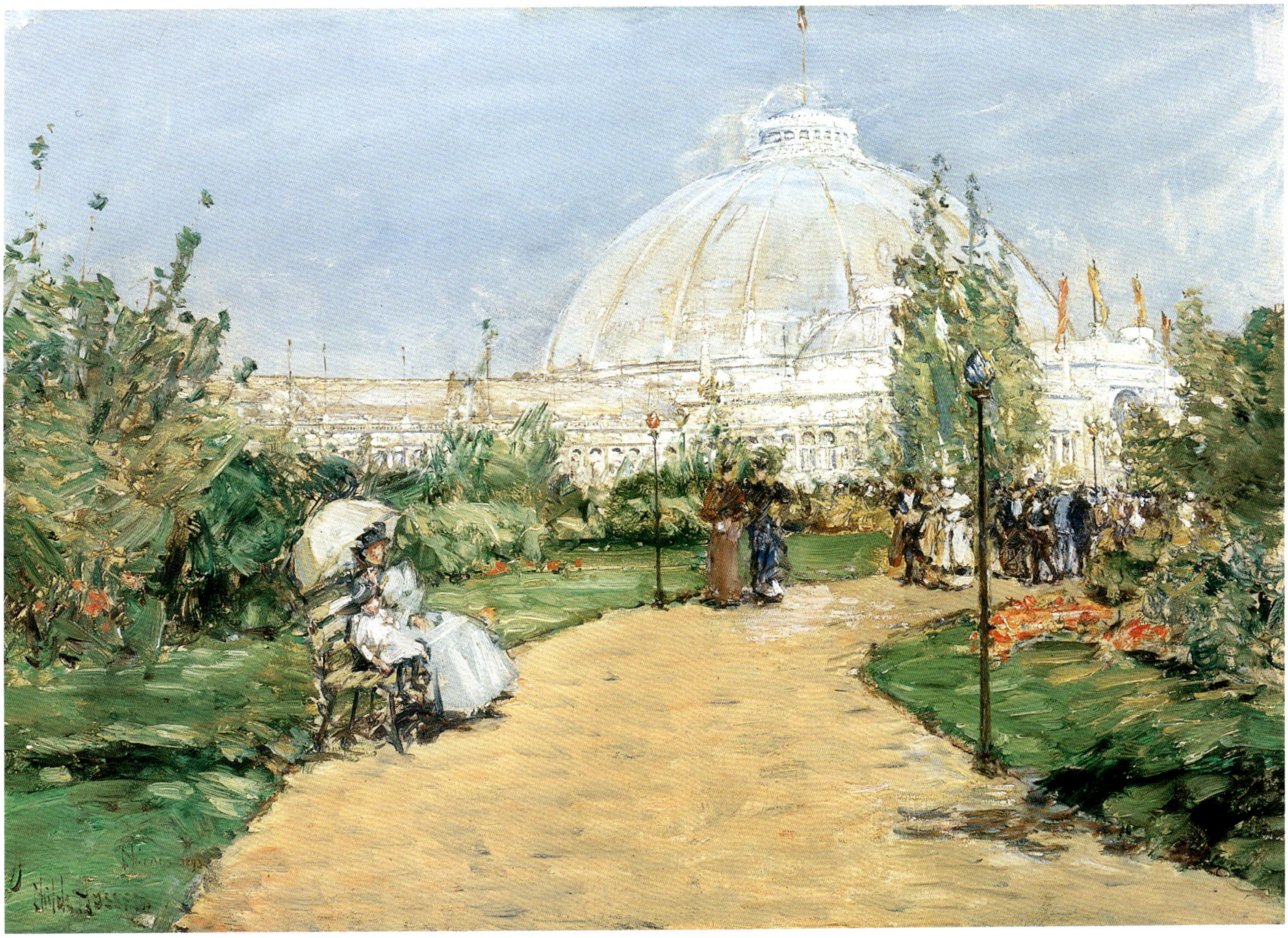

Fig. 192. Childe Hassam. *Horticulture Building, World's Columbian Exposition, Chicago,* 1893. Oil on canvas, 18½ x 26¼ in. (47 x 66.7 cm). Terra Foundation for the Arts, Chicago, Daniel J. Terra Collection

the many solid domes elsewhere on the fairgrounds, the Horticulture Building's dome had "a quality of fleeting and iridescent beauty, and seem[ed] to be blown like a bubble," to quote from the observations of a contemporary architect. The same writer remarked enthusiastically about the edifice as a whole: "No one can doubt the purposes of this building, and though its architecture has been gaily attuned to a much lighter mood than would be proper to its more serious companions, it does not forget the dignity and grace which belong to it as a work of art."[9] Hassam the Impressionist was attracted to the light, bright structure and its floral displays. Like its subject, his canvas is candid, informal, and fresh, particularly by comparison with romanticized images of the fair, among them John H. Twachtman's *Court of Honor, World's Columbian Exposition, Chicago* (fig. 194) and elaborate topographical views such as Theodore Robinson's *World's Columbian Exposition* (fig. 195).[10]

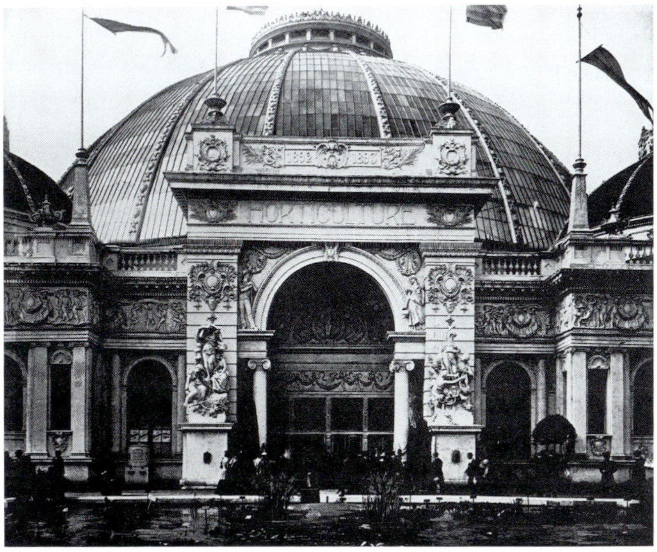

Fig. 193. View of the facade of the Horticulture Building, World's Columbian Exposition, Chicago, 1893

Although Hassam claims to have left Chicago before the fair opened,[11] he did exhibit five paintings there, including *Une Averse—rue Bonaparte* (fig. 54), *Grand Prix Day (Le Jour du Grand Prix)* (fig. 359), and *Fifth Avenue in Winter* (fig. 87), as well as five watercolors, and earned medals for the pictures in both media. There were not many French or American Impressionist works at the Chicago fair, but the few that were shown attracted substantial notice because they were so new and vivid in relation to the majority of paintings in the national installations. As Impressionist examples numbered no more than a handful within a predominantly academic American display and so many were by Hassam, he appeared to be a leader of the new movement.

The critic Hamlin Garland heard in the language of Impressionism local accents that reinforced his own quest for regional authenticity in American literature. Inspired by what he had seen at the Exposition, Garland presented a lecture on Impressionism in February 1894 that was published later that year in an anthology entitled *Crumbling Idols.* In this perceptive and influential defense of Impressionism, Garland lauded the style as appropriate for describing American locales and as an antidote to prevailing cosmopolitanism.[12] The works Hassam exhibited at the fair embodied Garland's beliefs, which, moreover, had been anticipated by the artist in his 1892 pronouncement that "the man who will go down to posterity is the man who paints his own time and the scenes of every-day life around him."[13]

In January 1895 Hassam went for his first and only visit to the Caribbean, traveling to Havana in the company of Frank Robinson, "an old friend . . . a bog coal merchant, who sold coal [to] the Electric Light people down there."[14] He spent more than a month in Havana, painting scenes near his hotel on the main square, in nearby neighborhoods, and at a sugar plantation. *Place Centrale and Fort Cabanas, Havana* (fig. 196) is one of the most significant works produced during the trip. Although Hassam depicted from his hotel window two of Havana's most monumental sites, he did so in a way that minimizes their grandeur. Rather than executing a picture-postcard view, he suggested a casual encounter. He rendered figures and vehicles freely and rapidly, emphasized brightly lit stucco walls undifferentiated by shadows, portrayed dark shadows on adjacent surfaces, and highlighted pink rooftops. Place Centrale, shown in the foreground, is Havana's Central Park; its north and south sides connect to the Prado, its Fifth Avenue. Lined with theaters, clubs, and hotels, in one of which Hassam stayed, Place Centrale was "in the very midst of Havana's social life," according to a 1905 travel writer. Hassam's painting portrays what that same writer described as the distinctive "laurel trees trimmed to formal shapes," which, "forming a green roof above the walks and flower beds and benches," shaded the square from the glaring sun.[15] Fort Cabanas, or La Cabaña, designed by a French engineer and constructed between 1763 and 1774, is the largest Spanish fort in the New World. By Hassam's time it served as a military barracks and prison.[16] Hassam knew the historical importance

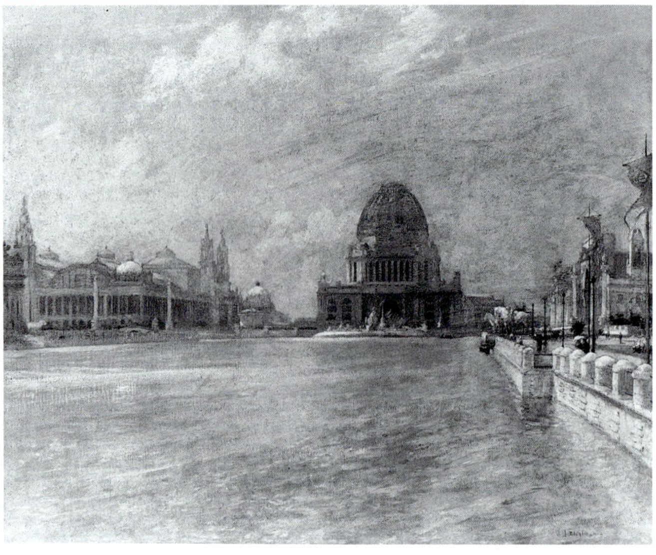

Fig. 194. John H. Twachtman. *Court of Honor, World's Columbian Exposition, Chicago,* 1893. Oil on canvas, 25 x 30 in. (63.5 x 76.2 cm). Columbus Museum of Art, Ohio: Bequest of Frederick W. Schumacher

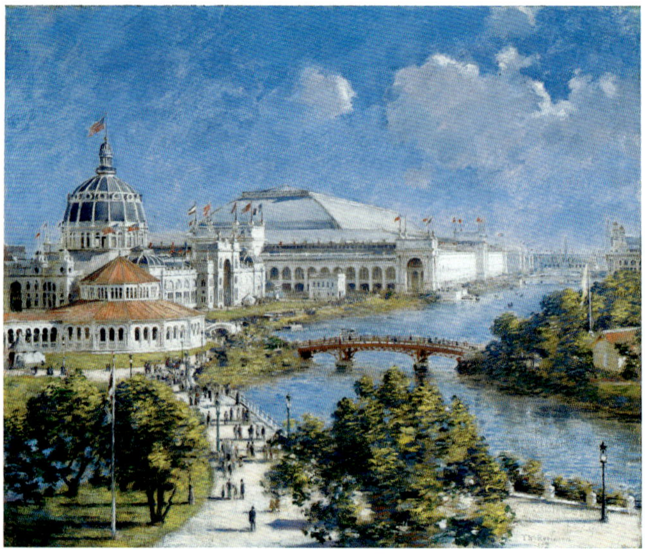

Fig. 195. Theodore Robinson. *World's Columbian Exposition,* 1894. Oil on canvas, 25 x 30 in. (63.5 x 76.2 cm). Private collection

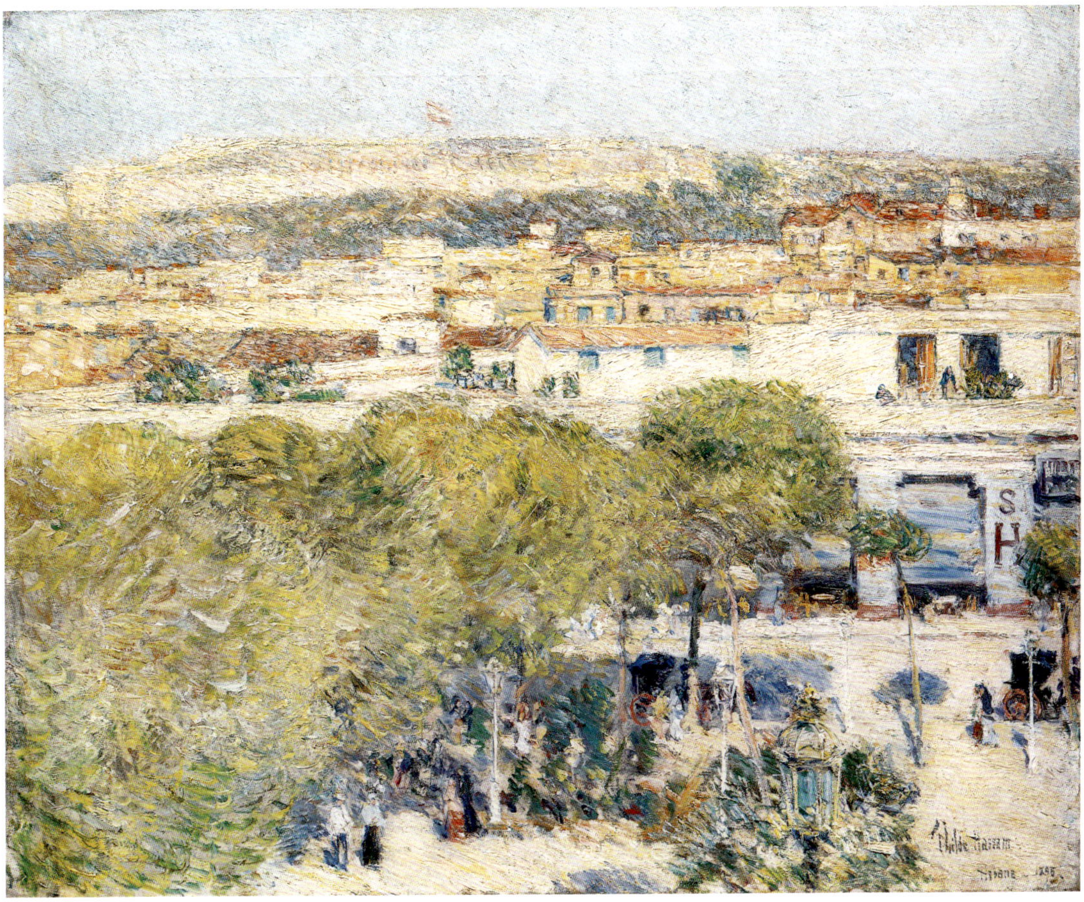

Fig. 196. Childe Hassam. *Place Centrale and Fort Cabanas, Havana*, 1895. Oil on canvas, 21¼ x 26¼ in. (54 x 66.7 cm). The Detroit Institute of Arts. City of Detroit Purchase

of the view and years later recalled his impression of the Spanish flag flying over Fort Cabanas: "We left Havana on the last day before the Cuban insurrection started. . . . It was the last time that the Spanish flag flew in the Eastern [*sic*] Hemisphere over a Spanish possession."[17] The painting marked significant professional milestones for Hassam, who received the Webb Prize for it at the 1895 exhibition of the Society of American Artists in New York and sold it to the Detroit Museum of Art (now the Detroit Institute of Arts) for $1,200 in 1911.[18]

Certain pictures painted before the trip to Cuba, such as *The Room of Flowers* (fig. 118), already signal Hassam's interest in pictorial experimentation but hold a balance between description and decoration. His Havana canvases, however, announce his willingness to tip that balance toward decoration.[19] An example of an earlier work showing a somewhat conventional approach is *The Manhattan Club (The Stewart Mansion)* (fig. 99), completed about 1891: here Hassam had created a spatial box, articulated by a massive architectural backdrop that recedes along a diagonal and inhabited by relatively solid figures whose diminishing size from foreground to background emphasizes the depth of the picture space. By contrast, in *Place Centrale and Fort Cabanas, Havana* panoramic chromatic bands proceed upward along the plane of the canvas, suggesting that he now preferred to distill from appearances and preserve only the pictorially useful elements. With its focus on abstract effects, *Union Square in Spring* (fig. 107), painted in New York the year after Hassam's Havana sojourn, implies that his Cuban experiments stimulated fresh investigations of compositional organization and pictorial pattern.

In December 1896, seven years after Hassam had returned home from his studies in Europe, he and his wife, Maud, sailed for Naples to begin a yearlong visit to Italy, France, and Great Britain that would be immensely productive.[20] Hassam had been able to paint only in watercolor when he first traveled in Italy, in 1883, and during his student years in Paris lack of money or fear of disease apparently prevented him from going there again.[21] Now Hassam finally had a chance to work in oil in Italy, and he began in earnest to view antiquities and works by the old masters in galleries and churches there. "I looked at the master pieces from every angle," he recalled.[22] Hassam painted through January 1897 in and around Naples, capturing views of Posilipo, Capri, and the Bay of Naples, and then went on to Rome and Florence. There he recorded counterparts of his American

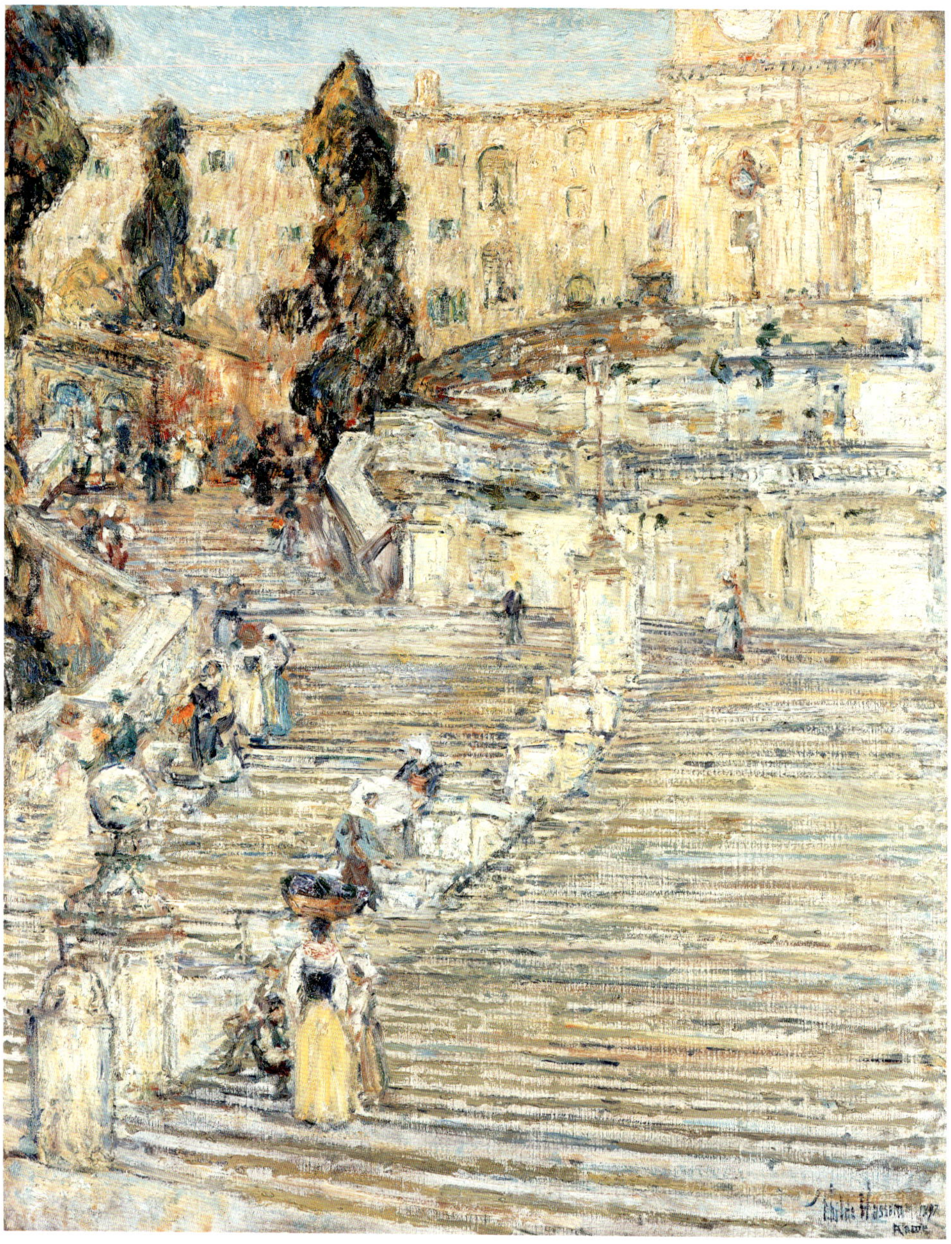

Fig. 197. Childe Hassam. *The Spanish Stairs, Rome,* 1897. Oil on canvas, 29¾ x 23⅜ in. (75.6 x 59.4 cm). Los Angeles County Museum of Art, William Randolph Hearst Collection

urban and suburban scenes and explored decorative composition, as he had in Cuba. The light palette and pictorial experiments apparent in his Italian canvases reiterate the color choices and formal solutions of both *Place Centrale and Fort Cabanas, Havana* and *Union Square in Spring.*

In *The Spanish Stairs, Rome* (fig. 197), a view of one of Rome's principal tourist attractions, Hassam was more concerned with arranging forms harmoniously on the picture plane than with suggesting naturalistic picture space.[23] Choosing a vertical format, he was attentive to the patterns of the striated steps of the monumental double stairway and its sweeping solid railings; the curvilinear contours of the parapet at the top of the stairs; the Church of Santa Trinità dei Monti and the adjacent buildings; and contrasts between the constructed forms and the quaintly costumed figures.[24] Hassam painted the site three more times under different light conditions, underscoring the notion that he was drawn not just to its picturesqueness but also, and primarily, to its pure pictorial potential.[25]

Probably in April 1897 Hassam and Maud left Italy for Paris, where he showed four paintings, including *The Room of Flowers* and a view of the Spanish Stairs, in the Salon of the Société Nationale des Beaux-Arts. Back in the city that had nurtured him in the late 1880s, he recapitulated the habits of his student years, searching for picturesque views along the Seine, on the boulevards, and in the parks. For some scenes, such as *Pont Royal* (fig. 330), he used the high vantage point he had adopted in Havana and had employed

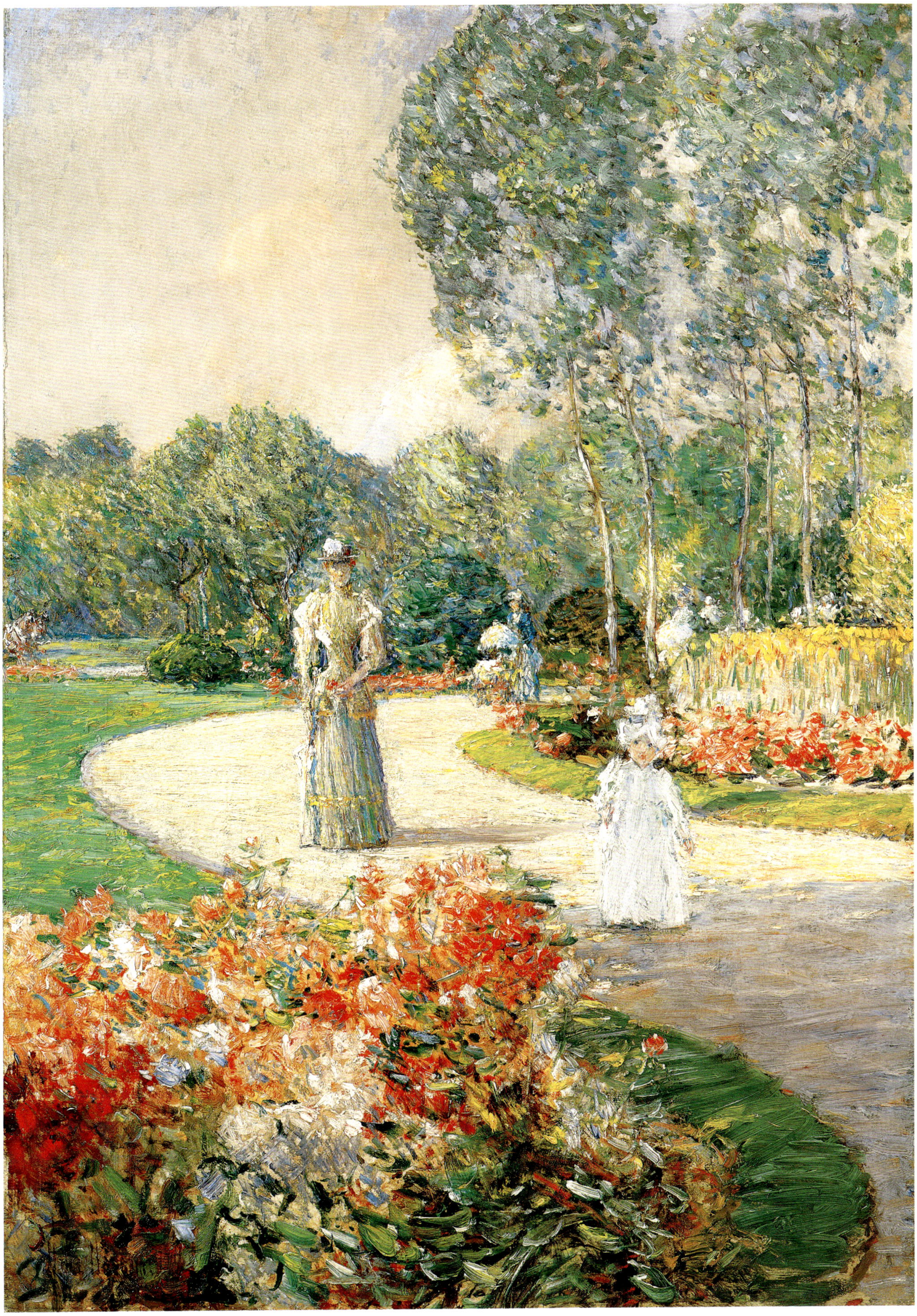

Fig. 198. Childe Hassam. *Parc Monceau, Paris,* 1897. Oil on canvas, 24⅛ x 17¾ in. (61.3 x 45.1 cm). Frye Art Museum, Seattle

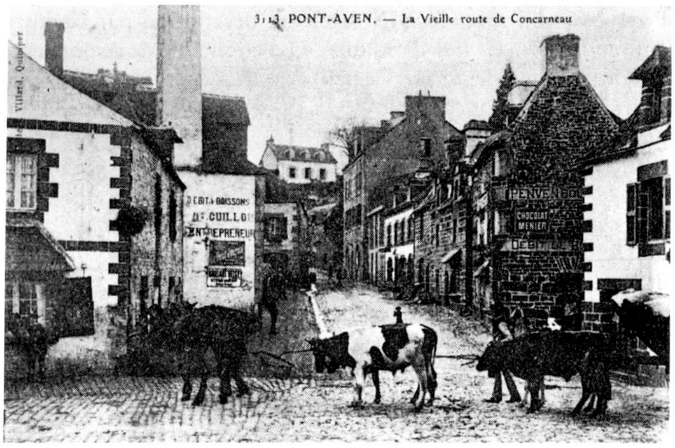

Fig. 199. "Pont-Aven,—La Vielle route de Concarneau." Undated postcard

for *Union Square in Spring*.[26] Many Paris pictures, as well as others from the 1897 trip, are marked by quick feathery brushwork and thin pigment, choices that have been attributed to Hassam's busy travel schedule.[27] In addition, the influence of Twachtman's evanescent works, which Hassam increasingly admired in this period, has been considered important in this regard.[28] Hassam's newly vibrant and translucent paint application can also be explained as a response to the inspiration provided by his return to the city that gave birth to Impressionism and by the models it provided in works by masters of the style.[29]

In *Parc Monceau, Paris* (fig. 198) Hassam announced his interest in two-dimensional decorative effects by emphasizing a sinuous pathway that curves simultaneously up along the picture plane and back into space.[30] The Parc Monceau, situated on the edge of the eighth arrondissement, was designed for Philippe d'Orléans in the late eighteenth century in the form of an English garden with winding paths, well-kept lawns, and pleasing flower beds.[31] Hassam had visited and painted the Parc Monceau during his student years and now returned to enjoy it and capture its quiet elegance. Hassam's contemporaries, including Gustave Caillebotte, Jean Béraud, and Claude Monet, had also found inspiration in this small, calm pleasure ground for upper-class Parisians whose mansions surrounded it.[32] After his return from Europe, in scenes such as *Spring in Central Park* (fig. 112), Hassam would recapitulate some of the frankly decorative devices he used in *Parc Monceau*.

During his stay in France, Hassam journeyed with his wife to Villiers-le-Bel, to work in the Blumenthals' garden, which he had painted during the summers of 1887 through 1889. He and Maud also visited London and the river Stour, the region identified with John Constable, and he spent two or three months in the late summer and early autumn at Pont-Aven, Port-Manech, and Le Pouldu on the coast of Finistère in Brittany. Like many French and American artists who frequented the well-known Pont-Aven artists' colony, Hassam found irresistible subjects for paintings in the area's quaint buildings, picturesque peasants, and other vestiges of old Breton culture.[33] One of the village's winding streets lined with its renowned stone houses (see fig. 199) provided the setting for *Pont-Aven, Noon Day* (fig. 200), a scene enlivened by people in traditional Breton costumes and a flock of chickens. *In Brittany* (fig. 201), filled with a whole catalogue of the features that attracted late-nineteenth-century artists to Pont-Aven, seems an emblem of the village, not a mere view. Perhaps energized by the legacy of Paul Gauguin's work at Pont-Aven, or Monet's at nearby Belle-Île, as David Sellin has suggested,[34] here Hassam enlisted tapestried brushwork and a vibrant palette. He combined in a decorative arrangement the flank of the Gothic chapel of Tremalo, which is perched on a hill above Pont-Aven, one of the great chestnut trees and the boulders that were common to the region, and two figures in traditional dress (see fig. 202).[35] Old-fashioned Breton subjects, an unusual diversion for a painter of modern life, inspired Hassam to create more than a dozen canvases; he left six of these—along with one produced in Rome and one produced in Paris—for exhibition in the new Salon Nationale des Beaux-Arts of 1898.

Hassam's sojourns in Old World sites may have encouraged both his appreciation of American historical architecture and artifacts and his sympathy for aspects of the modern urban scene upon his return home, as Ulrich W. Hiesinger has observed.[36] The trip abroad also supplied the studies upon which Hassam based his portrayals of Paris and London in his book *Three Cities*, published in 1899.[37]

In the summer of 1904 Hassam traveled to Portland, Oregon, where he installed a four-part mural he had painted in New York for the library in the home of Colonel Charles Erskine Scott Wood, a friend and patron whom he had met through J. Alden Weir.[38] Wood, a lawyer, soldier and explorer, poet, amateur painter, and connoisseur, was also a good friend to Olin Warner and Albert Pinkham Ryder, whose works he collected along with Weir's and Hassam's.[39] The largest section of the mural set, *The Bathers* (fig. 203), a four-by-twelve-foot composition reminiscent of ideal works by

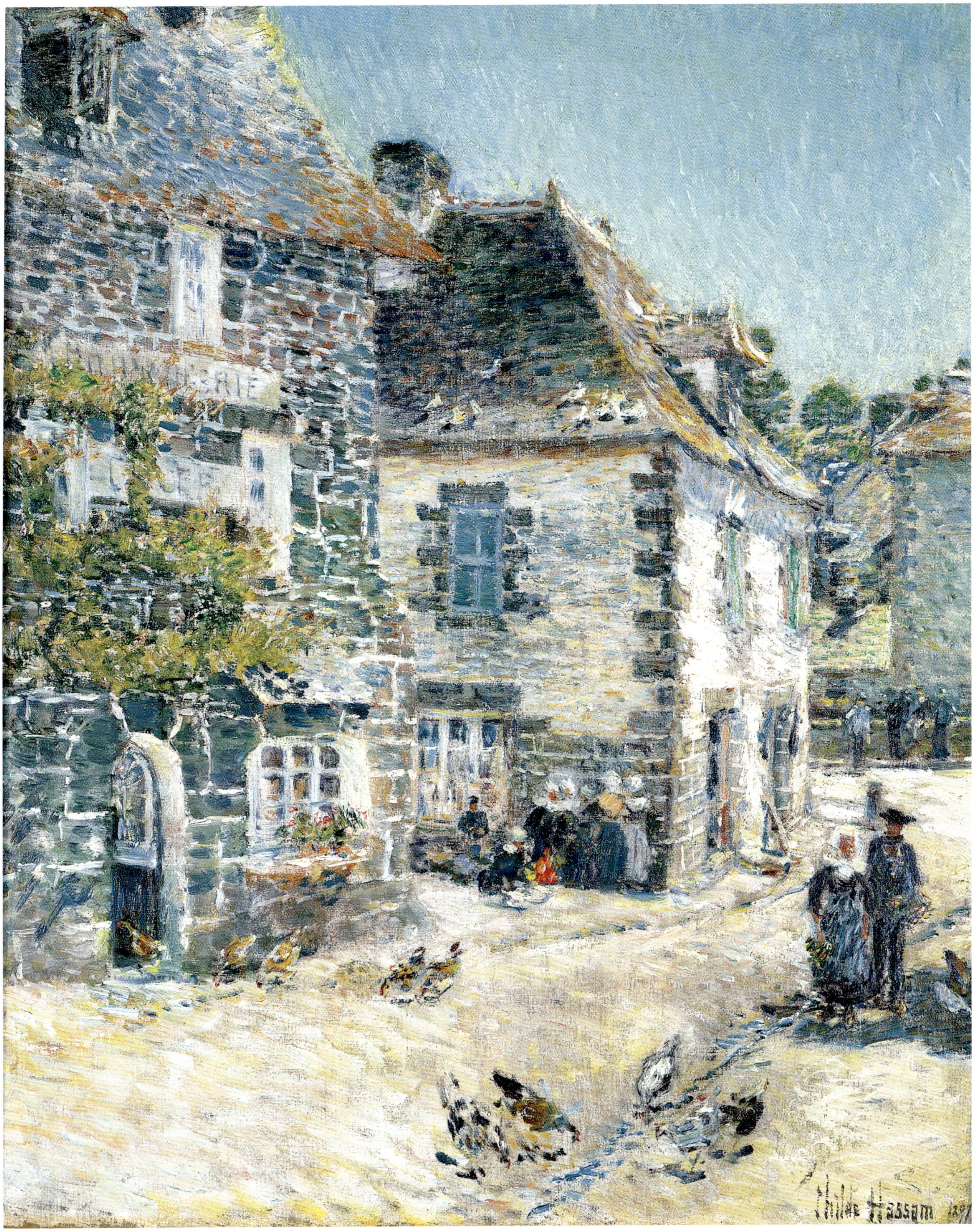

Fig. 200. Childe Hassam. *Pont-Aven, Noon Day,* 1897. Oil on canvas, 24⅛ x 19⅞ in. (61.3 x 50.5 cm). Private collection, New York

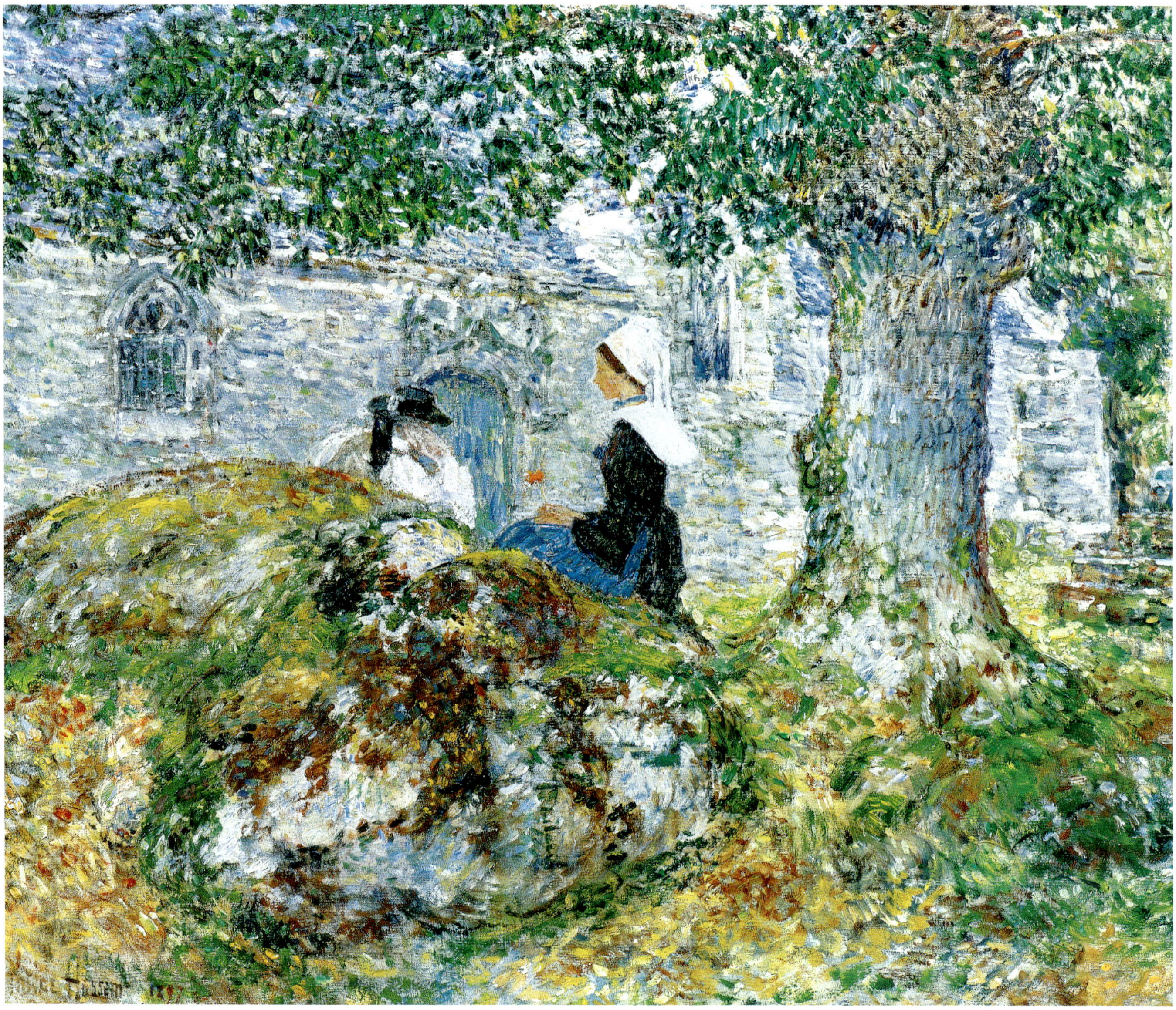

Fig. 201. Childe Hassam. *In Brittany,* 1897. Oil on canvas, 23¾ x 28⅛ in. (60.3 x 71.4 cm). Lord and Lady Ridley-Tree

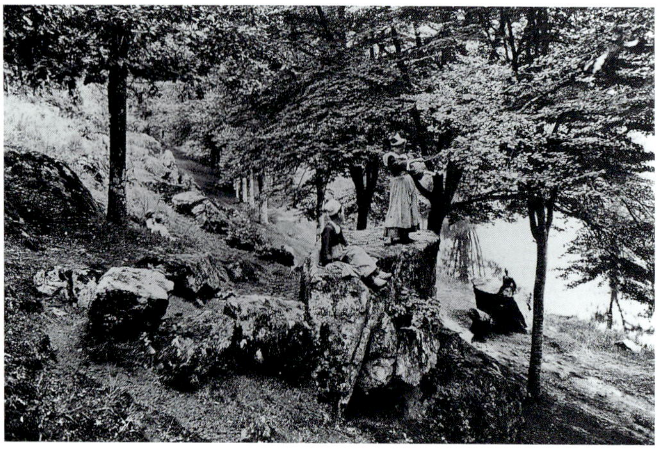

Fig. 202. Women on the rocks in Pont-Aven, ca. 1900

Pierre Puvis de Chavannes (see fig. 53), shows nude and lightly draped female figures in a landscape.[40] On the same excursion to Oregon, Hassam made portraits; painted watercolor views of Mount Hood, where he spent a week in a log cabin; worked along the seacoast and, with Wood, in the Harney desert region in eastern Oregon; and stopped in Seattle, San Francisco, and Monterey.[41]

In the fall of 1908, after he closed his studio residence on West Sixty-seventh Street and before he moved to West Fifty-seventh Street, Hassam visited eastern Oregon again. A local newspaper reported: "With Judge [Charles] Carey and C. E. S. Wood Mr. Hassam camped for two months this Summer on the Blitzen River, 40 miles from a post-office,

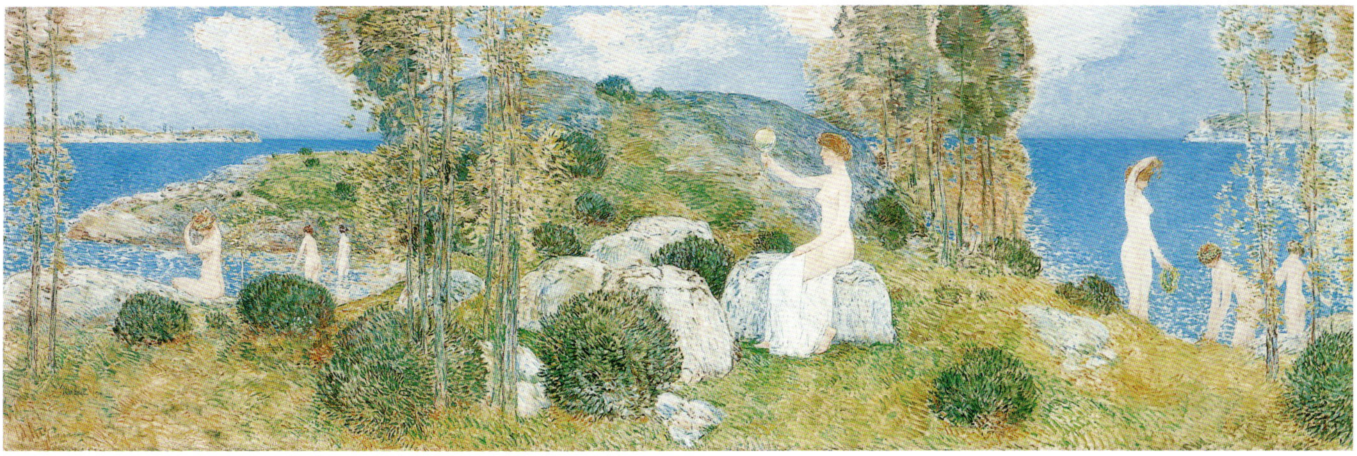

Fig. 203. Childe Hassam. *The Bathers,* 1904. Oil on canvas, 48¼ x 148¼ in. (122.6 x 376.5 cm). Memorial Art Gallery of the University of Rochester, New York. Gift of Mr. and Mrs. Ogden Phipps

hundreds of miles from any railroad, right in the heart of Harney and Malheur Counties, where he painted 40 canvasses [see fig. 204]."[42] Hassam was principally occupied with hunting and fishing on the high desert plateau, yet he responded to the locale's vast expanses, barren buttes, blazing light, and opalescent colors in about thirty canvases and watercolors and ten or a dozen cigar-box-size panels. These landscapes, "even the largest," Wood recalled, were "painted in one 'go'—say from two to five hours, with possibly some reconsideration or additional touches next day."[43] Hassam exulted in the remoteness of the desert—"It is an aspect of North America that has not been done (I think) except by me," he crowed to Wood.[44] And elsewhere he lauded its extraordinary look: "The air is limpid and liquid, the skies are stupendous and the distances amethystine."[45] *Golden Afternoon* (fig. 336), a panoramic view of Steens Mountain from the P Ranch, the party's headquarters, was described by Wood as "the most poetical thing" the artist had done.[46] Wood, who took credit for nagging Hassam into painting his desert views,[47] later echoed the spirit of *Golden Afternoon* in his own writing, as the opening lines of his 1915 poem *The Poet in the Desert* reveal:

I have entered into the Desert, the place of desolation.
The Desert confronts me haughtily and assails me with solitude.
She sits on a throne of light,
Her hands clasped, her eyes solemnly questioning.
I have come into the lean and stricken land
Which fears not God, that I may meet my soul
Face to face, naked as the Desert is naked;
Bare as the great silence is bare.[48]

Wood's purchase of four paintings from Hassam in May 1910 enabled the artist and Maud to spend almost six months in Europe, beginning in June.[49] Sailing on the SS *Saint Louis* for London on June 11, the Hassams went on from London to Holland and Belgium and arrived about July 7 in Paris, where they passed a few weeks.[50] At this time Hassam was exasperated with Paris, a feeling that mirrored his fading affection for New York. In a letter of July 21 to Weir written from the Hôtel de l'Empire, at no. 7, rue Daunou, where he and his wife were staying, he grumbled that the city had become "a huge Coney Island—noisy dirty. The streets are ankle deep in advertising cards and bills and when it rains the whole thing becomes a pulp. The town is all torn up like New York. Much building going on. They out American the

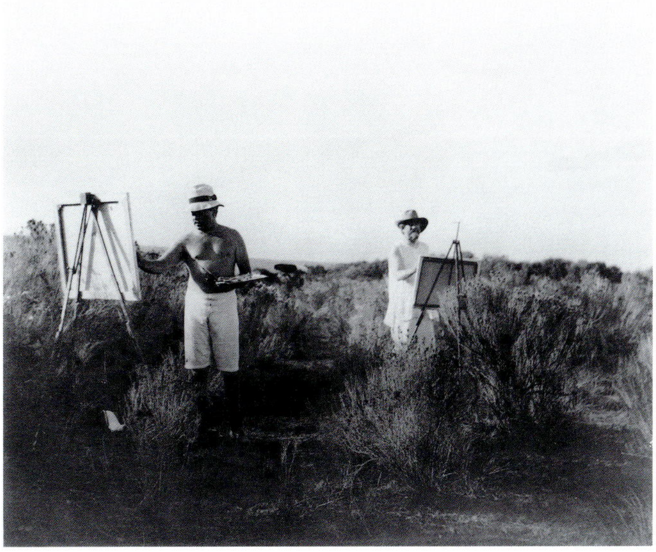

Fig. 204. Hassam painting in eastern Oregon with C. E. S. Wood, 1908. Oregon Historical Society, Portland

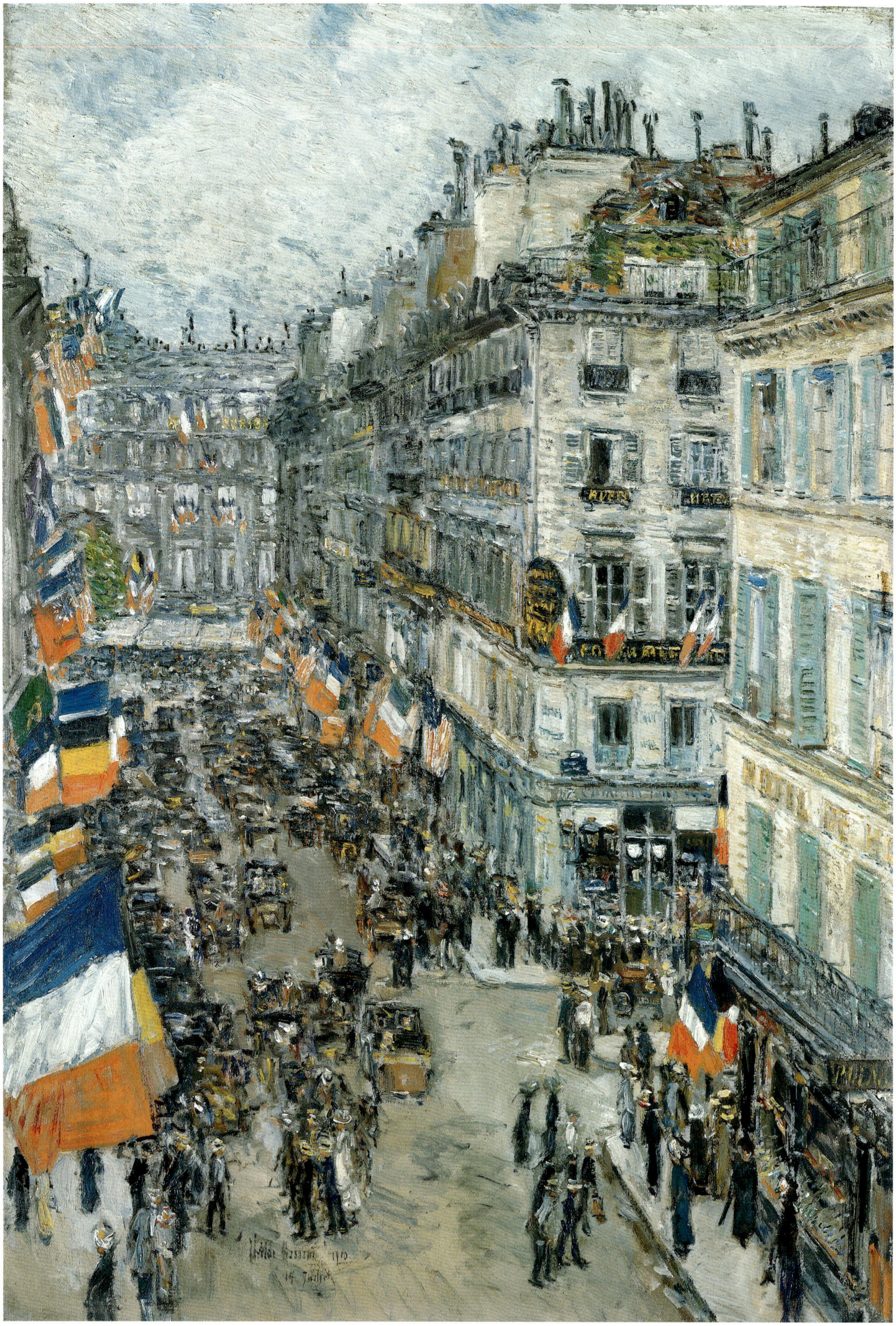

Fig. 205. Childe Hassam. *July Fourteenth, Rue Daunou, 1910*, 1910. Oil on canvas, $29\frac{1}{8}$ x $19\frac{7}{8}$ in. (74 x 50.5 cm). The Metropolitan Museum of Art, New York. George A. Hearn Fund, 1929 29.86

Americans!"[51] In the same letter Hassam reported, "I made a 14th July from the balcony here": the festive *July Fourteenth, Rue Daunou, 1910* (fig. 205), the most important canvas from the 1910 trip. This picture, like most of the paintings Hassam created in Paris and later on the same journey, reveals greater compositional deliberation and control and a richer, more complex application of pigment than the works from his European stay of 1897.

Hassam painted the visual delights of the Bastille Day celebrations from a hotel around the corner from photographer Nadar's former studio, where the first Impressionist exhibitions were held. He echoed in *July Fourteenth, Rue Daunou, 1910* the Impressionists' commitment to urban themes and enlisted their favored high vantage point.[52] In the same spirit in which he had portrayed New York's entertainment districts, he here focused on rue Daunou, the short street connecting the boulevard des Capucines and the avenue de l'Opéra in the heart of *"le Paris des plaisirs."*[53] Looking down on the rue Daunou's intersection with the rue de la Paix, he depicted in the distance the boulevard des Capucines, where awnings shade the familiar sidewalk cafés.

Hassam showed the rue Daunou adorned with flags for the *fête nationale* and filled with pedestrians, who were taking advantage of the closing of the streets to vehicles. Because Bastille Day so closely follows the Fourth of July, contemporary accounts of the French celebration often invoked the historical ties and parallel revolutions of France and the United States. For Hassam, the Fourteenth of July would have recalled the Fourth, prompting him to suffuse his view with a sense of his ardent nationalism and perhaps to exaggerate the number of American flags displayed. The repeated red, white, and blue of Old Glory and the French tricolor unify and enliven the composition and suggest shared national values. Belgium's black, yellow, and red flag, set out in honor of that nation's visiting monarchs, is also prominent, while Scotland, England, and Ireland are each represented by one flag.

July Fourteenth, Rue Daunou, 1910 had specific antecedents not only in Hassam's own works showing New York streets from elevated viewpoints but also in paintings by French Impressionists. Édouard Manet's *Rue Mosnier with Flags* (fig. 55), for example, employs a similarly high vantage point and plunging perspective and an analogous focus on humanity on the street. Monet's *Rue Montorgueil, Paris, during the Celebrations of June 30, 1878* (fig. 206), a more cheerful image, exerted an even more powerful influence on Hassam. Exhibited at the Galerie Georges Petit in Paris in early summer 1889, Monet's canvas may have inspired Hassam's first Paris flag paintings: two watercolors and a small oil depicting Montmartre on Bastille Day.[54] The paintings by Manet and Monet, Hassam's three initial explorations of the flag theme, and his *July Fourteenth, Rue Daunou, 1910* all anticipated the Flag series Hassam would paint in New York between 1916 and 1919.

To escape the summer heat in 1910, Hassam and his wife retreated from Paris to Lannion in the Côtes d'Armor department of Brittany and visited Grez-sur-Loing, the artists' colony south of Fontainebleau, where their friend Thomas Alexander Harrison had worked for many years.[55]

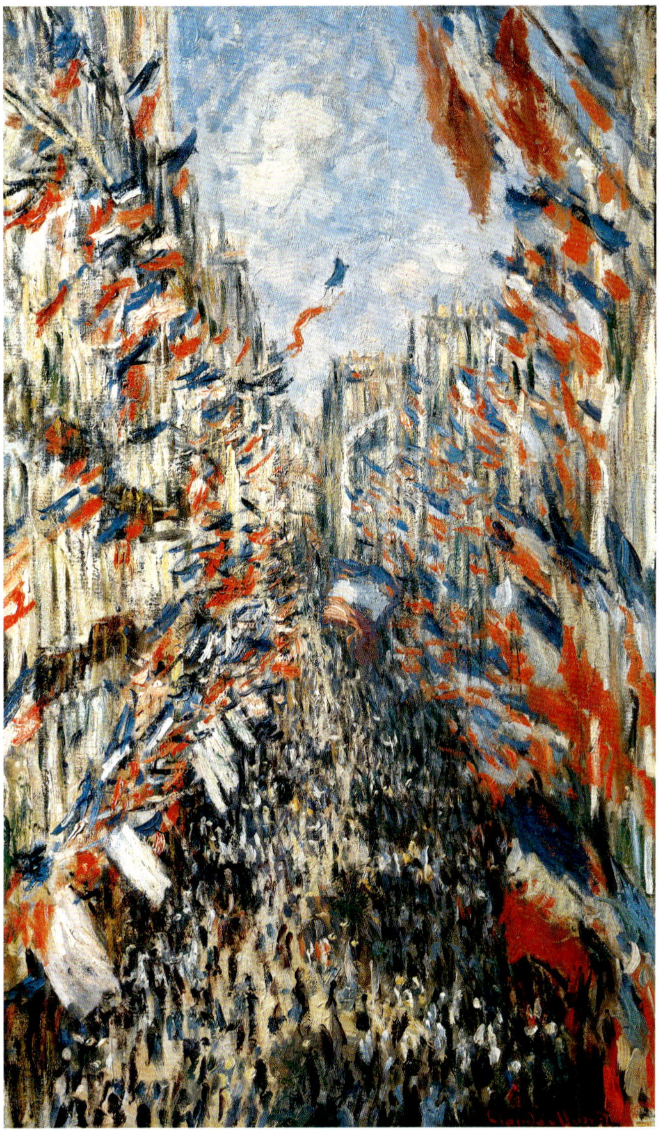

Fig. 206. Claude Monet. *La rue Montorgueil, Paris, during the Celebrations of June 30, 1878*, 1878. Oil on canvas, 31 ⅞ x 19 ⅞ in. (81 x 50.5 cm). Musée d'Orsay, Paris

Then, in the early fall, they made their way south through Nemours to Spain. Within a month the Hassams "came down through Spain," visiting Madrid, Toledo, Cordova, Seville, and Ronda, and on October 28 they returned to New York by way of Gibraltar.[56] Hassam had visited Spain, principally Granada, in 1883, on his way home from his first trip to Europe. He and Edmund Henry Garrett returned on a ship that, according to Hassam, "stopped at some of the Spanish ports. . . . to take on freight. So that we would sometimes stay for several days or a week at some of the ports. In that way we went through the Alhambra. . . . I made some water colors there in the Alhambra."[57] Hassam wished to return to Spain in 1910 so that he could work there in oil—"As I never painted in oil in Spain, I wanted to get some things in Spain," he recalled.[58] He did, however, also make watercolors and pastels once there. This journey may have been inspired not only by Hassam's desire to paint in oils in Spain but also by the popular 1909 exhibition of 350 works by Joaquín Sorolla y Bastida that he must have seen at the Hispanic Society of America in New York.[59]

Hassam's Spanish works eschew the romantic theatricality that informs many other American paintings of Iberian subjects.[60] His reticence was noticed by a writer for the *Newark Evening News* who described the "Spanish set," six oils Hassam showed among sixty-two assorted paintings, watercolors, pastels, and drawings at New York's Montross Gallery in February 1911; the critic observed: "These are handsome decorations, which is the true purpose of a painting: devoid of the kind of sentiment that thrives in the gloaming with whispering lovers going hand in hand down the shadowed lane and young mothers tossing their babes above their heads. An abstracted eye has seen the world in which we live; chosen choice spots at right moments; arranged his objects before his eye or before the eye of his imagination. Thus it has been painted—as it looks."[61]

Street of the Great Captain, Cordoba (fig. 207) is apparently the only view Hassam executed in the great historic city of Cordova in Andalusia's most northerly province.[62] The broad Paseo del Gran Capitán runs through Cordova's newer section, connecting the railway station with the old quarter and the Mezquita, a mile to the south. The Paseo was lined with cafés and hotels, in one of which Hassam may have stayed and from which he perhaps painted this view.[63] Hassam's sunlit scene focuses on a grand bell tower, likely that of the Colegiata de San Hipólito, built by Alfonso XI in 1348, modernized between 1726 and 1736, and enlarged by the addition of a tower in the 1770s. The Neoclassical palace to the left is the Gran Teatro. In the foreground Hassam suggested the boulevard's cafés and signaled with a few vivaciously rendered figures its role as a lively urban promenade.[64]

Square at Sevilla (fig. 208) evokes with the most economical means Seville's vibrancy, which a travel writer described in 1906: "From the deathlike stillness of Cordova it is a strange transition to the animation and bustle of the central part of Seville, with its brilliant shops and crowded streets, in which you would think that the whole population amused themselves all day long."[65] Characteristically, Hassam used a high vantage point, perhaps a hotel-room window, in this instance to create a dialogue between broad, sun-drenched architectural forms and knots of pedestrians in a composition not unlike that of *July Fourteenth, Rue Daunou, 1910*.[66] The plaza depicted, which defies precise identification, apparently was the site of hotels, such as the one from which he may have painted this scene, and included several picturesque elements: lines of trees shading the sidewalks; a stand for horse-drawn carriages; and a shop selling *coloniales,* or groceries.[67]

In Ronda, Hassam was likely ensconced at the Hotel Royal in the heart of the Mercadillo quarter, opposite the cathedral and near the Paseo de la Merced, from the end of which are breathtaking views over the Rio Guadalevín gorge.[68] However, he chose not to portray the dramatic vistas offered by one of picturesque Andalusia's most astonishing cities and instead concerned himself with the section of town in which he was staying. This "new" quarter, founded by merchants to avoid taxes levied in the old Ciudad after Ronda was retaken from its Muslim conquerors in 1485, contained most of the city's hotels and is marked by whitewashed stuccoed buildings and iron balconies. In *Cathedral at Ronda* (fig. 209), for example, he focused on the radiant light and the simple decorative shapes of the facade of the Iglesia la Merced, a sixteenth-century church that is not mentioned in either contemporary or recent guidebooks. Hassam showed a face-on view of the church and the trees and pedestrian activity in the foreground Plaza de la Merced, following his usual practice of working from his hotel window here, as in other Spanish canvases. Emphasizing surface pattern rather than rendering a tourist's souvenir, he cropped out of his composition the curious dome of the church's single tower. In so doing he repeated the format he had often employed to portray the First Congregational Church at Old

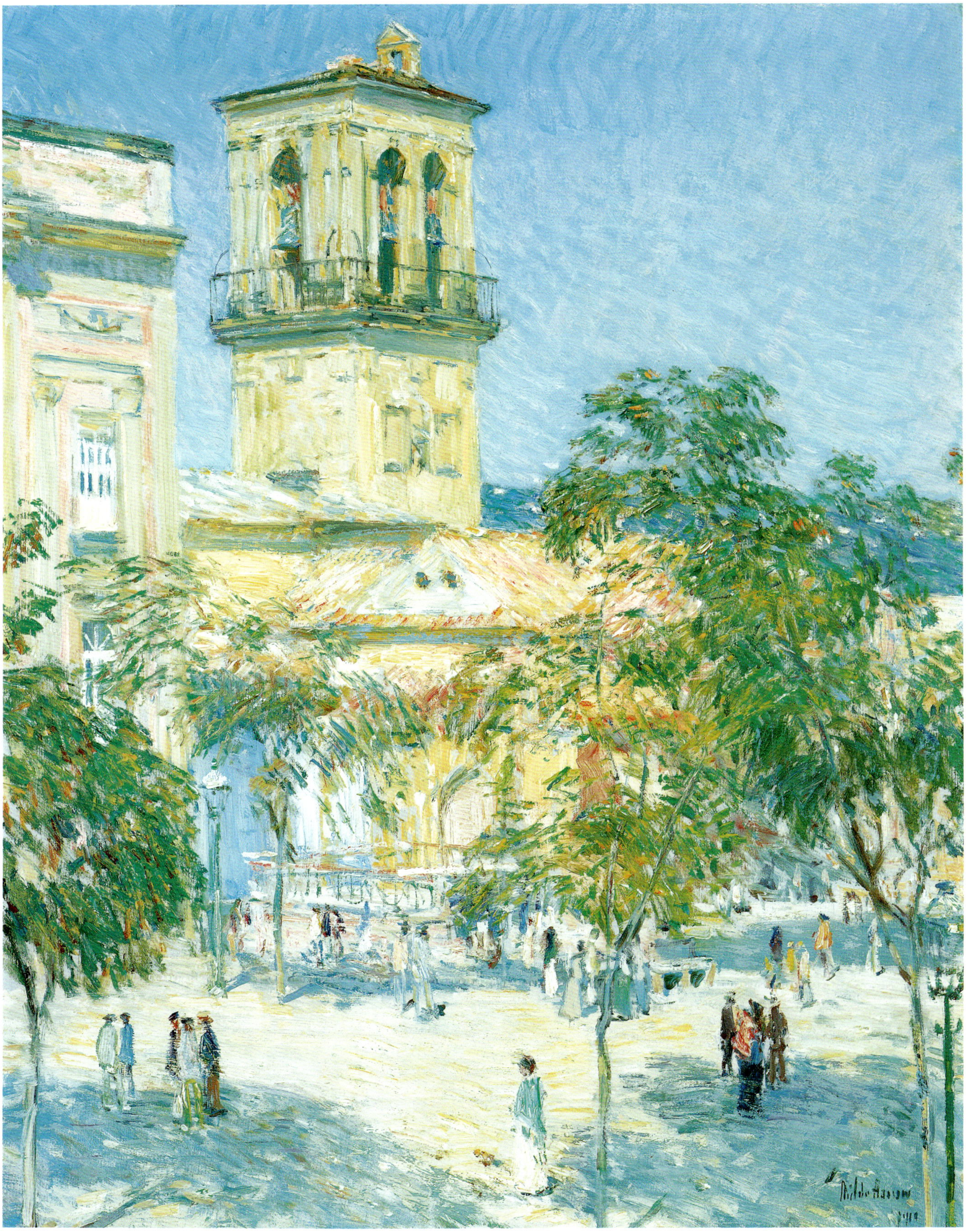

Fig. 207. Childe Hassam. *Street of the Great Captain, Cordoba,* 1910. Oil on board, 25½ x 20½ in. (64.8 x 52.1 cm). Saint Louis Art Museum, Gift of Mr. and Mrs. Mahlon Wallace

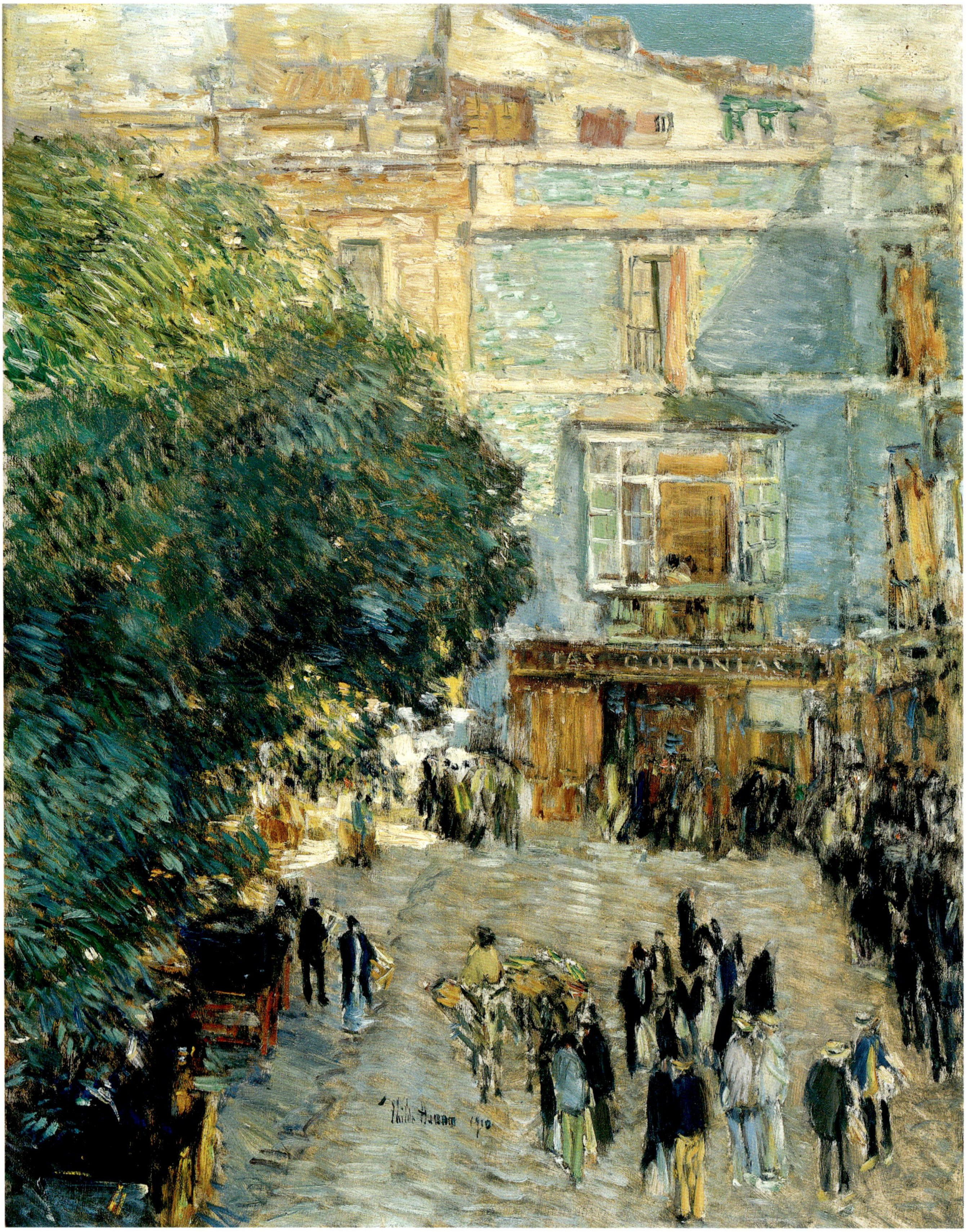

Fig. 208. Childe Hassam. *Square at Sevilla*, 1910. Oil on wood, 25⅝ x 20¾ in. (65.1 x 52.7 cm). Courtesy of The Hispanic Society of America, New York

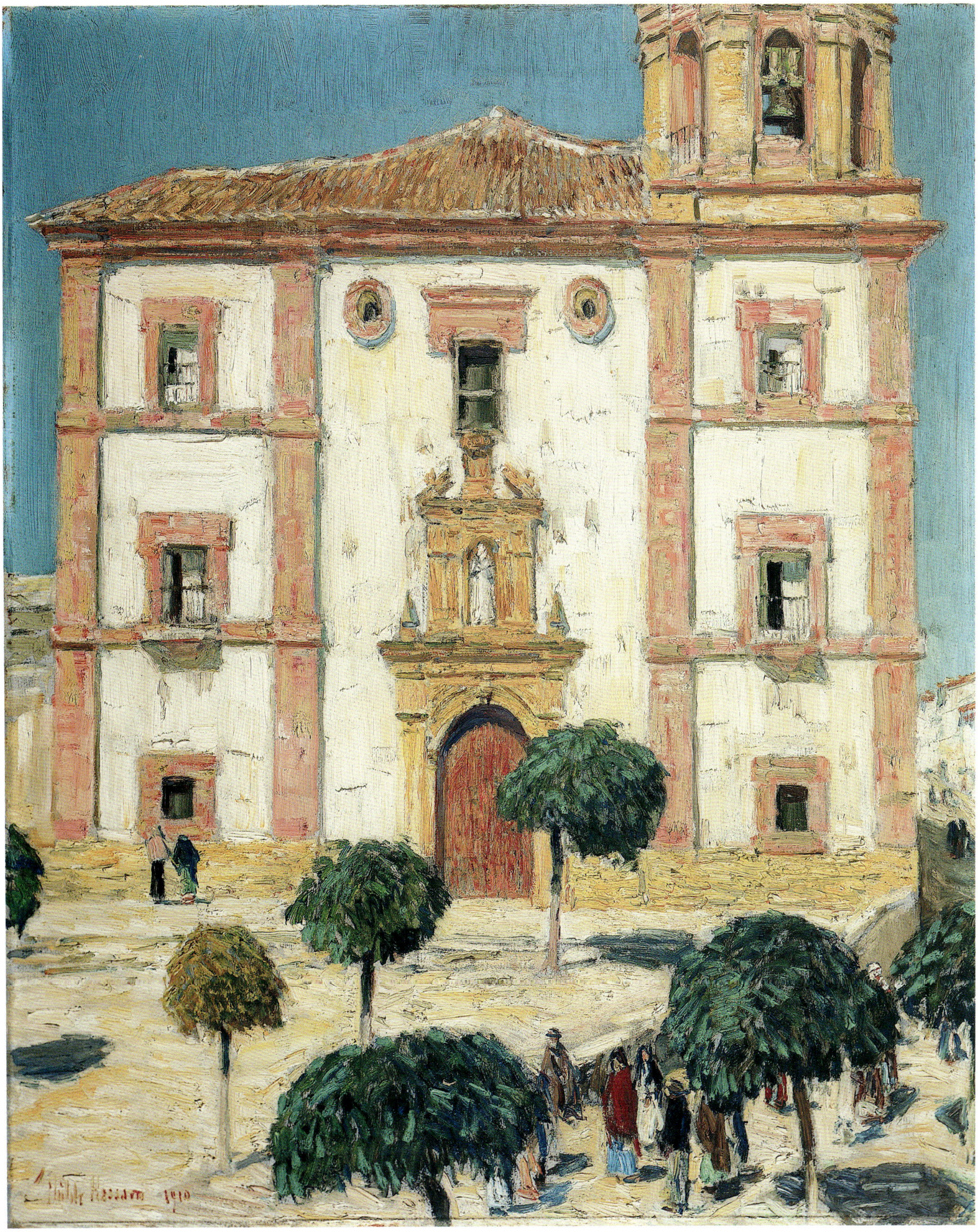

Fig. 209. Childe Hassam. *Cathedral at Ronda,* 1910. Oil on wood, 25⅝ x 21⅛ in. (65.1 x 53.7 cm). Courtesy of The Hispanic Society of America, New York

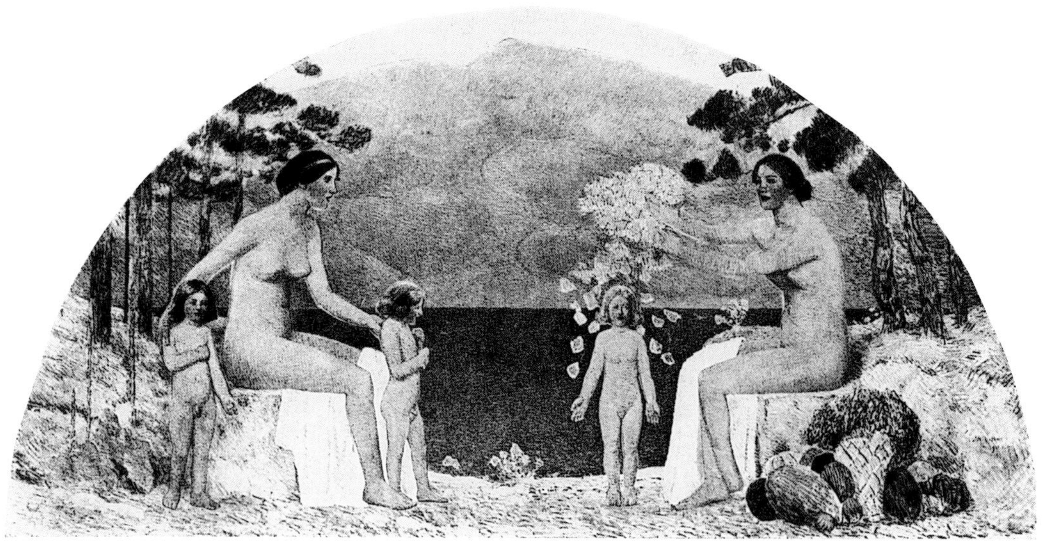

Fig. 210. Childe Hassam. *Fruits and Flowers,* 1915. Mural for the Court of Palms, Panama-Pacific International Exposition, San Francisco

Lyme (see figs. 176, 177) and anticipated its use in *The Church at Gloucester* (fig. 184). The writer for the *Newark Evening News,* referring to *Cathedral at Ronda* or a similar work in the "Spanish set" shown at the Montross Gallery, New York, in 1911, quoted an artist who had lived in Spain and had exclaimed upon encountering Hassam's picture: "The Piazza de la Merced! No one knows how difficult it is to paint unless he's tried it. But that's it. Yes! That's it. And that shadow in the street where the morning crowd has gathered."[69]

Hassam would make his fifth and last trip to Europe in May and June 1911, spending most of his time in Paris. He had, he recalled, "gone there . . . with the intention of going to Venice to paint. I found out that cholera had broken out and it was very hot in Paris, and I was a little disgusted and I went down to one of the steamship offices and said 'What is the quickest steamer that goes from Havre to New York.'"[70] The only known work that resulted from this trip is the sketchy watercolor *Pont Neuf, Paris,* 1911 (The Metropolitan Museum of Art, New York, 67.55.148).

In early summer 1913 Hassam was invited to execute a mural for the Panama-Pacific International Exposition, which would take place in San Francisco from February 20 through December 4, 1915. He wrote to Colonel Wood on June 10: "I have just received a commission to do a lunette for the San Francisco Exposition 21 x 10 feet. Send me a design—a motive—Quick now! You are a man of ideas. I am to secure the sum of twenty three hundred dollars for it."[71] Hassam interpreted the theme of the mural, *Fruits and Flowers* (fig. 210), with a female nude seated on a draped stone before which are heaped large fruits and a vase of flowers. She showers a nude girl with flower petals, while a second seated female nude and two nude boys look on. A critic enthused: "In its bright colors, clear atmosphere, and the charm of a masterly technician, this appropriate mural indicates the wealth of California in flowers and fruits."[72] Hassam began the mural in New York and went to San Francisco late in 1914 to complete it and supervise its placement over the entrance to the Palace of Education on the west side of the Court of Palms in Bernard Maybeck's colossal Palace of Fine Arts.[73] He stayed at the Bohemian Club along with Edward E. Simmons and possibly Robert Reid, and painted at sites along the nearby coast.

Point Lobos, Carmel (fig. 211), one of about a dozen California scenes Hassam produced, was probably based on a study made on a sketching trip with Francis J. McComas, a successful Australian-born San Francisco landscape watercolorist and muralist.[74] The pair worked at Point Lobos, just south of the Monterey Peninsula and Carmel on California's central coast, an area noted for its geological formations, rare flora, and astonishing beauty (and since 1933 a state reserve). According to Kent L. Seavey, McComas's widow—also a painter—recalled: "McComas was a meticulous painter and always worked, except for mural decoration, directly from nature. In this instance apparently Hassam studied the scene he intended to depict a while, then faced away from the sea and painted it from memory. When the two had finished their sketching for the day, Hassam asked McComas what he thought of his afternoon's work. The outspoken McComas, upset with Hassam's method of observation, suggested that he 'chuck it in the sea' thus bringing up short a rather pleasant weekend."[75] Hassam composed the brilliantly sunny, freely brushed *Point Lobos, Carmel* so that the view resembled one at Appledore, in the Isles of Shoals (see fig. 141), where he spent many summers. He must have done so either because he was painting from memory or because he wished to convey the analogy he perceived between the rugged California coast and the Isles of Shoals. Only the wind-sculpted Monterey cypress trees—a rare species indigenous to the region—announce the actual locale.

Hassam did not stay on in San Francisco to visit the Panama-Pacific International Exposition,[76] although his achievements were celebrated in a separate gallery filled with his paintings and drawings. This was one of several such installations in the United States section at the fair, which presented forty-five hundred catalogued works.[77] "I was given a room, which was considered honor enough," he recalled.[78] Beyond that honor, the thirty-eight works he showed were lauded by influential critics. Hassam's demonstration in his western scenes of the merits of Impressionism for depicting the region's forms, light, and atmosphere intersected with, and may even have stimulated, the development of California Impressionism.[79]

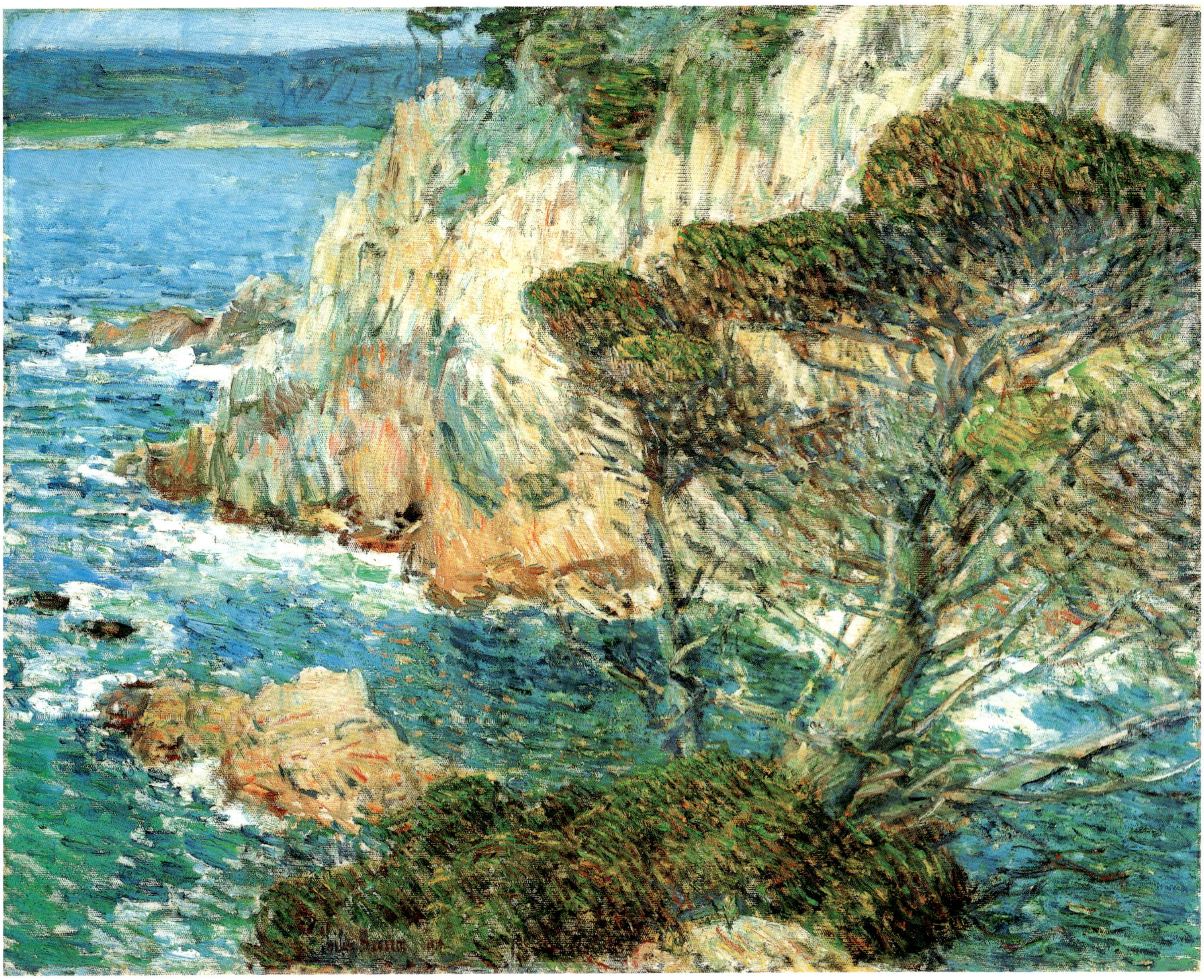

Fig. 211. Childe Hassam. *Point Lobos, Carmel,* 1914. Oil on canvas, 28⅜ x 36¼ in. (72.1 x 92.1 cm). Los Angeles County Museum of Art, Mr. and Mrs. William Preston Harrison Collection

1. Childe Hassam, New York, undated, to Florence Griswold, Old Lyme, Conn., archives, Florence Griswold Museum, Old Lyme, Connecticut. Hassam was complaining about frequent requests from journalists for interviews (and claiming that he doesn't read, much less save, press clippings). He wrote, "What they really want to know is about ones home life, whether you wear spates [*sic*] or puttees, whether you are married or divorced and how many times if so. What breakfast food you take too! You should begin now and write your book on some contemporary painters and their characteristics. I am the Marco Polo of the painters anyway—from Paris to Portland, Oregon and why not say Pekin—for Mrs Manners." The author thanks Susan G. Larkin for the reference.
2. Lockman interview, February 2, 1927, p. 28. Hassam, of course, frequented New England artists' colonies, as is detailed in Susan G. Larkin, "Hassam in New England, 1889–1918," in this publication.
3. Lockman interview, February 2, 1927, p. 24.
4. Travels that had less direct consequence for his work included a March 1925 journey through the South, including Charleston and Savannah, and a 1927 trip to California by way of New Orleans, Corpus Christi and El Paso, and finally Yuma, Arizona. In California he visited Los Angeles and Coronado Beach, and while he was there he may have spent a day in Tijuana.
5. William H. Gerdts, "Three Themes," in Adelson, Cantor, and Gerdts 1999, pp. 226–27, proposes that the verisimilitude of Hassam's illustration *The Jam of Street Cars at the Corner of Madison and State Streets, Chicago,* which was published in May 1892 in Thomas Curtis Clarke, "Rapid Transit in Cities. I.—The Problem," *Scribner's Magazine* 11 (May 1892), p. 568, indicates that the artist must have visited Chicago the year before the fair opened.
6. Lockman interview, January 31, 1927, pp. 39–40, and Hiesinger 1994, p. 93. Seven renderings in watercolor on cardboard and one in oil on paper from the lithographic project are in the Chicago Historical Society. Ulrich W. Hiesinger (ibid., p. 106, n. 32) records that the original watercolors and gouaches are in the Terra Museum of American Art, Chicago; the Fogg Art Museum, Harvard University Art Museums, Cambridge, Massachusetts; and on the art market.
7. *Paintings by Old Masters, and Modern Foreign and American Painters, Together with an Exhibition of the Work of Claude Monet the Impressionist . . . Loan Collection,* exh. cat. (New York: Union League Club, 1891), includes the first picture known to have been titled *Nocturne* by Hassam, according to Gerdts, "Three Themes," p. 227, n. 74. See also *Exhibition of Oil Paintings,* exh. cat. (New York: Union League Club, November 12–14, 1891), no. 45, *The Flower Girl–Nocturne.*
8. J[ames] W[illiam] Buel, *The Magic City* (Saint Louis and Philadelphia: Historical Publishing Company, 1894), unpaged.
9. Henry Van Brunt, "Architecture at the World's Columbian Exposition.—IV," *Century* 44 (September 1892), p. 729.
10. For a discussion by Marc Simpson of Robinson's *World's Columbian Exposition* (fig. 195), see *American Paintings from the Manoogian Collection,* exh. cat. (Washington, D.C.: National Gallery of Art; Detroit: Detroit Institute of Arts, 1989), pp. 154–57. Responses to the fair by some of the four dozen artists who painted it are the subject of Margaretta M. Lovell, "Picturing 'A City for a Single Summer': Paintings of the World's Columbian Exposition," *Art Bulletin* 77 (March 1996), pp. 40–55.
11. Lockman interview, January 31, 1927, p. 40: "I did not see the fair."
12. Hamlin Garland, "Impressionism," in *Crumbling Idols: Twelve Essays on Art Dealing Chiefly with Literature, Painting, and the Drama* (Chicago: Stone and Kimball, 1894; new ed., edited by Jane Johnson, Cambridge, Mass.: Belknap Press of Harvard University Press, 1960), p. 103.
13. Ives 1892, p. 116.
14. Lockman interview, January 31, 1927, p. 38. Our efforts to further identify Robinson have not been fruitful.
15. *Standard Guide to Havana: A Complete Handbook for Visitors, with Maps, Illustrations, History, and an English-Spanish Manual of Conversations* (New York: Foster and Reynolds; Havana: Diamond News Company, 1905), p. 40. In 1905 the Telegrafo Hotel, the Inglaterra Hotel, the Hotel Louvre, the American Club, and the Tacon Theater stood on the west side of the square. The Centro Asturiano clubhouse and the Albisu Theater were on the east side. The south side was home to the Pairet Theater, the Pasage Hotel, and the large Martí Theater–Centro Gallego Spanish Club.
16. María Luisa Lobo Montalvo, *Havana: History and Architecture of a Romantic City,* translated by Lorna Scott Fox (New York: Monacelli Press, 2000), p. 54. In 1990 La Cabaña was converted into a museum.
17. Lockman interview, February 2, 1927, p. 13. The "insurrection," which began on February 24, 1895, was the revolt against Spanish domination led by José Martí, who died in the struggle and became a martyr to Cuba's independence. Hassam's illustrations of "The Insurrection in Cuba" were published in *Harper's Weekly* 39 (May 18, May 25, June 8, 1895), pp. 458, 490, 543. The discrepancy between Hassam's claim that he departed from Havana on February 23, 1895, and his arrival with Robinson in the port of New York aboard the SS *Yumuri* on February 5, 1895, remains unexplained. See Ellis Island's on-line reference site (http://ellisisland.org). Elizabeth Broun, "Childe Hassam's America," *American Art* 13, no. 3 (fall 1999), p. 39, suggests that Hassam's patron Horatio S. Rubens, a New York lawyer and counsel to the Cuban Revolutionary Party, may have stimulated Hassam's interest in Cuba. Broun (ibid., pp. 40–41) further argues that Hassam's Cuban paintings "carry more political meaning than is at first evident in their creamy, colorful surfaces" and reflect "his ability to encode meaning into images that seem at first to be merely tourist views."
18. Undated minutes of the Picture Purchase Committee [1911] and related correspondence of August 1911 are in the Detroit Institute of Arts Archives. The author thanks Curator James Tottis for making them available to her.
19. Other Havana paintings that emphasize abstract values are *The Prado,* 1895 (Museo de Bellas Artes, Havana); and *Havana,* 1895 (private collection), a view of the Plaza de la Catedral, illustrated in Hiesinger 1994, p. 102.
20. Lockman interview, January 31, 1927, p. 33: "I sublet my apartment in the Rhembrandt [*sic*] to Miss Waring, a daughter of Colonel Waring, and we spent 1897 abroad. . . . We sailed for Naples in December 1896." Stuart P. Feld, "Childe Hassam—a Retrospective View in Progress," in Hassam (East Hampton) 1981, p. 9: "Throughout the '90s, viewed year by year, Hassam's output seems to have been modest, but suddenly in 1897, with a third trip abroad, Hassam seems to have become wildly prolific."
21. "Cholera Days in Europe," *New York Times,* September 20, 1886, p. 6, notes "the progress which the scourge is making toward Italy's western frontier and the absolute lack of all means to bar its advance give legitimate grounds for nervousness."

22. Lockman interview, January 31, 1927, p. 34. Asked whether they had "any effect on [his] art," he replied: "Not that I can see. They may have had, but I cannot see it. I have never changed since my Boston period. I have never changed my painting since my early days."

23. For additional information about the painting, see catalogue entry in Ilene Susan Fort and Michael Quick, *American Art: A Catalogue of the Los Angeles County Museum of Art Collection* (Los Angeles: Los Angeles County Museum of Art, 1991), pp. 207–8.

24. Hiesinger (1994, p. 109) indicates that these people were artists' models who gathered on the steps awaiting work.

25. See *Piazza di Spagna, Rome,* 1897 (Newark Museum); *The Spanish Steps of Rome* (Christie's, New York, sale cat., December 4, 1987, lot 208); and *Rome* (Christie's, New York, sale cat., June 3, 1983, lot 191). Fort and Quick (*American Art,* p. 208) note the differences between the noonday light in the Newark canvas and the late-afternoon light in the Los Angeles view (fig. 197). Hassam may have shown the latter picture in the 1897 Salon of the Société Nationale des Beaux-Arts, Paris, as *Le Soir, Piazza di Spagna (Rome).* For a discussion of the several versions of the scene, see Gerdts, "Three Themes," p. 227, n. 80.

26. Gerdts ("Three Themes," p. 159) writes that Hassam painted *Pont Royal* from his room in the Hôtel du quai Voltaire on the quai Voltaire, whose address he gave in the catalogue of the 1897 Salon of the Société Nationale des Beaux-Arts. The view extends across the Pont Royal to the Jardin des Tuileries. According to Donelson F. Hoopes (1979, p. 48), the painting was awarded the Temple Gold Medal at the Pennsylvania Academy of the Fine Arts in January 1899 and was acquired by the Cincinnati Art Museum six months later. Hassam's other pictures of the same district include *Tuileries Gardens,* 1897 (High Museum of Art, Atlanta), and *Le Louvre et le Pont Royal,* 1897 (MSC Forsyth Center Galleries, Texas A and M University, College Station).

27. Hiesinger 1994, p. 109: "Apparently intent on finishing as much work as possible, Hassam adjusted his method to a hurried schedule, laying down the pigment in extremely rapid, summary strokes. Hence, the painted surfaces are often quite thin, but, at their best, possess an engaging sense of impulsiveness and a striking immediacy of effect."

28. Hoopes (1979, p. 48) mentions Twachtman's influence.

29. See, for example, Camille Pissarro, *Le Pont Corneille à Rouen, Effet du matin,* 1896 (Sotheby's, New York, sale cat., May 19, 2001, lot 221).

30. *Parc Monceau, Paris,* ca. 1888–89 (private collection), illustrated in Hiesinger 1994, p. 44, also stresses the curving pathway but suggests deeper spatial recession through its more fully rendered trees and expansive sky.

31. The principal access gate to the Parc Monceau is on the boulevard de Courcelles; three other monumental entrances are on avenues named for Velázquez, Van Dyck, and Ruisdael.

32. See, for example, Gustave Caillebotte, *Le Parc Monceau,* 1877 (private collection), and *Le Parc Monceau,* 1878 (private collection), both illustrated in Anne Distel et al., *Gustave Caillebotte, 1848–1894,* exh. cat. (Paris: Galeries Nationales du Grand Palais; Chicago: Art Institute of Chicago, 1995), pp. 150–51; Jean Béraud, *At the Gates of the Parc Monceau* (Sotheby's, New York, sale cat., May 24, 1995, lot 249); Claude Monet, *Landscape, The Parc Monceau,* 1876 (The Metropolitan Museum of Art, New York, 59.206); and Claude Monet, *The Parc Monceau,* 1878 (The Metropolitan Museum of Art, New York, 59.142). Four other paintings of the Parc Monceau, all in private collections, are listed in Daniel Wildenstein, *Monet: Catalogue Raisonné,* 4 vols. (Cologne and Paris: Taschen, 1985), vol. 2, nos. 399, 400, 467, 468.

33. For artists in Pont-Aven, see David Sellin, *Americans in Brittany and Normandy, 1860–1910,* exh. cat. (Phoenix: Phoenix Art Museum, 1982), pp. 51–64; Michael Jacobs, *The Good and Simple Life: Artist Colonies in Europe and America* (Oxford: Phaidon, 1985), pp. 3–87; Denise Delouche, ed., *Pont-Aven et ses peintres à propos d'un centenaire* (Rennes: Presses Universitaires de Rennes, 1986); Julia R. Myers, "The American Expatriate Painters of the French Peasantry, 1863–1893" (Ph.D. diss., University of Maryland, College Park, 1989), pp. 48–182; David Sellin, "Peintres américains en Finistère," in David Sellin and Catherine Puget, *Peintres américains en Bretagne, 1864–1914,* exh. cat. (Pont-Aven: Musée du Pont-Aven, 1995), unpaged; and Julia Rowland Myers, "'Sympathy for Humanity': Robert Wylie and His Paintings of Breton Life," *American Art Journal* 28, no. 1–2 (1997), pp. 82–121. Robert Wylie, who first visited Pont-Aven in 1864, was the pioneer among the Americans who worked there.

34. David Sellin, "Pont-Aven: Innkeepers as Art Patrons," *Nineteenth Century* 2, no. 1–2 (1992), p. 29.

35. Henry Blackburn, *Breton Folk: An Artistic Tour in Brittany* (London: Sampson Low, Marston, Searle and Rivington, 1880), p. 132, describes Pont-Aven flora ("the cool avenues of beeches and chestnut trees, a distinctive feature of the country"), architecture ("an ancient chapel"), and models ("Pont-Aven has one advantage over other places in Brittany; its inhabitants in their picturesque costume . . . have learned that to sit as a model is a pleasant and lucrative profession"). Hassam's other paintings of Pont-Aven and surroundings in public collections include: *Afternoon in Pont-Aven, Brittany,* 1897 (Cummer Museum of Art and Gardens, Jacksonville, Florida); *Harvest Time, Brittany,* 1897 (Colby College Museum of Art, Waterville, Maine); *Pont-Aven, Brittany,* 1897 (Ruth Chandler Williamson Gallery, Scripps College, Claremont, California); *Street in Pont-Aven, Brittany,* 1897 (Museum of Art, Rhode Island School of Design, Providence).

36. Hiesinger 1994, p. 115.

37. Hassam 1899. The sketchy quality of the Paris scenes reproduced in *Three Cities* suggests their origin in the 1897 trip.

38. Childe Hassam, New York, March 1, 1904, to C. E. S. Wood: "The decoration is done—and it was with a very fine ration of 'Salmon Bellies' from Astoria Oregon that the last licks were put in. . . . When will you want the decoration sent out to you. It will be sent rolled. . . . It is on view perfectly by electric light. In fact I have worked on it in places at night. It will look as I want it to by electric light as daylight. I wish you could alight here and see it." Childe Hassam, New York, April 13, 1904, to C. E. S. Wood: "About your kind invitation for us to come out there. We would like to do so—very much." Both letters are in Wood Papers (Berkeley). Wood, writing to J. Alden Weir of Hassam, on May 23, 1904, asked if Weir had ever seen "such a cuss? Whirled in and painted me a whole wall for my studio. . . . It grew out of a remark of mine that I was tired of my bric-a-brac house, like a dealer's shop, and wanted to get back to Greek simplicity,—the whole room done as an intentional whole by one man." Quoted in Young 1960, p. 222. Price 1923, pp. 4–5: "Through Weir it was that Hassam met Colonel C. E. Wood." The author is indebted to Margaret Bullock, Associate Curator of American Art, Portland Art Museum, for sharing her expertise on Hassam in Oregon, which is the subject of her forthcoming exhibition.

39. For Wood, see *Collected Poems of Charles Erskine Scott Wood,* collected, with a foreword by Sara Bard Field (New York: Vanguard Press, 1949);

Portland Art Museum Bulletin 14 (March 1953), p. [2]; Edwin R. Bingham, "Experiment in Launching a Biography: Three Vignettes of Charles Erskine Scott Wood," *Huntington Library Quarterly* 35 (May 1972), pp. 221–39; and Robert Hamburger, *Two Rooms: The Life of Charles Erskine Scott Wood* (Lincoln: University of Nebraska Press, 1998). Bingham ("Experiment in Launching a Biography," p. 229) describes Wood's house: "The furnishings displayed the master's love of rare, exotic, and sumptuous things. The walls were hung with rich tapestries and with oils by Albert Pinkham Ryder, John [*sic*] Alden Weir, Childe Hassam, and Wood himself." In 1906 and 1909 Wood lent works by Hassam for exhibition at the Portland Art Museum, of which he had been a founder in 1892, and he occasionally lent individual works for showing in other museums and galleries.

40. Lockman interview, February 2, 1927, p. 3: "I went out again to Portland, Oregon, to put up a decoration. It was a classic—nude and landscape. I went out there to put it up and stayed several months." The murals in Wood's study were later dispersed among Wood's children. Hassam's *Bathers* passed to Wood's daughter, Nan Wood Honeyman; it was later sold to Mr. and Mrs. Ogden Phipps of New York, who gave it in 1963 to the University of Rochester Memorial Art Gallery. See William H. Gerdts, "California Impressionism in Context," in William H. Gerdts and Will South, *California Impressionism* (New York: Abbeville Press, 1998), p. 76, n. 75.

41. Albert P. Ryder, New York, September 22, 1904, to J. Alden Weir, Branchville, Conn.: "Wood says 'Hassam has been here for about six weeks and is still with us. He has been to the sea coast and painted some really beautiful pictures, some of which I think he will sell here.'" Ryder's letter is quoted in Young 1960, p. 223. Childe Hassam, New York, October 19, 1904, to C. E. S. Wood, Wood Papers (Berkeley): "I didn't see much of San Francisco for I went direct to Monterey—and the two days I was there before I started east it rained in torrents." See Eleanor H. Gustafson, "Museum Accessions," *Magazine Antiques* 163 (July 2003), p. 32.

42. "Hassam's Pictures Delight Lovers of Oregon Scenery," *Oregonian*, November 21, 1908, p. 100. Judge Charles Carey, vice president of the American Bar Association (1894–1914) and president of the Oregon Bar Association (1912–13, 1922–23), was a Portland lawyer who served as a municipal judge (1892–95). See "Judge Carey Dies; Northwest Jurist," *New York Times*, August 28, 1941, p. 19. Carey was also a patron of Hassam's, purchasing his *On the Snake River, Oregon* (fig. 334), along with a landscape C. E. S. Wood had painted of the same scene in Hassam's company; see Susan G. Larkin, "How Hassam Framed Hassams," in this publication, pp. 329–30. Both pictures are now in the Portland Art Museum.

43. Charles Erskine Scott Wood, "The Exhibition of Paintings of Eastern Oregon by Childe Hassam," *Pacific Monthly* 21 (February 1909), p. 142.

44. Childe Hassam, February 7, 1929, to C. E. S. Wood, Wood Papers (San Marino), quoted in Hiesinger 1994, p. 136.

45. Hassam quoted in "Desert Pictured by Mr. Hassam," *[New York] Herald*, [December] 1908, clipping, Hassam Papers, reel NAA1, frame 554.

46. C. E. S. Wood, [Portland, Oreg.], December 29, 1916, to J. Alden Weir, quoted in Young 1960, p. 254. Hassam sold the painting to The Metropolitan Museum of Art in 1911.

47. Ibid.: "But if I hadn't nagged Hassam, he would not have brought half that he did out of the Desert. That *Golden Afternoon* in the Metropolitan Museum, the most poetical thing of his—would never have existed if—(myself attracted by the brooding beauty of the day) I hadn't gone to the carpenter shop, made the stretcher, stretched the canvas and galvanized old Muley."

48. Charles Erskine Scott Wood, *The Poet in the Desert* (Portland, Oreg.: F. W. Baltes and Company, 1915), p. 3.

49. Wood Papers (San Marino) contains a document headed "Hassam's Statement / May 23, 1910 4 pictures," which lists a total cost of $5,500 and a payment on account of $2,500. Smaller installments to cover the balance were paid between May 1913 and October 1919.

50. Childe Hassam, New York, May 30, 1910, to [John W.] Beatty, Carnegie Institute Papers, file 673, Archives of American Art, Smithsonian Institution, describes Hassam's plan to sail on June 11. Childe Hassam, Paris, July 21, 1910, to J. Alden Weir, typescript copy of letter on Hôtel de l'Empire stationery, Hassam Papers, reel NAA2, frame 66: "We have been in Paris for two weeks."

51. Hassam, July 21, 1910, to Weir.

52. This account of *July Fourteenth, Rue Daunou, 1910* is indebted to the catalogue entry by Susan G. Larkin in H. Barbara Weinberg and Susan G. Larkin, *American Impressionists Abroad and at Home: Paintings from the Collection of The Metropolitan Museum of Art*, exh. cat. (New York: American Federation of Arts, 2000), pp. 34, 36. Nadar's given name was Gaspard Félix Tournachon. For the origin of his nickname, see Maria Morris Hambourg, "A Portrait of Nadar," in Maria Morris Hambourg et al., *Nadar*, exh. cat. (New York: The Metropolitan Museum of Art, 1995), pp. 5–6. The author thanks Jeff L. Rosenheim, Associate Curator, Department of Photographs, The Metropolitan Museum of Art, New York, for his assistance.

53. Paul Joanne, *Paris* (Paris: Librairie Hachette, 1913), p. 31, thus described the city's entertainment district. Catalogue entry by Larkin in Weinberg and Larkin, *American Impressionists Abroad and at Home*, p. 34: "Although rue Daunou was a relatively quiet side street, numerous stylish businesses filled its two-block length. Mrs. Hassam could choose among five hairdressers, four jewelers, a half-dozen lingerie shops, and at least eight dress boutiques. Five hotels, a florist, and several restaurants, bars, cafés and *confiseries* served an upscale clientele, while a British realtor catered to English-speaking foreigners."

54. See *Claude Monet, A. Rodin*, exh. cat. (Paris: Galerie Georges Petit, 1889), no. 38, *La Rue Montorgueil; Fête nationale du 30 Juin*, "appartient à Miele Bellio." One of Hassam's small watercolors is *14th July, Paris, Old Quarter*, (fig. 228). The location of the other, *July Fourteenth, Montmartre, Paris*, 1889, is unknown, as is that of his oil.

55. Scenes Hassam painted on this leg of the journey that are now in public collections include *Façade of an Old House at Lannion, France*, 1910 (Museum of Fine Arts, Boston); *Fête of Lannion*, 1910, watercolor (Saint Louis Art Museum); and *The Terre-Cuite Tea Set*, 1910 (Hunter Museum of American Art, Chattanooga).

56. Lockman interview, February 2, 1927, p. 28: "Went to Spain, came down through Spain and took a boat at Gibraltar and came home." Ellis Island's on-line reference site records Hassam's arrival on October 28, 1910, on the SS *Prinzess Irene* from Gibraltar. Childe Hassam, New York, November 10, 1910, to John W. Beatty, Carnegie Institute Papers, file 673: "I am just returned from Europe by way of Gibraltar."

57. Lockman interview, January 31, 1927, p. 8.

58. Ibid., February 2, 1927, p. 28.

59. *Catalogue of Paintings by Joaquín Sorolla y Bastida*, exh. cat. (New York: Hispanic Society of America, February 8–March 8, 1909). For the enthusiastic response to Sorolla's exhibition, see Priscilla E. Muller, "Sorolla and America," in Edmund Peel, *Joaquín Sorolla y Bastida*, exh. cat. (London: Philip Wilson Publishers, 1989), p. 55. Kenneth W. Maddox,

catalogue entry on *Street Scene, Ronda, Spain,* 1910 (formerly *Plaza de la Merced, Ronda*), in Tomás Llorens Serra, *Masterworks from the Carmen Thyssen-Bornemisza Collection: 60th Anniversary of the Opening of the Picture Gallery at the Villa Favorita,* exh. cat. (Geneva: Skira, 1997), p. 188, notes Sorolla's likely influence on Hassam, summarizes critics' comparisons between Hassam and Sorolla, and observes their tendency to deny that Sorolla influenced Hassam. "A Modern Master, Childe Hassam," *Newark Evening News,* February 4, 1911, clipping, Hassam Papers, reel NAA1, frames 558–59, remarks of the Spanish pictures Hassam showed at the Montross Gallery, New York, in February 1911: "What does Sorolla think of them? 'Tres bien!' he exclaimed as he stood before the Spanish pictures."

60. See M. Elizabeth Boone, "Vistas de España: American Views of Art and Life in Spain, 1860–1898" (Ph.D. diss., Graduate Center, City University of New York, 1996), and M. Elizabeth Boone, *España: American Artists and the Spanish Experience,* exh. cat. (New York: Hollis Taggart Galleries, 1998).
61. "Modern Master, Childe Hassam." See *Exhibition of Pictures by Childe Hassam,* exh. cat. (New York: Montross Gallery, February 1–14, 1911).
62. According to the Saint Louis Art Museum, this is likely the painting Hassam showed in the Montross Gallery, *Exhibition of Pictures by Childe Hassam,* no. 19, *Street of the Great Captain [*sic*], Cordova.*
63. Karl Baedeker, *Spain and Portugal: Handbook for Travellers,* 4th ed. (Leipzig: Karl Baedeker, 1913), p. 369, lists three hotels on the Paseo del Gran Capitán: Hotel de Oriente, Hotel Simon, and Hotel de España y Francia.
64. Ibid., p. 371; Ian Robertson, ed., *Spain, the Mainland,* 4th ed., The Blue Guides (London and Tonbridge: Ernest Benn; Chicago: Rand McNally and Company, 1980), p. 534.
65. Augustus J. C. Hare, *Wanderings in Spain* (London: George Allen, 1906), p. 95.
66. Baedeker, *Spain and Portugal,* pp. 25–26, lists a number of hotels in Seville. They were all on plazas, any one of which might be represented in Hassam's painting.
67. Nicolás Salas, the leading historian of Seville's urban morphology, has analyzed the painting in relation to the coexistence of hotels, lines of horse-drawn coaches, shops selling *coloniales,* and tree cover and has been unable to identify the plaza Hassam depicted. We are deeply grateful to him and to Ignacio Cano Rivero, Director, Museo de Bellas Artes, Seville, for their gracious assistance.
68. Baedeker, *Spain and Portugal,* p. 437, lists only one hotel near the church: the Hotel Royal, "near the Paseo de la Merced," noting that it is in "English hands" and is "good."
69. "Modern Master, Childe Hassam."
70. Lockman interview, February 2, 1927, p. 24. Maud Hassam remained in New York. See M. D. Hassam, New York, June 16, 1911, to A. H. Griffith, Detroit Museum of Art, Detroit Institute of Art Archives. Ellis Island's on-line reference site records Hassam's return on June 29, 1911, on the SS *Kronprinzessin Cecilie* from Cherbourg. Childe Hassam, Appledore, Isles of Shoals, N.H., July 10, 1911, to [J. Alden] Weir, Hassam Papers, reel NAA2, frame 66: "Here I am catching up on my swimming. I am very much behind-hand (none last year) and am attending strictly to it. . . . The cholera sidetracked me from Venice and in May and June Paris was hot."
71. Childe Hassam, New York, June 10, 1913, to C. E. S. Wood, Wood Papers (San Marino). Lockman interview, February 2, 1927, p. 21: "It was through my friend Henry Bacon, the Architect. He asked me how I would like to do a decoration."
72. Hamilton Wright, "Mural Decorations at the Panama-Pacific International Exposition," in *Art in California: A Survey of American Art with Special Reference to Californian Painting, Sculpture, and Architecture, Past and Present, Particularly As Those Arts Were Represented at the Panama-Pacific International Exposition* (San Francisco: R. L. Bernier, Publishers, 1916; reprint, Irvine, Calif.: Westphal Publishing, 1988), p. 136.
73. Lockman interview, February 2, 1927, p. 21: "I went out there to put up a lunette, an out-of-door decoration for one of the courts. I finished it out there." A plan of the Palace of Fine Arts appears in Bernard R. Maybeck, "Architecture of the Palace of Fine Arts at the Panama-Pacific International Exposition," in *Art in California,* p. 161. Fellow artists who made murals for the exposition include Edward E. Simmons, Robert Reid, and William de Leftwich Dodge from New York and Arthur Frank Mathews from California.
74. For additional information on the painting, see catalogue entry in Fort and Quick, *American Art,* pp. 208–9. For McComas, see *National Cyclopaedia of American Biography* 29 (1941), p. 473. Other California scenes by Hassam in public collections include: *Hill of the Sun, San Anselmo, California,* 1914 (Oakland Museum of California); *The Silver Veil and the Golden Gate,* 1914 (Brauer Museum of Art, Valparaiso University Center for the Arts, Valparaiso, Indiana); *California Hills in Spring,* 1914 (American Academy of Arts and Letters, New York); *Telegraph Hill,* 1914 (The White House, Washington, D.C.).
75. Kent L. Seavey, Director, Carmel Museum of Art, July 14, 1970, to Nancy Moure, Curatorial Aide, Los Angeles County Museum of Art, curatorial files, Los Angeles County Museum of Art.
76. Lockman interview, February 2, 1927, p. 21: "I did not see the Exhibition completed."
77. James McNeill Whistler (sixty-one works), Joseph Pennell (fifty), Howard Pyle (forty-two), Frank Duveneck (forty-two), William Merritt Chase (thirty-one), Gari Melchers (thirty), William Keith (twenty-eight), John H. Twachtman (twenty-five), Edward W. Redfield (twenty), Edmund C. Tarbell (nineteen), and John Singer Sargent (thirteen) also had one-artist displays. See *Official Catalogue of the Department of Fine Arts, Panama-Pacific International Exposition (with Awards), San Francisco, California, 1915* (San Francisco: The Wahlgreen Company, 1915), pp. 24–81; Eugene Neuhaus, *The Galleries of the Exposition: A Critical Review of the Paintings, Statuary and the Graphic Arts in the Palace of Fine Arts at the Panama-Pacific International Exposition* (San Francisco: P. Elder, 1915), pp. 68–69; and Christian Brinton, *Impressions of the Art at the Panama-Pacific International Exposition* (New York: John Lane Company, 1916), p. 92.
78. Lockman interview, February 2, 1927, p. 22.
79. Hassam's role in the development of California Impressionism is considered in John Caldwell, "California Impressionism: A Critical Essay," in *Impressionism, The California View,* exh. cat. (Oakland: Oakland Museum of Art, 1981), p. 14; Charles C. Eldredge, "American Impressionism Goes West," in *Crosscurrents in American Impressionism at the Turn of the Century,* edited by William U. Eiland (Athens: Georgia Museum of Art, University of Georgia, 1996), pp. 111–13; and Gerdts, "California Impressionism in Context," pp. 53–57. Hassam's work was shown in California before it was included in the Panama-Pacific International Exposition: in June 1914 eleven canvases were displayed, first at the Palace Hotel in San Francisco and then at an exhibition in Los Angeles. See Everett C. Maxwell, "Art," *Graphic,* June 20, 1914, p. 13, cited in Gerdts, "California Impressionism in Context," p. 57. See also *Panama-California Exposition,* exh. cat. (San Diego: Pictorial Publishing Co., January 1–December 31, 1915).

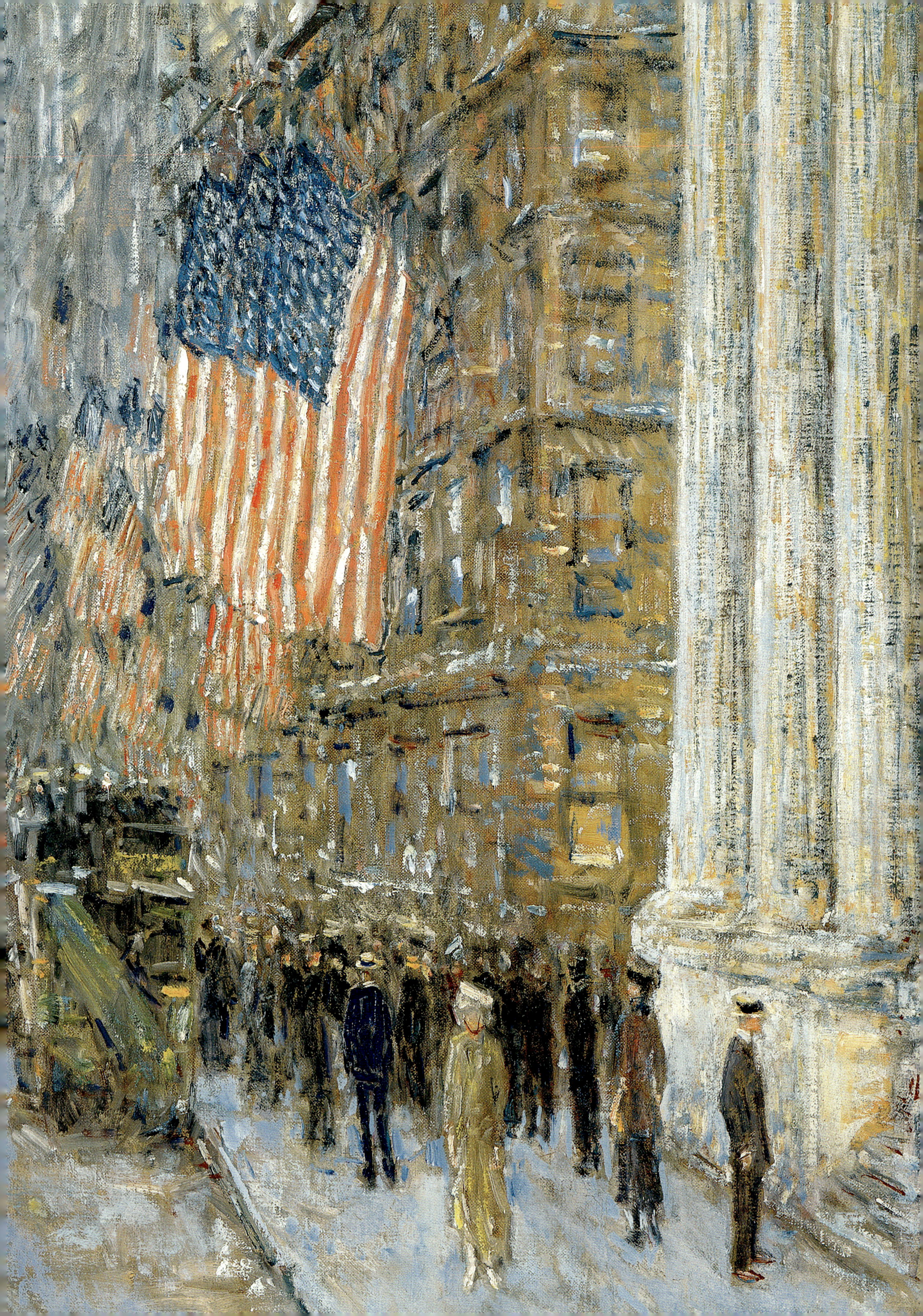

CHAPTER SIX

Hassam in New York, 1897–1919

H. Barbara Weinberg

In New York between 1889 and 1896 Hassam had specialized in painting anecdotal views of streets and parks in fashionable residential districts. The second phase of his work in the city began after he came home from his 1896–97 visit to Europe. On his return he was struck, perhaps more vividly than ever before, by New York's transformation into a distinctively modern metropolis, no longer merely a rival to Paris but now a unique urban center. The metamorphosis of New York's appearance, pace, and rhythm was rooted in innovations in steel-frame construction, which allowed the erection of skyscrapers; it was also the consequence of improvements in rail transportation—including the introduction of elevated lines—and the invention of the automobile. These changes captivated many artists and writers, among them John C. Van Dyke, whose 1909 book, *The New New York,* epitomized their sentiments. Van Dyke declared that New York was "more striking, more impressive, than any other city on the globe. It looms through the blue mist, not with any Oriental romance about it, but with a feeling of tremendous bulk and power."[1]

Responding to New York's new character, Hassam created a valuable iconography of the city during the complex first two decades of the twentieth century. He shifted his focus primarily to uptown commercial precincts and took notice of Manhattan's new skyscrapers aglow with electric light. He remained disengaged from urban realities, however, portraying looming towers only allusively and favoring anonymous examples over famous structures.[2] He avoided unpleasant imagery, often capturing evocative—almost romantic—weather conditions and times of day to veil ugliness. Hassam also sought out relatively remote sites such as the Battery, Wall Street, the Brooklyn Bridge, High Bridge in Washington Heights, and Brooklyn, from which he painted a few views of the Manhattan skyline.[3] Many of his post-1900 cityscapes seem to be studies of composition, color, and atmosphere rather than portraits of places; some verge on abstraction. This new emphasis on pictorial design may be a result of Hassam's association with the Ten American Painters (see fig. 20), which began in the autumn of 1897 and perhaps prompted him to reconsider his stylistic commitments.

Between 1909 and about 1922, seemingly threatened by burgeoning modernity, Hassam at times retreated from painting outdoor views to create a series portraying women isolated in their apartments. These works simultaneously encode the experience of living high up in modern buildings and romanticize that experience by showing other tall buildings only through curtained windows. And, from 1916 to 1919, as the sole major American Impressionist to depict the home front during World War I, Hassam produced the unprecedented Flag series, thirty or so canvases that represent Fifth Avenue as a vibrant skyscraper-lined stage decorated with patriotic banners.[4] In 1918 *New York Sun* critic Henry McBride could still crow that "Childe Hassam has been Fifth avenue's historian for years."[5]

Late Afternoon, New York: Winter (fig. 212) typifies Hassam's new approach to urban subjects. In this scene the poetic twilight hour and falling snow combine to soften harsh outlines, minimize details, obscure the upper portion of the skyscraper, and mute the sense of urban din. As Teresa A. Carbone has noted, the painting marks a rejection even of the "faint grittiness" of Hassam's earlier *Winter in Union Square* (fig. 89) and *Fifth Avenue in Winter* (fig. 87).[6] It also suggests

Detail, fig. 230. *Flags on the Waldorf, 1916*

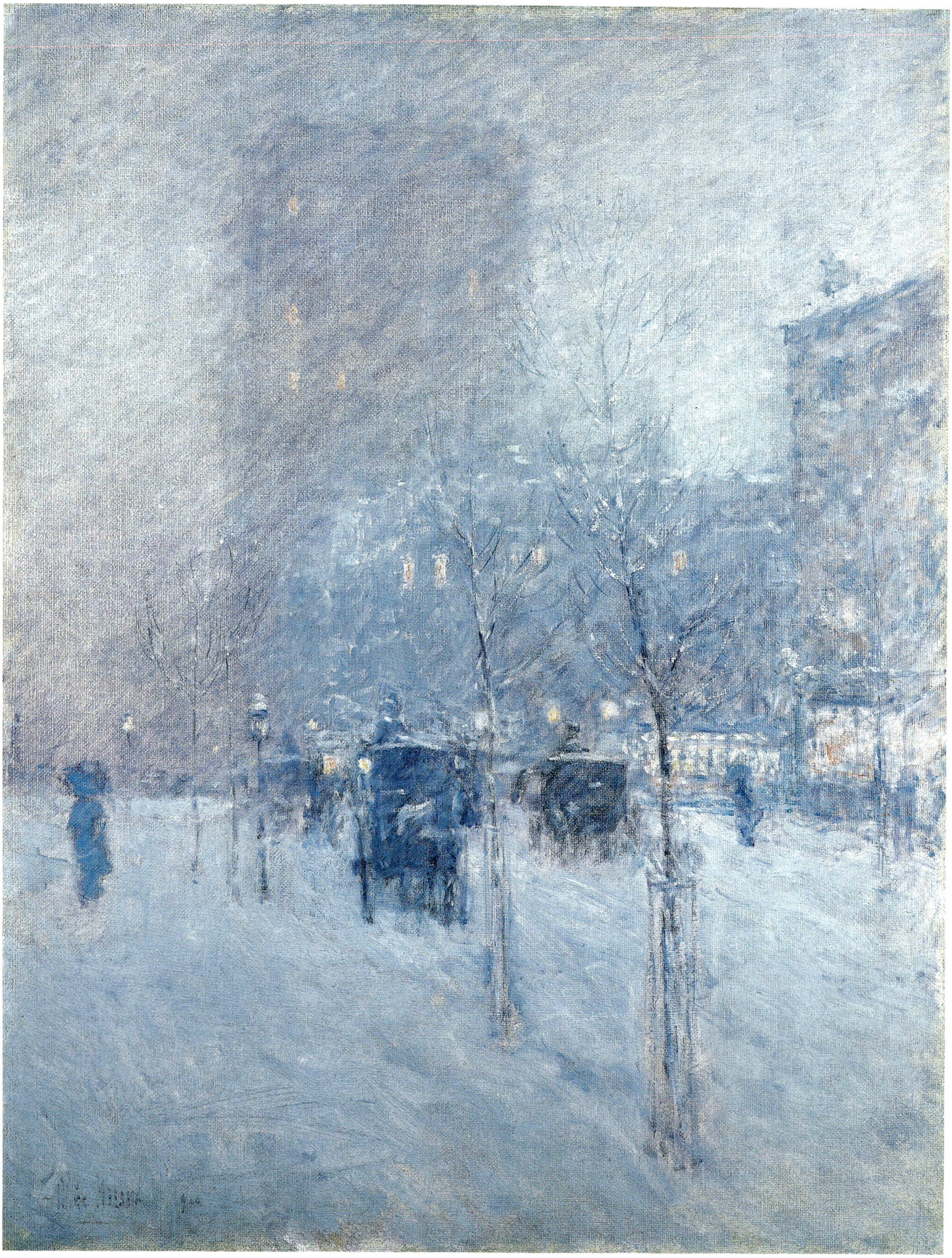

Fig. 212. Childe Hassam. *Late Afternoon, New York: Winter,* 1900. Oil on canvas, 37 x 29 in. (94 x 73.7 cm). Brooklyn Museum of Art, Dick S. Ramsay Fund 62.68

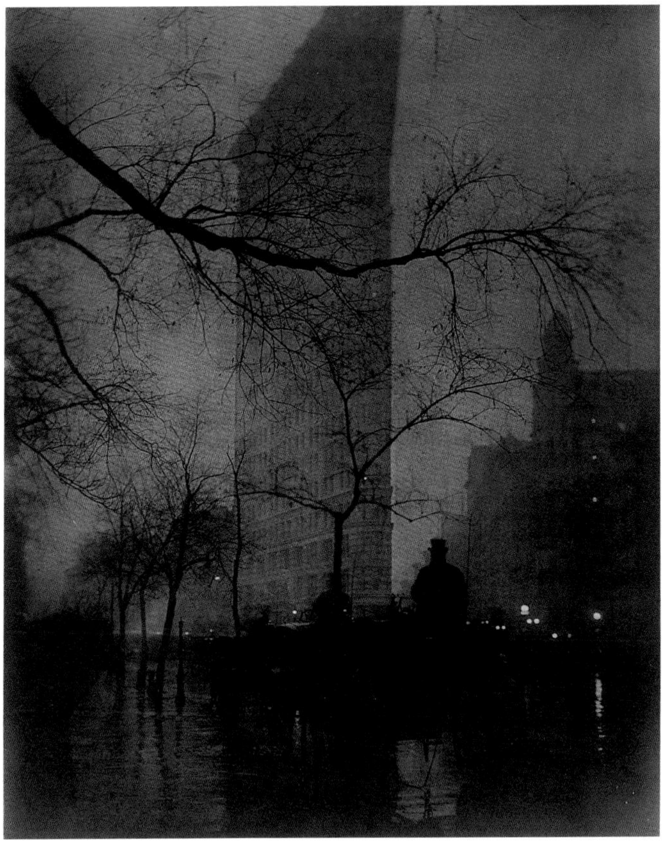

Fig. 213. Edward Steichen. *The Flatiron,* 1904. Gum bichromate over platinum print, 18 13/16 x 15 1/8 in. (47.8 x 38.4 cm). The Metropolitan Museum of Art, New York. Alfred Stieglitz Collection, 1933 33.43.39

his sympathy with contemporaneous Pictorialist cityscapes such as Edward Steichen's *Flatiron* (fig. 213).[7] Hassam's paintings and Steichen's photographs in turn echo the evanescent urban nocturnes that James McNeill Whistler painted beginning in the 1860s (see fig. 125). Indeed, the works of both artists recall Whistler's remarks on twilight's expressive potential in his 1890 "Ten O'Clock" lecture: "When the evening mist clothes the riverside with poetry, as with a veil, and the poor buildings lose themselves in the dim sky, and the tall chimneys become campanili, and the warehouses are palaces in the night, and the whole city hangs in the heavens, and fairy-land is before us . . . Nature, who, for once, has sung in tune, sings her exquisite song to the artist alone, her son and master."[8] Even though he favored Whistlerian urban poetry over prose in *Late Afternoon, New York: Winter,* Hassam articulated the dialogue between old and new New York in his canvas by juxtaposing horse-drawn cabs with the brightly lighted modern streetcar and contrasting gas lamps seen along the curb at the left with shop windows aglow with electric light.

In *Broadway and 42nd Street* (fig. 214) Hassam depicted Longacre Square, which became known as Times Square after the newspaper's headquarters opened there in 1904.[9] Here Hassam employed a dusky blue-black palette and glittering golden highlights to capture the allure of a winter evening in Manhattan's new commercial entertainment center. The opening, in 1883, on Broadway and Thirty-ninth Street of the new house for the Metropolitan Opera Company—which challenged and then supplanted the Academy of Music on East Fourteenth Street—had prompted the construction of several theaters in the district and announced the shift of the city's cultural center uptown from Union Square. By 1905 an observer could boast that Broadway's theaters "nightly suck in throngs of amusement seekers vaster than in any other of the world's thoroughfares."[10] Electric lights, installed in Longacre Square in 1895 and seen glowing in shop windows in Hassam's view, gave rise to the epithet the Great White Way. Trolley cars, introduced in 1891 and powered and illuminated by electricity, were called by one commentator "the greatest, . . . newest, menace to the wayfarer on Broadway."[11] As they pass lines of lantern-lit horse-drawn cabs, these trolley cars add another modern note to the scene. By 1911 Times Square was described as "the glowing, incandescent heart of the city."[12]

Hassam believed that skyscrapers of the sort that enframe the pedestrians in Longacre Square were "hideous" when seen individually. But "when silhouetted with a dozen or more other buildings against the sky," he claimed, they are "more beautiful than many of the old castles in Europe, especially if viewed in the early evening when just a few flickering lights are seen here and there and the city is a magical evocation of blended strength and mystery."[13] His intentional indifference to architectural details in *Broadway and 42nd Street* precludes identification of the particular street corner he portrayed.

Hassam eschewed the poetry of *Late Afternoon, New York: Winter* and the crepuscular glamour of *Broadway and 42nd Street* to create an unusual American cityscape, *The Hovel and the Skyscraper* (fig. 215). This picture he apparently painted from an east-facing window in his studio at 27 West Sixty-seventh Street, to which he had moved in late March 1903. Framing the view of Central Park are the backs of structures along Central Park West, of which the most distinctive is, at the left, the four-story granite and white marble Second Church of Christ, Scientist (Frederick R. Comstock, 1900), on the southwest corner of Sixty-eighth Street. These buildings

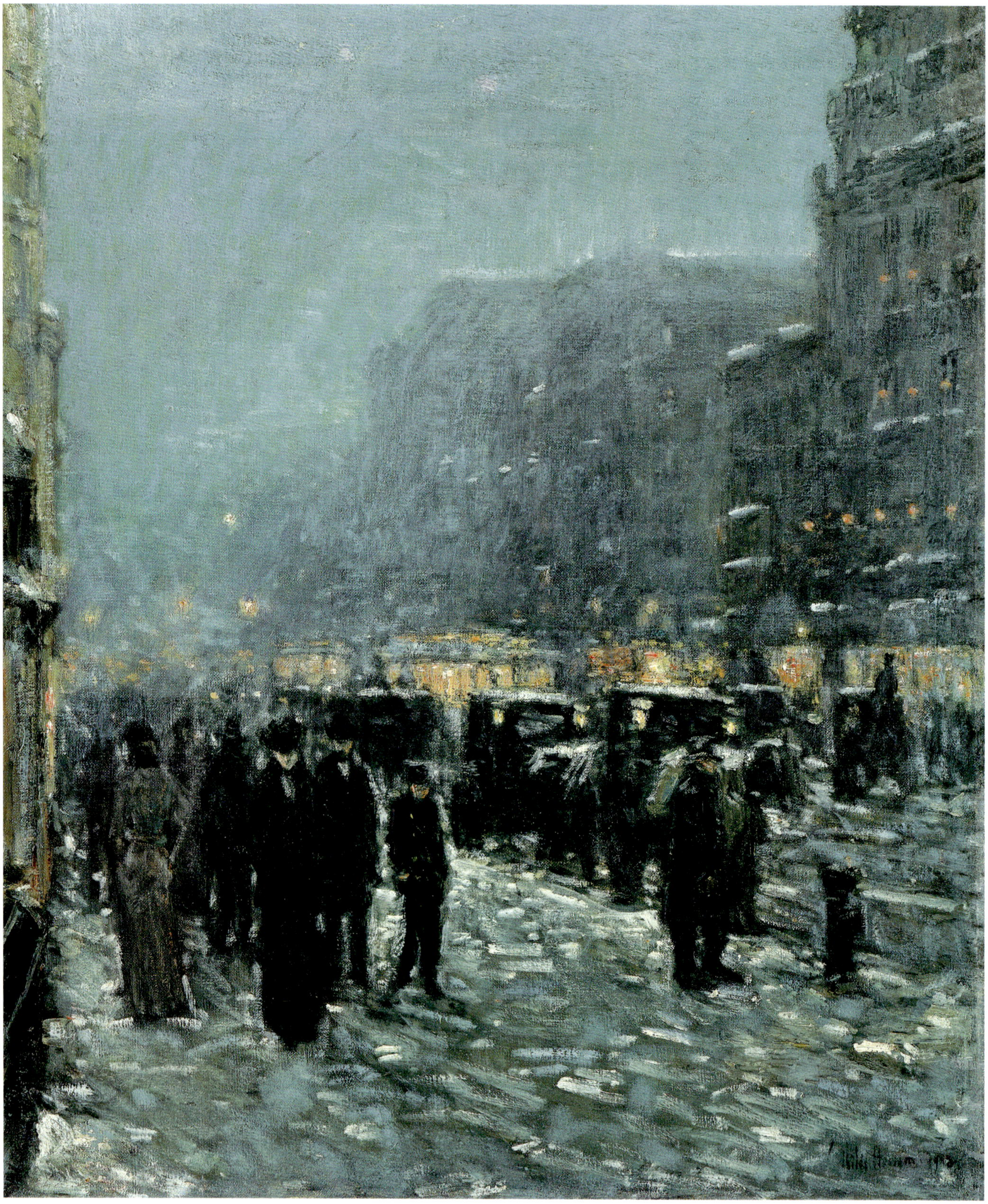

Fig. 214. Childe Hassam. *Broadway and 42nd Street,* 1902. Oil on canvas, 26 x 22 in. (66 x 55.9 cm). The Metropolitan Museum of Art, New York. Bequest of Miss Adelaide Milton de Groot (1876–1967), 1967 67.187.128

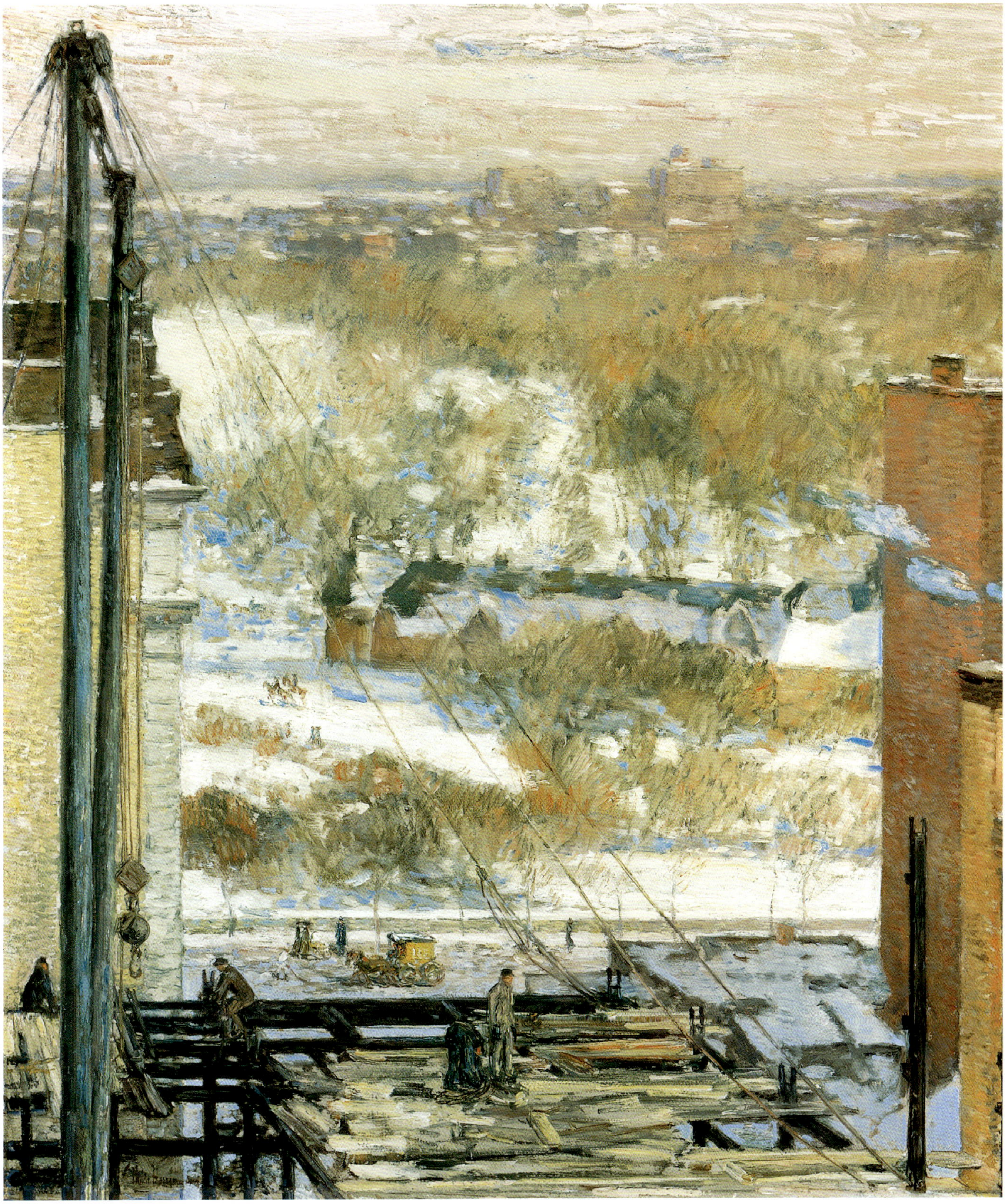

Fig. 215. Childe Hassam. *The Hovel and the Skyscraper,* 1904. Oil on canvas, 34¾ x 31 in. (88.3 x 78.7 cm). Courtesy of the Pennsylvania Academy of the Fine Arts, Philadelphia. The Vivian O. and Meyer P. Potamkin Collection. Bequest of Vivian O. Potamkin

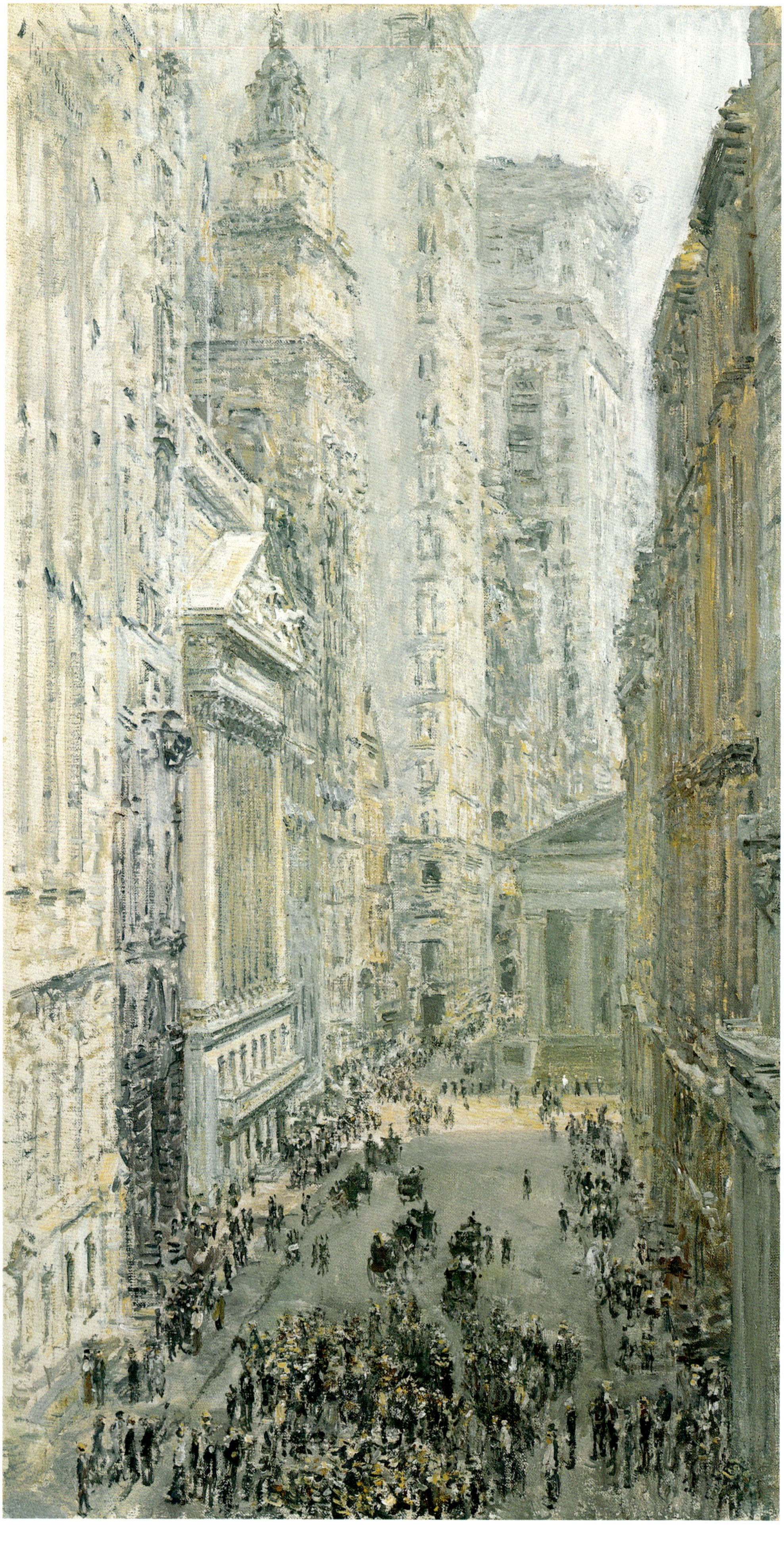

Fig. 216. Childe Hassam. *Lower Manhattan (View Down Broad Street)*, 1907. Oil on canvas, 30¼ x 16⅛ in. (76.8 x 41 cm). Herbert F. Johnson Museum of Art, Cornell University, Ithaca, New York. Gift of Leonard K. Elmhirst, Class of 1921, Cornell University

bracket the Sheepfold (Jacob Wrey Mould, 1870), built in the rural Victorian Gothic style, which accords with the romantic English quality that park designers Frederick Law Olmsted and Calvert Vaux intended. Erected just inside the entrance to the park, this picturesque barn housed the two hundred Southdown sheep that grazed in the adjacent Sheep Meadow. (The Sheepfold was converted by legendary parks commissioner Robert Moses to the Tavern on the Green restaurant, which opened in 1934.)

The "hovel" in the painting's title may refer to the Sheepfold; to a small wood-frame structure on Central Park West that would soon be overwhelmed by the adjacent steel-frame "skyscraper"—likely the new church parish house under construction in Hassam's view; or to the wood-frame structure that the parish house would replace.[14] The men on the foreground scaffolding are the urban counterparts of the workers Hassam had recorded on the piers of Gloucester. *The Hovel and the Skyscraper* distills a pointed urban story from the epochal changes Hassam witnessed in New York at the beginning of the twentieth century. In a city in transition, modern structures such as those along Central Park West will supplant smaller buildings and, in this view at least, obliterate the old-fashioned Sheepfold; such skyscrapers, towering over the park's verdant boundaries, will compromise the rural fantasy that Olmsted and Vaux had concocted; and the canopy of man-made steam and industrial pollution will spoil the pristine cleanliness of nature's fresh white snow.

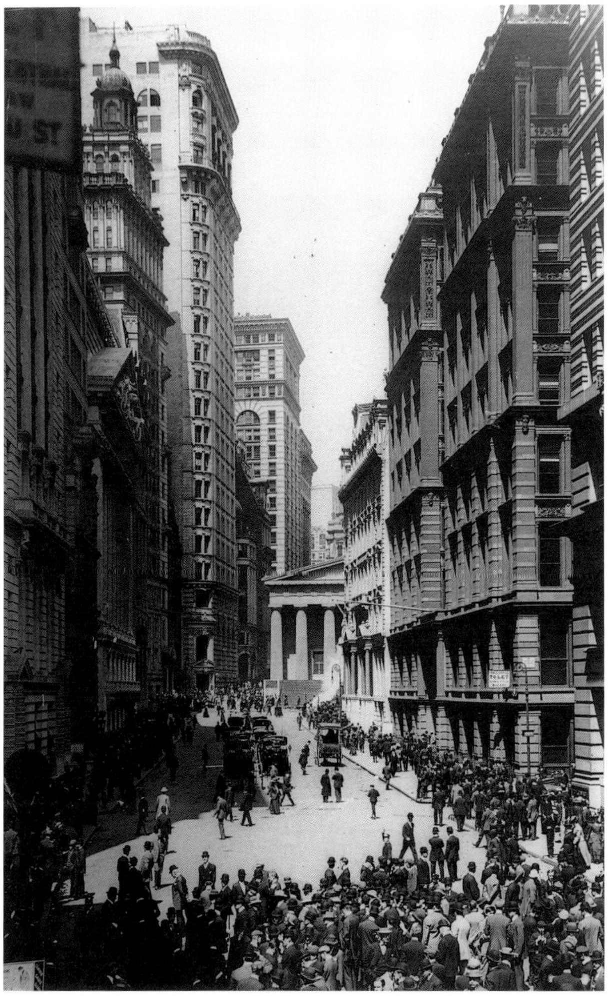

Fig. 217. View looking up Broad Street to Wall Street, 1900–1910. Collections of the Library of Congress, Washington, D.C.

Hassam conveyed New York's energy with a different visual vocabulary in *Lower Manhattan (View Down Broad Street)* (fig. 216), which portrays Broad Street looking north toward its intersection with Wall Street.[15] Seen on the west side of Broad Street in the heart of the financial district is the Neoclassical New York Stock Exchange (1903), designed by George B. Post with an immense Corinthian-style colonnade and a pediment sculpture by John Quincy Adams Ward. The Stock Exchange is bracketed by and faces tall banks and other commercial buildings.[16] On Wall Street is the Doric-style United States Sub-Treasury (now Federal Hall National Memorial), designed by Ithiel Town and Alexander J. Davis and erected in 1842 on the site of the old Federal Hall, where the first United States Congress met and George Washington was inaugurated as president. Filling the background are more skyscrapers, those lining Nassau Street, the continuation of Broad Street north of Wall.

Hassam's narrow vertical canvas—twice as high as it is wide—is a perfect format for this urban "landscape," whose compression and upward thrust contrast so markedly with his open, sprawling pastoral panoramas. The confined scene, elevated vantage point, and cropped cornices of the buildings on the west side of Broad Street emphasize the compacted quality of the financial district's shaded canyons and suggest an urban environment quite different from the parks and residential streets Hassam had painted during his first period in New York. His feathery brushstrokes in muted grays and dull reds describe the diverse buildings that set off the frenzied knot of the Curb Exchange—traders who had no places on the Stock Exchange. A reviewer commented in 1908: "The painter has given an impression of the asphaltic Eldorado. A slight mist obscures the features of the amateur golden fleece hunters. We cannot recognize any of the magnates of our acquaintance, but we do feel the soul of the quarter."[17] Hassam's skill in capturing "the soul of the quarter," with its teeming crowds of anonymous pedestrians, would inform the Flag series, which he began to paint nine years later.

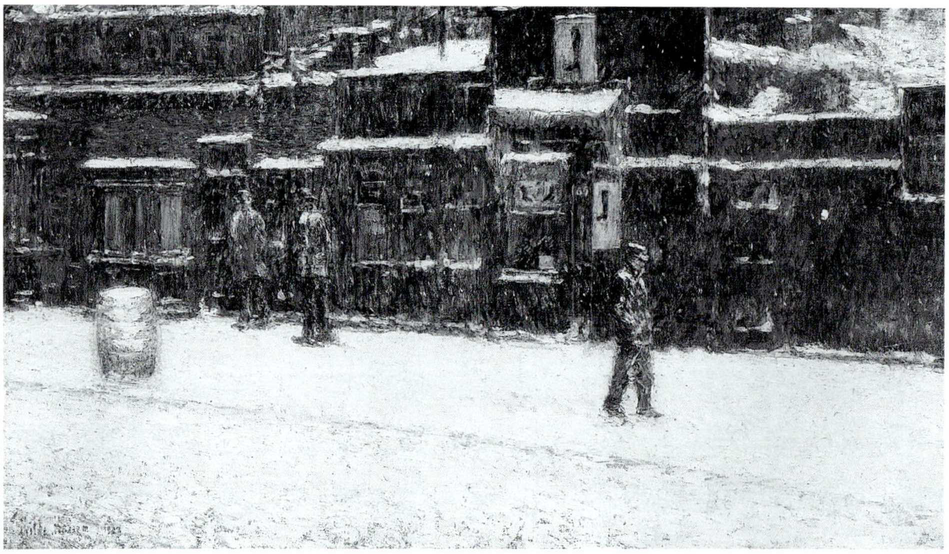

Fig. 218. Childe Hassam. *Messenger Boy,* 1902. Oil on canvas, 18½ x 32⅜ in. (47 x 82.2 cm). Museum of Art, Rhode Island School of Design, Providence; Jesse Metcalf Fund

In its composition *Lower Manhattan* is almost identical to a photograph of the site (fig. 217). Hassam may well have worked from this photograph, which would have helped him to delineate precisely the scene's architectural details. However, he had earlier strenuously claimed that he never relied on photographs, telling an interviewer in 1892: "I have been asked if I did not think photographic views were great helps to the artist in this branch of study. Undoubtedly they might be, but they have not been so to me. I never owned a camera or pressed the button of a Kodak in my life. . . . I think on the whole, I prefer to make my own studies right from the life, without any assistance from the camera."[18] It was perhaps to disguise the origin of his picture in the mechanical accuracy of a photograph that he created a tapestry-like surface for his canvas.

The vertical compression, deep vista, sense of urban energy, and nationally significant subject of *Lower Manhattan* have no place in Hassam's *Messenger Boy* (fig. 218) and *Little*

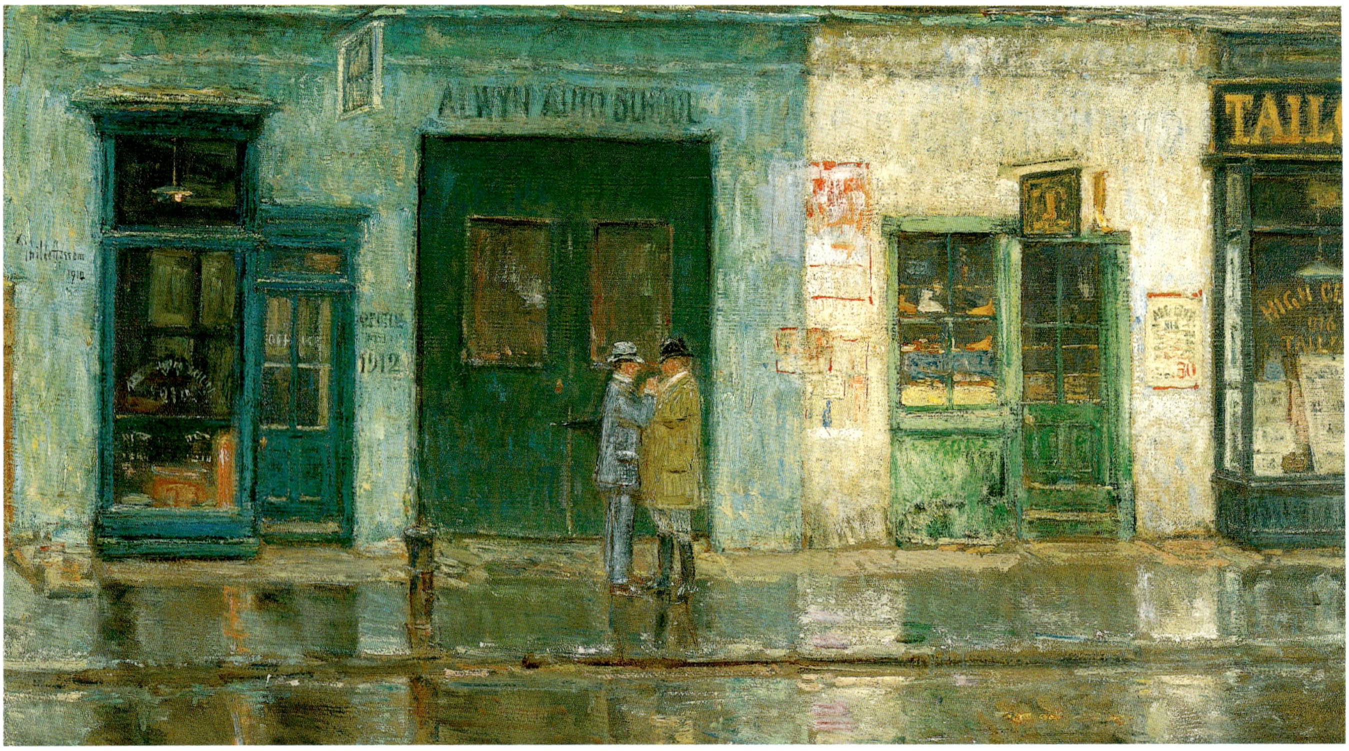

Fig. 219. Childe Hassam. *Little Cobbler's Shop,* 1912. Oil on canvas, 16½ x 30⅜ in. (41.9 x 77.2 cm). Addison Gallery of American Art, Andover, Massachusetts, gift of anonymous donor, by exchange

Cobbler's Shop (fig. 219). These two friezelike canvases provide intimate frontal views of ordinary streets lined with small shops and demonstrate a new, meditative approach to the modern urban scene. Both reiterate the geometric shop-front patterns of *La Bouquetière et la Laitière* (fig. 68), and both were inspired by Whistler's London streetscapes (see fig. 220), which Hassam admired in Charles Lang Freer's collection.[19]

Ulrich W. Hiesinger has reasonably suggested that Hassam's sale of *Fifth Avenue in Winter* (fig. 87) to the Carnegie Institute in 1900 and, perhaps, his nostalgia for his old neighborhood prompted him to quote the messenger from that painting's lower left foreground in *Messenger Boy* and in several other works in which "the former sense of dash and vitality is replaced by a slow, even mournful tempo."[20] That Hassam reconsidered and quoted from his own work reflects his willingness to emulate academic methods rather than insist upon unique, instantaneous impressions. He defended such an approach in a 1903 essay: "The definition so often given of the work of modern painters in landscape—which is that they take a *motif* anywhere, as if looking out of an open window, and paint it just as they see it—is partly erroneous, only a half truth. These painters do try to give you frankly the aspect of the thing seen in its fundamental and essential truths; but that they do not place things as they feel they should be placed to get the balance and beauty of the whole, well seen within the frame, is a mistaken idea."[21]

While *Little Cobbler's Shop* strikes a modern note by featuring at its center the Alwyn Auto School, located at 912 Seventh Avenue at about Fifty-eighth Street (around the corner from Hassam's studio), the intimacy of the view implies that the city can still feel like a small harmonious village.[22] The melancholy tone in both *Messenger Boy* and *Little Cobbler's Shop* expresses Hassam's waning appreciation of New York's dynamism. He wrote to Florence Griswold in December 1906: "I don't know that I wish a very large dose of New York for any of my friends."[23]

In his New York Window series (see figs. 226, 227) Hassam turned away from the city's lively boulevards to portray its hushed domestic interiors. The paintings, like most of Hassam's twentieth-century urban scenes, are far removed in their genteel spirit from the contemporaneous images of the Ash Can School. Although Hassam had depicted women against open windows as early as 1886, when he painted *Summer Evening* (fig. 115), he made a specialty of the theme in an urban context after he settled in his impressive studio residence at 130 West Fifty-seventh Street, just a few steps west of Sixth Avenue, in January 1909.[24] Hassam's recent financial success and long-standing preference for the most comfortable quarters available had prompted his move to this new cooperative building. As Hiesinger has explained: "The apartment was a large duplex on the top floor running the entire width of the building. Inside, a large two-story studio with a skylight and floor-to-ceiling windows faced north onto Fifty-seventh Street and offered what was then an open view of Central Park. A narrow iron balcony looked out onto the street below."[25]

Hassam created a sense of sanctuary in the Window series by anchoring his compositions in rectilinear grids composed of

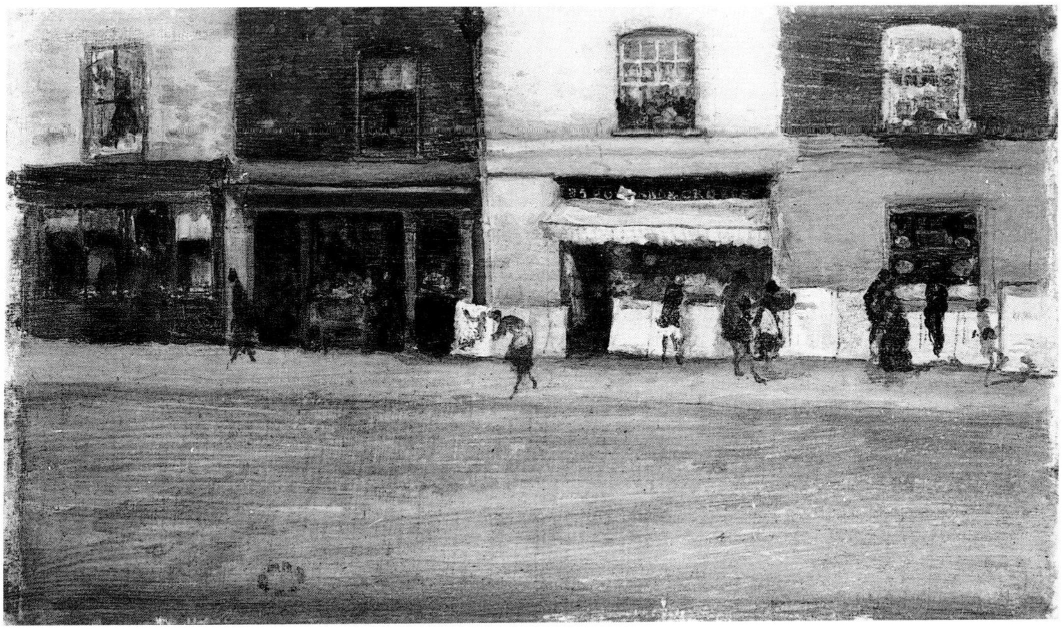

Fig. 220. James McNeill Whistler. *Chelsea Shops,* early 1880s. Oil on wood, 5¼ x 9¼ in. (13.3 x 23.5 cm). Freer Gallery of Art, Smithsonian Institution, Washington, D.C.: Gift of Charles Lang Freer F1902.149

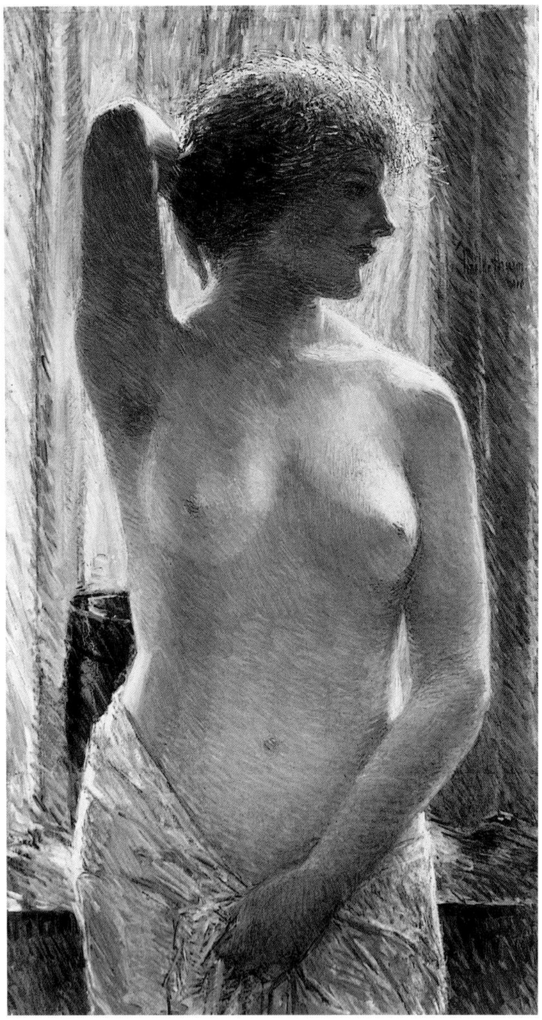

Fig. 221. Childe Hassam. *Against the Light,* 1916. Oil on canvas, 39 x 22 in. (99.1 x 55.9 cm). American Academy of Arts and Letters, New York

Fig. 222. James McNeill Whistler. *Caprice in Purple and Gold, No. 2: The Golden Screen,* 1864. Oil on wood panel, 19¾ x 27 in. (50.2 x 68.6 cm). Freer Gallery of Art, Smithsonian Institution, Washington, D.C.: Gift of Charles Lang Freer F1904.75

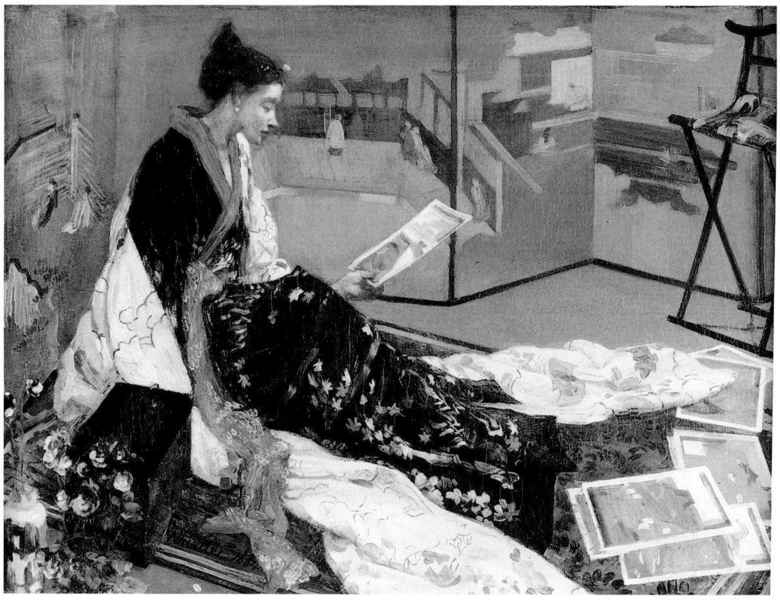

the walls, sunlit curtained mullioned windows, and luxurious furnishings of the intimate south-facing dining room or breakfast room at the back of his apartment. Painted contre-jour against these grids appear solitary women, often dressed in freely flowing garments made of Asian textiles and engrossed in reverie, reading, or examining objets d'art or flowers. Sometimes, as Hiesinger has observed, these works seem to be self-conscious efforts to combine outdoor and indoor views, figure painting and still life. *The Breakfast Room* (fig. 333), with its brilliantly lit, expansive cityscape beyond the window and several still-life elements, is an obvious example.[26]

In the Window series Hassam's emphasis on solitude and his tendency to generalize female forms and faces—in the manner of Archaic and Early Classical Greek sculpture—amplify the spirit of remoteness from the anxiety, and the exhilaration, of the modern era that informs much of his work. The classicizing figures in some of the Window canvases signal Hassam's apparent desire to affiliate himself with traditional artistic values after 1900, a desire also manifest in his increasingly numerous images of classical-style buildings and his paintings of nudes in idyllic settings or mythological guises. Homages to classical values are fundamental to many of his works of the period: examples are *Tanagra (The Builders, New York)* (fig. 311), depicting a stylized woman who holds a Tanagra figurine; *The Church at Gloucester* (fig. 184), celebrating classical-style New England architecture; and *Against the Light* (fig. 221), with its simplified, sculptural nude.[27] Classicism likewise infuses his 1914 self-portrait (fig. 356), in which the stretcher bars of a canvas form a grid like those of the mullions in the backdrops of the Window series and Hassam's erect posture seems to respond more to a will to pure geometric form than to natural appearance.[28]

Hassam's portrayals of contemplative women associated with precious objects in the Window series invoke timeless values and, perhaps, his long-standing taste for the art of Pierre Puvis de Chavannes (see fig. 53). They also recall paintings by Whistler such as *Caprice in Purple and Gold, No. 2:*

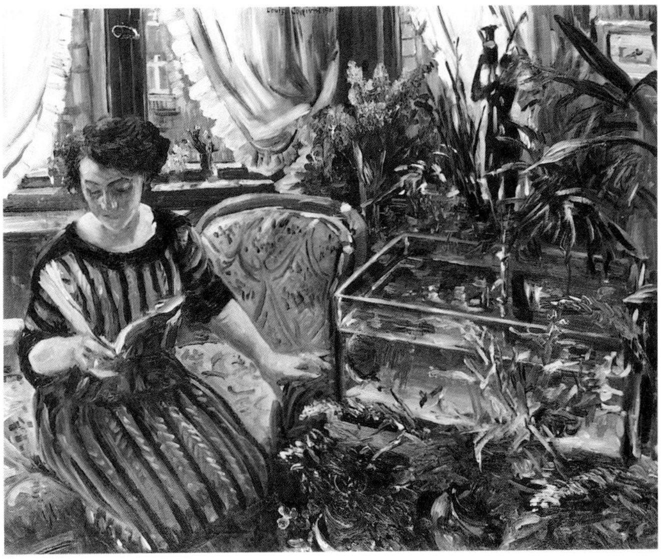

Fig. 223. Lovis Corinth. *Woman with Goldfish Bowl,* 1911. Oil on canvas, 29⅛ x 35⅝ in. (74 x 90.5 cm). Österreichische Galerie Belvedere, Vienna

The Golden Screen (fig. 222) and *Purple and Rose: The Lange Leizen of the Six Marks,* 1864 (Philadelphia Museum of Art, John G. Johnson Collection). They reveal as well the decorative approach to figural imagery of the Aesthetic Movement, in which Whistler participated. Hassam's use of Asian textiles in many Window paintings, among them *The Table Garden* (fig. 226), and Japanese screens in others, such as *Spring Morning* (fig. 10), specifically echoes Whistler's practices. Whether influenced by Greek antiquity, Puvis, Whistler, the Aesthetic Movement, or a combination of these sources, Hassam's Window series suggests that after 1900 he questioned the virtue of recording instantaneous impressions. In this respect Hassam was pursuing the kind of stylistic self-reform undertaken by other painters—including Pierre-Auguste Renoir, whom he admired—who had worked as Impressionists but explored traditional artistic values later in their careers.

About 1900, images of women isolated in quiet interiors from the turbulent city and engaged in genteel activity—or inactivity—preoccupied many artists in Europe and America. Intimate, peopled interiors painted by Pierre Bonnard, Édouard Vuillard, Henri Le Sidaner, and other French artists were often on display in New York and Paris. German painter Lovis Corinth studied the theme in canvases such as *Woman with Goldfish Bowl* (fig. 223). Boston's William MacGregor Paxton and other academic artists executed such scenes, and Bostonians Edmund C. Tarbell, Frank W. Benson, and Joseph R. DeCamp and New York–based Robert Reid, all members of Ten American Painters, also explored the subject and probably influenced Hassam.[29] Tarbell's *Josephine and Mercie* (fig. 224), Benson's *Rainy Day* (fig. 225), and DeCamp's *The Red Kimono,* ca. 1919 (Cummer Museum of Art and Gardens, Jacksonville, Florida) are typical of the genre. So, too, are Hassam's Window paintings, which are, however, distinguished from his contemporaries' works by their focus on life in modern apartment buildings. The privileged women who appear in all these paintings have literary

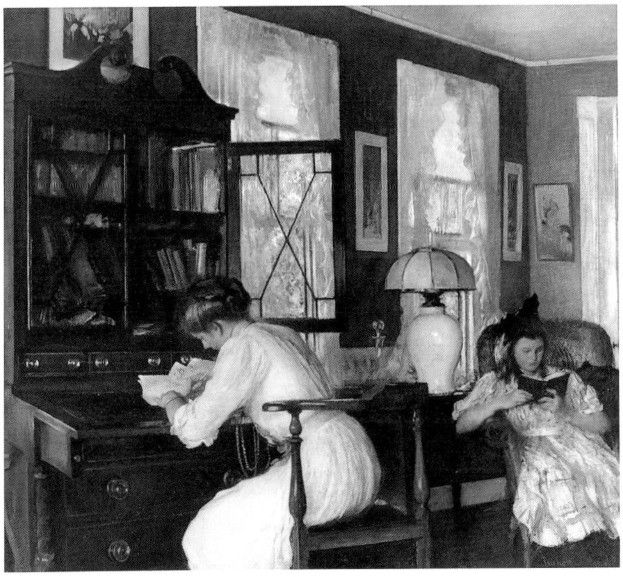

Fig. 224. Edmund C. Tarbell. *Josephine and Mercie,* 1907. Oil on canvas, 28¼ x 32¼ in. (71.8 x 81.9 cm). The Corcoran Gallery of Art, Washington, D.C., Museum Purchase, Gallery Fund 09.2

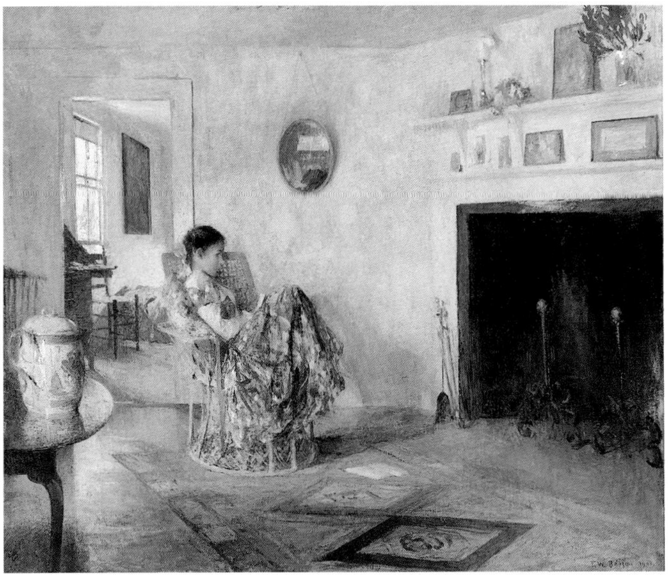

Fig. 225. Frank W. Benson. *Rainy Day,* 1906. Oil on canvas, 25 x 30 in. (63.5 x 76.2 cm). The Art Institute of Chicago, Friends of American Art Collection 1910.314

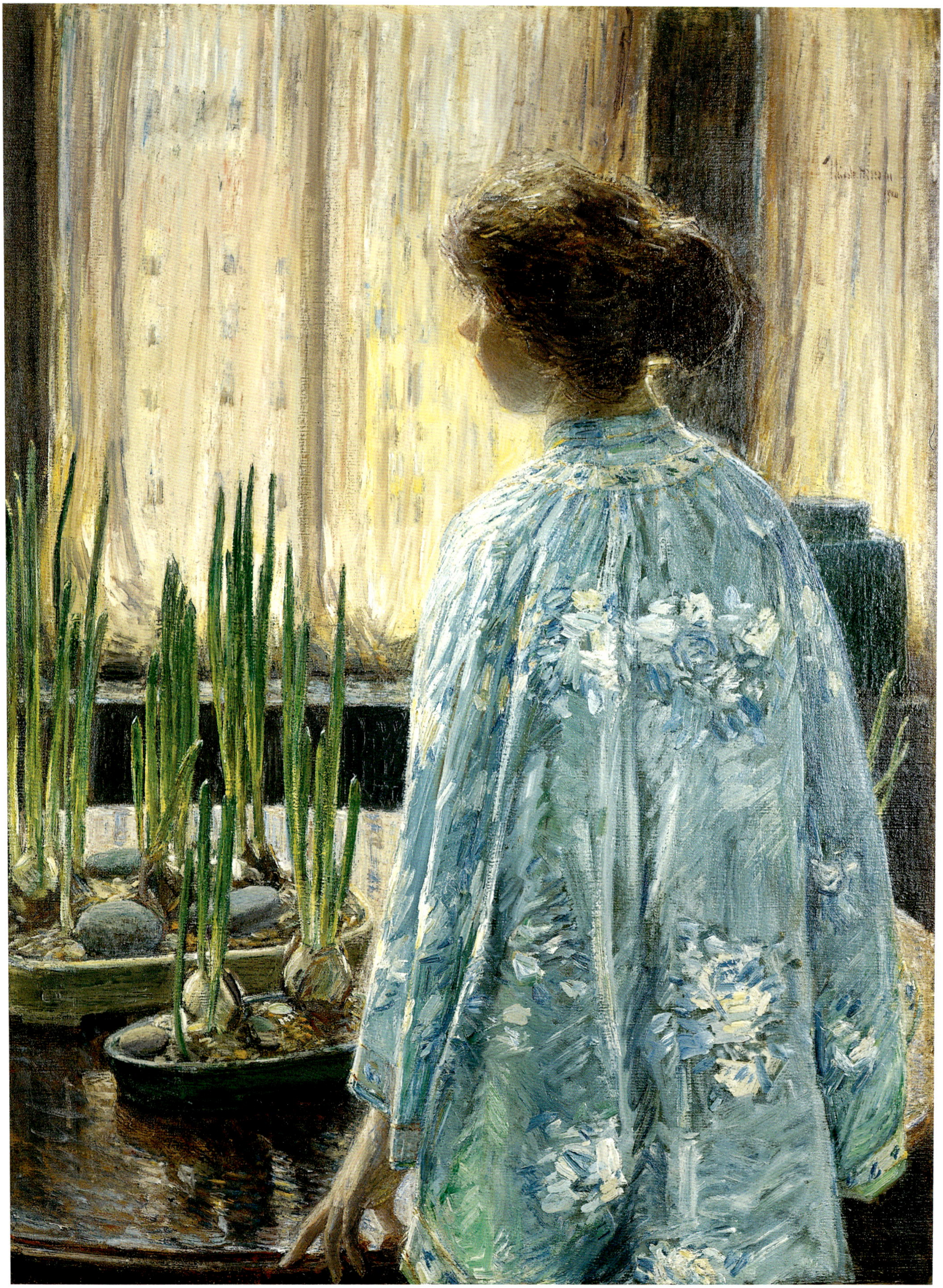

Fig. 226. Childe Hassam. *The Table Garden*, 1910. Oil on canvas, 39½ x 29¾ in. (100.3 x 75.6 cm). From the Collection of the Mitchell Museum at Cedarhurst, Mt. Vernon, Illinois. Gift of the John R. and Eleanor R. Mitchell Foundation

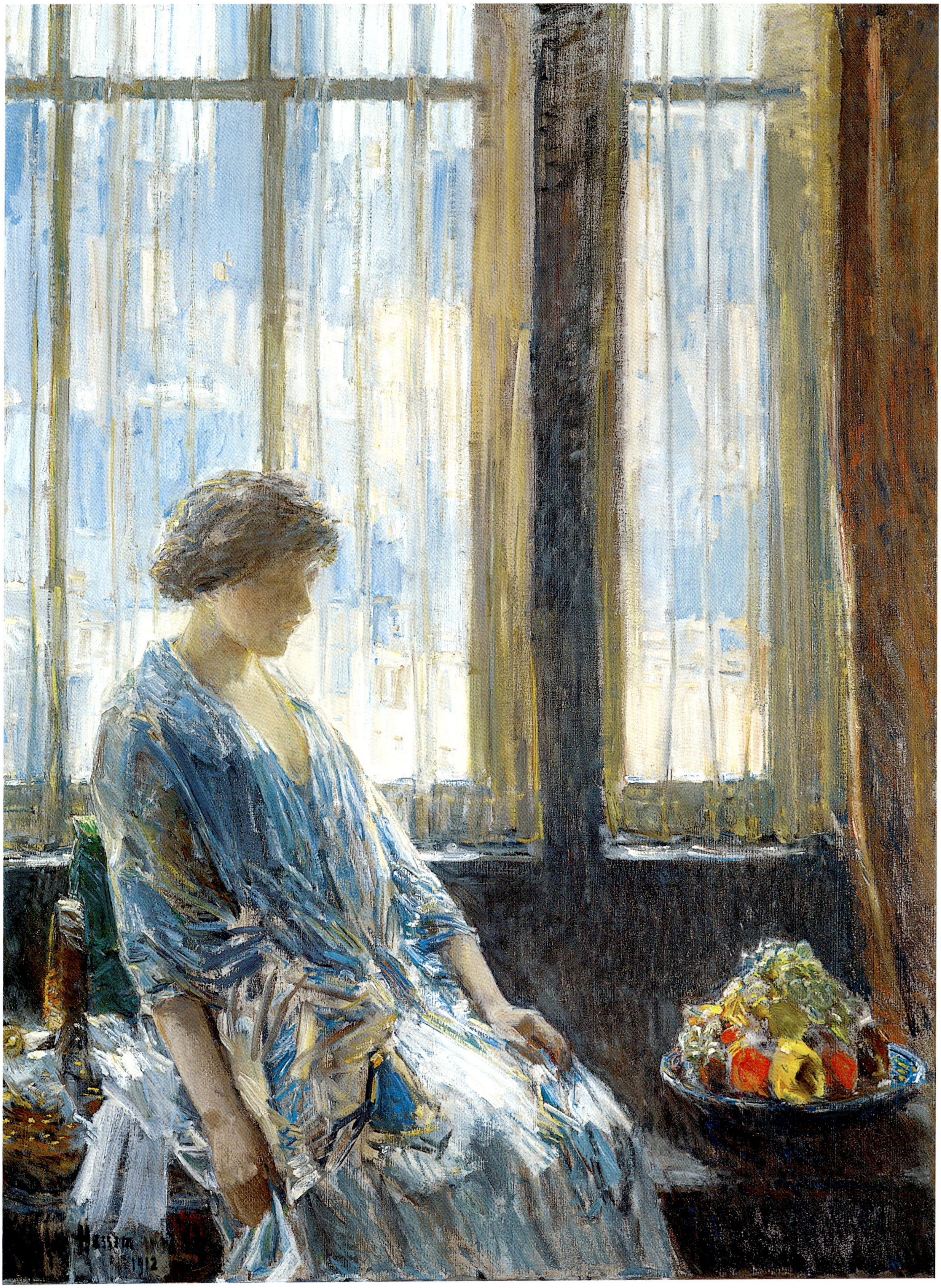

Fig. 227. Childe Hassam. *The New York Window,* 1912. Oil on canvas, 46⅛ x 35¼ in. (117.2 x 89.5 cm). The Corcoran Gallery of Art, Washington, D.C., Museum Purchase, Gallery Fund 12.10

counterparts in contemporary fiction by Henry James, Edith Wharton, and others, and reflect the notion, articulated in Thorstein Veblen's *Theory of the Leisure Class* (1899), that a woman at leisure announced her husband's or father's wealth and status.[30]

A young woman seen from behind, wearing a loose-fitting blue-and-white flower-patterned tea gown, perhaps made of kimono fabric, dominates Hassam's *Table Garden* (fig. 226).[31] The tea gown, which would have been acceptable attire for a proper woman only while she was entertaining in her own home, underscores the intimacy of the scene. The woman stands at a round table that holds two shallow dishes of paperwhite narcissus bulbs that are forced into bloom in winter; the green sprig to the right of the figure suggests another dish of bulbs. Painted on a large canvas, which is typical of the Window series, *The Table Garden* contrasts stark man-made buildings seen through the windows with natural elements that are abstracted in the robe's pattern and controlled in the table garden. *The Table Garden* thus revives the dialogue between artificial and natural that Hassam had explored in his garden paintings at Villiers-le-Bel in the late 1880s.[32] Describing similar motifs in *Tanagra (The Builders, New York),* Hassam remarked that "the background of New York building—one in the process of construction and the Chinese lilys [*sic*] [paperwhite narcissus] springing up from the bulbs is intended to typefy [*sic*] and symbolize groth [*sic*]—the groth [*sic*] of a great city hence the subtitle The Builders, New York."[33]

The enervated woman seated in a chair placed before the breakfast-room window seat in Hassam's *New York Window* (fig. 227) turns her back on modern life, symbolized by tall buildings seen through the curtained windows. Dressed in a flowing at-home garment of Asian fabric, she is as much a decorative still-life object as the large bowl of fruit that appears to the right. The conception here, like that of others in the series, allowed Hassam to remain committed to modern life as a subject while drawing a veil—pointedly embodied in curtains—over its vulgar actualities. Painter-critic Guy Pène du Bois applauded the painting's spirit, noting that it depicted "a woman whose beauty is doubled by a glorifying sheen of atmosphere. Behind her through faintly indicated curtains may be seen houses of the city that have become similar to the castles of the romanticist's fairyland without the bane of his mysticism and untruth."[34] An unidentified critic wrote: "Twilight has fallen, or it is afternoon of a gray day; through the window shadowy forms of great buildings loom as ghosts against the sky. It is the hour of rest, of meditation, and every line of the figure seated by the window conveys this suggestion."[35] The reception of other Window pictures was similarly positive; typical was the popularity and commercial success of *The New York Window,* exhibited in the winter of 1912–13 in Washington, D.C., at the Corcoran Gallery of Art, which awarded it the First William A. Clark prize of $2,000 and the Corcoran Gold Medal and purchased it.[36]

Hassam's disenchantment with New York as an artistic stimulus vanished in 1915–16, when he began to find in the city's streets, parks, and monuments fruitful subjects for etchings, drypoints, lithographs, and lithotints. His more than four hundred prints inspired by New York, as well as by New England and East Hampton, would preoccupy him from this time until the end of his life and would constitute one of his most important contributions to American art.

In 1916 Hassam embarked upon what proved to be among his most successful and appealing groups of paintings, the Flag series, which took as its theme the nationalistic displays of flags, banners, and bunting on the tall buildings that lined Fifth Avenue and nearby side streets in response to World War I.[37] Hassam's images of flag-bedecked New York were motivated by both patriotic and artistic imperatives. He told DeWitt McClellan Lockman, "I painted the flag series after we went into the war. There was that Preparedness Day, and I looked up the Avenue and saw these wonderful flags waving, and I painted the series of flag pictures after that."[38] Most of the series was made following the entry of the United States into the war, on April 6, 1917. The canvases reflect the spirit of a nation that was answering President Woodrow Wilson's appeal for self-sacrifice in what he deemed "a moment more critical perhaps than the history of the world has ever yet known"; singing the national anthems of the Allies at the close of church services; and participating in national patriotic song celebrations.[39]

Ilene Susan Fort has proposed that the Flag paintings' key motifs symbolize American pride and nationalistic resolve. Fifth Avenue was America's "most famous thoroughfare [and] it came to represent the nation's effort on the home front," she noted, observing also that "the skyscraper was the prime symbol of America's modernity, so by juxtaposing the image of the national banner and the dramatic sky line created by these tall buildings Hassam reinforced the patriotic motif of the flag with an example of the engineering expertise and ingenuity of Americans—the kind of technical facility that would win the war."[40] Hassam's own patriotism was manifest not only in his art but also in many other activities and in remarks, which Hiesinger has described: "Hassam had actively participated in the war effort from the beginning of the war in Europe in 1915, volunteering his services to various committees, contributing pictures to sales for war relief, and agreeing in one case to accept payment for his pictures in Liberty Bonds. His emotional commitment to the war was intense, as is shown by several angry statements he made condemning the Germans."[41]

Yet growing war sentiment—both America's and his own—motivated Hassam's Flag series only in part. The works also emerged from his longstanding commitment to portraying the urban scene, reflected the steady migration uptown of his New York subjects and residences, and responded to the sheer visual richness of the city's war-related ceremonies and festivities. Skyscrapers decorated with dynamic, chromatically diverse flags rekindled his Impressionist's impulse to experiment with vigorous brushwork and lively color. Hassam was familiar with similar French Impressionist scenes, including Manet's *Rue Mosnier with Flags* (fig. 55) and Monet's *Rue Montorgeuil, Paris, during the Celebrations of June 30, 1878* (fig. 206). As early as his student days in Paris he had responded to them with works such as *14th July, Paris, Old Quarter* (fig. 228), in which he offered a stenographic record of Parisian buildings displaying the tricolor for Bastille Day. And he had quoted their flag-decorated buildings and streets in *Church of the Paulist Fathers,* probably 1907 (private collection)[42] and echoed their vitality in *July Fourteenth, Rue Daunou, 1910* (fig. 205). The engaging compositional variations in Hassam's Flag canvases and the fact that he inscribed some of them with a date and time of day imply his awareness of Monet's series paintings. One critic applauded: "Mr. Hassam has done for the flag what Monet did for the haystack—shown it under all conceivable conditions of atmosphere and made beautiful by the caress of light."[43]

While Hassam used low perspectives in a few Flag canvases, he most often captured views from high up; he also usually rendered tall buildings as flat backdrops, and he suggested crowds with rapid notations. The visual results are quite different from the street-level or cab-level views in the majority of his earlier cityscapes. Yet, despite their unprecedented celebratory spirit and renewed Impressionist vivacity, the Flag paintings return to the candid aspects of Hassam's earlier New York genre scenes, showing ordinary pedestrians along Fifth Avenue and adjacent streets, rather than parades or other notable events.

Critics appreciated the dual appeal of war sentiment and visual richness that Hassam took from the actual flag displays and expressed in his paintings. For example, one reviewer remarked of a canvas shown at the Macbeth Gallery, New York, in June 1918:

> *There is something in the conjunction of flags and city buildings that stimulates the imagination. One gets from it the idea of the city, a place built by men for their satisfaction and activities, to be defended with passion from a destructive enemy. No fairer sight than the blonde wide lane of Fifth Avenue, with its innumerable banners, can well be imagined, and Mr. Hassam has precisely the vision and palette to commemorate its effect of stern gayety, of laughing beauty marching fearlessly to victory.*[44]

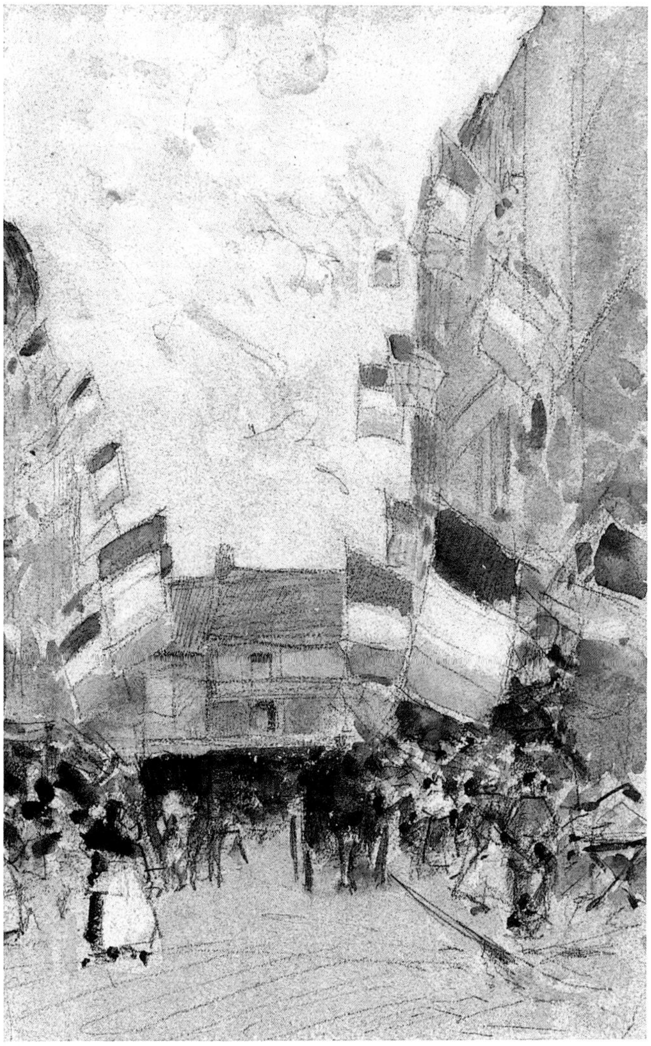

Fig. 228. Childe Hassam. *14th July, Paris, Old Quarter,* 1889. Watercolor and pastel on paper, 8½ x 5⅞ in. (21.6 x 14.9 cm). Carnegie Museum of Art, Pittsburgh; Andrew Carnegie Fund

The recent resurgence of American patriotic fervor has made the Flag paintings particularly cherished icons.

Hassam's first canvas painted in response to the war—*Just Off the Avenue, Fifty-third Street, May 1916,* May 1916 (Mr. and Mrs. Richard J. Schwartz)[45]—was, as he recalled, inspired by the Preparedness Day Parade held on Fifth Avenue on May 13, 1916. Its intimate composition and genre detail recall his earlier New York scenes. The absence of vehicles and the appearance of a street sweeper—who reiterates a figure in *Washington Arch, Spring* (fig. 97)—suggest a small-town spirit in the big city. By contrast with this initial picture, most of the Flag paintings feature large-scale banners and dynamic compositions, none more so than the second work in the series, *The Fourth of July, 1916* (fig. 229). One of only two sunny summer flag images by Hassam,[46] the canvas resulted from a trip in the summer—an unusual time for him to visit the city. While Hassam denoted the site as Fifth Avenue by showing its banks of skyscrapers and a green double-decker bus, he obscured the precise location, perhaps to imply that the entire length of the great boulevard was bedecked with flags. Deeming the painting "the climax that fairly shouts hurrah for Old Glory!" a commentator on Hassam's January 1917 display at the Montross Gallery, New York, noted the "sea of stars and stripes floating to the breeze from the skyscrapers on either side of the great American thoroughfare."[47]

For *Flags on the Waldorf, 1916* (fig. 230), Hassam used as a vantage point the west side of Fifth Avenue at Thirty-fourth Street and looked downtown along the canyon of the thoroughfare. In the right foreground appear the impressive Corinthian-style columns of the Columbia Trust Company, designed by Stanford White in 1903 as the Knickerbocker Trust Company on the site of the demolished Stewart mansion.[48] Just beyond is the flag-draped facade of the opulent Waldorf-Astoria Hotel, designed by Henry J. Hardenbergh in the German Renaissance style. Constructed between 1893 and 1897 as two buildings that functioned as a single unit, the hotel occupied the block between Thirty-third and Thirty-fourth Streets (see fig. 231).[49] Hassam inexplicably eliminated Thirty-fourth Street itself from the view, and he recessed the bank's white marble portico to align it with the hotel's red sandstone, brick, and terracotta facade—perhaps intrigued by the contrasts in color and texture presented by the two structures.[50] In *The Avenue in the Rain* (fig. 11), he combined the motif of layered American flags along Fifth Avenue with one of long-standing interest to him, reflections on wet pavements. These reflections, which multiply the panoply of red, white, and blue banners, allowed Hassam to investigate color variations, from deep red to pink, and cobalt blue to mauve.

After the United States entered World War I, the American flag was most often displayed in New York alongside those of Great Britain and France, our closest allies. *Allies Day, May 1917* (fig. 232) is one of Hassam's earliest expressions of the theme of Allied banners. His most famous Flag image, the painting was popularized by the sale of color reproductions to benefit the war effort and by its receipt of the Second Altman Prize for landscape from the National Academy of Design, New York, in March 1918. The acquisition of *Allies Day, May 1917* by the National Gallery of Art, Washington, D.C., in 1943 contributed to its reputation as Hassam's most overtly nationalistic canvas.

Fort has connected *Allies Day, May 1917* with the initial display of the Stars and Stripes alongside the Union Jack and the French tricolor in parades staged for the British and French war commissioners when they came to New York in early May 1917.[51] Unlike the generic buildings in most of the Flag paintings, the landmarks in *Allies Day, May 1917* are identifiable. The artist's vantage point was the northeast corner of Fifty-second Street on Fifth Avenue, looking north as the morning sunlight struck the facades on the west side of the avenue. Cram, Goodhue and Ferguson's Gothic Revival Saint Thomas Church (1913) stands at the northwest corner of Fifty-third Street; McKim, Mead and White's Renaissance palazzo built for the University Club (1899) appears a block to the north, with the Gotham (now Peninsula) Hotel and the Fifth Avenue Presbyterian Church visible beyond them. The ecclesiastical structures may suggest the "moral right of the Allied cause," as Fort has proposed.[52]

Groupings of the flags of America, Great Britain, and France are reiterated in several places, with the Union Jack also quoted in the Canadian Red Ensign in the left foreground. The harmony among the four nations is symbolized by the variations in pattern on the theme of red, white, and blue offered by their banners. But the American emblem is ascendant. Only one banner is uninterrupted by a flagpole or another flag: the American flag seen against the sky toward the upper center of the composition, in pictoral dialogue with the tower of Saint Thomas Church. This diagrammatic portrayal of the American banner at the pinnacle of the composition suggests the supremacy of the American spirit and strikes a powerfully nationalistic chord.

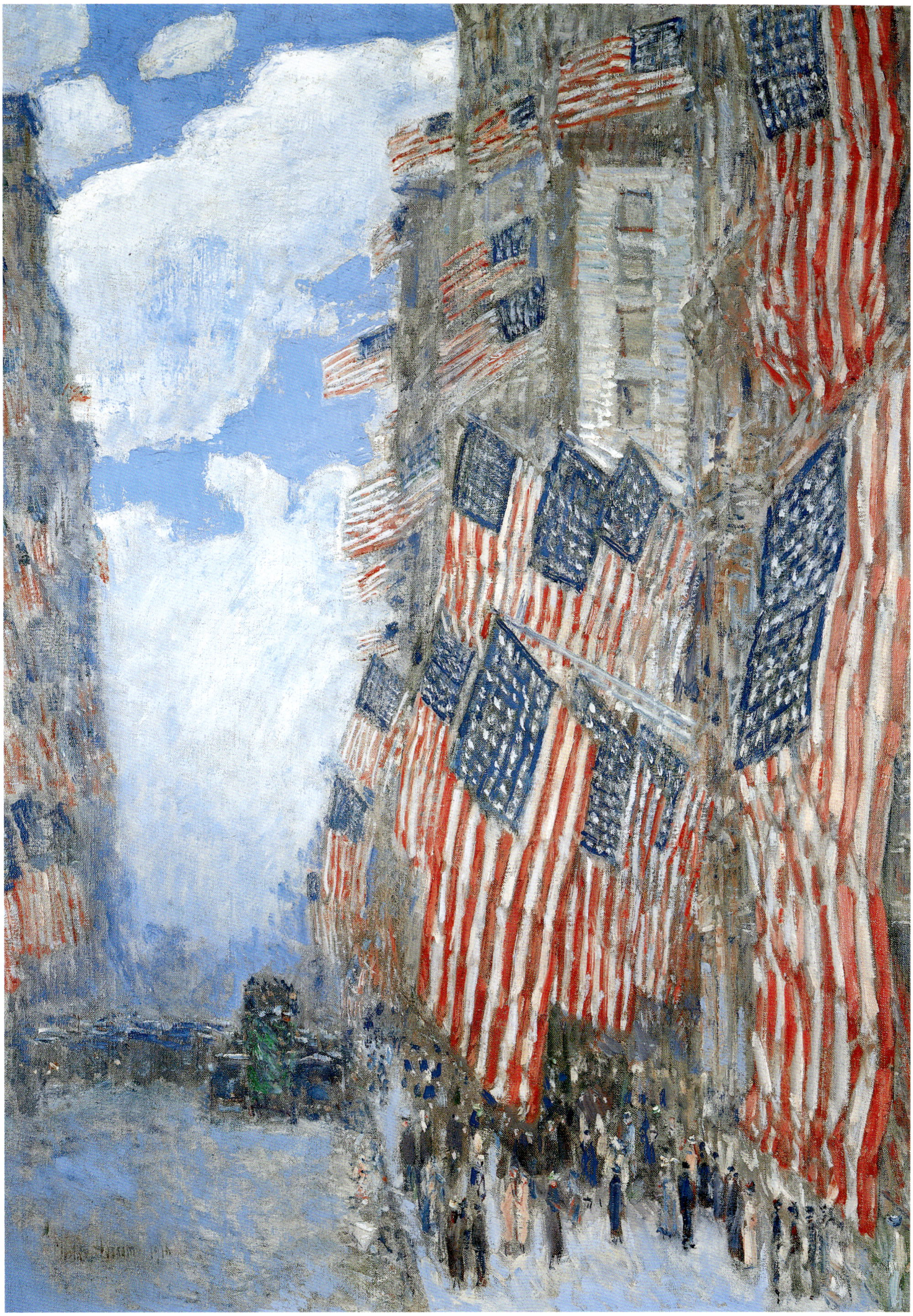

Fig. 229. Childe Hassam. *The Fourth of July, 1916 (The Greatest Display of the American Flag Ever Seen in New York, Climax of the Preparedness Parade in May)*, 1916. Oil on canvas, 36 x 26⅛ in. (91.4 x 66.4 cm). Private collection

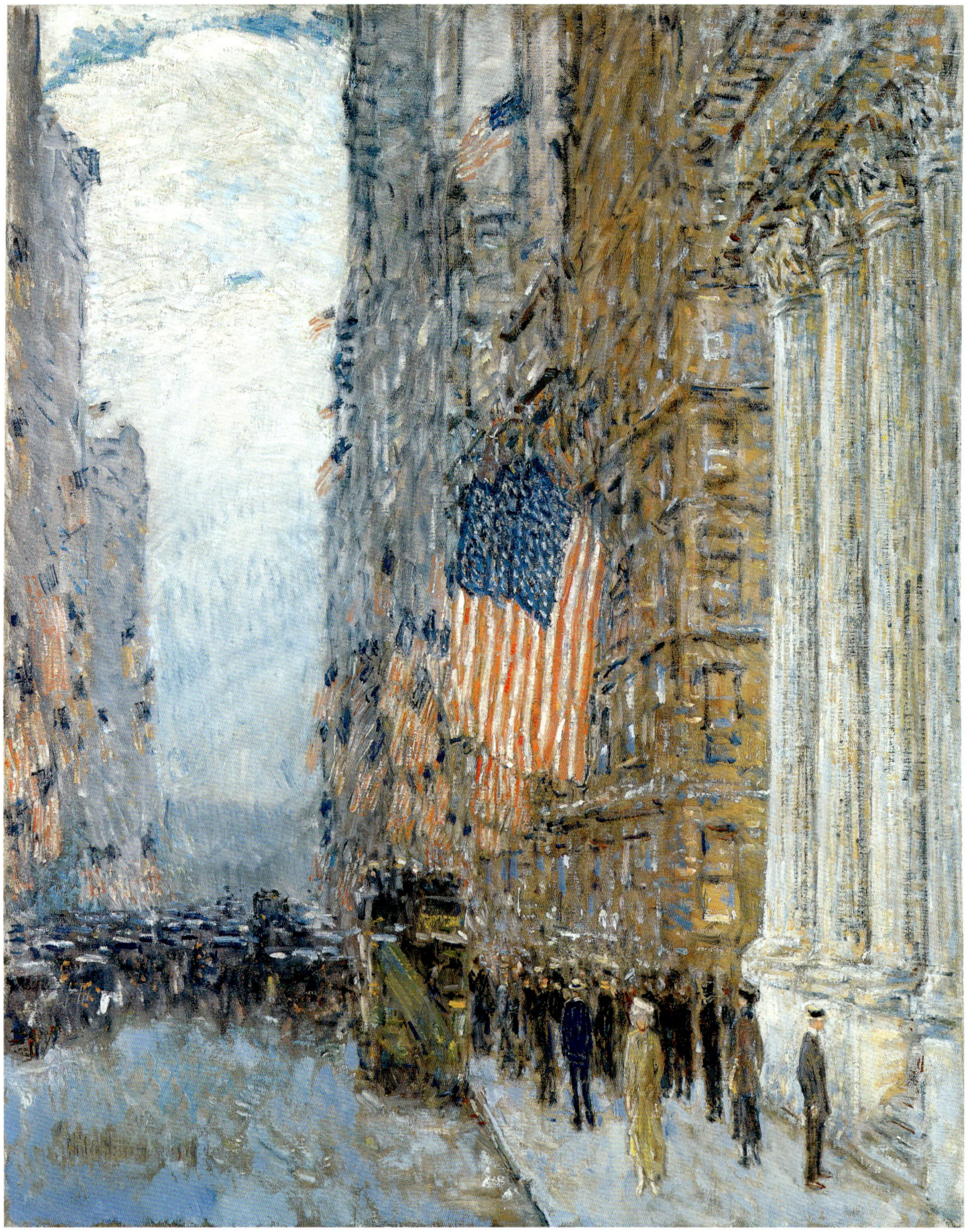

Fig. 230. Childe Hassam. *Flags on the Waldorf, 1916*, 1916. Oil on canvas, 36¼ x 31½ in. (92.1 x 80 cm). Amon Carter Museum, Fort Worth, Texas 1985.301

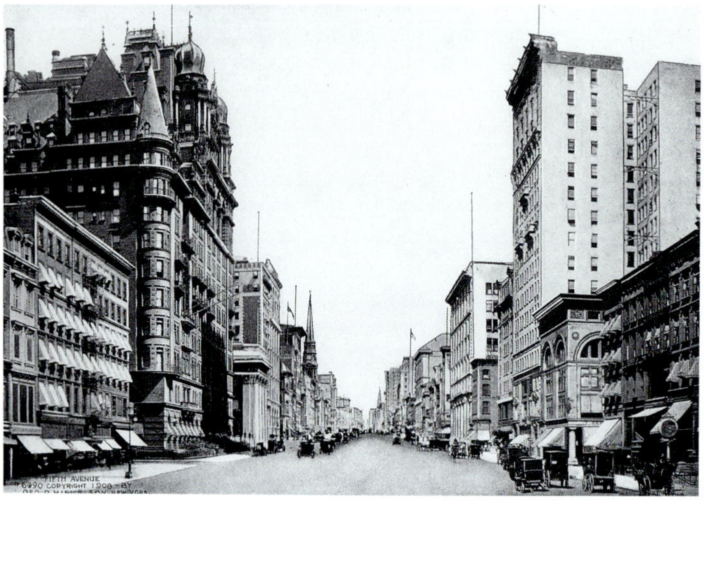

Fig. 231. Fifth Avenue looking north from 33rd Street, ca. 1908

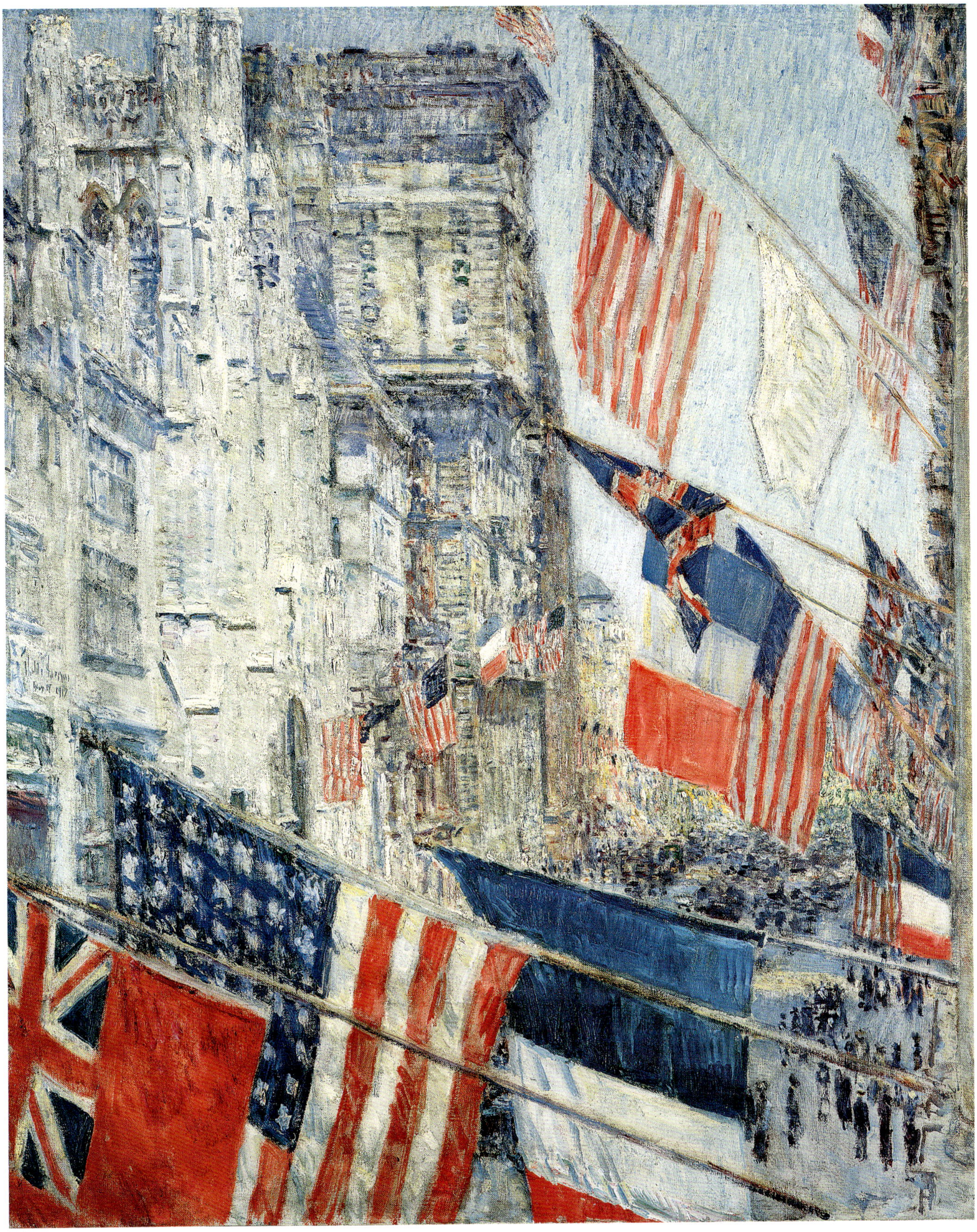

Fig. 232. Childe Hassam. *Allies Day, May 1917*, 1917. Oil on canvas, 36½ x 30¼ in. (92.7 x 76.8 cm). National Gallery of Art, Washington, D.C. Gift of Ethelyn McKinney in memory of her brother, Glenn Ford McKinney 1943.9.1

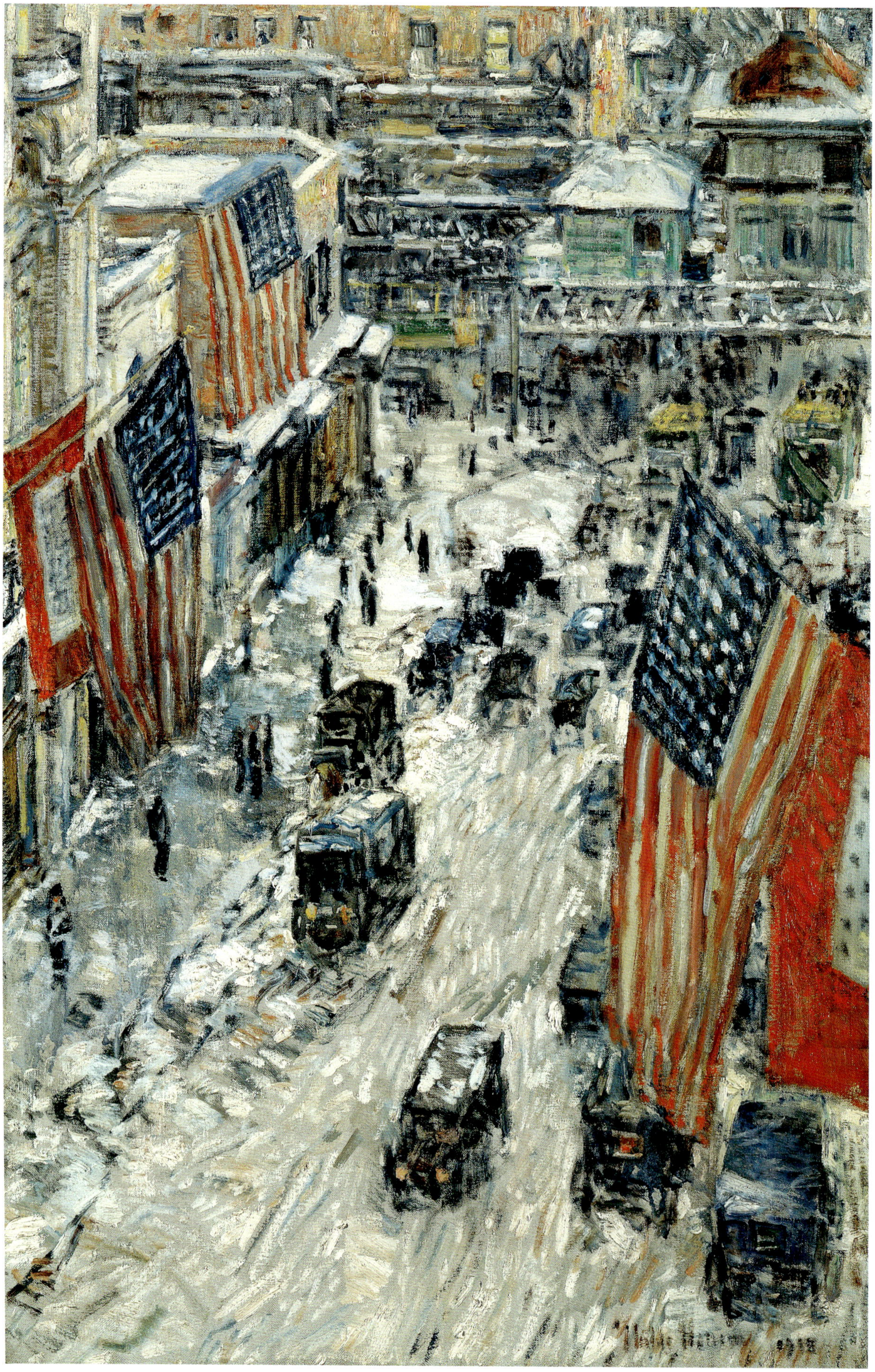

Fig. 233. Childe Hassam. *Flags on Fifty-seventh Street, The Winter of 1918,* 1918. Oil on canvas, 35¾ x 23¾ in. (90.8 x 60.3 cm). Collection of The New-York Historical Society, bequest of Julia B. Engel 1984.68

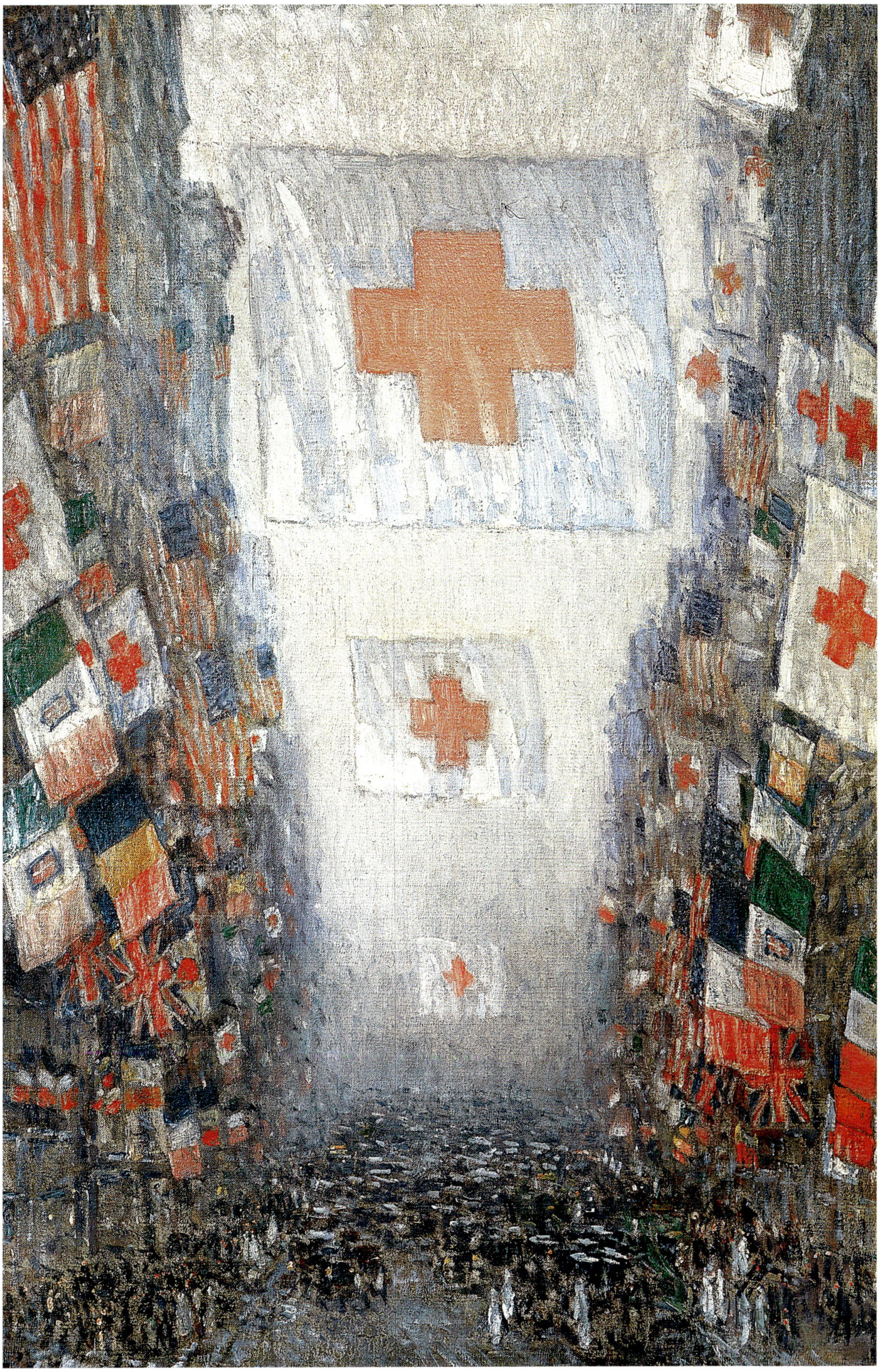

Fig. 234. Childe Hassam. *Red Cross Drive, May 1918 (Celebration Day)*, 1918. Oil on canvas, 35½ x 23½ in. (90.2 x 59.7 cm). May Family Collection, Christopher T. May, Sterling A. May, Meredith M. Smith, Laura May, Trustees

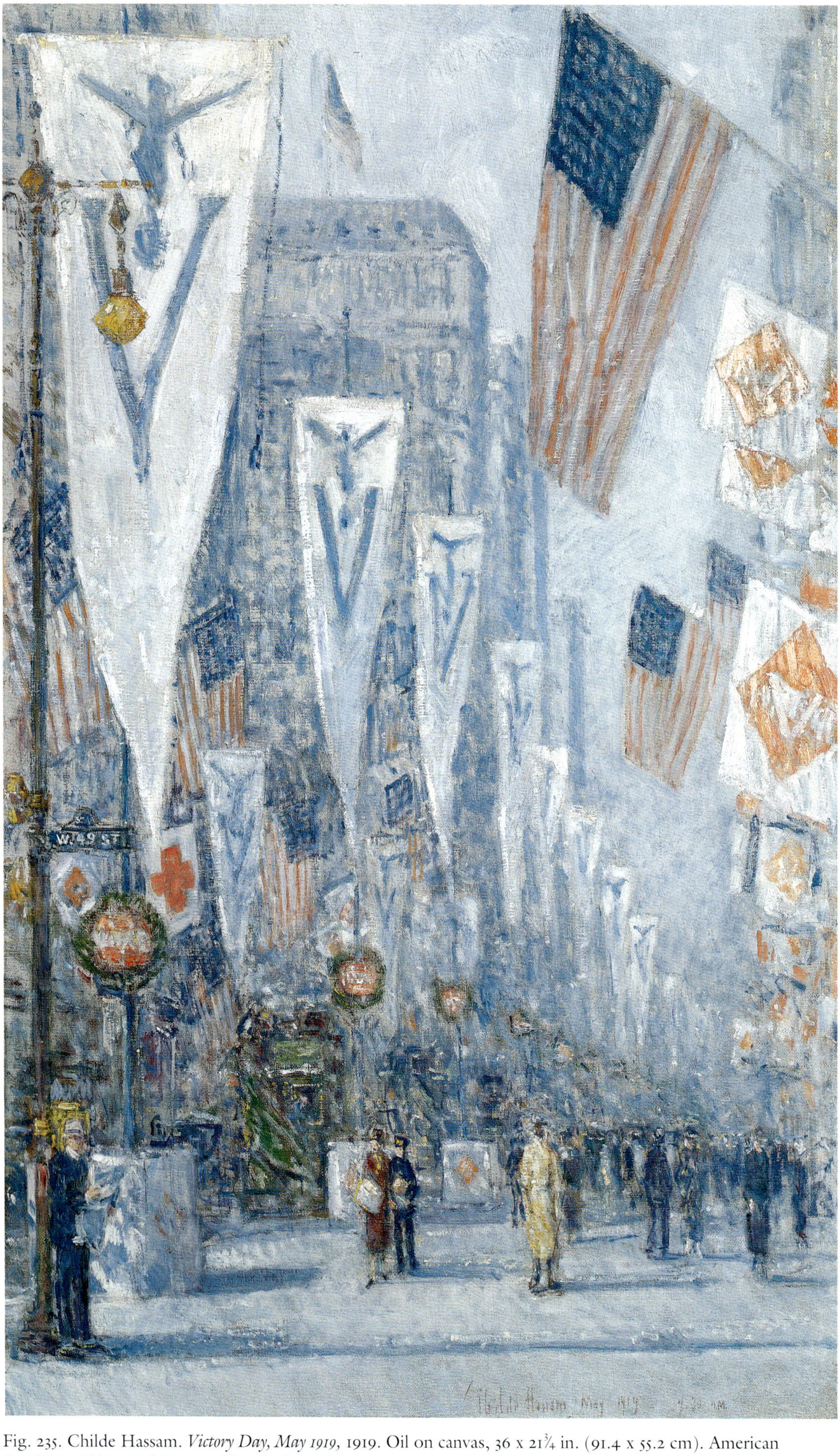

Fig. 235. Childe Hassam. *Victory Day, May 1919,* 1919. Oil on canvas, 36 x 21¾ in. (91.4 x 55.2 cm). American Academy of Arts and Letters, New York

Deborah Chotner has observed that *Allies Day, May 1917* "acts both as a patriotic rallying point, and as a symbol of three countries dear to the artist's heart: Great Britain, land of his ancestors; France, nurturing home to Hassam as a young artist; and the United States, the site of his greatest successes."[53]

From late 1917 to early 1918 Hassam experimented with new compositions for images of flag-lined city streets. *Flags on Fifty-seventh Street, The Winter of 1918* (fig. 233) departs from the long vistas presented by Fifth Avenue to portray the intersection of Fifty-seventh Street and Sixth Avenue as seen from Hassam's studio. As unusual as the locale are the winter setting, steep perspective, and presence of the Sixth Avenue El in the background.[54] Fifty-seventh Street was not a venue for ceremonial, patriotic displays, and the banners pictured were provided by commercial tenants. Thus, "Hassam's painting shows an ordinary winter day when few pedestrians have ventured out to brave the inclement weather," as Fort has written.[55]

Hassam recorded not only the flags of war but also some of the fund-raising events that organizations held throughout the conflict. *Red Cross Drive, May 1918 (Celebration Day)* (fig. 234) is a response to parades that highlighted and benefited the activities of the international humanitarian organization. Bracketed by kaleidoscopic cascades of Allied flags, the immense Red Cross banners displayed along Fifth Avenue provide the key motif in one of Hassam's most ambitious Flag paintings.[56]

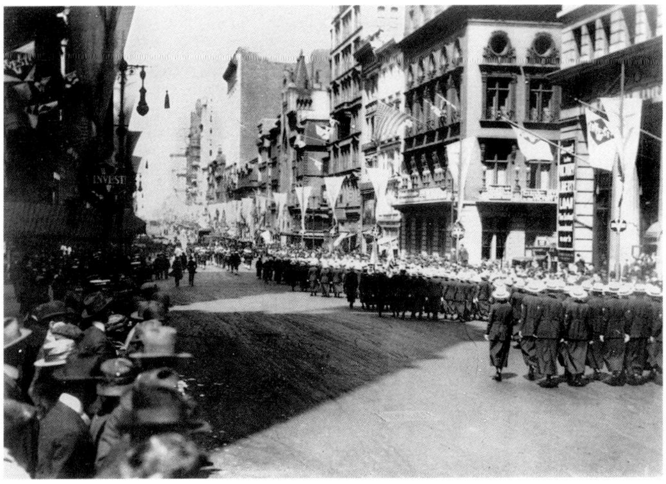

Fig. 236. Naval yeomen in Victory Loan Parade, New York, May 1919. Naval Historical Foundation, Washington, D.C.

Among Hassam's most impressive Flag compositions are five canvases inspired by the Fourth Liberty Loan Drive, organized by the federal government to raise money for wartime expenses by selling savings bonds. The Liberty Loan celebrations were the first events to evoke references to Fifth Avenue as the "Avenue of the Allies." The flags of all twenty-two allies were displayed, with the banners of an individual nation featured on a specific block between Twenty-sixth and Fifty-eighth Streets. American flags appeared at intervals throughout the route, and scarlet Liberty Loan banners bedecked lampposts all along the way. Typical of Hassam's representations of the Fourth Liberty Loan display is *Avenue of the Allies: Great Britain, 1918* (fig. 347), which compresses into a vibrant pattern a view of three blocks along Fifth Avenue looking north from Fifty-third Street. Hassam's vantage point was at the beginning of a block devoted to Great Britain, New Zealand, and Canada. The blocks to the north were dedicated to Brazil, whose green-and-yellow banner appears beyond the British flags, and Belgium. The Stars and Stripes is visible in the distance. Perhaps in emulation of Postimpressionist compositions, Hassam interpreted the flags more as abstract elements than as actual banners installed on Fifth Avenue facades, thereby emphasizing brilliant surface effects.

Four days after the armistice was signed, on November 11, 1918, Hassam showed twenty-three Flag paintings together for the first time, at New York's Durand-Ruel Galleries.[57] Proud of his accomplishment, he would exhibit the series five times, seeking, unsuccessfully, to sell the canvases as a group.[58] The last picture in the series, *Victory Day, May 1919* (fig. 235), is inscribed *May 1919—9:30 A.M.* Typically, Hassam avoided recording that month's most dramatic event: the May 6 parade of the returning Seventy-seventh Division up flag-lined Fifth Avenue from Washington Square to 110th Street, which was witnessed by at least a million spectators.[59] Instead of doing so, he commemorated the Victory Liberty Loan Drive. His canvas is dominated not by the throngs of marchers and spectators present on May 6 but by an array of large blue-and-white victory pennants and red-and-white banners urging purchase of victory bonds. Hassam also chose not to depict any of the other Victory Liberty Loan parades that were held along the avenue in May 1919 (see fig. 236), preferring to show citizens going about their ordinary morning activities.

An epilogue to the Flag series is *Fifth Avenue* (fig. 237), in which the avenue, seen at Forty-second Street,[60] is almost

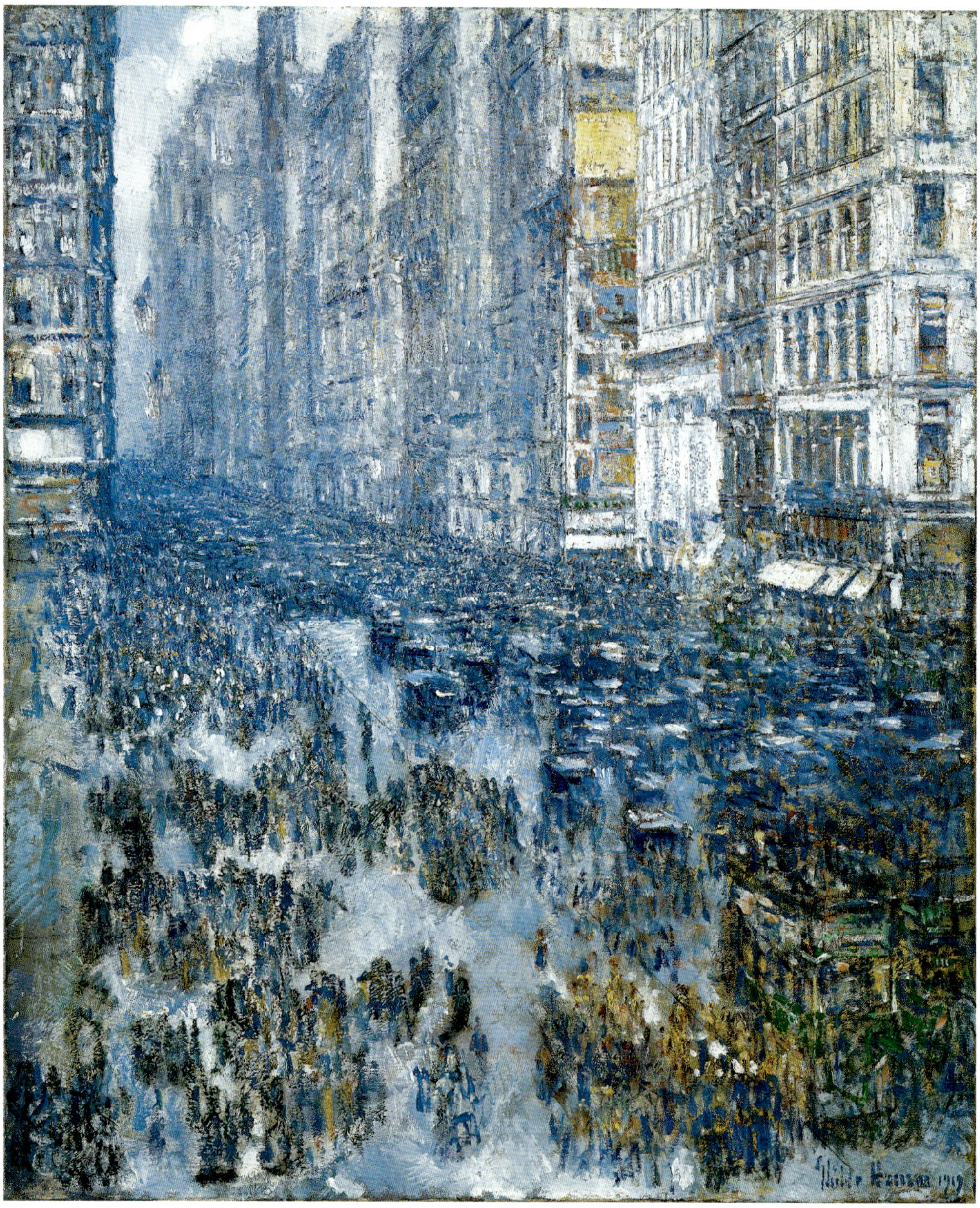

Fig. 237. Childe Hassam. *Fifth Avenue,* 1919. Oil on canvas, 24⅛ x 20¼ in. (61.3 x 51.4 cm). The Cleveland Museum of Art, 2003. Anonymous Gift 1952.539

devoid of colorful banners or references to human scale. Portrayed as a vast canyon created by intimidating towers, it is packed with vehicles and multitudes of pedestrians shown as mere ideographs. This gloomy view may reflect Hassam's disappointment at his inability to sell his Flag paintings as a series.[61] Whether or not this is so, Hassam surely meant the looming skyscrapers and undifferentiated knot of heterogeneous humanity to signify how New York had changed since he began painting intimate views of the bon ton in works such as *Lower Fifth Avenue* (fig. 95) and *Washington Arch, Spring* (fig. 97) and how he had literally distanced himself from the city. In 1919, the year Hassam painted *Fifth Avenue,* he purchased a colonial house in East Hampton and much more than ever before turned his attention to country life. In an essay of 1927 he articulated his disenchantment with New York, complaining that it had become garish and monstrously out of scale and that Times Square seemed like "a perfect machine shop."[62]

1. John C. Van Dyke, *The New New York: A Commentary on the Place and the People* (New York: Macmillan Company, 1909), p. 6. The responses of American Impressionists and early modernists to early-twentieth-century Manhattan are summarized in Wanda M. Corn, "The New New York," *Art in America* 61 (July–August 1973), pp. 58–65. Erica E. Hirshler, "The 'New New York' and The Park Row Building: American Artists View an Icon of the Modern Age," *American Art Journal* 21 (1989), pp. 26–45, offers a stimulating case study.
2. However, the Flatiron Building appears in Hassam's etching *Washington's Birthday, Fifth Avenue and 23rd Street* (fig. 18).
3. Hassam's painting of Wall Street (fig. 216) is discussed on pp. 209–10. See also *Brooklyn Bridge in Winter,* 1904 (Telfair Academy of Arts and Sciences, Savannah); *Bridge in Snow (Brooklyn Bridge in Winter),* ca. 1894 (Des Moines Art Center); *High Bridge,* 1922 (Santa Barbara Museum of Art); *Manhattan's Misty Sunset,* 1911 (Butler Institute of American Art, Youngstown, Ohio); and *Skyscrapers, Sunset,* 1918 (American Academy of Arts and Letters, New York). Some of these paintings embodied Hassam's belief, articulated in 1898, that "the very thing that makes New York irregular and topsy-turvy makes it capable of the most astounding effects. From the tops of the enormous buildings one can get magnificent sweeps along the rivers and over the tops of the buildings." Hassam quoted in "New York Beautiful" 1898, p. 9.
4. Milton W. Brown, *American Painting from the Armory Show to the Depression* (Princeton: Princeton University Press, 1955), pp. 71–76, summarizes "art activity" during the war years. Brown discusses posters; war reportage by Gifford Beal, Hassam, George Luks, and Joseph Pennell, among others; "inspirational" works by George Bellows, Edwin H. Blashfield, and Maxfield Parrish, for example; and "art for war" work, including the formation of committees and the organization of exhibitions. The author thanks Teresa A. Carbone for her remarks on this source.
5. Henry McBride, "Childe Hassam and the Americanization of Fifth Avenue," *New York Sun*, November 24, 1918, sec. 1, p. 10.
6. Teresa A. Carbone, catalogue entry (draft), for *American Paintings in The Brooklyn Museum of Art: Artists Born by 1876* (Brooklyn, forthcoming, fall 2004). Carbone proposes convincingly, although without conclusive proof, that the site of *Late Afternoon, New York: Winter* is "the north side of Central Park South, looking east from about Seventh Avenue."
7. For an introduction to Pictorial photography of New York, see Weston J. Naef, *The Collection of Alfred Stieglitz: Fifty Pioneers of Modern Photography,* exh. cat. (New York: The Metropolitan Museum of Art, 1978); Alan Trachtenberg, "Image and Ideology: New York in the Photographer's Eye," *Journal of Urban History* 10 (August 1984), pp. 453–64; William Sharpe, "New York, Night, and Cultural Mythmaking: The Nocturne in Photographs, 1900–1925," *Smithsonian Studies in American Art* 2 (fall 1988), pp. 2–21; and Alan Trachtenberg, "Camera Work/Social Work," in *Reading American Photographs: Images as History, Mathew Brady to Walker Evans* (New York: Hill and Wang, 1989), pp. 164–230. The author thanks Douglas Eklund, Assistant Curator, Department of Photographs, The Metropolitan Museum of Art, for his help with respect to this subject.
8. James A. McNeill Whistler, *"Ten O'Clock": A Lecture* (1885; Portland, Maine: T. B. Mosher, 1916), pp. 13–14. Donelson F. Hoopes (1979, p. 54) invoked this passage in connection with Hassam's *Late Afternoon, New York: Winter.*
9. This account of *Broadway and 42nd Street* is indebted to the catalogue entry by Susan G. Larkin in H. Barbara Weinberg and Susan G. Larkin, *American Impressionists Abroad and at Home: Paintings from the Collection of The Metropolitan Museum of Art,* exh. cat. (New York: American Federation of Arts, 2000), p. 32.
10. John Corbin, "The Lights and the Stars of Broadway," *Scribner's Magazine* 37 (February 1905), p. 129. For the development of Times Square, see Mary C. Henderson, *The City and the Theatre: New York Playhouses from Bowling Green to Times Square* (Clifton, N.J.: James T. White and Co., 1973).
11. "Broadway by Night," *Harper's Weekly,* January 20, 1894, p. 54.
12. Richard Le Gallienne, "The Philosopher Walks Up-Town," *Harper's Magazine* 123 (July 1911), p. 237. A picturesque tour of the nocturnal city that accords with the spirit of Hassam's *Broadway and 42nd Street* appears in James B. Carrington, "New York at Night," *Scribner's Magazine* 27 (March 1900), pp. 326–36.
13. Quoted in "New York the Beauty City," *New York Sun,* February 23, 1913, p. 16.
14. The first recorded display of the painting under the present title was *An Exhibition of Paintings, Etchings, Drawings, and Lithographs by Childe Hassam,* exh. brochure (East Hampton: Guild Hall, July 17 – August 8, 1932), no. 2, *The Hovel and the Skyscraper—Central Park West at 67th Street,* 1904. Hassam made a closer, verdant view of the Sheepfold the subject of the more bucolic *Across the Park,* 1904 (Art Museum of Western Virginia, Roanoke). Hoopes 1979, p. 62, and William H. Gerdts, *Impressionist New York* (New York: Abbeville Press, 1994), p. 14, suggest that the small building portrayed next to the steel-frame skyscraper under construction is the old riding stable. From the vast bibliography on Central Park, the following source was particularly helpful: Roy Rosenzweig and Elizabeth Blackmar, *The Park and the People: A History of Central Park* (Ithaca, N.Y.: Cornell University Press, 1992). The author thanks Dana Pilson, former Research Assistant, and Megan Holloway, Research Assistant, both Department of American Paintings and Sculpture, The Metropolitan Museum of Art, for investigating the site that Hassam depicted.
15. Much useful information about this picture is contained in William H. Gerdts, *American Impressionism: Masterworks from Public and Private Collections in the United States* (Lugano-Castagnola: Thyssen-Bornemisza Foundation, 1990), p. 68. The painting was reproduced as *Broad and Wall Streets* in White 1911, p. XXXII.
16. William H. Gerdts, "Three Themes," in Adelson, Cantor, and Gerdts 1999, p. 166, identified the buildings: "At the left is the twenty-one story Commercial Cable Building (1897); beyond the Stock Exchange is the ornate Gillender Building (1901) and then the tall Hanover Bank Building (1904). Across Broad Street, and also in the shade, is the long façade of the eleven-story Mills Building (1883)." See also Karl Baedeker, *The United States . . . Handbook for Travelers,* 4th ed., prepared by James F. Muirhead (Leipzig: Karl Baedeker, 1909), pp. 34–35.
17. "Among the Galleries," *New York Sun,* March 25, 1908, p. 6, quoted in Gerdts, *Impressionist New York,* pp. 102–3.
18. Hassam quoted in Ives 1892. See also Childe Hassam, 35, boulevard Rochechouart, Paris, May 28, 1889, to William Howe Downes, Boston, Downes Papers, MSS L337, transcribed in Hiesinger 1994, p. 179: "An artist should paint his own time and treat nature as he feels it, not repeat the same stupidities of his predecessors, for mechanical exactitude becomes stupid in art and tiresome, like all things photographic to the real artist." Yet Hassam believed that the camera could produce excellent

"impressions" because its mechanism was instantaneous. He was quoted to this effect in Sadakichi Hartmann, "Photographic Enquête," *Camera Notes* 5, no. 11 (April 1902), p. 236, cited in Fort 1993, p. xv, n. 35.

19. Lockman interview, February 2, 1927, p. 5: "I went to see his [Freer's] gallery once. . . . I admired his Whistler so much. The small street things are very interesting, [word probably omitted] the things that I have painted, the little shop windows and things like that." See also James McNeill Whistler, *An Orange Note: Sweet Shop,* 1884 (Freer Gallery of Art, Washington, D.C.). For additional information on Hassam's access to such paintings by Whistler, see Gerdts, "Three Themes," pp. 227–28, n. 89. In April 1910 Freer purchased Hassam's Portland genre scene, *Chinese Merchants,* 1909 (fig. 337), which in its composition is also similar to street scenes by Whistler in Freer's collection.

20. Hiesinger 1994, p. 128. The figure of the messenger boy also appears in three closely related paintings, all measuring 16 by 12 inches: *Street Scene in Winter* (signed and dated lower right: *1901;* formerly The Metropolitan Museum of Art, New York, deaccessioned February 1969, location unknown); *Fifth Avenue in Winter* (signed and dated lower left: *1901;* Sotheby's, New York, sale cat., December 10, 1981, lot 30); and *Snow Storm, Fifth Avenue, New York* (signed and dated lower right: *Jan. 1907;* R. H. Love Galleries, Chicago; illustrated in Adelson, Cantor, and Gerdts 1999, p. 77).

21. Childe Hassam in "John H. Twachtman: An Estimation," *North American Review* 176 (April 1903), sec. 2, p. 556.

22. Gerdts ("Three Themes," p. 164) cites the address of the school. Curatorial records, Addison Gallery of American Art, Phillips Academy, Andover, Massachusetts, include a stock disposition card from the Macbeth Gallery, New York, that gives an alternate title for the picture: *Little Shoemakers/Cobbler's Shop (7th Ave–58th St).* Fort (1993, p. ix) notes: "Despite the placement of the Alwyn Auto School in the center of *Little Cobbler's Shop,* both shop scenes [*Messenger Boy* and *Little Cobbler's Shop*] are about foot travel—as indicated by their titles and the inclusion of stores devoted to shoe repair—rather than motorized vehicles." She adds (p. xv, n. 18), "On the back of the stretcher of *Messenger Boy* is written 'little shoemaker's shop.'" The author of the present essay is greatly indebted to Fort for her incisive analyses of Hassam's work.

23. Childe Hassam, December 11, 1906, to Florence Griswold, archives, Florence Griswold Museum, Old Lyme, Connecticut, quoted in Hiesinger 1994, p. 131.

24. Another important precursor of the Window series is Hassam's *Two Children,* 1897 (Cincinnati Art Museum), as Hiesinger (1994, p. 145) has noted. Hiesinger (ibid.) indicates that the first work in the Window series is *Spring Morning* (fig. 10) (which is inscribed *1909* at center left and on the reverse at upper left) and that Hassam painted it in his studio on West Sixty-seventh Street. Hiesinger's apparent source is Lockman interview, February 2, 1927, p. 6, which quotes Hassam: "I was living then in 67th Street. Large apartment, beautiful studio. Larger than I ever had before. I painted along there in that studio. I painted pictures of Early Spring, A Woman Standing at a Window. It is owned by the Carnegie Institute. They paid me a very good price for it." The windows in *Spring Morning* differ from those in all the subsequent Window paintings made at West Fifty-seventh Street, suggesting that it was at least begun in the earlier studio, before Hassam moved to his new studio, in early January 1909. John Beatty, Pittsburgh, June 11, 1909, to Childe Hassam, New York, Carnegie Papers, file 673, Archives of American Art, Smithsonian Institution: "The Fine Arts Committee at its meeting, June 10, voted to purchase for the Institute's permanent collection, your painting now in the current exhibition, 'Spring Morning' at the price given by you on your entry blank, $6,000."

25. Hiesinger 1994, p. 141.

26. Ibid., p. 145.

27. See also *The Alders,* 1918 (American Academy of Arts and Letters, New York).

28. Hiesinger (1994, pp. 126–28) provides a good summary of Hassam's multifaceted classicism.

29. An excellent account of the American version of the genre is Bailey Van Hook, "Decorative Images of American Women: The Aristocratic Aesthetic of the Late Nineteenth Century," *Smithsonian Studies in American Art* 4 (winter 1990), pp. 45–68.

30. Thorstein Veblen, *The Theory of the Leisure Class: An Economic Study of Institutions* (1899; reprint, with a foreword by Stuart Chase, New York: The Modern Library, 1934), pp. 53–56.

31. The author thanks Elyssa Schram, Research Assistant, and Melinda Webber, Collection Assistant, Costume Institute, The Metropolitan Museum of Art, for information on the costumes in Hassam's Window series.

32. See H. Barbara Weinberg, "Hassam in Paris, 1886–1889," in this publication, pp. 75–78.

33. Childe Hassam, March 8, 1920, to John W. Beatty, Carnegie Institute Papers, file 673, quoted in Gail Stavitsky, "Childe Hassam and the Carnegie Institute: A Correspondence," *Archives of American Art Journal* 22, no. 3 (1982), p. 6.

34. Guy Pène du Bois, "National Academy Exhibit Decorous: Masterpiece of Show Is a Painting by Childe Hassam," *New York American,* March 11, 1912, quoted in David B. Dearinger, catalogue entry, in *Rave Reviews: American Art and Its Critics, 1826–1925,* exh. cat., edited by David B. Dearinger (New York: National Academy of Design, 2000), p. 259.

35. Untitled notice in *Art and Progress* 4, no. 4 (February 1913), unnumbered preliminary page, quoted in David R. Brigham, *American Impressionism: Paintings of Promise,* exh. cat. (Worcester, Mass.: Worcester Art Museum; San Francisco: Pomegranate, 1997), p. 23.

36. *Fourth Exhibition: Oil Paintings by Contemporary American Artists,* exh. cat. (Washington, D.C.: Corcoran Gallery of Art, December 1912–January 1913), no. 165. Hiesinger (1994, pp. 147–48) notes that *Spring Morning,* 1909 (fig. 10), was bought by the Carnegie Institute, Pittsburgh, in 1909; *Contre-Jour,* 1910, by the Art Institute of Chicago in 1910; and *The Breakfast Room,* 1911 (fig. 333), by the Worcester Art Museum in 1911. For further discussion of *The New York Window* and related canvases in the context of their rural counterparts, see Susan G. Larkin, "Hassam in New England, 1889–1918," in this publication, pp. 148, 150, 152, 154–55, 157, and Susan G. Larkin, *The Cos Cob Art Colony: Impressionists on the Connecticut Shore,* exh. cat. (New York: National Academy of Design; New Haven: Yale University Press, 2001), p. 150.

37. Hassam's Flag paintings have received admirable scholarly treatment in Fort 1988 and Ilene Susan Fort, "The Flag Paintings of Childe Hassam," *Magazine Antiques* 133 (April 1988), pp. 876–87.

38. Lockman interview, February 2, 1927, p. 26.

39. "President's Speech at Labor Convention," *New York Times,* November 13, 1917; see also, for example, "All Churches Offer War Thanksgiving," *New York Times,* November 30, 1917, p. 9: "After the recessional, the congregation stood while the national anthems of the United States, Great Britain, and France were played." "Nation Will Sing Patriotism Today," *New York Times,* December 9, 1917, p. 2: "At 4 o'clock tomorrow

afternoon 'The Star-Spangled Banner' will be sung by millions of Americans at community meetings throughout the country. The day has been set aside for the first national patriotic song service, and men, women, and children of every creed have been asked to join."

40. Fort, "Flag Paintings of Hassam," pp. 876, 879.
41. Hiesinger 1994, p. 156. Hassam contributed a drawing, *Girl Knitting*, to the portfolio of "Forty seven Fac-simile Drawings by American Artists," sold for $5 by the American Artists' War Emergency Fund in 1918. Among Hassam's anti-German statements, Hiesinger (ibid., p. 172, n. 39) cites "Hassam on the Huns," letter to the editor, *Boston Transcript*, July 31, 1916, clipping, MSS L337, Downes Papers.
42. *Church of the Paulist Fathers* is reproduced in Gerdts, *Impressionist New York*, p. 108, where the date is given as 1907. Elizabeth Broun, "Childe Hassam's America," *American Art* 13, no. 3 (fall 1999), pp. 41–43, mistakenly dates the painting 1892 (p. 42) and discusses it at length, interpreting the buildings depicted as emblematic of "fundamental aspects of turn-of-the-century New York—labor strife, commerce and tourism, and immigration." The painting appeared at Christie's, New York, sale, May 21, 1998, lot 59, with a date of 1907 specified.
43. "November Exhibitions in Great Variety, Art at Home and Abroad," *New York Times*, November 17, 1918, p. 7.
44. "Here and There in the Art Galleries," *New York Times*, June 16, 1918, p. 15.
45. *Just Off the Avenue, Fifty-third Street, May 1916* is reproduced in Fort 1988, p. 33.
46. Ibid., p. 34.
47. "New York Art Exhibitions and Gallery Notes," *Christian Science Monitor*, undated clipping [1917], Hassam Papers, reel NAA1, frame 566. See *Exhibition of Pictures by Childe Hassam*, exh. cat. (New York: Montross Gallery, January 4–20, 1917).
48. The Knickerbocker Trust Company and the Columbia Trust Company merged in 1914, and the new entity was thereafter called the Columbia Trust Company. Untitled notices, *New York Times*, December 4, 1914, p. 15, and December 21, 1914, p. 11.
49. See the discussion of *The Manhattan Club (The Stewart Mansion)* (fig. 99) in H. Barbara Weinberg, "Hassam in New York, 1889–1896," in this publication, pp. 103–6. For additional information on the Waldorf-Astoria Hotel, see Robert A. M. Stern, Gregory Gilmartin, and John Montague Massengale, *New York 1900: Metropolitan Architecture and Urbanism, 1890–1915* (New York: Rizzoli, 1983), pp. 254–61. *Avenue of the Allies (Flags on the Waldorf)*, 1917 (Telfair Academy of Arts and Sciences, Savannah), shows the same scene, but from the south, with the Waldorf-Astoria Hotel in the left foreground and the Columbia Trust Company beyond.
50. Materials of the hotel are specified in "The Hotel Waldorf-Astoria, New York," *American Architect and Building News* 60 (April 2, 1898), pp. 3–4. Fort (1988, p. 36) remarked that Hassam also eliminated the Fuller ("Flatiron") Building at Twenty-third Street, which, the present author believes, would not have been visible from Thirty-fourth Street in 1916—it cannot be seen from that vantage point today. The Waldorf-Astoria Hotel was demolished in 1929 to make way for the Empire State Building; the hotel opened in 1931 in a new building on Park Avenue between Forty-ninth and Fiftieth Streets. Kenneth T. Jackson, ed., *The Encyclopedia of New York City* (New Haven: Yale University Press, 1995), p. 1233.
51. Fort 1988, p. 46.
52. Fort, "Flag Paintings of Hassam," p. 885. Fort (1988, p. 46) noted that the brightness of the facade of Saint Thomas Church "metaphorically suggest[s] that the new union of Allies has divine blessing." Hiesinger (1994, p. 172, n. 41) countered Fort's symbolic reading by pointing out that the church was bright because it had only recently been completed.
53. Deborah Chotner, catalogue entry, in Franklin Kelly et al., *American Paintings of the Nineteenth Century, Part I* (Washington, D.C.: National Gallery of Art, 1996), p. 286. Maud Hassam's origins in Montreal may have prompted Hassam to feature the Canadian Red Ensign.
54. Enumerating the elements that enhanced New York's atmosphere, Hassam remarked in 1898: "Even the elevated railroad is at some times of day, in some lights, extremely effective. To see the thing shoot by, send[ing] off great spiral masses of smoke against the sky, is inspiring in the extreme." Hassam quoted in "New York Beautiful" 1898, p. 9.
55. Fort 1988, p. 56.
56. Ibid., p. 64.
57. *Exhibition of a Series of Paintings of the Avenue of the Allies by Childe Hassam*, exh. cat., foreword by William A. Coffin (New York: Durand-Ruel Galleries, November 15–December 7, 1918).
58. See exhibition history in this publication as follows: Durand-Ruel Galleries, New York, 1918; Carnegie Institute, Pittsburgh, 1919; Milch Galleries, New York, 1919; Parish House, Church of the Ascension, New York, 1919; Corcoran Gallery of Art, Washington, D.C., 1922. For Hassam's effort to sell the paintings as a group, see Hiesinger 1994, pp. 164–65.
59. "A Million Cheer 77th in Final Hike of War up 5th Av.," *New York Times*, May 7, 1919, p. 1. "2,000,000 Out to See Veterans Pass By," *New York Times*, May 7, 1919, p. 5, adds that a million viewed the parade, but "hundreds of thousands [were] held away from Fifth Avenue on either side."
60. Gerdts (*Impressionist New York*, p. 204, n. 23) indicates the location: "The open plaza at lower left marks the steps to the New York Public Library, just below Forty-second Street, and that location is confirmed by several other buildings." Gerdts adds, "But the omission, up one block at Forty-third Street, of Temple Emanu-el with its monumental façade—the most distinctive building on this section of Fifth Avenue—raises disturbing questions of Hassam's motivations and/or his perceptions of his potential clientele."
61. Broun ("Childe Hassam's America," p. 49) makes this suggestion.
62. *Catalogue of Etchings, Lithographs, Lithotints, Drawings, Water-colors and Pastels, by Childe Hassam*, exh. cat. (New York: Arthur Harlow and Co., January 22–February 11, 1927), p. 2.

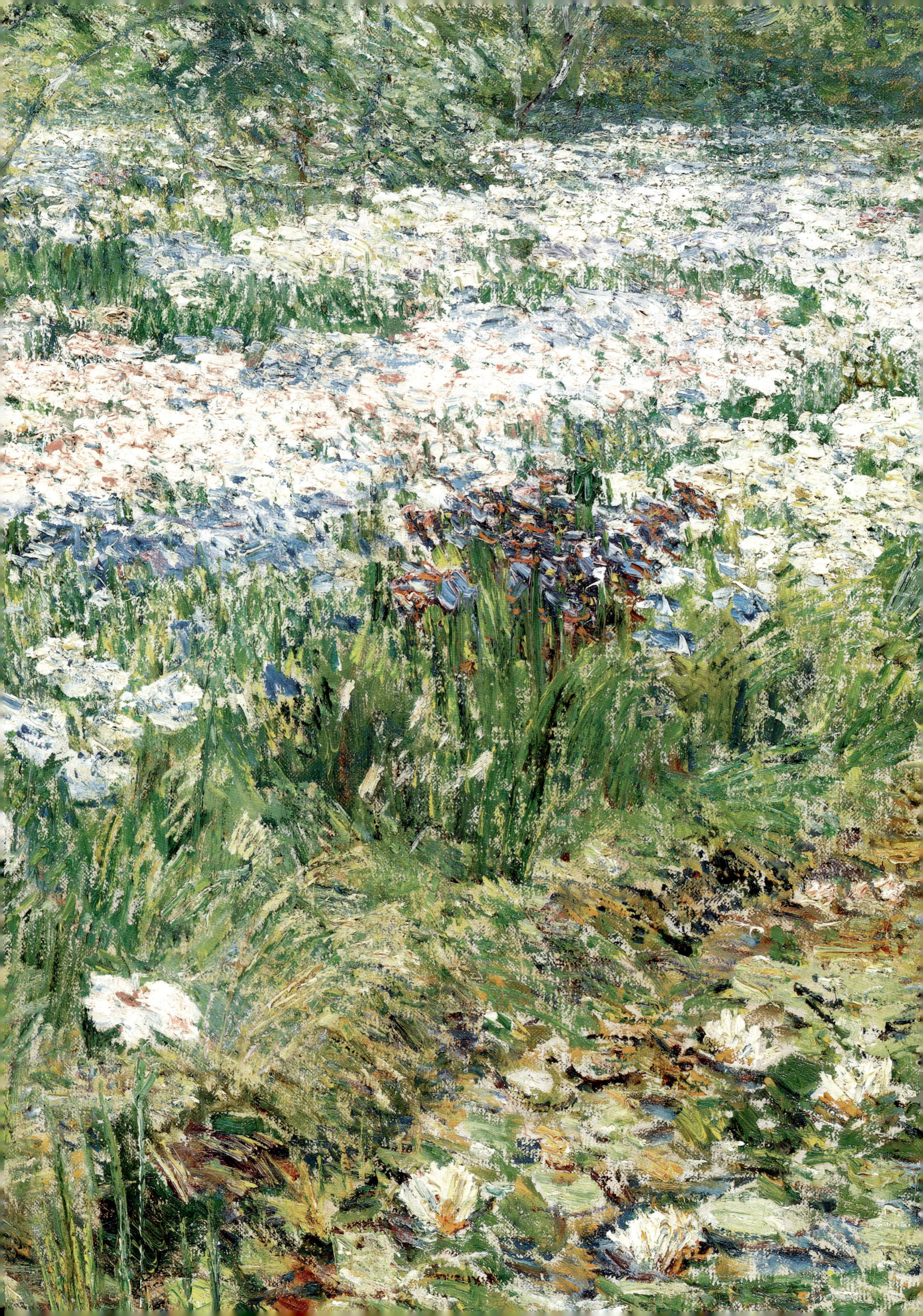

CHAPTER SEVEN

Hassam in East Hampton, 1898–1935

H. Barbara Weinberg

Between the summer of 1898 and his death in 1935, Hassam (fig. 238) enjoyed an association with East Hampton, an idyllic coastal village on the South Fork of Long Island, New York. East Hampton would inspire him to portray in paintings and prints gardens and old houses, meadows and beaches, still lifes, nudes, and golfers. In an interview of 1927 he recalled the circumstances of his first visit: "That was the Spanish war year, we did not go to the Shoals that year because it was supposed to be in an exposed position, and we did not know whether the house [Appledore House] would open, that I spent my days that summer at East Hampton. . . . I lived in one of the boarding houses there."[1]

Hassam was invited to East Hampton in 1898 by his artist friends G. Ruger Donoho and Thomas Alexander Harrison "who was living in his [Donoho's] house at that time."[2] Donoho had settled in East Hampton in 1891, the same year William Merritt Chase began teaching summer classes in neighboring Southampton. Throughout his life Donoho maintained New York studios, but he made East Hampton his principal residence after marrying Matilda Ackley in 1894. He built an impressive Colonial Revival house on Egypt Lane and laid out an ambitious old-fashioned garden over which his wife presided.[3] Donoho rented his carriage house to Harrison and other artists and, like Chase, attracted a number of painters to the region, encouraging them to work as Impressionists.

Like many unspoiled New England villages and towns with a New England flavor, East Hampton became a popular country retreat in the late nineteenth century. As urbanization and industrialization aroused nostalgia for simpler times, city dwellers sought occasional escape in communities associated with the periods of settlement and colonial growth, places redolent of cherished American fundamentals. Dona L. Brown, a scholar of the phenomenon, has noted: "Tourists eager to get a glimpse of 'Old New England' toured decaying towns and rural backwaters, looking for a world that seemed more old-fashioned, more virtuous, and

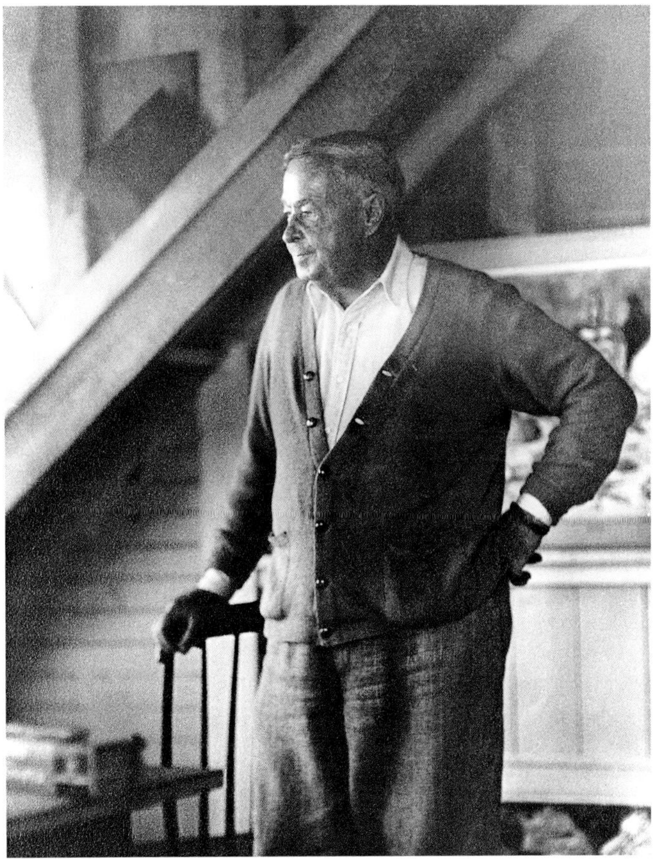

Fig. 238. Arnold Genthe. Hassam in his East Hampton studio, ca. 1925. Gelatin silver print, $9\frac{1}{4}$ x $7\frac{1}{8}$ in. (23.5 x 18.1 cm). National Portrait Gallery, Smithsonian Institution, Washington, D.C.

more comforting than their own worlds."[4] Artists participated in the quest for rustic reassurance in evocative American locales and simultaneously recapitulated the pleasures they had experienced in European country villages during their student years: inexpensive housing, picturesque scenery, camaraderie, and a mellow sense of place.[5]

For decades Hassam had found in coastal New England villages the old-fashioned values, virtues, and comforts that accorded with his proud family heritage and offered refuge from harsh urban actualities. The reasons he was drawn to East Hampton are clear: it was a beautiful village that had long combined summer social life with art, and it was filled with old houses, handsome gardens, nautical relics, and interesting wild flora. The town had, after all, been founded in 1648 by English Puritan immigrants, most from Lynn in the Massachusetts Bay Colony. There were remnants of early settlements in the indigenous architecture—which included weathered shingled houses and even windmills—and picturesque farmers, shipbuilders, and fishermen. Although East Hampton lacked attractive harbors like those Hassam had portrayed in Gloucester, Provincetown, and Newport, it boasted picturesque streets, lanes, and meadows. The observations made by a writer in 1872 were still relevant: "Perhaps no town in America retains so nearly the primitive habits, tastes, and ideas of our forefathers as East Hampton."[6] To Hassam and many others, the region must have seemed like the seventh New England state. Moreover, it was only 110 miles east of Manhattan. And it was not only East Hampton that attracted Hassam to the area—he would find an even more remote retreat at Montauk, a strip of glacier-honed land on the eastern tip of Long Island's South Fork.[7] Here he often camped and was moved to paint supremely nostalgic images: landscapes incorporating nude figures with biblical and classical allusions.

American painters had visited and found inspiration on Long Island's South Fork beginning in the 1860s.[8] Broader interest in the resources of the East End originated with the Tile Club, a group of New York artists, writers, and journalists who began to meet in 1877 to decorate ceramic tiles and seek professional companionship. In their first summer sketching trip, in June 1878, the Tilers took the Long Island Railroad to visit East End villages, including Bridgehampton, East Hampton, and Montauk. After a trip in the summer of 1879 to explore the upstate region that had been frequented by the artists of the Hudson River School and passing 1880 with no trip, they returned in the summer of 1881 to Long Island, this time on the tugboat *P. B. Casket*. The group, which included future Impressionists Chase, John H. Twachtman, and J. Alden Weir, visited the North Shore, studied vestiges of the shipbuilding industry around Port Jefferson, and honored the memory of William Sidney Mount by stopping in Stony Brook.

The Tilers announced Long Island's attributes in a series of illustrated articles in *Scribner's Monthly*. They reported in February 1879, for example, that East Hampton "consisted of a single street, and the street was a lawn. An immense 'tapis vert' of rich grass, green with June, and set with tapering poplar-trees [actually elms] . . . bordered on either side of its broad expanse by ancestral cottages."[9] Their several articles were later excerpted in a promotional publication for the Long Island Railroad, *The New Long Island: A Hand Book of Summer Travel*.[10]

The Tile Club's well-publicized enthusiasm for the area reinforced East Hampton's appeal to several painters working in traditional styles. Among them were topographical landscapist Thomas Moran, who, with his wife, painter Mary Nimmo Moran, began visiting East Hampton in 1878 and built a house and studio there in 1884. Other traditional artists who were village denizens included Bruce Crane, Walter Clark, Frederick Dielman, and Edward Lamson Henry. The "quaint old town" was described as "An Artist's Paradise" in the *American Art Journal* in September 1880 and dubbed the "American Barbison [*sic*]" in an article in *Lippincott's Magazine* in 1883.[11] In 1885 the writer Lizzie W. Champney claimed that East Hampton was "a true artist colony, and perhaps the most popular of adjacent sketching-grounds for New York artists."[12]

Hassam called East Hampton "a beautiful little town, with its wide main street,"[13] and already in 1898, on his initial visit, found inspiration there. That first year he made a series of views of the town's historic windmills and probably painted *July Night* (fig. 239), a memorable scene that shows Mrs. Hassam silhouetted against glowing Japanese paper lanterns in Donoho's garden on the Fourth of July.[14] The quaint old shingled and clapboarded houses of the sort that had long attracted Hassam and engaged many other American Impressionists abounded in East Hampton.[15] These Long Island cottages also began to figure in his paintings and prints as early as his first visit. "It has been my life-long aim to help

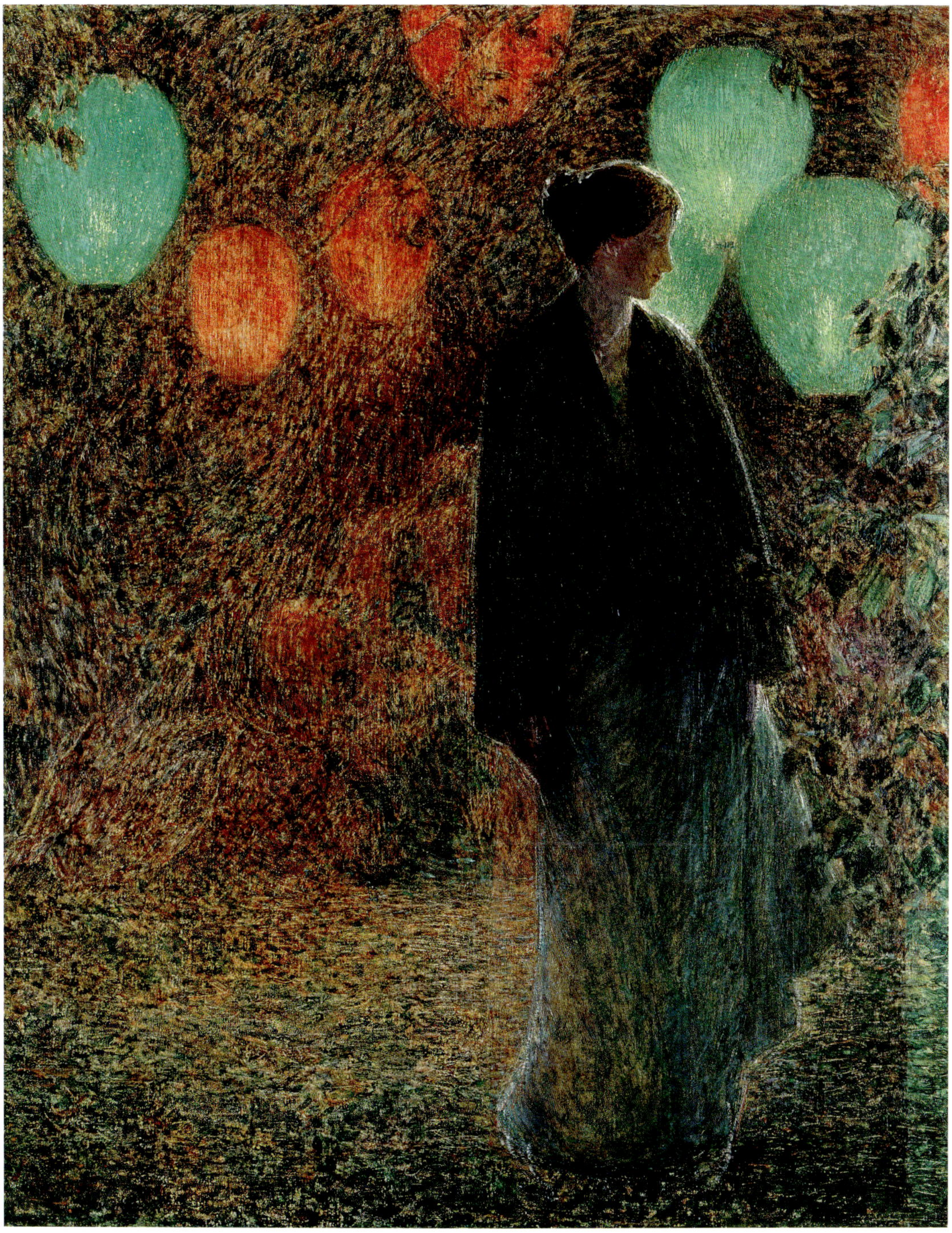

Fig. 239. Childe Hassam. *July Night*, 1898. Oil on canvas, 37½ x 30½ in. (95.3 x 77.5 cm). Private collection

retain the natural beauty and dignity of any fine old American community," he later wrote, adding, "I have always felt that to spare a fine old tree and to salvage fine old houses . . . from the hands of vandalists, constitutes the highest form of a civilized peoples' aim."[16]

The structure Hassam pictured in 1898 in *Old House and Garden, East Hampton* (fig. 240) was undoubtedly one of the "fine old houses" that had been salvaged in the town. An eighteenth-century timber-framed saltbox, it was clad in hand-shaved and squared three-foot-long cedar shingles weathered to a silver-gray color. The house featured six-over-six wood-muntin sash windows and a batten front door that opened out into a somewhat wild cottage-garden filled with old-fashioned roses and lilies.[17] Hassam had similarly combined old-fashioned architecture with old-fashioned gardens in oils, watercolors, and illustrations executed a few years

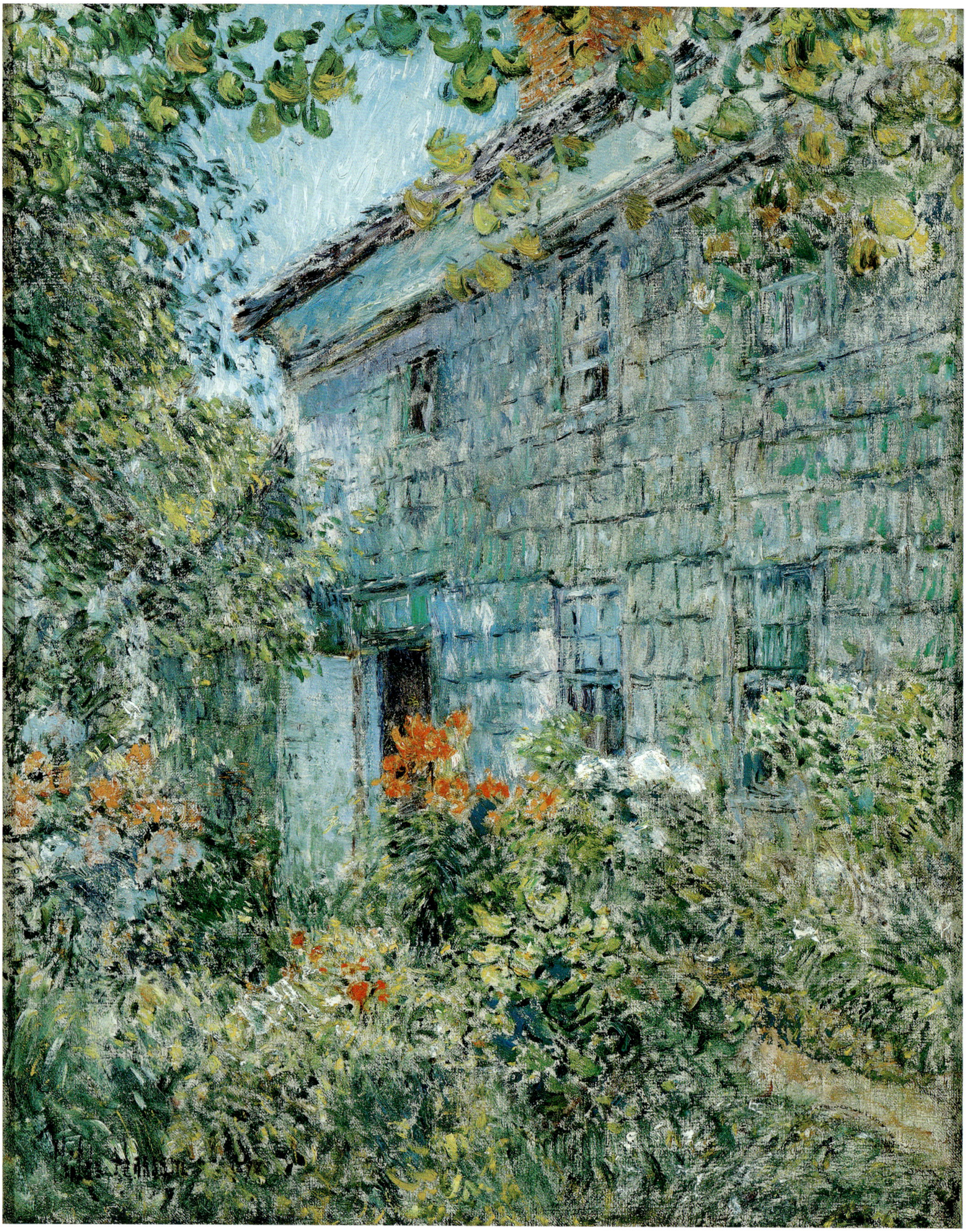

Fig. 240. Childe Hassam. *Old House and Garden, East Hampton,* 1898. Oil on canvas, 24⅛ x 20 in. (61.3 x 50.8 cm). Henry Art Gallery, University of Washington, Seattle, Horace C. Henry Collection

earlier at the Isles of Shoals, among them *The Garden in Its Glory* (fig. 129).

Old House and Garden, East Hampton, with its tapestried surface, is painted more thickly than most of Hassam's later East Hampton cottage-and-garden views. The canvas describes in detail the sort of architectural elements that most engaged him: old chimney brick, weathered shingles, and even a wrought-iron door latch. The view, which features a cropped facade and brings the observer into intimate contact with the old house, announces Hassam's usual compositional pattern for such images. It reflects as well his emphasis on a sense of domestic comfort rather than precise architectural documentation. The close-up view and profuse foliage make it difficult to identify the house, but the likeliest candidates are the Thomas Wickham House, whose address is now 134 Main Street, and the Osborne House, also known as Rowdy Hall, now 111 Egypt Lane.[18]

Hassam and his wife, Maud, went back to the Isles of Shoals in summer 1899[19] and again almost every year until about 1916. They spent time each year from 1896 to 1918 in Greenwich or Cos Cob, joined the art colony in Old Lyme most summers between 1903 and 1909, and visited Gloucester frequently in the 1890s and again in the teens. During this period they also returned occasionally to East Hampton as guests of Mr. and Mrs. Henry Keney Pomroy at Duneside near Georgica Pond in Wainscott, a hamlet in the town's southwest corner, as Hassam recalled.[20] And in midsummer 1919, soon after Hassam completed the Flag series, he bought a house in East Hampton. On August 9 he asked the Macbeth Gallery, one of his dealers, to send him "a check for my pictures sold," adding, "Mrs. Hassam has just bought a house at East Hampton, L.I. so make it as large as you conveniently can."[21]

Although Hassam favored colonial references and old-fashioned, sometimes overgrown cottage gardens for many East Hampton works, he was also enchanted by the more exotic Japanesque and Italianate gardens that engaged the interest, energy, and financial resources of several East Hampton residents.[22] An example was a Japanese-style water garden featuring a lily pond stocked with carp and surrounded by luxuriant plantings that Hassam's host Annie T. Pomroy had created at Duneside.[23] The Pomroys' garden was not, however, the only one that might have attracted Hassam's attention. Others belonged to his friends the artists Albert and Adele Herter, who also had a beautiful water garden as well as more formal Italianate "room" gardens at The Creeks, their property facing Georgica Pond. Adele Herter laid out these gardens soon after the house, designed by Grosvenor Atterbury, was completed in 1898.[24]

In 1901 Mrs. Lorenzo G. Woodhouse installed an ambitious Japanese water garden on almost four swampy acres adjacent to her estate, Greycroft, completed in 1894 on the south side of Huntting Lane in East Hampton. The Woodhouse Water Garden, which ran from Greycroft's formal lawns east to Egypt Lane, terminating just a block south of and across from the Donoho property, was said to be "the earliest documented Japanese water garden for a private home in the country."[25] It was flanked at the entrance by two teahouses and included streams, two oval lily ponds, several bridges, paths, and masses of naturalized native, German, and Siberian irises, along with Japanese varieties that Emma Woodhouse introduced to the United States.[26] These flowers, which flourish in wet soil, were at peak bloom in a blue-and-white carpet from May through July. One garden writer declared in 1910: "This garden has so completely embellished a low, far-stretching strip of marshy ground that it has become one of the most notable examples of iris planting in this country. It is a beacon light, attracting visitors from many directions; a water garden as well as an iris garden."[27] Another observed in 1915 that the Woodhouse Water Garden "is considered the best piece of work of its kind in the country. It is wonderfully composed with natural pools and streams, teahouses and rustic bridges suggestive of Japanese art, yet lovelier than the trim Oriental type of water garden because so delightfully wild and overgrown with massive plants, vines, and shrubs, without, however being disorderly in appearance."[28]

Emma Woodhouse's water garden, like those created by Mrs. Pomroy and Adele Herter, reflected the rage for Japanese art, design, architecture, and gardens aroused by the displays at the 1893 World's Columbian Exposition in Chicago and the 1894 California Midwinter Exposition in San Francisco.[29] The taste in East Hampton for such gardens, which were similar to Claude Monet's at Giverny, must also have been encouraged by their appropriateness to the topography. As garden historians have noted, "the shoreline of the East End is cut by river mouths, and many seaside ponds in the low, marshy landscape provide irresistable [*sic*] invitations for water gardeners."[30] In *July Night* Hassam had explored a formal arrangement influenced by Japanese principles, emphasizing the elegant, curvilinear shape of the female

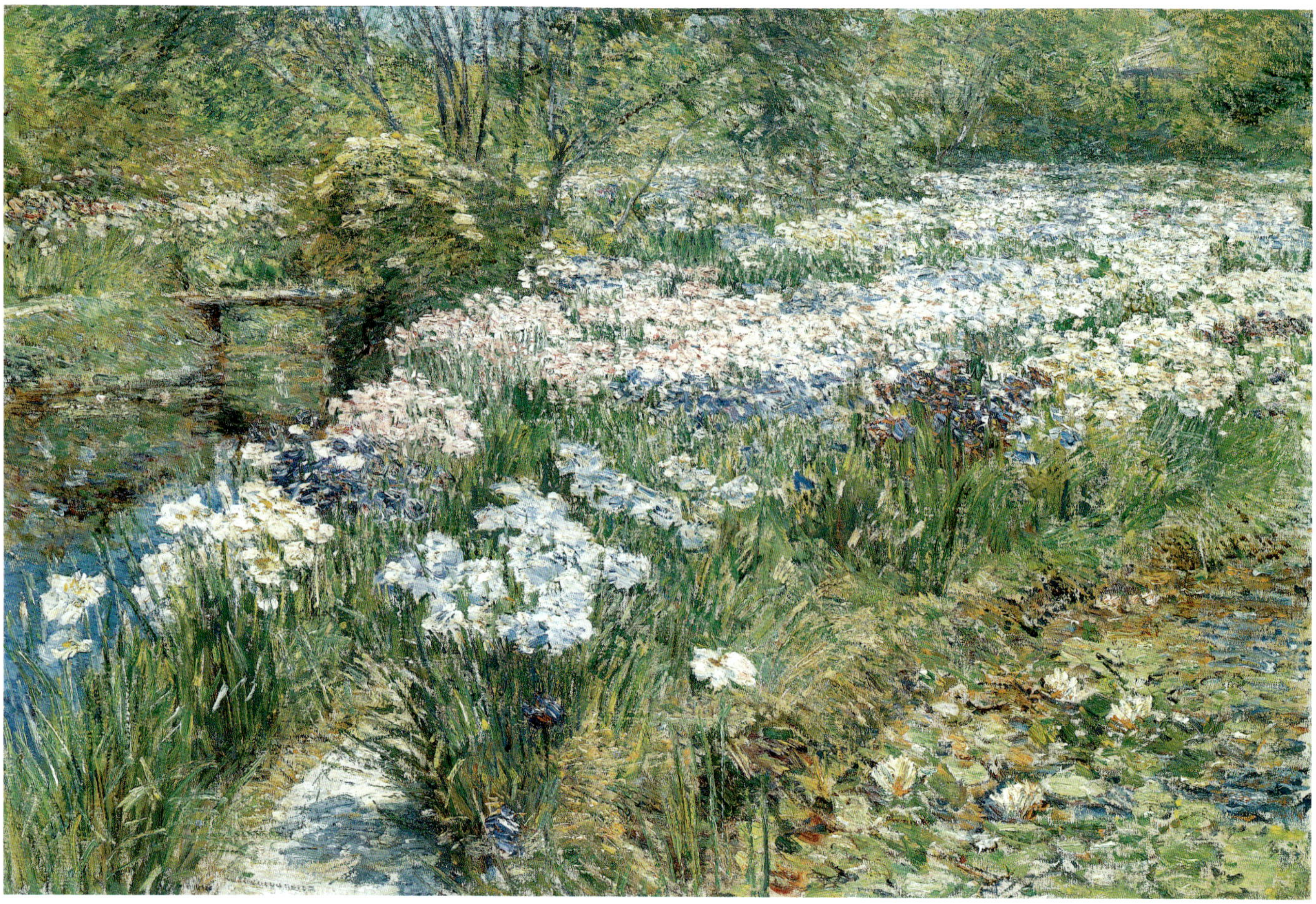

Fig. 241. Childe Hassam. *The Water Garden,* 1909. Oil on canvas, 24 x 36 in. (61 x 91.4 cm). The Metropolitan Museum of Art, New York. Partial and promised gift of Mr. and Mrs. Douglas Dillon, 1994 1994.450

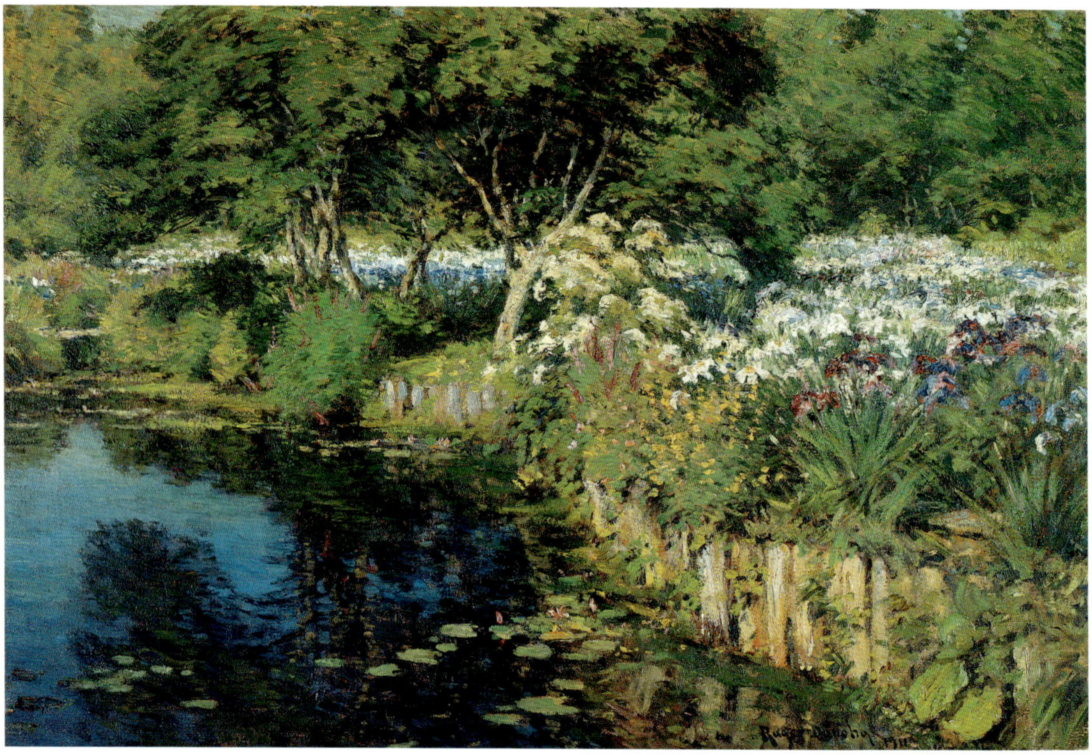

Fig. 242. G. Ruger Donoho. *Woodhouse Water Garden,* 1911. Oil on canvas, 24 x 34 in. (61 x 86.4 cm). Collection of the Guild Hall Museum, East Hampton, New York

figure placed asymmetrically against a flat, decorative backdrop of Japanese lanterns. Inevitably, in paintings inspired by East Hampton's water gardens, he also implicated Japanese design elements, balancing them with floral imagery that assumes a new importance.

The setting for Hassam's *Water Garden* (fig. 241) is almost certainly the Woodhouse Water Garden, whose vast waves of white, purple, and bluish Japanese irises along a water-lily pond are recorded in Donoho's more explicitly titled canvas *Woodhouse Water Garden* (fig. 242) and in photographs published in 1915 (see fig. 243).[31] A comparison of Hassam's and Donoho's paintings of what is presumably the same garden is instructive. Like Donoho, Hassam pictured a lily pond in the right foreground and a narrow stream traversed by a small footbridge in the left background. However, Hassam's vantage point allows the irises to obscure the receding stream and minimizes the suggestion of depth, which Donoho stressed. Instead of deep space, Hassam emphasized the abstract tapestry of color and brushstroke produced by the sunbathed floral maze. His lush, intimate canvas reveals formal discipline in its rhythmic composition, flattened space, and vigorous but orderly stitches of pigment. Hassam certainly intended this Japanese-inspired design to honor the Japanese water garden.

Hassam's *Lilies* (fig. 244) in all probability was painted in the Italianate garden Mrs. Lorenzo E. Woodhouse, the wife of Lorenzo G. Woodhouse's nephew, had constructed at her house, The Fens, which was built in 1904 on the north side of Huntting Lane.[32] While the elder Mrs. Woodhouse had chosen a natural and informal garden style in the manner of Andrew Jackson Downing and Frederick Law Olmsted, her niece Mary Leland Kennedy Woodhouse preferred the formal approach favored by later garden planners, including Olmsted's sons, John C. and Frederick Jr., and Charles Platt.[33] Concrete walls, trellis screens, and hedges divided the long rectangular garden of The Fens into "rooms" that were ornamented with flower beds, sculpture, seats, urns, and pools (see fig. 245). In *Lilies,* Hassam portrayed one such pool and a seated model in a classical gown appropriate to the Italianate setting. He also captured the distinctive way the garden was planted, with "Siberian iris, day lilies, and other typical perennials of the period . . . used, not in perennial borders, but massed at the foot of walls and around pools and garden ornaments."[34]

In the second decade of the twentieth century Hassam's visits to East Hampton continued to yield works of various kinds, among them several celebrations of the shapes, textures, and domestic details of the village's antique houses.

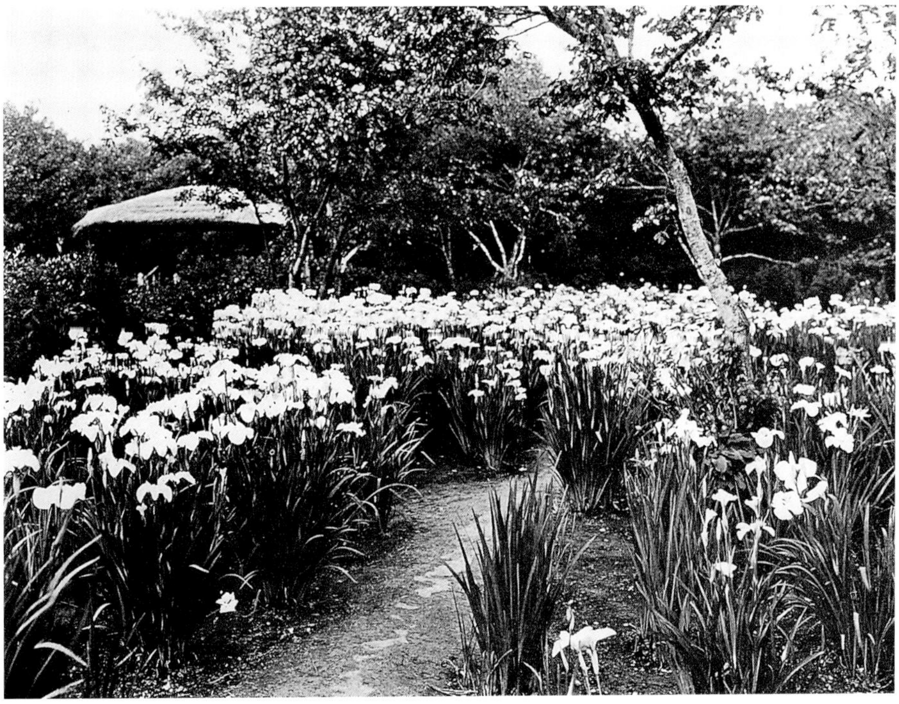

Fig. 243. Frances Benjamin Johnston and Mattie Edwards Hewitt. Woodhouse Water Garden at Greycroft, East Hampton

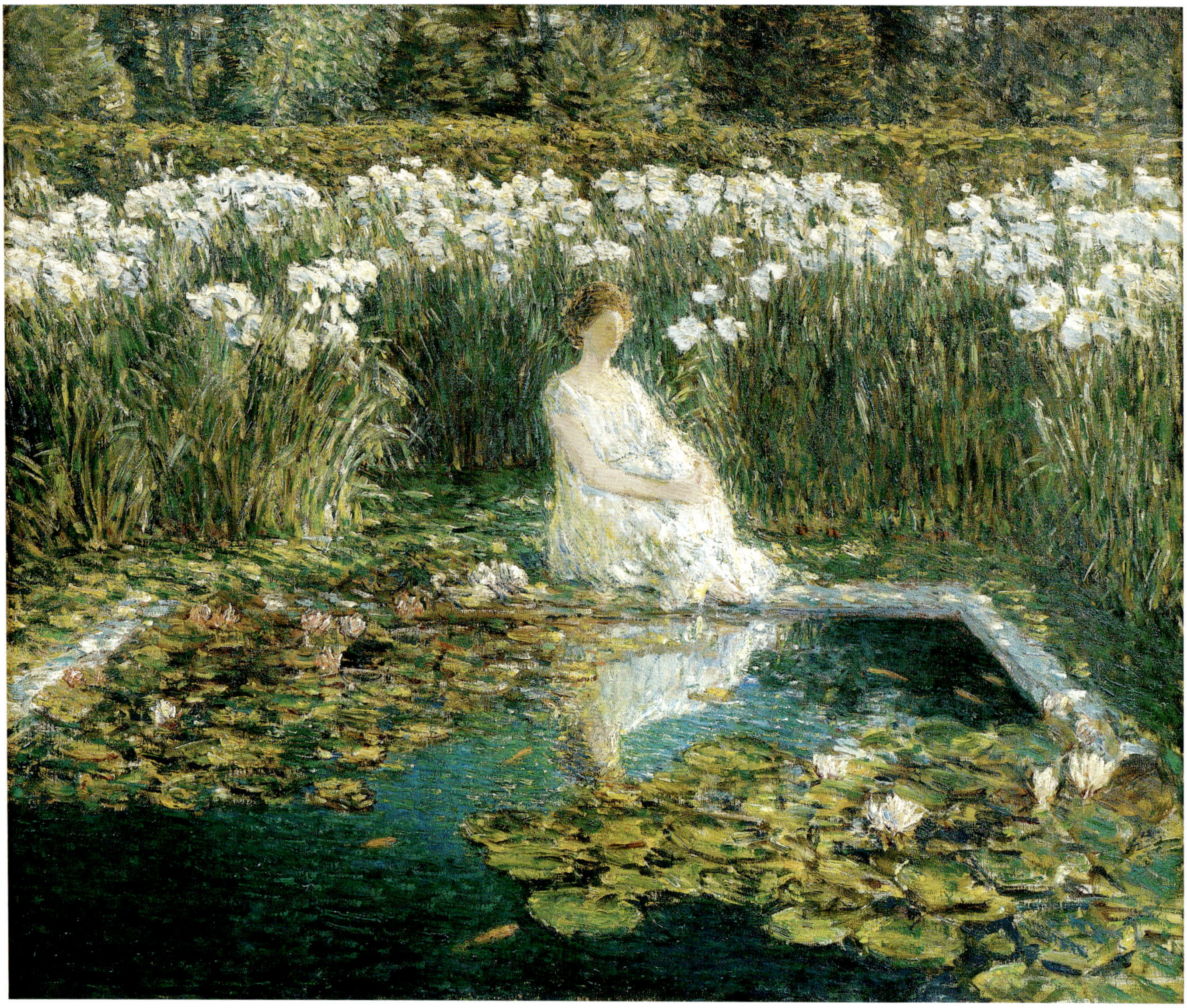

Fig. 244. Childe Hassam. *Lilies,* 1910. Oil on canvas, 27¼ x 33 in. (69.2 x 83.8 cm). Private collection

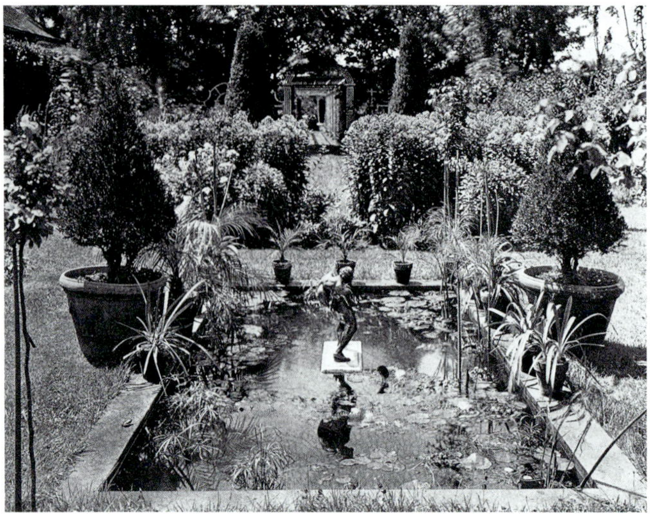

Fig. 245. Frances Benjamin Johnston and Mattie Edwards Hewitt. Mrs. Lorenzo E. Woodhouse's garden at The Fens, East Hampton

Little Old Cottage, Egypt Lane, East Hampton (fig. 246), for example, depicts a simple late-eighteenth-century timber-framed two-story saltbox. This house had been moved in 1900 by Sylvester Wines Hulse, a fisherman, from its original site at Three Mile Harbor, about five miles north of East Hampton, to Egypt Lane where it is intersected by Middle Lane. Although alterations and window rearrangements have changed the aspect of the building as it appears in the painting, it can be said that Hassam's view seems to show the principal east facade on Egypt Lane with its later one-story lean-to addition to the south. The house is covered in hand-shaved and squared three-foot-long cedar shingles weathered to a silver gray color.[35] Hassam hinted at domestic comforts by including a white cat and, next to the batten door, two ladder-back chairs that would invite conversation on the narrow porch. The small garden gate emphasizes the backyard's intimacy.

In East Hampton, Hassam frequently turned his attention to independent still lifes. Before he began to visit East Hampton, he had executed few such paintings, but he had often included still-life elements in a wide range of works focused on figures: French scenes such as *Geraniums* (fig. 79) and *Mrs. Hassam and Her Sister* (fig. 65); Appledore interiors, including *The Room of Flowers* (fig. 118) and *The Altar and Shrine* (fig. 121); Window series canvases, notably *The Table Garden* (fig. 226) and *The New York Window* (fig. 227); and pictures painted at various New England sites, for example, *Twenty-sixth of June, Old Lyme* (fig. 173), *Bowl of Goldfish* (fig. 159), and *Morning Light* (fig. 163).

The development of Hassam's independent still lifes—beginning with those he executed before he started to visit East Hampton—reflects his shifting stylistic commitments and documents his evolution from Impressionist candor to Postimpressionist deliberation. The delicate *Roses in a Vase* (fig. 247), perhaps painted at the Isles of Shoals during June—New England's Month of Roses—reiterates the colorful bouquets in clear glass vases that appeared in *Mrs. Hassam and Her Sister* and anticipates the sumptuous flower-filled glass vases Hassam would depict in *The Room of Flowers.* It also revises with an Impressionist's palette the many still-life paintings of roses that Hassam's new friend J. Alden Weir made during the 1880s.[36] Here, with an Impressionist's delight in capturing transparency and reflections, Hassam portrayed a vase of pale yellow roses, noting on its surface the reflection from a nearby window and on the shiny table the reflection of the vase and its contents.[37]

By the time he painted *Giant Magnolias* (fig. 248), probably in Old Lyme, fourteen years after he completed *Roses in a Vase,* Hassam had adopted more formal and abstract compositions and a more deliberate brushstroke. Appropriately

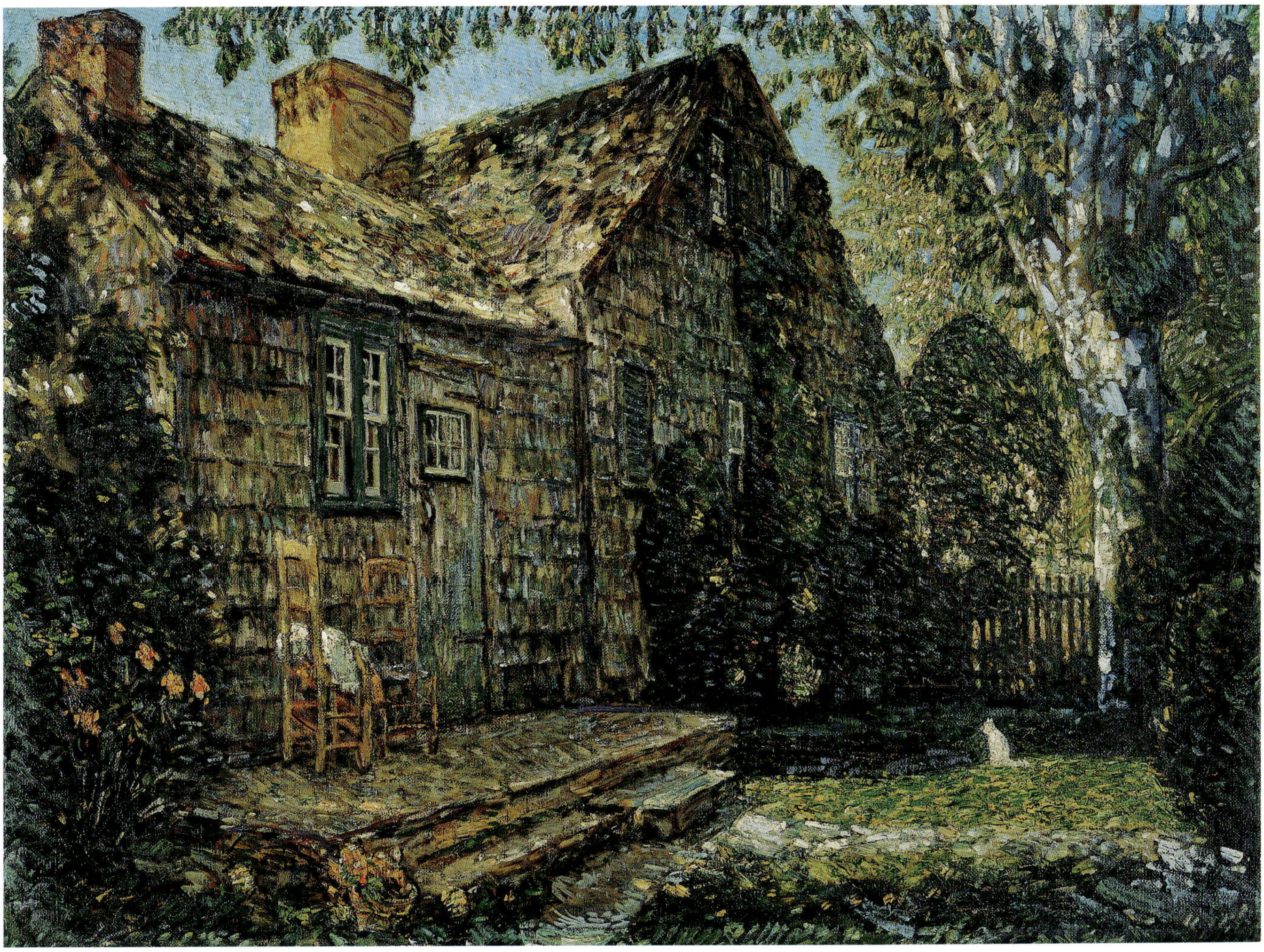

Fig. 246. Childe Hassam. *Little Old Cottage, Egypt Lane, East Hampton,* 1917. Oil on canvas, 32¾ x 45½ in. (83.2 x 115.6 cm). Collection of the Guild Hall Museum, East Hampton, New York

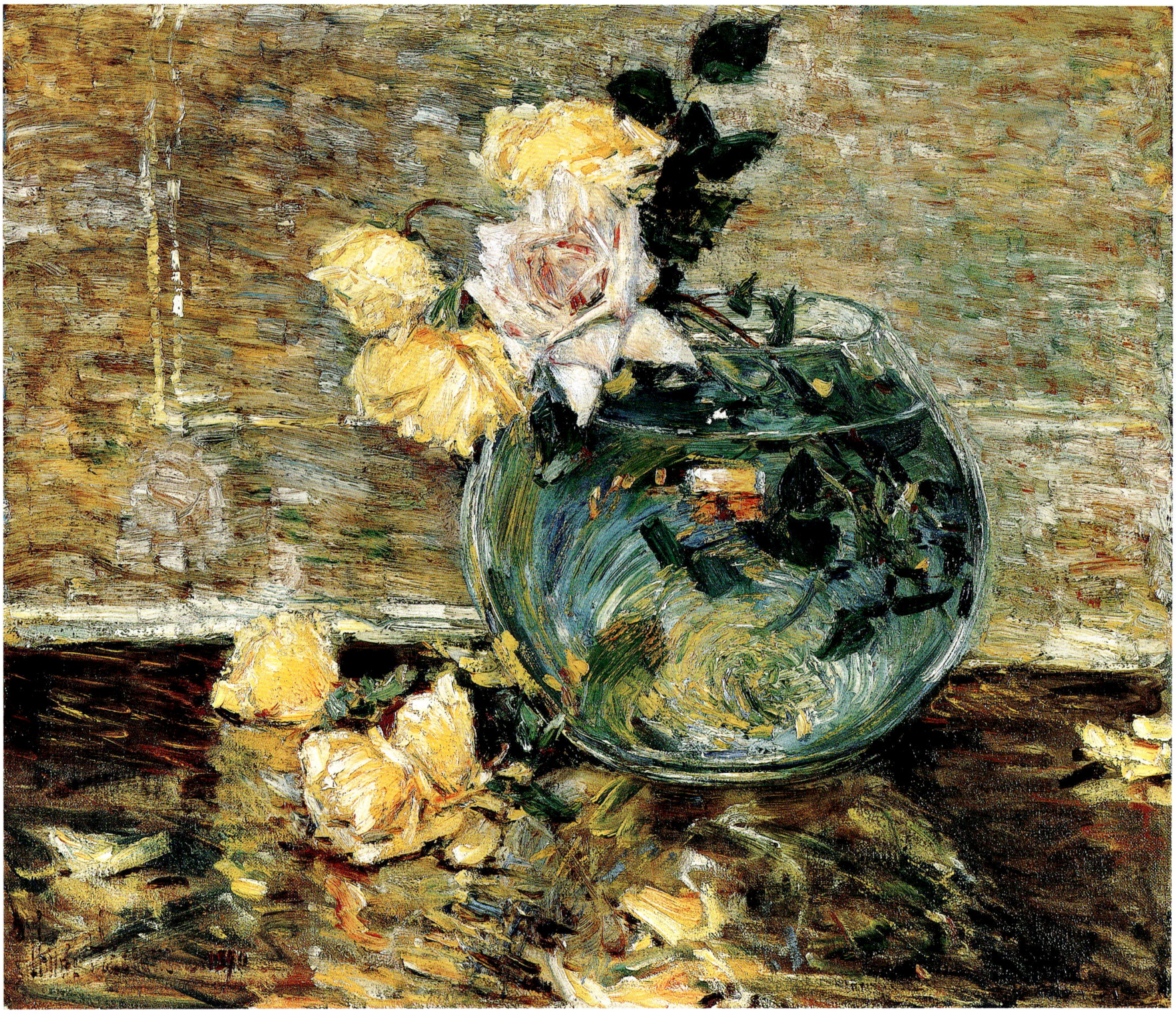

Fig. 247. Childe Hassam. *Roses in a Vase,* 1890. Oil on canvas, 20 x 24 in. (50.8 x 61 cm). The Baltimore Museum of Art: Helen and Abram Eisenberg Collection BMA 1967.36.3

for his new approach to composition, in the later picture he portrayed a trio of large, waxy magnolias in an erect triangular arrangement in place of the fragile roses with drooping stems, fallen blossoms, and scattered petals he had shown in *Roses in a Vase.* Instead of a thin glass vase, he depicted rugged stoneware and, in keeping with the nature of these objects, abandoned feathery paint application in favor of energetic strokes of viscous pigment. While Hassam once again showed reflections on a shiny tabletop, he emphasized the dynamic surface they created rather than transcribing an instantaneous impression of their effects.[38]

Winter Sickle Pears (fig. 249), which is inscribed *East Hampton Sept 24th, 1918,* presents familiar early autumn fruit scattered on a tabletop laid with a crisp white cloth. Hassam's deliberate, expressive cross-hatching of the pears and tablecloth suggests his awareness of Postimpressionist painters, including Vincent van Gogh, whose *Apples* (fig. 250) appeared at the 1913 Armory Show in New York.[39] The theme of fruit on a white cloth dynamically arranged on a tabletop also calls to mind Paul Cézanne's still lifes.

Hassam further mined Cézanne's example in another work painted in East Hampton, *Colonial Quilt* (fig. 349), which documents his embrace of formal experimentation in the early 1920s. Here he again investigated the relationship between solid forms and the flat canvas surface he had pursued in *Winter Sickle Pears.* Echoing devices Cézanne had explored, Hassam portrayed a tabletop draped with a Colonial Revival pieced or patchwork cotton quilt on which

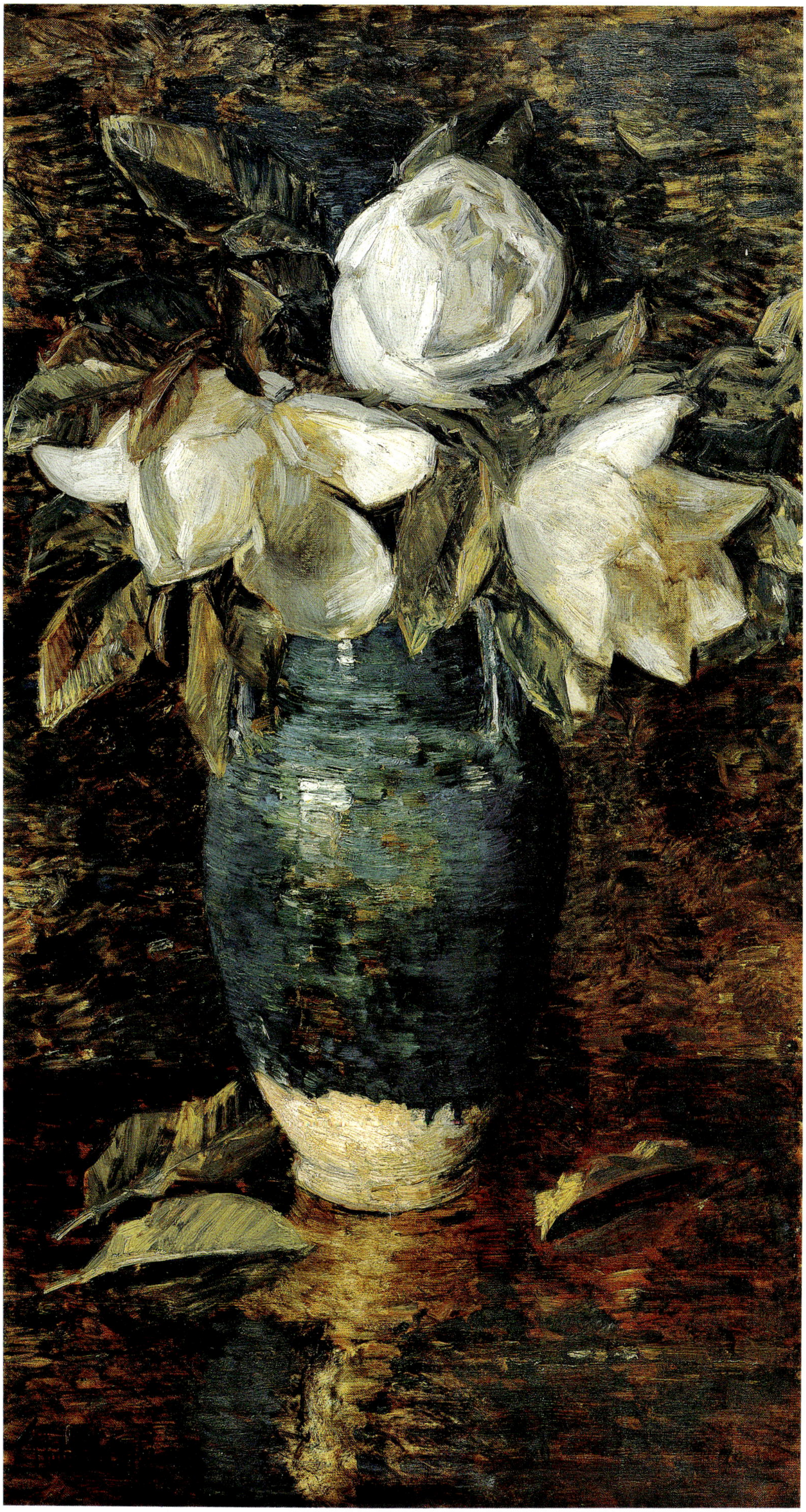

Fig. 248. Childe Hassam. *Giant Magnolias*, 1904. Oil on canvas, 35 x 20 in. (88.9 x 50.8 cm). Reynolda House, Museum of American Art, Salem, North Carolina. Original purchase fund from Mary Reynolds Babcock, Z. Smith Reynolds, ARCA, and Anne Cannon Forsyth

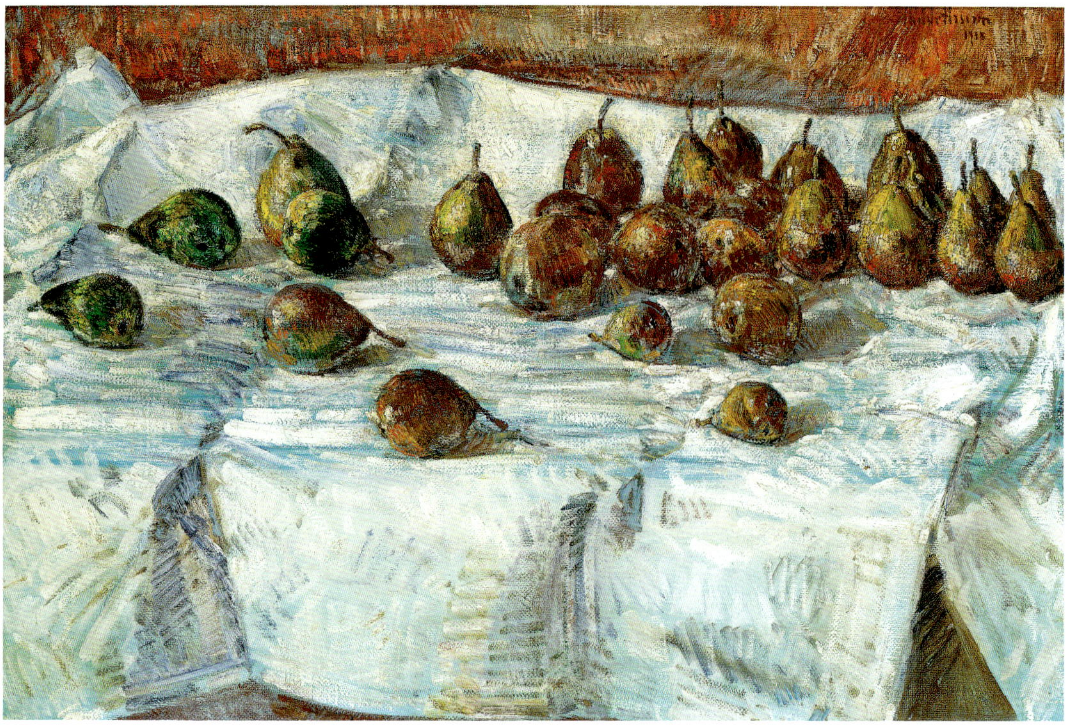

Fig. 249. Childe Hassam. *Winter Sickle Pears,* 1918. Oil on canvas, 20¼ x 30¼ in. (51.4 x 76.8 cm). Collection of Cornelia and Meredith Long

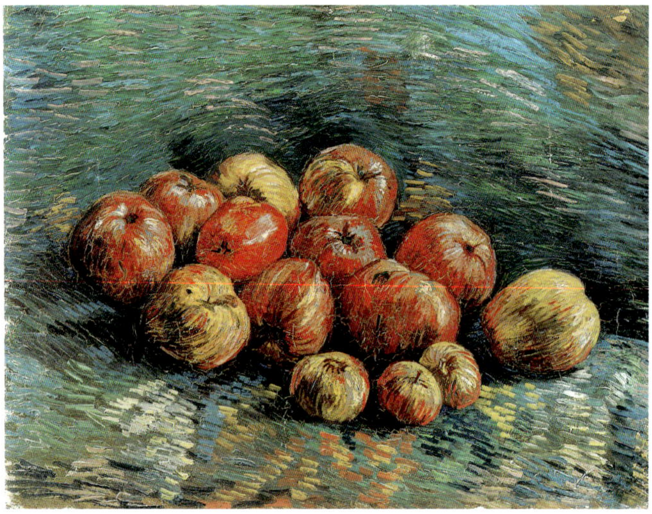

Fig. 250. Vincent van Gogh, *Apples,* 1887. Oil on canvas, 18⅛ x 24¼ in. (46 x 61.5 cm). Van Gogh Museum (Vincent van Gogh Foundation), Amsterdam

a plate of grapes is placed. The quilt and plate obscure the junction between the horizontal tabletop and vertical wall punctured by an open multipaned window. (The window is of the sort recorded in a slightly later photograph of Hassam in his East Hampton studio, which indicates this painting's origin.) The view outside the window, which would invite exploration of deep space in a traditional interior scene, insistently returns the viewer's eye to the canvas surface.

The tapestried effect of vines seen in the garden outside the window in *Colonial Quilt* is amplified in a later still life, *Heavenly Blues* (fig. 14), almost certainly painted at East Hampton. Hassam captured a wall of the China-blue trumpeting flowers and heart-shaped leaves of one of the most common varieties of morning glory and suggested the flowers' daily cycle: unfurling in the morning, closing, dying, and replacement by new blooms the next morning. In its decisive emphasis on surface patterning, *Heavenly Blues* represents a continuation and an intensification of the direction taken by Hassam's tabletop still lifes since the turn of the century. This evolution away from illusionism is apparent in other pictures as well, for example, *Long Island Pebbles and Fruit* (fig. 350) and *Formerly, Now, and Nevertheless,* 1933 (American Academy and Institute of Arts and Letters, New York).

In *Long Island Pebbles and Fruit* Hassam disposed on a monumental panel a classically balanced array of early-nineteenth-century mold-blown glass containers. The swirling patterns of these bowls and covered jars suggest their origin in glass manufactories in New England and other East Coast locales. These vessels are filled with a distinctive Long Island harvest: small quartz pebbles found on the beaches, and pears, peaches, melons, and apples that ripen in the region in late summer. The artist's focus on decorative concerns—assertive brushwork, faceted shapes, stylized forms, and certain arbitrary color choices—is echoed in the frame he designed and, apparently, constructed for the painting.[40]

The house Hassam bought in East Hampton in 1919 was Willow Bend (fig. 251), a shingled saltbox on Egypt Lane, five bays wide and with a central chimney, built about 1722 by William Barnes. Willow Bend had remained in the Barnes family until 1856, when William Barnes's great-grandson, also named William Barnes, moved to Illinois and sold it to Jeremiah Huntting. Huntting's son, David H. Huntting, sold the house to Donoho and his wife, Matilda, in 1904.[41] Hassam recalled the circumstances of his own purchase, relating that he and his wife had gone to East Hampton to visit Matilda Donoho. "The place next to her and which Ru[ger] had spent much time in remodeling, was one of the first houses ever built by one of the earliest English settlers there. It had hand hammered hinges, and if one was gone, Mr. Donoh[o] would say take this down to the village blacksmith and get another. It was filled with old furniture. Donoh[o] had rented it every year. She said now I am willing to sell this place. She named a price for us and we bought it."[42] From 1920 until the artist's death, in 1935, Willow Bend was the Hassams' residence from May through October each year.[43] In 1927 Hassam would summarize for DeWitt McClellan Lockman the way he and Maud had lived for the preceding ten years: "I have not moved out of New York, except to go to East Hampton. We have never even crossed over to New England to see our friends, which we have promised to do and might well do."[44]

The Hassams delighted in the antiquity of Willow Bend, the house that an interviewer for the *East Hampton Star* found "very lovely, with its old fireplaces and their simple mantels; old hand-made hinges on doors and cupboards; dark, rough-hewn beams left in what was the kitchen of Colonial days." The writer noted: "There are no paintings anywhere; only etchings. Mr. Hassam says they are better suited to such a house." The charm of East Hampton's 150-foot-wide main street also enchanted the Hassams. "It has a character all its own, may it never be changed!" the artist exclaimed. They loved the town's ancient byways too. "And Egypt lane—please register my protest against any 'cleaning up' of its tangle of evening primroses and blackberry," Hassam declared, warning: "East Hampton could very easily be made into a combed and manicured suburb—a New Rochelle—but it must not happen!"[45] His attraction to East Hampton's colonial buildings continued unabated. The *East Hampton Star* reported in 1925 that he was "often seen making sketches about the village," and he produced several views of the town's picturesque windmills and shingled houses.[46] He described his studio as being "on top of my garage, which is an old barn and looks out on what I call a beautiful old tree. It is very old and bent into a weird form. . . . I have used it several times." In 1922 Hassam bought four acres adjacent to his house to preserve that favored tree.[47]

Seeking to elevate the level of his art, Hassam had painted ideal nude or classically draped subjects since about 1898, often including them in his New England views. And now, during the 1920s, once he was established at Willow Bend, he often showed the familiar gardens, dunes, and beaches of East Hampton and environs as settings for antique themes or to suggest that the region was a Garden of Eden. Local people posed for the draped figures and professionals brought from New York modeled for the nudes who populated these landscapes.[48] As Stuart P. Feld has observed: "The same nymphs that had frolicked about his landscapes at Old Lyme and the cliffs at Appledore now roamed the dunes at Amagansett and Montauk. . . . Hassam had long been interested in the muses of antiquity and his Aphrodites of Appledore emerged again at Montauk in the company of other Classical and Biblical subjects."[49]

Notable among these curious hybrid works are canvases in which Hassam portrayed Montauk's barren landscape. Undertaken after he camped at Montauk with four artist friends, these paintings, like a group he executed in eastern Oregon in 1908, capture a rarely depicted locale. Inviting Hassam to exhibit his Montauk works, his dealer William

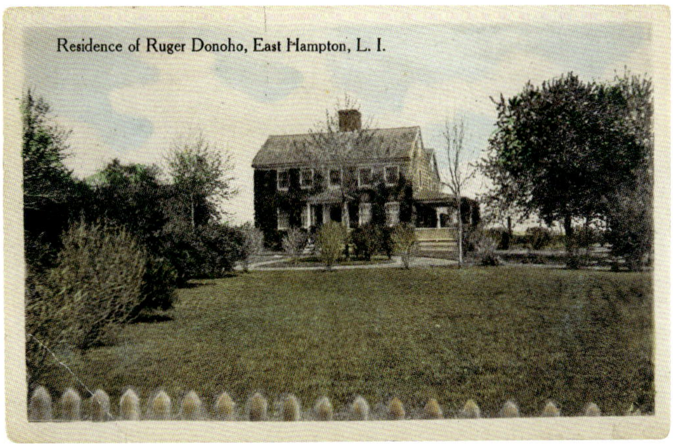

Fig. 251. Willow Bend, East Hampton. Undated postcard. Courtesy East Hampton Library, New York, Harvey Ginsberg Collection

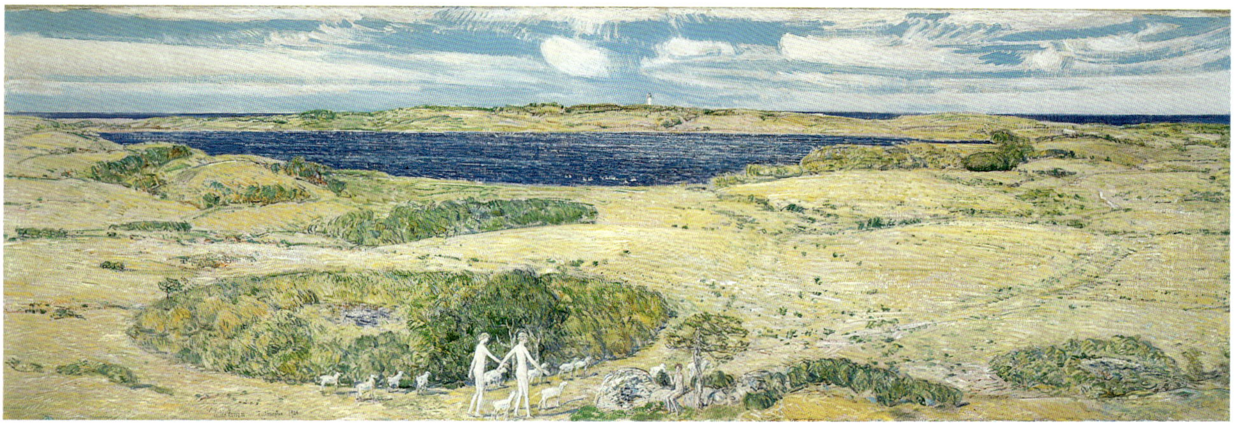

Fig. 252. Childe Hassam. *Adam and Eve Walking Out on Montauk in Early Spring,* 1924. Oil on panel, 33½ x 77 in. (85.1 x 195.6 cm). Collection of the Guild Hall Museum, East Hampton, New York

Macbeth wrote: "I believe you are the first to have painted there, and I claim at least some share of the credit because I urged it so strongly after my trip down there summer a year ago."[50]

In the introduction to the catalogue of the exhibition of Montauk pictures that opened at the Macbeth Gallery, New York, in late December 1924, collector Duncan Phillips remarked on Hassam's "eager desire to make us understand. . . . The Attica of the Age of Pericles can be made to live again on the shores of North America."[51] Critics were generally sympathetic to Hassam's attempts to restore the Age of Pericles on Long Island. Among the most supportive was Royal Cortissoz, the conservative critic for the *New York Herald Tribune,* who opined: "It has appealed to his fancy to visualize in this land of dunes and sea something of the form and movement which we associate with the age of Pericles. Nature and myth are conjoined in his work. . . . It is all rather daring—and successful."[52]

Encoded in such scenes was not only Hassam's desire to revive classical values but also his nativism, as he revealed in a newspaper interview in 1932, on the occasion of an exhibition of later images with nudes at East Hampton's Guild Hall. Hassam declared: "The Greek subjects were suggested by some of the formal East Hampton and Southampton gardens, and our blond and blue-eyed American girls made me think that it was all just the same as in the age of Pericles. For the Greeks were Nordics and their sculpture (their painting being lost) [w]as surely blue-eyed and blond, just as the people of the Renaissance in Italy were northern."[53]

The panoramic *Adam and Eve Walking Out on Montauk in Early Spring* (fig. 252) is one of Hassam's most ambitious Long Island landscapes featuring nude figures.[54] It "created a stir" at the opening of the hundredth annual exhibition of the National Academy of Design in New York in April 1925, according to one writer. "There was a throng around it most of the afternoon," this reporter noted, adding: "Adam and Eve are shown strolling hand-in-hand on the dunes in the foreground of the picture, with the blue sea and the Montauk lighthouse in the background. Round about them is a flock of lambs, some gamboling on the green, and nearby, under a tree, sits Pan with his pipes."[55] Painted in oil on a wood panel seventy-seven inches wide, the picture with Adam and Eve is typical of many of the East Hampton and Montauk scenes in its grandiose size and elongated format.[56] In their scale and subject these "decorative panels"[57] invoke the allegorical murals Hassam had painted years before for C. E. S. Wood's Portland library (fig. 203) and for the Panama-Pacific International Exposition (fig. 210) as well as contemporary ideal and symbolist works by Pierre Puvis de Chavannes.[58]

Hassam keenly appreciated Montauk's timeless, unspoiled beauty. In 1925 he remarked: "Montauk must look now as it looked countless ages ago, when . . . gods had played their last game of jack stones (the great boulders, erratics), the mosses and low flowers grew then as they do now and there could be no great forests, no higher than now, for the winds were always blowing. The gods were always there, too, and that favored people of the gods, the Greeks, were there."[59] He also revealed his feelings for the region in 1926, when he explained his intentions for his painting of Adam and Eve to its purchaser, Edward E. Bartlett, who would give it to East Hampton's Guild Hall Museum in 1938: "This spring landscape of mine, the spring of the year and the springtime of life (according to our early teaching anyway) is Montauk as it looked and must have looked for untold ages at that time of the year. There is no more beautiful or classic stretch of landscape anywhere: most barren—bare places if you will are always beautiful—they are like the nude, they contain the essence of beauty and are therefore classic."[60]

Although Hassam's identification of Montauk with the Edenic and antique spirit may now seem incongruous, the notion was, in fact, consistent with a description of the remote, uninhabited locale that appeared in a mundane contemporary source—a promotional brochure issued by the Long Island Railroad in 1921, which read:

> *For rugged scenery there is nothing to equal Montauk. The bluffs range from fifty to one hundred feet in height, and from these points of vantage the expanse of the sea is grand and inspiring. It is weird in its solitary isolation, scarred with winds and waves, having grandeur of outline, and yet its summit is softened with greenest grass, and all the tender grace that Nature gives. It is a place of dreams separated from the world's great life, with little around it but the silent reaches of land and the great mystery of the illimitable sea.*[61]

Hassam knew that Edenic Montauk would soon "change to just another American seashore settlement," as Duncan Phillips observed in the Macbeth Gallery catalogue that accompanied the artist's 1924–25 exhibition there.[62] Depicting Montauk peopled by biblical and classical figures would express its timeless virtues and preserve those virtues, even if only in paint.

Describing his ideal East Hampton works and implicitly answering hostile critics, Hassam invoked Kenyon Cox, an academic painter who disdained Impressionism and modernism and esteemed the human figure as the supreme subject of art. Hassam noted in 1927: "I painted the Montauk series, a landscape with figures, the nude, using models down there when possible and completing them here in New York. . . . That is the last group of things I did, that is treating the modern with the classic. My friend [K]enyon Cox, if he were alive, would understand my point of view."[63] It was not only the devout academic Cox who had responded to modern life by inventing mythical visions.[64] Images of ideal figures in generalized, imaginary landscapes were painted by Hassam's friends Thomas W. Dewing, Thomas Alexander Harrison (see fig. 253) and Albert Pinkham Ryder, as well as by Arthur B. Davies, Louis Michel Eilshemius, among numerous contemporary artists. Alfred Stieglitz and Clarence White made photographs in a similar spirit. Thomas Eakins (see fig. 254) painted Arcadian figures in naturalistic landscapes; muralist John La Farge portrayed allegorical figures against naturalistic backgrounds; other muralists, including Cox, Edwin H. Blashfield, Will H. Low, Robert Reid, and Abbott H. Thayer depicted ideal themes with abstract backgrounds.[65] Hassam's efforts differed from those of his contemporaries not in substance but in recording impressionistically rendered identifiable landscape settings for mythical characters.

By the time Hassam began to frequent East Hampton, increasing property values and gentrification were sapping its power as an artistic magnet. He remarked matter-of-factly in 1923: "Twenty-five years ago there were many artists here;

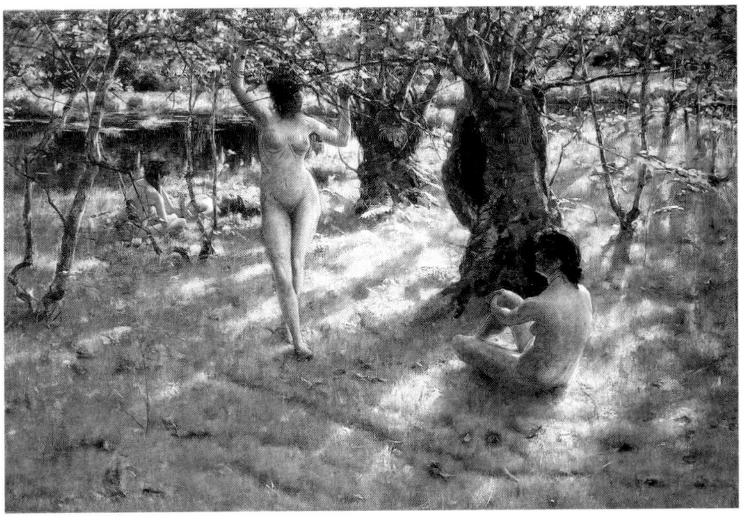

Fig. 253. Thomas Alexander Harrison. *In Arcadia,* ca. 1888. Oil on canvas, 77½ x 114½ in. (196.9 x 290.8 cm). Musée d'Orsay, Paris

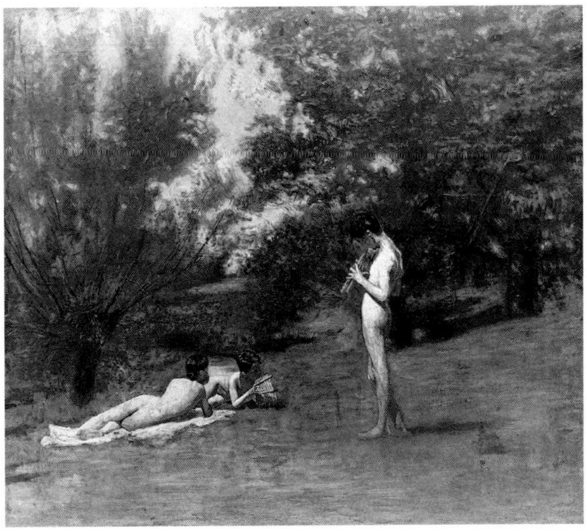

Fig. 254. Thomas Eakins. *Arcadia,* ca. 1883. Oil on canvas, 38⅜ x 45 in. (98.1 x 114.3 cm). The Metropolitan Museum of Art, New York. Bequest of Miss Adelaide Milton de Groot (1876–1967), 1967 67.187.125

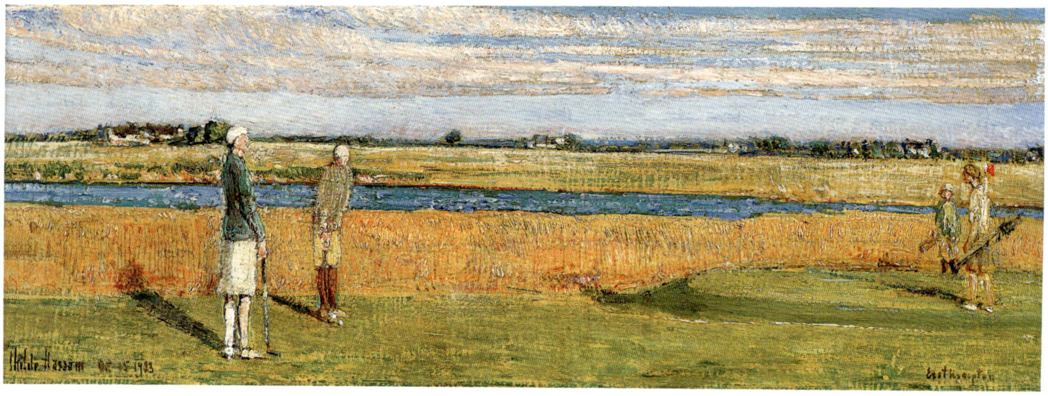

Fig. 255. Childe Hassam. *The Dome Green (Maidstone),* 1923. Oil on wood panel, 8 x 21 in. (20.3 x 53.3 cm). American Academy of Arts and Letters, New York

not so many now."[66] He had, however, become the leader of the town's small artists' community after Thomas Moran moved to California in 1922.[67] He also enjoyed East Hampton's social and recreational activities, especially the genteel Maidstone Club, founded in 1891, where he swam every day and on whose course at the end of Egypt Lane he played golf (see fig. 255). "I belong to the Golf Club, swim and paint when I feel like it," he told Lockman.[68] As an obituary notice stated, "He lived with gusto, smoked a pipe, played golf, kept a good cellar, buffeted the East Hampton surf with a great, bronzed body, and worked joyously until his last illness."[69]

Hassam's death at East Hampton on August 27, 1935, two months before his seventy-sixth birthday, "added a coda to the art colony's swan song," as art historian Helen Harrison has noted.[70] Not until the late 1940s, when the less affluent section known as Springs became a crucible for the development of Abstract Expressionism, did East Hampton again flourish as an artistic center.

1. Lockman interview, February 2, 1927, p. 10.
2. Ibid.
3. Mississippi-born Donoho (1857–1916) studied in the United States at Cooper Union, New York (1878–80), the Art Students League, New York (1878–80), and in France, where he showed in the Salons from 1881 through 1887. He established a reputation as a landscape painter upon his return to New York in 1887. See Stephanie L. Herdrich, "Hassam in Boston, 1859–1886," in this publication, p. 40. The principal source on Donoho is René Paul Barilleaux and Victoria J. Beck, *G. Ruger Donoho: A Painter's Path,* exh. cat. (Jackson: Mississippi Museum of Art in Association with University Press of Mississippi, 1995). See also Susan G. Larkin, catalogue entry on Donoho's *Windflowers,* 1912 (The Metropolitan Museum of Art, New York, 17.36), in H. Barbara Weinberg and Susan G. Larkin, *American Impressionists Abroad and at Home: Paintings from the Collection of The Metropolitan Museum of Art,* exh. cat. (New York: American Federation of Arts, 2000), p. 80, and Lisa N. Peters, catalogue entry on Donoho's *A Garden,* 1911 (Art Gallery of Ontario, Toronto), in Lisa N. Peters, *Visions of Home: American Impressionist Images of Suburban Leisure and Country Comfort,* exh. cat. (Carlisle, Pa.: Trout Gallery, Dickinson College, 1997), p. 120. Donoho's conversion from a painter of Barbizon-inspired landscapes to an Impressionist and his frequent emulation of Hassam's subjects, as, for example, in *Woodhouse Water Garden* (fig. 242) and *Windflowers,* was encouraged by his growing friendship with Hassam. Hassam led a group of artists who organized a memorial exhibition for Donoho, and he wrote the foreword to its catalogue. See *Memorial Exhibition, Paintings by the Late Ruger Donoho,* exh. cat. (New York: Macbeth Gallery, November 14–27, 1916). Maria Naylor, ed., *The National Academy of Design Exhibition Record, 1861–1900,* 2 vols. (New York: Kennedy Galleries, 1973), vol. 1, p. 245, lists Donoho's New York City address as 146 West 55th Street. In various years from 1909 to 1915 the *American Art Annual* lists his address as 130 West 57th Street, where Hassam had moved by January 1909. See *American Art Annual* 7 (1910), p. 119; 10 (1913), p. 250; 12 (1915), p. 362. "A Tribute to the Late Mrs. Ruger Donoho," *East Hampton Star,* August 3, 1939, p. 4, describes her passion for gardening and notes her charter membership in the Garden Club of East Hampton.
4. Dona L. Brown, "The Tourist's New England: Creating an Industry, 1820–1900" (Ph.D. diss., University of Massachusetts at Amherst, 1989), p. vii. See also Alan Axelrod, ed., *The Colonial Revival in America* (New York: W. W. Norton, 1985); Dona L. Brown, *Inventing New England: Regional Tourism in the Nineteenth Century* (Washington, D.C.: Smithsonian Institution Press, 1995); and Truettner and Stein 1999.
5. See Susan G. Larkin, "The Cos Cob Clapboard School," and Jeffrey W. Andersen, "The Art Colony at Old Lyme," in *Connecticut and American Impressionism,* exh. cat. (Storrs: William Benton Museum of Art, University of Connecticut, 1980), pp. 82–99, 114–37; Michael Jacobs, *The Good and Simple Life: Artist Colonies in Europe and America* (Oxford: Phaidon Press, 1985); Jeffrey W. Andersen, *En Plein Air: The Art Colonies at East Hampton and Old Lyme, 1880–1930,* exh. cat. (Old Lyme: Florence Griswold Museum; East Hampton: Guild Hall Museum, 1989); Weinberg, Bolger, and Curry 1994, pp. 88–133; Peters, *Visions of Home;* and Susan G. Larkin, *The Cos Cob Art Colony: Impressionists on the Connecticut Shore,* exh. cat. (New York: National Academy of Design; New Haven: Yale University Press, 2001).
6. O. B. Bunce, "Scenes in Eastern Long Island," in *Picturesque America,* edited by William Cullen Bryant, 2 vols. (New York: D. Appleton, 1872), quoted in Ronald G. Pisano, *Long Island Landscape Painting, 1820–1920* (Boston: Little, Brown, 1985), p. 8.

7. For East Hampton in general, see Jeannette Edwards Rattray, *East Hampton History, Including Genealogies of Early Families* (East Hampton: Star Press, 1953), and Averill Dayton Geus, *From Sea to Sea: 350 Years of East Hampton History* (West Kennebunk, Maine: Phoenix Publishers, 1999). For Montauk in general, see Jeannette Edwards Rattray, *Montauk: Three Centuries of Romance, Sport, and Adventure* (East Hampton: Star Press, 1938).
8. William H. Gerdts, "East Hampton, Old Lyme, and the Art Colony Movement," in Andersen, *En Plein Air*, p. 17, mentions East Hampton scenes by Gilbert Burling and William Magrath that were exhibited in New York in the late 1860s.
9. W. MacKay Laffan and Edward Strahan [Earl Shinn], "The Tile Club at Play," *Scribner's Monthly* 17 (February 1879), p. 464.
10. *The New Long Island: A Hand Book of Summer Travel Designed for the Use and Information of Visitors to Long Island and Its Watering Places* (New York: Rogers and Sherwood, 1879). The Tile Club's activities are summarized in Pisano, *Long Island Landscape Painting*, pp. 3–6, on the basis of their articles, published in *Scribner's Monthly* 17 (January and February 1879) and 19 (March 1880), and *Century* 23 (February 1882); and Edward Strahan [Earl Shinn] and F. Hopkinson Smith, *Book of the Tile Club* (Boston: Houghton Mifflin, 1887). A more extensive account is Ronald G. Pisano, *The Tile Club and the Aesthetic Movement in America*, with essays by Mary Ann Apicella and Linda Henefield Skalet, exh. cat. (New York: Harry N. Abrams in association with The Museums at Stony Brook, New York, 1999).
11. "From Week to Week. An Artist's Paradise—Easthampton, L.I.," *American Art Journal* 33 (September 18, 1880), p. 329, quoted in Gerdts, "East Hampton, Old Lyme, and the Art Colony Movement," p. 17; Charles Burr Todd, "The American Barbison [*sic*]," *Lippincott's Magazine*, n.s., 5 (April 1883), p. 323.
12. Lizzie W. Champney, "The Summer Haunts of American Artists," *Century* 30 (October 1885), p. 848, quoted in Pisano, *Long Island Landscape Painting*, p. 9. A helpful summary of the East Hampton art colony is Helen A. Harrison, "East Hampton's Artists, in Their Own Words," in Andersen, *En Plein Air*, pp. 49–55.
13. Lockman interview, February 3, 1927, p. 2.
14. See *Exhibition of Paintings by Childe Hassam, N.A., Covering the Period from 1888 to 1919, together with Etchings, Water Colors, and Pastels* (New York: Macbeth Gallery, April 1929), no. 10, *Old Hook Mill, Easthampton*—1898, and no. 25, *Windmill at Sundown, Easthampton*—1898. A painting (fig. 297) that bears the latter title is in the Huntington Museum of Art, Huntington, West Virginia. *Exhibition of the Works of Childe Hassam*, exh. cat. (New York: American Academy of Arts and Letters, April 21–October 21, 1927), no. 30, *July Night*, lent by Mrs. Hassam, was described (by Hassam): "Painted at Easthampton in Ruger Donoho's garden. Mr. Alexander Harrison and Mr. Donoho arranged these lanterns for a Fourth of July celebration in 1898. Portrait of Mrs. Hassam." *July Night* is signed and dated at the lower left *Childe Hassam 1900* and inscribed on the verso *C.H. 1898*. John Esten (1997, p. 8), notes: "The painting was first displayed publicly at the 76th annual exhibition of the National Academy of Design in January 1901. It is reasonable to speculate that Hassam dated the front of the canvas when he submitted it to the jury in late 1900 so it would appear to be a newly completed work."
15. For an account of the American Impressionists' interest in old dwellings and traditional landscapes, see David Schuyler, "Impressionist Artists and the Rediscovery of American Places," in Peters, *Visions of Home*, pp. 35–51.
16. Childe Hassam, "Foreword," in *An Exhibition of Paintings, Etchings, Drawings and Lithographs by Childe Hassam*, exh. brochure (East Hampton: Guild Hall, July 17–August 8, 1932). The last sentence in the copy of the "Foreword" preserved in the Hassam Papers, reel NAA2, frame 414, is annotated (probably in Hassam's hand) to read: "constitutes one of the highest forms of a civilized peoples' aim."
17. For the description of this house and others mentioned in this chapter, the author is grateful to Cynthia Schaffner, Research Assistant, Department of American Decorative Arts, The Metropolitan Museum of Art.
18. According to Dorothy King, Pennypacker Long Island Collection of the East Hampton Library, house numbers were assigned in 1954. See also "Carrier Mail May Be in Effect June 1," *East Hampton Star*, April 29, 1954, p. 1, which states: "The next step toward carrier delivery is to have all houses in the district numbered, and to secure four men to carry the mail." The Thomas Wickham House, said to have been built in 1663 for Captain Thomas Wickham, now possesses three of the distinguishing elements that appear in Hassam's picture: a central chimney, six-over-six windows, and a boxed cornice. See Jeannette Edwards Rattray, *Up and down Main Street: An Informal History of East Hampton and Its Old Houses* (East Hampton: *East Hampton Star*, 1968), pp. 31–32. The Osborne House originally stood on the east side of Main Street. Miss Annie Huntting opened the house to boarders in 1891, attracting young artists who earned it the appellation "Rowdy Hall." Soon after Miss Huntting established another boardinghouse in 1895, the Osborne House was moved to Gay Lane and from there was moved again, in 1925, to Egypt Lane. Distinguishing elements of the Osborne House seen in Hassam's view include: the off-center chimney, fascia board at the cornice, asymmetrical fenestration (which was changed in 1926, possibly from six-over-six), and the multiple-light dormer over the door. See Rattray, *Up and down Main Street*, pp. 35–36. Rattray's accounts are quoted in "Building-Structure Inventory Forms [1979]," completed by Robert Hefner and Alison Hoagland, in Incorporated Village of East Hampton and Ladies' Village Improvement Society, Long Island Collection, East Hampton Library, East Hampton, New York; retrieved by Cynthia Schaffner, Research Assistant, Department of American Decorative Arts, The Metropolitan Museum of Art, to whom the author is indebted.
19. *Social Register* 13, no. 9 (August 1899), p. 134, lists Hassam and his wife at "Isle of Shoals, NH."
20. "We used to visit the Pomroys every spring and autumn until I went to live there." Hassam in Lockman interview, February 2, 1927, pp. 23–24. Mr. and Mrs. Henry K. Pomroy appear in the *Social Register* for the first time in vol. 13, no. 9 (August 1899), p. 231, where they are listed as at Wainscott. The Pomroys are absent from the *Social Register, Summer* from 1905 to 1907. Mrs. Pomroy, whose maiden name is given as "Annie T. Moseley" in *Social Register, Summer* 29, no. 69 (June 1915), p. 219, apparently died before June 1920: only her widower is included in *Social Register, Summer* 34 (June 1920), p. 237, the first year in which Mr. and Mrs. Childe Hassam are listed (p. 113) at "Easthampton LI." The author thanks Cynthia Schaffner, Research Assistant, Department of American Decorative Arts, The Metropolitan Museum of Art, for her help with these records. Henry Keney Pomroy was elected to membership in the New York Stock Exchange in 1878 and was its vice-president (1901–4) and president (1904–7). See "H. K. Pomroy Dies; Veteran Broker," *New York Times*, December 24, 1925, p. 13.
21. Hassam, East Gloucester, Mass., August 9, 1919, to [Robert] McIntyre, Macbeth Gallery Papers, Archives of American Art, Smithsonian Institution, reel NMc51, frame 829.

22. Most of the information on the East Hampton gardens that attracted Hassam's interest was gathered by Lisa Miller, to whom the author is indebted.
23. Mrs. Chauncey B. Garver (née Virginia Rook), Mrs. Hassam's great-niece and the artist's secretary, telephone conversations with Judith Wolfe, Curator, Guild Hall Museum, East Hampton, January and February 1981, cited in Judith Wolfe, "Childe Hassam in East Hampton—a Note," in Hassam (East Hampton) 1981, p. 13. Warren Adelson, "Cosmopolitan and Patriot," in Adelson, Cantor, and Gerdts 1999, p. 56, notes Mrs. Pomroy's concern with gardening but gives her name as Gwendolyn.
24. Deborah Nevins, "The Triumph of Flora: Women and the American Landscape, 1890–1935," *Magazine Antiques* 127 (April 1985), pp. 908, 911.
25. Ellen R. Samuels, "The Woodhouse Landscapes of Huntting Lane," in Ellen R. Samuels et al., *East Hampton Invents the Culture of Summer: The Legacy of the Woodhouse Family of Huntting Lane* (East Hampton: East Hampton Historical Society, 1994), p. 49. The present account of the Woodhouse Water Garden also relies on Samuels's essay, pp. 49–55; a map of the Water Garden (p. 48); and maps of all the Woodhouse properties (pp. 34–35). See also Barilleaux and Beck, *Donoho: A Painter's Path,* p. 42, citing Enez Whipple, "The Japanese Water Garden and Nature Trail," October 15, 1984, manuscript, East Hampton [Free] Library. Lorenzo G. Woodhouse was the New York buyer for Marshall Field and Co. of Chicago for several years and had a significant financial interest in that firm. He was also an investor and held bonds and stocks of numerous cities and railroads. His estate was valued at $2,840,447.66 after he died at his East Hampton residence on September 4, 1903; see Obituary, *New York Times,* September 5, 1903, p. 7; "Funeral of L. G. Woodhouse," *New York Times,* September 8, 1903, p. 7; and "L. G. Woodhouse Estate," *New York Times,* January 6, 1904, p. 9.
26. For the history of the Japanese iris in the United States, see Currier McEwen, *The Japanese Iris* (Hanover, N.H.: University Press of New England for Brandeis University Press, 1990), pp. 8–15.
27. Alice Lounsberry, *Gardens near the Sea* (New York: Frederick A. Stokes Company, 1910), p. 193. See also ibid., pl. 56, a watercolor illustration captioned "The Water Garden."
28. Louise Shelton, *Beautiful Gardens in America* (New York: Charles Scribner's Sons, 1915), p. 129, quoted in Samuels, "Woodhouse Landscapes of Huntting Lane," p. 54. Pisano (*Long Island Landscape Painting,* p. 142), citing a letter from Enez Whipple, July 21, 1984, records that in 1934 Mrs. Donoho purchased eight acres of meadow across from her house and donated them to the town as a nature sanctuary in memory of her husband. The wife of Mrs. Woodhouse's nephew, Lorenzo E. Woodhouse, gave adjacent acreage on the northeast corner of Huntting Lane and Egypt Lane to the village in 1951. These parcels, along with a small lot added by May Rogers and the former Woodhouse Water Garden, were combined to create a twenty-three-acre nature trail and bird sanctuary, which has entirely reverted to wild vegetation.
29. Julian Ralph, *Harper's Chicago and the World's Fair* (New York: Harper and Brothers, 1893), p. 135, describing the Japanese display on the Wooded Island at the Chicago exposition, wrote: "The banks slope into the clear water of the lagoon in a very naturally ragged way, with sedge-grass and water-weeds and lilies wading out beyond the edges of the water. Little arms of vegetation and of land reach out here and there between tiny coves and bays, and the general effect is so natural and real that it amazes one to hear that it is not so. Yet the fact is that the island as we see it today is a work of art—the art of Frederick Law Olmstead [*sic*] and his partner, the landscape architects." These naturalistic effects did not, however, include an elaborate Japanese water garden, according to Robert Karr, Manager, Osaka Garden, Jackson Park, Chicago (telephone conversation, January 31, 2003), who notes that there was only minimal landscaping around the Hō-ō-den (Phoenix Temple, based on that of Byō-dō-in in Kyōto) and perhaps a small pond in front of the Tea House. The Japanese Village at the 1894 *California Midwinter Exposition* in San Francisco included a tea house and a temple set along stone-lined ponds, but not a full-dress water garden. See "Scene in the Japanese Village," in J[ames] W[illiam] Buel, *The Magic City* (Saint Louis: Historical Publishing Company, 1894; reprint ed., New York: Arno Press, 1974), unpaged.
30. Mac Griswold and Eleanor Weller, *The Golden Age of American Gardens: Proud Owners, Private Estates, 1890–1940* (New York: Harry N. Abrams in association with the Garden Club of America, 1991), p. 114.
31. Hiesinger (1994, pp. 165, 168) suggests that the subject of *The Water Garden* is the Pomroys' garden. William H. Gerdts ("Three Themes," in Adelson, Cantor, and Gerdts 1999, p. 196) maintains that although the canvas is "sometimes assumed to have been painted at East Hampton, probably also at Wainscott, there is no indication that Hassam was there that year."
32. This account of the garden at The Fens relies on Samuels, "Woodhouse Landscapes of Huntting Lane," pp. 55–60. Lorenzo G. Woodhouse was the brother of Charles W. Woodhouse, whose son was Lorenzo E. Woodhouse. Charles W. Woodhouse was the president of the Merchant's National Bank of Burlington, Vermont, until he died in 1914 and his son took over as president. Lorenzo E. Woodhouse resigned from the position in 1929 and spent his time traveling until he died, in 1935. In 1916 he and his wife donated a library to East Hampton, and in 1930 they bought land for the Guild Hall Museum, which they endowed and which opened in 1931. See Obituary, *New York Times,* January 24, 1935, p. 19, and "Mrs. Woodhouse Dead," *New York Times,* December 5, 1961, p. 43.
33. Samuels, "Woodhouse Landscapes of Huntting Lane," p. 49.
34. Ibid., p. 56. The same rectangular pool or another, similar one in the garden at The Fens appears in Hassam's *Long Island Garden,* 1922 ("property from the Kansas City Art Institute"); Sotheby's, New York, sale cat., November 29, 1995, lot 32. Adelson ("Cosmopolitan and Patriot," p. 56) and Gerdts ("Three Themes," p. 194) identify the garden in *Lilies* as being on the Pomroys' property. Gerdts adds (p. 229, n. 137) that the model for the figure was Margaret Fulton Spencer, wife of Pennsylvania Impressionist Robert Spencer, but supplies no source for this information. Margaret Fulton, an MIT-trained architect and a niece of painters Birge and Alexander Harrison, did not marry Spencer until 1914, so, if she was the model, her connection with Hassam is probably attributable to the Harrisons. We thank Thomas Folk for information on Fulton. Hassam painted an even more ambitious Italianate garden in *The Josiah Bartlett Garden, Amagansett* (dated *Aug. 1933;* Sotheby's, New York, sale cat., May 22, 2002, lot 45).
35. The current address of the house is 123 Egypt Lane. See also Lisa N. Peters, catalogue entry in Peters, *Visions of Home,* p. 92. Wolfe ("Hassam in East Hampton," p. 18, n. 11) mentions that Sylvester Hulse's grandson "knows from his father that Hassam had painted" the Hulse house and that, although it had been altered over the years, a former neighbor immediately recognized the subject when she first saw the painting at the Guild Hall in 1967.
36. See, for example, J. Alden Weir, *Roses,* probably 1880 (Addison Gallery of American Art, Phillips Academy, Andover, Massachusetts), and J. Alden Weir, *Roses,* 1883–84 (Phillips Collection, Washington, D.C.).

37. See catalogue entry in Sona K. Johnston, *American Paintings, 1750–1900, from the Collection of the Baltimore Museum of Art* (Baltimore: The Museum, 1983), p. 71.

38. See catalogue entry in *American Originals: Selections from Reynolda House, Museum of American Art*, exh. cat., essay by Charles C. Eldredge, catalogue by Barbara B. Millhouse (New York: Abbeville Press and American Federation of Arts, 1990), p. 96.

39. Association of American Painters and Sculptors, *Catalogue of International Exhibition of Modern Art, at the Armory of the Sixty-ninth Infantry . . .* (New York: Vreeland Advertising Press, 1913), no. 435; other still-life paintings by Van Gogh at the Armory Show were no. 431, *Souliers de bois;* no. 432, *Écrevisses;* no. 1049, *Red Flowers;* and no. 1050, *Lilies.*

40. For the frame, see the discussion by Susan G. Larkin in "How Hassam Framed Hassams," in this publication, p. 339. Hassam is shown working on *Long Island Pebbles and Fruit* in the documentary *Childe Hassam, Artist* (New York: The Metropolitan Museum of Art, 1932), one-reel silent film. Since the picture is placed on Hassam's easel already framed, he probably was only miming work on the panel. For mention of the film, see H. Barbara Weinberg, "Introduction," in this publication, pp. 21–22.

41. Jeannette Edwards Rattray, *Fifty Years of the Maidstone Club, 1891–1941* (East Hampton: Maidstone Club, 1941), p. 36; Rattray, *East Hampton History,* p. 36; Hefner and Hoagland, "Building-Structure Inventory Forms [1979]." Willow Bend was designated 48 Egypt Lane in 1954.

42. Lockman interview, February 2, 1927, p. 29. Robert J. Hefner, ed., *East Hampton's Heritage: An Illustrated Architectural Record* (New York: W. W. Norton and Company in association with the East Hampton Ladies Village Improvement Society, 1982), pp. 23–24, describes Donoho's renovations: "Although the fireplaces were left intact in the great chimney, the stairway was removed and the porch opened up to the adjoining front rooms. Partitions in the lean-to proper were taken out, and a free-standing open staircase of several flights was installed in the south end. An open porch on the left flank, and a gambrel-roofed ell in back equal to the original house in size, were added."

43. *Social Register, Summer* 34–49 (1920–35) list the Hassams at Willow Bend; Mrs. Hassam alone is listed in 1936. Wolfe ("Hassam in East Hampton," p. 13) notes that the couple usually remained in East Hampton until after Hassam's birthday, on October 17.

44. Lockman interview, February 3, 1927, p. 10. Adams 1938, p. 123: "Yet with all his love for movement, he had no wish to own a speed boat or to drive a car. His wife might drive, if she wished, but he himself, despite his remarkable manual control, steadfastly refused to touch a wheel. He saw that there were always plenty of other persons, young and old, ready to dash hell-for-leather through the beautiful countryside."

45. Quoted in Rattray 1923, p. 6.

46. *East Hampton Star* 40, no. 22 (April 10, 1925), p. 2, quoted in Wolfe, "Hassam in East Hampton," p. 13. See the following examples: *East Hampton House (Old Mulford House),* 1919 (New Britain Museum of American Art, Connecticut); *Hutchinson House, East Hampton, Long Island,* 1919 (New Jersey State Museum Collection, Trenton); *Old Long Island Landscape,* 1920 (American Academy and Institute of Arts and Letters, New York); *Old Mulford House, East Hampton,* 1930 (Brigham Young University Museum of Art, Provo, Utah).

47. Lockman interview, February 2, 1927, pp. 29–30.

48. Hassam mentioned "a young niece who poses for me for little Greek figures" and "several young girls who pose," and added, "if you want nude models, you have to take them down from New York." Ibid., p. 30.

49. Stuart P. Feld, "Childe Hassam—a Retrospective View in Progress," in Hassam (East Hampton) 1981, pp. 11–12. Very helpful for an understanding of Hassam's interpretation of Montauk is Linda Wassong, "Childe Hassam's *Montauk*" (research paper, Sotheby's Institute, New York, April 1998).

50. William Macbeth, New York, October 21, 1921, to Childe Hassam, New York [actually he was still in East Hampton], Macbeth Gallery Papers, reel NMc51, frame 852. The exhibition was held three years later; see *"Montauk" by Childe Hassam of the American Academy of Arts and Letters,* exh. cat. (New York: William Macbeth, Inc., December 30, 1924–January 19, 1925). Hassam's camping companions in September 1921 were painters Albert Smith, Gifford Beal, and Reynolds Beal, and sculptor Jack (John Heywood) Roudebush. See Childe Hassam, *Reynolds Beal Painting Montauk,* 1921, watercolor (private collection), reproduced in *Reynolds Beal, A.N.A., 1866–1951: Impressions of an American Artist, Paintings, Watercolors, and Drawings, Selections from the Haig Tashjian Collection,* exh. cat. (New York: Haig Tashjian Collection, 1984), p. 14. See Reynolds Beal, *Camping at Montauk with Childe Hassam,* 1921, oil on canvas, reproduced in *Reynolds Beal, 1867–1951, Paintings and Watercolors,* exh. cat. (New York: Hammer Galleries, 1976), unpaged. For Roudebush, see "J. H. Roudebush Dies in the West Indies," *New York Times,* April 24, 1925, p. 19.

51. Duncan Phillips, "Childe Hassam," in *"Montauk" by Hassam,* unpaged.

52. Royal Cortissoz, "Childe Hassam's Work on Long Island," *New York Herald Tribune,* December 28, 1924, sec. 8, p. 12.

53. Quoted in "Childe Hassam Exhibit Paintings, Etchings," *East Hampton Star,* July 22, 1932, p. 1. The article refers to *Exhibition of Paintings, Etchings, Drawings, and Lithographs by Hassam* (East Hampton, 1932), for which no checklist is available. Among the works mentioned are *The Distant Galley—Age of Pericles (Distant Galley, Montauk),* 1924 (Edwin A. Ulrich Museum of Art, Wichita State University), and *The Greeks Come Bearing Gifts—Age of Pericles,* 1924 (location unknown). The American Academy and Institute of Arts and Letters, New York, owns another work of the type, *Greek Garden—Age of Pericles,* 1924, which may also have been shown at the Guild Hall in summer 1932.

54. Related Montauk canvases include *Young Apollo and the Flying Swans* (fig. 326) and the following works in the collection of the American Academy of Arts and Letters, New York: *Georgica* (fig. 325); *Scuttle Hole Pond,* 1923; *Montauk,* 1924; *Spring on Long Island (Venus Genetrix)* (fig. 327); *Young Pan Piping,* 1928.

55. "Adam and Eve at Montauk," *East Hampton Star,* April 10, 1925, p. 2. The specific setting was Oyster Pond, in Indian Field, Montauk.

56. Cortissoz, "Hassam's Work on Long Island," p. 12: "Many of these designs are painted on long, low panels, and we find them again curiously beguiling. It is, of course, the extension of the horizon that chiefly counts, heightening our sense of romance through the always potent power of distance, but there is an indefinable element of fascination in these proportions. They have a distinction by themselves."

57. Receipt, dated January 7, 1936, for the 300 oils, 92 watercolors, 19 decorative panels, and 30 pastels that Hassam bequeathed to the American Academy of Arts and Letters, New York, Hassam Papers, reel NAA1, frame 323.

58. See, for example, Pierre Puvis de Chavannes, *The Sacred Grove, Beloved of the Arts and Muses* (fig. 53), a reduction of a large mural for the Musée des Beaux-Arts, Lyons, 1884; *A Vision of Antiquity—Symbol of Form,* ca. 1887–90 (Carnegie Museum of Art, Pittsburgh), a reduction of a large

mural for the Palais des Arts, Lyons, 1885; and *Summer,* 1891 (Cleveland Museum of Art). For Wood and the Panama-Pacific International Exposition, see H. Barbara Weinberg, "Hassam's Travels, 1892–1914," in this publication, p. 196.

59. Hassam quoted in R[obert] W. M[acIntyre], "Historical Note," in *"Montauk" by Hassam,* unpaged.

60. Childe Hassam, New York, January 20, 1926, to Edward E. Bartlett, quoted in "Bartlett Gives Hassam Picture to Guild Hall," *East Hampton Star,* June 16, 1938, p. 8.

61. *Out on Long Island* (New York: Long Island Railroad, General Passenger Department, F. M. Woodward, General Passenger Agent, 1921), col. 25.

62. Phillips, "Childe Hassam," unpaged.

63. Lockman interview, February 2, 1927, p. 27. Cox's commitment to the portrayal of the human figure is most fully articulated in Kenyon Cox, *The Classic Point of View* (New York: Charles Scribner's Sons, 1911). Cox believed (pp. 3–4), "The Classic Spirit is . . . above all, the love of permanence and of continuity. It asks of a work of art, not that it shall be novel or effective, but that it shall be fine and noble. . . . It strives for the essential rather than the accidental, the eternal rather than the momentary."

64. See Elizabeth Ewing Tebow, "Arcadia Reclaimed: Mythology and American Painting, 1860–1920" (Ph.D. diss., University of Maryland, College Park, 1987), p. 172: "As city dwellers looked to the country for respite from noise, crowding, and pollution, artists depicted rural and wilderness America as a new Arcadia, a refuge from the stress of civilized life and populated not only by noble Indians and healthy settlers, but also by nymphs, goddesses, and creatures from primitive nature myths." Tebow focuses on Hassam, pp. 95–99. The author thanks Linda Wassong for calling her attention to this source.

65. See, for example, Thomas W. Dewing, *Summer,* 1890 (Yale University Art Gallery, New Haven); Thomas W. Dewing, *In the Garden (Spring Moonlight),* ca. 1892–94 (Smithsonian American Art Museum, Washington, D.C.); Thomas Alexander Harrison, *In Arcadia* (fig. 253); Albert Pinkham Ryder, *Pegasus* (or *Pegasus Departing*), n.d. (Smithsonian American Art Museum, Washington, D.C.); Albert Pinkham Ryder, *Temple of the Mind,* 1885 (Albright-Knox Art Gallery, Buffalo); Arthur B. Davies, *A Measure of Dreams,* 1908 (The Metropolitan Museum of Art, New York, 09.72.4); Arthur B. Davies, *Girdle of Ares,* 1908–14 (The Metropolitan Museum of Art, New York, 14.17); Louis Michel Eilshemius, *Dancing in the Sunlight,* 1903 (Hirshhorn Museum and Sculpture Garden, Smithsonian Institution, Washington, D.C.); Louis Michel Eilshemius, *Figures in Landscape,* 1906 (Whitney Museum of American Art, New York); Thomas Eakins, *Arcadia* (fig. 254); John La Farge, *Music* and *Drama,* murals, 1887–88 (Whitelaw Reid Residence, now Palace Hotel, New York); John La Farge, *Athens,* mural, 1892–98 (Walker Art Building, Bowdoin College, Brunswick, Maine).

66. Quoted in Rattray 1923, p. 6.

67. Hassam recalled: "Thomas Moran was at East Hampton. Tom Moran, who I liked so much. I met him very early in my career. He was always so pleasant and courteous at East Hampton." Lockman interview, February 3, 1927, p. 3. Gerdts ("East Hampton, Old Lyme, and the Art Colony Movement," p. 16) notes that Moran moved to Santa Barbara in 1922. The Guild Hall Museum celebrated its fiftieth anniversary, in 1981, by organizing four exhibitions to honor East Hampton's key artists: Thomas Moran, Childe Hassam, Willem de Kooning, and Lee Krasner and Jackson Pollock. See Enez Whipple, "Foreword," in Hassam (East Hampton) 1981, p. 5.

68. Lockman interview, February 2, 1927, p. 29. Hassam's daily routine in East Hampton is summarized in Wolfe, "Hassam in East Hampton," pp. 15–16. Hassam's obsession with swimming is signaled by his watercolor *Through the Breakers on His Birthday* (American Academy and Institute of Arts and Letters, New York), a sheet signed and inscribed *Childe Hassam Oct. 17th—1933,* at which time the artist was seventy-four. Hassam made golf the subject of several works, including, in addition to *The Dome Green (Maidstone)* (fig. 255), *Great Peconic Bay, The National,* 1922; *The Dune Hazard [Maidstone],* 1922; *Morning on the Maidstone Links,* 1926 (all American Academy and Institute of Arts and Letters, New York).

69. "Childe Hassam, 75, Noted Artist, Dies," *New York Times,* August 28, 1935, p. 17.

70. Harrison, "East Hampton's Artists, in Their Own Words," p. 54. According to "Hassam, 75, Noted Artist, Dies," p. 17: "He was taken ill last October at his New York home, 130 West Fifty-seventh Street, and came to East Hampton in an ambulance early last Spring." By January 28, 1936, Maud Hassam had moved from Fifty-seventh Street to 850 Park Avenue in New York City, where she continued to live until her death, on October 13, 1946. See Maud Hassam, 850 Park Avenue, New York, January 28, 1936, to William Macbeth, Macbeth Gallery Papers, reel 2599, frame 43. "Mrs. Childe Hassam," *New York Times,* October 14, 1946, p. 22, notes that Mrs. Hassam "died yesterday at her residence, 850 Park Avenue, after a long illness." After her husband's death, Mrs. Hassam spent summers in East Hampton until 1942. She sold Willow Bend to Mrs. B. Mosley Stoddard in the fall of 1943. "Summer Colony," *East Hampton Star,* June 22, 1944, p. 5: "Mrs. Mosley B. [*sic*] Stoddard, who bought Mrs. Childe Hassam's house on Egypt Lane last fall [1943], will spend the summer there." "Mrs. Maude [*sic*] Hassam Widow of Artist Died Sunday in New York," *East Hampton Star,* October 17, 1946, p. 1: "The place [Willow Bend] is now owned by Mrs. B. Mosley Stoddard of New York." *East Hampton Social Guide,* annuals published by the *East Hampton Star,* in the Pennypacker Long Island Collection, East Hampton Library: (1942) Maud Hassam, Willow Bend, Egypt Lane; (1943) neither Mrs. Hassam nor Mrs. B. Mosley Stoddard is listed; (1944) Mrs. B. Mosley Stoddard, "Tobermory," Egypt Lane, E. H. [phone number] 924, 375 Park Avenue, New York.

MEDIA

SUBJECTS

PRESENTATION

MARKETING

CRITICAL RESPONSE

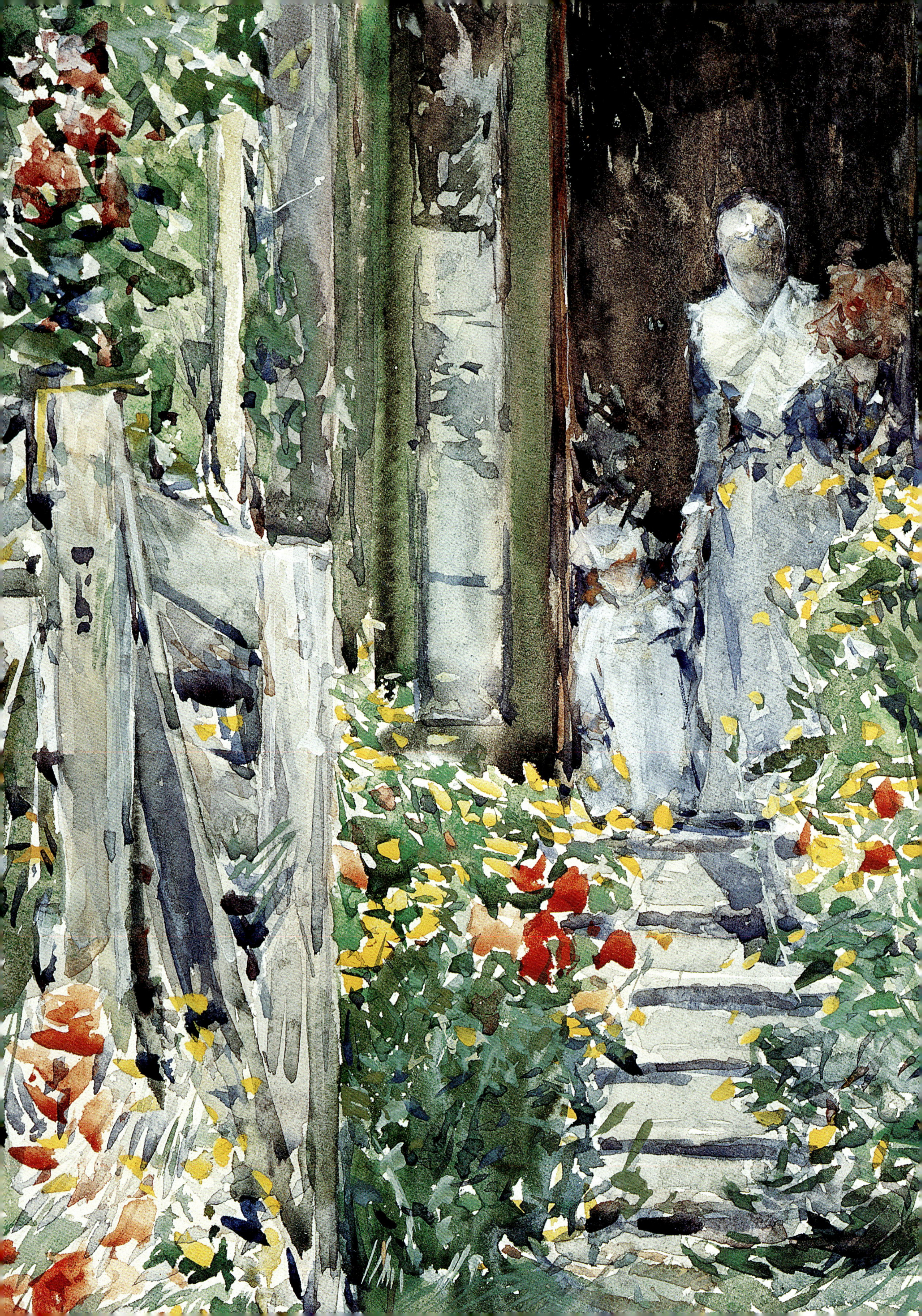

Hassam's Watercolors

Carol Troyen

In October 1912 Hassam wrote to a patron, Charlotte Buffington of Worcester, Massachusetts, concerning an early watercolor of his that she was considering: "I am glad that you like it, and that the Museum will possess it finally. To represent me well a museum must have several works and in different mediums—and this applies to a number of the modern paintings."[1] Mrs. Buffington took Hassam's advice to heart, eventually donating to the Worcester Art Museum two oils and, to stand for the "modern paintings," two additional watercolors from 1912.

Hassam's desire that museums own multiple examples and various types of his work reflects his continuing preoccupation with the marketing of his art. But more fundamentally it underscores his lifelong dedication to the so-called minor media—drawing, pastel, and especially watercolor. He began his career as an illustrator and a watercolor painter at the height of the Aesthetic Movement, which emphasized decorative values and media best suited to domestic display;[2] these concerns remained essential to his thinking throughout his career.

Hassam was an accomplished watercolor painter before he achieved proficiency in oil. His first one-man exhibition was a show of fifty-one watercolors and three drawings held at Boston's Williams and Everett Gallery in autumn 1882. This was the moment the watercolor movement in America was at its peak[3] and a time when watercolors were especially visible in Boston. Watercolors constituted nearly one-fifth of the works in the city's first major show of contemporary art, held at the Museum of Fine Arts in 1879;[4] featured were pictures by Jean-François Millet, Constant Troyon, J. Foxcroft Cole, John Appleton Brown, and others exemplifying the Barbizon aesthetic, as well as by American Pre-Raphaelites including Henry Farrer, and Charles Herbert Moore. In February 1880 a collection of watercolors by the British critic and painter John Ruskin went on view at the Museum of Fine Arts.[5] And perhaps most instructive for Hassam, in December 1880 Winslow Homer exhibited at Doll and Richards Gallery in Boston 112 watercolors and drawings, forty of which he sold for a total of $1,400.[6] Thus, just at the time Hassam was making his first sketching trips and beginning his professional studies, he saw that there was an audience and a market for watercolors. Furthermore, he became aware that this audience responded to a variety of watercolor styles and genres—the picturesque English school and the warm, intimate Barbizon manner; carefully finished, illustrative scenes and freer, sketchier landscapes; storytelling pictures and more impressionistic ones. These diverse models not only shaped his evolving watercolor style but also licensed the eclecticism that marked his work from the beginning.

Hassam's first watercolors take their lead variously from the English school and Homer. They are conventional and slightly old-fashioned yet show remarkable technical control for an artist barely in his twenties. These watercolors are relatively small; most are landscape studies, made en plein air. In their translucency and their emphasis on loose, dappled effects, enlivened with touches of red, some—for example, *Country Road* (fig. 23)—recall Homer's charming work of the late 1870s. Others, such as *Blossoming Trees* (fig. 309), are equally sketchy but use small strokes of gouache for highlights—a technique for which Homer's watercolors of the 1870s also provided an appealing precedent.[7] A group painted on Nantucket, among them *Old Doorway, Nantucket,* ca. 1882 (Collection Mr. and Mrs. Scott L. Probasco),[8] is tighter,

Detail, fig. 129. *The Garden in Its Glory*

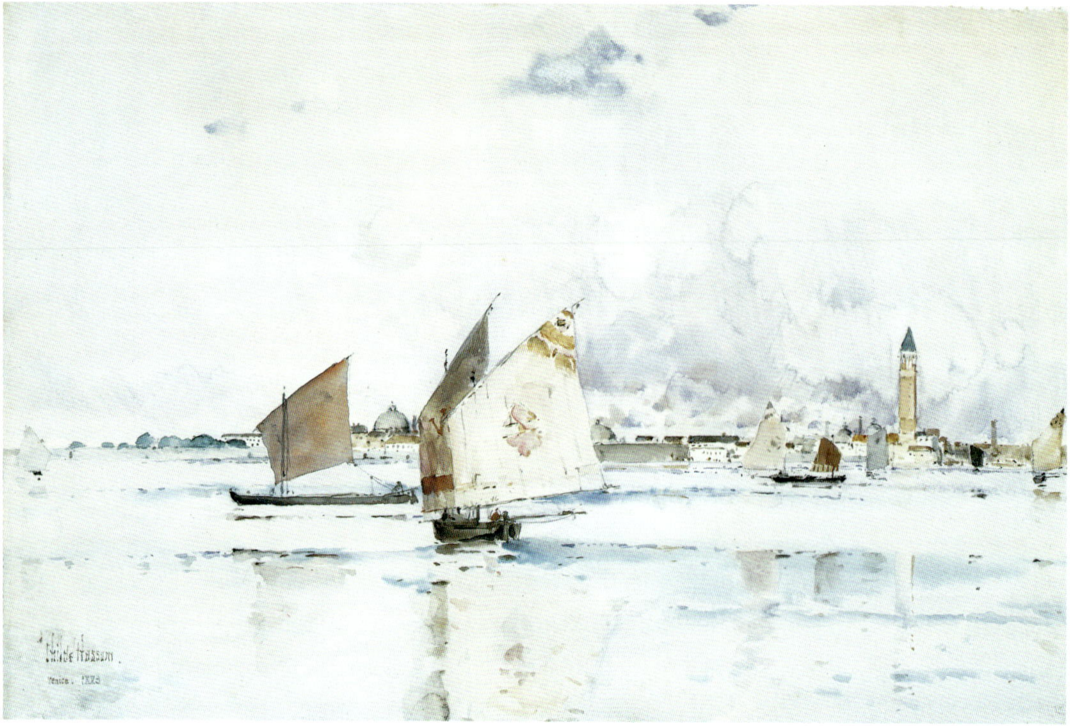

Fig. 256. Childe Hassam. *Venice,* 1883. Watercolor on paper, 12 x 18 in. (30.5 x 45.7 cm). Private collection

more finished, and more conventionally picturesque and reveals a certain awkwardness in rendering the human figure that Hassam would never entirely outgrow. Hassam's titles for these works and the penchant for old, tumbledown architecture displayed in them respond to the vogue for rural, nostalgic subjects that had emerged in the mid-1870s.[9] His enthusiasm for themes evoking New England's past would remain a constant in both his watercolors and his oils.

In 1883 Hassam made his first trip to Europe, where he fell under the spell of master watercolorists Richard Bonington, John Constable, and J. M. W. Turner. Like them, he followed the age-old practice of artists on the road and used watercolor to record his observations. He would later remember, not entirely accurately, "I made my sketches from nature in watercolor and I used no white. It was this method which led me into the paths of pure color. When I turned to oils, I endeavored to keep my color as vibrant in that medium as it was in water-color."[10] Shown at Williams and Everett in 1884 after Hassam's return to Boston, the European watercolors are generally wetter looking than his earlier works. They feature washes that are loose yet carefully managed, as well as a blonder tonality and more naturalistic skies than those seen in earlier sheets. The best of the watercolors Hassam produced in Europe—among them *On the Deck* (fig. 27)—are marked by a clarity that aspires to the brilliance of Bonington and Constable.

Despite his insistence that he worked exclusively in pure wash, Hassam used a variety of manners in his European watercolors, demonstrating his knack for adjusting his style to his subject even at this early stage.[11] His views of Venetian waterways, such as *Venice* (fig. 256), are especially free and suggestive and are indeed painted entirely with transparent washes. However, at the same time he was producing sheets of this kind, he painted larger, presentation watercolors in which he used white, that is, opaque pigment (gouache). These works may have been conceived on the spot but were likely completed in the studio. In some watercolors, for example *Promenade* (fig. 26), Hassam combined various techniques. Layers of transparent pigment are enlisted for sky and water at the left of *Promenade,* while reserved paper and subtle strokes of opaque color create highlights in the clearly silhouetted, tightly painted figures at right. This separation of styles—loose and transparent in one half of the picture, tight and opaque in the other—is somewhat artificial, but the watercolor nonetheless shows both Hassam's ambition and his growing understanding of the flexibility and evocative power of the medium.

No oil by Hassam from the period equals *Promenade* in scale or complexity. At this stage of his career, watercolors seem to have been Hassam's forum for the development of new themes and structures that would subsequently migrate to his oils. The compositional organization of *Promenade*—the division of the picture space by a dramatically plunging diagonal, with figures isolated on one side and a broad expanse of empty foreground on the other—and its theme—

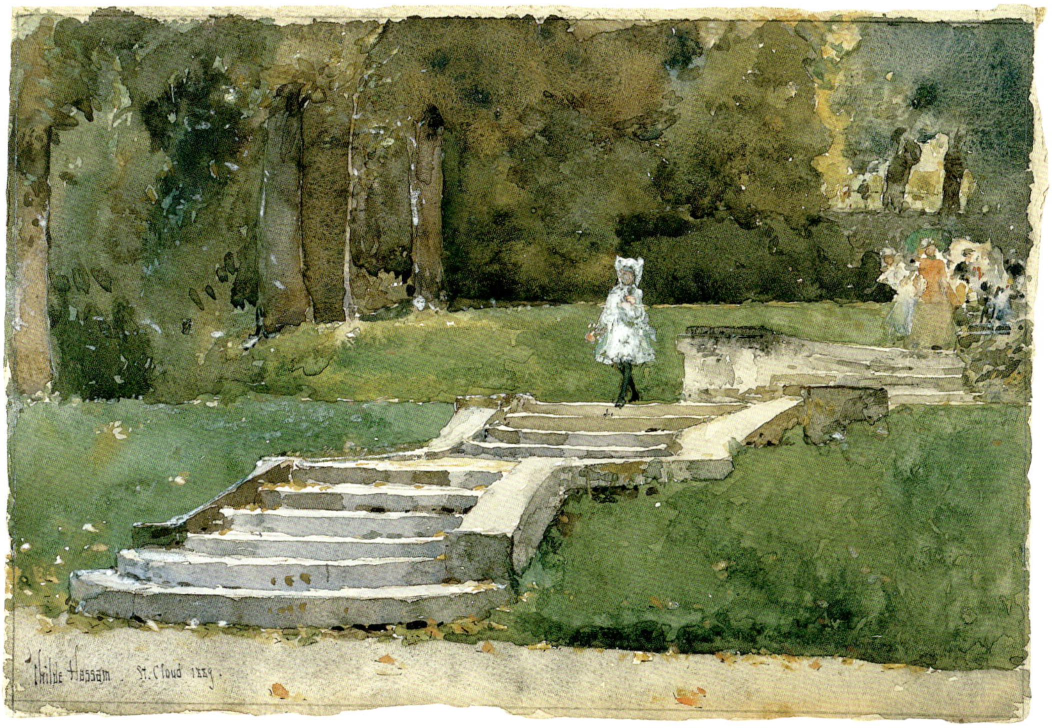

Fig. 257. Childe Hassam. *Saint Cloud,* 1889. Watercolor on paper, 7½ x 11⅛ in. (19 x 28.3 cm). The Art Institute of Chicago. Bequest of Marion E. Merrill 1978.481

the passing parade—recur frequently in Hassam's watercolors and oils of the mid-1880s, *Boston Common at Twilight* (fig. 39) being the best-known example.

In the mid-1880s, while supporting himself as an illustrator, Hassam maintained a high profile in many fine-arts organizations. On occasion, the two activities merged: in April 1884, for example, he provided a design in the arts-and-crafts manner for the cover of the catalogue of a Boston Art Club watercolor exhibition,[12] submitted works to the show, and served on its Jury of Admissions. He illustrated books by local authors,[13] joined the social Paint and Clay Club, was a founding member of the Boston Water-Color Society, went on sketching excursions (to Nantucket, Portsmouth, New Hampshire, and the Isles of Shoals), and, beginning in 1883, sent watercolors to the American Water Color Society's annual exhibitions in New York. The interrelationship of these disparate interests—involving both fine and applied art, professional and social pursuits—allies him with some of the most vital figures of what might be called the Aesthetic age.[14] Moreover, Hassam's stature in the art world was rising, as indicated by the fact that, as early as 1886, his watercolors began to be mentioned not just in local papers but in New York reviews as well (this year the critic for the *Nation* noted, for example, "Mr. Childe Hassam [shows] a very clever beach scene at Scheveningen").[15]

In the fall of 1886 Hassam returned to Europe, financing the trip with a sale of numerous oils and watercolors at Noyes, Cobb and Company held in March 1887. Many of the works on paper had appeared in shows at the Boston Art Club or the American Water Color Society of New York: his "clever beach scene" (*Gray Morning at Scheveningen,* location unknown) sold for $38; *September Clouds* (location unknown), ambitiously priced at $300 in the 1885 New York show, went for $49 at Noyes and Cobb. And *A Harvest Moonrise* (location unknown) brought $165, one of the best prices for a watercolor—a sum that surpassed that attained by many of his oils. Offered for $350 at the American Water Color Society a month earlier, it had been singled out by the reviewer in the *Nation* as "a richly-toned impression" and grouped with pictures by Dwight W. Tryon, Alexander H. Wyant, John Francis Murphy, and others working in a Barbizon vein that made up "a creditable showing in landscape."[16] Hassam worried that few pictures would sell and then only for low prices—"Expect to get a letter saying, Could not give your work away!!!," he wrote to a friend.[17] Yet his sale yielded nearly $4,000—more than Homer's sale had netted in 1880.

During Hassam's three years in France, his palette brightened, his brushwork became livelier, and he often turned his attention to subjects of urban leisure. However, as David Park Curry has noted, Hassam's work from this period shows no deliberate development toward an Impressionist style: "We will not find a clear progression from tight to loose brushwork or dark to blond palette in Hassam's Parisian period."[18] His watercolors may be freely rendered or highly finished, directly observed or thoughtfully conceived in the studio, painted entirely in transparent washes or with a great deal of opaque pigment. Some of the smaller ones, for example *Saint Cloud* (fig. 257), reveal that Hassam mastered the technique of combining transparent washes and gouache highlights to achieve the kind of luminous, sketchy effect popularized by Homer and others a decade earlier. At the same time Hassam was addressing themes of suburban recreation lately introduced by his French contemporaries. In a more adventurous picture, *Chatou near Bougival* (fig. 258), he applied his washes so thinly and smoothly that at first glance this surprisingly spare work seems to have been painted on tinted paper. He sketched in the houses along the horizon with small bright patches of color and improbably but effectively rendered the foliage at left in gray with an overlay of ocher. The most astonishing element is the bold stroke of cerulean blue, laid down dry and then softened with a second, damp stroke to describe the gentle wake on the placid river. The originality of Hassam's style here, particularly his manipulation of watercolor for expressive effect by making it masquerade as a support or as other media, represents one of the artist's most significant contributions to American watercolor painting.

At the end of his stay in France and before he returned to the United States in October 1889, Hassam went to England. There he painted tourist views that are modest in scale, well handled (usually incorporating a great deal of gouache), descriptive, and rather impersonal. These scenes are occasionally enlivened by an amusing incident such as the flock of pigeons dining in the middle of an otherwise empty foreground in *Gateway, Canterbury Cathedral Looking Out* (fig. 259).[19] If the travel watercolors of John Singer Sargent, Hassam's contemporary, can be described as autobiographical ("Other travelers wrote their diaries; [Sargent] painted his," observed one author)[20] and are notable for showing the unexpected view, Hassam's served another, more commercial, purpose: many would reappear as illustrations in the 1890s.

Perhaps the most ambitious watercolors Hassam produced during his three years in Europe were several large images of women selling flowers and other wares from the sidewalks and small shopfronts of Paris. In these works, which measure about 17 by 26 inches, the figures are pushed off center and the buildings and sidewalks are rendered in telling detail, as if the scenes were being taken in by approaching customers. Although designed to seem casually observed, these compositions are carefully structured and were clearly made in the studio as exhibition pieces. *La Bouquetière et la Laitière* (fig. 68), rendered in Hassam's by-now-characteristic transparent washes accented with gouache, shows adept manipulation of the wet-on-wet technique and judicious use of blotting to evoke, respectively, the damp pavement and the view through the shop windows. The heads of the women, by contrast, are described with fine, tiny strokes, in what is

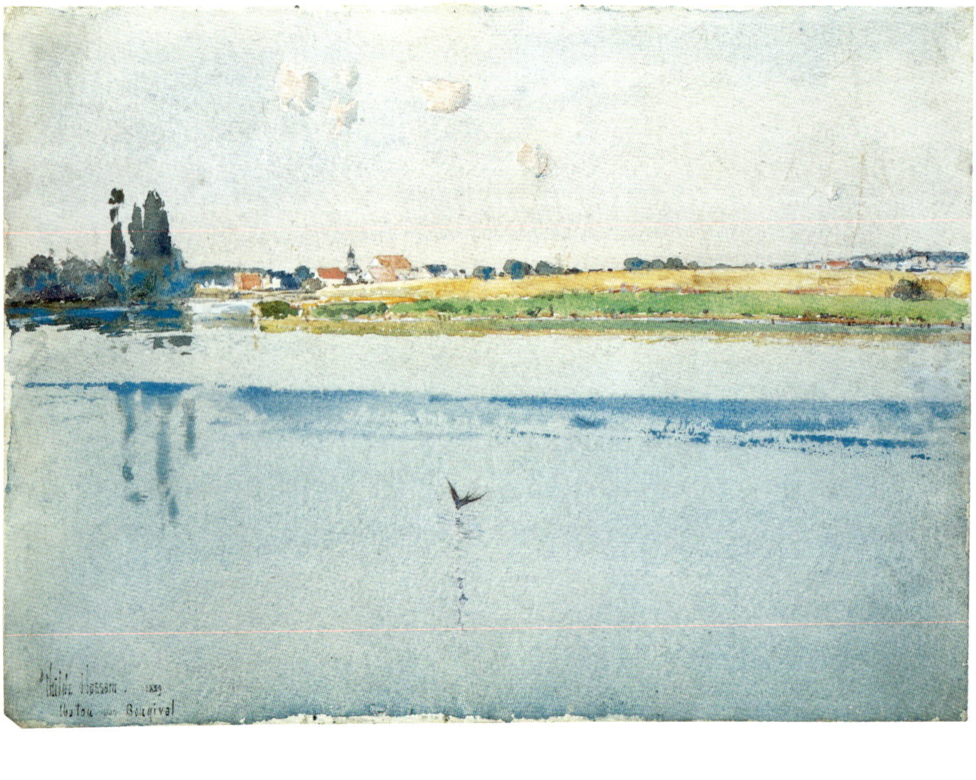

Fig. 258. Childe Hassam. *Chatou near Bougival*, 1889. Transparent and opaque watercolor on paper, 9¹⁵⁄₁₆ x 13⅞ in. (25.2 x 35.2 cm). The Museum of Fine Arts, Boston. Gift of Miss Kathleen Rothe 58.598

rable sketchy quality in the printed image—a laborious, and not always successful, operation. This problem led illustrators to encourage the development of the halftone process, a new technology that facilitated the transfer of tonal images to the printed page. By the late 1880s the halftone process had supplanted wood engraving as the principal method of reproducing images.[38] Increasingly, the prevailing taste was served by the process and printed illustrations were characterized by a gestural, suggestive, impressionistic quality, for which Hassam's watercolor style was well suited.

For his magazine assignments, Hassam both generated new images and reused old ones. This was an opportune way to put his work to multiple uses and to find new audiences for his designs. So, for example, in 1890 he sent *The Public Garden (Boston Common)* (fig. 41), a still-unsold major watercolor from the 1880s, to *Harper's Weekly* to complement an article entitled "Boston's Park and Parkway System."[39] *Fifth Avenue* was one of four watercolors and six oils he provided in 1893 for Mariana Griswold Van Rensselaer's article in *Century*, "Fifth Avenue."[40] Although any number of artists treated what are now considered Hassam's signature subjects—fashionable women promenading along sunny sidewalks or struggling prettily with umbrellas on rain-slicked streets, horse-drawn cabs moving through the snow, and so on[41]—his own renderings of these themes were especially appreciated.

Seeking to profit directly from the popularity of such pictures, in 1899 Hassam published his own illustrated book, *Three Cities*. This volume, containing forty-seven full-page scenes and several vignettes (but no text other than a brief caption beneath each picture), presented Hassam's three favorite cities, New York, London, and Paris, each in a separate section. In almost all of the views well-known buildings or intersections serve as backdrops to lively bits of street life—strolling pedestrians, moving cabs and trolley cars, vendors and laborers, and patrons of cafés and shops. Hassam derived the illustrations from old pictures or made new ones in several media, just as he had done for his magazine assignments.

Whether he reused compositions or created new ones, Hassam's activity as an illustrator affected his watercolor practice, encouraging him to produce images easily translated into print. The watercolor *Rainy Day on Fifth Avenue, New York* (fig. 262), for example, which would resurface in *Three Cities* as *Fifth Avenue at Central Park* (fig. 263), is based as much on tonal as on coloristic relationships. The range of washes in the picture—from virtually transparent in the sidewalk to completely opaque in the jackets of the figures—was readily converted into a range of black and white tones in the reproduction in the book. The opaque areas were painted with gouache: like many illustrators, Hassam tended to use a great deal of gouache in watercolors destined for reproduction, since it is a good medium for quick sketching and lively, expressive brushwork. And although sketchy images such as *Rainy Day on Fifth Avenue* appear to be informal and modern and to render freshly observed, momentary effects in the Impressionist manner, they were in fact deliberately designed to move the eye both into space and across the page. Hassam had the illustrator's knack for creating an impression of real life by including seemingly random details that are nonetheless carefully orchestrated. Thus, the telling touch of the foreground figure's lifted skirt flaring to the right looks true to life, but it also sets up a jaunty rhythm in combination with her umbrella, tilted the other way.

In fall of 1896 Hassam began staying at the Cos Cob art colony. Shortly thereafter, in December 1897 the thirty-eight-year-old artist banded together with colleagues to form Ten American Painters, or the Ten.[42] Few of his friends in either group were particularly active as watercolor painters. In part because of his involvement with these colleagues and in part because his paintings were selling well, after about 1900 Hassam stopped producing illustrations. These factors may also explain both his movement away from working in watercolors and certain changes in his style. Rarely would he experiment with complicated techniques and multimedia effects after the turn of the century.[43] In fact, when he did paint in watercolors, he worked almost exclusively on small sheets and with transparent washes, as for example in *Newfields, New Hampshire* (fig. 264), often indulging himself in the pleasures of painting out of doors.[44]

But if Hassam made few watercolors in the early years of the twentieth century, he continued to promote them. In January 1905 he had an exhibition at New York's Montross Gallery, the first of many solo shows there. In it, he presented twenty-five oils and fourteen watercolors and pastels, including a few recent pictures done at Cos Cob. That Hassam showed oils and watercolors together here—and would do so routinely and comfortably for the rest of his career—underscores his commitment to the latter medium, even though he was working in it only rarely. And while his oils from this period became increasingly formal and idealized, his watercolors, such as *Newfields, New Hampshire*, remained sunny

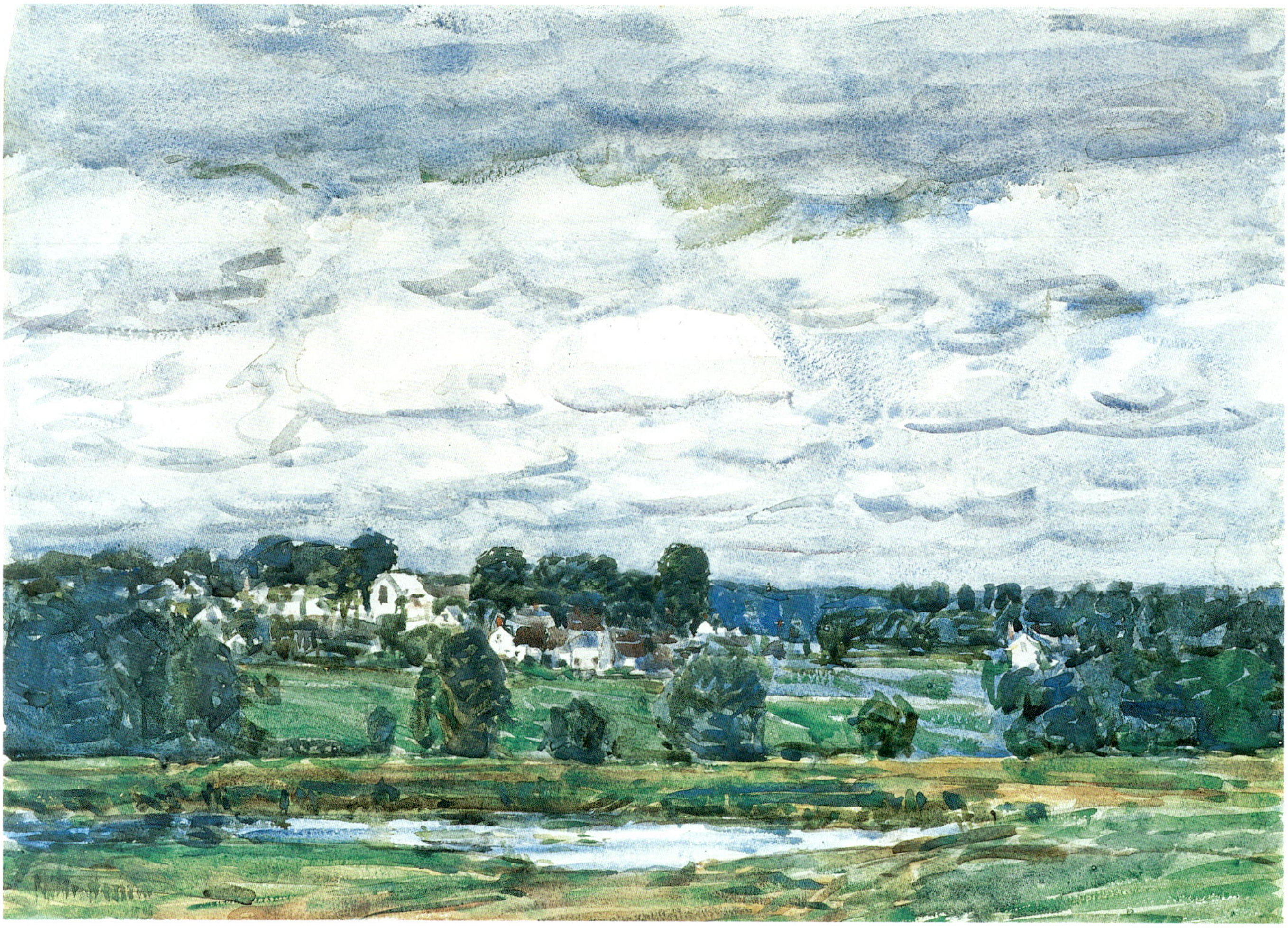

Fig. 264. Childe Hassam. *Newfields, New Hampshire,* 1906. Watercolor on paper, 13¾ x 19¾ in. (37.5 x 50.2 cm). Currier Museum of Art, Manchester, New Hampshire. Museum Purchase: Currier Funds 1963.1

and sometimes wistful, thus continuing to fill their accepted niche in America's visual culture at the turn of the century. As Charles Caffin wrote in 1898, "[Watercolors] are the gleanings of the summer vacation—fresh and spontaneous, with no suggestion of the heavier atmosphere of the studio. They make no strong appeal to the emotions, but entice one to gladsomeness, or that dreamy kind of sadness which is itself a pleasure."[45]

This sunny gladsomeness and dreamy sadness would be Hassam's legacy as a watercolor painter. While some have found his work old-fashioned and regretted his aversion to larger ideas,[46] others placed him with Sargent, Homer, and Whistler as a watercolorist of the first rank.[47] He may have cultivated such connections, referring to his watercolor series from the teens—pictures produced along the Hudson River, at Cos Cob, in Boston and Portsmouth, in Rockport, and at the Isles of Shoals—as "sets" in emulation of Whistler.[48] Three of these sets premiered at the Montross Gallery in January 1917; most of the works in them continue to display the bright and breezy manner of the earlier *Newfields, New Hampshire.* Done in pure wash with occasional charcoal or graphite underpinnings and lavish use of reserved white paper, like the earlier sheet, they convey the pleasure Hassam took in unpremeditated, summertime sketching. Some are casually, even awkwardly, cropped to create the sense of a momentary encounter. They tend to be devoid of figures, as though everyone in town had gone to the beach, leaving the site to the artist—and the viewer—alone (see fig. 190).

Hassam's watercolors, like the oils, sold well, but from the late teens, again like the oils, they ceased to advance. That Hassam was no longer achieving anything new in either medium was a fact critics recognized.[49] He nonetheless continued to show his watercolors regularly in New York at Montross and the Milch Galleries and to include them in surveys of his work presented at museums around the country.[50] He participated in the shows of the by-then-moribund American Water Color Society consistently in the teens and sporadically in the twenties, even winning that institution's Alexander M. Hudnut Prize in 1919 for a picture from the Hudson River set. *American Art News* announced the prize while describing that group of watercolors as "typical in brilliant color and . . . excellence."[51]

Excellence but not excitement. By this time a new generation of artists, including John Marin, Charles Demuth, and Georgia O'Keeffe, was creating the excitement in watercolor, making the medium not just an equal partner with oils but also a focus for many of their most original efforts.

However, in the first of his sets, Hassam had in fact achieved both excellence and excitement. In 1912 he had returned to the Isles of Shoals and produced this group of some twenty-two watercolors depicting the area's rocky ledges and its coves, headlands, and interior pools. These pictures were all produced in pure wash on relatively small sheets, yet they have a presence that far exceeds what we would expect from their modest scale. Again working with a limited palette—predominantly deep blue, green, and rust—Hassam created images that clearly evoke the area's appealing natural features and are at the same time intriguingly abstract. His characteristic staccato stroke is longer and more transparent now; it functions both decoratively and structurally. In *Looking into Beryl Pool* (fig. 265), for example, the layering of transparent strokes of gradated hues describes the mysterious depth of the pool and its shimmering surface while creating a pattern of interlocking shapes on the page. The brushstrokes in *The Cove* (fig. 17) attain an astonishing liquidity; in *Rocks at Appledore,* 1916 (private collection)[52]—a reprise of the images in the Isles of Shoals set—they become a kind of cubic calligraphy; and in each they have a life of their own on the surface of the sheet. Hassam's close cropping of both images enhances the evocation of nature: with no sense of scale, no vista into the distance, the viewer feels transported to a private, magical place. Yet the same device causes the pictures to read as flat, decorative, and abstract.

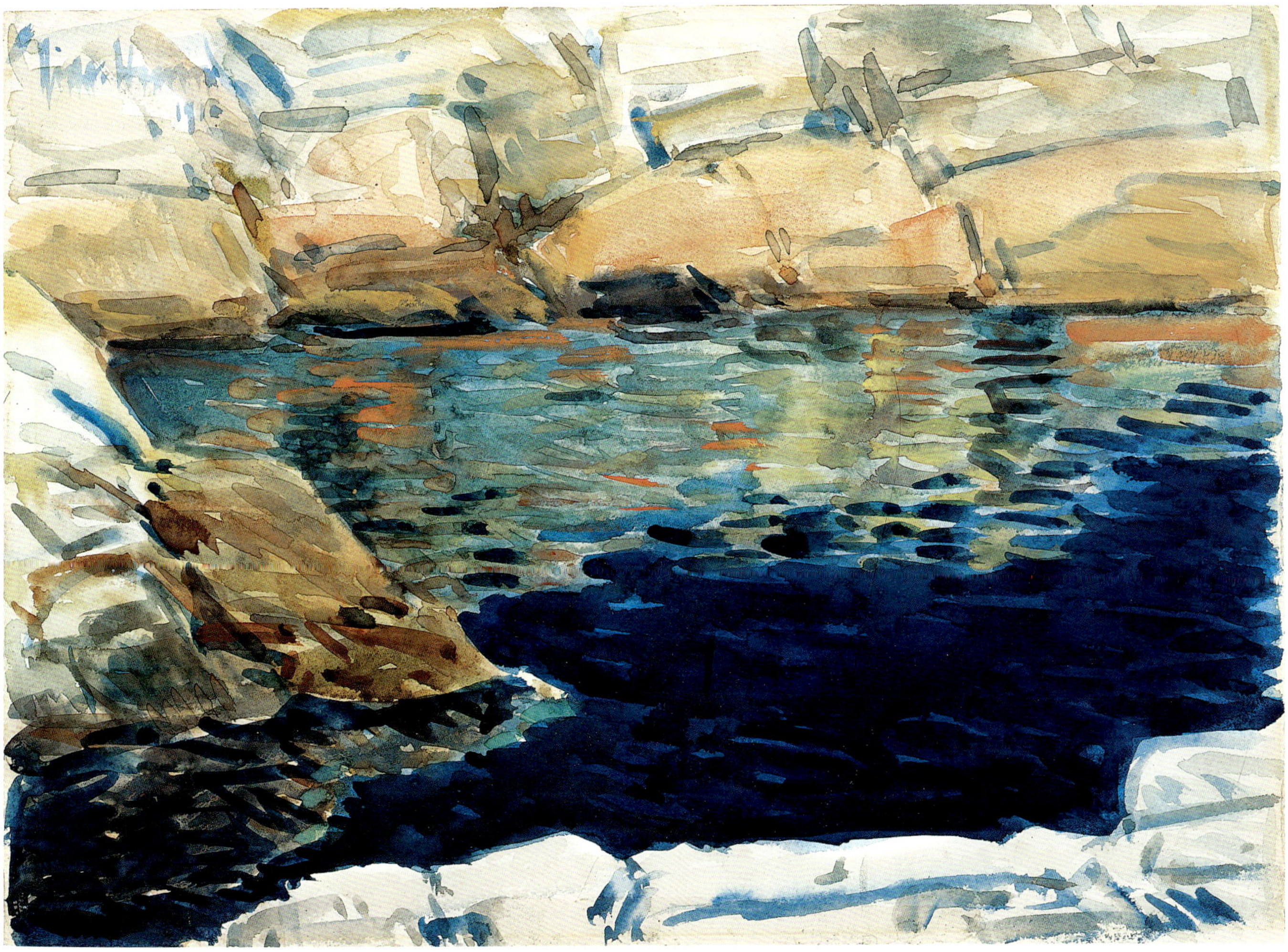

Fig. 265. Childe Hassam. *Looking into Beryl Pool,* 1912. Watercolor on paper, 10⅞ x 15¼ in. (27.6 x 38.8 cm). Worcester Art Museum, Massachusetts, Bequest of Mrs. Charlotte E. W. Buffington

On the strength of the Isles of Shoals sheets, the writer and collector of modernist art Albert Gallatin included Hassam in his 1922 publication *American Water-Colourists.* This was the first history of American watercolors, and it focused on the ten figures Gallatin considered "the chief exponents of the art." The criteria for inclusion were technical mastery, expressiveness, and "at least something of the spirit of modernity." Hassam's 1912 Isles of Shoals watercolors met those criteria, according to Gallatin, who responded to their forceful color, their "strong and bold strokes," their "freedom and gusto."[53] Hassam was, however, clearly among the old guard: even *The Cove,* perhaps the most abstract of the 1912 group, looks descriptive and placid next to Marin's contemporary watercolors, with their jazzy energy, telegraphic technique, and abstraction of natural forms, which Gallatin also discusses in his book.[54] Nonetheless, when Hassam's work in watercolor pushed the boundaries of the medium it did possess "the spirit of modernity." The Island Garden sheets and the nocturnes of the 1890s were among the most original watercolors of that era. The later Isles of Shoals watercolors, which a critic characterized in 1916 as "[exhibiting] the almost incredible strength, solidity, driving power attained in a medium which we had supposed essentially cursive and ephemeral,"[55] were equally inventive. As Hassam wrote to Mrs. Buffington, they are indeed "modern paintings."[56] And as Gallatin asserted, they qualify him for "an undisputed place with the masters of American watercolor."[57]

I am grateful to Kathleen A. Foster for her thoughtful reading of this essay.

1. Childe Hassam, Cos Cob, Connecticut, October 12, 1912, to Charlotte E. W. Buffington, Worcester, Massachusetts, Object files, Department of Prints and Drawings, Worcester Art Museum.
2. See Doreen Bolger Burke, "Painters and Sculptors in a Decorative Age," in Doreen Bolger Burke et al., *In Pursuit of Beauty: Americans and the Aesthetic Movement,* exh. cat. (New York: The Metropolitan Museum of Art, 1986), pp. 312–15.
3. Kathleen A. Foster, "Makers of the American Water Color Movement, 1860–1890" (Ph.D. diss., Yale University, New Haven, 1982), pp. 1–18.
4. See *Catalogue of an Exhibition of Contemporary Art, Held under the Direction of the Boston Art Club, the Boston Society of Architects, and the Schools at the Museum; also of the Paintings Shown by the Museum,* exh. cat. (Boston: Museum of Fine Arts; A. Mudge and Son, 1879).
5. *Notes on Drawings by Mr. Ruskin: Placed on Exhibition by Professor Norton of Harvard College,* exh. cat. (Boston: Museum of Fine Arts; Cambridge: University Press; John Wilson and Son, 1879).
6. Nicolai Cikovsky Jr. and Franklin Kelly, *Winslow Homer,* exh. cat. (Washington, D.C.: National Gallery of Art; New Haven: Yale University Press, 1995), p. 409.
7. See, for example, Homer's *Weary,* 1878, and *Apple Picking,* 1878 (both Terra Foundation for the Arts, Daniel J. Terra Collection, Chicago). By the time Hassam came under his influence, Homer was painting much more monumental, heroic subjects and had left behind the picturesque manner of the works in the 1880 Doll and Richards show.
8. Reproduced in Robert A. diCurcio, *Art on Nantucket: The History of Painting on Nantucket Island* (Nantucket, Mass.: Nantucket Historical Association, 1982), p. 147, fig. 173.
9. In response to both the widespread disillusionment that followed the Civil War and the excitement engendered by the centennial, many American artists—especially notable among them Homer and Eakins—took up old-fashioned themes in the 1870s. That much of their interest centered on New England was the subject of the exhibition and catalogue *Picturing Old New England: Image and Memory* (Truettner and Stein 1999).
10. Hassam, quoted in S. J. Woolf, "Hassam Speaks Out for American Art," *New York Times Magazine,* October 14, 1934, sec. 6, p. 7. As will become clear, Hassam's memory was rather selective—gouache, or opaque white, would become an important element in many of his watercolors. He did, however, accurately acknowledge the critical influence of the English school: "In England, during the eighteenth century, Bonnington [*sic*] turned out water-colors with colors as clear as those of any impressionist. The white of his paper showed through the filmy washes and made them vibrate. The pre-Raphaelites strove for the same effect. Constable carried on the tradition and the entire Barbizon school is an outgrowth of that English painter. As a young man, I was influenced by these Englishmen" (ibid.).
11. As perceptively noted by William H. Gerdts, "Hassam seems to have chosen to work in whatever manner best suited his purpose and his interpretation." William H. Gerdts, *American Impressionism* (New York: Abbeville Press, 1984), p. 96.
12. *30th Exhibition: Water Colors and Works in Black and White,* exh. cat. (Boston: Boston Art Club, [April 12–May 10] 1884).
13. See Stephanie L. Herdrich, "Hassam in Boston, 1859–1886," in this publication, pp. 30, 48, nn. 12, 13. A number of Hassam's illustrated books are listed in Hiesinger 1994, p. 28, n. 9.
14. These include not only artists who were clearly participants in the Aesthetic Movement, such as Louis Comfort Tiffany and John La Farge, but even some of their forerunners who were on its fringes, among them Edwin Austin Abbey and Winslow Homer.
15. "Fine Arts. American Water-Color Society," *Nation* 42 (February 4, 1886), p. 114.
16. "Fine Arts. The Water-Color Exhibition," *Nation* 44 (February 10, 1887), p. 129. Hassam and the other young painters showing in this annual may have benefited from the absence or indifferent participation of the two artists who usually claimed the lion's share of critical attention: Edwin Austin Abbey, who could usually be counted on to contribute a "sensation picture," but who did not show this year, and Winslow Homer, whose submissions to the 1887 show were called "unimportant and not particularly attractive sketches" (ibid., p. 128). The $350 price set for

A Harvest Moonrise was the highest Hassam ever put on a watercolor, which is indicative of his regard for the picture.

17. Childe Hassam, Paris, March 19, 1887, to Rose Lamb, Isles of Shoals Collection, Ms. 58, transcribed in Hiesinger 1994, p. 177.
18. Curry 1990, p. 96.
19. A picture titled *Gateway. Canterbury Cathedral, looking out* appeared as no. 40 in *Exhibition and Sale of Works in Oil and Water Color by Childe Hassam* (Boston: Noyes, Cobb, and Company, April 1–15, ca. 1890). It depicts a fifteenth-century gate to Christ Church Cathedral, looking out from the south porch of the cathedral. The subject was a popular one with artists: J. M. W. Turner, among others, depicted it. I am very grateful to Madeline Caviness, Mary Richardson Professor of Art and Art History, Tufts University, Medford, Massachusetts, for identifying the location shown here, and to Kathleen M. Burnside for supplying the information about the exhibition.
20. Mary Newbold Patterson Hale, "The Sargent I Knew," *World Today* 50 (November 1927), reprinted in Carter Ratcliff, *John Singer Sargent* (New York: Abbeville Press, 1982), p. 237.
21. As Hiesinger (1994, p. 44) remarks, that Hassam recognized the extraordinary quality of this watercolor is suggested by the little graffito that appears on the side of the building at left: a small stick figure that exclaims *ÉPATANT* (amazing!). The commentary is as charmingly self-congratulatory as Homer's famous notation on *The Blue Boat* (Museum of Fine Arts, Boston), his 1892 masterpiece: *This will do the business.* For another watercolor of this type by Hassam, see *The Flower Seller* (Christie's, New York, sale cat., November 30, 1999, lot 18).
22. "The attractive character both of the subjects and the methods of treatment, and the comparatively moderate prices at which water-colors are sold, commend them to the average picture buyer. Besides this, the aspect of the exhibition [the American Water Color Society exhibition of 1890] is decidedly a cheerful one, and is perhaps stimulating to the purchaser." "The Water-Color Exhibition," *Harper's Weekly* 34 (February 8, 1890), p. 111.
23. Hiesinger 1994, p. 183.
24. In fact, the watercolor was reprised in oil several years later, in *Sunday Morning*, 1897 (private collection), a charming panel about one-quarter the size of the original. *Sunday Morning* is reproduced in Adelson, Cantor, and Gerdts 1999, p. 34, fig. 33.
25. William A. Coffin, "Exhibition of the American Water-Color Society," *Harper's Weekly* 35 (February 7, 1891), p. 107.
26. "Fine Arts. Water-Colors and Etchings at the Academy," *Nation* 52 (February 19, 1891), p. 168.
27. "Fine Arts. American Water-Color Society," *Nation* 42 (February 4, 1886), p. 113. Later reviewers would be more accepting of variety in technique. The critic for *Harper's Weekly*, reviewing the 1894 American Water Color Society show, applauded the "healthy eclecticism" of the American watercolor school. "American Water-Colors," *Harper's Weekly* 38 (February 10, 1894), p. 128. For an illuminating analysis of this debate, see Foster, "Makers of the American Water Color Movement," esp. pp. 67–76.
28. "Telegraphic Brevities," *New York Times*, May 28, 1890, p. 5.
29. See, for example, a review of the first New York Water Color Club exhibition, which describes the close relationship between the effects of watercolor and of pastel: "The two arts have, as to the effects aimed at, much in common and some artists show a disposition to blend their techniques, so that it is not always possible to say, at a glance, whether a certain picture is in pastel or in watercolor." "The New York Water-Color Club," *Art Amateur* 24 (December 1890), p. 3.
30. The watercolor appeared as no. 45, *Nocturne at the Crossing*, in November 1893. When the work was acquired by the Museum of Fine Arts, Boston, in 1962, it was known as *Wet Night, Boston*. For a discussion of Hassam's debt to Whistler here (which is acknowledged in the title), see the entry on this picture in Sue Welsh Reed and Carol Troyen, *Awash in Color: Homer, Sargent, and the Great American Watercolor*, exh. cat. (Boston: Museum of Fine Arts in association with Bulfinch Press, Little, Brown and Company, 1993), pp. 133–36.
31. Curry 1990, p. 33.
32. Adelson, Cantor, and Gerdts 1999, p. 38, fig. 36.
33. Ibid., p. 189, fig. 198.
34. Sadakichi Hartmann, "Studio Talk," *International Studio* 29 (1907), pp. 267–70, quoted in Jane Calhoun Weaver, ed., *Sadakichi Hartmann, Critical Modernist* (Berkeley: University of California Press, 1991), p. 302.
35. "The Fine Arts. Watercolor Drawings by Childe Hassam at Doll and Richards," unidentified, undated clipping, [*Boston Evening Transcript*], Hassam Papers, reel NAA1, frame 490, quoted in Curry 1990, p. 86. In this section of his essay Curry offers an insightful caution against over interpreting Hassam's work.
36. William Dean Howells, *Venetian Life*, 2 vols. (1866; Boston: Houghton, Mifflin and Co., 1892). Hassam collaborated on *Venetian Life* with his friend Ross Turner, F. Hopkinson Smith, and fellow New York Water Color Club officer Rhoda Holmes Nicholls. Each provided several watercolors for the book, Hassam's seven images ranging in date from 1883 (*Rialto Market, Venice* [Mead Art Museum, Amherst College, Amherst, Massachusetts]) to about 1891 (*Gondoliers* [Adelson Galleries, New York, reproduced in Adelson, Cantor, and Gerdts 1999, p. 124, fig. 133]).
37. Thomas Curtis Clarke, "Rapid Transit in Cities, I.—The Problem," *Scribner's Magazine* 11 (May 1892), pp. 566–78; Philip G. Hubert Jr., "The Bicycle: The Wheel of To-day," *Scribner's Magazine* 17 (June 1895), pp. 692–702; Richard Harding Davis, "Three Gringos in Central America," *Harper's New Monthly Magazine* 91 (September 1895), pp. 490–505; Joseph H. Twichell, "Mark Twain," *Harper's New Monthly Magazine* 92 (May 1896), pp. 817–27. Among the other magazine stories illustrated by Hassam are: Royal Cortissoz, "Landmarks of Manhattan," *Scribner's Magazine* 18 (November 1895), pp. 531–44; A New Yorker, "Manhattan Day at the Fair," *Harper's Weekly* 37 (November 4, 1893), p. 1062; J. B., "Philosopher on Fifth Avenue," *Harper's Weekly* 41 (June 5, 1897), p. 568; Julian Ralph, "The City of Brooklyn," *Harper's New Monthly Magazine* 86 (April 1893), pp. 651–71; and "The Insurrection in Cuba," *Harper's Weekly* 39 (May 18, 1895), pp. 471–72.
38. Joshua Brown, *Beyond the Lines: Pictorial Reporting, Everyday Life, and the Crisis of Gilded-Age America* (Berkeley: University of California Press, 2002), p. 236.
39. Charles Pullen, "Boston's Park and Parkway System," *Harper's Weekly* 34 (September 27, 1890), pp. 745–48. Hassam's illustration appears on p. 747.
40. M[ariana] G[riswold] Van Rensselaer, "Fifth Avenue, with Pictures by Childe Hassam," *Century* 47, n.s. 25 (November 1893), pp. 5–18.
41. One of many similar examples is F. Stahl, *Unter den Linden*, which shows women on Berlin's main thoroughfare on a rainy day. The frontispiece (p. 530) for *Scribner's Magazine* 11 (May 1892), it relates to the article by Paul Lindau, "Unter den Linden," pp. 579–97.
42. For Hassam's colleagues in the Ten, see H. Barbara Weinberg, "Introduction," in this publication, fig. 20, p. 25, n. 46.
43. Some of the exceptions are significant. An example is the handsome watercolor *Yonkers from the Palisades*, 1916 (Worcester Art Museum), which

looks unpremeditated but is technically quite complex. In it Hassam combined colored pencil, layered washes, areas of reserved paper, and—to suggest the reflections dancing off the river—a kind of blotting process that left a shimmering pattern of yellow washes emerging from an overlayer of bright blue. And *White Mountains, Poland Springs,* 1917 (Fogg Art Museum, Harvard University Art Museums, Cambridge, Massachusetts) was painted on the back of the watercolor sheet, so that the pigment settled into the hollows of the coarse surface, creating an atmospheric effect. For further discussion of *Yonkers from the Palisades,* see Susan E. Strickler and Judith C. Walsh, "Technique in American Watercolors from the Worcester Art Museum, Worcester, Massachusetts," *Magazine Antiques* 131 (February 1987), pp. 412–25; and of *White Mountains, Poland Springs,* see Marjorie B. Cohn, *Wash and Gouache, A Study of the Development of the Materials of Watercolor,* exh. cat. (Cambridge, Mass.: Fogg Art Museum, 1977), p. 23.

44. Works such as *Newfields, New Hampshire* were lauded as "unsurpassed in the exhibition of deftness, vivacity of color, and force in the presentation of a vivid and authentic impression." However, the debate about the proper nature of watercolor continued, tiresomely, through the turn of the century. The writer who praised *Newfields, New Hampshire* contrasted it with the many works "not . . . above the average of mediocrity" that displayed the "effects of oil or pastel or lithograph" but rarely the "effect . . . most properly characteristic of the medium. "Art. The New York Water-Color Club," *Nation* 83 (November 15, 1906), pp. 422–23.

45. Charles H. Caffin, "The American Water-Color Society's Exhibition," *Harper's Weekly* 42 (February 12, 1898), p. 150.

46. The painter and critic Guy Pène du Bois, for example, noted that Hassam was "not the last word in modernity" and was rarely engaged by "intellectual considerations." Guy Pène du Bois, "An Almost Complete Exhibition of Childe Hassam," *Arts and Decoration* 6 (January 1916), p. 136.

47. See, for example, Buchanan 1916, p. LXXXIV: "The naked, primitive simplicity of Winslow Homer is duplicated in some of [Hassam's] water colours; Whistler, we believe, would have been happy to sign the *Chicago Nocturn* [*sic*]." See also Royal Cortissoz, "The Art of Childe Hassam Studied at Full Length," *New York Tribune,* Sunday, November 28, 1915, sec. 3, p. 3: "Sargent has done wonders with kindred themes [the 1912 Isles of Shoals watercolors]. But more satisfying than even his dazzling virtuosity is the sincere simplicity with which Mr. Hassam paints."

48. As Hiesinger (1994, pp. 150, 154) observed, the pictures in these so-called sets were often produced over several years and were not the products of deliberate creative campaigns.

49. One observer commented: "Hassam the Younger was an artist, one of the foremost in America, keen, sensitive, possessed of a brilliant color sense and fine powers of organization. He was, in the more accurate but less generally accepted sense, a modern painter. He was a good technician but never permitted his technique to dominate his art. His follower, Hassam the Elder, inherited the master's technique, and made a brilliant thing of it, but he became literary, arrogant and, finally, dull." "Childe Hassam. Macbeth Galleries," *Art News* 27 (April 20, 1929), p. 9. See also "A 'New' Hassam is Revealed in Exhibition of His Older Works," *Art Digest* 3 (mid-April 1929), p. 8: "Some of Hassam's admirers contend that he produced his best work between 1890 and 1910."

50. For example, his November 1916 exhibition at the Memorial Art Gallery of the University of Rochester, in which half the works were oils and half were watercolors and pastels, and his May 1917 exhibition *Paintings, Water Colors, Pastels, and Etchings* at the Saint Louis Art Museum, in which more than half were on paper.

51. "Watercolors by Childe Hassam," *American Art News* 17 (May 24, 1919), p. 2.

52. Adelson, Cantor, and Gerdts 1999, p. 83, fig. 90.

53. A. E. Gallatin, *American Water-Colourists* (New York: E. P. Dutton and Company, 1922), pp. vii–viii, 13–14.

54. Gallatin reproduces one of Marin's very wet, atmospheric Tyrolean watercolors of 1910 and three sheets painted in Maine between 1912 and 1915.

55. Buchanan 1916, p. LXXXIV.

56. See n. 1, above.

57. Gallatin, *American Water-Colourists,* p. 13.

"A truly learned weaving of light and dark" Hassam's Prints

Elizabeth E. Barker

"I began my career with the graphic arts and I am ending it with my greatest interest in graphic arts."
Childe Hassam, 1927

In 1915, at the age of fifty-six, the celebrated painter Childe Hassam turned his attention to etching. Tackling the medium with characteristic energy, he produced sixty-two etchings in that year alone, before embracing a second printmaking process, lithography, in 1917. Hassam's enthusiasm for making prints never waned. In the last two decades of his life he would create an impressive graphic legacy, numbering more than 400 printed works: 380 etchings and drypoints and 45 lithographs and lithotints. All reward close study. Technically accomplished and attentively printed, Hassam's etchings often repeat compositions from his painted oeuvre. But if the subjects appear *retardataire,* the style seems avant-garde. The bold articulation and strong surface patterns of Hassam's prints reveal a move toward expressionism that complements—and at times anticipates—the development of his oils.

Hassam's knowledge of prints and of printmaking techniques long preceded his activities as an independent etcher. He began his artistic career in the shop of the Boston wood engraver George E. Johnson.[1] There Hassam designed various commercial illustrations, including a panoramic view of Marblehead, Massachusetts, that served as the masthead for a local newspaper (fig. 266). To make this print Hassam followed his usual procedure: he observed his subject in nature—in this instance from a dory floating in the harbor—and drew it onto the surface of a block of boxwood. Back in the studio he (or, more likely, another, specially trained assistant) cut away the negative areas of the design, leaving the image raised above the surface for inking and printing, thereby transforming the piece of wood into a printing block.[2] Hassam does not appear ever to have attempted independent wood engravings, but soon after leaving Johnson's studio, in 1881, he began to experiment with other, intaglio (recessed-line) methods of printmaking.[3]

In the summer of 1883, while traveling in Europe and the British Isles with his good friend and fellow Johnson apprentice Edmund Henry Garrett, Hassam made his first mature attempts in etching.[4] Possibly inspired by the recent American lecture tour of the talented British etcher Francis Seymour Haden and presumably guided by Garrett (who had learned the technique in 1879), Hassam began five plates: three depicting Scottish subjects and two English ones.[5]

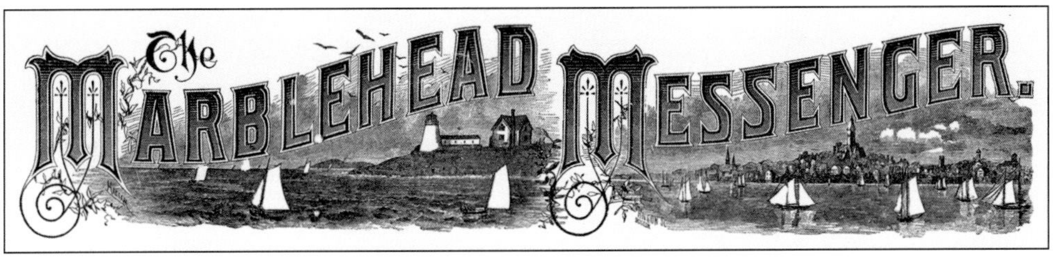

Fig. 266. Childe Hassam, designer, George E. Johnson, printer. *View of Marblehead, Massachusetts,* masthead of *The Marblehead Messenger,* 1882. Wood engraving. Collection of the *Marblehead Reporter,* Marblehead, Massachusetts

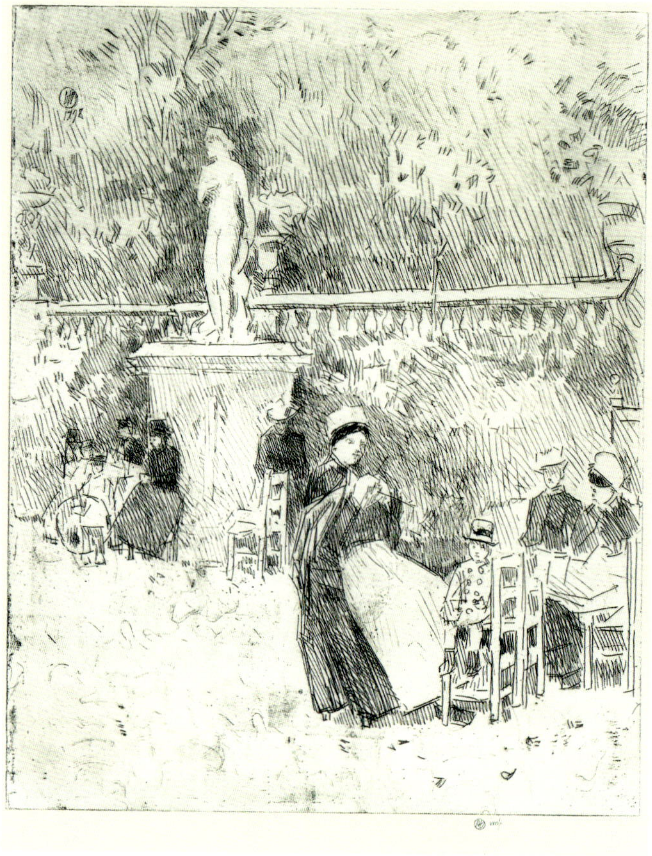

Fig. 267. Childe Hassam. *Garden of the Luxembourg*, 1898/1915. Etching and drypoint on white laid paper (Dutch, *Van Gelder Zonen* watermark), 10⅞ x 9 in. (27.7 x 22.7 cm) 40.30.2 (C2)

Hassam explained the challenging, chemically based printing process many years later, in a 1922 interview with the *New York Times:*

> *An etching . . . gets its name from the Dutch word "eten" (to eat). It is made by drawing lines, many or few, on a metal plate, usually copper, that has been covered with a ground of varnish. The lines so drawn on the plate expose the metal much or little, as the etching point or needle is fine or blunt. These lines are then eaten by an acid with an appetite for copper, so that the fine lines are just seen and the heavier lines may be seen across the room. The ground or varnish removed, the plate is cleaned, then covered with ink. The ink is wiped off and the plate put on the bed of a roller printing press. A sheet of linen paper, dampened, is laid over the plate and rolled through the press. The paper is pulled off with care and you have the print of the lines, and this is called an etching.*[6]

In 1883, however, he seems to have been rather less certain of the method. For reasons that remain insufficiently understood but which presumably involved technical problems, Hassam set all five of these early plates aside without finishing them.[7] (He would eventually complete and print them more than three decades later, in the late 1920s.)

During Hassam's second European sojourn—those fruitful years from 1886 to 1889 when he and his wife, Maud, resided in Paris—the young painter began to etch new plates: *Zola's House, Paris* (C84) and *Montmartre* (C85). Frustratingly, the original appearance of these etchings, like that of those he began in Britain, remains uncertain: no contemporaneous impressions of any of Hassam's etchings from the 1880s have been identified, and he subsequently reworked all his plates from this period. The somewhat later *Garden of the Luxembourg* (fig. 267), begun in 1898, provides a reasonable touchstone for Hassam's earliest style in etching, since it exhibits a stiffness in handling not encountered in his later prints.

In France, as in England and Scotland, Hassam used etching to record specific places rapidly observed, an approach that would characterize his later work in the medium as well. He prepared many etchings from nature—carrying his portable copper plates like sketchpads into the landscape, to be inscribed en plein air or occasionally from the windows of automobiles—and typically drew his figures from living models.[8] Hassam derived other designs from drawings but worked to ensure that the resulting etchings retained the immediacy of the initial sketches. Although he completed some plates at single sittings, most—such as the richly textured *Easthampton* (fig. 268)—required successive campaigns.[9]

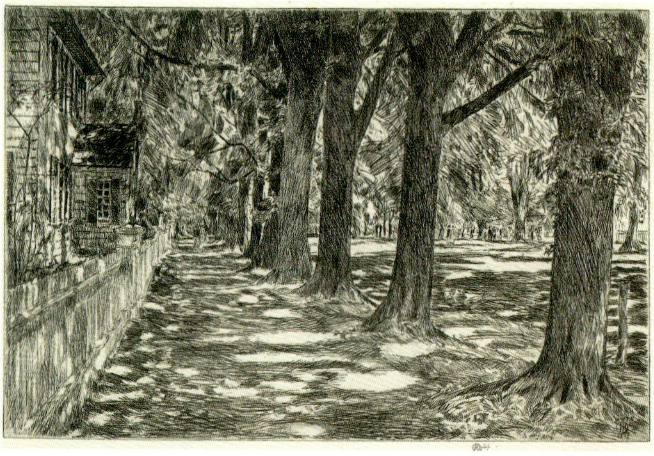

Fig. 268. Childe Hassam. *Easthampton*, 1917. Etching on buff laid paper, 7⅜ x 11¼ in. (18.8 x 28.7 cm). The Metropolitan Museum of Art, New York. Gift of Mrs. Gustavus S. Wallace, 1932 32.109.8 (C134)

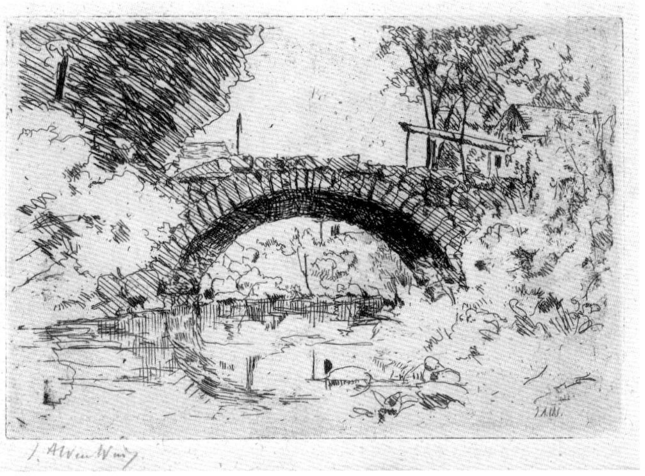

Fig. 269. Julian Alden Weir. *The Stone Bridge,* ca. 1887–88. Etching on blue laid paper, 4 x 5⅞ in. (10.1 x 15 cm). The Metropolitan Museum of Art, New York. Rogers Fund, 1918 18.59.28

Some campaigns were separated by decades: only in 1915–16 would Hassam complete the French and British plates he had abandoned in the 1880s.[10] Indeed, after Hassam moved to New York in 1889 and encountered a circle of like-minded artists—including those with whom he founded the Ten in 1897—painting in oils and watercolors dominated his creative activities to the exclusion of almost all printmaking for more than two decades.

Then, in the mid-teens (perhaps as early as 1912), Hassam began to etch again.[11] This time he persisted. He sought vital encouragement and crucial advice on materials from his close friend and fellow member of the Ten J. Alden Weir, whose etchings of the late 1880s, such as *The Stone Bridge* (fig. 269), must have provided an appealing model.[12] In the summer of 1915, Hassam focused his full attention on printmaking—and found success. Once he had mastered the difficult technique, in a matter of months he prepared a sizable group of works, many of which rank among the finest accomplishments of American graphic art. A review of Hassam's first exhibition of etchings, held at Frederick Keppel and Company in New York in November 1915, explained the circumstances that inspired this achievement: "A fellow artist, who etched, happened to be his neighbor in the country near Cos Cob, and placed his press and atelier at Mr. Hassam's service. There a number of plates were begun, and once fairly launched in these experiments Mr. Hassam caught the true etching fever, and gave almost his entire summer to making plates and printing them."[13]

That accommodating neighbor was Kerr Eby, a talented, apparently self-taught etcher who kept a press in his studio in Cos Cob, the Connecticut artists' colony on Long Island Sound.[14] The elegance of Eby's etching style—distinguished by fine lines, subtle tonalities, and skillfully abbreviated compositions—may well have inspired the refinement of Hassam's own graphic manner in 1915. Works such as Hassam's *Old Lace* (fig. 270)—in which the tiny figures crossing the iron-lattice bridge over the Cos Cob inlet dissolve within an intricate, weblike pattern of shimmering lines—exhibit a delicate, luminous quality not unlike that seen in Eby's *Morning Mists* (fig. 271).[15] Eby, who was only twenty-five in 1915, put his hard-won expertise, his press, his studio, and even his home at the older artist's disposal: when asked the secret for drying proofs without flattening the ink, Hassam confessed, "Well, as a matter of fact, I usually spread them out on Eby's bed."[16]

At first glance, Hassam's enthusiastic turn to etching in 1915 seems surprising. Why at middle age, having previously attempted and abandoned etching on various occasions—and having achieved tremendous success as a painter of light and color—did Hassam return with renewed focus to this technically complex, black-and-white medium? Considered with the benefit of hindsight, however, his decision seems inevitable. For a serious artist of Hassam's generation, etching simply could not be ignored.[17]

In the second half of the nineteenth century, countless artists on both sides of the Atlantic took up the etching needle, encouraged by the example of such celebrated *peintres-graveurs* (artist-printmakers) as the French etcher Charles Meryon, the French painters Jean-François Millet, Jean-Baptiste-Camille Corot, Camille Pissarro, and Edgar Degas, the British surgeon and amateur etcher Haden, and—above all—Haden's American brother-in-law, the painter James McNeill Whistler. Whistler's etchings (see fig. 274)—characterized by delicate, evocative lines and painterly, atmospheric tones of brown ink—reflect his distaste for the mirror-smooth look of reproductive prints and his admiration for the idiosyncratic character of Rembrandt's graphic work.

Inspired by Whistler's compelling example and attracted by the expressive sketchlike spontaneity that etching allowed, many American artists took up the medium in the last three decades of the nineteenth century.[18] By 1890 Boston, Cincinnati, New York, and Philadelphia all claimed

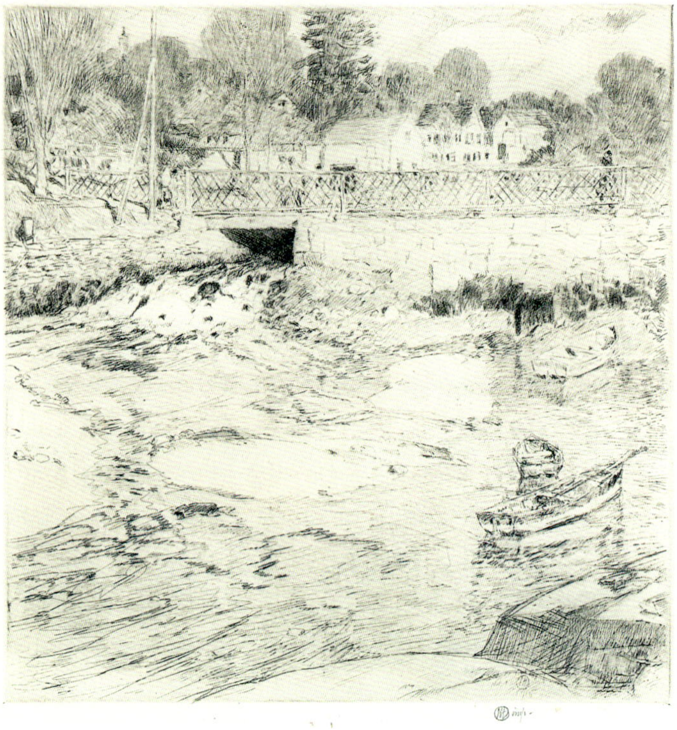

Fig. 270. Childe Hassam. *Old Lace,* 1915. Etching on a sheet of buff wove paper from a minister's Bible (text not shown), 6⅞ x 6¾ in. (17.5 x 17.3 cm) 40.30.16 (C56)

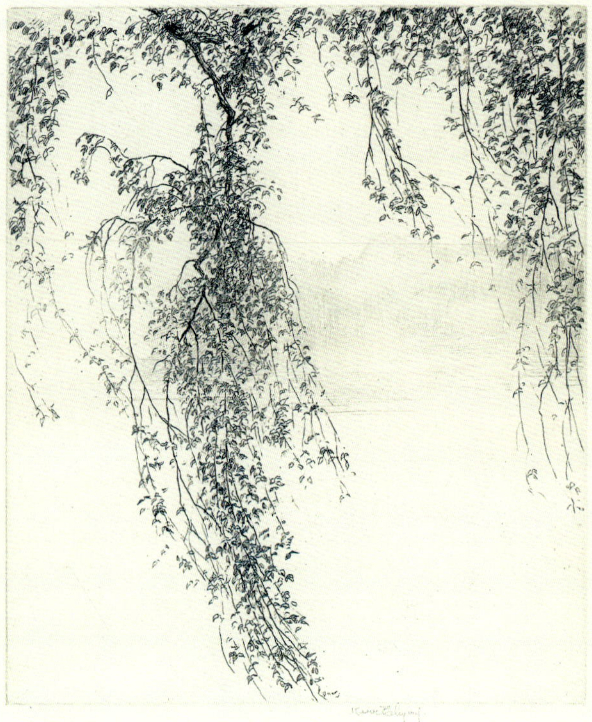

Fig. 271. Kerr Eby. *Morning Mists,* 1913. Etching on off-white laid paper (British, *FJ Head & Co* watermark), 7⅜ x 6½ in. (19.2 x 16.4 cm). The Metropolitan Museum of Art, New York. Gift of Phyllis Brevoort Eby, 1962 62.554.65

etching clubs and societies, formed to share expertise and pool expenses for publications and group exhibitions. In 1917, more than two decades after the heyday of the American etching revival, Hassam would become a founding member and the first chairman of another such association: the Painter-Gravers of America, which sought to encourage the development of the artist print in the United States and to educate a broad public through exhibitions and lectures.[19]

By the mid-teens, then, etching must have seemed a godsend to artists. Commonly practiced and widely taught, the method could be learned without inconvenience; increasingly popular and relatively inexpensive, the prints could be sold without difficulty. The latter consideration almost certainly influenced Hassam's decision to embrace etching when he did. In an economy successively weakened by a recession in the late 1890s, World War I, and the Great Depression, prints, less expensive to produce and purchase than paintings, would have held particular appeal for artists and collectors.[20] Hassam's decision to group his prints in sets of related views (featuring New England, New York, East Hampton, and the American Southwest) can be regarded not only as an homage

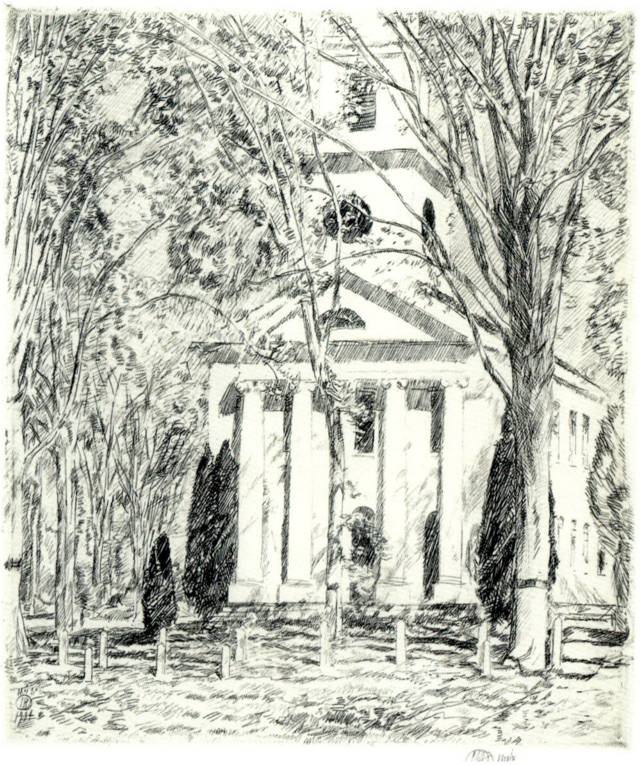

Fig. 272. Childe Hassam. *The Church at Old Lyme,* 1924. Etching on white wove paper, 7¼ x 6⅜ in. (18.3 x 16.2 cm) 40.30.35 (C233)

to Whistler, who established the practice with his celebrated sets of prints (depicting France, the Thames, and Venice), but also as a marketing strategy that demanded sustained financial commitment on the part of collectors.[21] Surprisingly, however, Hassam's graphic work proved a commercial failure, prompting the artist (whose paintings had made him prosperous) to lament, "Not doing ducks and dogs my prints are rarely very successful."[22]

Once he had begun to etch in earnest, Hassam would continue to make prints for the rest of his life. He did so not because it was fashionable (interest in etching was already in decline among the most creative printmakers of his day), nor because it offered a steady income (as we have seen, for Hassam it did not). Rather, it promised fresh aesthetic possibilities, allowing him to experiment with new visual effects in a medium other than painting. Specifically, Hassam used the black-and-white medium of etching (and later lithography) to reconsider his painted art in terms of line and plane (see fig. 272). The artist himself suggested as much when he defined the etching process in his 1922 interview with the *New York Times*. There he linked the medium explicitly to oil painting: "The linen [sheet of paper] is the same material as the painters' linen canvas, the ink is a black pigment oil like the painter's paint."[23] For Hassam, then, the processes of painting and printmaking seem to have been intertwined.

Throughout the last two decades of his life, Hassam's etching technique remained essentially unchanged. John Taylor Arms, first president of the Society of American Etchers (formerly the Brooklyn Society of Etchers, now the Society of American Graphic Artists), described Hassam's process with acuity:

> *[Hassam's technique] is based on a rather short, staccato line, thin and sensitive, capable of both strength and delicacy. He does not sweep around the contours of his forms with long, flowing lines, nor does his needle trace its path searchingly, hesitatingly, in and out through them. Rather does it build up the contours and values in short, sharp strokes, of a delightfully nervous and sentient quality, laid in groups of varying directions, sometimes hatched one over the other but more often than not with spaces between which seem to give forth light almost as from within. This consistent use of the short, cleanly etched line, and of the tiny passages of light let into even the darkest tones, contributes largely to the shimmering, palpitating effect of Hassam's work. And by the control of these things and the changing of their relation to each other, he is enabled, in his suggestion of light, to cover a wide range of effects.*[24]

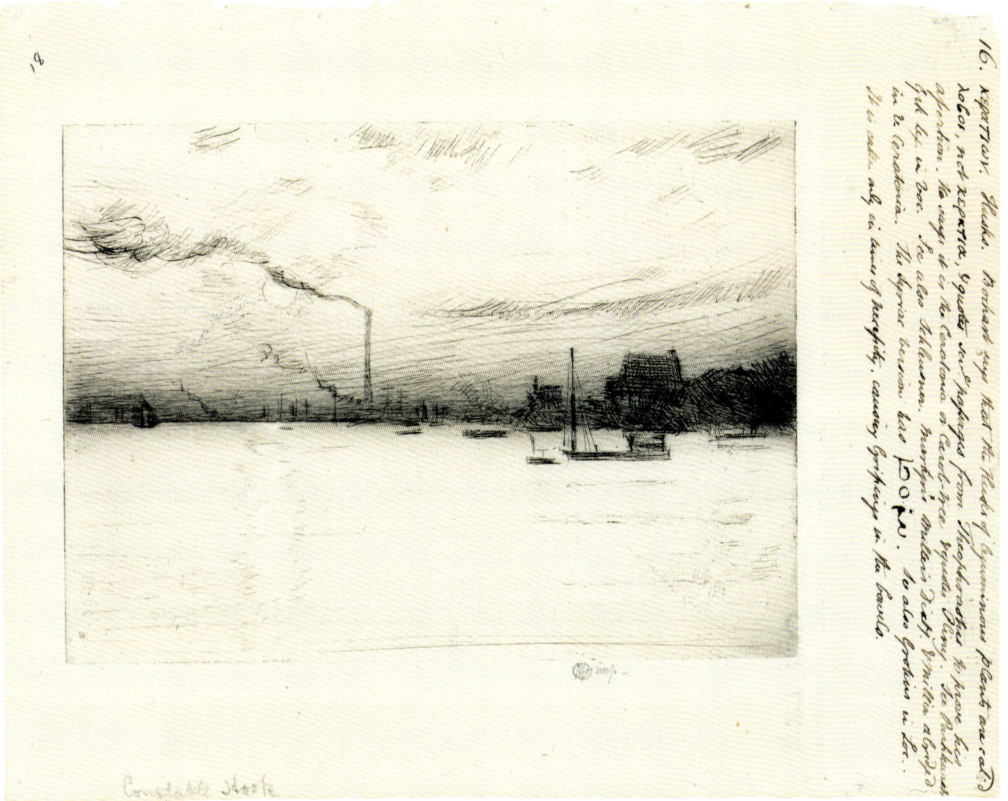

Fig. 273. Childe Hassam. *Sunset, Constable's Hook*, 1915. Etching and drypoint on a sheet of off-white laid paper from a notebook, 5 x 6⅞ in. (12.7 x 17.5 cm) 40.30.9 (C18)

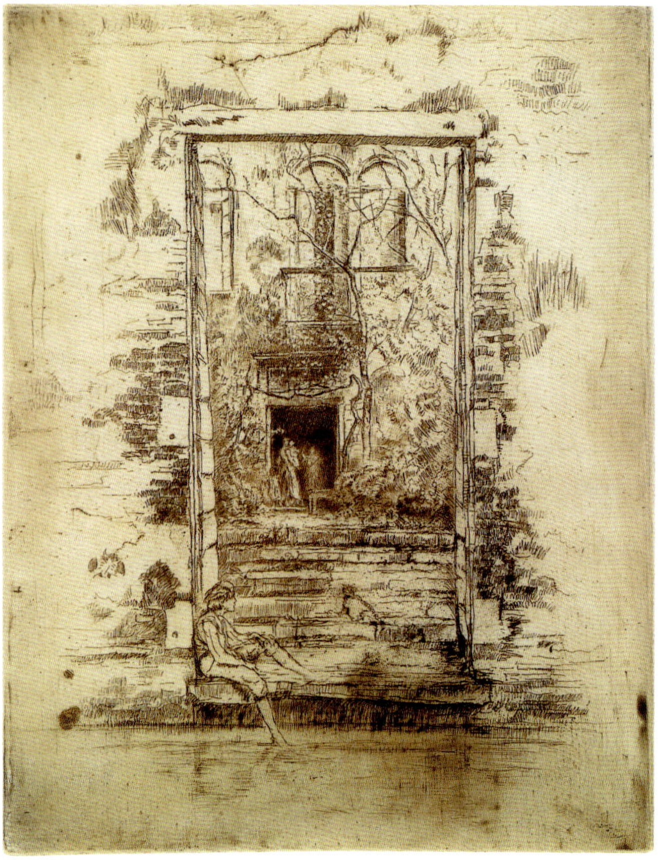

Fig. 274. James McNeill Whistler. *Garden* (from the *Twenty-Six Etchings*), 1879–80. Etching and drypoint on off-white laid paper, 4th state, plate 12 x 9¼ in. (30.5 x 23.5 cm). The Metropolitan Museum of Art, New York. Harris Brisbane Dick Fund, 1917 17.3.111

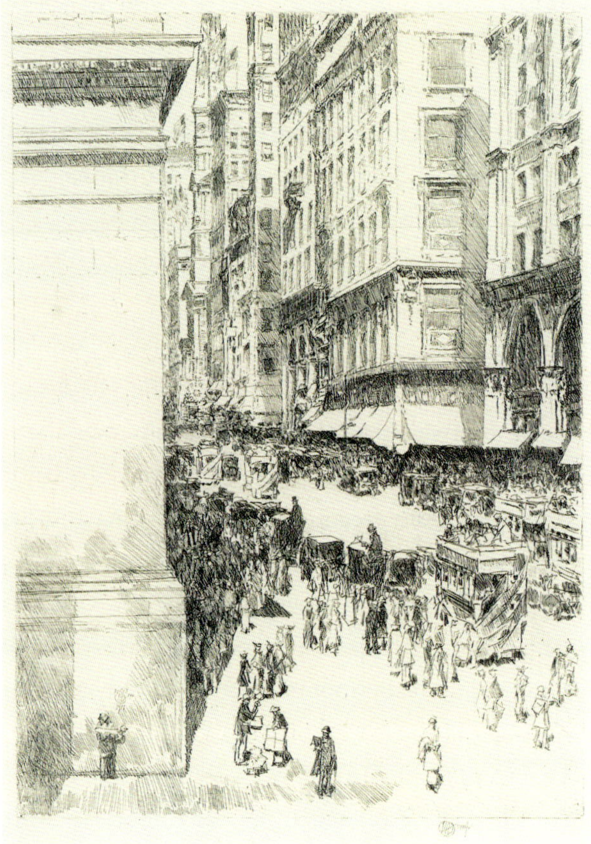

Fig. 275. Childe Hassam. *Fifth Avenue, Noon,* 1916. Etching on buff wove paper, 2nd state, 9⅞ x 7⅛ in. (25.1 x 18.2 cm) 40.30.25 (C77)

Occasionally, Hassam varied the quality of his line by adding drypoint to his etching plate. In drypoint, which is frequently combined with etching, the printmaker uses a pointed tool to gouge a furrow in the copper plate, thereby displacing the excess metal. The resulting burr thrown up alongside the scored line retains the ink in printing and lends the stroke a rich, almost furry appearance. On one such plate, *Sunset, Constable's Hook* (fig. 273), Hassam enlisted drypoint to articulate the wisps of smoke and edges of buildings and masts that reach into the wide, expansive sky.[25]

Hassam's decisive manner of etching contrasts notably with Whistler's, as demonstrated in that artist's view of a Venetian entranceway (fig. 274): *Garden* (which may have inspired Hassam's *Steps* [fig. 284]) displays light, wispy lines concentrated in the central areas of the scene that are typical of Whistler.[26] Initially some critics faulted the freshness and brightness of Hassam's line for its divergence from Whistler's; eventually, however, most found Hassam's energetic strokes to be the distinguishing strength of his prints.[27]

It did not take Hassam long to recognize this linear quality as the vital element of his etchings. Whereas Whistler and many of his followers left a film of ink tone on the plate to produce diffused, atmospheric effects and relied on retroussage (French for "dragging up")—the practice of drawing ink gently from the etched lines with a cloth before printing—to create an effect of softened edges, Hassam soon abandoned these practices. Unusually, he began to wipe his plates almost entirely clean before printing, allowing just enough ink to spill from the most delicate lines to strengthen them and leaving only the faintest natural tone (a thin residual film of ink) on his plates.[28] In *Old Lace* (fig. 270) Hassam's careful wiping of the plate to brighten areas of the water enhances an effect of motion. Similarly, in the impression of *Fifth Avenue, Noon* in the Metropolitan Museum's collection (fig. 275), he skillfully allowed the clean white sheet to shine uncolored, creating a spot of bright sunlight on the blank wall of the central building.[29]

As Hassam's early biographer, the painter and printmaker Ernest Haskell, succinctly put it: "He had things to express and he expressed them in his own manner, without fear of his medium. . . . He drew the plates cleanly letting each line remain to tell its story. He then printed the plates as few etchers dare to print, namely, with a clean wipe. This method reveals all to the experienced collector of prints. Nothing is hidden by false surface ink."[30]

Yet Hassam's attention to line did not deprive his etchings of texture and color: he supplied those elements by printing onto carefully selected sheets of paper. Just as Whistler and many of his American followers had printed on antique papers, so Hassam employed sheets from a variety of sources. These ranged widely, from "old English plate paper" to "Whatman paper"; from "yellowish woven paper" to "old handmade American paper"; from "old English note paper" to "yellowish Japan paper"; from "bluish linen paper" to "French line paper"; from "Spanish woven paper" to "French M.B.M. paper" and "bluish Holland paper"—to name only a few examples, all taken from the catalogue of Hassam's 1915 exhibition at Keppel.[31] Relics of an era when paper, made from linen rags rather than wood pulp, could be counted on to last, these sheets gave Hassam's prints a sense of permanence.[32]

By evoking an earlier age, these papers also linked Hassam's work to that of the old masters, with varying degrees of whimsy and solemnity. Hassam took one impression of *Montmartre* on ruled paper from an old ledger (C85), so that the image of a woman frying potatoes appeared flanked by an entry recording the purchase in 1777 of a dozen bottles of port for £17.7.4.[33] He printed the Metropolitan Museum's *Cos Cob Dock* (fig. 276) on a sheet taken from a minister's Bible in which the text is condensed into a single, narrow column on one side of the page, leaving the main space blank for notations. Here a verse addressing the cleansing power of water runs alongside the curving dock and calm, pellucid waters: "Then the priest shall wash his clothes, and he shall bathe his flesh in water" (Numbers 19:7). Hassam

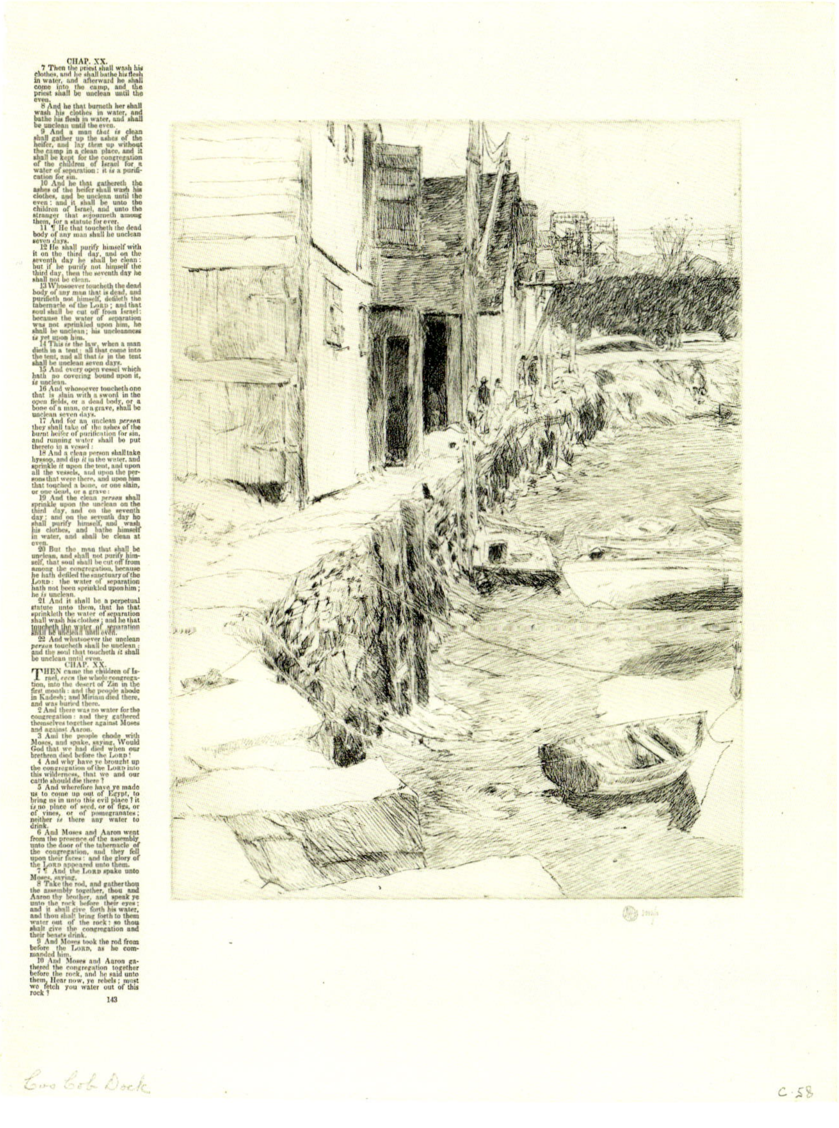

Fig. 276. Childe Hassam. *Cos Cob Dock,* 1915. Etching on a sheet of buff wove paper from a minister's Bible, 8⅜ x 6¼ in. (21.3 x 15.9 cm). The Metropolitan Museum of Art, New York. Harris Brisbane Dick Fund, 1917 17.3.511 (C58)

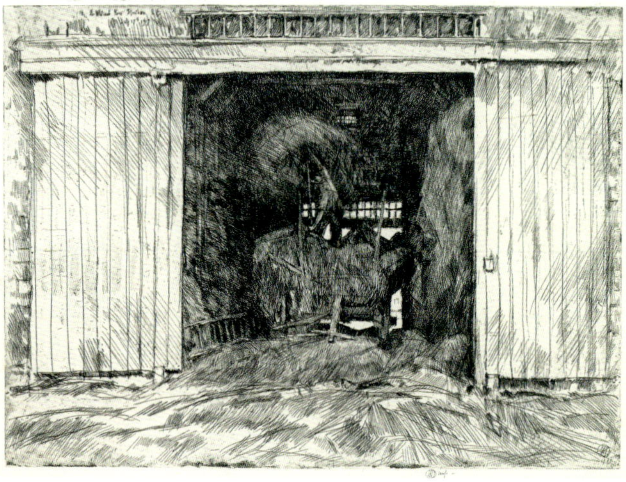

Fig. 277. Childe Hassam. *The Hay Barn,* 1920. Etching on white wove paper (British, *J Whatman* watermark), 10¼ x 14¼ in. (26.2 x 36.2 cm) 40.30.28 (C160)

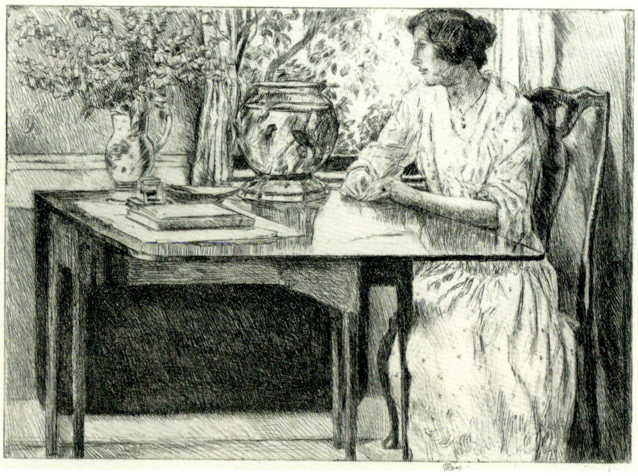

Fig. 278. Childe Hassam. *The Colonial Table,* 1915. Etching on off-white laid paper, 6⅞ x 9⅞ in. (17.5 x 25.1 cm) 40.30.33 (C51)

continued to print on old papers for many years, although in some later etchings, such as *The Hay Barn* (fig. 277), he would enlist bright wove papers that allowed him to create stronger contrasts of light and dark.

The subjects of Hassam's prints correspond closely to those of his paintings. In a few instances he reproduced specific oils in etchings or lithographs.[34] More typically Hassam explored anew, in black and white, the themes he had already addressed (or was currently addressing) in color in his oils, watercolors, and pastels: solitary women illuminated by windows (*The Colonial Table* [fig. 278]) or standing beside carved mantelpieces (*The White Kimono* [fig. 15]);

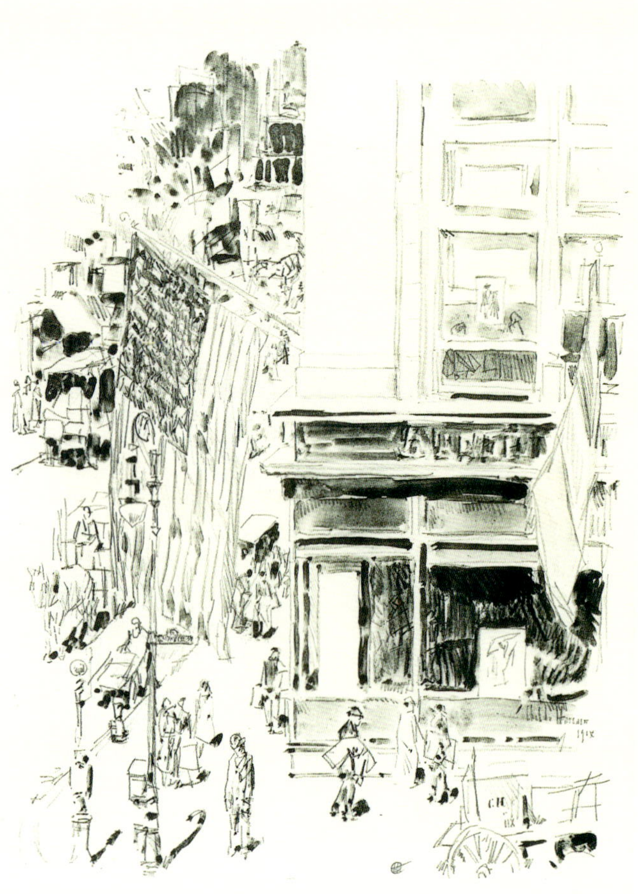

Fig. 279. Childe Hassam. *Lafayette Street,* 1918. Lithograph and lithotint on lightweight beige wove paper (Japanese, foliate watermark), 14½ x 11 in. (36.8 x 27.9 cm) 40.30.46 (G5)

Fig. 280. Childe Hassam. *The Chimneys, Portsmouth,* 1915. Etching on a sheet of buff wove paper from a minister's Bible (text not shown), 4⅞ x 8⅛ in. (12.3 x 20.7 cm) 40.30.3 (C16)

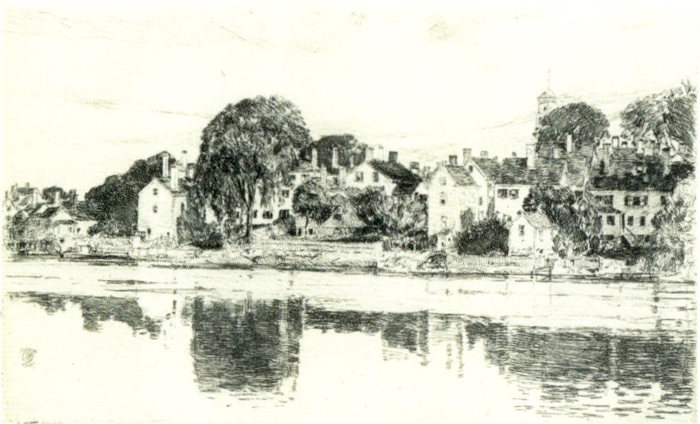

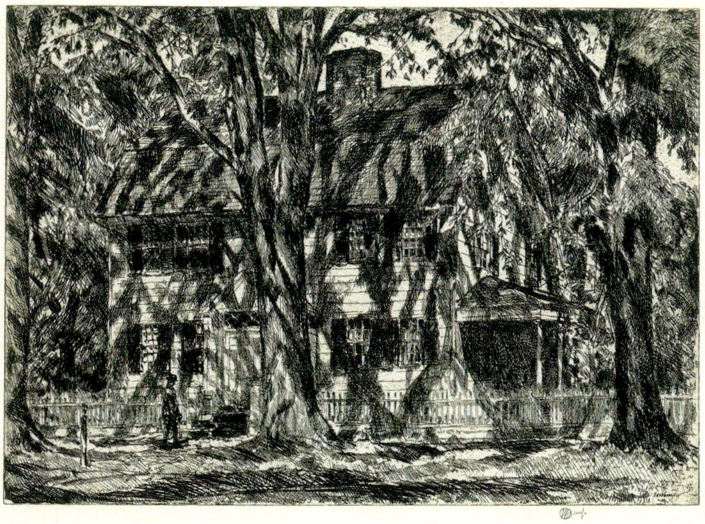

Fig. 281. Childe Hassam. *The Lion Gardiner House, Easthampton,* 1920. Etching on beige laid paper (French, *Michallet* watermark), 9¾ x 14 in. (24.8 x 35.6 cm) 40.30.36 (C159)

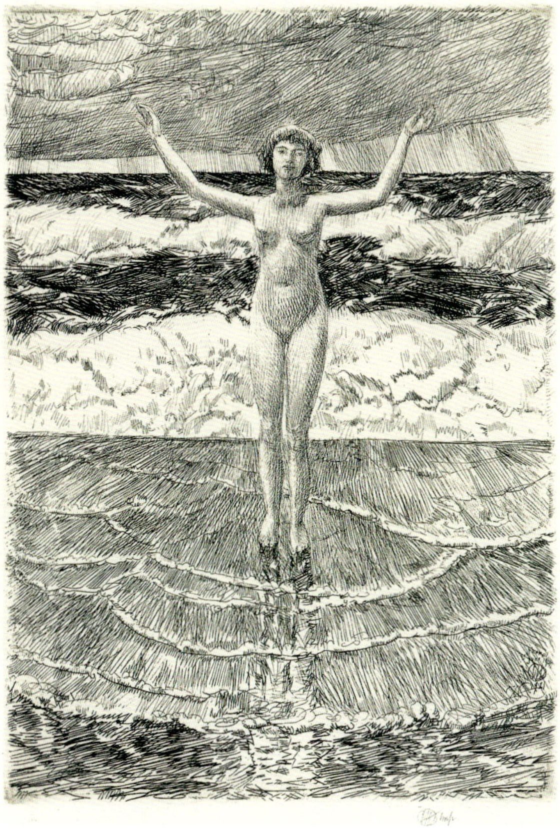

Fig. 282. Childe Hassam. *Rain Drops and Surf,* 1921. Etching on buff wove paper, 8½ x 6 in. (21.6 x 15.4 cm) 40.30.13 (C170)

city streets populated by distant figures (*Fifth Avenue, Noon*), soaring modern buildings (*Washington's Birthday, Fifth Avenue and 23rd Street* [fig. 18]), or massive flags (*Lafayette Street* [fig. 279]); expansive fields (*Newfields, New Hampshire* [fig. 285]) and quiet harbors (*The Chimneys, Portsmouth* [fig. 280]); ancient trees and colonial architecture (*The Lion Gardiner House, Easthampton* [fig. 281]); and classical nudes in idyllic landscapes (*Rain Drops and Surf* [fig. 282]).

Just as the subjects of Hassam's etchings and lithographs correspond closely to those of his paintings, so the compositions of his prints frequently repeat the structures of his oils. On paper, as on canvas, Hassam favored sweeping views of streets seen from an angle (*Union Square* [fig. 283]) or skyscrapers shown from an ennobling distance (*Washington's Birthday, Fifth Avenue and 23rd Street*). Hassam's prints also reveal the painter's long-standing interest in capturing fleeting effects of light and color. Some, for example, *Old Lace* and *The Chimneys, Portsmouth,* use carefully inked, intricate patterns of shimmering lines to suggest atmospheric vibration. Others, such as *Avenue of the Allies* and *The Little Church Around the Corner,* are inscribed with the time of day—a detail unquestionably linked to the Impressionists' attempt to record specific moments.[35]

General similarities of subject, composition, and effect between a given artist's prints and paintings might seem obvious; in Hassam's case, however, the specific relationships of the etchings and the lithographs to the oils are not straightforward. Some of Hassam's prints (such as the early Impressionist landscape etchings of 1915 to 1918, which correspond to oils of the 1890s) significantly postdate the comparable canvases. Others (such as the etched and lithographic views of flag displays of 1916 to 1918) are largely contemporaneous

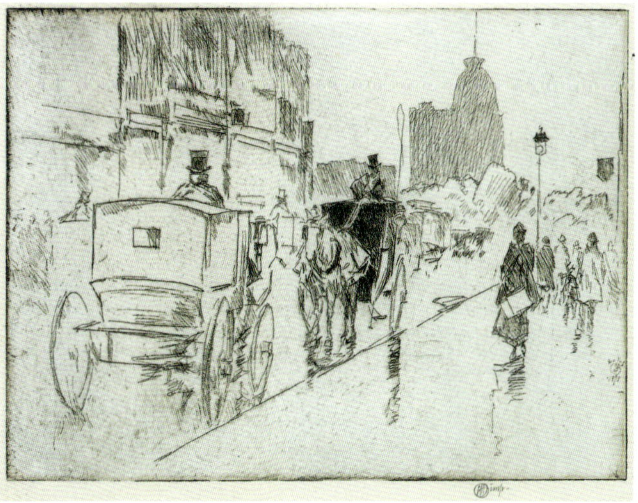

Fig. 283. Childe Hassam. *Union Square,* 1896/1916. Etching on blue laid paper, 4¼ x 5¾ in. (10.8 x 14.6 cm) 1940 40.30.7 (C89)

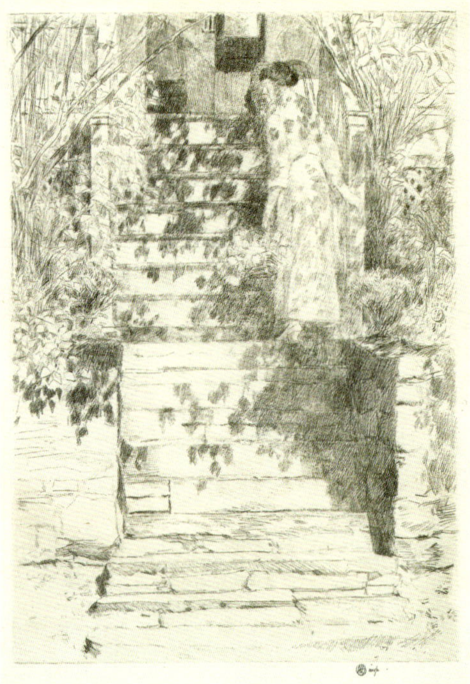

Fig. 284. Childe Hassam. *The Steps,* 1915. Etching on lightweight off-white paper, 10¾ x 7⅝ in. (27.4 x 19.4 cm). The Metropolitan Museum of Art, New York. Gift of Theodore De Witt, 1923 23.65.78 (C52)

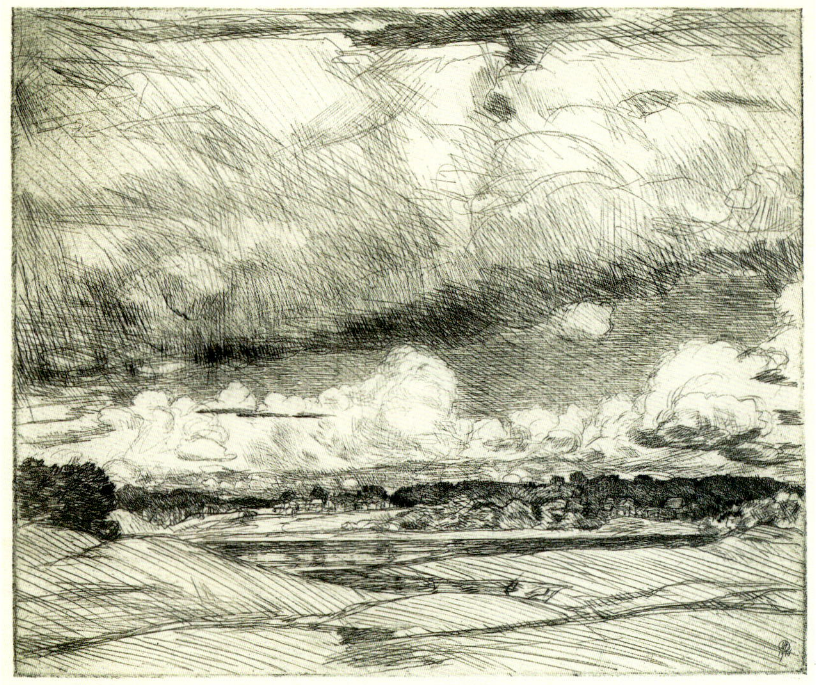

Fig. 285. Childe Hassam. *Newfields, New Hampshire,* 1916. Etching and drypoint on buff laid paper, 9⅜ x 11⅜ in. (24.8 x 29.8 cm) 40.30.23 (C106)

with their painted counterparts. Regardless of their chronological distance or proximity, however, Hassam's prints are never merely derivative of his paintings. The linear, monochromatic vocabulary specific to etching and lithography prompted him to attempt fresh artistic statements in print. As he struggled to master the challenging new visual language of prints, Hassam regained a sense of exploration that one critic (writing about the first exhibition of his etchings) had missed in his recent paintings:

> *In dropping the brush and taking up the more nervous needle, all these "phrases" [the conventions of his paintings], so to speak, dropped away from him, and it is amusing to see him putting down lines, as hopefully and directly as an infant, as though to say, "let this represent a tree," or "let's suppose this is to be a river bank." This sort of thing is so attractive in etching that there are times when one considers it to be the essential quality. . . . It is certainly to be wished that in gaining further experience Mr. Hassam will not lose this refreshing and etcher-like frankness.*[36]

Moreover, once Hassam had attained fluency in etching and lithography, he ceased to use those media primarily to translate oil paintings and began to make truly original statements in black and white. In the last two decades of Hassam's life, his paintings seem to have benefited as much from the prints as the prints did from the paintings. Indeed, Hassam's oils would begin to reflect developments in his etchings as early as 1916, when he devised the concept for his Flag paintings initially as a printmaking project: as Carl Zigrosser observed, Hassam intended to capture on copper a single view of Fifth Avenue "at varying hours and seasons."[37] More profoundly, by 1917 the insistent repetition of line characteristic of Hassam's prints had become a central concern for all his art (see figs. 11, 237, 310, 316).[38]

Even the most casual glance at Hassam's mature prints reveals the change in style. In some, bold patterns of dark and light, so intense as to obscure their ostensible subjects, replace the earlier effects of flickering illumination. In *The Lion Gardiner House, Easthampton* (fig. 281), massive trees cast looming, veinlike shadows onto a colonial house; the dark striations animate the building and lend it a far livelier aspect than that of the small man standing frozen at the gate. Other mature prints place objects in flat planes parallel to the picture surface or in vertical arrangements receding from it. In *The Steps* (fig. 284)—executed in Cos Cob

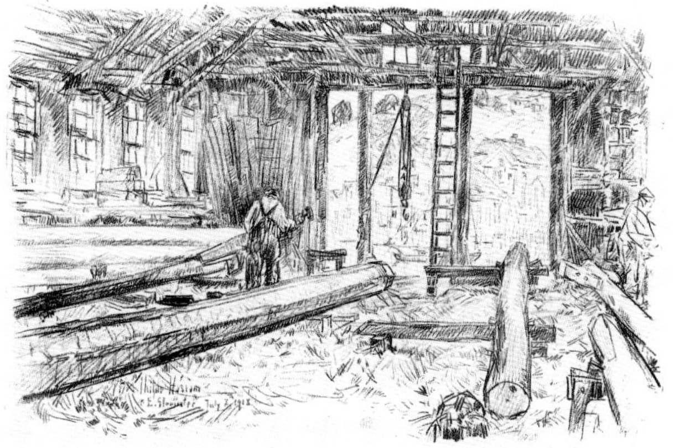

Fig. 286. Childe Hassam. *The Spar Shop, Gloucester,* 1918. Lithograph on lightweight beige wove paper (Japanese, foliate watermark), 7⅛ x 12 in. (18.1 x 30.5 cm) 40.30.44 (G23)

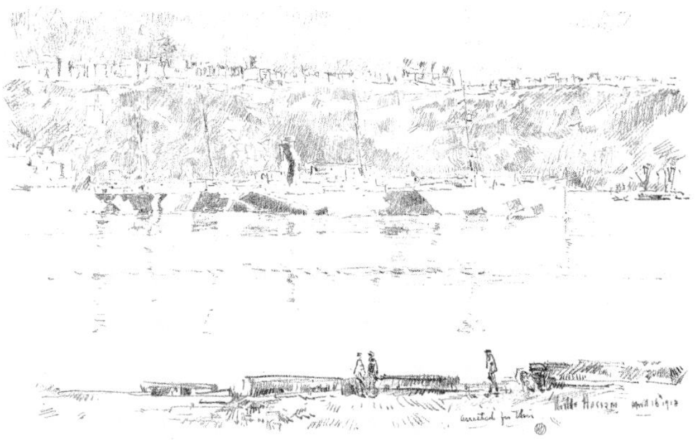

Fig. 287. Childe Hassam. *Camouflage,* 1918. Lithograph, 6⅛ x 11 in. (17.3 x 27.9 cm). Print Collection, Miriam and Ira D. Wallach Division of Art, Prints, and Photographs, The New York Public Library, Astor, Lenox, and Tilden Foundations G8

and Hassam's first work of this kind—clustered masses of fine, densely hatched strokes convey the effect of dappled sunlight and distract attention from the woman who stands on the steep steps, holding a basket of cuttings in one hand and reaching for the banister with the other.[39] Hassam may have borrowed this scaffoldlike, asymmetrical composition from Japanese prints, which were widely collected by his contemporaries and enthusiastically studied by his associates in Cos Cob.[40] Seen from a slight distance, the scene dissolves into a field of dark shapes falling into light lines. As John Taylor Arms put it, Hassam's prints of this kind "may equally be considered not only as lines and values cunningly disposed on white paper, but as designs of white on dark backgrounds, thus proving the perfect interrelation of solids and blank spaces in each." Consequently, Arms continued, the works appear almost to be "abstractions, yet the forms are those of reality and their relation, one to another, is such as exists in nature."[41]

Strong, expressive patterns would come to dominate Hassam's designs, even those that seem explicitly tied to real subjects. In *Newfields, New Hampshire* (fig. 285)—to take an example named for its geographic location—broadly spaced lines represent open fields; densely packed strokes form trees and distant farms; and rough, rapid dashes chart a fast-approaching storm that forces a layer of small white cumulus clouds to gather at the horizon.

Not surprisingly, Hassam's shift toward a bolder style coincided with his adoption, at the end of 1917, of the planographic medium of lithography. For an artist concerned with articulating rich patterns of dark strokes against light grounds, it must have seemed a natural step. Indeed, Hassam's most attentive critics urged him to it. In 1918 Frank Weitenkampf, chief of the Art and Prints Division of the New York Public Library, observed that "subjects, such as 'The Steps' and others, fairly cry for the lithographic crayon."[42]

In 1918 Hassam confined almost all of his printmaking activities to lithography, and his experience with the medium encouraged him to move still further in the direction of abstract pattern. Hassam presumably learned the technique from his friend Joseph Pennell, whose successful series of lithographs documenting the construction of the Panama Canal and the war effort in Britain and America did much to promote the medium in the United States. In 1922 Pennell provided a clear description of the lithographic process: "Lithographs are surface prints from flat stones or metal plates on which a drawing in greasy ink or chalk has either been made or transferred. The stone or plate is dampened and ink rolled on it: the dampness repels the ink only on the undrawn parts and adheres only to the greasy drawing. Paper is then laid on the inky stone and both run through a press, and the greasy design comes off the stone on the paper."[43]

Hassam made his lithographs using transfer paper, onto which he drew his designs before applying each sheet to the zinc plate or lithographic stone. (The texture of this transfer paper remains visible as a slight tone on some of the resulting prints, such as *The Spar Shop, Gloucester* [fig. 286].)[44] This technique allowed Hassam to continue his practice of

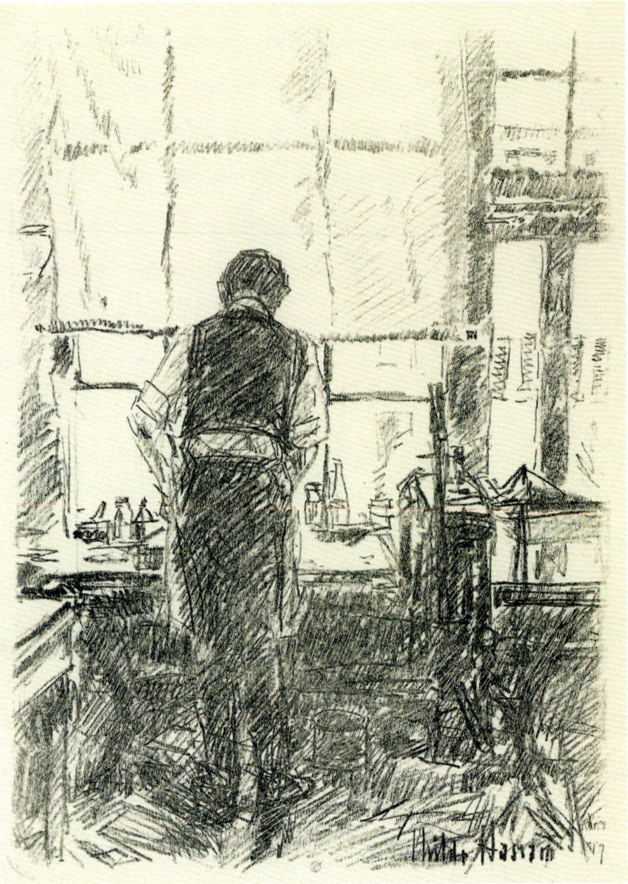

Fig. 288. Childe Hassam. *Portrait of Joseph Pennell,* 1917. Lithograph on lightweight beige wove paper (Japanese, foliate watermark), 15⅜ x 11¼ in. (39.1 x 28.6 cm) 40.30.39 (G3)

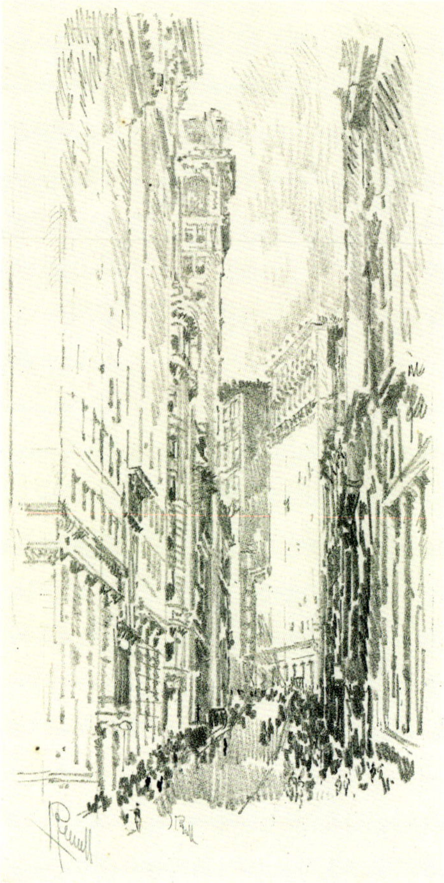

Fig. 289. Joseph Pennell. *William Street,* from the portfolio *Lithographs of New York in 1904 Drawn by Joseph Pennell* (The Society of Iconophiles, New York, 1905). Lithograph on lightweight beige wove paper, 11⅛ x 7¼ in. (28.4 x 18.4 cm). The Metropolitan Museum of Art, New York. Gift of Mrs. William Loring Andrews, 1921 21.74.125

drawing on the spot after nature; as a result, his lithographs retain the immediacy of his sketches. Hassam's fondness for drawing from the motif once got him into trouble with the authorities: in the spring of 1918, while sketching a camouflaged American transport vessel anchored in the Hudson River, he was mistaken for a spy and arrested.[45] Apparently amused by the misunderstanding, the artist inscribed the completed lithograph, *Camouflage* (fig. 287), at the lower right: *Childe Hassam April 18, 1918 / arrested for this.*

In *Camouflage,* as in his *Portrait of Joseph Pennell* of the previous year (fig. 288), Hassam applied the lithographic crayon in brusque, summary marks that recall the broad, unblended strokes of his pastels (see fig. 155). Such bold handling may also reveal the inspiration of Pennell's lithographic style; in that artist's *William Street* (fig. 289) similarly brisk, decisive marks delineate the tall buildings of early-twentieth-century New York and indicate the crowds in front of them. Hassam's decisive handling prompted one critic to describe his lithographs as "crisp renderings of fearless decision."[46] At times Hassam's crispness must have seemed at odds with his subject. In a *Nude* of 1918 (fig. 290), for example, a slim, angular young woman presents the viewer with her back, scored by sharp, parallel lines and fine passages of scratching out. With a gesture that suggests self-defense more than seduction, the figure raises her elbows against the jagged, slashing lines of shadow (or foliage) that encroach upon her space. For viewers accustomed to the soft, yielding curves of most late-nineteenth-century female nudes—favored equally by academic and avant-garde painters from Bouguereau to Renoir—the distinctly unsensuous body of Hassam's figure may well have been unsettling.[47] Pennell, however, detected a certain admirable expressiveness in such unconventional depictions of

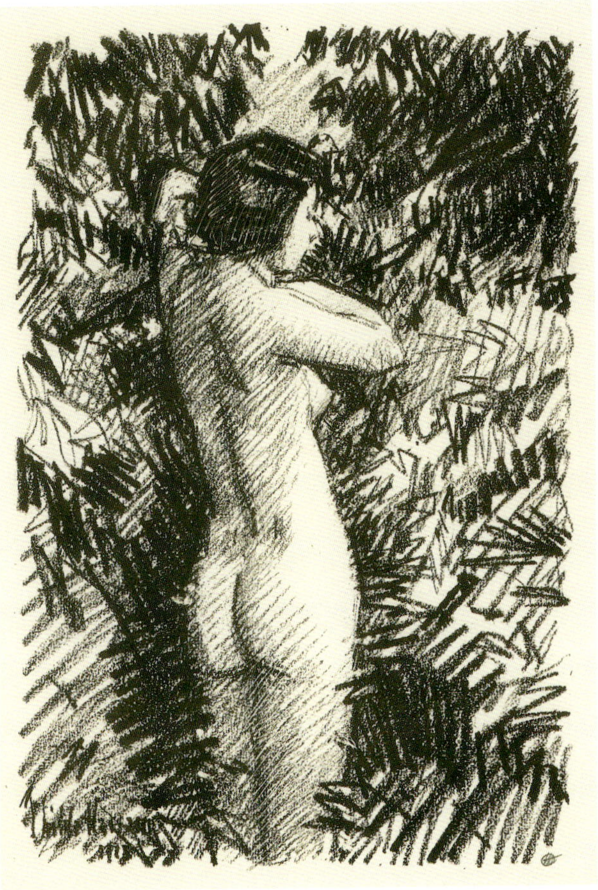

Fig. 290. Childe Hassam. *Nude,* 1918. Lithograph on lightweight beige wove paper (Japanese, foliate watermark), 14⅜ x 9 in. (36.5 x 22.8 cm) 40.30.49 (G38)

female anatomy and cited Hassam's nudes as "proof that . . . there are American women still left who do not look like flappers, [and] that there are other methods besides tracing photographs, of drawing nudes."[48]

In addition to lithography, Hassam explored the related technique of lithotint, in which the artist uses a brush to apply washes of tusche (a black liquid made of the same materials as the lithographic crayon). Hassam prepared his lithotints—unlike his lithographs—directly on the stone.[49] His last, *Storm King* (fig. 291), ranks as a masterpiece of the form: the ominous mountains that pierce the cloudy sky and dwarf the minuscule ship may reveal Hassam's own emotions in wartime. Just as the marks in Hassam's lithographs recall the strokes of his pastels, so the large, flat masses that characterize his lithotints resemble the fluid washes of his watercolors.[50] In lithotint, as in watercolor, pigments of the liquid medium pool at the edges of strokes; large passages display a grainy texture (caused by partial evaporation of the medium); and scratching out of already pigmented areas yields highlights. The resulting effects are dark, in striking contrast to the blond tonalities favored by Whistler and his followers. Hassam's lithotints stirred one admiring critic to proclaim them "brunette beauties, dark Rosaleens with their fearless brush strokes like the stroke of a disciplined oar."[51]

Today Hassam's bold late printmaking style may suggest links to modern European art. The powerful linear forms of his lithographs resemble the interlocking planes that structure paintings by Paul Cézanne. His emphatic patterns recall the decorative surfaces created by the Nabis Pierre Bonnard and Édouard Vuillard. And his flattened, sometimes vertically stepped designs that stress surface decoration over recession into depth seem to correspond to the shallow, fragmented spaces presented in the Cubist works of Pablo Picasso and Georges Braque.

Hassam, however, disdained modernism. Royal Cortissoz, the artist's friend and the cataloguer of his prints, recalled hearing him fling "his criticisms in a kind of noble rage" against "the bizarre muddles of the cubists, the abstractionists and such like."[52] In Hassam's own day, then, the severe late style he developed in conjunction with his printmaking did not resonate with advanced European art. Rather, for Hassam's contemporaries, this late style embodied a distinctly American vigor, which one critic characterized as

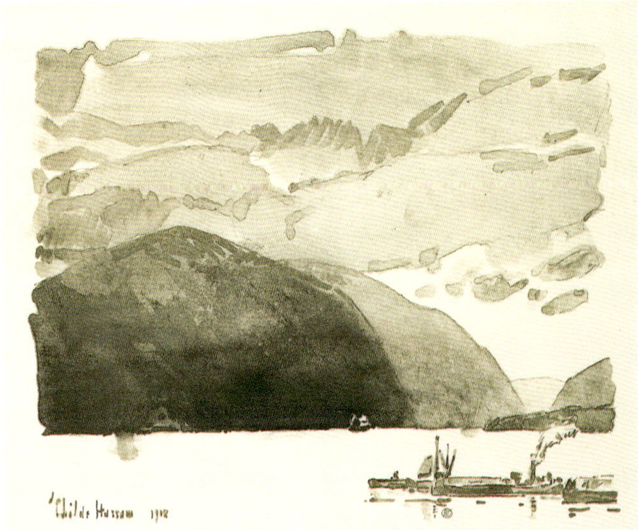

Fig. 291. Childe Hassam. *Storm King,* 1918. Lithotint on lightweight beige wove paper, 10¾ x 12⅛ in. (27.3 x 30.8 cm). Print Collection, Miriam and Ira D. Wallach Division of Art, Prints, and Photographs, The New York Public Library, Astor, Lenox, and Tilden Foundations G45

"athletic."[53] For some Hassam's art more specifically bespoke his Yankee heritage. As Haskell observed: "His Puritan ancestry, with the downright qualities that such ancestry engenders, has had much to do in shaping his career. . . . Bred into his art is this vigorous quality, this New England thoroughness. And how essentially American his work is! He has absorbed the European influence of his younger days and stands alone profoundly American. This 'national integrity' is without doubt the great need of American art to-day."[54]

Hassam himself probably regarded the style in similar terms. Significantly, he chose to display only prints at Willow Bend, his early-eighteenth-century East Hampton summer house, claiming that they were better suited to the rustic colonial setting than were paintings.[55] Like other American artists who participated in the etching revival movement, he regarded his original handmade prints as an alternative to slick photomechanical methods of reproduction. More distinctively, he appears to have associated the boldly articulated, densely patterned, antivolumetric style of his prints with notions of American nationalism.[56]

For viewers today, Hassam's prints provide a key with which to begin to unlock the secrets of his later art. Formally ambitious, technically assured, and briskly articulated, they reveal a vision of the world far darker and bolder than that expressed in the bright glory of such early paintings as *Grand Prix Day* (fig. 58). More enticing than ominous, the dark and bold world of Hassam's etchings and lithographs is well worth exploring.

The title phrase of the essay is from "Art at Home and Abroad. Childe Hassam's Work in Various Mediums," *New York Times Magazine*, November 16, 1919, p. 12. The author is presumably Elisabeth Luther Cary, art critic for the *New York Times*. The epigraph is taken from Lockman interview, February 3, 1927, p. 21.

Unless otherwise noted, the prints reproduced in this essay are in the collection of The Metropolitan Museum of Art, Gift of Mrs. Childe Hassam, 1940.

The catalogue raisonné of Hassam's etchings and drypoints is Royal Cortissoz and the Leonard Clayton Gallery, *Catalogue of the Etchings and Dry-Points of Childe Hassam, N.A. of the American Academy of Arts and Letters*, rev. ed. (San Francisco: Alan Wofsy Fine Arts, 1989). The revised edition includes Cortissoz's 1925 catalogue of Hassam's etchings (through 1924); the Clayton Gallery's 1933 catalogue of his subsequent etchings (through October 1933), with an introduction by Paula Eliasoph; and entries for four etchings completed in the remaining two years of his life. In the present essay, prints included in this source are identified with the initial C and the number given to the work, enclosed in parentheses: for example (C1). The dating presented in this essay follows the catalogue raisonné, with particular attention to Eliasoph's authoritative introduction, which provides the most thorough discussion of the chronology of Hassam's etched work; Cortissoz 1989, pp. 147–55, originally published as Paula Eliasoph's introduction to *Handbook of the Complete Set of Etchings and Drypoints of Childe Hassam, N.A.* . . . (New York: The Leonard Clayton Gallery, 1933), pp. v–viii. Eliasoph, herself an artist, prepared her account with the assistance of Hassam and his wife's grandniece, Virginia Rook (later Mrs. Chauncey B. Garver). Two dates separated by a slash, for example 1898/1915, indicate the starting and completion dates of a given plate.

The catalogue raisonné of Hassam's lithographs is Fuller Griffith, *The Lithographs of Childe Hassam: A Catalog*, United States National Museum, Bulletin, no. 232 (Washington, D.C.: Smithsonian Institution, 1962; reprinted, New York: M. Gordon, 1980). In the present essay, lithographs included in this source are identified with the initial G and the number given to the work, enclosed in parentheses, for example (G3).

The following sources were consulted in addition to those cited in the notes below: Royal Cortissoz, *The Etchings and Dry-Points of Childe Hassam, N.A.* (New York: Charles Scribner's Sons, 1925); Janet A. Flint, *J. Alden Weir: An American Printmaker, 1852–1919*, exh. cat. (Washington, D.C.: National Collection of Fine Arts, Smithsonian Institution, and Brigham Young University; Provo, Utah: Brigham Young University Press, 1972); Hassam (Tucson) 1972; Rona Schneider, "The Birth of American Painter-Etching, 1866–1882" (M.A. thesis, Queens College, City University of New York, 1978); Ellen S. Jacobowitz and George H. Marcus, *American Graphics, 1860–1940*, exh. cat. (Philadelphia: Philadelphia Museum of Art, 1982); Rona Schneider, *American Painter Etchings, 1853–1908*, exh. cat. (New York: Grolier Club, 1989); Curry 1990; Hildegard Cummings, Helen K. Fusscas, and Susan G. Larkin, *J. Alden Weir: A Place of His Own*, exh. cat. (Storrs, Conn.: William Benton Museum of Art, University of Connecticut, 1991); Fort 1993; Reba White Williams, "Greetings from Weyhe," *Print Quarterly* 10, no. 4 (December 1993), pp. 408–12; Weinberg, Bolger, and Curry 1994; Kit Basquin, "A Member Muses: 'Italian Barque' by Childe Hassam," *University Club Bulletin*, 8, no. 3 (February 1995), p. 4; Esten 1997; Truettner and Stein 1999; Eric Denker and Herbert L. Cooper, "The Prints of Childe Hassam," *American Art Review* 15, no. 3 (May–June 2003), pp. 92–95.

The author acknowledges with gratitude Donelson F. Hoopes, who generously shared an annotated copy of his 1979 monograph on Hassam that assisted us greatly in our search for primary source materials. At The Metropolitan Museum of Art, the following individuals in the Department of Drawings and Prints deserve thanks: intern Kate Kooistra looked for documentary references to Hassam's printmaking activities with characteristic energy and intelligence, and helped compile the bibliography; Taube Greenspan, a dedicated volunteer, undertook useful preliminary research; Kit Basquin, our Administrative Assistant, shared her knowledge—and love—of works by Hassam in New

York private collections; and Connie McPhee, Study Room Supervisor, and Liz Zanis, Study Room Assistant, tirelessly helped with various matters concerning the Metropolitan's own holdings of Hassam's prints. In the Department of Paper Conservation, Margaret Lawson, Associate Conservator, brought her expertise to bear on the close examination of the Metropolitan's Hassam prints. At the New York Public Library, Paul LeClerc, Director; Roberta Waddell, Curator of the Print Collection; Roseann Panebianco, Loan Administrator; and the staff of the Miriam and Ira D. Wallach Division of Art, Prints and Photographs gave valuable assistance. At the Philadelphia Museum of Art, Rena M. Hoisington, Curatorial Fellow in the Department of Prints, Drawings, and Photographs, shared important information. And at the Archives of American Art, Smithsonian Institution, Washington, D.C., Joy Weiner and Judy Throm provided crucial guidance in navigating their repository's rich collections.

1. For Hassam's early work and training, see Stephanie L. Herdrich, "Hassam in Boston, 1859–1886," in this publication, pp. 29–42.
2. Hassam recounted the circumstances of his design in 1924, when the 1882 masthead of the *Marblehead Messenger* was still in use; "Old Woodcut Work of Childe Hassam," *East Hampton Star*, November 28, 1924, p. 1. Hassam described his apprenticeship with Johnson further, in Lockman interview, January 25, 1927, p. 9.
3. The term derives from the Italian *intagliare*, meaning to engrave or to cut.
4. Hassam also recalled making etchings "as a boy in the Art Students League [in Boston]. For a part of a winter." Lockman interview, January 31, 1927, p. 35.
5. *Reid's Close* (C285), *Plainstone Close* (C286), *The End of Plainstone Close* (C374), *English Cottages* (C307), and *Hogarth's House* (C327). Hassam's attendance at Haden's Boston lectures is not recorded, but the importance of that artist's 1882–83 American tour in promoting etching is uncontested. See Richard S. Schneiderman, *A Catalogue Raisonné of the Prints of Sir Francis Seymour Haden* (London: Robin Garton, 1983), p. 29. Garrett had learned to etch at the urging of Robert Swain Gifford, the gifted painter-printmaker who was an early American Fellow of the Society of Painter-Etchers in London and became a founding member of The New York Etching Club.
6. Hassam was interviewed by the *New York Times* on the occasion of the first exhibition of graphic arts at the American Academy of Arts and Letters. "America to Show Its Graphic Arts. First Exhibit of Etchings and Engravings to Open at Academy's Galleries March 16," *New York Times*, March 5, 1922, p. 14.
7. Areas on the somewhat later plates for *Porte St. Martin*, 1898/1915 (C1), and *Garden of the Luxembourg* (fig. 267), for example, appear to have been burnished out, presumably to replace earlier, unsatisfactory work. Hassam may have had such prints in mind when he recalled, in 1927: "My earliest etchings were disastrous failures. It all depends on the physical condition of the medium and the chance of biting a plate." Lockman interview, February 2, 1927, p. 20.
8. *The Athenaeum, Portsmouth*, 1915 (C14), for example, was reportedly "done from nature in Miss Dorothy Whitcomb's car" (Cortissoz 1989, p. 25). Hassam employed professional models (usually for nudes, often in the studio), and also asked the women in his artistic circle to pose for him (particularly at Cos Cob and East Hampton). Maud Hassam, his wife; Carolyn Mase, Twachtman's pupil; Constant Holley MacRae, the daughter of a Cos Cob innkeeper and wife of the painter Elmer MacRae; Helen Burke, the daughter of a Cos Cob barkeeper; and Virginia Rook, Mrs. Hassam's grandniece, have all been identified in his etchings. The last recalled posing for Hassam in East Hampton during the summers, sometimes with friends following a tennis match—but never, she insisted (dismissing rumors to the contrary), wearing a toga! Judith Wolfe, "Childe Hassam in East Hampton—a Note," in Hassam (East Hampton) 1981, p. 14.
9. *The Little Piano* (C30), according to Cortissoz, was made from life using the model Muse Costello "in an impromptu sitting at New York" (Cortissoz 1989, p. 31). Hassam described completing *Easthampton* (fig. 268) "from nature in three sittings"; quoted in Frank Weitenkampf, "Childe Hassam and Etching," *American Magazine of Art* 10 (December 1918), p. 49.
10. Confusingly, the dates Hassam inscribed on his prints do not always refer to the dates of their completion. In some instances they indicate the years in which he began work on the plates (C1, C2, C84, C85); in others they correspond to the dates of the preliminary drawings on which they were based (C5, C6, C19, C43, C82, C83, C86–C89, C92, C94, C95, and probably C201). For the method of recording the dates of Hassam's prints used here, see the text preceding these endnotes.
11. The exact date of Hassam's return to etching is uncertain; in 1927 he recalled, "I did not take up etching until about 1912. And then in 1915 being in Cos Cob in the Fall and there being Mr. K. Ebbey [Kerr Eby] there who had a press there, it made it very pleasant to take up etching then and get proofs of my work," and "I never quite got at it just right until about 1912, when I went to Cos Cob." Lockman interviews, January 31, 1927, p. 35, and February 2, 1927, p. 20, respectively. The Long Island architect Lars de Lagerberg wrote that he remembered witnessing Hassam's first attempts at drypoint, made in "1912–13 or 14 or 1911," on the occasion of a Cos Cob sketching and swimming party also attended by the illustrator and cartoonist Oscar Howard. Lars de Lagerberg, March 16, 1959, to Richard H. Howland of the National Trust for Historic Preservation, who forwarded it to Anson Lowitz, president of the Historical Society of the Town of Greenwich, which owns the Bush-Holley House, where Hassam stayed in Cos Cob. The letter is in the collection of the Historical Society of the Town of Greenwich, Cos Cob, Connecticut. I am grateful to Susan G. Larkin for drawing my attention to this delightful, little-known missive and for providing me with a copy of it. Finally, it should be noted that Hassam might have begun to etch again as early as 1910. His comment "You shall have a proof of the first etching I make," in a letter to John W. Beatty dated January 6, 1910, suggests that he was at least considering the prospect at that date; Carnegie Institute Papers, box 42 of 255, file 673, Carnegie Institute Museum of Art Records, 1896–1940, Archives of American Art, Smithsonian Institution.
12. On August 7, 1914, Hassam wrote to Weir from Appledore, Isles of Shoals, asking him where he might find portable copper etching plates: "I really intended to make some etchings this summer and that morning in town when you were in such a rush I wanted to ask you about getting some plates—I want to take plates around in my pocket." Weir Family Papers Vault Mss. 511, box 3, folder 10, L. Tom Perry Special Collections, Harold B. Lee Library, Brigham Young University, Provo, Utah. Weir is likely to have known the answer: at the height of his interest in etching (about 1890), he and his friend John H. Twachtman

began carrying in their pockets "a half dozen plates which would fill up odd moments." Walter Pach, "Peintres-graveurs contemporains: M. J. Alden Weir," *Gazette des beaux-arts,* ser. 4, 6 (September 1911), pp. 214–15, translated by and quoted in Doreen Bolger Burke, *J. Alden Weir: An American Impressionist* (Newark: University of Delaware Press; New York, London, and Toronto: Cornwall Books, 1983), pp. 178–80. On the occasion of Hassam's first exhibition of etchings, Weir wrote: "I have always felt that so direct an observer [as Hassam] would add a new note in etching, and I have, with others in the past several years, tried to awaken his interest in the needle." J. Alden Weir, foreword, *Catalogue of an Exhibition of Etchings and Dry Points by Childe Hassam* (New York: Frederick Keppel and Co., November 30–December 18, 1915), p. 7.

13. "What Is Happening in the World of Art," *New York Sun,* December 12, 1915, sec. 5, p. 8. The first sentence of the passage quoted appears to support 1912 as the date of Hassam's return to etching (see n. 11 above): "Three years ago the painter made a few etchings, but it was not until the past summer that accident more than design impelled him to try again with the needle."

14. Eby's uncle was Frederick Keppel Sr., founder of the gallery that (not coincidentally) held Hassam's first exhibition of etchings, in 1915; Bernadette Passi Giardina, *Kerr Eby: The Complete Prints* (Bronxville, N.Y.: M. Hausberg, 1997), pp. 3–4. In Lockman interview, February 2, 1927, p. 20, Hassam recalled that Eby had arranged for the dealer David Keppel to visit Cos Cob to see his etchings. Carl Zigrosser—the influential critic, director of New York's Weyhe Gallery (1919–40), and first curator of prints and drawings at the Philadelphia Museum of Art (1940–63)—remembered the circumstances of Hassam's introduction to the Keppel Gallery differently. Zigrosser wrote that he was working at Keppel and acted as Hassam's advocate when Eby brought the artist and his etchings into the gallery during the summer of 1915; see "The Keppel Gallery," in Carl Zigrosser, *A World of Art and Museums* (Philadelphia: Art Alliance Press, 1975), p. 19. Hassam portrayed himself in Eby's studio in *The Etcher,* 1915 (C27); Eby surrounded by his materials in *The Illustrator,* 1915 (C31); and the picturesque location of Eby's studio in *Cos Cob,* 1915 (C32) and in the watercolor *Casa Eby, Cos Cob,* 1916 (private collection); see Susan G. Larkin, *The Cos Cob Art Colony: Impressionists on the Connecticut Shore,* exh. cat. (New York: National Academy of Design; New Haven: Yale University Press, 2001), pp. 132–33, pl. 80; Kathleen M. Burnside with Jeffrey W. Andersen, *Childe Hassam in Connecticut,* exh. cat. (Old Lyme, Conn.: Lyme Historical Society, Florence Griswold Museum, 1987), p. 30, no. 27; and Larkin in Harold Spencer, Susan G. Larkin, and Jeffrey W. Andersen, *Connecticut and American Impressionism,* exh. cat. (Storrs: William Benton Museum of Art, University of Connecticut, 1980), p. 96. Eby's article on the technique of etching, first published in *Print* 2, no. 2 (1941), pp. 41–51, is reprinted as Appendix A of Giardina, *Kerr Eby,* pp. 157–64.

15. For more on *Morning Mists,* see Giardina, *Kerr Eby,* p. 35, no. 18.

16. Hassam quoted in Dorothy Keppel, "Kerr Eby," *Print Collector's Quarterly* 6 (February 1939), p. 91, quoted by Larkin in Spencer, Larkin, and Andersen, *Connecticut and American Impressionism,* p. 96. Keppel recalled that Eby worked with Hassam in Cos Cob in 1919, but the two might also have worked together in 1915.

In later years the professional New York printer Peter J. Platt pulled Hassam's etchings. Works printed by Platt—such as the impression of Hassam's *Cos Cob Dock* in The Metropolitan Museum of Art (fig. 276)—can be identified by the distinctive series of small holes in their margins, formed when the dampened prints were pinned down to dry. Hassam depicted Platt—who also assisted Pennell and John Sloan—standing at his press in the 1934 etching *The Plate Printer, Peter J. Platt* (C379). If not through Pennell, Hassam could have met Platt through Frederick Keppel and Company or Kennedy and Company, two of his New York dealers, for both of whom Platt worked. See Emma Platt, *In Memoriam: Peter J. Platt* (New York: N.p., 1935); "Keppel Gallery," in Zigrosser, *World of Art and Museums,* p. 18; and Burke and Kiehl 1977, no. 12. Another professional printer, George C. Miller, also of New York, pulled Hassam's lithographs. Fuller Griffith, *The Lithographs of Childe Hassam: A Catalog,* United States National Museum, Bulletin, no. 232 (Washington, D.C.: Smithsonian Institution, 1962; reprinted, New York: M. Gordon, 1980), p. 5. For more on Miller, see "George C. Miller," *American Artist* 30, no. 5 (1966), pp. 12–13, 63.

17. One unnamed critic characterized Hassam's copperplate work as a concession to fashion: "One benefit in a fashion is that everybody follows it. . . . The present enthusiasm for etching got under way quietly some time ago, branching out no doubt from the successes of certain living English etchers, and now we may almost begin to boast of an American school. . . . Every day new volunteers rally to the flag. Mr. MacLaughlin, Mr. Andre-Smith, Mr. Pennell and Mr. Plowman have been rejoiced recently by the accession of two new and worthy comrades. Childe Hassam and Frank W. Benson, who are both academicians and members of the [*sic*] 'The Ten,' have become etchers. Who will be next?" "What Is Happening in the World of Art," p. 8.

18. Inevitably, Hassam's etchings would be compared to those of his famous predecessor. Zigrosser linked the two artists as early as 1915: "To him who is interested in discovering artistic kinships and tracing family trees (futile task generally), one would say that Childe Hassam and Whistler have much in common. There is the same untiring pursuit of the beauty of the world, the same preference for the decorative over the human element in picture-craft, the same broad culture, and the same genius of creative taste." Carl Zigrosser, introduction, *Catalogue of Exhibition of Etchings and Dry Points by Hassam,* p. 5. Henry McBride later faulted Hassam for addressing superficial, popular, and insufficiently profound subjects, which he characterized as Whistlerian; Henry McBride, "News and Comment in the World of Art," *New York Sun,* January 7, 1917, sec. 5, p. 12.

19. Other members included J. Alden Weir, John Marin, John Sloan, George Bellows, and Kerr Eby; "'Painter-Gravers' Aim to Cultivate American Taste for Graphic Art," *New York Times,* March 25, 1917, p. XX2. Hassam's disenchantment with commercial attempts to reproduce his paintings may have strengthened his resolve to reach a wider collecting audience through original artist's prints. As Hassam complained in a letter to John W. Beatty, he became furious when Harper and Brothers reproduced *The Sea,* 1898 (Adelson Galleries, Inc., New York), without his permission and noticeably cropped the image; Childe Hassam, New York, December 26, 1898, to John W. Beatty, Philadelphia, Carnegie Institute, Carnegie Institute Papers, box 42 of 255, file 673, Carnegie Institute Museum of Art Records, 1896–1940.

20. As one critic wrote in 1917: "The print is more in keeping with the democratic tendencies of today. It can be brought within the means of a greater number, and fifty or more collectors may enjoy their separate

impressions of one print." "'Painter-Gravers' Aim to Cultivate American Taste for Graphic Art," p. XX2. Hassam evidently shared this view. In 1927 he said: "I have used the medium of etching as one of the means of artistic expression. It is the most democratic means, because the price of etchings being so low, they are within the reach of everybody." Lockman interview, February 2, 1927, p. 20.

21. Hassam's earliest sets comprised originally discrete works assembled for sale as groups; Elisabeth Luther Cary, "The New York and East Hampton Sets Now on Exhibition: Many and Diverse Prints from the '90s to the Present Day," *New York Times,* February 26, 1933, p. X12. Sets of course commanded higher prices than individual works. But in a typewritten sheet dated February 7, 1933, pertaining to Hassam's exhibition of prints at the Leonard Clayton Gallery that year, filed in the Department of Drawings and Prints, The Metropolitan Museum Art, Paula Eliasoph claimed that Hassam sold his prints in sets because he felt that "an artist's interpretation of a town or city can best be conveyed by a group arrangement of etchings of that particular town." Eliasoph provides complete lists of Hassam's sets in the index to her 1933 catalogue; Paula Eliasoph, *Handbook of the Complete Set of Etchings and Drypoints, with 25 Illustrations, of Childe Hassam, N.A. of the American Academy of Arts and Letters; His Complete Work in This Medium from 1883 till October 1933* (New York: Leonard Clayton Gallery, 1933), pp. 70–76, reprinted in Cortissoz 1989, pp. 151–55. For Hassam's marketing of his work, see Dana Pilson, "'On the crest of the wave': Childe Hassam and the Marketing of His Art," in this publication, pp. 343–54.

22. Childe Hassam, February 7, 1932, to [Frederic Newlin] Price, Ferargil Galleries, New York, Ferargil Galleries Records, 1900–1963, Archives of American Art, Smithsonian Institution, reel N68–14, frame 115. Ultimately, the failure of Hassam's prints to sell has benefited a broad public, since, in the years following his death, his wife donated many of them to forty museums and libraries. Her generous gift of thirty-eight etchings and twelve lithographs to the Metropolitan Museum in 1940 transformed the collection into a major repository of Hassam's printed oeuvre. See Mayor 1940, pp. 138–39. Most of the prints included in the present exhibition have been drawn from Maud Hassam's donation.

23. Hassam quoted in "America to Show Its Graphic Arts," p. 14.

24. John Taylor Arms, "Childe Hassam, Etcher of Light," *Prints* 4, no. 1 (November 1933), pp. 4, 6.

25. Hassam also made pure drypoints, including C130, C133, C138, C140, C141, C147, C206, and C214.

26. A. Hyatt Mayor, *Prints and People: A Social History of Printed Pictures* (New York: The Metropolitan Museum of Art, 1971), fig. 703 and facing text.

27. As an early reviewer noted, "Among the etchers who use the medium in the spirit of the painter are Childe Hassam, whose line is asked to translate light, an even more daring essay than Whistler's, who filled blank spaces with tone"; "Art at Home and Abroad. Exhibitions for the Print Collector," *New York Times,* June 8, 1919, p. 81. And an unnamed critic described "his crisp sparkling technique [as] so annoying to the purists, so entrancing to everyone else"; "The World of Art: French Paintings and American Prints," *New York Times,* March 20, 1921, p. BRM11. Cary repeated the thought some years later: "Even in this enlightened day one hears now and again that Childe Hassam's line is 'not an etcher's line,' and gains no favor by uttering sincerest thanks that it isn't." Elisabeth Luther Cary, "Tendencies in Etching: Many Men of Many Minds Show Work Comparing Favorably with European Standards," *New York Times,* June 3, 1928, p. XX20.

28. Hassam may have felt encouraged by critics to forgo surface tone. Already in 1920 Cary identified Hassam's strength as a linear etcher, remarking: "It is only necessary to wipe his plates clean and refrain from tricks to get beautiful impressions. His clear dark pleasant greys and light-suffused darks are made with lines and depend hardly at all upon the printing." Elisabeth Luther Cary, "Collecting American Etchings," *American Magazine of Art* 11, no. 7 (May 1920), p. 238.

29. Burke and Kiehl 1977, introduction and no. 8. Hassam took his view from an upper-story window of a building on the southeast corner of Fifth Avenue and Thirty-fourth Street; the scene has been reversed in printing. The large column at the left is part of the newly completed B. Altman and Company department store (now occupied by the Graduate Center of the City University of New York). For the history of the site, see H. Barbara Weinberg, "Hassam in New York, 1889–1896," in this publication, pp. 105, 116, n. 91.

30. Ernest Haskell, introduction to Pousette-Dart 1922, p. ix.

31. *Catalogue of Exhibition of Etchings and Dry Points by Hassam,* pp. 9–12, nos. 1, 2, 19, 21, 22, 32, 41, 59, 65, 67, 68. Hassam's friends Eby, Weir, Twachtman, and Pennell all printed on old papers; see Giardina, *Kerr Eby,* p. 13; Burke, *J. Alden Weir,* p. 183; Mary Welsh Baskett, *John Henry Twachtman: American Impressionist Painter as Printmaker; a Catalogue Raisonné of His Prints* (Bronxville, N.Y.: M. Hausberg, 1999), pp. 43–45; and Joseph Pennell, *The Graphic Arts: Modern Men and Modern Methods* (Chicago: University of Chicago Press, 1921), p. 215.

32. Hassam reused certain sheets when taking proofs. The Metropolitan Museum's impression of *The Colonial Table* (fig. 278), for example, is printed on antique laid paper with an indecipherable watermark and bears a proof impression of *The Greek Dance,* 1916 (C91), on the reverse.

33. Cary, "Collecting American Etchings," p. 238.

34. Three lithographs made in 1918 copy paintings: *The Court, Gloucester* (G30), *End of the Court, Gloucester* (G31), and *Avenue of the Allies* (G43); as do three etchings made in 1924: *Fire Opals* (C232), *The Church at Old Lyme* (fig. 272), and *The Jonathan Baker Farm* (C234). One etching made in 1915 copies a pastel: *Young Pan Piping* (C61). Most of Hassam's prints that reproduce paintings, however, date to 1916 and follow earlier drawings of specific places made between 1887 and 1911: *Paris* (C82–C85), *London* (C86), *New York* (C76, C87–C89), *San Francisco* (C95), *Toledo, Spain* (C94), and *Old Lyme* (C92).

35. *Avenue of the Allies,* 1918 (G43) is inscribed *Oct. 19th, 1918 4 pm; The Little Church Around the Corner,* 1923 (C220) is inscribed *11 am July 31st 1923.* Catherine Green, in the pamphlet accompanying the exhibition *The Graphic Art of Childe Hassam* (Buffalo: Albright-Knox Art Gallery, July 31–October 18, 1981), linked such inscriptions to an Impressionist concern with times of day. Hassam may also have associated the practice with late-eighteenth- and early-nineteenth-century British watercolor painters—artists who occupied a pivotal position in his outline of the development of modern painting; see Hassam 1928, pp. 27–28. For two of the best-known British plein-air painters who annotated their sketches with the times and dates of their execution, see Timothy Wilcox, *Francis Towne,* exh. cat. (London: Tate Gallery, 1997), and Edward Morris, ed., *Constable's Clouds: Paintings and Cloud Studies by John Constable,* exh. cat. (Edinburgh: National Galleries of Scotland, 2000).

36. "What's Happening in the World of Art," *New York Sun,* December 12, 1915, sec. 5, p. 8.
37. Carl Zigrosser, *Childe Hassam* (New York: Frederick Keppel and Co., 1916), p. 22.
38. For more on Hassam's change of style between 1915 and 1935, see Fuller Griffith's introduction to Griffith, *Lithographs of Hassam,* and David W. Kiehl's introduction to Burke and Kiehl 1977.
39. Constant Holley MacRae posed for the figure on the steps of Holley House, Cos Cob.
40. Larkin, *Cos Cob Art Colony,* pp. 41–45.
41. Arms, "Childe Hassam, Etcher of Light," pp. 8, 10.
42. Weitenkampf, "Childe Hassam and Etching," p. 51. For Hassam's relationship to his critics, see Kathleen M. Burnside, "'Man Sass'Em': Hassam and His Contemporary Critics," in this publication, pp. 355–63.
43. Quoted in "America to Show Its Graphic Arts," p. 14.
44. Grant Reynard, "The Prints of Childe Hassam, 1859–1935," *American Artist* 24 (November 1960), p. 45.
45. "Childe Hassam Arrested: Policeman Congratulated by Artist for His Alertness in Riverside Park," *New York Times,* April 17, 1918, p. 24.
46. Haskell, introduction to Pousette-Dart 1922, p. x.
47. For Hassam's late nudes, see Kimberly Orcutt, "'The subject that I am known for': Hassam's Pursuit of a Legacy," in this publication, pp. 319–21.
48. Joseph Pennell, February 23, 1923, to Childe Hassam, published as the foreword to the *Catalogue of Exhibition of Etchings and Dry Points by Hassam.*
49. Griffith, *Lithographs of Childe Hassam,* p. 9.
50. Kiehl, introduction to Burke and Kiehl 1977; Hoopes 1979, p. 17. For Hassam's work as a watercolor painter, see Carol Troyen, "Hassam's Watercolors," in this publication, pp. 253–66.
51. Elisabeth Luther Cary, "Childe Hassam's Lithographs and Lithotints," *New York Times,* June 16, 1935, p. X8. Cary's readers would have recognized the reference to "Dark Rosaleen," a well-known poem by James Clarence Mangan (1803–1894), which characterized Ireland as a dark-haired beauty.
52. [Royal Cortissoz], "Childe Hassam," *New York Herald Tribune,* August 29, 1935, p. 16.
53. Elisabeth Luther Cary, "Exhibition of Works by Childe Hassam. Many Mediums. Oil Paintings, Pastels, Water Colors and Prints," *New York Times,* May 1, 1927, p. X9.
54. Haskell, introduction to Pousette-Dart 1922, p. vii.
55. Rattray 1923, p. 6.
56. For the popular association of American nationalism in general and colonial history in particular with early-twentieth-century antimodernism, see Thomas Andrew Denenberg, *Wallace Nutting and the Invention of Old America,* exh. cat. (Hartford, Conn.: Wadsworth Atheneum Museum of Art; New Haven: Yale University Press, 2003).

Hassam's Pride in His Ancestry

Elizabeth Broun

"Hassam is a Puritan and he paints American pictures," wrote Ernest Haskell in 1922, noting that the artist had a "sturdy background" and "national integrity."[1] Haskell was neither first nor last to sound this "Puritan" refrain,[2] nor was Hassam the only artist cast as patriotic exemplar. But in the 1920s Hassam did align his art with a large national purpose, a wave of conservative nativism similar to the spirit of the Colonial Revival initiated a half-century earlier.

Hassam does not at first seem to fit the conventional idea of a Puritan, for he was not religious or abstemious, nor were his works antiquarian in style or subject, as were many during the Colonial Revival period. He lived his modern creed: "I believe the man who will go down to posterity is the man who paints his own time and the scenes of every-day life around him."[3] He made his reputation in the 1880s and 1890s as the painter of Boston's fashionable Back Bay, Haussmann's reconstructed Paris, and New York's new commercial avenues. He celebrated New York as "the most beautiful city in the world," saying he preferred the new parts with their character and force to the older sections of the city.[4]

Hassam usually spent summers painting in New England villages as a diversion from the urban subjects he depicted during the rest of the year. But in August 1919 he purchased an early colonial house called Willow Bend in East Hampton, Long Island, and began spending six months of each year there. This move recentered his art on the island's old sites and landscapes; it meant stepping back into America's storied past and delving into his English ancestry. With this move, he adjusted his art in subtle ways to bring his personal and family history in line with broader national concerns. Throughout his career Hassam produced many paintings that encode "past and present" as a theme and range widely in mood, encompassing nostalgia, pride, anxiety, and regret.[5] After 1919 his pleasurable life on Long Island tipped the balance toward the positive, and he focused on the world of the colonial past viewed as an American Eden.

Childhood in Dorchester

Hassam grew up surrounded by the Puritan past in Dorchester, Massachusetts. Dorchester was New England's third settlement, founded in 1630 after Plymouth (1620) and Salem (1628). He attended the historic Mather School, which prided itself on being America's first public school. It sat on Meeting House Hill, where the first town meetings were convened, pointing the way to America's participatory democracy. In unpublished notes probably made in 1934, Hassam described his Dorchester childhood as idyllic. "Dorchester was a most beautiful and pleasant place for a boy to grow up and go to school—from Meeting House Hill and Milton hill looking out on Dorchester bay and Boston harbor with the white sails and the blue water of our clear and radiant North American weather, that electric and living quality of clear blue of certain times of the year could not be surpassed anywhere, if you like as fair as the isles of Greece—as blue at times as the Mediterranean."[6]

Harper's Weekly celebrated the 250th anniversary of the town in 1880 with an article entitled "Ancient Dorchester" and an illustration, *Old and New Dorchester*[7] (fig. 292), although there is nothing new in the image. It features the landing of the Dorchester settlers, vignettes of the old cemetery, the last meeting house, the old harbor, and two colonial

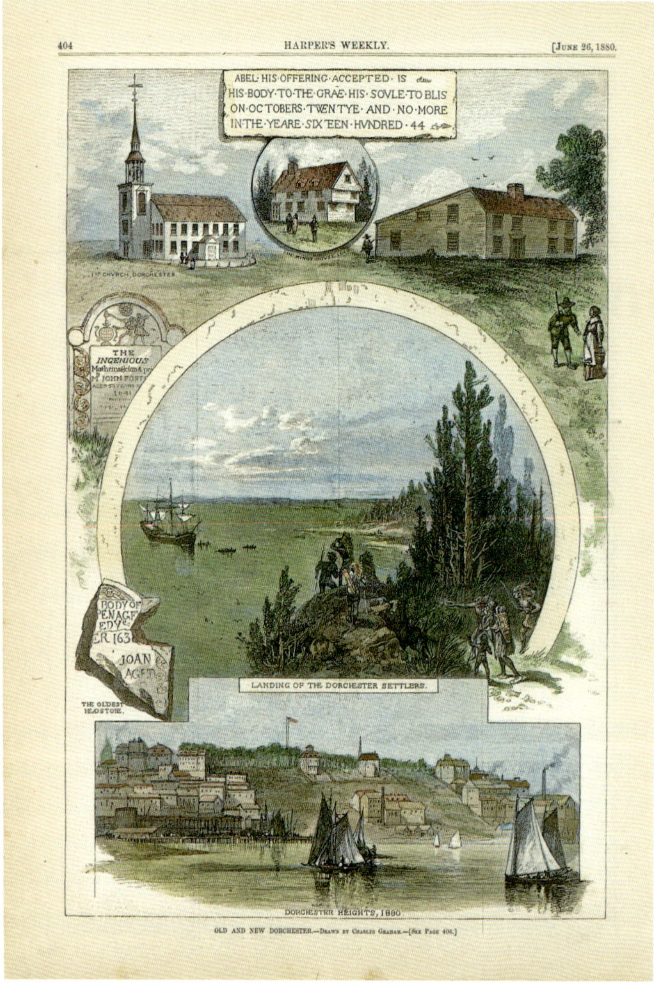

Fig. 292. Charles Graham. *Old and New Dorchester,* from *Harper's Weekly* 24 (June 26, 1880), p. 404

homes. This anniversary was bittersweet, coming a decade after Dorchester was annexed to Boston. The debate about annexation had raged from 1867 to 1869, beginning when Hassam was eight. It divided Dorchester's Yankee traditionalists—many of them descendants of the original settlers—from those advocating the economic advantages of Boston's railroads, trolleys, water resources, and real-estate development. Annexation passed by a vote of 928 to 726, and Dorchester's last town meeting was held on December 28, 1869.[8]

Historian William Dana Orcutt noted that at the time of Dorchester's annexation there was not a single almshouse or liquor saloon within the town limits,[9] a statement that reflects the strong anti-Irish sentiments of the time. A fundamental issue in the annexation debate was whether Dorchester would be overrun by recent Irish immigrants if it became part of Boston. During the 1840s and 1850s more and more Irish had found work in Dorchester's factories and mills. When Boston's Bishop John Fitzpatrick bought land to establish a parish for Dorchester's growing Catholic population, he kept the purpose of his purchase unclear by using a straw buyer, hoping to prevent protests at what was thought to be an encroachment of Papists. Still, nativist ruffians burned the Church of Saint Gregory during its construction, which was finally completed in 1854. When the annexation debate began in 1867, a fifth of the townspeople were from Ireland.[10]

About 1877–78 Hassam left high school to take a job in the accounting department of Little, Brown and Company in Boston, moving quickly to a wood-engraving firm. At least one of his early biographers claimed that he gave up school for love of art,[11] but Ulrich W. Hiesinger has suggested that it was the failure of his father's cutlery business that forced Hassam from his rural village to the commercial city.[12] His youth was cut short by necessity, and his halcyon memories were buried in Boston's sprawl. He wrote later: "Dorchester now is merely the ugly suburb of a large city all the old estates have been cut up the good houses have gone and it is nothing at all like what it was when I knew it, that part of Boston now has anything but an American population. . . . none of the old English names of families persist."[13]

Family History

Hassam wrote often and sometimes defensively about his early English origins. "The reply to queries about my surname is that it is one of the most Saxon names that you may come up with Horsham is probably first Horseham and 'ham' is the commonest ending of all Anglo-Saxon names, they are almost without number."[14] This etymology is recorded in the Hassam family history, published by John Tyler Hassam, a distant cousin, in 1870.[15] The history gives Hassam's earliest New England ancestor as William Horsham, who settled in Manchester, Massachusetts, by 1684 and obtained three land grants there. He appears in town records under thirteen variant spellings as constable (1693), highway surveyor (1696), fish culler (1705), and guard on the town's common land (1706). An 1880 addendum to the family history includes Horsham's petition for leniency, filed after arrest and sentencing for abusing a rate collector while drunk.

Childe Hassam's paternal ancestors include mariners and soldiers, but, as he often noted, no clergy. Frequently, an ancestor is listed as lost at sea or drowned. One was a privateer;

one was seized by a press gang and served five years on a British frigate during the Revolutionary War; another ran British blockades to reach Mediterranean ports. Another was in General Amherst's army for the invasion of Canada in 1759. There was enough to be proud of, if service to country and kinship with Saxon yeomen can be counted—the "sturdy background" cited by Ernest Haskell—though there was no business success, intellectual refinement, or religious attainment to decorate the family tree. Hassam wrote of his lineage with pride in its Saxon plainness, saying: "All of my people for eight generations back were obscure sailors and farmers and few could read or write. There was not one clergyman on either side. There was at least one pirate."[16]

One lineal ancestor, Hassam's great-grandfather, stood out. Stephen Hassam was born about 1761 and served as a powder monkey in the Revolutionary War, loading charges as well as taking water to the soldiers of the Copps Hill Battery and watching the Battle of Bunker Hill from a church steeple. He learned the trade of clockmaker in Worcester, then married up in status to Theodosia Hastings and settled in Charlestown, New Hampshire, where the couple had five children. (The fifth child, Stephen Danforth Hassam, was Childe Hassam's grandfather.) When Theodosia died, Stephen, then eighty years old, married twenty-three-year-old Lucy Miller, and they also had five children. In 1861, at age one hundred, Stephen carved and inscribed his own headstone. He lived another four years, long enough to bury his own son, a soldier killed in the Civil War.

This history fascinated Childe Hassam, who admired his great-grandfather's Revolutionary War experiences, virility, and longevity, calling him a "biological wonder."[17] But the Hassam side of the family provided no artistic progenitors,[18] so he turned to the distaff side for antecedents. His father's mother was a Hunt, so he could claim a distant relationship to architect Richard Morris Hunt and painter William Morris Hunt, who first brought Barbizon pictures to Boston. His own mother's ancestors were Hathornes, who arrived in New England a half-century before the Hassams. Patriarch William Hathorne came to Salem in 1630 and to Dorchester in 1631, before the family migrated to Maine. The most famous and literary Hathorne was Nathaniel, who changed the family name to Hawthorne, believing it to be an earlier, more authentic spelling. Although Hassam often cited his ties to Nathaniel Hawthorne and the two Hunts, they were distant relations at best and ones he apparently never met.[19]

About 1883 Hassam dropped his first name, Frederick, as well as the familiar Fred and the initial F in his signature. He insisted that "Childe" implied high status, saying: "Childe as it was invariably spelled in the earlier times is the Saxon word for shield or knight."[20]

Biographer Adeline Adams wrote: "What could be more English than Childe, and seemingly, what more Arabian than Hassam?"[21] Rumors of Near Eastern origins followed Hassam throughout his life. His physical appearance lent plausibility to the idea of a Turk or Arab ancestor; he was stocky with a bronzed complexion, perhaps from his lifelong love of ocean swimming. He preceded his signature with a crescent—a meticulous moon shape in the early days, reduced to an angled slash later in his career. Artist friends called him Muley after a fictional character in Washington Irving's *Alhambra*. After Hassam's death, painter Albert Rosenthal wrote about having visited Hassam's father in 1888, when the old man supposedly said: "After 150 years of intermarriage with New England people, look at me, I am still the Arab."[22]

During the Gilded Age English bloodlines and class distinctions became increasingly important to the emerging aristocracy of wealth. Hassam wrote of his humble ancestors with a complicated mixture of pride and apology, parading his English pedigree while betraying anxiety over its low social status. His worry was surely heightened by his father's business failures and his own truncated education. "The Hassams and Hathorns [*sic*] were sailors and farmers, some were Salem shipwrights, soldiers in every war for human liberty," he proudly stated. But he also declared defensively, "Hathorne is one of the names of the old yeoman families of England and like many of the other old yeoman farmer families it is older and more important than some of the titles dating from the time of Charles the second bestowed by him on gamblers and prostitutes."[23]

Hassam's concerns about lineage sharpened his sensitivity to class issues in modern life. This artist of yeoman descent painted street sweepers, coachmen, hod carriers, construction workers, and messenger boys alongside the social elite in modern urban views. Yet these workers are rarely protagonists, never reaching for the heroic humanism of the peasants depicted by Millet. They remain integrated into the scene, knowing their place.

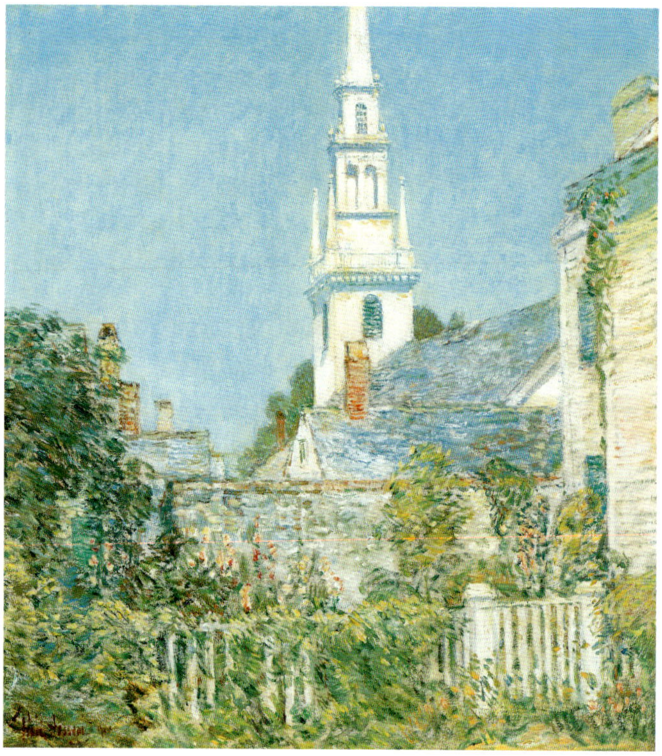

Fig. 293. Childe Hassam. *White Church at Newport,* 1901. Oil on canvas, 26 x 24 in. (66 x 61 cm). Private collection. Courtesy Sotheby's, Inc.

Exploring Old New England

At the very beginning of Hassam's painting career, about 1881 to 1884, he began visiting New England villages and painting picturesque colonial homes with sheltering trees, both symbolizing stability and continuity. *Old House, Dorchester,* 1884 (private collection),[24] shows deep shadows enveloping the ancient home, while dappled sunlight dances on grass and tree blossoms. Here as in many of Hassam's portrayals of such New England subjects past and present, memory and oblivion are in dialogue. Just a few years after leaving Dorchester, Hassam submerged personal memory in a broader historical context, presenting the stable geometry of Puritan craftsmanship as a solid anchor for a changing America.

Change was occurring throughout New England, but Hassam's views were carefully selected and edited to avoid acknowledging it. *The Old Fairbanks House, Dedham, Massachusetts* (fig. 31) shows the oldest surviving timber-frame home in North America, built in 1636 and already in Hassam's day emblematic of a New England that was rapidly fading. In the early 1870s, a decade before Hassam painted the Fairbanks House, Dedham's large, old agricultural holdings had mostly been subdivided into areas for immigrant newcomers.[25] *The Old Fairbanks House* and other evocative paintings of old sites were Hassam's contributions to the Colonial Revival, which was characterized by a passion for preserving old New England homes and village squares. About fifty years later Hassam seemed almost to be speaking of his own people when he hailed the plain virtues and enduring values he found in these surviving structures: "The square squat houses of the first settlers from England with their backs to the north wind long sloping roofs to shed the snow built by ships carpenters, these migrants took care to have builders of ships in their number and when they built a fine house . . . the inside finish

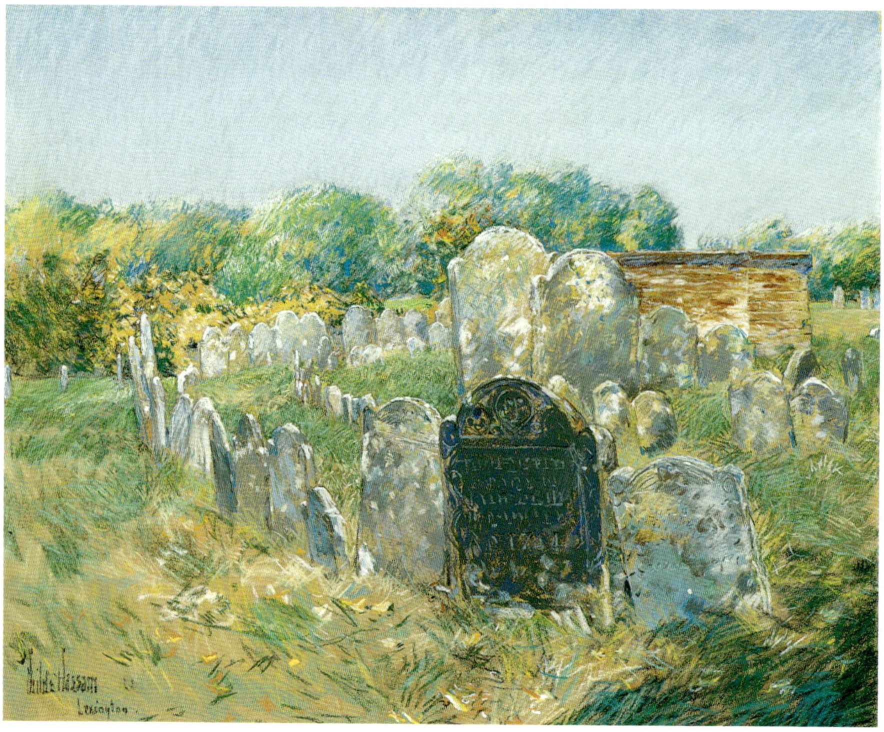

Fig. 294. Childe Hassam. *Colonial Graveyard at Lexington,* ca. 1891. Pastel on paper, $17\frac{3}{4}$ x $21\frac{1}{2}$ in. (45.1 x 55.3 cm). Smithsonian American Art Museum, Washington, D.C. Gift of John Gellatly

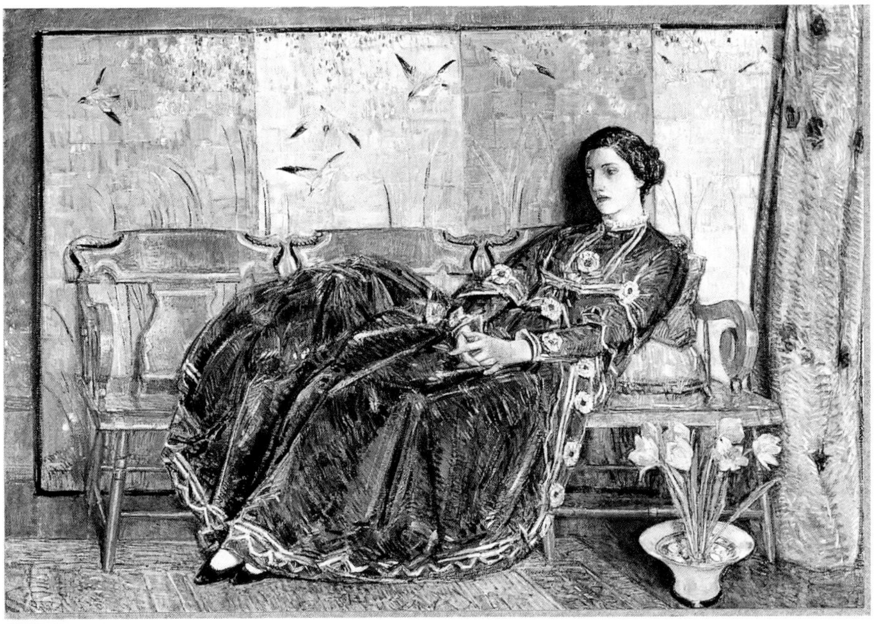

Fig. 295. Childe Hassam. *April (The Green Gown)*, 1920. Oil on canvas, 56 x 82¼ in. (142.2 x 208.9 cm). Gibbes Museum of Art/ Carolina Art Association, Charleston, South Carolina 1936.09.01

is such as would have been made for a ships cabin, and very fine it was of pine without a flaw straight long panels to last for all time."[26]

Hassam's extensive rambles throughout decades, beginning in the 1880s, from Maine to Long Island yielded a wide range of subjects evoking the past. In Gloucester he focused on the harbor and shipyards. In Sudbury he painted the tree-lined path to the Old Wayside Inn. In Newport and Old Lyme he sought out white churchs with towering steeples guarded by sentinel-like fences (see fig. 293); in Lexington he portrayed the colonial graveyard with headstones arrayed like regiments in formation (fig. 294). In Cos Cob he rendered the interior of the Holley House; in East Hampton he painted windmills and stone bridges. The ambitious summer itineraries through New England and Long Island villages reflected in these pictures suggest a search for lost innocence and the vanished village of his youth.

Hassam's approach to New England subjects centered on the surviving material culture, especially the skilled craftsmanship of early builders. In cherishing these relics, Hassam was echoing his father's interest in Americana. Frederick Fitch Hassam's barn was filled with old furniture, Indian artifacts, firearms, Eskimo harpoons, sporting prints, and a carriage used by Lafayette before business reversals forced a sale in the early 1870s. Hassam's notes make clear that his father was viewed as a "crank" because of his "mania" for "old furniture." He admitted that "you had to . . . bear with the comments of your friends and relatives it was not all so easy."[27] Obituary writers and biographers usually upgraded his father's status to "lover of antiques" and "collector."[28] The barn full of old furniture that had embarrassed Hassam as a youth became a point of pride.

Merging Personal and National

In 1920 Hassam painted a reflective young woman in an old-fashioned dress, reclining on an old-fashioned bench, with potted bulbs blooming nearby (fig. 295). Originally titled *April 1859*, this painting is unusual in Hassam's art for re-creating a specific moment in the past. His other pictures of women invariably show them as living in the present, whether placed in modern or historical interiors. But *April 1859*, now known as *April (The Green Gown)*,[29] with its vintage costume and blooming flowers symbolizing growth, appears to be a staged re-creation of the imagined private moment when the artist's mother realized she was with child. In April 1859 Rosa Hathorne Hassam was just in the third month of pregnancy with the son who would become America's Puritan artist, born on October 17.

What accounts for this departure from Hassam's preference for depicting modern life? Was he merely painting the happiness any soon-to-be new mother would experience? Or was he more subtly commemorating his own impending birth, which would be of such unusual significance for the nation? His autobiographical notes show that he did in fact link his birth to epochal events in America and beyond:

> *Frederick Childe Hassam came into the world at about half past eight on October 17th 1859 in the old town of Dorchester since 1870 a part of the city of Boston and in the old Bay State of Massachusetts. Words making a message*

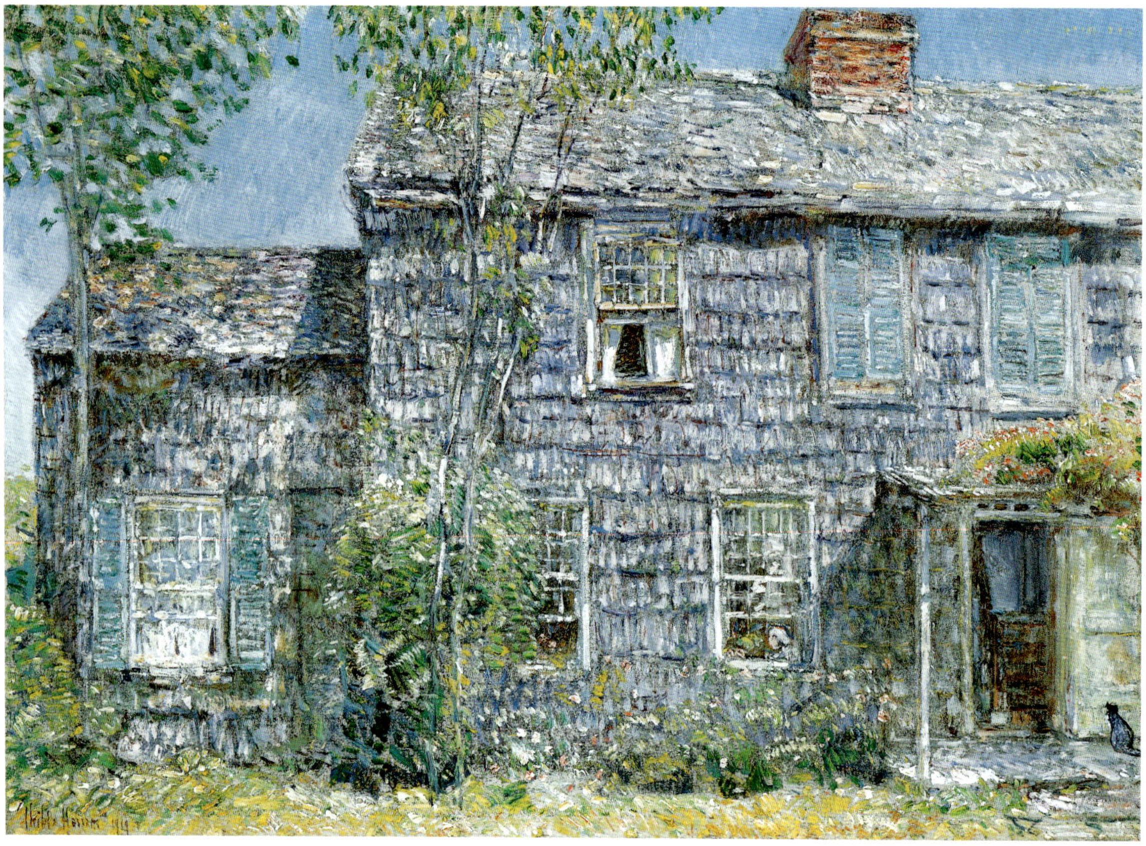

Fig. 296. Childe Hassam. *East Hampton, L.I. (Old Mumford House),* 1919. Oil on canvas, 21⅜ x 30 in. (54.4 x 76.2 cm). Charles and Elizabeth Buchanan Collection, New Britain Museum of American Art, Connecticut 1989.25

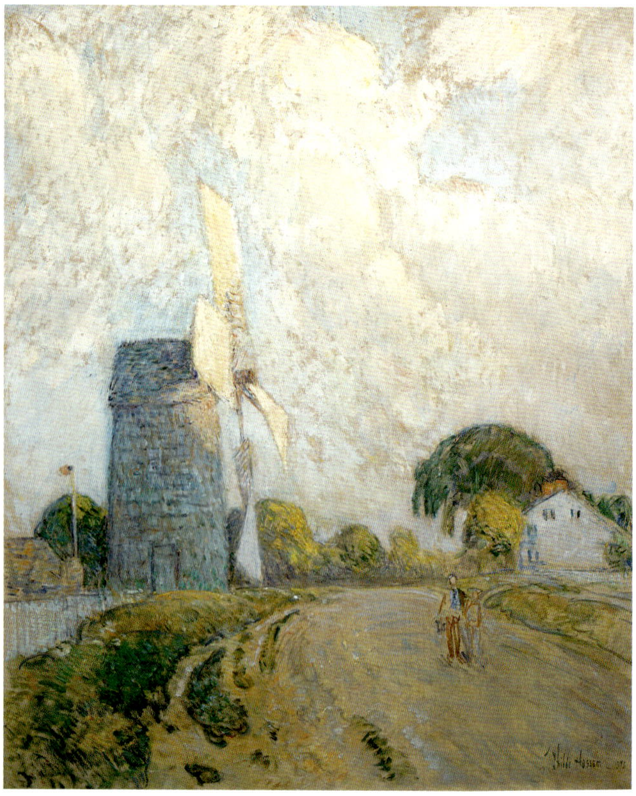

Fig. 297. Childe Hassam. *Windmill at Sundown, East Hampton,* 1898. Oil on canvas, 29 x 22¾ in. (73.7 x 57.8 cm). Huntington Museum of Art, West Virginia

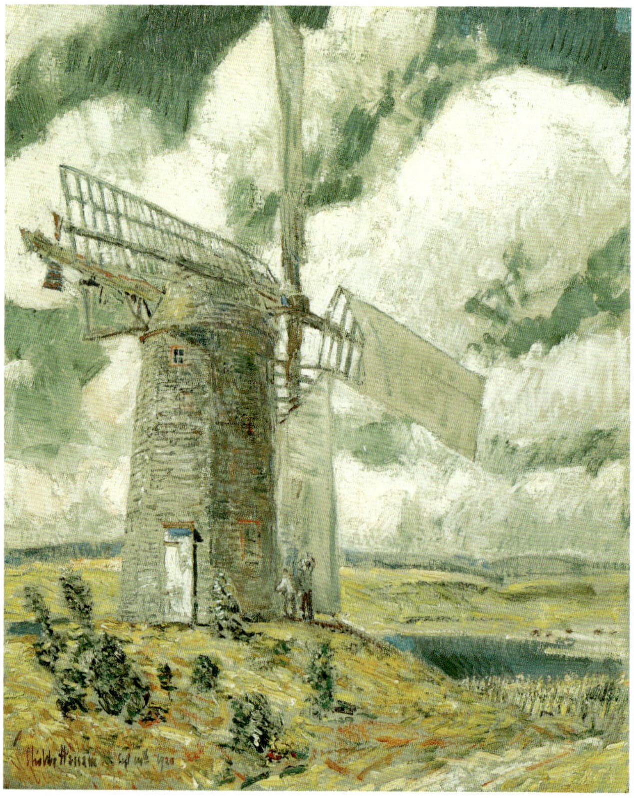

Fig. 298. Childe Hassam. *Bending Sail on the Old Mill,* 1920. Oil on canvas, 24 x 20 in. (61 x 50.8 cm). Private collection. © Christie's Images Inc. 2004

at that moment were being flashed over wires strung on poles telling the world of John Brown's raid on Harper's Ferry. . . . This raid was to lead in less than two years to what seems to us now as one of the poor old world's biggest blunders, the American Civil War. Another event of that year that shook the English speaking world to its foundations was the publication of a book by Charles Darwin called "The Origin of Species." The one event was to free the world of human slavery and the other was to free it from theological slavery of thought or mental slavery.[30]

It is significant that *April 1859* was painted in 1920, just at the moment Hassam began spending six months each year in his newly purchased home in East Hampton. For decades he had divided his year between the city and the country, but with the purchase of Willow Bend in 1919 he relocated his home base to the country, while continuing to spend time in New York City. This shift in primary domicile coincided with a shift in his self-image and a change in his art. Increasingly, he linked his life and art to debates about the nation's past and future. As Hassam aligned personal and national stories, he encoded subtle meanings and references in his work, as in the autobiographical allusion concealed in the short-lived title *April 1859*. Meditating on his birth and returning to a country idyll similar to that of his childhood, Hassam experienced around 1919 and 1920 an emotional renewal or a rebirth as the Puritan, the worthy successor to his yeoman ancestors and to all American colonists who built the nation. Relieved of his longtime goal of painting modern life, Hassam was freed to turn his art to new purposes, transforming it into a symbolic emblem of enduring values and the founders' vision.

In the early 1920s Hassam increasingly painted a mythologized New England "Puritan" past rather than the modern city. In East Hampton he turned his hand and skill to reclaiming through his art his cherished family legacy, magnifying the significance of the old shingle houses, churches, and windmills that early Americans like his ancestors had erected with their own hands and skill. He recycled the quaint, picturesque New England subjects of his earlier works into more formal, declarative images, with most detail erased in favor of a grand simplicity. The subjects are presented in self-consciously frontal compositions, sacrificing quaint charm to a new bold urgency. His subjects take on new status as tributes or elegies, in effect becoming icons of what America had lost or was in danger of losing.

In East Hampton Hassam rediscovered the idyllic colonial village of his childhood, a place that had luckily escaped Dorchester's fate and seemed almost to have been preserved in amber. East Hampton's English settlers had come to Long Island in 1648 from Lynn, Massachusetts, not far from Dorchester, so Hassam found in his new town many familiar echoes of his youth. The early English and Dutch founders of Long Island—with names such as Josiah Hobart, Samuel Mulford, Lion Gardiner, and Samuel Hutchinson—had left their legacy of "national integrity" there in the shingle houses and windmills.[31]

As Hassam immersed himself in the world of old East Hampton, he increasingly traced English and Dutch influence in his art, despite his years of study in France. He had grown disenchanted with Paris by 1910–11, but it was only after his move to Long Island that he revised the lineage of modern art to relate to Long Island's Anglo-Dutch history. While most scholars credited the French with inventing Impressionism and modern art, Hassam insisted that the Dutch artist Jongkind and English watercolorists had created the first modern, light-filled landscapes and had been his inspiration.[32]

He had painted shingle houses during his first visit to Long Island in August 1898, as in *Old House and Garden, East Hampton* (fig. 240). Two decades later he treated similar homes in a bolder, more forceful manner, making them not just elements in scenes but rather iconic centerpieces. In *East Hampton, L. I. (Old Mumford House)* (fig. 296), for instance, the chimney aligns with the top canvas edge and the house sits parallel to the picture plane, emphasizing "truthful" right angles of windows and doorways and making the structure consonant with that of the painting. The imposing house fills the frame and picturesque details are reduced. Hassam retained one favorite detail—an open door revealing a wooden staircase, perhaps hewn by an English ship's carpenter—to suggest a fine interior.

In 1898 Hassam had portrayed the Hook Mill in *Windmill at Sundown, East Hampton* (fig. 297), a typically charming view of a quaint relic, well integrated into the landscape. Painted two decades later, *Bending Sail on the Old Mill* (fig. 298) strikes a more majestic note, with the vast arms of the mill forming a gigantic cross in the landscape and making Hayground Mill the symbolic equivalent of Notre Dame in Paris, a powerful emblem of spiritual values and cultural identity.

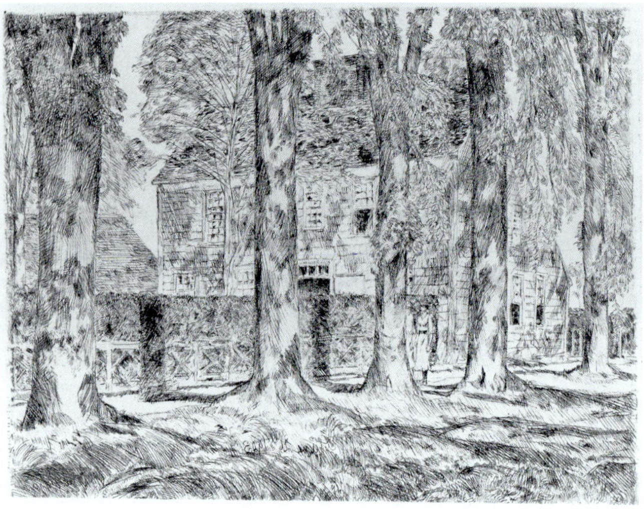

Fig. 299. Childe Hassam. *The Village Elms, Easthampton,* 1923. Etching, 6⅞ x 8⅞ in. (17.4 x 22.5 cm). Smithsonian American Art Museum, Washington, D.C. Transfer from the National Museum of American History, Division of Graphic Arts, Smithsonian Institution (C 222)

About 1919 Hassam similarly invested his images of trees with deep meaning about heritage. Avoiding the pictorialism of earlier decades, he portrayed oaks, elms, and hickories as silent guardians of America's "origin myth." He made the ancient English oaks near the historic Wayside Inn the subject of a 1926 etching and celebrated the aged American elms standing guard outside East Hampton's old homes in oils and etchings of the 1920s (see fig. 299). One of his most formally composed paintings is *The Two Hickory Trees (Golf Player)* of 1919 (fig. 300), in which a thoroughly modern woman stands between two towering hickories that rise to the top edge of the canvas. Hickory trees could grow to 100 feet and live to be 250 years old—as old as Long Island's shingle houses were then. Native to North America, the hickory's dense, strong wood was used by settlers for ax and hatchet handles and wagon wheels. Its close grain made it a natural choice for fine furniture and wall panels, and in Hassam's day, for golf-club shafts. The woman golfer[33] depends on the same strong material that her forebears relied upon, as she stands front and center gripping her club and flanked by living witnesses to the past. Once more, Hassam encoded in this painting a link from past to present.

Hassam's move to East Hampton has the feel of a retreat. It is significant that he purchased Willow Bend in August 1919, soon after plans for showing the Flag series in Paris fell through and when he was feeling frustrated because no buyer for the complete series had come forward. His work on Long Island in the 1920s has been viewed, then and now, as representing a decline, a reaction against aesthetic revolutions inspired by the 1913 Armory Show.[34] Conservative concepts dominate his work in this decade, when he awkwardly inserted strange classical nudes into contemporary landscapes (see figs. 252, 325). The results were deemed "bizarre" by almost every critic. The best of Hassam's works of the 1920s, however, have a stronger formal arrangement and bolder meaning than earlier renderings of similar subjects. On Long Island Hassam may have been increasingly out of touch with the art world, but he was more in touch with his own past.

He was also attuned to the broad celebration of American art and history that took place during the 1920s, which was part nostalgia, part self-discovery. The East Hampton Historical Society was founded in 1921. *The Magazine Antiques* was

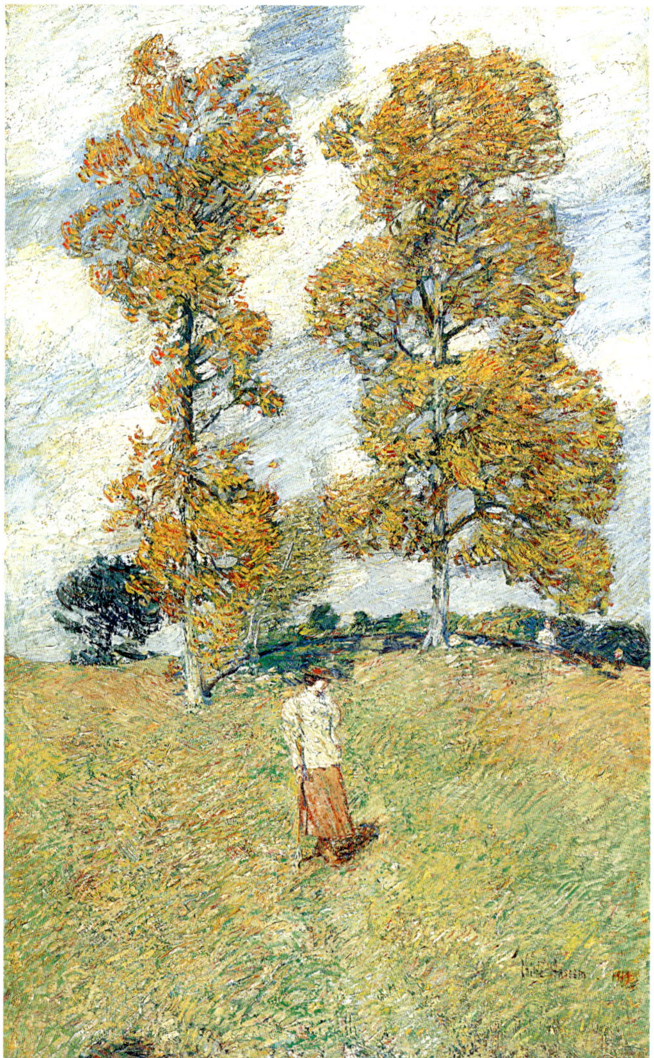

Fig. 300. Childe Hassam. *The Two Hickory Trees (Golf Player),* 1919. Oil on canvas, 36 x 22 in. (91.4 x 55.9 cm). Private collection. Courtesy Sotheby's, Inc.

begun in 1922. The American Wing of the Metropolitan Museum opened in 1924. John D. Rockefeller Jr. began the restoration of Colonial Williamsburg in 1926. Henry Francis du Pont inherited Winterthur in 1927 and began preparing it as a showcase for early American furnishings. Gutzon Borglum began sculpting Mount Rushmore in 1927. This passion for looking inward and backward at America's early history reflected many factors, including a generation of peak immigration, a reaction to the self-confident internationalism of the Gilded Age, and the nation's debut as a military power in World War I.

Although Hassam came to America's heritage from a humble vantage point quite different from the perspective of a du Pont or a Rockefeller, he had long championed New England villages, finding deep-rooted childhood memories there. His 1919 purchase of Willow Bend, in East Hampton, was as close as he would come to going home again. One of his most curious and perplexing images, *Adam and Eve Walking Out on Montauk in Early Spring* (fig. 252), is best understood as signifying Hassam's readmission to his childhood paradise, now transported to Long Island. Since his expulsion from Edenic Dorchester more than forty years earlier, he had wandered through Europe, New England, and far Oregon deserts, garnering awards and recognition but not satisfying a deeper yearning. On Long Island he finally found the special qualities he cherished in Dorchester memories, among them "that electric and living quality of clear blue of certain times of the year could not be surpassed anywhere, if you like as fair as the isles of Greece—as blue at times as the Mediterranean."[35]

1. Ernest Haskell, "Introduction," in Pousette-Dart 1922, pp. x, vii.
2. See White 1911, pp. XXIX–XXXVI; Price 1923, pp. 3–7; and Adeline Adams, "A Puritan's Quest," in Adams 1938, pp. 1–22.
3. Ives 1892, p. 116.
4. Childe Hassam quoted in "New York, the Beauty City," *New York Sun*, February 23, 1913, p. 16. See also "New York Beautiful" 1898, p. 9.
5. See discussions about encoded past and present themes in Elizabeth Broun, "Childe Hassam's America," *American Art* 13, no. 3 (fall 1999), pp. 32–57.
6. Childe Hassam, Autobiographical notes, 1934, Hassam Papers, reel NAA1, frame 741.
7. "Ancient Dorchester," *Harper's Weekly* 24 (June 26, 1880), p. 406.
8. Peter F. Stevens, "Dorchester's Ultimate Turf War," parts 1 and 2, *Dorchester Reporter*, December 7 and 14, 2000, www.dotnews.com/annex-part1.html and www.dotnews.com/annex-part2.html.
9. Cited in ibid., part 2.
10. Peter F. Stevens, "Dorchester's 'Wearing of the Green' Did Not Come Easily," *Dorchester Reporter*, March 15, 2001, www.dotnews.com/dotirish.html. Stevens tells how Dorchester's reputation as the "Chocolate Village" is owed ironically to an Irish immigrant. In 1764 Irishman John Hannon gave the secret of grinding chocolate to Dorchester's Dr. James Baker, who founded Baker's Chocolate.
11. "Childe Hassam declined the University education offered to him by an uncle. That box of water colors appealed to him more strongly than the Greek verbs then considered an advisable prelude to collegiate success. . . . With characteristic independence, this young New Englander left the Dorchester High School on the eve of his expected graduation. . . ." Adams 1938, pp. 13–14. Hassam wrote, "About the Dorchester High School it was as I have been assured since, one of the best schools in a city of good schools—and taking a course there *then* was equivalent to going to college *now*." Hassam, Letter to Miss Farmer, 1933, p. 3, Hassam Papers, reel NAA1, frame 746.
12. Hiesinger 1994, p. 28, n. 5.
13. Hassam, Autobiographical notes, 1934, Hassam Papers, reel NAA1, frame 740.
14. Ibid., frame 741.
15. J. T. Hassam 1870. An addendum was published in J. T. Hassam 1880. The final edition, J. T. Hassam 1896, includes additional notes. Unless otherwise noted, information is taken from the 1870 edition.
16. Hassam, Letter to Miss Farmer, 1933, p. 7, Hassam Papers, reel NAA1, frame 748.
17. Hassam, Autobiographical notes, 1934, Hassam Papers, reel NAA1, frame 690.
18. The Hassam family history does not mention Stephen Hassam's career as a master builder in Charlestown, New Hampshire, although Hassam speaks briefly about it in interviews, calling him an "architect" and a "builder." Lockman interviews, January 25, 1927, p. 3, and February 3, 1927, p. 23. Six surviving houses, a bank, and the Unitarian Church that Stephen Hassam built in the town center contribute to its designation as the Charlestown Main Street Historic District. The National Register Nomination Information for this Historic District (http://members.valley.net/~connriver/N06-17.htm) says Stephen Hassam "appears to have acted as one of the primary vehicles for transporting all of these styles [Federal, Greek Revival, Gothic] to Charlestown and is responsible for the delicate woodcarving adorning many Charlestown buildings." Similarly, there is no mention that Stephen Hassam's second wife was judged insane before the birth of her fifth child and spent the remainder of her life in a poorhouse, dying in 1905 at age eighty-seven. Her aged husband turned to drink, and his once-considerable estate was auctioned to benefit his creditors, among whom were several of his own children. See Donn Haven Lathrop, "Lucy Amy Hasham Miller, 1818–1905," 1995, http://members.aol.com/donnl/lucy.html.
19. Nathaniel Hawthorne died in 1864, when Hassam was only five. Of William Morris Hunt, who lived until 1879, Hassam wrote: "My kinsman William Hunt I never actually met, but I saw him once walking through his studio where he had on exhibition his Niagara Falls picture. He was my relative but I did not pay any attention to it at all." Lockman interview, January 31, 1927, pp. 2–3. He also notes (ibid., p. 24) that Celia Thaxter found Hunt's body in her pond and considered him a suicide.

The widely recognized architect Richard Morris Hunt lived in New York City during his mature career, dying in 1895, but there is no indication that Hassam met him.

20. Hassam, Autobiographical notes, 1934, Hassam Papers, reel NAA1, frame 739.
21. Adams 1938, p. 4.
22. Albert Rosenthal, letter to the *New York Times,* September 2, 1935, p. 16, quoted in Hiesinger 1994, p. 28, n. 2.
23. Hassam, Autobiographical notes, n.d. and 1934, Hassam Papers, reel NAA2, frame 229, and reel NAA1, frame 740.
24. Reproduced in Christie's, New York, sale cat., May 22, 1991, lot 244.
25. "The town fell away from its traditional associations with agriculture; increased mobility for local residents, and an increased rate of immigration by newcomers spelled the inevitable destruction of open, agricultural areas. The Whiting Farm was the first large subdivision, becoming Oakdale in 1871. The Farrington Farm became Endicott in 1872, and the Turner/Whiting tract became Ashcroft in 1873." "A Capsule History of Dedham," Dedham Historical Society, 2004, www.dedhamhistorical.org/html/history.shtml. This echoes the development of Hassam's Dorchester: "I remember the old times . . . I used to walk across the fields to the Dorchester High School. Of course the fields are now built up into apartment houses." Lockman interview, February 3, 1927, p. 4.
26. Hassam, Autobiographical notes, n.d., Hassam Papers, reel NAA1, frame 690.
27. Ibid., frame 688, and Lockman interview, January 25, 1927, p. 7.
28. "His father was a well-to-do merchant and lover of antiques." "Childe Hassam, 75, Noted Artist, Dies," *New York Times,* August 28, 1935, p. 17. "His father was a prosperous Boston merchant. . . . A lover of beauty, he collected domestic Americana. . . ." Adams 1938, p. 10.
29. The photograph negative in the Peter A. Juley Collection (Smithsonian American Art Museum, Washington, D.C.) is inscribed *April 1859* and *Spring Academy 1921,* indicating the painting's original title and that it was photographed as documentation of the National Academy of Design exhibition that year. It was exhibited under this same title in Los Angeles in 1925–26. On other occasions in the 1920s the painting was published as *April,* without the year reference. When the work was acquired by the Gibbes Museum from Mr. and Mrs. Archer Huntington in 1936, the name had been changed to *The Green Dress.* I am indebted to H. Barbara Weinberg for this information.
30. Hassam, Autobiographical notes, 1934, Hassam Papers, reel NAA1, frame 739.
31. In fact, East Hampton's Puritan charms and its waters made the town a destination for summering New Yorkers by the 1870s, which led to the extension of the railroad from Bridgehampton to East Hampton in 1895. The absence of a nearby metropolis spared it from industrialization. It was incorporated in 1920.
32. "Take the actual history of the modern movement. It is not French. It is English. The English watercolor painters cleared up the palettes of the painters in oil. . . . Look at the work of the modern Dutch painter, Jongkind; look at his watercolors, if you can see one or two you will find out who first tried for light, and large form out of doors. . . . Modern landscape painting, as any one can learn, was taken to England from Holland, cleared in tone by the English school of watercolor painters, highly developed by such masters as Turner and Constable." Excerpts from Hassam 1928, p. 27.
33. Golf flourished on Long Island, where it "set the standard for all golf across the country." The first incorporated club was the Shinnecock Hills Golf Club, founded in 1891. It was the first golf club to allow women full membership, which it granted from its founding. Hassam played most often at the Maidstone Club, founded before 1900 by a group including Thomas Moran. Jeff Williams, "Shinnecock: A Crucial Link," http://www.newsday.com/extras/lihistory/specspor/golf.htm.

    The Maidstone Club was named for the town in Kent, England, from which most of East Hampton's first families emigrated. These families initially lived in Lynn, Massachusetts, and then came to Long Island in 1648. The town they founded there was called Maidstone for fourteen years and was subsequently renamed East Hampton. Tom Morris, "East Hampton Village: The First Resort of the Wealthy," http://www.newsday.com/extras/lihistory/spectown/histo06b.htm.
34. Hiesinger 1994, pp. 168, 174, nn. 59, 60. The exception is Donelson F. Hoopes, who wrote enthusiastically of the East Hampton works as "youthful" in spirit and representing the end of a long search. "If, in fact, Hassam had been searching for the ideal landscape, as his travels of thirty summers suggest, he found it at last on the eastern end of Long Island. . . . He created some of his most chromatically brilliant work during his East Hampton years. The size of his pictures became correspondingly large, as if to embrace the whole of nature. . . . There is an exuberance about these Long Island landscapes that speaks of a youthful spirit, in spite of the fact that the artist was approaching his seventieth year." Hoopes 1979, p. 19.
35. Hassam, Autobiographical notes, 1934, Hassam Papers, reel NAA1, frame 741.

Hassam and American Architecture

Erica E. Hirshler

Childe Hassam rejoiced in depicting architecture. His images of white New England churches flanked by elm trees and his determinedly modern, flag-bedecked New York views were celebrated as exemplars of artistic achievement in the United States and praised as "profoundly American."[1] Those same scenes are often regarded by scholars today as manifestations of the defensive cultural nationalism of an aging artist anxious to maintain his privileged position in the shifting hierarchies of early-twentieth-century American art and society. Described by both his advocates and his detractors as a puritan and a patriot, Hassam crafted pictures that seem calculated to endorse two characteristically American principles: faith and progress. His views on those subjects were Protestant and positive and, for whatever reasons, in his art he ignored the social diversity and problems of an increasingly urban and multicultural country.[2]

The patriotic and reactionary declarations about American society that Hassam made in the 1920s can easily be applied retrospectively to his earlier pictures of New England and New York. Those paintings seem to spring and develop from his growing conservatism. As Hassam continued to promote an elitist agenda that favored the Academy and a socially correct colonial heritage (thus preserving his own superior position both as a painter and as an individual), he appeared to turn increasingly to subjects that can be seen to incorporate those same standards. In the Protestant temples of New England and in the commercial avenues of New York, Hassam found distinctly American motifs that stood for both traditional religious affiliations and an established community of culture and business. But these themes were not confined to his late work, and thus they cannot be securely linked only to the political and social views the painter expressed in his later years. When Hassam was a young painter, this same imagery would have been considered quite modern.

From the very start of his career and throughout the period in which he produced his most avant-garde work, Hassam portrayed architecture that was both new and old. His interest in this subject may have been stirred by his experience as an illustrator in the early 1880s: he recalled that one of his first jobs was to make "very careful architectural designs" for John A. Lowell and Company, a Boston engraver.[3] Whatever the inspiration, he chose to paint images of buildings when he was seeking to establish himself as an artist. The decisions Hassam made about what to paint during this period reveal a young man wrestling with new subjects and new ideas. At this time, colonial architecture had only recently won the attention of America's tastemakers, and American artists were just beginning to explore its motifs. The modern city was not considered an appropriate subject for fine art, and none of Hassam's compatriots who did paint urban views embraced the theme as completely as he did. Thus, Hassam's treatment of architecture and city views at this time signifies his engagement with the most up-to-date cultural concerns.

Among Hassam's first known works are depictions of colonial houses, which had largely been ignored until a wave of nostalgia engulfed Americans after the Civil War. This nostalgia took the form of a preoccupation with America's rural past, and together with the patriotism and nationalism that accompanied the 1876 centennial celebrations, it gave rise to the Colonial Revival movement. Among the many manifestations of this movement was a new interest in architectural preservation. Significant interest in America's old buildings became widespread only in the last quarter of the nineteenth century.

In Hassam's native Boston, history had always been important. There the Colonial Revival emerged and coexisted with colonial survival. The city's fledgling architectural-preservation movement had failed to stop the demolition of patriot John Hancock's house in 1863, but that event galvanized future support for the cause. It gained momentum in the 1870s with the centennials of various Revolutionary battles and the "evacuation" of the British army, when Boston's "historic points and buildings were noted and decorated" as part of the celebration.[4] Many of the city's most influential citizens rallied to save the Old South Meeting House (1729), in which the tax on tea had been debated in 1773. This church had survived the great fire of 1872, but its existence was threatened when its congregation, in a controversial action, sold the building and moved to newer quarters. Oliver Wendell Holmes penned a verse declaring "Woe to the three-hilled town, / When through the land the tale is told— / 'The brave "Old South" is down!'"[5] Harvard president Charles William Eliot, educator and philanthropist Mary Hemenway, abolitionist Wendell Phillips, minister Edward Everett Hale, and writers Ralph Waldo Emerson, Julia Ward Howe, Henry Wadsworth Longfellow, James Russell Lowell, and John Greenleaf Whittier all joined the campaign to save the building. When the Old South Ball of 1877, a fundraising dance, was described as the "social event of the season," it was clear that preservation of the icons of the colonial past had become the latest fashion.[6]

Boston's preservation efforts were matched in many smaller towns in Massachusetts, where old houses were beginning to attract new attention and visitors. Hassam certainly meant his images of such structures to appeal to an elite among these sightseers, educated consumers who not only were seeking out old New England but also had the resources to purchase art. At the Williams and Everett Gallery, Boston, in the fall of 1882, Hassam exhibited what one journal described as "quaint studies at Nantucket . . . old cottages, with glimpses of sea and sky" (see fig. 24).[7] Nantucket citizens had been marketing their island as a tourist destination whose main attraction was its past. Its promoters offered visitors a romanticized vision of rural America in colonial days, banking on their historic architecture to bring in tourist dollars.[8]

Hassam no doubt hoped his work would share the commercial appeal of his subjects; thus he painted not only Nantucket's cobbled streets and wooden houses but also several historic sites in small towns near Boston that were well-known exemplars of the American colonial past. These included the ancient oak-lined road leading to the Wayside Inn in Sudbury in a watercolor (location unknown), which was exhibited at Williams and Everett in 1882; the slump-shouldered Fairbanks House in Dedham (fig. 31); and a rambling seventeenth-century house in Dorchester in *Old House, Dorchester*, 1884 (private collection).[9] The Wayside Inn, the Fairbanks House, and the Pierce House in Dorchester had all been pictured in Edwin Whitefield's *Homes of Our Forefathers*, a guidebook published in Boston in 1880, when Hassam was working in the city as an illustrator.[10] Featured were the "oldest and most interesting buildings" in Massachusetts and texts embellished with prints from "original drawings made on the spot."[11]

Constructed early in the eighteenth century as a public house on the Boston Post Road, the Wayside Inn had been immortalized by Longfellow in his *Tales of a Wayside Inn* (1863).[12] The inn and its surroundings were familiar and beloved, even though the inn was not open to tourists until 1897, when antiques collector Edward Rivers Lemon bought the building and restored it as a "retreat for literary pilgrims."[13] Many years after he depicted it, Hassam recalled working there "with one or two other artists" when he was "about twenty," drawing and painting the interior, the exterior, and the bucolic country lane that was preserved as the main approach to the inn.[14]

The Fairbanks House (1636) was also a local favorite. One of the nation's oldest surviving timber-frame houses, it was described by a writer in a journal of 1889 as an "integral part of its natural surroundings." Observing that "it must strongly attract the eye of every wandering landscape-painter," the author declared it a "little New England home . . . [with its] characteristically American shape and material" and noted that "time can sanctify and beautify even a wooden house of the humblest proportions."[15] By 1894, when Alvin Jones wrote *Under Colonial Roofs*, the Fairbanks House was so overrun with "devotees of the easel and sketching-block" and "the more numerous camera 'fiends'" that Miss Fairbanks had difficulty keeping "the dooryard clear of these budding 'Raphaels.'"[16] In his view Hassam emphasized the bulky mass of the house, which hugs the sloping meadow like a beached hulk.

Hassam was one of many Boston artists who responded to the new antiquarian taste. Working in and around the city

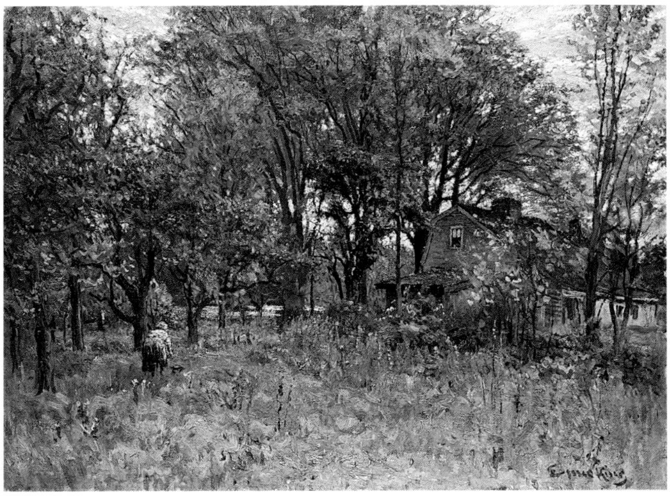

Fig. 301. John J. Enneking. *The Old Roundy House on the Neponset River,* ca. 1890. Oil on canvas, 26¼ x 36¼ in. (66.7 x 92.1 cm). The Museum of Fine Arts, Boston. Gift of Morton C. Bradley in memory of Robert C. Vose 1975.753

and in other New England towns, they took delight in the irregular shapes and romantic, deserted appearance of the old houses they depicted. John J. Enneking, who was primarily a landscape painter and knew Hassam as a neighbor in the Studio Building on Tremont Street in Boston, portrayed several such houses in the Boston area, including a gambrel-roofed structure on the Neponset River then known as the Roundy House (fig. 301).[17] Like Enneking and in contrast to Frank Millet, Edwin H. Blashfield, and some other contemporaries, Hassam as a rule did not attempt to re-create the past in his portrayals of colonial settings.[18] His views are most often unpopulated, and the figures that occasionally appear are too generalized to be assigned to a particular era. In *The Old Fairbanks House,* for example, a woman with a heavy bucket walks across the yard. She could have lived in the house at any point in its history; her task is timeless and her costume plain enough to span the centuries.

In their interpretations of New England sites, Hassam and his fellow artists were not only appealing to the new interest in the region's history; they were also responding to the well-established local predilection for the rural and vernacular subjects of the French Barbizon painters. This taste had been popularized by the influential artist, teacher, and collector William Morris Hunt, who favored the rustic subjects of the Barbizon style. Hunt encouraged Boston collectors to buy pictures by Jean-François Millet (see fig. 29), Thomas Couture, Jean-Baptiste-Camille Corot, and other Barbizon artists. He also adopted their rustic subjects and direct technique and echoed their distaste for complex narrative in his own work (see fig. 30), and he encouraged his students and fellow painters to do the same (see fig. 302). Hunt died in 1879, but most of Hassam's artist acquaintances were former colleagues and friends of Hunt's. Like them, Hassam attempted to Americanize the French aesthetic, replacing the stone farmhouses of Normandy with the distinctive wooden architecture of New England. He and his fellow artists largely ignored the social commentary of their French models to focus on a romantic and nostalgic vision of country life (see figs. 31, 35).

In contrast to his colleagues, however, and most significantly, Hassam was interested in more than nostalgia. The most exceptional paintings he made during the 1880s were of Boston, where a powerful sense of the present coexisted with the evident past. Hassam did not depict the city of Paul Revere and John Hancock, despite intense local interest in the sites and streets they had inhabited. He was inspired by Boston's future instead of its past, and in his art he celebrated a distinctly new metropolis. Writers too were struck by the changes taking place there. Among them were the authors of *King's Hand-book of Boston,* who declared in 1881, "A great, far-reaching, imposing modern city has taken the place of the bustling, quaint, picturesque town," adding proudly that "the new Boston, with its wealth of magnificent buildings . . . [is] most attractive."[19] Another was Henry James: Basil Ransom, hero of his novel *The Bostonians* (1885–86), found the view west toward the Back Bay from Olive Chancellor's Beacon Hill home "impressive [in its] extreme modernness."[20]

The transformation of Boston had started only twenty years before the first of these observations was made.

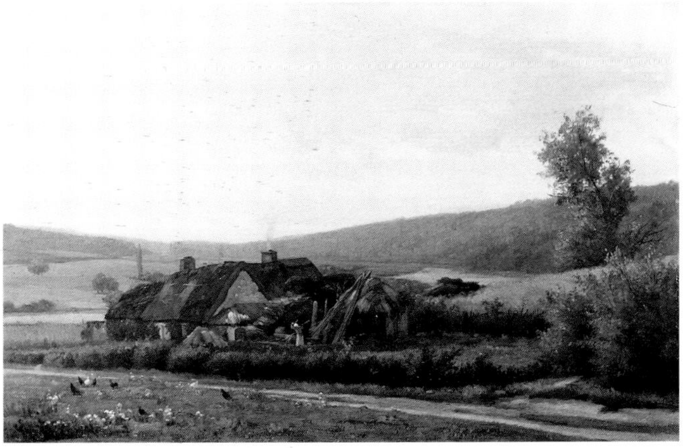

Fig. 302. Joseph Foxcroft Cole. *Valley of the Rambouillet, France,* late 1860s. Oil on canvas, 22¼ x 35⅞ in. (56.5 x 91.1 cm). The Museum of Fine Arts, Boston. Gift of Misses Louisa W. and Marian R. Case 20.597

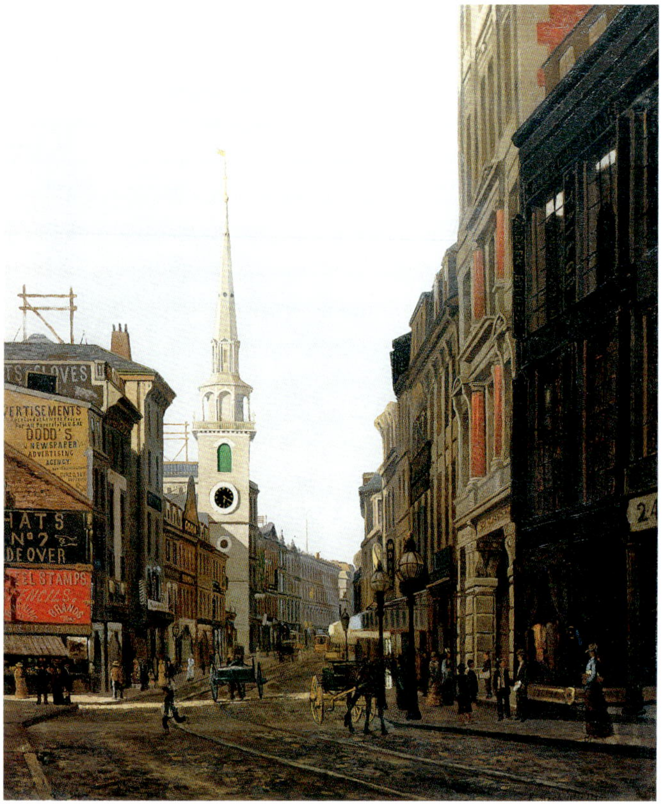

Fig. 303. Enrico Meneghelli. *Boston, Massachusetts,* 1879. Oil on canvas, 30 x 25 in. (76.2 x 63.5 cm). Private collection

Beginning in 1855, the brackish mud flats west of Charles Street were reclaimed with a carefully planned landfill and development project. The original business district was also substantially rebuilt in the wake of the 1872 fire that destroyed sixty-five acres of commercial buildings. The two projects, the one deliberate and the other the result of accident, led to an unprecedented building boom and an extensive redevelopment of the city that doubled its size.

Hassam's focus on views of the modern city was unusual, for while Bostonians were inordinately fond of their town, artists rarely painted it. Moreover, very few of the oil paintings of Boston that do exist are comparable to Hassam's unremittingly modern street scenes. Among the handful of Hassam's contemporaries who produced views of Boston that took its modern aspect into account were Enrico Meneghelli and Theodore Robinson. In 1879 the elusive Italian-born Meneghelli, best known for his images of museum interiors, painted Washington Street looking toward the Old South Meeting House, showing its slender spire rising above the commercial bustle that surrounded it (fig. 303). And in 1884 Robinson executed a view of Beacon Street, looking up the hill toward the State House (fig. 304). Here the elegant row houses facing the Common form a parti-colored backdrop to the cluster of horses and the pile of cobblestones that

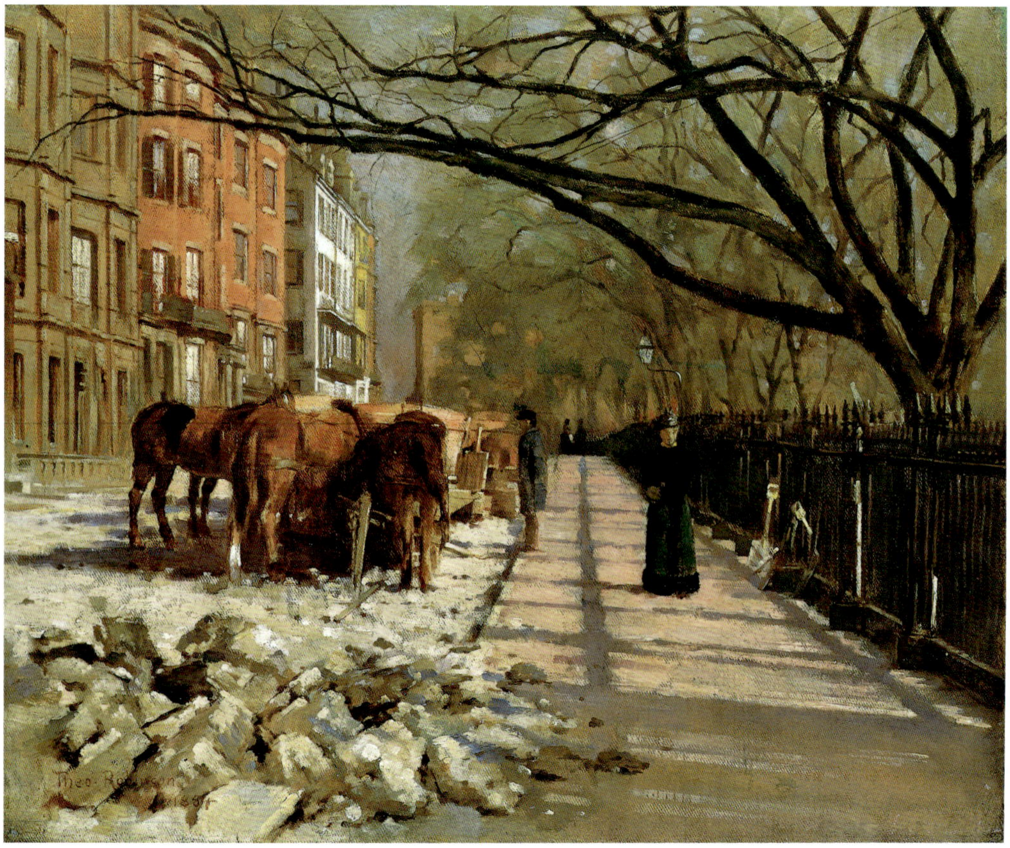

Fig. 304. Theodore Robinson. *Beacon Street, Boston,* 1884. Oil on canvas, 17 x 21 in. (43.2 x 53.3 cm). Wadsworth Atheneum, Hartford. The Ella Gallup Sumner and Mary Catlin Sumner Collection Fund

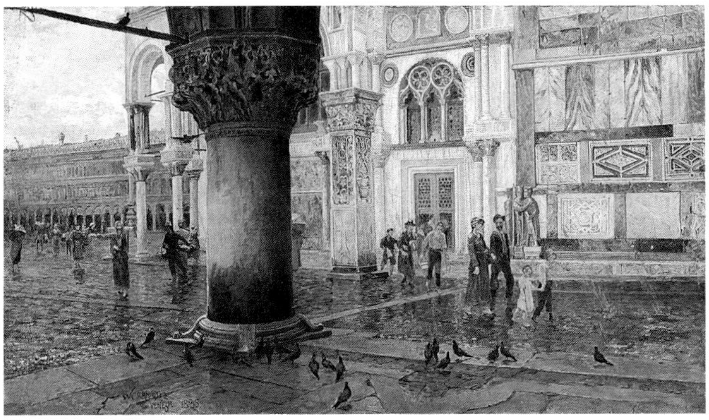

Fig. 305. William Graham. *A Rainy Day in the Piazzetta, Venice,* 1885. Oil on canvas, 16¼ x 28½ in. (41.3 x 72.4 cm). The Museum of Fine Arts, Boston. Bequest of Miss Mary Felton 96.656

engage the workman at center, while a well-dressed woman strolls down the brick sidewalk. These city views are anomalies in the work of Meneghelli and Robinson, while Hassam, by contrast, painted more than a dozen urban images with modern content in the 1880s, many of them in large formats. Indeed, their number provoked one critic to remark in 1886 that the artist had "follow[ed] his newly found fancy of Columbus-avenue subjects to the bitter end."[21] Often included in Hassam's exhibitions, these city scenes were an integral part of his early artistic production and presentation.

Hassam was perhaps inspired to undertake contemporary urban subjects during his travels abroad in 1883. European painters Giuseppe de Nittis, Jean Béraud, and Atkinson Grimshaw, as well as the American Frank Boggs, have all been proposed as providing models of such themes.[22] Although these artists were not represented in the Boston collections that Hassam may have known, their work had been reproduced and was familiar to American artists and critics. What exactly Hassam saw during his first visit to Europe remains unknown, and in interviews of many years later he admitted to no transformative experience from that journey. It seems unlikely that he could have found models in Boston. Although several of the French Impressionists painted city streets, none of their urban scenes were shown in the 1883 *Foreign Exhibition* in Boston. Moreover, local collectors, despite their early and enthusiastic embrace of Impressionism, preferred rural imagery. Perhaps a determining factor in Hassam's adoption of urban subjects is his encounter with Venice, a city beloved by Bostonians, who collected and created images of it in a variety of weather conditions (see fig. 256). Hassam's scenes of lively Venetian piazzas tightly bounded by architecture earned him some acclaim when they were shown at the Williams and Everett Gallery in 1884, and he may have seen Boston's wet or snowy streets as a comparably picturesque but more novel motif.[23] It is also possible that Hassam was influenced by the work of William Graham, an American who lived in Venice and painted views of the streets of Italy (see fig. 305) and Egypt; these were popular with Boston collectors and were, moreover, shown at Williams and Everett in the 1880s. The inspiration of contemporary images of European street scenes (see fig. 307) and of photographs of Boston, particularly stereographs, should also be considered in the search for Hassam's sources.[24]

Soon after his marriage, on February 1, 1884, Hassam moved into the relatively new Hotel Albemarle at 282 Columbus Avenue, a residential apartment building erected in 1876 on the corner of Clarendon Street. The Albemarle was designed as "French flats," in which each unit spread across a single floor (rather than up and down several levels).[25]

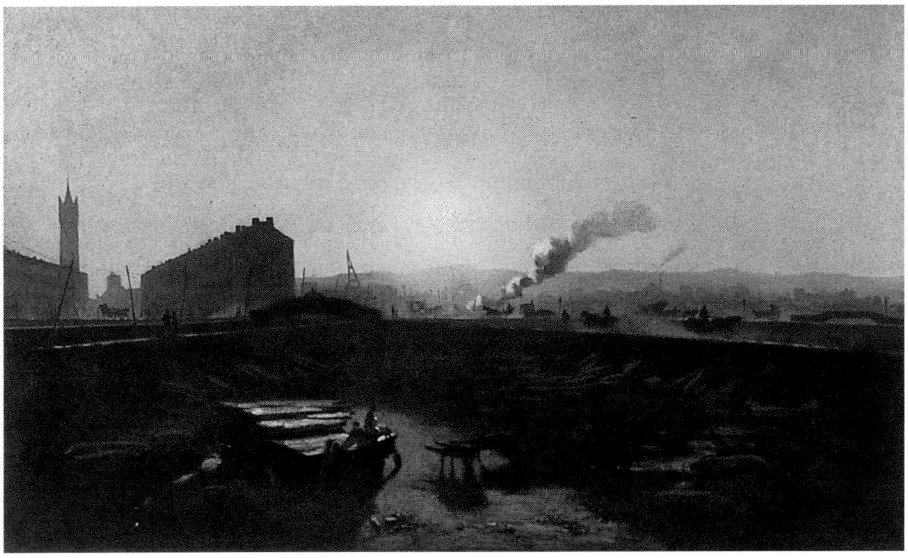

Fig. 306. Frederick Dickinson Williams. *A View of Boston, The First Block of Columbus Avenue and the Providence–Boston Railroad,* 1868. Oil on canvas, 18 x 30 in. (45.7 x 76.2 cm). Skinner, Inc., Boston

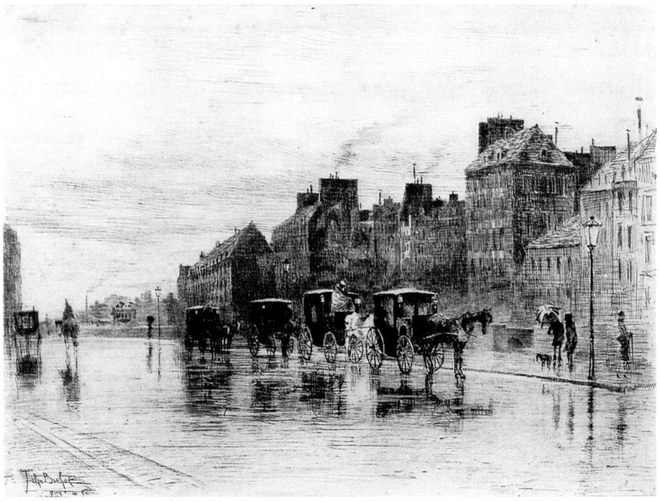

Fig. 307. Félix Hilaire Buhot. *Une Matinée d'hiver au Quai de L'Hôtel Dieu*, 1876. Etching on paper, 9⅜ x 12⅝ in. (23.8 x 14.9 cm.). Skinner, Inc., Boston

After 1865 such buildings were constructed in great numbers in Boston, many of them in the new neighborhoods of the Back Bay and the South End. Most included modern conveniences—the Albemarle boasted full bathrooms, elevators, and central heating. The Albemarle was comparable to the more expensive residential hotels on Commonwealth Avenue, in the city's most exclusive district. It was in such establishments that many of Boston's wealthiest citizens had chosen to dwell, preferring communal luxury to single-family homes. Apartment living had now become tremendously fashionable.

Not only were Hassam's own building and his style of living modern, his entire neighborhood was also new. Columbus Avenue had been conceived just twenty years before he moved there, on land slated to be reclaimed from the Back Bay, a receiving basin of the Charles River that extended south to Tremont Street and west from the edge of the Public Garden to the nearby town of Brookline. Crisscrossed by dams, dikes, and railroad lines, the Back Bay had become a festering swamp by 1849. Various schemes were proposed for filling it to create a new section of the city, and the ambitious project began in 1855. Columbus Avenue was added to the plan in 1864 (see fig. 306). Intended to be the major southwest road through the newly built neighborhood, it was not as fashionable or luxurious as the streets to the north of the Boston and Providence railroad tracks.[26] Nevertheless, Columbus Avenue was planned and developed as a boulevard in emulation of those in Baron Haussmann's Paris. The avenue boasted elegantly uniform architecture, providing a stately enfilade of doorways, steps, and rooflines. It ran in a straight line, affording long vistas that the curving warrens of streets in the older sections of Boston could not provide. The cobblestones of the old city were exchanged for a smooth new pavement wide enough to accommodate modern horse-drawn trolleys, ensuring that Columbus Avenue would remain a busy thoroughfare lively with both vehicular and pedestrian traffic.

Many of Hassam's earliest urban scenes feature the active streets of his new neighborhood. In *Rainy Day, Columbus Avenue, Boston* (fig. 36), for example, he showed the intersection of Columbus Avenue with West Canton and Appleton Streets, a few blocks from his home. By 1870 developers had forced the brackish bay north and west, opening the area for building, and Appleton Street first appeared on the city map. Its elegant row houses, some of which are visible on the right of Hassam's composition, were all constructed between 1870 and 1880. The yellow trolley Hassam depicted heading toward Park Square was a recent addition to the city's expanding public transportation system, which linked the neighborhood to the newly built Boston and Providence Railway Station (1872); the station's clock tower stood at the end of the avenue and appears in the background of Hassam's composition. Here Hassam created a painting of great beauty from what one critic described as "silent piles of brick and stone houses whose façades looked so moist and grim," transforming the raw, ordinary modernity of a middle-class neighborhood into art.[27]

Hassam also painted the area near the Boston Common, using the park to provide a tranquil contrast to the activity of the street in his ambitious *Boston Common at Twilight* (fig. 39). Despite its seemingly old-fashioned charm, this too is a distinctly modern scene. Once a residential area of handsome Federal row houses, the neighborhood west and south of the Common had become a lively business district during the 1870s. The red brick buildings visible at the left of Hassam's composition were mostly new; the traffic of trolley cars and carriages on the road signals the bustle of commerce on a winter afternoon, and artificial light glows from gas streetlights and shops, to which electricity had been introduced in 1881. Hassam enhanced his expression of the fast pace of city life by using a perspective scheme in which the verticals of the fence, lampposts, and trees recede rapidly into the distance, coming closer and closer together.

The calm, snowy park that Hassam contrasted with the hurried movement at left seems timeless. But the Common, like the streets near it, had been altered substantially during the nineteenth century. Originally a reserve for cattle grazing and military gatherings, it had been manicured into an oasis of elm trees and graceful promenades in emulation of the great parks of Paris and London. The area shown here is the Tremont Street Mall, one of five broad tree-lined walkways created to provide pedestrians with an elegant, tranquil alternative to the city's congested thoroughfares.

Although he selected conspicuously modern urban subjects, Hassam tempered them by softening the hard edges of new buildings and noisy streets with an illusion of natural effects and the skillful handling of painterly devices. Thus he used a variety of reds to unify *Boston Common at Twilight,* bringing the brick buildings, the glow of the lamps, and even the brilliant end of a lit cigarette in the hand of a passerby into harmony with the sky and snow, both tinged pink by the sunset. And, similarly, in *Rainy Day* he showed the wet streets reflecting the rosy glow of brick. Years after he painted the Boston pictures, Hassam recalled his fascination with light effects of this kind, remembering that Columbus Avenue "was all paved in asphalt, and I used to think it very pretty when it was wet and shining, and caught the reflections of passing people and vehicles."[28] He continued to explore effects of weather and light in his Paris scenes and, after 1889, in his New York views. In these paintings Hassam sometimes obscured specific details of buildings with veils of rain or fog, yet he emphatically did not lose his interest in depicting modern architecture.

However, Hassam was more concerned with people than with buildings in his images of Paris of 1887 to 1889. He was fascinated by the life of the street—the parades of cabs and carriages, the groceries and other goods set out along the sidewalk, the interplay of pedestrians on crowded boulevards. Sometimes identifiable landmarks, such as the Arc de Triomphe or Notre Dame, served as backdrops to the pageantry of the street (see figs. 58, 66). But it was only upon his return to the United States in late October 1889 and his relocation to New York City that Hassam again devoted much of his attention to architecture.

Still a young man when he moved there, Hassam was entranced with New York, which he later described as "the most beautiful city in the world."[29] For him, New York combined the vivacity of urban life he had encountered in Paris with the energy of a rapidly changing architectural environment, and he painted it repeatedly. In New York, as in Boston, Hassam's devotion to picturing the metropolis was unmatched. Most of his colleagues—among them William Merritt Chase and Thomas Dewing—turned inward while they were living in New York, painting figures shown in the comfortable and carefully controlled environments of their studios. If they ventured out of doors, they usually confined their subject matter to the city's parks and esplanades, seldom concerning themselves with its ambitious architecture. Chase, for example, depicted only the city's bucolic public spaces (see fig. 111), declaring that it would be much easier to explain where the beautiful places to sketch in the New York area were not than to say where they were.[30] But Hassam painted the streets, buildings, and crowds of the city: "He sees beauty in what many would reject as unworthy of serious art," as one critic noted in 1901.[31]

Inspired by writings of the French critic Edmond Duranty and their echoes in American periodicals, Hassam maintained that "the man who will go down to posterity is the man who paints his own time and the scenes of every-day life around him."[32] In 1876, about fifteen years before Hassam made this pronouncement, Duranty had called for painters to "take away the partition separating the studio from the community" and charged them with recording the modern world, including its railroads, shops, construction sites, gaslights, and omnibuses.[33] Hassam had first explored Duranty's agenda in Boston and later experimented with it in Paris, but he pursued it most completely in New York, prompted at least in part by the city's energetic and ceaseless architectural reinvention. New buildings replaced old ones, towers grew to unprecedented heights, streets changed from open boulevards to chasms constricted by skyscrapers, and electric lights turned night into day. The architectural transformations provided Hassam with new subjects and also with new vantage points from which to paint them.

Hassam's response to New York's dynamism was enthusiastic. And in his embrace of the new New York he stood apart not only from his fellow painters but also from such writers as Henry James, whose picturesque descriptions once seemed well matched to Hassam's own vision. James's portrait of an appealing Boston in *The Bostonians,* for example, with its busy streets, red brick buildings, and gray skies, parallels Hassam's painted impressions. But James was not as sanguine about New York. Although he admired the city's energy, in 1907 he disdained its distinctive new skyline as "some colossal hair comb turned upward and . . . deprived of half its teeth"; he considered its skyscrapers "monsters of the mere market . . . grossly tall and grossly ugly" and deplored its proliferation of lights and signs.[34] In the 1890s William Dean Howells had already complained that New York's long vistas were "architecturally like nothing so much as a horse's jaw bone, with the teeth broken or dislodged at intervals."[35] Indeed, just as few painters apart from Hassam were inspired to look beyond picturesque locations in New York and find in its new architecture appropriate and exciting subject matter, few writers praised the city's modern buildings until after the turn of the century.

Hassam was attracted to skyscrapers and other new architecture that his contemporaries specifically disliked. He painted a number of scenes that included tall new buildings, among them Madison Square Garden with its distinctive tower (1890)[36] and the nearby Knickerbocker apartments (1883) (fig. 91). He often depicted buildings in mist, rain, or snow and in artificial light, as he had done in Boston and Paris. But his motivation never seems to have been to deny the reality of the city's modern architecture by veiling it with atmospheric effects. Rather, after the manner of Whistler, the Impressionists, and many of his contemporaries, Hassam was exploring the aesthetic variety that changing weather conditions and artificial illumination could impose upon static subjects. Snow, night, rain, and mist had always inspired painters, but Hassam's investigations of innovations such as electric lights and streetcars are of a piece with his portrayals of the new architecture: already in the 1890s both demonstrated his enthusiasm for the artistic possibilities modern developments could offer. As early as 1891 he displayed works entitled "An Electric Car in the Suburbs," "Effect of Electric Light in the Snow (Madison Square)" (fig. 102), "A Broadway Nocturne," and "Rain, Mist, and Electric Light (Madison Square)."

Hassam also explored other transformations that were taking place in New York, focusing exclusively on their aesthetic aspects and shunning the social commentary that would concern a younger generation of painters. In compositions such as *The Hovel and the Skyscraper* (fig. 215) he recorded the contrasts between new and old that were apparent along the city's streets. Scholars have identified the buildings in question, noting that they are not a hovel and a skyscraper but are possibly the Sheepfold, a small wood-frame structure in Central Park at West Sixty-seventh Street and the new steel-frame parish house for a church.[37] Hassam's title is significant not for the veracity of its references but for the way it invites viewers to compare the two structures. They are old and new, brick and steel, small and large, but Hassam did not judge their relative merits: he simply presented the contrast.[38] Similarly, in *Union Square in Spring* (fig. 107) he eschewed social content and concerned himself with formal values. He took delight in using an elevated vantage point, permitted only by the construction of tall buildings, to produce a composition in which abstract elements predominate: above all, Hassam's subject is a pattern of circles and rectangles arranged across the surface of a square canvas.

In his devotion to formal concerns, Hassam demonstrated his continuing allegiance to the artistic philosophy of the Aesthetic Movement, which had engaged his colleagues in Ten American Painters. According to this philosophy, graceful rhythm, color contrast and harmony, and skillful arrangements of shapes did not have to bear the burden of narrative content or moral instruction but could be appreciated for their beauty alone. Along with several of his fellow painters, Hassam followed these precepts in producing a series of canvases featuring kimono-clad women with Asian art objects in interiors, arranging and rearranging them to achieve designs that emphasize abstract values (see figs. 226, 227). Unlike his colleagues, however, he was able to find that same formal beauty in the geometric patterns he saw in the modern city. These urban views are in fact similar to the work of some of the avant-garde artists of his day, including photographers Alvin Coburn and Alfred Stieglitz, who both explored the formal patterns revealed by elevated vantage points and exploited the theme of contrasting building types (see fig. 308). The kinship of Hassam's imagery to that of his modernist contemporaries complicates the characterization of Hassam as an uncompromisingly conservative, even reactionary painter and demonstrates some of the complexities of early-twentieth-century American art.

After 1900 Hassam expanded his repertoire to include images not only of the city's skyline but also of the dense, congested streets of lower Manhattan, two of the most characteristic visual features of the new New York (see figs. 18, 216). Favorite subjects of contemporary literature, social criticism, and architectural reviews, they were variously praised and denounced by authors.[39] As usual, Hassam eschewed such judgments, mining New York for its aesthetic qualities and always finding in the city's architecture inspiration for his explorations of form and atmosphere. "One must stand off at a proper angle to get the right light . . . when taken in groups with their zig zag outlines towering against the sky . . . skyscrapers are truly beautiful," he declared in 1913.[40]

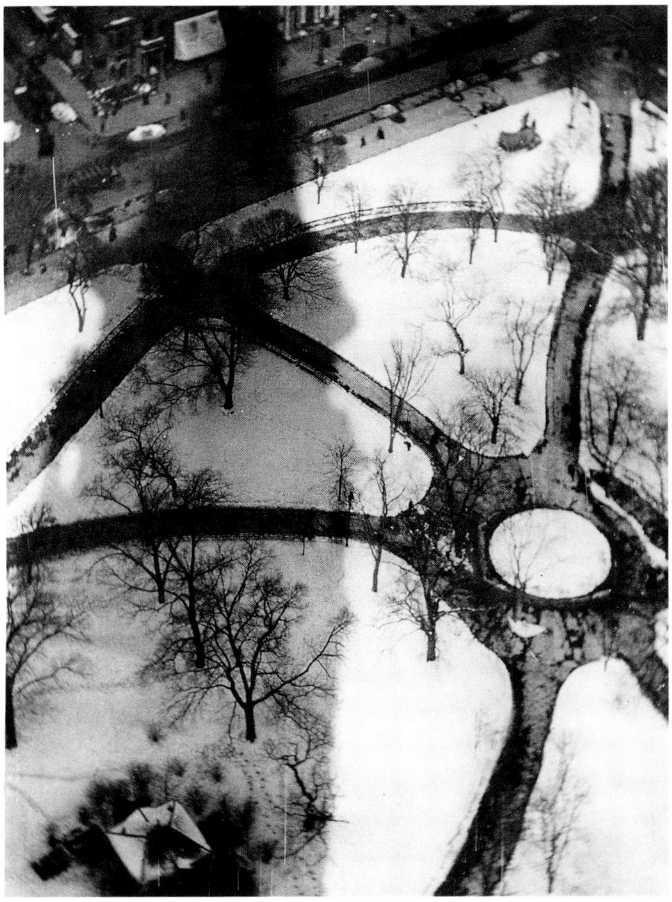

Fig. 308. Alvin Langdon Coburn. *The Octopus,* 1912. Platinum print, 16⁷⁄₁₆ x 12½ in. (41.8 x 31.8 cm). The Metropolitan Museum of Art, New York. Ford Motor Company Collection, Gift of Ford Motor Company and John C. Waddell, 1987 1987.1100.13

Hassam continued to depict New York for the rest of his career, alternating urban subjects with the views of rural colonial architecture he had never abandoned. Along with his images of busy streets, storefronts, and squares, he painted white steepled churches in New England, irregular wooden houses in small villages from Portsmouth to Easthampton, and the old buildings in southern Connecticut that he dubbed the icons of the "Cos Cob Clapboard School" (see figs. 154–57).[41] Thus, Hassam's approach is distinguished by his long-standing commitment to both rural and urban subjects and his abiding interest in both ancient and modern themes. As such, his outlook resonates with the analysis of the American mind that poet and philosopher George Santayana published in 1911: "America . . . is a country with two mentalities, one a survival of the beliefs and standards of the fathers, the other an expression of the instincts, practice, and discoveries of the younger generations . . . one-half of the American mind . . . has floated gently in the back-water, while alongside, in invention and industry and social organization the other half of the mind was leaping down a sort of Niagara Rapids." Santayana continued, "this division may be found symbolically in American architecture . . . a colonial mansion . . . stands beside the sky-scraper."[42] Deliberately embracing both conservative and modern states of mind and subjects, Hassam's architectural images epitomize the quintessentially American art the painter so ardently promoted.

1. Ernest Haskell, "Introduction," in Pousette-Dart 1922, p. vii.
2. See, for example, Julia B. Rosenbaum, "Childe Hassam's Church at Old Lyme, Connecticut: A Transformative Vision of Place," Paper presented to the College Art Association, 84th Annual Conference, Boston, February 1996; Julia B. Rosenbaum, "Local Views, National Visions: Art, New England, and American Identity, 1890–1920" (Ph.D. diss., University of Pennsylvania, Philadelphia, 1998); and Elizabeth Broun, "Childe Hassam's America," *American Art* 13, no. 3 (fall 1999), pp. 32–57.
3. Lockman interview, January 31, 1927, p. 11.
4. *King's Hand-book of Boston* (Cambridge, Mass.: Moses King, 1881), p. 18.
5. Oliver Wendell Holmes, "An Appeal for 'The Old South,'" 1877, in *The Complete Poetical Works of Oliver Wendell Holmes* (Boston: Houghton Mifflin and Company, 1895), p. 237.
6. *King's Hand-book of Boston,* p. 18.
7. Unidentified clipping, Hassam Papers, reel NAA1, frame 508.
8. For Nantucket and tourism, see Dona L. Brown, *Inventing New England: Regional Tourism in the Nineteenth Century* (Washington, D.C.: Smithsonian Institution Press, 1995), pp. 105–34. See also Truettner and Stein 1999.
9. Reproduced in Christie's, New York, sale cat., May 22, 1991, lot 244. Hassam's hometown of Dorchester, described in *King's Hand-book of Boston,* pp. 29–30, as "quite rural . . . [with] fine country residences," also offered rich potential for subject matter. Among the "fine country residences" were two suitably picturesque seventeenth-century survivors, the Blake House and the Pierce House. The house has not yet been securely identified, but Hassam later noted that the building he depicted in *Old House, Dorchester* was "two hundred years old." *Old House, Dorchester* is signed and dated 1884; Hassam inscribed his comments about the location on the back of the painting in 1930. The three-over-three window fenestration pattern Hassam records matches neither the Blake House nor the Pierce House, the two remaining seventeenth-century structures in Dorchester.
10. Edwin Whitefield, *The Homes of Our Forefathers, Being a Selection of the Oldest and Most Interesting Buildings in Massachusetts* (Boston: A. Williams and Company, 1880).
11. Ibid., title page.
12. Henry Wadsworth Longfellow, *Tales of a Wayside Inn* (Boston: Ticknor and Fields, 1863). This book included Longfellow's popular poem "The Midnight Ride of Paul Revere." Whitefield used Longfellow's verses in his text for *Homes of Our Forefathers.*
13. *Boston Herald,* July 3, 1897, as quoted in the history of the Wayside Inn at http://www.wayside.org. In 1923 Lemon's widow sold the property to Henry Ford, who restored the site further.
14. Childe Hassam, Autobiographical notes, n.d., Hassam Papers, reel NAA1, frame 689. Hassam noted approvingly that "the preservation and restoration of this old building is enough to justify anybody for most anything."

15. "The Fairbanks House at Dedham," *Garden and Forest* 2, no. 79 (August 28, 1889), pp. 411, 415.
16. Alvin Lincoln Jones, *Under Colonial Roofs* (Boston: C. B. Webster, 1894), p. 184.
17. The so-called Roundy House may have been built about 1700. In the mid-eighteenth century it was sold (together with the nearby paper mill) to George and Richard Clark. The Roundy family owned the house at the time Enneking painted it; the name is no longer associated with the house.
18. In at least two paintings, however, Hassam deviated from his usual practice and catered to an antiquarian taste: the costume piece *Indian Summer in Colonial Days*, 1899, reproduced in Susan G. Larkin, *The Cos Cob Art Colony: Impressionists on the Connecticut Shore*, exh. cat. (New York: National Academy of Design; New Haven: Yale University Press, 2001), p. 106; and *The Stairway: A Plot of the Revolution*, shown in the *Second Exhibition and Competition of Colonial Pictures Under the Auspices of The Colonial Dames of Massachusetts*, Boston Art Club, December 2–16, 1899, no. 25.
19. *King's Hand-book of Boston*, p. 21. Edwin M. Bacon, who later published several local guides of his own, and William Howe Downes, best known as an art critic for the *Boston Evening Transcript*, are credited with the text.
20. Henry James, *The Bostonians* (1886; New York: New American Library, 1979), p. 11. *The Bostonians* was first published in serialized form in *Century* 29–31 (February 1885–February 1886).
21. "Art Notes," *Boston Evening Transcript*, January 27, 1886.
22. See, for example, Bienenstock 1980, pp. 168–71, and Teresa A. Carbone's entry for Hassam's *Late Afternoon, New York: Winter*, in *American Paintings in the Brooklyn Museum of Art: Artists Born by 1876*, forthcoming 2004. I am grateful to Dr. Carbone for sharing her manuscript with me.
23. William H. Gerdts, "Three Themes," in Adelson, Cantor, and Gerdts 1999, p. 122. Hassam's 1884 exhibition of watercolors at Williams and Everett featured watercolors painted in Europe and also included street scenes.
24. Mary Felton, a Beacon Hill resident, bought Graham's *A Rainy Day in the Piazzetta, Venice* in January 1887. Another Graham, *Snowing in Campo S.S. Giovanni e Paolo, Venice*, 1879 (Museum of Fine Arts, Boston), belonged to the Bartol family, members of Hunt's circle and likely known to Hassam. For the influence of stereographs on Hassam, see Sarah Vure, "Childe Hassam's Paintings of Boston Architecture" (seminar paper, Boston University, 1990), curatorial files, Museum of Fine Arts, Boston.
25. The first American example of an apartment building consisting of French flats was Boston's Hotel Pelham, built in 1857 on Boylston Street near the Common. For French flats and apartment living in Boston, see Douglass Shand-Tucci, *Built in Boston: City and Suburb, 1800–1950* (Boston: New York Graphic Society, 1978), pp. 101–20. See also Elizabeth Prindle, "Childe Hassam, South End Impressionist," *South End Historical Society Newsletter* 29, no. 1 (April 2001), p. 2. The Hotel Albemarle is listed at 282 Columbus Avenue on maps and in city directories of the 1880s. Gerdts ("Three Themes," p. 125), however, has identified Hassam's residence not as the Hotel Albemarle but as the Copley Chambers, across the street.
26. Boston's original South End was confined to the southern part of the Shawmut peninsula, once the defining geographical boundary of the city and connected to the mainland only by a narrow neck of land. Early in the nineteenth century landfill projects enlarged the South End to include new streets parallel to Washington Street, which ran along the neck. In 1861 the South End's northern edge was Tremont Street. To the north and south of the neck was water: Back Bay and South Bay. Once the waters of the Back Bay were entirely filled in and the land was developed, the line of the Boston and Providence railroad tracks made it easier to distinguish the new neighborhoods of the Back Bay and the South End. Everything north of the tracks was called "Back Bay," and everything south of the tracks (including Columbus Avenue) was considered the "South End." For full details of the city's growth, see Alex Krieger et al., *Mapping Boston* (Cambridge, Mass.: MIT Press, 1999), and Nancy S. Seasholes, *Gaining Ground: A History of Landmaking in Boston* (Cambridge, Mass.: MIT Press, 2003).
27. Frank T. Robinson, "F. Childe Hassam," in Frank T. Robinson, *Living New England Artists* (Boston: Samuel E. Cassino, 1888), p. 102.
28. Hassam quoted in Ives 1892, p. 117.
29. Hassam quoted in "New York the Beauty City," *New York Sun*, February 23, 1913, p. 16.
30. Chase quoted in A. E. Ives, "Suburban Sketching Grounds," *Art Amateur* 25 (September 1891), p. 80, as excerpted in William H. Gerdts, *Impressionist New York* (New York: Abbeville Press, 1994), p. 31.
31. Frederick W. Morton, "Childe Hassam, Impressionist," *Brush and Pencil* 8, no. 3 (June 1901), p. 147.
32. Hassam quoted in Ives 1892, p. 116.
33. Louis Emile Edmond Duranty, "La Nouvelle Peinture," 1876, translated and reprinted in *The New Painting: Impressionism, 1874–1886*, exh. cat. (San Francisco: Fine Arts Museums of San Francisco, 1986), pp. 38–47. The original French version is reprinted on pp. 447–84.
34. Henry James, *The American Scene* (1907; New York: Charles Scribner's Sons, 1946), pp. 139, 80, 87.
35. William Dean Howells, *Letters of an Altrurian Traveller, 1893–94*, a series of 23 essays originally published in *Cosmopolitan*, November 1892–September 1894, as quoted in Merrill Schleier, *The Skyscraper in American Art, 1890–1931* (New York: Da Capo Press, 1986), pp. 9–10.
36. See *Madison Square in Snow*, 1893 (Peabody Art Collection, Maryland Commission on Artistic Property of the Maryland State Archives).
37. See H. Barbara Weinberg, "Hassam in New York, 1897–1919," in this publication, pp. 205, 209.
38. Some scholars have interpreted Hassam's image as celebrating progress, while others believe it expresses disapproval of the changes taking place in the city. See, for example, Jay E. Cantor, "Beyond Impressionism: Hassam's Twentieth-Century Work," in Adelson, Cantor, and Gerdts 1999, p. 99; Gerdts, "Three Themes," p. 162; and Schleier, *Skyscraper in American Art*, p. 28, among many. It should be noted that the word "skyscraper" did not necessarily have a positive connotation when Hassam compared it with "the hovel" in his title. Henry James (*American Scene*, p. 92), for example, defined a skyscraper in 1907 as a "fifty-floored conspiracy against the very idea of the ancient graces."
39. See Schleier, *Skyscraper in American Art*.
40. "New York the Beauty City," p. 16.
41. Hassam 1928, p. 28, repeated in Adams 1938, p. 93, and quoted in Larkin, *Cos Cob Art Colony*, p. 103.
42. George Santayana, "The Genteel Tradition in American Philosophy," 1911, in *The Genteel Tradition: Nine Essays by George Santayana*, edited by Douglas L. Wilson (Cambridge, Mass.: Harvard University Press, 1967), pp. 39–40.

Hassam's Gardens

Lisa Miller

Childe Hassam celebrated gardens and flowers from the beginning to the end of his long career. He started in 1882 with Barbizon-influenced landscapes such as *Blossoming Trees* (fig. 309), a delicate watercolor of a cherry tree in spring, its pink petals fluttering amid the surrounding foliage. He finished in his own front yard in 1934—during the last summer in which he was well enough to work—with *Mrs. Hassam's Garden at East Hampton* (fig. 310), a tightly cropped view of a border of lemon-yellow daylilies (*Hemerocallis*), some of which are gathered in a vase and arranged on a tree bench with a platter of peaches and a patterned textile. The evolution of Hassam's style can be traced in these works, as the early Tonalist washes give way to a full-blown Impressionism that in some later works embraces elements of Postimpressionism.

Two groups of Hassam's floral paintings stand out, both in number and quality: first the images produced during a stay in France from 1886 to 1889, which feature women posed in parks and gardens or selling flowers on the streets; second, and most famously, the exuberant outpouring of flower-filled scenes from Celia Thaxter's garden and parlor on Appledore Island, Maine. Whatever the ostensible subject, Hassam's brush never strayed far from dabs of green or dots of bright flower colors.[1] Park scenes executed on

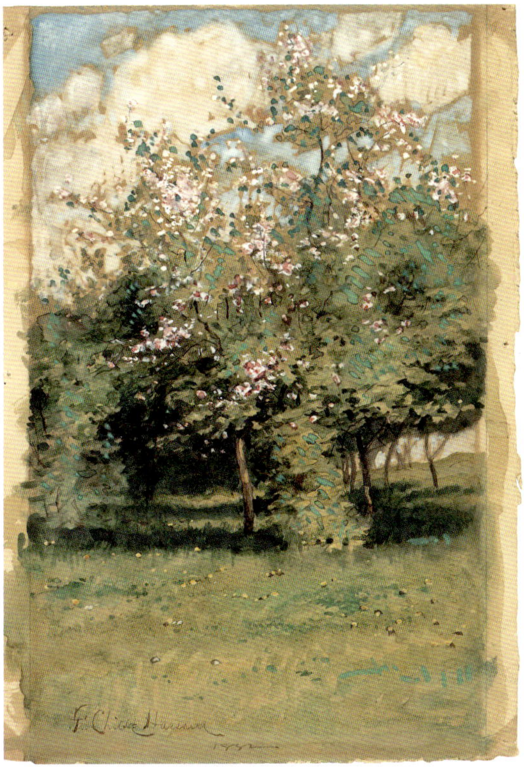

Fig. 309. Childe Hassam. *Blossoming Trees,* 1882. Opaque watercolor on brown paper, 10½ x 9 in. (26.7 x 22.9 cm). The Museum of Fine Arts, Boston. Bequest of Kathleen Rothe 65.1301

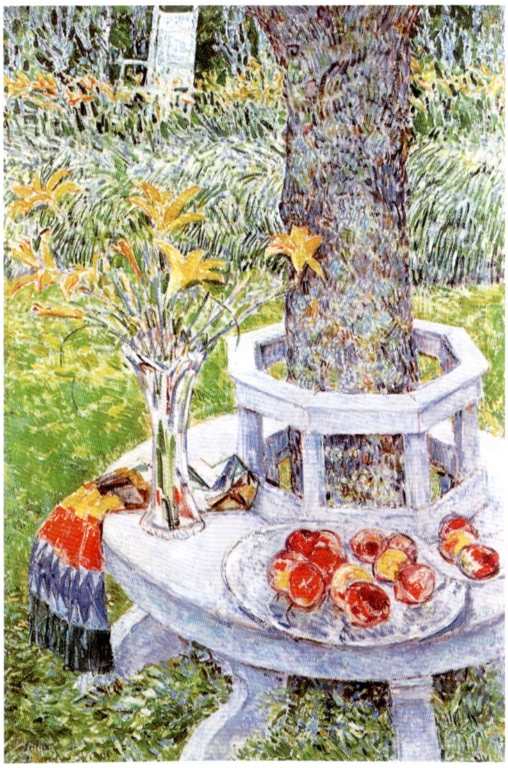

Fig. 310. Childe Hassam. *Mrs. Hassam's Garden at East Hampton,* 1934. Oil on canvas, 40¾ x 28½ in. (103.5 x 72.4 cm). Private collection

both sides of the Atlantic include horticultural tableaux, and paintings of city life detail trees in spring bud or showy leaf and offer peeks at front-yard flower beds. Depictions of eighteenth-century vernacular architecture in New England coastal towns portray buildings swagged with vines or surrounded by shrub and flower borders and native trees. In a series of images painted from 1909 to about 1922 a woman stands in front of a window located sometimes in the country and sometimes in the city. The country compositions, set in Cos Cob and Old Lyme, Connecticut, typically reveal a garden through the window—a verdant backlighting for the figure—or, at the least, a glimpse of a flower-filled window box on the porch.[2] In each of the city paintings—the New York Window series—buildings of a fast-rising metropolis are seen through a veiled windowpane of Hassam's studio, while the garden comes inside in the form of troughs of paperwhite narcissus, spring bouquets, bowls of roses, or floral decoration seen on painted screens or a woman's slinky garments (see figs. 226, 311).

Flowers appear in other pictures as well: Hassam occasionally painted floral still lifes (see figs. 247, 248). There are also images of the bouquets in Celia Thaxter's parlor (see fig. 121), and he rarely included a mantelpiece or a piano in a composition without adding a floral note (see figs. 160, 312).

Although he was not a gardener himself, or even a garden tourist, Hassam had a lifelong affinity for the transient beauty of flowers. Many of his most moving canvases study the subject. In his French floral and garden pictures Hassam used flowers as one part of a multi-faceted narrative that includes figures and a built environment. In the Appledore paintings the flowers have become the focus of intimate attention and are seen as part of the natural world. These differences not only reflect the differences between elegant French garden architecture and Thaxter's wind-whipped island flower patch but also demonstrate Hassam's desire to paint Thaxter's flowers as she herself perceived them.

Gardens were, of course, a key Impressionist motif, affording artists an ideal opportunity to explore the play of

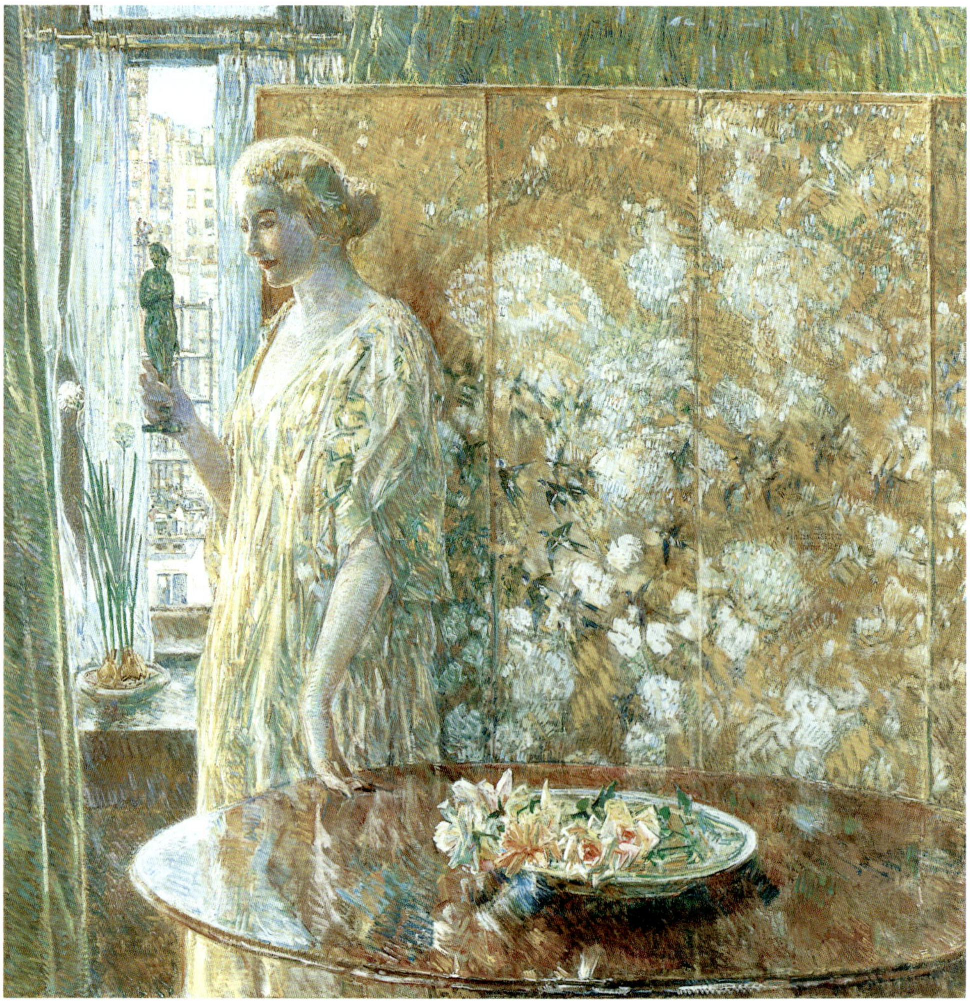

Fig. 311. Childe Hassam. *Tanagra (The Builders, New York)*, 1918. Oil on canvas, 58¾ x 58¾ in. (149 x 149 cm). Smithsonian American Art Museum, Washington, D.C. Gift of John Gellatly

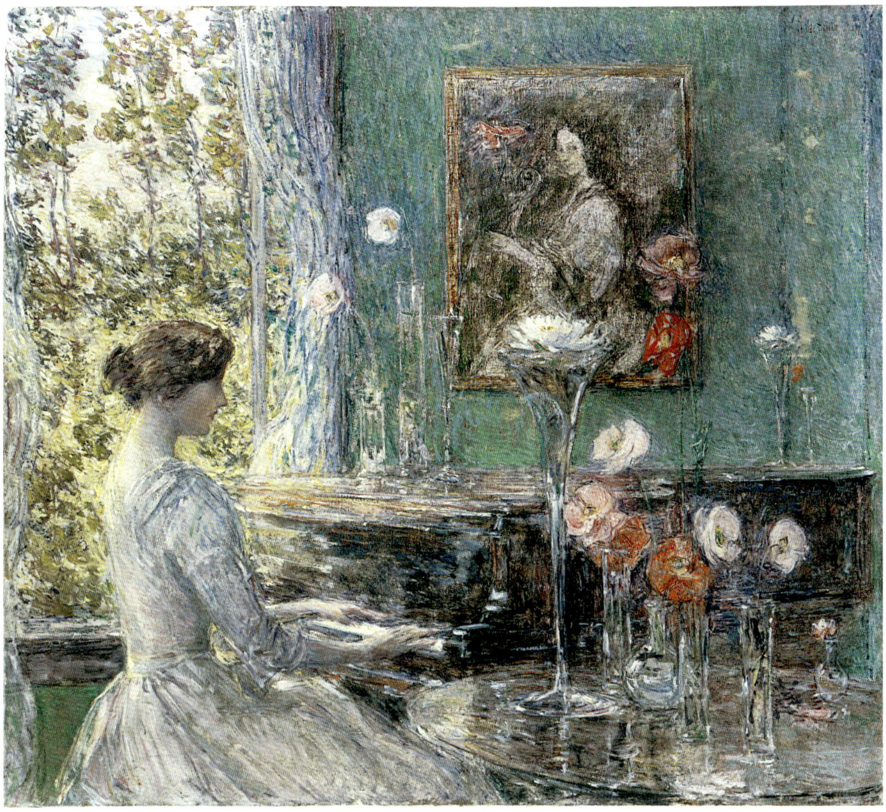

Fig. 312. Childe Hassam. *Improvisation,* 1899. Oil on canvas, 30 x 33⅞ in. (76.3 x 86.2 cm). Smithsonian American Art Museum, Washington, D.C. Gift of John Gellatly

light on animated colored surfaces. Hassam as well as other Americans knew the lush garden paintings of Monet and Renoir, and he was not the only American Impressionist who was concerned with gardens. William Merritt Chase painted in New York City's parks as early as 1886. Willard Metcalf, John Leslie Breck, and Theodore Robinson depicted the gardens at Giverny, where they were early members of the art colony surrounding Monet. Robinson also worked at Cos Cob with John H. Twachtman, J. Alden Weir, and Hassam, all of whom painted the flowering landscape.

By the late nineteenth century, Americans were building houses with extensive and lavish landscapes or smaller cottage gardens; in addition, books and periodicals on gardening proliferated during the period. As a man of his time, Hassam was aware of these developments, but it was apparently his deep relationship with Thaxter, gardener and garden writer extraordinaire, that gave him his garden fever. Under the sway of her enthusiasms, he became as passionate a painter of gardens as she was a gardener.[3] The most compelling of Hassam's garden pictures, whether painted in France or on Appledore, are from the decade of their friendship. The only garden other than Thaxter's on Appledore that has ever been explored in such depth by a major artist is Monet's at Giverny.

Celia Thaxter was a member of the Laighton family, which had turned the bare windswept rocks of Appledore Island, one of the Isles of Shoals, into a summer resort (fig. 114). Thaxter took over her parents' cottage, a three-story frame house next to Appledore House, the summer hotel that her family owned and operated (figs. 126, 127). There she established a salon that was visited by New England's artistic and intellectual elite.[4] She was a poet and an essayist, a painter who illustrated her books with her own watercolors and decorated china with botanical motifs, a lover of music and art, a devoted admirer of artists, a moralist, and above all a rapturous flower gardener. Hassam met Thaxter about 1879, when he was "not much past twenty,"[5] and she was nearly forty-four. About his visits to Appledore Hassam reminisced in 1927:

> *Celia Thaxter had a salon there, which was as fine as anything could be. . . . I had known her before I went to Paris and had spent a few days at the Shoals[.] I met her in Boston. But she had the most interesting people with her in the summer time. William Hunt went there. . . . She was a great friend of Hunt's. . . . He spent all his time in her little salon, which was a big room in the Thaxter cottage. . . . The world is small and the arts and letters of*

> *the artists quarters is a world in itself. . . . William Mason, the musician was there. I met Whittier there. . . . Mrs. Thaxter was interested in painting and literature. She was a woman of the finest culture. Her famous garden was there. . . . I have painted many times the Island Garden. . . . The Isles of Shoals bring up some of the pleasantest memories.*[6]

If Hassam looked to Thaxter as a spiritual mentor and a champion—as well as the only hands-on gardener among his close friends—she was equally enthusiastic about him. She wrote poems extolling his gifts, and it was she who suggested that he drop his given name, Frederick, in favor of his more unusual and heroic middle name, Childe (Byron's *Childe Harold* still had romantic currency). When Hassam added a crescent-moon cipher to his signature, he took the device from the similarly shaped silver barrette that Thaxter always wore like a tiara in her hair (see fig. 1).[7]

Hassam's first documented visit to Appledore was in the summer of 1886, not long before he sailed to Paris with his wife, Maud. Looking at the French capital through Thaxter's eyes, he produced a steady stream of flower-filled pictures during this European stay. Under the influence of Impressionism, in these paintings of French parks, gardens, and flower vendors he employed a quick brushstroke and lighter, brighter colors than those of his earlier works.

The French garden canon, with its formal aesthetic of containment and control, was the antithesis of Thaxter's casual-looking style. Nevertheless, Hassam responded to the French tradition, which, going back to André Le Nôtre in the seventeenth century, called for woody and herbaceous plants to be used as architectural elements. Rather than being prized for their natural form, these plants were trained as lollipop-shaped standards, grafted into weeping cascades, or displayed in tubs and pots. Tree canopies were sheared (pleached) into hedges or pollarded into spheres; packed earth, paving, and gravel were the preferred surfaces for garden terraces and park paths.

About 1888 Hassam painted his wife and her sister Mrs. George H. Cotton on the roof terrace of the couple's building at 35, boulevard Rochechouart in Paris in *Twilight (Le Crépuscule)* (fig. 313). Both figures are presented in profile, a pose he favored. They are dressed in white (the color of Thaxter's summer gowns) and share the terrace with a pot garden composed of white hydrangeas, lilies, and pale

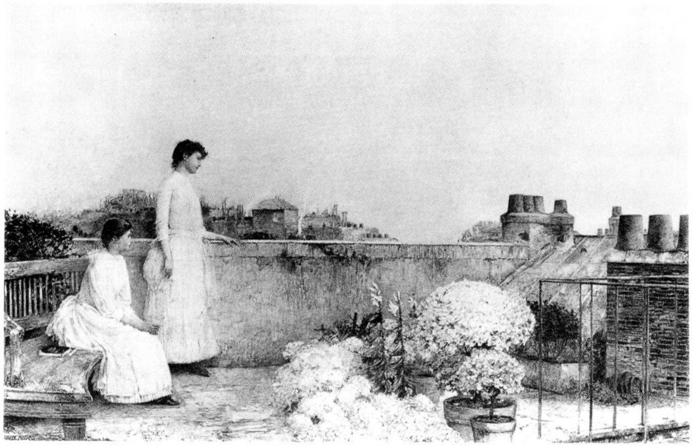

Fig. 313. Childe Hassam. *Twilight (Le Crépuscule)*, ca. 1888. Oil on canvas, 50 x 77 in. (127 x 195.6 cm). Location unknown

pink and white azalea standards. Hassam gave the only horticulturally detailed description he had ever given of one his garden paintings, when he recalled *Twilight* as "a picture of the rough [*sic*] tops of Paris. . . . The top of the building on this roof top was filled with flowers in pots. Those azaleas—the French do it there beautifully. [Y]ou might call them a dome of flowers growing out of a pot, and it had some of those hydrangia [*sic*] . . . and these azaleas—you might call them dome like shrubs all in flower. All of them are in this picture. That was my motif."[8] *Twilight* is not painted in the new Impressionist style but is instead bathed in an overall hazy pink Tonalist wash.

During Mrs. Cotton's visit, Hassam again portrayed the two women dressed in white, this time in his studio (fig. 65).[9] Their floral complement, bouquets of roses on the piano at which Mrs. Cotton is seated, is an echo from Thaxter's parlor, which always featured music as well as flowers.[10] In both paintings of the sisters, as in so many of the artist's confections portraying women and flowers, the figures are impassive, having no more contours, color, or animation than the flowers. The beauty of the flowers and gardens paraphrases and extends the beauty of the women, although the blooms are often the more fragrant, vibrant, voluptuous presence.[11]

Every summer during their stay in France, the Hassams visited Ernest Blumenthal and his wife—a close friend of Maud's—at Villiers-le-Bel, ten miles northeast of Paris. The Blumenthals' walled garden was the subject of more than two dozen works and Hassam's first sustained treatment of a garden motif.[12]

The Thaxter and Blumenthal gardens were different in every way except perhaps in their need for constant skilled attention. Thaxter sowed her own seeds each spring and grew a wild-looking garden that seemed to tumble off the end of the earth. The Blumenthal garden was paved as well as walled, its many levels of paths and terraces displaying plants not native to northern Europe (geraniums, oleanders, dracaena, rhododendrons) and not all hardy in its climate. At least five paintings of the Blumenthal garden portray Mrs. Hassam and other women tucked in among the plants, lounging, sewing, reading, dreaming, dripping a little water into a potted oleander: *After Breakfast* (fig. 76); *Geraniums* (fig. 79); *The Artist's Wife in a Garden, Villiers-le-Bel,* 1889 (private collection);[13] *In the Garden* (fig. 80); and the undated *Reading* (Nelson-Atkins Museum of Art, St. Louis). All display the same deep diagonal space, sun-brightened reds and earth tones, and garden accoutrements. The well-tended plants, cared for by a professional gardener, are placed in pots around the paved terraces, to be admired one by one, as precious objects.[14] This closed and private world, surrounded by high walls and hedges,[15] is meant for leisure, and the women are garden ornaments, luxuriating like cats in the strong summer light.

Hassam's Villiers-le-Bel images reveal close affinities with paintings Monet produced in the 1880s of the enclosed world of his blossoming garden at Argenteuil. Monet's *Luncheon,* 1873 (Musée d'Orsay, Paris), *Artist's House at Argenteuil,* 1873 (Art Institute of Chicago), and *Gladioli,* 1876 (Detroit Institute of Arts), for example, all foreshadow the red palette of the flowers, the deep space with receding diagonals, and the languorous mood of the women who are present but not prominent in the gardens of Hassam's Villiers-le-Bel pictures.

In 1872–73 Monet painted four canvases featuring fashionably dressed women relaxing near the flower-laden branches of a stand of old lilac trees at his first Argenteuil house, among them *The Garden,* 1872 (private collection),[16] and *Lilacs, Gray Day,* 1872 (Musée d'Orsay, Paris). Perhaps inspired by Monet, in a number of paintings whose precise setting has not been determined, Hassam, too, paired women and lilacs. One example is his *In the Garden*, in which

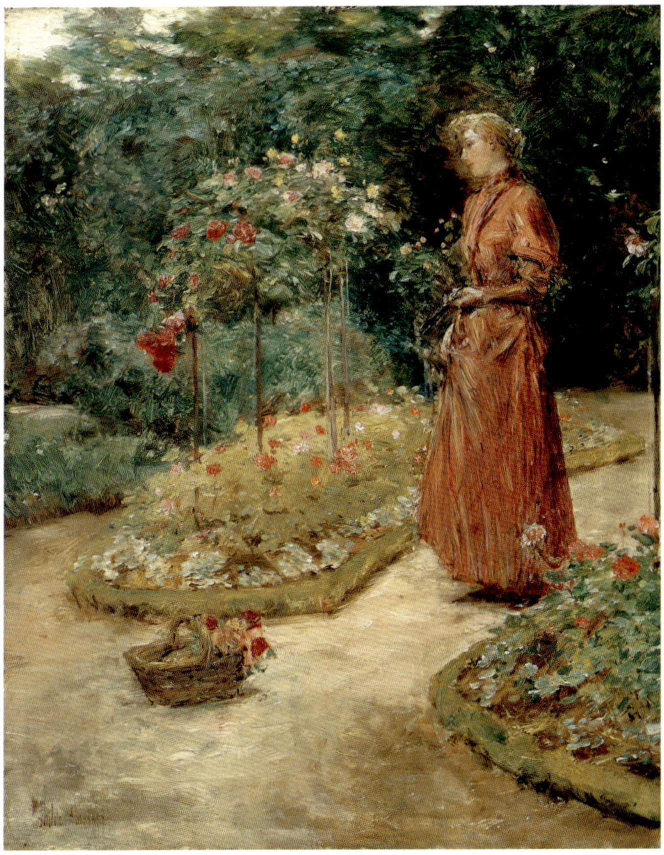

Fig. 314. Childe Hassam. *Woman Cutting Roses in a Garden,* ca. 1888–89. Oil on panel, 18⅛ x 14⅜ in. (46.1 x 36.6 cm). Collection of The Newark Museum, Bequest of Diana Bonnor Lewis, 1988 88.7

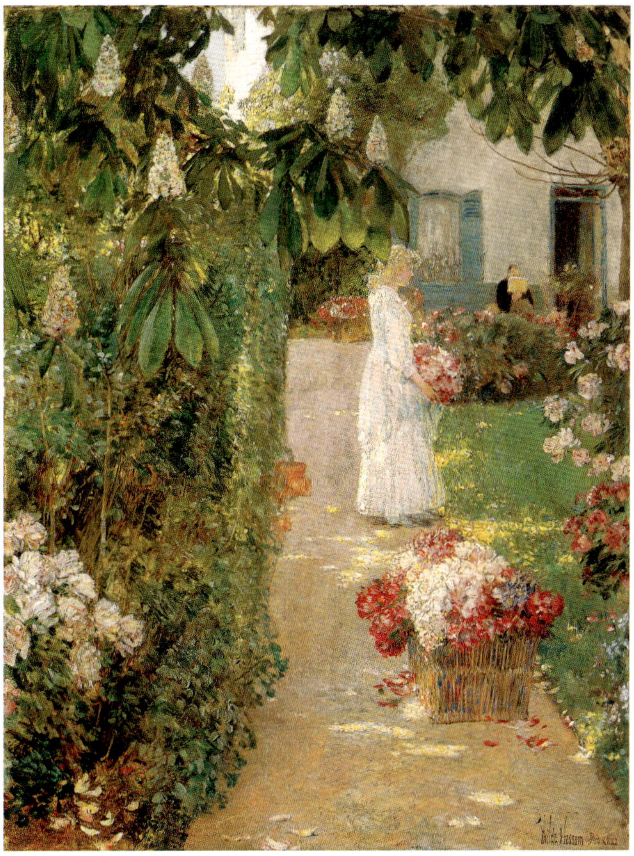

Fig. 315. Childe Hassam. *Gathering Flowers in a French Garden,* 1888. Oil on canvas, 28 x 21¾ in. (71.1 x 55.1 cm). Worcester Art Museum, Massachusetts, Theodore T. and Mary G. Ellis Collection

he posed a woman sitting on a low wall in front of blooming lilac trees. Unlike the figures in the Villiers-le-Bel compositions, which are embedded deep into the background, the women in the lilac paintings have been placed close to the picture plane. Two other canvases, *Woman Cutting Roses in a Garden* (fig. 314) and *Gathering Flowers in a French Garden* (fig. 315) also show women collecting flowers, bouquets in hand and full baskets at their feet.[17]

When Hassam painted in Paris, the structure of the enclosed gardens gave way to the openness of the streets. In works such as *Flower Girl* (fig. 71) and *Rue Montmartre*, 1888 (private collection),[18] attractive young women offer bouquets pulled from their sidewalk baskets, which billow with peonies and flowering bulbs. Each vendor stands at a curb in the foreground as pedestrians bustle around her. Painting with loose brushstrokes and rich impasto, Hassam offset the subdued colors of the streets with the brilliant hues of the flowers.[19] These women are not contained in floral surrounds but instead vividly punctuate the hard gray streets. They are working-class girls, selling their beautiful blooms to earn their keep.

Hassam's depiction of a flower seller that most emphatically emphasizes ornamental effects is the fanciful *Rose Girl* (fig. 72), in which the artist adopted some of the same compositional strategies Manet used in his *Bar at the Folies-Bergère* (fig. 73). Hassam's highly decorative triptych, gilded and tightly cropped, portrays a half-length figure with a delicately realized face and crocheted shawl. More animated and individualized than Hassam's typical flower seller, she stands behind her stock, a tumble of multicolored roses, and clasps a smaller bouquet that she is making up for immediate sale. Like Manet's barmaid, she is directly engaged with her customer (visible in the French painting but only implied here). And, as with Manet's painting, our pleasure in admiring the woman's beauty suggests the pleasure to be had from sampling her wares.

At the Florist (fig. 75) was the last large exhibition work that Hassam painted in Paris.[20] Its friezelike format and flattened space are unusual for the artist's floral compositions, and, except for its highly colored Impressionist palette, the picture is executed in a more academic style, using firm outlines and crisp drawing.[21] For the first time Hassam included a specific customer for his sidewalk vendor, a smartly dressed matron in a flower-trimmed bonnet. The three young women tending the stall are nothing like the saucy Parisians in the other works. They are country girls in simple gray gowns with clean white caps and aprons, and their attire is echoed by the fresh white paper wrapper on each bouquet and flowering plant. Like the plants at Villiers-le-Bel, each one stands alone, complete in itself. In *At the Florist* Hassam balanced the verticality of the plants arrayed along the sidewalk with the horizontal ranks of bouquets stretching up the back wall in repeating circles.

At the start of Hassam's first Parisian summer he wrote longingly to a friend who was visiting Thaxter's cottage: "You are at the Shoals and you are enjoying it I am sure. Same sun, same moonlight, and the same flowers in Mrs. Thaxter's garden. And as all these things are charming always, and the best to be had in the world, of course you are enjoying the lovely place. I wouldn't dare to say how many times I have wished to be there this summer."[22] By June 1890 the artist was back at Appledore, and until Celia Thaxter's death, in 1894, he spent part of every summer there, painting her garden and relishing the atmosphere.

Thaxter herself planned and tended her garden, which lives on in all its summer beauty in Hassam's many paintings, watercolors, and pastels.[23] Her cottage garden was laid out in a simplified Colonial Revival style. It featured rectilinear beds and borders filled with heirloom annuals, old perennials, roses, and vines, all growing together in a tangle of form and color. The taste for such old-fashioned gardens, which replaced the high Victorian craze for island beds filled with newly hybridized or exotic annuals, was inspired by the writings of John Ruskin and William Morris, leaders of the English Arts and Crafts Movement. The fashion was spread through William Robinson's influential books *The Wild Garden* and *The English Flower Garden*,[24] and popularized by the American Centennial Exposition of 1876. In *The American Flower Garden* (1909), Neltje Blanchan praised the seventeenth-century colonial New England garden, the prototype for Colonial Revival garden ideas: "We like to remember that the beautiful as well as the utilitarian had a place in the gardens of those hard times that tried men's souls: that hollyhocks stood like cheerful sentinels beside the cabin door in the Plymouth Plantation and Massachusetts Bay Colony; that roses looked in at the windows; . . . that gilly flowers, feverfew and honesty, with its mother-of-pearl seed vessels for the winter bouquet, grew freely among the comfortable variety of simples, vegetables and pot herbs."[25]

The seemingly natural, uncomposed colonial garden style Blanchan described suited Appledore's rustic location, harsh climate, and short growing season. It also accorded with Thaxter's taste for old-fashioned gardens, which was shared by many of her educated and talented contemporaries. As May Brawley Hill wrote in *Grandmother's Garden:* "Grandmother's garden was eagerly adopted by creative amateurs across the country, including artists and crafts workers, taken as much with the aesthetic possibilities of an exuberant and informally planted garden of hardy flowers that could be maintained by one person as by its links to America's past."[26] Candace Wheeler, textile designer and founder of the New York Society of Decorative Art, developed a half-acre garden at her Catskill retreat at Onteora and wrote about it in her *Content in a Garden* (1901).[27] Adeline Robineau, the great art potter from Cincinnati, had an extensive garden filled with roses, and Fidelia Bridges and Maria Oakey Dewing grew the flowers they painted. Here it is relevant to note that Hassam's strong attraction to Thaxter's garden was in keeping with his fondness for all things colonial.

Thaxter was besotted with flower gardening—she not only grew them but also painted them on her pottery and featured them in her poems. In *An Island Garden*, published the year of her death and lavishly illustrated with Hassam's watercolors (see figs. 123, 137), Thaxter described her gardening life in detail. She wrote:

> *this little island garden of mine is so small that the amount of pure delight it gives in the course of a summer is something hardly to be credited. It lies along the edge of a* piazza, *forty or fifty feet long, sloping to the south, not more than fifteen feet wide, sheltered from the north winds and open to the sun. The whole* piazza *is thickly draped with vines . . . [which] make a grateful green shade, doubly delightful for that there are no trees on my island, and the shade is most welcome in the wide brilliancy of sea and sky.*[28]

Thaxter created her garden with cutting in mind and planted flowers that she could snip each morning and bring into her parlor in small, fragrant bouquets. Not particularly interested in garden design, she grew mostly home-propagated flowers in simple rectangular beds, and she surrounded her 50-by-15-foot plot with a plain board fence to protect it from the wind. Poppies abounded, as did hollyhocks and honeysuckle, sweet peas and sweet william, coreopsis and helianthus; the roses often survived the harsh winters, and each summer she replaced the water lilies in her large garden tubs.

Responding to Thaxter's aesthetic, Hassam painted his purest, most effusive interpretations of flowers at Appledore. Monet was an obvious stylistic inspiration, as David Park Curry points out: "No matter how tiresome Hassam must have found his early twentieth-century pigeonhole as the American Monet, the Shoals pictures bear eloquent witness to Monet's fertilization of Hassam's painting style. The most memorable Appledore images, like Monet's finest works, combine great delicacy with resonant strength."[29]

Thaxter encouraged her flowers, particularly the poppies, to seed outside the garden's perimeter and to spill down the rocky slope to the harbor.[30] No longer constrained to portray cultivated plants in a built environment, Hassam plunged into the task of painting Thaxter's poppies, lithe and floaty little flowers strewn about to look as if they grew wild.[31] Poppies, an emblem of the Art Nouveau movement, were in vogue among both French and American painters.[32] The European corn poppy that is sprinkled through the fields of France was a favorite subject of many French Impressionists, among them Monet, who painted it during the 1870s and 1880s. Hassam might well have seen at least one work by Monet featuring poppies in New York in 1886 at Durand-Ruel's exhibition of Impressionist paintings and during his years in Paris at several Monet shows there.[33] American Impressionist Robert Vonnoh, renowned for his poppy paintings, was Hassam's friend and a fellow student at the Académie Julien in Paris in 1887. Both Vonnoh, who painted his first poppy studies in 1888, and Hassam, who began his in 1890 on Appledore, were surely responding to Monet's example in taking up the subject.[34] Other Americans who were avid poppy painters include Willard L. Metcalf, George Hitchcock, Frank Millet, Walter Shirlaw, and Maria Oakey Dewing.[35]

Hassam often pictured the poppies growing alone and wild on the slopes of Appledore, as in the oil *Poppies, Isles of Shoals* (fig. 134), which shows a wide foreground swath of the pink, red, and white flowers falling away to rocks, sea, and a North Atlantic sky. In the vertical raked-angle view of the watercolor *Flower Garden, Isles of Shoals* (fig. 133), poppy heads bobbing over the boldly stroked green mass of their stems and leaves are set against waving larkspur, deep blue against the fainter blue of sea and sky.[36] The same poppies and larkspur appear in *Home of the Hummingbird* (fig. 131), but weathered fence boards indicate that the setting is not uncultivated. Hassam would even bury himself in a flowery bank to paint frog's-eye views of it: in *Celia Thaxter's*

Garden, Isles of Shoals, Maine (fig. 9), and *Poppies,* ca. 1890 (private collection),[37] the immediacy of the flowers engulfs the viewer. These Appledore pictures reveal the artist replacing the cerebration and complex compositions of his French work with a sort of untethered rapture, freeing the flowers from the hand of a gardener and showing off their natural habits. With this ecstatic visual imagery, Hassam matched Thaxter's rapturous floral prose and poetry.

Poppies play a part in two portraits of the gardener in her garden. Painted as an illustration for *An Island Garden,* the watercolor entitled *The Garden in Its Glory* (fig. 129), catches Thaxter descending from her house, grandson Eliot in one hand, a bouquet of her signature scarlet poppies in the other. She is about to step through the vine-laden piazza into her garden, which is lush with high summer's hollyhocks and poppies. *In the Garden (Celia Thaxter in Her Garden)* (fig. 130) presents Thaxter dressed in a white gown and crowned with her distinctive crescent-moon barrette.[38] Surrounded by her kingdom, she rises like Venus Anadyomene from a foam of poppies, framed on either side by columns of hollyhocks, as the Shoals sea and sky fade into the distance.

In 1894 Hassam re-created Thaxter's parlor, the scene of her animated salon, in his magnificent *Room of Flowers* (fig. 118). Writing to John W. Beatty, Director of the Carnegie Institute, a year later, he described the work as "a picture of Mrs. Thaxter's house here which was the most unique setting and wholly characteristic of her remarkable love for flowers. It was painted just before her death and I think it one of my best things."[39] In this elegiac homage to his muse, the artist envisioned Thaxter as the presiding spirit of the house, symbolized by a young woman stretched out with a book on her green-pillowed sofa. The slanted deeply receding space, the vacant foreground half blocked with flowers, and the woman partially hidden among the blooms are familiar devices from the Villiers-le-Bel pictures. Here the dainty woman is subsumed into her flowers, embowered by her books and pictures, in a room bathed in green-tinged sunlight shining through the vines. The fluted glass vase bisecting her figure is filled with a swirling sheaf of yellow nasturtiums.[40] The artist chose to eulogize Thaxter with a cornucopia of these flowers, which, like Thaxter herself, were tough and stalwart yet still flamboyant. In the Victorian language of flowers, the nasturtium signified patriotism,[41] and for Hassam his friend embodied all the best of the American spirit that he held most dear.

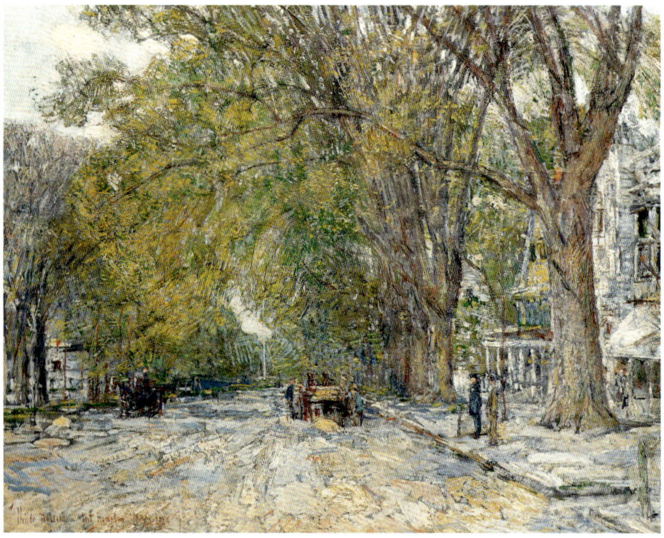

Fig. 316. Childe Hassam. *Main Street, East Hampton,* 1920. Oil on canvas, 16 x 20 in. (40.6 x 50.8 cm). Private collection

After Thaxter's death Hassam spent less time at the Shoals, finding artistic stimulation during summer interludes in other New England villages. He had visited East Hampton, New York, regularly since 1898, and in 1919 he and Maud settled there in a colonial house on Egypt Lane. He painted the luxuriant cottage gardens that clung to the old shingled houses in *Old House and Garden, East Hampton* (fig. 240) and the towering stand of elm trees on Main Street (see fig. 316).[42] The Woodhouse family gardens were depicted in 1909 and 1910 in Hassam's stunning *Water Garden* and *Lilies* (figs. 241, 244).[43]

The Water Garden portrays Emma (Mrs. Lorenzo G.) Woodhouse's naturalistic Japanese water garden, lush with creamy white iris (*Iris enstata*) at peak bloom.[44] The iris form a diagonally spreading arc that flows between a curved wedge of water lilies floating at the lower right and a small rustic bridge at the upper left. This enchanted vision of plants and water, so tightly focused that there is no sky, harks back to Hassam's high-horizon flowery meads at Appledore (see fig. 132).

In *Lilies,* which shows Mary (Mrs. Lorenzo E.) Woodhouse's Italianate garden, the same Japanese iris and pink water lilies are employed for a different effect. The downward angle of *The Water Garden* is exchanged for an upward view of a rectilinear lily pond with a naiad seated at its edge. The nymph's reflection shimmers among the lily pads and goldfish, while her pale filmy gown is all of a piece with the tall white iris that encircle her. The painting returns to the enclosed world of

Hassam's French gardens, where the women do not so much use the garden as decorate it. Both Woodhouse canvases combine an Impressionist focus on light and color with the Postimpressionist device of overall floral patterning.[45]

In a late work, *Heavenly Blues* (fig. 14), Hassam painted a portrait of morning glories flowering on the vine. Seen in a flattened-out close-up, the saffron-centered blue trumpets nestle against their heart-shaped leaves in a continuous design. Morning glories were another of Celia Thaxter's most beloved flowers.[46] She grew them on her trellised piazza and picked them to drape over a whelk shell suspended from a chandelier in her parlor. Hassam must have walked under them many times a day during his happy summer idylls at Appledore and remembered them with love.

1. For a discussion of Hassam's garden paintings as they relate to contemporary depictions of the same subject, see William H. Gerdts, *Down Garden Paths: The Floral Environment in American Art* (Rutherford, N.J.: Fairleigh Dickinson University Press; Cranbury, N.J.: Associated University Presses, 1983).
2. For a complete discussion of Hassam in Cos Cob, including this series, see Susan G. Larkin, *The Cos Cob Art Colony: Impressionists on the Connecticut Shore*, exh. cat. (New York: National Academy of Design; New Haven: Yale University Press, 2001).
3. Hassam rarely painted trees and other woody plants in settings other than gardens. *Blossoming Trees* (fig. 309) and *Peach Blossoms–Villiers-le-Bel* (fig. 81) are among the exceptions, as is *Laurel on the Ledges*, 1906 (Senator and Mrs. John D. Rockefeller IV), reproduced in Adelson, Cantor, and Gerdts 1999, p. 194, a woodland image depicting mountain laurel (*Kalmia latifolia*) in its natural habitat.
4. For a discussion of the Laighton family at the Shoals, see John M. Kingsbury's introduction to Thaxter 1894 (1985 ed.), p. vii. Thaxter entertained Longfellow and Richard Henry Dana, among others, and counted as her close friends John Greenleaf Whittier, Annie and James Fields, and Sarah Orne Jewett. See Sharon Paiva Stephan, *One Woman's Work: The Visual Art of Celia Laighton Thaxter*, exh. cat. (Portsmouth, N.H.: Portsmouth Atheneum in association with Isles of Shoals Historical and Research Association; Peter E. Randall Publisher, 2001), p. 40.
5. Hassam, Letter to Miss Farmer, 1933, p. 5.
6. Lockman interviews, January 31, 1927, pp. 24–25, and February 2, 1927, p. 15.
7. Summer visitor Charlotte Goodrich described Thaxter in her diary: "She was graceful and had an exquisite head and beautiful hair, in which she wore a silver crescent." Charlotte Goodrich, Diary, MS. 547.1, Jessie Donahue Collection, Vaughan Cottage Museum and Library, Star Island, Isles of Shoals, New Hampshire.
8. Lockman interview, January 31, 1927, p. 14. Hydrangeas are a prominent element in the undated *Afternoon in Nantucket* (Senator and Mrs. John D. Rockefeller IV), reproduced in Adelson, Cantor, and Gerdts 1999, p. 26, in which a diagonally receding porch is lined with plump white hydrangeas that reinforce the whiteness of the seated woman's summer gown. They appear again, interspersed with geraniums, on the balcony of the Hotel Bartholdi in *View of Broadway and Fifth Avenue* (fig. 93).
9. Thaxter wore only white or black with white, as do many of the women Hassam depicted. According to Charlotte Goodrich, "Celia's dresses had a black underbody with white over. The gowns were of wash[ed] materials in the morning and silk at night—black and white, or just white." Goodrich, Diary, MS. 547.1, Jessie Donahue Collection.
10. Thaxter, who was as enthusiastic about music as she was about flowers, made a practice of surrounding her piano with small bouquets. Among the many works by Hassam that show a piano and flowers are *The Sonata* (fig. 122), with a rose lying on the piano and a picture of spring blossoms hanging on the wall to the left; *Improvisation* (fig. 312), with poppies, which had been one of Thaxter's favorite flowers, and water lilies arranged singly in narrow vases around the room; and *At the Piano*, 1908 (Cincinnati Art Museum), with roses on the piano and the side table and a large pittosporum in a blue ceramic jug on the floor.
11. Substituting "Hassam's flowers" for "Cézanne's apples" in Meyer Schapiro's discussion of Cézanne's still lifes offers a thought-provoking view of Hassam's garden pictures: "Cézanne's apples . . . are often the objects of a caressing vision. . . . He loves their finely asymmetrical roundness and the delicacy of their rich local color which he sometimes evokes through an exquisite rendering rarely found in his painting of nude flesh. . . . In paintings of the apples he was able to express through their more varied colors and groupings a wider range of moods, from the gravely contemplative to the sensual and ecstatic." "The Apples of Cézanne: An Essay on the Meaning of Still-Life," in Meyer Schapiro, *Modern Art, 19th and 20th Centuries: Selected Papers* (New York: George Braziller, 1978), pp. 28, 30.
12. Warren Adelson, "Childe Hassam: Cosmopolitan and Patriot," in Adelson, Cantor, and Gerdts 1999, p. 23.
13. Reproduced in ibid., p. 172, pl. 179.
14. Tender plants like those depicted in the Villiers-le-Bel paintings would have to overwinter in a greenhouse.
15. *The Artist's Wife in a Garden, Villiers-le-Bel* gives the clearest sense of the size and layout of the Blumenthal garden. It shows curving beds with in-ground planting as well as potted geraniums.
16. Reproduced in Paul Hayes Tucker, *The Impressionists at Argenteuil* (New Haven: Yale University Press in association with the National Gallery of Art, Washington, D.C., 2000), pl. 17.
17. Rose standards such as those in *Woman Cutting Roses in a Garden* were particularly popular in Hassam's time even outside France. William Morris's utopian novel *News from Nowhere; or, An Epoch of Rest, Being Some Chapters from a Utopian Romance* (Boston: Roberts Brothers, 1890) was illustrated with drawings of rose standards the author grew at his Gloucestershire home, Kelmscott Manor.
18. Reproduced in Adelson, Cantor, and Gerdts 1999, p. 175, pl. 182.
19. Another of these works, *Flower Girl by the Seine, Paris*, 1889 (private collection), reproduced in ibid., p. 38, is painted with the same pinkish Tonalist wash used in *Twilight (Le Crépuscule)* (fig. 313) and includes the azalea standards and hydrangeas Hassam dubbed "dome like shrubs all in flower" (see p. 308 and n. 8, above) and which he liked so much.

20. Hassam left the painting in Paris to be exhibited at the Salon of 1890.
21. For a full discussion of *At the Florist,* see Weinberg, Bolger, and Curry 1994, pp. 15ff. See also H. Barbara Weinberg, "Hassam in Paris, 1886–1889," in this publication, p. 75.
22. Childe Hassam, 11, boulevard de Clichy, Paris, July 21, 1887, to Rose Lamb, Thaxter Cottage, Isles of Shoals, Isles of Shoals Collection, transcribed in Hiesinger 1994, p. 178.
23. David Park Curry (1990, p. 193) has identified approximately four hundred Shoals images. Not all the images are floral, for Hassam also painted the island's rocky landscape, especially after Thaxter's death.
24. William Robinson, *The Wild Garden; or, Our Groves and Shrubberies Made Beautiful by the Naturalization of Hardy Exotic Plants, with a Chapter on the Garden of British Wild Flowers* (London: J. Murray, 1870), and William Robinson, *The English Flower Garden: Style, Position, and Arrangement* (London: J. Murray, 1893), influenced garden design and plant selection on both sides of the Atlantic.
25. Neltje Blanchan [pseud.], *The American Flower Garden* (New York: Doubleday, Page and Company, 1909), p. 47. Gillyflower is *Dianthus,* feverfew *Chrysanthemum parthenium,* and honesty *Lunaria.*
26. May Brawley Hill, *Grandmother's Garden: The Old Fashioned American Garden, 1865–1915* (New York: Abrams, 1995), p. 9.
27. Wheeler visited Thaxter's garden at Appledore and criticized its lack of a cohesive color scheme. However, she praised the color harmonies of Thaxter's parlor flower arrangements (Wheeler, quoted in ibid., p. 123).
28. Thaxter 1894, p. 18. The piazza Thaxter mentioned was a covered front porch. In *Art Out-of-Doors,* Mariana Griswold van Rensselaer informed her readers that, "when well arranged, the piazza always becomes the very focus of domestic life and social intercourse . . . an American country house without a piazza is in every sense a mistake and a failure." Mrs. Schuyler [Mariana Griswold] van Rensselaer, *Art Out-of-Doors: Hints on Good Taste in Gardening* (1893; new, enl. ed., New York: Charles Scribner's and Sons, 1925), p. 126.
29. Curry 1990, p. 94.
30. Thaxter was enthralled with poppies. *An Island Garden* devotes eleven consecutive pages (Thaxter 1894, pp. 75–86) to them, including long quotations from Ruskin and Browning. Her watercolors of poppies illustrated several of her poems, and the plant was one of those used as a motif on her painted china. An avid propagator, Thaxter grew poppies from seed each year, naming as her favorite varieties the Oriental (*Papaver orientale*), the Iceland (*Papaver nudicaule*), the Thorn (*Argemone pleiacantha*), the California (*Eschscholzia californica*), and the Shirley (see n. 31, below).
31. The domesticated version, the Shirley poppy (*Papaver rhoeas*), was named after the Anglican clergyman Reverend Wilks of Shirley, who in the late nineteenth century selectively pollinated poppies of the species *rhoeas* and bred them for color variation.
32. Curry 1990, p. 77.
33. For a full discussion of Hassam's and Monet's depictions of poppies, see ibid., pp. 94ff.
34. Gerdts, *Down Garden Paths,* p. 61.
35. Ibid., p. 81.
36. Annual larkspur (*Delphinium consolida*), a turn-of-the-century favorite, would have grown tall encouraged by the cool nights at Appledore.
37. Curry 1990, p. 103, pl. 44.
38. *In the Garden* was used as the frontispiece for *An Island Garden.* Thaxter strikes the same pose she holds in a photograph taken that summer, which was most likely shot for Hassam to work from (fig. 114).
39. Childe Hassam, September [i.e. August] 31, 1895, to John W. Beatty, Carnegie Institute Papers, file 81A00, Archives of American Art, Smithsonian Institution, quoted in Hiesinger 1994, p. 92; Hiesinger (ibid., p. 106, n. 29) discusses the correct date of the letter.
40. Thaxter cultivated many varieties of this flowering annual, which she cherished for its abundant growth and drought tolerance, as well as for its curving beauty. Nasturtiums were regularly featured in her drawing-room arrangements, and she described their colors in *An Island Garden*: "The shelves of the tall mantel are splendid with massed Nasturtiums like a blazing torch, beginning with the palest yellow, almost white, and piled through every deepening shade of gold, orange, scarlet, crimson, to the blackest red." Thaxter 1894, p. 94.
41. Mary K. Moulton, ed., *The Language of Flowers: Ancient and Modern* (Saint Charles, Ill.: Kennington House, 1962), unpaged.
42. Despite Dutch elm disease that has wiped out most stands of the great American elm, these trees still flourish in East Hampton today. In *Old House and Garden* the splashes of orange, blue, and white breaking out through the greenery are most likely daylilies, hydrangeas, and phlox.
43. For discussion of the Woodhouse gardens, see H. Barbara Weinberg, "Hassam in East Hampton, 1898–1935," in this publication, pp. 235–38.
44. For photographs of the garden, see Louise Shelton, *Beautiful Gardens in America,* rev. ed. (New York: Charles Scribner's Sons, 1924), pls. 105, 106. Shelton incorrectly identifies Greycroft as Grey Gables, and S. S. Cummins as Mrs. Woodhouse's first husband, not her second.
45. *A Long Island Garden,* 1922 (reproduced in Sotheby's, New York, sale cat., November 29, 1995, lot 32: "property from Kansas City Art Institute"), presents a different view of the pool seen in *Lilies.* An empty stone bench at the water's edge is backed by a border of white lilies (*Lilium candidum*). No longer painting an enclosed world, Hassam included the farm fields of Suffolk County, which stretch out in the distance.
46. Thaxter 1894, p. 99.

"The subject that I am known for" Hassam's Pursuit of a Legacy

Kimberly Orcutt

In 1927, when DeWitt McClellan Lockman asked Childe Hassam what type of work he had been engaged in during the previous twelve years, he replied, "I have been doing the subject that I am known for. Mostly the figures and the landscape."[1] This remark might sound puzzling to twenty-first-century ears, since Hassam's best-known works are not concentrated on figures. His late oeuvre, however, is dominated by figural compositions such as his 1924 *Adam and Eve Walking Out on Montauk in Early Spring* (fig. 252). In this painting a man and a woman, stiff, elongated, and nude, stroll hand in hand in a Montauk field amid a flock of sheep; the distant lighthouse identifies the setting as a site that is both recognizable and contemporary. The iconography is further complicated by the presence of the mythological god Pan, piping under a nearby tree.

It is hardly surprising that Hassam's departure from his familiar landscapes and cityscapes represented by the *Adam and Eve* and like pictures was dismissed by scholars as an aberration and consequently neglected. Recent accounts of Hassam's oeuvre either downplay or condemn such works, or both. In the catalogue of a 1965 retrospective exhibition, Charles Buckley described Hassam's late paintings as "almost perfunctory" works in which "classical mythology and Long Island landscape were brought into uneasy relationship."[2] In 1990 David Park Curry called Hassam's mythological landscapes a "failure" and his Adam and Eve "nothing more than out-of-place, underdressed tourists."[3] In his 1994 monograph on Hassam, Ulrich W. Hiesinger noted "an undeniable lessening of creativity" and the emergence of "strange, even bizarre elements" in the artist's late paintings.[4]

Such responses to Hassam's late oeuvre range from bewilderment to embarrassment. Yet in identifying his late works as depicting "the subject I am known for," Hassam suggested that this was the subject he *wished* to be known for. Why did Hassam paint such subjects? What were his hopes for these paintings? And how do they illuminate his late career?

By painting nudes with allegorical associations, Hassam used an enduring genre in an attempt to create a legacy as a serious painter. He seems to have adopted themes common to murals and history painting in order to affiliate himself with the old master tradition. However, along with many of his contemporaries, Hassam was also engaged in a struggle to reconcile timeless subject matter with his "modern" technique. By "treating the modern with the classic" (as he characterized his intention),[5] Hassam strove to create a lasting form of "modernism" in response to the burgeoning radical modernism he disparaged.

Becoming an Established and "Establishment" Artist

In the first decades of the twentieth century, Hassam appeared to be settling into a comfortable and prosperous middle age. In 1917 he wrote that he was "quite free" financially and could even help out artist friends who needed assistance.[6] In August 1919 he purchased a house in East Hampton, a Long Island village then noted for its "conservative and decorous" art community.[7] His income from painting in 1920 was said to have been $100,000, an astounding figure even if exaggerated.[8] Most remarkable is the fact that, unlike his colleagues, Hassam made his living almost entirely from the sale of his works and never depended on teaching or commissions for portraits or murals.[9]

With fortune came honors. Hassam sold his first picture to a museum in 1899; by 1911 he was represented in most major American museums. He was given a one-man exhibition at the Fourteenth Carnegie International Exhibition, Pittsburgh, in 1910, and another at the Panama-Pacific International Exposition, San Francisco, in 1915. Along with prestigious exhibitions came numerous medals and awards; in 1920 he was, for example, presented with a medal of honor for lifetime achievement by the Pennsylvania Academy of the Fine Arts, Philadelphia, and was elected a member of the American Academy of Arts and Letters, New York.

Hassam valued these awards but, priding himself on being modern, he may have been troubled by their eulogizing quality. The one-man exhibition at the Panama-Pacific International Exposition hinted at mortality; of the seven other American artists similarly honored, three were already dead and two more died soon afterward.[10] And the Pennsylvania Academy award for lifetime achievement implied that his most productive years were over. In 1916 Hassam and his lifelong friend J. Alden Weir were introduced at an artists' dinner as "prehistoric," "the mammoth and the mastodon of American art";[11] Weir died three years later.

In the face of such intimations of mortality, it is not surprising that Hassam became increasingly preoccupied with constructing his legacy. As early as October 1909 he expressed his hope for a one-man exhibition at The Metropolitan Museum of Art, which would signal his admission into the pantheon of great artists.[12] He showed keen interest in the public perception of his work, and he insisted on selecting which of his paintings would be displayed in exhibitions and on installing them himself.[13] Extremely revealing is a short film about Hassam produced by the Metropolitan Museum in 1932 that apotheosizes him as the consummate gentleman artist. He is successful: the film opens with him pulling up to his house in a chauffeured car. He is masculine: he golfs and swims in the ocean (although he struggles a bit against the waves). Most importantly, he adheres to the "old master" tradition of careful preparation, rather than painting with the Impressionists' perceived dash and spontaneity. He is seen carefully outlining a form on a panel (fig. 317), with a subtitle reading, "Pencil sketches are carefully made and critically studied." The film ends with Hassam strolling through a gallery at the Metropolitan containing his own paintings.[14] Although commissioned by the Museum, the film was roundly criticized as a transparent attempt on Hassam's part to shape his image, or, as a writer for the *New York World-Telegram* put it, his "bid for fame."[15]

The Dilemma of Modernism

At the same time that Hassam was establishing his legacy, he was taking his stand as a bitter antagonist of the "new art" of the early twentieth century—that is, the modernism that followed his generation's version of modernism. Hassam was strongly identified with Impressionism throughout his career, and, like many of his contemporaries, he reacted to ensuing styles with skepticism bordering on hostility. The Armory Show of 1913 introduced Americans to the European avant-garde and was the object of harsh criticism. Hassam, despite exhibiting six oils, five pastels, and one drawing there, led the charge. Later he ridiculed the more radical pieces on display as "not very beautiful things, with one eye in the top of the head and the other in the chin, and all the absurdities in an attempt to attract attention."[16] Others joined in the attack, among them the prominent painter and writer Kenyon Cox, who deemed the exhibition "heartrending and sickening" as well as "silly" and, like the muralist Edwin Howland Blashfield, decried the exhibitors' lack of discipline and training.[17]

Hassam greatly admired Cox, calling him "one of the most brilliant minds of any one whoever wrote about the fine arts."[18] In *The Classic Point of View,* published in 1911, Cox extolled "above all, the love of permanence and continuity" and a "striving for the essential rather than the accidental,

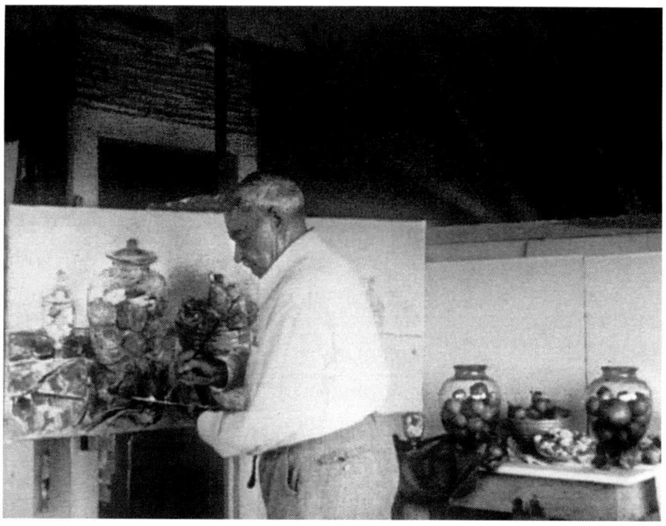

Fig. 317. Hassam in his studio in East Hampton, with *Long Island Pebbles and Fruit* on the easel, 1932. Still from The Metropolitan Museum of Art's film *Childe Hassam, Artist,* 1932

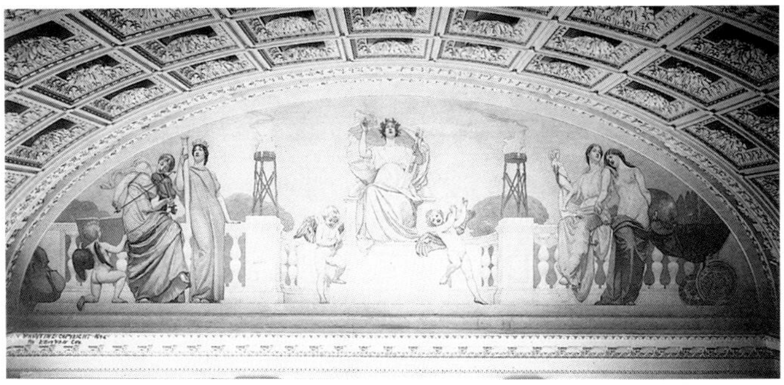

Fig. 318. Kenyon Cox. *The Arts,* 1896. Mural, Thomas Jefferson Building, Library of Congress, Washington, D.C.

the eternal rather than the momentary"—goals that were diametrically opposed to those of Impressionism.[19] Consistent with his esteem for tradition was Cox's belief that "the highest subject for the exercise of the greatest powers of a painter is the human figure, the subject of the Greeks and of Michelangelo."[20]

While Cox was a steadfast devotee of tradition and worked in a conservative style throughout his career (see fig. 318), Hassam was driven by two simultaneous desires: to leave a lasting legacy, and to be among the modernists. An obituary would recall that more important to him than honors and awards was "the knowledge that his art . . . remained in the vanguard with the paintings of much younger men, who regarded him as a contemporary."[21] Yet Hassam's stake in modernism was complicated by the fact that modernism was changing, while his approach to painting remained the same. To explain this contradiction, he distinguished between "good" and "bad" modernism, declaring: "Modern art is fine. But when I say modern art, I am drawing a clear line between the good and the bad. Many of the so-called modern painters are nothing more or less than fakers."[22] Of his contributions to the Armory Show, Hassam remarked in 1927, "You might say they were modern, well they were modern but they are now considered as of the classic period spirit, as Kenyon Cox would say."[23] He realized that the word "modern" had been co-opted by younger artists.

Hassam faced a dilemma that many of his generation shared. How would he remain current as he moved toward the end of his career and also ensure that his work left a lasting imprint? How would he combine the momentary with the timeless, the local with the universal? Hassam's awareness of the competing imperatives of timeliness and timelessness can be traced to the late 1870s, when the American Renaissance movement emerged. He must surely have noticed his contemporaries' increasing involvement with mural painting and their new preoccupation with allegorical, biblical, and mythological themes for the decoration of churches, government buildings, and private residences.[24] As the movement flourished, hundreds of murals were executed throughout the country, many by Hassam's friends and colleagues. Fellow members of the group known as the Ten—notably Weir, Edward E. Simmons, Willard L. Metcalf, and Robert Reid—worked on numerous mural commissions, including ones for the World's Columbian Exposition, Chicago, the Library of Congress, state capitol buildings, the New York Appellate Division Courthouse, and the Panama-Pacific International Exposition.[25]

In carrying out these commissions, artists employed two different approaches. One was to interpret modern subjects with a traditional academic vocabulary. The result could be slightly awkward, as in the 1896 mural *The Spirit of Physics* painted for the Boston Public Library by Puvis de Chavannes (whom Hassam greatly admired), which shows two draped figures flying over a telegraph line that recedes into the distance. Or it could sometimes be laughable, as demonstrated by Blashfield's mural spandrel executed for the Mahoning County Courthouse in Youngstown, Ohio, *The Law in Modern Times* (fig. 319), in which an idealized young girl wears both a toga and a jarringly anachronistic headset for telegraphing.[26]

The alternative approach was to render mythological and allegorical themes in a contemporary manner. Classical subjects were painted in this way by Thomas Eakins, Albert Pinkham Ryder, Thomas Wilmer Dewing, John La Farge, J. Alden Weir, and Arthur B. Davies (see fig. 320), in personal styles that range from academic to naturalistic, Impressionist, or Symbolist.[27] In 1911 the artist Elliott Daingerfield waxed lyrical on the value of arcadian subjects and challenged colleagues of all kinds to paint them: "Surrounded on every side with beautiful material for artistic interpretation, with a landscape opulent, tender, rugged, and vast . . . with a woodland peopled anew by Pan and the nymphs (I see no reason for disbelief!); the minds of men fatigued in the hourly struggle for wealth and its keeping, seeking relief from the prosaic . . . what is it we lack? What then but the interpreter?"[28] In canvases such as *June* (fig. 321), Hassam anticipated Daingerfield's call, applying his familiar Impressionist technique to allusive themes by conjoining his usual rapid brushwork and broken stroke to myth and allegory.

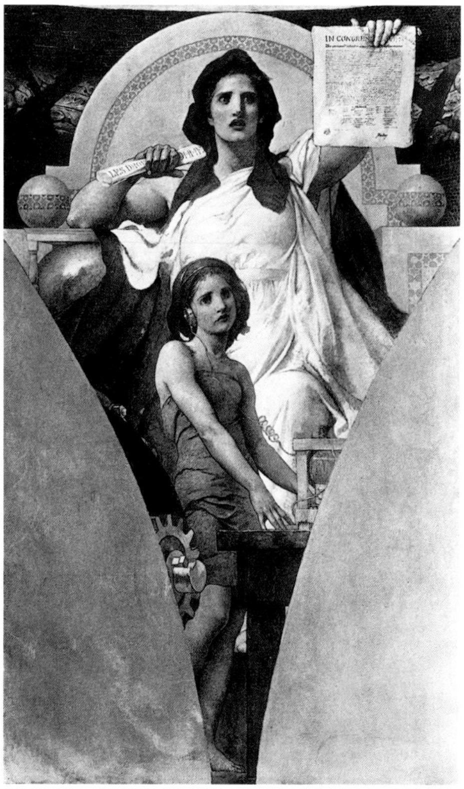

Fig. 319. Edwin Howland Blashfield. *The Law in Modern Times,* ca. 1910. Mural, Mahoning County Courthouse, Youngstown, Ohio

Fig. 320. Arthur B. Davies. *Unicorns (Legend—Sea Calm),* ca. 1906. Oil on canvas, 18¼ x 40¼ in. (46.4 x 102.2 cm). The Metropolitan Museum of Art, New York. Bequest of Lillie P. Bliss, 1931 31.67.12

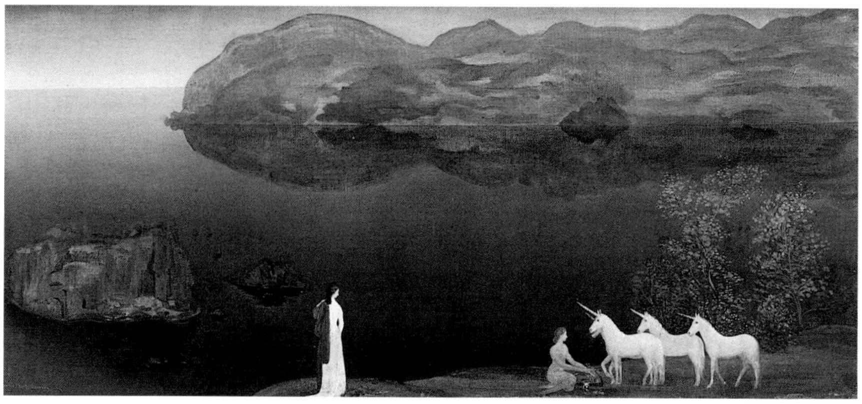

Embracing Academicism

The turn to the figure and the academic tradition was a distinct reversal for Hassam, who had built his reputation on paintings of contemporary landscapes and cityscapes. His artistic training had consisted of little more than brief study at the Lowell School of Practical Design and its Drawing Class in Boston, a few life classes at the Boston Art Club in 1883, and a short stay at the Académie Julian in Paris. The French training system emphasized the study of the nude, with an eye toward the goal of painting large-scale biblical, historical, or allegorical subjects. But Hassam was impatient and left the Parisian school after about a year and a half, although the usual course of study could take several years. He had concluded, a reporter quipped in 1901, that his art education in Boston was preliminary and his instruction in Paris was superfluous.[29] Hassam was a member of the last American generation to value French academic training, yet he had chosen to minimize it. Later in life he was ill equipped to take on its traditional subject matter.

Although Hassam lacked much formal training, he worked to develop and publicize his involvement with traditional art. During his 1897 trip to Europe he claimed to have spent a great deal of time studying old master paintings in galleries and museums.[30] In 1903 he wrote, "The business of the good painter is to carry on tradition as every one of the good painters have done always and without deviation from the well beaten path."[31] In subsequent years he reinvented his past to match his new allegiance to tradition. The artist recalled that in 1918 a collector had asked him to paint portraits of his daughters, asserting that as long as the pictures were by Hassam, he did not care whether or not they were good likenesses. "If I paint them it will be an absolute likeness. I have had an academic training," was Hassam's reply.[32] By 1927 his memory of his time at the Académie Julian had changed. He recalled starting with "very careful academic drawing," adding, "I believed in a careful academic training whatever you are going to do."[33] Finally, abandoning—at least momentarily—his well-known advocacy of American art and American subjects, in 1932 he declared his link to the old masters: "One of those writers discovered the other day that some of our painting is European. Silly ass! All of our painting is European."[34]

Hassam immersed himself in classical literature, according to his biographer Adeline Adams; his preferred reading was in the areas of history, philosophy, and biography.[35] He was fond of quoting Thoreau's remark "the Greeks were boys in the sunlight" to emphasize that classical culture was steeped in notions of light and an appreciation of the outdoors.[36] Hassam professed that every artist and critic should be familiar with the culture of the Middle Ages, the Italian and French Renaissance, and the Spanish and Dutch masters.[37] This apparent high-mindedness and love of erudition contradict the usual image of Hassam as a bluff, outdoorsy fellow dashing off paintings of his immediate surroundings. They signal an unexpected aspect of his persona: if he was not a true intellectual, he at least wished to be perceived as one.

"I have painted against the light the figure nude"

When asked in 1927 what he had been working on recently, Hassam answered loftily, "I have painted against the light the figure nude."[38] His elevated tone conveys the utter seriousness with which he approached his subject. Having begun painting nudes as early as 1898,[39] he undertook two major projects—murals in 1904 and a large canvas in 1905—that he must have hoped would signal a new departure in his career.

Colonel Charles Erskine Scott Wood, a lawyer from Portland, Oregon, whom Hassam probably met through Weir, commissioned him to execute a series of murals for the library of his home.[40] Hassam painted the murals on canvas in New York and in 1904 brought them to Portland, where he installed them himself.[41] One of them, entitled *The Bathers* (fig. 203), suggests the scale of Hassam's ambition. Approximately four feet high and twelve feet wide, the painting depicts a group of nudes at various stages of their toilette. The figures are elongated, their depiction generalized; with its stylized, primitive quality, the scene suggests a Greek frieze. Hassam later articulated his intention, calling the piece "a classic—nude and landscape."[42] Wood must have been pleased with Hassam's work, since the two remained friends for many years.[43]

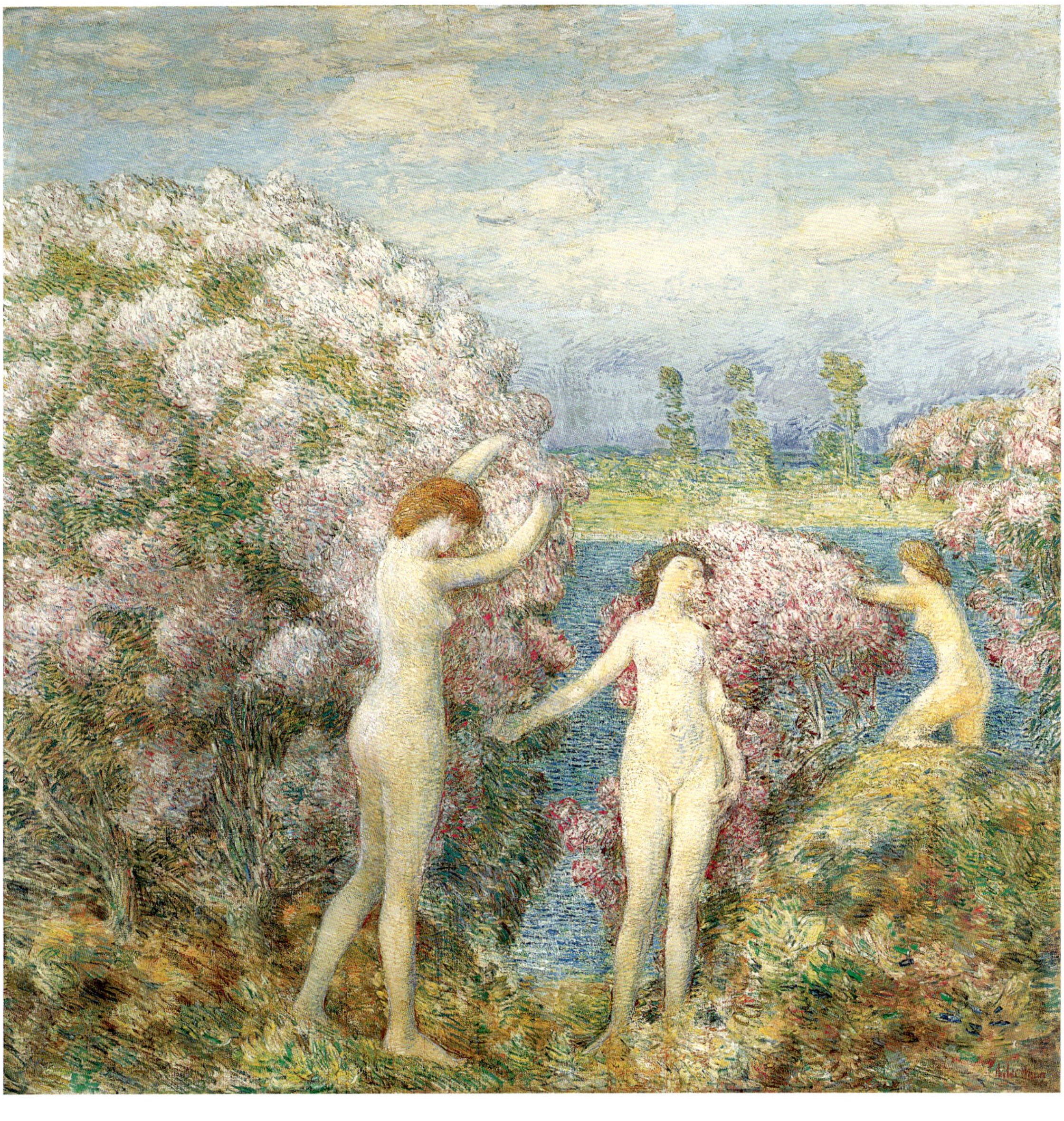

Fig. 321. Childe Hassam. *June,* 1905. Oil on canvas, 84 x 84 in. (213.4 x 213.4 cm). American Academy of Arts and Letters, New York

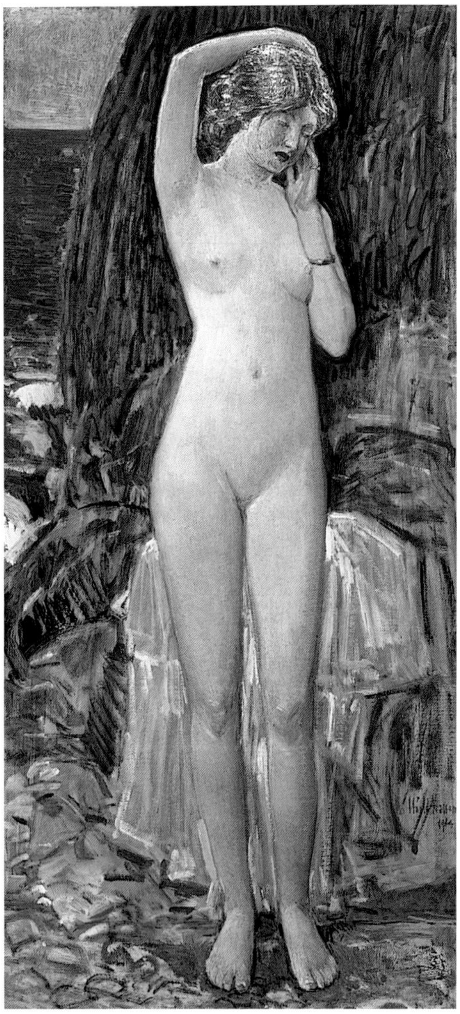

Fig. 322. Childe Hassam. *The Nymph of the Beryl Gorge,* 1914. Oil on canvas, 34⅛ x 16½ in. (86.7 x 41.9 cm). The Art Institute of Chicago, Gift of Mr. and Mrs. Carter H. Harrison 1935.312

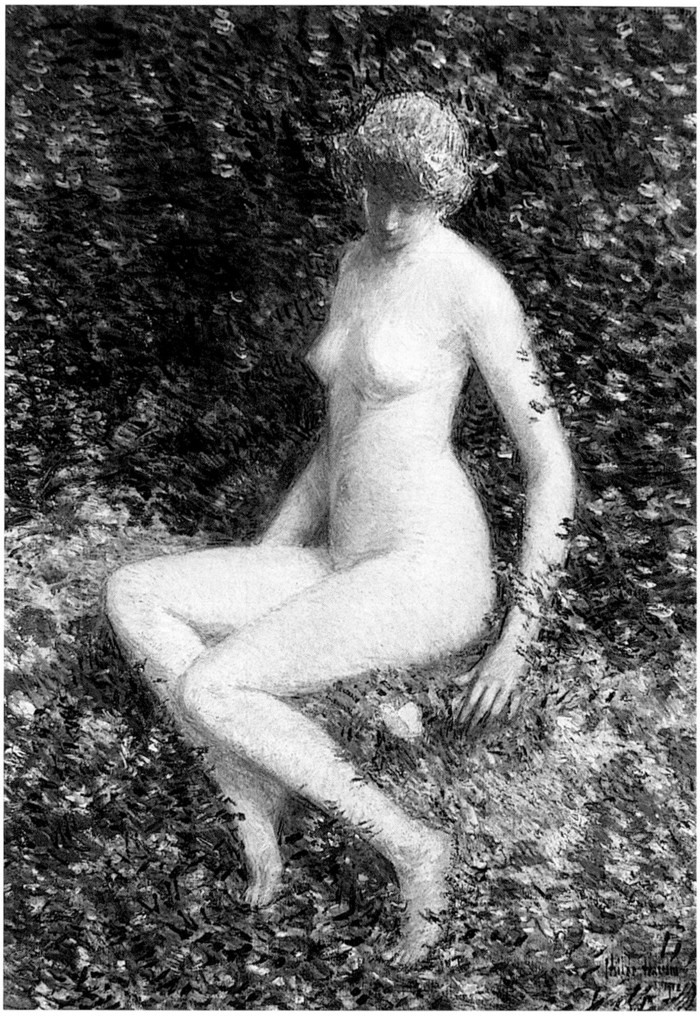

Fig. 323. Childe Hassam. *The Butterfly,* 1912. Oil on canvas, 27¼ x 20¼ in. (69.2 x 51.4 cm). The Huntington Museum of Art, West Virginia. Gift of Herbert Fitzpatrick, 1952 52.374

The next year Hassam painted *June,* a seven-foot-square canvas showing three nudes in a landscape. Despite its grand scale, *June* was not carried out on commission and was still in the artist's studio at his death. Rather than following his usual practice of suggesting deep space, here Hassam placed foliage prominently in the foreground and forced the figures toward the picture plane, creating a schematic, flat effect that echoes that seen in paintings by Puvis de Chavannes (see fig. 53). He considered the work a masterpiece and described the care with which he put it on a panel-back stretcher, "relined" it, and installed it in "an Italian hand-carved frame." "It will last forever," he said.[44] Clearly he intended the work to endure as a statement of artistic values as well as a monument to himself. Although little known today, *June* was acclaimed in its time, receiving a third-class medal at the Tenth Annual Exhibition of the Carnegie Institute, Pittsburgh, in November 1905 and the Carnegie Prize from the Society of American Artists, New York, in March 1906.

Between 1905 and 1920 Hassam's production was punctuated by images of nudes in various settings. In many instances the figures were placed in familiar landscapes, as in *Aphrodite, Appledore* (fig. 12). Hassam also experimented with reducing the scale of the figures and placing them in forest scenes, as in *Dawn* (fig. 339). He often underlined his classical intent by using titles with mythological associations, such as *Nymph Bathing,* 1904 (private collection);[45] *The Nymph of the Beryl Gorge* (fig. 322); *Pomona in the Rose Bower,* 1919 (location unknown);[46] and even *Nymph with Ducks,* n.d. (location unknown, formerly collection of Duncan Phillips).[47]

A few of Hassam's nudes, such as *The Butterfly* (fig. 323), are particularized enough to suggest the use of a model. But the vast majority reveal his meager training and share a similar elongated, highly simplified body type that can be attributed to his working from memory. The critics noticed this of course, remarking that "figures in Mr. Hassam's paintings are only occasionally happy," and "so long as Mr. Hassam paints landscape he is on safe ground . . . With the figure he takes his chances."[48] One writer grasped Hassam's aim early on, observing in 1908, "It looks very much as if Hassam were seeking to hand his name down to posterity as a great academical man, rather than a painter of light and air."[49]

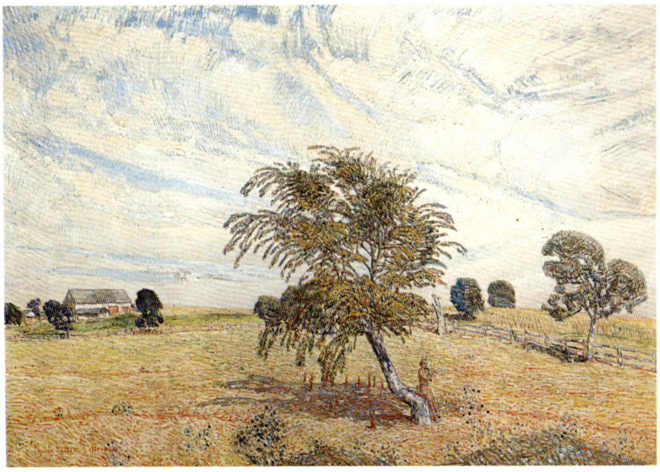

Fig. 324. Childe Hassam. *The Mares Tail Sky,* 1920. Oil on canvas, 53 x 76 in. (134.6 x 193 cm). American Academy of Arts and Letters, New York

East Hampton and the Montauk Series

In 1919 Hassam purchased a house in East Hampton, and he spent half of each year there until his death. The region's unspoiled landscape and expansive beaches became the principal setting for his compositions. In 1920 he painted *The Mares Tail Sky* (fig. 324), in which a horned Pan sits beneath a tree playing a flute and several rabbits stand at attention, mesmerized by his music. Oddly, this scene is set in the back field of some East Hampton residence; farm buildings appear in the background, and a rail fence recedes along one side. While the anachronism is startling, it parallels the telegraph wires in Puvis de Chavannes's Boston Public Library murals and Blashfield's toga-clad girl wearing a headset.

In September 1921 Hassam went camping in Montauk, at the eastern tip of Long Island's south fork, with his artist friends Albert Smith, the brothers Reynolds and Gifford Beal, and Jack (John Heywood) Roudebush. In Montauk, still wild and uninhabited, the men hunted, fished, hiked, and sighted wild ponies roaming on the dunes, and Hassam painted.[50] "There is no more beautiful or classic stretch of landscape anywhere" was Hassam's appraisal; he was particularly captivated by what seemed to him the region's primeval quality.[51]

At the end of December 1924 Hassam presented an exhibition at the Macbeth gallery, New York, entitled *Montauk*. The show was his boldest and most focused effort to re-create himself as a figure painter and even a history painter. The titles of all but two works in the exhibition allude to classical, biblical, or mythological subjects. Most prominent was the painting *Adam and Eve Walking Out on Montauk in Early Spring* (fig. 252). Another large canvas, *Georgica* (fig. 325), depicts, in front of East Hampton's Georgica Pond, three nude female figures with hands upraised and joined in a pose that identifies them as the Three Graces. Rabbits like those in *The Mares Tail Sky* stand on their hind legs to watch the dancers, signaling that the scene takes place in an innocent realm. In another work, *Young Apollo and the Flying Swans* (fig. 326), a nude male stands on a dune looking up at the sleek, streamlined forms of swans passing overhead.

Hassam offered a rambling and not entirely coherent meditation on Montauk in the exhibition catalogue, perhaps by way of explaining the anachronisms in his paintings: "Montauk must look now as it looked countless ages ago. . . . The gods were always there, too, and that

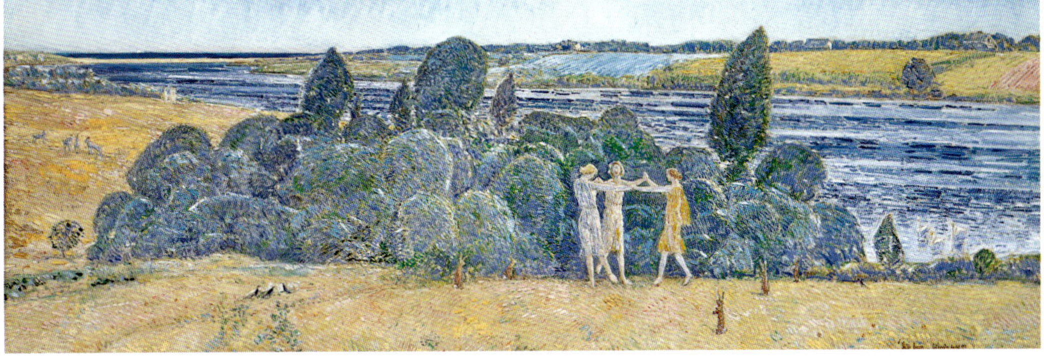

Fig. 325. Childe Hassam. *Georgica,* 1923. Oil on canvas, 27 x 78 in. (68.6 x 198.1 cm). American Academy of Arts and Letters, New York

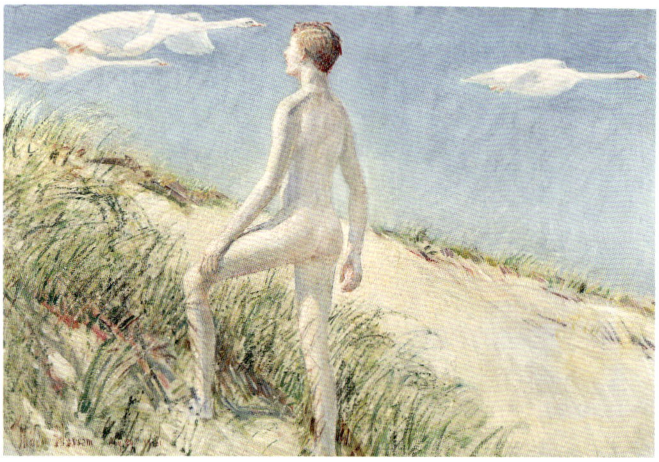

Fig. 326. Childe Hassam. *Young Apollo and the Flying Swans,* 1921. Oil on canvas, 19½ x 30 in. (49.5 x 76.2 cm). Guild Hall Museum, East Hampton, New York, Gift of Mrs. Victor Harris

favored people of the gods, the Greeks were there. As for time[,] compared to the ages that have passed since Montauk was made by the last glacial age or period, the age of Pericles was but day before yesterday."[52] He would explain in 1927 that he began his Montauk paintings on site using models and finished them in New York, "treating the modern with the classic." And he added that his "friend, Kenyon Cox, if he were alive, would understand my point of view."[53] Throughout his late career, a significant part of Hassam's production consisted of mythological and biblical figures shown in naturalistic settings, such as *Adam and Eve on Shelter Island,* 1925 (American Academy of Arts and Letters, New York), or *Spring on Long Island (Venus Genetrix)* (fig. 327), in which a nude woman stands in the foreground, untroubled by the presence of a (clothed) farmer planting seeds in a nearby field.

Hassam's Montauk series and related works received surprisingly positive reviews, although, perhaps out of respect for a great artist in his dotage, many of these were restricted to polite descriptions and quotations of the artist's stated aims. The *New York Times* critic called the Macbeth gallery exhibition pleasant and colorful and blandly suggested, "We cannot all go to Palm Beach for the Winter, but we can all visit this Fifty-seventh Street Arcadia."[54] Royal Cortissoz seemed sincere in his appreciation of the Montauk show: "His work celebrates one of those fortunate periods in a painter's life in which he takes a fresh grasp upon nature, with a new creative zest . . . It is all rather daring—and successful."[55] One writer mentioned, perhaps dubiously, Hassam's "highly individual interpretation of modernism."[56]

"A dangerous experiment to an artist's reputation"

The last ten years of Hassam's life were filled with retrospective exhibitions. In a preface to the catalogue of the March 1929 exhibition at the Albright Art Gallery in Buffalo, William M. Hekking described retrospectives in general as "a dangerous experiment to an artist's reputation"; indeed, they were for Hassam. Many of them offered opportunities to compare his early and late works as well as his landscapes and figural scenes. Because of his excellence in landscapes, the same author suggested in the Albright catalogue, "we might overlook his ability to portray the figure."[57] However, the critic of *Art News* identified two Hassams, the Younger and the Elder, and lamented that the Elder "inherited the master's technique . . . but he became literary, arrogant, and finally, dull."[58] In some late exhibitions, such as one held at the Macbeth gallery in April 1929, the question was avoided altogether by including few figural works or none at all.[59]

Criticism of Hassam's late oeuvre turned even less favorable after his death in 1935. In his obituary in the *New York Times* it was frankly stated that "often he painted bizarre subjects."[60] Even his loyal supporter Cortissoz, writing in 1939, dismissed his arcadian fantasies as a momentary "playful indulgence."[61] Hassam bequeathed to the American Academy of Arts and

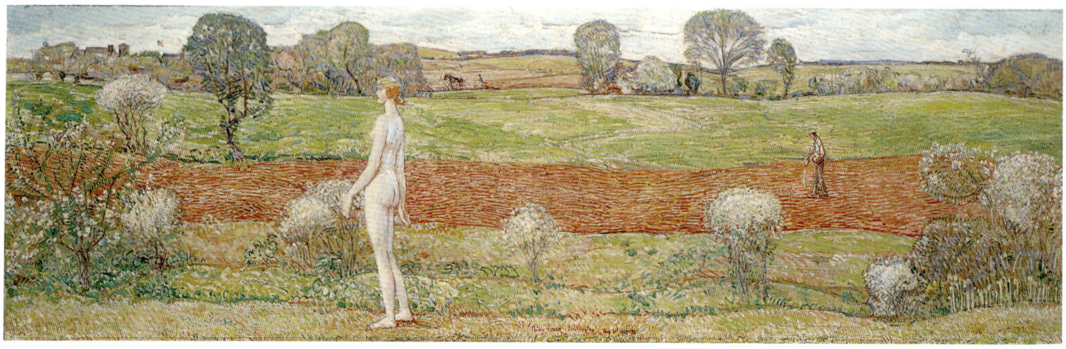

Fig. 327. Childe Hassam. *Spring on Long Island (Venus Genetrix),* 1926. Oil on wood panel, 24 x 49 in. (61 x 124.5 cm). American Academy of Arts and Letters, New York

Letters his artistic estate, consisting of 326 oil paintings (including 19 decorative panels), 89 watercolors, and 33 pastels. The majority of these works were from his late period. That so many of these were unsold at his death speaks volumes about their appeal in comparison to that of his earlier pictures.

Whatever one thinks of Hassam's late paintings, his effort to reinvent himself must inspire respect. At a time when his success was already assured, and many of his colleagues were settling into styles that had become outmoded, Hassam made an audacious bid to continue as a modernist. He attempted not only to reshape his legacy but also to unite modernism and academicism. In so doing, he revealed a more complex and more idealistic personality than was previously apparent, even if his reach exceeded his grasp. Hassam may well have subscribed to the advice of his friend Kenyon Cox: "Fix your eye on the highest, gird yourself for the journey, and God speed! If you fall by the way you may at least fall face forward. And it may be that you, too, may find yourself, in the end, among that small but glorious company whose work the world will cherish and whose memory the world will not let die."[62]

I am grateful for assistance I received when preparing this essay from Diana Dayton and Dorothy King of the East Hampton Library; Christina Strassfield of the Guild Hall, East Hampton, and Elizabeth Mann, formerly of the Guild Hall; Margaret Bullock of the Portland Art Museum; Sara Jablon of the Fogg Art Museum, Harvard University Art Museums, Cambridge, Massachusetts; and Lisa Miller and Megan Holloway of The Metropolitan Museum of Art. I am particularly indebted to Kathleen Kienholz for her generosity with the resources of the American Academy of Arts and Letters, New York. I would also like to thank Theodore E. Stebbins, Jr., H. Barbara Weinberg, Stephanie L. Herdrich, and Dana Pilson for their advice and suggestions.

1. Lockman interview, February 3, 1927, p. 8.
2. "Nevertheless," Buckley conceded, Hassam's career "extended over fifty years and [for] nearly thirty-five of these he had produced a large and varied body of work." Charles Buckley in Hassam (Washington, D.C.) 1965, p. 21.
3. Curry 1990, pp. 145, 148.
4. Hiesinger 1994, p. 168.
5. Lockman interview, February 2, 1927, p. 27.
6. Childe Hassam, New York, December 15, 1917, to C. E. S. Wood, Wood Papers (San Marino).
7. Helen A. Harrison, "Guild Hall and East Hampton: A History of Growth and Change," in *Crosscurrents*, exh. cat. (East Hampton: Guild Hall Museum; Provincetown, Mass.: Provincetown Art Association and Museum, 1986), p. 44.
8. "Art Fund Created by Hassam's Will," *New York Times,* November 13, 1935, p. 18.
9. In 1883 Hassam taught watercolor briefly to one student, Celia Laighton Thaxter, substituting for his friend Ross Turner. See Susan G. Larkin, "Hassam in New England, 1889–1918," in this publication, p. 121. He also taught at the Art Students League in New York from late December 1898 to May 1899, probably filling in for the absent Frank Duveneck. See Dana Pilson, "'On the crest of the wave': Hassam and the Marketing of His Art," in this publication, p. 343. He painted no more than eight or ten portraits, mostly of friends, and only a few on commission. See "'The Lady in Furs' Shows Hassam's Portrait Skill," *[New York Herald Tribune,* July 3, 1932], unidentified clipping, Hassam Papers, reel NAA1, frame 605.
10. See H. Barbara Weinberg, "Hassam's Travels, 1892–1914," in this publication, pp. 197, 201, n. 77.
11. Walter Pach, *Queer Thing Painting: Forty Years in the World of Art* (New York: Harper and Brothers, 1938), p. 236, quoted in Hiesinger 1994, p. 153.
12. Childe Hassam, October 18, 1909, to Miss Cornelia B. Sage, archives of the Albright-Knox Gallery, Buffalo, quoted in Hiesinger 1994, p. 141. See H. Barbara Weinberg, "Introduction," in this publication, pp. 20–21.
13. "A 'New' Hassam Is Revealed in Exhibition of His Older Works," *Art Digest* 13, no. 14 (mid-April 1929), p. 8.
14. *Childe Hassam, Artist* (New York: The Metropolitan Museum of Art, 1932), one-reel silent film.
15. "Childe Hassam Plays Lead in Film of Artist's Real Life," *New York World-Telegram,* Friday, January [1932], clipping, artist files, Department of American Painting and Sculpture, The Metropolitan Museum of Art; see also "On Location," *Time,* February 8, 1932, p. 22, and "Metropolitan Gets Film on Childe Hassam's Work," *New York Herald Tribune,* January 18, 1932, p. 15.
16. Lockman interview, February 2, 1927, p. 25. See also Hassam 1928, p. 22.
17. Kenyon Cox, "The 'Modern' Spirit in Art," in *Three Papers on "Modernist Art"* (New York: American Academy of Arts and Letters, 1924), pp. 5, 9–10; Edwin Howland Blashfield, "The Painting of To-Day," in *Three Papers on "Modernist Art,"* pp. 50–51.
18. Lockman interview, February 2, 1927, p. 17.
19. Kenyon Cox, *The Classic Point of View* (New York: Charles Scribner's Sons, 1911), pp. 3–4, 17. Paradoxically, Cox praised Hassam's use of Impressionist technique (p. 17).
20. Ibid., p. 43.
21. "Brilliant Career of Childe Hassam Comes to a Close," *Art News* 3, no. 40 (September 14, 1935), p. 12.
22. "Death Stills Brush of Childe Hassam," clipping, labeled "*Boston Ev. Transcript,* August 27, 1935," and "Childe Hassam," clipping, labeled "*Boston Herald,* August 28, 1935," Hassam Papers, reel NAA1, frames 657, 660.
23. Lockman interview, February 2, 1927, p. 25.
24. Richard Guy Wilson, "The Great Civilization," in Richard Guy Wilson et al., *The American Renaissance, 1876–1917,* exh. cat. (Brooklyn: Brooklyn Museum, 1979), p. 45.
25. William H. Gerdts, "Edward Simmons," in Gerdts et al. 1990, pp. 118, 120.
26. Henry B. Fuller lampooned such themes in his book *Under the Skylights* (New York: D. Appleton, 1901), p. 172, suggesting ideas for a mural in a residence: "It will be a low relief in bronze: 'The Genius of the West Lighting the Way to Further Progress,' or else, 'Commerce and Finance United to Do Something or Other'—don't know what just yet, but shall hit on some notion or other in due time."

27. Elizabeth Ewing Tebow, "Arcadia Reclaimed: Mythology and American Painting, 1860–1920" (Ph.D. diss., University of Maryland, College Park, 1987), pp. 27–31, summarizes these varied approaches.
28. Elliott Daingerfield, "Nature vs. Art," *Scribner's Magazine* 49 (February 1911), p. 256.
29. Frederick W. Morton, "Childe Hassam, Impressionist," *Brush and Pencil* 8 (June 1901), p. 146.
30. See Weinberg, "Hassam's Travels, 1892–1914," in this publication, p. 183.
31. Manuscript fragment, 1903, Hassam Papers, reel NAA1, frame 488.
32. Lockman interview, February 3, 1927, p. 17.
33. Ibid., January 31, 1927, p. 13.
34. Quoted in Thomas Sugrue, "Childe Hassam Hits America's Art Gullibility," clipping, labeled "*East Hampton Press,* October 15, 1932, p. 1," artist files, Department of American Painting and Sculpture, The Metropolitan Museum of Art.
35. Adams 1938, p. 116.
36. Childe Hassam in "John Twachtman: An Estimation," *North American Review* 176 (April 1903), p. 556.
37. Cortissoz 1939, p. 8.
38. Lockman interview, February 2, 1927, p. 27.
39. See H. Barbara Weinberg, "Introduction," in this publication, pp. 10, 12–13.
40. See Mahonri Sharp Young, "Treasures from Rochester," *Art News* 76 (May 1977), p. 132, and Price 1923, pp. 4–5. See also Weinberg, "Hassam's Travels, 1892–1914," in this publication, pp. 186, 188–89, and Susan G. Larkin, "How Hassam Framed Hassams," in this publication, p. 329.
41. Priscilla C. Colt, "Childe Hassam in Oregon," *Portland Art Museum Bulletin* 14 (March 1953), unpaged.
42. Lockman interview, February 2, 1927, p. 3.
43. They maintained a lively correspondence that continued through the 1920s. See Wood Papers (San Marino) and Wood Papers (Berkeley).
44. Lockman interview, February 2, 1927, p. 17.
45. For a reproduction of *Nymph Bathing,* see advertisement for The Albany Gallery in *Magazine Antiques* 134 (September 1988), p. 414.
46. A photograph of this painting is in the Frick Art Reference Library, New York.
47. For a reproduction of *Nymph with Ducks,* see Pousette-Dart 1922, unpaged, fig. [38].
48. "A Leader of the Open-Air School," *Evening Post* (New York), clipping, labeled "December 12, 1907," Hassam Papers, reel NAA1, frame 537; "The Personal Touch Versus Academic Discipline," *New York Daily Tribune,* November 23, 1919, p. 11.
49. Pattison 1908, p. 19.
50. Linda Wassong, "Childe Hassam's *Montauk*" (research paper, Sotheby's Institute, New York, April 1998), pp. 3–4; Harrison, "Guild Hall and East Hampton," p. 58.
51. Childe Hassam, New York, January 20, 1926, to Edward E. Bartlett, quoted in "Bartlett Gives Hassam Picture to Guild Hall," *East Hampton Star,* June 16, 1938, p. 8.
52. Hassam quoted in R[obert] W. M[acIntyre], "Historical Note," in *"Montauk" by Childe Hassam of The American Academy of Arts and Letters,* exh. cat. (New York: William Macbeth, Inc., December 30, 1924–January 19, 1925), unpaged.
53. Lockman interview, February 2, 1927, p. 27.
54. "Art: Exhibitions of the Week: Sun and Summer," *New York Times,* January 4, 1925, p. XII.
55. Royal Cortissoz, "Childe Hassam's Work on Long Island," *New York Herald Tribune,* December 28, 1924, sec. 8, p. 12.
56. Ralph Flint, unidentified clipping, with the byline "New York, Jan. 25," Hassam Papers, reel NAA1, frame 631, in reference to a ca. 1926 exhibition.
57. *Exhibition of a Retrospective Group of Paintings Representative of the Life Work of Childe Hassam, N.A.,* exh. cat. (Buffalo, N.Y.: Buffalo Fine Arts Academy, Albright Art Gallery, March 9–April 8, 1929), p. 11.
58. "Childe Hassam, Macbeth Galleries," *Art News* 27 (April 20, 1929), p. 9.
59. *Exhibition of Paintings by Childe Hassam, N.A., Covering the Period from 1888 to 1919, Together with Etchings, Water Colors and Pastels,* exh. cat. (New York: Macbeth Gallery, April 1929).
60. "Childe Hassam, 75, Noted Artist, Dies," *New York Times,* August 28, 1935, p. 17.
61. Cortissoz 1939, p. 8.
62. Cox, *Classic Point of View,* pp. 231–32.

How Hassam Framed Hassams

Susan G. Larkin

Among American artists, Childe Hassam is most active in designing the frame to fit the picture," a critic wrote in 1921. Unlike artists who relied on their dealers to select frames, the writer observed, Hassam "sees to it personally that his canvases are placed in a harmonious setting."[1] By the time that commentary appeared, Hassam had been a professional artist for four decades. Over the course of his long career, he used a wide variety of frames, patronized numerous craftsmen, customized moldings for specific paintings, adopted initialed frames unique in American art, and created modernist frames that minimized the aesthetic barrier between the canvas and its surround. With each of his choices, Hassam manipulated the viewer's perception of his paintings, presenting them as either European or American, heir to a long tradition or defiantly new, akin to works by other artists or entirely his own. Hassam's decisions also reveal his attention to the preferences of individual collectors, trends in interior design, and regional differences in taste.

Hassam seems to have spared no expense on his frames. For an artist who exhibited as extensively as he, the cost was considerable. His friend John H. Twachtman declined an invitation from the director of the Pennsylvania Academy of the Fine Arts to participate in the institution's prestigious annual exhibition because he could not pay for the necessary frames. "You know very well that I should like to send to your show," Twachtman wrote, "but I don't see how I can afford to. I can not afford to buy frames for one tenth of the things I have. My pictures have been sent to all the cities in the land and are returned after an absence of from three to six months. Pray tell me what benefit there is to me. I have been doing this stunt for the last twenty five years with large frame bills unpaid. This very month three of my pictures will be sold at auction to pay part of a frame bill contracted six years ago."[2] Hassam, however, could justify the expense because he sold many more paintings than Twachtman. Although he moved frames from picture to picture and negotiated with suppliers for favorable prices, Hassam usually specified gold-leaf, rather than the less costly metal-leaf, and always insisted on the highest-quality surrounds.

Hassam's concern with the presentation of his work is revealed in the frames he chose for paintings that museums acquired during his lifetime or just after his death. The American Academy of Arts and Letters in New York, to which Hassam bequeathed all the works in his estate, is an especially rich resource for study of Hassam's frames. Many of the four-hundred-odd works in the bequest have been sold, as he directed, to buy paintings from living artists for dispersal to American and Canadian museums. The pictures that remain in the Academy's collection retain the frames that, for the most part, Hassam selected. Archival records provide further evidence of his taste: the orders Hassam placed with the Carrig-Rohane shop and the Milch Galleries are preserved on microfilm at the Archives of American Art. In addition, Hassam's correspondence and quoted remarks offer glimpses of his preferences. In this vein, the outspoken artist once warned his friend J. Alden Weir that "his frames were getting too ornate"; Weir, reportedly, was "grateful to have his attention called to it."[3]

A photograph of Hassam in his studio about 1896 (p. 366) shows him with at least three distinct styles of frames. The two propped on a chair at the left exemplify the kind of

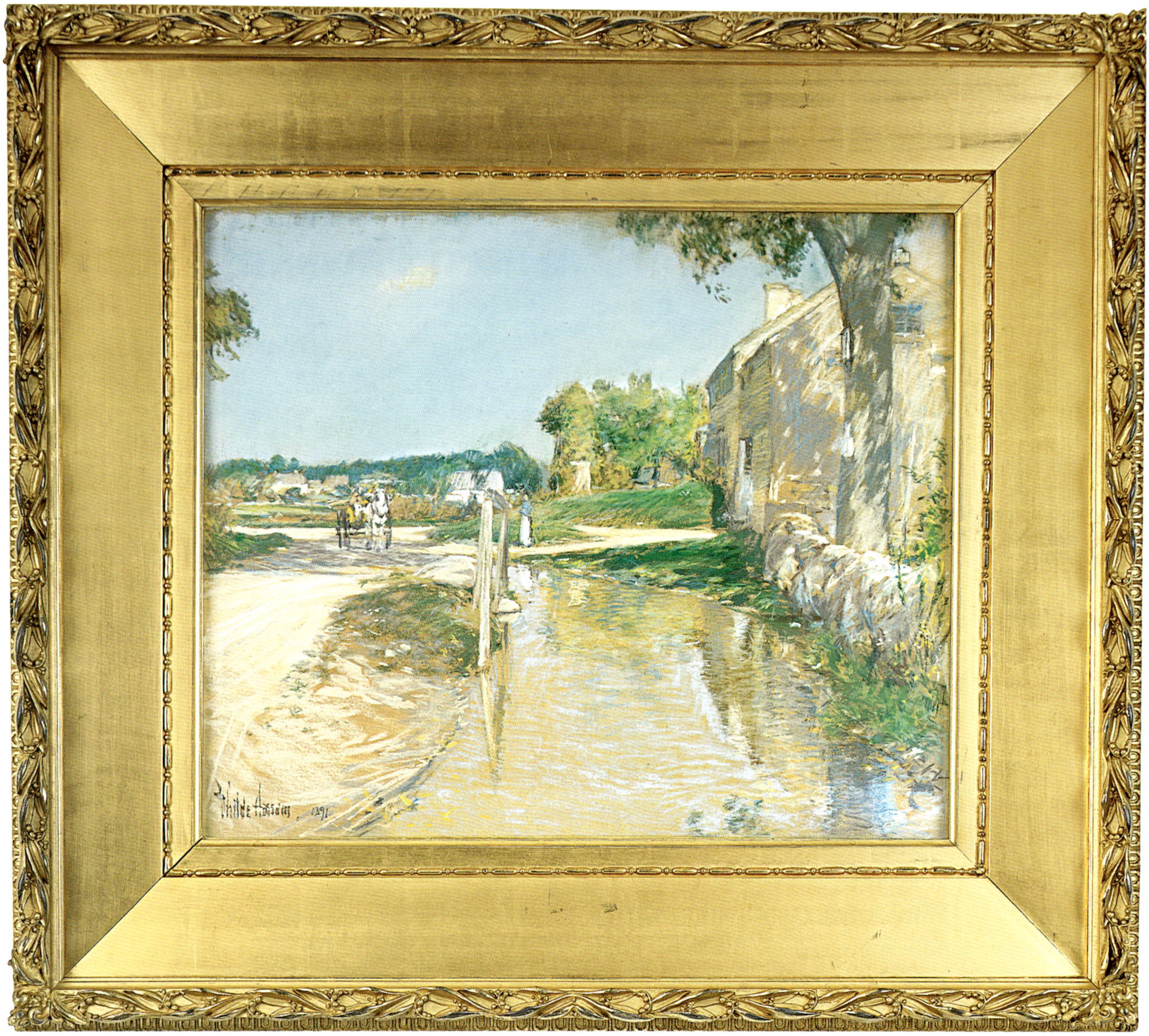

Fig. 328. Childe Hassam. *A Country Road,* 1891. Pastel on paper, 17⅝ x 21¼ in. (44.8 x 54 cm). Private collection. Frame: wood, applied composition ornament, gilded; made by F. J. LeCount Jr., Brooklyn

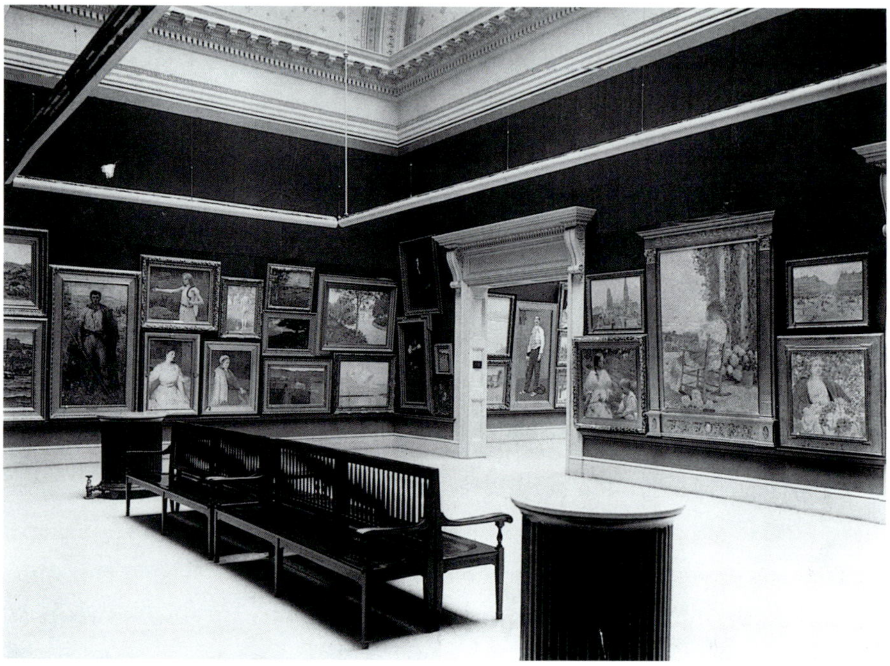

Fig. 329. Installation view, *Third Carnegie International Exhibition,* 1898. Carnegie Museum of Art, Pittsburgh. Hassam's *The Sea* is the large vertical painting on the right wall

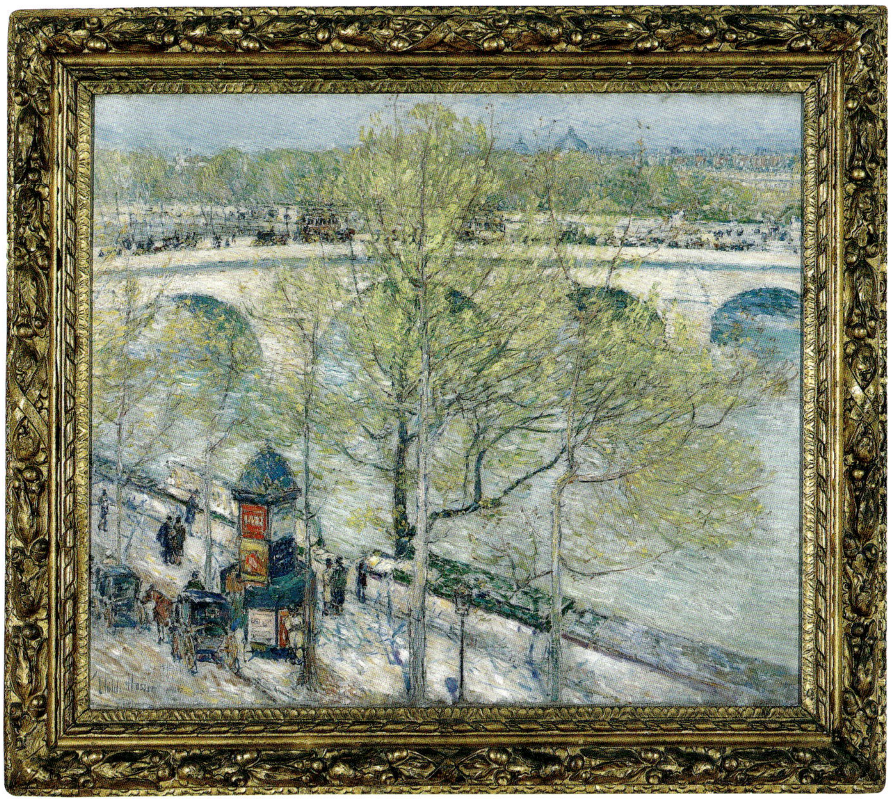

Fig. 330. Childe Hassam. *Pont Royal,* 1897. Oil on canvas, 24½ x 28½ in. (62.2 x 72.4 cm). Cincinnati Art Museum, Israel and Caroline Wilson Fund 1899.68. Frame: wood, applied composition ornament, gilded; made in France, ca. 1897

high-relief molded ornament fashionable in the late nineteenth century. Such surrounds were mass-produced not by carving but by pressing a composition material, called "compo," into a mold and then applying it to a wooden frame. Behind the artist's head is a typical 1890s frame with a wide unembellished frieze. Finally, the frame on the painting on the upper shelf resembles the one on the picture-within-the-picture in Hassam's *Sonata* (fig. 122). In that canvas the work over the piano is displayed in a wide gilded frame with ribbon-and-stick trim bordering a flat sight edge. A similar frame survives today on the pastel *A Country Road* (fig. 328). The pastel's frame, however, has a reeded outer edge succeeded by a leaf-and-berry trim, whereas the frames in the photograph and on the picture-within-the-picture, with their unadorned outer edges, are simpler.[4]

With other framing choices, Hassam connected his work to the international Aesthetic Movement. The American expatriate artist James McNeill Whistler, a leader of that movement, profoundly influenced the presentation and display of art. Together with his friend the Pre-Raphaelite painter Dante Gabriel Rossetti, in the 1860s Whistler introduced frames whose broad, flat surfaces stood in marked contrast to the ornate, high-profile borders fashionable among their Victorian contemporaries.[5] Whistler's later designs, featuring a finely reeded molding, are commonly called "Whistler frames." Hassam, who greatly admired the older artist, employed that late style throughout his career. *The Children,* 1897 (Cincinnati Art Museum), a panel depicting two of the Twachtman children, is framed in a reverse-ogee, beaded-course, Whistlerian molding.[6]

American architect and interior designer Stanford White collected antique frames, which he used as inspiration for new designs that combined classical and Renaissance elements.[7] White often employed the form known as the tabernacle frame, composed of an entablature supported by pilasters or columns, which had been devised in the late Middle Ages for devotional images. He probably designed the impressive tabernacle frame visible on Hassam's oil *The Sea,* 1898 (Adelson Galleries, New York), in an installation photograph of the *Third Carnegie International Exhibition* (fig. 329). By enshrining his portrayal of a young woman relaxing on a veranda in a molding associated with depictions of saints, Hassam implied that his secular American altarpiece demanded the same reverent attention due to sacred art.

Hassam sometimes patronized European frame makers. When he returned to New York in November 1897 after his third trip to the Continent, he left behind a group of canvases to be framed in Paris.[8] One of them, *Pont Royal* (fig. 330), won a gold medal at the annual exhibition of the Pennsylvania Academy of the Fine Arts, Philadelphia, held in

January–February 1899 and was purchased by the Cincinnati Art Museum from its Sixth Annual Exhibition of American Art of May–July 1899. Today it retains its original Barbizon-style frame, which features a convex-profile outer molding of oak leaves and acorns, a ribbon-and-stick banderole, and a gadrooned sight edge.[9] In choosing a frame of this type, Hassam claimed for his work the esteem that, he believed, Americans reserved for European art. He may also have been catering to Philadelphia taste: *Cat Boats, Newport* (fig. 187) and *Cliff Rock, Appledore,* 1903 (Indianapolis Museum of Art), included in the Pennsylvania Academy's annuals in 1902 and 1906, respectively, were both presented in ornate French-style frames, in which they are still shown.[10] Hassam's personal distaste for the style may have been betrayed in his outburst to a collector who had reframed one of his paintings: "For the love of Art, take off that Schuylkill moulding."[11]

By selecting frames derived from European sources other than Paris, Hassam proclaimed his cosmopolitanism. Short of funds on his return from Paris in November 1897, he arranged with a New York "framemaker, Mr. Le Brock [*sic*], to procure so many frames in exchange for so many pictures," collector John Gellatly's curator recalled later.[12] The firm referred to would be Jacobson and Le Brocq of New York, whose label appears on a frame in the Metropolitan Museum's collection (fig. 331). A penciled inscription on the back of the frame suggests that it was intended for Hassam's *Winter, Midnight* (fig. 104).[13] The frame's wide flat panels and geometric ornament were inspired by a seventeenth-century crossetted-corner Dutch design. However, the prototype would typically have been ebony, whereas the American variation is gold-leafed poplar. Hassam's choice of this design reveals his preference for simple borders, a taste he shared with his friend Weir, whose *Ice Cutters,* 1895 (Portland Art Museum), retains a frame of the same type.

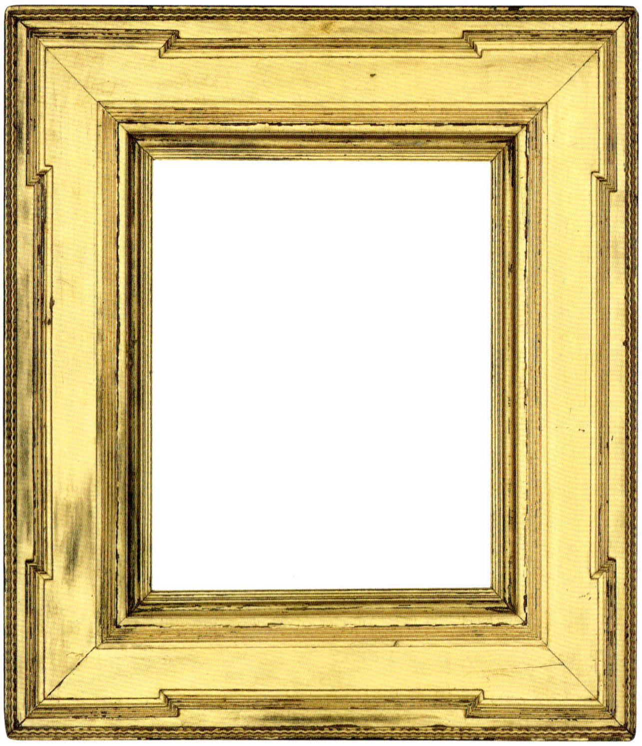

Fig. 331. Thomas Jacobson and William C. Le Brocq. Frame, ca. 1897. Carved wood (poplar), with gold leaf applied over gray bole, 38 x 34⅛ in. (96.5 x 86.7 cm). Inscribed in pencil on verso: *Winter Midnight / Childe Hassam / 12 West 57th St New York.* The Metropolitan Museum of Art, New York. Gift of Stuart P. Feld, 1969 Inst.69.16.3

When Hassam, Weir, and eight of their colleagues mounted the first exhibition of their group Ten American Painters in New York in the spring of 1898, the understated galleries won the admiration of visitors accustomed to the floor-to-ceiling installations then common. One critic observed "how discreetly all the things are framed" and dubbed the group "the Plain Frame School." "I don't mean to say I noticed these frames first off," he explained, "it is merely that the frames are modest enough to play into the pictures' hands."[14] The new look of the group's frames had not come about by accident; not only Hassam and Weir but also several other members of the Ten were known for their explorations of the aesthetic possibilities of frames. Twachtman had used white frames to harmonize with the subtle pastels and winter landscapes in his solo exhibition at the Wunderlich gallery in New York in March 1891.[15] Thomas W. Dewing often commissioned frames from Stanford White.[16] Edmund C. Tarbell insisted on using distinctive hand-crafted frames.[17] During the first two decades of the twentieth century their demands were often met by Boston artist Hermann Dudley Murphy.

In 1903 Murphy began making frames in the basement of his home in Winchester, Massachusetts, which he named Carrig Rohane (Gaelic for "red cliff"). By 1906 he and his business associates, Charles Prendergast and Walfred Thulin, moved the enterprise to Boston.[18] Although the firm was not officially known as Carrig-Rohane until 1914, from the beginning Murphy incised that name on the red-painted back of each of his frames, together with the year of its execution, his circled initial, and, usually, an inventory number corresponding to the order number in the shop's account books (see fig. 332).[19] Discriminating artists and collectors prized Murphy's frames. Among them were Hassam and other American Impressionists, who favored the designs Murphy

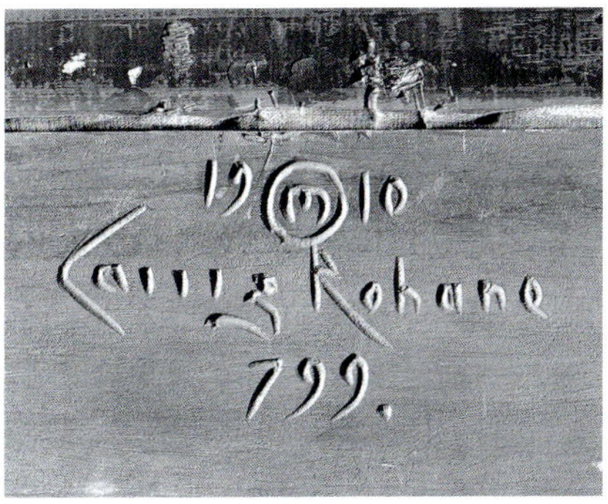

Fig. 332. Inscription on verso of frame on *Golden Afternoon* (fig. 336)

based on fifteenth-century Venetian cassetta frames, which have wide flat panels edged by raised inner and outer moldings.[20] (*Cassetta* means "little box" in Italian.)

Hassam patronized Carrig-Rohane from 1904 to 1912. His first order was for two frames: one in pattern number 2, the earliest of Murphy's cassetta designs, and the other in the Tarbell pattern, which in the firm's parlance signifies a design with basket-weave or grillwork corners.[21] In its style and dimensions the frame in pattern number 2 matches the frame that now surrounds *The Breakfast Room* (fig. 333), painted in 1911 and acquired that year by the Worcester Art Museum.[22] Its floral and grillwork corners and the shallow channels on its outer molding would recur frequently on Hassam's frames, whereas its bellflower-rope sight edge, rippled cove, and bead-and-reel outside molding are elaborations that he eliminated in most subsequent orders.

The frames in this first order were shipped on December 14, 1904, to Charles Erskine Scott Wood in Portland, Oregon, whom Hassam had visited earlier that year.[23] Wood, a lawyer, poet, amateur painter, and art patron, counted Hassam among his numerous artist friends. His preferences may have influenced the framing of a painting Hassam produced during his 1904 visit. *On the Snake River, Oregon* (fig. 334) is displayed in delicate filigreed panels with anthemion corners; this is a classical motif likely to have pleased Wood, who had commissioned Hassam to decorate his library with "Greek simplicity" (see fig. 203) and urged Weir to paint more "ideal pictures" in the spirit of "the old Greeks."[24] A matching frame surrounds a canvas Wood painted in Hassam's company. Today, his untitled picture and *On the Snake River, Oregon* hang together in the Portland Art Museum.[25]

Hassam's orders from Carrig-Rohane reveal that he was attentive to finish as well as design, seeking to harmonize the

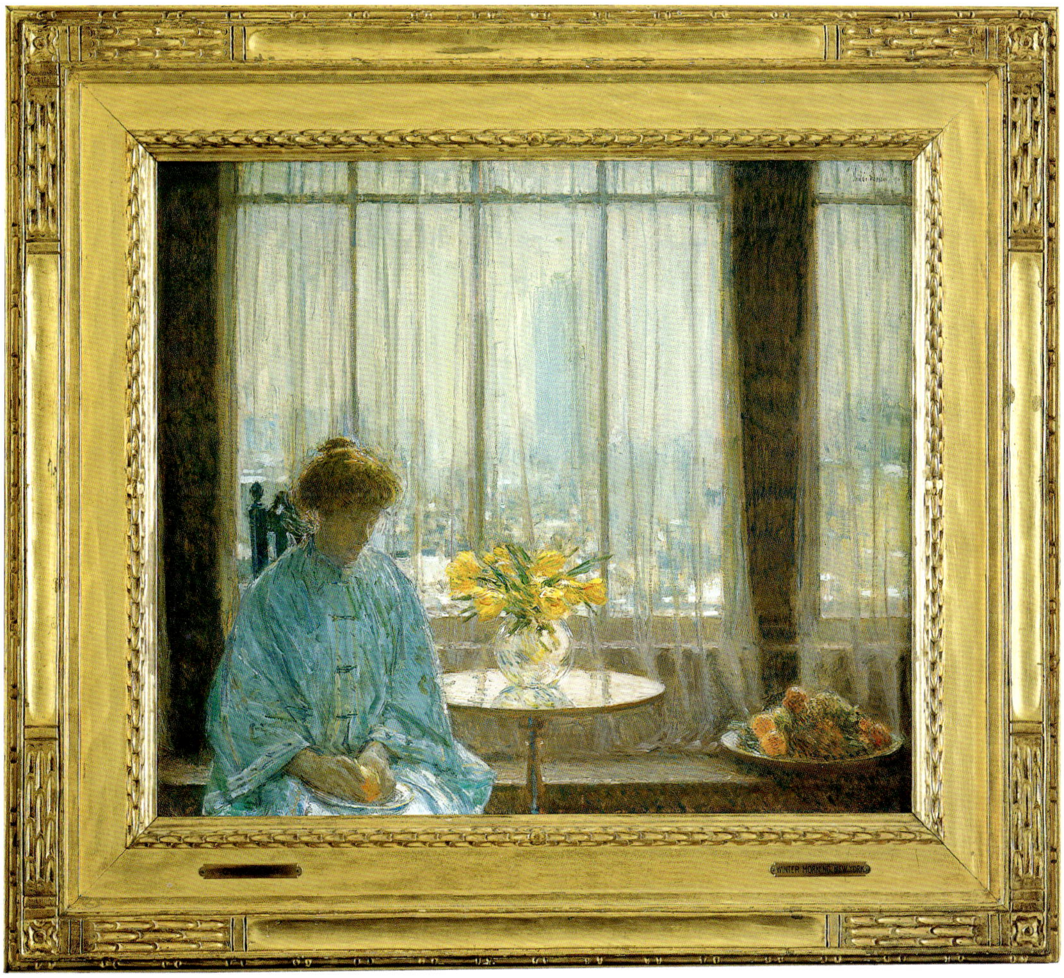

Fig. 333. Childe Hassam. *The Breakfast Room,* 1911. Oil on canvas, $25\frac{1}{8}$ x $30\frac{1}{8}$ in. (63.8 x 76.5 cm). Worcester Art Museum, Massachusetts, museum purchase. Frame: carved and gilded wood, inscribed on verso: *19(M)04 / Carrig Rohane*

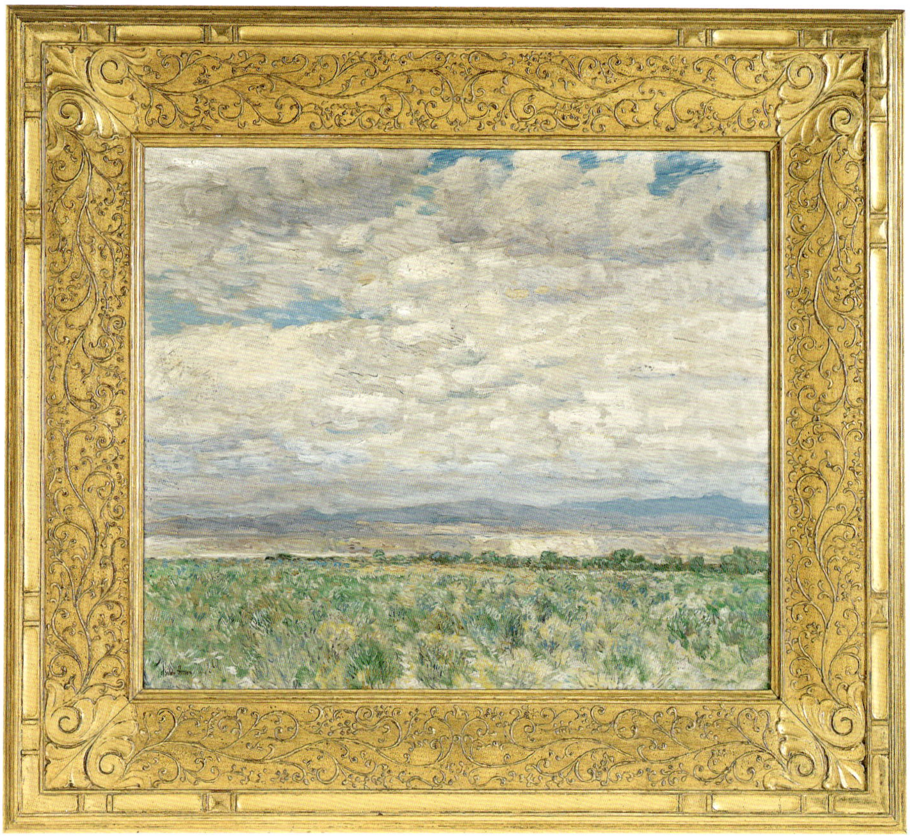

Fig. 334. Childe Hassam. *On the Snake River, Oregon,* 1904. Oil on canvas, with frame, 37½ x 42½ in. (95.3 x 108 cm) Portland Art Museum, Oregon. Museum purchase. Frame: carved and gilded wood, inscribed on verso: *19(M)06 / Carrig Rohane / 307*

frame with the painting for which it was intended. In one of his earliest orders, he specified two Tarbell-pattern frames, one "old gold toned gray for green landscape," the other with a "very silvery effect for pink landscape with laurel."[26] Other orders required various different finishes, including "gray gold for moonlight," pale gold, and old gold toned light, dark, or light gray.[27]

The Carrig-Rohane staff designated number 33 the "Hassam pattern." Introduced in 1903, number 33 is an elegant cassetta form with a flat sight edge, reeded inner molding, smooth concave cove, and graceful foliate corners (fig. 335). It is first identified with Hassam in his order dated September 13, 1906, for "Pattern 33–Hassam / for Moonlight picture, tone of which is purple & pearl–Pale Gold."[28] Four of his orders from 1907 call for "#33 Hassam pattern," all in pale gold but with corner variations; subsequent orders refer simply to "Hassam pattern." No painting by Hassam framed in an original Carrig-Rohane pattern 33 has been located.[29]

The frame on *Golden Afternoon* (fig. 336), which Hassam commissioned from Carrig-Rohane in 1910, exemplifies the basic vocabulary he employed most frequently: wide panels and restrained ornament that create a spacious, elegant

Fig. 335. Carrig-Rohane frame no. 33, Hassam pattern. Courtesy Eli Wilner and Company, New York

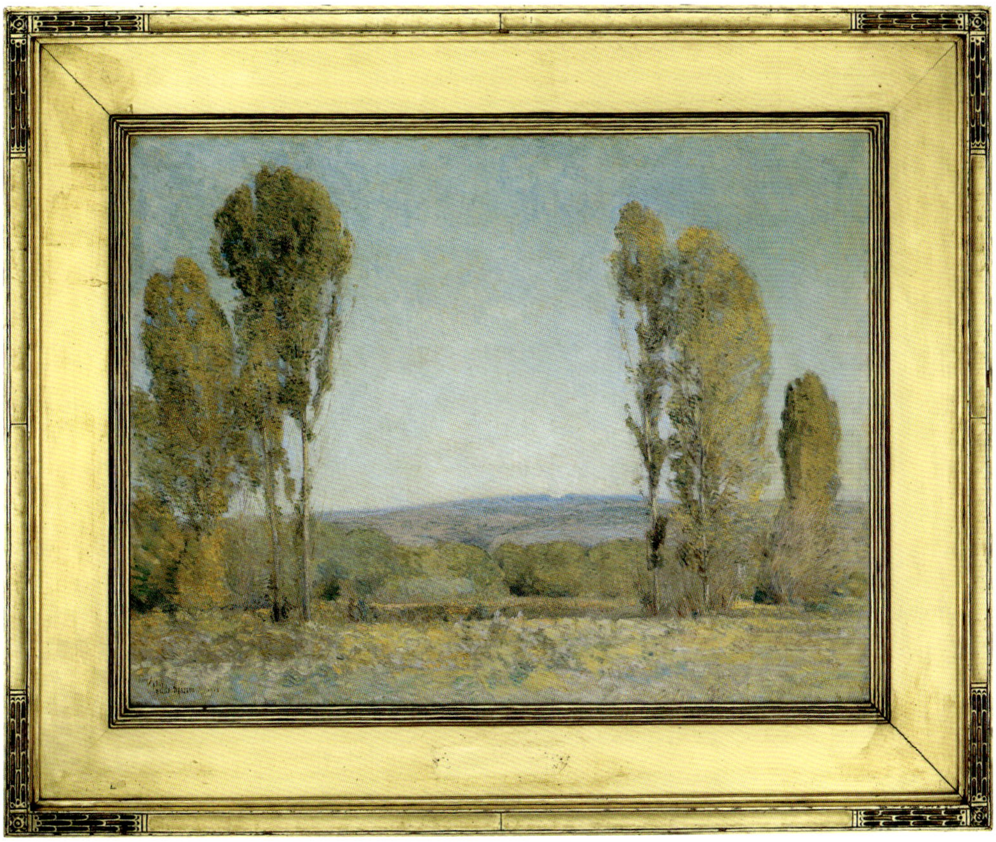

Fig. 336. Childe Hassam. *Golden Afternoon,* 1908. Oil on canvas, 30⅛ x 40⅜ in. (76.4 x 102.6 cm). The Metropolitan Museum of Art, New York. Rogers Fund, 1911 11.40. Frame: carved and gilded wood, inscribed on verso: *19(M)10 / Carrig Rohane / 799*

environment for the canvas. An identical frame Hassam ordered on the same day now surrounds *The New York Window* (fig. 227), a painting the Corcoran Gallery purchased in 1912 after it won a gold medal in the institution's fourth biennial.[30]

Hassam modified the elements in the frames on *Golden Afternoon* and *The New York Window* to customize a surround for *The Chinese Merchants* (fig. 337). Describing a scene in the Chinese section of Portland, the composition was influenced by Whistler's sketches of shop fronts in London

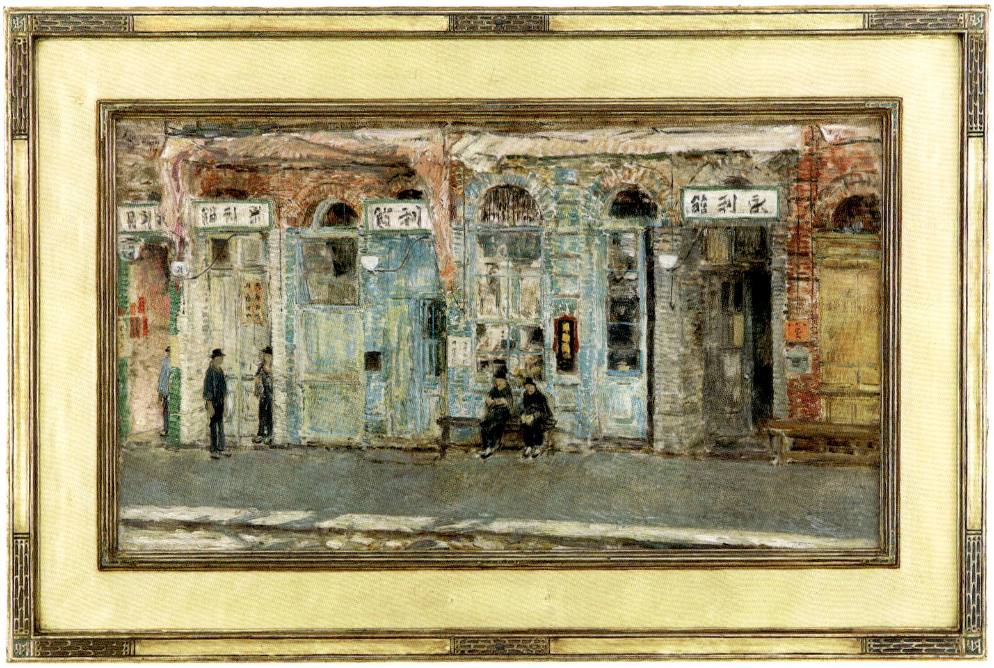

Fig. 337. Childe Hassam. *The Chinese Merchants,* by 1906 (inscribed *1909*). Oil on canvas, 19⅞ x 33⅛ in. (50.4 x 84 cm). Freer Gallery of Art, Smithsonian Institution, Washington, D.C.: Gift of Charles Lang Freer F1910.22. Frame: carved and gilded wood with blue pigment, inscribed on verso: *19(M)10 / Carrig Rohane / 755*

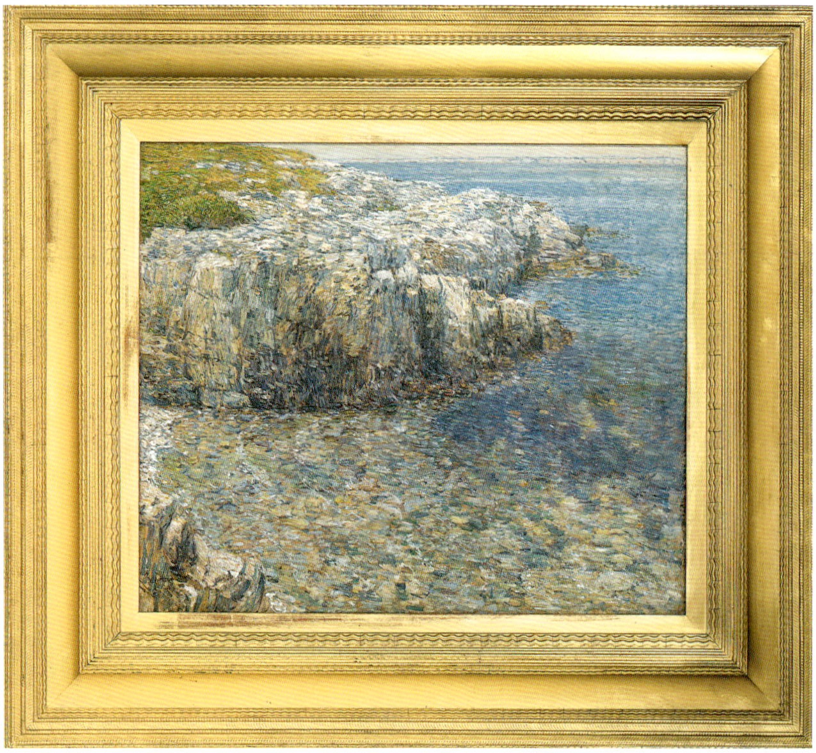

Fig. 338. Childe Hassam. *Isles of Shoals,* 1907. Oil on canvas, 24½ x 29¾ in. (62.2 x 75.6 cm). Portland Art Museum, Oregon. Gift in memory of William Maxwell Wood IV. Frame: carved and gilded wood, made by Zimmerman and Mossmann, New York, ca. 1907

Fig. 339. Childe Hassam. *Dawn,* 1914. Oil on canvas, 49 x 52 in. (124.5 x 132.1 cm). American Academy of Arts and Letters, New York. Frame: carved and gilded wood, designed by Hassam and made by Milch Galleries, New York, ca. 1921

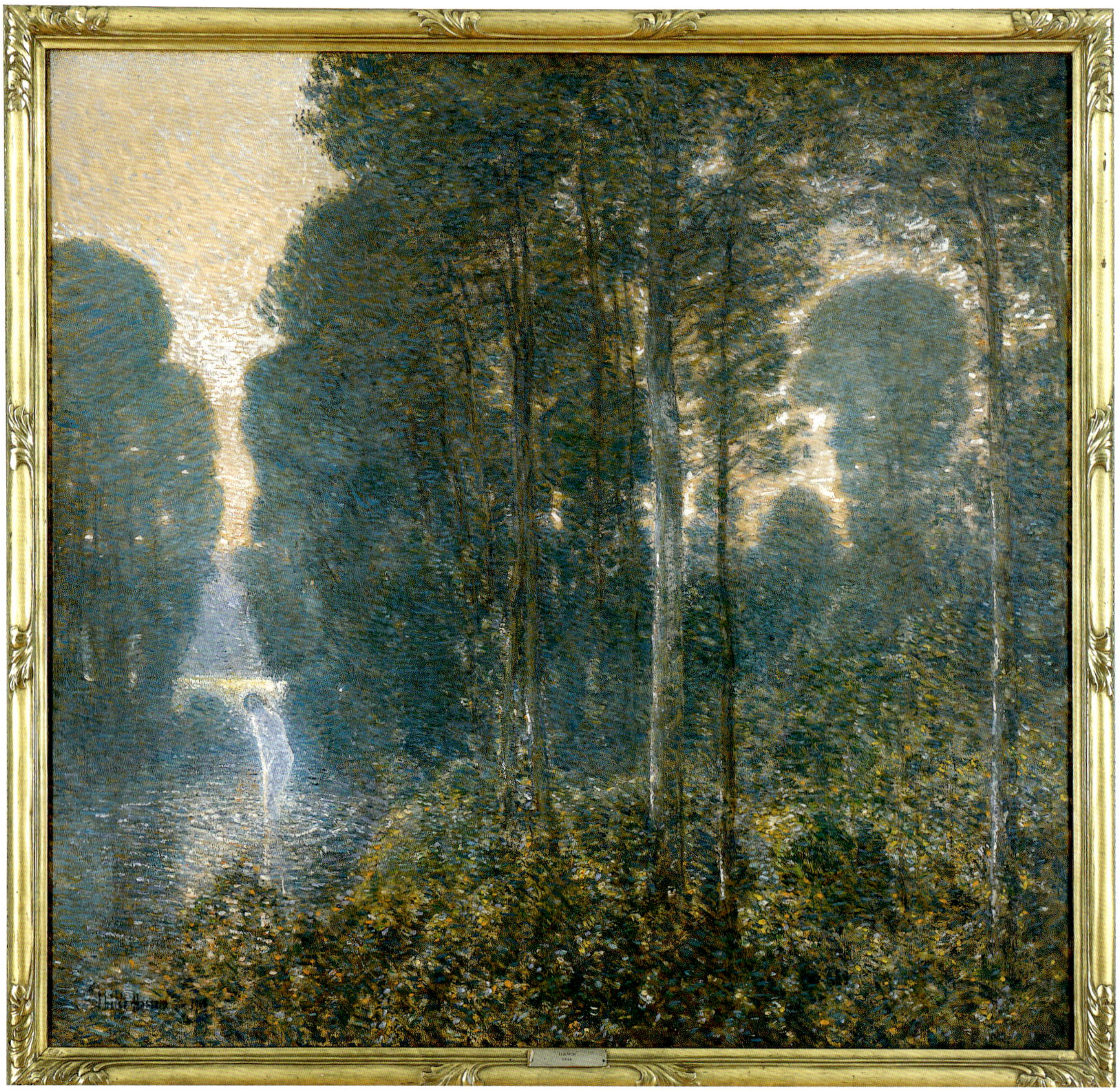

(see fig. 220) and Venice. The frame may have been inspired by the one Whistler designed for *Purple and Rose: The Lange Lijzen of the Six Marks,* 1864 (Philadelphia Museum of Art), which is embellished with six Chinese characters.[31] The floral corners of the frame on *Golden Afternoon* are replaced in the surround for *The Chinese Merchants* with pseudo-Chinese characters raised above blue pigment that echoes the color of the shop doors in the picture. Additional touches of blue accent the corners of the reeded inner molding and create the illusion of gemstones in the center of the horizontal rails. Hassam placed his order with Carrig-Rohane on February 12, 1910, in preparation for the exhibition of Ten American Painters at the Montross Gallery the following month. Charles Lang Freer, the noted patron of Whistler and collector of Asian art, purchased the painting on April 23, 1910.[32]

Although Carrig-Rohane was Hassam's principal frame maker in the first decade of the twentieth century, he also used other workshops during this period.[33] He ordered two cassetta frames for watercolors from New York dealer William Macbeth, stipulating that he "wanted no paper passe-partouts [mats]."[34] A fragmentary label on the back of *Isles of Shoals* (fig. 338) identifies its frame as the product of the Manhattan firm Zimmerman and Mossmann.[35] Hassam probably ordered the handsome reverse-ogee molding before C. E. S. Wood purchased the painting.

In early 1912 Hassam began patronizing New York's Milch Galleries, established that year. Brothers Edward and Albert Milch not only sold paintings but also framed them; in fact, members of the originally Austrian family had been in the framing business in New York since 1898.[36] Hassam's first documented order from Milch, dated March 22, 1912, launched a relationship that would endure for the rest of the artist's life. He had devised new patterns in cooperation with the workers at Carrig-Rohane, and now Hassam did so again with the Milch artisans. On November 7, 1918, he ordered a large square frame in the "special Hassam pater [*sic*]," to be delivered to the National Academy of Design. That frame was undoubtedly intended for *Tanagra (The Builders, New York)* (fig. 311), which was shown at the Academy's *Winter Exhibition* in December 1918. *Tanagra* has since been reframed, but a sketch on the order form resembles the pattern of the molding on *Dawn* (fig. 339), which retains Milch labels.[37] Both *Tanagra* and *Dawn* are monumental renderings of the female figure, suggesting that Hassam considered scale and subject matter in selecting similar frames for the two paintings.

After decades of modifying frames to suit his shifting needs, Hassam began to state clearly his involvement in framing by incorporating his initials in his designs. Although Whistler had ornamented a few frames with his butterfly emblem, Hassam is, to this date, the only American artist to place his initials on the front of his frames.[38] The first record of a frame initialed in this way is Hassam's Milch Galleries order of April 23, 1919. Several subsequent orders from Milch also specify a frame with a monogram, an H, or initials.[39] The order of October 20, 1919, for example, stipulates "Hassam patt with initial" and includes a sketch of a flat molding with two Hs on top and bottom and a single H on each side.[40] In a letter dated October 13, 1920, Hassam asked E. and A. Milch to "put through . . . an H frame . . . *at once*."[41] And in a letter of August 3, 1925, he commissioned "an H frame" from Milch for a picture he was exhibiting "at the Academy" that year.[42]

No initialed frame with a Milch label has been located. However, one reproduced "courtesy of the Milch Galleries" in an article published in 1921 was undoubtedly made by the firm.[43] A surviving unlabeled frame (fig. 340) strongly resembles the one in that reproduction. Its basic elements repeat those introduced years earlier by Carrig-Rohane, but the H punctuating the outer molding is new and makes the frame emphatically Hassam's. A rare variant of that design seen, for example, on a frame at the Metropolitan Museum (fig. 341) includes both of the artist's initials enclosed in a circle—a

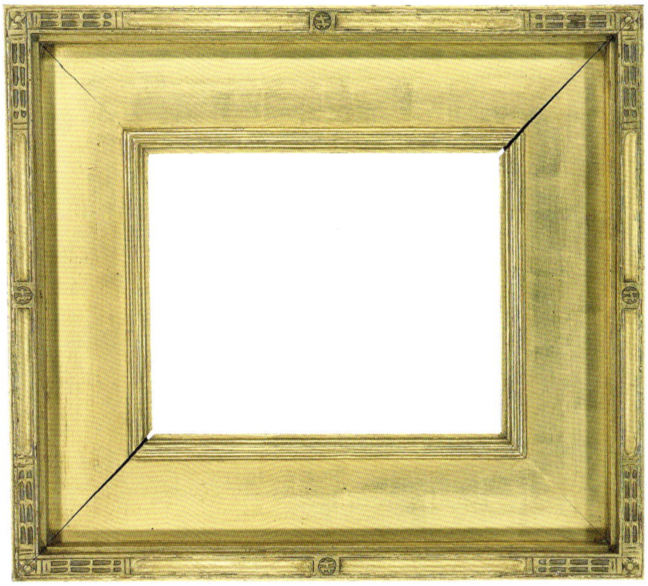

Fig. 340. Frame designed by Childe Hassam, ca. 1919. Carved and gilded wood, with Ⓗ in center of outer moldings. Julius Lowy Frame and Restoring Company, New York

Fig. 341. Frame designed by Childe Hassam, ca. 1919. Wood (poplar), with gold leaf applied over gesso and red bole, with (CH) in center of outer moldings. The Metropolitan Museum of Art, New York. Gift of Stuart P. Feld, 1971 Inst.1971.4.4

mark much like his signature on etchings of the 1910s and 1920s (see figs. 270, 272). This cursive monogram enhances the elegance of the beautifully crafted frames on which it appears.

The Royal Art Framing Company as well as Milch produced initialed frames for Hassam. First listed at 970 Sixth Avenue in the 1920 New York City directory, the firm had moved to 115 West Fifty-fourth Street by 1922.[44] One of the earliest frames Royal Art made for Hassam surrounds his painting *The Far Horizon* (fig. 342).[45] That frame and others bearing the Royal Art label, unlike those illustrated in figures 340 and 341, can be oriented either vertically or horizontally, which allowed Hassam to move them freely from painting to painting as his exhibition schedule demanded. Another Royal Art innovation was the introduction of a crescent moon (fig. 343) that replaced the floral corner; this motif was, in effect, an additional monogram, as it reiterated the crescent Hassam had been inscribing in front of his signature since about 1883.

The initialed frames, whether produced by Royal Art, Milch, or other workshops, vary in the quality of their carving and in subtle details. In some, the H is enclosed in a circle; in others it forms a bold, blocky square. The grillwork corners differ in the number and arrangement of the incised lines. Sometimes Hassam eliminated them entirely to produce a molding ornamented only by the crescent and his initial. Delicate variations in gilding lend a quiet sophistication

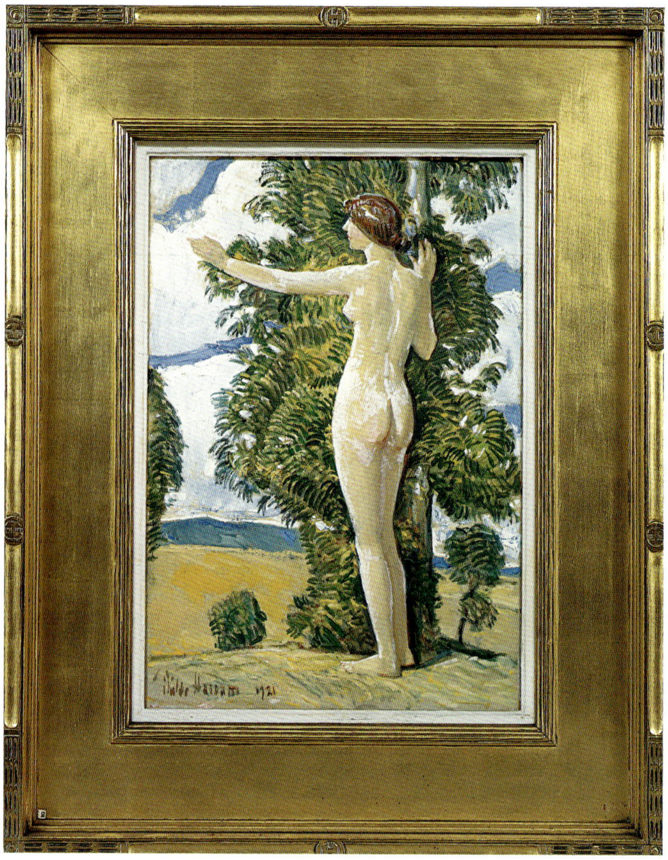

Fig. 342. Childe Hassam. *The Far Horizon,* 1921. Oil on canvas, 20 x 14 in. (50.8 x 35.6 cm). American Academy of Arts and Letters, New York. Frame: carved and gilded wood, designed by Hassam and made by Royal Art Framing Company, New York, ca. 1921

Fig. 343. Detail, frame on *The Far Horizon* (fig. 342), showing crescent and grillwork corner

Fig. 344. Frame designed by Childe Hassam and made by Royal Art Framing Company, New York, ca. 1922. Carved wood (poplar), with metal leaf applied over gesso and red bole, with crescent corners and Ⓗ in outer moldings. The Metropolitan Museum of Art, New York F.1990.46

to one such Royal Art frame in the Metropolitan Museum (fig. 344).

Once Hassam adopted the initialed frame, he used it only selectively and continued to rely on a variety of types, sometimes choosing an antique or an import. Speaking of *June* (fig. 321), a seven-foot-square painting of three nudes in the open air, Hassam proudly told interviewer DeWitt McClellan Lockman in 1927, "I have an Italian hand-carved frame for it."[46] A short film on the artist, produced by the Metropolitan in 1932, shows him viewing his paintings in the Museum's galleries. *The Church at Gloucester* (fig. 184) and *July Fourteenth, Rue Daunou, 1910* (fig. 205), both acquired by the Museum in the 1920s, appear in the film in frames of dramatically different styles. The New England scene is displayed in a simple cassetta molding that perfectly accords with the church's quiet grace. The Parisian streetscape, by contrast, is presented in an ornate French-style frame in which rich ornamentation alternates with smooth, shiny reserves. Today both canvases retain their original frames.

Hassam frequently commissioned Whistler frames, ordering that style from the Milch Galleries at least ten times between 1918 and 1920. *Back of the Fishkill Mountains* (fig. 345) retains such a surround.[47] He also continued to use frames based on Stanford White's designs, which were produced after White's death in 1906 by the Milch Galleries, William C. Le Brocq, and the Chicago firm Newcomb Macklin.[48] When the Detroit Museum of Art (now the Detroit Institute of Arts) purchased *Place Centrale and Fort Cabanas, Havana* (fig. 196) from Hassam in 1911, the painting arrived in a frame of Stanford White design with a nearly flat profile and fine reeding that harmonize with its horizontal composition and delicate broken brushwork. Eight years later, when the Detroit museum purchased *Surf and Rocks,* 1906, Hassam dispatched it in another Stanford White frame. His decision to frame that rugged Postimpressionist canvas in an elegant earlier style may have been prompted by a consideration of how the picture would relate to *Place Centrale and Fort Cabanas, Havana* when the two paintings hung together in the museum's galleries.

Hassam's concern with the aesthetic impact of frames is evident in his treatment of his Flag paintings. An installation photograph of the first exhibition of the series, at New York's Durand-Ruel Galleries in November 1918, shows the canvases uniformly framed (fig. 346). That strategy encouraged gallery visitors to view the works as an ensemble, promoting Hassam's ultimately unfulfilled dream that the entire group would be acquired by New York City or an American museum.[49] The style of the handsome frame is deceptively simple, with many light-catching surfaces that enhance the paintings' lively colors and broken brushwork. Three of the Flag paintings in the present exhibition, *Avenue of the Allies, Great Britain, 1918* (fig. 347), *Flags on Fifty-seventh*

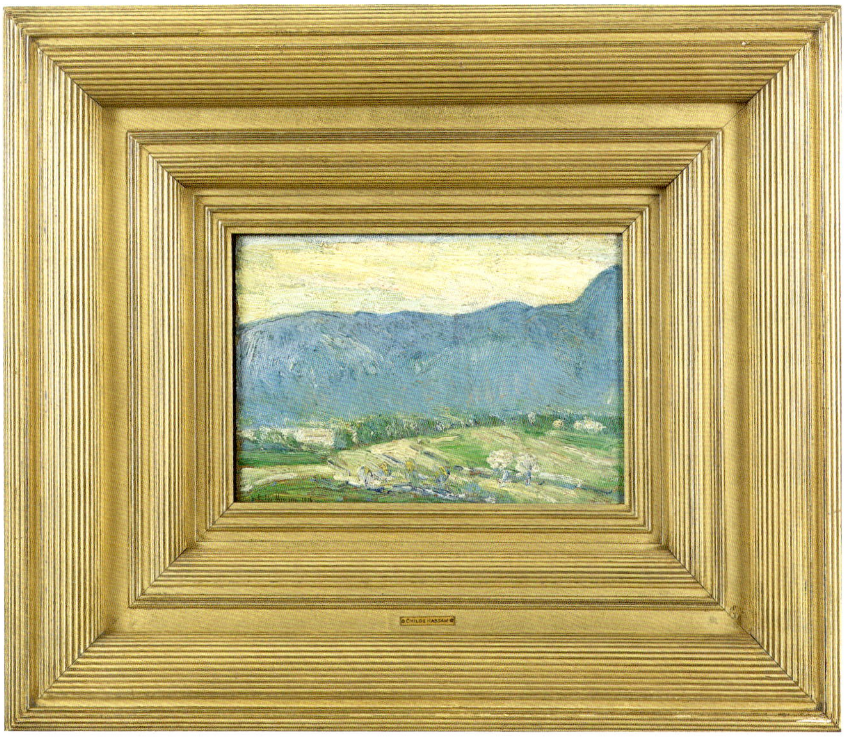

Fig. 345. Childe Hassam. *Back of the Fishkill Mountains,* 1916. Oil on wood panel, 6½ x 9½ in. (16.5 x 24.1 cm). American Academy of Arts and Letters, New York. Frame: carved and gilded wood, Whistler style, made by Albert Milch Company, New York, ca. 1918

Street, The Winter of 1918 (fig. 233), and *Victory Day, May 1919* (fig. 235) retain their original frames.

Whereas Hassam chose a uniform presentation for the Flag series, late in his career he employed three different frames that are integral to the paintings they surround. *Greek Altar to Autumn* (fig. 348), depicting two toga-clad women bringing fruit to a marble altar over which a zephyr-like figure floats, is presented in a tabernacle frame inscribed on the right outer edge *Carv. by gregory Kirchner 1924 n.y.c.* Kirchner was a Russian-born craftsman based in Brooklyn. In his design for *Greek Altar to Autumn* he updated delicate classical architectural elements by rendering them more boldly and on a larger scale than usual. The carver stated his allegiance to the Aesthetic Movement by placing one of its emblems, sunflowers, on each pilaster. He distressed the surface, rubbing off the gold leaf in some areas to expose the red bole (clay base), which repeats the colors in Hassam's painting: the hue of the apples, the crimson of one woman's robe, and the auburn hair of both figures.

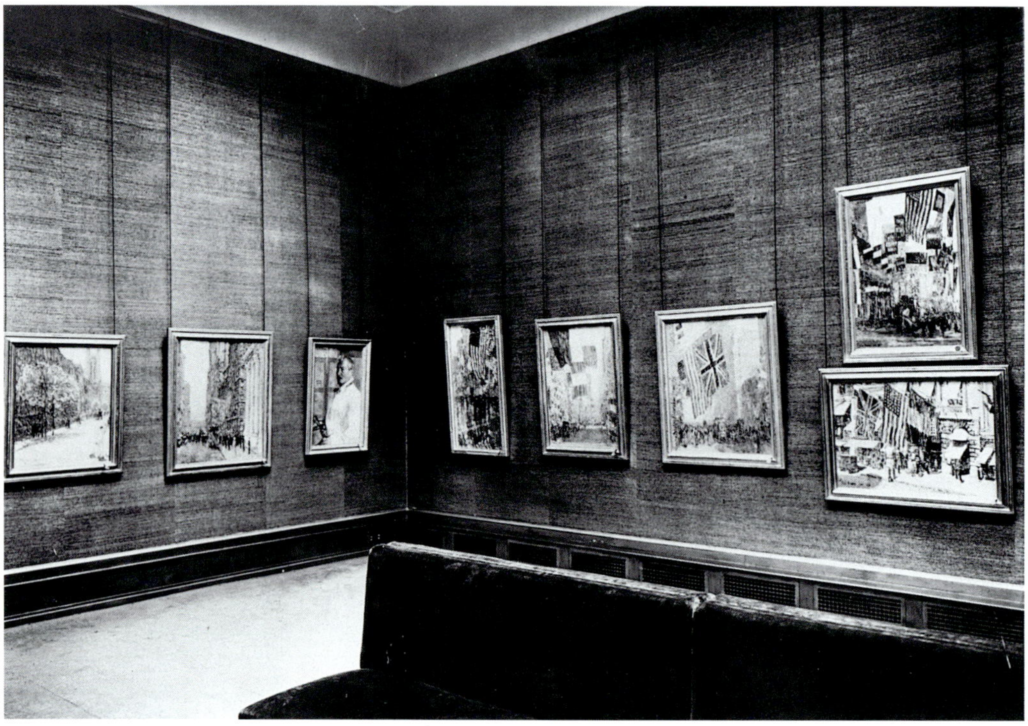

Fig. 346. Installation view, *Exhibition of a Series of Paintings of the Avenue of the Allies by Childe Hassam,* Durand-Ruel Galleries, New York, November 15–December 7, 1918

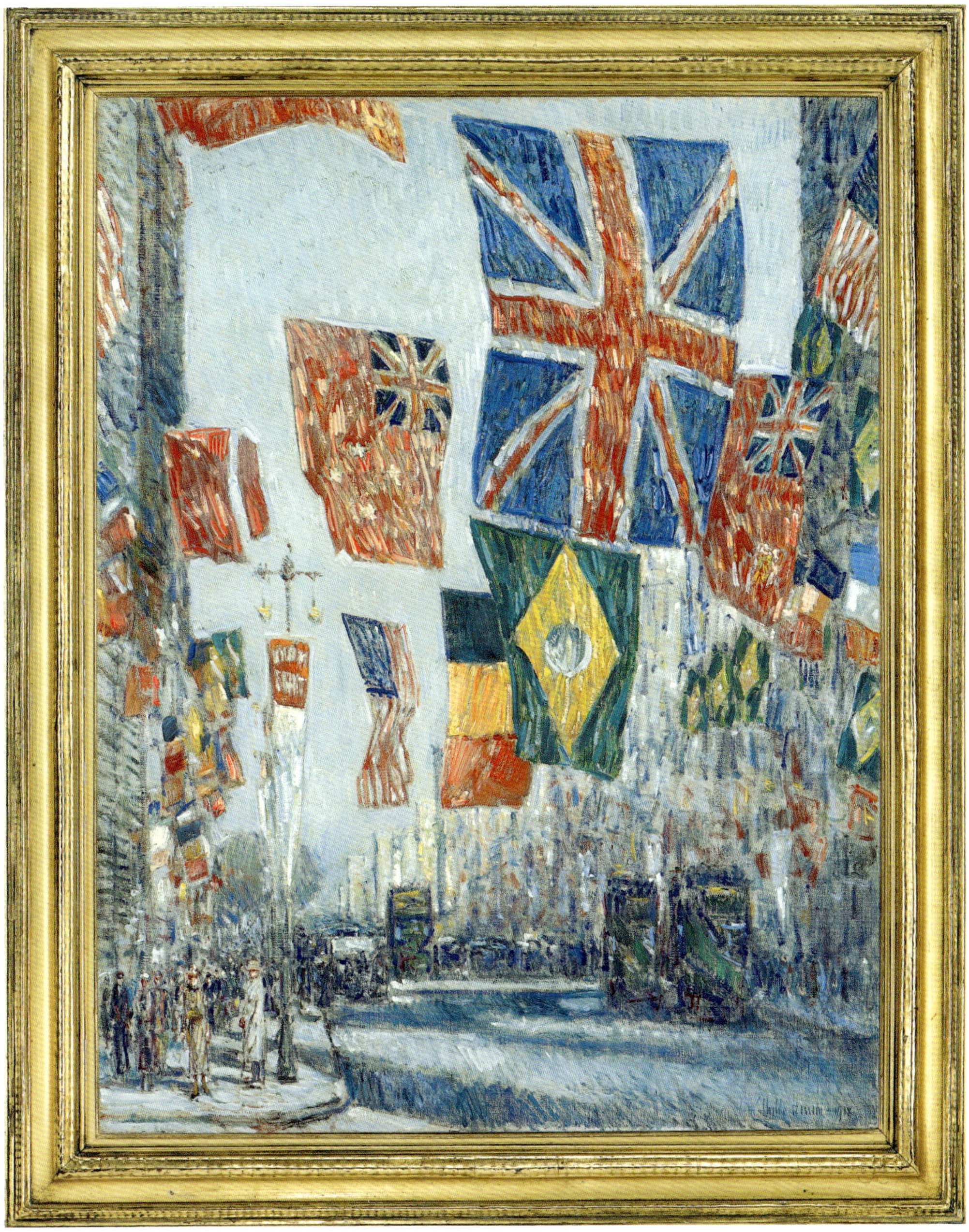

Fig. 347. Childe Hassam. *Avenue of the Allies, Great Britain, 1918,* 1918. Oil on canvas, 36 x 28⅜ in. (91.4 x 72.1 cm). The Metropolitan Museum of Art, New York. Bequest of Miss Adelaide Milton de Groot (1876–1967), 1967 67.187.127. Frame: carved and gilded wood, ca. 1918

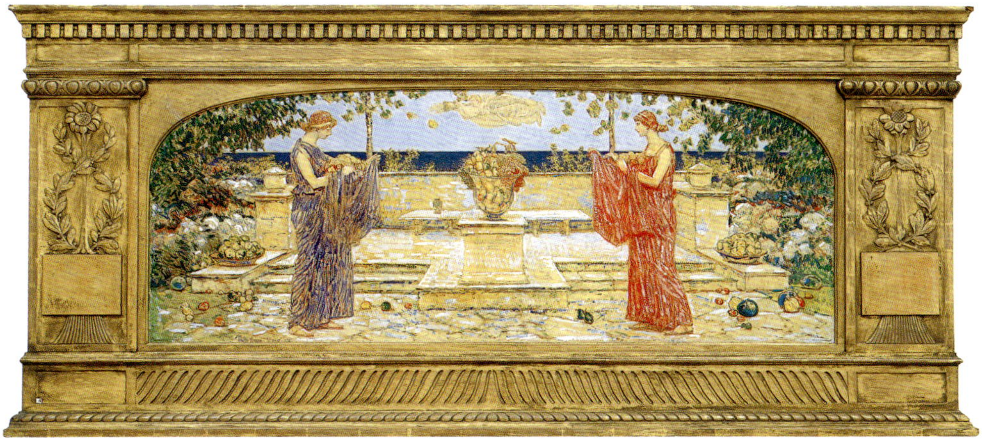

Fig. 348. Childe Hassam. *Greek Altar to Autumn,* 1924. Oil on wood panel, 16 x 43 in. (40.6 x 109.2 cm). American Academy of Arts and Letters, New York. Frame: carved wood with gold leaf applied over red bole, made by Gregory Kirchner, New York, 1924

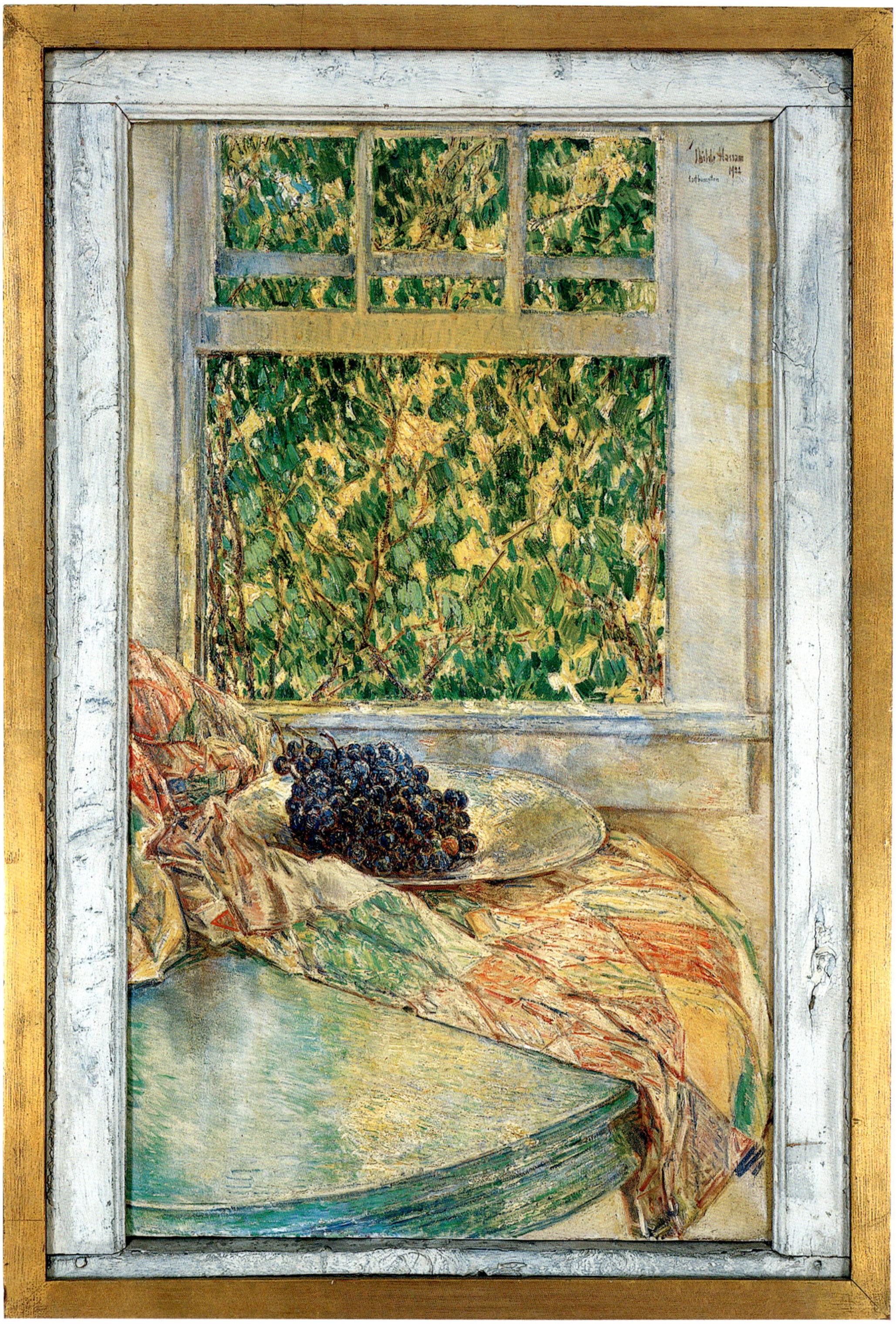

Fig. 349. Childe Hassam. *Colonial Quilt,* 1922. Oil on canvas, 42 x 26 in. (106.7 x 66 cm). American Academy of Arts and Letters, New York. Inner frame: painted wood window frame from an old house, incorporated into the composition by Hassam, 1922. Outer frame: gilded wood, made by Royal Art Framing Company, New York, ca. 1922–35

Kirchner carved frames for collector John Gellatly as well as for Hassam.[50] When Gellatly donated his extensive collection to the Smithsonian Institution in Washington, D.C., in 1929 (today, it is in the collection of the Smithsonian American Art Museum in Washington, D.C.), seven of the paintings— including Hassam's *Improvisation* (fig. 312)— arrived in Kirchner frames.[51] Hassam may have commissioned the frame for *Greek Altar to Autumn* from Kirchner in a bid for Gellatly's continued patronage. He probably ordered it in preparation for his solo exhibition, composed mainly of works inspired by Greek mythology, which opened at the Macbeth Gallery at the end of December 1924. *Greek Altar to Autumn* is most likely the work shown there as *The Great Altar to Ceres and the West Wind.*[52]

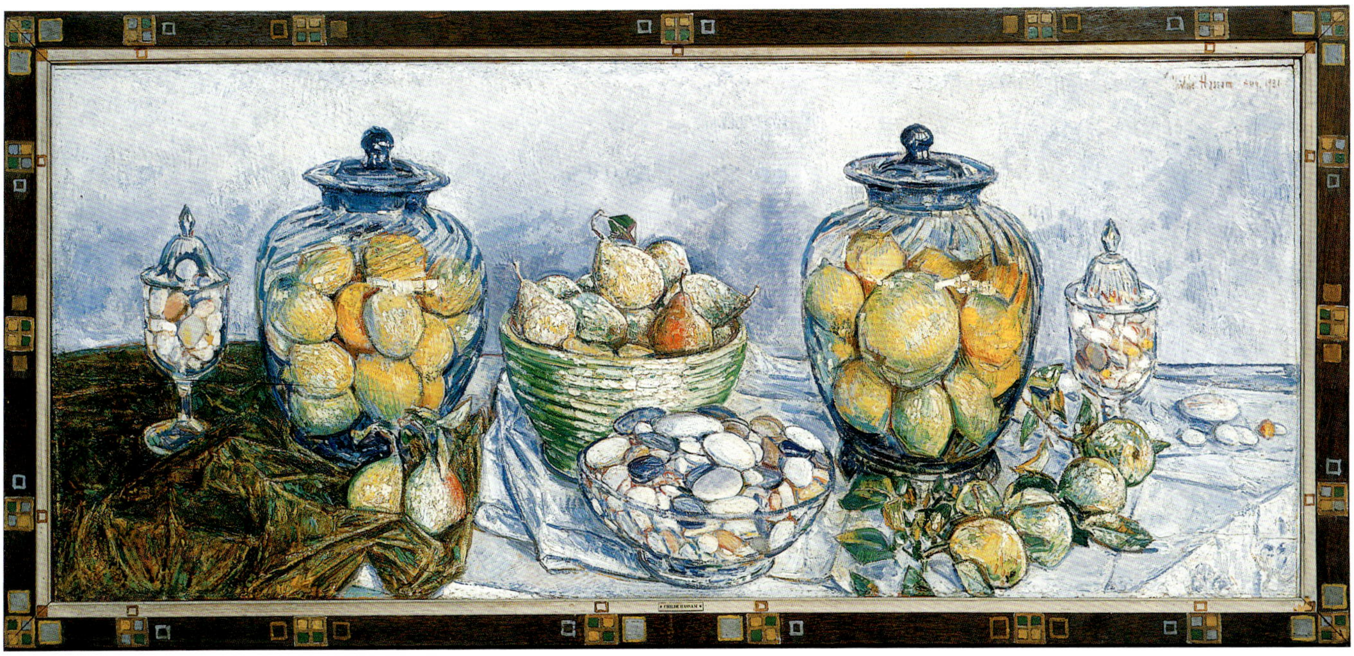

Fig. 350. Childe Hassam. *Long Island Pebbles and Fruit,* 1931. Oil on wood panel, 23¼ x 56½ in. (59.1 x 143.5 cm). American Academy of Arts and Letters, New York. Frame: stained and painted wood, designed and made by Childe Hassam, 1931

A companion piece to that painting in the Macbeth exhibition was probably *Colonial Quilt* (fig. 349), displayed there under a title that links American and Greek antiquity: *Grapes for the Great Altar, A Window Frame of Swamp Cedar, out of the Old Church hand hewn by the early English settlers of Easthampton and Montauk.* Hassam told an interviewer, "I have used old window panels that are out of old houses" and connected that practice to his classical subjects.[53] In *Colonial Quilt* a heavy bunch of Concord grapes—a variety developed in Hassam's native Massachusetts—rests like an offering on an iridescent platter. Playing on the age-old conceit that a painting is a view seen through a window,[54] the frame of *Colonial Quilt* is an actual window frame. The viewer becomes a voyeur, standing outside an old house and peering through a window across a small room to another open window. Foliage screens the landscape beyond, focusing attention on the two windows, one "real," the other painted. The recycled window's knotty wood, rustic construction, and weathered finish convey age more vividly than does the quilt of the title. A narrow gold band enframing the old window tempers Hassam's arresting experiment, but a Royal Art label on its reverse suggests that he himself—or perhaps his wife, before she relinquished the picture in his bequest to the American Academy of Arts and Letters—chose to frame the window frame.

Like *Colonial Quilt, Long Island Pebbles and Fruit* (fig. 350) extends Hassam's composition beyond the confines of the picture in a modernist manner astonishing for an artist whose antipathy to advanced contemporary art is well documented.[55] *Long Island Pebbles and Fruit* is displayed in narrow flat strips of wood, painted white on the liner, stained dark brown on the outer molding. Using the same colors he had employed for the still life they enclose, Hassam brushed a geometric design on the liner and frame.[56] The treatment is as daring as the contemporary framing innovations of the early American modernists Arthur Dove, Marsden Hartley, John Marin, and Georgia O'Keeffe—all much younger than the septuagenarian Hassam.[57]

Critics have noted the remarkable range of Hassam's work; his framing choices were equally diverse. Throughout his career he selected forms, most of them simple, that create elegant settings for his pictures; chose embellishments, most of them understated, that capture and reflect light; and for each frame specified a finish, usually subtle, that enhances the tonal harmonies of the painting it surrounds. Hassam used frames to shape viewers' perceptions of his works, locating them at different points on the continuum of art history. His sophisticated approach to framing illuminates his surprising complexity and shrewd but sensitive presentation of his art.

In researching this topic, I enjoyed the gracious assistance of many people. Suzanne Smeaton of Eli Wilner and Company generously shared her wealth of knowledge about American frames. Kathleen Kienholz and Souhad Rafey at the American Academy of Arts and Letters, New York, helped me inspect many Hassams in their collection and patiently answered my numerous queries. Carrie Rebora Barratt of The Metropolitan Museum of Art reviewed the manuscript and offered constructive criticism. Directors, curators, registrars, and conservators in other institutions made my research both enjoyable and productive. I would like to thank Heather Lineberry and Tiffany Fairall, Arizona State University Art Museum, Tempe; Judith Barter, Art Institute of Chicago; Alain Joyaux, Ball State University Museum of Art, Muncie, Indiana; Louise Lippincott, Carnegie Museum of Art, Pittsburgh; Julie Aronson, Cincinnati Art Museum; Sarah Cash and Dare Hartwell, Corcoran Gallery of Art, Washington, D.C.; James W. Tottis and Justin Clark, Detroit Institute of Arts; Lynn M. Turner, Diplomatic Reception Rooms, U.S. Department of State, Washington, D.C.; Elizabeth F. Duley, Paul Jett, and Kenneth Myers, Freer Gallery of Art, Washington, D.C.; Jeffrey W. Andersen, Florence Griswold Museum, Old Lyme; Marcus Burke, Hispanic Society of America, New York; Harriet Warkel, Indianapolis Museum of Art; Jeremy Adamson, Library of Congress, Washington, D.C.; Sue Canterbury, Minneapolis Institute of Arts; Erica E. Hirshler, Museum of Fine Arts, Boston; Emily Neff, Museum of Fine Arts, Houston; Kim Sajet, Pennsylvania Academy of the Fine Arts, Philadelphia; Margaret Bullock, Portland Art Museum, Oregon; Elizabeth Broun, Eleanor Harvey, Martin Kotler, and Richard Murray, Smithsonian American Art Museum, Washington, D.C.; and Rita Albertson, Worcester Art Museum. I extend my gratitude as well to Laurie Bradt; Linda Merrill; the late Vance Jordan; Larry Shar and Brad Shar, Julius Lowy Frame and Restoring Company, New York; and Terry Vose, Vose Galleries, Boston.

1. Peyton Boswell, "When the Frame Fits the Picture," *House and Garden* 39 (February 1921), pp. 38 (photo caption), 66. I am grateful to Suzanne Smeaton for bringing this article to my attention. Hassam delegated the selection of a frame to his dealer on at least one occasion: he wrote to Albert Milch in 1930, instructing him to "get hold of a good frame for me (one of my finest canvases) a period if possible and if not too exorbitant in price. *Borrow one, steal one* or *buy one* [emphasis original]." Childe Hassam, [East Hampton], October 20, 1930, to Albert Milch, [New York], Milch Gallery Records, 1911–1980, Archives of American Art, Smithsonian Institution, reel 4420, frame 330. Hassam was in East Hampton and would not return to the city in time to choose the frame before the painting in question was sent to an exhibition.
2. John H. Twachtman, November 11, 1900, to Harrison S. Morris, Director, Pennsylvania Academy of the Fine Arts, Director's correspondence, archives, Pennsylvania Academy of the Fine Arts, Philadelphia, quoted in Hiesinger 1991, pp. 156–57, 171, n. 21.
3. Hassam made the remark at the Holley House in Cos Cob. Typescript (probably by Dorothy Weir Young) of notes from an undated interview with Elmer and Constant MacRae, Dorothy Weir Young Research Papers, tub 3, "Holley Farm" folder, archives, Weir Farm National Historic Site, Wilton, Connecticut.
4. The label on the pastel's frame reads: *FROM / F. J. LeCOUNT, JR. / MANUFACTURER OF / GOLD, BRONZE, OAK AND EBONY / PICTURE FRAMES / OF EVERY DESCRIPTION, / 411 Bedford Avenue, / Brooklyn, N.Y. / BY-GILDING A SPECIALTY.* I am grateful to Suzanne Smeaton for calling this frame to my attention.
5. Whistler also took a radical approach to gilding, ordering the gold leaf applied directly to oak, without the usual underlayer of gesso or bole. Although Whistler is often given sole credit for his innovative frame designs, scholars have established that Rossetti was responsible for many of them. See Suzanne Smeaton, *The Art of the Frame: An Exhibition Focusing on American Frames of the Arts and Craft Movement, 1870–1920*, exh. cat. (New York: Eli Wilner and Co., 1988), pp. 6–7, and Linda Merrill, *The Peacock Room: A Cultural Biography* (New Haven: Yale University Press in association with Freer Gallery of Art, 1998), pp. 55–56, 65. Merrill's splendid study provides information on Whistler's frames.
6. According to Curator Julie Aronson, *The Children* came to the Cincinnati Art Museum in 1940 in a bequest from Ruth Harrison, who had purchased it out of the museum's *Annual Exhibition of American Art,* held from May to July 1904. (In the catalogue the painting, no. 10, is titled *Twachtman's Children.*) Although the frame seems to be the original one, it does not bear a label from the 1904 exhibition. I am grateful to Dr. Aronson for this information.
7. For more on White's frames, see Susan A. Hobbs, "A Note on Frames," in Susan A. Hobbs, *The Art of Thomas Wilmer Dewing: Beauty Reconfigured,* exh. cat. (Washington, D.C.: Smithsonian Institution Press in association with the Brooklyn Museum, 1996), pp. 83–85; William Adair, "Stanford White's Frames," *Magazine Antiques* 151, no. 3 (March 1997), pp. 448–57; and Nina Gray, "Within Gilded Borders: The Frames of Stanford White," in *The Gilded Edge: The Art of the Frame,* edited by Eli Wilner (San Francisco: Chronicle Books, 2000), pp. 82–103.
8. In a letter to Harrison S. Morris, director of the Pennsylvania Academy of the Fine Arts, Philadelphia, dated June 29, 1898, Hassam said of the paintings he intended to send to the institution's next annual exhibition, "All these things were done last year abroad. . . . They were left over there to be framed so they have never even seen this side." Director's correspondence, archives, Pennsylvania Academy of the Fine Arts, quoted in Hiesinger 1991, p. 170, n. 602.
9. No frame maker's labels survive on *Pont Royal,* but a fragmentary label from a French shipping company was originally attached to the back of the canvas or the frame. The torn label reads: *Guinchard Fourniret, Emballeurs / 76 Rue Blanche, Paris / Exposition* [—]. I am grateful to Julie Aronson, Curator of American Art, Cincinnati Art Museum, for providing this information. The painting was shown at the Salon of the Société Nationale des Beaux-Arts, Paris, in May 1898, as no. 602.
10. *Cat Boats, Newport* was purchased from the January–March 1902 annual by the Pennsylvania Academy of the Fine Arts. A torn label on the back of the frame reads: *WM. SCHILL, / GILDER / Looking Glass & Picture Frame Ma[-]er. / 47 University [—] / N.E. Cor. St. / Pictures Cleaned and Varnis[—]. Cliff Rock, Appledore* was exhibited at the Pennsylvania Academy of the Fine Arts from January–March 1906 and at the *Inaugural Exhibition* of the John Herron Art Institute, Indianapolis, held from November—December 1906. It was purchased by the new art institute after the exhibition closed. For further information on this painting, see Alain G. Joyaux, Brian A. Moore, and Ned H. Griner, *Childe Hassam in Indiana,* exh. cat. (Muncie, Ind.: Ball State University Art Gallery, November 3–December 8, 1985), p. 37.
11. Quoted in Price 1923, p. 6. Price does not identify the painting, nor is it clear from the context what Hassam meant by a "Schuylkill moulding." However, the similar frames on three paintings originally exhibited at Pennsylvania Academy of the Fine Arts annuals suggest that

Philadelphia collectors—or Pennsylvania Academy of the Fine Arts' managing director, Harrison S. Morris—favored that style. The connection to Philadelphia is supported by the fact that the Schuylkill River runs through the city.

12. "Information provided by John Gellatly's curator Ralph Seymour," ca. 1932, typewritten notes from the curatorial files for Hassam's *In the Garden (Celia Thaxter in Her Garden)* (fig. 130), Smithsonian American Art Museum, Washington, D.C. According to this source, Gellatly purchased Hassam's *Ponte Santa Trinità* (fig. 353), one of the paintings in the exchange, from Le Brocq in 1898.
13. The label reads: *TH. JACOBSON, / Picture Frames For Artists / MADE TO ORDER. / 136 W. 30th STREET, / NEW YORK. / / W. C. Le BROCQ, / FRAMES GILDED / in METAL LEAF or GOLD LACQUERED and / toned to harmonize with paintings. / Plate Glass Furnished. / 136 W. 30th Street / NEW YORK.* The inscription on the back of the frame reads: *Winter Midnight / Childe Hassam / 152 West 57th St New York.*
14. Orson Lowell, "Three Important New York Exhibitions," *Brush and Pencil* 2 (May 1898), p. 89. Unfortunately, no installation photographs of the exhibitions of the Ten have been found.
15. *Paintings in Oil and Pastels by J. H. Twachtman* (New York: H. Wunderlich and Company, March 1891). For the design of the exhibition, see Lisa N. Peters, "Twachtman's Greenwich Paintings: Context and Chronology," in Deborah Chotner, Lisa N. Peters, and Kathleen A. Pyne, *John Twachtman: Connecticut Landscapes,* exh. cat. (Washington, D.C.: National Gallery of Art, 1989), p. 24.
16. See Hobbs, "Note on Frames," pp. 83–85.
17. For Tarbell's interest in frames, see Erica E. Hirshler, "'Good and Beautiful Work': Edmund C. Tarbell and the Arts and Crafts Movement," in Susan Strickler, Linda J. Docherty, and Erica E. Hirshler, *Impressionism Transformed: The Paintings of Edmund C. Tarbell,* exh. cat. (Manchester, N.H.: Currier Art Gallery, 2001), pp. 102–3.
18. For the history of Murphy's framemaking enterprise, see Jill Lundin, "Historical Note," in Jill Lundin, "A Finding Aid to the Carrig-Rohane Shop Records, 1903–1962, in the Archives of American Art," 1994, http://artarchives.si.edu/findaids/carrrohs/carrrohs.htm, and the Carrig-Rohane Shop Records, 1903–1962, Archives of American Art, Smithsonian Institution, reels 4974–82. See also Suzanne Smeaton, "On the Edge of Change: Artist-Designed Frames from Whistler to Marin," in *Gilded Edge,* pp. 64, 69, and Eli Wilner and Mervyn Kaufman, *Antique American Frames: Identification and Price Guide* (New York: Avon Books, 1995), pp. 124–26. Vose Galleries, Boston, acquired Carrig-Rohane in 1915 and operated it until 1939.
19. The firm's name was recorded inconsistently over the years. Early frames seem to have been inscribed Carrig Rohane, without a hyphen, like the name of Murphy's home; later ones were marked Carrig-Rohane. Since the hyphenated form appears on the firm's account books, now at the Archives of American Art, I have used it in this essay.
20. Smeaton, "On the Edge of Change," p. 64.
21. Photographs of pattern number 2, dated 1903, appear in Carrig-Rohane Shop Records, 1903–1962, reel 4974, frames 3, 5, 105. A reference to "Tarbell cuts" appears on Hassam's order no. 816, ibid., frame 951. I am grateful to Jeremy Adamson of the Library of Congress for identifying the Tarbell corner as the distinctive grillwork that Hassam used so frequently.
22. The dimensions of *The Breakfast Room,* a horizontal canvas, match those of the frame specified in order no. 16 in the Carrig-Rohane Shop Records, 1903–1962, reel 4974, frame 824. The Worcester frame is inscribed *19*Ⓜ*04 / Carrig Rohane* but lacks the inventory number that would make absolute identification possible. The numerous empty screw holes on the back of the frame indicate that Hassam had used it on other canvases, including vertical ones. I am grateful to Rita Albertson, Paintings Conservator, Worcester Art Museum, for inspecting the frame and sharing her discoveries.
23. Hassam told Wood that the frames, intended for paintings entitled *Souvenir of Shoshone* and *Magnolias,* "are really works of art." Childe Hassam, [New York], November 23, 1904, to C. E. S. Wood, [Portland, Oreg.], Wood Papers (Berkeley). For more on Wood, see H. Barbara Weinberg, "Hassam's Travels, 1892–1914," in this publication, pp. 186, 188–89, 199–200, nn. 38–49.
24. Wood's instructions to Hassam are quoted in Young 1960, p. 222. His advice to Weir is quoted in ibid., p. 221. This source provides extensive information on Wood.
25. The frame of *On the Snake River* is inscribed with the name Carrig-Rohane and the number 307, corresponding to Hassam's order for a frame in pattern 24; Carrig-Rohane Shop Records, 1903–1962, reel 4974, frame 868. Hassam ordered the frame in 1906, just before Judge Charles Carey of Portland purchased his painting and the related one by Wood. The two pictures descended in the Carey family until the Portland Art Museum purchased them in 2002. The frame on Wood's landscape is inscribed with the Carrig-Rohane name and the year of its manufacture, but no inventory number appears. I am grateful to Margaret Bullock, Associate Curator of American Art, Portland Art Museum, for information on the paintings' provenance. For more on Carey, see Weinberg, "Hassam's Travels, 1892–1914," in this publication, pp. 188–89, 200, n. 42.
26. Carrig-Rohane Shop Records, 1903–1962, reel 4974, frame 824. This order is dated December 21, 1904.
27. See, for example, Carrig-Rohane order nos. 309, 313, 399–401, 910, 928, 929; Carrig-Rohane Shop Records, 1903–1962, reel 4974, frames 868–69, 879, and reel 4975, frames 965, 968.
28. Ibid., reel 4974, frame 869.
29. *Isles of Shoals,* 1899 (Minneapolis Institute of Arts), is framed in a copy of pattern 33. The back of this frame lacks the Carrig-Rohane inscription; I am grateful to Sue Canterbury, Assistant Curator, Minneapolis Institute of Arts, for examining the frame.
30. The frames on *Golden Afternoon* and *The New York Window* are, respectively, order nos. 799 and 800 in the Carrig-Rohane Shop Records, 1903–1962, reel 4974, frame 948.
31. For a reproduction of Whistler's painting in its frame and a discussion of the work, see Merrill, *Peacock Room,* pp. 53–55.
32. Elizabeth F. Duley, Registrar, Freer Gallery of Art, Washington, D.C., kindly provided a copy of the receipt and other information about the frame. Acting as Hassam's agent, Wood had tried unsuccessfully to find a purchaser for the unframed painting as early as June 1906. When the picture did not sell in Portland, Wood shipped it back to Hassam. See letters dated June 7, 1906, September 7, 1906, and September 20, 1907, from Childe Hassam, [New York], to C. E. S. Wood, [Portland, Oreg.], Wood Papers (Berkeley).
33. Hassam's last documented order from Carrig-Rohane is dated January 18, 1912, Carrig-Rohane Shop Records, 1903–1962, reel 4974, frame 972. Although others commissioned frames from Carrig-Rohane for his works, Hassam himself seems not to have used the Boston firm after that date.

The following paintings by Hassam that are not discussed in this essay are in frames he ordered from Carrig-Rohane and have been located in museums (the order number cited in each entry is from the Carrig-Rohane Shop Records, 1903–1962, reel 4974): *Isles of Shoals,* 1906 (Florence Griswold Museum, Old Lyme, Connecticut), order no. 399 (frame 879): *Afternoon Sky, Harney Desert,* 1908 (Portland Art Museum), order no. 620 (frame 920); *Mount Hood,* 1908 (Portland Art Museum), order no. 761 (frame 938); and *Cathedral at Ronda* (fig. 209), order no. 821 (frame 952).

34. Childe Hassam, New York, November 6 and 11 (no year given), to William Macbeth, New York, Macbeth Gallery Papers, Archives of American Art, Smithsonian Institution, reel NMc7, frames 379–80.
35. The label reads: *ZIMMERMAN & MOSSMANN, / [-]uccessors to WM. SCHILL / [-]TIC PICTURE FRAMES, / [-] FRAMES RE-GILT, ETC. / [-]0 WEST 18TH ST. / [-]70 Chelsea NEW YORK.* Another frame maker he patronized was William Schill, who produced the frame for *Cat Boats, Newport* (see n. 10, above).
36. Information from the New York City directories, courtesy of Suzanne Smeaton. See also Alexander W. Katlan, *American Artists' Materials,* vol. 1, *Suppliers Directory. Nineteenth Century: New York,* 1810–1899*; Boston, 1823–1887* (Park Ridge, N.J.: Noyes Press, 1987), p. 180.
37. Two labels on the back of the frame on *Dawn* read: *Albert Milch / Manufacturer / High Grade / Picture Frames / 101 West 57 Street / New York City.* I am grateful to Kathleen Kienholz for examining the back of this frame. The frames on *South Window,* 1916 (American Academy of Arts and Letters, New York), and *April (The Green Gown),* 1920 (fig. 295), also resemble the one on *Dawn,* but they retain no framer's labels. Both of these paintings, like *Tanagra* and *Dawn,* depict the female figure.
38. Suzanne Smeaton kindly verified this observation.
39. See, for example, Milch Gallery Records, 1911–1980, reel 4437, frames 1456, 1466, 1493, 1498, 1551, 1578; reel 4438, frame 523.
40. Ibid., reel 4437, frame 1551.
41. Childe Hassam, East Hampton, October 13, 1920, to E. and A. Milch Co., New York, Milch Gallery Records, 1911–1980, reel 4420, frame 325. A sketch in the letter shows a horizontal cassetta frame with two Hs on each horizontal side and one H on each vertical side.
42. Childe Hassam, East Hampton, August 3, 1925, to [illegible], Milch Gallery Records, 1911–1980, reel 4420, frame 299.
43. Boswell, "When Frame Fits Picture," p. 38.
44. In the directories, Isaac Polatinsky is identified as the firm's president, Benjamin Diamond as secretary-treasurer, and D. Mott as vice-president.
45. Paper labels with the earlier, Sixth Avenue, address have been found on two initialed frames at the American Academy of Arts and Letters: *The Far Horizon* (fig. 342) and *Over the Great Divide,* 1908. The initialed frame on another painting at the American Academy of Arts and Letters, *Moonrise at Sunset, Harney Desert,* 1908, has a paper label with the Fifty-fourth Street address. Many other H frames on paintings at the Academy bear no frame maker's label. An empty frame at The Metropolitan Museum of Art (F1990.46) is stamped with Royal Art's Fifty-fourth Street address.
46. Lockman interview, February 2, 1927, p. 17.
47. Hassam ordered Whistler frames on February 18, May 14, July 16, and October 12, 1918; February 3, March 29, May 8, and December 20, 1919; and January 27 and February 25, 1920. Milch Gallery Records, 1911–1980, reel 4436, frames 823, 1265, 1480, and 1674; reel 4437, frames 456, 797, and 1008; and reel 4438, frames 54, 208, and 313. A label on the reverse of *Back of the Fishkill Mountains* reads: *Albert Milch / Manufacturer / High Grade / Picture Frames / 101 West 57 Street / New York City.*
48. Hobbs, "Note on Frames," p. 83.
49. Fort 1988, pp. 112–13. See also H. Barbara Weinberg, "Hassam in New York, 1897–1919," in this publication, pp. 225–26.
50. According to the 1930 census, Kirchner, then fifty-two, had been born in Russia, spoke Yiddish as his native language, came to the United States in 1902, was a naturalized citizen, and was employed as a furniture carver. His address was given as 14 Clara Street. In the Brooklyn city directory for 1933–34, he was listed at 304 Park Avenue. This information was provided by Paula Baxter of the New York Public Library to Martin Kotler, Frame Conservator, Smithsonian American Art Museum, Washington, D.C. I am indebted to them both. An article in the *New York Times* lists Kirchner as the carver of an altar in the Chapel of Saint Cornelius the Centurion on Governors Island in New York City; "Bishop Blesses Altar at Governors Island," *New York Times,* November 20, 1931. Martin Kotler kindly sent me a copy of that article.
51. The other Kirchner frames on Gellatly paintings at the Smithsonian American Art Museum surround *In the Stable,* before 1911, *Jonah,* ca. 1885, and *Pastoral Study,* before 1904, by Albert Pinkham Ryder; *Cornish Headlands,* 1898, by Abbott Handerson Thayer; *The Brook, Greenwich, Connecticut,* ca. 1890–1900, by John H. Twachtman; and *The Magic Mirror,* attributed to Giovanni Battista Piazzetta (Italian, 1682–1754). Kirchner's address is given as 305 Pennsylvania Avenue, Brooklyn, N.Y., in a card file kept by Gellatly's curator, Ralph Seymour. I am grateful to Richard Murray at the Smithsonian American Art Museum for providing this information and also thank Eleanor Harvey for her help on this subject.
52. Hassam also showed *Greek Altar to Autumn*—under that title—in his retrospective exhibition at Buffalo Fine Arts Academy, Albright Art Gallery, Buffalo, in March 1929 (it was number 65). For a discussion of Hassam's allegorical late works, see Kimberly Orcutt, "'The subject that I am known for': Hassam's Pursuit of a Legacy," in this publication.
53. Lockman interview, February 3, 1927, p. 7.
54. Leon Battista Alberti codified that belief in 1435. See Shirley Neilsen Blum, "The Open Window: A Renaissance View," in *The Window in Twentieth-Century Art,* edited by Suzanne Delehanty, exh. cat. (Purchase, N.Y.: Neuberger Museum, 1986), p. 9.
55. For Hassam's aversion to modernism, see H. Barbara Weinberg, "Introduction," in this publication, pp. 18–19; Hiesinger 1994, p. 153; and Jay E. Cantor, "Hassam's Twentieth-Century Work," in Adelson, Cantor, and Gerdts 1999, pp. 99–103.
56. For another discussion of *Colonial Quilt* and *Long Island Pebbles and Fruit,* see H. Barbara Weinberg, "Hassam in East Hampton, 1898–1935," in this publication, pp. 240, 242–43.
57. For frames designed by these younger artists, see Smeaton, "On the Edge of Change," pp. 73, 81, and figs. on pp. 42, 76, 78, 79. For Hartley's framing choices, see Stephen Kornhauser and Ulrich Birkmaier, "Notes on Frames," in *Marsden Hartley,* edited by Elizabeth Mankin Kornhauser, exh. cat. (Hartford, Conn.: Wadsworth Atheneum Museum of Art; New Haven: Yale University Press, 2003), pp. 274–76.

"On the crest of the wave"
Hassam and the Marketing of His Art

Dana Pilson

Childe Hassam began his painting career with great anxiety as to whether his art would sell. Yet by about 1900, he had established a formidable reputation as a leader of American Impressionism through aggressive marketing of his pictures and his image. Dealers eagerly sought his works, and he was able to charge higher and higher prices. However, Hassam occasionally felt conflicted about the art market, considering himself underappreciated by the art world; at such times he mocked the dealers who flocked to his studio. Yet he persevered boldly, painting images he knew would appeal to collectors and carving out a comfortable niche for his work.

Unlike many of his contemporaries who taught in art schools on a regular basis, Hassam had only a short stint as an instructor at New York's Art Students League, from late December 1898 to May 1899.[1] And he claimed that he had "never taken any money for teaching."[2] While some of his colleagues relied on painting portraits or mural decorations for income, Hassam accepted only a few such commissions.[3] Except for these commissions and some early efforts as an illustrator, he depended upon sales of his works, and his letters reveal that throughout his career he was preoccupied with exhibiting and selling. Hassam's output was immense: he produced over two thousand oil paintings, pastels, watercolors, and drawings. He often proposed small shows of his work to museums and enlisted museum directors to help him attract patrons. Several dealers represented him simultaneously: in New York City they included William Macbeth, his son Robert W. Macbeth, and his nephew Robert G. McIntyre of Macbeth Gallery; Newman Emerson Montross of the Montross Gallery; Edward and Albert Milch of the Milch Galleries.

Frederick Childe Hassam received his first marketing advice in the 1880s from the poet Celia Laighton Thaxter. She persuaded him to create a more exotic, more marketable persona by dropping his first name in favor of his unusual middle name. About 1883, when he began signing his work "Childe Hassam,"[4] he placed a crescent before his signature. At first Hassam carefully drew the motif, but over the years he made it increasingly sketchy and ultimately reduced it to a quick slash. The artist called the crescent the "secret part" of his "true signature," and it became important when forgeries appeared.[5]

Although many of his contemporaries enhanced their reputations through exhibitions, Hassam surpassed them all in the number of his shows and the intensity of his marketing effort. Winslow Homer and John Singer Sargent were inveterate exhibitors, but their records seem thin when we compare their recently published exhibition chronologies to the one devoted to Hassam in this volume.[6]

When Hassam was in his early twenties, he contributed works to shows and sales, beginning with the Boston Art Club's February 1882 exhibition.[7] In December 1885, when Hassam participated in the first exhibition of the Boston Water-Color Society, he was noted by a critic to be the "chief contributor."[8] In March 1887, when Hassam was in Paris, the Boston gallery Noyes, Cobb and Company organized an auction of his oils and watercolors. Hassam's correspondence from Paris expresses his anxiety about the sale. To Boston writer William Howe Downes he wrote: "I . . . ask you to do what you could towards the success of my auction in February. I knew you would do it up as kindly as you always do but what I mean is if you and [Frank T.?] Robinson and Weeks can't lead the attention of the public by a few short notices 'au premier'. . . . I wouldn't bother you if it was an exhibition simply but you know an auction in Boston is a beastly venture ie. a matter of life and death. . . . I depend a good deal on the success of that sale."[9]

Hassam's anxiety was unwarranted. Although most works sold for under $100, the auction yielded almost $4,000.[10] Two examples did especially well: *Springtime in the City* sold for $245 and *Springtime in a City Park,* for $190.[11] A review in the *Boston Evening Transcript* noted: "Mr. Hassam, in the midst of so many good, bad and indifferent art currents, seems to be paddling his own canoe with a good deal of independence and method."[12] In 1888, a year after the auction, Hassam was described in Frank T. Robinson's *Living New England Artists* as "one of the best painters [of outdoor life] in the country."[13]

Hassam also began to show in New York City. In January 1883 *Corner of a Studio* was included in an exhibition of Boston artists at the American Art Galleries on Madison Square. In February the American Water Color Society included three of Hassam's watercolors in its annual display. At $65 to $70 each, his pictures were moderately priced, neither the least nor the most expensive.[14] Hassam sought higher prices for his early oils: *A City Fairyland* (fig. 3) was exhibited in December 1886 at New York's National Academy of Design and sold for $375, an impressive sum considering that J. Alden Weir's *After a Day's Rain,* dubbed "a good picture" by the *New York Times,* brought $450.[15] Prices for Hassam's watercolors increased thereafter: the 1887 American Water Color Society exhibition included *A Harvest Moonrise* at $350 and *In the Country* and *In the Town* at $300 each.[16]

After his return from Paris in late October 1889, Hassam, believing that Boston offered "a doubtful market," settled in New York.[17] The city had emerged as a major cultural capital and a hub of activity for ambitious young artists. However, the prospects of making a career as a painter anywhere in the country were difficult. As Hassam's colleague landscapist John J. Enneking stated: "Art has always had a hard time in America. 'No one buys an American picture,' the dealers say, and they're about right. We all have to teach or paint potboilers to make a living."[18] Hassam did not share Enneking's pessimism, and he continued optimistically to build his reputation through exhibitions.

In New York Hassam became enthralled by the modern urban environment. His city scenes of the 1890s gloss over the darker, seamier aspects of progress and focus on the fashionable squares and avenues. A writer in *Brush and Pencil* exclaimed in 1901 that Hassam was "indeed . . . one of the very few artists who have found beauty in the teeming busy streets of New York."[19] Hassam infused his cityscapes with a sense of optimism, gentility, and nostalgia. A growing number of collectors who preferred to have their world recorded in that manner began to notice them.

In January 1890 Hassam sold a watercolor to artist Samuel Colman on the opening night of the American Water Color Society exhibition. Hassam must have felt that the sale would benefit his reputation, as he later commented: "Of course, the painters are the ones who make the reputation of the artist, it is not the dealers, it is not the public."[20] The opening night was "the Social Art event of the year," according to Hassam. "They sold most of the pictures the first night. . . . It was the only time that American art was popular. . . . People came and bought."[21] By the spring of 1890 Hassam was fully immersed in the New York art world and a member of the most prestigious clubs and artists' societies. He was the first president of the New-York Water Color Club, founded to provide an alternative venue for young artists returning from Europe. He later explained: "Water colors were so low in price," and "It was a more democratic art, as water colors could be sold for much lower prices than the oild [*sic*] paintings."[22] Hassam's leadership abilities, astute marketing sense, and optimism enabled him to enter the New York art world with ease and panache.

In the 1890s Hassam contributed works to many of the major New York exhibitions. He also sought to broaden his market by sending paintings to large annual shows at the Pennsylvania Academy of the Fine Arts and the Art Institute of Chicago, as well as to exhibitions in Denver, Saint Louis, Cleveland, and Minneapolis. He participated in many group shows and was given one-man exhibitions in Saint Louis (1891) and Boston (1893, 1896). He received numerous medals and awards.[23] Hassam sent five watercolors and five oils, including several Salon pictures, to the 1893 World's Columbian Exposition in Chicago, and took home medals in oil painting and watercolor.

Hassam was always on the lookout for new venues as well as new patrons. In July 1894, for example, he visited Gloucester, Massachusetts; soon after he arrived, he asked his dealer, William Macbeth, to "please get a number of water colors and water color mats . . . box them as light as you can . . . I am in a hurry."[24] Hoping to attract vacationers, Hassam may have intended to display these pictures in the lobby of the Delphine Hotel in East Gloucester. He was probably inspired by Celia Thaxter, who understood the spending habits of wealthy people on holiday. A photograph from about 1890 shows at least three, and possibly more, works by Hassam on display in her Isles of Shoals hotel parlor, where pictures were available for purchase (figs. 117, 120).[25] No locale was too small or too remote to provoke Hassam's interest while he was building his reputation during the 1890s. For example, in February 1899 he contributed a work entitled *Summer* to the midwinter exhibition at the Haydon Art Club in Lincoln, Nebraska.

Hassam seems to have suffered something of a setback in February 1896, when his paintings found buyers but did not fare well at an American Art Galleries sale, his first important one-man show in New York. The auction of more than two hundred oils, watercolors, and pastels included many major pictures by Hassam: *Une Averse—rue Bonaparte* (fig. 54); *Twilight (Le Crépuscule)* (fig. 313); *Geraniums* (fig. 79); *The Rose Girl* (fig. 72); *Autumn* (fig. 74); and *The Manhattan Club (The Stewart Mansion)* (fig. 99). There was much advance publicity. The American Art Galleries ran a notice of the sale in the *New York Times* that featured quotations from other newspapers (fig. 351).[26] In the end, however, the publicity proved ineffectual, and the pictures failed to achieve high prices. The *Times* reported that "the majority of those present had come as spectators," and the sale was considered a "financial disaster" with proceeds totaling about $9,600, an average of just $47 per picture.[27] The highest price during the first night was $115 for *In the Garden in June.* As there were no bidders for *Une Averse—rue Bonaparte,* its sale was postponed until the second night.[28] A week later, portraitist J. Carroll Beckwith noted in his diary that the only pictures selling in New York were "modern French or eighteenth century English."[29] Possibly disillusioned by his lack of success, Hassam decided to spend time away from the city and traveled around the Northeast. During this, a period of economic slowdown, prospects for American artists did not improve; *Scribner's Magazine* described New York artists as a group of "discouraged limners and carvers."[30] In December 1896 Hassam departed for a year-long trip to Europe.

Hassam returned to New York in November 1897, renewed by his stay in Europe. He hoped to energize his own career and assist fellow American Impressionists Weir and John H. Twachtman, who had fared poorly at the Society of American Artists. Although they were members, their works were not selling well at the exhibitions. Hassam recalled that he "proposed the idea [of a breakaway group] to Weir. . . . 'The Ten' was my idea entirely."[31] The Ten American Painters insisted that they hoped to "create a sympathetic venue"[32] for their work and to preserve the "integrity of the movement in their devotion to the principles of beauty and taste."[33] Yet they were, ultimately, more interested in marketing and selling their paintings. As Ulrich W. Hiesinger has suggested, the Ten were "too much business and too little art."[34] Their works sold well, and they were, as Linda Skalet has noted, "fortunate in inaugurating their group shows at a time when the market in American painting was clearly on the rise and interest in contemporary American art was growing."[35] Hassam took a leading role throughout the Ten's lifespan and did not miss a single exhibition. In 1905 the Ten began an affiliation with New York's Montross Gallery; the director, Newman Emerson Montross, took a personal interest in Hassam and eventually owned eight of his pictures.[36]

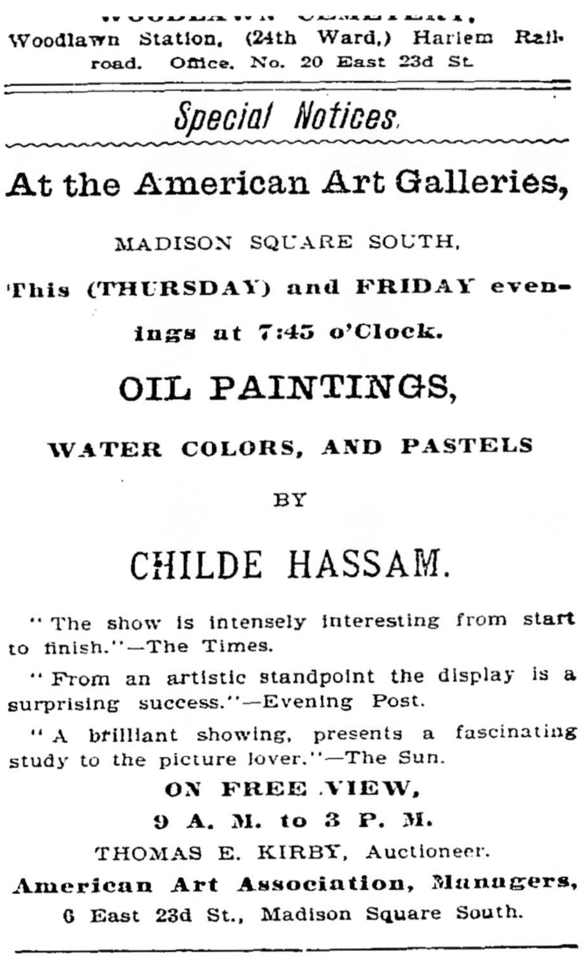
Woodlawn Station, (24th Ward,) Harlem Railroad. Office, No. 20 East 23d St.

Special Notices.

At the American Art Galleries,

MADISON SQUARE SOUTH.

This (THURSDAY) and FRIDAY evenings at 7:45 o'Clock.

OIL PAINTINGS,

WATER COLORS, AND PASTELS

BY

CHILDE HASSAM.

"The show is intensely interesting from start to finish."—The Times.

"From an artistic standpoint the display is a surprising success."—Evening Post.

"A brilliant showing, presents a fascinating study to the picture lover."—The Sun.

ON FREE VIEW,

9 A. M. to 3 P. M.

THOMAS E. KIRBY, Auctioneer.

American Art Association, Managers,

6 East 23d St., Madison Square South.

Fig. 351. "At the American Art Galleries, Madison Square South . . . ," *The New York Times,* February 6, 1896, p. 5

About the turn of the century Hassam saw the burgeoning of American museums' interest in his paintings. In 1899 the Cincinnati Art Museum made one of the earliest purchases of an American Impressionist work for a public collection when it bought his *Pont Royal* (fig. 330). And in 1900 the Carnegie Institute acquired his *Fifth Avenue in Winter* (fig. 87) for $800, according to Hassam, "a large price for a painting in those days."[37]

During this period Hassam, as usual, astutely gauged the market. Seeing that images of women in interiors by Frank W. Benson and Edmund C. Tarbell sold well from the Ten's exhibitions, Hassam began to paint them. Early in 1909 the Carnegie Institute purchased the first of the Window series, *Spring Morning* (fig. 10), and called attention to the acquisition in May 1910 with a special showing of Hassam's works. By 1910 many major American museums owned at least one Hassam. Other canvases from the Window series purchased by museums between 1910 and 1912 include *Against the Light (Contre-Jour),* 1910 (Art Institute of Chicago); *The Breakfast Room* (fig. 333); and *The New York Window* (fig. 227), which won a gold medal at the Corcoran's fourth biennial in 1912 and was purchased for the gallery.

When Hassam began his career, as now, dealers facilitated sales to museums and private collectors, printed catalogues, generated publicity, and promoted their artists through group and solo exhibitions. But few dealers engaged in selling and promoting American art existed until April 1892, when William Macbeth opened a gallery in New York City. Macbeth set up shop just north of Madison Square at 237 Fifth Avenue, near Twenty-seventh Street, and announced his intentions: "The work of American artists has never received the full share of appreciation it deserves, and the time has come when an effort should be made to gain for it the favor of those who have hitherto purchased foreign works exclusively."[38]

In the early twentieth century more dealers entered the American art market. In 1911, as prices for American paintings continued to rise, brothers Edward and Albert Milch opened the Milch Galleries at 939 Madison Avenue. Both Macbeth and the Milches recognized that a market for American Impressionism existed and profited from it. Hassam benefited from his affiliation with Macbeth, the Milches, and also Newman Emerson Montross, who began selling in 1885 and became well-known for handling American art after 1889. The Montross Gallery presented exhibitions by the Ten, as well as large one-man shows of Hassam's pictures in 1905, 1909, 1911, 1914, 1915, and 1917.

Hassam took a great interest in the purchasers of his works. Many letters preserved in the Macbeth Gallery Papers indicate his wish to cultivate relationships with them. For instance, in April 1907 Hassam wrote to William Macbeth: "We can all work together and I am very pleased indeed that you have sold a picture to Dr. Humphrey [probably Alexander Humphreys] whom I have never met. If at anytime there is anything of mine that you want I am sure that we can arrange to send it to your gallery."[39]

When most wealthy collectors were concentrating on European art, several patrons of American painting were acquiring works through dealers and seeking out artists in their New York studios. Harrison S. Morris, secretary and managing director of the Pennsylvania Academy of the Fine Arts, cited William T. Evans, George A. Hearn, Thomas B. Clarke, Dr. Alexander Humphreys, and John Gellatly as men who had "courage enough to choose the best then produced [in America] and buy it."[40]

Evans was introduced to American art in 1879, when his wife gave him George William Sheldon's book *American Painters,* which included engravings by Winslow Homer, William Merritt Chase, and George Inness.[41] In 1890 Evans sold his European paintings and focused first on American Tonalism. Eventually, he began acquiring American Impressionist works. He encouraged other wealthy collectors to patronize American artists and cultivated close relationships with Twachtman, Theodore Robinson, Robert Reid, and Hassam. Evans purchased paintings directly from Hassam, including *Leda and the Swan,* 1902; *At the Piano,* 1908; *Spring, Navesink Highlands* (fig. 352); *October Haze, Manhattan,* 1910; and *The Butterfly* (fig. 323). Through dealers and other sources he acquired a pastel, *Summer at Cos Cob* (fig. 155), in 1902; *Isles of Shoals* (Minneapolis Institute of Arts) by 1908; and *The Victorian Chair* (fig. 172) by 1911.[42] Between 1907 and 1915 Evans donated 150 paintings, including Hassam's *Spring, Navesink Highlands* and *The Victorian Chair,* to the National Gallery of Art, Washington, D.C. (now the Smithsonian American Art Museum, Washington, D.C.). He sold five paintings by Hassam at auction in 1913; *At the Piano* brought the highest price, $2,050.[43]

Thomas Benedict Clarke, according to Hassam, "did so much to stimulate American art,"[44] building a notable collection of American paintings that included pictures by Hassam, Chase, Reid, and Twachtman. Hassam recalled: "When I was practically a boy I sent some pictures to an open exhibition of American painters in New York, . . . and very much to my surprise they were sold. Of course, the price was very low. Thomas B. Clarke bought two: One was a little nocturne and the other *Night on Columbus Avenue.*"[45]

Clarke purchased *Rainy Day* by March 1887 and sold it in the 1899 dispersal of his collection.[46] This enormous sale, which included works by Chase, Inness, and Homer, set record prices for contemporary American paintings. It was, as Skalet has observed, "a manifestation of a dramatic upswing in the market for American painting."[47] Contemporary critic Charles de Kay, writing in the *New York Times Magazine,* seized the opportunity to promote American art: "American paintings are as much a part of our National birthright as our patriotic songs and our literature. They are an expression of American feeling and thought—varied, superficial, deep, naïve, or complex. The public ought to realize that an art like that of our painters, which has struggled to the front against the peculiar obstacles of European rivalry, is worthy of the most searching study and of encouragement."[48] Clarke may have counted on a rising market for American paintings, which was perhaps linked to a surge of patriotism during the Spanish-American War. H. Barbara Weinberg has suggested that Clarke might have been speculating, building a collection and publicizing, exhibiting, and boosting it in order to sell it for high prices at the right time; this hypothesis is supported by the fact that Clarke did not resume collecting works by living artists after the 1899 sale.[49]

John Gellatly, one of the most enthusiastic supporters of American Impressionism, amassed sizable holdings of paintings by Hassam and, in 1929, donated many of them to the National Gallery of Art, Washington, D.C. (now the Smithsonian American Art Museum, Washington, D.C.). Gellatly's oils included early and late works from the Isles of Shoals: *In the Garden (Celia Thaxter in Her Garden)* (fig. 130); *The South Ledges, Appledore* (fig. 146); an ideal subject, *Pomona,* 1900; and interiors, *Marechal Niel Roses,* 1919; *Tanagra (The Builders, New York)* (fig. 311); and *Improvisation* (fig. 312), all of which are now at the Smithsonian. Gellatly also owned a work from Hassam's 1897 trip to Italy, *Ponte Santa Trinità* (fig. 353), which the artist considered "among the finest things I did."[50]

The Detroit industrialist Charles Lang Freer purchased *The Chinese Merchants* (fig. 337) through N. E. Montross in 1910. Donelson Hoopes has speculated that this painting may have been Hassam's "calculated gesture" toward attracting Freer's patronage.[51] Freer had assembled a collection of works by James McNeill Whistler and was attracted to American paintings that had a Whistlerian look. Thus in *The Chinese Merchants* Hassam may have incorporated Whistler's design

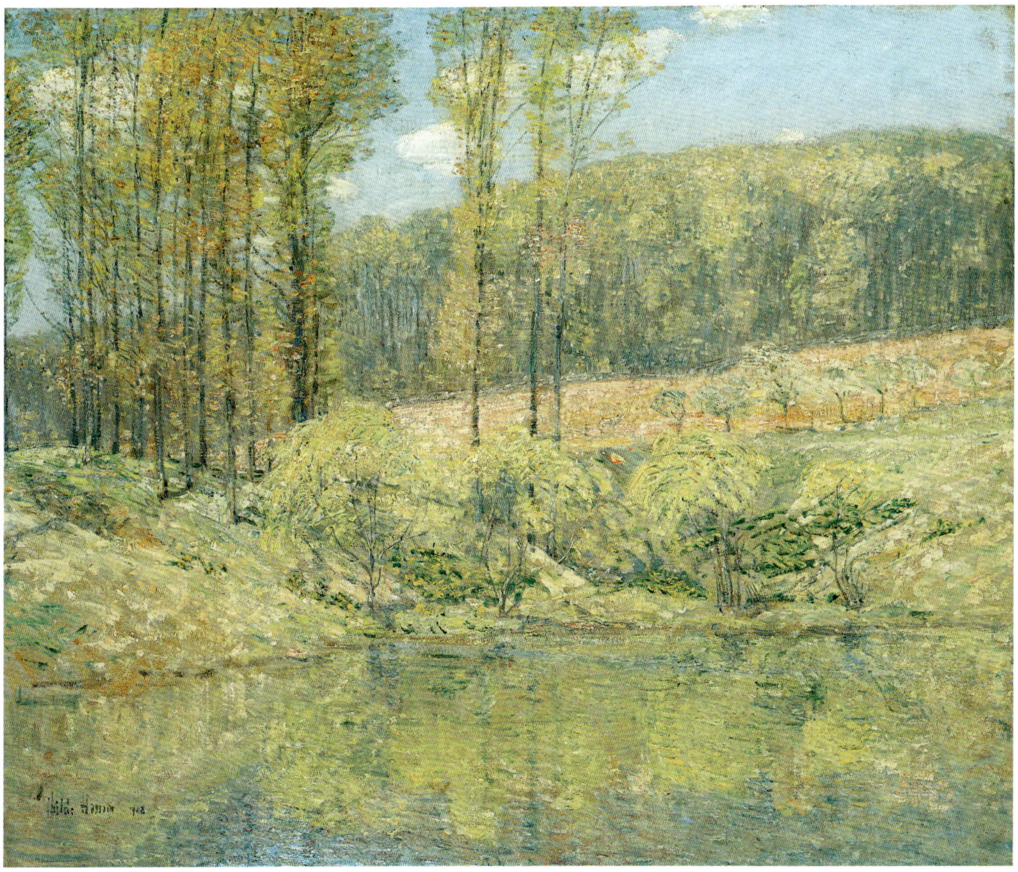

Fig. 352. Childe Hassam. *Spring, Navesink Highlands,* 1908. Oil on canvas, 25 x 30⅛ in. (63.6 x 76.6 cm). Smithsonian American Art Museum, Washington, D.C. Gift of William T. Evans

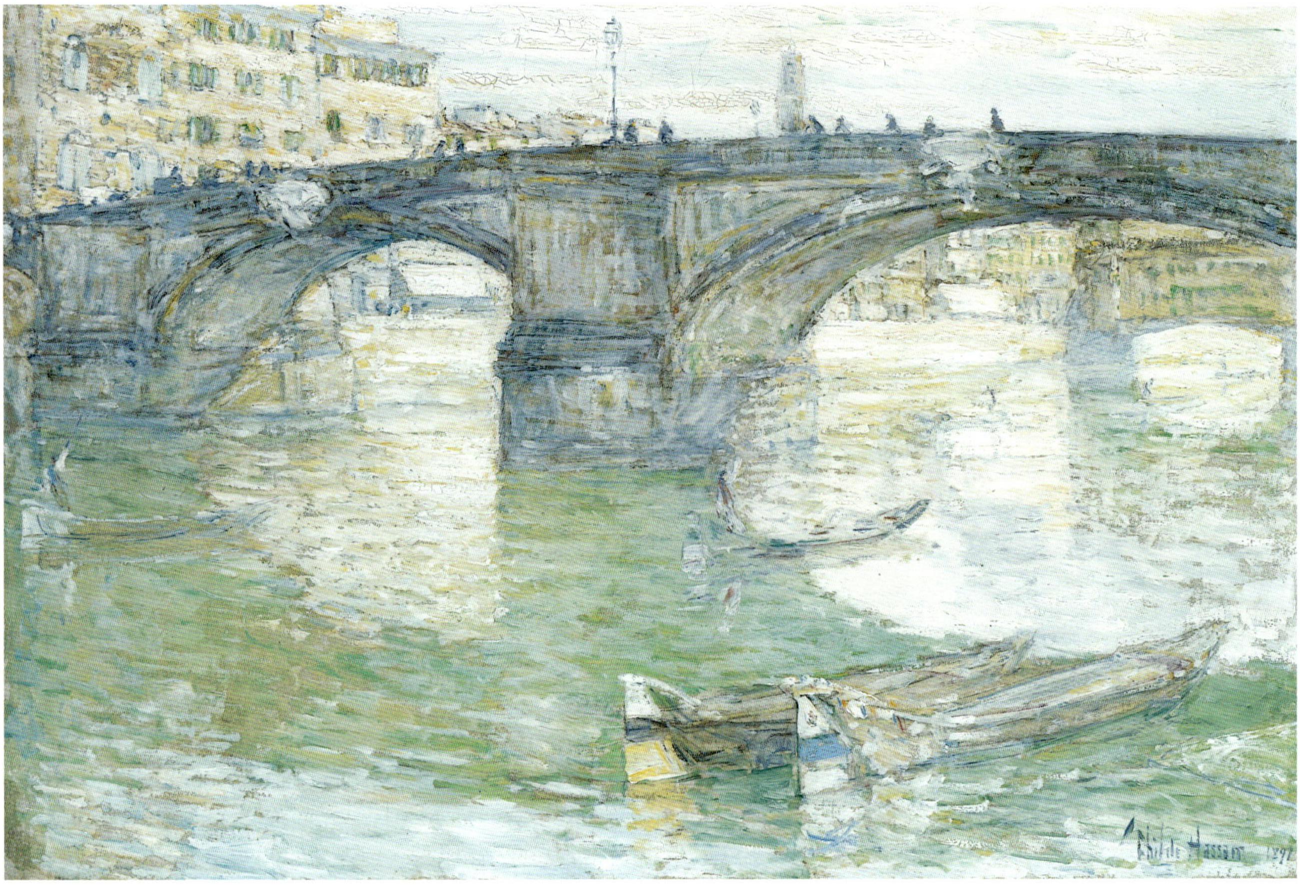

Fig. 353. Childe Hassam. *Ponte Santa Trinità,* 1897. Oil on canvas, 22½ x 33⅝ in. (57 x 85.3 cm). Smithsonian American Art Museum, Washington, D.C. Gift of John Gellatly

principles to make his picture appealing to Freer. As Freer had given his collection to the nation in 1906, Hassam was probably eager to be represented in Washington. The artist regretted that Freer had become interested in his works too late in life: "It is interesting to know that at the time of his last illness, he said, 'as soon as I get out [of the hospital] I am going to add to my Hassam's' [*sic*] and he never got out."[52]

Other collectors of Hassam's works included Gertrude Cowdin, who owned *A Winter Day*; George A. Hearn, who championed American art and who purchased *Coast Scene, Isles of Shoals* (fig. 22) in 1908 and gave it to The Metropolitan Museum of Art; Mrs. William Bliss; Desmond Fitzgerald, an ardent collector of French Impressionism; industrialist Henry Clay Frick; and philanthropist Dorothy Whitney.[53] Architect Stanford White's collection, auctioned in 1907 following his death, included three paintings by Hassam: a *Bois de Boulogne* that may be the picture of that title now in the

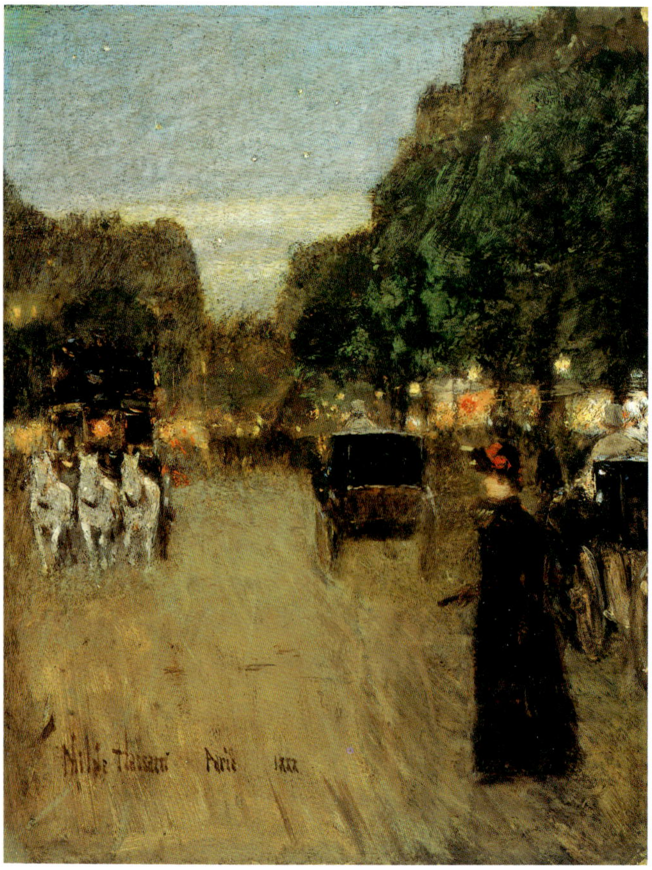

Fig. 354. Childe Hassam. *The Bois de Boulogne,* 1888. Oil on canvas, 12 x 9⅜ in. (30.6 x 23.8 cm). Mead Art Museum, Amherst College, Massachusetts AC 1953.10

Mead Art Museum, Amherst College (fig. 354), *Moonlight*, and *The Bathers*.[54]

Nine Hassams were included in a sale of one hundred pictures owned by H. Wood Sullivan, who was described in his obituary in 1903 as "a steadfast patron of . . . younger artists, notably J. Francis Murphy and Childe Hassam."[55] One painting, *Isles of Shoals*, prompted a comment in the *New York Times* that "at a proper distance—and the distance that is proper is a long one—the bit of rock and stretch of sunlit sea in 'Isles of Shoals' stand out in brilliant colors that might well embellish the dark rooms of a city house."[56] Another picture, *Spring Morning, Fifth Avenue and Fifty-sixth Street*, sold for $320 to A. Augustus Healy.[57] Healy sent it back to auction four years later, and Alexander Morten purchased it for $625.[58] Morten eventually owned twelve paintings by Hassam, and in the 1916 sale of his collection, *Spring Morning, Fifth Avenue and Fifty-sixth Street* brought $1,275.[59] That picture, which sold three times between 1903 and 1916, demonstrated the steady appreciation of Hassam's works.

Interest in Hassam extended to the West Coast. Charles Erskine Scott Wood, a Portland, Oregon, attorney and patron of American art, established a close and mutually beneficial friendship with the artist. Hassam installed murals in Wood's library and painted with him in eastern Oregon in late summer 1904; he made another visit to paint in Wood's company in autumn 1908. In May 1910 Wood bought four paintings from Hassam for $5,500: *Hollows in Spring*, *Moonlight—Isles of Shoals*, *Diamond Cove*, and *Oregon Valley*.[60] Hassam found a following in Portland: in 1900 Mr. I. N. Fleischman bought *Road in New England*, and in 1908 the Portland Art Association's first purchase was Hassam's *Afternoon Sky, Harney Desert* (fig. 355). In 1909 the association held a one-man show of Hassam's eastern Oregon canvases, and about this time Portland-area residents C. S. Adams, Judge Charles Carey, Elliott Corbett, Henry L. Corbett, Miss Henrietta E. Failing, and the Misses Flanders purchased his works.[61]

In a letter of May 1907 to Wood, Weir commented that "our mutual friend Hassam has been in the greatest of luck and merited success . . . [more] I think, than ever before and is really on the crest of the wave."[62] And in a November 1910 letter, Weir again wrote about their friend, noting: "He produces more canvases than any man I know, thirty or forty in a season seem nothing to him."[63]

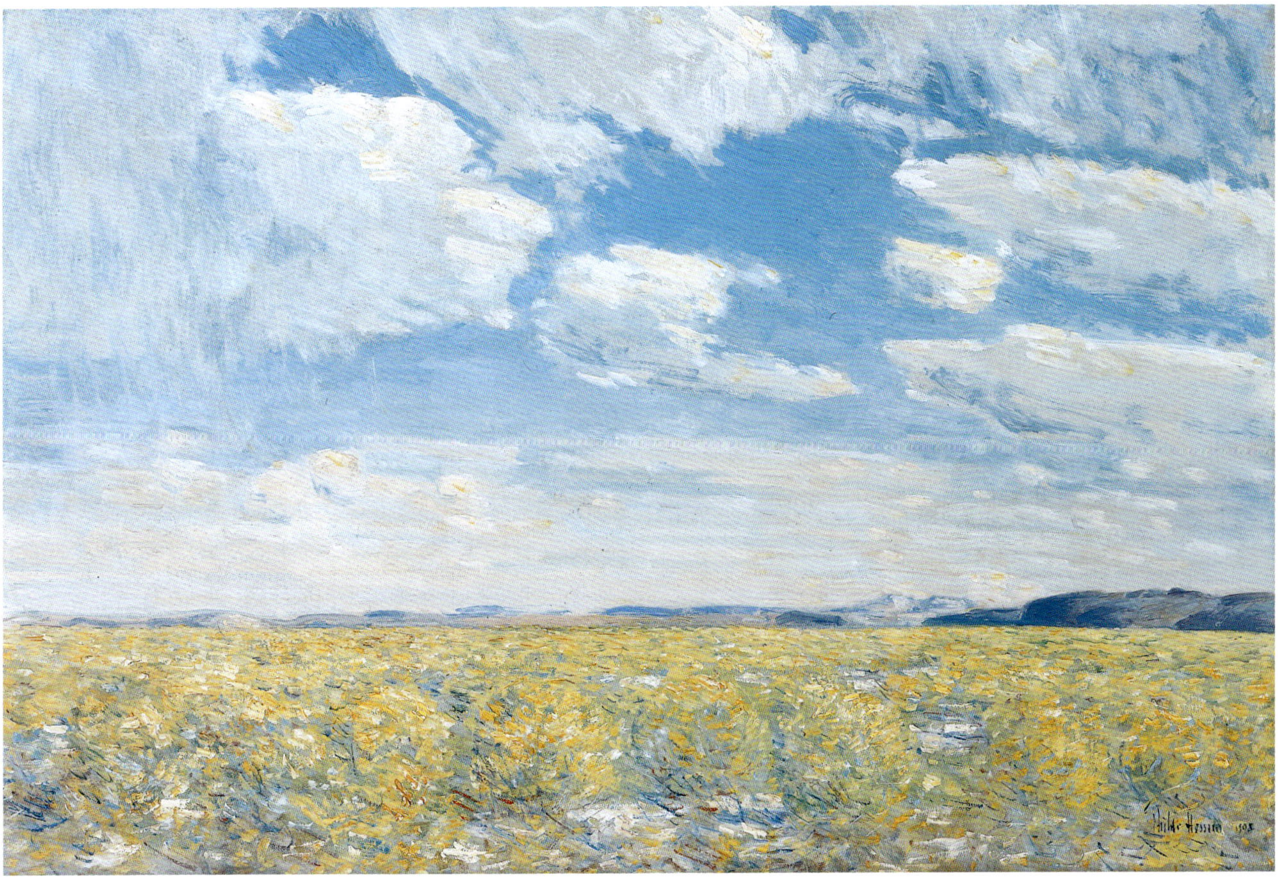

Fig. 355. Childe Hassam. *Afternoon Sky, Harney Desert*, 1908. Oil on canvas, 20⅛ x 30⅛ in. (51.1 x 76.5 cm). Portland Art Museum, Oregon. Gift of August Berg, Henrietta E. Failing, Winslow B. Ayer, William D. Wheelwright, I. N. Fleischner, estate of D. F. Thompson

About 1911 a writer in the *Mail and Express* lamented Hassam's overproduction: "Think of the appalling number of Hassam pictures there will be in the world by the time the man is seventy years old!"[64] Hassam may have flooded the market, but his canvases still sold briskly to collectors and museums, and he was always able to supply new paintings to exhibitions.[65] However, Jerome Myers has commented that while Hassam was " a brilliant but incessant painter," he suspected that the artist's huge, inevitably uneven, output, combined with high prices, stimulated the activity of forgers.[66] In March 1911 Hassam complained to William Macbeth: "When there are two canvases painted alike by the same painter it is of course true that of the two one is worth less (possibly worthless) than the other. Now of these two you have one and a Mrs. Edward H. Thomas of Fishkill Landing, N.Y. has the other. Since, as you know, they have done me the honor to forge my work (I had two destroyed only a week ago at the American Art Galleries) it is just as well to record this for me, unusual fact, for I do not ever make replicas of my pictures."[67]

Forgeries did in fact plague Hassam throughout his mature career. In 1923 an unidentified newspaper's headline, describing an incident that took place at the Macbeth Gallery, announced, "Childe Hassam Rips Name Off Fake Art, Painter Takes One Look at Pictre [*sic*] Here, Then Uses Knife on It."[68]

In 1912 American Impressionist Robert Vonnoh remarked: "American artists against much odds are making good and are rapidly coming to their own. . . . When ten years ago such men as Weir, Hassam, Crane, Alexander, Ranger, Tarbell, Benson, Metcalf, Chase . . . Dewing . . . Reid . . . Redfield and many others of note brought hundreds, now they bring thousands."[69] Indeed, by this time Hassam's prices had far surpassed the $1,000 mark. In April Hassam submitted three works to an exhibition of the Ten at the Rhode Island School of Design. Handwritten notes in a copy of the catalogue seem to indicate that dealers asked $1,200 for *Autumn Bouquet;* $6,500 for *Strawberry Tea Set,* 1912 (Los Angeles County Museum of Art); and $3,500 for *Summer Sea,* 1906 (Grand Rapids Art Museum).[70] In February–March 1913 Hassam exhibited twelve works at the *International Exhibition of Modern Art* in New York (the Armory Show). Two paintings, *Nude Woman with Mirror* and *The Spanish Stairs, Rome* (fig. 197), were offered for $6,000 each.[71]

By the second decade of the twentieth century, Hassam's reputation was firmly established in the United States. Through the efforts of his dealers, his paintings brought handsome sums and sold rapidly. Hassam and his dealers continued to work together to seek new venues and markets. In September 1913 Hassam requested that William Macbeth "ask Mr. Montross to deliver to you for the Los Angeles exhibition the picture of the nude with little silver poplars. I forget what title I have on it—the price is 3500. . . . I want very much to exhibit in that part of the country."[72] In September 1922 Robert Macbeth asked Hassam if he could take two paintings to Dallas for "an exhibition showing the historical development of American painting. . . . There is slight chance of sale but it will give me an important picture by an important man whom I am very anxious to include."[73]

The letters exchanged between Hassam and his dealers document a symbiotic, though sometimes tense, relationship and illustrate Hassam's confidence in the present and future value of his works. In October 1918 Hassam wrote to William Macbeth from Cos Cob: "The prices that you have on my canvases are the lowest that I will sell them for. I am as I said last winter willing to make my prices fit the times somewhat. . . . In fact some of the canvases that you have of mine I shall ask more for in the near future."[74]

Throughout his career, Hassam was not only consumed with marketing his paintings; he also cared deeply about his image. In 1918 he asked Robert Macbeth to include in an exhibition a self portrait (possibly *Self-Portrait* [fig. 356]), which he felt showed him in a patriotic, and thus positive, manner. As Hassam described it, joking about imaginary Arabian ancestry:

> *[The self-portrait] portrays me in a sport shirt instead of stripped to the waist as Henry Poore painted me at Old Lyme a few years ago. My face is red, my shirt is white and my hair is blue! My bandanna tie . . . displays all the colors of the allied flags. I have always stood for these colors. As you know I am decended [*sic*] from that pure Arabian stock that landed in Dorchester in 1631. My mothers name was Hathorn of the same decent [*sic*] as the great Arabian romancer who went back to the early spelling of the name Hawthorne. My male ancestor back in those early days was John Horsham, a real Arabian name so you see I have good reason for being red white and blue.*[75]

Hassam's dealers were often able to make extremely expeditious sales. Robert Macbeth wrote in 1917 to Hassam in Portsmouth, New Hampshire: "I hope you were pleased with the sale of the 'South West Wind' You can't accuse us of having it on our hands very long."[76] In 1919 the Milch Galleries sold out an entire show of Hassam's paintings held from November 7 to December 6.[77] Other times, however, works lingered. In 1914 Robert Macbeth wrote to Hassam: "I think it well to return to you the 'Fisherman's Cottage' and 'The Window Curtain' from our last exhibition, as well as 'The Music Room' and nine water colors most of which have just come back from the Boston exhibition. Needless to say I am sorry that these all have to go back to you unsold."[78] Apparently, Hassam's obsessive productivity had temporarily created a supply in excess of the demand.

After World War I prices for Hassam's most desirable paintings exceeded $10,000. In July 1919 he sent *The Alders* to an exhibition, asking $12,000 for it.[79] Hassam, however, did not always obtain the sums he sought. He hoped Milch Galleries would sell his entire Flag series for $100,000.[80] The group did not find a buyer, and Hassam expressed his frustration in a letter to the gallery: "Nobody has heard of New York subscribing anything for the Fine Arts—unless it was for some God damned foreign mediocrity for some God damned third rate American native painters—they will probably be sold in the West some where—and the enthusiastic New Yorkers will have to pay railroad fare—to go and see them!"[81]

Hassam purchased a house in East Hampton, Long Island, in August 1919 but continued to spend time in New York City. He actively exhibited his East Hampton paintings, and these popular works added cachet to his reputation and marketability. In 1935, looking back on Hassam's career, the *New York Times* reported that "in 1920 he said the revenue from his brush that year was $100,000."[82] (This would be roughly the equivalent of earning $896,000 in 2002.)[83] Indeed, Hassam's prices were high for the time. Landscapes averaged $2,500 to $3,500, and larger figure pictures $6,500 or more.[84]

In December 1928 the Milch Galleries held an "exhibition of Hassam's early and recent work." Handwritten notes on a copy of the catalogue may indicate the prices: *The Island Garden* and a self-portrait were offered for $12,000 each; *Against the Light, Out-of-Door Portrait, The Room of Flowers* (fig. 118), and *Venetian Brocade* for $18,000 each; and *June* (fig. 321) for $75,000. These were sizable sums in 1928.[85]

Throughout the 1920s Hassam's paintings continued to appeal to some of the country's most important collectors, including Duncan Phillips, who stated: "I do not collect American paintings just because they are American, but because they are good and often great."[86] In 1921 Phillips purchased *Washington Arch, Spring* (fig. 97) from the Macbeth Gallery and *The Sonata* (fig. 122) through the Milch Galleries. Hassam had written to the Milch Galleries that he was "always willing to oblige and aid in [Phillips's] efforts to make a good collection of pictures."[87] But later he asserted in an interview that Phillips "does not know anything. He is as ignorant in the arts as he can be. He has the money to buy pictures without the mind to appreciate them."[88] And in April 1928 Hassam wrote an article in *Art News* that was highly critical of certain wealthy patrons, especially Phillips.[89] In December 1928 Phillips reluctantly put *The Sonata* up for sale through Mrs. Gerald Thayer in New York, hoping to get $10,000 but willing to accept $7,500. He claimed that the painting was "not a discard," but that he was forced to sell some of his finest things "because of their very saleability and

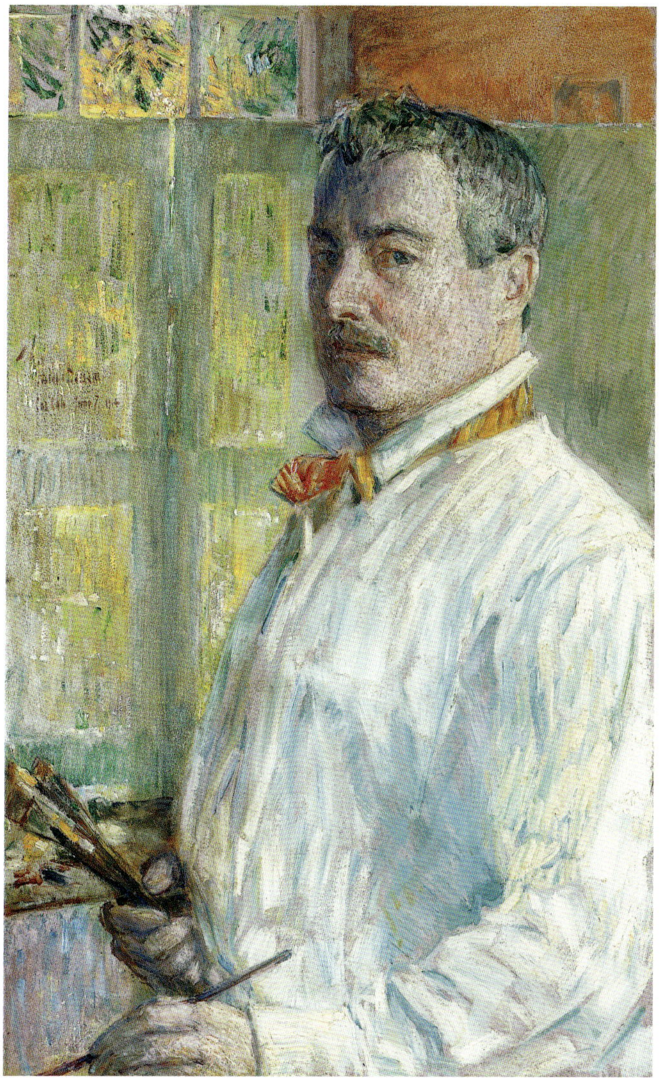

Fig. 356. Childe Hassam. *Self-Portrait,* 1914. Oil on canvas, 32⅞ x 20¾ in. (83.4 x 52.7 cm). American Academy of Arts and Letters, New York

celebrity."[90] Perhaps Hassam's venomous attack made it easier for Phillips to part with *The Sonata.*

Many scholars feel that Hassam was in an artistic decline after World War I. Yet his current as well as his early works were bringing high prices, and dealers were constantly at his doorstep. In 1926 Hassam complained to Royal Cortissoz about their avidity: "I'm away for six months and they get after me as soon as I get back to town and annoy the life out of me for small drawings, water colors, small and less expensive paintings. They might have done all this when I was younger. I'm showing some of the larger and more expensive paintings at Durand-Ruel on January 14th. . . . I use the word 'expensive' advisedly for they all seem to want to make money. . . . Americans are now worth something!"[91]

In 1940, five years after the artist's death, Jerome Myers provided a fitting assessment of Hassam's success:

Childe Hassam . . . commanded the art dealers, issuing his orders of the day, supervising the galleries, a general whose word was law to 57th Street. He was an artist to salute for his excellent record, in full possession of his power of production and—what is a major point—with a keen knowledge of distribution, the tactical ability to place his work. . . . Childe Hassam seems to me to represent an aristocracy of American art that has passed away, one might say our Golden Period—for reputations, high remuneration and consistent evaluations. It was the day when American collectors were proud of their compatriots' work, when auction sales were competitive struggles for the ownership of American celebrities. These great auctions had all the keen interest of a horse race. How many thousands would this bring? . . . What was the last price? . . . The applause when the bidding shot up higher and higher.[92]

Many titles mentioned in this essay are taken from exhibition records, letters between Hassam and his dealers, and Hassam's recollections as recorded in interviews with Lockman. The author has made every effort to link these titles with located works, for which the current title, date, and collection are indicated.

1. According to the archivist at the Art Students League of New York, Hassam was most likely a midyear substitute for Frank Duveneck. His tenure began sometime at the end of December 1898 and was probably intended to be temporary. In April 1899 the League's Board of Control noted that Hassam would continue as Duveneck's replacement for the rest of the season.
2. Lockman interview, February 3, 1927, p. 15.
3. For example, in 1918, when Hassam was in Gloucester, Harry W. Jones of Independence, Oklahoma, asked him to paint portraits of his two daughters. Hassam told him that he "was doing other things" and was not painting portraits, but Jones insisted. Hassam later told Lockman: "I finished the portraits and [Mr. Jones] said 'I have never spent any money that I enjoyed spending so much and to have these two little childrens' portraits.[']He paid me $1500 each for them." Ibid., pp. 16–17. For Hassam's murals, see H. Barbara Weinberg, "Hassam's Travels, 1892–1914," in this publication, pp. 186, 188–89, 196.
4. Hiesinger 1994, p. 17. See also, Stephanie L. Herdrich, "Hassam in Boston, 1859–1886," in this publication, p. 49, n. 25.
5. Childe Hassam, 1927, to Robert Macbeth, Macbeth Gallery Papers, Archives of American Art, Smithsonian Institution, reel NMc51, frame 933.
6. See Nicolai Cikovsky Jr. and Franklin Kelly, *Winslow Homer,* exh. cat. (Washington, D.C.: National Gallery of Art; New Haven: Yale University Press, 1995), pp. 407–13, and Stephanie L. Herdrich and H. Barbara Weinberg, *American Drawings and Watercolors in The Metropolitan Museum of Art: John Singer Sargent,* exh. cat. (New York: The Metropolitan Museum of Art, 2000), pp. 377–93.
7. See Janice H. Chadbourne, Karl Gabosh, and Charles O. Vogel, eds., *The Boston Art Club: Exhibition Record, 1873–1909* (Madison, Conn.: Sound View Press, 1991), p. 206.
8. "Art Notes," *New York Times,* December 13, 1885, p. 4.
9. Childe Hassam, 11, boulevard de Clichy, Paris, January 11, 1887, to William Howe Downes, Downes Papers, MSS L337, transcribed in Hiesinger 1994, p. 177.
10. Handwritten note in an annotated copy of *Exhibition and Sale of Works in Oil and Water Color by Childe Hassam,* exh. cat. (Boston: Noyes, Cobb and Company, March 9–10, 1887), American Art Auction Catalogs, 1785–1942, Archives of American Art, Smithsonian Institution, reel D140, frames 1078–88.
11. Ibid., frames 1086, 1088.
12. "Fine Arts. Exhibition of Mr. Hassam's Paintings at Noyes, Cobb & Co.'s Gallery," undated clipping, labeled "*Boston Transcript,*" Hassam Papers, reel NAA1, frame 509.
13. Frank T. Robinson, *Living New England Artists: Biographical Sketches* (Boston: Samuel E. Cassino, 1888), p. 103.
14. Hassam's *Spring-time* and *Nantucket Architecture* were both priced at $65 and *Cider Apples* at $70. *Sixteenth Annual Exhibition, Including the Exhibition of the New York Etching Club,* exh. cat. (New York: American Water Color Society, 1883), nos. 69, 79, 566, Macbeth Gallery Papers, reel NMc16, frames 1278, 1308, 1319.
15. "Autumn Academy Prices, Buyers Governed Little by Artistic Taste: An Exhibition Wherein May be Found a Large Number of Paintings Open to Severe Criticism," *New York Times,* December 6, 1886, p. 5.
16. *American Water Color Society Illustrated Catalogue of Twentieth Annual Exhibition,* exh. cat. (New York, 1887), Macbeth Gallery Papers, reel NMc16, frames 1406, 1409.
17. Childe Hassam, 35, boulevard Rochechouart, Paris, June 13, 1888, to Celia Thaxter, Isles of Shoals, private collection, transcribed in Hiesinger 1994, p. 178.
18. Enneking quoted in Hamlin Garland, *Roadside Meetings* (New York: Macmillan and Company, 1930), p. 27, cited in Hiesinger 1994, p. 63.
19. "Childe Hassam, Impressionist," *Brush and Pencil* 8, no. 3 (June 1901), p. 147.

20. Lockman interview, February 2, 1927, p. 16.
21. Opening night was January 31, 1890. Ibid., January 31, 1927, p. 21.
22. Ibid., February 3, 1927, p. 5. The New York Water Color Club was founded to provide a rival to the American Water Color Society, whose "apparent purpose is to encourage sociability," according to "Art Notes," *New York Times,* June 5, 1890, p. 12.
23. Hiesinger 1994, p. 183.
24. Childe Hassam, July 8, 1894, to William Macbeth, Macbeth Gallery Papers, reel NMc7, frame 385.
25. For further discussion of this subject, see Susan G. Larkin, "Hassam in New England, 1889–1918," in this publication, pp. 124, 126.
26. Notice in the *New York Times,* February 6, 1896, p. 5, where quotations from various New York newspapers include: "'The show is intensely interesting from start to finish.'—*The Times;* 'From an artistic standpoint the display is a surprising success.'—*Evening Post;* 'A brilliant showing, presents a fascinating study to the picture lover.'—*The Sun.*"
27. "First Night Sale of Hassam Pictures, Canvases Go for Little—Attendance Good, but Bidding Slow," *New York Times,* February 7, 1896, p. 3. Hiesinger (1994, pp. 102, 104) discusses the financial debacle.
28. "First Night Sale of Hassam Pictures," p. 3.
29. J. Carroll Beckwith, Diary, entry for February 13, 1896, National Academy of Design, New York, quoted in Hiesinger 1994, p. 106, n. 48.
30. "The Field of Art: Social Art Gatherings in New York," *Scribner's Magazine* 20 (December 1896), p. 783, quoted in Hiesinger 1994, p. 104.
31. Childe Hassam, "Reminiscences of Weir," in Duncan Phillips et al., *Julian Alden Weir: An Appreciation of His Life and Works,* Phillips Publications, no. 1 (1921; New York: E. P. Dutton and Company, 1922), pp. 67–68.
32. Susan G. Larkin, *The Cos Cob Art Colony: Impressionists on the Connecticut Shore,* exh. cat. (New York: National Academy of Design; New Haven: Yale University Press, 2001), p. 59.
33. Donelson Hoopes, "American Impressionism," *Portfolio* 3 (January–February 1981), p. 60.
34. Ulrich W. Hiesinger, "Impressionism and Politics: The Founding of The Ten," *Magazine Antiques* 140 (November 1991), p. 783, quoting *New York Herald,* January 11, 1898.
35. Linda Henefield Skalet, "The Market for American Painting in New York, 1870–1915" (Ph.D. diss., Johns Hopkins University, Baltimore, 1980), p. 62.
36. Burnside 1990, p. 104.
37. Lockman interview, January 31, 1927, p. 23.
38. Macbeth Gallery's printed opening announcement, quoted in Malcolm Goldstein, *Landscape with Figures: A History of Art Dealing in the United States* (Oxford and New York: Oxford University Press, 2000), p. 64.
39. Childe Hassam, April 1907, to William Macbeth, Macbeth Gallery Papers, reel NMc7, frame 391–92.
40. Harrison S. Morris, *Confessions in Art* (New York: Sears Pub. Co., 1930), p. 146, quoted in William H. Truettner, "William T. Evans, Collector of American Paintings," *American Art Journal* 3, no. 2 (fall 1971), pp. 53–54.
41. George William Sheldon, *American Painters, with Eighty-three Examples of Their Work Engraved on Wood* (New York: D. Appleton and Company, 1879).
42. Truettner, "Evans, Collector of American Paintings," p. 75.
43. *Illustrated Catalogue of the Collection of American Paintings Formed by . . . William T. Evans, Esq.*, sale cat. (New York: American Art Association, March 31–April 2, 1913), lot 51. William Macbeth purchased *Isles of Shoals* (lot 54) and *October Haze, Manhattan* (lot 186) for $1,500 each, N. E. Montross purchased *The Butterfly* (lot 178) for $1,000, and Hugo Reisinger purchased *Leda and the Swan* (lot 124) for $1,300. See *American Art Annual* 11 (1914), pp. 417, 437. Reisinger also owned Hassam's *Brooklyn Bridge in Winter,* 1894, and *Dryads,* 1906. *Dryads* was included in the 1916 sale of Reisinger's collection, *Illustrated Catalogue of the Valuable Pictures by Foreign and American Masters Collected by the Late Hugo Reisinger,* sale cat. (New York: American Art Association, January 18, 1916), lot 6. See Teresa A. Carbone, "A Discussion of the Early Patronage of American Impressionism" (unpublished research paper, Ph.D. program in Art History, Graduate Center, City University of New York, 1985), p. 17.
44. Lockman interview, February 3, 1927, p. 3.
45. Ibid., pp. 2–3. I have been unable to determine the name, date, and location of this exhibition.
46. *Private Art Collection of Thomas B. Clarke, Part II—Objects of Art,* sale cat. (New York: American Art Association, February 15, 1899), lot 134.
47. Skalet, "Market for American Painting," p. 56.
48. Charles de Kay, "Great American Paintings," *New York Times Magazine,* February 5, 1899, p. 7.
49. H. Barbara Weinberg, "Thomas B. Clarke: Foremost Patron of American Art from 1872 to 1899," *American Art Journal,* 8, no. 1 (May 1976), p. 70.
50. Lockman interview, January 31, 1927, p. 27.
51. Hoopes 1979, p. 74.
52. Lockman interview, February 2, 1927, p. 5.
53. Carbone, "Discussion of Early Patronage of American Impressionism," p. 9; Hiesinger 1994, p. 141.
54. *Old and Modern Paintings, Water Colors, and Drawings*, sale cat. (New York: American Art Association, April 11–12, 1907), lots 13, 44, 53; *American Art Annual, 1907–1908* (1908), p. 36.
55. "Wood-Sullivan Pictures, Early Paintings by American Artists—The Rosa Bonheurs—Recent Work by Murphy and Kost," *New York Times,* April 1, 1903, p. 8. The H. Wood Sullivan collection was sold at American Art Galleries, New York, April 3, 1903. "Pictures at Auction: The H. W. Sullivan Collection of One Hundred Canvases Sold for $25,270," *New York Times,* April 4, 1903, p. 8.
56. "Wood-Sullivan Pictures," p. 8.
57. Sullivan sale, 1903; *American Art Annual, 1903–1904* (1903), pp. 60–61. Other works by Hassam sold at the auction were: *Snowy Day in the City,* to John Zimmerman, $110; *Gloucester Dock,* $160; *Spring Morning, The White Dory,* $170; *Isles of Shoals,* $140; *Snowstorm in the City, Seventh Avenue and Fifty-seventh Street,* $180; and *Moonrise at Sunset,* $160.
58. *Catalogue of Valuable Paintings and Water Colors, Mostly of the Modern, Dutch School, Forming the Private Collection of A. Augustus Healy, Esq.*, sale cat. (New York: American Art Association, February 15, 1907), lot 56; *American Art Annual 1907–1908* (1908), p. 27.
59. *Illustrated Catalogue of Nearly Three Hundred Valuable Paintings . . . the Property of . . . Mrs. Benjamin Thaw, Mr. Alexander Morten,* . . . sale cat. (New York: American Art Association, May 9–10, 1916), lot 116; *American Art Annual* 13 (1917), p. 356.
60. Document headed "Hassam's Statement / May 23, 1910 4 pictures," Wood Papers (San Marino).
61. Priscilla C. Colt, "Childe Hassam in Oregon," *Portland Art Museum Bulletin* 14 (March 1953), unpaged.
62. J. Alden Weir, late May 1907, to C. E. S. Wood, quoted in Young 1960, p. 225.
63. J. Alden Weir, Windham, Connecticut, November 13, 1910, to C. E. S. Wood, Wood Papers (San Marino).
64. "The Abounding Childe Hassam: An American Painter's Remarkable Output of Recent Pictures," *Mail and Express,* undated clipping [ca. 1911],

Hassam papers, reel NAA1, frame 541, review of *Paintings in Oil, Water Color and Pastels by Childe Hassam,* Montross Gallery, New York, February 1–15, 1911.

65. Elizabeth Broun, "Childe Hassam's America," *American Art* 13, no. 3 (fall 1999), p. 33.
66. Myers 1940, p. 83. Myers continued: Hassam was "painting still another landscape from nature when Alden Weir said, in his genial way, 'Well, Muley, I see you're still pumping nature.' I have often thought of that word, 'pumping,' not only in the sense in which Weir addressed Hassam, but in general relation to the process of pumping away more or less blindly to get results—results that lead to such an accumulation that it becomes at times an acute problem to those concerned. Almost at random, an artist can become a subject for exploitation by the multitude through methods of publicity, which extol him in terms of greatness."
67. Childe Hassam, March 7, 1911, to William Macbeth, Macbeth Gallery Papers, reel 2598, frame 138.
68. "Childe Hassam Rips Name off Fake Art," unidentified clipping, 1923, artist files, Department of American Paintings and Sculpture, The Metropolitan Museum of Art. According to the article, "The fake that bore the signature of Hassam had been made, according to an art dealer, by taking several printed reproductions of works by Hassam, cutting them up and piecing them like a picture puzzle into a new composition, which the faker copied in oil on canvas." Hassam was surprised by this fake and called it "a clever piece of work."
69. Robert W. Vonnoh, "Increasing Values in American Paintings: An Academician's Estimate of Contemporary Art," *Arts and Decoration* 2 (May 1912), pp. 254, 256.
70. Annotated copy of *Catalogue of Paintings by "Ten American Painters,"* exh. cat. (Providence: Rhode Island School of Design, April 17–May 1, 1912), departmental files, Department of American Paintings and Sculpture, The Metropolitan Museum of Art.
71. *Catalogue of International Exhibition of Modern Art, at the Armory of the Society of the Sixty-ninth Infantry,* exh. cat. (New York: Association of American Painters and Sculptors, February 15–March 15; New York: Vreeland Advertising Press, 1913), nos. 71, 72.
72. Childe Hassam, Cos Cob, Conn., September 8, 1913, to William Macbeth, Macbeth Gallery Papers, reel NMc7, frame 398.
73. [Robert] Macbeth, September 11, 1922, to Childe Hassam, Macbeth Gallery Papers, reel 2599, frame 27. Macbeth requested Hassam's *Spring, Ft. George,* and *The Sky-scraper Window.*
74. Childe Hassam, Cos Cob, Conn., October 1918, to William Macbeth, Macbeth Gallery Papers, reel NMc51, frame 793.
75. Childe Hassam, November 4(?), 1918, to Robert Macbeth, Macbeth Gallery Papers, reel 2598, frame 1398. The portrait by Poore to which Hassam referred appeared in *The Fox Chase,* a lampoon of the Old Lyme artists painted between 1901 and 1905 as an overmantel in the dining room in the Florence Griswold House; illustrated in Harold Spencer, Susan G. Larkin, and Jeffrey W. Andersen, *Connecticut and American Impressionism,* exh. cat. (Storrs, Conn.: William Benton Museum of Art, 1980), pp. 134–35.
76. [Robert] Macbeth, September 5, 1917, to Childe Hassam, Portsmouth, N.H., Macbeth Gallery Papers, reel NMc51, frame 803. *South West Wind* is possibly *Southwest Wind,* 1905, in the collection of the Worcester Art Museum, Massachusetts.
77. M[aude] R[iley], "Noted American Impressionists—Lawson, Robinson, Hassam—Exhibited," *Art Digest* 17, no. 14 (April 15, 1943), p. 7.
78. Robert Macbeth, January 28, 1914, to Childe Hassam, Macbeth Gallery Papers, reel NMc7, frame 403.
79. Childe Hassam, The Moorland, Bass Rocks, Gloucester, Massachusetts, July 15, 1919, to Milch Brothers, Milch Gallery Records, 1911–1980, Archives of American Art, Smithsonian Institution, reel 4420, frame 269.
80. Fort 1988, p. 112.
81. Childe Hassam, The Moorland, Bass Rocks, Gloucester, Massachusetts, August 19, 1919, to Milch Brothers, Milch Gallery Records, 1911–1980, reel 4420, frames 272–73.
82. "Art Fund Created by Hassam's Will," *New York Times,* November 13, 1935, p. 18; see also "Brilliant Career of Childe Hassam Comes to a Close," *Art News* 14 (September 14, 1935), p. 12.
83. Inflation calculator: http://www.eh.net/ehresources/howmuch/dollarq:php.
84. Annotated picture lists from the Milch Galleries offer a gauge of the prices Hassam sought. Alternatively, these numbers may indicate insurance values. "Paintings in stock of Mr. Childe Hassam," May 10, 1928, Milch Gallery Records, 1911–1980, reel 4420, frame 317.
85. Annotated copy of *Important Exhibition of Early and Recent Works by Childe Hassam of the American Academy of Arts and Letters,* exh. cat. (New York: Milch Galleries, December 3–24, 1928), nos. 4, 11, 14, 32, 20, 19, 1, Milch Gallery Records, 1911–1980, reel NM2. Inflation calculator: http://www.eh.net/ehresources/howmuchdollarq:php.
86. Duncan Phillips, "Original American Paintings of Today," *Formes* 21 (January 1932), p. 197, quoted in Elizabeth Tebow, "The American Vision, Part I: The American Tradition and American Impressionism," in Erika D. Passantino, ed., *The Eye of Duncan Phillips: A Collection in the Making* (Washington, D.C.: Phillips Collection, in Association with Yale University Press, 1999), p. 127.
87. Childe Hassam, East Hampton, June 30, 1921, to Milch Brothers, Milch Gallery Records, 1911–1980, reel 4420, frames 274–75.
88. Lockman interview, February 3, 1927, p. 5.
89. Hassam 1928, p. 27. Hassam comments on the use of the term "Impressionism": "Unnumbered, soon to be forgotten asses, like the author of *A Collection in the Making,* are even now using it with the rest of their stock stupidities though in that book the really clean-cut type of opinionated ignorance has never been surpassed." Hassam is referring to Duncan Phillips, *A Collection in the Making; a Survey of the Problems Involved in Collecting Pictures, together with Brief Estimates of the Painters in the Phillips Memorial Gallery* (New York: E. Weyhe; Washington, D.C.: Phillips Memorial Gallery, 1926).
90. Duncan Phillips, December 3, 1928, to Mrs. Gerald Thayer, and Duncan Phillips, December 14, 1928, to Mrs. Gerald Thayer, Phillips Collection Papers, Archives of American Art, Smithsonian Institution, reel 1937, frames 330, 333. Hassam bought the painting back from Mrs. Thayer, and it was later part of his bequest to the American Academy of Arts and Letters Bequest.
91. Childe Hassam, December 18(?), 1926, to Royal Cortissoz, Royal Cortissoz Papers, The Beinecke Rare Book and Manuscript Library, Yale University, New Haven, Connecticut, quoted in Hiesinger 1994, p. 169.
92. Myers 1940, pp. 101–2.

"Man Sass'Em"
Hassam and His Contemporary Critics

Kathleen M. Burnside

On April 15, 1891, a peculiar little art exhibition opened at Chase's Gallery, Boston, under the auspices of the Paint and Clay Club. Called in its catalogue the club's *Great Moral Show,* it was described on the title page as "Consisting of Marvellous Hand-Painted Pictures, Designed to Edify, Entertain, Instruct, Illuminate, and Illustrate in a Most Striking and Pertinent Manner the Numerous Art Eccentricities, Incoherencies, Vagaries, Isms, Fads, and Fashions of the Fin-de-Siecle; the Collection is For Exhibition Only, and the Works are Not For Sale; the Pictures should be Viewed from as Great a Distance as Possible—say One Furlong; they are by The Most Eminent Artists."[1]

The *New York Times* explained that in the exhibition paintings by "Whistler, Monet, Sisley, Delacroix, . . . Childe Hassam, Sargent . . . and Tarbell are caricatured in various ways; the catalogue indulges in appropriate witticisms."[2] Thus, no. 21 was listed as the work of "McJ., McNeil, McWhistler: *A Monotony in Black. One of a Four Hundred.*" No. 23 was a quartet of Barbizon pictures "From our own factory" at prices that "defy competition." The "Rousseau" could be had for 50¢, while the putative Corot was a bargain at $2.50. Claude Monet ("Claude Monnaie," no. 13) and Alfred Sisley (contributing "A Sissler" of a painting, no. 25) were similarly lampooned, and the origins of Impressionism were elucidated through entry no. 12, by "Artist Unknown, The Earliest Impressionist."[3]

Although he was not yet thirty-two and had only recently left his professional base in Boston, Childe Hassam had already gained notoriety there with his art. His boldness and penchant for tonal cityscapes earned him a listing (no. 6) in the exhibition's catalogue as "Man Sass'Em," with a painting entitled *Dry Day* that was explicated as "City of B——n Street Department."

Hassam's inclusion in this parodic exhibition demonstrates the commanding position he had assumed at a young age within the artistic community. His was not an easy personality to ignore, and the versatility, virtuosity, and sheer volume of his production demanded critical notice. As early as 1890 Hassam was cited in the *New York Times* for his "astonishing" command of medium; he seemed "equally at home in oils, water colors, and pastels."[4] The *Times* critic wrote of him in 1896, "Few of our native painters have succeeded in so many directions. Sea, landscape, architecture, flowers, still life, animals and figures. . . . He seems able to paint anything his fancy dictates, in any particular manner he chooses. He can be as finished, as broad, as impressionistic, as colorful as the best of them, and all at will."[5]

During his lifetime Hassam completed over two thousand works in oil, watercolor, pastel, and pencil. At the age of fifty-six he took up printmaking in earnest and subsequently produced more than four hundred etchings and drypoints, lithographs and lithotints. Colleagues and critics alike were struck by Hassam's productivity. His good friend J. Alden Weir, for example, envied the seeming ease with which Hassam painted, as Weir explained in a letter to their mutual friend and patron, Colonel Charles Erskine Scott Wood.[6] While Hassam's range of subjects and facility with varied media awed some critics, not all of them admired his prodigious output; one review concluded, "probably Mr. Hassam paints too many pictures."[7]

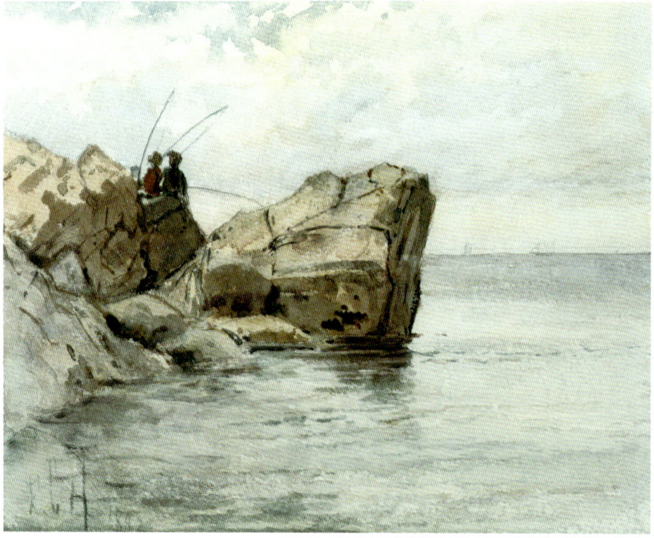

Fig. 357. Childe Hassam. *Young Fishermen,* 1882. Watercolor on paper, 11⅜ x 9 in. (28.9 x 22.9 cm). Private collection

Born in Dorchester, Massachusetts, in 1859, Frederick Childe Hassam was the son of a cutlery merchant, although he had a more artistic ancestry as well: both Nathaniel Hawthorne and William Morris Hunt were distant relatives.[8] By the early 1880s he had established a substantial reputation in Boston as an illustrator, specializing in children's stories and contributing to various magazines. His earliest independent work was in watercolor, the medium that gained him his first critical attention. His initial one-man exhibition, *Water Colors by Fred C. Hassam,* was held in 1882 at the Williams and Everett Gallery in Boston and included such works as *Young Fishermen* (fig. 357). The debut elicited this notice in a Boston paper:

> *The collection of watercolors now on view in Williams & Everett's Fine Art Rooms introduces to the public a young artist of exceptional talent and of more than ordinary promise. For a number of years Mr. Hassan [*sic*] has been quietly at work . . . preparing himself by diligent study and earnest work for a professional career. . . . He now invites attention to a collection of fifty watercolors, a department of art of which he is specially fond and for which . . . he has rare gifts. The best feature about the collection is its fresh "outdoor" feeling. . . . Many of the subjects are quaint studies at Nantucket—bits of beach, with boats and figures; old cottages, with glimpses of sea and sky; others give sections of woods, with brooks and paths; . . . all happily selected subjects.*[9]

Hassam's freely washed renderings of the Massachusetts countryside were succeeded in the mid-1880s by Tonalist paintings of Boston streets, typically seen in the poetic atmosphere created by gray, rain-laden skies. These canvases earned Hassam some notice in the press (witness the lampooning of such a work in the Paint and Clay Club exhibition). In November 1886 Hassam showed one of his cityscapes in the autumn exhibition of the National Academy of Design. The *New York Times* critic reported that "*A City Fairyland* [fig. 3], a study of Boston's new streets through a Winter Fog," was sold from the exhibition for $375.[10]

In early 1887 an exhibition and auction of 120 works by Hassam was held at the Boston galleries of Noyes, Cobb and Company.[11] The collection included many of his tonal Boston cityscapes, such as *At Dusk,* now known as *Boston Common at Twilight* (fig. 39), and *Arlington Street through the Rain* (fig. 358). The critic for the *Boston Advertiser* considered these urban views "impressions, in the best sense" that give "a good notion of local color, life, movement and atmosphere." The writer continued: "They usually represent the effect of rainy weather, and in the description of wet pavements, mist and mud, the confused gleam of lights in long vistas as evening draws on, and the many reflections and furtive flashes of brilliancy that night discloses in the streets of a busy town, they manifest not only an extraordinarily clever perception, and an original way of seeing, but also an artistic grasp of fleeting effects which is little short of masterly."[12]

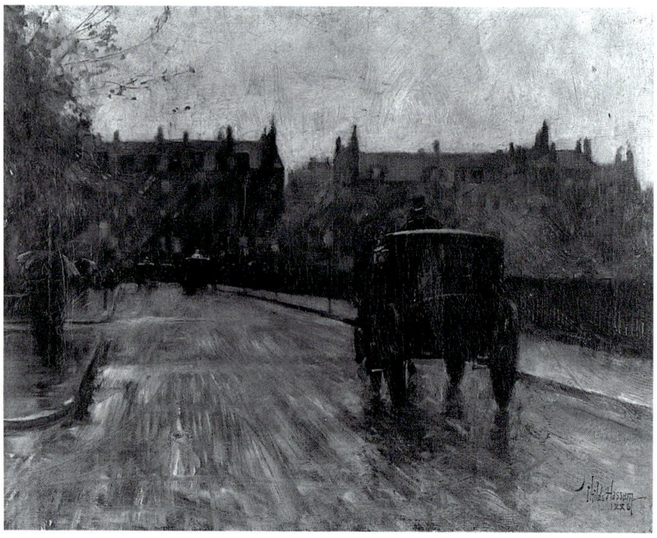

Fig. 358. Childe Hassam. *Arlington Street through the Rain,* 1886. Oil on canvas, 14⅛ x 18⅛ in. (25.9 x 46 cm). The Charles P. Russell Collection of Deerfield Academy, Massachusetts

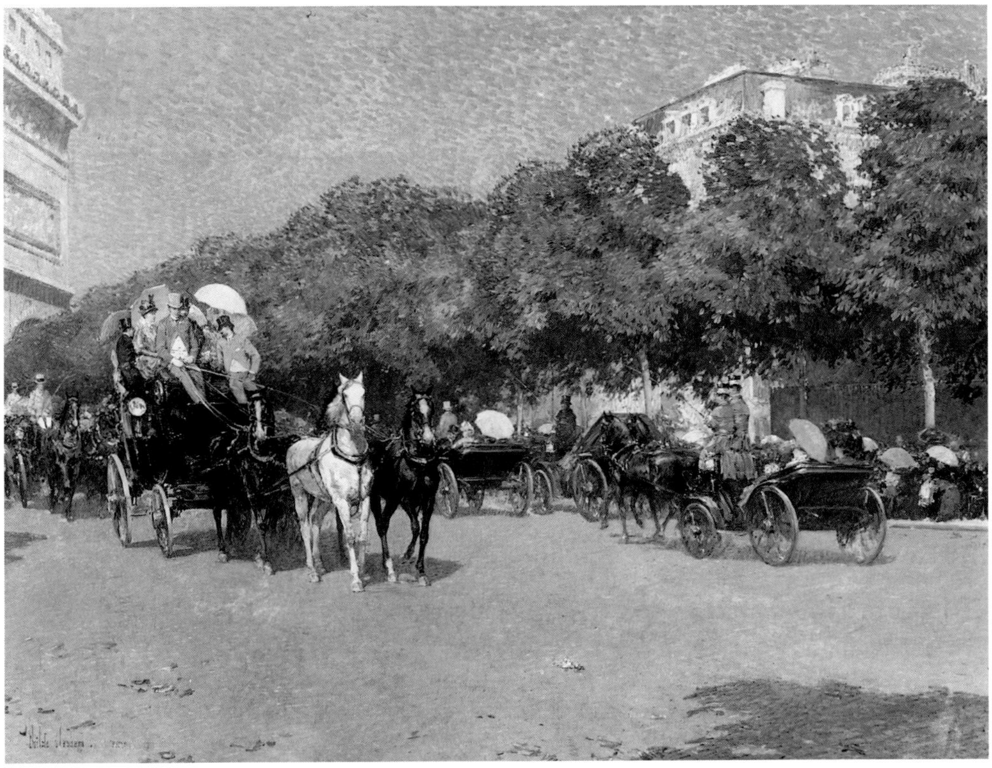

Fig. 359. Childe Hassam. *Grand Prix Day (Le Jour du Grand Prix)*, 1887–88. Oil on canvas, 36 x 48 in. (91.4 x 121.9 cm). New Britain Museum of American Art, Connecticut, Grace Judd Landers Fund

The auction at Noyes and Cobb was actually held after Hassam and his wife had departed Boston for what would become a three-year residence in Paris, where he studied under Gustave-Rodolphe Boulanger and Jules-Joseph Lefebvre at the Académie Julian. Particularly at first, Hassam continued to specialize in tonal cityscapes. His contributions to the 1887 Paris Salon included a large canvas titled *Une Averse—rue Bonaparte* (fig. 54). The *New York Sun* critic took note of him:

> *Mr. Childe Hassam, who went abroad . . . after having won a certain reputation as a painter of street scenes in Boston, has changed his sky but not his mood. Now he paints street scenes in Paris, and if his brush has lost something of the individuality in touch and color which once it possessed, it has gained in every other way. He has four pictures here, all of them good and one (showing a long perspective of cabs ranged against a dead wall and a few pedestrians plodding ahead in the rain) quite remarkably clever.*[13]

But not everyone applauded Hassam's facility in his chosen genre. Reviewing the same Salon exhibition, the critic of the generally appreciative *Boston Evening Transcript* was sarcastic: "Childe Hassam ought to 'come in out of the rain.' But I know of no one who can picture a city street in a rain with the fidelity and skill that he shows. His 'Shower—Rue Bonaparte,' is a very clever piece of work, but unless the subject is changed soon, one will have to take a dose of quinine as an antidote against the dampness that pervades Mr. Hassam's artistic environment."[14]

Perhaps Hassam took this criticism to heart, for he began to paint with greater frequency the effects of sunlight on his modern subjects (see fig. 76). It is commonly said that Hassam converted to Impressionism during his stay in Paris, but the truth is far less tidy. Even his earliest Boston-period watercolors were projected and perceived as plein air impressions; and in his post-Paris work, tonal, poetic, or symbolic concerns were often emphasized. What does seem legitimate to observe, however, is that in Paris Hassam's brushwork acquired a pronounced staccato rhythm. For the most part, Hassam's handling of paint would remain impressionistic through the many succeeding years of his long career. Critics agreed that he was a practitioner of Impressionist methods, and his work was even described in a 1905 review as in the "best style of the pointillists."[15]

The new developments in Hassam's work found critical favor. A painting entitled *Grand Prix Day (Le Jour du Grand Prix)* (fig. 359), his contribution to the 1888 Salon, was, a *Chicago News* writer asserted, "even superior" to *Une Averse—rue Bonaparte* of the preceding year, being "a very brilliant picture, full of life and light and movement, and instinct with the gayety of the bright French capital."[16] The

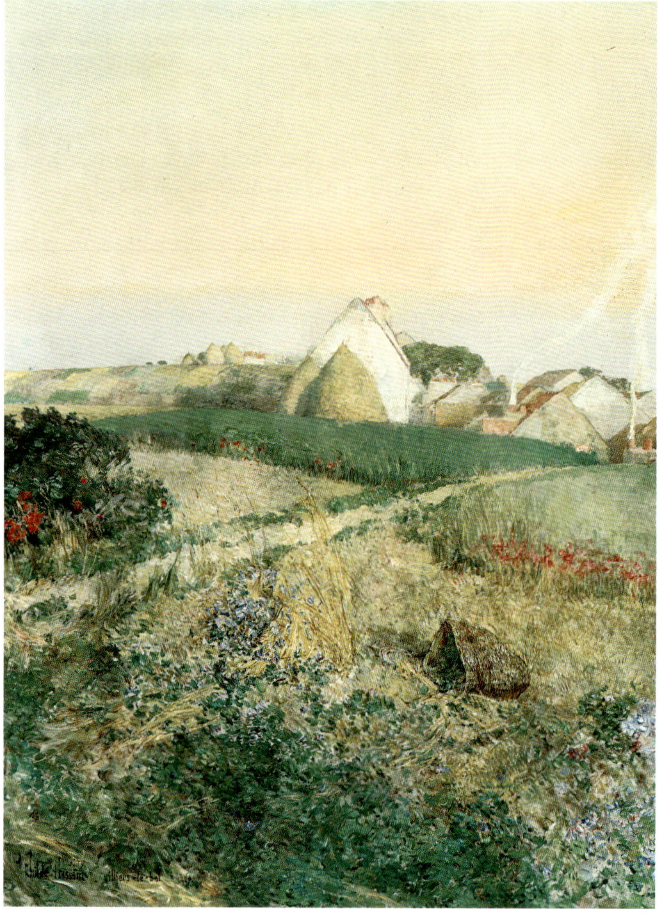

Fig. 360. Childe Hassam. *Villiers-le-Bel (The Enchanted Hour)*, 1889. Oil on canvas, 51 x 38½ in. (129.5 x 97.8 cm). Spanierman Gallery LLC, New York

sampling of his French work that Hassam sent home to Boston, exhibited in March 1889 at Noyes, Cobb and Company, was well received.[17] Wrote one reviewer, "Since he left Boston he has made a very noticeable gain, especially in color, and he has never painted so well as now."[18]

Despite the hospitality of Boston's critics, Hassam established himself in New York on his return to America, in late October 1889, and promptly began to exhibit with art organizations both locally and out of town. He was a regular contributor, for example, to the annual exhibitions of the American Water Color Society, the New-York Water Color Club (which he cofounded in 1890),[19] the National Academy of Design, and the Society of American Artists. The latter group, composed of younger artists, was closely identified with modern French tendencies. As one critic wrote in 1890, "That the sympathies of the leading members of the Society of American Artists go with the later school of French impressionists is plain enough from the number of paintings more or less touched by the new fashion which have been accepted this year. . . . The French extremists have already won the dignity of a nickname in Paris. . . . They are called the Lentillists, because they put figures and landscapes together out of dabs of bright paint about the size of a lentil grain."[20]

Hassam was only one of numerous American artists painting in the Impressionist style. Others with whom he was mentioned in reviews of the early 1890s included Weir, Edmund C. Tarbell, Robert Reid, Theodore Robinson, John H. Twachtman, Dwight W. Tryon, William Merritt Chase, and Theodore Wendel. Although Impressionist paintings were often greeted with disdain, Hassam's work of the kind was rarely dismissed out of hand. Sometimes a critic lambasted one of his paintings while applauding another on view in the same exhibition or across town at a different annual. In the *New York Times,* Hassam's work was characterized on various occasions as "shrill" and "stringy,"[21] "wild and weedy,"[22] and "deft and pleasing."[23] His range of subjects, even within one exhibition, was always noted, as in this review of the twelfth annual exhibition of the Society of American Artists:

> *The versatility of Mr. Childe Hassam is indeed surprising. "The Rose Girl" [fig. 72] is a composition in the manner of James Tissot, the flower girl and her masses of flowers, the yellow cab and passers-by being painted with a solid insistance* [sic] *not generally found in Mr. Hassam's other works. . . . The picture is in a wonderful frame, which takes under its wings two smaller panels with flowers. . . . "The Enchanted Hour" [fig. 360] is the nooning near a small village with red roofs. The yellow haystacks, the poppies mixed with blue cornflowers, the vegetables and abandoned basket tell of work interrupted by the midday bell. Less solidly painted than these, but more attractive, are street scenes in Winter, one from Paris, the other from New-York.*[24]

The impact of French art was strong in New York in the 1890s. Exhibitions of the work of Monet, Sisley, Camille Pissarro, and Pierre-Auguste Renoir were mounted, notably at the Fifth Avenue galleries of the Parisian dealer Durand-Ruel and at the American Art Association. In addition, many American artists came back from studying in France eager to experiment with French techniques. In 1892 it was reported in the *New York Times* that many "young painters" had returned to America inspired by "Neo-Impressionism" and that "the most obvious general effect of all this upon our exhibitions is that air of gayety produced by strong colors in

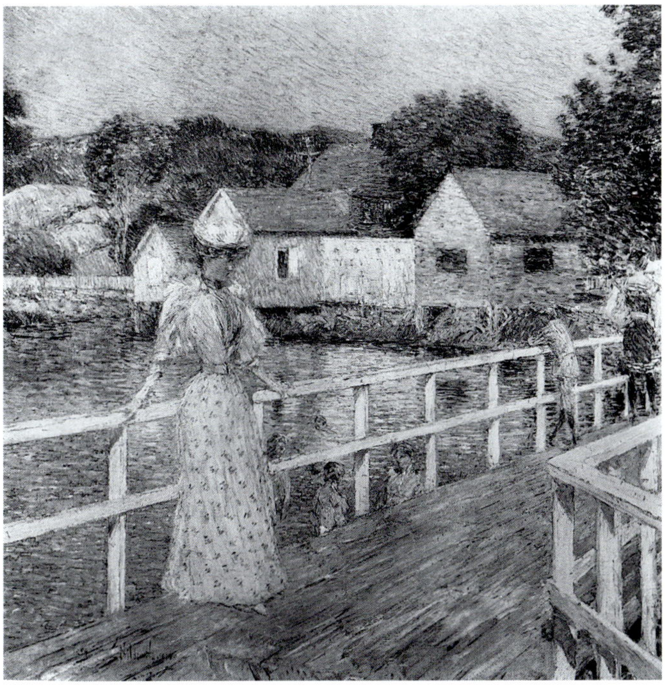

Fig. 361. Childe Hassam. *Midsummer Girl,* 1894. Oil on canvas, 32 x 32 in. (81.3 x 81.3 cm). Private collection

a high key, which must strike the least observant visitor of such shows as those offered to the public by the National Academy and the Society of American Artists."[25]

By 1895 Hassam had clearly been placed in the camp of the American Impressionists. The *New York Times* reviewer, after observing that the seventeenth annual Society of American Artists show had "been struck by a great wave of Impressionism," had this to say on the subject:

> *The impressionistic bent of the show is emphasized by the award of the Webb landscape prize to Mr. Hassam's picture, or more properly, sketch, "Plaza Central, Havana" [fig. 196].*
>
> *Upon what grounds the jury could have selected this canvas out of all the collection is difficult of comprehension. There is not even a slight suggestion of composition about it, the color is not at all distinguished, nor does it show the artist at his best. We must admit frankly that it is not as eccentric as the sketch by the same artist of "Quincy" (No. 153), on the opposite side of the room, a work which easily distances every other canvas in the exhibition by its abnormal and erratic rendition of nature. It may be possible that Mr. Hassam sees the world in this manner and that through his eyes the landscape occasionally takes on this aspect. If this really be so, an oculist is surely his affair. Happily, Mr. Hassam has lucid intervals, and in some of these he has painted "The Midsummer Girl" [fig. 361], which is vibrant, colorful, and very artistic.*
>
> *It may have been the influence of the Manet, the Raffaëlli, and art shows of a similar nature that have had so strong an effect on the men, apparent here, but whatever the reason, the work surpasses any previous years in its rampant, wild schemes of vibrating color, and in its straining after high, light tones, that end too frequently in utter chalkiness.*[26]

This review notwithstanding, the critical response to Hassam's style (and to American Impressionism in general) was gradually becoming less strident during the 1890s. As one critic put it in 1893, the "American artists who took Neo-Impressionism like the scarlet fever a few years ago have sensibly modified their use of the method."[27] Hassam's style was accepted and even, within bounds, applauded. His picturesque *The White Dory* (fig. 362), shown in the 1895 National Academy of Design annual, was praised in the *New York Times* for its "brilliancy" and "realism of sunlight."[28] The following year a critic noted in the same paper that "of the steadily increasing band of impressionists, Mr. Hassam is a priest high in the councils. But," he opined, "if some will quarrel with this artist for his very advanced notions of the

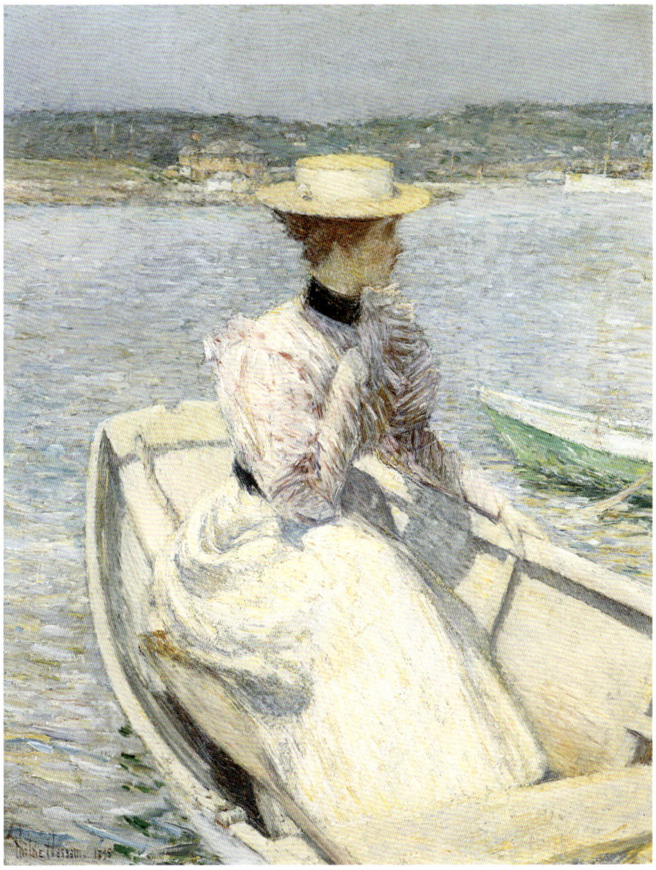

Fig. 362. Childe Hassam. *The White Dory,* 1895. Oil on canvas, 26 x 21 in. (66 x 53.3 cm). Private collection

importance of certain qualities at the expense of others, he must be credited with excellent draughtsmanship, happy composition at times, and occasionally remarkably brilliant color schemes that are very alluring and excuse much eccentricity."[29]

By the close of the nineteenth century, Hassam, then just forty, was playing a large and influential role in the world of contemporary art. In addition to exhibiting numerous works with almost every American art society, he was honored with many one-man shows at commercial galleries in New York, Boston, and even Paris. He was one of the organizers of the Ten, the band of painters who in December 1897 seceded from the Society of American Artists in order to assume more control over their own exhibitions. Hassam contributed amply to each of the Ten's annuals, which were held until 1919. His "alluring" canvases achieved a measure of critical and popular success. Yet just as some critics had judged Hassam's Impressionist style harshly in the 1890s, they were less than encouraging about his later pursuit of a more symbolic, expressive, and decorative art.

In 1897 Hassam visited Italy, Spain, and France. He spent time in both Paris and the provinces of Normandy and Brittany and was particularly engaged by the rituals of peasants in the Breton village of Pont-Aven, a locale favored by Paul Gauguin. He returned to New York with a new enthusiasm for heightened color, exaggerated brushwork, linear patterning, and the art of the European Symbolists.

The twentieth century saw Hassam embark upon his own form of symbolic painting. He developed a genre of poetic landscape peopled with nudes and often bearing mythological titles (see figs. 12, 322). Some critics interpreted Hassam's new subjects as manifestations of his own artistic "elasticity" and "variety."[30] Arthur Hoeber called Hassam "a most interesting art personality, searching, as it would seem, continually in many directions, a painter astonishingly well equipped technically, with a highly developed pictorial instinct."[31] But writers increasingly questioned the merit of Hassam's symbolic work and praised only his virtuoso renditions of "real" subjects. Reviewing the spring 1902 exhibition of the Ten, to which Hassam had submitted both city scenes and symbolic compositions of nudes, the critic for the *New York Sun* declared, "Probably, we shall find ourselves viewing Childe Hassam's group with qualified acceptance. Two . . . [works] we must dismiss as the amiable vagaries of a painter who insists upon sandwiching in between his wonderfully truthful pictures examples of how things do not appear to average sane minds."[32]

Most critics respected Hassam's abilities and prestigious position but shared the view that his new ventures were mere "amiable vagaries." In his reviews of a major one-man show at New York's Montross Gallery in December 1907, Joseph Edgar Chamberlin observed: "We have to take Mr. Hassam's affectations along with his genius." Chamberlin was not "inspired" by Hassam's mythical figure painting *Leda and the Swan* (fig. 363), finding the model "more highly endowed with avoirdupois than grace."[33] The dual strain of Hassam's production was also alluded to by the *New York Herald* columnist who reviewed the March 1908 exhibition of the Ten. Praising the painting *Lower Manhattan (View Down Broad Street)* (fig. 216), he noted that "Childe Hassam, who usually wanders in groves and dells inhabited by nymphs and lambs, has been to Wall Street. One of the most striking of the pictures he shows is the canon [*sic*] about which men pile up dollars or capitalize their conversation, as seen by the impressionist."[34]

Despite adverse criticism, Hassam continued to produce poetic and decorative figural work from 1900 until shortly before his death, in 1935. Like other American artists working in the early twentieth century, he embraced a classical revival that seemed to transform the aestheticism of Impressionism and at the same time to offer defense against the challenge of European modernism. Reviewing a 1907 exhibition of the recently merged Society of American Artists and National Academy of Design, one critic wrote:

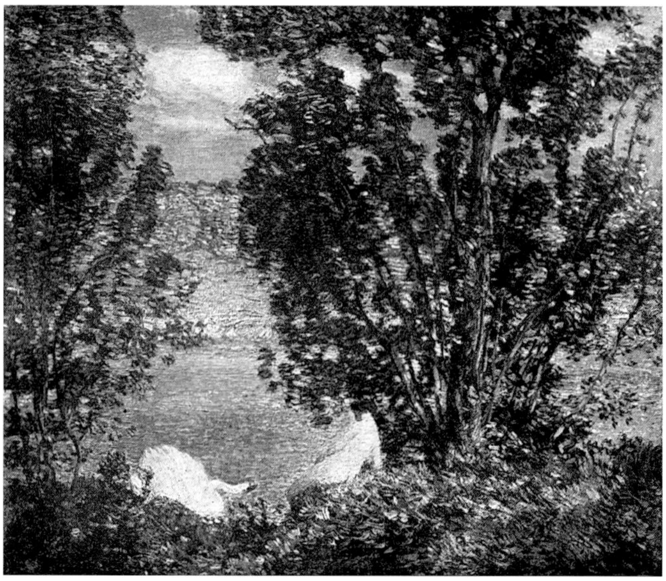

Fig. 363. Childe Hassam. *Leda and the Swan*, ca. 1907. Oil on canvas. Location unknown

That an American school of painting, with characteristics of its own, is disengaging and affirming itself, there can no longer be any doubt. . . . The excesses of Impressionism, for instance, are already of the past. Almost the only work in the exhibition which shows the Impressionist influence in a noticeable degree is that of Childe Hassam, and Mr. Hassam has profoundly modified the Impressionist method, has bent it to new ends and to the expression of a new personality, so that his production is essentially original as it is essentially artistic. There is nothing in him of Monet's temper of scientific demonstration—it is beauty he is after, . . . not a theory of light.[35]

This commentary reveals several characteristic features of Hassam criticism as it evolved during the early twentieth century. It underlines Hassam's stalwart (some would say anachronistic) adherence to an Impressionist style of painting. It asserts a somewhat defensive, nativist pride at a time when European painters were beginning once again to challenge accepted aesthetic notions, demonstrating anew the dynamism of European art. And by praising Hassam's originality it disavows the influence of French sources on his work.

During the first decades of the twentieth century, Hassam was championed by critics such as Albert Gallatin, Royal Cortissoz, Israel White, and Frederic Newlin Price, all of whom devoted entire essays to his work. Cortissoz closely followed the last twenty years of Hassam's career and offered posthumous praise for him. According to Cortissoz, Hassam's study abroad was useful for "training his hand" but above all he was to be commended as an "honest technician" whose art "rebukes the slipshod workmanship and the vulgar tastes so often encountered to-day."[36] Hassam's American character was a dominant theme. Gallatin emphasized the artist's native heritage, writing in 1907, "Hassam only went to France to learn the technique of his art. Above all he is typically American, and a painter who never finds it necessary to leave New York in winter, or certain spots of New England in summer, to make a grand tour in search of the picturesque."[37] Both White and Price also drew attention to Puritan ancestry, and Price reminded readers that a Puritan was "a true aristocrat with democratic sympathies."[38] White praised Hassam as the "best exponent" of the modern movement.[39]

However, not all observers of Hassam's art were so respectful; while usually acknowledging his abilities, some writers made it clear that they regarded him as a lightweight. Reviewing a major show of Hassam's work held at the Montross Gallery in November–December 1915, a columnist for *Arts and Decoration* wrote: "In a country in which the good art is very apt to be consciously serious, a matter for worship and admiration, but not love, Mr. Hassam's work stands out as a happy, disinterested spot. Indeed, there are few painters anywhere in whom affinity with nature is less sullied by technical, fashionable or intellectual considerations."[40]

And when yet another large annual exhibition of Hassam's work was mounted at the same gallery in January 1917, Henry McBride, reviewer for the *New York Sun,* began his critique this way: "There is no American artist now before the public that the American reviewer is called upon to consider so frequently as Mr. Hassam. In consequence it is sometimes difficult to have new things to say in regard to him, particularly as Mr. Hassam doesn't seem to have new things to say for himself. . . . He doesn't trouble us with profound things nor ask us questions we cannot answer."[41]

Although praise for Hassam's painting had dwindled over time, even some of his harsher critics continued to admire his watercolors. One reviewer remarked regarding the watercolors in a show at Montross, "Sometimes here he showed the force, and directness and largeness of brush of a Sargent, a linguistic virility, and at others a minute consciousness of the sparkle to be derived from the detailing of nature's color."[42] And despite his rather insulting assessment of Hassam's work, McBride found: "As has happened in many of Mr. Hassam's recent exhibitions, he reaches a more general level of success with his water colors than with the oils; . . . a number of the water colors are gay affairs, and one of them, the 'Back of the Old House, Cos Cob' [fig. 364], is Mr. Hassam at his best. The touches are swift and sure, the color attractive and the subject simply adorable. Mr. Hassam does a real service in drawing these fine old New England cottages for us." Hassam should be placed, McBride concluded, "among the three or four best water colorists now in the country."[43]

A separate study might be made of Hassam's own art criticism, set forth in his later years with increasing frequency in letters, interviews, and articles.[44] Hassam's views were always forcefully articulated in language filled with colorful imagery. He had developed his own understanding of art and art history and had little regard for critics and art experts. Asked to comment about a proposed book project on Robert Henri, Hassam wrote to the publisher, "Your idea of getting out a series of books on American artists is a good one, I am

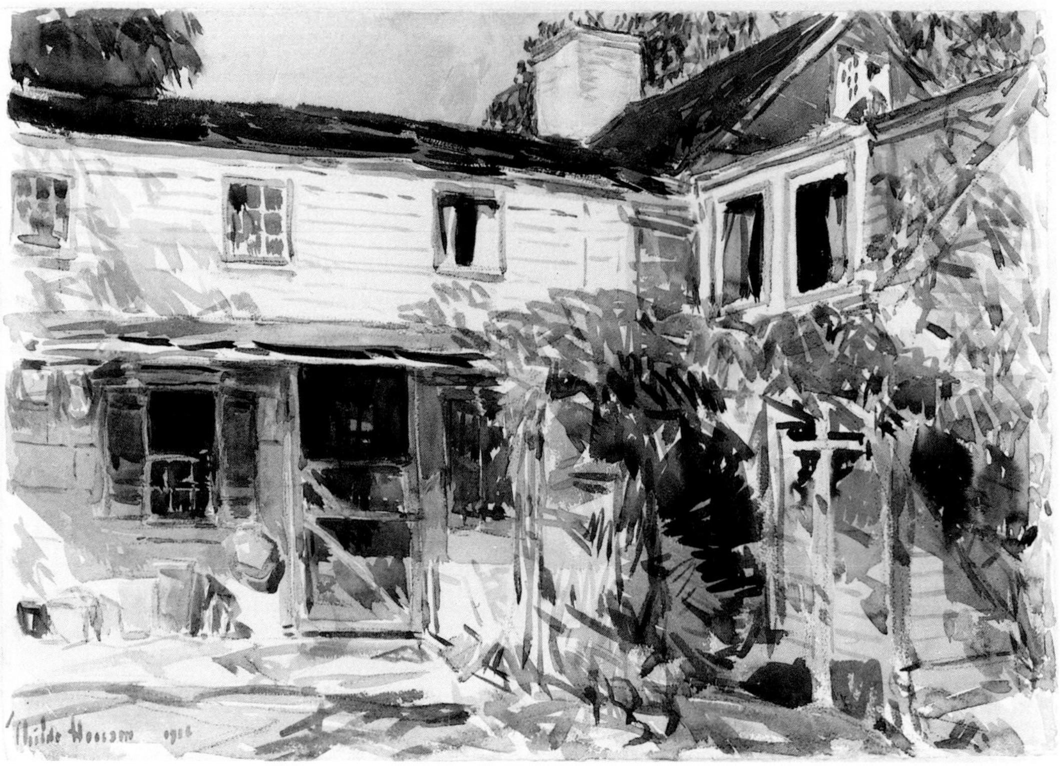

Fig. 364. Childe Hassam. *Back of the Old House,* 1916. Watercolor over brown chalk on wove paper. 15¼ x 22 in. (38.5 x 55.9 cm). Yale University Art Gallery, New Haven, Gift of George Hopper Fitch, B.A. 1932 and Mrs. Fitch

sure. I have said for some years past there are books on all the modern European mediocrities in art, and none on really great modern artists, who have worked and passed their lives in America, notably my old friend Twachtman. . . . I might make a wicked epigram now—There are books on all the European mediocrities in art, and now we are going to have some on the Americans."[45]

Hassam acknowledged the ascendancy of modern art but subjected it to stringent scrutiny and a jaundiced eye. His antagonism is clear in a 1934 interview: "Modern art is fine, but when I say 'modern art,' I am drawing a clear line between the good and the bad. Many of the so-called modern painters are nothing more or less than fakers. . . . Critics unable to understand the mystical outpourings and fearing to acknowledge their ignorance [about the new cult of modernism] write about metaphysical meanings, and all the while designing dealers laugh up their sleeves and rake in the [money]."[46]

Irascible and irreverent to the end, Hassam always defended with a ferocious loyalty what he considered to be true art and true artists. In a letter to his friend Colonel Wood he lamented the fact that Weir's art went unappreciated and unsold, and he lashed out at all the "prattling art boobys" and "amiable old ladies" who run "art matters."[47] And the artist who loved to "Sass'Em" cast a final vote of confidence for art and artists rather than critics when, in 1935, shortly before his death, he willed his entire estate to the American Academy of Arts and Letters, stipulating that the proceeds from the gradual sale of his work be devoted to a fund supporting contemporary American and Canadian artists.

1. *Descriptive Catalogue of the Paint and Clay Club's Great Moral Show,* . . . exh. cat. (Boston: Chase's Gallery, April 15–29, 1891), unpaged. The cover title reads: *Descriptive Catalogue. International Salon. In Bond, under the "Protection" of the Paint and Clay Club.*
2. "Art Notes," *New York Times,* April 19, 1891, p. 13, col. 7.
3. *Paint and Clay Club's Great Moral Show,* unpaged.
4. "Painters in Pastel," *New York Times,* May 5, 1890, p. 4, col. 7.
5. "Pictures by Childe Hassam," *New York Times,* February 2, 1896, p. 21, col. 7.
6. J. Alden Weir, Windham, Conn., November 13, 1910, to C. E. S. Wood, Wood Papers (San Marino), quoted in Young 1960, p. 228.
7. "Annual Show of The Ten American Painters," *New York Evening Mail,* March 21, 1906, p. 7, col. 5.
8. See Adams 1938, chap. 1, for an anecdotal history of Hassam's origins and early career. See also H. Barbara Weinberg, "Introduction," in this publication, pp. 3–5; Stephanie L. Herdrich, "Hassam in Boston, 1859–1886," in this publication, pp. 29–30; and Elizabeth Broun, "Hassam's Pride in His Ancestry," in this publication, pp. 285–87.
9. Unidentified clipping, [autumn 1882], Hassam Papers, reel NAA1, frame 508.
10. "Autumn Academy Prices," *New York Times,* December 6, 1886, p. 5, col. 6.
11. The exhibition opened on February 28, 1887; the auction was held on March 9 and 10. *Exhibition and Sale of Works in Oil and Water Color by Childe Hassam* (Boston: Art Galleries of Noyes, Cobb and Company, 1887).
12. "Mr. Hassam's Exhibition," undated clipping, labeled "*Boston Advertiser,*" Hassam Papers, reel NAA1, frame 508.
13. Untitled clipping, labeled "*New York Sun,* 1887," Hassam Papers, reel NAA1, frame 509.
14. Untitled clipping, signed E. W. M., labeled "*Boston Transcript,* 1887," Hassam Papers, reel NAA1, frame 509.
15. "A Pointillist's Paintings. Landscapes by Childe Hassam at the Montross Gallery," *New York Times,* December 27, 1905, p. 8, col. 6.
16. In the article, the titles of the paintings are given in English. Untitled clipping, labeled "*Chicago News,* 1888," Hassam Papers, reel NAA1, frame 509.
17. See *Exhibition and Private Sale of Paintings by Mr. Childe Hassam* (Boston: Noyes, Cobb and Company, March 11–23, 1889).
18. "Fine Arts. Exhibition of Mr. Hassam's Paintings at Noyes, Cobb & Co.'s Gallery," clipping, labeled "*Boston Transcript,* 1889," Hassam Papers, reel NAA1, frame 509.
19. See "City and Suburban News: New-York," *New York Times,* May 23, 1890, p. 3, col. 3, for an announcement of the incorporation of the New-York Water Color Club. Hassam was president of the club, which held its first exhibition in November 1890. For a commentary on the first exhibition, see "New-York Water-Color Club," *New York Times,* November 7, 1890, p. 4, col. 6.
20. "Society of American Artists," *New York Times,* May 11, 1890, p. 4, col. 7.
21. "The Water-Color Society," *New York Times,* February 3, 1894, p. 2, col. 6.
22. "Group Exhibits of Painting," *New York Times,* July 7, 1894, p. 5, col. 4.
23. "New-York Water-Color Club," p. 4, col. 6.
24. "Society of American Artists," *New York Times,* May 23, 1890, p. 4, col. 6.
25. "The Neo-Impressionists," *New York Times,* June 19, 1892, p. 19, col. 7.
26. "Society of American Artists," *New York Times,* March 23, 1895, p. 4, col. 7.
27. "The Society of Artists," *New York Times,* April 24, 1893, p. 4, col. 6.
28. "The Academy of Design," *New York Times,* March 29, 1895, p. 5, col. 5.
29. "In the World of Art," *New York Times,* February 2, 1896, p. 12, col. 7.
30. See "The Ten American Painters," *Mail and Express,* April 20, 1903, p. 6, and "Ten American Painters," *Art Interchange* 52 (May 1904), p. 116.
31. Arthur Hoeber, "Art and Artists," *Globe and Commercial Advertiser,* March 13, 1913, p. 8.
32. "Exhibition of Ten American Painters," *New York Sun,* April 1, 1902, p. 6.
33. Joseph Edgar Chamberlin, "Childe Hassam's Pictures: The Heights and Limitations of an Artist's Power—Fine Pictures of Florence and Manhattan," *Evening Mail* (New York), December 18, 1907, clipping, Hassam Papers, reel NAA1, frame 550.
34. "'Ten Painters' Show Pictures. Each Man His Own Jury and Space the Final Arbiter at Montross Galleries. Wall Street and 'Curb.' William M. Chase, Childe Hassam, Robert Reid and Others Display Interesting Works," *New York Herald,* March 18, 1908, p. 9.
35. "The Winter Academy," unidentified clipping, labeled "1907," Hassam Papers, reel NAA1, frame 533. Regarding the classical revival, see Kimberly Orcutt, "'The subject that I am known for': Hassam's Pursuit of a Legacy," in this publication, pp. 317–18.
36. Royal Cortissoz, "An Important Figure in American Art. An American Painter. The Work of Childe Hassam Seen in Retrospect," *[New York Herald Tribune],* undated clipping, labeled "12-16-26," but more likely dating to December 1928 (when Hassam had a Milch Gallery exhibit matching that described by Cortissoz), artist files, Department of American Painting and Sculpture, The Metropolitan Museum of Art. The clipping was originally in the files of Harold Milch, Milch Galleries, New York. Cortissoz's posthumous articles on Hassam include "Impressionistic Types of American Art," *New York Herald Tribune,* October 17, 1937, sec. 7, p. 8, and Cortissoz 1939.
37. A[lbert] E. G[allatin], "Childe Hassam: A Note," *Collector and Art Critic* 5 (January 1907), p. 103.
38. Price 1923, p. 4.
39. White 1911, p. xxx.
40. "An Almost Complete Exhibition of Childe Hassam," *Arts and Decoration* 6 (January 1916), p. 136.
41. Henry McBride, "News and Comment in the World of Art," *New York Sun,* January 7, 1917, sec. 5, p. 12.
42. "Almost Complete Exhibition of Hassam," p. 136.
43. McBride, "News and Comment in World of Art," p. 12.
44. See, for example, feature interviews by John Kimberly Mumford, "Who's Who in New York—No. 75," *New York Herald Tribune,* August 30, 1925, sec. 2, p. 3, and S. J. Woolf, "Hassam Speaks Out for American Art," *New York Times Magazine,* October 14, 1934, sec. 6, pp. 7, 17.
45. Quoted in Price 1923, p. 6.
46. Woolf, "Hassam Speaks Out," p. 7.
47. Childe Hassam, East Hampton, June 19, 1929, to C. E. S. Wood, Wood Papers (San Marino).

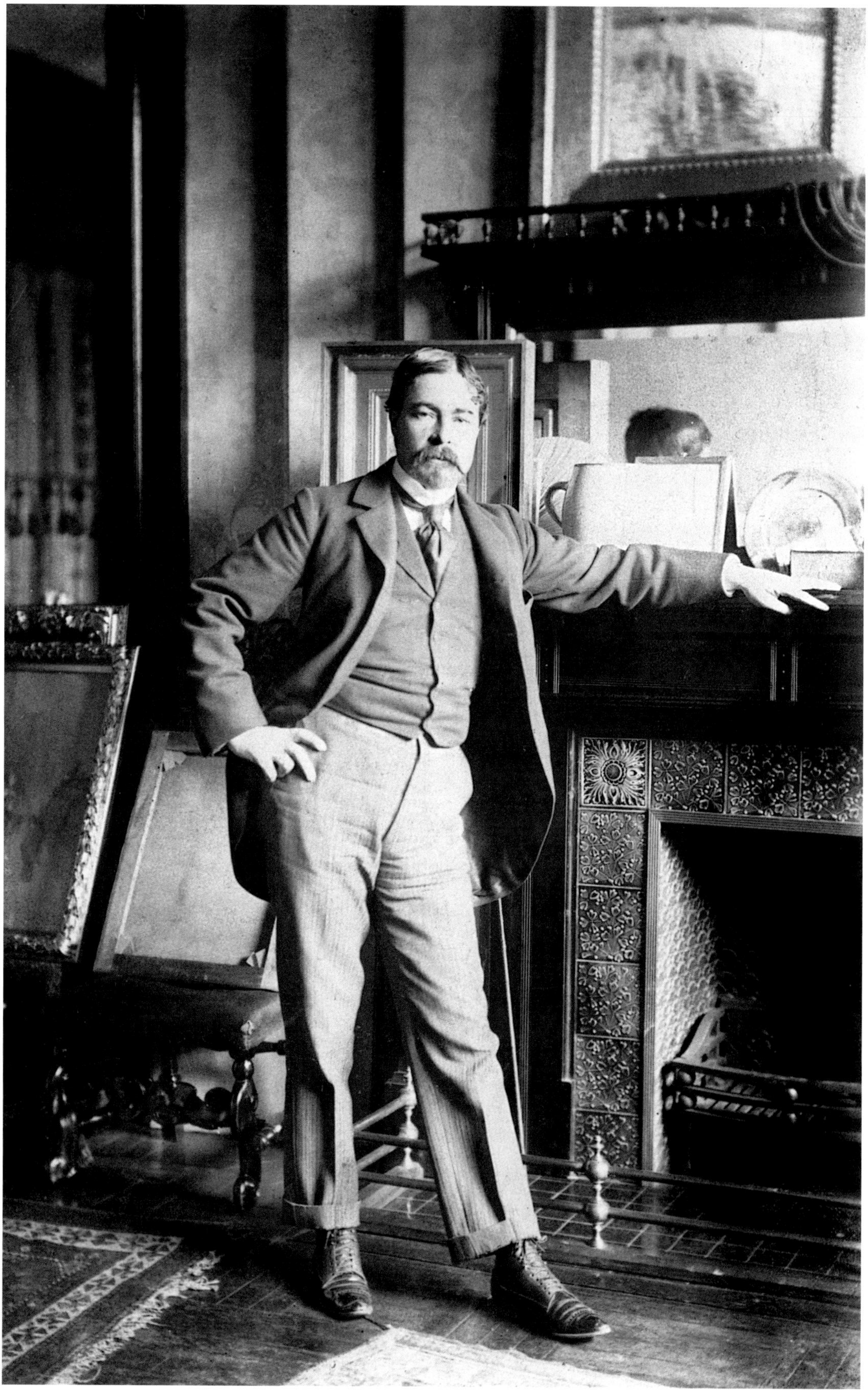

Hassam in his studio, ca. 1896

Chronology

Stephanie L. Herdrich, Megan Holloway

Only the most important solo exhibitions are listed. Hassam's participation in a recurrent group show of a major institution is cited only on his first appearance in the series or if he received an award. For a complete listing, see Exhibitions in Hassam's Lifetime in this volume.

1859
October 17 Born on Olney Street in Dorchester, Massachusetts, a suburb of Boston, to Rosa Delia Hathorne Hassam (1834–1891/92) and Frederick Fitch Hassam (1825–1912), both descendants of seventeenth-century Massachusetts settlers. Frederick works as a cutlery merchant and collects American antiques.

Attends Sunday school and services at Unitarian Church. Sketches and paints in watercolor in father's antique-filled barn.

1872
November 9–10 Father loses cutlery business in Great Boston Fire.

1875/76
Graduates from Mather School, Meeting House Hill, Dorchester.

Ca. 1875/76–77/78
Attends Dorchester High School, which was then a military school; studies drawing, watercolor, Latin, French, Greek, and German. Excels at rugby, swimming, boxing.

Lives near family of future artist Walter Gay; is friendly with Gay's brothers.

Ca. 1877
Leaves Dorchester High School in third year, without graduating, to work in accounting room at Little, Brown and Co., Boston publishers. Dismissed after three weeks. His supervisor recommends that he pursue a career in art.

Ca. 1878–81
Apprentices in shop of wood engraver George E. Johnson at 9 Milk Street, Boston. Boards first on Michigan Avenue in Dorchester, then in suburb of Hyde Park.

1879, 1880
Appears in *Boston Directory . . .* (Boston: Sampson, Davenport, and Company, 1879, 1880) as " Fred C. Hassam, draughtsman."

Ca. 1880
Perhaps through his friend watercolor painter Ross Turner, meets poet Celia Laighton Thaxter in Boston. Thaxter will become an important figure in his early career. She winters in Kittery, Maine, and hosts artists, writers, and musicians at her summer home at Appledore, Isles of Shoals.

1880/81
Summer First paints in Gloucester, Massachusetts, accompanied by Turner. There he meets artists Kenyon Cox, John Leslie Breck, Will Hicok Low, and Louis Ritter.

Ca. 1881
Begins work as free-lance illustrator, specializing in children's stories.

Designs masthead of *The Marblehead Messenger* (fig. 266).

Studies drawing and anatomy at Lowell Institute, Boston. Knows painter, sculptor, and anatomist William Rimmer, who teaches there. Takes evening class in anatomy and dissection from student of Rimmer.

1881
Before October Probably visits Thaxter in Kittery; sketches her house.

1882
February 11–March 11 *25th Exhibition of Oil Paintings,* Boston Art Club. First known public exhibition. Has already sold works in local shops.

By July 1 Has studio at 28 School Street, Boston, but boards in Hyde Park, where he will live until early 1884. Appears in *Boston Directory . . .* (Boston: Sampson, Davenport, and Company, 1882) for first time as "artist."

Summer Visits Nantucket, Medway, Sudbury, and neighboring towns in Massachusetts.

Autumn *Water Colors by Fred C. Hassam,* Williams and Everett Gallery, Boston. First one-man exhibition, includes work done during summer.

Designs illustrations for William H. Thomes, *The Belle of Australia; or, Who Am I?* and *On Land and Sea; or, California in the Years 1843, '44 and '45*, serial in *Ballou's Monthly Magazine* (published as book by De Wolfe, Fiske and Co., Boston, 1883).

At Thaxter's suggestion, discards prosaic given name in favor of unusual, presumably more marketable middle name. After signing himself "F. Childe Hassam" for a while, in 1883 begins to drop initial and becomes "Childe Hassam."

1883
By January Has rented large studio at 149A Tremont Street, Boston, for about $250 per year. Meets painter George Fuller, who also has studio in building.

From January 15 *Exhibition of Paintings by an Association of Boston Artists,* American Art Galleries, New York. New York exhibition debut

Until February 25 *16th Annual Exhibition,* American Water Color Society, New York

April 2–May 12 *58th Annual Exhibition of Paintings,* National Academy of Design, New York

Possibly travels to New York to see these exhibitions.

Late spring/early summer Makes documented stay in Portsmouth, New Hampshire, and from there probably takes first trip to Isles of Shoals to visit Thaxter at her summer cottage on Appledore.

June 30 Sails to Europe on SS *Anchoria* with fellow illustrator Edmund Henry Garrett.

July–August Travels through Europe with Garrett. Exact itinerary unknown. Visits Great Britain (Glasgow, Edinburgh, London), Netherlands (Scheveningen), France (Brittany, Auvers-sur-Oise, Paris briefly), Italy (Venice, Naples, Pompeii, Florence), Switzerland (Ouchy), and Spain (Granada, Denia, Malaga, San Sebastian). Attends bullfight in Malaga. Later recalls he was impressed by English watercolorists, particularly J. M. W. Turner, whose works he sees in cellar of National Gallery, London. Studies Dutch masterpieces in Netherlands and Spanish pictures in Prado, Madrid. Visits major galleries in Venice. Paints in watercolor throughout trip. First attempts at etching

Late August–early September Sails from Naples to New York on SS *Alsatia*, which stops at several Spanish ports before crossing Atlantic. Visits and paints at Alhambra, Granada. Paints in watercolor aboard ship (see fig. 27). Works in studio at 12 West Street, Boston, on return.

From September 3 *Foreign Exhibition,* Massachusetts Charitable Mechanics' Association, Boston. Perhaps sees the seventeen works by leading French Impressionists included and is inspired by them.

From December 4 *Pedestal Fund Art Loan Exhibition,* National Academy of Design, New York. Possibly attends or hears about this four-week exhibition, which includes French Impressionist works.

December School of Drawing at Boston Art Club opens. Enrolls in classes taught by Tommaso Juglaris, Italian artist who had worked under Thomas Couture in Paris.

Substitutes for Turner as Thaxter's watercolor instructor.

Meets Emil Carlsen.

Joins Paint and Clay Club, Boston, along with Garrett.

Jean Ingelow, *The High Tide on the Coast of Lincolnshire* (Boston: Roberts Brothers), with illustrations by Hassam, published.

1884
February 1 Marries Montreal-born Kathleen Maud Doane (1862–1946), known as "Maud."

Early in year Moves to The Albemarle, at 282 Columbus Avenue on corner of Clarendon Street in Boston's newly expanded South End. Begins painting urban street scenes. Keeps studio at 12 West Street.

October 30–December 11 *55th Annual Exhibition,* Pennsylvania Academy of the Fine Arts, Philadelphia

December First appearance of illustrations by Hassam in *Wide Awake*, periodical to which he will contribute regularly until 1887.

Water Colors by Hassam, Williams and Everett Gallery, Boston

Contributes illustrations to *The Poetical Works of Lord Byron* and *Favorite Poems Selected from English and American Authors* (both New York: Thomas Y. Crowell and Co.), as well as *Doll Rosy's Days* (Boston: D. Lothrop and Co.), all published this year.

1885
April 11–May 2 *32nd Exhibition, Water Colors, Black and White Drawings, and Sculpture,* Boston Art Club. Includes *The Public Garden* (fig. 41), first Boston street scene he has exhibited.

E. S. Brooks, *In No Man's Land, A Wonder Story* (Boston: D. Lothrop and Co.), children's book with illustrations by Hassam, published.

Places before his signature a crescent, at first rendered carefully and later more cursorily.

1886
From April 10 *Special Exhibition. Works in Oil and Pastel by the Impressionists of Paris. Exhibition under the management of the American Art Association of the city of New York,* American Art Association, New York. May visit exhibition here or at its second venue, National Academy of Design, New York, where it opens on May 25.

May 5–October 15 *8th Exhibition of the Society of American Artists,* The Metropolitan Museum of Art, New York

August First recorded visit to Appledore, Isles of Shoals. Paints watercolor series of White Island lighthouse.

Summer Probably visits Nantucket.

Autumn With Maud sails for Europe to study in Paris. Before departure, announces intention to remain abroad for three years.

By November 20 Has moved into apartment with adjoining studio at 11, boulevard Clichy. Other residents include painters Puvis de Chavannes, Giovanni Boldini, Henri Pille, and American Frank Boggs.

By end of year Has enrolled in Académie Julian, where he works under Gustave Boulanger and Jules-Joseph Lefebvre in studio at 48, rue de faubourg Saint-Denis in tenth arrondissement. Is introduced into studio by Albert Henry Munsell. Meets Ernest L. Major there. Remains friendly with Garrett, who had been studying there with Boulanger, Lefebvre, and Jean-Paul Laurens since 1879. His tenure overlaps with that of Boston colleague Breck.

Later recalls contact with American painters Boggs, Gari Melchers, Edward Simmons, Ogden Wood, and Moses White.

M. E. Blake, *Youth in Twelve Centuries* (Boston: D. Lothrop and Co.), with illustrations by Hassam, published.

Charles Stuart Pratt, *Bye-o-baby Ballads* (Boston: D. Lathrop and Co., ca. 1886), with illustrations by Hassam, published.

1887
January 11 Writes from Paris to Boston art critic William Howe Downes, encouraging him to promote upcoming auction of his works at Noyes, Cobb and Co., noting that he depends "a good deal on the success of that sale." Writes, "I am drawing like a slave at Julians and shall until Spring" (transcribed in Hiesinger 1994, p. 177). Will later maintain he worked at Julian's for a year and a half, until spring 1888 (Lockman interview, January 31, 1927, p. 14).

March 9–10 *Exhibition and Sale of Works in Oil and Water Color by Childe Hassam,* Noyes, Cobb and Co., Boston. Sale grosses $3,957.50, which helps finance stay abroad.

From May 1 Paris Salon. First salon in which he exhibits. His entry, *Une Averse—rue Bonaparte* (fig. 54), shown at Goupil's, Paris, for a week after Salon closes.

Summer Begins Grand Prix series. Travels to Normandy. Visits Villiers-le-Bel, about ten miles northeast of Paris in Oise Valley near Ecouen, as guest of businessman Ernest Blumenthal and his wife, who has befriended Maud, and paints in their garden. Their house stands on property owned by a daughter of Couture.

By November 29 Has moved to 35, boulevard Rochechouart, Paris.

November Having sold first *Grand Prix Day* (fig. 58) to a Mr. Williams, is working on second and larger version (fig. 359).

Sarah Chauncey Woolsey, *Ballads of Romance and History* (Boston, D. Lothrop and Co.), with illustrations by Hassam and others, published.

1888
Spring Probably leaves Académie Julian.

June Visits Le Havre.

Summer Visits Villiers-le-Bel and again paints in Blumenthals' garden. Also goes to Ecouen and Auvers-sur-Oise and possibly Sannois and Ermont.

1889
March 11–23 *Exhibition and Private Sale of . . . Mr. Childe Hassam,* Noyes, Cobb and Co., Boston, is a critical and financial success.

May 5–October 31 Exposition Universelle, Paris; bronze medal. Attends exhibition, admires American section.

July Paints small series of works recording Bastille Day celebrations.

Summer Visits Blumenthals at Villiers-le-Bel and paints in garden. Travels to Bougival, Saint-Cloud, and Suresnes, all on outskirts of Paris, perhaps also to Brittany. Travels to England, where he stays for half of summer, visiting London, Broadstairs, Canterbury, Chiswick, and other places, and paints watercolors.

Late summer–early autumn In preparation for return to United States, moves temporarily to smaller studio and apartment at 35, boulevard Rochechouart previously occupied by Renoir.

October 17 Spends thirtieth birthday aboard ship in transit to United States with Maud and her sister.

Late October Docks in New York. Immediately travels to Boston, where he spends about one month.

Before December Moves to New York and rents apartment and studio at 95 Fifth Avenue, at southeast corner of Seventeenth Street; building also occupied by painter Bruce Crane. Befriends painter and sculptor Frederic Remington.

1890
January Exhibition at Doll and Richards Gallery, Boston, first of many solo shows held there through 1895.

February 3–March 1 *23rd Annual Exhibition,* American Water Color Society, New York. At opening makes first sale of a watercolor in New York, to painter Samuel Colman. At exhibition, meets painters John H. Twachtman and J. Alden Weir, who will become his closest friends.

March 19 Elected member of American Water Color Society at its annual meeting; will remain member for rest of his life.

May 22 New York Water-Color Club incorporated. Hassam a founding member and first president, a position he retains until 1896.

June, July, and part of September Stays at Appledore, Isles of Shoals, marking beginning of pattern of making long visits to New England locales. Paints first of series showing poppies in bloom in Thaxter's garden. Probably builds painting studio to which he will frequently return during summers until about 1916. At Appledore during 1890s will meet Richard Watson Gilder, editor of *Century,* and Henry M. Alden, editor of *Harper's New Monthly Magazine,* among others.

Summer Travels to Gloucester, Massachusetts.

Autumn Bedford, Massachusetts

Joins Society of American Painters in Pastel in New York and shows in its final exhibition.

Joins Society of American Artists; will remain member for rest of his life.

Accepts invitation to join Players Club, New York; will remain member until 1931.

Boston Art Club purchases *Winter Nightfall in the City,* 1889 (private collection).

With F. Hopkinson Smith, Rhoda Holmes Nicholls, and Turner, makes watercolor illustrations for new edition of William Dean Howells, *Venetian Life* (Boston and New York: Houghton, Mifflin and Co., 1892), originally published in 1866.

1891
June 4–July 13 *Exposition de Peintures et Sculptures d'Artistes Américains,* Galerie Durand-Ruel, Paris

Summer Isles of Shoals

September, October Lexington, Concord, Bedford, and Belmont, Massachusetts

1891/92
His mother dies.

1892
March *2nd Annual Exhibition of Water Colors and Pastels,* Art Club of Philadelphia; gold medal for watercolor for *La Bouquetière et la Laitière* (fig. 68).

May Publication in *Scribner's Magazine* of illustration depicting Chicago suggests he had visited the city by this time in connection with World's Columbian Exposition.

June 1–October Accepts painter Charles F. Ulrich's invitation to exhibit in sixth *Internationalen Kunst-Ausstellung,* Königliche Glaspalaste, Munich; Second Medal

July, August Isles of Shoals. Paints series of garden scenes, mostly watercolors, that will become illustrations in Thaxter's, *Island Garden* (see 1894, below).

Autumn Lexington, Lenox, and Quincy, Massachusetts

Late in year Moves apartment and studio to Chelsea Hotel, 222 West Twenty-third Street, New York.

Late 1892–early 1893 Chicago. Adds skies and groups of figures to other artists' architectural drawings of World's Columbian Exposition buildings; these are intended for reproduction in limited edition set of chromolithographs *Gems of the White City.* Hired by Frank Millet to create original drawings of exposition buildings. Meets businessman and collector Charles Deering and golf expert Charles B. McDonald. Returns to New York before exposition opens.

1893
April–May Executes commission for series of drawings that will appear in Mariana Van Rensselaer, "Fifth Avenue with Pictures by Childe Hassam," *Century* 47 (November 1893).

From May 1 World's Columbian Exposition, Chicago; prizes in painting and watercolor, including Department of Fine Arts Medal. Does not visit exposition.

July Isles of Shoals

November 8–29 *2nd Annual Exhibition of Water Colors by American Artists,* Macbeth Gallery, New York. First exhibition at gallery that will become his primary New York dealer.

Moves to Rembrandt Building, 152 West Fifty-seventh Street, New York.

Award from Cleveland Art Association

1894
May 30 Visits Twachtman at his home in Greenwich, Connecticut, probably not for first time.

July Gloucester. Holds small exhibition of watercolors at his hotel cottage.

August Isles of Shoals

August 26 Thaxter dies suddenly at Appledore, after Hassam has departed.

Publication of Celia Laighton Thaxter, *An Island Garden,* with watercolor illustrations by Hassam (Boston and New York: Houghton, Mifflin and Co.).

Named corresponding member of Munich Secession.

1895
January 22–March 2 *1st Annual Exhibition,* Cleveland Art Association; first prize ($350) for watercolor *Fifth Avenue, New York* (fig. 260)

January Travels to Havana with friend Frank Robinson, coal merchant who does business in Cuba. Paints in Cuba for at least one month.

February 5 Arrives in New York with Robinson aboard SS *Yumuri.*

March 25–April 27 *17th Annual Exhibition of the Society of American Artists*, New York; Webb Prize for *Place Centrale and Fort Cabanas, Havana* (fig. 196)

May and June "The Insurrection in Cuba," with illustrations by Hassam, published in *Harper's Weekly* 39 (May 18), p. 458 (May 25), p. 490, (June 8), p. 543. Based illustrations on drawings made during stay in Cuba, although he had returned to New York before the revolt against Spanish domination, led by José Martí, began on February 24, 1895.

July Gloucester with Willard L. Metcalf

August Isles of Shoals. Following Thaxter's death and the deterioration of her garden, turns increasingly to island's rocks and surrounding sea for subject matter.

November First exhibition at Carnegie Art Galleries, Pittsburgh, as part of dedication program for Carnegie Library

Mid–late 1890s
Meets Albert Pinkham Ryder, through Weir, and Abbott H. Thayer.

1896
January 13–February 15 *53rd Exhibition, Oil Paintings and Sculpture*, Boston Art Club; second prize ($1,500) for *Summer Sunlight*, 1892 (Israel Museum, Jerusalem)

February 6–7 American Art Galleries, New York. Exhibition and auction of 205 works including oils, watercolors, and pastels from his entire career, considered financial disaster, with proceeds totaling about $9,600, or about $47 per picture (Hiesinger 1994, p. 104).

March Serves on New York jury for *8th Annual Exhibition of Water Colors, Pastels, and Miniatures by American Artists* at Art Institute of Chicago.

June Gloucester

Summer Isles of Shoals

September In Winter Harbor, Maine, paints views of Ironbound Island and Cadillac Mountain.

Autumn Visits Twachtman in Greenwich, Connecticut, and makes first of many visits to neighboring Cos Cob.

November–January 1897 Shows in *1st Annual Exhibition*, Carnegie Art Galleries, Pittsburgh; serves as member of jury for subsequent annuals.

By December 8 Sublets studio in Rembrandt Building, New York, to Miss Waring, a daughter of Colonel George E. Waring Jr., commissioner of city's Street-Cleaning Department. Relocates temporarily to Hotel Grenoble, on Seventh Avenue between Fifty-sixth and Fifty-seventh Streets, before sailing for Naples with Maud. On ship meets Charles Francis Adams, a brother of historian Henry Adams.

1897
Through January In and around Naples, paints views of Posilippo, Capri, and Bay of Naples, then travels north to Rome and Florence. Visits Charles Francis Adams at his villa outside Florence. Studies old master paintings in Florence.

By April 27 In Paris in time for opening of Paris Salon. Stays at hotel on Quai Voltaire.

May Elected associate member of Société Nationale des Beaux-Arts, Paris.

Late spring/early summer Visits Blumenthals at Villiers-le-Bel and paints in their garden.

Summer Visits London and paints along River Stour in English countryside.

Late summer, early autumn Pont-Aven and Le Pouldu in Brittany

October 20 Back in New York. Sends telegram to John W. Beatty, director of Carnegie Art Galleries, presumably referring to the year's annual exhibition, asking, "Is it too late to send some [of] my best pictures [?]" (Carnegie Papers, letter 132, division H, file 7).

Autumn Greenwich

December 17 Resigns from Society of American Artists and with Twachtman and Weir establishes Ten American Painters, or the Ten. Other members are Frank W. Benson, Joseph R. DeCamp, Thomas W. Dewing, Metcalf, Robert Reid, Simmons, and Edmund C. Tarbell. Twachtman will die in 1902 and be replaced by William Merritt Chase in 1905 (see fig. 20).

1898
January 7 Breaks silence that had surrounded founding of Ten American Painters by relating the story to reporter friend Hutchins Hapgood, who publishes account on front page of *Commercial Advertiser* on January 8. The secession of the Ten from the Society of American Artists sparks acrimony among some members of the latter group and controversy in the New York art world.

March 31–April 16 *1st Exhibition, Ten American Painters*, Durand-Ruel Galleries, New York. No. 26, *The Bather* (location unknown) presumably depicts a nude and is one of the first of many Hassam will paint.

Summer Does not visit Isles of Shoals, fearing attack related to Spanish-American War.

By July 4 First visit to East Hampton, New York, where he spends time with friend painter G. Ruger Donoho. Paints *July Night* (fig. 239), apparently on July 4 in Donohos' garden.

Autumn Cos Cob, where he visits the Holleys.

November 3, 1898–January 1, 1899 *3rd Annual Exhibition*, Carnegie Institute, Pittsburgh; Second Class (silver) medal for *The Sea* (see fig. 329), displayed in tabernacle-style frame probably designed by Stanford White

Late December 1898–May 1899 Teaches at Art Students League, New York, as midyear substitute for Frank Duveneck (course unknown).

One of first 250 members elected to National Institute of Arts and Letters, founded in New York this year; will remain member for rest of his life.

1899
January 16–February 25 *68th Annual Exhibition*, Pennsylvania Academy of the Fine Arts, Philadelphia; Temple Gold Medal for *Pont Royal* (fig. 330).

June–July Negotiates sale of *Pont Royal* to Cincinnati Art Museum: his first sale to a museum.

Summer Gloucester; Duveneck, DeCamp, and Metcalf also there. Also visits Isles of Shoals.

By September 20 New York

Autumn, Greenwich

November 2, 1899–January 1, 1900 *4th Annual Exhibition*, Carnegie Institute, Pittsburgh; two awards, one for *Fifth Avenue in Winter* (fig. 87), which Carnegie Institute purchases for $800 early in 1900, the other for *White Island Light*, 1899 (Smith College Museum of Art, Northampton, Massachusetts).

Publication of *Three Cities* (New York: R. H. Russell) comprising forty-nine of Hassam's views of New York, Paris, and London, executed in various media (see fig. 263).

1900
April 14–November 12 Exposition Universelle, Paris; Silver Medal for *Fifth Avenue in Winter* (fig. 87), the only painting he shows

April 23 Attends celebration of Shakespeare's birthday at Players Club, New York.

Summer Provincetown, Massachusetts

August, September Isles of Shoals, Gloucester

September 25 Returns to New York.

Joins Salmagundi Club, New York; will remain member for rest of his life.

1901
Winter Visits Chicago.

May 1–October 31 Pan-American Exposition, Buffalo; Gold Medal from exposition's Department of Fine Arts

August Isles of Shoals

September Cos Cob. Back in New York by September 27.

Late September–October Newport, Rhode Island

October Moves to Holbein Studio Building, 139 West Fifty-fifth Street, New York.

1902
Spring Unclear whether he makes repeated visits to Cos Cob from spring through November or makes it his base for most of year. Moves apartment and studio about this time and may use Holley House in Cos Cob as interim home.

Summer New Canaan and Cos Cob

August 8 Twachtman dies.

September–November Cos Cob. Other visitors include Charles Ebert, Elmer Livingston MacRae, Walter Fitch, Carolyn Mase, and possibly Weir.

November Joins artists who plan to build cooperative studio building at 27 West Sixty-seventh Street, New York; others include Allen Butler Talcott, Robert Sewell, Frank Vincent DuMond, and Henry Ward Ranger.

Elected Associate of National Academy of Design, New York.

1903
Late March After short stay at Sherwood Studio Building, 58 West Fifty-seventh Street, has moved to 27 West Sixty-seventh Street.

July First of many visits to Old Lyme, Connecticut, probably at suggestion of other artists in West Sixty-seventh Street studio building. Will become friendly with Florence Griswold, proprietor of Old Lyme boardinghouse, where he stays with DuMond, William Henry Howe, Henry Rankin Poore, and Ranger. Metcalf and Simmons join him on subsequent sojourns in Cos Cob.

August Isles of Shoals

Autumn Cos Cob and probably Branchville, Connecticut, to visit Weir

October Old Lyme. Travels to Pittsburgh to serve as a juror for *8th Annual Exhibition*, Carnegie Institute.

1904
June, July Old Lyme

August, September Travels to Portland, Oregon, to install murals in library of friend Colonel C. E. S. Wood. Paints on seacoast and in Harney desert area of eastern Oregon. Visits Seattle and San Francisco.

August–October Louisiana Purchase Exposition, Saint Louis; two gold medals from Department of Fine Arts, one for oils, the other for pastels

October 17 Returns to New York.

October Juror for *9th Annual Exhibition*, Carnegie Institute, Pittsburgh. Writes to Wood from New York on December 13: "That is my last service on that jury!" (Wood Papers [Berkeley]).

October, November Old Lyme

By November 23 Back in New York.

December 31, 1904–January 30, 1905 *80th Annual Exhibition*, National Academy of Design, New York; Thomas B. Clarke Prize for *Lorelei*, 1904 (Walters Art Gallery, Baltimore)

Late in year Places first order for frames with Carrig-Rohane, shop founded in Winchester, Massachusetts, in 1903 by Hermann Dudley Murphy, who worked with Charles Prendergast and Walfred Thulin.

1905
January 12–28 *Exhibition of Paintings by Childe Hassam,* Montross Gallery, New York, first of many solo exhibitions there

April Old Lyme

July Old Lyme, Isles of Shoals, and, by July 25, Windham, Connecticut, to visit Weir.

August–September 2 Isles of Shoals

October Old Lyme

November 2, 1905–January 1, 1906 *10th Annual Exhibition,* Carnegie Institute, Pittsburgh; Third Class Medal for *June* (fig. 321)

1906
Early in year Plans spring trip to Bermuda; excursion apparently canceled.

January 22–March 3 *101st Annual Exhibition,* Pennsylvania Academy of the Fine Arts, Philadelphia; Walter Lippincott Prize for *Rock Cliff: Appledore,* 1903 (Indianapolis Museum of Art), and award for *Summer Morning: Isles of Shoals* (location unknown)

March 17–April 22 *28th Annual Exhibition of the Society of American Artists,* Galleries of the American Fine Arts Society, New York. Final exhibition of Society of American Artists, which will be subsumed into National Academy of Design, New York. The Ten invited to contribute. Submits *June* (fig. 321) and wins Carnegie Prize ($500).

April 1906–April 1907 Negotiates sale of thirty drawings to Carnegie Institute, Pittsburgh.

May Old Lyme

May 31–September 23 *9th Annual Exhibition of Oil Paintings, Summer Exhibition,* Worcester Art Museum, Massachusetts; Third Prize for *Rock Cliff, Appledore,* 1903 (Indianapolis Museum of Art)

By June 7 Old Lyme

June 9 Travels to Branchville, Connecticut, to visit Weir.

By July 7 Old Lyme

Ca. July 25–August 20/22 Isles of Shoals

Late August New London, Connecticut

By September 7 In Wainscott, Long Island, visiting friends Henry Keney Pomroy, president of New York Stock Exchange, and his wife, Annie T.

September 13 Places first order with Carrig-Rohane for its frame number 33, introduced in 1903, a cassetta form that will become known as the "Hassam pattern" (fig. 335).

By October 8–early November Old Lyme

Elected Academician of National Academy of Design, New York.

1907
January 8 Writes from New York to Wood that he has "just returned from Philadelphia" (Wood Papers [Berkeley]).

June Wainscott, Long Island

July 11–late August Isles of Shoals. Also spends few days at Cornish colony, New Hampshire.

By September 25 In New York, writes to Wood: "I'll be in the country somewhere through October" (Wood Papers [Berkeley]).

Paints at Cos Cob. Travels to Phoenicia in Catskill Mountains, New York. Possibly visits Old Lyme.

1908
Spring Bedford Hills, New York, and possibly Old Lyme

April 11 Visits Philadelphia for opening of *Paintings by Ten American Painters,* group's tenth anniversary exhibition.

July, August Isles of Shoals and Old Lyme

August 28 Stratham, New Hampshire

Late August–early September *7th Annual Exhibition,* Public Library, Old Lyme. May visit when his paintings are shown here.

Autumn Vacates 27 West Sixty-seventh Street while new studio and apartment at 130 West Fifty-seventh Street are still under construction. Maud stays in Hotel Gregorian on West Thirty-fifth Street while Hassam travels west.

September 3 Meets Wood in Ontario.

September–October Visits San Francisco and Portland, Oregon. With Judge Charles Carey and Wood, camps for two months on Blitzen River in heart of Harney and Malheur counties of eastern Oregon, where he paints forty canvases.

November Returns to Portland with Wood. Paints several portraits of Wood's family members and friends.

Late November Returns to New York. Serves on jury of selection for *Winter Exhibition,* National Academy of Design, New York.

December 1 Moves to studio and apartment in new cooperative building at 130 West Fifty-seventh Street, which he will retain for rest of his life.

1909
April 8–21 *Exhibition of Paintings of Eastern Oregon by Childe Hassam,* Montross Gallery, New York

April 19 The Metropolitan Museum of Art acquires its first work by Hassam, *Coast Scene, Isles of Shoals* (fig. 22), as gift from George A. Hearn, who had purchased the painting in 1908.

May–June Yarmouth, Massachusetts, and Portland, Maine

June 10 From its *13th Annual Exhibition,* Carnegie Institute purchases *Spring Morning,* 1909 (fig. 10), first painting of Window series, for permanent collection for $6,000.

July–August Isles of Shoals

Summer Visits East Hampton.

September Spends week in Portsmouth, New Hampshire. Travels to Gloucester.

Late September–October Returns briefly to New York.

Autumn Visits Old Lyme and New Haven. With Beatty begins planning retrospective exhibition to coincide with Carnegie Institute's *14th Annual Exhibition* in spring 1910.

Late October Visits Remington at Ridgefield, Connecticut.

Joins Lotos Club, New York; remains member until 1916 or 1917.

1910
January 6 Indicates interest in printmaking in letter to Beatty: "You shall have a proof of the first etching I make" (Carnegie Papers, file 673).

January 23–March 20 *105th Annual Exhibition,* Pennsylvania Academy of the Fine Arts, Philadelphia; Jennie Sesnan Gold Medal for *Summer Sea,* 1906 (Grand Rapids Art Museum)

Spring To Wainscott, Long Island, to visit Pomroys.

May 2–June 30 *14th Annual Exhibition,* Carnegie Institute, Pittsburgh, includes showing of thirty-eight of Hassam's works.

May 23 Sells four paintings to Wood for total of $5,500. First payment of $2,500 allows Hassams to travel to Europe that summer and fall; smaller installments covering balance paid between May 1913 and October 1919.

June 11 Departs for Europe with Maud on SS *Saint Louis,* which will dock in London.

Late June–early July Travels and visits museums in Netherlands (Haarlem, Amsterdam, The Hague), also goes to Antwerp. By July 2 in Haarlem. By July 4 in Amsterdam.

July–October Paints in Paris, Côte du Nord, Lannion, Brélévenez, Perros-Guirec, Nemours, La Clarté, Grez-sur-Loing. Later travels and paints in Spain (Madrid, Toledo, Ronda, Cordova, Seville). By about July 7 at Hôtel l'Empire, 7, rue Daunou, Paris. From hotel balcony paints *July Fourteenth, Rue Daunou, 1910* (fig. 205), important precursor of his New York Flag series of 1916–19. On July 21 "about to move on to the Côte du Nord by the sea," according to letter to Weir (Hassam Papers, reel NAA2, frame 66). By August 3 in Côte du Nord. By September 7 at Hôtel Chevillon, Grez-sur-Loing. Writes to Wood: "I am leaving here soon for Paris " and "Mrs. Hassam has been in Paris for a week." (Wood Papers, Berkeley). By September 27 at Gran Hotel Imperial, Toledo. Writes to Wood that Toledo is "tremendously interesting and one could paint here forever" (Wood Papers (Berkeley).

By October 17 In Gibraltar. Departs for New York today, his birthday.

October 28 Arrives in New York aboard SS *Prinzess Irene.*

November 17 Attends funeral of John La Farge at Church of Saint Francis Xavier, New York.

December 8 Attends annual meeting of American Academy of Arts and Letters at New Theatre, New York.

December 13, 1910–January 22, 1911 *3rd Exhibition of Oil Paintings by Contemporary American Artists,* Corcoran Gallery of Art, Washington, D.C.; Corcoran Bronze Medal for *Springtime* (location unknown)

1911
February Sells *Contre-Jour,* 1910, to Art Institute of Chicago.

May–June Travels alone to Europe. Visits Paris but cancels planned trip to Venice because he fears outbreak of disease; returns to New York on SS *Kronprinzessin Cecilie* via Cherbourg.

June 29 Arrives in New York.

July East Hampton

By July 20–August Isles of Shoals

Early September Rockingham, New Hampshire, then possibly Branchville, Connecticut

September 10 Goes to Cos Cob to visit Twachtman.

September 12 New York

December 28, 1911–January 15, 1912 *Exhibition of Oil Paintings, Water Colors, Pastels and Drawings by Childe Hassam,* Corcoran Gallery of Art, Washington, D.C., includes fifty-nine works.

Paints at Cos Cob. Sells *The Breakfast Room* (fig. 333) to Worcester Art Museum, Massachusetts.

1912
January 18 Places last order for frames from Carrig-Rohane.

March 22 Places first documented order for frames from Milch Gallery, New York, launching relationship that will endure for rest of his life.

April 25–May 12 *45th Annual Exhibition,* American Water Color Society, New York; W. T. Evans Prize ($300) for *The Minuet* (location unknown)

June In Old Lyme, paints *Twenty-sixth of June, Old Lyme* (fig. 173) to honor Maud's fiftieth birthday.

July In Isles of Shoals, begins series of watercolors he will call "The Isles of Shoals Set, 1912–16."

Summer Cos Cob

October Cos Cob

December 17, 1912–January 26, 1913 *4th Exhibition of Oil Paintings by Contemporary Artists*, Corcoran Gallery of Art, Washington, D.C.; First William A. Clark Prize and Corcoran Gold Medal ($2,000) for *The New York Window* (fig. 227), which Corcoran purchases for its permanent collection.

Autumn Takes up etching and is encouraged by printmaker Kerr Eby, with whom he works in Cos Cob. Introduced to David Keppel, who will exhibit his prints at Frederick Keppel and Co., New York, from 1915 until 1932.

Late in year Declines offer of membership in Association of American Painters and Sculptors, formed in 1911 to exhibit work of progressive living American and foreign artists. The association, at odds with conservative National Academy of Design, will present Armory Show in February 1913.

Father dies.

1913
January Through friend architect Henry Bacon receives commission for mural, *Fruits and Flowers* (fig. 210), for Panama-Pacific International Exposition to be held in San Francisco in 1915.

February 17–March 15 Shows twelve works in *International Exhibition of Modern Art, at the Armory of the 69th Infantry*, Association of American Painters and Sculptors, New York; shows thirteen works when exhibition travels to Art Institute of Chicago in March–April.

Summer Probably Isles of Shoals

September Spends week or two in Cos Cob.

1914
February–March Travels to San Francisco to complete and install *Fruits and Flowers* at Panama-Pacific International Exposition. Mural is placed over entrance to Palace of Education on west side of Court of Palms in Bernard Maybeck's colossal Palace of Fine Arts. Stays at Bohemian Club. Falls ill and is briefly hospitalized. Later visits San Anselmo, Sausalito, Point Lobos, and Carmel.

June Cos Cob. Paints *Self-Portrait* (fig. 356).

August Isles of Shoals and Boston

Late summer Cos Cob. Travels to Belfast, Maine.

September 13 Fire sweeps Appledore, destroying hotel and cottages, including Hassam's studio.

November 7 Old Lyme

1915
February 20–December 14 Panama-Pacific International Exposition, San Francisco, includes separate gallery with thirty-eight paintings by Hassam, as well as his *Fruit and Flowers*.

May–June Visits painters Gifford Beal and Reynolds Beal at Newburgh, New York. Visits West Point, Mount Kisco, Poughkeepsie, Fishkill, and other places in area. Paints " Hudson River Set" of watercolors.

June–August Cos Cob. Begins serious work in etching. Writes to Wood on July 14: "I am making etchings—Weir has been starting me for years—So this year I am in it—I would like to have you see some proof—There is a press out here and I am surprised that I can print so well." (Wood Papers [Berkeley]).

August Long Ridge, Connecticut, and Portsmouth, Exeter, and Stratham, New Hampshire. Possibly visits Isles of Shoals.

September Old Lyme

Mid-September Cos Cob, after brief visit to Boston

October, November Cos Cob

November 27–December 11 *Exhibition of Pictures by Childe Hassam*, Montross Gallery, New York, includes "Hudson River Group," "California Group," "Mount Hood Group," and "Isles of Shoals Group."

November 30–December 18 *Exhibition of Etchings and Dry Points by Childe Hassam*, Frederick Keppel and Co., New York, his first show of prints.

Late November–early December Sits on jury of selection for *Winter Exhibition*, National Academy of Design, New York.

Possibly visits Gloucester.

1916
April Buffalo

April 27 Attends 91st Annual Dinner of National Academy of Design at Delmonico's, New York.

May 13 Preparedness Day Parade held in New York, first major public demonstration in support of World War I. Flag displays inspire Hassam to paint Flag series.

June, July New York. Paints first major canvas of Flag series: *The Fourth of July, 1916* (fig. 229).

July Cos Cob, Newburgh, and Gloucester

Summer Probably makes last visit to Isles of Shoals.

August East Hampton, Newport, and Portsmouth, New Hampshire

September Boston, Newfields, and Stratham, New Hampshire

October Chicago

December Washington, D.C.

Joins Coffee House, New York; will be resident member until 1927 and nonresident member 1928–35.

1917
January 4–20 *Exhibition of Pictures by Childe Hassam*, Montross Gallery, New York, includes two of earliest Flag paintings.

Early in year Becomes founding member and first chairman of Painter-Gravers of America, association seeking to encourage development of artist-print in United States and to educate public about prints through exhibitions and lectures. Other founding members include George Bellows, John Marin, John Sloan, and Weir.

June Catskills, New York, and Exeter, New Hampshire

July East Hampton

August Newfields

August–September Stratham and Portsmouth

September Poland Spring, Maine

October One of thirty-three artists who sign petition opposing erection of replicas of George Grey Barnard's statue of Abraham Lincoln in Paris and London, calling image an "unworthy representation" (*New York Times*, October 26, 1917, p. 14).

Late in year Begins to make lithographs.

1918
March 13–April 21 *93rd Annual Exhibition*, National Academy of Design, New York; Second Altman Prize ($500) for *Allies Day, May 1917* (fig. 232).

April 16 Arrested in Riverside Park, New York, for sketching camouflaged American transport ship anchored in Hudson (see fig. 288).

June Bethel, Connecticut, and Boston

July–September Gloucester. Poses for bust-length portrait by sculptor Charles Grafly (plaster, 1918, Wichita State University; bronze, 1918, Philadelphia Museum of Art).

Summer Visits East Hampton.

September East Hampton. *Winter Sickle Pears* (fig. 249) inscribed *East Hampton Sept 24th, 1918*.

October Cos Cob

November 15–December 7 *Exhibition of a Series of Paintings of the "Avenue of the Allies" by Childe Hassam*, Durand-Ruel Galleries, New York, first major exhibition of Flag series (see fig. 346)

Works as printmaker, producing only lithographs.

1918–20
Places at least ten orders for Whistler-style frames from Milch Gallery, New York.

1919
February 6–27 *Exhibition of Pictures by Ten American Painters*, Corcoran Gallery of Art, Washington, D.C., group's last exhibition.

February 6–28 *52nd Annual Exhibition of the American Water Color Society*, New York; Alexander M. Hudnut prize ($200) for *Mt. Beacon from Broadway, Newburgh*, 1916 (Colby College Museum of Art, Waterville, Maine)

February 27 A guest of honor at tea at Ritz-Carlton Hotel, New York, held by Book Committee of the Art War Relief. Also honored is Alfred Noyes, whose poems "The Avenue of the Allies" and "Victory" book committee is publishing with Hassam's *Allies Day, May 1917* (fig. 232), as volume's frontispiece.

February Serves on jury of selection for *94th Annual Exhibition*, National Academy of Design, New York, and on Advisory Board of Society of Independent Artists, New York.

April 23 Orders frame that incorporates his initial into design from Milch Gallery, New York, his first recorded order of this type and first such design by an American artist.

May Completes last picture in Flag series, *Victory Day, May 1919* (fig. 235).

July Southampton and East Hampton

Late July, September Gloucester

August Purchases Willow Bend, at 48 Egypt Lane, East Hampton, house built in 1722. Starting in 1920 and for rest of his life lives there from about May through October each year.

September Rockport, Massachusetts, Boston, and East Hampton

October Newburgh and vicinity

November Sues art dealer Frank K. M. Rehn to recover possession of painting *Flower Girl Selling Peonies*, 1890 (location unknown), which Hassam claims was stolen from him in 1903. Rehn believes he purchased painting in good faith.

November 9–December 14 *17th Annual Philadelphia Water Color Exhibition, and the 18th Annual Exhibition of Miniatures*, Pennsylvania Academy of the Fine Arts, Philadelphia; Philadelphia Water Color Prize

December 8 Weir dies.

1920
February 8–March 28 *115th Annual Exhibition*, Pennsylvania Academy of the Fine Arts, Philadelphia; Gold Medal of Honor for lifetime achievement

October Montauk, Long Island, and Bethel, Connecticut

November 17 Elected to American Academy of Arts and Letters, New York, chair number 41; remains member for rest of his life.

"In 1920 he said the revenue from his brush that year was $100,000" ("Art Fund Created by Hassam's Will," *New York Times,* November 13, 1935, p. 18). 2002 equivalent is $896,502.

1921
February 7 Attends dinner and reception in honor of British sculptor Claire Sheridan hosted by Condé Nast and Frank Crowninshield at Coffee House, New York.

April Sits on jury for sixth competition of John Armstrong Chaloner Concours at National Academy of Design, New York.

September 22 With Cass Gilbert, Edwin H. Blashfield, Herbert Adams, Daniel Chester French, and William C. Brownell, appointed to Art Committee of American Academy of Arts and Letters, on which he will serve for many years.

September Camps at Montauk Point, Long Island, with artist friends Jack Roudebush, Albert Smith, Reynolds Beal, and Gifford Beal.

1922
Spring Member of committee, with Joseph Pennell and Timothy Cole, at American Academy of Arts and Letters to choose works for large show of American graphic arts to be held at Academy's building, 15 West Eighty-first Street, March 16–April 16. *New York Times* (March 5, 1922) reports that exhibition aims "to demonstrate that America in this branch of art, although not generally known, occupies a far more distinguished place than other countries which for years past have been holding annual exhibits."

April 25 Attends dinner at American Academy of Arts and Letters, New York, in honor of critic André Chevrillon and dramatist Maurice Donnay.

1923
February 22 Attends reception celebrating opening of new building of American Academy of Arts and Letters on West 155th Street.

Autumn Serves as Assistant Commissioner of Painting of American Section of 2nd Roman Biennial Exposition, November 4, 1923–April 30, 1924. Selects paintings along with Cecilia Beaux, Frederick Dielman, Frank Dumond, Gari Melchers, and Charles Hawthorne.

Purchases four acres of land adjacent to Willow Bend.

Probably visits Peacham, Vermont.

1924
April Baltimore

November 15–December 7 Winter Exhibition, National Academy of Design, New York; First Altman Prize ($1,000) for *Miss Ingram,* 1923 (private collection)

December 22 Attends luncheon at Hotel Astor, New York, part of campaign supporting completion of Cathedral Church of Saint John the Divine in upper Manhattan.

1925
Late March–early April Travels to Savannah, stopping at Baltimore, Richmond, and Charleston.

December 18 Attends dinner hosted by Nicholas Murray Butler, president of Columbia University, in honor of John St. Loe Strachey, former editor of *London Spectator.*

Limited edition of *Catalogue of the Etchings and Dry-Points of Childe Hassam,* with introduction by Royal Cortissoz, published (New York: Charles Scribner's Sons).

1926
March 20–April 11 101st Annual Exhibition, National Academy of Design, New York; First Altman Landscape Prize for *Flight Into Egypt,* 1925 (American Academy of Arts and Letters, New York)

March Washington, D.C.

April Harper's Ferry, West Virginia

June 1–December 1 Sesqui-Centennial International Exposition, Philadelphia; Gold Medal in painting from Department of Fine Arts for *Miss Ingram,* 1923 (private collection)

1927
January 25–February 10 Sits for five interviews with DeWitt McClellan Lockman, New York portrait painter, later recording secretary, New-York Historical Society, and president, National Academy of Design.

Early February Sets out for California, stopping in New Orleans, Corpus Christi and El Paso, and Yuma, Arizona. Visits Los Angeles, Coronado Beach, and Santa Barbara and spends one day in Tijuana. By February 12 at Saint Charles, New Orleans. On February 19 traveling aboard Sunset Limited on Southern Pacific Line. By February 21 at Hotel Paseo del Norte, El Paso. By March 2 at Hotel Mayfair, Los Angeles. By March 16 at Hotel del Coronado, Coronado Beach. By March 25 at El Mirasol Hotel, Santa Barbara.

By April 7 New York

April 21–October 21 Exhibition of the Works of Childe Hassam, American Academy of Arts and Letters, New York. Hassam attends the opening with his wife (see figs. 16, 19).

1928
February Visits Atlantic City, New Jersey.

Summer Sponsors memorial exhibition of paintings and etchings by Thomas Moran at Clinton Academy, East Hampton.

Visits Annapolis, Maryland.

Joins Union Club, New York; remains member for rest of his life.

1929
March 9–April 8 Exhibition of a Retrospective Group of Paintings Representative of the Life Work of Childe Hassam, N.A., Albright Art Gallery, Buffalo

April Williamsburg, Virginia

1930
September Andover, Massachusetts

Autumn Serves on jury of selection and awards and hanging committee for *12th Annual Exhibition,* Corcoran Gallery of Art, Washington, D.C.

1931
January 10–February 9 15th Annual Exhibition of Contemporary Etchings, Brooklyn Society of Etchers; Nathan I. Bijur Prize of $25 for best print, for *Skimhampton Road,* 1929

Ca. May–November East Hampton. The Metropolitan Museum of Art begins filming scenes there for one-reel silent film *Childe Hassam, Artist.*

June Lends group of his recent East Hampton etchings to East Hampton Free Library.

August 19 Opening ceremonies at Guild Hall Museum, East Hampton. Hassam dedicates main gallery to memory of Thomas Moran, whom he credits with establishing the village as an artists' retreat.

November 1–December 6 Shows only prints in *29th Annual Philadelphia Water Color Exhibition and 30th Annual Exhibition of Miniatures,* Pennsylvania Academy of the Fine Arts, Philadelphia; Joseph Pennell Memorial Gold Medal for Etching

1932
January Release of *Childe Hassam, Artist,* first film in series on important American artists produced by The Metropolitan Museum of Art. Hassam shown swimming, painting (see fig. 317), and golfing in East Hampton and looking at his own paintings in Museum.

By February 3 Group of 100 Etchings by Childe Hassam, Leonard Clayton Gallery, New York

March 11 Contributes decorative panel of "baroque" design to Abstract Ball, benefit held by Contemporary Arts, organization that supports the work of young artists.

September 14 "The Bicentennial Pageant of George Washington," portfolio of twenty original etchings by American artists, presented to President Hoover at White House. Final etching, *Washington at Mount Vernon,* by Hassam. Portfolio later published in edition of 1,000 by George Washington Memorial Association, Inc.

1933
By February 12–March 15 Etchings by Childe Hassam, Adam Clayton Gallery, New York, shows "East Hampton Set" (forty) and "New York Set" (thirty-four).

October 17 Celebrates birthday by "reviewing with satisfaction his ability to continue his work and to take a dip in the ocean the age of 74" (*New York Times,* October 22, 1933, p. N3).

November Travels to Boston.

December 8, 1933–February 1, 1934 Complete Etched Work of Childe Hassam, Leonard Clayton Gallery, New York. Includes 376 plates and coincides with gallery's publication of its illustrated catalogue raisonné of Hassam's etchings and drypoints, *Handbook of the Complete Set of Etchings and Drypoints of Childe Hassam, N.A. . . .*

1934
May–ca. October 19 East Hampton

May 8 Awarded Gold Medal for Distinguished Services to Fine Art by American Art Dealers Association, New York. Does not attend awards dinner.

October 17 Spends seventy-fifth birthday "walking through the fields, motoring in the near-by woods, enjoying the autumnal coloring." Does not take his regular swim because of the "low temperatures" (*New York Times,* October 18, 1934, p. 24).

October Taken ill in New York, remains unwell through winter.

1935
March 13–April 9 110th Annual Exhibition, National Academy of Design, New York; Saltus Medal for Merit for *Evening: Pont Aven,* 1897 (private collection)

Early April Hassam, seriously ill, and wife leave New York for East Hampton.

August 27 Dies at Willow Bend at age seventy-five.

August 28 Funeral services held at Willow Bend for small group of family and friends. Reverend William Grainger, rector of Saint Luke's Episcopal Church, East Hampton, presides. Burial at Cedar Lawn Cemetery, East Hampton

November 13 Public announcement of Hassam's bequest to American Academy of Arts and Letters, New York, of his studio contents—326 oil paintings (including 19 decorative panels), 89 watercolors, and 33 pastels—and his recommendation that proceeds from their sale enrich The Hassam Fund, with which works by American and Canadian artists would be purchased for presentation to American and Canadian museums.

Before her death in 1946 Maud Hassam will distribute groups of her husband's prints to museums throughout the country.

Awarded John Elliot Memorial Prize, Newport Art Club.

1936
April Hassam's gross estate, made up mainly of stocks and bonds—and exclusive of works of art bequeathed to American Academy of Arts and Letters—appraised at $212,710, equivalent to about $2,757,034 in 2002.

November 12 American Academy of Arts and Letters formally establishes The Hassam Fund.

Exhibitions in Hassam's Lifetime

Elizabeth Block, Stephanie L. Herdrich, Megan Holloway, Dana Pilson

Both solo and group exhibitions are listed; exhibitions devoted exclusively to prints are not included. Original sources of information are catalogues, checklists, annual reports, correspondence, ephemera, contemporary newspaper and periodical articles, reviews, and advertisements. Key collections of these materials are listed in Frequently Cited Sources in this publication. Secondary sources include exhibition catalogues and monographs, exhibition indexes for institutions and artists' organizations, and "Childe Hassam," *Index of Twentieth Century Artists* 3, no. 1 (October 1935) (College Art Association), pp. 461–75.

Exhibition titles and venues are transcribed from original sources when possible. However, "exh." and other abbreviations (see list below) are used in exhibition titles and for some venues. These titles are set in italics. If the exact title is unknown, a descriptive title is taken from a contemporary source, identified in brackets. If quoted, the title appears in roman type with quotation marks; if paraphrased, there are no quotation marks. Non-contemporary sources are not cited. Titles of some foreign exhibitions are simplified or translated. Unless otherwise noted, the location is New York City. Only the originating venue is given; traveling schedules are not listed.

Titles of works, including those in foreign languages, and their catalogue numbers are transcribed from the original sources when possible and given in italics. The few descriptions of works taken from reviews are in roman and quotation marks. Unless otherwise noted, works are oils (these are either designated so in the original sources or appear to be oils to the best of our knowledge). Other media are identified by abbreviations: (d) drawing, (p) pastel, (wc) watercolor. Exhibitions in which media are not specified are marked as such. Prints included in exhibitions of works in other media are not listed.

Subdivisions transcribed from exhibition catalogues or checklists appear in quotation marks. Dates of works, awards, and any other annotations are transcribed from the original sources. Lenders' names and credit lines are transcribed, although "loaned by" is changed to "lent by," states are abbreviated, and the institutions in the following list are abbreviated as indicated.

Abbreviations

AIC (The Art Institute of Chicago)
AWCS (American Water Color Society)
BAC (Boston Art Club)
BE (*Brooklyn Eagle*)
BFAA (Buffalo Fine Arts Academy, Albright Art Gallery; now Albright-Knox Art Gallery)
CAM (Cincinnati Art Museum)
CAMSL (City Art Museum, Saint Louis; now The Saint Louis Art Museum)
CI (Carnegie Institute, Pittsburgh); now Carnegie Museum of Art
Corcoran (The Corcoran Gallery of Art, Washington, D.C.)
DMA (Detroit Museum of Art; now The Detroit Institute of Arts)
DRG (Durand-Ruel Galleries)
JHAI (John Herron Art Institute; now Indianapolis Museum of Art)
Knoedler (M. Knoedler and Company)
Macbeth (Macbeth Gallery)
Milch (Milch Galleries)
Montross (Montross Gallery)
NAD (National Academy of Design)
NYT (*New York Times*)
NYWCC (New York Water Color Club)
PAA (Portland Art Association, Oregon)
PAFA (Pennsylvania Academy of the Fine Arts, Philadelphia)
PSAG (Poland Spring Art Gallery, Maine)
RISD (Rhode Island School of Design, Providence)
SAA (Society of American Artists)
SB (St. Botolph Club, Boston)
ULCNY (Union League Club, New York)
WAM (Worcester Art Museum)

1882

Feb. 11–Mar. 11, BAC, *25th Exh. of Oil Paintings.*
65. *May Morning*
187. *A Daisy Field*

Apr. 28–May 27, BAC, *26th Exh. of Water Colors and Works in Black and White.*
50. *Harbinger of Spring—In the City and in the Country* (d)
239. *Bit of Autumn* (wc)

Autumn, Williams and Everett Gallery, Boston, *Water Colors by Fred C. Hassam.*
(1–51 wcs)
1. *Rocks, Nahant*
2. *September Morning*
3. *Brant Point*
4. *Edge of Meadow*
5. *On the Beach, Nantucket*
6. *March*
7. *Winter Twilight*
8. *Shelling Peas*
9. *Road Leading to Wayside Inn, Sudbury*
10. *Old House, Nantucket*
11. *The River-Bank*
12. *Pride of the Meadow*
13. *Cider-Apples (Beverly)*
14. *Close of a June Day*
15. *A Glimpse from the Roadway, Nantucket*
16. *Old Mill, Nantucket*
17. *Sunlight and Shadows*
18. *In Other Days*
19. *The Harvest Moon*
20. *An Impression*
21. *Two Friends*
22. *Dolce Far Niente*
23. *The First Greens—March*
24. *Banks of the Saco, North Conway*
25. *Beeches*
26. *Town-Pump, S'conset*
27. *Digging Bait*
28. *One Afternoon*
29. *A Winter Morning*
30. *Sunday Morning*
31. *Fishing Dories, Nantucket*
32. *A Summer Retreat, Nantucket*
33. *A Back Road—September*
34. *A Hot Morning*
35. *Banks of the Neponset*
36. *No!*
37. *Study of an Apple-Tree*
38. *Old House—Brickyards*
39. *Sheep Pasture*
40. *A Fisherman's Home, S'conset*
41. *Where the Lilies Grow*
42. *Over the Fence*
43. *Early Blossoms*
44. *Hauled Up—Swampscott*
45. *Spring*
46. *Young Fisherwoman*
47. *A Wet Day—Nantucket*
48. *Apple Blossoms*
49. *Nantucket Architecture*
50. *A Bit of Autumn*
51. *Mote Mountain, North Conway*
52. *Pen Sketch* (d)
53. *Pencil Sketch* (d)
54. *Summer* (d)

Dec. 1–22, Salmagundi Sketch Club, NAD, *5th Annual Black and White Exh.*
406. *Thought* (d)

1883

From Jan. 15, American Art Galleries, *Exh. of Paintings by an Association of Boston Artists.*
41. *Apple Blossoms*
89. *Corner of a Studio*

Jan. 25–Feb. 17, BAC, *27th Exh. of Oil Paintings.*
15. *Spring-time*
105. *At the Concert*

Until Feb. 25, AWCS, *16th Annual Exh.*
(all wcs)
69. *Spring-time*
79. *Nantucket Architecture*
566. *Cider Apples*

Mar. 13–24, Brooklyn Art Association, Brooklyn Museum of Art, *Winter Exh., 46th Reception.*
176. *On the Beach, Nantucket* (wc)

Apr. 2–May 12, NAD, *58th Annual Exh. of Paintings.*
536. *Spring Blossoms*

Apr. 14–May 12, BAC, *28th Exh. of Water Colors and Works in Black and White.*
(wcs)
24. *Autumn Greys*
139. *Convalescent*

1884

Jan. 19–Feb. 16, BAC, *29th Exh. of Oil Paintings.*
12. *Wood Interior*

Feb.–Mar. 1, AWCS, *17th Annual Exh.*
(all wcs)
176. *Autumn Greys*
306. *Getting Well*
598. *Hillside—October*

Apr. 12–May 10, BAC, *30th Exh., Water Colors and Works in Black and White.*
(all wcs)
50. *Gate of an Old Chateau, near Paris*
132. *Grey Morning. Spring*
161. *The Red Horse Tavern (Longfellow's "Wayside Inn")*

Oct. 30–Dec. 11, PAFA, *55th Annual Exh.*
93. *Springtime on an Old Neglected Place*
94. *In the Fields Back of an Old Place*
95. *Still Life*
282. *A Steamer's Deck* (wc)
283. *Castello dell'Novo [sic], Naples* (wc)
284. *Grey Morning: Venice* (wc)

Nov. 10–Dec. 10, American Art Galleries, *Inauguration of New Galleries, Works from the Salon of '84 and Other American Paintings Contributed by the Artists.*
57. *A Back Road—New England*
86. *The Old Place—Springtime*

Dec. 11–23, Salmagundi Sketch Club, *7th Annual Black and White Exh.*
206. *On the Beach, Nantucket* (d)

Williams and Everett Gallery, Boston, *Water Colors by Hassam.*
(all wcs)
1. *From a Hotel Window, Geneva, Switzerland*
2. *Morning off Valencia, Spain*
3. *Cottages near Antwerp*
4. *Mediterranean Boats*
5. *On the River Oise*
6. *On the Leven, Dumbarton*
7. *Fruit Steamer leaving Spanish Port*
8. *Old Church—Denia*
9. *Spanish Gypsy*
10. *Towing—Holland*
11. *Street at Noon—Denia, Spain*
12. *Square and Fountain—Denia, Spain*
13. *Rainy Day—Brighton, England* (In this town lived and died the ancestors of George Washington)
14. *Cottage—Brighton, England*
15. *Dutch Fishing Boat*
16. *Street in Grenada*
17. *Overflow of Brook—Spring*
18. *Court-Yard, France*
19. *On the River, near Rotterdam*
20. *Morning*
21. *On the Mediterranean*
22. *On the Beach—Scheveningen*
23. *The Promenade, Ouchy, Switzerland*
24. *Grand Canal, Venice*
25. *San Giorgio, Venice*
26. *Dutch Fishing-Boat and Crew, Scheveningen*
27. *On the Lagoon, Venice*
28. *English Boats at Rochester*
29. *Street—Auvers sur L'Oise*
30. *French Cottage—same village*
31. *The Brook*

32. *Gray Day—Denia, Spain*
33. *On the Pier—Rotterdam*
34. *Dutch Fisherman*
35. *Barn-Yard*
36. *"White Bait" Vender—Malaga*
37. *English Kitchen Garden*
38. *A Rough Day on the Mediterranean*
39. *Fishing-Boats—New Haven, Scotland*
40. *Street—Denia, Spain*
41. *English Farm-House*
42. *Gossips—Holland*
43. *Café Entrance—Denia*
44. *Alhambra, Spain*
45. *On the River Maas, Holland—Early Morning*
46. *Noon—Auvers sur L'Oise*
47. *In the Fields*
48. *A Warm Day—March*
49. *Weeding a Brook—Holland*
50. *A Spanish Town by the Sea*
51. *Beacon Street and Public Garden—Morning*
52. *Tower San Marco and Doge's Palace, Venice*
53. *Fruit Steamers Riding out a Gale—Coast of Spain*
54. *Off Venice*
55. *Venetian Fishing-Boats—Morning*
56. *Dutch Fisherman*
57. *Roadway—Auvers*
58. *Cherokee Rose*
59. *Roses*
60. *Gates at Pompeii—Early Morning*
61. *On the Thames, near London*
62. *Old Church—Auvers*
63. *Dumbaron Rock and Castle, Scotland*
64. *Sunday—Scheveningen*
65. *River Oise*
66. *Castello dell'Ouvo [sic], Naples*
67. *Thunder Storm—Spanish*

1885

Jan. 17–Feb. 14, BAC, *31st Exh. Oil Paintings.*
63. *A Back Road*
104. *An Old House, Springtime*
136. *Little Pigs*

Until Feb. 28, AWCS, *18th Annual Exh.*
219. *September Clouds* (wc)

Apr. 11–May 2, BAC, *32nd Exh., Water Colors, Black and White Drawings, and Sculpture.*
(all wcs)
35. *A Gondolier*
95. *The Fisher*
129. *In the Public Garden*

May 5–June 2, Museum of Fine Arts, Boston, *5th Annual Exh. of Contemporary American Art.*
46. *A Seedy Old Place in Spring*
115. *A Warm Day in September*
149. *September Clouds*

Sept. 2–Oct. 17, Inter-State Industrial Exposition of Chicago, *13th Annual Exh.*
123. *A Very Old Place*
215. *Some Nantucket Architecture*
302. *A Back Road, New England*

Oct. 29–Dec. 10, PAFA, *56th Annual Exh.*
130. *The Haystack*

Nov., American Art Galleries, *Fall Exh.*
201. *Moonrise, October*
257. *A Seedy Old Place*

From Dec. 1, Boston Water-Color Society, *1st Exh.*
1. *Springtime in the City*
2. *The Beach at Scheveningen (Holland)*
3. *Autumn Afternoon on Copp's Hill*
4. *The River Oise*
5. *Wet Decks*
6. *Rainy Day, Columbus Avenue*

1886

Jan. 15–Feb. 13, BAC, *33rd Exh., Oil Paintings.*
45. *A Wet Day in the City*
61. *Columbus Avenue in the Rain*

Until Feb. 27, AWCS, *19th Annual Exh.*
333. *Gray Morning at Scheveningen*
354. *Autumn*
585. *Wet Decks*
766. *The River Oise*
788. *June*

Apr. 5–May 15, NAD, *61st Annual Exh.*
160. *Rainy Day*

Apr. 10–May 8, BAC, *34th Exh., Water Colors, Works in Black and White, and Sculpture.*
(all wcs)
75. *Distant Venice*
76. *English Kitchen Garden*
96. *Copley Square, Rainy Morning After a Snow Fall*

Apr. 15–May 1, SB, Spring Exh.
40. *The Public Garden (Spring)*
41. *Wet Night Effect*
42. *Dutch Village*

Apr., American Art Association, *2nd Prize Fund Exh.*

May 5–Oct. 15, SAA, The Metropolitan Museum of Art, *8th Exh. of SAA.*
58. *A Rainy Day*

Nov. 22–Dec. 18, NAD, *Autumn Exh.*
405. *A City Fairyland*
610. *Showery Day, Nantucket*

Nov., American Art Galleries, *Fall Exh.*
91. *A City Park in Spring*
92. *When the Lights Glimmer Out, wet afternoon*

1887

Jan. 14–Feb. 12, BAC, *35th Exh., Oil Paintings.*
21. *At Dusk*

Until Feb. 26, AWCS, *20th Annual Exh.*
(all wcs)
83. *A Harvest Moonrise*
123. *To-day and Yesterday*
125. *In the Country—Companion to No. 131*
131. *In the Town—Companion to No. 125*
248. *The Country Boarder*

Mar. 9–10, Noyes, Cobb and Co., Boston, *Exh. and Sale of Works in Oil and Water Color by Childe Hassam.*
30–60; 92–120 (wcs)
1. *A Street Corner*
2. *A Woodland Pool*
3. *A Daisy Field*
4. *An Artist at Work*
5. *A Brook after Rain*
6. *Arlington Street, through the Rain*
7. *Twilight*
8. *An Old Homestead*
9. *Vanishing Daylight. September*
10. *Haystacks and Barn*
11. *A Passing Shower in Early Spring*
12. *Willows in Spring*
13. *Study for the Haystack*
14. *Study in an Old House*
15. *Looking across the Common. Winter evening*
16. *A Dandelion Field*
17. *A Lane in May*
18. *Early Spring*
19. *Apple Blossoms*
20. *Declining Day*
21. *Corner of a Garden. Nantucket*
22. *Pigs*
23. *Moonrise in a Quiet Place*
24. *Quince Blossoms*
25. *Old Fruit Trees. Nonquitt*
26. *The Last Load*
27. *Moonrise in Spring*
28. *A Wet Day. Berkeley Street Bridge*
29. *At Dusk*
30. *Harvest. Moonrise*
31. *Sunday Afternoon. Scheveningen*
32. *Winter*
33. *Old Trees at Beverly*
34. *A Spanish Street*
35. *An Old Gateway*
36. *The Blue Skies of Spain*
37. *Dumbarton Rock*
38. *Thames Boats*
39. *The Bay of Naples*
40. *Stone Alley. Nantucket*
41. *Old Buildings. Milton*
42. *Low Tide*
43. *Early Morning. Venice*
44. *Morning. Gates of Pompeii*
45. *Wet Decks*
46. *Dutch Fisherman*
47. *On the Thames above London*
48. *In the Public Garden*
49. *The Beach. Scheveningen*
50. *Study in the Alhambra*
51. *In the Mediterranean*
52. *Wild Apple Tree*
53. *Idle Hours*
54. *The Gossips*
55. *Street in Denia, Spain*
56. *Wind and Rain*
57. *A Back Yard. France*
58. *A Swiss Lake*
59. *Grey Morning. Beach at Scheveningen, Holland*
60. *September Clouds*
61. *Mid-Summer*
62. *A Shady Place*
63. *Tender Morning*
64. *Sunset. Nantucket*
65. *A Breezy Day*
66. *A Hillside in September*
67. *Across the River*
68. *Ode to a Water Fowl*
69. *Boats at Sunset*
70. *French Cottages*
71. *A Showery Day. Nantucket*
72. *Old Fairbanks House. Dedham*
73. *A Morning in June*
74. *April*
75. *Last Rays*
76. *Union Square. Spring*
77. *Early April*
78. *Still Life*
79. *Dutch Village*
80. *Wet Night. Columbus Avenue*
81. *A Crab*
82. *A Wood Interior*
83. *Springtime in a City Park*
84. *Mid-Summer. Nantucket*
85. *A New England Farm Yard*
86. *Early Spring Twilight*
87. *Sundown. A French Village*
88. *Moonrise. September*
89. *A Rainy Day in the City*
90. *The Haystack*
91. *Through the Rain*
92. *The Nahant Rocks*
93. *By the Lily-Pond*
94. *Dutch Weeding. Holland*
95. *Spring*
96. *Fishing Skiffs. Nantucket*
97. *A French Carpenter's Shop*
98. *Venice*
99. *Study of Sunlight. French Village*
100. *Distant Venice*
101. *Doge's Place and Tower of St. Mark*
102. *Roses*
103. *The Brook after a Rain*
104. *Copley Square in Winter*
105. *White Bait Vendor. Malaga*
106. *A Short Cut. Anyers [sic] sur Oise*
107. *An English Kitchen Garden*
108. *A Chateau Garden near Paris*
109. *A "Shoals" Day*
110. *Castello Dell Noro [sic]. Naples*
111. *Fishing Boats. New Haven, Scotland*
112. *An English Cottage*
113. *Copp's Hill*
114. *Springtime in the City*
115. *River Oise. France*
116. *A Rainy Day in an English Village*
117. *Fish House at Swampscott*
118. *June*
119. *The Steamer's Deck*
120. *Old Fortress. Naples*

Apr. 4–May 14, NAD, *62nd Annual Exh.*
104. *Snow Storm on the Boulevard*
187. *Winter Morning in Paris*
357. *Through the Rain*

From May 1, Paris Salon.
1181. *Une averse;—rue Bonaparte*
Painting exhibited at Goupil's for a week after the close of the Salon [CH, Paris, 7/21/1887, to Rose Lamb, Isles of Shoals Collection].

Sept. 7–Oct. 22, Inter-State Industrial Exposition of Chicago, *15th Annual Exh.*
208. *A Shower;—Rue Bonaparte, Paris*
209. *Autumn in the Garden of the Luxembourg, Paris*

Nov.–Dec., American Art Galleries, *Fall Exh.*
140. *A Shower—Rue Bonaparte, Paris,* Salon '87
141. *Midsummer Day*
142. *Vespers at the Madeleine*
143. *The Coming Night,* Place de l'Europe

Paint and Clay Club, Boston, *6th Annual Exh. of Paint and Clay Club Held at the Gallery of BAC.*
59. *A Snow-Storm on the Boulevards*
60. *Winter Morning in Paris*
61. *Impression Champs-Élysées*

Boston Society of Water Color Painters

1888

Feb. 16–Mar. 29, PAFA, *58th Annual Exh.*
156. *A Shower: rue Bonaparte, Paris*
157. *Back from the Garden*
446. *La Blanchisseuse* (wc)
447. *Going to the Race: Paris* (wc)
448. *At the Race: Paris* (wc)

From May 1, Paris Salon.
1270. *Le Jour de Grand-Prix*, gold medal

Internationalen Kunst-Ausstellung, Munich. Catalogue distributed mid-July
1162. *Dämmerung*
1163. *Im Garten*

Boston Society of Water Color Painters

1889

Jan. 19–Feb. 16, BAC, *39th Exh., Oil Paintings.*
6. *La rue Bonaparte*

Jan. 24–Mar. 7, PAFA, *59th Annual Exh.*
104. *On the Way to the "Grand Prix"*

Until Mar. 2, AWCS, *22nd Annual Exh.*
(all wcs)
143. *Le Marché aux Fleurs*

247. *Un Anglais*
348. *La Fête à Montmartre*

Mar. 11–23, Noyes, Cobb and Co., Boston, *Exh. and Private Sale of [illeg.] Mr. Childe Hassam.*
1. *Notre Dame de Paris*
2. *A French Kitchen Garden, Midday*
3. *Spring Blossoms*
4. *Le Beau Temps*
5. *Tow Horses, Old Street in the Latin Quarter*
6. *Idylle*
7. *The Gardener's Daughter*
8. *The Evening Star*
9. *Roses*
10. *A Village Byway*
11. *A l'heure*
12. *La Fruetière [sic]*
13. *A House-top Garden, April Morning*
14. *Souvenir of Venice*
15. *Communion Morning*
16. *The Champs Elysées, Day of the Grand Prix*
17. *The Eastern Sky at Sundown*
18. *In Lilac Time*
19. *Moonrise at Sunset*
20. *A Sun Batch*
21. *Pear Blossoms*
22. *A little Old Shop on Montmartre*
23. *Amongst the Flowers, Chateau Blumenthal*
24. *The Little Gardener*
25. *Feeding the Pigeons*
26. *A Street in Granada, Spain*
27. *Idle Hours*
28. *Moonrise behind the Towers of Notre Dame*
29. *Twilight*
30. *Public Gardens, Boston*
31. *Vespers at the Madelaine [sic]*
32. *A Midsummer Day, Paris*
33. *Snow-storm on the Boulevards*
34. *In Town*
35. *In the Country*

By Apr. 26–until after June 9, American Art Galleries, *5th Prize Fund Exh.*
144a. *Returning from the Grand Prix Races*

From May 1, Paris Salon.
1304. *L'automne*
1305. *Soleil et fleurs*

May 5–Oct. 31, Exposition Universelle, Paris, bronze medal.
149. *Le crépuscule*
150. *La rue Lafayette, un soir d'hiver*
151. *Après déjeuner*
152. *Lettre d'Amérique*

May 30–June 30, AIC, *2nd Annual Exh. American Oil Paintings.*
87. *Rainy Day—Boston Street*

Sept. 5–Oct. 20, Inter-State Industrial Exposition of Chicago, *16th Annual Exh.*
194. *"Grand Prix" Day, Paris*
195. *Church of St. Germain de l'Auxerrois, Paris*
196. *The Coming of Night*
197. *Midsummer*
198. *Vespers at the Madeleine*
199. *La Blanchisseuse* (wc)
200. *The Races—"Grand Prix de Paris"* (wc)
201. *On the Way* (wc)

Mid-Nov., Doll and Richards Gallery, Boston.
14 ps, 16 wcs

DMA, *2nd Exh., Paintings, Water Colors, Drawings, Etchings, and Collection of Corean Antiques.*
50. *A Shady Lane—Nantucket*

Galerie Georges Petit, Paris.

1890

Jan. 18–Feb. 15, BAC, *41st Exh., Oil Paintings.*
27. *Winter Nightfall in the City*
29. *The Rose Girl*
93. *The Back Bay Towers from Berkeley Street Bridge—Souvenir of Boston.*

Jan. 30–Mar. 6, PAFA, *60th Annual Exh.*
87. *L'Automne*
88. *Twilight*
89. *The Flower Girl*

Jan., Doll and Richards Gallery, Boston. (12 wcs)

Feb. 3–Mar. 1, AWCS, *23rd Annual Exh.* (all wcs)
91. *Along the Seine, Bougival*
262. *Paris and the Eiffel Tower from Montmartre*
301. *Under the Obelisk, Thames Embankment*
430. *The Thames, Victoria Embankment*
488. *The Edge of the Chalk Cliffs at Broadstairs, England*
640. *The Bathing Hour, Broadstairs, England*
641. *A Bit of New York*

Feb. 13–15, ULCNY, *Pictures by American Figure Painters, Together with an Exh. of Persian and Indian Art.*
38. *After the Rain*

Apr. 5–26, BAC, *42nd Exh., Water Colors.* (all wcs)
86. *The Hollyhock Cottages*
95. *Farm Cottages in Kent*
102. *Bleak House*

Apr. 10–May 17, NAD, *65th Annual Exh.*
100. *After Lunch*
391. *Winter Evening in Paris*
424. *The Peony Girl*
598. *The Last Gleam, after the Rain*

Apr. 28–May 24, SAA, 5th Avenue Art Galleries, *12th Exh. of SAA.*
93. *The Enchanted Hour*
94. *The Rose Girl*
95. *Fifth Avenue and the Snow*
96. *Winter Evening—rue Lafayette, Paris*

Spring, Denver, Colo.
"a group of pastel portraits of fair ladies" [Adams 1938, p. 76]

May 1–24, Hermann Wunderlich Gallery, *4th Exh. of Society of American Painters in Pastel.* (all ps)
September Afternoon from a Paris Café
At the Races
A New York Blizzard
and "three…scenes at the Grand Prix de Paris," and "view… into the Bois de Boulogne" [*Art Amateur* 23, no. 1 (June 1890), p. 4.]

From May 1, Paris Salon.
1178. *Chez la fleuriste*
2978. *Une Cremière* (wc)

May 26–June 4, Rochester Art Club, *11th Annual Exh.*
97. *The Last Gleam after the Rain*
98. *Corner of a French Garden*

June 9–July 13, AIC, *3rd Annual Exh. of American Oil Paintings.*
92. *The Enchanted Hour*
93. *The Rose Girl*
94. *Fifth Avenue and the Snow*
95. *Winter Evening, Rue Lafayette, Paris*

Sept. 4–Oct. 19, Inter-State Industrial Exposition of Chicago, *17th Annual Exh.*
236. *Autumn—A Paris Boulevard*
237. *Starting Out, Early Morning in April*
238. *April Showers, Paris*
239. *Girl with Peonies*
240. *Gathering Peonies for the "Fête des Fleurs"*

Nov. 3–Dec. 7, Art Club of Philadelphia, *2nd Special Exh.*
33. *Corner of a French Garden*
84. *The Last Gleam*

From Nov. 6, NYWCC, *1st Annual Exh.* (all wcs)
175. *A Paris Market*
176. *September at the Isles of Shoals*
177. *A Gloucester Street*
178. *Gloucester Harbor, September Morning*
179. *Rain and Mist, Gloucester Harbor*
180. *Portico of the Union Club, Rainy Night*
181. *A Corner of Reha [sic]Thaxter, Isle of Shoals*

Nov. 24–Dec. 20, NAD, *9th Autumn Exh.*
60. *Autumn Sunlight (Fifth Avenue)*
64. *Winter Morning, Union Sq.*
73. *Fifth Avenue at Washington Square (May)*
120. *Broadway and Madison Square, from a balcony, May*

Until Dec. 7, Fellowcraft Club, "Exhibition of sketches" [*NYT*, 12/7/1890, p. 12.]
Hassam included in "sketches of landscape" section.

Apr. 1–15, ca. 1890, Noyes, Cobb and Co., Boston, *Exh. and Sale of Works in Oil and Water Color by Childe Hassam.*
26–46 (wcs)
1. *A City Evening.* Place Pigal[l]e, Paris
2. *Along the Seine.* Late afternoon in April
3. *Lamplight and Afterglow.* Paris
4. *A Street on the Top of Montmartre*
5. *Under the Lilacs.* Chateau Blumenthal
6. *A Montmartre "Impasse"*
7. *April Afternoon on the Boulevard*
8. *Paris Flower-store.* Spring
9. *Summer Midnight on the Boulevards*
10. *La Blanchisseuse*
11. *Winter in Paris*
12. *Paris Flower-girls*
13. *Autumn Twilight.* Exterior Boulevards
14. *The Return from the "Bois"*
15. *A Little Republican*
16. *A New York "Blizzard"*
17. *White Horses and Wet Street*
18. *The Old Flower-woman*
[19.] *A Voter*
20. *July 14th.* Decoration of a little Paris shop
21. *Afternoon in a French Garden*
22. *A Corner of a Studio Table*
23. *French Roses*
24. *Pear Blossoms*
25. *Alhambra*
26. *Under the Chalk Cliffs.* Broadstairs, England
27. *Distant Venice*
28. *The Cottage Window*
29. *Spires of Canterbury Cathedral*
30. *The Burlington Arms.* Chiswick
31. *Hogarth's House.* Chiswick
32. *Old Church in Canterbury*
33. *A Spanish Port on the Mediterranean*
34. *Sketch.* The Beach at Broadstairs
35. *The Joss Farm Cottages.* Broadstairs
36. *Under the Chalk Cliffs at Low Tide*
37. *Tourists in the Gardens of St. Cloud*
38. *Head at the Races*
39. *The Edge of the Cliffs at Broadstairs*
40. *Gateway.* Canterbury Cathedral, looking out
41. *Low Tide at Broadstairs*
42. *The Coming Storm*
43. *A Broadstairs Hamlet*
44. *A Dorchester Wall*
45. *St. Peter's Church and Graveyard.* Broadstairs
46. *The Seine at Bougival*

1891

Jan. 17–Feb. 14, BAC, *43rd Exh., Oil Paintings.*
48. *The Peony Girl*
138. *Winter Night on the Common*

Jan. 26–Feb. 10, Brooklyn Art Club, *Annual Exh.* (wcs)
89. *September Moonrise*
90. *The Last of Summer, Isle of Shoals*

Jan. 29–Mar. 6, PAFA, *61st Annual Exh.*
129. *A Paris Flower Market*
130. *Autumn Sunlight: Fifth Avenue, New York*
131. *Church of St. Germain de l'Auxerrois, Paris*
132. *Sundown in the Parc Monceau*
133. *Early Spring, Union Square, New York*
134. *In Lilac Time*
135 *Springtime in a City Park: Boston Public Garden*

Feb. 2–28, AWCS, *24th Annual Exh.* (all wcs)
75. *A Street in Gloucester*
145. *September, Isles of Shoals*
211. *In the Garden, Minster, England*
423. *Fisherman Mending His Net*
466. *Fifth Avenue*
571. *Morning Isles of Shoals*
603. *Thistledown, Isles of Shoals*

Feb. 6–18, Doll and Richards Gallery, Boston, *Exh. and Private Sale of Oil Paintings and Water Color and Pastel Drawings by Childe Hassam.*
30–39 (wcs), 40–48 (ps)
1. *The Enchanted Hour*
2. *In the Rain [Union Square, New York]*
3. *Winter Evening [Rue Lafayette, Paris]*
4. *Fifth Avenue and the Snow*
5. *Sunday Morning [Union Square, NY]*
6. *The Heart of the City [Broadway and Madison Square, from a balcony]*
7. *The Idlers*
8. *A Paris Roof-top Garden in April*
9. *After Lunch [A French Garden near Paris]*
10. *Spring Morning [Montmartre, Paris]*
11. *Evening in the City*
12. *Fifth Avenue, late afternoon in April*
13. *Copps Hill Burial Ground*
14. *In the Garden, early evening*
15. *Commonwealth Avenue*
16. *After the Shower*
17. *In the New Park*
18. *A Back Bay Street*
19. *A Little Graveyard at the Isles of Shoals*
20. *The Dame of the Val de Grâce*
21. *Dawn*
22. *Communion Meeting [A Montmartre Street]*
23. *Cloud Shadows*
24. *Along the Banks of the Seine in April*
25. *Flower Girls*
26. *Moonrise [Isles of Shoals]*
27. *A Republican*
28. *The Little Orphan*
29. *Summer Seas*
30. *Market Day*
31. *An Electric Car in the Suburbs*

32. *Promenade on the Cliff-tops [Broadstairs]*
33. *The Bathing Hour [Broadstairs]*
34. *Under the Obelisk [Thames Embankment]*
35. *Wet Night on the Boulevards*
36. *Rain and Mist [Gloucester Harbor]*
37. *Surf [Isles of Shoals]*
38. *Gloucester Harbor, September morning*
39. *A Gloucester Street*
40. *Celia Thaxter's Garden*
41. *Midsummer*
42. *The Dying Poppies, September*
43. *At the "Grand Prix de Paris"*
44. *Group at the Races*
45. *Head at the Races*
46. *A Carriage*
47. *From a Café*
48. *A Corner of the Garden*

By Feb. 12, 3 Hamilton Place, Boston, "Paintings by Childe Hassam, Miss Ellen Day Hale, and her brother, Phillip Hale" [*NYT*, 2/12/1891, p. 4].

Mar. 2–Apr. 4, Brooklyn Art Association, *Spring Exh.*
64. *Street Scene in Paris*
medium not specified

Mar. 23–Apr. 19, AIC, *Spring Exh. of Water Colors.*
(all wcs)
114. *A Street in Gloucester*
115. *Fifth Avenue*
116. *In the Gardens of St. Cloud*
118. *September, Isle of Shoals*
119. *A Spanish Port in the Mediterranean*
120. *English Cottage, Minster*

Apr. 6–May 16, NAD, *66th Annual Exh.*
463. *Idlers*

Apr. 27–May 23, SAA, 5th Avenue Art Galleries, *13th Exh. of SAA.*
109. *Moonlight*
110. *Midsummer*, owner—Eugene R. Knapp
111. *Isle of Shoals—June*
112. *Spring Morning in the Heart of the City*
113. *Electric Light*
114. *The Hod-Carrier*
115. *Afternoon Sunlight—Top of Montmartre, Paris*

May 25–June 3, Rochester Art Club, *12th Annual Exh.*
116. *April Showers, (Ave de Villiers, Paris, France)*

June 4–July 5, Museum of Fine Arts, Boston, *13th Annual Exh. of SAA.*
Moonlight
Midsummer
Spring Morning in the Heart of the City
Electric Light
The Hod-carrier
Afternoon Sunlight—Top of Montmartre, Paris
Autumn in the City—Marlborough Street

June 4–July 13, Galerie Durand-Ruel, Paris, *Exposition de Peintures et Sculptures d'Artistes Américains.*
74. *Fifth Avenue in Winter.* La Cinquième en hiver.
75. *Autumn sunshine.* Soleil d'automne.

Sept. 2–Oct. 17, St. Louis Exposition and Music Hall Association, *8th Annual Exh.*
"The Hassam Collection"
134. *"Nocturne"*
135. *"A Paris Cocher"*
136. *"The Enchanted Hour"*
137. *"After Lunch"—A French Garden*
138. *"A Cab Stand"—Rue Bonaparte, Paris*
139. *"Roses in Irridescent [sic] Glass Globe"*
140. *"Return from the 'Bois'—Twilight"*
141. *"Evening in Paris"*
142. *Head of a Young Girl*
143. *"Reading The Bills"—Paris*
144. *"Wet Evening"*
145. *"In a French Garden"*
146. *"Pear Trees in Blossom"*
147. *"Church of St. Germain de l'Auxerrois"*
148. *"Moonrise on the Seine at Bougival"*
149. *"Twilight"*
150. *"Early Spring in Central Park"*
151. *"Harvest Moonrise"*
152. *"Springtime in the City." Boston Public Garden*
153. *"The Eastern Sky at Sunset." French Farm*
154. *"Sunset"*
155. *"French Kitchen Garden"*
156. *"Moonrise Near the Seashore"*
157. *"In the Rain." Union Square Park, New York*
158. *"The Coming Storm"—Gloucester Harbor*
159. *"On the Beach at Broadstairs"*
160. *Under the Chalk Cliffs at Low Tide. Broadstairs, England*
161. *"St. Peter's Church, Broadstairs"*
162. *"The Chestnut Vendor, Paris"*
163. *"Group at the Races." Grand Prix de Paris*
164. *"A Carriage at the Races"*
165. *"From a Paris Café—September"*
166. *"A Corner of Celia Thaxter's Garden." Isles of Shoals*
167. *"The Dying Poppies of September"*
168. *"Midsummer"*
169. *"Surf—Isles of Shoals"*
170. *"Cloud Shadows"*
171. *"Moonrise at Sunset—Isles of Shoals"*
172. *"The Flower Girl by the Seine"*

Nov. 12–14, ULCNY, *Exh. of Oil Paintings.*
45. *The Flower Girl—Nocturne*

Nov. 13–25, Doll and Richards Gallery, Boston, *Exh. and Private Sale of Pastel and Water Color Drawings by Childe Hassam.*
1–19 (ps), 20-35 (wcs)
1. *October [Lexington Common]*
2. *The Old Burial Ground [Lexington]*
3. *An Autumn Stroll*
4. *September Clouds*
5. *Study of a Young Girl*
6. *The Concord Road [Lexington Common]*
7. *A Wet Day on Broadway*
8. *Eternity*
9. *An Avenue [Lexington Common]*
10. *Waverly Oaks*
11. *An Old Bedford Tavern*
12. *A Meadow Brook*
13. *The Pool [Waverly Oaks]*
14. *Nocturne [Lexington]*
15. *The Battle Ground [Lexington]*
16. *In the Park*
17. *A New England Roadside*
18. *Reflections*
19. *Souvenirs [Nocturne]*
20. *Fifth Avenue*
21. *Wet Night on the Boulevards*
22. *The Bathing Hour*
23. *An Electric Car*
24. *Under the Obelisk [Thames Embankment]*
25. *A Gloucester Street*
26. *Promenade on the Cliff-tops [Broadstairs]*
27. *Gloucester Harbor, September Morn'g*
28. *Montmartre*
29. *West Gate [Canterbury]*
30. *English Cottages*
31. *St. Peter's, near Broadstairs*
32. *Canterbury Cathedral in the Afternoon Haze*
33. *The Village of Suresnes, distant Paris across the "Bois de Boulogne"*
34. *Celia Thaxter's Garden*
35. *The Garden and a Morning Mirage*

Nov. 16–Dec. 13, Art Club of Philadelphia, *3rd Annual Exh. of Oil Paintings and Sculpture.*
62. *A French Garden*
207. *Winter Morning in the City*

From Nov. 18, NYWCC, *2nd Annual Exh.*
(all wcs)
160. *Rain, Mist and Electric Light*
161. *Broadway at Union Square, Rainy Evening*
162. *Surf—Isles of Shoals*
163. *English Coast—Guardsmen on the Chalk Cliffs*
164. *Moonrise—Eastern Point, Gloucester*

Nov. 23–Dec. 20, NAD, *10th Autumn Exh.*
111. *Copps Hill Burial-Ground, Boston*
168. *Flower Girl*

Dec. 16, Union League Club, Brooklyn, "Loan exhibition of oil and watercolors by American artists" [*BE*, 12/17/1891, p. 1].
Moonlight, the Towers of Notre Dame de Paris (Childe Hassam, owner)

By Dec. 27, Blakeslee galleries, "Exhibition of Childe Hassam's Oils, Aquarelles and Pastels" [*BE*, 12/27/1891, p. 9].
"forty-three little pictures, seven of which are in oils and the others about equally divided between pastel and acquarelle."
Eternity
and "group of children playing among the flowers in Central park," "midnight view of the Champs Elysee from a balcony," "a picture of the Manhattan club"

1892

Jan. 14–16, ULCNY, *Paintings by American Artists . . . Exhibited at ULCNY, Annual Meeting.*
29. *Late Afternoon on the Avenue*

Jan. 21–Mar. 5, PAFA, *62nd Annual Exh.*
349–353 (ps)
106. *Fifth Avenue on a Winter Day*
349. *In Central Park*
350. *A New England Roadside*
351. *The Waverly Oaks*
352. *The Battle-ground: Lexington Common*
353. *Surf: Isles of Shoals*

Jan. 25–Feb. 15, Brooklyn Art Club, *Annual Exh.*
media not specified
100. *In the Parc Monceau, Paris*
101. *In the Rain, Union Square*
102. *After Lunch, a French Garden*
103. *Snowy Night, Boston Common*

Feb. 1–27, AWCS, *25th Annual Exh.*
88. *The West Gate, Canterbury*
152. *The White Mist of December, Madison Square*
348. *La Bouquetière et la Laitière, Paris*
459. *A Walk up the Avenue*
473. *Autumn in Central Park*
485. *St. Peter's Church, Broadstairs*
631. *A New Year's Nocturne, New York, 1892*

Feb. 13–15, ULCNY, *Exh. of Oil Paintings by American Artists.*
20. *Au Lion d'Or*

Mar. 10–12, ULCNY, *Monthly Loan Exh... Old Masters and Modern Oil Paintings.*
24. *An April Lady*

Mar. 21–Apr. 17, Art Club of Philadelphia, *2nd Annual Exh. of Water Colors and Pastels.*
(all wcs)
36. *La Bouquetiere et la Latiere* [sic], gold medal for watercolor
55. *English Farms, Broadstairs*
252. *Fifth Avenue*

Mar. 21–Apr. 17, AIC, *Spring Exh. of Water Colors.*
(all wcs)
77. *New* Year[']s *Nocturne, New York, 1892*
78. *Fifth Avenue, Evening*
79. *St. Peter's Church, Broadstairs, England*

Apr. 2–23, BAC, *46th Exh., Water Colors.*
(all wcs)
161. *Indian Summer*
209. *Thistledown—Isles of Shoals*
255. *The White Mist of December—Madison Square, New York*

Apr. 4–May 14, NAD, *67th Annual Exh.*
3. *"Sehnsucht"*

Apr. 14–16, ULCNY, *Annual Loan Exh. of Water Color Paintings.*
39. *Springtime* (wc)

May 2–28, SAA, 5th Avenue Art Galleries, *14th Annual Exh. of the SAA.*
111. *An April Lady*
112. *A June Morning in the City*
113. *Midsummer Morning, Celia Thaxter's Garden, Isles of Shoals*
114. *First Steps, a City Park in June*
115. *The Girl with a Red Book*

May 25–June 4, Rochester Art Club, *13th Annual Exh.*
101. *Moonlight—the Towers of Notre Dame*
102. *La Cremiere et la Bouquetiere*

June 1–end of Oct., *Internationalen Kunst-Ausstellung*, Munich, award.
718. *Das Blumenmädchen (Erinnerung an Paris)*
719. *Die 5. Avenue im Schnee*
720. *Ein alter Friedhof*

By Sept. 26, Portland, Oreg., "Exhibition of oils and water colors" [*NYT*, 9/26/1892, p. 4].

Oct.–Nov., Massachusetts Charitable Mechanic Association, Boston, *18th Triennial Exh. of the Massachusetts Charitable Mechanic Association.*
52. *Day of the Grand Prix de Paris*

Nov. 14–Dec. 25, Art Club of Philadelphia, *4th Annual Exh. of Oil Paintings and Sculpture.*
39. *An April Lady*
40. *Springtime—Madison Square, New York*

Nov. 21–Dec. 17, NAD, *11th Autumn Exh.*
111. *Blossoms, Central Park*
415. *Autumn Celebration in a New England Village*

Dec. 5–25, SAA, Galleries of American Fine Arts Society, *Retrospective Exh. of SAA.*
162. *Fifth Avenue at the Manhattan Club*
163. *Midsummer, An Island Garden*
164. *La Rue Bonaparte, Paris*

165. *A Snowstorm in the City, Union Square*
166. *Flower Girls*

Dec. 19–Jan. 7, 1893, NYWCC, *3rd Annual Exh.*
129A. *Night in the City*
130. *A Rainy Day on B'way*
131. *Night*
132. *A Rainy Evening*
133. *Village of Suresnes*
133A. *A Midsummer Garden*
133B. *The Setting Moon*

1893

Jan. 27–Feb. 8, Doll and Richards Gallery, Boston, *Exh. and Private Sale of Paintings by Childe Hassam.*
1. *The Heart of the City (Madison Square in Spring)*
2. *An Autumn Celebration in a New England Village*
3. *May Day in Central Park*
4. *Nasturtium*
5. *Winter in the City (Union Square)*
6. *The Girl with the Red Book*
7. *Union Square. An Afternoon in the Early Summer*
8. *My "Flower Girl"*
9. *The Hod Carrier*
10. *Banana Boy (Fifth Avenue)*
11. *An Island Garden*
12. *A Summer Day by the Sea*
13. *Winter. Parc Monceau, Paris*
14. *Springtime in the Park*
15. *Montmartre Roof-top. Moonrise at Sunset*
16. *Fifth Avenue*
17. *Effect of Electric Light on the Snow (Madison Square)*
18. *Moonlight*
19. *The Back Door of the Old House*
20. *Early Spring Morning (Central Park)*
21. *Flowers by the Sea*
22. *The Landing at Low Tide (Isles of Shoals)*
23. *Spring Sunlight in the City (16th Street, Union Square)*
24. *Autumn Day (Fifth Avenue at the Park)*
25. *The Ocean*
26. *Low Tide at Appledore (Isles of Shoals)*
27. *Charles River and Beacon Hill*
28. *A Broadway Nocturne*
29. *Rainy Night in front of a White Café*
30. *Coming up the Avenue, Late Afternoon*
31. *Nocturne (23rd Street)*
32. *Crocus Gatherers (Scene in a French Village)*
33. *Wet Day on the Boulevards*

Jan. 30–Feb. 5, AWCS, *26th Annual Exh.*
168. *The Beach at Broadstairs*
357. *Indian Summer—Madison Square*
368. *The Rain*
380. *Visiting*
546. *Montmartre*

Jan. 30–Feb. 21, Brooklyn Art Club, *Annual Exh.*
92. *In the Light, Rainy night on Broadway*
93. *In Central Park*
94. *Union Square, Spring*
95. *Rainy Day, Broadway* (wc)
96. *Celia Thaxter's Garden, Isles of Shoals* (p)
97. *Flower Girls, Parc Monceau, Paris* (p)

Apr. 13–15, ULCNY, *Annual Loan Exh. of Paintings in Water Colors.*
33. *Visitors* (wc)

Apr. 17–May 13, SAA, Galleries of American Fine Arts Society, *15th Annual Exh. of SAA.*
139. *An Island Garden*
141. *Last Light on the City*
145. *Music*

May 1–Oct. 30, *World's Columbian Exposition*, Chicago, awarded medals in painting and watercolor. List taken from *World's Columbian Exposition, Official Publications, Revised Catalogue, Department of Fine Arts, Published by W.B. Conkey Company, Chicago, 1893.*
326. *Mid-summer Morning*
337. *A Snowy Day on Fifth Avenue, New York*
666. *Autumn*
833. *Cab Station, Rue Bonaparte, Paris*
931. *On the Way to the Grand Prix*
1297. *Indian Summer, Madison Square, New York* (wc)
1399. *Springtime in the City* (wc)
1427. *Montmartre* (wc)
1470. *The Rain* (wc)
1503. *Fifth Avenue, New York* (wc)

Munchener Jahreausstellung von Kunstwerken aller Nationen, Munich. catalogue issued Aug. 12
592. *Frühling (New-York)*
593. *Nocturne*

Munich Secession.
catalogue issued Aug. 22
229. *Winter (Union Square, New York)*
230. *Eine April-Lady (New-York 1892)*

Nov. 8–29, Macbeth, *2nd Annual Exh. of Water Colors by American Artists.*
(all wcs)
34. *Rain, Union Square*
35. *A Misty Night, Wabash Avenue*
36. *The Surf, Isles of Shoals*
37. *Coast Guardsmen, Broadstairs*

Nov. 20–Dec. 8, NYWCC (held at Fine Arts Society), *4th Annual Exh.*
28. *A Play in a City Park* (wc)
39. *Broadway, Riany Day* (p), owned by Mr. Blaney
45. *Nocturne at the Crossing* (wc)
119. *At the Florist's, Rainy Night* (p)
139. *Seventeen* (p)
149. *Moonlight—The Old Boston Road* (wc)

Nov. 23–Dec. 31, Art Club of Philadelphia, *5th Annual Exh. of Oil Paintings and Sculpture.*
151. *Cab Station, Rue Bonaparte*

Dec. 4–Jan. 13, 1894, NAD, *Loan Collection 1893 Including 12th Autumn Exh.*
172. *Christmas Morning—Fifth Avenue*
208. *Flower Girl*

By Dec. 9, "Alpha Delt" Club, Exh. of 50 "oils and water colors by American artists...lent by the artists" [*NYT*, 12/9/1893, p. 8].
"A big blond view of Villiers-le-Bel on the Normandy coast, the white gables, red roofs, and yellow hayricks shining in the soft sunshine"

By Dec. 10, Frederick Keppel and Co., "water colors...show of eighty pictures" [*BE*, 12/10/1893, p. 17]

Dec. 18–Feb. 24, PAFA, *63rd Annual Exh.*
18. *On the Way to the Grand Prix*
63. *Harvest Celebration in a New England Village*
315. *Paris Coaches*

Knoedler Gallery

St. Louis Art Museum, *10th Annual Exh.*
110. *The Last Light of the City*

1894

Jan. 11, ULCNY, *Loan Exh. of Paintings by American Artists.*
44. *Fifth Avenue and the Snow*

Feb. 5–Mar. 3, AWCS, *27th Annual Exh.*
(all wcs)
172. *The Union League Club*
173. *Venetian Street*
226. *Rainy Evening*
246. *A Modern Minuet*
278. *New England Village Street*
279. *Sunset in the City*
410. *Delmonico's*
511. *Reflections*

Feb. 8–10, ULCNY, *Loan Exh. of Paintings.*
40. *Dusk*

Mar. 12–Apr. 14, SAA, Galleries of American Fine Arts Society, *16th Annual Exh. of SAA.*
4. *The Center of a Western Town*
108. *An Island Landscape—Evening*
115. *Dusk*
151. *Snow Halos—Midnight*
302. *Union Square—Springtime*

Mar., ULCNY, *Exh. of Paintings.*
48. *The Arch—Springtime*

Apr. 3–May 6, AIC, *6th Annual Exh. of Watercolors.*
(all wcs)
112. *A Modern Minuet*
113. *Rainy Evening*
114. *Visiting*
115. *Sunset, a City Street*

Apr. 7–12, Klackner Gallery, Exh. and sale of sketches in water colors, oils, pastel, and black and white for benefit of unemployed poor [*NYT*, 4/11/1894, p. 8], "show of artists' sketches and studies contributed to the Emergency Fund" [*Art Amateur* 30, no. 6 (May 1894), p. 156].

Apr., ULCNY, *Exh. of Water Colors.*
(wcs)
59. *Union League Club*
60. *The Rain*

By July 7, Fine Arts Society, *Group Exh. of American Paintings* [*NYT*, 7/7/1894, p. 5].
Street View, Top of Montmartre, Paris and others

July, Gloucester, Mass., Private exh. at hotel cottage.
(some wcs)

Munich Secession.
catalogue issued Aug. 12
104. *Hochsommermorgen. — Eine Mohnpflanzung am Meer.*

Nov. 2–14, Doll and Richards Gallery, Boston, *Exh. and Private Sale of Water Color Drawings by Childe Hassam.*
(all wcs)
1. *Nocturne [At the Crossing]*
2. *Children at Play [Union Square]*
3. *Rain, Mist and Electric Light [Madison Square]*
4. *December Morning. Cab Stand [Madison Square]*
5. *Pale, Warm, Morning Mist*
6. *The Bride*
7. *The Cottage Gate and Garden*
8. *Larkspur and Lilies*
9. *The Little Table*
10. *The "Altar and Shrine" [Mrs. Thaxter's arrangement of poppies]*
11. *The Gold Sunset*
12. *The Ashes of Roses Sunset*
13. *The Romanza Sunset*
14. *The Ocean*
15. *The Great Lakes [October Morning]*
16. *Autumn Harmony [Isles of Shoals]*
17. *The Northwest Wind*
18. *Old Boat Landing [Gloucester]*
19. *Gloucester Street*
20. *The Old Yacht*
21. *Sunset Light on the Willows*
22. *The Union League Club [New York]*
23. *Fifth Avenue at Delmonico's*
24. *Venetian Streets*
25. *Sunset [Fifth Avenue at Washington Square]*
26. *A Modern Minuet*
27. *Surf at the Shoals*
28. *Girl and Rainy Night*
29. *Seines and Old Houses [Gloucester]*
30. *Mist. The Distant Shore*
31. *Nocturne [A Balcony in Venice]*
32. *Rain and Fog [Gloucester Outer Harbor]*
33. *Gloucester Fish Houses*
34. *Rainy Evening [A Fifth Ave. Flower Shop]*
35. *Rainy Day [Fifth Avenue at the Park]*

Nov. 19–Dec. 16, Art Club of Philadelphia, *6th Annual Exh. of Oil Paintings and Sculpture.*
21. *The Girl in the White Dory, Gloucester Harbor*

Dec. 3–22, NYWCC, *5th Annual Exh.*
(all wcs)
35. *The Girl in a Grey Gown*
185. *A Gloucester Street*
194. *Mid-Summer Morning Mist*
205. *Celia Thaxter's Garden and Cottage at the Isles of Shoals*

Dec. 17–Feb. 23, 1895, PAFA, *64th Annual Exh.*
147. *Winter: Union Square, New York*
148. *Dusk: Central Park West, New York*
149. *The Hod-carrier*
150. *Afternoon Sunlight: Top of Mont-Martre, Paris*
151. *A Summer Morning*
152. *Girl in Gray Light: Central Park West*

Dec., ULCNY, *Exh. of Paintings.*
47. *Gloucester*
48. *Union Square in Spring*

1895

Jan. 22–Feb. 22; extended to Mar. 2, Cleveland Art Association, *1st Annual Exh. of Cleveland Art Association.*
92. *Flower Girl of Paris*
134. *Celia Thaxter's Room at the Isles of Shoals*
331. *The Rain* (Michigan Ave., Chicago)
429. *Fifth Ave., New York,* 1st prize for wcs [*Cleveland Plain Dealer*, 2/7/1895, n.p]

Feb. 4–Mar. 2, AWCS, *28th Annual Exh.*
(all wcs)
54. *"The Mysterious City"*
110. *Nocturne—A Balcony in Venice*
176. *Under the Chalk Cliffs at Low Tide, Broadstairs, Eng.*
298. *The Old Yacht, Gloucester*
304. *Sunset Light on the Willows*
471. *Rain and Mist, Gloucester Harbor*

Feb. 23–Mar. 6, Doll and Richards, Boston, *Exh. and Private Sale of Oil Paintings by Mr. Childe Hassam.*

1. *Midsummer*
2. *Celia Thaxter's Room at the Isles of Shoals*
3. *The Poppies. Summer Morning*
4. *Washington Square in June*
5. *The Prado, Havana, Cuba*
6. *Quincy, Massachusetts*
7. *The North River, after the Naval Parade, April 1893*
8. *Gloucester at Sunset*
9. *An Island Garden*
10. *Plaza Montserrate, Havana*
11. *Snowstorm and the Midnight Cabs*
12. *The Pond Lily and Nasturtiums*
13. *Rocks at Appledore*
14. *A Fisherman's Cottage, Gloucester*
15. *Fifth Avenue and the Washington Arch in May*
16. *A New England Street in Summer*
17. *Gloucester*
18. *Spring Morning, Fifth Avenue*
19. *Lilacs*
20. *The Cathedral and Fifth Avenue in June*
21. *The Old Flower Merchant of 23rd Street*
22. *Golf Players*
23. *Poppies and the Sea at Noonday*
24. *Rainy Midnight*
25. *September. The Gloucester Repair Docks*
26. *Centre of a Western Town*
27. *Sundown and Evening Mist*
28. *Nocturne, the 6th Avenue Elevated*
29. *Spring Rain. Paris*
30. *The Landing, East Gloucester*
31. *The Old Bottle Man*
32. *"La Cabana" and "Plaza Centrale," Havana*
33. *Summer Afternoon at the Isles of Shoals*

Mar. 25–Apr. 27, SAA, Galleries of American Fine Arts Society, *17th Annual Exh. of SAA.*
45. *The Midsummer Girl*
153. *Quincy, Massachusetts*
183. *A Fisherman's Cottage, Gloucester*
191. *Summer*
236. *Place Centrale and Fort Cabanas, Havana*, Webb prize

Apr. 1–May 11, NAD, *70th Annual Exh.*
159. *The Girl in the White Dory*

Apr. 11–May 16, AIC, *7th Annual Exh. of Water-Colors and Pastels by American Artists.*
155–159 (wcs)
155. *The Mysterious City*
156. *The Old Yacht, Gloucester*
157. *Sunset Light on the Willows*
158. *The Beach at Broadstairs, England*
159. *Under the Chalk Cliff at Low Tide, Broadstairs*
160. *The White Birches* (p)

May 6–ca. May 20, Pratt Institute Museum, Exh. of "original drawings in black and white" [*BE*, 5/12/1895, p. 8]. "picturesque drawing by Childe Hassam of the old Park street church in Boston"

By June 9, Hartford Art Society [*NYT*, 6/9/1895, p. 28].

Sept., St. Louis Exposition and Music Hall Association, *12th Annual Exh.*
238. *Summer*
239. *Plaza Centrale and Fort Cabanas, Havana*, Webb Prize, SAA, 1895
240. *Winter, New York*

Nov. 11–23, NYWCC, *6th Annual Exh.*
173. *Grey Morning, Madison Square*

Nov., Cincinnati Museum Association, *Paintings Exhibited in the West Gallery of the Art Museum during Nov. 1895.*
8. *Summer*
9. *Plaza Centrale, and Fort Cabanas, Havana*, Webb Prize, SAA, 1895
10. *Winter, New York*
all lent by the artist

Nov., *Program and Exh. in Dedication of Carnegie Library; Pittsburgh, PA.*
128. *Summer*
129. *The Girl in a Dory*
130. *The Room of Flowers*, Celia Thaxter's Parlor at the Isle of Shoals
131. *Paris in Winter*, lent by John Caldwell

Dec. 23–Feb. 22, 1896, PAFA, *65th Annual Exh.*
150. *Plaza Central and Fort Cabañas, Havana*
151. *The White Cottage*
152. *Old Age*
153. *Summer*
154. *The Room of Flowers*
155. *Girl in a Dory*
492. *A Gray Morning* (wc)

1896

Jan. 13–Feb. 15, BAC, *53rd Exh., Oil Paintings and Sculpture.*
2. *Summer Sunlight*, 2nd prize

Jan. 27–Feb. 15, SB, *Exh. of Paintings by Childe Hassam.*
1. *The Girl in a White Dory*
2. *The Old Fisherman*, owned by Mrs. John Lowell
3. *Nocturne, Fifth Avenue*
4. *The Spar Yard. Sunlight and fog*
5. *June Afternoon*
6. *The Princess in Pink*
7. *Midsummer*
8. *Snowstorm in the City (Union Square)*
9. *September. Suite in gold and purple*
10. *June Morning in gold and blue*
11. *The Mist Harmony*
12. *The Fisherman's Family*
13. *The Rainy Day*
14. *The Schooner with Purse Nets*
15. *The Old Coaster*
16. *The Girl in a Green Gown*
17. *The Willows*
18. *A New England Street*
19. *The Sea Mist Sunset*
20. *Spring Sunlight in the City*
21. *August*
22. *Winter in Gramercy Park*
23. *The Isles of Shoals*
24. *Dryade*
25. *Plaza Montserrate, Havana*
26. *Winter, Madison Square*
27. *Appledore. Suite in grey*

Feb. 3–29, AWCS, *29th Annual Exh.* (all wcs)
22. *The Blue Caribbean*
64. *An Island Garden*
122. *Hogarth's House, Chiswick*

Feb. 6–7, American Art Galleries, *Paintings, Pastels and Water Colors by Childe Hassam.*
1st Night Sale: February 6
41–48 (ps), 49–65 (wcs)
1. *Isles of Shoals, Morning*
2. *In the Kitchen Garden, France*
3. *Autumn Twilight*
4. *Study of Poppies against the Sea*
5. *Harvest Moonrise, France*
6. *Morning from a Balcony, New York*
7. *Evening*
8. *In New England*
9. *Afternoon in the Lane Villiers-le-bel*
10. *Evening in the Garden, French Chateau*
11. *Winter, Latin Quarter*
12. *Summer, Place Clichy*
13. *The Girl in Gray*
14. *Early Spring, Union Square*
15. *Crab*
16. *A Lane in Brittany*
17. *Sweeping the Stoop*
18. *The Pear Trees in Blossom*
19. *Surf at the Isles of Shoals*
20. *The Railway*
21. *Midsummer*
22. *Sundown, Rocky Neck, Gloucester*
23. *Sunset, from the Isles of Shoals*
24. *In Old Nantucket*
25. *Evening, Return from the Fields*
26. *Spring Dawn*
27. *Feeding the Pigeons*
28. *The Doorway, French Cottage*
29. *The Garden of Sun*
30. *Winter Midnight*
31. *The Misty Sunset and Autumn Elms*
32. *Afternoon, Isles of Shoals*
33. *The Distant Village on the Plain*
34. *Noontime, Shanty Town*
35. *Moonrise, over the Ocean*
36. *Apple Blossoms*
37. *A Gloucester Garden*
38. *Poppies and Marigolds*
39. *The Road over the Downs*
40. *Early Sunday Morning, Union Square*
41. *An Autumn Afternoon*
42. *Old Burial Ground, Lexington*
43. *The Old Bedford Tavern*
44. *In the Park*
45. *The Pool*
46. *Little Girl with a Pear*
47. *The Poppy Garden in June*
48. *In the Bois, Opening of the Paris Exposition, 1889*
49. *Seines and Old Fish Houses, Gloucester*
50. *Rocks and Surf*
51. *Venice*
52. *Study of Poppies*
53. *The Yellow Car*
54. *Autumn on the Great Lakes*
55. *Lilies*
56. *The Sea Mist, Gloucester Harbor*
57. *Wet Night, Fifth Avenue*
58. *Evening*
59. *Autumn on the Shore*
60. *The Little Tables with Poppies*
61. *A Gloucester Street*
62. *A Broadway Nocturne*
63. *The Union Club*
64. *Rainy Night, Broadway*
65. *The Rain*
66. *On the Ways, Gloucester, Mass.*
67. *Gathering Flowers in a French Garden*
68. *The West Wind and the Oak Branch*
69. *Autumn in New England*
70. *Lilac and Gold*
71. *Evening, Gloucester Harbor*
72. *In Central Park*
73. *Shanty Town Residence*
74. *Sunset, Nantucket*
75. *The Little Apple Tree*
76. *The Blue Caribbean*
77. *In the New Park, Boston*
78. *The Little Cherry Tree, at Evening*
79. *Evening and the Lilacs*
80. *October, Marlborough Street, Boston*
81. *In Shanty Town*
82. *Study of Poppies, Celia Thaxter's Garden*
83. *The Old Flower Merchant of Twenty-third Street*
84. *Along the Seine, Evening*
85. *The Girl in White, Entrance to the Park*
86. *In an English Park*
87. *Springtime, a Montmartre Street*
88. *Return from the Bois, Place d'Etoile*
89. *The Battle-ground, Lexington*
90. *September Afternoon, from a Café*
91. *Moonlight Sky, Isles of Shoals*
92. *The Manhattan Club*
93. *Nasturtiums*
94. *Afternoon in the Park*
95. *The Rose Girl*
96. *The Book Collector, Paris*
97. *Spring Morning, Rue Mt. Cenis, Montmartre*
98. *Nocturne, the Balcony*
99. *In the Garden, June*, Exposition Universal, 1889
100. *La rue Bonaparte*, Salon, 1887
2nd Night Sale: February 7
131–136 (ps), 137–155 (wcs)
101. *Morning, Isles of Shoals*
102. *Fire and Rainy Night*
103. *Afternoon, Isles of Shoals*
104. *Summer Afternoon, the Cottages*
105. *Nocturne*
106. *Cloud Shadows*
107. *The White Pair, Wet Night*
108. *The Banana Boy*
109. *The Girl in a Gray Jacket*
110. *The Little Old Shop on Montmartre*
111. *In a Paris Park*
112. *Along the Seine, near Paris*
113. *Doorways, Montmartre Street*
114. *Copps Hill, Boston*
115. *Christmas Morning, Fifth Avenue*
116. *The Flower Girl, Parc Monceau, Paris*
117. *Springtime, Paris*
118. *Nocturne, Boston Common*
119. *Wet Night, Paris*
120. *Winter Morning, Fifty-ninth Street*
121. *Early Spring, the Distant City*
122. *Nocturne, Notre Dame de Paris*
123. *Effect of Electric Light on the Snow, Madison Square*
124. *The Rocks of the Isles of Shoals*
125. *Over the Seine*
126. *The Yellow Cab, Place d'Anvers*
127. *The Garden in Gray*
128. *The Little New England Bar-room*
129. *A Roof-top Garden, Montmartre*
130. *Head of a Young Girl*
131. *September Clouds*
132. *Elm Avenue, Lexington*
133. *The Waverly Oaks*
134. *October, Lexington Common*
135. *Nocturne, Lexington*
136. *The Concord Road, Lexington Common*
137. *Celia Thaxter's Garden at the Isles of Shoals*
138. *The Old Landing*
139. *The Chalk Cliffs, Broadstairs, England*
140. *Arrangement of Poppies*
141. *Moonrise*
142. *Thistledown*
143. *Among the Fish Houses*
144. *Coming up the Avenue*
145. *Sunset from the Shoals*
146. *Larkspur and Lilies*
147. *Hollyhocks*
148. *Surf, Isles of Shoals*
149. *Old Fishing Schooner, Gloucester Harbor*
150. *Lovage*
151. *Delmonico*
152. *Venetian Streets*
153. *New England Village Street*
154. *Fifth Avenue*, Awarded a prize of $300 at Cleveland, 1895
155. *Springtime in the City*
156. *September Sunlight, Paris*
157. *Nocturne, Montmartre, Paris*
158. *Rainy, Late Afternoon, Union Square*
159. *Italian Barks, Gloucester Harbor*
160. *Commonwealth Avenue, Boston*
161. *Morning on the Quais*
162. *The Flower Market, Paris*
163. *At the Fair, Chicago, 1893*
164. *The Road to the Sea*
165. *Pear Blossoms*
166. *Flower Fête*
167. *Moonlight, Isles of Shoals*
168. *French Roses*
169. *In the Conservatory*
170. *Beauty and the Beast*
171. *Moonlight at Sunset, Isles of Shoals*
172. *The Girl and the Geraniums*, Salon, 1889
173. *Blossoms in Central Park*
174. *The Girl with the Red Book*
175. *Late Afternoon, Union Square*

176. *White Moonlight, Isles of Shoals*
177. *Girl in Pink*
178. *Winter in Central Park*
179. *Spanish Street*
180. *Under the Lilacs*
181. *White Island Light, from Appledore*
182. *The Cloud*
183. *The Moonrise in Silver and Gold*
184. *Early Spring Morning, Central Park*
185. *September, the Marshes*
186. *Summer Clouds*
187. *Nocturne, la Place Pigalle*
188. *Dusk, Central Park, West*
189. *In the Park, Girl with a Cloak*
190. *Flower Girl, Paris*
191. *Low Tide*
192. *Late Afternoon in the Park*
193. *The Main Land, from the Isles of Shoals*
194. *Winter Morning, Forty-second Street*
195. *Fish Houses*
196. *Commission Day, Montmartre*
197. *The Church of St. Germain d'* [sic] *l'Auxerrois*
198. *Nocturne, a Night in Paris*
199. *Midsummer Morning, the Island Garden*
200. *The Fiacre*
201. *The Enchanted Hour*
202. *The Red Geraniums,* Exposition Universal, 1889
203. *Sunday in Central Park*
204. *Twilight over the City; a Roof-top Garden, Paris,* Awarded Third Medal, Exposition Universal, 1889
205. *Autumn,* Salon, 1889. Awarded medal. World's Columbian Exposition, 1893

Mar. 28–May 2, SAA, Galleries of American Fine Arts Society, *18th Annual Exh. of SAA.*
39. *The Room of Flowers*
186. *The Girl in a Green Gown*
197. *Through the Willow Branches*
198. *Old Age*

Mar. 30–May 16, NAD, *71st Annual Exh.*
158. *The Lilacs*
164. *Summer*

Apr. 11–May 2, BAC, *54th Exh., Water Colors, etc.*
(all wcs)
102. *The Rain — Michigan Avenue, Chicago*
123. *Nocturne — Broadway*
191. *At Play — Union Square*

Apr. 16–June 7, AIC, *8th Annual Exh. of Water-Colors, Pastels and Miniatures by American Artists.*
(all wcs or ps)
178. *The Blue Caribbean*
179. *Gray Morning*
180. *Gloucester Street*
181. *Fifth Avenue Near the Park — Rainy Day*

May 16–June 13, CAM, *Spring Exh. in the Art Museum.*
6. *Summer Sunlight*

From May 25, Madison Square Garden, *Cuban-American Fair* [*BE*, 5/25/1896, p. 2].

Nov. 5–Jan. 1, 1897, Carnegie Art Galleries, Pittsburgh, *1st Annual Exh.*
128. *Spring*
129. *Lady with Yellow Rose*
130. *Under the Willows*

Dec. 5–Jan. 9, 1897, BAC, *55th Exh., Oil Paintings and Sculpture.*
22. *The Ferry Landing — Gloucester*

Dec. 7–19, Cleveland Picture Exh. Society, *Some American Plein Air Painters, Theodore Robinson, Childe Hassam.*
28. *Spar-Yard, Gloucester*
29. *The Willows*
30. *Spring Morning*
31. *Peonies*
32. *Rainy Day, Fifth Avenue, New York*
33. *Boston (Charles River and Beacon Hill)*
34. *June Morning*
35. *Nocturne, Fifth Avenue*
36. *The Morning Mist*
37. *The Promenade, Isles of Shoals*
38. *Flower Girl, Paris*
39. *Afternoon, Montmartre, Paris*
40. *Union Square, Spring, New York City*
41. *Winter Twilight on the Champa-Elysee* [sic]
42. *The Fisherman Family*

Dec. 21–Feb. 22, 1897, PAFA, *66th Annual Exh.*
137. *The Girl in Pink*
137 [sic]. *Summer Sunlight*
138. *The Lilac*
139. *The Green Gown*
140. *The Lady with Yellow Roses*

St. Louis Exposition and Music Hall Association, St. Louis, *13th Annual Exh.*
229. *The Room of Flowers*
230. *The Lilacs*
231. *The Green Gown*
232. *A Girl in Pink*
233. *The Stoop in Winter*
234. *Waverly Oaks* (p)

1897

Mar. 28–May 1, SAA, Galleries of the American Fine Arts Society, *19th Annual Exh. of SAA.*
56. *The Ship-Yard*
196. *Girl and Snow*

Apr. 5–May 15, NAD, *Annual Exh.*
396. *A Street in Gloucester*
397. *Quincy, Mass.*
400. *Girl and the Rocks*

From Apr. 24, Salon of the Société Nationale des Beaux-Arts, Paris.
288. *Vieillard*
289. *Chambre avec fleurs*
290. *Jeune fille dans les rochers*
622. *Le soir Piazza di Spagna (Rome)* and others

June 1–ca. Oct. 31, International Art Exh., Munich.
654. *Sommer*
655. *Unter den Weiden*
656. *Morgen, Neapel*
657. *Vesuv, Abend*

Nov. 2–Dec. 12, AIC, *10th Annual Exh. of Oil Paintings and Sculpture by American Artists.*
167. *The Room of Flowers*
168. *Old Age*
169. *Summer Sunlight*
170. *The Spanish Stairs, Rome*

1898

Jan. 10–Feb. 22, PAFA, *67th Annual Exh.*
199. *The Spanish Stairs: Rome*
200. *The Gold Player*
201. *Morning*
202. *Midsummer*
203. *Iron Bound*

Jan. 22–Feb. 19, BAC, *57th Exh., Oil Paintings and Sculpture.*
59. *New England Village Street*
70. *Montmartre — Paris*
221. *Pont-Aven*

Jan. 31–Feb. 26, AWCS, *31st Annual Exh.*
(all wcs)
8. *Poppies Against the Sea*
30. *The Silver Cloud*
74. *Alice in Wonderland, Isle of Shoals*
146. *The Brownstone Stoop*
193. *Sky and Rooftops, Paris*
298. *The Yellow Rose*
392. *Early Summer, Lake George*
405. *Evening, Paris*

Feb. 1–28, Gill's Art Galleries, Springfield, Mass., *The Best Work of Eminent American Artists Resident in America and Europe.*
44. *The Fisherman's Cottage*

Feb. 24–Apr. 1, La Libre Esthétique, *La Cinquième Exposition à Bruxelles.*
163. *Été*
164. *Sous les saules*
165. *Naples le matin*
166. *Le Vésuve vers le soir*

Mar. 7–27, Boston Art Students Association, Copley Hall and Allston Hall, Boston, *Loan Exh. of Pictures by Modern Painters.*
43. *Old Age*

Mar. 28–May 14, NAD, *73rd Annual Exh.*
335. *Springtime*

Mar. 31–Apr. 16, DRG, *1st Exh., Ten American Painters.*
23. *Haymaking, Pont-Aven*
24. *Spanish Stairs*
25. *The Arno*
26. *The Bather*
27. *St. Germain l'Auxerrois*
28. *Pont-Aven Finistere*
45. *The Rain — New York*

Apr. 2–23, BAC, *58th Exh., Water Colors, etc.*
105. *The Yellow Rose* (wc)

Apr. 19–June 5, AIC, *10th Annual Exh. of Water-Colors, Pastels and Miniatures by American Artists.*
(all wcs)
158. *The Silver Cloud*
159. *The Brown Stone Stoop*
160. *Evening, Paris*

Apr. 25–May 14, SB, *An Exh. of Painting by Ten American Painters.*
1. *The Arno*
2. *Pont Aven, Finisterre*
4. *The Spanish stairs*
5. *St. Germain de l'Auxerrois*
12. *Haymaking. Pont Aven*
13. *The Rain. New York*
28. *The bather*

From May 1, Salon of the Société Nationale des Beaux-Arts, Paris.
595. *Le village de Pont-Aven*
596. *Le soir en Bretagne*
597. *Le clocher de Pont-Aven*
598. *Une rue à Pont-Aven*
599. *Une rue à Pont-Aven*
600. *Bretonnes du Pouldu*
601. *Rome*
602. *Pont Royal (Paris)*

Until May 17, New York Athletic Club, "Exhibition of sixty-five American paintings, selected from among those which have been awarded the various prizes at the annual Spring Academy, Water Color Society, and the Society of American Artists' exhibitions during the past ten years" [*NYT*, 5/16/1898, p. 7].
Plaza, Havana

May 21–July 5, CAM, *5th Annual Exh. of Works by American Artists.*
182. *Sky and Rooftops, Paris*
183. *New England Village Scene*

June 1–Nov. 1, Mississippi and International Exposition, Omaha, Neb., *Fine Arts Exhibit.*
257. *Autumn*
258. *The Rain*

June, WAM, *1st Exh. of WAM with the Cooperation of Worcester Art Society.*
17. *The Spanish Stairs*
18. *The Summer Girl,* Mr. James Logan

Sept. 14–Oct. 29, St. Louis Exposition and Music Hall Association, *15th Annual Exh.*
202. *Haymaking, Pont Aven, Finistere*
203. *St. German l'Auxerrois*
204. *Springtime*
205. *The Arno*
206. *The Spanish Stairs, Rome*

Nov. 3–Jan. 1, CI, *3rd Annual Exh.*
23. *The Sea,* Medal of the Second Class (silver)
24. *Night Piece to Julia*

Nov. 5–26, NYWCC, *9th Annual Exh.*
27. *English Landscape* (wc)

Nov. 14–Dec. 11, Art Club of Philadelphia, *10th Annual Exh. of Oil Paintings and Sculpture.*
3. *Easter Morning*

Nov. 15–Dec. 18, AIC, *11th Annual Exh. of Oil Paintings and Sculpture by American Artists.*
116. *Summer*
117. *The Willows*
118. *Naples*
119. *Vesuvius, Winter Evening*

Dec. 6–17, BAC, *An Exh. and Competition of Colonial Pictures under the Auspices of Colonial Dames of Massachusetts.*
22. *The old Boston Road*
23. *Quincy, Massachusetts*
24. *The Cider Jugs*

1899

Jan. 16–Feb. 25, PAFA, *68th Annual Exh.*
40. *The Sea*
213. *Night-piece to Julia*
214. *Road to Pont-Aven*
215. *Pont Royal, Paris,* Temple Gold Medal
216. *Peasant Women*
219. *The Village of Pont-Aven*
221. *Rome*
222. *Road to Pont-Aven*
224. *Evening in Brittany*
404. *Clock Tower of Pont-Aven*

Feb. 1–Mar. 1, Haydon Art Club, Lincoln, Neb., *Midwinter Exhibit.*
14. *Summer*

By Feb. 7, American Art Galleries, "Picture show…each is the work of an American painter…," sale held the following week [*BE*, 2/7/1899, p. 4].

Feb. 11–Mar. 4, Architectural League of New York, *14th Annual Exh.*
108. *Decorative Panel — September*

Feb. 13–Mar. 11, AWCS, *32nd Annual Exh.*
(all wcs)
165. *A Cottage in Kent*

284. *A Garden by the Sea*
302. *Riverbend on the Thames*
303. *Gleaners*
325. *The Water Lily*

Feb. 16–Mar. 16, Art Club of Erie, Pa., *2nd Annual Exh. of Art Club of Erie.*
22. *The Old Boston Road. (Colonial Times)*
23. *Quincy, Massachusetts.*
24. *The Cider Jugs.*

Mar.–Apr., DMA, *Special Exh. of Paintings by Henry Mosler, Together with one each by Childe Hassam, Jules Guerin, Louis Paul Dessar, George H. Smillie, Paul Lazerges, Robert Hopkins, Etc., Etc.*
15. *The Autumn of Life*

Apr. 3–May 13, NAD, *74th Annual Exh.*
177. *The Sea*

Apr. 4–15, DRG, *Ten American Painters.*
In the Sun, Brittany
Down the Spanish Stairs, Rome
Morning Mist
The Brook

May 2–June 11, AIC, *11th Annual Exh. of Water-Colors, Pastels and Miniatures by American Artists.*
(wcs)
153. *Cottage in Kent*
154. *The Gleaners*

May 20–July 10, CAM, *6th Annual Exh. of American Art.*
2. *The Sea*
3. *Pont Royal, Paris*
4. *Down the Spanish Stairs, Rome*
5. *Noonday, — Pont-Aven*
6. *The Wood Brook*
7. *River Bend on the Thames* (wc)

Nov. 1–Dec. 2, Art Club of Philadelphia, *11th Annual Exh. of Oil Paintings and Sculpture.*
117. *The Pale Green Gown*
139. *Evening, Appledore*

Nov. 2–Jan. 1, 1900, CI, *4th Annual Exh.*
112. *Improvisation*
113. *White Island Light*, award
114. *Charlotte*
115. *Fifth Avenue in Winter*, award

Nov. 5–25, NYWCC, *10th Annual Exh.*
(wcs)
6. *The Park at St. Cloud*
103. *The Shade of the Cliff*

Nov. 6–Dec. 17, AIC, *12th Annual Exh. of Oil Paintings and Sculpture by American Artists.*
145. *The Sea*
146. *The Wood Brook*
147. *Noonday. Pont Aven*
148. *River Bank on the Thames*

Dec. 2–16, BAC, *A 2nd Exh. and Competition of Colonial Pictures under the Auspices of Colonial Dames of Massachusetts.*
25. *The Stairway: A Plot of the Revolution*
26. *Early Colonial Gravestones at Lexington*
27. *Indian Summer in Colonial Days*

1900

Jan. 1–27, NAD, *75th Annual Exh.*
206. *The Flower Shop*

Jan. 6–Feb. 3, BAC, *61st Exh., Oil Paintings and Sculpture.*
35. *Beacon Hill*
74. *Montmartre*

By Jan. 13, Macbeth, *Exh. of Works by Childe Hassam of New York, London and Paris Subjects.*
"Twenty-seven drawings of New York, London, and Paris streets" [*NYT*, 1/13/1900, p. BR9]

Jan. 15–Feb. 24, PAFA, *69th Annual Exh.*
61. *Charlotte*
62. *The Mediterranean*
66. *Improvisation*
67. *Summer*
81. *Fifth Avenue in Winter*

Jan. 17–Feb. 14, Art Club of Erie, Pa., *Works of American Artists. Water Colors, 3rd Annual Exh. of Art Club of Erie.*
(all wcs)
46. *The Rain*
47. *The Divan*
48. *Mist and Rain*

Feb. 5–17, AWCS, *16th Annual Exh.*
(all wcs)
40. *Rainy Midnight*
48. *Children in the Park*
169. *Rain, Mist, and Electric Light*
174. *The Dewey Arch*

By Feb. 7, Union League Club, Brooklyn, *Annual Exh.* [*BE*, 2/7/1900, p. 13].

Mar. 15–31, DRG, "Exhibition of Paintings by Ten American Painters."
Gloucester
Improvisation
September

Mar. 27–Apr. 15, Minneapolis Society of Fine Arts, *1st Annual Art Exh.*
70. *The White Dory*
71. *The Old Fisherman. (A Street in Glaucester [sic], Mass.)*

Apr. 14–16, National Arts Club, "exhibition of paintings, water colors, pastels, etchings, and bronzes...for the benefit of the widowed mother of the late Ernest Tarleton..." [*NYT*, 4/14/1900, p. BR15].

Apr. 14–Nov. 12, Exposition Universelle, Paris, *Exposition des Beaux-Arts États-Unis d'Amérique Exposition Universelle de Paris 1900.*
145. *Jour de Neige dans Fifth Avenue*, Propriété de l'Institut Carnegie, [silver medal]

Apr. 16–30, SB, *Exh. of Paintings by Ten American Painters.*
5. *September. A Decoration*
6. *Improvisation*
7. *Gloucester*

Apr. 24–June 10, AIC, *12th Annual Exh. of Water Colors, Pastels and Miniatures by American Artists.*
(all wcs)
148. *Rain, Mist, and Electric Light*
149. *Children in the Park*
150. *Rainy Midnight*

May 10–19, Art Students League, Fine Arts Building, *Retrospective Exh., 1875–1900, Works by Members, Students and Instructors of the Art Students' League of New York.*
87. *Summer Sunlight*

May 14–28, Albert Roullier Art Galleries, Chicago, *Exh. of Twenty-seven Drawings by Childe Hassam.*
(all ds)
"New York"
1. *The Up-tide on the Avenue*
2. *The Blizzard*
3. *Riverside Drive*
4. *The Organ-grinder*
"London"
5. *Westminster Bridge*
6. *London Bridge*
7. *The Thames*
8. *The Guild Hall*
9. *Along the Embankment*
10. *Fleet Street*
11. *Birdcage Walk*
12. *Regent Street*
13. *Little English Girl*
"Paris"
14. *The Madeleine*
15. *The Luxembourg Gardens*
16. *Au Café*
17. *Porte St. Denis*
18. *The Drinking Fountain*
19. *Outside the Café*
20. *Gossip*
21. *Old Clothes*
22. *Street Vendors*
23. *Returning from Market*
24. *Street Sweeper*
25. *Latin Quarter Café*
26. *The Chestnut Vendor*
27. *Coryphée*

From May 14, Press Artists' League, at the Astoria Hotel, *1st Annual Exh.* [*NYT*, 5/15/1900, p. 6].

May 19–July 9, CAM, *7th Annual Exh. of American Art.*
82. *A Fisherman's Family, Gloucester*
83. *Noonday, Pont Aven, Brittany*
84. *St. Germain l'Auxerrois*
85. *Union Square in Spring*

June 11–26, Richmond Art Association, Richmond, Ind., *4th Annual Exh.*
87. *The White Dory*
88. *June Morning*

Summer, WAM, *Oil Paintings, Summer of 1900, Prize Exh.*
70. *Improvisation*
71. *Gloucester*, honorable mention

Oct. 29–Nov. 17, SB, *Exh. of Paintings by Childe Hassam.*
1. *The Hod Carrier*
2. *Beacon Hill*
3. *Au Park Monceau*
4. *The Laborer*
5. *Nocturne, "Big Ben"*
6. *June*
7. *Appledore, August*
8. *Beacon Street — October Morning*
9. *The Rocks of Appledore*
10. *Provincetown*
11. *Snowstorm in the City*
12. *Building the Schooner*
13. *The Dunes*
14. *The Old Chapel*
15. *A Brittany Cottage*
16. *Gloucester, Morning*
17. *Washington Arch, May*
18. *The Bather*
19. *The Room of Flowers*
20. *The Fruit Shop*
21. *A New England Street*
22. *The Ferry Landing*
23. *The Nut Tree*
24. *Rainy Midnight*
25. *Nocturne*
26. *The Children*
27. *Summer Afternoon, Isles of Shoals*
28. *The Blue Sky and the White Church*
29. *Boston Common, September*
30. *Gloucester, Evening*
31. *The Old Bottle Man*
32. *The Cathedral and Fifth Avenue in June*
33. *In Brittany*
34. *Nocturne, The "Tenderloin"*
35. *Houses of Parliament*
36. *Grande Boulevarde*
37. *The Little Piano*
38. *The White Church*

Oct. 30–Dec. 9, AIC, *13th Annual Exh. of Oil Paintings and Sculpture by American Artists.*
111. *A Fisherman's Cottage*
112. *Midday, Pont Aven*
113. *Saint Germain, Paris*

Nov. 1–Jan. 1, 1901, CI, *5th Annual Exh.*
114. *Penelope*
115. *Madison Square in Spring*

Nov. 10–Dec. 2, NYWCC, *11th Annual Exh.*
214. *The Silver Cloud* (wc)

Nov. 21–Dec., Boston Art Students' Association, Copley Hall, *1st Annual New Gallery Exh. of Contemporary American Art.*
54. *The Ferry Landing, Gloucester*

Dec. 26–Jan. 16, 1901, Nebraska Art Association, Lincoln, *7th Annual Exh. of Oil Paintings, Sculpture, and Ceramics by American Artists.*
54. *A Fisherman's Cottage*
55. *Midday, Pont Avon [sic]*
56. *Saint Germain, Paris*

PSAG, *6th Annual Exh. of Paintings by Prominent Artists.*
45. *Gloucester Fisherman*
46. *English Landscape*

1901

Jan. 5–Feb. 2, BAC, *63rd Exh., Oil Paintings and Sculpture.*
9. *The Great Dunes*

Jan. 5–Feb. 2, NAD, *76th Annual Exh.*
171. *July Night*
262. *Winter Morning on Broadway*
269. *White Island Light*

Jan. 14–Feb. 23, PAFA, *70th Annual Exh.*
317. *Gloucester*
401. *Penelope*

Feb. 11–Mar. 28, AWCS, *34th Annual Exh.*
(all wcs)
132. *The Horizon of the Poor*
247. *The Minuet*
266. *Westminster Bridge*
420. *London Bridge*

Feb. 15–Mar. 15, Art Club of Erie, Pa., *Oil Paintings by American Artists, 4th Annual Exh. of Art Club of Erie.*
23. *White Island Light.*
24. *Winter Morning on Broadway*

From Feb. 17, Salmagundi Club, *Annual Black and White Exh.* [*BE*, 2/17/1901, p. 40].

From ca. Feb. 21, Lotos Club, "Exhibition of paintings by artist members of the club" [*BE*, 2/22/1901, p. 9].
Noonday, Pont-Aven, Brittany

Feb., William Clausen Galleries, *Childe Hassam.*
"landscapes, townscapes, and flower pieces" [*NYT*, 2/27/1901, p. 9]

Mar. 18–30, DRG, "Exhibition of Paintings by Ten American Painters."
Blue Sea
Highland Light
Midday — Pont Aven

Mar. 22–31, Salmagundi Club, *Annual Exh. of Oil Paintings.*
36. *Poppies and Grasses*

Mar. 25–Apr. 15, Minneapolis Society of Fine Arts, *2nd Annual Exh. of Paintings.*
54. *Penelope*
55. *Sand Dunes of Cape Cod*

Mar. 28–Apr. 13, Society of Washington Artists, Washington, D.C., *11th Annual Exh. of Society of Washington Artists.*
50. *Indian Summer in Colonial Days*
52. *Morning, Sea and Sky*

Apr. 6–27, BAC, *64th Exh., Water Colors, Etc.*
165. *The Horizon of the Poor* (wc)

Apr. 22–Oct. 31, Venice Biennale.
15. *Il Mare (The Sea)*

Apr. 25–June 9, AIC, *13th Annual Exh. of Water Colors, Pastels and Miniatures by American Artists.*
(all wcs)
156. *Westminster Bridge*
157. *The Bride (Celia Thaxter's Garden at the Isle of Shoals)*
158. *The Garden Gate (Celia Thaxter's Garden at the Isle of Shoals)*

May 1–Oct. 31, Department of Fine Arts, Pan-American Exposition in Buffalo, N.Y., *Exh. of Fine Arts.*
Awarded gold medal
65. *The Hod Carrier*
556. *Plaza Centrale, Havana*
557. *White Island Light*
558. *September*
559. *Summer*
560. *July Night*
561. *Union Square in Spring*
562. *Gloucester*

May 18–July 8, CAM, *8th Annual Exh. of American Art.*
38. *Spring Morning on 5th Avenue*
39. *New England Village*
40. *Poppies and Grasses*
41. *Indian Summer*
42. *Morning Sea and Sky*

June 3–Oct. 14, WAM, *3rd Annual Exh. of Oil Paintings, Summer Exh., 1901.*
87. *New England Headlands*
96. *Evening, The Rose of Sharon*

Sept. 9–19, Galerie Durand-Ruel, Paris, One-man exhibition.
1. *Naples, le matin*
2. *Le quai Voltaire, Paris*
3. *La Promenade, après-midi*
4. *L'Escalier des Espagnols, Rome*
5. *Jardin à Ermont*
6. *Pommiers et Pruniers en Fleurs*
7. *Pont-Aven*
8. *Le Soir: Gloucester*
9. *Le Calfatage*
10. *Fleurs: Nasturtium et nymphea*

Oct. 22–Nov. 12, RISD, *Autumn Exh.*
16. *New England Village Street*
17. *The Old Bottle-Man*

Oct. 29–Dec. 8, AIC, *14th Annual Exh. of Oil Paintings and Sculpture by American Artists.*
154. *The Bather*

Dec. 26–Jan. 16, 1902, Nebraska Art Association, Lincoln, *8th Annual Exh. of Oil Paintings, Sculpture, and Ceramics by American Artists.*
45. *White Island Light*

1901–02, South Carolina Inter-State and West Indian Exposition, Department of Fine Arts, Charleston, *Exh. of Fine Arts.*
116. *Plaza Centrale, Havana*

1902

Jan. 3–Feb. 1, NAD, *77th Annual Exh.*
12. *Penelope*

Jan. 4–Feb. 1, BAC, *65th Exh., Oil Paintings and Sculpture.*
34. *The Northeast Gorge—Appledore*

By Jan. 12, Macbeth [*BE*, 1/12/1902, p. 8].
"a scene on a rocky coast and a city square at night with the lights reflected in a wet pavement"

Jan. 20–Mar. 1, PAFA, *71st Annual Exh.*
71. *The Cat-boats, Newport*
75. *Union Square in Spring*
77. *Broad Cove*

Feb. 25–Mar. 17, Minneapolis Society of Fine Arts, *Special Exh. of Paintings by Max Bohm, Alexis J. Fournier, Herbjorn Gausta, Agnes Harrison, Childe Hassam, Robert Koehler, G. Sangster Truesdell, Lionel Walden, Cadwallader Washburn.*
61. *The Room of Flowers*
62. *Moonrise at Sunset*
63. *The open Window*
64. *Parc Monceau*
65. *Golden Rod*
66. *The Cliffs at Newport*
67. *Yellow Roses*
68. *Sunset in August Mist*
69. *October Gold*
70. *Exterior Boulevard*
71. *The Horizon of the Poor*
72. *Summer Breeze*
73. *Nocturne—Provincetown*
74. *Blue Sky and White Church*
75. *Boston Common*
76. *Brittany Cottage*
77. *Stair Case*
78. *White Church and Flag*
79. *In Brittany*
80. *The Dunes*
81. *The Laborer*
82. *Nocturue [sic], Hyde Park Corner*
83. *The Children*
84. *June*
85. *Houses of Parliament*
86. *The Little Piano*

Mar. 31–Apr. 14, DRG, *Ten American Painters.*
5. *In Summer Sunlight*
6. *Summer*
7. *The Bather*
8. *Mountain Brook*
9. *Little Shoemaker's Shop*
10. *Washington Bridge*

Mar., PAA, *Paintings by American Artists*
18. *A Road in New England*, lent by Mr. I. N. Fleischner

Apr. 5–25, BAC, *66th Exh., Water Colors, Etc.*
46. *Westminster Bridge* (wc)

Apr. 10–12, ULCNY, *A General Exh. of Paintings*
21. *Summer Afternoon, Isles of Shoals*, lent by the artist

From Apr. 20, Salon of the Société Nationale des Beaux-Arts, Paris
583. *Premières feuilles (quai Voltaire)*
584. *L'Escalier des Espagnols à Rome*
585. *Pommiers et poiriers en fleurs*
586. *Jardin à Ermont*
587. *Fleurs*

Apr. 21–May 4, AWCS, *35th Annual Exh.*
178. *The Bride*
179. *In the Park at St. Cloud*
180. *The Beach at Broadstairs*
181. *The Garden Gate*
182. *Hogarth House, Chiswick*

Apr. 21–May 12, SB, *Exh. of Paintings by Ten American Painters.*
(all wcs)
1. *The Bather*
2. *Summer Sunlight*
3. *Mountain Brook*
4. *Summer*
5. *Little Shoemaker's Shop*
6. *Washington Bridge*

Apr. 22–June 8, AIC, *14th Annual Exh. of Water-Colors, Pastels and Miniatures by American Artists.*
206. *Venice* (wc)

May 17–July 7, CAM, *9th Annual Exh. of American Art.*
249. *Mountain Brook*
250. *Little Shoemaker Shop*
251. *Summer Sunlight*

May 29–Sept. 15, WAM, *4th Annual Exh. of Oil Paintings, Summer Exh., 1902.*
71. *Moonrise at Sunset*
168. *Broad Cove, Appledore*

Sept. 20–Oct. 12, Minneapolis Society of Fine Arts, *3rd Annual Art Exh.*
70. *The Shoe Maker's Shop*
71. *Mountain Brook*
72. *Mountain Brook*

Oct. 28–Nov. 18, RISD, *Autumn Exh.*
16. *Plaza, Central, Havana*
17. *Cottage in Brittany*

Oct. 28–Dec. 7, AIC, *15th Annual Exh. of Oil Paintings and Sculpture by American Artists.*
176. *The Jonquils*
177. *Washington Bridge*

Nov. 22–Dec. 14, NYWCC, *13th Annual Exh.*
(all wcs)
173. *Suresnes*
174. *Canterbury*
365. [no title indicated]

Nov., Doll and Richards Gallery, Boston. *Exh. and Private Sale of Water Color Paintings By Mr. John LaFarge, Mr. Childe Hassam, Miss Lucy S. Conant.*
(all wcs)
23. *Under the Cliffs*
24. *Venice*
25. *The Garden Gate*
26. *A Gloucester Street*
27. *Ten Pound Island*
28. *Rain Mist and Electric Light (Madison Square)*
29. *The Bride*
30. *Hogarth's House, Chiswick*
31. *The Minuet*
32. *Children in the Park*
33. *At Sundown*
34. *In the Park at St. Cloud*
35. *The Obelisk. Thames Embankment*
36. *From the Top of the Cliffs*
37. *Evening, the Seine at Bougival*
38. *The Chestnut Vendor*
39. *Kathleen*
40. *Westminster Bridge*
41. *London Bridge*
42. *Regent Street*
43. *Early Evening on the Thames*
44. *The Madeline and Rue Royale*
45. *Au Café*
46. *In the Luxembourg Garden*
47. *The Guild Hall*
48. *Porte St. Denis*
49. *Fleet Street*

Dec. 1–13, Louis Katz Galleries, "Exhibition of seventeen pastels by Childe Hassam" [*NYT*, 11/30/1902, p. 24].
17 ps

PSAG, *8th Annual Exh. of Paintings by Prominent Artists.*
3. *Summer Afternoon, Isles of Shoals*
94. *The Bride*

1903

Jan. 3–30, NAD, *78th Annual Exh.*
169. *Building the Schooner*

Jan. 3–31, BAC, *67th Exh., Oil Paintings and Sculpture.*
29. *Cottage in Brittany*

Jan. 19–Feb. 28, PAFA, *72nd Annual Exh.*
63. *Washington Bridge*
65. *Moonrise at Sunset*
67. *Scarlet Tanager*
78. *Oyster Sloop*
667. *Broadstairs*

Until Feb. 26, Salmagundi Club, *Annual Exh. of Oil Paintings.*
Moonrise at Sunset

Feb. 27–Mar. 14, Water Color Club, *16th Annual Exh. at BAC.*
(all wcs)
26. *Night*
27. *Old Graveyard*
28. *Autumn*
29. *Hollyhocks*
30. *Landscape*

From Feb. 28, Lotos Club, *Exh. of Paintings by the Artist Members of Lotos Club.*
18. *Near the Sea*

Apr. 4–25, BAC, *68th Exh., Water Colors, Etc.*
9. *Suresnes* (wc)

Apr. 15–30, Waldorf Art Galleries, *Spring Exh. of Modern American Art.*
27–29 (ps)
23. *"The Little Shoemaker's Shop"*
24. *"Nocturne," Provincetown*
25. *"The Bathers—Moonrise at Sunset"*
26. *"The Little Piano"*
27. *"October"*
28. *"White Birches"*
29. *"The Concord Meadows"*

From Apr. 16, Salon of the Société Nationale des Beaux-Arts, Paris.
661. *Naples (le matin)*
662. *La promenade (après-midi)*
663. *Les calfats*
664. *Pont-Aven*

Apr. 18–May 2, DRG, *Ten American Painters.*
15. *Newport*
16. *The Scarlet Tanager*
17. *The Jonquils*
18. *Sunlight*
19. *Snow Storm in the City*

Apr. 23–June 7, AIC, *15th Annual Exh. of Water-Colors, Pastels and Miniatures by American Artists.*
(all wcs)
132. *An Island Garden*
133. *Antares*
134. *November, Cos Cob*

135. *Up the River, Late Afternoon, October*
136. *The Old Bridge*
137. *The Salt Hay Marshes*
138. *Last Leaves and Old Buildings*

By Apr. 26, AWCS, *36th Annual Exh.*
113. *Thames Embankment*
114. *The Squall, Gloucester Outer Harbor*
115. *Afternoon*
116. *Rainy Night*
117. *Evening Breeze*
118. *English Landscape*
119. *West Gate, Canterbury*

May 1–Oct. 4, Royal Academy, Berlin, Germany, *Grosse Berliner Kunst-Ausstellung.*
331. *Washington-Brücke, New York City*

May 23–July 6, CAM, *10th Annual Exh. of American Art.*
237. *Plaza Centrala, Havana*
238. *The Laborer*
239. *Near the Sea*

May 29–Oct. 4, WAM, *6th Annual Exh. of Oil Paintings, Summer Exh., 1903.*
12. *The Jonquils*
82. *Union Square in Spring*

Summer, DMA, *Paintings Exhibited During Summer, 1903, at DMA.*
1. *Autumn of Life*
2. *Moonlight*
3. *In the Sunlight*
4. *The Rocky Shore*
5. *The Old House*
6. *Moonlight on the Coast*

Sept. 3–5, Public Library, Old Lyme, *Recent Pictures Painted in Lyme and the Surrounding Country.*
The Old Lyme Bridge, 1903

Sept. 20–Oct. 11, Minneapolis Society of Fine Arts, *4th Annual Art Exh.*
90. *Near the Sea*
91. *Summer Sunlight*
92. *Plaza Centrale and Fort Cabanas (Havana)*

Oct. 20–Nov. 25, AIC, *16th Annual Exh. of Oil Paintings and Sculpture by American Artists.*
194. *Plaza Central and Fort Cabanas, Havana*
195. *Summer sunlight*

Oct. 28–Nov. 18, RISD, *Autumn Exh.*
21. *The Messenger Boy*
22. *Newport Harbor*

Nov. 5–Jan. 1, CI, *8th Annual Exh.*
68. *The Jonquils*
69. *Moonrise at Sunset*

Dec. 26–Jan. 16, Nebraska Art Association, Lincoln, *10th Annual Exh. of Oil Paintings, Sculpture, and Ceramics by American Artists.*
45. *Summer Evening*
46. *October Silver and Gold*

PSAG, *9th Annual Exh. of Paintings by Prominent Artists.*
75. *October*

1904

Jan. 1–30, BAC, *69th Exh., Oil Paintings and Sculpture.*
48. *Plaza — Winter Morning*

Jan. 2–30, NAD, *79th Annual Exh.*
107. *Springtime: Central Park*
305. *Moonrise at Sunset*

Jan. 25–Mar. 5, PAFA, *73rd Annual Exh.*
89. *Summertime*
241. *The Church at Old Lyme, Connecticut*
244. *Gray Morning: Newport Harbor*

Feb. 11–Mar. 5, Stadden's Art Galleries, Springfield, Mass., *Gill's 27th Annual Exh. of American Artists' Pictures.*
53. *A Nocturne*

Feb. 15–27, Salmagundi Club, *Annual Exh. of Oil Paintings.*
29. *The Old Violinist*

Mar. 19–Apr. 2, DRG, *Ten American Painters.*
9. *Moonrise at Sunset*
10. *Whispering Leaves*
11. *Winter — Union Square*
12. *The Sunken Rock*
13. *Bather*
14. *Winter — Fourth Ave. and Twenty-First St.*
15. *Nocturne — Boulevard Clichy*
16. *Nocturne — Hyde Park Corner*
17. *Spring Morning — Twentieth Street*
18. *Winter Evening — Bois de Boulogne*
19. *Idyl of Early Summer*
20. *The Church of Old Lyme, Connecticut*

Mar. 28–Apr. 16, PAFA, *Philadelphia Water Color Exh.*
(wcs)
93. *Up the River, Late Afternoon in October*
94. *October*

Apr. 28–June 5, AIC, *16th Annual Exh. of Water-Colors, Pastels and Miniatures by American Artists.*
163. *The West Gate, Canterbury* (wc)
164. *October* (p)

Apr. 29–May 13, AWCS, *37th Annual Exh.*
(all wcs)
126. *Connecticut Barns*
127. *After Rain, Connecticut Hills*
128. *Surf, Isle of Shoals*
129. *Gate of the Alhambra*
130. *Rainy Night, Broadway*

May 21–July 11, CAM, *11th Annual Exh. of American Art.*
4. *Winter Evening, Bois de Boulogne*
5. *Summer Idyl*
6. *Nocturne, Hyde Park Corner*
7. *Early Spring, New York*
8. *Nocturne, Boulevard Clichy*
9. *Spring Morning, 20th Street, New York*
10. *Twachtman's Children*
11. *Nocturne, Provincetown*
12. *Winter, Calvary Church, New York*

May 29–Sept. 26, WAM, *7th Annual Exh. of Oil Paintings, Summer Exh., 1904.*
146. *The Milldam*
153. *Newport Harbor*

June–Oct., PSAG, *10th Annual Exh. of Paintings by Prominent Artists.*
77. *The Little Piano*
113. *The Squall, Gloucester, Outer Harbor*

Aug.–Oct., Department of Fine Arts, Louisiana Purchase Exposition, St. Louis, *Universal Exposition.*
Awarded a gold medal for oils and a gold medal for pastels. Two catalogues issued. Original edition is indicated by "orig. ed." Revised edition is indicated by "rev. ed."
283. (341 in rev. ed) *Whispering Leaves*
284. (342 in rev. ed) *The Sea*
285. (343 in rev. ed) *Moonrise at Sunset*
286. (344 in rev. ed) *Golden October*
287. (345 in rev. ed) *Church of Old Lyme, Connecticut*
346. (rev. ed only) *In the Garden*
927. (orig. ed. only) *Nocturne, Rainy Midnight* (wc)
928. (orig. ed. only) *An Island Garden* (p)
929. (orig. ed. only) *November* (p)

Sept. 1–3 and 5, Public Library, Old Lyme, *3rd Annual Exh. of Pictures Painted in Old Lyme and the Surrounding Country.*
A June Morning

Oct. 20–Nov. 27, AIC, *17th Annual Exh. of Oil Paintings and Sculpture by American Artists.*
183. *Newport Harbor*

Oct. 26–Nov. 16, RISD, *Autumn Exh. of Work by American Painters.*
18. *Washington Bridge, New York*
19. *Evening*

Nov. 3–Jan. 1, CI, *9th Annual Exh.*
125. *June Morning*
126. *Across the Park — New York in Early Spring*
127. *Amaryllis*

Nov. 5–19, BAC, *Semi-Centennial Exh.*
52. *Provincetown*

Nov. 15–Dec. 11, Society of Art Collectors, American Fine Arts Society, *Comparative Exh. of Native and Foreign Art.*
70. *The Arno*, lent by Mr. John Gellatly

Dec. 31–Jan. 30, 1905, NAD, *80th Annual Exh.*
77. *Lorelei*, Thomas B. Clarke prize
166. *Mt. Desert*
170. *The Apple Blossoms*

1905

Jan. 6–Feb. 4, BAC, *71st Exh., Oil Paintings and Sculpture.*
94. *Newport*

Jan. 12–28, Montross, *Exh. of Paintings by Childe Hassam.*
1. *The Stairway, Spring Morning*
2. *Lady in White*
3. *Summer Sunlight*
4. *Union Square in Spring*
5. *The Bed of the Brook, November*
6. *October Morning, the Sinking Moon*
7. *Capri*
8. *Smelt Fishing, Cos Cob*
9. *Plaza Centrale and Fort Cabañas, Havana*
10. *In the Sun*
11. *The Mulberry Tree*
12. *Spring Brook*
13. *Through the Trees — June*
14. *The Evening Gown*
15. *In Pale Yellows*
16. *The Old Violinist*
17. *Summertime*
18. *Twelve O'Clock*
19. *In Acadia*
20. *Nocturne — Hyde Park Corner*
21. *Riverbank*
22. *Madison Square in Snow*
23. *20th Street, Spring Morning*
24. *The Cider Jugs*
25. *Under the Alders*
and
1–14 (wcs and ps)
1. *Rainy Night*
2. *Connecticut Hills*
3. *Weir's Barn*
4. *Appledore, Isles of Shoals*
5. *Autumn Haze*
6. *Up the River*
7. *The Birches*
8. *Salt Hay*
9. *The Concord Meadows*
10. *Back of the Old House*
11. *Smelt Fishers, Cos Cob*
12. *The Old House*
13. *Cos Cob Docks*
14. *Cedric's Garden, Isles of Shoals*

Jan. 23–Mar. 4, PAFA, *100th Annual Exh.*
576. *The Jonquils*
577. *The Rockweek Pool*
740. *The Milldam*

From Jan. 28, Lotos Club, *Exh. of American Figure Paintings.*
16. *Messenger Boy*
17. *The Bathers, Moonrise at Sunset*

Feb. 11–Mar. 4, Stadden's Art Galleries, Springfield, Mass., *Gill's 28th Annual Exh., Original Paintings.*
55. *A Nocturn*

Mar. 10–27, AWCS, *38th Annual Exh.*
(wcs)
25. *The Pale Green Gown in Rose Light*
26. *Nocturne, The Times Building*

Mar. 22–Apr. 13, Society of Washington Artists, Corcoran, *15th Annual Exh. of Society of Washington Artists.*
29. *Moonrise at Sunset*

Mar. 25–Apr. 13, Montross, *Ten American Painters.*
8. *The Opal*
9. *Spring Morning*
10. *The Laurel*
11. *Listening to the orchard Oriole*

Apr. 3–29, PAFA, *2nd Annual Philadelphia Water Color Exh.*
(all wcs)
44. *The Concord Meadows*
47. *Autumn Haze*
301. *Cos Cob Docks*
322. *Back of the Old House*
621. *The Pale Green Gown in Rose Light*
624. *Nocturne: The Times Building*

Apr. 8–30, CAM, *Water Colors by Members of AWCS.*
34. *Gate of the Alhambra*
35. *Rain, Mist and Electric Light*

From Apr. 14, Salon of the Société Nationale des Beaux-Arts, Paris.
Printemps (le Central-park, New York)
La Neige à New York, Juin
La Petite Maison blanche (Nouvelle-Angleterre)

Apr. 24–May 6, Artists' Club, Denver, *11th Annual Exh.*
29. *Washington Bridge*

Apr. 26–May 13, SB, *Exh. of Paintings by the "Ten American Painters."*
8. *The Opal*
9. *Spring Morning*
10. *The Laurel*
11. *Listening to the Orchard Oriole*

Apr. 27–May 18, New Haven Paint and Clay Club, Conn., *5th Annual Exh.*
30. *October's Silver and Gold*

May 20–July 10, CAM, *12th Annual Exh. of American Art.*
(wcs)
7. *Smelt Fishing, Cos Cob*
8. *The Old Violinist*
9. *Twelve O'clock*
10. *Riverbank*
11. *The Old House*

May 31–July 1, BFAA, *Inaugural Loan Collection of Paintings.*

18-f. *The Bridge*, owner, Mr. John Gellatly, New York

June 2–Sept. 24, WAM, *8th Annual Exh. of Oil Paintings, Summer Exh., 1905.*
47. *Lorelei*

July–Aug., BFAA, *Special Exh. of Water Colors by Members of AWCS.*
(wcs)
30. *Gate of the Alhambra*
31. *Rain, Mist, and Electric Light*

Aug. 31 and Sept. 1, 2, 4, and 5, Public Library, Old Lyme, *4th Annual Exh. of Pictures Painted in Old Lyme and the Surrounding Country.*
Spring Brook
Old Lyme
and one or two others

Oct. 19–Nov. 26, AIC, *18th Annual Exh. of Oil Paintings and Sculpture by American Artists.*
164. *Smelt Fishing, Cos Cob*
165. *The Old Violinist*
166. *Twelve O'clock*
167. *River Bank*
168. *Lorelei*

Oct. 26–Nov. 16, RISD, *Autumn Exh.*

Nov. 2–Jan. 1, 1906, CI, *10th Annual Exh.*
108. *June*, medal of the third class, CI, 1905

Dec. 13–31, Montross, *Paintings by Childe Hassam.*

Dec. 23–Jan. 20, 1906, NAD, *81st Annual Exh.*
79. *October in New England*
282. *Moonrise at Sunset*

Lewis and Clark Centennial Exposition, Portland, Oreg., *Department of the Fine Arts, Section A, Including Paintings in Oil, Water Colors, Pastels, Together with Miniatures, Pictures in Photography and Works in Sculpture.* catalogue in three sections.
"Paintings"
1. *A North East Headland*
2. *Near the Sea*
3. *The Jonquils*
4. *The Golf Players*
5. *The Rock Weed Pool*
6. *Golden October*
74. *Bathers, Moonrise at Sunset*
"Water Colors, Pastels and Studies for Decorations"
36. *Nocturne: The Times Building*
71. *Concord Meadows*
78. *The Last Leaves and Old Buildings*
80. *Autumn Haze*
84. *The Pale Gown in Rose Light*
94. *Back of the Old House*
99. *Cos Cob Docks*
"Water Colors, Original Illustrations and Sketches from Nature"
117. *The Thames Embankment*

New Bond Street Gallery, London, *1st Exh. of NYWCC.*

PSAG, *11th Annual Exh. of Paintings by Prominent Artists.*
43. *Bather, Moonrise at Sunset*

Toledo Museum of Art, *American Paintings from St. Louis Exposition.*
51. *October Gold*

1906

Jan. 6–Feb. 3, BAC, *73rd Exh.*
38. *Summer Afternoon, Isles of Shoals*

Jan. 22–Mar. 3, PAFA, *101st Annual Exh.*
16. *June Morning*
208. *Summer Morning: Isle of Shoals*, award
209. *Rock Cliff: Appledore*, Walter Lippincott Prize
221. *At Sunset in the October Haze*

Jan.–Feb., DMA, *1st Annual Exh. of Paintings by American Artists.*
29. *The Laurel*
30. *Summertime*

Feb. 1–24, Gill's Art Galleries, Springfield, Mass., *29th Annual Exh. of American Artists' Pictures.*
55. *Summer Afternoon*

Feb. 7–25, RISD, *Ten American Painters.*
October in New England

Feb. 9–Mar. 11, Art Club of Erie, Pa., *Water Colors by American Artists, 9th Annual Exh. of Art Club of Erie.*
42. *Gate in the Alhambra* (wc)

Feb. 26–Mar. 17, PAA, *Loan Exh. of Paintings.*
142. *A New England Road*
143. *Near Shoshone*
144. *Pomona*
145. *Magnolias*
146. *Ecola, on the Oregon Coast*

Mar. 14–31, Montross, *Ten American Painters.*
11. *June Idylle*
12. *The Butterfly*
13. *Early Spring—Central Park*
14. *Bather*

Mar. 17–Apr. 22, SAA, Galleries of American Fine Arts Society, *28th Annual Exh. of SAA.*
352. *June*, Carnegie Prize

Mar. 19–Apr. 7, Society of Washington Artists, Washington, D.C., *16th Annual Exh. of Society of Washington Artists.*
10. *Summer Morning Isles of Shoals*

Mar. 26–Apr. 21, PAFA, *3rd Annual Philadelphia Water Color Exh.*
(all wcs)
139. *Jardin du Luxembourg*
143. *The Guildhall*
144. *Porte St. Denis*
244. *The Madelaine [sic]*
399. *Bleak House: Broadstairs*
400. *London Bridge*
401. *The Minuet*
402. *Venetian Night*
403. *The Children*
404. *Park of St. Cloud*
405. *Exterior Boulevard: The Chestnut Vendor*
406. *On the Thames*
584. *Les Anglais*
585. *Kathleen*

From Mar. 31, Lotos Club, *Exh. of American Paintings From the Collection of William T. Evans, Esq.*
27. *Isles of Shoals*

Apr. 15–June 30, Salon of the Société Nationale des Beaux-Arts, Paris
643. *L'Opale*
655. *Juin, le matin*
645. *La Mer au grand matin*

May 3–26, AWCS, *39th Annual Exh.*
(all wcs)
372. *Les Anglais*
409. *Kathleen*
433. *The Letter Box*
447. *Ticonderoga*
469. *London Bridge*
491. *The River*
531. *The Trio*
540. *The Turquoise Sea*
569. *The Minuet*
573. *The Children*
579. *The Chestnut Vendor*

May 3–June 10, AIC, *18th Annual Exh. of Water-Colors, Pastels and Miniatures by American Artists.*
(all wcs)
144. *The Guildhall*
145. *The Madeleine*
146. *Garden of the Luxembourg*

May 19–July 16, CAM, *13th Annual Exh. of American Art.*
280. *Morning Sea*
281. *Spring Morning*
282. *Summer Morning Sea*
283. *Connecticut Hills* (wc)
284. *Appledore, Isle of Shoals* (wc), lent by N. E. Montross, Esq. 372 5th Ave., N.Y.

May 31–Sept. 2, BFAA, *1st Annual Exh. of Selected Paintings by American Artists.*
52. *June Idylle*, lent by Mr. N. E. Montross, New York
53. *Lorelei*, lent by Mr. N. E. Montross, New York
54. *The Blue Robe*

May 31–Sept. 23, WAM, *9th Annual Exh. of Oil Paintings, Summer Exh., 1906.*
94. *June Morning*
130. *Rock Cliff, Appledore*, third prize
148. *June*
168. *Summer Morning, Isles of Shoals*

June 12–26, Art Association of Richmond, Ind., *10th Annual Exh.*
63. *The Old Violinist*

June, PSAG, *12th Annual Exh. of Paintings by Prominent Artists.*
72. *Spring Brook, Old Apple Orchard*
100. *Weir's Barn*

Aug. 13–Sept. 13, Saint Louis Museum of Fine Arts, *Annual Exh. of Water Colors by American Artists.*
(all wcs)
32. *The Letter Box*
33. *Venetian Night*
34. *London Bridge*
35. *The River*
36. *The Turquoise Sea*
37. *The Minuet*
38. *The Children*

Aug. 31–Sept. 4, Public Library and Town Hall, Old Lyme, *5th Annual Exh. of Pictures Painted in Old Lyme and the Surrounding Country.*
First Leaves
and another oil depicting nudes in landscape

Sept. 17–Oct. 7, Minneapolis Society of Fine Arts, *7th Annual Art Exh.*
30. *Silver Cloud*
31. *Spring Morning*
32. *Connecticut Hills* (wc)
33. *Appledore, Isle of Shoals* (wc)

Oct. 16–Nov. 29, AIC, *19th Annual Exh. of Oil Paintings and Sculpture by American Artists.*
160. *Rock Cliff, Appledore*
161. *June*

Nov. 6–17, Kimball Gallery, Boston, *The Ten.*
Apple Orchard
A June Idyl
Moonrise at Sunset
Moonrise, Isles of Shoals

Nov. 10–Dec. 2, NYWCC, *17th Annual Exh.*
(all wcs)
7. *Maine Coast—Low Tide*
15. *Appledore Rocks*
348. *Newfields Village*

Nov. 20–Dec. 31, Art Association of Indianapolis, Ind., JHAI, *Catalogue of Inaugural Exh.*
90. *Morning Sea*
91. *Summer Morning Sea*
91a. *Cliff Rock, Appledore*, purchased for the Permanent Collection of the Art Association
91b. *Portland, Oregon*, lent by Collier and Company, New York

Nov. 22–Dec. 4, Museum of Art, RISD, *Ten American Painters.*
June Idyll
Moonlight
Moonrise at Sunset
A Spring Brook

Nov., BFAA, *2nd Annual Exh. of Selected Water Colors by American Artists.*
(all wcs)
32. *The Letter Box*
33. *Venetian Night*
34. *London Bridge*
35. *The River*
36. *The Turquoise Sea*
37. *The Minuet*
38. *The Children*

Dec. 7–29, Montross, *Paintings by Childe Hassam.*

Dec. 13–26, DMA, *Ten American Painters.*
June Idylle
Moonlight—Isle of Shoals
Moonrise at Sunset
A Spring Brook

Dec. 22–Jan. 19, 1907, NAD, *Winter Exh.*
50. *Portrait*
278. *The Little June Idylle*

Dec. 29–Jan. 1907, M. O'Brien and Sons, Chicago, *The Ten.*
Apple Orchard
June Idylle
Moonlight—Isle of Shoals
Moonrise at Sunset
A Spring Brook

BFAA, *Collection of Paintings, Carlton T. Chapman, A. N. A. and others.*
94. *The Stoop in Winter*

1907

Jan. 4–16, Art Association of New Orleans, *6th Annual Exh.*
128. *Rainy Day*

Jan. 19–29 (?), Bressler Gallery, Milwaukee, *The Ten.*
Apple Orchard
A June Idylle
Moonlight—Isle of Shoals
Moonlight at Sunset

Jan. 21–Feb. 24, PAFA, *102nd Annual Exh.*
251. *The Lorelei*
257. *Idylle: Sunlight in June*
259. *Golden October*
261. *The Bridge: Old Lyme*
272. *Ironbound*

Feb. 4–16, Noonan-Kocian Gallery, St. Louis, *The Ten.*
Apple Orchard
A June Idylle
Moonlight—Isle of Shoals
Moonrise at Sunset
A Spring Brook

Feb. 7–Mar. 9, Corcoran, *1st Biennial Exh. Oil Paintings by Contemporary American Artists.*
227. *The Blue Kimono*
235. *June*
237. *Up the River—October*
240. *North East Headlands—New England Coast*

Feb. 18–Mar. 4, J. J. Gillespie Galleries, Pittsburgh, *Exh. of The Ten.*
Apple Orchard
A June Idyll
Moonlight—Isle of Shoals
Moonrise at Sunset
A Spring Brook

From Feb. 23, Lotos Club, *Exh. of Paintings by Artist Members of Lotos Club.*
22. *Shimmering Sunlight*

Mar. 2–10, Minnesota State Art Society, Fergus Falls, *4th Annual Exh.*

Mar. 11–23, McClees Galleries, Philadelphia, *The Ten.*
11. *Moonlight: Isles of Shoals*
13. *Moonrise at Sunset*
14. *Spring Brook*
15. *June Idyl*

Mar. 15–Apr. 6, BAC, *76th Exh.*
46. *Afternoon, Appledore* (wc)

Mar. 16–Apr. 20, NAD, *82nd Annual Exh.*
71. *Winter: New York*
284. *The Church at Old Lyme*
304. *Spring*

Mar. 19–Apr. 6, Montross, *Ten American Painters, 10th Annual Exh.*
12. *The Music Room*
13. *Dawn*
14. *The Alders*
15. *The Bowl of Nasturtiums*

Apr. 1–27, PAFA, *4th Annual Philadelphia Water Color Exh.*
(all wcs)
59. *Spring Idylle*
97. *Weir's Barns*
98. *Canterbury*
102. *Ticonderoga*
109. *The Letter Box*
114. *Mackerel Fleet: Gloucester Outer Harbor*
151. *Flood-tide: Appledore*

Apr. 11–June 30, CI, *11th Annual Exh.*
206. *Aphrodite*
207. *Idyl; Sunlight in June*
208. *Moonlight; The Old House*

Late Apr.–May, Goldwin Smith Hall, Cornell University, Ithaca, "Exhibition of Paintings by Childe Hassam" [*Cornell Daily Sun*, 5/1/1907, p. 1].
June
Golden October
Moonlight, Isles of Shoals
Lorelei
Moonrise at Sunset
Spring Brook and Old Orchard
The June Idylle
Moonlight, Appledore
June Morning
Under the Cliffs, Newport
The Church Nocturne, Old Lynne [sic]
The Golf Players
The Butterfly
Late Afternoon, Appledore

Apr., Charleston Art Association, *Annual Spring Exh.*

May 2–26, AWCS, *40th Annual Exh.*
(all wcs)
29. *The Chalk Cliffs of England*
403. *McTaggart's Field*
446. *Katydid Lane*
467. *Aphrodite*

May 7–June 16, AIC, *19th Annual Exh. of Water-Colors, Pastels and Miniatures by American Artists.*
135. *Spring Idylle* (wc)

May 18–July 17, CAM, *14th Annual Exh. of American Art.*
3. *Dawn*
4. *The Bowl of Nasturtiums*
5. *The Music Room*
6. *The Alders*

May 31–Sept. 1, BFAA, *2nd Annual Exh. of Selected Paintings by American Artists.*
47. *Winter in New York*

May 31–Sept. 22, WAM, *10th Annual Exh. of Oil Paintings, Summer Exh., 1907.*
35. *The Church at Old Lyme*
118. *The Blue Kimono*

May, St. Louis Museum of Fine Arts, *Exh. of The Ten.*

June–Sept., St. Louis Museum of Fine Arts, *2nd Annual Exh. of Water Colors by American Artists.*
(all wcs)
53a. *The Chestnut Vender*
53b. *The Road to the Sea at Sundown*
53c. *Mackerel Fleet, Gloucester*

From Sept. 26, St. Louis Museum of Fine Arts, *Annual Exh. of Selected Paintings by American Artists.*
47. *Winter in New York*

Oct. 14–Nov. 11, American Art Society of Philadelphia, Haseltine Art Galleries, *Annual Exh. of Oil Paintings.*
98. *Madison Square, New York City*
250. *Isles of Shoals*

Oct. 22–Dec. 1, AIC, *20th Annual Exh. of Oil Paintings and Sculpture by American Artists.*
171. *Bowl of Nasturtiums*
172. *Dawn*
173. *The Elders*
174. *Music Room*
175. *Aphrodite*

Nov. 2–24, NYWCC, *18th Annual Exh.*
52. *The Bath* (wc)

Dec. 2–28, PAFA, *5th Annual Water Color Exh.*
(wcs)
603. *Poppies*
611. *The Chalk Cliffs of England*

Dec. 11–28, Montross, *Exh. of Pictures by Childe Hassam.*
1. *The Jonquils*
2. *Moonlight—Isles of Shoals*
3. *June Morning—The Laurel Bush*
4. *Winter—New York*
5. *The North Shore Moonlight*
6. *Diamond Cove*
7. *The Flower Shop*
8. *The Bloom of June*
9. *The Northeast Wind*
10. *In the Sun—Lower Brittany*
11. *Florence*
12. *New York*
13. *Sylphs' Rock—Appledore*
14. *Leda*
15. *The Church at Old Lyme*
16. *The Hemlock Ledge*
17. *Bonnie Moore*

Dec. 12–Jan. 12, 1908, BFAA, *3rd Annual Exh. of Selected Water Colors by American Artists.*
(all wcs)
61. *The Chestnut Vender*
62. *The Road to the Sea at Sundown*
63. *Mackerel Fleet, Gloucester*

Dec. 14–Jan. 11, 1908, NAD, *Winter Exh..*
241. *Evening Bells*

PSAG, *13th Annual Exh. of Paintings by Prominent Artists.*
51. *In Brittany*
124. *West Gate, Canterbury*

1908

Jan. 20–Feb. 29, PAFA, *103rd Annual Exh.*
379. *The Church at Provincetown*
381. *The Aspens*
466. *Leda*
713. *Aphrodite*

Jan., BFAA, *3rd Annual Exh., Selected Water Colors by American Artists.*

Feb. 6–20 or Feb. 13–27, PAA, *Loan Exh. of Water Colors.*
Two catalogues issued with differing dates.
104. *The Hammock*, lent by Miss Frances Lewis

Feb. 18–Mar. 3, SB, *Pictures by Childe Hassam.*
1. *Diamond Cove, Isles of Shoals*
2. *Morning*
3. *Hilltop. October*
4. *Bowl of Nasturtiums*
5. *Newport. October Sundown*
6. *Room of Flowers*
7. *The Butterfly*
8. *South Wind on the Sea*
9. *Jonquils*
10. *Washington Bridge*
11. *Lorelei*
12. *The Ledges*
13. *The North Shore Moonlight*
14. *Moonlight. The Old House*
15. *The North West Wind*
16. *Flower Shop. Piccadilly*
17. *Church at Old Lyme, Connecticut*
and 7 "studies of Sunset at the Isles of Shoals"

Feb., Art Lovers' Guild, Columbia, Mo., *2nd Annual Exh. of Paintings.*
32. *Old Lyme*, lent by Mr. Robert C. Hall, Pittsburgh, PA.

Mar. 14–Apr. 18, NAD, *83rd Annual Exh.*
60. *Moonlight: Isles of Shoals*

Mar. 17–Apr. 4, Montross, *11th Annual Exh., Ten American Painters.*
15. *Broad and Wall Streets*
16. *Moonlight—The Old House*
17. *Newport—October Sundown*
18. *The Bower*

Mar., Carolina Art Association, Charleston, S.C., *Annual Spring Exh.*

Mar., DMA, *3rd Annual Exh. of Selected Water Colors by American Artists.*
(all wcs)
61. *The Chestnut Vender*
62. *The Road to the Sea at Sundown*
63. *Mackerel Fleet, Gloucester*

Apr. 11–May 3, PAFA, *Exh. of Paintings by Ten American Painters.*
38. *Aphrodite*
39. *Lyman's Ledge, Appledore*
40. *The South Wind on the Sea*
41. *June Morning*
42. *Washington Bridge*
43. *Lorelei*
44. *The Opal*
45. *The Little June Idyl*
46. *The Room of Flowers*, Celia Thaxter's Room at the Isles of Shoals, 1894
47. *The Jonquils*

Apr. 28–June 7, AIC, *20th Annual Exh. of Water-Colors, Pastels and Miniatures by American Artists.*
(all wcs)
366. *The Chestnut Vender*
367. *The Road to the Sea at Sundown*
368. *Mackerel Fleet, Gloucester*

Apr. 30–May 24, AWCS, *41st Annual Exh.*
15. *Autumn Haze* (p)
33. *October* (p)
62. *Bridge at Cos Cob* (p)
69. *Autumn Day* (p)
495. *Morning, Isle of Shoals* (wc)
508. *The Green Jade Gown* (wc)
544. *Bougival* (wc)

Apr. 30–June 30, CI, *12th Annual International Exh.*
127. *The Bowl of Nasturtiums*
128. *October, Old Lyme*, award

Apr. 30–Aug. 30, BFAA, *3rd Annual Exh. of Selected Paintings by American Artists.*
67. *North East Headlands, Massachusetts Coast*, lent by Corcoran
68. *The Bower*
69. *The Old House, Moonlight*

May 23–July 20, CAM, *15th Annual Exh. of American Art.*
1. *Sunset, Isles of Shoals*
2. *The Willows*
3. *Peonies*
4. *The Aspens*

May 29–Sept. 20, WAM, *11th Annual Exh. of Oil Paintings, Summer Exh.*
19. *The Butterfly*
31. *Sylph's Rock, Appledore*, Property of the Museum

From June 1, St. Louis Museum of Fine Arts, *3rd Annual Exh. of Water Colors by American Artists.*
37–39 (ps), 40–41 (wcs)
37. *Autumn Haze*
38. *October*
39. *Bridge at Cos Cob*
40. *Borgival*
41. *Morning, Isle of Shoals*

June 9–23, Art Association of Richmond, Ind., *12th Annual Exh.*
55. *The Rocks of Appledore—Isles of Shoals*
56. *The Church Spire—Provencetown* [sic]

June 20–July 7, Minnesota State Art Society, Duluth, *5th Annual Exh.*

Aug. 13–Oct. 13, CI, *Summer Loan Exh. of Painting.*
31. *Idyl: Sunlight in June*
32. *October, Old Lyme*
33. *The Bowl of Nasturtiums*, lent by the Artist

Late Aug.–early Sept., Public Library, Old Lyme, *7th Annual Exh.*
The Ledges
and "...church at Lyme...1906"

Sept. 9–Oct. 18, BFAA, *4th Annual Exh. of Selected Water Colors by American Artists.*
35–37 (ps), 38–39 (wcs)
35. *Autumn Haze*
36. *October*
37. *Bridge at Cos Cob*
38. *Borgival*
39. *Morning, Isle of Shoals*

From Sept. 15, 1908, St. Louis Museum of Fine Arts, *3rd Annual Exh. of Selected Paintings by American Artists.*
68. *North East Headlands, Massachusetts Coast,* lent by the Corcoran
69. *The Bower*
70. *The Old House, Moonlight*

Nov. 23–Dec. 20, PAFA, *6th Annual Philadelphia Water Color Exh.*
(wcs)
96. *Rocks: Isles of Shoals*
100. *Rocks: Isles of Shoals*

Nov., Portland Art Museum, *Exh. of Paintings of Eastern Oregon by Childe Hassam.*
1. *Morning in the Desert*
2. *Painted Butte. Harney Desert*
3. *Wagontire and Squaw Cap*
4. *Burns, Harney Valley*
5. *Afternoon Sky, Alkali and Grusewood*
6. *The Rabbit Brush in Bloom, October*
7. *Stein Mountains from the Tula Marshes*
8. *Hassam Butte. Harney Desert*
9. *Rainbow Trout*
10. *Malheur Butte, Grey Morning*
11. *Stormy Sky, Harney Valley*
12. *The Malheur Desert*
13. *The Magpie, Oasis and Desert*
14. *Moonrise at Sunset, the Oasis*
15. *The Rainbow in the Desert*
16. *Hanley's Prairie, Harney Valley*
17. *The Malheur Butte*
and "nine studies of desert sky effects"

Dec. 6–Jan. 4, 1909, Art Association of Indianapolis, Ind.: JHAI, *24th Annual Exh.*
35. *Northeast Headlands, New England Coast,* lent by Corcoran

Dec. 8–Jan. 17, 1909, Corcoran, *2nd Exh. Oil Paintings by Contemporary American Artists.*
60. *The Little June Idyll*
214. *The Bowl of Nasturtiums*
231. *Isles of Shoals,* lent by Mr. William T. Evans
277. *Aphrodite*

Dec. 12–Jan. 9, 1909, NAD, *Winter Exh.*
122. *Winter*

By Dec. 22–until Dec. 31, Montross, *Exh. of Paintings by Childe Hassam* [*NYT,* 12/22/1908, p. 4; 12/27/1908, p. X6].
Seaweed, Low Tide
Little June Idylls
The Rainbow in the Desert
Painted Butte: Harney Desert
Wagon Tire and Squaw Cap
Stormy Sky: Harney Desert
and "portrait... of a young girl in a yellow hat trimmed with yellow flowers"

Dec. 24–Jan. 16, 1909, DMA, *4th Annual Exh. of Selected Water Colors by American Artists.*
35–37 (ps), 38–39 (wcs)
35. *Autumn Haze*
36. *October*
37. *Bridge at Cos Cob*
38. *Borgival*
39. *Morning, Isle of Shoals*

1909

Jan. 30–Feb. 21, CAM, *Special Exh. of Selected Water Colors by American Artists, 4th Season.*
35–37 (ps), 38–39 (wcs)
35. *Autumn Haze*
36. *October*
37. *Bridge at Cos Cob*
38. *Borgival*
39. *Morning, Isle of Shoals*

Jan. 31–Mar. 14, PAFA, *104th Annual Exh.*
404. *The Mountain Laurel at Old Lyme*
440. *The Golden Afternoon*
457. *June: Under the Willows*
511. *The Church at Old Lyme*
531. *Headlands*

Feb. 2–27, BAC, *79th Exh.*
63. *Golden Head, Isles of Shoals*

Feb. 16–Mar. 13, Art Gallery, Charles Hall Building, Springfield, Mass., *Gill's 32nd Annual Exh. of Paintings by American Artists.*
64. *Bowl of Nasturtiums*

Mar. 13–Apr. 17, NAD, *84th Annual Exh.*
266. *Sunlight Through the Leaves*

Mar. 17–Apr. 7, Montross, *12th Annual Exh., Ten American Painters.*
8. *Summer Idyl*
9. *The Music Room*
10. *Neptune's Hall—Appledore*
11. *The Black Hat*

Apr. 8–21, Montross, *Exh. of Paintings of Eastern Oregon by Childe Hassam.*
1. *Morning in the Desert*
2. *Painted Butte. Harney Desert*
3. *Wagon Tire and Squaw Cap*
4. *Burns*
5. *Roaring Spring Canyon*
6. *The Rabbit Brush in Bloom*
7. *Storm at the Ranch*
8. *Hassam Butte. Harney Desert*
9. *Moonrise at Sunset—Stein Mountain*
10. *Malheur Butte—Grey Morning*
11. *The Storm*
12. *The Malheur Desert*
13. *The Magpie—Oasis and Desert*
14. *Moonrise—The Oasis*
15. *The Rainbow in the Desert*
16. *Hanley's Herds—Harney Valley*
17. *Malheur Butte*
18. *The Golden Afternoon*
19. *Cloud Shadows and Canyons*
20. *The P Ranch*
21. *Sunrise in the Desert*
22. *The Distant Canyon from the Mesa*
23. *The Rim-Rock of the Desert*
24. *Painted Butte—Afternoon*
25. *Thunder Storm on Stein Mountain*
26. *Early Morning—Harney Valley*
27. *Snow on the Mountains*
28. *Sunset on Cat-Nap Valley (Elevation 5200 Ft.)*
29. *Mountain Home—Idaho*
30. *Moonlight in an Alkali Desert—Squaw Cap Mountain*
31. *Moonlight—Malheur Desert*
32. *Clouds and Mountains*
33. *Moonrise at Sunset—Malheur Lake*
34. *First Snow on the Mountains*
35. *The Blizzard—Burns*
36. *Sunset*
37. *Afternoon Sky*

Apr. 12–24, Copley Society, Boston, *Exh. of The Ten.*
The Music Room
Neptune's Hall—Appledore
Summer Idyl

Apr. 29–May 23, AWCS, *42nd Annual Exh.*
452. *Rocks, Isles of Shoals* (wc)

Apr. 29–June 30, CI, *13th Annual Exh.*
137. *The Church at Old Lyme,* award
138. *Spring Morning*

By May 2–until May 8, Montross, "Twenty one pictures by American painters" [*NYT,* 5/2/1909, p. X6].
"two little marines," "a New York street in Winter"

May 10–Aug. 30, BFAA, *4th Annual Exh. of Selected Paintings by American Artists.*
85. *The Music Room*
86. *Summer Idyls*
87. *Neptune's Hall*

May 11–June 13, AIC, *21st Annual Exh. of Water-Colors, Pastels and Miniatures by American Artists.*
371–373 (ps), 374–375 (wcs)
371. *Autumn Haze*
372. *October*
373. *Bridge at Cos Cob*
374. *Borgival*
375. *Morning, Isle of Shoals*

May 28–Sept. 19, WAM, *12th Annual Exh. of Oil Paintings, Summer Exh., 1909.*
10. *Sylph's Rock, Appledore,* Property of the Museum
72. *The Black Hat*

June 1–Oct. 16, Department of Fine Arts, *Alaska-Yukon-Pacific Exposition,* Seattle.
122. *The Blue Kimono*
137. *June Morning, Sunlight Through the Leaves*
148. *June*
207. *Aphrodite*
269. *Golden Head, Isle of Shoals*
290. *The Oasis—Twilight Moonlight*

June 20–Sept. 1, St. Louis Museum of Fine Arts, *4th Annual Exh. of Water Colors by American Artists.*
60. *Rocks, Isles of Shoals* (wc)

July 5–Aug., National Arts Club, "Works from the collection of William T. Evans" [*NYT,* 7/4/1909, p. 3].
Isles of Shoals

Summer, PAA, *Loan Exh. of Paintings.*
66. *Portrait*
89. *Landscape*
90. *Figure*
93. *Portrait*
94. *Figure*
95. *Marine*
99. *Landscape*
100. *Fruit. Decorative Design*
101. *Mt. Hood*
111. *Landscape*
112. *Magnolias*
113. *Mt. Hood*
114. *Afternoon*
115. *New England Road*
116. *Oregon Coast*
117. *Marine*
118. *Marine*
141. *Pomona*
182. *Summer*
193. *Marine*
194. *Landscape*
207. *Marine*
211. *Evening*

Aug. 2–Oct. 31, CI, *A Summer Loan Exh. of Paintings.*
34. *Winter Evening in Paris,* lent by Mr. John Caldwell
35. *The Church at Old Lyme,* lent by the artist

Sept. 10–Oct. 10, BFAA, *5th Annual Exh. of Selected Water Colors by American Artists.*
(all wcs)
71. *Rocks, Isles of Shoals*
72. *Venetian Night*
73. *Corner of a Garden—Isles of Shoals*
74. *Ticonderoga*

From Sept. 12, Museum of Fine Arts, St. Louis, *4th Annual Exh. of Selected Paintings by American Artists.*
85. *The Music Room*
86. *Summer, Idyls*
87. *Neptune's Hall*

Oct. 30–Dec. 5, Philadelphia Art Club, *20th Annual Display of Oil Paintings and Sculpture.*

Nov. 8–Dec. 19, PAFA, *7th Annual Philadelphia Water Color Exh.*
(wcs)
395. *Spring Maples*
407. *The Seine at Chatou*

By Nov. 8, Montross, "Watercolors and pastels by American painters" [*NYT,* 11/8/1909, p. 6].
The Mulleins: Appledore (p)

From Nov. 14, CAMSL, *An Historical Collection of Pictures in Water Color by American Artists, Assembled by George H. Buek, Esq., of Brooklyn, New York, and by Him Lent for Exh. at the Forest Park Art Building.*
64. *A Bit of New England Coast* (wc)

Dec. 2–22, Montross, *Exh. of Pictures by Childe Hassam.*
1. *The Green, New Haven*
2. *The Waterfall*
3. *Bornero Hill, Old Lyme*
4. *The Old Elm*
5. *The Park and the Plaza, April Evening*
6. *The Blue Kimono*
7. *The Dell, Early Spring*
8. *Schooner with Purse Nets, Gloucester*
9. *Provincetown*
10. *Village of Yarmouth, May*
11. *The Sirens' Grotto, Appledore*
12. *Naiad*
13. *Sunlight Brook*
14. *The Oaks at Hardscrabble, Early Spring*
15. *Wainscott Links*
16. *Young Girl Reading*
17. *The Iris Pool*

Dec. 11–Jan. 9, 1910, NAD, *Winter Exh.*
101. *Aphrodite*

Dec. 20–Jan. 20, 1910, Fort Worth Museum of Art, *A Collection of Oil Paintings by American Artists Assembled by the American Federation of Arts, Washington, D.C., For Exh. at the Carnegie Public Library Building.*
18. *Summer Sea; Isle of Shoals*

Esposizione Internazionale d'Arte Della Città de Venezia, Venice.
22. *La vecchia chiesa di Lyme*

PSAG, *15th Annual Exh. of Paintings by Prominent Artists.*
58. *Storm on Stein Mountain*
60. *Early Spring*

1910

Jan. 8–31, CAM, *5th Annual Exh. of Selected Water Colors by American Artists.*
65. *Rocks, Isles of Shoals*

By Jan. 16, Katz Galleries, "Collection of American Pictures" [*NYT,* 1/16/1910, p. SM14].
Madison Square

By Jan. 17, M. O'Brien and Sons, Chicago, *Paintings by Childe Hassam.*

Jan. 23–Mar. 20, PAFA, *105th Annual Exh.*
416. *Bornero Hill*

419. *The Old Elm*
667. *The Sirens' Grotto*
678. *Summer Sea*, Jennie Sesnan Gold Medal

From Feb. 26, Newark Museum Association, held in the Public Library Building, Newark, N.J., "...celebrated the opening of its Museum ...with the exhibition of a loan collection of pictures and of the permanent possessions of the museum" [*NYT*, 2/27/1910, p. 9].
October's Gold

Mar. 12–Apr. 17, NAD, *85th Annual Exh.*
273. *Diamond Cove*

Mar. 13–Apr. 1, DMA, *5th Annual of Selected Water Colors by American Artists.*
65. *Rocks, Isles of Shoals*

From Mar. 17, National Gallery of Art, Washington, D.C., *Catalogue of Paintings and Other Art Objects Exhibited on the Occasion of the Opening of the Gallery in the New Building of the United States National Museum, Mar. 17, 1910.*
39. *Spring, Navesink Highlands*

Mar. 18–Apr. 13, BFAA, *A Collection of Paintings by Childe Hassam.*
1. *The Waterfall*
2. *Village of Yarmouth, May*
3. *L'Opale*
4. *The Blue Kimono*
5. *Wainscott Links*
6. *Schooner with Purse Nets, Gloucester*
7. *The Dell, Early Spring*
8. *The Park and the Plaza, April Evening*
9. *Young Girl Reading*
10. *The Bridge at Old Lyme*
11. *Ridgefield*
12. *Building the Schooner, Provincetown*

Mar. 24–Apr. 16, Montross, *13th Annual Exh., Ten American Painters.*
12. *The Table Garden*
13. *Summer Sea*
14. *The Chinese Merchants*
15. *Spring Garland*

Mar., Royal Academy, Berlin, *Ausstellung Amerikanischer Kunst.*
Alte Kirche in Lyme
New Haven
Dame mit Vase
Najade

Apr. 18–May 5, Montross, *Special Exh., Selected Paintings.*
6. *The North Shore Moonlight*

Apr. 28–May 22, AWCS, *43rd Annual Exh.*
542. *Arethusa*

May 2–June 30, CI, *14th Annual Exh.*
113. *Ecola*
114. *Isles of Shoals*
115. *Winter Nightfall in the City*
116. *Gloucester Inner Harbor*
117. *Isles of Shoals*
118. *The Mulberry Tree*
119. *Brooklyn Bridge*
120. *Fifth Avenue*
121. *Bornero Hill*
122. *The Old Elm*
123. *Paris; Winter Day*
124. *Village of Old Lyme*
125. *Cat Boats, Newport*
126. *Mt. Hood from Portland, Oregon*
127. *Plaza Centrale and Fort Cabanas, Havana*
128. *Sunlight though the Leaves*
129. *The Cider Jugs*
130. *Across the Park*
131. *Morning in the Desert*
132. *October*
133. *Entrance to the Siren's Grotto, Isle of Shoals*
134. *Northeast Headlands*
135. *Spring, Navesink Highlands*
136. *Cliffe Rock, Appledore*
137. *Sylph's Rock, Appledore*
138. *The Messenger Boy*
139. *Sunrise in the Desert*
140. *Afternoon Sky; Harney Desert*
141. *Portrait of Mrs. David J. Honeyman*
142. *Portrait of Liza*
143. *Malheur Butte*
144. *Evening, Appledore*
145. *Pont Royal*
146. *Northeast Headlands: Appledore*
147. *The Bather*
148. *The Mist*
149. *The Blue Sea and the Bather*
150. *Ironbound*

May 10–June 8, AIC, *22nd Annual Exh. of Water-Colors, Pastels and Miniatures by American Artists.*
359. *Rocks, Isles of Shoals*

May 11–30, Ann Arbor Art Association, Mich., *Exh. of Oriental and American Art Under the Joint Auspices of the Alumni Memorial Committee and the Ann Arbor Art Association.*
47. *The Chinese Merchants*, lent by the National Gallery of Art, Washington, D.C. – Freer Collection
48. *The North Shore Moonlight*, lent by the artist
49. *Sundown — Newport*, lent by the artist

May 11–Sept. 1, BFAA, *5th Annual Exh. of Selected Paintings by American Artists.*
107. *The Table Garden*
108. *Summer Sea*
109. *Autumn — Ridgefield, Connecticut*
110. *The Bridge — Old Lyme, Connecticut*
111. *Schooner with Purse Nets, Gloucester*

May 21–July 20, CAM, *17th Annual Exh. of American Art.*
9. *East Gloucester, — the end of the Trolley*
10. *Bathers, — Moonrise at Sunset*
11. *Moonlight, Isles of Shoals*
12. *The Caulkers, Gloucester*

May, Munich, *Exh. of American Art.*

June 3–Sept. 19, WAM, *13th Annual Exh. of Oil Paintings, Summer Exh., 1910.*
36. *Spring Garlands*

July 12–Sept. 1, Buenos Aires, Argentina, *Exposición Internacional de Arte del Centenario,* United States section, awarded hors concours.
45. *El ópalo*
46. *Las flores del manzano*
Traveled: from Sept. 17, Santiago, Chile, as *International Fine Arts Exposition,* United States section [*NYT*, 10/2/1910, p. SM15; *American Art Annual*, 1910–1911], and to Montevideo, Uruguay.

July 26–Aug. 28, AIC, *A Historical Collection of Pictures in Water Color by American Artists, Assembled by Gustav H. Buek, Esq., of Brooklyn, New York, and by Him Lent for Exh.*
70. *A bit of New England coast*

Aug. 31–Sept. 6, Phoebe Griffin Noyes Library, Old Lyme, *9th Annual Exh. of Pictures.*
16. *The Oaks at Hardscrabble*

Sept. 15–Oct. 24, BFAA, *6th Annual Exh. of Selected Water Colors by American Artists.*
60. *The Mulleins — Appledore*

Sept. 15–Nov. 15, CAMSL, *5th Annual Exh. of Selected Paintings by American Artists.*
76. *Evening in Connecticut*
109. *Young Girl Reading — Spring*
110. *Summer Sea*
111. *Autumn — Ridgefield, Connecticut*
112. *The Bridge — Old Lyme, Connecticut*
113. *The Schooner with Purse Nets, Gloucester*

Oct. 15–30, Art Department, State Fair of Texas.
41. *The Country Fair*
42. *In the Pasture*

Oct. 18–Nov. 27, AIC, *23rd Annual Exh. of Oil Paintings and Sculpture by American Artists.*
114. *La Pivione*
115. *New Haven, the Green*
116. *Springtime*

Oct.–Apr. 1911, PAA, *Paintings Exhibited by PAA.*
16. *Afternoon Sky: Harney Desert*, owned by PAA
18. *Mount Hood*

Nov. 28–Jan. 2, 1911, Fort Worth Museum of Art, *2nd Annual Exh. of Selected Paintings by American Artists.*
14. *The Bridge – Old Lyme, Connecticut*

Dec. 10–Jan. 8, 1911, NAD, *Winter Exh.*
354. *Summer Idyl*

Dec. 13–Jan. 22, 1911, Corcoran, *Third Exh. Oil Paintings by Contemporary American Artists.*
53. *La Pivoine*
57. *New Haven — The Green*
120. *Springtime*, Third William A. Clark Prize and Corcoran Bronze Medal

Dec. 17–Jan. 7, 1911, BAC, *Informal Exh. by Artist Members of the Club.*
20. *Isle of Shoals*
21. *Late October*
22. *The Brook*

From Dec. 17, Lotos Club, *Exh. of Paintings by French and American Luminists.*
7. *The Bowl of Nasturtiums*, lent by the artist
8. *The Georgian Chair,* William T. Evans Collection, National Gallery
9. *Leda and the Swan*, lent by Mr. William T. Evans
10. *October Haze, Manhattan*, lent by Mr. William T. Evans
11. *Isles of Shoals*, lent by Mr. William T. Evans

PSAG, *16th Annual Exh. of Paintings and Sculpture by Prominent Painters and Sculptors.*
54. *Neptune's Hall*
86. *Early Spring*

1911

Feb. 1–14, Montross, *Exh. of Pictures by Childe Hassam.*
1. *The Ancient Window of Nemours*
2. *Castles in Spain*
3. *August Moonlight, Grez*
4. *The Old Bridge at Grez*
5. *The Terre-cuite Tea Set*
6. *Grez*
7. *The Open Window*
8. *Mt. Desert*
9. *Ironbound — At Sunset*
10. *Contre-jour*
11. *The Black Hat*
12. *The Gray Screen*
13. *Bonnie Moore*
14. *The Piano*
15. *Lilies*
16. *The Grapevine*
"Spanish Set"
17. *El Zocodover, Toledo*
18. *Morning, Sevilla*
19. *Street of the Great Captain, Cordove*
20. *Plaza del Duque de la Victoria, Sevilla*
21. *La Merced, Ronda*
22. *Plaza de la Merced, Ronda*
"Water Colors, Pastels and Drawings"
1. *Calle del Alcazar*
2. *Balconies and Roofs, Madrid*
3. *Street in Lannion, Côtes du Nord*
4. *Puerta del Sol, Toledo (within)*
5. *Street in Haarlem*
6. *Diamond Cove, Appledore*
7. *The Park St. Sebastian*
8. *La Clarté — From a Grain Field*
9. *The Duet*
10. *La Clarté — Afternoon Sky*
11. *La Clarté — With Blue Sky*
12. *The Cathedral, Antwerp*
13. *Mt. Hood from the Perpetual Snow Line*
14. *Puerta del Sol, Toledo (without)*
15. *Iron-workers, New York*
16. *The Bridge and Church, Lannion*
17. *The Fête of Lannion, Gray Evening*
18. *The Bridge and Convent, Lannion*
19. *La Clarté from Perros-Guirec*
20. *Lannion from the Quai*
21. *Evening on the River, Grez*
22. *The Bridge at Grez — Evening*
23. *The Bridge at Grez — Rainy Day*
24. *St. Botolph's, Without, London*
25. *Fifth Avenue at the Waldorf — Fourth of July*
26. *La Clarté — Rainy Sky*
27. *The Convent and the Bridge, Lannion*
28. *Old Houses, Lannion*
29. *La Clarté — Spire and Roof*
30. *Brelévénez Lannion*
31. *Drawing for "June"*
32. *Calle Venancio Gonzalez, Toledo*
33. *The Bridge at Old Lyme*
34. *Houses on the Place, Lannion*
35. *The Fête of Lannion — The Quai*
36. *Fuenta de Alcantara, Toledo*
37. *Gothic Gateway, Toledo*
38. *Moonrise on the Oregon Trail*
39. *Old House, Grez*
40. *Mt. Hood — The End of the Timber Line*
41. *Drawing for "Aphrodite"*
42. *Happy Valley, Harney Desert*
43. *Plaza del Duque de la Victoria, Sevilla*
44. *St. Mathurin's, Morlaix*
45. *Café, Toledo*
46. *The Thunder Storm, Malheur Desert*
47. *The Church at Grez*
48. *Der Groot Haus, Haarlem*
49. *Drawing for the "Moonrise at Sunset"*
50. *La Clarté — Early Morning*
51. *La Clarté*
52. *Drawing for "Thalassa"*
53. *Madrid — Arenal y Puerta del Sol*
54. *Houses in Haarlem*
55. *Puente del Alcantara, Toledo*
56. *Lannion — The Sand Quais*
57. *Chaumière, Perros-Guirec*
58. *Brooklyn Bridge*
59. *Landscape in the Land of Nod*
60. *St. Michael's, Lannion*
61. *Old House of Lannion*
62. *La Clarté — The Church Door*

Feb. 5–Mar. 26, PAFA, *106th Annual Exh.*
405. *The Abalone Shell*
413. *The Schooner with Purse Nets:*

Gloucester
420. *New Haven: The Green*

By Feb. 11, City Club, Exh. by various artists of paintings of the City of New York [*NYT*, 2/11/1911, p. 10].
Union Square

By Feb. 24, Lotos Club, Exh. by artist members [*NYT*, 2/24/1911, p. 9].
Golden Afternoon, Harney Desert

Mar. 9–11, ULCNY, *Art Exh., Paintings by American Artists and Opening of the Gallery containing Antique Objects of Art belonging to the Club or loaned by its Members.*
9. *The Piano*

Mar. 11–Apr. 16, NAD, *86th Annual Exh.*
237. *Springtime in the City*

Mar. 17–Apr. 8, Montross, *14th Annual Exh., Ten American Painters.*
7. *The Breakfast Room — Winter Morning, New York*
8. *The Times Building — Nocturne*
9. *Gloucester*

Mar. 20–Apr. 15, Carolina Art Association, Gibbes Memorial Art Building, Charleston, South Carolina, *Annual Exh. of Paintings.*
21. *Washington Arch Spring*

Mar. 30–Apr. 6, Lotos Club, *Exh. of Paintings by Living American Artists.*
21. *The Ancient Window of Nemours*, lent by the artist

Apr.–Oct., DMA, *Special Exh. of Paintings by Childe Hassam.*
1. *October*
2. *Sunlight Through the Leaves*
3. *Plaza Centrale and Fort Cabanas, Havana*
4. *The Waterfall*
5. *Village of Yarmouth*
6. *Wainscott Links*
7. *The Dell, Early Spring*
8. *Young Girl Reading*
9. *Building the Schooner, Provincetown*
10. *Sea Weed, Low Tide, Isles of Shoals*
11. *June Morning*
12. *Northwest Wind*
13. *The North Shore, Moonlight*
14. *Wagon-Tire and Squaw Cap, — The Old Oregon Trail*
15. *Sunlight Brook*
16. *The Iris Pool*
17. *The Enchanted Hour*
18. *Moonlight, Isle of Shoals*
19. *Bathers, Moonrise at Sunset*
20. *East Gloucester, — End of the Trolley Line*
21. *The Bowl of Nasturtiums*

Apr. 27–May 21, AWCS, *44th Annual Exh.*
142. *The Thunderstorm* (wc)

Apr. 27–June 30, CI, *15th Annual Exh.*
116. *The Terre-cuite Teaset*, award
117. *The Open Window*, award

May 11–31, Brooklyn Institute of Arts and Sciences, held at Art Association Galleries, *Brooklyn Loan Exh., with the Cooperation of the Brooklyn Art Association, Rembrandt Club and Little Italy Settlement.*
54. *Moonrise at Sunset*, lent by George D. Pratt
medium not specified

May 12–Aug. 28, BFAA, *6th Annual Exh. of Selected Paintings by American Artists.*
57. *Grez*
58. *El Zocodover*
59. *Springtime*

May 20–July 22, CAM, *18th Annual Exh. of American Art.*
137. *New Haven — The Green*
138. *Schooner Drying Purse Nets, Gloucester*
139. *The Abalone Shell*
"Drawings"
140. *The Fête of Lannion — The Quai*
141. *The Church at Grez*
142. *The Cathedral — Antwerp*
143. *The Duet*
144. *La Clarté — Early Morning*
145. *La Clarté — With Blue Sky*
146. *Old House, Grez*
147. *Chaumière — Perros — Guirec*
148. *Lannion — The Sand Quais*
149. *Mt. Hood — End of the Timber Line*
150. *St. Botolph's, (without) London*
151. *La Clarté — Afternoon Sky*
152. *Fuenta de Alcantara, Toledo*
153. *Café, Toledo*
154. *Old Houses of Lannion*
155. *Calle Venaucio Gonzalez, Toledo*, owned by CAM

May 28–Sept. 18, WAM, *14th Annual Exh. of Oil Paintings by American Painters, Summer, 1911.*
23. *The Breakfast Room, Winter Morning, New York*

Aug. 1–Sept. 22, JHAI, *3rd Annual Exh. of the Indiana Circuit, Oils, Water Colors, Pastels and Prints.*
18. *Autumn in New England*
19. *The Shoals Rocks*

Aug. 1–Dec. 30, CI, *A Loan Exh. of Paintings in Oil, Watercolor, and Pastel, from the Collection of Mr. Burton Mansfield, of New Haven, Connecticut.*
26. *Church at Old Lyme: Spring*

Aug. 26–Sept. 11, Canadian National Exh., Toronto, *Department of Fine Arts.*
68. *The Black Hat*

Sept. 17–Nov. 17, CAMSL, *6th Annual Exh. of Selected Paintings by American Artists.*
51. *Grez*
52. *El Zocodover*
53. *Springtime*

Oct. 4–Dec. 1, Portland Museum of Art, Portland, Oreg., *Paintings, Pastels and Bronzes by Childe Hassam, J. Alden Weir and A. Phiminster Proctor.*

Oct. 10–29, Art Association of Richmond, Ind., *15th Annual Exh.*
18. *Autumn in New England*
19. *The Shoals Rocks*

Oct. 14–29, Art Department, State Fair of Texas.
57. *Old House*
58. *White Church, Provincetown*

Oct. 14–29, Montross, *Opening Exh., Season 1911–1912, Selected Paintings.*
5. *June Night*, 1906
6. *Village Street — Old Lyme*, 1906
7. *The Hudson in Winter*, 1908

Oct. 28–Nov. 29, NYWCC, *22nd Annual Exh.*
(all wcs)
129. *The Grove of Aphrodite*
130. *Ten Pound Island, Gloucester*
131. *At Sunrise, Isles of Shoals*
132. *Madison Square, Winter Mist*
133. *Sylph's Rock, Appledore*
134. *The Rain, Connecticut Hills*

Nov. 8–30, Newark Museum Association, Newark, N.J., *Paintings by Childe Hassam.*
1. *October*
2. *Sunlight Through the Leaves*
3. *The Waterfall*
4. *Village of Yarmouth*
5. *Wainscott Links*
6. *The Dell, Early Spring*
7. *Young Girl Reading*
8. *Building the Schooner, Provincetown*
9. *Sea Weed, Low Tide, Isles of Shoals*
10. *June Morning*
11. *Northwest Wing*
12. *The North Shore, Moonlight*
13. *Wagon-Tire and Squaw Cap — The Old Oregon Trail*
14. *Sunlight Brook*
15. *The Iris Pool*
16. *The Enchanted Hour*
17. *Moonlight, Isles of Shoals*
18. *Bathers, Moonrise at Sunset*
19. *East Gloucester — End of the Trolley Line*
20. *The Bowl of Nasturtiums*
21. *Sunset, Isles of Shoals*
22. *Sunset, Isles of Shoals*
23. *Bather*
24. *Afternoon, Harney Desert*

Nov. 13–Dec. 17, PAFA, *9th Annual Philadelphia Water Color Exh.*
(all wcs)
332. *Pont Neuf*
334. *The Squall: Gloucester*
336. *Broadstairs*
337. *The Blue Sea*
338. *Under the Chalk Cliffs: Broadstairs*

Nov. 14–Dec. 27, AIC, *24th Annual Exh., Exh. of American Paintings and Sculpture.*
164. *The Opal*
165. *Reflected Sunlight*

Dec. 9–Jan. 7, 1912, NAD, *Winter Exh.*
338. *Manhattan's Sunset Towers*

Dec. 16–Jan. 13, 1912, Isaac Delgado Museum of Art, New Orleans, *Inaugural Exh. Collected and Arranged for the Isaac Delgado Museum of Art by the Art Association of New Orleans.*
272. *Old Violinist*

Dec. 28–Jan. 15, 1912, Corcoran, *Exh. of Oil Paintings, Water Colors, Pastels and Drawings by Childe Hassam.*
media not specified
1. *Northwest Wind*
2. *Bathers: Moonrise at Sunset*
3. *The Enchanted Hour*
4. *Sunlight Brook*
5. *The North Shore, Moonlight*
6. *Young Girl Reading, Spring*
7. *Wagon-Tire and Squaw Cap*
8. *Northeast Headlands, New England Coast*, owned by Corcoran
9. *Wainscott Links*
10. *June Morning*
11. *October*
12. *Sunlight Through the Leaves*
13. *Building of the Schooner, Provincetown*
14. *Sea Weed, Low Tide, Isle of Shoals*
15. *The Iris Pool*
16. *The Waterfall*
17. *Moonlight, Isle of Shoals*
18. *Village of Yarmouth, May*
19. *The Bowl of Nasturtiums*
20. *The Dell, Early Spring*
21. *East Gloucester, End of the Trolley Line*
22. *The Park St. Sebastian*
23. *Drawing for "June"*
24. *The Fête of Lannion — The Quai*
25. *Moonrise on the Oregon Trail*
26. *Drawing for "Thalassa"*
27. *Houses on the Place, Lannion*
28. *Lannion — The Sand Quais*
29. *Der Groot Haus, Haarlem*
30. *Fuenta de Alcantara, Toledo*
31. *Café, Toledo*
32. *Mt. Hood — The End of the Timber Line*
33. *La Clarté — Early Morning*
34. *Fifth Avenue at the Waldorf — Fourth of July*
35. *The Cathedral, Antwerp*
36. *Houses in Haarlem*
37. *Chaumière, Perros-Guirec*
38. *Sunset, Isles of Shoals*
39. *The Fête of Lannion, Gray Evening*
40. *La Clarté from Perros-Guirec*
41. *Calle del Alcazar*
42. *Sunset, Isles of Shoals*
43. *The Bridge at Grez — Rainy Day*
44. *St. Botolph's, Without, London*
45. *La Clarté — Afternoon Sky*
46. *La Clarté — Spire and Roof*
47. *La Clarté — With Blue Sky*
48. *Old House, Grez*
49. *Old Houses of Lannion*
50. *Happy Valley, Harney Desert*
51. *The Church at Grez*
52. *Brélévez*
53. *Old Houses, Lannion*
54. *Gothic Gateway, Toledo*
55. *Brélévez, Lannion*
56. *The Duet*
57. *St. Michael's, Lannion*
58. *Afternoon, Harney Desert*
59. *Bather*

Dec. 31–Jan. 29, 1912, JHAI, *27th Annual Exh.*
53. *The Opal*

PSAG, *17th Annual Exh. of Paintings and Sculpture by Prominent Painters and Sculptors.*
56. *Early Spring*
60. *Spring, Union Square*

Roman Art Exposition, Rome, *Collection of Pictures and Sculpture in the Pavilion of the United States of America*
55. *June*
68. *Newport, Rhode Island*
278. *The Bather*

1912

Jan. 17–Feb. 12, Toledo Museum of Art, *Inaugural Exh.*
37. *The Ancient Window of Nemours*, lent by the artist
38. *The Little June Idyl*, lent by the artist
39. *Moonlight in a French Village*, lent by the artist

Jan. 20–Feb. 10, BAC, *Modern American Pictures.*
22. *Springtime*

Jan. 22–Feb. 20, Fort Worth Museum of Art, *3rd Annual Exh. of Selected Paintings by American Artists.*
19. *The Old Violinist*

Feb. 4–Mar. 24, PAFA, *107th Annual Exh.*
525. *The Open Window*
526. *Mount Desert*
534. *Village Street: Old Lyme*
537. *The Sunset Sea*

Week of Feb. 9, ULCNY, "General Exhibition of American and European Paintings" [*NYT*, 2/9/1912, p. 7].
Manhattan's Sunset Towers

Feb. 12–24, Montross, *Exh. of Pictures by Childe Hassam.*
1. *The Jonquils*, 1903
2. *The Room of Flowers*, 1894
3. *The Opal*, 1905
4. *Oscar Laighton*, 1911
5. *The Plaza, December Morning*, 1902

6. *Washington Bridge*, 1902
7. *The Silver Poplar Pool*, 1912
8. *The Little Piano*, 1891
9. *Brooklyn Bridge*, 1894
10. *Early Morning Calm*, 1901
11. *Sunlight on an Old House*, 1897
12. *The Late Afternoon Walk*, 1895
13. *Early Spring in Maine*, 1909
14. *Golden Rod*, 1907
15. *The July Night*, 1898
16. *Across the Park, Early Spring*, 1904
17. *The Sirens' Grotto*, 1906
18. *Laurel in the Woods*, 1906
19. *Bather*, 1905
20. *Boulevard Clichy*, 1889
21. *The Northwest Wind, 2nd*, 1909
22. *Spring Morning, New York*, 1892
23. *Manhattan's Misty Sunset Towers*, 1911
24. *Union Square*, 1891

Mar. 9–Apr. 14, NAD, *87th Annual Exh.*
235. *The New York Window*

Mar. 15–Apr. 6, Montross, *15th Annual Exh., Ten American Painters.*
10. *The Little Shoemaker's Shop*
11. *The Strawberry Tea-set*
12. *Lady with Black Furs*
13. *Autumn Bouquet*
41. *Le Pont-Neuf*
42. *Gold Point*
43. *Broadstairs*

From Apr. 7, CAMSL, *A Collection of Paintings and Drawings by Mr. Childe Hassam, N. A.*
media not specified
1. *Reflected Sunlight*
2. *Northwest Wind*
3. *Bathers: Moonrise at Sunset*
4. *The Enchanted Hour*
5. *The North Shore: Moonlight*
6. *Young Girl Reading: Spring*
7. *Wagon-Tire and Squaw Cap*
8. *Wainscott Links*
9. *June Morning*
10. *October*
11. *Sunlight Through the Leaves*
12. *Building the Schooner, Provincetown*
13. *Sea-Weed, Low Tide, Isles of Shoals*
14. *The Iris Pool*
15. *The Waterfall*
16. *Moonlight, Isles of Shoals*
17. *Village of Yarmouth*
18. *The Bowl of Nasturtiums*
19. *The Dell: Early Spring*
20. *East Gloucester: End of the Trolley Line*
21. *Sunset, Isles of Shoals*
22. *Sunset, Isles of Shoals*
23. *Afternoon, Harney Desert*
24. *Bather*
25. *Oscar Larghton [sic]*
26. *The Park. St. Sebastian*
27. *Drawing for "June"*
28. *The Fete of Lannion: The Quai*
29. *Moonrise on The Oregon Trail*
30. *Drawing for "Thalassa"*
31. *Houses on the Place, Lannion*
32. *Lannion: The Sand Quais*
33. *Der Groot Haus, Haarlem*
34. *Fuenta de Alcantara, Toledo*
35. *Café, Toledo*
36. *Mount Hood: The End of the Timber Line*
37. *La Clarte: Early Morning*
38. *Fifth Avenue at the Waldorf: Fourth of July*
39. *The Cathedral, Antwerp*
40. *Houses in Haarlem*
41. *Chaumiere, Perros-Guirec*
44. *Calle del Alcazar*
45. *The Bridge at Grez: Rainy Day*
46. *St. Botolph's Without, London*
47. *La Clarte: Afternoon Sun*
48. *La Clarte: Spire and Roof*
49. *La Clarte: With Blue Sky*
50. *Old Houses of Lannion*
51. *Happy Valley, Harney Desert*
52. *The Church at Grez*
53. *Brelevenez*
54. *Old Houses, Lannion*
55. *Gothic Gateway, Toledo*
56. *Brelevenez, Lannion*
57. *The Duet*
58. *St. Michael's, Lannion*

Apr. 14–May 12, WAM, *Exh. of Paintings from the Collection of Burton Mansfield, Esq., New Haven, Conn.*
22. *Church at Old Lyme; Spring*

Apr. 15–27, Macbeth, *Group of Selected Paintings by American Artists.*
25. *Fifth Avenue Nocturne*

Apr. 17–May 1, RISD, *Ten American Painters.*
3. *Autumn Bouquet*
4. *Strawberry Tea-set*
5. *Summer Sea*

Apr. 25–May 12, AWCS, *45th Annual Exh.*
(all wcs)
2. *Lannion from the Quai*
15. *Balconies and Roofs, Madrid*
34. *The Letter-box*
38. *Street in Lannion*
87. *Venetian Night*
94. *Ticonderoga*
100. *The Minuet*, 1912 W. T. Evans Prize
106. *The Turquoise Sea*

Apr. 25–June 30, CI, *16th Annual Exh.*
137. *A Room of Flowers*
138. *Reflected Sunlight*

By May 19–until end of May, Montross, "Collection of pictures in oil, water color and pastel by American artists" [*NYT*, 5/19/1912, p. SM15].
Newport

May 21–Sept. 2, BFAA, *7th Annual Exh., Selected Paintings by American Artists.*
68. *The Breakfast Room, New York City, Winter*, lent by WAM
69. *The Little Shoemaker's Shop*
70. *Autumn Bouquet*
71. *Strawberry Tea-set*
72. *Summer Sea*
73. *Lady with Black Furs*

May 25–July 27, CAM, *19th Annual Exh. of American Art.*
186. *The Enchanted Hour*
187. *Sunlight through the Leaves*
188. *The Bowl of Nasturtiums*
189. *Oscar Larghton [sic]*
"Drawings and Studies"
190. *The Park, St. Sebastian*
191. *Drawing for June*
192. *The Fête of Lannion: The Quai*
193. *Moonrise on the Oregon Trail*
194. *Drawing for Thalassa*
195. *Houses on the Place, Lannion*
196. *Lannion: The Sand Quais*
197. *Der Groot Haus, Haarlem*
198. *Fuenta de Alcantara, Toledo*
199. *Café, Toledo*

May–Sept., Syracuse Museum of Fine Arts, *Summer Exh.*

June 7–Sept. 15, WAM, *15th Annual Exh. of Oil Paintings, Summer Exh., 1912.*
25. *Bridge at Grez*

From June 16, CAMSL, *Annual Exh. of Selected Water Colors by American Artists.*
(wcs)
45. *Venetian Night*
46. *The Letter Box*

June 21–July 5, Hackley Gallery of Art, Muskegon, Mich., *Inaugural Exh.*
29. *A Bit of New England Coast*

July 19–28, Art Association of Newport, R.I., *1st Annual Exh. of Pictures by American Painters.*
51. *The Ancient Window, Nemours*

Late Aug. to early Sept., Old Lyme, *11th Annual Exh.*
Village Street

From Sept. 15, CAMSL, *7th Annual Exh., Selected Paintings by American Artists.*
52. *The Little Shoemaker's Shop*
53. *Strawberry Tea-Set*
54. *The Room of Flowers*

Sept. 22–Nov. 22, PAA, *Loan Exh. of Paintings.*
1. *Landscape — Eastern Oregon*
2. *Mount Hood*
3. *Moonlight*
4. *Landscape*
7. *Camellias*
8. *"On the Porch"*
9. *Landscape with Poplars*
10. *In the Luxembourg Gardens*
11. *Moonlight, New England Coast*
12. *On the Snake River, Oregon*

Oct. 5–27, CAM, *7th Annual Exh. of Selected Water Colors by American Artists.*
(wcs)
45. *Venetian Night*
46. *The Letter Box*

Oct. 12–27, Art Department, State Fair of Texas.
63. *Village Street, Old Lyme*
64. *Smutty-Nose from Appledore*

Oct. 12–27, Minneapolis Society of Fine Arts, *Exh. of Paintings by Childe Hassam, N. A.*
1. *Northwest Wind*
2. *Bathers: Moonrise at Sunset*
3. *The North Shore: Moonlight*
4. *Young Girl Reading: Spring*
5. *Wagon-Tire and Squaw Cap*
6. *Wainscott Links*
7. *June Morning*
8. *October*
9. *Building the Schooner, Provincetown*
10. *Sea-Weed, Low Tide, Isles of Shoals*
11. *The Iris Pool*
12. *The Waterfall*
13. *Moonlight, Isles of Shoals*
14. *Village of Yarmouth, May*
15. *The Dell; Early Spring*
16. *East Gloucester; End of the Trolley Lines*
17. *Sunset, Isles of Shoals*
18. *Sunset, Isles of Shoals*
19. *Afternoon; Harney Desert*
20. *Bather*
21. *Mount Hood; the End of the Timber line*
22. *La Clarte; Early Morning*
23. *Fifth Avenue at the Waldorf; Fourth of July*
24. *The Cathedral, Antwerp*
25. *Houses in Haarlem*
26. *Chaumiere, Perros-Guirec*
27. *The Fete of Lannion; Gray Evening*
28. *La Clarte from Perros Guirec*
29. *Calle del Alcazar*
30. *The Bridge at Grez: Rainy Day*
31. *St. Botolph's Without, London*
32. *La Clarte: Afternoon Sky*
33. *La Clarte: Spire and Roof*
34. *La Clarte: With Blue Sky*
35. *Old Houses of Lannion*
36. *Happy Valley, Harney Desert*
38. *Brelevenez*
39. *Old Houses, Lannion*
40. *Gothic Gateway, Toledo*
41. *Brelevenez, Lannion*
42. *The Duet*
43. *St. Michael's, Lannion*

Nov. 2–24, NYWCC, *23rd Annual Exh.*
177. *The Invitations* (wc)

Nov. 5–Dec. 8, AIC, *25th Annual Exh. of American Oil Paintings and Sculpture.*
110. *Laurel*
111. *Naiad*
112. *In the Woods*

Dec. 9–21, Copley Gallery, Boston, *Pictures by Childe Hassam.*
1. *Reflected Sunlight*
2. *Summer Idyl*
3. *The Enchanted Hour*
4. *Oscar Laighton*
5. *The Beryl Pool*
6. *Summer Sea*
7. *The East Headland Pool*
8. *The Spanish Ledges*
9. *The Beryl Gorge*
10. *Neptune's Hall*
11. *The Trap-Dyke Gorge*
12. *North Headland Pools*
13. *The South Gorge*
14. *Kalmia*
15. *The Open Window*
16. *The Naiad's Pool*
17. *Woodland Brook*
18. *The Lady of the Gorge*, lent by Mr. J. P. Lyman

Dec. 14–Jan. 12, 1913, NAD, *Winter Exh.*
357. *The Butterfly*

By Dec. 15, Montross, "Representative paintings" [*NYT*, 12/15/1912, p. SM14].

Dec. 17–Jan. 26, 1913, Corcoran, *4th Exh. Oil Paintings by Contemporary Artists.*
136. *The Bowl of Gold Fish*
165. *The New York Window*, First William A. Clark Prize and Corcoran Gold Medal

Dec. 17–Feb. 3, 1913, JHAI, *28th Annual Exh. of Oil Paintings by American Artists.*
35. *Laurel*

PSAG, *18th Annual Exh. of Paintings and Sculpture by Prominent Painters and Sculptors.*
61. *Autumn*
90. *Early Spring*

1913

Jan. 22–31, Empire Art Galleries, Rochester.
Lady with Black Furs

Feb. 9–Mar. 30, PAFA, *108th Annual Exh.*
453. *The Strawberry Tea Set*
527. *The Afternoon Walk*
531. *Kalmia*

Feb. 11– Mar. 9, Peabody Gallery, Baltimore, *4th Annual Exh. of Contemporary American Art, under the auspices of the Charcoal Club and the Peabody Institute.*
49. *The Spanish Ledges, Appledore*

Feb. 13–27, DMA, *Loan Exh. of Pictures Owned in Detroit.*
10. *The Chinese Merchants*, lent by the National Gallery of Art, Washington, D.C. (Freer Collection)

By Feb. 16–until Mar. 1, St. Mark's-in-the-Bowerie, "Exhibition of water colors and oil paintings by Arthur W. Dow, Louise B. Hancock, Childe Hassam,

Emily N. Hatch, Luis Mora, and Francis Newton" [*NYT*, 2/16/1913, p. 55].

Feb. 17–Mar. 15, Association of American Painters and Sculptors, Inc., *International Exh. of Modern Art, at the Armory of the Society of the 69th Infantry*.
71. *Nude Woman with Mirror*
72. *The Spanish Stairs*
73. *Naples*
74. *Vesuvius*
75. *Posilippo*
76. *Cos Cob*
96. *Cos Cob, Old House* (p)
97. *Cos Cob, Old House* (p)
98. *Cos Cob, Old House* (p)
99. *Sylph Rock, Appledore* (p)
100. *The Rain, Connecticut Hills* (p)
101. *Drawing for Moonrise at Sunset* (d)
Traveled: Mar. 24–Apr. 16, AIC, *International Exh. of Modern Art*.
156. *Naples*

Mar. 12–Apr. 5, Montross, *16th Annual Exh., Ten American Painters*.
12. *Young Woman Reading a Letter*
13. *Summer Idyl*
14. *Fruit and Chinese Jars*
15. *Mrs. Holly of Cos Cob*, small panel
16. *The A. I. News Depot, Cos Cob*, small panel
17. *The Fireplace*, small panel
18. *The Fireplace, 2nd*, small panel
19. *The Fireplace, 3rd*, small panel
20. *The Butterfly*, small panel
47. *The Times Building—Nocturne*
48. *Lake Leman*
49. *Rain, Mist and Electric Light*

Mar. 15–Apr. 20, NAD, *84th Annual Exh.*
229. *Reflected Sunlight*

Mar. 24–Apr. 16, AIC, *International Exh. of Modern Art*.
156. *Naples*

Mar. 25–Apr. 27, AIC, *25th Annual Exh. of Water Colors, Pastels and Miniatures by American Artists*.
243. *Venetian Night*
244. *The Letter Box*

Until Mar. 29, Cottier Galleries, "Thirty-one pictures by modern French, Dutch, and American artists" [*NYT*, 3/23/1913, p. SM15].
View of Portland, Ore.
and one other

Apr. 14–May 5, Copley Society, Boston, Exh. of The Ten.
Beacon Hill
Fruit and Chinese Jars
Summer Idyl
Young Woman Reading a Letter

Apr. 24–June 30, CI, *17th Annual Exh.*
121. *The East Window*
122. *Mt. Desert*

Apr., O'Brien's Gallery, Chicago, *Exh. of Paintings by Childe Hassam*.

May 10–Aug. 31, BFAA, *8th Annual Exh. of Selected Paintings by American Artists*.
48. *Improvisation*, lent by Mrs. Chauncey J. Blair, Chicago, Ill.
49. *Posilippo*
50. *Nude Woman Holding a Mirror*
51. *The Spanish Stairs*
52. *The North West Wind*
53. *Vesuvius*

May 24–July 26, CAM, *20th Annual Exh. of American Art*.
123. *Young Woman Reading a Letter and Sunlight Without*
124. *Fifth Avenue at the Waldorf* (wc)
125. *Ticonderoga* (wc)
126. *Balconies and Roofs* (wc)
127. *Street Sweeper, Paris* (d)
128. *Street in Lannion* (wc)
129. *St Michaels, Lannion* (wc)
130. *La Voune, Paris* (d)
131. *Drinking Fountain* (d)
132. *The Squall* (wc)

From June 15, CAMSL, *8th Annual Exh. of Selected Water Colors by American Artists*
(all wcs)
40. *Café, Toledo*
41. *The Fete of Lannion*
42. *Connecticut Hills*

June 16–Sept., Syracuse Museum of Fine Arts, *Summer Exh.*

July 26–Sept. 6, CI, *A Summer Loan Exh. of Paintings*.
26. *The Grapevine*, lent by Mr. William Smith Stimmel
27. *New England Hilltop: Autumn*, lent by Mr. W. J. Johnson

July–Nov., CAMSL, *A Collection of Works Owned in St. Louis and Lent to the Museum*.
30. *A Street in Seville*, lent by Mr. Edward A. Faust

Aug. 23–Sept. 8, Canadian National Exh., Toronto, Canada, *Department of Fine Arts*.
242. *The Children*
243. *Early Morning, Appledore*

Oct. 8–29, Memorial Art Gallery, Rochester, *Inaugural Exh.*
51. *The Jonquils*

By Nov. 13, Macbeth, "Thirty paintings by thirty artists" [*NYT*, 11/13/1913, p. 10].
Board Cove: Appledore

Nov. 14–Dec. 25, AIC, *26th Annual Exh. of Oil Paintings and Sculpture by American Artists*.
165. *Posilippo*
166. *The East Window*
167. *The Lady with Black Furs*

Week of Dec. 5, Lotos Club, "Eighty-one pictures from the collection of Dr. Alexander C. Humphreys" [*NYT*, 12/5/1913, p. 10].
Messenger Boy
one other from the "street scene period"

By Dec. 12, ULCNY, "Exhibition of the work of American artists" [*NYT*, 12/12/1913, p. 10].
White Sloop: Cos Cob
and one other

Dec. 20–Jan. 18, 1914, NAD, *Winter Exh.*
274. *Diana's Bath*
304. *The South Ledges, Appledore*

Los Angeles (?) [CH, Cos Cob, Conn., 9/8/1913, to Mr. Macbeth, Macbeth Gallery Papers, AAA, reel NMc7, frame 398.]

Michigan State Federation of Arts, Kalamazoo, *1st Circuit Exh.*

PSAG, *19th Annual Exh. of Paintings and Sculpture by Prominent Painters and Sculptors*.
24. *Early Spring*
57. *The Old Violinist*

1914

Jan. 1–Feb. 1, JHAI, *29th Annual Exh. of Paintings and the Sculpture of the Art Association of Indianapolis*.
33. *The East Window*

Jan. 5–19, Water Color Club, *27th Annual Exh. at the BAC*.
(all wcs)
44. *Street in Lannion*
45. *The Church at La Closte*
46. *Lannion Côtes du Nord*
47. *The Square Tower*
48. *Twilight*
49. *Balconies and Roofs, Madrid*
50. *La Closte*
51. *Gateway, Toledo*

Jan. 6–19 (extended to Jan. 26), Macbeth, *Paintings by Emil Carlsen, Paul Dougherty, Frederick C. Frieseke, Childe Hassam, Willard L. Metcalf, Kenneth H. Miller, J. Alden Weir.*
15. *Church at Provincetown*
16. *Fisherman's Cottage, Gloucester*
17. *April; Glow of the Swamp Maple*
18. *The Window Curtain*

Jan. 8–28, AIC, *Friends of American Arts, Loan Exh. of American Paintings*.
22. *Morning Light*, lent by Mr. A. H. Marks
24. *Improvisation*, lent by Mr. Chauncey J. Blair
36. *The Pool*, lent by Mr. A. H. Marks
73. *A Parisian Afternoon*, lent by Mr. Walter H. Wilson
75. *Quai Voltaire*, lent by Mr. William O. Goodman

Jan. 14–16, ULCNY, *Landscapes by Eight American Artists*.

Jan. 24–Feb. 8, CAM, *46th Annual Exh. of AWCS of New York*.
(all wcs)
41. *Café, Toledo*
42. *The Fête of Lannion*
43. *Connecticut Hills*

Jan. 30–Mar. 1, BAC, *80th Annual Exh. of Contemporary American Oil Paintings*.
14. *Union Square and 16th Street, New York, Spring*

Feb. 5–23, PAA, *Exh. of Paintings by American Artists Sent by the American Federation of Arts*.
8. *The Spanish Ledges, Isles of Shoals*

Feb. 5–Mar. 7, National Arts Club, *Exh. Contemporary Art*.
(all ps)
171. *The Squall*
172. *Fifth Avenue*
173. *November Evening*
174. *Brelevenez, Cote du Nord*
175. *Old Houses—Haarlem*

Feb. 8–Mar. 29, PAFA, *109th Annual Exh.*
148. *The Young Woman and a Plate of Apples*
308. *The Swimmer: Appledore*
310. *Rainy Day: The Oyster Sloop*

Feb. 21–June 23, CI, *Exh. of Paintings Lent by Dr. Alexander C. Humphreys*.
55. *Fifth Avenue: Snow Scene*
56. *Messenger Boy*
57. *Across the Park*

Mar. 18–Apr. 7, Montross, *17th Annual Exh., Ten American Painters*.
12. *Clarissa's Window*
13. *The Model Disrobing*
14. *The Golden Window*
15. *The Gorge—Appledore*

Apr. 4–26, PAA, *An Exh. of Paintings by the Mural Painters of the Panama-Pacific Exposition*.
57. *Kalmia*
58. *The Grotto*
59. *Spring Mood*
60. *Woodland Brook*
61. *The Siren's Grotto*
62. *East Headland Pool*
63. *The Alders at Sunset*
64. *The Granite Rocks, Cape Ann*
65. *The Ledges, October in Old Lyme*
66. *Northeast Headland, Isles of Shoals*
67. *Old House and Garden, Long Island*

Apr. 5–May 10, WAM, *Exh. of Contemporary American Paintings Owned in Worcester County*.
21. *The Gardener's Daughter*, lent by Mr. James Logan
22. *Columbus Ave., Rainy Day*, lent by Mrs. E. D. Buffington
23. *Headlands at Appledore*, lent by Mrs. Sydney R. Mason, Whitinsville

Apr. 8–26, New Haven Paint and Clay Club, Conn., *13th Annual Exh.*
35. *Church at Old Lyme*, lent by Mr. Burton Mansfield

From Apr. 14, Montross, *Special Exh. of Pictures by American Artists*.
6. *The Butterfly*
25. *Pont Neuf*
26. *The Bridge at Grez*

Apr. 30–June 30, CI, *18th Annual Exh.*
148. *The Morning Room*
149. *Venetian Glass*

May 16–Aug. 31, BFAA, *9th Annual Exh. of Selected Paintings by American Artists*.
56. *The Chinese Merchants*, lent by the Smithsonian Institution (Freer Collection), Washington, D.C.
57. *Summer Sea*
58. *The Golden Window*

May 23–July 31, CAM, *21st Annual Exh. of American Art*.
52. *The Lady with Black Furs*
53. *The Yachts*
54. *Sunset—Ironbound Mt. Desert*
55. *The Afternoon Walk, East Gloucester*

June 20–Aug. 2, Bruce Museum, Greenwich, Conn., *Greenwich Society of Artists' 3rd Annual Exh. of Oil Paintings and Sculpture*.
28. *The Jonquils*

July 20–30, Art Association of Newport, R.I., *3rd Annual Exh. of Pictures by American Painters*.
51. *Sunlight on an Old House*

Summer, Fine Arts Palace at Shepherd's Bush, London, *Anglo-American Exposition*.
181. *Room of Flowers*
184. *Young Woman Reading*
185. *Moonlight Landscape*
186. *Diana's Bath*
188. *The South Ledges*
190. *At the Window*

From Sept. 6, CAMSL, *9th Annual Exh. of Selected Paintings by American Artists*.
87. *The Morning Room*
88. *Venetian Glass*

Oct. 25–Nov. 23, RISD, *Autumn Exh.*
12. *Summer Sea*

Oct. 27–Nov. 16, Macbeth, Group Exh. of Paintings [*NYT*, 11/1/1914, p. SM11].
In the Old House

Nov. 3–Dec. 6, AIC, *27th Annual Exh. of American Oil Paintings and Sculpture*.

145. *Venetian Glass*
146. *Morning Room*
147. *Summer Sea*

Nov. 7–29, NYWCC, *25th Annual Exh.* (all wcs)
108. *Old Houses, Haarlem*
109. *The Church Tower, Lannion, Cotes du Nord*
110. *Puerta Del Sol (within)*
111. *Spire of Antwerp Cathedral*
112. *Little Church in Brittany*
113. *Fete Day of Lannion*

Nov. 12–28, Montross, *Exh. of Pictures by Childe Hassam.*
21–44 (wcs)
1. *Capri*
2. *The Couch on the Porch*
3. *Water Lily*
4. *The West Indian Girl*
5. *Girl Reading a Letter*
6. *Cloud Reflections, Gloucester*
7. *The Breakfast Room in the Old House*
8. *Rose Hawthorne*
9. *Young Girl Reading*
10. *New England Peaches and Grapes*
11. *The County-fair Still Life*
12. *Helen Burke*
13. *The View of Central Park—April*
14. *Young Girl in a Greek Dress*
15. *The Beryl Gorge*
16. *Self Portrait*
17. *Virginia*
21. *Duck Island, Isles of Shoals*
22. *Lanion, Cotes du Nord*
23. *Brélévenez*
24. *Brélévenez, 2nd*
25. *Rainy Night*
26. *Fish Houses, Gloucester*
27. *La Clarté, Cotes du Nord*
28. *The Blue Sea, Appledore*
29. *The Rain, Weir's Farm*
30. *On the Marne*
31. *The Fisherman, The Marne*
32. *Grez—sur Loing*
33. *Bleak House, Broadstairs*
34. *The Old House, November*
35. *Moonrise at Sunset*
36. *November, Old Lyme*
37. *Old Houses in Haarlem*
38. *The Back of an Old House*
39. *Cos Cob*
40. *The Madeleine*
41. *The Old House, September*
42. *The Squall, Gloucester Outer harbor*
43. *The Pont Neuf*
44. *Broadstairs*

Dec. 15–Jan. 24, 1915, Corcoran, *5th Exh. Oil Paintings by Contemporary American Artists.*
56. *Dawn in the Valley of the Marne*
179. *The Little Shoemaker's Shop*
223. *Morning Light*

Dec. 19–Jan. 17, 1915, NAD, *84th Annual Exh.*
190. *The East Window*
293. *The Beryl Pool*

PSAG, *20th Annual Exh. of Paintings and Sculpture by Prominent Painters and Sculptors.*
11. *Early Spring*
70. *Sunset, Near Seattle, Puget Sound*

1915

Jan. 1–Dec. 31, San Diego, Calif., *Panama-California Exposition.*
33. *The Beryl Gorge, Appledore*
34. *Moonrise at Sunset*
35. *The Squall, Cape Ann*
36. *In Brittany*

By Jan. 3, Daniel Gallery, *Special Exh.* [*NYT*, 1/3/1915, p. SM11].

Jan. 7–Feb. 7, Minneapolis Institute of Arts, *Inaugural Exh.*
189. *Church at Old Lyme*, lent by BFAA
190. *The Isle of Shoals*, The Martin B. Koon Memorial Collection—Gift of Mrs. C. C. Bovey and Mrs. C. D. Velie, 1914

Jan. 26–Feb. 14, Macbeth, *30 Oils by 30 Artists.*

Feb. 7–Mar. 28, PAFA, *110th Annual Exh.*
394. *The Breakfast Room in the Old House*
395. *Portrait*
396. *The Rose Hawthorne*

Feb. 20–Mar. 11, Corcoran, *19th Annual Exh. of Washington Water Color Club.* (all wcs)
216. *St. Botolph, Bishopsgate, London*
221. *Old Gateway, Toledo*
226. *La Clarté, Côtes du Nord*
227. *Fifth Avenue at The Waldorf, 4th of July*

Feb. 20–Dec. 14, San Francisco, *Panama-Pacific International Exposition.*
"Paintings and Drawings"
2000. *Puerta del Sol: Toledo*
2001. *Isles of Shoals: Duck Island*
2002. *Newfields: New Hampshire*
2003. *The Old Home with Elms*
2004. *The Old House: September*
2005. *The Squall: Gloucester*
2006. *Lannion*
2007. *Moonrise at Sunset*
2008. *Brittany Cottage*
2009. *Happy Valley: Harney Desert*
2010. *Skull Springs: Oregon*
2011. *Der Groot House: Haarlem*
2012. *The Quais:Lannion*
2013. *The Fete of Lannion: Grey Evening*
2014. *Brelevenez: 2nd*
2015. *Aphrodite*
2016. *St. Michaels': Lannion*
2017. *La Clarte*
2018. *Brelevenez*
2019. *Street in Haarlem*
2020. *The Blue Sea: Appledore*
2021. *Weir's Farm: the Rain*
2022. *Cathedral Spire: Antwerp*
2023. *The Terre Cuit[e] Tea Set*
2024. *The Strawberry Tea Set*
2025. *The Woman with Black Furs and Fire Opals*
2026. *Sunset: New England Coast*
2027. *In the Shadow of the Vine*
2028. *The South Ledges*
2029. *The Yachts: Gloucester Harbor*
2030. *Diana's Bath*
2031. *Portrait of a Young Girl*
2032. *The Ancient Window of Nemours*
2033. *The West Indian Girl*
2034. *New England Peaches and Grapes*
2035. *Couch on the Porch: Cos Cob*
2036. *Reading the Letter*
2037. *California Hills in Spring*

Mar. 15–27, Knoedler, *Paintings by The Ten American Painters.*
16. *Morning Light*
17. *The Sea*
18. *Dawn*
19. *Road in the Land of Nod*

Mar. 20–Apr. 25, NAD, *90th Annual Exh.*
85. *Portland, Oregon*

Apr. 4–May 3, Brooklyn Museum of Art, *Contemporary American Painting.*
44. *Breakfast Room in the Old House*
45. *The View of Central Park*

Apr. 9–May 31, DMA, *1st Annual Exh. of Selected Paintings by American Artists.*
4. *The Sea*
14. *Road in the Land of Nod*
16. *Dawn*
18. *A Summer Sea*

May 7–June 9, Vassar College, Poughkeepsie, *Founder's Day Loan Exh. of American Paintings.*
46. *The Snowstorm, Brooklyn Bridge*

May 22–July 31, CAM, *22nd Annual Exh. of American Art.*
54. *Northeast Headland, Isles of Shoals*
55. *November, the Ledges*
56. *The Siren's Grotto, Appledore*

May 22–Aug. 30, BFAA, *10th Annual Exh. of Selected Paintings by American Artists.*
74. *Dawn*
75. *The Sea*
76. *The Road in the Land of Nod*

June 27–July 26, WAM, *Exh. of Paintings by Contemporary American Artists, lent by Folsom Galleries of New York and Doll and Richards of Boston.*

July–Oct., CAMSL, *5th Annual Exh. of Paintings Owned in St. Louis, A Collection of Works from St. Louis Homes Lent to the Museum.*
29. *The Old Fisherman*, lent by Mr. Philip B. Fouke

Aug. 1–30, WAM, *Exh. of Oil Paintings by American Artists, Lent by M. Knoedler and Co., New York City.*
9. *Summer Idyl*

Summer, Knoedler, *8th Annual Summer Exh. of Paintings by American Artists.*
20. *Morning Light*

From Sept. 12, CAMSL, *10th Annual Exh. of Selected Paintings by American Artists.*
71. *Dawn*
72. *The Sea*

Nov. 16–Jan. 2, 1916, AIC, *28th Annual Exh. of American Oil Paintings and Sculpture.*
164. *Down in the Valley of the Marne*
165. *The Sea*

Nov. 27–Dec. 11, Montross, *Exh. of Pictures by Childe Hassam.*
1. *Morning Light*
2. *The White Mantel—Portrait of Miss E.*
3. *Janet*
4. *Portrait*
5. *The Christmas Basket*
"Hudson River Group"
6. *The Destroyers*
7. *Constable Hook—Sunset*
8. *Back of the Fishkill Mountains*
9. *Mount Beacon in Winter*
10. *Sunset on the Hudson below Fishkill*
11. *Mount Beacon in Spring*
"California Group"
12. *Madroñes Hill*
13. *The California Hills—The Little Vineyard*
14. *Spring Morning in California*
15. *Telegraph Hill*
16. *The Eucalyptus in Blossom*
17. *The Silver Veil and the Golden Gate*
18. *Spring Afternoon in the California Hills*
19. *The Hill of the Sun—San Anselmo*
20. *Eucalyptus Trees—Spring*
21. *San Anselmo*
22. *Point Lobos*
"Pastels"
23. *The Smelt Fishers*
24. *Moonrise at Sunset in November*
25. *Dawn—The Cos Cob Docks*
26. *Brook Back of New Canaan*
27. *The Secular Cedars*
28. *The Holley Homestead—November Haze*
29. *Indian Summer*
30. *The Old Brush House—Cos Cob*
31. *The Wood Chopper*
32. *Moonrise at Sunset*
33. *The Old Brush House and Store*
34. *Marsh Haymakers*
35. *The Mill-dam*
36. *The Boston Post Road*
37. *Church at Old Lyme*
38. *Thalassa*
39. *Study for the Diver*
40. *Maud*
"Water Colors"
41. *Venice—San Giorgio*
42. *The Bather*
43. *Veranda of the "Old House"*
44. *Old Barns at Grez*
45. *Perros Guirec*
46. *Weir's Barn*
47. *Terrace on the Hudson*
48. *Back of the Old Barn*
49. *In Holland*
50. *Boulevard Haussmann*
51. *Autumn*
52. *Church—Star Island*
53. *The Bridge at Grez*
54. *On Fifth Avenue*
55. *Broadstairs*
56. *Lannion—La Place*
57. *Chicago Nocturn [sic]*
58. *The Shoals Garden*
59. *Sunset at Lannion*
60. *Fishkill Mountains*
61. *Mount Beacon*
62. *Lannion*
63. *The Convent*
64. *Hudson at Newburg [sic]*
65. *Weir's Garden*
66. *Cape Ann*
67. *Ethel*
68. *The House on the Cliffs—Broadstairs*
69. *The Dance*
70. *Seattle Harbor*
71. *Remington Canoes—Lake George*
72. *Hickorynut Trees*
73. *Stein Mountain*
74. *The Gardener*
75. *The Alhambra*
76. *Church at Kingston*
77. *Old House at Kingston*
78. *Girl Reading*
79. *The River—Nude*
80. *Buttermilk Falls*
"Mount Hood Group"
81. *Mount Hood*
82. *End of the Timber Line—Mt. Hood*
83. *Adams and St. Helens—Early Morning*
84. *Looking toward Adams from Mt. Hood*
"Isles of Shoals Group"
85. *Appledore*
86. *Smutty Nose Island*
87. *Southeast Headland*
88. *Appledore*
89. *Diamond Cove*
90. *Sunday Morning—Appledore*
91. *Afternoon at Appledore*
92. *The Gorge*
93. *Looking into Beryl Pool*
94. *Evening—Turtle Rock*
95. *Sirens Grotto*
96. *The Deep Pool*
97. *The East Headland*
98. *Babbs Cove*
99. *Lymans Pool*
100. *South Ledges*
101. *The Trap-dyke Gorge*
102. *Haddock Head*
103. *The Dark Pool*
104. *The Dark Pool, 2nd*
105. *Rocks at Appledore*
106. *Nathalies Gorge*

Nov. 30–Dec. 18, Frederick Keppel and Co., *Exh. of Etchings and Dry Points by Childe Hassam.*

Dec. 18–Jan. 16, 1916, NAD, *Winter Exh.*
208. *A Town in France*

Dec. 31–Jan. 20, 1916, Corcoran, *20th Annual Exh. of the Washington Water Color Club.*
(all wcs)
154. *The Dutch Door*
154a. *The White Kimono*
155. *Elms in May*
156. *Toby's Cos Cob*
156a. *The Colonial Table*
157. *The Steps*
158. *Kitty Resting*
160. *The Dance*
161. *The Dock, Low Tide*
162. *Cos Cob*

Dec., Hackley Art Gallery, Muskegon, Mich., *Exh. of Paintings by 12 American Artists.*

Philadelphia Art Club
Awarded gold medal

PSAG, *21st Annual Exh. of Paintings and Sculpture by Prominent Painters and Sculptors.*
68. *The Musician*
105. *Early Spring*

1916

Jan. 1–May 1, San Francisco Art Association, *Post-Exposition Exh. in the Department of Fine Arts.*
5523. *The Yachts: Gloucester Harbor,* purchased by the San Francisco Society of Artists for presentation to the San Francisco Art Association
5524. *Jonquils*
5525. *Sunset: New England Coast*
5526. *The Woman with Black Furs and Fire Opals*
5527. *Nymph with Ducks*
5528. *Couch on the Porch: Cos Cob*
5529. *Peonies*
5530. *In the Shadow of the Vine*
5531. *The Little River in June*
5532. *The West Indian Girl*
5533. *The Ancient Window of Nemours*
5534. *California Hills in Spring*
5535. *The Strawberry Tea Set*
5536. *Spring Morning in California*
5537. *Telegraph Hill*
5538. *The Terre Cuit Tea Set*
5539. *Aphrodite*
5540. *The South Ledges*
5541. *Nude*

By Jan 2, Daniel Gallery, *Group Exh.* [*N Y I*, 1/2/1916, p. SM21].
Boulders in Winter

Jan. 4–29, Fort Worth Museum of Art, *7th Annual Exh. of Selected Paintings Assembled by American Federation of Arts, Washington, D.C.*
25. *Bridge at Grez*

Jan. 11–Feb. 13, JHAI, *31st Annual Exh. of Paintings at JHAI, Art Association of Indianapolis, Indiana.*
17. *Miss Florence's Garden*
18. *The Siren's Grotto*
19. *Nocturne*
20. *Moonlight, Old Lyme*

Jan., Albert Roullier Art Galleries, Chicago, *Etchings and Drypoints by Childe Hassam.*

Jan., DMA, *Selected Paintings from Albright Art Gallery and a Collection of Recent Work by British Artists.*
12. *Church at Old Lyme*

Feb. 3–27, AWCS, National Arts Club, *49th Annual Exh.*
(all wcs)
134. *The Fishkill Mountain*
135. *The Bather*
136. *Seattle Harbor*
137. *Old Barns at Grez*
138. *The Poppies*
139. *The Bridge at Grez*

Feb. 6–Mar. 26, PAFA, *111th Annual Exh.*
99. *A Town in France*
256. *The East Window*
295. *Sonata*
320. *The Sea*

Feb. 14–25, SB, *Paintings, Pastels and Etchings by Childe Hassam.*
media not specified
1. *Lannion*
2. *The Smelt Fishers*
3. *Moonrise at Sunset*
4. *The Secular Cedars*
5. *Siren's Grotto*
6. *Afternoon at Appledore*
7. *Terrace on the Hudson*
8. *The Dark Pool—2nd*
9. *Autumn*
10. *Appledore*
11. *The Mill-dam*
12. *Moonrise at Sunset in November*
13. *Girl Reading*
14. *The Boston Post Road*
15. *The Wood Chopper*
16. *The Old Brush House—Cos-Cob*
17. *Weir's Barn*
18. *The Dark Pool*
19. *The Gardener*
20. *Remington's Canoes—Lake George*
21. *Cape Ann*
22. *Appledore—No. 2*
23. *The Christmas Basket*
24. *Portrait*
25. *Madrones Hill*
26. *The Open Window*
27. *The Silver Veil and the Golden Gate*
28. *The White Mantel (Portrait of Miss B)*
29. *The Hill of the Sun—San Anselmo*
30. *The Eycalyptus [sic] in Blossom*
31. *Adams and St. Helen's—Early Morning*
32. *Looking towards Adams from Mt. Hood*
33. *The Trap-dike Gorge*
34. *Back of the Barn*
35. *Babb's Cove*
36. *Veranda of the "Old House"*
37. *Haddock Head*
38. *Church—Star Island*
39. *Smutty Nose Island*
40. *In Holland*
41. *Diamond Cove*
42. *Church at Old Lyme*
43–73. etchings

Mar. 6–18, Knoedler, *Exh. of Paintings by The Ten.*
6. *Manhattan*
7. *Half Tide*
8. *Oregon Apples*
9. *Naples*
10. *The Alcantara Fountain, Toledo*
11. *The Top of the Cliff*

Mar. 18–Apr. 23, NAD, *91st Annual Exh.*
399. *The Old Elm*

Apr. 4–24, PAA, *Exh. of Paintings by a Group of New York Artists.*
24. *The Beryl Gorge, Appledore*
25. *Moonrise at Sunset*
26. *The Squall, Cape Ann*
27. *In Brittany*

Apr. 15–May 7, BFAA, *Exh. of Paintings, Water Colors, Pastels and Etchings by Childe Hassam, N. A.*
1–71 media not specified
1. *The Open Window*
2. *Eucalyptus Trees in Blossom*
3. *The Christmas Basket*
4. *The White Mantel—Portrait*
5. *The Silver Veil*
6. *Portrait*
7. *Madrones Hill*
8. *Hill of Sun, San Anselmo*
9. *The Smelt Fishers*
10. *The Secular Cedars*
11. *Moonrise at Sunset*
12. *Church at Old Lyme*
13. *The Old Brush House, Cos Cob*
14. *The Boston Post Road*
15. *The Milldam*
16. *The Wood Chopper*
17. *Moonrise at Sunset*
18. *The Church at Star Island, Isles of Shoals*
19. *Adams and St. Helens*
20. *Lannion*
21. *Back of the Old Barn*
22. *Looking Towards Adams*
23. *In Holland*
24. *Autumn*
25. *Girl Reading*
26. *Weir's Barn*
27. *Terrace on the Hudson*
28. *The Gardener*
29. *Frederic Remington's Canoes*
30. *Cape Ann*
31. *Veranda of the Old House*
32. *The Sirens Grotto*
33. *Appledore*
34. *Appledore, Second*
35. *The Trapdyke Gorge*
36. *The Dark Pool*
37. *The Dark Pool, Second*
38. *Haddock Head*
39. *Babbs Cove*
40. *Afternoon at Appledore*
41. *Diamond Cove*
42. *Church at Kingston*
43. *Hudson at Newburg*
44. *Mount Beacon*
45. *Lannion—La Place*
46. *Broadstairs*
47. *Perros Guirec*
48. *Chicago Nocturn [sic]*
49. *The House on the Cliffs—Broadstairs*
50. *Evening—Turtle Rock*
51. *Venice—San Gorgio [sic]*
52. *On Fifth Avenue*
53. *Old House at Kingston*
54. *Boulevard Haussmann*
55. *End of the Timber Line—Mt. Hood*
56. *The Alhambra*
57. *Stein Mountain*
58. *The Holly Homestead—November Haze*
59. *Dawn—The Cos Cob Docks*
60. *Brook Back of New Canaan*
61. *Maud*
62. *Study for the Diver*
63. *Indian Summer*
64. *San Anselmo*
65. *Eucalyptus Trees—Spring*
66. *Constable Hook—Sunset*
67. *Mount Beacon in Winter*
68. *The Destroyers*
69. *Mount Beacon in Spring*
70. *Sunset on the Hudson, below Fishkill*
71. *Back of the Fishkill Mountains*
72–150 etchings

Apr. 25–May 13, Montross, *Exh. of Pictures by a Selected Group of American Artists.*
32. *The Back of An Old House*
33. *Old Houses in Haarlem*

Apr., DMA, *Exh. of Paintings by Men Who Paint the Far West, Twelve American Artists and Sandor Landeau.*
47. *Miss Florence's Garden*
48. *The Siren's Grotto*
49. *Nocturne*
50. *Moonlight, Old Lyme*

May 5–June 4, DMA, *2nd Annual Exh. of Selected Paintings by American Artists and Sculpture by Anna V. Hyatt.*
42. *In the Old House,* lent by Macbeth
43. *Town in France*
44. *Manhattan*

May 27–July 31, CAM, *23rd Annual Exh. of American Art.*
77. *The Village of Pont-Aven, Brittany*
78. *The East Headland Pool, Appledore, Isles of Shoals*

May, Memorial Art Gallery, Rochester, *Exh. of Paintings by Twelve Contemporary American Artists.*
17. *Miss Florence's Garden*
18. *The Siren's Grotto*
19. *Nocturne*
20. *Moonlight, Old Lyme*

June 6–Sept. 20, Cleveland Museum, *Inaugural Exh.*
60. *Young Woman Reading a Letter*

June–Aug., Toledo Museum of Art, *Annual Summer Exh. of Selected Paintings by American Artists.*
135. *In the Old House,* lent by Macbeth
136. *Town in France*
137. *Manhattan*

From Sept. 3, CAMSL, *11th Annual Exh. of Selected Paintings by American Artists.*
11. *St. Michael Lannin [sic], Cotes du Nord, France*
73. *A Town in France*
74. *The East Window*

Oct. 14–29, Art Department, State Fair of Texas.
56. *The Last Light of the City*
57. *The Ledges, November*

Nov. 2–Dec. 7, AIC, *29th Annual Exh. of American Oil Paintings and Sculpture.*
134. *The Rocky Shore of New England*
135. *Against the Light*

Nov. 3–Dec. 3, Montclair Art Museum, N.J., *Exh. of Oils, Water Colors, and Etchings by Childe Hassam.*
18–35 (wcs), 36–38 (ps)
1. *The Lovers, Brittany*
2. *Moonrise at Sunset, the Mountain Laurel*
3. *Woman in blue and white standing by a mirror*
4. *Fire Opals*
5. *The Squall, Appledore*
6. *Manhattan, Sunset Towers*
7. *Manhattan, at Sunset in the October haze (1907)*
8. *Spring Lyric*
9. *The Gorge, Appledore*
10. *The East Headland Pool, Appledore*
11. *The Village of Pont-Aven, Brittany*
12. *Early Spring in New England*
13. *The Big Cloud, Isles of Shoals*
14. *Young Girl in a Greek Dress*
15. *The Bather in Cloud Reflections*
16. *The Beryl Gorge, Appledore*
17. *Spring, Yarmouth, Maine*
18. *The Island Garden*
19. *Morning Calm, Appledore*
20. *Weir's Barn*
21. *Connecticut Hills*
22. *Terrace on the Hudson*
23. *Back of the Old Barn*
24. *The Gardener*
25. *Remington's Canoes, Lake George*
26. *The Veranda of the Old House*
27. *Lake Leman*
28. *Spring Maples*
29. *Boulevard Hausmann*
30. *Venetian Night*
31. *In Holland*

32. *La Clarté, Rainy Sky*
33. *Mt. Hood, end of timber line*
34. *Winter the Chalk Cliffs, Broadstairs*
35. *La Clarté, Côtes du Nord*
36. *Street Sweeper, Paris*
37. *Wallace Drinking Fountain, Paris*
38. *La bonne, Paris*
and 60 etchings

Nov. 5–Dec. 10, PAFA, *14th Annual Philadelphia Water Color Exh., and 15th Annual Exh. of Miniatures.*
(all wcs)
405. *Sunday Morning: Appledore*
406. *The Dark Pool*
407. *Autumn*
408. *Babbs Cove*
409. *East Headland*
410. *Lyman's Pool*
411. *Buttermilk Falls*
412. *Appledore*
413. *The Gorge*
414. *Appledore, Number 2*
415. *Church: Star Island*
416. *Diamond Cove*
417. *Newfield, NH*

Nov. 16–Dec. 2, Frederick Keppel and Co., *Etchings and Drawings by Childe Hassam.*
68. *Malheur Desert* (wc)
69. *Malheur Desert* (wc)
70. *Squaw's Cap, Haney [sic] Desert* (wc)
71. *Chestnuts, Old Lyme* (wc)
72. *Snow in Connecticut Hills* (pen and wc)
73. *Appledore* (p)
74. *Appledore* (p)
77. *14 Juillet, Monmartre* (wc)
78. *Perros Guirec* (wc)
79. *Brittany Barns, Perros Guirec* (wc)
80. *Outer Gate, Toledo* (wc)
82. *Seville* (wc)
83. *Toledo* (wc)
85. *Madonna of the North End, Boston* (wc)
86. *Malcolm Street, Boston* (wc)
87. *Acorn Street, Boston* (wc)
88. *Old House, Newburgh* (wc)
89. *Coytesville* (wc)
90. *On the Palisades* (wc)
and 59 etchings

Nov. 20–Dec. 2, Tilden-Thurber Co., Providence, The Ten.
A Serene Grotto

Nov., Memorial Art Gallery, Rochester, *An Exh. of Paintings, Pastels, and Etchings by Childe Hassam.*
27–41 (wcs), 42–54 (ps)
1. *Portrait of a Young Girl*
2. *In the Shadow of the Vine*
3. *The Ancient Window of Nemours*
4. *California Hills in Spring*
5. *Spring Morning in California*
6. *Young Woman Reading a Letter*
7. *Portrait of a Young Girl by a White Mantel*
8. *Portrait of a Young Woman with a Violet*
9. *The Christmas Basket*
10. *The Bridge at Grez*
11. *Summer Idyl*
12. *At Breakfast*
13. *14th of July*
15. *The Eucalyptus Trees in Bloom, California*
16. *The Little Piano*
17. *The Jonquils*
18. *The Beryl Gorge*
19. *Janet*
20. *Spring Afternoon in the California Hills*
21. *Plaza de la Merced, Ronda*
22. *Virginia*
23. *Sunlight on an Old House*
24. *The Butterfly*
25. *The Water Lily*
26. *The Model Disrobing*
27. *St. Michael's—Lannion*
28. *Broadstairs, England*
29. *The Fisherman on the Marne*
30. *Mount Hood*
31. *Broadstairs*
32. *Skull Springs, Harney Desert*
33. *The Squall, Gloucester*
34. *The Convent*
35. *Weir's Garden*
36. *The Hickory Nut Tree*
37. *The Shoals Garden*
38. *Gloucester Street*
39. *Rain, Mist, and Electric Light*
40. *The Chalk Cliffs of England*
41. *Drawing for "Thelassa [sic]"*
42. *Happy Valley, Idaho*
43. *The Back of an Old House*
44. *Brélévénez*
45. *Old Houses in Haarlem*
46. *La Clarté*
47. *Street in Haarlem*
48. *Brélévénez, 2nd*
49. *The Old House with Elms*
50. *The Shrimp Fishers*
51. *The Old House, September*
52. *Salt Marsh Haymakers*
53. *The Old Brush House and Store, Cos Cob*
54. *The Groot Haus, Haarlem*

Dec. 16–Jan. 14, 1917, NAD, *Winter Exh.*
201. *The Northeast Headland*
298. *The South Window*

Dec. 17–Jan. 21, 1917, Corcoran, *6th Exh. Oil Paintings by Contemporary American Artists.*
46. *The Old Elm*
67. *Moonrise at Sunset—the Laurel*
85. *Against the Light*
92. *Young Woman Standing by a Cheval Glass*

PSAG, *Exh. of American Art.*
26. *Early Spring*
77. *North East Gorge, Isles of Shoals*

1917

Jan. 4–20, Montross, *Exh. of Pictures by Childe Hassam.*
1. *The Goldfish Window*
2. *The Old House at East Hampton, L.I.*
3. *The Spanish Stairs*
4. *The Opal*
5. *The Stone Cottage, Old Lyme*
6. *The 17th of October*
7. *Ponte Vecchio*
8. *The 4th of July—Fifth Avenue*
9. *The 4th of July—2d*
10. *Posilippo*
11. *Florence*
12. *The "Home Sweet Home" Cottage East Hampton, L.I.*
13. *Nude Woman with Sandals*
14. *Morning in May, 1916*
15. *The 14th of July, Paris, 1889*
16. *The 14th of July, Montmartre*
"Harney Desert Group"
17. *Cloud Shadows—Harney Desert*
18. *Sage Brush and Willows*
19. *The Rainbow in the Desert*
20. *Malheur Butte*
21. *Desert Clouds*
"Group of Small Panels"
22. *Mrs. Holly of Cos Cob*
23. *The A-1 News Depot, Cos Cob*
24. *The Fireplace*
25. *The Fireplace—2d*
26. *The Fireplace—3d*
27. *The Butterfly*
"Pastels"
28. *Colonial Gravestones at Lexington*
29. *The Concord Meadows*
30. *The Star*
31. *The Island Garden*
32. *The Old Bridge at Cos Cob*
33. *The Birches*
"Water Colors"
34–81 (wcs)
34. *The Plains of France*
35. *The Lieutenant River, Old Lyme*
36. *The Seven-branched Cherry Tree*
37. *The 4th of July—Fifth Avenue*
38. *The Art Institute, Chicago*
39. *Michigan Avenue and Dearborn, Chicago*
40. *Sunset, Old Lyme*
41. *The Garden, Appledore*
42. *Moonlight, Old Lyme*
43. *Appledore Reef*
44. *Douglas Firs—Oregon*
"Hudson River Set"
45. *Old Dutch Church, Fishkill Village*
46. *Storm King*
47. *Early Morning Above Newburgh*
48. *Scarface*
49. *Bull Hill and Breakneck*
50. *At Sunset Above Newburgh*
51. *Mt. Beacon from Broadway, Newburgh*
52. *The Loom of Storm King*
53. *Newburgh Elms on the Steep Street*
54. *Storm King in the Afternoon*
55. *Noon Above Newburgh*
56. *Yonkers from the Palisades*
57. *Old House on the Hudson*
58. *Sunset from Fishkill Landing*
59. *Fishkill Landing*
60. *Sunset, Little Hill*
61. *Upper Manhattan from Fort Lee*
62. *Tows on the River*
63. *The Top of the Town from Coytesville*
"Cos Cob Set"
64. *Back of the Old House*
65. *The Mirror*
66. *The Boboli Gardens, Cos Cob*
67. *The Kitchen Door*
68. *The Red Store*
69. *The Weather Side of an Old House*
70. *The Brush House*
71. *Casa Eby, Cos Cob*
72. *The Dock at Noon*
"Boston and Portsmouth Set"
73. *Boston from Beacon Hill*
74. *The State House Dome*
75. *Mt. Vernon Street*
76. *Castle Island, Boston Harbor*
77. *Portsmouth Stoop*
78. *The White Fence*
79. *Street in Portsmouth*
80. *Doorway of the Warner House*
81. *Court Street, Portsmouth*

Jan. 5–28, AIC, *Exh. of Paintings, Water Colors, Pastels and Etchings by Childe Hassam.*
29–55 (wcs), 56–68 (ps)
1. *Portrait of a Young Girl*
2. *In the Shadow of the Vine*
3. *The Ancient Window of Nemours*
4. *California Hills in Spring*
5. *Spring Morning in California*
6. *Young Woman Reading a Letter*
7. *Portrait. Young Girl by a White Mantel*
8. *Portrait. Young Woman with a Violet*
9. *The Christmas Basket*
10. *The Bridge at Grez*
11. *Summer Idyl*
12. *At Breakfast*
13. *Fourteenth of July*
14. *Point Lobos, Monterey*
15. *The Eucalyptus Trees in Bloom, California*
16. *The Little Piano*
17. *The Jonquils*
18. *The Beryl Gorge*
19. *Janet*
20. *Spring Afternoon in the California Hills*
21. *Plaza de la Merced, Ronda*
22. *Virginia*
23. *Sunlight on an Old House*
24. *The Butterfly*
25. *The Water Lily*
26. *The Model Disrobing*
27. *A Town in France*
28. *The Val-de-Grâce, Paris*
29. *St. Michael's, Lannion*
30. *Broadstairs, England*
31. *The Fisherman of the Marne*
32. *Mount Hood*
33. *Broadstairs*
34. *Skull Springs, Harney Desert*
35. *The Squall, Gloucester*
36. *The Convent*
37. *Weir's Garden*
38. *The Hickory Nut Tree*
39. *The Shoal's Garden*
40. *Gloucester Street*
41. *Rain, Mist and Electric Light*
42. *The Chalk Cliff of England*
43. *Drawing for "Thelassa [sic]"*
44. *The Dark Pool*
45. *Appledore*
46. *Diamond Cove*
47. *Appledore*
48. *Sunday Morning, Appledore*
49. *Church, Star Island*
50. *Autumn*
51. *Buttermilk Falls*
52. *Lyman's Pool*
53. *East Headland*
54. *The Gorge*
55. *Babb's Cove*
56. *Happy Valley, Idaho*
57. *The Back of an Old House*
58. *Brélévénez*
59. *Old Houses in Haarlem*
60. *La Clarté*
61. *Street in Haarlem*
62. *Brélévénez II*
63. *The Old House with Elms*
64. *The Shrimp Fishers*
65. *The Old House, September*
66. *Salt Marsh Haymakers*
67. *The Old Brush House and Store, Cos Cob*
68. *The Groot Haus, Haarlem*

Jan. 5–Feb. 4, *JHAI, 32nd Annual Exh. of Paintings and Bronzes at JHAI, Art Association of Indianapolis.*
28. *The rocky shore of New England*

Jan. 8–22, Albert Roullier Art Galleries, Chicago, *Exh. of Etchings and Drawings by Childe Hassam.*
1–54 (etchings), 55–66 (ds)
55. *Elms in May*
56. *Church Doorway, Snow*
57. *The Organ Grinder*
58. *Madonna of the North End, Boston*
59. *A Figure Study*
60. *The Steps*
61. *Toledo*
62. *Portal, Toledo*
63. *Portsmouth, Doorway*
64. *Seville*
65. *Malheur Desert*
66. *Swimmer, Morning*

By Jan. 15–Feb. 5, Macbeth, "Thirty pictures by thirty painters" [*NYT*, 1/21/1917, p. SM7].
depiction of Bailey's Beach

Jan. 28–Feb. 25, WAM, *Water-colors by Childe Hassam.*
9 wcs

Jan. 29–Feb. 12, Mrs. H.P. Whitney's Studio, *3rd Exh. of Portraits.*
2. *Oscar Laighton*

Jan., Dayton Gallery, Washington, D.C., *Exh. of Etchings by Childe Hassam.*

Feb. 1–24, AWCS, *50th Annual Exh. of AWCS.*
(all wcs)
119. *Old House—Lannion*
120. *Rainy Day, 5th Avenue and Central Park*
121. *The Letter Box, East Gloucester*
122. *Balconies and Roofs, Madrid*
123. *Ticonderoga*
124. *Old Fifth Avenue, 1898*

Feb. 1–28, Women's University Club, *Paintings and Etchings by Childe Hassam.*

Feb. 2–15, Corcoran, *21st Annual Exh. of the Washington Water Color Club.*
(all wcs)
149. *Café in Toledo*
178. *The Alhambra*
182. *Spring Maples*
284. *The Almond Tree*
286. *Washington's Birthday, 5th Ave. and 23rd St. N. Y.*
288. *Church Doorway, Snow*

Feb. 4–Mar. 25, PAFA, *112th Annual Exh.*
267. *South Window*
286. *Moonrise at Sunset*
344. *Young Woman Standing by a Cheval Glass*
415. *Against the Light*
438. *Northeast Headland*

Feb. 15–Mar. 3, Knoedler, *Exh. of American Painters.*
19. *Venetian Glass*

Feb., Copley Hall, Boston, *Watercolors by Childe Hassam.*

Mar. 1–15, Ferargil Galleries, *Intimate Studies by great American artists, chiefly from the studios of Childe Hassam, William L. Lathrop, Emil Carlsen, J. Francis Murphy.*

Mar. 4–30, Brooks Memorial Art Gallery, Memphis, *Loan Exh. and Local Artist Exhibit.*
23. *Landscape,* collection of Mrs. Justina Alcorn Swift

Mar. 6–24, Montross, *20th Annual Exh., Ten American Painters.*
13. *The Window with Skyscrapers*
14. *Kitty Hughes*
15. *The 57th Street Window*
16. *Side Street, Provincetown*
17. *Fifth Avenue February, 1917*
18. *Sunset, Isles of Shoals* (wc)
19. *Place de la Trinité, Paris* (wc)
20. *The Harness-maker's Shop,* London (wc)
21. *Broadstairs—Under the Cliffs* (wc)
22. *Doorway of Warner House, Portsmouth* (d)

Mar. 17–Apr. 22, NAD, *92nd Annual Exh.*
4. *Fifth Avenue: Fourth of July*
5. *Dawn*

Mar. 27–Apr. 14, Montross, *Special Exh., Important Works by American Artists.*
8. *New England Peaches and Grapes*
9. *The Cliffs at Forty Steps, Newport*
10. *Spire of Antwerp Cathedral* (wc)

Mar., Peabody Gallery, Baltimore, *21st Annual Exh., Baltimore Water Color Club.*

Apr. 9–20, SB, *Ten American Painters, 20th Annual Exh.*
5. *Side Street, Provincetown*
10. *The 57th St. Window*
13. *The Window with Skyscrapers*
21. *Fifth Avenue—February 1917*
26. *The Harness Maker's Shop, Lannion*
27. *Broadstairs—Under the Cliffs*
28. *Sunset—Isles of Shoals*
29. *Place de la Trinité, Paris*
30. *Doorway of Warner House, Portsmouth*

Apr. 9–May 30, DMA, *3rd Annual Exh. of Selected Paintings by American Artists.*
56. *The Trap-dyke Gorge*
57. *The 17th of October*

Apr. 10–May 6, SAA, Grand Central Palace, *1st Annual Exh. of Society of Independent Artists.*
41. *Diana's Pool, Appledore*
42. *The County Fair, Still Life*

Apr. 17–May 5, Montross, *Exh. of Pictures by Modern American Masters.*
8. *At the Piano*
9. *The Gorge—Appledore*
10. *Peonies*

From May 6, CAMSL, *Paintings, Water Colors, Pastels and Etchings by Childe Hassam, N. A.*
32–64 (wcs), 65–79 (ps)
1. *Portrait of a Young Girl*
2. *In the Shadow of the Vine*
3. *The Ancient Window of Nemours*
4. *California Hills in Spring*
5. *Spring Morning in California*
6. *Portrait: Young Girl by a White Mantel*
7. *Portrait: Young Woman With Violet*
8. *The Christmas Basket*
9. *The Bridge at Grez*
10. *Summer Idyl*
11. *At Breakfast*
12. *Fourteenth of July*
13. *Point Lobos, Monterey*
14. *The Eucalyptus Trees in Bloom, California*
15. *The Little Piano*
16. *The Jonquils*
17. *The Beryl Gorge*
18. *Janet*
19. *Spring Afternoon in the California Hills*
20. *Plaza de la Merced, Ronda*
21. *Virginia*
22. *Sunlight on an Old House*
23. *The Butterfly*
24. *The Water Lily*
25. *The Model Disrobing*
26. *A Town in France*
27. *Aphrodite*
28. *The West Indian Girl*
29. *Telegraph Hill*
30. *Strawberry Tea Set*
31. *Terre Cuite Tea Set*
32. *St. Michael's, Lannion*
33. *Broadstairs, England*
34. *The Fisherman on the Marne*
35. *Mount Hood*
36. *Broadstairs*
37. *Skull Springs, Harney Desert*
38. *The Squall, Gloucester*
39. *The Convent*
40. *Weir's Garden*
41. *The Hickory Nut Tree*
42. *The Shoal's Garden*
43. *Gloucester Street*
44. *Rain, Mist and Electric Light*
45. *The Chalk Cliffs of England*
46. *Drawing for "Thalassa"*
47. *The Dark Pool*
48. *Appledore*
49. *Diamond Cove*
50. *Appledore*
51. *Sunday Morning, Appledore*
52. *Church, Star Island*
53. *Autumn*
54. *Buttermilk Falls*
55. *Lyman's Pool*
56. *East Headland*
57. *The Gorge*
58. *Babb's Cove*
59. *The Dance*
60. *The River*
61. *New Fields, N. H.*
62. *Isle of Shoals*
63. *The Quais Lannion*
64. *The Fete of Lannion*
65. *Happy Valley, Idaho*
66. *The Back of an Old House*
67. *Brélévénez*
68. *The Old House With Elms*
69. *The Shrimp Fishers*
70. *Old Houses in Haarlem*
71. *La Carte*
72. *Street in Haarlem*
73. *Brélévénez II*
74. *The Old House, September*
75. *Salt Marsh Haymakers*
76. *The Old Brush House and Store, Cos Cob*
77. *The Groot Haus, Haarlem*
78. *Thalassa*
79. *Old Dutch Church*
80–139 etchings

May 12–Sept. 17, BFAA, *11th Annual Exh. of Selected Paintings by American Artists.*
65. *The South Window*
66. *Against the Light*
67. *Moonrise at Sunset*
68. *Young Woman Standing at a Cheval Glass*

By May 13–June 1, Milch, Group Exh. of American paintings [*NYT,* 5/13/1917, p. SM8].
Nymph in the Woods

May 26–July 31, CAM, *24th Annual Exh. of American Art.*
(all wcs)
57. *Old House on the Hudson*
58. *Sunset from Fishkill Landing*
59. *Bull Hill and Breakneck*
60. *Sunset above Newburgh*
61. *Casa Eby, Cos Cob*
62. *Storm King*
63. *The Plains of France*
64. *Fishkill Landing*

Summer, Brooks Memorial Art Gallery, Memphis, *Summer Exh., 1st Anniversary Opening of 1st Exh., Memphis Art Association.*
146. *Rainy Day*

Summer, Knoedler, *10th Annual Summer Exh. of Paintings by American Artists.*
15. *The Allied Flags*

Summer, Macbeth, *Summer Exh.*
31. *Moonlight*
32. *The South-west Wind*

Aug. 15–28, Mystic Art Association, Mystic, Conn., *4th Annual Exh. of Oil Paintings* [*NYT,* 8/12/1917, p. SM7].

Sept. 23–Oct. 28, CAMSL, *12th Annual Exh. of Paintings by American Artists.*
99. *Northeast Headland*

Oct. 3–24, RISD, *Autumn Exh.*
17. *February, 1917,* lent by Montross

Oct., Macbeth, *Opening Exh. of our 2nd Quarter-Century.*
11. *Old House at East Hampton*

Nov. 4–Dec. 9, PAFA, *15th Annual Philadelphia Water Color Exh., and 16th Annual Exh. of Miniatures.*
(all wcs)
129. *Portsmouth Stoop*
612. *Boston: From Beacon Hill*
614. *Scarface*
615. *The Top of the Town from Coyotesville [sic]*
616. *Doorway of the Warner House*
617. *Appledore Reef*
618. *Storm King in the Afternoon*
619. *Tows on the River*
620. *The Dock at Noon*

Nov. 8–Jan. 2, 1918, AIC, *30th Annual Exh. of American Oil Paintings and Sculpture.*
95. *The Goldfish Window*
96. *The South Window*

Nov. 17–Dec. 5, Corcoran, *22nd Annual Exh. of Washington Water Color Club.*
(all wcs)
135. *Long Island Landscape*
136. *Three Hickories*
137. *Chimneys, Portsmouth*
178. *East Hampton*

By Dec. 14, Montross, *Water Color Exh.* [*NYT,* 12/14/1917, p. 12].
Fifth Avenue – April Morning (wc)

Dec. 15– Jan. 13, 1918, NAD, *Winter Exh.*
190. *Winter: Union Square*
222. *Looking Into the Little South Room*

Dec., Philadelphia Art Alliance, *Group of Works of Childe Hassam.*

1918

Jan. 2–Feb. 2, Bourgeois Galleries, *Modern Paintings, Drawings, &c. For the Benefit of the American War Relief.*
5. *Shoveling Snow—New England*
55. *The Dark Pool* (wc)

Jan. 10–12, ULCNY, *Exh. of Paintings By American Artists from the Collection of C. Lansing Baldwin, Esq.*
20. *Little Old Shops, New York City*
21. *Rocks, Isles of Shoals*

Jan. 15–Feb. 12, Fort Worth Museum of Art, *9th Annual Exh. of Selected Paintings by American Artists.*
16. *Brooklyn Bridge, Winter*

Feb. 3–27, WAM, *Exh. of Water Colors Arranged by American Federation of Arts.*
42. *Isles of Shoals* (wc)

Feb. 3–Mar. 24, PAFA, *113th Annual Exh.*
383. *Flags at the Waldorf, 1917*
384. *Paris: July 14th, 1889*
385. *The Willow Pool*
387. *Fifth Avenue Flags, 1916*
390. *Montmartre: July 14, 1889*
424. *The Sweeper*

By Mar. 12, Macbeth, *Thirty Paintings by Thirty Artists* [*NYT,* 3/12/1918, p. 12].
New Haven Green

Mar. 13–Apr. 21, NAD, *93rd Annual Exh.*
282. *Allies Day, May 1917,* 2nd Altman prize

Apr. 9–May 30, DMA, *4th Annual Exh. of Selected Paintings by American Artists.*
122. *Spring in France*
123. *The Venetian Glass*
124. *In a French Garden*
125. *Improvisation*
126. *Old House at Easthampton*
127. *The Enchanted Hour*
128. *Old Bridge at Grez*
129. *The Rainbow in the Desert*

Apr. 18–May 4, Montross, *Special Exh.*
5. *Paris, 14th July, 1889*
6. *Flags at the Waldorf, 1917*
7. *Fifth Avenue Flags*
8. *Fifth Avenue, February 1917*
9. *Three Flags*

Apr. 25–June 25, CI, *Founder's Day Exh., Private Collection of Mr. W. S. Stimmel, Paintings by Modern American and Foreign Painters.*
35. *The Grapevine*
36. *The Messenger Boy*

May 11–Sept. 9, BFAA, *12th Annual Exh. of Selected Paintings by American Artists.*

39. *Ponte Vecchio*
40. *Allies' [sic] Day*
41. *June*

By June 16, Macbeth, "Exhibition of war pictures" [*NYT*, 6/16/1918, p. 65].
The Flags of the Allies

July 1–Sept. 9, Museum of History, Science and Art, Los Angeles, *Summer Exh. of Paintings.*
24. *Landscape*, lent by Mrs. James Erwin

Aug. 15–Sept. 5, Gallery-on-the-Moors, East Gloucester, Mass., *3rd Annual Exh. of Paintings, Sculpture and Drawings.*
7 lithographs

Aug., Mystic, Conn..
Allied Flags

Sept. 15–Oct. 28, CAMSL, *13th Annual Exh. of Paintings by American Artists.*
31. *Allies Day*

Sept. 28–Nov. 3, Montclair Art Museum, N.J., *Exh. of Sketches.*
media not specified
57. *Seattle Harbor*
58. *Bridge at Grez*
59. *Barns at Grez*
60. *October, 1917*

Oct. 18–Dec. 9, CI, *27th Annual International Exh. of Paintings.*
101. *The Nine Muses, Indian Corn in Flower*
102. *Long Island Poppy Garden*
103. *Goldenrod, Montauk*
104. *Trees of Heaven*
105. *Lilac and Laburnum*

Nov. 7–Jan. 1, 1919, AIC, *31st Annual Exh. of American Oil Paintings and Sculpture.*
97. *Allies Day, May 1917*

Nov. 10–Dec. 15, PAFA, *16th Annual Philadelphia Water Color Exh., and 17th Annual Exh. of Miniatures.*
(all wcs)
414. *Mt. Beacon: from Broadway, Newburgh*
550. *Newburgh Elms on the Steep Street*
557. *Bull Hill and Breakneck*
569. *Casa Eby, Cos Cob*
573. *Noon Above Newburgh*

Nov. 15–Dec. 7, DRG, *Exh. of a Series of Paintings of the "Avenue of the Allies" by Childe Hassam.*
1. *Avenue of the Allies—France, 1918*
2. *Avenue of the Allies—Great Britain, 1918*
3. *Avenue of the Allies, 1918*
4. *Avenue of the Allies, 1918*
5. *Avenue of the Allies—Brazil, Belgium, 1918*
6. *Italian Day—May, 1918*
7. *Red Cross Drive—May, 1918*
8. *Lincoln's Birthday—1918*
9. *Flags on Fifty-seventh Street—The Winter of 1918*
10. *The Flag—Fifth Avenue—across Central Park at Fifty-ninth Street, 1918*
11. *The Union Jack, April Morning, 1918*
12. *Across the Avenue in Sunlight, June, 1918*
13. *The Flag Outside Her Window, April, 1918*
14. *March, 1917*
15. *Up the Avenue from Thirty-fourth Street, May, 1917*
16. *Afternoon on the Avenue, 1917*
17. *Early Morning on the Avenue in May, 1917*
18. *The New York Bouquet—West Forty-second Street, 1917*
19. *The High Balcony, 1917*
20. *The Avenue in the Rain, 1916*
21. *Just off the Avenue, Fifty-third Street, May 1916*
22. *Flags on the Waldorf, 1916*
23. *The Fourth of July, 1916*
24. *Self-Portrait*

Nov. 22–Dec. 29, Minneapolis Institute of Arts, *Exh. of Paintings by French, Dutch and English Artists, and by Contemporary American Artists From the Galleries of R.C. and N.M. Vose, Boston.*
64. *The Music Room*

Dec. 9–24, American Art Galleries, *Allied War Salon.*
257. *Early Morning on Fifth Avenue, May, 1917*
257A. *Flags of the Allies*

Dec. 11–Jan. 12, 1919, NAD, *Winter Exh.*
161. *To the 101st Massachusetts Infantry*
258. *Tanagra: The Builders, New York*

Dec. 18–Jan. 16, 1919, Milch, *Annual Holiday Exh. of Selected Paintings of Limited Size by American Artists.*
27. *Thousand Houses, Gloucester*
28. *Flags at the Waldorf, New York*
29. *Notre Dame, Paris*
30. *Le Pont Neuf, Paris*

Dec., Macbeth, *2nd Exh. of "Intimate Paintings."*
34. *Hawk's Nest, Old Lyme*
35. *A Head*
36. *Old House at Newfields*
37. *Beach in France*
38. *Street Musicians*

Brooks Memorial Art Gallery, Memphis, *Exh. of Water Colors from New York, Philadelphia and Washington Water Color Clubs.*
162. *Isles of Shoals* (wc)

Macbeth
6. *Goldfish Window*
7. *Highland Light, Cape Cod*
8. *Madison Square*, 1890
9. *Pont Royal and Louvre*
10. *Winter Morning, Broadway and 72nd Street*

1919

Jan. 1–Feb. 12, DMA, *Exh. of Watercolors by American Artists.*
(all wcs)
25. *The Mirror, Cos Cob*
26. *The Boboli Gardens, Cos Cob*
27. *At Sunset Above Newburgh*
28. *Portsmouth Stoop*
29. *Boston from Beacon Hill*
30. *Back of the Old House*
31. *Fishkill Landing*
32. *Storm King*
33. *Doorway of the Warner House*
34. *Sunset from Fishkill Landing*
35. *The Lieutenant River, Old Lyme*
36. *Scarface*

Jan. 19–Mar. 2, JHAI, *34th Annual Exh. of Paintings and Sculpture of Art Association of Indianapolis, Indiana, at JHAI.*
120. *Allies Day, May, 1917*

Feb. 6–28, AWCS, *52nd Annual Exh. of AWCS.*
(all wcs)
146. *Elms on the Steep Street, Newburgh*
147. *Bull Hill and Breakneck*
148. *Casa Ely [sic], Cos Cob*
149. *Mt. Beacon from Broadway, Newburgh*, Hudnut Prize
150. *Old House on the Hudson*
151. *The Kitchen Door*

Feb. 6–27, Corcoran, *Exh. of Pictures by Ten American Painters.*
14. *The Little River, June*
15. *The West Indian Girl*
16. *Rock Weed Pools, Appleton*
17. *The Allied Flags*

Feb. 9–Mar. 30, PAFA, *114th Annual Exh.*
196. *Tanagra*
240. *Venetian Glass*
260. *Self Portrait*

Feb. 15–Apr. 1, CI, *Exh. of Paintings of the Flags of All Nations and of the Avenue of the Allies by Childe Hassam.*
1. *March, 1917*
2. *Afternoon on the Avenue*
3. *Italian Day, May, 1918*
4. *The Avenue in the Rain, 1916*
5. *The High Balcony, 1917*
6. *Up the Avenue from Thirty-fourth Street, May, 1917*
7. *Flags on Fifty-seventh Street, the Winter of 1918*
8. *Red Cross Drive, May, 1918*
9. *Avenue of the Allies, France, 1918. The Czecho-Slovak Flag in the Foreground—Greek Beyond*
10. *Just off the Avenue, Forty-third Street, May, 1916*
11. *The Union Jack, April Morning, 1918*
12. *Across the Avenue. In Sunlight, June, 1918*
13. *Avenue of the Allies, 1918. Haitian, Guatemalian [sic], Greek. French beyond.*
14. *The Flag—Fifth Avenue across Central Park at Fifty-ninth Street. 1918*
15. *Avenue of the Allies, 1918. Allied Flags in front of St. Patrick's Cathedral. Service Flag on the Union Club. Chinese, British, Belgian beyond.*
16. *Lincoln's Birthday, 1918. The Flag of the City of New York above*
17. *Avenue of the Allies, Great Britain, 1918. The Flags of the Colonies, Canada and Anzac, Brazilian, Belgian beyond*
18. *Avenue of the Allies. Brazilian, Belgian, 1918.*
19. *The New York Bouquet, West Forty-second Street, 1917*
20. *The Fourth of July, 1916. The Greatest Display of the American Flag Ever Seen in New York. Climax of the Preparedness Parade, in May*
21. *The Flag outside her Window, April, 1918*
22. *Flags on the Waldorf, 1916*

By Feb. 19, Macbeth, *Thirty Paintings by Fifteen Painters* [*NYT*, 2/19/1919, p. 12].
13. *Pont Royal*, 1897

Mar. 20–Apr. 21, PAA, *An Exh. of Portraits Lent by Residents of Portland.*
23. *Portrait*, lent by Mrs. C. E. S. Wood
24. *Portrait*, lent by Mrs. Henry L. Corbett

Mar. 22–Apr. 27, NAD, *94th Annual Exh.*
161. *The Alders*
163. *October in New England*

Apr. 8–30, Milch, *Special Exh. of Paintings by Leading American Artists.*
11. *Tea in a French Garden*

Apr. 16–May 31, DMA, *5th Annual Exh. of Selected Paintings by American Artists.*
80. *Surf and Rocks*
86. *Rockwood Pool*

May 15–June 15, AIC, *31st Annual Exh. of Water-Colors, Pastels and Miniatures by American Artists.*
(all wcs)
306. *The Mirror, Cos Cob*
307. *The Boboli Gardens, Cos Cob*
308. *At Sunset above Newburgh*
309. *Portsmouth Stoop*
310. *Boston from Beacon Hill*
311. *Back of the Old House*
312. *Fishkill Landing*
313. *Storm King*
314. *Doorway of the Warner House*
315. *Sunset from Fishkill Landing*
316. *The Lieutenant River, Old Lyme*
317. *Scarface*

May 18–Oct. 19, Bruce Museum, Greenwich, Conn., *Greenwich Society of Artists Exh. of Painting, Sculpture and Arts and Crafts.*
22. *Spanish Ledges*

May 20–June, Milch, *New York Street Scenes and Flag Pictures by Childe Hassam* [*NYT*, 5/18/1919, p. 40; 5/25/1919, p. 38; 6/1/1919, p. 36; 6/15/1919, p. 39].
3. *Flags on the Waldorf*
8. *Red Cross Drive—May 1918*

May 24–July 31, CAM, *26th Annual Exh. of American Art.*
136. *Spring Landscape*
137. *Autumn in Connecticut*
138. *St. Patrick's Day*
139. *The New Flag*

May 24–Sept. 8, BFAA, *13th Annual Exh. of Selected Paintings by American Artists and a Group of Small Selected Bronzes by American Sculptors.*
48. *The East Indian Girl*
49. *The Allied Flags*
50. *The Little River—June*

May, Macbeth, *Comparative Exh.*
18. *La Val de Grâce*. 1888
19. *Washington Arch*. 1898, lent
20. *New York Landscape*. 1918

May, Macbeth, *Thirty Paintings by Thirty Arists.*
14. *Calvary Church—New York*

ca. June 22–Aug. 3, 1919, Milwaukee Art Institute, *Watercolors by Gifford Beal, Paul Dougherty, Childe Hassam, Hayley Lever, J. Alden Weir, and Mahonri Young* [*Wisconsin News*, 6/28/1919, n.p, *Sentinel* (Wisconsin), 7/19/1919, n.p].
(all wcs)
Sunset from Fishkill Landing
Back of the Old House
Doorway of the Warmer [sic] House
The Mirror, Cos Cob
The Boboli Gardens, Cos Cob
At Sunset Above Newburgh
Boston from Beacon Hill
Fishkill Landing
Storm King
Scarface
Old Lyme

June–Aug., Toledo Museum of Art, *8th Annual Exh. of Selected Paintings by American Artists.*
32. *Rockwood Pool*
33. *Young Woman with a Rose*

July 1–Sept. 30, Museum of History, Science and Art, Los Angeles, *Summer Exh. of Paintings.*
20. *Landscape*, lent by Mrs. James Erwin

By July 20, Knoedler, *Summer Exh. of Work by American Painters* [*NYT*, 7/20/1919, p. 71].

July 24–Aug. 11, Gallery-on-the-Moors, East Gloucester, Mass., Group Exh.
The Alders
Indian Summer—Colonial Days
and two portraits

Sept. 14–Oct. 28, CAMSL, *14th Annual Exh. of Paintings by American Artists.*
63. *Autumn in Connecticut*
64. *The Cliff at Forty Steps, Newport*

Oct. 27–Nov. 27, Parish House, Church of the Ascension, *Patriotic Street Scenes by Childe Hassam and Verdun Church Relics (Loaned by the French High Commission).*
1. *Flags on Fifty-Seventh Street—Winter*, 1918
2. *April Morning, The Union Jack, 1918*
3. *Flags on the Waldorf*, 1916
4. *Avenue of the Allies, 1918 Allied Flags In Front of Saint Patrick's, Great Britain, Belgian Flag Beyond*
5. *Italian Day—May*, 1918
6. *Lincoln's Birthday—Flag of the City of New York*
7. *Afternoon on the Avenue*, 1917
8. *Red Cross Drive—May*, 1918
9. *Avenue of the Allies, 1918—Haiti, Guatemala, Greece; French Flag Beyond*
10. *Avenue of the Allies—Brazil, Belgium*, 1918
11. *Avenue of the Allies—France, 1918 Czecho-Slovak Flag in Foreground, Greek Beyond*
12. *Across the Avenue in Sunlight, June*, 1918
13. *Fourth of July, 1917—The Climax of the Preparedness Parade in May*
14. *The New York Bouquet*
15. *Just Off the Avenue, Fifty-Third Street—May*, 1916
16. *Avenue of the Allies, Great Britain, 1918—Flags of the Colonies, Canada, Australia, Brazil and Belgium Beyond*
17. *March, 1917*
18. *Flag Outside Her Window, April*, 1918
19. *The Flag—Fifth Avenue, Across Central Park at Fifty-ninth Street*, 1918
20. *The High Balcony*, 1917
21. *Avenue in the Rain*, 1916
22. *Victory Won*

Oct.–Nov., Musée National du Luxembourg, Paris, *Exposition d'Artistes de L'École Américaine, organisée avec the concours d'un Comité Américain et Français.*
131. *Coup d'oeil dans la petite chambre du sud.* Looking into the little south room.

Nov. 3–22, E. Gimpel and Wildenstein, *1st Annual Exh. of the American Painters Sculptors and Gravers.*
57. *Silver Beach Grass*
58. *Boston, Acorn Street in War Time* (wc)
59. *July Leafage*
60. *Summer Morning, Gloucester, 1919*
61. *A Town in France* (p)
62. *The Same Town in France* (p)

Nov. 6–Dec. 10, AIC, *32nd Annual Exh. of American Oil Paintings and Sculpture.*
99. *Nude Woman with Sandals*
100. *The Alders*
101. *The New Model*

Nov. 9–Dec. 14, PAFA, *17th Annual Philadelphia Water Color Exh., and 18th Annual Exh. of Miniatures.*
awarded Philadelphia Water Color Prize (all wcs)
332. *Rockport Quarry Series or "Set"*
324. *Rockport Quarry Set*
326. *Rockport Quarry (Series) "Set"*
328. *Rockport Quarry, Series or "Set"*
330. *Rockport Quarry, Series or "Set," No. 2*

Nov. 10–Dec. 6, Macbeth, *3rd Exh. of "Intimate Paintings."*
36. *Gloucester Church*
37. *Harbor of a Thousand Masts*
38. *Gloucester Street*

Nov. 15–29, Concord Art Association, Concord, Mass., *4th Annual Exh.*
In the Shadow of the Vines
and etchings

Nov. 17–Dec. 6, Milch, *Exh. of Works in the Various Mediums By Childe Hassam.*
"Paintings"
1. *The Marshall [sic] Neil [sic] Rose*
2. *Autumn*, Salon picture 1888
3. *Lilly Thorpe*
4. *Fire Opals*
5. *Kitty Hughes*
6. *The Little Flower Shop*
7. *Oregon Apples*
8. *Seckle and Winter Pears*
9. *The Sea Gull*, 1906
10. *Youth*
11. *Spring Garland*
12. *The West Indian Girl*
13. *Summer Sunlight*, 1892
14. *Bonnie Moore*, 1906
15. *October Woods*
16. *New England Fair*, 1890
17. *Willow Pool*
18. *The Laurel in the Ledges, Appledore*
19. *The Good Harbor Beach*
20. *The Hod Carrier*
21. *The Fishkill Mountains* (group)
Mount Beacon
Mount Beacon Back of Fishkills
Mount Beacon in Spring
"Water Colors, Pastels, Etchings Lithographs and Drawings"
1. *The Graveyard at Lexington, Mass.*
2. *The Marshes at Concord, Mass.*
3. *The Boston Post Road*
4. *The Old House at Cos Cob*
5. *Broadstairs*
6. *The Bridge at Grey [sic]*
7. *Old Barns at Grey [sic]*
8. *Perras [sic] Guirec*
9. *Columbus Circle*
10. *Girl in Red Gown*
11. *Maud*
12. *The Dutch Door*
13. *The White Kimono*
14. *Fifth Avenue—noon*
15. *Fifth Avenue and Twenty-Third Street*
16. *Public Library*
17. *Cos Cob Docks at Low Tide*
18. *The Old House, Cos Cob*
19. *The Far Horizon*
20. *The Almond Tree*
21. *Diana's Pool*
22. *Colonial Church, Gloucester*
23. *Plumb Street, Gloucester*
24. *Haskell Street, Gloucester*
25. *St. Thomas' Church*
26. *Avenue of the Allies*
27. *New York Bouquet*

Nov. 18–27, Dallas Art Association, *1st Annual Exh. of Contemporary International Art.*
34. *Sandy Road, Sunset*
35. *Window in France*

Dec. 2–20, Galleries of Henry Reinhardt and Son, *Exh. of Contemporary American Landscape.*
27. *Dawn*

Dec. 6–Jan. 5, 1920, BFAA, *1st Annual Exh. of Society of American Painters, Sculptors and Gravers.*
29. *Silver Beach Grass*
30. *Boston, Acorn Street in War Time* (wc)
31. *July Leafage*
32. *Summer Morning, Gloucester, 1918*
33. *A Town in France* (p)
34. *The Same Town in France* (p)

Dec. 13–Jan. 11, 1920, NAD, *Winter Exh.*
293. *The New York Winter Window*

Dec. 21–Jan. 25, 1920, Corcoran, *7th Exh. Oil Paintings by Contemporary American Artists.*
94. *Tanagra*
102. *Old House at Easthampton*
106. *Sylvia Jewell*

Dec.–Jan. 28, 1920, College of the City of New York, Exh. of Childe Hassam's flag paintings.

1920

Jan. 10–Feb. 15, BFAA, *Exh. of Important Works by a Number of America's Leading Painters.*
24. *Isles of Shoals*, lent by Minneapolis Institute of Arts, Minneapolis, Minn.
25. *The Caulker*, lent by CAM Association, Cincinnati, Ohio
26. *The Table Garden*, lent by Mrs. Charles H. Larkin
27. *Evening Light*, lent by C. E. S. Wood, Esq., Portland, Ore.
28. *Surf and Rocks*, lent by DMA
29. *Morning Light*, lent by William A. Rogers, Esq., Buffalo, N. Y.
30. *Josephine and Duke*

Jan. 15–25, Detroit Institute of Arts, *Exh. of Society of American Painters, Sculptors, and Engravers.*
29. *Silver Beach Grass*
30. *Boston, Acorn Street in War Time* (wc)
31. *July Leafage*
32. *Summer Morning, Gloucester*, 1918
33. *A Town in France* (p)
34. *The Same Town in France* (p)

Feb. 5–27, AWCS, *53rd Annual Exh. of AWCS.*
(all wcs)
118. *Rockport Quarry, The Docks*
119. *Rockport Quarry, Gray Morning*
120. *Rockport Quarry, The Granite Arch*
121. *Rockport Quarry, The Big Squall*
122. *Rockport Quarry, Afternoon*

Feb. 8–Mar. 28, PAFA, *115th Annual Exh.*
Awarded gold medal of honor for lifetime achievement
209. *The Japanese Iris*
219. *The New York Winter Window*
224. *Sylvia Jewell*

Mar. 9–Apr. 1, AIC, *Exh. by Society of American Painters Sculptors and Gravers.*
29. *Silver Beach Grass*
30. *Boston, Acorn Street in War Time* (wc)
31. *July Leafage*
32. *Summer Morning, Gloucester, 1918*
33. *A Town in France* (p)
34. *The Same Town in France* (p)

Mar. 11–18, PAA, at the Museum of Art, *Loan Exh. of Paintings.*
16. *Moonlight*, lent by Mrs. Helen Ladd Corbett
17. *Portrait*, lent by Mrs. David T. Honeyman
18. *Landscape*, lent by Mrs. Elliot Corbett
19. *Ecola*, lent by Miss Flanders
20. *Sunset*, lent by Miss Crocker
21. *Magnolias*, lent by Mrs. Helen Ladd Corbett
22. untitled (p), lent by Mrs. David T. Honeyman

Mar. 11–Apr. 1, SAA, Waldorf Astoria, *4th Annual Exh. of Society of Independent Artists.*
328. *The New Model*
329. *Midsummer*

Apr. 6–May 9, NAD, *95th Annual Exh.*
265. *Shingling the First Baptist Church: East Gloucester*
266. *Beacon Street: Boston*
267. *Mount Hood and the Valley of the Willamette*

Apr. 20–May 31, Detroit Institute of Arts, *6th Annual Exh. of Selected Paintings by American Artists.*
77. *Table Garden*, lent by Mrs. Charles H. Larkin, Buffalo, NY
78. *Church at Old Lyme*, lent by Albright Art Gallery
79. *New Haven Green*, lent by the Detroit Athletic Club

Apr. 22–May 1, Vose Galleries, Boston, *Exh. of Water Colors by Childe Hassam.*
(all wcs)
1. *Boston from Beacon Hill*
2. *Back of the Old House*
3. *Storm King in the Afternoon (Hudson River Series)*
4. *Old House on the Hudson*
5. *The Big Squall (Rockport Quarry Series)*
6. *The Docks Æ " "*
7. *Afternoon " "*
8. *Grey Morning " "*
9. *The Granite Arch " "*
10. *The Kitchen Door*
11. *Bull Hill and Break Neck*
12. *The Mirror*
13. *Newburgh Elms on the Steep Street (Hudson River Series)*
14. *Earl [sic] Morning above Newburgh " "*
15. *Fishkill Landing " "*
16. *Sunset From Fishkill Landing " "*
17. *A Sunset above Newburgh " "*
18. *Mt. Beacon from Broadway Newburgh " "*
19. *Noon above Newburgh " "*
20. *Scarface " "*
21. *The Weather Side of an Old House*
22. *The Boboli Garden, Cos Cob*
23. *Isle of Shoals, Duck Island*
24. *Doorway of the Warner House*
25. *Newfields, New Hampshire*
26. *Casa Eby, Cos Cob*
27. *Portsmouth Doorway*
28. *Storm King (Hudson River Series)*
29. *The Dock at Noon*
30. *The State House Dome*
31. *The Plains of France*
32. *The Lieutenant River Old Lyme*

Apr. 29 – June 30, 1920, CI, *19th Annual International Exh. of Paintings.*
142. *The New York Winter Window*, award
143. *Tanagra, The Builders, New York*

May 10–June 1, Ferargil Galleries, *Mr. Russell presents selected examples of Four Great American Artists: Carlsen, Hassam, Davies, The Late Julian Alden Weir, P.N.A.*
media not specified
1. *Strawberry Teaset*
2. *Scarlet Tananger*
3. *The Gorge*
4. *Daffodils*
5. *The Dell in Autumn*
6. *Bridge at Old Lyme*

May 29–July 31, CAM, *27th Annual Exh. of American Art.*
9. *Rainbow in the Desert*

May 29–Sept. 7, BFAA, *14th Annual Exh. of Selected Paintings by American*

Artists and a Group of Small Selected Bronzes by American Sculptors.
54. *Japanese Iris*
55. *Sylvia Jewell*
56. *Fire Opals*

By June 13, Milch, "Summer Exh."
[*NYT*, 6/13/20, p. 64].
Beacon Street, Boston

June 24–Sept. 30, Museum of History, Science and Art, Los Angeles, *Summer Exh. of Paintings.*
19. *Connecticut Hills in Winter*, lent by Miss Augusta Senter
20. *Landscape*, lent by Mrs. James Erwin

Summer, Knoedler, *13th Annual Summer Exh. of Paintings by American Artists.*
7. *The New Flag, March 1919*
10. *St. Patrick's Day, March 17, 1919*

Oct. 6–28, RISD, *Autumn Exh.*
9. *Strawberry Tea Set*

Nov. 4–Dec. 12, AIC, *33rd Annual Exh. of American Oil Paintings and Sculpture.*
62. *The New York Winter Window*

Nov. 7–Dec. 12, PAFA, *18th Annual Philadelphia Water Color Exh., and 19th Annual Exh. of Miniatures.*
(all wcs)
406. *New York from the Hudson*
407. *Avenue of the Allies*
408. *Sunset, Constable Hook*
409. *The Same Town in France*
410. *Midsummer*
411. *Acorn Street in Wartime*
412. *The Greek Pageant*
413. *A Town in France*
414. *Newfields, N.H.*
415. *The Avenue*
544. *Madonna of the North End*

Nov. 8–27, E. Gimpel and Wildenstein, *2nd Annual Exh. of New Society of Artists.*
57. *July Night*
58. *Peony Girl*
59. *Central Park 1890*

Nov. 15–27, Milch, *Exh. of Water Colors by Childe Hassam.*
(all wcs)
"Rockport Quarry Set"
1. *The Granite Arch*
2. *Gray Morning*
3. *The Docks*
4. *The Big Squall*
5. *Afternoon*
"Hudson River Set"
6. *Storm King*
7. *Storm King—Afternoon*
8. *Early Morning—Above Newburgh*
9. *Noon—Above Newburgh*
10. *Sunset—Above Newburgh*
11. *Broadway—Newburgh*
12. *Newburgh Elms on Steep Street*
13. *Sunset from Fishkill Landing*
14. *Scar Face*
15. *Old House on the Hudson*
16. *Bull Hill and Break Neck*
"New England Set"
17. *Newfields—New Hampshire*
18. *The Lieutenant River—Lyme, Conn.*
19. *A Portsmouth Stoop*
20. *Doorway of the Warner House*
21. *The Weatherside of an Old House*
22. *The State House Dome*
23. *Boston from the Hill*
24. *Back of the Old House*
25. *The Kitchen Door*
26. *The Boboli Garden—Cos Cob*
27. *The Dock at Noon*
28. *Casa Eby—Cos Cob*
29. *The Mirror*
30. *Isles of Shoals—Duck Island*
31. *Plains of France* [not part of a set]

Nov. 30–Dec. 31, Macbeth, *4th Exh. of "Intimate Paintings."*
38. *Easthampton Street*
39. *Old Lyme Church, Moonlight*

By Dec. 5, Century Club, "Group of Paintings from Phillips Memorial Art Gallery" [*NYT*, 12/5/1920, p. 55].
The Willow Pool

AWCS, London, *53rd Annual Exh.*

BAC, *An Exh. of Painting by the Honorary Members of BAC.*
15. *Kitty Hughes*
16. *Sylvia Jewell*
17. *Boston*

Brooks Memorial Art Gallery, Memphis, *Exh. of Paintings Collected by Macbeth.*
171. *Bouquet of Oaks*

Venice Biennale.
22. *Il passeggio del pomeriggio*
23. *Gli ontani (The Alders)*

1920 or later, Milch, *Important Works in Paintings and Sculpture by Leading American Artists.*
undated catalogue
Gloucester Harbor

1921

Jan. 8–31, 1921, BFAA, *A Collection of Paintings Lent by Messrs. R. C. and N. M. Vose of Boston, Mass.*
31. *The Bowl of Nasturtiums*

Jan. 8–Feb. 6, Art Gallery of Toronto, *Paintings by Contemporary American Artists.*
38. *The New York Winter Window*

Jan. 10–29, Milch, *Exh. of Paintings by George De Forest Brush, Bruce Crane, Thomas E. Dewing, Childe Hassam, Willard L. Metcalf, J. Francis Murphy.*
13. *The Hudson*
14. *Shingling the First Baptist Church, Gloucester*
15. *Montauk*
16. *St. Patrick's Day, 1919*

Feb. 3–24, AWCS, *54th Annual Exh. of AWCS.*
(all wcs)
147. *Casa Eby*
149. *The Mirror*
150. *Sunset from Fishkill Landing*

Feb. 6 Mar. 27, PAFA, *116th Annual Exh.*
79. *The Old Long Island Landscape*
176. *Autumn: Old Lyme*
416. *The Portrait and the Bust*
462. *Early Spring: 'Way Up Town*

Mar. 5 –Apr. 3, NAD, *96th Annual Exh.*
22. *April*
221. *May: Fort George*

By Mar. 12–Apr., Grafton Galleries, London, *Exh. of Contemporary American Art* [*Times* (London), 3/12/ 1921, p. 13].
3. *The Isles of Shoals*
23. *Against the Light*
26. *Afternoon of* [sic] *the Avenue*
89. *The Alders*

By Mar. 27, Powell Galleries, "Group Exh." [*NYT*, 3/27/21, p. X8].

Apr. 7–21, Dallas Art Association, *2nd Annual Exh. American and European Art.*
149. *The Hudson*

Apr. 20–May 31, Detroit Institute of Arts, *7th Annual Exh., Detroit Institute of Arts of City of Detroit.*
55. *The New York Winter Window*

Apr. 28–June 30, CI, *20th Annual International Exh. of Paintings.*
129. *The Play of Light*
130. *The Easthampton Elms in May*, award

By May 1, Ehrich Galleries, *Modern Paintings* [*NYT*, 5/1/1921, p. 85].
The Melting Snow: Fifth Avenue
The South Window

May 6–21, Junior Art Patrons of America at Fine Arts Building, *Retrospective Exh. of American Art.* [*NYT*, 4/24/1921, p. X8].

May 28–July 31, CAM, *28th Annual Exh. of American Art.*
38. *Gloucester Inner Harbor*
39. *"Home, Sweet Home" Cottage*
40. *The South Gorge, Appledore*

June 2–Sept. 6, BFAA, *15th Annual Exh. of Selected Paintings by American Artists, a Group of Small Selected Bronzes by American Sculptors and an Exh. of Early American Portraits.*
54. *Beacon Street*
55. *The Portrait and the Bust*
56. *Autumn, Old Lyme*
57. *April*

June 10–July 10, Cleveland Museum of Art, *1st Exh. of Contemporary American Paintings.*
The Poet's Garden

July 4–30, Galeries Georges Petit, Paris, *Exposition d'un Groupe de Peintres Américains.*
56. *The Alders*—Les Aulnes
57. *Afternoon on the avenue*—L'Après-midi dans l'avenue
58. *Isles of Shoals*—Les Iles de Shoals
59. *Against the light*—A contre-jour

July 22–Sept. 5, Los Angeles Museum of History, Science and Art, *Summer Exh. of Paintings.*
30. *Landscape*, lent by Mrs. James Erwin

Summer, Knoedler, *14th Annual Summer Exh. of Paintings by American Artists.*
21. [no title listed]

Summer, The Metropolitan Museum of Art, Exh. of the Museum collection of watercolors.

By Aug. 21, Milch, Summer Group Exh. [*NYT*, 8/21/1921, p. 38].
Winter, 1900

Sept. 15–Oct. 25, CAMSL, *16th Annual Exh. of Paintings by American Artists.*
44. *April*

Oct. 10–31, Galleries of Junior Art Patrons of America, *Opening Exh. of Junior Art Patrons of America.*
17. *Fishkill Landing*
18. *Café Toledo*
19. *Mount Beacon*
20. *Morning Calm (Appledore)*
21. *Rainy Day*

Oct. 11–30, Macbeth, *Opening Exh., Season of 1921–1922, Group of Selected Paintings.*
7. *Over the Harbor*

Nov. 2–15, Whitney Studio Club, Overseas Exh. of Contemporary American Paintings Shown in Venice, London, and Paris from May 1920–Nov. 1921 [*NYT*, 11/3/1921, p. 19].

Nov. 3–Dec. 11, AIC, *34th Annual Exh. of American Oil Paintings and Sculpture.*
87. *Home Sweet Home Cottage*

Nov. 6–Dec. 11, PAFA, *19th Annual Philadelphia Water Color Exh., and 20th Annual Exh. of Miniatures.*
519. *Land's End* (wc)

Nov. 8–Dec. 18, Brooklyn Museum, *A Group Exh. of Water Color Paintings by American Artists.*
(all wcs)
"Rockport Quarry Set"
96. *The Granite Arch*
97. *Grey Morning*
98. *Afternoon*
99. *The Docks*
100. *The Squall*
101. *The Dock at Noon*

Nov. 15–Dec. 15, Wildenstein and Co., *3rd Annual Exh., New Society of Artists.*
24. *Nude Bathing*
25. *Nude with Red Hair*
26. *Seated Nude*
27. *On the Beach*
28. *Nude Study*
29. *The Surf*
30. *Self Portrait—1898*
and 5 etchings

Nov. 19–Dec. 18, NAD, *Winter Exh.*
156. *Easter Morning: New York Window Series*
272. *The East Headland Pool: Appledore*

Nov.–Dec., New Society of Artists, *3rd Annual Exh.*

Dec. 18–Jan. 22, 1922, Corcoran, *8th Exh. of Oil Paintings by Contemporary American Artists.*
13. *The Play of Light*
154. *The Easthampton Elms in May*

Dec. 31–Jan. 15, 1922, NYWCC and AWCS, American Fine Arts Building, *1st Combined Exh., NYWCC and AWCS.*
(all wcs)
387. *Back of the Old House*
388. *Scarface*
389. *At Sunset Above Newburgh*
390. *Weather Side of an Old House*
391. *Kitchen Door*
392. *Old House on the Hudson*

American Academy of Arts and Letters, *Exh. of the Works of Childe Hassam.*
26. *The Room of Flowers*

Brooks Memorial Art Gallery, Memphis, *Exh., Collected by American Federation of Art.*
107. *Northwest Wind*

1922

Jan. 1–29, JHAI, *37th Annual Exh. of Paintings and Sculpture by American Artists at JHAI.*
22. *April*

Jan. 3–28, Fort Worth Museum of Art, *13th Annual Exh. of Paintings by American Artists, Assembled by the American Federation of Arts Washington, D.C.*
17. *Moonrise at Sunset*

Jan. 6–28, Tiffany Gallery and The Art Centre, Louis Comfort Tiffany Foundation Exh. of the Works of Its Advisory Art Committee [*NYT*, 1/1/1922, p. 72].

By Jan. 15, Division of Home Economics, Kansas State Agricultural College, Manhattan, Kans., "Exh. of Paintings by Contemporary American Artists" [*NYT*, 1/15/1922, p. 77].

Jan. 24–Feb. 13, Macbeth, *Thirty Paintings by Thirty Artists, 12th Annual Exh.*
13. *May, Fort George*

Feb. 5–Mar. 26, PAFA, *117th Annual Exh.*
235. *Fire Opal*

Feb. 7–28, Corcoran, *Exh. of the Series of Flag Pictures by Childe Hassam.*
1. *Avenue in the Rain*, 1916
2. *Avenue of the Allies*, Great Britain, 1918 — Flags of the Colonies, Canada, Australia, Brazil, and Belgium Beyond
3. *Avenue of the Allies — Front of St. Thomas's*
4. *Avenue of the Allies*, 1918, Allied Flags in Front of St. Patrick's, Great Britain, Belgian Flag Beyond
5. *Allied Flags, April*, 1917
6. *Flags on the Waldorf*, 1916
7. *Across the Avenue in Sunlight, June*, 1918
8. *The New York Bouquet*
9. *Just off the Avenue, Fifty-third Street, May*, 1916
10. *Afternoon on the Avenue*, 1917
11. *The High Balcony*, 1917
12. *Italian Day, May*, 1918
13. *Flag Outside Her Window, April*, 1918
14. *Victory Won*
15. *Lincoln's Birthday — Flag of the City of New York*
16. *Red Cross Drive, May*, 1918
17. *Avenue of the Allies*, France, 1918 — Czecho-Slovak Flag in Foreground, Greek Beyond
18. *Fourth of July*, 1917, The greatest display of the American Flag ever seen in New York — Climax of the Preparedness Parade in May
19. *Avenue of the Allies*, 1918, Haiti, Guatemala, Greece, French Flag Beyond

Mar. 25–Apr. 23, NAD, *97th Annual Exh.*
178. *The Winter River*
245. *The Easthampton Elms in May*

Apr. 15–May 21, AIC, *2nd International Water Color Exh.*
(all wcs)
49. *Scarface*
50. *The Kitchen Door*
51. *Back of the Old House*
52. *Weatherside of an Old House*
53. *Old House on the Hudson*
54. *At Sunset above Newburgh*

Apr. 27–June 15, CI, *21st Annual International Exh. of Paintings.*
73. *April*

May 7–Oct. 15, Bruce Museum, Greenwich, Conn., *Greenwich Society of Artists 6th Annual Exh.*
21. *Street in Easthampton*

June 8–July 8, Cleveland Museum of Art, *2nd Exh. of Contemporary American Painting.*
Clearing the Snow

June 18–July 31, CI, *Exh. of Art and Science in Gardens.*
73. *Flower Shop*
74. *Japanese Iris*, lent by Milch

July 8 – Sept. 14, Museum of History, Science and Art, Los Angeles, *Summer Exh.*
13. *Yacht Harbor*, lent by the San Francisco Museum of Art
14. *Landscape*, lent by Mrs. Jas. Erwin

Summer, Knoedler, *15th Annual Summer Exh. of Paintings by American Artists.*
34. *Central Park from the Plaza, December Morning*

Oct. 10–Nov. 5, RISD, *Autumn Exh.*
16. *The Stone Cottage*

Nov. 2–Dec. 10, AIC, *35th Annual Exh. of American Oil Paintings and Sculpture.*
95. *Gloucester, Massachusetts*
96. *Spring, the Dogwood Tree*

Nov. 16–30, Dallas Art Association, *3rd Annual Exh., American Art From the Days of the Colonists to Now.*
90. *Church at Old Lyme*, lent by the Albright Art Gallery
91. *At Easthampton, L. I.*
92. *Skyscraper Window*

Nov. 17–Dec. 17, NAD, *Winter Exh.*
25. *The Sun Room*, Second Altman Prize
49. *The North East Gorge Appledore*

Dec. 20–Jan. 30, 1923, Minneapolis Institute of Arts, *An Exh. of Modern American Paintings from Annual Exh. of AIC*
10. *Spring, The Dogwood Tree*

1923

Jan. 1–28, JHAI, *38th Annual Exh. of Paintings and Sculpture by Contemporary American Artists, at JHAI.*
17. *Gloucester*

Jan. 4–Feb. 5, Fort Worth Museum of Art, *14th Annual Exh. of Paintings by American Artists, Assembled by the American Federation of Arts, Washington, D.C.*
16. *The Fisherman*, lent by Milch

Jan. 18–Feb. 17, CI, *An Exh. of Studies by Well-known Artists.*
168. *Deep Sea Bathers*
169. *Elms in May*
170. *Girl in May*
171. *Portsmouth Doorway*
172. *The Old House, Cos Cob, Connecticut*
173. *Toledo*

Jan. 23–Feb. 12, Macbeth, *Thirty Paintings by Thirty Artists, 13th Annual Exh.*
13. *Listening to the Orchard Oriole*

Jan. 27–Mar. 4, Art Gallery of Toronto, *Paintings by Contemporary American Artists.*
32. *The Shortest Day in the Year*

By Jan. 28, Montross, Special Exh. of Contemporary Art [*NYT*, 1/28/1923, p. X7].
"an early Childe Hassam"

Feb. 4–Mar. 25, PAFA, *118th Annual Exh.*
70. *Portland: Oregon*

Feb. 12–Mar. 3, Milch, *Water Colors, Etchings, Lithographs by Childe Hassam* [*NYT*, 2/11/1923, p. X7; 2/18/1923, p. X7; 2/25/1923, p. X7] .
"small picture of an autumn landscape" [*NYT*, 2/25/1923, p. X7]

Feb. 22–Apr. 1, Baltimore Museum of Art, *Inaugural Exh.*
216. *Loralei [sic]*, lent by Mr. Henry Walters

Mar. 1–30, CAMSL, *International Water Color Exh., selected from 2nd International Water Color Exh. at AIC.*

Mar. 7–24, Frederick Keppel and Co., *Exh. of Etchings and Dry Points by Childe Hassam, National Academician, Member of American Academy of Arts and Letters.*

Mar. 17–Apr. 15, NAD, *98th Annual Exh.*
28. *A Long Island Garden*
249. *Althea*

Mar. 20–Apr. 22, AIC, *3rd International Water Color Exh.*
(all wcs)
118. *End of Timber Line, Mt. Hood*
119. *Looking towards Adams from Mt. Hood*
120. *Cafe in Toledo*
121. *Tows on the River*
122. *Appledore Reef*
123. *Dark Pool*
124. *Sunday Morning, Appledore*
125. *East Headland*
126. *Weir's Garden*
127. *The Gardener*
128. *Bab[b]'s Cove*
129. *Rockport Quarry Set; Afternoon*
130. *Rockport Quarry, No. 4*
131. *Loom of the Storm King*
132. *Old Dutch Church*
133. *Adams and St. Helena, Early Morning*
134. *Top of the Town, Coytesville*
135. *Michigan Avenue and Dearborn Street, Chicago*
136. *Appledore, No. 1*
137. *The Gorge*
138. *Appledore, No. 2*
139. *Diamond Cove*
140. *Isles of the Shoal's Garden*
141. *Cape Ann*
142. *Hickory Nut Tree*
143. *Rockport Quarry Set; Big Squall*
144. *Rockport Quarry Set; the Docks*
145. *Seven-branched Cherry Tree*
146. *Newburgh Elms*
147. *The Red Store*

Apr. 8–June 18, BFAA, *17th Annual Exh. of Selected Paintings and Small Bronzes by American Artists.*
81. *The Marshall [sic] Niel Rose*, lent by Duncan Phillips, Esq., Washington, D.C.

Apr. 11–May 31, Detroit Institute of Arts, *9th Annual Exh.*
49. *Table Garden*

Apr. 16–30, Scott and Fowles, *Water Colors by Childe Hassam* [*NYT*, 4/15/1923, p. X10].
A Street, Boston
Base Rocks
The Cherry Tree
Brick Mansions, Portsmith [sic]
and other unnamed works

Apr. 26–June 17, CI, *22nd Annual International Exh. of Paintings.*
68. *The Sun Room*

By May 6, Milch, Paintings by American Painters [*NYT*, 5/6/1923, p. X8].
Arch[e] de Triomphe

May 6–June 3, Art Association, Concord, Mass., *7th Annual Exh. of Paintings and Sculpture.*
19. *The Church at Gloucester*

May 26–July 31, CAM, *30th Annual Exh. of American Art.*
3. *Caulkers, Inner Harbor, Gloucester*
4. *April*

June 1–Aug. 31, Corcoran, *Paintings, mostly American, lent by Mr. Charles V. Wheeler.*
14. *Gloucester*

By June 17, Macbeth, *Summer Exh.* [*NYT*, 6/17/1923, p. E5].
"a new England town painted by Childe Hassam, stimulating with its clear salt air"

By July 22, Knoedler, *Summer Exh.* [*NYT*, 7/22/1923, p. BR16].
"Childe Hassam paints Central Park West, in 1804, street lamps lighted, horse cabs ambling along, women in huge sleeves and little hats…"

Oct. 13–28, State Fair of Texas, Dallas, *18th Annual Loan Collection of American Paintings.*
53. *Union Square*

Oct. 27–Nov. 30, Corcoran, *28th Annual Exh. of Washington Water Color Club.*
39. *Mt. Beacon, Broadway, Newburgh*

Nov. 4–Dec. 9, PAFA, *21st Annual Philadelphia Water Color Exh., and 22nd Annual Exh. of Miniatures.*
(all wcs)
422. *East Headland*
423. *The Top of the Town from Coyotesville [sic]*
424. *Diamond Cove*
425. *New England Barn*
426. *The Knolls: New Hampshire*
427. *Appledore*
428. *Appledore No. 2*
429. *Tows on the River*

Nov. 4–Apr. 30, 1924, Seconda Biennale Romana: United States Section, Mostra Internazionale di Belle Arti, Rome.

Nov. 14–28, Dallas Art Association, *4th Annual Exh.*
41. *Marine, Isle of Shoals*
42. *Central Park West*

Nov. 17–Dec. 16, NAD, *Winter Exh.*
75. *The Quarry Pool: Cape Ann*
153. *Venetian Brocade*

Dec. 3–29, Milch, *Recent Paintings, Water Colors and Etchings by Childe Hassam, N.A.* [*NYT*, 12/2/1923, pp. SM7; X12].
Little Peconic Bay
Morning
Evening
The Year's [sic] at the Spring
In the Garden
Georgica
and other unnamed works: "[Mr. Hassam] calls them 'Recent Canvases of Long Island,' but for the most part they are panels of heavy wood, not canvas, and two, at least, came from Cape Ann…"

Dec. 16–Jan. 20, 1924, Corcoran, *9th Exh. of Contemporary American Oil Paintings.*
117. *Spring — The Dogwood Tree*
175. *Central Park From the Plaza, December Morning*

Dec. 30–Jan. 19, 1924, Macbeth, *Two Dozen Recent Canvases of Childe Hassam*

1923–24, Macbeth, *Opening Exh., Season 1923–1924.*
12. *Calvary Church*
13. *Little Old Shops*

1924

Feb. 3–Mar. 23, PAFA, *119th Annual Exh.*
293. *The Sun Room*

Feb. 7–25, Macbeth, *Thirty Paintings by Thirty Artists, 14th Annual.*
18. *The Cedar Lot, Old Lyme*

Mar. 3–15, Galleries of Frank K.M. Rehn, *Paintings of Golf Subjects by Childe Hassam.*
1. *The 14th Tee—Virginia*
2. *May on the Maidstone Links*
3. *The Dune Hazard*
4. *The Water Hazard (Virginia and Fran)*
5. *Wainscott Links*
6. *The Sand and Water Trap at the 4th Green—Maidstone Links*
7. *Down the Steps from the Dune Hazard*
8. *The Trap at the 15th*
9. *Great Peconic Bay—The National*
10. *Approach to the Dome Green*
11. *Amagansett Links*

Mar. 22–Apr. 20, NAD, *99th Annual Exh.*
27. *Winter*
349. *The Skyscrapers*
359. *The Mares-Tail Sky*

Mar., Milwaukee Art Institute, *Etchings by Childe Hassam.*

Apr. 20–June 30, BFAA, *18th Annual Exh. of Selected Paintings and Small Bronzes by American Artists.*
106. *The Sun Room*
107. *Listening to the Oriole*

Apr. 24–June 15, CI, *23rd Annual International Exh. of Paintings.*
57. *The Skyscraper Window*

May 24–July 31, CAM, *31st Annual Exh. of American Art.*
1. *Easthampton Street*
2. *Central Park West*

June 13–July 13, Cleveland Museum of Art, *4th Exh. of Contemporary American Paintings. Union Square*

June, Brooklyn Museum of Art, Group Exh. of water colors [*NYT*, 6/15/1924, p. SM12].
"big Maine subjects" by Childe Hassam

Oct. 7–27, Macbeth, *Selected Group of Paintings by Thirty American Artists.*
15. *Little Old Shops*
20. *Summer Afternoon*

Oct. 14–Nov. 9, RISD, *Annual Exh. of Recent American Paintings.*
15. *Little Flower Shop*

Nov. 8–30, Corcoran, *29th Annual Exh. of Washington Water Color Club.*
(wcs)
13. *Diamond Cove, Appledore*
16. *Appledore, Number 2*

Nov. 15–Dec. 7, NAD, *Winter Exh.*
316. *Miss Ingram,* First Altman Prize

From Nov. 15, New York Public Library, Exh. of works representing scenes from the old and new Fifth Avenue, in honor of Centennial Week [*NYT*, 11/15/1924, p. 15].

From Nov. 20, Brooklyn Museum of Art, *Loan Exh. of Brooklyn Art Treasures and Original Drawings by American Artists.*
138. *Still Life*
191. *The Gorge* (wc)

Nov., RISD, *Annual Fall Exh. of Recent American Paintings.*

Nov., State Fair, Dallas, *19th Annual Loan Collection of American Paintings.*

Dec. 12–Jan. 2, 1925, Los Angeles Museum of History Science and Art, *Exh. by Childe Hassam, Joseph Pennell, Maurice Sterne.*
"Original Drawings for Etchings"
1. *Raindrops and Surf*
2. *The Beach, East Hampton*
3. *Home Sweet Home Cottage*
4. *East Hampton*
5. *New York and the Hudson*
6. *The Bather, Morning*
7. *Elms in May*
8. *The Old House*
9. *Fifth Avenue, Noon*
10. *The Steps*

Dec. 30–Jan. 19, 1925, Macbeth, *"Montauk" by Childe Hassam, N. A. of American Academy of Arts and Letters.*
1. *Adam and Eve Walking out on Montauk in Early Spring*
2. *The Dance of the Dryads*
3. *The Grove of Aphrodite, The White Poplars on Great Pond*
4. *The Nine Muses Celebrating the Indian Corn in Flower*
5. *Ariadne and Artemis*
6. *Diana the Huntress Finding Graffiti of Poseidon*
7. *A Montauk Garden in the Age of Pericles*
8. *The Little Altar to Ceres*
9. *The Great Altar to Ceres and the West Wind*
10. *Dance of the Autumn Zephyrs*
11. *A Montauk Villa in the Age of Pericles*
12. *Pomona in the Rose Bower*
13. *The Hours*
14. *The Little Garland for Pan*
15. *Young Apollo and the Flying Swans*
16. *Sunset from the Grove of Nemesis*
17. *The Strange Galley, Old Hook Pond at Sundown*
18. *The Wild Swans, Sacred to Apollo*
19. *Nereid*
20. *Diana as Spring, The Beach Plum and the Dogwood*
21. *Georgica*
22. *The Festival of Poseidon*
23. *Montauk*
24. *Lace of the Goddesses, Queen Ann's Lace or Wild Carrot*
25. *The Blue of the Eyes of the Goddesses, The Wild Chicory*
26. *Grapes for the Great Altar, A Window Frame of Swamp Cedar, out of the Old Church hand hewn by the early English settlers of Easthampton and Montauk*
27. *The Wild Flowers of Montauk by Moonlight*

Late Dec.–Jan. 15, 1925, The Metropolitan Museum of Art, *Drawings Given and Lent by A.E. Gallatin.*

Venice Biennale.
Primavera

1925

Jan. 14–Feb. 2, PAA, at the Museum of Art, *Exh. of Drawings, Lithographs, Etchings and Watercolors by Childe Hassam and Joseph Pennell, Drawings, Paintings and Sculpture by Maurice Sterne.*
"Original Drawings for Etchings"
1. *Raindrops and Surf*
2. *The Beach, East Hampton*
3. *Home Sweet Home Cottage*
4. *East Hampton*
5. *New York and the Hudson*
6. *The Bather, Morning*
7. *Elms in May*
8. *The Old House*
9. *Fifth Avenue, Noon*
10. *The Steps*

Jan. 24–Feb. 5, Art Students League, *50th Birthday Jubilee Exh.*
no checklist in original catalogue

Feb. 7–Mar. 2, Art Gallery of Toronto, *2nd Annual Exh. of Canadian Society of Graphic Art and a Collection of American Paintings.*
4. *Church at Old Lyme*, lent by the Albright Art Gallery, Buffalo, from their permanent collection

Feb. 8–Mar. 29, PAFA, *120th Annual Exh.*
91. *Virginia*

Apr. 1–24, NAD, *100th Annual Exh.*
362. *The Little Altar: Montauk*
399. *Adam & Eve Walking Out on Montauk in Early Spring*

ca. Apr. 12–28, Phillips Memorial Gallery, Washington, D.C., *Paintings by Childe Hassam.*
Bailey's Beach, Newport
Marshall [sic] Neil [sic] Rose
Nude Among the Rocks
Spring—Washington Arch, New York
Washington Square
The Willow Pool
and 6 others

Apr. 19–June 15, BFAA, *19th Annual Exh. of Selected Paintings by American Artists.*
78. *Isle of Shoals*

May 2–July 31, CAM, *32nd Annual Exh. of American Art.*
2. *Grove of Aphrodite*

June 12–July 12, Cleveland Museum of Art, *5th Exh. of Contemporary American Paintings.*
Adam and Eve Walking out on Montauk in Early Spring

Oct. 1–Dec. 6, CI, *24th Annual International Exh. of Paintings.*
309. *Spring in a New York Skyscraper*

Oct. 10–20, Art Department, State Fair of Texas, Dallas, *20th Annual Loan Collection of American Paintings.*
36. *Church of the Paulist Fathers*

Oct. 17–Nov. 15, Corcoran, *Commemorative Exh. by Members of NAD, 1825–1925.*
192. *Arcady*
and 4 etchings

Oct. 29–Dec. 13, AIC, *38th Annual Exh. of American Oil Paintings and Sculpture.*
85. *Adam and Eve on Shelter Island*

Nov. 8–Dec. 13, PAFA, *23rd Annual Philadelphia Water Color Exh. and 24th Annual Exh. of Miniatures.*
154. *Catskill; Grant House* (wc)
155. *West Brookfield, Massachusetts* (wc)
156. *Sunrise; The Knolls, New Hampshire* (no medium indicated)
157. *Old House; East Hampton, Long Island* (wc)
158. *Three Pines* (wc)
159. *Acorn Street; Boston* (no medium indicated)
161. *Mt. Vernon; Boston* (wc)
163. *Street in Belfast; Maine* (wc)
and 12 etchings

Nov. 16–Dec. 1, Dallas Art Association, *5th Annual Exh.*
60. *Easthampton,* lent by Macbeth
61. *Autumn,* lent by Milch

Nov. 27–Feb. 28, 1926, Los Angeles Museum, *1st Pan-American Exh. of Oil Paintings.*
19. *April, 1859,* lent by E. and A. Milch

Dec. 1–Jan. 3, 1926, Grand Central Art Galleries, *Commemorative Exh. by Members of NAD (1825–1925).*

Dec. 8–Jan. 4, 1926, Macbeth, *Exh. of Water Colors by Distinguished American Artists.*
(all wcs)
29. *Madonna of the North End*
30. *Plaza, Seville*
31. *Street in Toledo*

1926

Jan. 25–Feb., DRG, *Exh. of Paintings by Childe Hassam.*
1. *The New York Winter Window*, 1919
2. *Looking into the Little South Room, East Hampton*, 1917
3. *The Portrait and the Bust*, 1920
4. *The Opal*, 1905
5. *The Room of Flowers*, 1894
6. *Against the Light*, 1916
7. *Miss Ingram Reading a Letter*, 1913
8. *The Sun Room*, 1922
9. *Posilippo*, 1897
10. *Naples*, 1897
11. *Vesuvius*, 1897
12. *Phryne*, 1912
13. *Portrait in the Park*, 1890
14. *Portrait Out of Doors, Miss W.*, 1909
15. *Portrait at a New York Window*, 1921
16. *Gloucester*, 1899
17. *Pierce's Stable*, 1900
18. *July Night*, 1898
19. *The Purple Trail (Motor Parkway, Long Island)*, 1925
20. *The Beyrl [sic] Pool*, 1912
21. *The Window at Appledore*, 1910
22. *June 26th, Old Lyme*, 1912
23. *The Flower Shop*, 1893
24. *Pomona in the Rose Bower*, 1919
25. *The Beyrl [sic] Gorge*, 1912
26. *Self Portrait*, 1898

Jan. 26–Feb. 15, Wildenstein Gallery, Exh. of Tri-National Art-French, British and American.
44. *Easthampton*

Jan. 31–Mar. 21, PAFA, *121st Annual Exh.*
67. *New England Snow*
204. *A Montauk Garden in the Age of Pericles*

By Feb. 7–until Feb. 20, Montross, Group Exh. of pictures selected from the Montross "Sanctum" [*NYT*, 2/7/1926, p. X14].
Gloucester Harbor

Feb. 26–Mar. 31, Fine Arts Gallery of San Diego, *Inaugural Exh.*
28. *Spring Morning,* lent by the Carnegie Institute of Arts and Sciences, Pittsburgh

Mar. 20–Apr. 11, NAD, *101st Annual Exh.*
57. *Flight Into Egypt,* First Altman Landscape Prize
266. *The Play of Light*

Mar. 22–Apr. 10, Milch, *Water Colors and Drawings, Recent Etchings by Childe Hassam.*

Apr. 4–May 2, WAM, *Exh. of Water Color Paintings in the Museum Collection, by Frank W. Benson, Childe Hassam, Winslow Homer, Dodge MacKnight, John Singer Sargent, Charles Collings and Auguste Rodin.*

Apr. 4–May 16, Corcoran, *10th Exh. of Contemporary American Oil Paintings*.
203. *Great Peconic Bay*
205. *Diana, The Huntress, Montauk*
207. *The Grove of Aphrodite*

By Apr. 25–May 8, Ferargil Galleries, *American Paintings* [*NYT*, 4/25/1926, p. X12].
"a few selected pictures from the collection of a Wall Street collector…who has known the artists personally."

June 1–Dec. 1, Department of Fine Arts, Philadelphia, *Sesqui-Centennial International Exposition*.
72. *The Beryl Gorge*
73. *Diana – Huntress*
75. *Miss Ingram*, gold medal in painting
76. *Grove – Appledore*
77. *Diana as Spring*
538. *Greek Garden – Age of Pericles*

July 22–Sept., Los Angeles Museum, Exposition Park.
43. *The Church at Gloucester*, lent by Mr. and Mrs. Sherman Stevens

Summer, Toronto Art Gallery, *National Exh.*

Oct. 12–Nov. 8, RISD, *Annual Exh. of Recent American Paintings*.
13. *Easthampton, 1922*

Oct. 14–Dec. 5, CI, *25th Annual International Exh. of Paintings*.
71. *Venetian Brocade*

Oct. 28–Dec. 12, AIC, *39th Annual Exh. of American Oil Paintings and Sculpture*.
99. *The Flight into Egypt*
100. *Pep[p]eridge Trees and Wind in the Grain, Southampton*

Nov. 7–Dec. 12, PAFA, *24th Annual Philadelphia Water Color Exh. and 25th Annual Exh. of Miniatures*.
782. *Afternoon in Promised Land* (wc)

Nov. 15–Jan. 30, 1927, California Palace of the Legion of Honor, San Francisco, *1st Exh. of Selected Paintings by American Artists*.
77. *The Table Garden*, lent by Mr. and Mrs. Herbert Fleishhacker, San Francisco
78. *The Caulker*, lent by CAM Association, Cincinnati, Ohio
79. *Breakfast Room*, lent by WAM, Worcester, Mass.
80. *Nymph Bathing*, lent by C.E.S. Wood, San Francisco
81. *Catalow Valley*, lent by C.E.S. Wood, San Francisco
82. *Roses*, lent by C.E.S. Wood, San Francisco
83. *The Hod Carrier*, lent by C.E.S. Wood, San Francisco
84. *Clouds*, lent by C.E.S. Wood, San Francisco
85. *Nymph Overlooking Sea*, lent by C.E.S. Wood, San Francisco
86. *Still Life*, lent by C.E.S. Wood, San Francisco
87. *Landscape*, lent by C.E.S. Wood, San Francisco
88. *Nude Figure Seated*, lent by C.E.S. Wood, San Francisco
89. *Katydid Lane* (p), lent by C.E.S. Wood, San Francisco
90. *Italian Barque*
91. *Avenue of the Allies*
92. *Sun Room*
93. *Spring — The Dogwood Tree*

Nov. 27–Dec. 19, NAD, *Winter Exh.*
110. *Virginia*
327. *An Easthampton Garden*

Dec. 8–Jan. 4, Macbeth, *Exh. of Water Colors by Distinguished American Artists*.
(all wcs)
29. *Madonna of the North End*
30. *Plaza, Seville*
31. *Street in Toledo*

1927

Jan. 11–31, Macbeth, *15th Annual Exh. of Thirty Paintings by Thirty Artists*.
14. *Rue Lafayette*

Jan. 22–Feb. 11, Arthur Harlow and Co., *Etchings, Lithographs, Lithotints, Drawings, Water-Colors and Pastels by Childe Hassam*.
1–76 prints
77–130 (wcs), 131–54 (ds), 155–59 (ps)
77. *Old Delmonico's*
78. *An Island Garden*
79. *Belfast, Maine*
80. *The Mare's-tail Sky*
81. *Young Pan*
82. *Young Pan (2nd)*
83. *Stratham Hill*
84. *September Sky*
85. *The Brownstone Stoop, New York*
86. *The Auditorium, Chicago, 1893*
87. *Thunderstorm on the Oregon Trail*
88. *Portrait of Lily, 1898*
89. *Hiram Sherrill's Field, Easthampton*
90. *The Birches*
91. *The Aspens, Bass Rocks*
92. *Bass Rocks Beach*
93. *Bear Mountain, Catskills*
94. *Georgica*
95. *"Home Sweet Home"—Cottage, Easthampton*
96. *Acorn Street in War-time, Boston*
97. *General Lee's House in Richmond*
98. *Old Washington (1st)*
99. *Old Washington (2nd)*
100. *Old Washington (3rd)*
101. *Old Washington (4th)*
102. *The Capitol, Early Morning*
103. *Washington Monument*
104. *Washington Monument*
105. *Washington Monument from High Street*
106. *St. John's, Washington (1st)*
107. *St. John's, Washington (2nd)*
108. *Lafayette Park, Washington*
109. *Lafayette Park, Washington*
110. *In Lafayette Park*
111. *General Andrew Jackson*
112. *Harper's Ferry (1st)*
113. *Harper's Ferry (2nd)*
114. *Harper's Ferry, Afternoon*
115. *Big Sycamore, Harper's Ferry*
116. *Serpentine Wall, University of Virginia*
117. *University of Virginia*
118. *Potomac in Spate*
119. *Natural Bridge, Virginia*
120. *In the Shenandoah Valley*
121. *Monticello*
122. *Repairing the First Presbyterian Church, Staunton*
123. *Sycamore Tree*
124. *Sammy's Beach, Easthampton*
125. *Big Barn, Stratham, N. H.*
126. *Frame Mansion, Portsmouth, N. H.*
127. *Brick Mansion, Portsmouth, N. H.*
128. *The Rum Cherry Tree*
129. *Brick Mansion, Portsmouth, N. H.*
130. *The Flagstones, Portsmouth, N. H.*
131. *Julia*
132. *Harriette*
133. *The Piano Duet*
134. *The Window Seat*
135. *The Old Mulford House*
136. *The Old Mulford House (2nd)*
137. *Young Sappho*
138. *The Stock Exchange*
139. *Washington Monument*
140. *Washington Monument (2nd)*
141. *Washington Monument (3rd)*
142. *St. John's, Washington*
143. *The White House*
144. *Richmond, Virginia*
145. *The Washington Elms*
146. *Mt. Vernon*
147. *Plaza de la Constituçion, St. Augustine*
148. *Easthampton Elms in May*
149. *A Live Oak Growing in the South*
150. *The Old Fort, St. Augustine*
151. *St. Michael's, Charleston*
152. *Spring in Charleston*
153. *The Viaduct at 138th Street*
154. *St. Philip's, Charleston*
155. *Au Grand Prix de Paris*
156. *Four-in-hand at the "Grand Prix"*
157. *Cedric's Garden*
158. *Court Street, Portsmouth*
159. *Old Dutch Church, Fishkill*

Feb. 6–Mar. 27, WAM, *Exh. Showing the Development of American Painting*.
The Breakfast Room

Feb. 8–26, Anderson Galleries, *Exh. of Works by American Artists Selected by Associated Dealers in American Paintings, Inc., First Cooperative Exh.*
39. *Isles of Shoals*
40. *Miss Ingham*

Feb. 28–Mar. 19, Macbeth, *16th Annual Exh. Thirty Paintings by Thirty Artists*.
13. *Pont Aven*

Mar. 16–Apr. 6, Gordon Dunthorne, Washington, D.C., *Exh. of Water Colours and Etchings by Childe Hassam*.
(1–28 wcs)
1–11 "Washington"
1. *In Lafayette Park*
2. *Lafayette Park No. 1*
3. *Lafayette Park No. 2*
4. *Old Washington No. 2*
5. *Old Washington No. 3*
6. *Washington Monument from "H" Street*
7. *Capitol; Early Morning*
8. *Washington Monument No. 1*
9. *Washington Monument No. 2*
10. *General Andrew Jackson*
11. *St. John's Washington*
12. *The Potomac in Spate*
13. *Monticello*
14. *General Lee's House, Richmond*
15. *Harper's Ferry, Afternoon*
16. *Harper's Ferry No. 1*
17. *Harper's Ferry No. 2*
18. *Big Sycamore, Harper's Ferry*
19. *Natural Bridge, Virginia*
20. *University of Virginia*
21. *Sycamore Tree*
22. *In the Shenandoah Valley*
23. *Repairing the First Presbyterian Church, Staunton*
24. *Brick Mansion, Portsmouth, N. H., No. 1*
25. *Brick Mansion, Portsmouth, N. H., No. 2*
26. *Frame Mansion, Portsmouth, N. H.*
27. *Street in Belfast, Maine*
28. *Four in Hand at the Grand Prix*
29–48 etchings

Mar. 23–Apr. 17, NAD, *102nd Annual Exh.*
73. *October*

Apr. 21–Oct. 21, American Academy of Arts and Letters, *Exh. of the Works of Childe Hassam*.
Extensive notes are provided in original catalogue.
1. *June*, lent by Mrs. Hassam
2. *Bay of Naples*
3. *The Opal*
4. *Beacon Street, Boston*
5. *The Open Window*
6. *Portrait in the Park*
7. *The Evening Hour*
8. *Self Portrait*, lent by Mrs. Hassam
9. *Still Life*
10. *Against the Light*, lent by Miss R. B. Moore
11. *Looking into the Little South Room*, lent by Mrs. Hassam
12. *Portrait of Miss Ingram*
13. *Posilippo*, lent by Miss R. B. Moore
14. *The New York Winter Window*
15. *Service Flags, Philadelphia*
16. *Malheur Butte*, lent by Mrs. Hassam
17. *Phryne*
18. *Outdoor Portrait*
19. *The Top of the Cliffs*
20. *Oscar Leighton [sic]*
21. *Winter*
22. *The Beryl Gorge*
23. *The Bowl of Nasturtiums*
24. *The Pretty Pool*
25. *Tanagra*, lent by John Gellatly, Esquire
26. *The Room of Flowers*, lent by Mrs. Hassam
27. *Easter Morning, 1921*
28. *Arcady*
29. *Venetian Brocade*
30. *July Night*, lent by Mrs. Hassam
31. *Pomona*, lent by John Gellatly, Esquire
32. *The Dogwood Tree*
33. *The Sun Room*
34. *Still Life*
35. *The Play of Light*
36. *Colonial Crocks*
37. *October, 1918*, lent by Miss R. B. Moore
38. *Against the Light*
39. *Vesuvius*
40. *Appledore, Isles of Shoals*
41. *Rhonda [sic]*
42. *Nude on the Bank*
43. *White Island Light*
44–67 (wcs)
44. *Afternoon, Promised Land*
45. *Old Delmonicos, 1892*
46. *Court Street, Portsmouth, N. H.*
47. *The Brownstone Stoop, New York*
48. *The Island Garden*
49. *Thunderstorm on the Oregon Trail*
50. *Auditorium, Chicago, 1890*
51. *Hiram Sherrill's Field*
52. *Sammie's Beach*
53. *Georgica*
54. *Young Pan*
55. *Thalassa*
56. *Young Pan*
57. *Court Street Corner, Portsmouth, N. H.*
58. *Suresnes*
59. *Stratham Hill*
60. *The Mare's Tail Sky*
61. *Courtyard, Toledo*
62. *Church Tower, Broadstairs, England*
63. *Lannion, Brittany*
64. *Canterbury Cathedral*
65. *Winter, 1918, Columbus Circle*
66. *Broadstairs*
67. *Broadstairs, Bleak House*
68–78 (ps)
68. *Old House, Cos Cob*
69. *Old House, Cos Cob*
70. *Old Dutch Church, Fishkill*
71. *The Tidal Dam and Bridges*
72. *Moonrise at Sunset, Cos Cob*
73. *Boston Post Road, Greenwich*
74. *Cedric's Garden*
75. *The Salt Hay Makers*
76. *The Old Brush House, Cos Cob*
77. *Wood Chopper, Cos Cob*
78. *The Shrimpers, Cos Cob*
79–99 (ds)
79. *Julia*
80. *Harriette*
81. *The Old Mulford House*
82. *The Floor of the Stock Exchange*
83. *St. Philips, Charleston*
84. *Spring in Charleston*
85. *Richmond, Virginia*
86. *Young Sappho*

87. *Washington Monument, 1st*
88. *The Washington Elms*
89. *The Duet*
90. *St. John's, Washington*
91. *Washington Monument, 3rd*
92. *St. Michael's, Charleston*
93. *Washington Monument, 2nd*
94. *The Viaduct at 138th Street*
95. *Easthampton Elms in May*
96. *Mt. Vernon*
97. *The White House*
98. *The Old Fort, St. Augustine*
99. *A Live Oak Growing in the South*
100–182 prints

May 28–July 30, CAM, *34th Annual Exh. of American Art.*
138. *Crimson Rambler* (wc)

July and Aug., Macbeth, *Summer Exh.*
26. *Melting Snow, Fifth Avenue*

Summer, Babcock Galleries, *Watercolors and Paintings by American Artists.*
15. *Street Scene*

Aug. 23–Sept. 5, Parrish Memorial Hall, Southampton, "American art exhibition" [*NYT*, 8/23/1927, p. 30].
"Paintings of Montauk Point"
and prints

Oct. 8–23, Art Department, State Fair of Texas, Dallas, *42nd Annual Exh.*
76. *Riggers Shop*

Oct. 11–Nov. 6, RISD, *Annual Exh. of Recent American Paintings.*
14. *Laurel in the Woods*

Oct. 12–31, O'Brien Art Galleries, Chicago, *Exh. of Paintings by American Artists (1870–1927).*
5. *Early Spring, Ft. George*

Oct. 20–Nov. 1, Association of the Junior Leagues of America, "Exhibition of American art loaned by the Associated Dealers in American Paintings" [*NYT*, 10/21/1927, p. 17].

Dec., Toledo Museum of Art, *An Exh. of Paintings by American Artists.*
19. *Early Spring, Fort George*
20. *Street in East Hampton*

1928

Jan. 24–Feb. 12, Downtown Gallery, *75 Years of American Landscapes.*
Putnam Cottage (oil or wc)

Jan. 29–Mar. 18, PAFA, *123rd Annual Exh.*
231. *South Ledges: Isle of Shoals*

Feb. 21–Mar. 10, Anderson Galleries, *Exh. of Works by American Artists Selected by the Associated Dealers in American Paintings, Inc. The 1928 Exh.*
64. *Italian Barque*
65. *The Mantelpiece*
66. *The Cove — Isle of Shoals*
67. *Summer Afternoon*
167. *Broadstairs* (wc)
168. *Broadstairs, Bleak House* (wc)

Feb. 28–Mar. 19, Macbeth, *16th Annual Exh.: 30 Paintings by 30 Artists.*

Feb.–May, Phillips Memorial Gallery, Washington, D.C., *Tri-Unit Exh. of Paintings and Sculpture.*
Noon on the Rocks

Mar. 21–Apr. 8, NAD, *103rd Annual Exh.*
279. *Incoming Tide*

Apr. 29–June 24, BFAA, *22nd Annual Exh. of Selected Paintings by American Artists.*
50. *Shingling the Baptist Church*

By May 13–end of summer, Milch, "Summer exhibition of paintings" [*NYT*, 5/13/1928, p. 143].
"a number of luminously treated small landscapes"

Spring, Macbeth, *American Paintings for Home Decoration.*
16. *Brush House, Cos Cob* (p)

By June 17, Dudensing Galleries, "Invited group from the twenty-sixth Carnegie International, though none of the pictures here exhibited was included in the last Carnegie show" [*NYT*, 6/17/1928, p. 137].

Summer, Babcock Galleries, *Exh. by American Artists.*
29. *Street Scene*

Oct. 18–Dec. 9, CI, *27th Annual International Exh. of Paintings.*
101. *The Nine Muses, Indian Corn in Flower*
102. *Long Island Poppy Garden*
103. *Goldenrod, Montauk*
104. *Trees of Heaven*
105. *Lilac and Laburnam*

Oct. 28–Dec. 9, Corcoran, *11th Exh. of Contemporary American Oil Paintings.*
130. *Shingling the First Baptist Church, Gloucester*
249. *In a French Garden*
258. *Spring in New York*
318. *Peaches and Damsons*

Oct., Museum of Fine Arts, Syracuse, *Etchings by Childe Hassam.*

Nov. 10–14, ULCNY, *Exh. of Paintings by Modern Artists.*
9. *Trees and Meadow*

Nov., John Hanna Gallery, Detroit, *Exh. of Work by Childe Hassam.*

Dec. 3–24, Milch, *Important Exh. of Early and Recent Works by Childe Hassam of the American Academy of Arts and Letters.*
1. *June*
2. *The Old Bottle Man*
3. *The Square, Pont-Aven*
4. *The Island Garden*
5. *The Flag, 1918*
6. *Portrait Arrangement*
7. *Quinces and Long Island Pebbles*
8. *Overmantel*
9. *Gardens at Villier-le-bel, France*
10. *Old Farmhouse, Long Island*
11. *Self Portrait*
12. *The Fountain of Alcantara, Toledo*
13. *Top of the Cliff — Montauk*
14. *Against the Light*
15. *Down the Steps, Central Park*
16. *Building the Schooner*
17. *Nude*
18. *Flags, Philadelphia*
19. *Venetian Brocade*
20. *The Room of Flowers*
21. *The French Window*
22. *Portrait*
23. *The Salt Meadow Haystack*
24. *Vesuvius, Evening*
25. *Spring Morning*
26. *Quincy, Massachusetts*
27. *The Bridge, on-the-Stour*
28. *Christ Church, on-the-Stour*
29. *Putnam Cottage, Greenwich*
30. *The Bowl of Nasturtiums*
31. *The Opal*
32. *Out-of-door Portrait*
33. *Fish Nets, le Pouldu, Brittany*
34. *Appledore*
35. *The Birches, October*
36. *Spray of Quinces*
37. *The "Alpes Maritimes" — Still Life*

1–12 (wcs), 13–28 (ps), 29–37 (ds)
1. *Rockport Quarry*
2. *The Bridge*
3. *The Quarry*
4. *The Port*
5. *Appledore*
6. *The White Fence, Portsmouth, N. H.*
7. *The Kitchen Door*
8. *Weir's Garden at Branchville, Conn.*
9. *Fishkill Landing*
10. *Sunset, The Hudson above Newburgh*
11. *Lake Leman*
12. *The Old Mulford House, Easthampton*
13. *The Bridge, Cos Cob*
14. *An Old House*
15. *Moonrise, the Bridge*
16. *The Old House, Cos Cob*
17. *The Shrimpers*
18. *Autumn Haze*
19. *The Wood Chopper*
20. *Old House, October*
21. *Moonrise and Sunset*
22. *The Tidal Dam*
23. *Summer Night, Isles of Shoals*
24. *Evening Star, Appledore*
25. *November Haze*
26. *The Concord Meadows*
27. *Spring at Easthampton, 1928*
28. *Autumn, Old Lyme*
29. *Old House, Court Street, Portsmouth*
30. *Giants and Pigmies*
31. *Court Street, Portsmouth*
32. *Road to Promised Land*
33. *Floor of the Stock Exchange*
34. *Helen Wills at Easthampton*
35. *Helen Wills (No. 3) at Easthampton*
36. *Julia*, "Drawings for Portraits"
37. *Harriet*, "Drawings for Portraits"
and etchings, dry points, lithographs and lithotints

By Dec. 23–ca. Dec. 31, Babcock Galleries, "small selected group of paintings by prominent American artists" [*NYT*, 12/23/1928, p. 94].

Dec., Gatterdam Gallery, *Paintings by 12 American Artists.*

1929

Jan. 1– 31, California Palace of the Legion of Honor, San Francisco, *26 Recent Paintings by Childe Hassam.*

Jan. 10–Feb. 24, Memorial Art Gallery, Rochester, *Contemporary American Paintings and Sculpture Selected from Recent Exhibitions in American Art Centers.*
18. *Listening to the Orchard Oriole*

By Jan. 13, Arts Council at Hotel Barbizon, *New York by Painters and Graphic Artists* [*NYT*, 1/13/1929, p. 121].

Jan. 27–Mar. 27, PAFA, *124th Annual Exh.*
372. *Trees and Meadow*

Jan., Brooks Memorial Art Gallery, Memphis, *Etchings by Childe Hassam.*

Feb. 19–Mar. 4, Macbeth, *Thirty Paintings by Thirty Artists.*
11. *Windmill at Sundown*

Mar. 9–Apr. 8, BFAA, *Exh. of a Retrospective Group of Paintings Representative of the Life Work of Childe Hassam, N. A.*

1. *A Street in Provincetown*, 1911
2. *Spring*, 1908
Both lent by Mr. Charles D. Armstrong, Pittsburgh
3. *Capri*. 1897, lent by Mr. E. L. Ballard, New York
4. *The Lady of the Gorge*, 1912, lent by Museum of Fine Arts, Boston
5. *Still Life*, 1904, lent by Brooklyn Museum
6. *Church at Old Lyme*, 1905
7. *Brook Back of New Canaan*, 1902
Both owned by BFAA
8. *Old Bridge at Lyme*
9. *Provincetown*
Both lent by Canajoharie Library, N.Y.
10. *Fifth Avenue in Winter*
11. *Spring Morning*, 1909
Both lent by CI
12. *Against the Light*, 1910
13. *Cathedral Spires, Spring Morning*, 1900
14. *The Willows*, 1912
All lent by AIC
15. *Pont Royale*, 1897
16. *The Caulker*, 1895
17. *Houses on the Place Lannion* (p), 1911
All lent by CAM
18. *In the Old House*, 1914
19. *Little Good Harbor Beach*, 1919
Both lent by Mrs. Emily J. Clark, Grand Rapids, Mich.
20. *September*, 1906, lent by Mr. M. H. Cohen, Des Moines
21. *New Haven Green*, 1909, lent by Detroit Athletic Club
22. *Place Central and Fort Cabanas, Havana*, 1895
23. *Surf and Rocks*, 1906
Both lent by Detroit Institute of Arts
24. *The Flags on Fifty-seventh Street, Winter*, 1918
25. *The Union Jack, April Morning*, 1918
Both lent by DRG
26. *Quai, St. Michel*
27. *Gloucester Harbor*, 1909
28. *Men o' War — "The Black" and "The Boston,"* 1893
29. *Wild Swans Sacred to Apollo*, 1924
30. *Pepperidge Tree*, 1921
31. *Appledore, August*, 1910
32. *Gloucester, Grey Morning*, 1918
33. *Gloucester*, 1919
34. *At the Piano*
35. *Quarry Pool*, 1918
36. *Central Park, South*, 1913
37. *Norman's Woe, Gloucester*, 1918
All lent by Mr. Hersey Egginton, New York
38. *The Southwest Wind*, 1905
39. *Gathering Flowers*, 1888
Both lent by Mr. Theodore T. Ellis, Worcester, Mass.
40. *Old Fisherman*, 1879, lent by Mr. Philip Bond Fouke, New York
41. *Fireplace in Old Holly House*
42. *Haskell Street, East Gloucester*
43. *Winter, Central Park*, 1918
44. *Old Washington, No. 4* (wc)
45. *Old Washington, No. 1* (wc)
46. *Street Musicians* (wc)
47. *Coytesville from New York* (wc) (withdrawn from exh.)
48. *Egypt Lane* (wc) (withdrawn from exh.)
49. *The Hudson* Above Newburgh (wc) (withdrawn from exh.)
All lent by Mr. George A. Gay, Hartford, Conn.
50. *Quai Voltaire*, April 1897, lent by Mr. William O. Goodman, Chicago
51. *Leda and the Swan*, 1907, lent by Mrs. Charles Greenough, New York
52. *Isles of Shoals*, 1911
53. *The Square, Pont Aven*, 1897
Both lent by Mr. and Mrs. A. C. Griffin, Brooklyn
54. *Fine Arts Building, World's Fair, from the Costa Rica Landing*
55. *Gloucester Harbor*, 1895

Both lent by Mrs. Ernest A. Hammill, Chicago
56. *The Birches*, October 1928
57. *Venetian Brocade*, 1926
58. *Long Island Poppy Garden*, 1924
59. *Golden Rod, Montauk*, 1927
60. *Lilac and Laburnam*, 1926
61. *Wildflowers by Moonlight, Montauk*, 1922
62. *Peaches and Damsons*, 1928
63. *The Young Sappho*, 1925
64. *Trap Dyke Gorge, Isle of Shoals*, 1916
65. *Greek Altar to Autumn*, 1924
66. *Daphne, Montauk*, 1921
67. *Overmantel*, 1928
68. *Trees of Heaven*, 1927
69. *Summer Sunlight, Isle of Shoals*, 1892
70. *The Skyscraper Window, New York*, 1923
71. *Spray of Quinces*, 1928
72. *Flags on the Union League Club*, April 1917
73. *July Fourteenth, Rue Daunou*, 1910
74. *Quinces and Long Island Pebbles*, 1928
75. *The Sea*, 1921
76. *Against the Light*, 1916
77. *Self Portrait*, 1914
78. *Moonlight, Isles of Shoals*, 1911
79. *The Beryl Pool, Appledore*, 1912
80. *The Hudson at Newburgh*, 1919
81. *East Gloucester*, 1918
82. *Japanese Iris*, 1916
All lent by the artist
83. *Val de Grace, Spring Morning*, 1888
84. *Duck Island*, 1906
85. *Harbor of a Thousand Masts*, 1919
86. *Along the Seine, Winter*
All lent by Mr. Joel T. Howard, Dallas
87. *Clifferock [sic], Appledore*, 1903, lent by Art Association of Indianapolis, JHAI, Indianapolis, Ind.
88. *The English Girl*, 1919, lent by Mr. W. J. Johnson, St. Davids, Pa.
89. *Sunshine*, 1896
90. *Indian Summer, Colonial Days*, 1899
Both lent by Estate of Harry W. Jones, courtesy of Mr. Albert R. Jones, Kansas City, Mo.
91. *Isles of Shoals*, lent by Mrs. D. M. Keith, Rockford, Ill.
92. *Pears*, 1928
93. *Quinces*, 1928
94. *Sickle Pears and Long Island Pebbles*, 1928
95. *West Wind, Isle of Shoals*, 1909
96. *East Headland Pool*, 1912
All lent by the C. W. Kraushaar Galleries
96a. *San Pietro, Venice*, 1884, lent by Mr. and Mrs. E. H. Letchworth, Buffalo
97. *Beethoven's Sonata Appassionata*, 1893, lent by Mr. Robert W. Macbeth, New York
98. *Old Indian Trail to the Sea*, 1906
99. *Church at Old Lyme, Spring*, 1906
Both lent by Mr. Burton Mansfield, New Haven
100. *Little Old Shops, New York*, 1927
101. *Union Square*. 1890
Both lent by Mr. G. F. McKinney, New York
102. *Calvary Church in Snow*, 1903
103. *Fifth Avenue in Rain, with Flags*, 1916
104. *Montmartre*, 1888
105. *Nude*, 1909
All lent by Mr. Albert E. McVitty, Bryn Mawr, Pa.
106. *In a French Garen*, 1897
107. *Winter Sickle Pears*, 1918
108. *Isles of Shoals*
109. *St. Thomas' Avenue of the Allies*, 1917
All lent by Milch
110. *Isles of Shoals*, 1899, lent by Minneapolis Institute of Arts
111. *A Street in Gloucester*, 1896, lent by Honorable Walton Mitchell, Pittsburgh
112. *Daphne*, 1919
113. *Miss Ingram Reading a Letter*, 1913
Both lent by Miss Rosa B. Moore, New York
114. *Isles of Shoals*, 1905, lent by Mrs. C. T. Palmer, Stamford, Conn.
115. *The Old Paris Cab Stand*, 1889, lent by Miss Julia Peck, New York
116. *Catboats, Newport*, 1901, lent by PAFA
117. *Nymph with Ducks*, 1906, lent by Mr. Duncan Phillips, Washington, D.C.
118. *The Outer Harbor, Gloucester*, 1919, lent by Mr. E. M. Plunkett, Detroit
119. *Isle of Shoals*, 1912, lent by Mr. John L. Porter, Pittsburgh
120. *Montauk*, 1920, lent by Mr. George Roberts, New York
121. *Isles of Shoals*, 1907, lent by Mr. Frank P. Rush, Scottsdale, Pa.
122. *Kelp-covered Rocks, Isles of Shoals*, 1908, lent by Mr. Charles F. T. Seaverns, Hartford, Conn.
123. *American Elm*, 1905, lent by Mr. Ray L. Skofield, New York
124. *The Cab*, 1888, lent by Mrs. David W. Smyth, New York
125. *The East Window*, 1913
126. *The Fete of Lannion*, 1910
Both lent by CAMSL
127. *The Dry Northeaster, Isle of Shoals*, 1906, lent by Mrs. S. E. Stokes, Moorestown, N.J.
128. *In the Doorway*, 1888, lent by Syracuse Museum of Fine Arts
129. *Summer Sea*, 1902, lent by Toledo Museum of Art
130. *Diamond Cove, Isles of Shoals*, 1908, lent by Washington University, St. Louis
131. *The Breakfast Room, Winter Morning*, 1911
132. *Sylphs Rock, Appledore*, 1907
133. *Yonkers from the Palisades* (wc), 1916
All lent by WAM
134. *Highland Light*, 1900
135. *Model Disrobing*, 1918
136. *Street in Pont Aven, Brittany*, 1897
All lent by General E. C. Young, New York

Apr. 16–29, Macbeth, *Exh. of Paintings by Childe Hassam, N. A. Covering the Period from 1888 to 1919, Together with Etchings, Water Colors and Pastels*.
1. *Havana*, 1895
2. *Along the Seine*, 1888
3. *Spring Song*, 1918
4. *The Little Pond, Appledore*, 1890
5. *Bridge at Old Lyme*, 1903
6. *Little Old Shops, New York*, 1907
7. *The Bathing Pool, Appledore*, 1907
8. *The Quai, Pont Aven*, 1897
9. *Twilight, Madison Square*, 1902 (Looking North toward Delmonico's)
10. *Old Hook Mill, Easthampton*, 1898
11. *Old Lyme Church, Moonlight*, 1905
12. *The South Room, Easthampton*, 1919 (Portrait of Mrs. Hassam in Living Room of Mrs. Ruger Donohoe's [sic] House)
13. *Along the Park, Winter*, 1902
14. *April, Quai Voltaire*, 1897
15. *The Turquoise Sea*, 1901
16. *The Southwest Wind*, 1905
17. *Northeast Headland, Isles of Shoals*, 1909
18. *Marché St. Pierre, Montmartre*, 1888
19. *Early Morning Calm, Appledore*, 1901
20. *Over the Hill, East Gloucester*, 1919
21. *The Harbor of a Thousand Masts*, 1919
22. *Duck Island*, 1906
23. *Church at Old Lyme, Spring*, 1906
24. *Isles of Shoals, Moonlight*, 1906–7
25. *Windmill at Sundown, Easthampton*, 1898
26. *Les Grands Boulevards*, 1897
27. *Incoming Tide*, 1911
28. *Val de Grace, Spring Morning*, 1888
29. *Capri*, 1897
30. *St. Mark's in the Bowery*, 1910 (Horsechestnuts in Bloom after a Shower)
31. *July Fourteenth, Rue Daunou*, 1910
32. *Provincetown*, 1900
33. *The Rigger's Shop, Provincetown*, 1909
34. *Isles of Shoals*, 1908

May 16–June 3, JHAI, *Childe Hassam, Etchings and Watercolors and a Color Print by Mary Cassatt.*
(wcs)
Brick Mansion, Portsmouth, N.H.
New Fields, N.H.
Both lent by Macbeth
and 12 etchings

By May 19–Summer, Babcock Galleries, *Exh. of Paintings, Watercolors, Etchings by American Artists.*
19. *Landscape and Nude*

By Aug. 4–ca. Sept. 1, Lime Rock, Conn., "Some well-known Lime Rock painters, in collaboration with the Milch Galleries, have arranged an exhibition" [*NYT*, 8/4/1929, p. X7].

By Aug. 18, The Metropolitan Museum of Art, "Recent accessions" [*NYT*, 8/18/1929, p. X10].
July 14, Rue Daunou

Aug. 19–Sept. 2, Clinton Academy, East Hampton, "A group show of the work of Southampton and East Hampton artists" [*NYT*, 8/18/1929, p. X13].

From ca. Sept. 22, Arnold, Constable and Co., "An exhibition of pictures, medals, prints and other historical material depicting the growth of Fifth Avenue from its dirt-road days to the present" [*NYT*, 9/15/1929, p. N1].

Oct. 8–Nov. 3, RISD, *Annual Exh. of Recent American Paintings.*
10. *Church of the Paulist Fathers, New York*

Oct. 24–Dec. 8, AIC, *42nd Annual Exh. of American Oil Paintings and Sculpture.*
87. *Bailey's Beach*

Dec. 10–Jan. 31, 1930, National Gallery of Art, Washington, D.C., *An Exh. of Paintings by Contemporary American Artists Purchased by the Council of the National Academy of Design from the Henry Ward Ranger Fund in Accordance with the Provision of the Ranger Bequest Dated January 21, 1914.*
34. *A Long Island Garden*, lent by Kansas City Art Institute, Mo.

Dec., Toledo Museum of Art, *19 American Paintings.*
43. *South Room, Easthampton*

1930

Jan. 26–Mar. 16, PAFA, *125th Annual Exh.*
372. *The River Pont-Aven*

Feb. 4–17, Macbeth, *Thirty Paintings by Thirty Artists.*
11. *Spring in West 78th Street*

Mar. 15–Apr. 7, Royal Academy, Stockholm, *Unställning av Amerikansk Konst.*
44. *Kyrkan; Old Lyme*, lent by BFAA
45. *Klipporna vid middagstid*, lent by the Phillips Memorial Gallery, Washington, D.C.

Mar. 22–Apr. 8, Milch and Vogel, Inc., *Childe Hassam Early and Recent Etchings* [*NYT*, 3/23/1930, p. X12].

Mar., Mauk-Murray Gallery, Providence, R.I., *Etchings by Childe Hassam.*

Apr. 16–May 2, SB, *American Artists—Second in the Series 1890–1910.*
29. [no title given], lent by Mrs. Phillips Ketchum

By Apr. 23–Apr. 26, Ferargil Galleries, "Small pictures by a dozen American painters" [*Wall Street Journal*, 4/23/1930, p. 4].

May 3–22, Carlsberg glyptothek, Copenhagen, *Unställning av Amerikansk Konst.*
44. *Kyrkan; Old Lyme*, lent by BFAA
45. *Klipporna vid middagstid*, lent by the Phillips Memorial Gallery, Washington, D.C.

By May 11–June, Milch, "Summer exh." of "selected paintings by American artists" [*NYT*, 5/11/1930, p. 128; 5/25/1930, p. 123; 6/8/1930, p. 121]. "Early paintings by Childe Hassam are made a special feature and date from 1889 to 1901" [*NYT*, 6/8/1930, p. 121].

By June 15–July 3, Art Centre, "An exh. of nearly fifty paintings, showing various aspects of New York" [*NYT*, 6/15/1930, p. X9].

July 12–Aug. 2, Art Association of Newport, R.I., *Exh. of Contemporary American Painting and Sculpture.*
6. *Evening, Pont Aven*
7. *Hickory Trees*
8. *Old Tidal Dam, Cos Cob*

Summer, Babcock Galleries, *Exh. of Paintings, Watercolors, Etchings by American Artists.*
34. *Landscape and Nude*

By Oct. 5–Oct. 11, Pascal M. Gatterdam, "A small but excellent group of canvases by Chase, Davies, Childe Hassam, Blakelock, J. Francis Murphy, Twachtman, Inness and Bruce Crane" [*NYT*, 10/5/1930, p. X11].

Oct. 11– 26, Art Department, State Fair of Texas, Dallas, *45th Annual Exh. of Paintings, Sculptures and Art Objects Assembled and Exhibited by the State Fair of Texas in the Art Department.*
61. *Duke Street*

By Oct. 12, Ovington's, The Art Gallery, *Important Exh. of Original Paintings* [*NYT*, 10/12/1930, p. X13].

Nov. 13–May 13, 1931, American Academy of Arts and Letters, Exh. of "works in whatever medium of the living artists of the National Institute of Arts and Letters."
The Sonata (*The Marechal Niel Rose*) and others

By Nov. 16, Macbeth, *Paintings of Museum Importance* [*NYT*, 11/16/1930, p. X12].

By Nov. 23–Nov. 29, Milch, "A group of important Americans" [*NYT*, 11/23/1930, p. 121].

Nov. 25–Dec. 21, NAD, *Special Exh. of Members' Work.*
187. *Aphrodite, Appledore*

Nov. 30–Jan. 11, 1931, Corcoran, *12th Exh. of Contemporary American Oil Paintings.*
110. *The Old Abbott House at Andover, Mass.*
112. *Building the Art Museum, Andover, Mass.*
250. *Solarium*

Dec. 2–Jan. 20, 1931, Museum of Modern Art, *Paintings and Sculpture by Living Americans, 9th Loan Exh.*
45. *Val de Grace*, 1888, collection Joel T. Howard, Dallas, Tex.
46. *Spring in West 78th Street*, 1905, private collection, New York
47. *Flags on 57th Street, Winter*, 1918, collection of the Artist

Venice Biennale.
36. *Fifth Avenue d'inverno*, app. al CI

1931

Jan. 13–Feb. 15, Fort Worth Museum of Art, *22nd Annual Exh. of Paintings and a Collection of Prints by American Artists.*
19. *Surf, Appledore*

Jan. 25–Mar. 15, PAFA, *126th Annual Exh.*
206. *The Old Peasant: Brittany*

Mar. 15–Apr. 5, NAD, *106th Annual Exh.*
152. *The Amagansett Links, Long Island*
188. *West Hills: Long Island*

Apr. 14–May 17, Detroit Institute of Arts, *17th Annual Exh. of American Art.*
114. *Little Cobbler's Shop*

Summer, Babcock Galleries, *Exh. of Paintings, Watercolors, Etchings by American Artists.*
15. *Landscape and Nude*

Sept. 19–Nov. 1, CAMSL, *26th Annual Exh. of Paintings by American Artists.*
41. *The Old Abbott House at Andover, Massachusetts*, lent by Mr. George D. Pratt, Glen Cove, L.I.

By Oct. 7–ca. Oct. 31, Macbeth, "30 paintings by American artists selected from the stock of the gallery" [*Wall Street Journal*, 10/7/1931, p. 4].
"a New York street scene"

Oct. 13–31, Macbeth, "Water-colors by four American artists" [*NYT*, 10/15/1931, p. 25].
"sunny landscapes and a delightful grocery store."

Oct. 15–Dec. 6, CI, *30th Annual International Exh. of Paintings.*
149. The Framemaker
156. *Portrait of John Gellatly*

Oct. 29–Dec. 13, AIC, *44th Annual Exh. of American Paintings and Sculpture.*
79. *The Old Peasant, Brittany*

Nov. 25–Dec. 21, NAD, *Winter Exh.*
279. *Spring in a Skyscraper*

1932

Jan. 14–24, ULCNY, *Exh. of Paintings by American Artists.*
9. *Gloucester Harbor*

Jan. 24–Mar. 13, PAFA, *127th Annual Exh.*
299. *Building the Art Gallery*

Feb. 1–28, Maurel Gallery, *Paris and Its People* [*NYT*, 2/5/1932, p. 18; *NYT*, 2/7/1932, p. X10].

By Feb. 3, Leonard Clayton Gallery, *Group of 100 Etchings by Childe Hassam.*

Feb. 8–Mar. 5, Milch, *Important 19th and 20th Century American Painters.*
15. *Pont Aven, Evening*

Feb.–Mar. 11, CI, *Exh. of Drawings by Childe Hassam.*
(24 ds)
"Many...are sketches made at Newport, Cos Cob, or Gloucester" [*Carnegie Magazine*, 2/5/1932, p. 264].

Mar. 27–Apr. 17, NAD, *107th Annual Exh.*
206. *The Mares-Tail Sky*

Mar. 28–Apr. 9, Macbeth, *Small Paintings of Museum Importance.*
7. *Little Cobbler's Shop*

Apr. 11–30, Macbeth, *Forty Years of American Art.*
7. *Madison Square*, 1890

Apr. 12–30, Frederick Keppel and Co., "Water-colors and drawings, including not only 'etchers' drawings' more or less tinted with color, but also water-colors in the usual sense" [*NYT*, 4/17/1932, p. X11].

Apr. 24–May 21, Art Association, New Rochelle, N.Y. *13th Annual Exh., The Painters.*

By May 8–ca. May 30, Leonard Clayton Gallery, *Drawings by Childe Hassam and Augustus Vincent Tack* [*NYT*, 5/8/1932, p. X8].

June 5–Aug. 28, Toledo Museum of Art, Ohio, *20th Annual Exh. of Selected Paintings by Contemporary American Artists.*
22. *Moonlight, Isles of Shoals*
23. *Old Hutchinson House, Easthampton*

July 17–Aug. 8, Guild Hall, East Hampton, N.Y., *An Exh. of Paintings, Etchings Drawings and Lithographs by Childe Hassam.*
1. *Montauk*
2. *The Hovel and the Skyscraper—Central Park West at 67th Street*, 1904
3. *The Lily Pond, East Hampton*
4. *The Amagansett Links*
5. *Afternoon at Devon*
6. *The Distant Gallery—Age of Pericles*
7. *Uncle Benny's Dune*
8. *Maidstone Links*
9. *Liriodendron Tulipifera*
10. *Adam and Eve in an East Hampton Garden*
11. *Lemon Lilies and Long Island Pebbles*
12. *Goldenrod, Montauk*
13. *Nasturtiums and Long Island Pebbles*
14. *In the Old House, East Hampton*
15. *The Yacht Race, Devon*
16. *The Riding Club, East Hampton*
17. *Fourth of July, Devon*
18. *Quinces and Long Island Pebbles*
19. *The Greeks Come Bearing Gifts—Age of Pericles*
and "various other still-life and flower paintings just completed"

By July 17, Knoedler, "Summer exh. of American painters" [*NYT*, 7/17/1932, p. XX8].
Blue Sea Bather

Summer, Babcock Galleries, *Exh. of Paintings, Watercolors, Etchings by American Artists.*
8. *Outskirts of Pont Aven*

Sept. 19–Oct. 3, Jersey City Museum Association, Bergen Branch Library, Jersey City, N.J., "Exh. of paintings and sculptures" [*NYT*, 9/19/1932, p. 15].

Oct. 3–15, Gatterdam Gallery, "Paintings by 11 Americans" [*NYT*, 10/7/1932, p. 18].
Peconic

October 10–30, Springfield Art Museum, Mass., *Entering the Twentieth Century, Oils, Watercolors, Drawings Assembled by the College Art Association.*
23. *Bailey's Beach*, lent by Milch

By Oct. 26, Macbeth, "Special sale exhibition" [*Wall Street Journal*, 10/26/1932, p. 4].

By Oct. 28–Nov. 24, Kleemann-Thorman Galleries, "Exh. of drawings by American artists" [*NYT*, 10/28/1932, p. 17].

Oct. 31–Jan. 31, 1933, Museum of Modern Art, *American Painting and Sculpture (1862–1932).*
43. *Church at Old Lyme*, collection Albright Art Gallery, Buffalo

Nov. 6–Dec. 11, PAFA, *30th Annual Philadelphia Water Color Exh. and 31st Annual Exh. of Miniatures*
(wcs)
387. *Scarface; Hudson River*
395. *The Mirror; Cos Cob*

Nov. 18–Jan. 2, 1933, PAA, *Loan Exh. of Paintings Held in the New Museum of Art.*
44. *Portrait*, lent by Mrs. David T. Honeyman
45. *Clouds*, lent by Mrs. Robert H. Strong
46. *Landscape*, lent by Mrs. Elliott R. Corbett
47. *The Beach at Newport*, lent by Mr. Walter J. Burns
48. *On the Umatilla*, lent by Mrs. Henry L. Corbett
49. *The Snake River*, lent by Mrs. Charles H. Carey
50. *Ecola*, lent by the Misses Flanders
51. *Portrait*, lent by Mrs. Henry L. Corbett
52. *New England Road*, lent by Mrs. Harold F. Wendel
53. *Moonlight*, lent by Mrs. C. E. S. Wood
54. *Boston*
55. *Nude in Sunlit Wood*, lent by Mrs. Hold Wilson Berni

Nov. 22–Jan. 5, 1933, Whitney Museum of American Art, *1st Biennial Exh. of Contemporary American Painting.*
82. *Listening to the silent, the inner voice*

Nov. 26–Dec. 21, NAD, *Winter Exh.*
278. *The Framemaker*

Dec. 4–Jan. 15, 1933, Corcoran, *13th Exh. of Contemporary American Oil Paintings.*
91. *Street in Pont Aven—Evening*
173. *The Old Peasant, Brittany*

Addison Gallery, Phillips Academy, Andover, Masschusetts, *One Man's Taste in Contemporary Art.*
39. *Oyster Sloop, Cos Cob*

1933

Jan. 29–Mar. 19, PAFA, *128th Annual Exh.*
298. *Listening to the Silent, the Inner Voice*

From Feb. 2, Grand Central Galleries, *Background of American Painting*, organized by College Art Association [*NYT*, 2/2/1933, p. 15].

Week of Feb. 14, Taft School, Watertown, Conn., "Representative works by a number of leading American painters...by the Macbeth Gallery" [*NYT*, 2/14/1933, p. 13].

By Mar. 12, Howard Young Galleries, "A group of paintings (sponsored ... by the College Art Association...)...to bring forward the work that ushered in the present century and followed it along its tumultuous course. The group comprises 100 examples...only thirty-eight of them to be shown here" [*NYT*, 3/12/1933, p. X8].
Bailey's Beach

Mar. 25–Apr. 18, NAD, *108th Annual Exh.*
126. *Long Island Pebbles and Fruit*

June 1–Nov. 1, AIC, *A Century of Progress, Exh. of Paintings and Sculpture, Lent from American Collections.*
561. *New England Headlands*, lent by AIC, Walter H. Schulze Memorial Collection

Week of June 19, Lawrence Hall, Williamstown, Mass., "Painting exhibition of leading American artists" presented by Professor Karl E. Weston [*NYT*, 6/19/1933, p. 12].

From June 23, National Gallery of Art, Washington, D.C., *American and European Paintings in the Gellatly Collection.*
51. *Appledore, No. 2.* (wc)
52. *Celia Thaxter in Her Garden*
53. *Colonial Graveyard at Lexington* (p)
54. *Dexter's Garden* (wc)
55. *Improvisation*
56. *Isle of Shoals Garden* (wc)
57. *Lily (Lily Langtry)* (wc)
58. *Marechal Neil Roses* or *Let There Be Light*
59. *Noon Above Newburgh* (wc)

July 9–25, Four Fountains, the Ethel Hunt Tyng Memorial, Southampton, N.Y., *Loan Exh. of American Landscapes* [*NYT*, 7/9/1933, p. XX10].
Old Hook Mill

Oct. 7–22, Art Department, State Fair of Texas, Dallas, *1933 Exh. Showing the Changes in Painting for the last hundred years in Europe and America.*
33. *A Lady in Furs*
34. *Quai Book Stalls*
From Macbeth

Nov. 2–19, AWCS, *67th Annual Exh.*
(all wcs)
151. *Diana Coming Over the Great Dune at Easthampton with the Young Apollo*
153. *Maidstone Club*
154. *Out of Door, Self Portrait*
155. *In the Surf, Easthampton*

Nov. 9–30, Whitney Museum of American Art, *20th Century New York in Paintings and Prints* [*NYT*, 11/9/1933, p. 24].

Nov. 15–Dec. 10, PAFA, *31st Annual Philadelphia Water Color Exh. and 32nd Annual Exh. of Miniatures.*
(all wcs)
420. *In the Surf: Easthampton*
423. *In Promised Land*
426. *The Great Dune and the Golf Players; Easthampton*

Dec. 5–Jan. 11, 1934, Whitney Museum of American Art, *1st Biennial Exh. of Contemporary American Sculpture, Watercolors and Prints.*
(all prints)

Dec. 10–Feb. 1, 1934, William Rockwell Nelson Gallery of Art, Kansas City, *A Loan Exh. of American Paintings Since 1900.*
Lady in Furs, lent by Macbeth
Little Cobbler's Shop, lent by Macbeth
Old Bridge—Lyme, lent by Macbeth

1934

By Jan. 11, Kleemann-Thorman Galleries, "Exh. representing various nineteenth and twentieth century artists and including work in several mediums" [*NYT*, 1/11/1934, p. 19].
Diana the Huntress

Jan. 29 – Feb. 17, SB, *Exh. of American Art.*
19. *Boys Bathing*

By Feb. 1, Dudensing's Galleries, "Twenty-five canvases by American artists, selected from the collection of Frank Dudensing" [*NYT*, 2/1/1934, p. 17].

Feb. 5–17, Goodspeed's Book Shop, Inc., Boston, *Childe Hassam, Drawings and Etchings.*

Feb. 28–Mar. 31, Rockefeller Center, R.C.A. Building, *First Municipal Art Exh.; Paintings, Sculpture, Drawings, Prints by Living American Artists identified with the New York Art World.*
424. *Spring Garland*, 1932
425. *The Maidstone Club, Easthampton* (wc)
and 1 etching

Mar. 14–Apr. 15, NAD, *109th Annual Exh.*
54. *The Birches in October*

By Mar. 30–Apr. 7, Walter M. Grant Gallery, *Dealer's Choice* [*NYT*, 3/30/1934, p. 24].
The Bridge at Old Lyme, Connecticut (wc), selected by Albert Milch

By May 3, Kleemann-Thorman Galleries, "Group exhibition" [*NYT*, 5/3/1934, p. 17].

June 1– Nov. 1, AIC, *A Century of Progress, Exh. of Paintings and Sculpture.*
449. *Bailey's Beach, Newport, R.I.*, 1901, lent by Milch
450. *In a Cove, Isles of Shoals*, 1912, lent by Mr. Horatio S. Rubens, New York

Oct. 6–21, State Fair of Texas Art Gallery, Dallas, *48th Annual Exh. of Paintings, Water Colors, Sculpture, Graphic Arts.*
65. *Landscape*
66. *Pont-Aven*

Oct. 13–Nov. 3, Wanamaker Gallery, *The Wanamaker Regional Art Exh. of Contemporary American Painting.*
105. *Gloucester Harbor*

Oct. 16–30, Macbeth, *An Exh. of "Collector's Examples" of American Painting, Received for Sale from Private Owners and Estates.*
16. *Old Fisherman, Gloucester*
17. *Bill Boards*

Oct. 18–Dec. 9, CI, *International Exh. of Paintings.*
75. *A New York Winter Window*

1935

Jan. 27–Mar. 3, PAFA, *130th Annual Exh.*
127. *Laurel Ledges*

Feb. 5–Mar. 10, CI, *Paintings which Have Received Prize Awards in International Exhibitions at the Carnegie Institute.*
2. *The Sea*, lent by the artist

Mar. 5–18, Macbeth, *Loan Exh.*
6. *Mt. Vernon Street, Boston*

Mar. 13–Apr. 9, NAD, *110th Annual Exh.*
260. *Evening: Pont-Aven*, 1897, Saltus Medal for Merit

Mar. 24–May 5, Corcoran, *14th Biennial Exh. of Contemporary American Oil Paintings.*
178. *Montauk Point: Early Spring*
184. *Pont Aven*

Apr. 1–20, Guy E. Mayer Gallery, *Childe Hassam Etchings and Pastels* [*NYT*, 4/7/1935, p. X8].

May 6–28, Detroit Institute of Arts, *8 Modes of Modern Paintings, A College Art Association Exh.*
1. *Church of the Paulist Fathers*, collection Milch

By May 19–June 3, Macbeth, "Watercolors and pastels by American artists" [NYT, 5/19/1935, p. X9].
"a Childe Hassam New England scene"

June 7–July 7, M. H. de Young Memorial Museum, California Palace of the Legion of Honor, San Francisco. *Exh. of American Painting.*
120. *Bailey's Beach, Newport*, 1901, lent by Milch
121. *Old House at Easthampton*, lent by Corcoran

July 13–Aug. 3, Art Association, Newport, R.I., *24th Annual Exh. of American Contemporary Art.*
Shingling the First Baptist Church, John Elliott Prize

Symphony Hall, Boston.
Boston Common at Twilight

Frequently Cited Sources

Adams 1938
Adeline Adams. *Childe Hassam.* New York: American Academy of Arts and Letters, 1938.

Adelson, Cantor, and Gerdts 1999
Warren Adelson, Jay E. Cantor, and William H. Gerdts. *Childe Hassam, Impressionist.* New York: Abbeville Press, 1999.

Bienenstock 1980
Jennifer A. Martin Bienenstock. "Childe Hassam's Early Boston Cityscapes." *Arts Magazine* 55 (November 1980), pp. 168–71.

Boyle 1974
Richard J. Boyle. *American Impressionism.* Boston: New York Graphic Society, 1974.

Buchanan 1916
Charles L. Buchanan. "The Ambidextrous Childe Hassam." *International Studio* 57 (supplement) (January 1916), pp. LXXXIII–LXXXVI.

Burke 1980
Doreen Bolger Burke. *American Paintings in The Metropolitan Museum of Art, Volume III: A Catalogue of Works by Artists Born between 1846 and 1864.* Edited by Kathleen Luhrs. New York: The Metropolitan Museum of Art, 1980.

Burke and Kiehl 1977
Doreen Bolger Burke and David W. Kiehl. *Childe Hassam as Printmaker: A Selection in Various Media.* Exh. cat., The Metropolitan Museum of Art, New York, June 28–September 11, 1977. New York: The Metropolitan Museum of Art, 1977.

Burnside 1990
Kathleen M. Burnside. "Childe Hassam." In Gerdts et al. 1990, pp. 103–8.

Cortissoz 1939
Royal Cortissoz. "The Life and Art of Childe Hassam." *New York Herald Tribune,* January 1, 1939, sec. 6, p. 8.

Cortissoz 1989
Royal Cortissoz and the Leonard Clayton Gallery. *Catalogue of the Etchings and Dry-Points of Childe Hassam, N.A., of the American Academy of Arts and Letters.* Reprints Cortissoz's 1925 catalogue of etchings and the Clayton Gallery's 1933 catalogue of etchings; new introduction by Paula Eliasoph and 4 additional etchings completed after 1933. San Francisco: Alan Wofsy Fine Arts, 1989.

Curry 1990
David Park Curry. *Childe Hassam: An Island Garden Revisited.* Exh. cat., Yale University Art Gallery, New Haven, April 4–June 10, 1990; Denver Art Museum, July 4–September 9, 1990; National Museum of American Art, Washington, D.C., October 5, 1990–January 7, 1991. Denver: Denver Art Museum, 1990.

Downes Papers
William H. Downes Papers, Letters received, 1874–1922. Special Collections Department, Boston Athenaeum.

Esten 1997
John Esten. *Childe Hassam: East Hampton Summers.* Exh. cat., Guild Hall Museum, East Hampton, N.Y., August 9–October 12, 1997. East Hampton, N.Y.: Guild Hall Museum, 1997.

Fairbrother 1986
Trevor J. Fairbrother. *The Bostonians: Painters of an Elegant Age, 1870–1930.* Contributions by Theodore E. Stebbins Jr., William L. Vance, and Erica E. Hirshler. Exh. cat., Museum of Fine Arts, Boston, June 11–September 14, 1986; Denver Art Museum, October 25, 1986–January 18, 1987; Terra Museum of American Art, Chicago, March 13–May 10, 1987. Boston: Museum of Fine Arts, 1986.

Fort 1988
Ilene Susan Fort. *The Flag Paintings of Childe Hassam.* Exh. cat., National Gallery of Art, Washington, D.C., May 9–July 17, 1988; Los Angeles County Museum of Art, August 25–November 13, 1988; Amon Carter Museum, Fort Worth, January 7–March 12, 1989; New-York Historical Society, April 20–June 25, 1989. Los Angeles: Los Angeles County Museum of Art, 1988.

Fort 1993
Ilene Susan Fort. *Childe Hassam's New York.* San Francisco: Pomegranate Artbooks, 1993.

Gerdts 1980
William H. Gerdts. *American Impressionism.* Exh. cat., Henry Art Gallery, University of Washington, Seattle, January 3–March 2, 1980; Frederick S. Wight Gallery, University of California at Los Angeles, March 9–May 4, 1980. Seattle: Henry Art Gallery, University of Washington, 1980.

Gerdts et al. 1990
William H. Gerdts et al. *Ten American Painters.* Exh. cat., Spanierman Gallery, New York, May 8–June 9, 1990. New York: Spanierman Gallery, 1990.

Hassam 1899
Childe Hassam. *Three Cities.* New York: R. H. Russell, 1899.

Hassam 1928
Childe Hassam. "Twenty-five Years of American Painting." *Art News* 26 (April 14, 1928), pp. 22, 27–28.

Hassam, Letter to Miss Farmer, 1933
Childe Hassam. Letter to "Miss Farmer, who was making a record of the Graduates of the Dorchester High School." New York, February 22, 1933. An appendix to Hassam's Autobiographical notes, 1934, Hassam Papers, reel NAA1, frames 743–49.

Hassam Papers
Childe Hassam Papers and Correspondence. Owned by the American Academy of Arts and Letters, New York. Microfilmed by the Archives of American Art, Smithsonian Institution, American Academy of Arts and Letters Records, 1864–1942, reels NAA1, NAA2. Hassam's Autobiographical notes are on reel NAA1, frames 688–90 (undated manuscript), frames 739–42 (manuscript from 1934, a date based on Hassam's statement [frame 739] that his mother "would be one hundred years old this year as Mr. Whistler [born 1834] would be if he were living"), frames 755–56 (dated on frame 755: "now in 1934"), and reel NAA2, frames 227–29 (undated typescript, with handwritten corrections).

Hassam (East Hampton) 1981
Stuart P. Feld, with the assistance of Kathleen M. Burnside; coordinated by Judith Wolfe. *Childe Hassam, 1859–1935.* Exh. cat., Guild Hall Museum, East Hampton, N.Y., March 21–May 10, 1981. East Hampton, N.Y.: Guild Hall Museum, 1981.

Hassam (Tucson) 1972
Childe Hassam, 1859–1935. Exh. cat., University of Arizona Museum of Art, Tucson, February 5–March 5, 1972; Santa Barbara Museum of Art, March 26–April 30, 1972. Tucson: University of Arizona Museum of Art, 1972.

Hassam (Washington, D.C.) 1965
Childe Hassam: A Retrospective Exhibition. Introduction by Charles E. Buckley. Exh. cat., Corcoran Gallery of Art, Washington, D.C., April 30–August 1, 1965; Museum of Fine Arts, Boston, August 17–September 19, 1965; Currier Gallery of Art, Manchester, N.H., September 28–October 31, 1965; Gallery of Modern Art, New York, November 16–December 19, 1965. Washington, D.C.: Corcoran Gallery of Art, 1965.

J. T. Hassam 1870
John T. Hassam. *The Hassam Family.* Boston: David Clapp and Son, 1870.

J. T. Hassam 1880
John T. Hassam. *Notes and Queries Concerning the Hassam and Hilton Families.* Boston: David Clapp and Son, 1880.

J. T. Hassam 1889
John T. Hassam. "The Hassam Family, Additional Notes." *New-England Historical and Genealogical Register,* July 1889, pp. xliii, 320.

J. T. Hassam 1896
John T. Hassam. *The Hassam Family.* Boston: Privately printed [David Clapp and Son], 1896.

Hiesinger 1991
Ulrich W. Hiesinger. *Impressionism in America: The Ten American Painters.* Exh. cat., Jordan-Volpe Gallery, New York, May 18–June 28, 1991. Munich: Prestel-Verlag, 1991.

Hiesinger 1994
Ulrich W. Hiesinger. *Childe Hassam, American Impressionist.* Exh. cat., Jordan-Volpe Gallery, New York, May 20–July 1, 1994. Munich: Prestel-Verlag, 1994. Reprint ed., 1999.

Hoopes 1972
Donelson F. Hoopes. *The American Impressionists.* New York: Watson-Guptill, 1972.

Hoopes 1979
Donelson F. Hoopes. *Childe Hassam.* New York: Watson-Guptill, 1979.

Isles of Shoals Collection
Isles of Shoals Collection, Portsmouth Athenaeum, Portsmouth, New Hampshire. Manuscript Collections, Ms. 58: Hassam/Lamb correspondence, typewritten transcriptions of unlocated letters.

Ives 1892
A. E. Ives. "Talks with Artists: Mr. Childe Hassam on Painting Street Scenes." *Art Amateur* 27 (October 1892), pp. 116–17.

Lockman interview
DeWitt McClellan Lockman. Five interviews with Childe Hassam, January 25, 31, February 2, 3, 10, 1927. DeWitt McClellan Lockman Papers, New-York Historical Society. Archives of American Art microfilm, reel 503.

Mayor 1940
A. Hyatt Mayor. "Childe Hassam." *Bulletin of The Metropolitan Museum of Art* 35, no. 7 (July 1940), pp. 138–39.

Myers 1940
Jerome Myers. *Artist in Manhattan.* New York: American Artists' Group, Inc., 1940.

"New York Beautiful" 1898
"New York Beautiful." *New York Commercial Advertiser,* January 15, 1898, p. 9. Transcribed in Hiesinger 1994, p. 178.

Pattison 1908
James William Pattison. "The Art of Childe Hassam." *House Beautiful* 23 (January 1908), pp. 19–20.

Pousette-Dart 1922
Nathaniel Pousette-Dart, comp. *Childe Hassam.* Introduction by Ernest Haskell. Distinguished American Artists series. New York: Frederick A. Stokes, 1922.

Price 1923
Frederick Newlin Price. "Childe Hassam—Puritan." *International Studio* 77 (April 1923), pp. 3–7.

Rattray 1923
[Jeannette E. Rattray]. "Looking Them Over." *East Hampton Star* 38, no. 42 (August 31, 1923), p. 6.

Saint-Gaudens 1941
Homer Saint-Gaudens. *The American Artist and His Times.* New York: Dodd, Mead and Company, 1941.

Thaxter 1894
Celia Laighton Thaxter. *An Island Garden.* Pictures and illuminations by Childe Hassam. Boston and New York: Houghton Mifflin, 1894. Reprinted, with a new introduction by John M. Kingsbury, Bowie, Md.: Heritage Books, 1978, and Ithaca, N.Y.: Bullbrier Press, 1985; with a new introduction by Allen Lacy, Boston: Houghton Mifflin, 1988; and with a new introduction by Tasha Tudor, Boston: Houghton Mifflin, 2001. There is also a full text electronic version at http://digital.library.upenn.edu/women/thaxter/garden/garden.html

Truettner and Stein 1999
William H. Truettner and Roger B. Stein, eds. *Picturing Old New England: Image and Memory.* Exh. cat., National Museum of American Art, Smithsonian Institution, Washington, D.C., April 2–August 22, 1999. Washington, D.C.: National Museum of American Art, Smithsonian Institution; New Haven: Yale University Press, 1999.

Weinberg, Bolger, and Curry 1994
H. Barbara Weinberg, Doreen Bolger, and David Park Curry, with the assistance of N. Mishoe Brennecke. *American Impressionism and Realism: The Painting of Modern Life, 1885–1915.* Organized by The Metropolitan Museum of Art, New York, and the Amon Carter Museum, Fort Worth. Exh. cat., The Metropolitan Museum of Art, New York, May 10–July 24, 1994; Amon Carter Museum, Fort Worth, August 21–October 30, 1994; Denver Art Museum, December 3, 1994–February 5, 1995; Los Angeles County Museum of Art, March 12–May 14, 1995. New York: The Metropolitan Museum of Art, 1994.

White 1911
Israel L. White. "Childe Hassam—A Puritan." *International Studio* 45 (December 1911), pp. XXIX–XXXIII.

Wood Papers (Berkeley)
Charles E. S. Wood Papers, 1884–1920. BANC MSS 72/28 c. The Bancroft Library, University of California, Berkeley.

Wood Papers (San Marino)
C. E. S. Wood Papers. Henry E. Huntington Library and Art Gallery, San Marino, California.

Young 1960
Dorothy Weir Young. *The Life and Letters of J. Alden Weir.* New Haven: Yale University Press, 1960.

Works in the Exhibition

The list is in alphabetical order.

1. *After Breakfast*, 1887. Oil on canvas, 28 x 39⅝ in. (73 x 100.6 cm). Collection of Fayez Sarofim

2. *Allies Day, May 1917*, 1917. Oil on canvas, 36½ x 30¼ in. (92.7 x 76.8 cm). National Gallery of Art, Washington, D.C. Gift of Ethelyn McKinney in memory of her brother, Glenn Ford McKinney 1943.9.1

3. *The Almond Tree*, 1916. Etching, 11 x 5¾ in. (27.9 x 14.6 cm). Print Collection, Miriam and Ira D. Wallach Division of Art, Prints, and Photographs, The New York Public Library, Astor, Lenox, and Tilden Foundations

4. *Along the Seine, Winter*, 1887. Oil on cardboard, 8 x 11 in. (20.3 x 27.9 cm). Dallas Museum of Art, bequest of Joel T. Howard

5. *The Altar and Shrine*, 1892. Watercolor on paper, 15½ x 12¼ in. (39.4 x 31.1 cm). Private collection, loaned Courtesy Spanierman Gallery

6. *Apple Trees in Bloom, Old Lyme*, 1904. Oil on panel, 25 x 30½ in. (63.5 x 77.5 cm). Private collection, New York

7. *April Showers, Champs Élysées, Paris*, 1888. Oil on canvas, 12½ x 16⅝ in. (31.8 x 42.2 cm). Joslyn Art Museum, Omaha JAM1946.30

8. *At the Florist*, 1889. Oil on canvas, 36¾ x 54¼ in. (93.4 x 137.8 cm). Chrysler Museum of Art, Norfolk, Virginia; Gift of Walter P. Chrysler, Jr. This work of art is dedicated by the Museum Trustees to Linda Kaufman in gratitude for the time, talent and resources she has so generously given to the Chrysler. June 1999

9. *Avenue of the Allies, Great Britain, 1918*, 1918. Oil on canvas, 36 x 28⅜ in. (91.4 x 72.1 cm). The Metropolitan Museum of Art, New York. Bequest of Miss Adelaide Milton de Groot (1876–1967), 1967 67.187.127

10. *Une Averse—rue Bonaparte*, 1887. Oil on canvas, 40⅜ x 77½ in. (102.6 x 196.9 cm). Terra Foundation for the Arts, Chicago, Daniel J. Terra Collection

11. *A Back Road*, 1884. Oil on canvas, 31¼ x 25 in. (79.4 x 63.5 cm). Brooklyn Museum of Art, Caroline H. Polhemus Fund 47.122

12. *Boston Common at Twilight*, 1885–86. Oil on canvas, 42 x 60 in. (106.7 x 152.4 cm). The Museum of Fine Arts, Boston. Gift of Miss Maud E. Appleton

13. *Bowl of Goldfish*, 1912. Oil on canvas, 25⅛ x 30¼ in. (63.8 x 76.8 cm). Ball State University Museum of Art, Muncie, Indiana, Frank C. Ball Collection, partial gift and promised gift of the Ball Brothers Foundation

14. *Broadway and 42nd Street*, 1902. Oil on canvas, 26 x 22 in. (66 x 55.9 cm). The Metropolitan Museum of Art, New York. Bequest of Miss Adelaide Milton de Groot (1876–1967), 1967 67.187.128

15. *The Brush House*, 1916. Watercolor and graphite on off-white wove paper, 15 5/16 x 22 5/16 in. (38.9 x 56.7 cm). The Metropolitan Museum of Art, New York. Rogers Fund, 1917 17.31.1

16. *Cab Stand at Night, Madison Square*, 1891. Oil on paper, 9 x 14⅜ in. (22.9 x 36.5 cm). Smith College Museum of Art, Northampton, Massachusetts. Bequest of Annie Swan Coburn (Mrs. Lewis Larned Coburn)

17. *Carriage Parade*, 1888. Oil on canvas, 15 x 12 in. (38.1 x 30.5 cm). The Haggin Collection, The Haggin Museum, Stockton, California

18. *Carriage, Rue Bonaparte*, 1888. Oil on canvas, 41 x 30½ in. (104.1 x 77.5 cm). Private collection

19. *Cat Boats, Newport*, 1901. Oil on canvas, 24⅛ x 26⅛ in. (61.3 x 66.4 cm). Courtesy of the Pennsylvania Academy of the Fine Arts, Philadelphia. Joseph E. Temple Fund

20. *Cathedral at Ronda*, 1910. Oil on wood, 25⅝ x 21⅛ in. (65.1 x 53.7 cm). Courtesy of The Hispanic Society of America, New York

21. *Celia Thaxter's Garden, Isles of Shoals, Maine*, 1890. Oil on canvas, 17¾ x 21½ in. (45.1 x 54.6 cm). The Metropolitan Museum of Art, New York. Anonymous Gift, 1994 1994.567

22. *Central Park*, 1892. Oil on canvas, 18 x 22½ in. (45.7 x 57.2 cm). Private collection

23. *Charles River and Beacon Hill*, ca. 1892. Oil on canvas, 16⅛ x 18 in. (41 x 45.7 cm). Museum of Fine Arts, Boston. Tompkins Collection

24. *The Chimneys, Portsmouth*, 1915. Etching on a sheet of buff wove paper from a minister's Bible, 4⅞ x 8⅛ in. (12.3 x 20.7 cm). The Metropolitan Museum of Art, New York. Gift of Mrs. Childe Hassam, 1940 40.30.3 (C16)

25. *The Church at Gloucester*, 1918. Oil on canvas, 30 x 25 in. (76.2 x 63.5 cm). The Metropolitan Museum of Art, New York. Arthur Hoppock Hearn Fund, 1925 25.206

26. *Church at Old Lyme*, 1905. Oil on canvas, 36¼ x 32¼ in. (92.1 x 81.9 cm). Albright-Knox Art Gallery, Buffalo, Albert H. Tracy Fund, 1909

27. *Church at Old Lyme*, 1906. Oil on canvas, 30⅛ x 25¼ in. (76.5 x 64.1 cm). The Parrish Art Museum, Southampton, New York, Littlejohn Collection

28. *The Church at Old Lyme*, 1924. Etching on white wove paper, 7¼ x 6⅜ in. (18.3 x 16.2 cm). The Metropolitan Museum of Art, New York. Gift of Mrs. Childe Hassam, 1940 40.30.35 (C233)

29. *A City Fairyland*, 1886. Oil on canvas, 20 x 33 in. (50.8 x 83.8 cm). Mr. and Mrs. Samuel P. Peabody

30. *Clearing Sunset (Corner of Berkeley Street and Columbus Avenue)*, 1890. Oil on canvas, 25 x 30½ in. (63.5 x 77.5 cm). Marie and Hugh Halff

31. *Coast Scene, Isles of Shoals*, 1901. Oil on canvas, 24⅞ x 30⅛ in. (63.2 x 76.5 cm). The Metropolitan Museum of Art, New York. Gift of George A. Hearn, 1909 09.72.6

32. *Colonial Quilt*, 1922. Oil on canvas, 42 x 26 in. (106.7 x 66 cm). American Academy of Arts and Letters, New York

33. *The Colonial Table*, 1915. Etching on off-white laid paper, 6⅞ x 9⅞ in. (17.5 x 25.1 cm). The Metropolitan Museum of Art, New York. Gift of Mrs. Childe Hassam, 1940 40.30.33 (C51)

34. *Conversation on the Avenue*, 1892. Oil on board, 15¾ x 12½ in. (40 x 31.8 cm). Private collection

35. *Cos Cob Dock*, 1915. Etching on a sheet of buff wove paper from a minister's Bible, 8⅜ x 6¼ in. (21.3 x 15.9 cm). The Metropolitan Museum of Art, New York. Harris Brisbane Dick Fund, 1917 17.3.511 (C58)

36. *A Country Road*, 1891. Pastel on paper, 17⅝ x 21¼ in. (44.8 x 54 cm). Private collection

37. *Country Road (Wayside Inn, Sudbury, Massachusetts)*, 1882. Watercolor on paper, 9½ x 14 in. (24.1 x 35.6 cm). Private collection

38. *The Cove*, 1912. Watercolor on paper, 14 x 20 in. (35.6 x 50.8 cm). Wichita Art Museum, Kansas, The John W. and Mildred L. Graves Collection

39. *Duck Island from Appledore*, 1911. Oil on canvas, 28¼ x 35¾ in. (71.8 x 90.8 cm). Private collection

40. *Easthampton*, 1917. Etching on buff laid paper, 7⅜ x 11¼ in. (18.8 x 28.7 cm). The Metropolitan Museum of Art, New York. Gift of Mrs. Gustavus S. Wallace, 1932 32.109.8 (C134)

41. *The Evening Star*, 1891. Pastel on tan paper, 20 x 24 in. (50.8 x 61 cm). Yale Collection of American Literature, Beinecke Rare Book and Manuscript Library, Yale University Library, New Haven

42. *Fifth Avenue in Winter*, ca. 1890. Oil on canvas, 21⅝ x 28 in. (54.9 x 71.1 cm). Carnegie Museum of Art, Pittsburgh; purchase 1900

43. *Fifth Avenue, Noon*, 1916. Etching on buff wove paper, 2nd state, 9⅞ x 7⅛ in. (25.1 x 18.2 cm). The Metropolitan Museum of Art, New York. Gift of Mrs. Childe Hassam, 1940 40.30.25 (C77)

44. *Flags on Fifty-seventh Street, The Winter of 1918*, 1918. Oil on canvas, 35¾ x 23¾ in. (90.8 x 60.3 cm). Collection of The New-York Historical Society, bequest of Julia B. Engel 1984.68

45. *Flags on the Waldorf, 1916*, 1916. Oil on canvas, 36¼ x 31½ in. (92.1 x 80 cm). Amon Carter Museum, Fort Worth, Texas 1985.301

46. *Flower Garden*, 1893. Watercolor on paper, 19⅝ x 13⅞ in. (49.8 x 35.2 cm). Mrs. George M. Kaufman

47. *Flower Garden, Isles of Shoals*, 1893. Watercolor on paper, 19½ x 13½ in. (49.5 x 34.3 cm). Private collection, New York

48. *Flower Girl*, ca. 1887–89. Oil on canvas, 14¼ x 8⅝ in. (36.2 x 21.9 cm). Senator and Mrs. John D. Rockefeller IV

49. *The Fourth of July, 1916 (The Greatest Display of the American Flag Ever Seen in New York, Climax of the Preparedness Parade in May)*, 1916. Oil on canvas, 36 x 26⅛ in. (91.4 x 66.4 cm). Private collection

50. *French Peasant Girl,* ca. 1883. Oil on canvas, 21⅝ x 13⅞ in. (54.9 x 35.2 cm). Terra Foundation for the Arts, Chicago, Daniel J. Terra Collection

51. *La Fruitière,* ca. 1888–89. Oil on composition board, 14¼ x 10¼ in. (36.2 x 26 cm). Curtis Galleries, Minneapolis

52. *The Garden in Its Glory,* 1892. Watercolor on paper, 19⅞ x 13⅞ in. (50.5 x 35.2 cm). Smithsonian American Art Museum, Washington, D.C. Gift of John Gellatly

53. *Garden of the Luxembourg,* 1898/1915. Etching and drypoint on white laid paper (Dutch, *Van Gelder Zonen* watermark), 10⅞ x 9 in. (27.7 x 22.7 cm). The Metropolitan Museum of Art, New York. Gift of Mrs. Childe Hassam, 1940 40.30.2 (C2)

54. *Geraniums,* 1888–89. Oil on canvas, 18¼ x 13 in. (46.4 x 33 cm). The Hyde Collection, Glens Falls, New York

55. *Giant Magnolias,* 1904. Oil on canvas, 35 x 20 in. (88.9 x 50.8 cm). Reynolda House, Museum of American Art, Winston-Salem, North Carolina. Original purchase fund from Mary Reynolds Babcock, Z. Smith Reynolds, ARCA, and Anne Cannon Forsyth

56. *Gloucester,* 1899. Oil on canvas, 32 x 32 in. (81.3 x 81.3 cm). Collection of The Newark Museum, Gift of Mr. and Mrs. J. Russell Parsons, 1973

57. *Gloucester Harbor,* 1899. Oil on canvas, 24½ x 22½ in. (62.2 x 57.2 cm). Private collection

58. *Gloucester Harbor,* 1899 (inscribed *1909*). Oil on canvas, 25 x 26 in. (63.5 x 66 cm). Norton Museum of Art, West Palm Beach, Florida

59. *Golden Afternoon,* 1908. Oil on canvas, 30 x 40⅜ in. (76.4 x 102.6 cm). The Metropolitan Museum of Art, New York. Rogers Fund, 1911 11.40

60. *The Gorge, Appledore,* 1912. Watercolor on paper, 13¾ x 19⅞ in. (34.9 x 50.5 cm). The Brooklyn Museum of Art, Museum Collection Fund 24.103

61. *Grand Prix Day,* 1887. Oil on canvas, 24⅛ x 31 in. (61.3 x 78.7 cm). Museum of Fine Arts, Boston. Ernest Wadsworth Longfellow Fund

62. *The Hay Barn,* 1920. Etching on white wove paper (British, *J Whatman* watermark), 10¼ x 14¼ in. (26.2 x 36.2 cm). The Metropolitan Museum of Art, New York. Gift of Mrs. Childe Hassam, 1940 40.30.28 (C160)

63. *Home of the Hummingbird,* 1893. Watercolor on paper, 13¾ x 10⅛ in. (34.9 x 25.7 cm). Manoogian Collection

64. *Horticulture Building, World's Columbian Exposition, Chicago,* 1893. Oil on canvas, 18½ x 26¼ in. (47 x 66.7 cm). Terra Foundation for the Arts, Chicago, Daniel J. Terra Collection

65. *The Hovel and the Skyscraper,* 1904. Oil on canvas, 34¾ x 31 in. (88.3 x 78.7 cm). Courtesy of the Pennsylvania Academy of the Fine Arts, Philadelphia. The Vivian O. and Meyer P. Potamkin Collection. Bequest of Vivian O. Potamkin

66. *In Brittany,* 1897. Oil on canvas, 23¾ x 28⅛ in. (60.3 x 71.4 cm). Lord and Lady Ridley-Tree

67. *In the Garden,* ca. 1888–89. Oil on canvas, 18 x 10¾ in. (45.7 x 27.3 cm). Private collection

68. *In the Garden (Celia Thaxter in Her Garden),* 1892. Oil on canvas, 22¼ x 18 in. (56.5 x 45.7 cm). Smithsonian American Art Museum, Washington, D.C. Gift of John Gellatly

69. *In the Old House,* 1914. Oil on canvas, 31¼ x 48 in. (79.4 x 121.9 cm). Lewis and Ali Sanders

70. *In the Park,* 1889. Oil on canvas, 12¾ x 16⅜ in. (32.4 x 41.6 cm). Lewis and Ali Sanders

71. *The Isles of Shoals,* 1912. Oil on canvas, 22 x 18 in. (55.9 x 45.7 cm). Virginia Museum of Fine Arts, Richmond, The Adolph D. and Wilkins C. Williams Fund

72. *Jelly Fish,* 1912. Oil on canvas, 20¼ x 24¼ in. (51.4 x 61.6 cm). Wichita Art Museum, Kansas, The John W. and Mildred L. Graves Collection

73. *July Fourteenth, Rue Daunou, 1910,* 1910. Oil on canvas, 29⅛ x 19⅞ in. (74 x 50.5 cm). The Metropolitan Museum of Art, New York. George A. Hearn Fund, 1929 29.86

74. *Lafayette Street,* 1918. Lithograph and lithotint on lightweight beige wove paper (Japanese, foliate watermark), 14½ x 11 in. (36.8 x 27.9 cm). The Metropolitan Museum of Art, New York. Gift of Mrs. Childe Hassam, 1940 40.30.46 (G5)

75. *Late Afternoon, New York: Winter,* 1900. Oil on canvas, 37 x 29 in. (94 x 73.7 cm). Brooklyn Museum of Art, Dick S. Ramsay Fund 62.68

76. *Lilies,* 1910. Oil on canvas, 27¼ x 33 in. (69.2 x 83.8 cm). Private collection

77. *The Lion Gardiner House, Easthampton,* 1920. Etching on beige laid paper (French, *Michallet* watermark), 9¾ x 14 in. (24.8 x 35.6 cm). The Metropolitan Museum of Art, New York. Gift of Mrs. Childe Hassam, 1940 40.30.36 (C159)

78. *Little Cobbler's Shop,* 1912. Oil on canvas, 16½ x 30⅜ in. (41.9 x 77.2 cm). Addison Gallery of American Art, Andover, Massachusetts, gift of anonymous donor, by exchange

79. *Little Old Cottage, Egypt Lane, East Hampton,* 1917. Oil on canvas, 32¾ x 45½ in. (83.2 x 115.6 cm). Collection of the Guild Hall Museum, East Hampton, New York

80. *Long Island Pebbles and Fruit,* 1931. Oil on wood panel, 23¼ x 56½ in. (59.1 x 143.5 cm). American Academy of Arts and Letters, New York

81. *Lower Fifth Avenue,* 1890. Oil on canvas, 25¼ x 21 in. (64.1 x 53.3 cm). Private collection

82. *Lower Manhattan (View Down Broad Street),* 1907. Oil on canvas, 30¼ x 16⅛ in. (76.8 x 41 cm). Herbert F. Johnson Museum of Art, Cornell University, Ithaca, New York. Gift of Leonard K. Elmhirst, Class of 1921, Cornell University

83. *The Manhattan Club (The Stewart Mansion),* ca. 1891. Oil on canvas, 18¼ x 22⅛ in. (46.4 x 56.2 cm). Santa Barbara Museum of Art, Gift of Mrs. Sterling Morton to the Preston Morton Collection

84. *Morning Light,* 1914. Oil on canvas, 34 x 34 in. (86.4 x 86.4 cm). Howard and Susan Sosin

85. *Mrs. Hassam and Her Sister,* 1889. Oil on canvas, 9⅞ x 6⅛ in. (25.1 x 15.6 cm). Terra Foundation for the Arts, Chicago, Daniel J. Terra Collection

86. *Newfields, New Hampshire,* 1916. Etching and drypoint on buff laid paper, 9⅜ x 11⅜ in. (24.8 x 29.8 cm). The Metropolitan Museum of Art, New York. Gift of Mrs. Childe Hassam, 1940 40.30.23 (C106)

87. *A New York Blizzard,* ca. 1890. Pastel on gray paper, 13¾ x 9½ in. (34.9 x 24.1 cm). Isabella Stewart Gardner Museum, Boston

88. *The New York Window,* 1912. Oil on canvas, 46⅛ x 35¼ in. (117.2 x 89.5 cm). The Corcoran Gallery of Art, Washington, D.C.

89. *Nocturne, Railway Crossing, Chicago,* 1893. Watercolor on paper, 16 x 11¾ in. (40.6 x 29.8 cm). Museum of Fine Arts, Boston. The Hayden Collection. Charles Henry Hayden Fund

90. *Notre Dame Cathedral, Paris, 1888,* 1888. Oil on canvas, 17½ x 21½ in. (44.5 x 54.6 cm). The Detroit Institute of Arts. Founders Society Purchase, Robert H. Tannahill Foundation Fund

91. *Nude,* 1918. Lithograph on lightweight beige wove paper (Japanese, foliate watermark), 14⅜ x 9 in. (36.5 x 22.8 cm). The Metropolitan Museum of Art, New York. Gift of Mrs. Childe Hassam, 1940 40.30.49 (G38)

92. *The Old Fairbanks House, Dedham, Massachusetts,* ca. 1884. Oil on canvas, 22⅛ x 22 in. (56.2 x 55.9 cm). Museum of Fine Arts, Boston. Bequest of Kate Talbot Hopkins

93. *Old House and Garden, East Hampton,* 1898. Oil on canvas, 24⅛ x 20 in. (61.3 x 50.8 cm). Henry Art Gallery, University of Washington, Seattle, Horace C. Henry Collection

94. *Old Lace,* 1915. Etching on a sheet of buff wove paper from a minister's Bible, 6⅞ x 6¾ in. (17.5 x 17.3 cm). The Metropolitan Museum of Art, New York. Gift of Mrs. Childe Hassam, 1940 40.30.16 (C56)

95. *On the Deck,* 1883. Watercolor on paper, 18⅞ x 12¼ in. (47.9 x 31.1 cm). Ms. Cheryl Chase and Mr. Stuart Bear

96. *Oyster Sloop, Cos Cob,* 1902. Oil on canvas, 24⅜ x 22⅜ in. (61.9 x 56.8 cm). National Gallery of Art, Washington, D.C. Ailsa Mellon Bruce Collection 1970.17.100

97. *Parc Monceau, Paris,* 1897. Oil on canvas, 24⅛ x 17¾ in. (61.3 x 45.1 cm). Frye Art Museum, Seattle

98. *Peach Blossoms—Villiers-le-Bel,* ca. 1887–89. Oil on canvas, 18⅛ x 21½ in. (46 x 54.6 cm). The Metropolitan Museum of Art, New York. Gift of Mrs. J. Augustus Barnard, 1979 1979.490.9

99. *Point Lobos, Carmel,* 1914. Oil on canvas, 28⅜ x 36¼ in. (72.1 x 92.1 cm). Los Angeles County Museum of Art, Mr. and Mrs. William Preston Harrison Collection

100. *Pont-Aven, Noon Day,* 1897. Oil on canvas, 24⅛ x 19⅞ in. (61.3 x 50.5 cm). Private collection, New York, courtesy Rita Krauss Fine Art

101. *Poppies, Isles of Shoals,* ca. 1890. Pastel on paper, 9 x 12 in. (22.9 x 30.5 cm). Private collection

102. *Poppies, Isles of Shoals,* 1891. Oil on canvas, 19¾ x 24 in. (50.2 x 61 cm). National Gallery of Art, Washington, D.C. Gift (Partial and Promised) of Margaret and Raymond Horowitz 1997.135.1

103. *Portrait of Joseph Pennell,* 1917. Lithograph on lightweight beige wove paper (Japanese, foliate watermark), 15⅜ x 11¼ in. (39.1 x 28.6 cm). The Metropolitan Museum of Art, New York. Gift of Mrs. Childe Hassam, 1940 40.30.39 (G3)

104. *Promenade,* 1883. Watercolor, gouache, and graphite on off-white wove paper, 16¹⁵⁄₁₆ x 25¹³⁄₁₆ in. (43 x 65.6 cm). The Metropolitan Museum of Art, New York. Gift of Mr. and Mrs. Arthur G. Altschul, 1971 1971.246.2

105. *Promenade at Sunset, Paris,* 1888–89. Oil on canvas, 18⅛ x 15⅛ in. (46 x 38.4 cm). Tom James Company / Oxxford Clothes

106. *The Public Garden (Boston Common),* ca. 1885. Watercolor on paper, 26⅛ x 38⅛ in. (66.4 x 96.8 cm). Slavin Family

107. *Rain Drops and Surf,* 1921. Etching on buff wove paper, 8½ x 6 in. (21.6 x 15.4 cm). The Metropolitan Museum of Art, New York. Gift of Mrs. Childe Hassam, 1940 40.30.13 (C170)

108. *Rainy Day, Columbus Avenue, Boston,* 1885. Oil on canvas, 26⅛ x 48 in. (66.4 x 121.9 cm). The Toledo Museum of Art; Purchased with funds from the Florence Scott Libbey Bequest in Memory of her Father, Maurice A. Scott

109. *Red Cross Drive, May 1918 (Celebration Day),* 1918. Oil on canvas, 35½ x 23½ in. (90.2 x 59.7 cm). May Family Collection, Christopher T. May, Sterling A. May, Meredith M. Smith, Laura May, Trustees

110. *The Room of Flowers,* 1894. Oil on canvas, 34 x 34 in. (86.4 x 86.4 cm). Private collection

111. *The Rose Girl,* ca. 1888. Center panel, oil on canvas with gold leaf, 21¾ x 30⅛ in. (55.2 x 76.5 cm); side panels, oil on wood with gold leaf, each 15¼ x 6¼ in. (38.7 x 15.9 cm). Senator and Mrs. John D. Rockefeller IV

112. *Roses in a Vase,* 1890. Oil on canvas, 20 x 24 in. (50.8 x 61 cm). The Baltimore Museum of Art: Helen and Abram Eisenberg Collection BMA 1967.36.3

113. *The Sonata,* 1893. Oil on canvas, 32 x 32 in. (81.3 x 81.3 cm). The Nelson-Atkins Museum of Art, Kansas City, Missouri (Gift of Mr. and Mrs. Joseph S. Atha) 52–5

114. *The South Ledges, Appledore,* 1913. Oil on canvas, 34¼ x 36⅛ in. (87 x 91.8 cm). Smithsonian American Art Museum, Washington, D.C. Gift of John Gellatly

115. *The Spar Shop, Gloucester,* 1918. Lithograph on lightweight beige wove paper (Japanese, foliate watermark), 7⅛ x 12 in. (18.1 x 30.5 cm). The Metropolitan Museum of Art, New York. Gift of Mrs. Childe Hassam, 1940 40.30.44 (G23)

116. *Spring in Central Park (Springtime),* 1898. Oil on canvas, 29½ x 37½ in. (74.9 x 95.3 cm). Robert Rubin

117. *Spring Morning in the Heart of the City,* 1890, reworked 1895–99. Oil on canvas, 18⅛ x 20¾ in. (46 x 52.7 cm). The Metropolitan Museum of Art, New York. Gift of Miss Ethelyn McKinney, in memory of her brother, Glenn Ford McKinney, 1943 43.116.1

118. *Square at Sevilla,* 1910. Oil on wood, 25⅝ x 20¾ in. (65 x 52.8 cm). Courtesy of The Hispanic Society of America, New York

119. *The Steps,* 1915. Etching on lightweight off-white paper, 10¾ x 7⅝ in. (27.4 x 19.4 cm). The Metropolitan Museum of Art, New York. Gift of Theodore de Witt, 1923 23.65.78 (C52)

120. *Storm King,* 1918. Lithotint on lightweight beige wove paper, 10¾ x 12⅛ in. (27.3 x 30.8 cm). Print Collection, Miriam and Ira D. Wallach Division of Art, Prints, and Photographs, The New York Public Library, Astor, Lenox, and Tilden Foundations G45

121. *Street in Portsmouth,* 1916. Watercolor on off-white wove paper, 15⅛ x 22 in. (38.4 x 55.9 cm). The Metropolitan Museum of Art, New York. Rogers Fund, 1917 17.31.2

122. *Street of the Great Captain, Cordoba,* 1910. Oil on board, 25½ x 20½ in. (64.8 x 52.1 cm). The Saint Louis Art Museum, Gift of Mr. and Mrs. Mahlon Wallace

123. *Summer at Cos Cob,* 1902. Pastel on paper, 22 x 18 in. (55.9 x 45.7 cm). The Montclair Art Museum, Gift of William T. Evans 1915.24

124. *Summer Evening,* 1886. Oil on canvas, 12⅛ x 20⅜ in. (30.8 x 51.8 cm). Florence Griswold Museum, Old Lyme, Connecticut; Gift of the Hartford Steam Boiler Inspection and Insurance Company

125. *Summertime,* 1891. Pastel on canvas, 20 x 24 in. (50.8 x 61 cm). Private collection

126. *Sunset at Sea,* 1911. Oil on canvas, 34 x 34 in. (86.4 x 86.4 cm). Collection of The Rose Art Museum, Brandeis University, Waltham, Massachusetts, Gift of Mr. and Mrs. Monroe Geller

127. *Sunset, Constable's Hook,* 1915. Etching and drypoint on a sheet of off-white laid paper from a notebook, 5 x 6⅞ in. (12.7 x 17.5 cm). The Metropolitan Museum of Art, New York. Gift of Mrs. Childe Hassam, 1940 40.30.9 (C18)

128. *Surf, Isles of Shoals,* 1913. Oil on canvas, 28¼ x 35¼ in. (71.8 x 89.5 cm). The Metropolitan Museum of Art, New York. Gift of Dr. and Mrs. Sheldon C. Sommers, 1996 1996.382

129. *Sylph's Rock, Appledore,* 1907. Oil on canvas, 25 x 30 in. (63.5 x 76.2 cm). Worcester Art Museum, Massachusetts, Gift of Charlotte E. W. Buffington in memory of her husband

130. *The Table Garden,* 1910. Oil on canvas, 39½ x 29¾ in. (100.3 x 75.6 cm). From the Collection of the Mitchell Museum at Cedarhurst, Mount Vernon, Illinois

131. *Twenty-sixth of June, Old Lyme,* 1912. Oil on canvas, 31¾ x 24½ in. (80.6 x 62.2 cm). Mr. and Mrs. Theodore N. Lerner

132. *Union Square,* 1896/1916. Etching on blue laid paper, 4¼ x 5¾ in. (10.8 x 14.6 cm). The Metropolitan Museum of Art, New York. Gift of Mrs. Childe Hassam, 1940 40.30.7 (C89)

133. *Union Square in Spring,* 1896. Oil on canvas, 21½ x 21 in. (54.6 x 53.3 cm). Smith College Museum of Art, Northampton, Massachusetts. Purchased

134. *The Victorian Chair,* 1906. Oil on wood, 30⅛ x 25 in. (76.5 x 63.5 cm). Smithsonian American Art Museum, Washington, D.C. Gift of William T. Evans

135. *Victory Day, May 1919,* 1919. Oil on canvas, 36 x 21¾ in. (91.4 x 55.2 cm). American Academy of Arts and Letters, New York

136. *View of Broadway and Fifth Avenue,* 1890. Oil on canvas, 13¾ x 10½ in. (34.9 x 26.7 cm). Private collection, Pennsylvania

137. *Village Scene,* 1883–85. Oil on canvas, 17¼ x 22¼ in. (43.8 x 56.5 cm). Mr. and Mrs. Thomas A. Rosse

138. *Washington Arch, Spring,* ca. 1893 (inscribed *1890*). Oil on canvas, 27⅛ x 22½ in. (68.9 x 57.2 cm). The Phillips Collection, Washington, D.C.

139. *Washington's Birthday, Fifth Avenue and 23rd Street,* 1916. Etching, 12⅞ x 8¼ in. (32.7 x 21 cm). Print Collection, Miriam and Ira D. Wallach Division of Art, Prints, and Photographs, The New York Public Library, Astor, Lenox, and Tilden Foundations

140. *The Water Garden,* 1909. Oil on canvas, 24 x 36 in. (61 x 91.4 cm). The Metropolitan Museum of Art, New York. Partial and Promised Gift of Mr. and Mrs. Douglas Dillon, 1994 1994.450

141. *The West Wind, Isles of Shoals,* 1904. Oil on canvas, 15 x 22 in. (38.1 x 55.9 cm). Yale Collection of American Literature, Beinecke Rare Book and Manuscript Library, Yale University Library, New Haven

142. *The White Kimono,* 1915. Etching and drypoint on cream laid paper (French, Ingres d'Arches, *MBM* watermark), 7⅜ x 10⅞ in. (18.7 x 27.6 cm). The Metropolitan Museum of Art, New York. Harris Brisbane Dick Fund, 1917 17.3.494 (C47)

143. *Winter in Union Square,* 1889–90. Oil on canvas, 18¼ x 18 in. (46.4 x 45.7 cm). The Metropolitan Museum of Art, New York. Gift of Miss Ethelyn McKinney, in memory of her brother, Glenn Ford McKinney, 1943 43.116.2

144. *Winter, Midnight,* 1894. Oil on canvas, 21½ x 17½ in. (54.6 x 44.5 cm). Private collection

145. *Winter Sickle Pears,* 1918. Oil on canvas, 20¼ x 30¼ in. (51.4 x 76.8 cm). Collection of Cornelia and Meredith Long

Index

Page numbers in *italics* refer to illustrations. Unless otherwise noted, works cited are by Hassam.

Photograph Credits

Most photographs were supplied by the owners of the works and are reproduced by their permission; their courtesy is gratefully acknowledged.

New photography of works in the Metropolitan Museum collection by Mark Morosse, Juan Trujillo, and Peter Zeray, the Photograph Studio, The Metropolitan Museum of Art. Additional credits appear under some illustreations and in the following list.

© Addison Gallery of American Art, Phillips Academy, Andover, Massachusetts. All Rights Reserved: fig. 219

Courtesy Adelson Galleries, Inc., New York: figs. 6, 27, 95, 112, 113, 200, 244

Amon Carter Museum, Fort Worth: fig. 346

© The Art Institute of Chicago: figs. 37, 52, 53, 106, 225, 257, 322

Courtesy Babcock Galleries, New York: fig. 175

From James W. Buel, *The Magic City* (Saint Louis: Historical Publishing Company, 1894): fig. 193

Carnegie Museum of Art, Pittsburgh: fig. 329

Carrig-Rohane Shop Records 1903–1962, Archives of American Art, Smithsonian Institution, Washington, D.C.: fig. 335

Glenn Castellano: figs. 189, 342, 345, 349

© Christie's Images Inc., 2004: figs. 70, 110, 298

Geoffrey Clements: fig. 221

© The Cleveland Museum of Art, 2004: fig. 237

From Royal Cortissoz, *The Works of Edwin Howland Blashfield* (New York: Charles Scribner's Sons, 1937): fig. 319

© 1988 The Detroit Institute of Arts: figs. 66, 196

Courtesy Fotostudio Otto, Vienna: fig. 223

Michael Fredericks: fig. 79

© The J. Paul Getty Museum, Los Angeles: fig. 55

Erik Gould: fig. 218

From Ulrich W. Hiesinger, *Childe Hassam, American Impressionist* (1994; reprint, Munich: Prestel, 1999): figs. 43, 48

Courtesy Hirschl and Adler Galleries, New York: figs. 361, 363

From *Illustrated Catalogue of the Twenty-fifth Annual Exhibition of the American Water Color Society* (New York: 1892): fig. 261

From Michael Jacobs, *The Good and Simple Life, Artist Colonies in Europe and America* (Oxford: Phaidon, 1985): fig. 202

Courtesy Vance Jordan Fine Art, New York. Photograph by Camerarts Inc., New York: figs. 68, 256, 316, 362

From Moses King, *King's Views of New York 1896–1915 and Brooklyn 1905* (New York: B. Blom, 1974): fig. 231

© Erich Lessing / Art Resource, New York: figs. 51, 206

Collections of the Library of Congress, Washington, D.C.: fig. 318

Jamison Miller: fig. 122

© 2004 Museum Associates / LACMA: figs. 109, 197, 211

© 2004 Museum of Fine Arts, Boston: figs. 30, 31, 39, 58, 62, 84, 109, 136, 191, 258, 259, 301, 302, 305, 309

© Board of Trustees, National Gallery of Art, Washington, D.C.: figs. 134, 150, 158, 230

National Portrait Gallery, Smithsonian Institution / Art Resource, New York: fig. 238

Robert Newcombe: fig. 60

The New-York Historical Society, negative 9063: fig. 94; negative 54156: fig. 100; negative 75871: fig. 88; negative 75872: fig. 96

Richard Nicol, 2003: fig. 240

Offenbach, New York: figs. 16, 19

Photograph Studio, The Metropolitan Museum of Art, New York: figs. 43, 48, 74, 193, 199, 202, 210, 231, 243, 245, 261, 263, 292, 313, 319

From Bruce Porter et al., *Art in California* (Irvine: Westphal Publishing, 1988): fig. 210

© Portland Art Museum, Oregon: figs. 334, 338, 355

Tom Powel: figs. 12, 14, 235, 321, 324, 325, 327, 339, 348, 350

From Bertrand Quéinec, *Pont Aven 1800–1914* (Pont-Aven, France: Quéinec, 1983): fig. 199

© Réunion des Musées Nationaux / Art Resource, New York: figs. 40, 44, 253

Noel Rowe: fig. 177

From George W. Sheldon, *Recent Ideals of American Art* (ca. 1888; reprint, New York: Garland Publishing, 1977): figs. 74, 313

Louise Shelton, *Beautiful Gardens in America* (New York, 1915): figs. 243, 245

Courtesy Sotheby's, Inc., New York: figs. 38, 93, 160, 239, 293, 300

Courtesy Spanierman Gallery, LLC, New York: fig. 121

Richard A. Stoner: fig. 188

© Tate, London 2004: figs. 45, 162

James Via: fig. 203

Courtesy Vose Galleries of Boston: fig. 23

Katherine Wetzel. © Virginia Museum of Fine Arts, Richmond: fig. 147

Yale University Art Gallery, New Haven: figs. 124, 148